WISDEN
Anthology 1963-1982

WISDEN
Anthology 1963-1982

EDITED BY BENNY GREEN

Queen Anne Press
Macdonald & Co · London & Sydney

First published in Great Britain in 1983 by
Queen Anne Press, a division of
Macdonald & Co (Publishers) Ltd
Maxwell House
74 Worship Street
London EC2A 2EN
ISBN 0 356 09379 4

Typeset by Spottiswoode Ballantyne Ltd.,
Colchester and London.
Printed and bound in Great Britain
by Hazell Watson and Viney, Aylesbury

FOREWORD

As a friend of mine – not wont to be demonstrative – assured me the other day that he had no pleasanter evenings in the whole year than when the appearance of *Wisden* enabled him to fight the battles of the cricket season over again, I am fortified in the belief that the Almanack fulfils its mission and preserves in a readable and attractive form a record of all that is essential in connection with our glorious game. Lest there should seem to be any suspicion of vanity or egotism in my saying this, I may point to the ever-increasing favour with which *Wisden* is received, and to a constantly-growing circulation.

Sydney H. Pardon 1893

To Natasha

CONTENTS

Introduction

On May 1st, 1963, English cricket stepped out of its battered fortress into the bleak world of the twentieth century. There was to be no going back. The castle was being abandoned once and for all, although it is doubtful if the garrison realised that as it stepped gingerly out into the open market. "What Manchester does today the rest of the country does tomorrow" is a claim often heard, especially in Manchester, so perhaps it was fitting that the scene of the great departure was Old Trafford, for a match between Lancashire and Leicestershire. May 1st was a Sunday, which represented the abandonment of a tradition which was not so much religious as sentimental. Nor was it the breach of sabbatarian rectitude which defined the watershed, but the nature of the event itself. English professional cricket was about to become English commercial cricket. The great figures of its hierarchy were now about to bear on their backs the name of a sponsor who openly avowed his intention of pushing his product by advertising cricket. But not even that was the factor which cut off the garrison's retreat. Neither the name of the day nor of the paymaster could alone have threatened the game as generations had come to know it. There was a third factor. Perhaps on that day at Old Trafford the garrison believed it was going out for a brief spree. But whatever it believed, it never came back. This was not a sortie but a surrender, rendered more poignant than otherwise by the fact that almost nobody suspected it. On Sunday May 1st, 1963, there took place the first ever first-class limited-overs one-day match in England.

The reasons justifying this heretical course were impressive, and perfectly plain to anyone capable of standing back and assessing the true nature of what had once been the national game. For at least a century English cricket had been an institution underwritten by patronage. Because of the historical accident that once upon a time the landowning patrician had fallen in love with the game, its economic future was not so much taken for granted as rendered irrelevant. Other pastimes and entertainments might have to pay their way, but not cricket, which, when faced with an imminent fall from economic grace, could always anticipate happy landings on the silken cushion of patronage. Let a County club fall into debt, and some local member of the landed gentry could be relied upon to gallop to the rescue. Let there be a rain-ruined season, or a crumbling pavilion roof, or a calamitous benefit match, or a mortgage about to be foreclosed, and the squirearchy would answer for it. In administration, too, the patricians had always performed nobly in the cause, not simply by accepting the drudgery of clerical responsibility, but rushing to embrace it, a self-sacrificial tendency exquisitely rendered by the story of the Reverend George William Gillingham, padre, as it were, to the aristocracy, who, after slaving for some years as honorary secretary to Worcestershire, saw one day that the River Severn had flooded the county ground, dived into the waters, swam into the pavilion and swam back again carrying the accounts books between his teeth. While the reverend gentleman's devotion to the cause might be thought by a more utilitarian age to have been somewhat excessive, it was by no means untypical. The governors of cricket gave much time to bookkeeping, much counsel on investment, much guidance on the husbanding of slender resources. They proselytised on behalf of the game in the most unlikely corners of the earth, moving mountains in their resolve that whether in the remote South Seas or in the New World, the great game should not go under. They did not always succeed. Canada and the United States proved a sore disappointment. But generally the success of cricket's major-generals was prodigious. There is no question that without them, the first-class game could hardly have evolved.

Naturally in return for this patronage, the benefactors demanded some sort of control, and took it, not always quite in the most diplomatic way. Sometimes they exercised their power in a style not quite commensurate with their gentlemanly pretensions. It might, for example, require a nice sense of the absurd to decide which of two experiences would be the more unfortunate, to be marooned on a desert island with Lord Harris, or rescued from it by Lord Hawke. But whatever their faults, the patricians kept afloat a game which, as professionalism advanced, came to rely to an ever-growing extent on charity. In one sense the predicament of the County club was analagous to that of a newspaper. Circulation, or in the case of cricket, gate money, might contribute towards revenues but it would always fall short of minimal requirements. The newspaper bridged the gap with advertising, the cricket club with patronage, which gave cricket an immense strength, because unlike the newspaper proprietor, who dare not offend his advertisers, it could offend anyone it pleased. Except the patricians. When pressures were brought to bear by the outside world, cricket could afford to ignore them. And ignore them it did, which is how it came about that an essentially Victorian garrison found itself suddenly exposed to the rigours of a neo-Elizabethan market-place.

For the patricians had all gone, taxed out of existence by Death Duties, killed in wars, spurred by social conscience, out-manoeuvred by events. The great estates were broken up; stately homes which had once echoed to the plock-plock of country house strokeplay now rang to the steady tramp of sightseers on conducted tours. By one of those neat coincidences which bring a smile to the historian's face, the advent of the one-day game marked also the abolition of the Gentleman-Player differentiation. No longer supported by the landed gentry, cricket was obliged to earn its living. No more the divisive prefix "Mr" and the rubric of triple initials on the matchcard, no more the panache of what Richard Tyldesley had described as "coloured caps", no more the capacity crowds for Eton-Harrow and Oxford-Cambridge. We were all professionals now, and some way had to be found to reconcile the cost of running a County club with the empty seats at County Championship matches. The game's administrators could not afford to luxuriate in protracted deliberations. By 1963 the crisis had become grave enough to threaten the very existence of the first-class game. Ever since the golden summer of 1947 attendances had been falling. Once over two million in an English season, they were now roughly one-third of that number. Something had to be done.

What alternatives were available? Raising the price of admission? But that would have driven away customers even as it attracted revenue. Increasing the cost of membership of County clubs? But membership drives had been tried and tried again without solving the problem. Asking for government subsidy? Apparently nobody thought of that, but even if they had, they might have considered the implications of ministerial control and opted for oblivion instead. An all-out attempt to bring television fees up from the currently derisory level? But cricket had only one customer, the BBC, and without the bargaining weapon of rival bidders, its power at the negotiating table was marginally less than nil. There was one last refuge. Subsidy. Advertising. The linking of the game with the name of some manufacturer. And this meant transforming the game as it stood into a spectacle with sufficient commercial appeal to attract the cash of patrons. And so the one-day game arrived.

After all, argued the sophists, almost all the cricket ever played in this world has been one-day cricket, in the sense that it lasts only one day. Clubs everywhere have been contesting one-day matches happily enough for centuries without ever blemishing either the game or their own relish for it. All Muggleton and Dingly Dell managed to complete their transactions within the compass of a single day. So did Tillingfold and Raveley and so did Mr Hodge's eleven against Fordenden. If these paragons were content to play under these conditions, why not the professionals? The speciousness of this argument obscured the most vital truth of all, which is that a match which begins and ends in one day is not at all the same thing as a one-day match. Three years before the great departure, Kent had defeated Worcestershire by an innings and 101 runs in a Championship match which began and ended on June 15th. But Worcestershire were put in and out twice in that day, a fate quite impossible under the new rules. In any case, the reason why weekend cricketers find the first-class game so fascinating is precisely because it is not played by weekend cricketers, but by virtuosi. In cricket as in music, great executants create their own rhythms and tempi in performance. Those rhythms and tempi require for their full expression certain conditions of performance. An opera-lover confronted by the prospect of a production of "Boris Godunov" limited to a duration of ten minutes might understandably conclude that the outcome would not be "Boris Godunov" at all, but some scrambled parody not worth listening to. For he would know that in order to perform so complex a work in so short a span of time, essential elements would have to be flung overboard. Among the possibilities which those members of the Lancashire and Leicestershire sides were leaving behind them as they marched out to do brief battle were the death-defying second innings recovery, the gallant last-ditch fight for a draw, the gradual accelerando of an individual double century, the parabolic allure of leg-break bowling content to buy its wickets at a price, the frisson of the unknown which attaches to any innings whose duration remains uncertain until the fall of the last wicket. No more the obduracy of a Barlow or a Bailey, the profligacy of an Arthur Mailey or a Douglas Wright, the perversity of Banerjee and Sarwate, no more nightwatchman whimsicalities, no more overnight speculation, no more daft declarations by Machiavellian captains.

But if all this was to be jettisoned, the dispassionate observer might well be pardoned for wondering what was left. A generation later the question remains unanswered. Often when discussions are mounted on the technical decline of Enghlish cricket, the case is heard that too many counties have opted for imported stars at the expense of home-grown talent, although curiously enough the obverse of this argument, that a Sobers or a Zaheer achieves more for English cricket by precept than he damages it by intrusion, is rarely heard. It is one of the most crushing of all cricketing ironies that during the period under review in this volume, a period fraught with domestic crises, looming bankruptcies, shrinking three-day attendances and the steady erosion of English excellence, the County Championship, in terms of individual virtuosity, enjoyed a dazzling passage which one day will be seen as a golden age in which the great stars of all nations were in daily contention, Sobers against Intikhab, Kanhai against Procter, Glenn Turner against Roberts. In the last seven seasons covered by this volume, of the twenty one names filling the first three places in the batting averages, sixteen belong to overseas players, in the bowling analyses twelve.

But whatever the strengths or weaknesses of the lobby which would introduce tariff walls to the world of cricket and exclude all but the English from the English game, history will certainly pronounce its verdict that the most damaging single factor in the tragic decline of the domestic game has been the advance of the one-day idea, which has, within the compass of a generation, advanced so far in newsworthiness and popularity as to have transformed the etiquette of the game, its laws, its procedures, its rituals, its very personality. By dangling prize money and insisting on a Man of the Match, by courting cup final hysteria, by splitting itself, amoeba-like, from one competition into two, and then three, it pushed the County Championship into the background, and would appear to have damaged the fabric of the domestic game so seriously as to have rendered any prospect of recovery remote indeed. In order to accommodate new competitions, the County Championship has been cut back and cut back again, with the result that the double of a thousand runs and a hundred wickets, the scoring of 3000 runs or the taking of 200 wickets in a season, all have become things of the distant past. Instead we are vouchsafed the spectacle of grown men kissing each other like troupes of light-headed chorus girls at the fall of every wicket, of international sides clothed in hues which even those chorus girls would have found unbecoming, of technical solecism so widespread and so outrageous as to have rendered all the text books obsolete and all canons of judgment passé.

As to the moral justification for all this, whether rape, so to speak, is justified by expediency, that is a question outside the compass of this volume. But there is one other corruption for which the one-day game must answer, a corruption especially perplexing to the anthologist. The speed of the action and the inevitability of a result in one-day matches have combined to destroy all previous concepts of what constituted a thrilling or unusual or comic or otherwise noteworthy match. The riot of slogging and the selling of cheap wickets have, so to speak, debased the currency of sensationalism. Where once the anthologist looked for the occasional freak among the general mass of ordinary matches, now he is very nearly pushed by his confusion to find the occasional ordinary match in a sea of lurid freaks. When it comes to assessing the intrinsic worth of the one-day game, and the validity of its claims to be counted as part of the first-class programme, each man must come to his own conclusions, and the editor of this volume, having come to his, has followed the dictates of his cricketing conscience and included only as much one-day cricket as he finds historically revealing as well as genuinely thrilling and good cricket. That is, very little.

In the sense that the decline of a patrician class inclined to the distribution of largesse is a political rather than sporting development, the necessity to court commercial subsidy must be accounted a classic example of the way in which politics cannot be kept out of organised sport. It is one of the little whimsies of cricket history that the cry to keep the game free of political entanglements has usually been raised by the very people responsible for causing those entanglements. The customary sequence of events is for someone to perform an act which is in its nature blatantly political, and then, when the opposition musters, to accuse the enemy of dragging politics into sport. There then follows a long and acrimonious debate which so begs the question as to evoke thoughts of the ancient argument about the efficacy of manufacturing cucumbers out of sunbeams. The real issue is not whether to keep politics out of cricket is desirable, but whether it is possible. In the light of post-war events, the answer is so blatantly obvious that any attempt to ignore it can only lead to chaos and disaster. Wherever there are international contests between representatives of societies with ideologies so conflicting that they cannot even agree what politics are, then already the issue is joined, even if it takes some specific incident to bring the fight out into the open, at which point the air is murmurous with nostalgic sighs for the good old days.

But there never were any good old days. Politics have always been with us. When English University graduates decreed that only English University graduates were qualified to select and lead the national side, they were bringing politics into cricket. When Maharajahs who should have been taking rest cures at health farms insisted on captaining touring sides, they were bringing politics into cricket. When Lord Hawke insisted on vetting the prospective wives of his professionals but not of his amateur colleagues, he was bringing politics into cricket as well as into the boudoir. When in 1933 the raging waters of Bodyline lapped against the very doors of the Colonial Office, who could deny that cricket had very nearly BECOME politics? Cricket, like everything else, is a part of the real world, and cannot hope to avoid political imbroglios from time to time. Nor is this involvement necessarily a bad thing. That passionate ideologue and anti-colonialist C. L. R. James has often paused in his exposition of the joys of Marxism to pay eloquent tribute to the English Public schoolboys who came to his island and introduced Newboltian concepts of Fair Play which were destined to enrich the life of the entire community. And there have been times when the calculated deployment of cricket as an imperial policy had an effect of sublime benignity, as those will know who have followed Arthur Grimble's account of cricket in the Gilbert and Ellice Islands, which progressed within a generation from contests involving "considerable slaughter" to genuine sporting occasions in which the participants were "the fighters who love each other".

The D'Oliveira dispute is one of the most sensational cause célèbres in the history of any game, and is laid out in some detail elsewhere in this volume. But it may be worth providing, as a useful background to that extraordinary sequence of events, a few historical notes which suggest that politics, so far from suddenly deciding to rear an ugly head in 1968, had been rearing it for many years before. In 1896 K. S. Ranjitsinhji was omitted from the England side to play Australia at Lord's because Lord Harris disapproved of overseas players representing England. Lord Harris, captain of England in 1878-79, was born in Trinidad. Two years earlier a South African side had visited England without selecting the outstanding black cricketer T. Hendricks. In 1929 Ranji's nephew, K. S. Duleepsinhji, was selected for the English side to play in the first Test against South Africa in 1929, but withdrew after objections from the tourists. Nor did he appear in the four subsequent matches against the visitors, nor was he ever picked for an English tour of South Africa.

Now the perceptive reader will notice a distinct difference between the cases of Ranji and Hendricks on the one hand, and Duleep on the other, and that this difference is fundamental to any rational assessment of the D'Oliveira affair. Ranji and Hendricks were being snubbed by their own side, Duleep by his opponents. However blackguardly the motives of those who victimised the cricketers Ranji and Hendricks for non-cricketing reasons, and no matter how blatantly they were dragging politics into cricket as they did so, they were at any rate befouling nobody's nest but their own. The case of Duleep is of a different order altogether, because it was rendering invalid the very tenet on which the philosophic basis of all sporting competition stands, that each side in the contest will not expect to dictate the rules to the other. A prize fight in which the challenger insists on his opponent's bootlaces being tied together, a Wimbledon final in which one player is handicapped by the removal of the strings from his racket, a foot race in which the favourite is required to run backwards, all these hypotheses are so ludicrous as to be beyond the bounds of rational discussion. And yet in the cases of Duleepsinhji and D'Oliveira, English cricket was being asked to take the field with sides selected by their opponents. The Ranji and Hendricks incidents merely made the cricket ridiculous; the Duleep and D'Oliveira affairs made it impossible. The point is worth making because while the D'Oliveira argument was raging, it was not always easy for the protagonists to see where they were going. Some of the disputants even evoked Soviet Russia, asking why, if we could compete against one totalitarian state, we could not compete against another, overlooking the distinction that not even in its most rampant imperial mood did the Soviet regime dare to attempt to select the sides of foreign sporting challengers. Ethics apart, the case of D'Oliveira was the moment when politics had obtruded so far into sport as to have destroyed it utterly. In other words, although the D'Oliveira affair embodied a vital issue of political morality, it remained perfectly possible to reach conclusions about the crisis within a frame of reference which excluded politics altogether. When one side in a cricket match insists on the right to select both sides, then reality has degenerated into Mad Hatterism.

As the D'Oliveira affair, but not its implications, gradually faded from the immediate consciousness, lovers of the game were tempted to think that perhaps at last, having learned to live with one-day gaucherie and the intervention of governments in team selection, that nothing worse could happen. They were wrong. If the D'Oliveira affair was bitter and impassioned, it centred about a small group of men. The Packer Affair embroiled the entire cricketing world. It bought up entire teams, it spanned continents, it dismantled the first-class structures of four continents, and when at last it was taken into an English court of law, it routed its opponents with a casual ease which dismayed some administrators and reduced others to a lickspittle subservience which would once have seemed impossible. So far as English cricket was concerned, the fates were malignant indeed, because the Packer revolution was an Australian domestic argument which just happened to spill over into the embarrassed laps of Australia's cricketing opponents. Nor was the revolution about cricket, nor about the rights of players to move in a free market, nor about Trade Unionism nor about Restraint of Trade. It was about television, and the fact that the game could be turned on its head because of a fight between entrepreneurs looking for Ratings is an indication of what had happened to that wandering garrison now that the sanctuary of the castle no longer existed. When the Packer Case was over and the new lines of battle had subsided back into a more conventional landscape, the crowds were back inside the cricket grounds. At last the magic act had been performed.

But in the modern commercial world miracles usually have strings attached, and those attached to the new conditions in which cricket thrives may yet strangle it. For the nature of cricket has been altered so drastically that the nature of the audiences it attracts has altered with it. Many members of that new audience come to watch a fight to a finish rather than a cricket match. Very often they get it. Conduct on the field has become, in its own sly way, as loose as that of the people who pay for tickets. There are new charlatan techniques involving electronic gadgets purporting to measure pitch moisture but none which measure fatuousness. Cricket, like the world in which it is obliged to operate, has entered the New Age, and it would of course be unreasonable to expect it to resemble the old one. Indeed, the cricket-lover is sometimes pleasurably surprised to find how much of the old world does survive. English cricketers, like Englishmen generally, have altered their patterns of speech and behaviour since the days when monied eccentrics pedalled tricycles over

London Bridge, or camouflaged themselves in white night-shirts in the snowy dawn as they stalked partridge, or expressed a desire to be laid in the coffin wearing an umpire's coat and clutching a cricket ball. But it is doubtful if a purer fast bowling action has ever been seen that Dennis Lillee's, or a more comprehensive all-round genius than Sir Garfield Sobers', or a more awesome spectacle than Ian Botham on a good day. The period encompassed by this volume saw the apotheosis of John Arlott, a poet whose radio commentaries elevated a useful social function to an English art form; they saw the passing of the most gifted prose master ever to turn his attention to the game, Sir Neville Cardus; they saw, in Zaheer and Barry Richards and Vivian Richards and Graeme Pollock, some of the greatest batsmen of the century, and in Michael Holding, Imran Khan, and Lillee and Thomson some of the greatest bowlers. They saw a last late flowering of the old patrician style in the beauty of Ted Dexter's style, the advent of one of the most comprehensive of all all-rounders in Michael Procter, and the inspired Pure Reason of captaincy in the person of Michael Brearley.

And as a valedictory, there are the Obituaries, through whose paragraphs there echoes the march of the generations. The last of the Fosters passes on. One cricketer is assassinated, another dies while shovelling snow. Hobbs, Hammond, Grimmett, John Barton King, oddest of all great cricketers in that he lived on the wrong continent, Rhodes, Strudwick, Woolley, all of them pass on in an age preoccupied with slow-motion reruns and paperback residuals. I am particularly attached to the character of the Lieutenant-Colonel whose big hitting was so destructive that the pavilion at High Wycombe exhibited a photograph of the damage he had inflicted. But there are three other moments in this volume which symbolise the unchanging wellsprings of the game. Two are obituaries, one a forgotten fact. Among the deaths will be found that of the divine whose religious status helped his bowling figures, and the bizarre follower of the game whose greatest pleasure it was to go "prowling on the field of play" while the cricket was in progress. The third and last whimsicality worth remarking concerns that very first one-day match between Lancashire and Leicestershire. Because of rain it lasted two days.

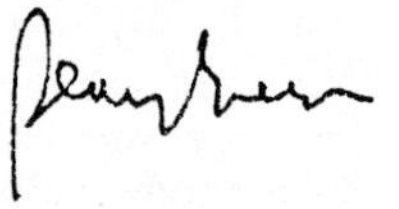

THE PLEASURES OF READING WISDEN [1964]

By Rowland Ryder

As my father was secretary of the Warwickshire County Cricket Club from 1895 to 1944, it is not altogether surprising that the game was a frequent topic of conversation at the family meal table: cricket was our bread and butter.

Reaching double figures in the early 1920s, I naturally heard a good deal about the achievements of Hobbs and Sutcliffe, and, in the cricketless winters, learnt from my father, and from the yellow-backed pages of *Wisden*, about Grace and Spofforth; "Ranji" and Fry and Jessop; Blackham and Lilley; and, of course, "My Hornby and my Barlow long ago". I knew about the cricketing giants of the past before I had learnt about Gladstone and Disraeli, and, looking back on those days of enchantment, and with all respect to those eminent statesmen, I have no regrets.

We had in our living-room a formidable Victorian bookcase, its shelves protected by glass shutters. In one of these shelves, overspilling into a second, were editions of *Wisden*, in strict chronological order – and woe betide anyone who took out a copy and put it back into the wrong place: a bad school report might on some rare occasion be forgiven, but to cause havoc in the thin yellow line of *Wisdens* – that was another matter!

It was always a red letter day for me when our stock was increased by a new volume, and father announced "I've got the new *Wisden*!" with the same quiet pride that Disraeli – whom I eventually did get to hear about – would have announced that he had secured shares in the Suez Canal. My excited request to peruse the magic pages was always countered by my father with dark allusions to homework; but the reply deceived neither of us, for we both knew that he wanted to read *Wisden* first.

We all have our foibles about the Almanack. For each, of course, his own county. We study our own side's home matches times without number, paying scant attention to the achievements of the other counties. Sir Arthur Conan Doyle, who played for the MCC and for Sussex, who had "W.G." as one of his victims, and who wrote *The Missing Three-quarter*, might well have written a cricket detective story, entitled, say, *The Missing Mid-on*. It would go perhaps something like this.

"Did you not observe, my dear Watson, that in the library were 37 editions of *Wisden*?"

This makes Watson forget the Afghan campaign. "By heavens, Holmes, then the man was possibly interested in cricket?"

"More than that, my dear Watson. I noticed that in all these editions the home matches of Loamshire were heavily thumbed. This puts me on the scent of the miscreant." The possibilities seem endless!

Sherlock Holmes, in any case, is not unconnected with *Wisden*. In the Births and Deaths section of earlier editions will be found the names of Shacklock, F. (Derbyshire, Nottinghamshire and Otago) and Mycroft, Thomas (Derbyshire), who inspired Conan Doyle to use the names Sherlock and Mycroft Holmes for his detective stories. Perhaps Sir Arthur played against them: certainly the line "Doyle, Sir A. C. (MCC) b. May 22, 1859" appeared for many years in *Wisden*. Incidentally, could not space be found for the famous though fictitious Raffles in the Births and Deaths? He would enjoy being on the same page as Ranjitsinhji!

For each, too, his favourite editions of *Wisden*. If I were permitted to take eight editions of the Almanack with me to some remote desert island, I would find the task of selection an extremely difficult one. To choose the first half-dozen, recording the most absorbing of the England v Australia Test match series, would be a tricky enough problem in all conscience.

What of the final pair? The first of all the *Wisdens*? – the current issue? – the copies recounting Warwickshire's Championship triumphs of 1911 and 1951? – the 1915 edition, in which batsmen were laconically recorded as "Absent" during the fateful first week in August? – how does one choose only a couple from these?

But if on my desert island I could have one *Wisden* and one only, then there be not the faintest tremor of hesitation: I would plump for the issue of 1903, recording that superb vintage year (1902) when the Australians came over with Darling, Trumper, Noble, Clem Hill and Warwick Armstrong, and when, during the course of the series, the English selectors could actually leave out G. L. Jessop, C. B. Fry and Ranjitsinhji, from sides that were to do battle for England.

This, the fortieth edition of *Wisden*, informs us of marquees to be bought for £10, tents for £5, lawn tennis nets for five shillings. Lord Harris eulogises Bartlett's "Repercussive" cricket bats, on sale at prices varying from nine and six to a guinea. Cricket balls can be bought for tenpence, leg guards for three and six. Peru House Private Hotel, Russell Square (for convenience, quietude, comfort and economy) offers Bedroom and Meat Breakfast for four and six.

The real feast, of course, is provided in the Test match accounts. Of the first Test match, played at Edgbaston, on Thursday, Friday and Saturday, May 29, 30 and 31, the *Wisden* chronicler writes most evocatively, and many authorities have since considered that the team that played for England in this game was the greatest ever to represent the Mother Country – A. C. MacLaren, C. B. Fry, K. S. Ranjitsinhji, F. S. Jackson, J. T. Tyldesley, A. A. Lilley, G. H. Hirst, G. L. Jessop, L. C. Braund, W. H. Lockwood, W. Rhodes.

"A beautiful wicket had been prepared," says *Wisden*, "and when MacLaren beat Darling in the toss for innings, it was almost taken for granted that England would make a big score. In the end expectation was realised, but success came only after a deplorable start, and after the Australians had discounted their chances by two or three palpable blunders in the field. Fry was caught by the wicket-keeper standing back in the third over; a misunderstanding for which Ranjitsinhji considered himself somewhat unjustly blamed, led to MacLaren being run out, and then Ranjitsinhji himself, quite upset by what had happened, was clean bowled, three of the best English wickets being thus down for 35 runs."

England recovered and finished the day with 351 for 9, Tyldesley scoring 138 and Jackson 53. Owing to rain the game did not commence until 3 o'clock on the second day. "Some people expected", continues *Wisden*, "that MacLaren would at once declare the English innings closed, but acting, it was understood, on Lilley's advice, he decided to let his own side go on batting for a time, so that his bowlers might not have to start work on a slippery foothold. He declared when the score had been raised to 376 and then followed one of the chief sensations of the cricket season of 1902, the Australians being got rid of in less than an hour and a half for 36, Trumper, who played fine cricket for seventy minutes, alone making a stand." Trumper made 18. Wilfred Rhodes returned the extraordinary figures:

O	M	R	W
11	3	17	7

In 1961, when Australia were batting against England once again at Edgbaston, I had the privilege of meeting Wilfred Rhodes, sole survivor of the twenty-two players in that struggle of 1902, and observed that we sorely needed his 7 for 17.

"Ah, yes," said Wilfred Rhodes reflectively, "you know how we got them out, don't you? We changed over!" Len Braund, who made an immortal slip catch to dismiss Clem Hill, had bowled one over to allow Hirst (3 for 15) and Rhodes to change ends. Following on, the Australians had scored eight for no wicket at close of play.

Writing in *Wisden*, 1936 (Trials of a County Secretary) the writer's father has this to say about the third day: "Torrents of rain fell overnight, and at 9 a.m. the ground was a complete lake. Not a square yard of turf was visible and play was, of course, out of the question that day. The head groundsman agreed; I paid off half my gatemen and dispensed with the services of half the police. It proved to be a 'penny wise pound foolish' action. The umpires arrived; the players arrived – the captains were there. I have never known any men more patient, more hopeful than those umpires and captains. They just sat still and said nothing most effectively. At two o'clock the sun came out and a great crowd assembled outside the ground. What I hadn't thought of was that two umpires and two captains would sit and wait so long without making a decision. The crowd broke in, and to save our skins we started play at 5.20 on a swamp." The game ended as a draw with Australia 46 for 2.

The second Test match, says *Wisden*, was "utterly ruined by rain", the third "a severe disaster for England" and we lost by 143 runs. Of the last agonizing over in the fourth Test, when England had nine wickets down and eight to win, *Wisden* relates: "Tate got a four on the leg-side from the first ball he received from Saunders, but the fourth, which came a little with the bowler's arm and kept low, hit the wicket and the match was over."

For the fifth Test match Ranjitsinhji was left out! England, set 263 to win, were saved by G. L. Jessop with possibly the most superb innings of his life. "He scored", says *Wisden*, "in just over an hour and a quarter, 104 runs out of 139, his hits being a five in the slips, seventeen 4s, two 3s, four 2s and seventeen singles." Hirst and Rhodes, the last pair, scored the necessary fifteen runs to win. It was of this occasion that the apocryphal story "We'll get them in singles, Wilfred!" is told. *Wisden*, preferring accuracy to romance, records "Rhodes sent a ball from Trumble between the bowler and mid-on, and England won the match by one wicket."

Yorkshire's victory over the Australians, who were dismissed for 23 in their second innings, is described as "a big performance"; an Australian victory over Gloucestershire is chronicled in a burst of Edwardian prose – "the Colonials had no great difficulty in beating the western county in a single innings"; and of a match against Surrey we are told "Trumper and Duff hit up 142 in an hour and a quarter" – this against Richardson and Lockwood! The historian is chatty and informative about the match with Cambridge University. "So greatly were the Australians weakened by illness that they had to complete their side by playing Dr R. J. Pope, a cricketer, who it will be remembered, appeared several times for H. J. H. Scott's eleven in 1886. Dr Pope came over from Australia for a holiday mainly to see the cricket, and was a sort of general medical adviser to the eleven." Anyway, he made 2 not out!

The 1923 edition contains the saga of the Warwickshire–Hampshire match at Edgbaston; surely the most extraordinary game of county cricket ever played. Warwickshire, batting first, were out for a mediocre 223 on a good wicket. They then proceeded to dismiss their opponents in 53 balls for 15. The analyses of Howell and Calthorpe speak for themselves:

	O	M	R	W
Howell	4.5	2	7	6
Calthorpe	4	3	4	4

Hampshire followed on, and lost 6 wickets for 186. However, as *Wisden* observes, "Brown batted splendidly for four hours and three-quarters and Livsey made his first hundred without a mistake." Brown made 172, and Livsey 110 not out; Hampshire made 521, got Warwickshire out for 158 and won by 155 runs. "The victory, taken as a whole", says *Wisden*, "must surely be without precedent in first-class cricket." And has there been anything like it since?

Not along ago I had the good fortune to discuss the match with the late George Brown in his house at Winchester, where, appropriately enough, a framed score-card of the conflict hung in the hall. He contended that Hampshire should have been out for 7 in their first innings, explaining that "Tiger" Smith, while unsighted, had let a ball go for four byes, and that Lionel Tennyson was missed at mid-on, the ball then travelling to the boundary.

The chief joy of reading *Wisden* is also the chief snare – once you have picked up a copy you cannot put it down. How many wives have become grass-widowed on account of the limp-covered, yellow-backed magician it is impossible to say.

A teasing problem crops up – when was W.G.'s birthday? Who captained the Australians in 1909? Who won the championship in 1961? "I won't be a minute", says the cricket enthusiast, "I'll just look it up in *Wisden*" – and he disappears in search of his treasures. And, of course, he isn't a minute: he may be away for an hour or for the rest of the day. He may even never return.

There is one thing that you can be quite certain of in "looking it up in *Wisden*" and that is that you will pick up a whole miscellany of information before you find the thing you have been looking for.

Suppose, for instance, that you want to look up the match between Kent and Derbyshire at Folkestone in 1963. You pick up your *Wisden* for 1964, open it at random, believing firmly that the problem will be solved in a matter of seconds, and you find yourself confronted with a Lancashire-Yorkshire match at Old Trafford.

The result is a draw. Forgetting now altogether about Kent and Derbyshire at Folkestone, you next turn up the Table of Main Contents to see if you can find out how Yorkshire and Lancashire have fared over the years in their Roses battles. On skimming down the Table of Contents, however, you come across a heading about Test Cricketers (1877-1963). This immediately starts you off on a new track, and you turn to the appropriate section to find how many cricketers have played for their country. The names Clay, Close, Coldwell, Compton, Cook, Copson leap up at you from the printed page: memories of past Test matches dance in bright kaleidoscopic colours before you. *Wisden*, you feel, is as exciting as a Buchan thriller. The word "Buchan" leads logically enough to Midwinter.

Midwinter – of course! – now, didn't he play for England v Australia, and also for Australia v England? Research confirms that such was indeed the case. You look him up in Births and Deaths; but this entails searching an earlier edition. At random you select the issue for 1910; and sailing purposefully past an offer on page 3 of a free sample of Oatine (for Men after Shaving) you find that Midwinter, W. E. was also a regular player for Gloucestershire and for Victoria. Meanwhile, you have hit upon another Test match series.

In the first of this series of Tests England were trying out a twenty-six year old opening batsman named Hobbs (Cambridgeshire and Surrey). He made a "duck" in his first innings, but did better in the second. "England wanted 105 to win, and as it happened, Hobbs and Fry hit off the runs in an hour and a half without being separated."

There are now two tracks that lie ahead. You can follow the Australians on their tour, to find that they won the Ashes but came close to defeat against Sussex and Somerset, and also played some unusual sides – Western Union (Scotland), South Wales, two rain-ridden draws against combined Yorkshire and Lancashire elevens, and, towards the end of the tour, Mr. Bamford's eleven at Uttoxeter.

The other track, of course, is the golden trail of the Master's 197 centuries!

Wisden's attractions are endless. A county cricketer of former days recently told me how much he enjoyed browsing over the Public Schools averages "So that I can see how my friends' sons are getting on."

Even the briefer obituaries are always interesting to read, and, when occasion demands, amusing – as surely obituaries should be. To return again to the 1903 edition, we read of the Reverend Walter Fellows, described in Scores and Biographies as "a tremendous fast round-armed bowler". For Westminster against Rugby (1852) he took nine wickets in the first innings and six in the second. However, in the course of so doing he bowled 30 wides, "thereby giving away as many runs as Westminster made in their two innings combined". In 1856 he hit a ball 175 yards "from hit to pitch. . . . In 1863 he emigrated to Australia, and joined the Melbourne Club the following year. He was interested in the game to the last. Height 5 ft. 11 ins., and playing weight as much as 16 st. 4 lbs."

And again, in the 1961 edition there is the superb obituary of Alec Skelding. Of the many selected tales *Wisden* recounts of him, perhaps this is the loveliest: "In a game in 1948 he turned down a strong appeal by the Australian touring team. A little later a dog ran on to the field, and one of the Australians captured it, carried it to Skelding and said: 'Here you are. All you want now is a white stick!'"

Wisden is indeed better than rubies. *Wisden* is an inexhaustible gold mine in which lies embedded the golden glory of a century of cricketing summers. In the 1964 edition (page 1024) we read the brief statement "*Wisden* for cricket". I think that sums it up.

NOTES BY THE EDITOR, 1964

Wisden itself made an indelible contribution to the summer by the appearance on April 19 of the 100th edition of "The Cricketers' Bible". The newspapers, television and sound radio were lavish in their praise and they treated it as a national event. I don't think I am giving away any secrets when I say that even the publisher was surprised by the public demand for the Almanack. It ran into three impressions by the printers before everyone was satisfied. Naturally, *Wisden*, which specializes in cricket facts and records, established its own record of sales.

The firm of John Wisden and Co. Ltd. commemorated the event by launching The Wisden Trophy, with the approval of MCC and the West Indies Cricket Board of Control, to be played for perpetually between England and West Indies in the same way as England and Australia contest the Ashes. West Indies have become the first holders of the trophy, which is being kept permanently in the Imperial Cricket Museum at Lord's. All the members of the West Indies touring team received a silver replica and, as a personal souvenir to mark the efforts of the Editor, the directors of the firm presented me with a replica suitably inscribed. It has a prominent place in my home and is something I and my family will always treasure.

BETTER CRICKET COMPETITION

The *Daily Express* treated the One Hundredth Edition of *Wisden* generously by launching a Better Cricket Competition. It was possibly the widest inquiry on cricket conducted during the lifetime of the Almanack. Their readers were invited to make five suggestions to improve cricket. The top entry received tickets for one of the Tests between England and West Indies and one hundred others each received a copy of the hundredth *Wisden*. Three judges, D. J. Insole, A. V. Bedser and myself, shared the task of perusing over 2,000 letters and we were astonished at the quality of the comments these contained. An analysis showed that the reformers wanted:

(1) A return to bonus points for faster run-rates.
(2) Sunday cricket – after church – plus two divisions with promotion and relegation.
(3) Limitation of time, or overs, for first innings in county games and cash bonuses for wins and 6-hits.
(4) Permission for overseas stars to play immediately – one per county – and a speed-up of over-rates to 19 or 20 an hour.
(5) Batsmen to be given out for deliberate pad play.
(6) The elimination of all types of time-wasting by (a) limiting the fast bowlers' run up to 15 paces and (b) increasing the overs to eight or 10 balls.

In the opinion of the judges, the most constructive letter came from Mr H. Ball, of Worcester. This was his letter:

My five suggestions to improve cricket for the spectators are as follows:

(1) In addition to the Championship Shield there should also be a Runners-up Trophy, and the award of talent money for third place.
(2) Bonus points for first-innings lead.
(3) A minimum number of overs per hour's average. I suggest 19.
(4) A maximum distance fixed for a bowler's run-up to the wicket.
(5) Disciplinary action where players waste time deliberately to prevent the other side winning. Add time wasted.

I suggest that 1, 3, 4 and 5 should be implemented immediately. They would create more interest within the clubs having little hope of the Championship and prevent sides trying to gain an unfair advantage when going for a win.

Spectators would enjoy the game being speeded up and the wider competition would attract more.

All three judges agreed that the great need in the modern game was to eliminate time-wasting.

AUSTRALIANS IN ENGLAND

ENGLAND v AUSTRALIA

Fourth Test Match

Played at Old Trafford, July 23, 24, 25, 27, 28, 1964

For all the remarkable personal achievements in the match, a bad taste was left in the mouth of the cricket enthusiasts who saw Australia retain the Ashes. Simpson's strategy, with his team one up and two to play, was to make certain that Australia did not lose. Dexter, with England kept in the field until the third morning was well advanced, had no hope of winning and so a boring situation resulted in which twenty-eight and a quarter hours of play were needed to produce a decision on the first innings! Both sides were to blame for frequent periods of needlessly tiresome batting on a perfectly-made closely-cut firm pitch of placid pace which gave neither quick nor spin bowlers the slightest help. The intention to win was never once apparent after Simpson, for the first time in the series, won the toss, and only rarely were the justifiable expectations of the spectators for entertainment realized.

The match yielded these records:

Lawry and Simpson made 201 for the first wicket – an Australian record against England. *The previous best was 180 by W. Bardsley and S. E. Gregory in the Fifth Test at The Oval, 1909.*

Simpson's score of 311 was the highest ever made at Old Trafford.

His innings, lasting twelve and three-quarter hours, was the longest ever played against England. *It beat F. M. Worrell's 197 not out in eleven hours and twenty minutes in the First Test at Bridgetown, Barbados, January, 1960.*

Australia's total of 656 for eight declared and England's 611 were their highest at Old Trafford.

Barrington's score of 256 was England's highest at Old Trafford.

Other notable performances were:

Simpson scored his first Test century in 30 matches.

Barrington made his first Test century in England after hitting nine abroad.

McKenzie took seven wickets for 153 in a total of 611.

Veivers bowled 95.1 overs, only 17 balls short of the record number of 588 balls bowled in an innings by S. Ramadhin for West Indies against England, at Birmingham, in 1957.

Australia made one change from their victorious Third Test team, bringing back O'Neill in place of Cowper, and England, who had to win to retain a chance of recovering the Ashes, took the drastic step of omitting Trueman and Cowdrey. The Selectors picked three seam bowlers – Cartwright and Rumsey were new to Test cricket – and two off-spin bowlers, and eventually left out M. J. K. Smith from the chosen twelve. Price played in his first Test in England.

What would have happened had Dexter won the toss can only be conjectured, for McKenzie, following a severe stomach upset a few days earlier, was not at his fittest. On the easy-paced turf Australia, setting themselves to build a formidable total to stop England winning, scored 253 for two wickets on the first day. There was no encouragement to bowlers from the opening delivery sent down by Rumsey to his rival left-hander Lawry, and although Cartwright, by control of length at medium-pace with some movement off the pitch occasionally worried the batsmen – he had Simpson when 33 missed at the wicket on the leg side – the attack posed no real danger. Lawry adept in hooking, took a 6 apiece off Price, Cartwright and Rumsey before hitting his first four with his score at 64, but the stroke-play generally was far from forceful.

Methodically, the batsmen wore down the toiling bowlers in sunshine. Titmus had a long bowl, but Dexter who set largely defensive fields did not employ Mortimore until twenty past three with the score 173 and Lawry, with a cover-drive off the Gloucestershire bowler, reached his third hundred against England out of 179 in five minutes under four hours. His sound, but unenterprising innings, ended three-quarters of an hour later when, for the third time in Tests in the current series, and for the fifth time in the season, he was run out when Mortimore, the bowler, made a brilliant stop. The partnership produced 201, and Lawry included five 4s besides the three 6s, in his 106.

Dexter, for the first time, crowded the batsmen when Redpath arrived, but Simpson, after five and a half hours at the crease with only six 4s among his neat but far from strong strokes, completed his century out of 232. Cartwright gained reward for his steadiness when beating Redpath off the pitch for leg-before at 233. At the close Australia were 253 for two with Simpson 109, and O'Neill 10.

On the second day, Simpson and his colleagues maintained their dominance yet seldom became free-scoring. Simpson again batted in subdued, if almost faultless, fashion and was barracked before displaying some of his characteristic cuts and drives. O'Neill had given promise of brightening proceedings before a ball which swung across knocked back his leg-stump at 318. Burge did not settle down before Price smartly caught him at backward square leg at 382. From that point, at ten minutes to three, the England bowlers strove without compensation.

In company with Booth, Simpson, who had reached 160 at rather less than 20 an hour since he began, at last decided to open his shoulders. He took 11 in an over off Price with the new ball, but soon reverted to his sedate mood. When 203, Simpson could have been run out backing-up if Titmus, about to bowl, had not been chivalrously inclined, and the Middlesex bowler inappropriately suffered when the Australian captain, bestirring himself again, hit 14 off him in one over. At the end of another hot day, Simpson had been in twelve hours for 265 out of a score of 570 for four, and Booth, who had scored with firm strokes, was 82 in an unfinished partnership of 188. Cartwright, England's best bowler, had sent down 77 overs for 118 runs and two wickets.

Simpson continued Australia's and his own innings next morning and in the light of subsequent events his policy, however, unpalatable it was to cricket lovers, proved correct. Had he declared the previous evening and managed to snatch a couple of wickets a way to victory might have been open to him, but that again is mere surmise. In the event, Simpson made sure that Australia would not lose by extending his team's innings for another hour and raising the total to 656 for eight before declaring. In that time, the batting, for the first time in the match, was consistently entertaining, bringing 86 runs for four wickets.

Simpson had a chance of passing the world record Test score of 365 not out by G. S. Sobers, but this did not affect his attitude. He made no attempt to play safe for the purpose and after straight-driving Mortimore for 6 and hitting four more 4s he fell at the wicket paying the penalty for a slashed stroke played off Price with rather reckless abandon. The crowd, having overlooked the dull spells of his batting, generously gave him an ovation for his score of 311 out of 646 for six. He defied England for three minutes under twelve and three-quarter hours, and in addition to his 6 he hit twenty-three 4s. His stand with Booth, fifth to leave, well caught off a stiff return at 601, added 219 in just over three and a half hours. Booth, who missed a hundred by two, hit one 6 and ten 4s. The innings lasted thirteen hours. Price took three for 183. He, like his team-mates, had his edge blunted by the unresponsive pitch. Barrington, with his leg-breaks, was never tried, a tactical shortcoming by Dexter.

When England began batting at twenty to one on Saturday, there seemed little hope of them making 457 to avoid following-on, and what optimism did exist soon received a check when Edrich edged the now full-recovered fast-medium McKenzie to second slip with the score 15. Then came a renewal of hope with Boycott and Dexter driving and cutting excellently. Simpson unavailingly challenged Dexter with spin and flight and the second wicket brought 111 before Boycott, having stayed three hours, played too soon at a slower ball from McKenzie and was bowled.

A shaky start sent Barrington into his shell and Dexter, too, became so restrained that slow handclapping broke out. At one stage Barrington's disinclination to make a forcing stroke encouraged Simpson to employ four short-legs, for Veivers. With the score carried to 162 for two, Dexter 71 and Barrington 20, bad light stopped play fifty minutes early – a disappointing end to the day for a crowd of 30,000.

Wanting 295 more to make Australia bat again, England had by far their best day on Monday when Dexter carried his score to 174 and Barrington reached 153 not out. Dexter, who hit his eighth Test hundred, was missed twice by McKenzie at backward short leg when 74 and 97, and narrowly escaped being given out at 108 when Burge said he did not really know whether he had made a catch low down at cover, but the later part of Dexter's innings provided much pleasure for the onlookers. From lunch, taken at 247 for two, the batsmen were masters. In turn they forced the game with drives, square-cuts, late-cuts and full-blooded leg-side strokes which punished quick and slow bowlers alike. Poor fielding swelled the scoring and Barrington was fortunate, when 99, that McKenzie, at short-slip failed to hold a cut.

Barrington had played 44 Test innings in England without making more than 87. In one spell of ten overs, Simpson conceded 38 runs and the partnership passed 200 in ten minutes over four hours. Dexter, with a majestic cover-drive off Veivers, exceeded K. S. Ranjitsinhji's 154 not out for England at Old Trafford in 1896, and at tea, with 111 runs having come since lunch, England wanted 99 more to save the follow-on.

Afterwards, England's rising hopes received an unexpected setback in the dismissal of Dexter, third out, at 372. Hawke and Veivers, doing sufficient to keep the batsmen watchful, made runs scarce enough to set impatient onlookers slow handclapping, and whether or not Dexter had his concentration disturbed he eventually played across, in somewhat casual style, at a ball pitched well up to him and was bowled. He, too, was given an ovation for his fine innings, including twenty-two 4s, for which he had kept the Australians at bay for eight hours. The stand of 246 in five hours and twenty-five minutes fell 16 short of the record England third-wicket partnership against Australia of 262 by W. R. Hammond and D. R. Jardine at Adelaide in 1928-29.

Barrington suffered a painful blow on his left shoulder from a bouncer by Corling, but recovered after treatment on the field and he remained unbeaten, with fifteen 4s to his credit, at the close when England, 411 for three, needed 46 more to make Australia go in again.

The fifth and last day proved the most disappointing for England supporters, for lack of enterprise by the batsmen when conditions were all in their favour threw away a golden chance of passing the massive Australian total. Dexter's example counted for nothing. Barrington pushed and deflected when he could have driven powerfully and the opportunity to encourage his partners and thoroughly discourage his rivals was lost. Parks hit only three 4s in his 60 which occupied three hours and twenty minutes, Titmus made nine runs in almost an hour and when Barrington was lbw, seventh to go, at 594 he had been at the crease for eleven hours and twenty-five minutes. He hit twenty-six 4s in his 256.

With McKenzie enlivened and Veivers still pitching a length, the issue was soon settled after Barrington's departure on the stroke of tea, and England, though having kept Australia in the field over two hours longer than the tourists had kept them, finished 45 behind. McKenzie's late successes, achieved by change of pace and deceptive movement, gave him a fine analysis in such a huge total, but the endurance of Veivers, who sent down 46.1 overs unchanged on the last day, was just as remarkable.

The Australians had to bat a second time for the closing five minutes, and it was a suitable ending, seeing what indecisive cricket had gone before, that Simpson and Lawry were bowled to by Barrington and Titmus using an old ball. Simpson, who square-cut Barrington for the four runs obtained, was on the field for all but a quarter of an hour of the match which, over the five days, was watched by an estimated attendance of 108,00(who paid £36,340 3s. 6d. On the second afternoon, Mr Harold Wilson, Leader of th(Opposition, was present and next evening Sir Alec Douglas Home, the Prime Minister saw some cricket. No interruption occurred through rain during the match which took place in almost unbroken sunny weather.

Australia

W. M. Lawry run out	106	– not out (
*R. B. Simpson c Parks b Price	311	– not out 4
I. R. Redpath lbw b Cartwright	19	
N. C. O'Neill b Price	47	
P. J. Burge c Price b Cartwright	34	
B. C. Booth c and b Price	98	
T. R. Veivers c Edrich b Rumsey	22	
*A. T. W. Grout c Dexter b Rumsey	0	
G. D. McKenzie not out	0	
B 1, l-b 9, n-b 9	19	
1/201 2/233 3/318 4/382 5/601 6/646 7/652 8/656	(8 wkts dec.) 656	(no wkt) 4

N. J. N. Hawke and G. E. Corling did not bat.

Bowling: *First Innings*—Rumsey 35.5–4–99–2; Price 45–4–183–3; Cartwright 77–32–118–2; Titmus 44–14–100–0; Dexter 4–0–12–0; Mortimore 49–13–122–0; Boycott 1–0–3–0. *Second Innings*—Barrington 1–0–4–0; Titmus 1–1–0–0.

England

G. Boycott b McKenzie	58
J. H. Edrich c Redpath b McKenzie	6
*E. R. Dexter b Veivers	174
K. F. Barrington lbw b McKenzie	256
P. H. Parfitt c Grout b McKenzie	12
†J. M. Parks c Hawke b Veivers	60
F. J. Titmus c Simpson b McKenzie	9
J. B. Mortimore c Burge b McKenzie	12
T. W. Cartwright b McKenzie	4
J. S. E. Price b Veivers	1
F. E. Rumsey not out	3
B 5, l-b 11	16
1/15 2/126 3/372 4/417 5/560 6/589 7/594 8/602 9/607	611

Bowling: McKenzie 60–15–153–7; Corling 46–11–96–0; Hawke 63–28–95–0; Simpson 19–4–59–0; Veivers 95.1–36–155–3; O'Neill 10–0–37–0.

Umpires: J. S. Buller and W. F. Price.

KENT v AUSTRALIANS

Played at Canterbury, August 17, 18, 19, 1968

The Australians won by nine wickets. Kent, having won the toss and elected to bat made a bad start, losing their first two wickets for eight runs. After McKenzie had got rid of Denness, Freeman and Connolly had half the side out for 112. Shepherd, however, came to the rescue. He hit hard and reached his 50 in seventy-six minutes, finally claiming fourteen boundaries in his very useful innings. The best support came from Leary, most of the other batsmen being troubled by Gleeson's spin. On the Sunday the tourists entertained the crowd with some attractive batting, and McKenzie reached his 50 in seventy-four minutes, hitting two 6s and seven 4s. When Kent batted again, McKenzie started them on the slide and Gleeson once more proved troublesome. The Australians were left to score 44 to win, a task they easily accomplished.

Kent

M. H. Denness lbw b McKenzie	2	– lbw b McKenzie	37
B. W. Luckhurst c Chappell b Connolly	21	– c Taber b McKenzie	9
Asif Iqbal c Taber b Freeman	0	– c Taber b McKenzie	10
*M. C. Cowdrey lbw b Connolly	17	– c Taber b Gleeson	20
J. N. Shepherd c Chappell b Freeman	84	– lbw b Chappell	25
†A. P. E. Knott c Taber b Freeman	18	– lbw b Gleeson	22
S. E. Leary lbw b Gleeson	39	– lbw b Gleeson	15
D. L. Underwood b Gleeson	8	– c Inverarity b Gleeson	0
A. L. Dixon c Taber b Gleeson	6	– c Walters b Gleeson	5
A. Brown not out	8	– c Taber b Connolly	1
J. N. Graham st Taber b Gleeson	0	– not out	0
L-b 3, n-b 4	7	B 1, l-b 3, n-b 4	8
1/3 2/8 3/38 4/51 5/112 6/165 7/186 8/194 9/204	210	1/13 2/23 3/63 4/85 5/121 6/134 7/138 8/147 9/148	152

Bowling: *First Innings*—McKenzie 16–7–33–1; Freeman 19–6–41–3; Connolly 20–11–53–2; Gleeson 25.2–10–61–4; Chappell 3–0–15–0. *Second Innings*—McKenzie 15–4–44–3; Freeman 11–1–38–0; Connolly 9–4–18–1; Gleeson 16.3–4–29–5; Chappell 5–2–15–1.

Australians

*W. M. Lawry c Luckhurst b Shepherd	46		
R. J. Inverarity run out	17	– not out	14
I. R. Redpath b Dixon	18	– not out	14
I. M. Chappell c Knott b Brown	57		
K. D. Walters c Asif b Graham	3	– c Shepherd b Graham	16
A. P. Sheahan lbw b Dixon	46		
E. W. Freeman c Denness b Dixon	37		
†H. B. Taber c Leary b Shepherd	29		
G. D. McKenzie c Asif b Shepherd	50		
J. W. Gleeson c Knott b Shepherd	0		
A. N. Connolly not out	7		
B 1, l-b 8	9		
1/44 2/65 3/107 4/124 5/161 6/229 7/229 8/292 9/296	319	1/27	(1 wkt.) 44

Bowling: *First Innings*—Graham 18–3–58–1; Brown 20–4–53–1; Dixon 18–3–72–3; Shepherd 12.4–0–47–4; Underwood 14–1–50–0; Leary 2–0–13–0; Asif 3–0–17–0 *Second Innings*—Graham 7–2–20–1; Brown 7–0–24–0.

Umpires: J. Arnold and O. W. Herman

WELCOME AUSTRALIA [1972]

By E. R. Dexter

No English cricketer bred since the war has so captured the imagination of those inside, outside and far from the boundary ropes of our big cricket grounds than Ted Dexter, stated Wisden *in his biography in the 1961 edition. He was captain of Cambridge University, Sussex and England and he led England in the quest for the Ashes in Australia in 1962-63 and here at home in 1964. It is a privilege to air his views on the past, present and future of this great game and to thank him for not dwelling on what who did to whom! – N.P.*

I have on occasions taken a quite unreasonable dislike to Australians. Sorry, but it is the truth. And if I blush at the thought, let alone the telling of it publicly, I derive a certain amount of comfort from the knowledge that I am not alone amongst England's cricketers in my feelings, highly reprehensible though they of course are.

Given suitable circumstances – and there can be few so absolutely right for a spot of disliking than a Test match between us Pommies and our most respected cricketing foes – the opposition from down under. Whether players, partisan spectators or mere uncommitted natives of that distant continent, can without much effort it seems either on their part or ours, change radically from the affable earthy folk they most times are into creatures every bit as dreadful as the Hydra; as multi-headed and indestructible now as the day when Hercules received a helping hand from Iolaus to despatch the brute.

The story goes that Iolaus stopped new heads from growing by applying a burning iron to the wound as each neck was severed – oh! would that in moments of severe temptation I had had such an iron readily to hand and coals to heat it! I would have shown less mercy than an IRA Provisional or a guerrilla of Bangladesh, I can tell you.

Entirely irrational I know. But I take further comfort from having long ago learned that this barbaric level of response is not entirely directed from us to them.

Under provocation no greater certainly than is needed to stimulate our own aggression Australians can, and do, quite readily and often in my experience, throw off all their 180 years of civilised nationhood; they gaily revive every prejudice they ever knew, whether to do with accent, class consciousness or even the original "convict" complex, and sally forth into battle with a dedication which would not disgrace the most committed of the world's political agitators.

To try to give adequate reasons for this intensity of reaction, as quick, positive and predictable a process as when photographic paper is first exposed to light, would be to attempt the arduous, if not the impossible. Psychology, history, politics, sport, religion and many factors besides would need thorough investigation.

However, I cannot help feeling that an almost complete lack of guilt on both sides is a primary cause.

Like puppies from the same litter we feel perfectly entitled to knock hell out of one another for as long as we like, until passions burn themselves low and we continue once more, for a limited period, to display outward signs of peaceful co-existence.

The indisputable fact is that we come from the same stock and can therefore indulge ourselves rather splendidly in an orgy of superficial hate which neither our consciences, nor Panorama (whichever of them it was that came first) can possibly allow in relation to any of the other cricketing nations with whom we consort.

However much we may be infuriated by Indians: annoyed by Pakistanis: get angry with West Indians: niggle New Zealanders (who are just too much like our better selves for us to care about them so strongly): or get upset by South Africans (South Africans more than any): we are honour bound to maintain a more formal diplomatic front.

Not so with the "Diggers". Little, if anything, is sacrosanct in the feuding, and no point remains too small or insignificant not to be turned to advantage if humanly possible.

So what of this opportunity, golden as it clearly is, to implant a few fertile seeds of propagands in the path of the 1972 tourists?

"Welcome Australia" we say. Do we mean it? And if so is it just because we think we can beat them!? Answers? Probably yes on both counts.

Illingworth's side was never fully extended in Australia in 1970-71 and the general attitude is that advancing age will not be a sufficient hindrance over here to prevent the same somewhat venerable side from dishing out the same medicine again.

Let them bring all their old players, under whatever captain, and, furthermore, regardless of what happened in the series against a World 3rd XI, and they will still start second favourite, I'm afraid. I can hardly be more presumptuous than that and simply beg the printers of *Wisden* to use digestible paper in case I have to eat my words.

It is a relief to have the matter so cut and dried. Had it really been in the balance then I would have felt it my duty to compare in detail the relative merits of the two probable sides.

Can the Australian batsmen survive a fast bowling assault on our pitches better than they did on their own? Is John Snow still a force to be reckoned with? What of their new boy Dennis Lillee? Can he repeat his remarkable analysis at Perth during the winter?

Happily the whole thing is academic and I need not give the answers. Suffice to say that I personally hope to see instead a whole lot of new faces in both sides. Then the issue could be a live one.

It is extraordinary to me that some spectators take an opposite view. They want to see Bill Lawry & Co. over here again. They would like to bring everyone out of retirement and prove to themselves that the old players really were better than the current lot. I, on the other hand, shudder at the thought.

Not only at the theory being proved horribly wrong in most cases, but at the dismal prospect of knowing beforehand exactly what a good hundred from, say, Neil Harvey will look like; no better than seeing a film for the umpteenth time if he does happen to oblige, and merely leaving one with a vague sense of disappointment if he fails.

What thrills me is the performance which suddenly stamps a man as having a future ahead of him. And the less pre-publicity such a player receives the more striking the impact when it comes.

Nobody, for instance, had taken much notice of a certain Zaheer Abbas before the first Test against Pakistan played at Edgbaston in 1971. Gangly, bespectacled and too ready with a smile to promise much in the way of dedication to big scores, he dished out a double-hundred as though he was a teller in the bank – doing it every day.

That was the best of cricket watching for me, giving as it did a continuing and growing delight as the innings grew. Zaheer can, and probably will, play many more just as good as that one, but for me the clearest memory will be of that first impressive statement of his great ability.

I remember Seymour Nurse doing the very same thing in Barbados in 1959 – 213 for his Island against the full might of MCC including Trueman and Statham – although the pleasure was not without its painful side on that occasion since I had much of the bowling and fielding to do as well.

When last did this happen in an England side? Or, dare I say it, when last was anyone given a chance to prove that a touch of class and character can triumph in an international setting without giving more than the odd glimpse of itself in a more mundane setting?

I fear Australian selectors are becoming less adventurous also; less far sighted for instance than when they sent the raw Alan Davidson on his first tour in 1953, or the 20-year-old Graham McKenzie on his in 1961. By contrast, in their hour of need at Sydney last February they dropped Lawry, not for some bright youngster but for another left hander, Eastwood, of similar age and half the skill just because he had been "getting runs" in State matches.

We must hope that 1972 is not entirely given over to the Redpaths and Boycotts; that an Evonne Goolagong will do for Australian cricket what that gorgeously graceful young lady did for their tennis last year and that England selectors will be so carried away with the romance of the moment that they will actually pick someone under thirty years of age.

A special welcome is due surely to every Australian who is new to us over here and if he can show us what he can do without too much delay then he need not fear this pen being dilatory or grudging in recognising him.

The next question seems to me to ask ourselves just what sort of scene we are welcoming the visitors to.

It was back in 1964 that Bobby Simpson, the then Australian captain, went home to Australia and wrote about "Swinging England" in a cricketing sense.

The Gillette Cup had been christened the year before, it is true, and there was Cavaliers Cricket on television just beginning, but in all honesty there was precious little to justify such eager description of this minor breeze of change as it was then.

How the breeze became a fully fledged wind is a story worth telling on its own and is not my subject here. Its effect on the 1972 Australians is however pertinent.

As I write, the once great and now great again Lancashire County Cricket Club has disclosed an operating profit for 1971 of more than £20,000, ninety-nine per cent of which is directly due to their success in the one-day competitions.

Almost simultaneously the fixture list for the Australians is available in the MCC Diary and it is a shock to read the heading which states firmly that "unless otherwise stated, these matches are of three days' duration".

The only reference to one-day matches – there are the usual complement of five five-day Tests – is in respect of the mini-series against England in August, comprising three one-day "Tests".

This is a bold and well conceived plan to set international one-day cricket off on the right foot, but I can't help feeling that there should be an even greater response generally by the administration to the public's present appetite for quick-fire win or lose cricket, and in particular towards involving visiting teams more in our highly successful new structure.

The trouble with the Australian itinerary is that for more than half the time they will be playing what can only be considered "friendly" games with the counties. Not so long ago this gentlemanly basis of sporting competition was sufficient to keep the crowds amused but with the advent of sponsorship, win-money, man-of-the-match awards, etc., etc., the old format now seems hopelessly outmoded. Honour and glory, artistry and skills are now only given their due by your potential spectator if something depends on the outcome thereof. Not necessarily money; an extra point or two towards some goal may be quite acceptable. On the other hand a dozen or more games following one another in a pattern, each one played in a vacuum as on this tour, gives your cricket fan far too good an excuse to stay away if the weather is poor, if the star players are being rested or for any other minor reason.

The writing was on the wall last time Australia toured England. Since then Illingworth's team in Australia has signally failed to halt the trend of dwindling gates for State matches. In fact it seemed that neither the State sides nor the MCC could do more than go through the motions when there was literally nothing to play for. In no time at all the lack of interest on the field communicated itself to the watchers and I honestly think they swore to a man that they wouldn't be taken for suckers a second time.

Surely it is not beyond the wit of man to involve a visiting team in the hurly burly of our own competitions. Points would need to be averaged up to decide how the maverick side was placed in relation to the others – either this or a concerted attempt made to find sponsors to put up prize-money – or, the ultimate in daring, to put up the prizes and promote the matches from within cricket and thus gamble a little on achieving a better return.

Otherwise I fear a situation where already hard-worked county players will be ever more content to take it easy against the tourists; the tourists will be just practising for the Tests and only the hardiest of cricket-watchers will pay to see them do so.

I hate to sound so gloomy because, overall, I count myself the greatest enthusiast for cricket in all its many forms. I won't have a word said against the game whether it is played for four hours on a Sunday afternoon, village or county doesn't matter with me, or whether it is played for five days or a week. What does concern me is that whereas the good name of the game clearly depends on masses of ordinary people being given the opportunity to share that enthusiasm by following the game and watching it, at the same time chances are missed like open goals when it comes to encouraging them to do so.

I remember for instance how marginal a decision it was to hold a one-day match in Melbourne when the ill-fated Test was washed out there last winter.

One felt that but for the happy coincidence which brought the then President of MCC Sir Cyril Hawker, the Treasurer G. O. Allen, and Sir Donald Bradman, Chairman of the Australian Board, all to lunch together on the ground, there might so easily have been no such match arranged. As it was the circumstances were so novel that the England players found themselves committed to appearing without prior consultation or any agreement as to their pay! – but that was a small price to pay for the pleasure of seeing 40,000 spectators turn out for a match that could so easily have been stillborn.

To be fair, there has been one leap forward after another in recent years and those, like Billy Griffith, secretary of MCC who have been in the thick of all the changes have been pretty sound (other than in the handling of the International Cavaliers) in keeping pace with what has gone on. It's nice to be able to say so here, for had I been writing this in 1962 instead of 1972 I doubt I could have even found enough of interest to cover the pages this far.

As it is we can look forward now to a decade of rapid growth and some consolidation – including acceptance, perhaps, of the one-day game for what it is in itself without continuous comparison with the other forms of the game it has superseded.

That is my view of our own situation here in England. Maybe there are more difficult paths towards a flourishing game in other parts of the world.

I can't help thinking though that for the good of the game it will be a matter of some importance for the various countries who play the game to make some attempt at keeping in step with each other.

England may need to maintain longer games for longer than she would like in order to keep faith with India and Pakistan where they are still acceptable. By the same token Australia may perhaps consider with profit adapting her ways more quickly to ours.

There is clearly a long way to go yet before cricket can settle down again to anything like the calm and unruffled existence it led through the early part of the twentieth century, but at least so long as Australia and England continue to see eye to eye occasionally, in between these other eyeball to eyeball confrontations, then progress is reasonably assured.

ENGLAND v AUSTRALIA

Second Test Match

Played at Lord's, June 22, 23, 24, 26, 1972

Australia won by eight wickets on the fourth day with nine and a half hours to spare. So Australia soon avenged their defeat at Manchester in a contest which will be remembered as Massie's match. The 25-year-old fast bowler from Western Australia surpassed all Australian Test bowling records by taking sixteen wickets for 137 runs; in all Tests only J. C. Laker, nineteen for 90 for England against Australia in 1956 and S. F. Barnes, seventeen for 179 for England against South Africa in 1913-14, stand above him. Moreover, Massie performed this wonderful feat on his Test début, the previous best by a bowler on his first appearance for his country being as far back as 1890 when at The Oval, Frederick Martin, a left-arm slow to medium pacer from Kent, took twelve for 102 for England against Australia on a pitch that had been saturated by rain.

Not for the first time, particularly in recent years, England were badly let down by their specialist batsmen, who failed lamentably in all respects. From the start they allowed the Australian bowlers to take the initiative and their excessive caution met with fatal results. Illingworth won the toss for the seventh consecutive time and one must admit that the hard fast pitch – it remained true to the end – was ideal for men of pace. During the first three days, too, the atmosphere was heavy and ideally suited to swing. Massie maintained excellent length and direction and his late swing either way always troubled the England batsmen. The conditions would also have suited Arnold, but England's best bowler at Manchester was suffering from hamstring trouble and on the morning of the match was replaced by Price, who proved rather disappointing. That was England's only change, whereas Australia brought in Edwards and Massie, who had recovered from a strain. Both were making their Test début and for the first time Western Australia had four representatives in the Test XI.

One must also stress the important part Lillee played in Australia's victory. Perhaps he was inspired by his six for 66 in England's second innings at Manchester. Anyhow, although this time his reward was confined to two wickets in each innings he looked a far better bowler. He had tidied his long fast approach of 22 strides, he was truly fast and he sent down far fewer loose deliveries. Massie capitalized on the hostility of his partner.

A light drizzle delayed the toss and the start for twenty-five minutes. Australia lost little time in taking the initiative, Boycott, Luckhurst and Edrich being removed for 28 runs before any substantial resistance was offered. At times Massie bowled round the wicket, but Smith and D'Oliveira raised the score to 54 for three at lunch. Afterwards, D'Oliveira struck three fine boundaries only to be leg-before to Massie's slower ball, whereupon Greig proceeded to hit his third successive fifty for his country.

Greig and Knott enabled England to make a satisfactory recovery in their stand of 96, but immediately after tea at 147 Knott spooned Gleeson gently to mid-wicket where to everyone's amazement Francis dropped the catch. In the end both batsmen fell to casual strokes, but Illingworth and Snow played well so that at the close of a momentous and exciting first day England were 249 for seven.

Next morning the new ball was due after two overs and Massie snatched the remaining three wickets and led his team back to the pavilion. Of the 36 bowlers *Wisden* lists who have taken eight wickets in a Test innings, only A. E. Trott, for Australia against England at Adelaide in 1895 and A. L. Valentine, for West Indies against England at Manchester, 1950 had previously accomplished the performance on their Test début.

A superb century by G. S. Chappell made the second day memorable after Australia had received early shocks in the loss of Francis and Stackpole for seven runs. Ian Chappell set a noble example as captain, leading the recovery with an agressive display. He used his favourite hook to some purpose while his brother remained strictly defensive. Ian struck one 6 near Smith before he fell to a fine running-in catch that Smith held rolling over near his ankles.

Snow, if not so fast as Lillee, bowled splendidly and soon induced a catch from Walters, but Greg Chappell, in for three hours before he hit his first boundary, now took charge, excelling with the off drive. Edwards gave valuable support, but with the light murky Illingworth brought on Gifford and then himself, tempting Edwards into indiscretion for Smith to bring off another fine running catch on the leg side. Chappell duly completed his hundred on the stroke of time and Australia wound up 71 behind with half their wickets intact.

On Saturday the gates were closed at 11.10 a.m. with 31,000 inside. Greg Chappell lasted another hour and a half, batting altogether for six and a quarter hours and in his splendid upright style hit fourteen 4s. Australia, who did not wish to face a huge target in the fourth innings, went ahead through another gallant display of powerful hitting by Marsh. He struck two 6s and six 4s in his 50, which came in seventy-five minutes and Australia gained a useful lead of 36. Snow, five for 57, alone of the England bowlers excelled.

Only the most optimistic Australian could have anticipated the success which so soon attended the efforts of Lillee and Massie. The England collapse – half the side were out for 31 – began when a fast shortish ball from Lillee lifted and Boycott, instead of dodging, preferred to let it strike his body while his bat was lifted high. It bounced off his padded front left ribs over his shoulder and dropped behind him on to the off bail. It was most unlucky for Boycott as well as England. Obviously, the Australians, having captured so valuable a wicket so cheaply, now bowled and fielded like men inspired. Luckhurst had no positive answer to Lillee's pace and soon went, to be followed by Edrich who was compelled to flick at a late outswinger (to him) that would have taken his off stump.

Again, Smith, getting right behind the ball, kept up his end, but the remainder were bemused by Massie's accuracy and late swing which meant that at the end of a miserable Saturday for England they stood only 50 runs ahead with nine wickets down.

It remained only for the weather to stay fine on Monday for Australia to gain their just reward. Gifford and Price put on 35 in the best stand of the innings but Australia needed only 81 to win and Stackpole saw them comfortably home.

With 7,000 present on the last day, the match was watched by just over 100,000 (excluding television viewers) and the receipts of £82,914 were considered to be a world record for a cricket match with the possible exception of India. N.P.

England

G. Boycott b Massie	11	b Lillee	6
J. H. Edrich lbw b Lillee	10	c Marsh b Massie	6
B. W. Luckhurst b Lillee	1	c Marsh b Lillee	4
M. J. K. Smith b Massie	34	c Edwards b Massie	30
B. L. D'Oliveira lbw b Massie	32	c G. S. Chappell b Massie	3
A. W. Greig c Marsh b Massie	54	c I. M. Chappell b Massie	3
†A. P. E. Knott c Colley b Massie	43	c G. S. Chappell b Massie	12
*R. Illingworth lbw b Massie	30	c Stackpole b Massie	12
J. A. Snow b Massie	37	c Marsh b Massie	0
N. Gifford c Marsh b Massie	3	not out	16
J. S. E. Price not out	4	c G. S. Chappell b Massie	19
L-b 6, w 1, n-b 6	13	W 1, n-b 4	5
1/22 2/23 3/28 4/84 5/97 6/193 7/200 8/260 9/265	272	1/12 2/16 3/18 4/25 5/31 6/52 7/74 8/74 9/81	116

Bowling: *First Innings*—Lillee 28–3–90–2; Massie 32.5–7–84–8; Colley 16–2–42–0; G. S. Chappell 6–1–18–0; Gleeson 9–1–25–0. *Second Innings*—Lillee 21–6–50–2; Massie 27.2–9–53–8; Colley 7–1–8–0.

Australia

K. R. Stackpole c Gifford b Price	5	not out	57
B. C. Francis b Snow	0	c Knott b Price	9
*I. M. Chappell c Smith b Snow	56	c Luckhurst b D'Oliveira	6
G. S. Chappell b D'Oliveira	131	not out	7
K. D. Walters c Illingworth b Snow	1		
R. Edwards c Smith b Illingworth	28		
J. W. Gleeson c Knott b Greig	1		
†R. W. Marsh c Greig b Snow	50		
D. J. Colley c Greig b Price	25		
R. A. L. Massie c Knott b Snow	0		
D. K. Lillee not out	2		
L-b 7, n-b 2	9	L-b 2	2
1/1 2/7 3/82 4/84 5/190 6/212 7/250 8/290 9/290	308	1/20 2/51 (2 wkts)	81

Bowling: *First Innings*—Snow 32–13–57–5; Price 26.1–5–87–2; Greig 29–6–74–1; D'Oliveira 17–5–48–1; Gifford 11–4–20–0; Illingworth 7–2–20–0. *Second Innings*—Snow 8–2–15–0; Price 7–0–28–1; Greig 3–0–17–0; D'Oliveira 8–3–14–1; Luckhurst 0.5–0–5–0.

Umpires: D. J. Constant and A. E. Fagg.

ENGLAND v AUSTRALIA

First Test Match

Played at Birmingham, July 10, 11, 12, 14, 1975

Australia won by an innings and 85 runs with a day and half to spare after Denness, the England captain, had won the toss and sent them in to bat. It was a gamble which the majority of the England team supported on a dull grey morning, but the weather forecast for the next days predicted rain and Denness took the risk of his batsmen being caught on a wet wicket and this was exactly what happened. The general opinion was that the

England batsmen were not anxious to face Lillee and Thomson. They preferred to postpone the evil hour.

This was the tenth time in 215 Tests that England had put in Australia and only once had England won – at Melbourne in February 1912 when heavy rain had left the ground soft and J. W. H. T. Douglas told Clem Hill to bat. Seven times now England have lost and two Tests have been drawn. Australia have put in England twelve times to date and won three, lost five and drawn four.

Obviously, England hoped that the ball would move about under a cloudy sky, but the four seam bowlers found no response either through the air or off a lifeless pitch. Occasionally, McCosker and Turner (in his first Test) looked in difficulty, but they saw their side safely through the first two hours before lunch, scoring 77. Later the bowlers obtained some movement, but the ball never rose awkwardly, yet by five o'clock England were happier with five wickets down for 186. Then Edwards held firm while Marsh in his swashbuckling way hit 47 out of 57 added before rain stopped play seventeen minutes early with Australia 243 for five. Curiously, Underwood was given only six overs on this first day when beside the opening pair, Ian Chappell played well, excelling with the drive.

The second day, Friday, also went in Australia's favour. Edwards had a charmed life when Snow and Arnold took the second new ball and altogether he stayed four hours for his 56, but the main value of his great effort was that Australia put on 197 runs while he was at the crease. Marsh made 61 out of 79 added for the sixth wicket and showed much displeasure at his dismissal which followed next ball after a delay of five minutes when the ball had lost its shape within eight overs of first coming into use. Thomson swung his bat to good purpose until at last England remembered Underwood and in his only over for 24 hours he promptly ended Thomson's frolics.

No sooner had Edrich and Amiss begun England's reply at a quarter to three than after one over a thunderstorm drenched the whole ground. The hold up lasted one hour, forty minutes, but with the late extra hour now added in such circumstances there remained two and three-quarter hours and in that time Australia, through Lillee and Walker, captured seven wickets for a paltry 83 runs, including five wides by Thomson in his first two overs and one no-ball.

Thomson was so erratic that Chappell allowed him only two overs before turning to the more reliable Walker. Lillee, in great form, caused the ball to lift awkwardly, but while Edrich defended gallantly until five minutes before the close, his partners were helpless against two splendid bowlers whose analysis at the end of the day read:

Lillee 12–6–13–3; Walker 15–5–35–4.

Australia never released their tight grip on the game. They took the last three England wickets in twenty-five minutes on Saturday morning, Lillee and Walker each finishing with five victims. The match must have been completed that day, but for two more hold-ups through rain. This time, Thomson found proper length and direction to add to England's problems.

The first setback when England followed on 258 behind came in Lillee's third over. Amiss turned his back on a short ball and it struck him a painful blow just below the left elbow that made him quite ill. Fletcher alone managed to survive, his runs coming mainly through skilful leg strokes and square cutting over the slips, until Walters at third slip juggled and held a difficult catch.

Gooch, in his first Test, survived only three balls in the first innings and seven in the second when he received a horrible lifter from Thomson, but he was only one failure among so many in a nightmare situation. England had lost five wickets on Saturday night for 93 runs.

A thunderstorm in the early hours of Monday morning delayed the resumption by twenty minutes and further hindrance soon occurred, but only forty-five minutes cricket was lost before lunch and by three o'clock England had suffered their first defeat in 17 Tests at Edgbaston. Amiss, now recovered, soon fell, caught off the glove from a lifting ball in the leg trap, but Knott and Snow offered resistance and Snow drove Mallett over mid-off for 6.

Thomson took the second innings bowling honours with five wickets for 38 and true to their reputation for splendid fielding the Australians brought off many remarkable catches in a victory they so thoroughly deserved. Attendance 44,391, receipts £40,943.

Australia

R. B. McCosker b Arnold	59	J. R. Thomson c Arnold b Underwood	49
A. Turner c Denness b Snow	37	D. K. Lillee c Knott b Arnold	3
*I. M. Chappell c Fletcher b Snow	52	A. A. Mallett not out	3
G. S. Chappell lbw b Old	0	B 1, l-b 8, n-b 9	18
R. Edwards c Gooch b Old	56		——
K. D. Walters c Old b Greig	14	1/80 2/126 3/135	359
†R. W. Marsh c Fletcher b Arnold	61	4/161 5/186 6/265 7/286	
M. H. N. Walker c Knott b Snow	7	8/332 9/343	

Bowling: Arnold 33–3–91–3; Snow 33–6–86–3; Old 33–7–111–2; Greig 15–2–43–1; Underwood 7–3–10–1.

England

J. H. Edrich lbw b Lillee	34	– c Marsh b Walker	5
D. L. Amiss c Thomson b Lillee	4	– c sub b Thomson	5
K. W. R. Fletcher c Mallett b Walker	6	– c Walters b Lillee	51
*M. H. Denness c G. S. Chappell b Walker	3	– b Thomson	8
G. A. Gooch c Marsh b Walker	0	– c Marsh b Thomson	0
A. W. Greig c Marsh b Walker	8	– c Marsh b Walker	7
†A. P. E. Knott b Lillee	14	– c McCosker b Thomson	38
D. L. Underwood b Lillee	10	– b Mallett	3
C. M. Old c G. S. Chappell b Walker	13	– c Walters b Lillee	7
J. A. Snow lbw b Lillee	0	– c Marsh b Thomson	34
G. G. Arnold not out	0	– not out	6
L-b 3, w 5, n-b 1	9	B 2, l-b 5, n-b 2	9
	——		——
1/9 2/24 3/46 4/46	101	1/7 2/18 3/20 4/52	173
5/54 6/75 7/78 8/87 9/97		5/90 6/100 7/122 8/151 9/167	

Bowling: *First Innings*—Lillee 15–8–15–5; Thomson 10–0–21–0; Walker 17.3–5–48–5; Mallett 3–1–8–0. *Second Innings*—Lillee 20–8–45–2; Walker 24–9–47–2; Thomson 18–8–38–5; Mallett 13.2–6–34–1.

Umpires: A. E. Fagg, H. D. Bird, A. S. M. Oakman and T. W. Spencer.

ESSEX v AUSTRALIANS

Played at Chelmsford, August 23, 25, 26, 1975

Australia won by 98 runs. In a match contested in festival mood, Hobbs, better known for his deeds with the ball, stole the show with a century on the final day in only forty-four minutes. It was the quickest for fifty-five years and the fourth fastest ever – and contained seven 6s and twelve 4s. Higgs and Mallett were the sufferers from Hobbs' assault. His last 50 arrived in the astonishing time of twelve minutes and came off 15 balls. On a perfect batting wicket, the match produced four centuries. Laird and Edwards reached this landmark as the tourists totalled a healthy 365 for six declared in their first innings and Alan Turner made 118 in Australia's second innings. Boyce, McEwan and Gooch all batted with aggressive enterprise in the Essex first innings – and then came Hobbs' moment of glory, but his spectacular display was not enough to save the depleted Essex from defeat. Illness and injury, respectively, prevented Edmeades and Fletcher batting a second time, and Hardie was left stranded with 88 when the end came.

Australians

A. Turner lbw b Hobbs	33 – c Acfield b Turner	118
B. M. Laird c Edmeades b Lever	127 – c Smith b Turner	72
*R. W. Marsh lbw b Acfield	30 – not out	39
R. Edwards run out	101 – c and b Acfield	19
G. J. Gilmour b Lever	2	
K. D. Walters c Hardie b Hobbs	10 – not out	61
†R. D. Robinson not out	39	
M. H. N. Walker not out	4 – lbw b Lever	1
B 2, l-b 11, n-b 6	19 B 2, l-b 6, n-b 7	15
1/103 2/169 3/243 4/247 5/289 6/350	(6 wkts dec.) 365 1/185 2/192 3/202 4/257	(4 wkts dec.) 325

J. R. Thomson, J. D. Higgs and A. A. Mallett did not bat.

Bowling: *First Innings*—Boyce 8–0–39–0; Lever 12–2–35–2; Acfield 31–7–96–1; Turner 11–0–38–0; Edmeades 6–1–22–0; Hobbs 33–5–116–2. *Second Innings*—Lever 17–6–48–1; Acfield 22–4–86–1; Turner 20–3–62–2; Hobbs 11–0–73–0; Gooch 13–2–41–0.

Essex

B. E. A. Edmeades lbw b Walker	15 – absent ill	0
B. R. Hardie b Thomson	8 – not out	88
K. S. McEwan b Walker	71 – hit wkt b Thomson	3
*K. W. R. Fletcher retired hurt	24 – absent hurt	0
G. A. Gooch st Robinson b Mallett	68 – lbw b Walker	0
S. Turner b Walker	9 – c Turner b Walker	11
K. D. Boyce run out	79 – c Robinson b Walker	11
†N. Smith st Robinson b Mallett	46 – c Higgs b Thomson	24
R. N. S. Hobbs c Gilmour b Higgs	5 – c Laird b Higgs	100
J. K. Lever not out	1 – c Thomson b Higgs	0
D. L. Acfield (did not bat)	– st Robinson b Mallett	10
L-b 2, n-b 10	12 L-b 4, w 1, n-b 2	7
1/15 2/23 3/150 4/194 5/212 6/279 7/324 8/338	(8 wkts dec.) 338 1/42 2/58 3/65 4/95 5/109 6/242 7/243 8/254	254

Bowling: *First Innings*—Thomson 12–1–64–1; Walker 19–3–61–3; Higgs 15–1–103–1; Gilmour 2–0–9–0; Mallett 18–2–89–2. *Second Innings*—Thomson 7–0–35–2; Walker 12–2–45–3; Higgs 13–0–91–2; Mallett 7.1–0–76–1.

Umpires: A. Jepson and P. B. Wight.

NOTES BY THE EDITOR, 1976

HOBBS HITS FASTEST HUNDRED

Well over forty years ago this would have been no surprise banner-line when Jack Hobbs was in his heyday. Yet it was no relation of the "Master", but Robin Hobbs, of Essex, who caught the headlines towards the end of August when he scored a century in 44 minutes against the Australians at Chelmsford. It was the fastest hundred since Percy Fender's all-time record of 35 minutes at Northampton for Surrey in 1920 and according to my reckoning the fourth fastest in the history of first-class cricket. Following Fender's rapid hundred, come two by Gilbert Jessop: 100 in 40 minutes against Yorkshire at Harrogate, 1897 and 100 in 42 minutes for Gentlemen of the South against Players of the South at

Hastings, 1907. Some record books place A. H. Hornby, son of A. N. Hornby fourth; his 100 against Somerset at Old Trafford in 1905 is given in 43 minutes, but the official history of Lancashire, published in 1954 with statistics by C. M. Oliver, gives Hornby's time as 48 minutes.

Earlier in the summer, Keith Boyce hit the fastest Championship hundred for 38 years when he reached three figures for Essex against Leicestershire, also at Chelmsford, in 58 minutes. Most of Hobbs's runs came off two spin bowlers, Mallett (off-breaks) and Higgs (leg-breaks), and Hobbs said afterwards that he had no idea of time. He just went out determined to have a good slog and entertain the crowd, which he certainly did. His benefit in 1974 realised £13,500.

SOMERSET v AUSTRALIANS

Played at Bath, May 18, 19, 20, 1977

Somerset won by seven wickets off the first ball of the final 20 overs. A splendid match played in superb weather, punctuated with fine cricket throughout brought Somerset their first win over the Australians in 22 fixtures played since 1893. After Garner took a wicket with his fifth ball for Somerset, Chappell, reaching 99 before lunch, and hitting three 6s and twelve 4s in a brilliant display of under two and a half hours dominated a third wicket stand of 120. Then Garner and Burgess caused a collapse as the last eight wickets fell for 55 runs. Thomson bowled 15 no-balls in seven overs as Denning led a fine opening stand of 81. Botham hit three 6s and six 4s and Slocombe, missed when 3, hit one 6 and ten 4s. All the while Rose batted patiently and steadily, hitting fifteen 4s while escaping difficult chances at 63 and 96. After the loss of two early wickets with his side still 90 behind, Hookes batted superbly. Making 85 not out in ninety minutes overnight, he reached 100 in 81 balls, eventually making 108 with four 6s and fifteen 4s. There was good support from Serjeant, Walters, Chappell and O'Keeffe. Somerset needed 182 to win in three and three-quarter hours. Denning again led a brisk opening of 50 in an hour; Rose played patiently for two hours; Richards hit eleven 4s while racing to 53 and then Botham struck boldly to finish their memorable match with an hour to spare.

Australians

R. B. McCosker c Botham b Garner	2	– run out	2
C. S. Serjeant st Taylor b Burgess	13	– c Garner b Botham	50
*G. S. Chappell b Garner	113	– c Garner b Botham	39
G. J. Cosier b Garner	44	– c Taylor b Botham	2
K. D. Walters c Denning b Burgess	23	– b Botham	25
D. W. Hookes b Botham	3	– b Burgess	108
†R. W. Marsh b Garner	3	– b Garner	0
K. J. O'Keeffe c Denning b Burgess	11	– c Denning b Moseley	20
J. R. Thomson b Burgess	0	– c Botham b Garner	0
M. F. Malone b Burgess	2	– c Richards b Breakwell	17
G. Dymock not out	0	– not out	6
B 10, w 2, n-b 6	18	B 4, l-b 10, w 1, n-b 5	20
1/2 2/57 3/177 4/197 5/200 6/204 7/223 8/223 9/231	232	1/16 2/18 3/141 4/172 5/183 6/214 7/251 8/252 9/271	289

Bowling: *First Innings*—Garner 20–8–66–4; Moseley 16–5–52–0; Burgess 9.3–2–25–5; Botham 15–2–48–1; Breakwell 7–0–23–0. *Second Innings*—Garner 23–6–71–2; Moseley 17–6–55–1; Botham 22–6–98–4; Burgess 9–3–41–1; Breakwell 0.3–0–4–1.

Somerset

B. C. Rose not out	110	– c Marsh b Thomson	27
P. W. Denning c Marsh b Dymock	39	– b Chappell	34
I. V. A. Richards c Hookes b Malone	18	– c Cosier b O'Keeffe	53
*D. B. Close c McCosker b Malone	0		
D. Breakwell c Chappell b O'Keefe	23		
I. T. Botham c McCosker b O'Keefe	59	– not out	39
P. A. Slocombe not out	55	– not out	8
B 4, l-b 6, n-b 26	36	B 4, l-b 3, w 3, n-b 11	21
1/81 2/116 3/117 4/146 5/228	(5 wkts dec.) 340	1/50 2/129 3/129	(3 wkts) 182

G. I. Burgess, †D. J. S. Taylor, J. Garner and H. R. Moseley did not bat.

Bowling: *First Innings*—Thomson 16–2–60–0; Dymock 17–7–48–1; Malone 22–4–70–2; O'Keeffe 35–15–114–2; Chappell 2–0–11–0; Walters 2–1–1–0. *Second Innings*—Thomson 12–1–57–1; Malone 9–2–18–0; Chappell 8–4–29–1; Dymock 5–0–25–0; O'Keeffe 5.1–0–32–1.

Umpires: H. D. Bird and T. W. Spencer.

ENGLAND v AUSTRALIA

Third Test Match

Played at Nottingham, July 28, 29, 30, August 1, 2, 1977

England won by seven wickets ten minutes after tea on the last day. It was England's first victory against Australia at Trent Bridge since 1930 when Bradman made his first Test appearance in England and was on the losing side the only time after he had hit a century.

Blessed with fine weather, the ground was packed on the first four days and made a wonderful sight. Moreover, The Queen was in the Midlands for the Silver Jubilee celebrations and visited the ground on the first day. Play was interrupted briefly at 5.30 p.m. when the players and officials were presented to Her Majesty in front of the pavilion.

Memorable mostly from a cricket point of view was the return of Boycott to the England team after three years of self-imposed absence. Naturally, Boycott hoped for success and he exceeded all expectations by scoring 107 and 80 not out. He had the singular experience of batting on all five days of the match and altogether spent over twelve hours at the crease, his second innings taking five and a quarter hours.

Among several other splendid personal achievements, Botham distinguished his Test Match début by taking five wickets for 74. He moved the ball each way and at one time took four for 13 in 34 balls. It was this feat which put England in the ascendancy on the first day after Chappell had won the toss and Australia gained first use of batting on a fast, hard pitch. Again England supported their bowlers brilliantly in the field, especially behind the stumps, where Hendrick held three catches. Outstanding was the way he dived to his left and held one-handed a slash by Hookes.

With the gates closed before lunch for the first time at Trent Bridge since 1948 when 22,000 were present, McCosker and Davis gave Australia a sound start and although McCosker edged Botham's second ball through a gap where England had dispensed with their third slip, the Somerset all-rounder strayed too much on the leg side during his first spell. The opening stand had produced 79 when twenty minutes before lunch Underwood in his third over offered a slower ball to Davis who lifted it to Botham at mid-on.

After lunch when Australia were 101 for one, Hendrick and Willis renewed their attack and soon McCosker touched a ball that left him, for Brearley at first slip to snap up a low catch. For a time Chappell and Hookes looked safe, but after an hour drinks were taken and then came Botham's devastating spell. His first ball was short and Chappell, intending a fierce drive, played on and with Walters, Marsh and Walker also falling to Botham's varied swing, Australia were reduced to 155 for eight, Willis and Greig accounting for Hookes and Robinson.

Then O'Keeffe stood firm and receiving staunch support from Thomson and Pascoe he played the major part while the last two wickets put on 88. At the end of the day Brearley and Boycott negotiated three overs while taking the score to nine.

Australia fought back on the second day and had England reeling at 82 for five thanks to some splendid pace bowling by Pascoe and Thomson, who were well supported by Walker. Boycott kept his end shut but no sooner had he been joined by Knott, after batting three hours for 20, than he was dropped off Pascoe by McCosker at second slip which would have made the position 87 for six. Earlier, Brearley had been caught brilliantly in the gully and Woolmer went leg-before to the third ball he received. Randall began in great style but he was run out when Boycott went for an impossible single after stroking the ball down the pitch where Randall was backing up. In the end Randall sacrificed his wicket to save Boycott, who stood dejected covering his face with his hands. Boycott freely admitted that he was to blame, and he continued to defend with the utmost resolution.

With Australia now on top, Knott rose to the occasion in his own impudent style. When bad light ended the contest half an hour early that evening the Boycott–Knott stand had yielded 160 in two hours fifty minutes and left England only one run behind with half their wickets in hand: Boycott 88, Knott 87.

On Saturday, Australia were able to claim the new ball first thing and Knott was first to his hundred in three hours, twenty-two minutes. Boycott soon followed him, having occupied six hours, eighteen minutes. The pair had just equalled the previous sixth-wicket stand of 215 by Hutton and Hardstaff at The Oval, 1938 when Boycott was caught at slip, having batted seven hours and hit eleven 4s.

Knott went on to make the highest score by an England wicket-keeper against Australia, beating 120 by Ames at Lord's, 1934. He batted four hours, fifty-five minutes for his 135 and hit one 5 and eighteen 4s.

By mid-afternoon Australia were batting again, 121 runs behind. Willis soon disposed of Davis, held at second slip, but McCosker played confidently only to see his captain, Chappell, fall to a very fine ball by Hendrick which he edged as it came back rather low. Hookes then stayed with McCosker till the close when Australia were 112 for two.

The two Australian batsmen continued their solid resistance on Monday, but having stayed over three hours while 94 runs were added Hookes left leg-before to Hendrick. Walters lasted an hour before he lofted a half-volley to cover. Underwood had sent down sixteen overs for only 18 runs and then the new ball was taken after 91 overs whereupon McCosker completed his excellent hundred. Willis, fast and accurate, immediately had McCosker taken at first slip. He batted just over six hours and hit one 6 and ten 4s. There was further resistance by Robinson and O'Keeffe, but Willis would not be denied and he finished with five wickets for 88.

England needed 189 to go two up in the series and before the close Brearley and Boycott made 17 from seven overs. On the last day, with the pitch true but slow, the only problem was the weather, as thunder showers had been forecast. With much of the bowling outside the offstump and ignored by the batsmen, progress was still slow. Eventually, Brearley accelerated, until trying to force Walker off the back foot, he played on. As England now needed to hurry, Knott and Greig went to the crease. Both failed and Walker claimed the three wickets which fell in six balls. Finally, Randall took charge and he made the winning hit. He walked off arm in arm with Boycott, the run out completely forgotten.

With over 20,000 present on each of the first four days and 8,000 on the fifth, the takings amounted to £152,000, the biggest ever for a match outside London and £80,000 more than the previous Trent Bridge record of 1976. Moreover, the large crowds were perfectly behaved – a pleasant contrast to the rowdyism and noise which had so often prevailed in recent years at some Test Matches.

Australia

R. B. McCosker c Brearley b Hendrick	51	c Brearley b Willis	107
I. C. Davis c Botham b Underwood	33	c Greig b Willis	9
*G. S. Chappell b Botham	19	b Hendrick	27
D. W. Hookes c Hendrick b Willis	17	lbw b Hendrick	42
K. D. Walters c Hendrick b Botham	11	c Randall b Greig	28
R. D. Robinson c Brearley b Greig	11	lbw b Underwood	34
†R. W. Marsh lbw b Botham	0	c Greig b Willis	0
K. J. O'Keeffe not out	48	not out	21
M. H. N. Walker c Hendrick b Botham	0	b Willis	17
J. R. Thomson c Knott b Botham	21	b Willis	0
L. S. Pascoe c Greig b Hendrick	20	c Hendrick b Underwood	0
B 4, l-b 2, n-b 6	12	B 1, l-b 5, w 1, n-b 17	24
1/79 2/101 3/131 4/133 5/153 6/153 7/153 8/155 9/196	243	1/18 2/60 3/154 4/204 5/240 6/240 7/270 8/307 9/308	309

Bowling: *First Innings*—Willis 15–0–58–1; Hendrick 21.2–6–46–2; Botham 20–5–74–5; Greig 15–4–35–1; Underwood 11–5–18–1; *Second Innings*—Willis 26–6–88–5; Hendrick 32–14–56–2; Botham 25–5–60–0; Greig 9–2–24–1; Underwood 27–15–49–2; Miller 5–2–5–0; Woolmer 3–0–3–0.

England

*J. M. Brearley c Hookes b Pascoe	15	b Walker	81
G. Boycott c McCosker b Thomson	107	not out	80
R. A. Woolmer lbw b Pascoe	0		
D. W. Randall run out	13	not out	19
A. W. Greig b Thomson	11	b Walker	0
G. Miller c Robinson b Pascoe	13		
†A. P. E. Knott c Davis b Thomson	135	c O'Keeffe b Walker	2
I. T. Botham b Walker	25		
D. L. Underwood b Pascoe	7		
M. Hendrick b Walker	1		
R. G. D. Willis not out	2		
B 9, l-b 7, w 3, n-b 16	35	B 2, l-b 2, w 1, n-b 2	7
1/34 2/34 3/52 4/65 5/82 6/297 7/326 8/357 9/357	364	1/154 2/156 3/158	(3 wkts) 189

Bowling: *First Innings*—Thomson 31–6–103–3; Pascoe 32–10–80–4; Walker 39.2–12–79–2; Chappell 8–0–19–0; O'Keeffe 11–4–43–0; Walters 3–0–5–0. *Second Innings*—Thomson 16–6–34–0; Pascoe 22–6–43–0; O'Keeffe 19.2–2–65–0; Walker 24–8–40–3.

Umpires: H. D. Bird and D. J. Constant.

ENGLAND v AUSTRALIA

Fourth Test Match

Played at Leeds, August 11, 12, 13, 15, 1977

England won by an innings and 85 runs, completing a crushing victory at 4.40 p.m. on the fourth day to regain the Ashes. The completeness of their triumph, following wins by nine wickets at Manchester and seven wickets at Nottingham, left no room for doubt as to which was the superior side. It was the first year since 1886 that England had won three tests in a home series against Australia.

A historic game was made more memorable by Boycott who, on the opening day, became the first player to score his hundredth century in a Test Match. The Yorkshire crowd seemed to regard the achievements of this landmark as inevitable and Boycott batted with such ease and assurance that he gave his loyal supporters few qualms and the Australian bowlers scant hope. His was a remarkable feat, for he was only the eighteenth cricketer to reach this goal. Two of the others, Herbert Sutcliffe and Sir Leonard Hutton, were present for at least part of the match. By the time Boycott was finally out for 191, Australia had lost any hope of saving the series.

A strong local conviction that cricket history was about to be made helped to fill the ground close to overflowing on the first two days when the gates were shut well before the start. England, who won the toss, included Roope for Miller, while Australia also limited themselves to a single change, Bright being entrusted with the spin bowling in place of O'Keeffe.

Although Brearley was caught at the wicket off Thomson's third ball, Boycott soon took the measure of the attack and apart from one edged stroke off Walker, which nearly carried to Marsh, looked well nigh invincible. Partners came and went, Woolmer, Randall and Greig contributing briskly, while Boycott proceeded at his own measured pace. Thirty-four runs before lunch, another 35 by tea. He had been in for five hours twenty minutes when a full throated roar from the crowd told those for miles around that the local hero had done it. An on-driven boundary off Chappell, his fourteenth 4 from the 232nd ball he had received, took the Yorkshire captain to three figures and brought the inevitable invasion of the middle. Happily this did not cause a lengthy hold up in play or cost Boycott his cap, which was sheepishly returned by a would-be souvenir hunter.

England finished the first day already strongly placed at 252 for four with Boycott 110 and Roope 19. The match was virtually settled on the Friday, truly a Glorious Twelfth for England, who carried their score to 436 and then captured five wickets for 67 in the last eighty-five minutes. Boycott succeeded in his objective of batting England into an invincible position and when he was last out he had hit twenty-three 4s in his second best score for his country. As at Trent Bridge, Knott was again his best partner and they put on 123 in three hours before Knott got out as England sought to accelerate. The three Australian pace bowlers performed tirelessly but Walker would assuredly not have finished wicketless had he bowled to a fuller length with better direction.

After their long stint in the field, the Australians batted like men in a state of shock after bowling at Boycott for twenty-two and a half hours since his return to the England side. With the ball swinging under evening cloud the batting was taxed beyond its resources. Hendrick claimed victims with his second and thirteenth balls and McCosker, who was making a staunch fight, was brilliantly run out by Randall when backing up a shade too eagerly.

Hendrick and Botham combined to complete the destruction of the first innings on Saturday morning. The last five wickets went for 36 runs in forty-five minutes. The Australian score of 103 was their lowest against England since Lord's in 1968 when they were put out for 78, but were saved by rain after following on. Botham, who took five for 21 to follow his successful début at Trent Bridge, soon removed Marsh and the rest went quietly. When two wickets in the second innings had been captured by lunch England had high hopes of repeating a three-day win on the same ground as in 1961 and 1972. Greig made the breakthrough, Knott catching Davis down the leg-side for his 250th Test success before diving in front of first slip to send back McCosker with a marvellously athletic effort.

An object lesson on how to play the swinging ball was provided by Chappell throughout Saturday afternoon when the light was often dim. Brearley, with five bowlers of medium pace or above, allowed the batsmen little respite and more wickets would have fallen had some of the seamers bowled a more attacking line. Nevertheless, despite the loss of almost all the final session through rain and bad light Australia at 120 for four were in a dreadful plight.

Monday dawned wet but play was possible at two o'clock. Chappell, having added but seven runs, prodded forward at Willis to be caught at second slip. Marsh hit fiercely and with Walker put on 65 for the eighth wicket. With Botham injured and Hendrick resting,

England struggled for a wicket for the only time in the match. The new ball, taken at 243 for seven, brought a speedy end.

Willis wrecked the stumps first of Walker and then Thomson, the latter being his 100th Test wicket. The honour of taking the final wicket went deservedly to Hendrick, who had done so much to undermine the opposition. Marsh skied him to wide mid-off where Randall wheeled to get under an awkward catch. Most of the England players set off for the dressing rooms and Randall did not let them down. The catch safely completed he threw the ball high in the air and did a joyous victory cartwheel before joining his colleagues on the players' balcony to acknowledge the cheers of thousands. Attendance 78,000. Receipts £140,000.

England

*J. M. Brearley c Marsh b Thomson	0
G. Boycott c Chappell b Pascoe	191
R. A. Woolmer c Chappell b Thomson	37
D. W. Randall lbw b Pascoe	20
A. W. Greig b Thomson	43
G. R. J. Roope c Walters b Thomson	34
†A. P. E. Knott lbw b Bright	57
I. T. Botham b Bright	0
D. L. Underwood c Bright b Pascoe	6
M. Hendrick c Robinson b Pascoe	4
R. G. D. Willis not out	5
B 5, l-b 9, w 3, n-b 22	39
1/0 2/82 3/105 4/201 5/275 6/398 7/398 8/412 9/422	436

Bowling: Thomson 34–7–113–4; Walker 48–21–97–0; Pascoe 34.4–10–91–4; Walters 3–1–5–0; Bright 26–9–66–2; Chappell 10–2–25–0.

Australia

R. B. McCosker run out	27	– c Knott b Greig	12
I. C. Davis lbw b Hendrick	0	– c Knott b Greig	19
*G. S. Chappell c Brearley b Hendrick	4	– c Greig b Willis	36
D. W. Hookes lbw b Botham	24	– lbw b Hendrick	21
K. D. Walters c Hendrick b Botham	4	– lbw b Woolmer	15
R. D. Robinson c Greig b Hendrick	20	– b Hendrick	20
†R. W. Marsh c Knott b Botham	2	– c Randall b Hendrick	63
R. J. Bright not out	9	– c Greig b Hendrick	5
M. H. N. Walker c Knott b Botham	7	– b Willis	30
J. R. Thomson b Botham	0	– b Willis	0
L. S. Pascoe b Hendrick	0	– not out	0
L-b 3, w 1, n-b 2	6	B 1, l-b 4, w 4, n-b 18	27
1/8 2/26 3/52 4/57 5/66 6/77 7/87 8/100 9/100	103	1/31 2/35 3/63 4/97 5/150 6/167 7/179 8/244 9/245	248

Bowling: *First Innings*—Willis 5–0–35–0; Hendrick 15.3–2–41–4; Botham 11–3–21–5. *Second Innings*—Willis 14–7–32–3; Hendrick 22.5–6–54–4; Greig 20–7–64–2; Botham 17–3–47–0; Woolmer 8–4–8–1; Underwood 8–3–16–0.

Umpires: W. L. Budd and W. E. Alley.

THE PACKER CASE

By Gordon Ross

First news of what was to become, virtually, "The Packer Explosion", came from South Africa towards the end of April 1977 when South Africa's *Sunday Times* broke the news that four South African cricketers had signed lucrative contracts to play an eight-week series of matches throughout the world. It was said that when the team visited South Africa and played local teams it would have immeasurable benefits for the game there.

In the middle of May, *The Bulletin*, Australia's 97-year-old magazine owned by The Australian Consolidated Press Limited (Chairman, Kerry Packer) announced the completion of a huge sporting deal in which thirty-five top cricketers had been signed for three years to play specially arranged matches, beginning with a series of six five-day Test matches, six one-day games, and six three-day round robin tournaments in Australia in 1977-78. Prize money would be $100,000. The deal had been put together by JP Sports and Television Corporation Limited, proprietors of Channel 9 in Sydney (Chairman, Kerry Packer).

The thirty-five players signed up were:

Eighteen Australian and seventeen from Overseas, chosen by Ian Chappell and Tony Greig; I. M. Chappell (Captain), R. J. Bright, G. S. Chappell, I. C. Davis, R. Edwards, G. J. Gilmour, D. W. Hookes, D. K. Lillee, M. F. Malone, R. W. Marsh, R. B. McCosker, K. J. O'Keeffe, L. S. Pascoe, I. R. Redpath, R. D. Robinson, J. R. Thomson, M. H. N. Walker, K. D. Walters.

A. W. Greig (Captain), Asif Iqbal, E. J. Barlow, D. L. Hobson, M. A. Holding, Imran Khan, A. P. E. Knott, C. H. Lloyd, Majid Khan, Mushtaq Mohammad, R. G. Pollock, M. J. Procter, B. A. Richards, I. V. A. Richards, A. M. E. Roberts, J. A. Snow, D. L. Underwood.

G. Boycott was invited to take part in the scheme but declined. Richie Benaud and his Sports Consultancy Company were engaged in the management of the series. Many of the signings were carried out during the Centenary Test match in Melbourne, and the New Zealand-Australia series. Austin Robertson and John Kitto (Secretary and Attorney of the Television Corporation Group) flew to West Indies where West Indies were playing Pakistan, and then to Britain to finalise the arrangements with the English and South African players.

The Australian team was already in England. The Manager, Len Maddocks, was quoted as having said: "I do not envisage the present development having a detrimental effect upon this tour. But if any of them play for a side contrary to the jurisdiction of the Australian Board, they will place their careers in jeopardy."

On May 13 The Cricket Council issued a statement at the end of an emergency meeting to the effect that Greig was not to be considered as England's captain in the forthcoming series against Australia. The statement went on: "His action has inevitably impaired the trust which existed between the cricket authorities and the Captain of the England side." F. R. Brown, Chairman of the Council, added: "The captaincy of the England team involves close liaison with the selectors in the management, selection and development of England players for the future and clearly Greig is unlikely to be able to do this as his stated intention is to be contracted elsewhere during the next three winters."

On May 25 it was announced from Lord's that a special meeting of full and foundation members of the International Cricket Conference would be held at Lord's on June 14 to discuss the situation, and the next day the Test and County Cricket Board said that the selection committee should "pick England sides this summer strictly on merit," which obviously meant that Greig, Knott and Underwood could play.

At the end of May, Packer arrived in England, and at a Press Conference, said: "It is not a pirate series but a Super-Test Series. I have sent telegrams to all the cricketing bodies but they don't reply. I am willing to compromise but time is running out." He referred to cricket as the easiest sport in the world to take over, as nobody had bothered to pay the players what they were worth.

At this point the only cricketing subject being discussed from the highest Committee Room in the land to the Saloon Bar of the tiniest inn, was "Packer", and from all the multifarious points raised, one was likely to be proved the dominant factor in the end. In this age of extreme partisanship, had non-partisanship cricket any future? Does the world not want to see England beat Australia, or Arsenal beat Tottenham, or England beat Wales at Twickenham – or vice versa. According to particular loyalties? Could a collection of players, however great, stimulate public interest, when there was nothing on the end of it, except a considerable amount of money for the participants? The fact that tennis players and golfers are a constant attraction was irrelevant; they are individuals playing for no-one but themselves. And moreover, the whole crux of this matter was linked to big business – the business of television, and not so much to the furtherance of cricket or cricketers.

Mr Packer, as Chairman of Channel 9 in Australia, was bitterly disappointed that an offer he had made to the Australian Board of Control for television rights for conventional test cricket had not been given the due consideration which Mr Packer felt the offer had merited. Out of this frustration, his scheme was born and nurtured. Meanwhile, unanimous agreement on their attitude to Packer's television "circus" was reached at the emergency meeting of the International Cricket Conference on June 14. Mr Packer, who left Heathrow that evening for the United States, was to be invited to discuss his plans with representatives of the ICC at the earliest possible moment. This meeting was arranged for June 23, but negotiation was not found possible on one salient point – Mr Packer demanded exclusive television rights from the Australian Board of Control from 1981 when their present contract with the Australian Broadcasting Commission ended. The ICC representatives told him that it would be totally wrong in principle if this were taken as a condition of agreement. The representatives of all the countries present were unanimous that no member country should be asked to submit to such a demand. The ICC's five conditions were:

1 – Programme and venues of the "circus" to be acceptable to the home authority, and the length of programme not to exceed six weeks. Matches under home authority and the laws of cricket.

2 – No player to participate without the permission of his home authority, who would not withhold it unreasonably.

3 – No teams to be represented as national. That is, not Australia, possibly "an Australian XI".

4 – Players contracted to Mr Packer to be available for Tests, first-class fixtures and other home-authority sponsored matches.

5 – The home authority must be able to honour all contractual commitments to existing sponsors and advertisers.

Afterwards, Packer said: "I will take no steps at all to help anyone. It isn't 40 players, it's 51." It seemed clear that his purpose in signing up the players was essentially as a bargaining weapon to help him to secure the exclusive television rights he so badly wanted. Names of other players to have joined Packer were being announced from day to day – D. L. Amiss, A. I. Kallicharran, C. L. King, B. D. Julien, C. G. Greenidge. At the crucial meeting at Lord's on July 26 the ICC tabled three principal resolutions:

1 – No player, who after Oct. 1, 1977, has played or has made himself available to play in a match previously disapproved by the Conference, shall thereafter be eligible to play in any Test match without the express consent of the Conference, to be given only on the application of the governing body for cricket of his country.

2 – Any match arranged or to be arranged by J. P. Sports (PTY) Ltd., Mr Kerry Packer, Mr Richie Benaud or associated companies or persons, to take place in Australia or elsewhere between Oct. 1, 1977 and March 31, 1979 is disapproved.

3 – Matches are liable to be disapproved if so arranged as to have the probable result that invitations to play in such matches will conflict with invitations which have been or may be received to play in first-class matches.

Zaheer Abbas was yet another to defect from cricketing authority, making the known total at that time forty-one, except that it was announced that Jeff Thomson had withdrawn, as indeed had Kallicharran, according to Mr David Lord, the Australian agent for them both. Packer swiftly answered this possible damage to his cause by setting out for England to talk to them. Lord, who also acted for Vivian Richards, said: "I shall be offering them the same advice that I have given to Jeff. I am going to make it my job to see as many players as I can to try and persuade them to follow this example."

Mr Packer then announced that he would apply for an injunction and damages in the High Court against the International Cricket Conference and Test and County Cricket Board, and a similar action was to be started against Mr David Lord, claiming that Mr Lord had wrongfully induced players to break their contracts with the Company. A temporary injunction was granted against Lord but the TCCB gave an undertaking that no Packer player would be banned until the Court hearing.

The meeting at Lord's on August 10 produced the following conditions:

The TCCB's new sub-rules to meet the ICC request concerning players who are members of the Packer group are:

1. No player who, after October 1, 1977, has played or made himself available to play in a match previously disapproved by the Conference shall thereafter be eligible to play in any Test match without the express consent of the Conference.

2. No county shall be entitled to play in any competitive county cricket match, any cricketer who is and remains precluded from playing in a Test match on the above grounds before the expiration of a period of two years immediately following the date of the last day of the last match previously disapproved by the ICC in which he has played or made himself available to play.

This, of course, was subject to any High Court ruling which might follow. The name of Bob Woolmer was added to the list of Packer players. On Monday September 26 the High Court hearing began, and it lasted 31 days, the judgment, occupying 221 foolscap pages, took five and half hours to deliver. Herewith are extracts from this massive document, summarised from *The Times*:

THE JUDGMENT

Mr Justice Slade granted three English cricketers who had contracted to play for Mr Kerry Packer's World Series Cricket Pty Ltd. declarations that all the changes of the rules of the International Cricket Conference and all their resolutions banning them from Test cricket are ultra vires and void as being in unreasonable restraint of trade. So, too, are the Test and County Cricket Board's proposed rules governing qualification and registration of cricketers in Test and competitive county cricket.

His Lordship also granted similar declarations to World Series Cricket.

The three cricketers, the individual plaintiffs, were Mr Tony Greig, Mr John Snow and Mr Michael Procter.

His Lordship said that as a result of the entry of World Series Cricket into cricket promotion, the International Cricket Conference in July, 1977, changed its rules in a manner which, if implemented, was likely effectively to disqualify any of the individual plaintiffs from playing in official international Test cricket for an indefinite time if he played in any cricket match organized by WSC. The TCCB proposed, subject to the court's decision, to change its rules in a manner which was likely to disqualify any of the plaintiffs from playing in English county cricket for at least several years if he played WSC cricket.

In both actions the plaintiffs claimed that the new or proposed new rules would be legally invalid, and sought orders which would effectively prevent the ICC and TCCB from implementing them. WSC further claimed that those rules were or would be an unlawful inducement to a number of players who had entered into contracts to break them.

His Lordship considered that there were nine principal questions for ultimate decision.

(A) Are the contracts between WSC and its players void?

(B) Has WSC established that, as at August 3, and subject to any statutory immunity conferred by the 1974 Act, it has a good cause of action in tort against the ICC based on inducement of breach of contract?

(C) Has WSC established that as at August 3 and subject as aforesaid, it had a good cause of action in tort against the TCCB based on the same grounds?

(D) Subject to the provisions of the 1974 Act, are the new ICC rules void as being in restraint of trade?

(E) Subject to aforesaid, are the proposed new TCCB rules void as being in restraint of trade?

(F) Is the ICC an "employers' association" within the 1974 Act?

(G) Is the TCCB an "employers' association"?

(H) If either the ICC or TCCB or both be "employers' associations", does this itself bar any cause of action that would otherwise exist?

(I) In the light of the answers, what relief (if any) should be given to (i) the individual plaintiffs and (ii) WSC?

Summarizing the evidence, his Lordship commented that the evidence relating to the conditions under which cricketers worked, particularly in the United Kingdom, would have filled a book and would doubtless provide useful raw material for cricket historians of the future.

His Lordship could see the possible force of criticism directed against Mr Greig, who, when he signed his contract with WSC and recruited others to do so, had just completed a tour of Australia as captain of the England team, was still generally regarded as its captain and could have looked forward with reasonable confidence to his formal reappointment as such. There was obviously a case for saying that his responsibilities to the TCCB were of a rather special nature.

However, two points had to be borne in mind in regard to him and all the other United Kingdom players. (1) Neither the Cricket Council (the governing body of cricket in England recognized by the ICC) nor the TCCB had themselves entered into any kind of commitment, legal or otherwise, ever to offer employment to any of those players again. (2) The players themselves had entered into no contractual commitment with the Cricket Council or the TCCB precluding them from playing cricket for a private promoter.

In conclusion his Lordship said that Mr Michael Kempster, in his opening speech for the defendants, generously but correctly, acknowledged five positive beneficial effects which, on the evidence, had already been produced by the emergence of WSC as a promoter of cricket. First it had offered the promise of much greater rewards for star cricketers. Indeed, it had gone farther – it had offered secure, regular, remunerative employment in cricket to more than 50 cricketers, in most cases for three English winter seasons, at a time when most of them would otherwise have no guarantee of regular employment in the game. Secondly, it had already stimulated new sponsors for traditional cricket. Thirdly, it has brought back to the game in Australia several talented players. Fourthly, it, or the group of companies of which it formed part, had initiated a useful coaching scheme for young players in New South Wales. Fifthly, it had increased public interest in the game.

For all those acknowledged benefits, the defendants had held the strong opinion that ICC's effective monopoly in the promotion of first-class cricket at international level had been good for the game and that the emergence of WSC into the promotion field was bad for it. However, whether or not that opinion was correct had not been the question for the court. The question for decision had been whether the particular steps which the ICC and the TCCB took to combat what they regarded as the threat from WSC were legally justified. The long investigation had satisfied his Lordship that the positive demonstrable benefits that might be achieved by introducing the ICC and TCCB bans and applying them to players who had already committed themselves to contracts with WSC were at best somewhat speculative.

On the other hand there were demonstrable disadvantages if the bans were to be applied in that way. They would preclude the players concerned from entry into important fields of professional livelihood. They would subject them to the hardships and injustice of essentially retrospective legislation. They would deprive the public of any opportunity of seeing the players concerned playing in conventional cricket, either at Test or at English county level; for at least a number of years. By so depriving the public they would carry with them an appreciable risk of diminishing both public enthusiasm for conventional cricket and the receipts to be derived from it. Furthermore, the defendants by imposing the bans, in the form which they took and with the intentions which prompted them, acted without adequate regard to the fact that WSC had contractural rights with the players concerned, which were entitled to the protection of the law. The defendants acted in good faith and in what they considered to be the best interests of cricket. That, however, was not enough to justify in law the course which they had taken.

Judgment was given for the plaintiffs in both actions with costs.

BEARING THE COSTS

It was estimated that the costs to the defendants were likely to be about £200,000, and whilst this sort of figure was a severe blow to any organisation – certainly to the game of cricket, there were three cardinal factors to be borne in mind in connection with the financial administration of Test and County Cricket in this country. First, since the International Cricket Conference were co-defendants, it is assumed that they would bear some of the costs. Secondly, as a result of the Packer intervention, Cornhill moved in to sponsor Test cricket in England, a sum of one million pounds spread over five years was mentioned, and not, apparently, being far from the mark, and thirdly, the Test and County Cricket Board received £150,000 from Mr Packer for the television rights for his Channel 9 coverage of the England v Australia Test matches during the 1977 summer.

Whatever the net loss to the TCCB, it would be spread over the various beneficiaries from the TCCB's income for 1977 such as the seventeen first-class counties, the Minor Counties, Universities, and so on. Admittedly, the county budgets could not readily accommodate any deduction from their share, but overall the blow divided by at least twenty was brought down to more bearable proportions.

The defendants were given six weeks from the date of entering of the order to consider the possibility of an appeal. They no doubt took account of three important factors – the total lack of crowds at Packer's early matches in his series, and, although Packer brushed this aside as having no consequence because he was only interested in television reaction and ratings, one must take the ramifications of a lack of interest on the part of paying customers as being important. Secondly, that Australia beat a very good Indian side in three tests without their Packer players, and thirdly that the England side held their own in Pakistan where both sides were without their Packer players. A good deal of water will have to flow under the bridge before a total clarification of all the implications, short, and long-term, is possible.

Early in February 1978, the International Cricket Conference and the TCCB decided not to appeal and agreed to share their burden of the costs.

In the documentation of the Packer case in last year's Wisden *[1978] it was possible only at the last minute to add the words: "Early in February, 1978, the International Cricket Conference and the TCCB decided not to appeal and agreed to share their burden of the costs." The story, therefore, is taken up at the point of this decision, but in greater detail, as it was not possible to elaborate on the appeal decision at the time.*

It was announced from Lord's on Thursday, February 2, 1978 that an appeal against the High Court ruling by Mr Justice Slade the previous November in favour of Mr Kerry Packer and some of his players would not be in the best interests of international cricket. Mr Jack Bailey, secretary of the International Cricket Conference, said that once the delegates had agreed there should be no appeal – the first item on the agenda – all discussions that followed were in the light of the High Court judgment. No pressure could be brought to bear upon member countries about whom they should select to play; the ICC could not make stipulations concerning this aspect. Mr Bailey told a Press conference that, though it was felt that both the ICC and the TCCB had reasonable grounds for appeal, there was no guarantee of success, and to appeal just for the sake of appeal would be churlish.

The selectors of individual countries will, as now, be responsible for making their own decisions and there may be different criteria used – consideration of the short-term or long-term requirements of that particular country.

As far as the TCCB were concerned, Peter Lush, the spokesman on their behalf, said that the selection by counties of World Series Cricket players was a matter for individual members; just as, in the case of the ICC, the TCCB was not in a position to make recommendations. At this moment, six England players were under contract to WSC – Greig, who had just been relieved of the Sussex captaincy because of derogatory remarks made about Boycott – Amiss, Snow, Knott, Underwood, and Woolmer. The ICC meeting, which lasted two days, agreed that the costs of the High Court hearing would be divided between the ICC and the TCCB. The question of making contractual arrangements with players had been aired, but no collective decision was taken. If individual countries were approached by WSC, any discussion would have to be with the ICC as a whole.

Meanwhile, WSC were continuing to sign up players; or rumour had it that they were. On February 3 *The Sydney Sun* claimed that Sunil Gavaskar and Bishan Bedi were to be offered lucrative contracts for the next season, though Bedi said he knew of no such offer, and was loath to comment further until he did. On February 7 it was revealed that Greig and Sydney promoter David Lord had had lengthy discussions with a view to effecting a compromise between WSC and the ICC, with a new international series, under the auspices of the ICC, to be played in addition to scheduled Test series. In what struck observers as a most curious finale to their discussions, it was stated that Greig had not signed the "joint statement" because it did not constitute a perfectly true expression of his views. The Australian Board's view has never wavered from its original course; that if WSC wished to re-open talks with the Board, it should do so through the ICC in London. On this they stood firm.

In any event, a joint statement not signed by the second party hardly constituted the basis for serious discussion. On the same day, in England, a meeting of Kent's full committee decided to have back all their four Packer players should they wish to return. Hampshire announced at the same time that Greenidge, Richards, and Roberts would again be playing for them in the summer. Inevitably, all shades of opinion were being expressed. A letter to *The Times* from Surrey's chairman, Raman Subba Row, advocated a genuine discussion between the ICC and the rival system; two days later, Oliver Popplewell, QC, in a letter to the same newspaper, stated that the authorities should stand firm and beware the siren song of compromise until such time as Kerry Packer notified them that players signed by him would be released for the whole of the England tour of Australia in 1978-79.

During these diverse expressions of opinion, the WSC Packer matches were taking place in Australia to attendances considerably smaller than Packer would have hoped for. The exceptions were matches played in floodlight, which obviously had a novelty attraction and were well patronised. Before a crowd of 2,716 WSC Australia prevented a run of three defeats at the hands of the WSC World XI by winning by 41 runs. Comparative failure by Australia, in any sport, is something that appeals less to Australian crowds than to those in most other cricketing countries, and the Australian team's performance clearly could not have aided the Packer cause.

The true financial picture of this first series may not emerge for some time – if ever – but estimates put the loss in excess of £2,000,000; derived from an outlay of some three and a half million, with receipts from advertising revenue about a million, and gate receipts of a shade under half a million. Packer's comment was: "We are still amateurs, but we are more professional than we were, and will become even more professional."

It was said that the prize-money, worth $A201,500, had gone into a provident fund for three years, after which it would be paid out with interest. Still on the question of finance, it was apparently agreed, at a meeting between the Victorian Football League and Kerry Packer, that the mobile pitches at VFL Park would stay in place throughout the football season at an additional cost to WSC, who paid VFL $A850,000 for the use of the ground for three summers, with an original agreement to remove the pitches before the start of each football season.

When the dust was allowed to settle on this first adventure, followers of traditional cricket throughout the world had some comfort that this adventurer, Mr Kerry Packer, had clearly not met with the resounding success for which he had hoped. On the other hand, any new enterprise is subject to teething troubles. Moreover, Mr Packer's make-up is such that he was most unlikely to throw in the towel after a disastrous first round, and suffer a loss of pride as well as of money. In the end, of course, he may have to decide how much money he can afford to spend on pride. At a much later date a new managing director, Andrew Caro, emerged, clearly with the brief to make WSC pay, and to fight what, at that stage, appeared to be a battle with authority.

In Australia, one factor in the whole affair had remained constant – the unwavering line pursued by the Australian Board. Any opinion suggesting that the Australian Board might have taken a more conciliatory view of this rather ugly menance thrust upon them, holds little water when it is accepted that the Board, even if somewhat reluctantly, were party to the working arrangement proposed at the ICC meeting, which Packer turned down, out of hand. The Board knew well enough, after this, that they had a fight on their hands, and they prepared for the fray. Who could blame them? Australia's point of view was fairly and comprehensively put by Mr E. W. Swanton, in an article in *The Cricketer* of May 1978 entitled "'Bob' Parish pumps home the facts". Mr Parish, chairman of the Australian Cricket Board, was at great pains to point out, in a speech in his home state of Victoria, the enormous improvements in payments made to their players in recent years; long before Packer's arrival. The following is worth quoting:

"In 1974 the Board resolved that it would pay to the players the maximum it could afford after taking into consideration its overall responsibility to Australian cricket at all other levels. The Board has honoured the undertaking. In 1974-75, Test match payments were $A250 per Test. In 1975-76 this was increased to $A475 plus a bonus of $A400, a total of $A875 per Test. In 1976-77 the match fee was maintained at $A475 and a bonus of $A250 was paid, a total of $A725 per Test. In 1977-78 the match fee payment was $A800.

Sponsorship was introduced to cricket in the 1974-75 season. The Board decided that 30 per cent of the sponsorship should go to the players as prize-money. Sponsorship of first-class cricket in Australia by the Benson and Hedges Company has increased from the initial $A50,000 to a massive $A250,000 this season [1977-78] and $A350,000 next year. This season a total of $A175,000 was provided as prize-money for the five Tests against India and the Sheffield Shield matches. Each of the tests carried a winners' prize of $A6,000 and a losers' prize of $A3,000. In addition to the prize-money there was a team sponsorship fee of $A802 per Test. This is provided by the Benson and Hedges Company from a team sponsorship arranged by the Board with the approval of the players in January 1977. So, for each of the Tests against India, Australian Test players received from the Board $A1,852 if the match was lost or $A2,102 if the match was won. Australia won three and lost two Tests this season. So a player who played in all five Tests received from the Board $A10,010. Sheffield Shield and Gillette Cup earnings would together total another $A4,000 to $A5,000, and add to this another $A7,000 for the West Indies tour and the total for the 1977-78 season would exceed $A20,000 (£12,000)."

Mr Parish, with a touch of irony, substantiated the improvement in the lot of the Australian cricketer by quoting from a book recently published by Greg Chappell, in which the former captain of Australia wrote: "Cricketers' rewards have increased dramatically in a comparatively short time. In a matter of just two seasons the base Test payment doubled from $A200 to $A400. Sizeable bonuses have been handed out at the end of the past two series, provident fund money has been increased, cash endorsements are flowing as never before, and the Test team is now sponsored for three years. It's hardly surprising that Australia leads the way in providing a far better deal for cricketers."

Chappell's words seem to make a mockery of the well-worn cry that Establishments do little to improve the lot of the first-class cricketer. However, it is only fair to say that the advent of Packer was clearly instrumental in substantially improving the lot of the England Test player. Not, of course, from the purse of Mr Packer, but in the way the surrounding controversy brought into the public gaze the fact that perhaps the England Test player was inadequately rewarded for his labours on behalf of his country. So in one way, Greig's cry that what he was doing was for the good of all cricketers, and not just the élite, had a ring of truth about it; but possibly not in the precise way that Greig had contemplated.

Just as Australia was firm, Pakistan, too, was doing its best to follow the hardline. When the Board of Control for Cricket in Pakistan announced the names of about 30 players to attend the training camp in preparation for the tour of England, Majid, Imran, Mushtaq, and Zaheer were omitted. The Board stated they were prepared to consider the Packer players, provided they could guarantee their availability to play for Pakistan, not only on the tour of England but for all future commitments. This, they could not give; and there followed a raging controversy, the result of which was a meeting called on March 26 under the chairmanship of the Chief Martial Law Administrator and attended by former Pakistan captains, prominent cricket organisers, and representatives from every province. At the end of it, the Administrator ruled that Packer players would not be included in the Pakistan team. There, it seemed, the matter was closed, but shortly before the team were due to leave, rumours spread that Miandad, Haroon, and Sarfraz had signed Packer contracts. This was at once denied by the Board, but suspicion lingered on. In the end, the air was cleared when a Packer representative announced that neither Miandad nor Haroon had signed any form of contract, and Sarfraz, in due course, announced that neither had he. The poor showing of the Pakistan team, deprived of the Packer players, was later to generate some re-thinking.

West Indies, perhaps the most vulnerable of all ICC members in the matter of cricket finance, was placed in an increasingly difficult position. The distance between the islands – 1,200 miles, for instance, between Jamaica and Barbados – and multifarious other problems have made it an intense struggle for any treasurer of the West Indies Board to make ends meet: and a West Indies team that was virtually a second team would impair this rickety financial structure even more. It is not surprising, therefore, that West Indies had taken the most moderate line with Packer players. The Board were against the original ICC ban, although subsequently voting for it in the interests of unity, and they decided to continue to play their Packer men, provided they made themselves available. Anyone with first-hand knowledge of West Indies cricket will readily understand their thinking.

In the series beginning in the Caribbean in March, West Indies included the Packer players; Australia did not. As a result, West Indies won the first two Tests with some ease – by an innings and 106 runs, and by nine wickets. But just before the third Test, at Georgetown, Guyana, a balloon of sizeable dimensions went up. When the West Indies team was announced, three Packer players – Haynes and Austin, recently signed, and Deryck Murray, secretary of the West Indies Players Association – were dropped and replaced by non-Packer players. Clive Lloyd made an immediate protest and resigned as captain, although the Board stated they had not been officially informed by Lloyd of his decision. Lloyd then sought a meeting between the Board and the Packer players, but by the time the Board's president, Jeffrey Stollmeyer, arrived in Guyana, the Packer set had already written to the Board withdrawing from the Test; which was due to start the day after Stollmeyer's arrival.

The result was that West Indies took the field for the third Test with six players new to Test cricket. Williams joined the cricketing élite by scoring a century in his first Test, and Gomes, another of the original triumvirate, also scored a hundred in a huge second innings total of 439. This looked to have secured the match, but for the second time in a 1977-78 series Australia scored more than 300 in the fourth innings to win a Test; they had done so to win the second Test aginst India in Perth.

Australia's dramatic recovery provided the West Indies Board with another headache. A match had been narrowly lost; the presence of the Packer players in the West Indies side would almost certainly (as certain as a game of cricket can be) have produced a different result. The Board, understandably, had already announced that the Packer players would take no further part in the series; because the players had been unable to give an assurance that they would be available for the tour of India and Sri Lanka.

The Board had set March 23 as the date for a decision from the players. Packer himself flew to Georgetown and held a Press conference. And in the grand manner, he sent his jet aircraft to pick up former West Indies players who had problems in getting flights to a dinner party he gave at the Sandy Lane Hotel, Barbados, using his visit to put his case on television, and to win over his receptive audience. Events followed events and immeasurably widened the gulf between the Board and the Packer players. The West Indies Board, so far the only ICC member to play their Packer men, were now realising they were on a collision course. There was precious little evidence that Packer was looking for an amicable compromise.

The international position at this moment was that Australia, England, and Pakistan were not playing Packer players, West Indies, though having done so, were now in line with the others; India, New Zealand and South Africa were not specifically concerned, though India and New Zealand could conceivably be in the future. South Africa, not playing Test cricket, would not.

An important factor was to affect the thinking of both the West Indies and Pakistan Boards; the opinion of cricket followers in both countries. Clearly, throughout the Caribbean, sympathy was with the Packer players; or more precisely with West Indies always fielding the best available side in Test cricket. The same applied in Pakistan; if anything, feeling was heightened by the palpably poor performance of the Pakistan side in England. Attempts were made by Pakistan's supporters to make martyrs out of the discarded Packer players and ridicule the team, at a time when it needed firm support. Clearly, something had to be done, especially by the West Indies Board who faced the stark reality of a huge financial loss on the series with Australia; it was rumoured to be in the region of £100,000.

It was not so much a turn-about, therefore, as facing reality when the West Indies Board recommended that dialogue between the International Cricket Conference and World Series Cricket be re-opened at the earliest opportunity; and, if necessary, on the initiative of the ICC. The second resolution offered the Board's services to initiate such discussions. Meanwhile, WSC, which had named Deryck Murray as its Caribbean representative, was writing to the clubs responsible for the major grounds in West Indies, plus Antigua and St Lucia, to set up a West Indies v Australia WSC series in 1978-79. The West Indies Board were to have the enemy on their doorstep – if enemy they were to be – doing irreparable damage to the future of organised cricket in West Indies. It left the Board with virtually no option but to seek a peaceful solution.

World opinion and interest was now focussed on the International Cricket Conference meeting that was to begin at Lord's on Tuesday, July 25, and this was not without its dramatic overture. On the eve of proceedings, Mr David Clark, president of MCC and thus chairman of the ICC, resigned from the Kent County Cricket Club committee, on which he had served for 30 years, following Kent's decision to offer new contracts to the three

WSC players; Asif, Woolmer and Underwood. Mr Clark's position, in the light of this decision, left him with no option but to resign, otherwise he could have been accused of double-dealing.

Kent's decision to make their policy known when they did was considered by many to have political implications; it was felt they were trying to influence ICC thinking, and perhaps give the impression that all English counties felt the same way. There were also rumours that the players concerned were bringing pressure to bear on Kent during the week before the Benson and Hedges Cup final at Lord's; Kent were finalists and obviously would not want disruptions during the run-up to a final. The county had previously met legal requirements by offering contracts of only one year to Packer employees; Knott, being one of them, withdrew (for the time being at any rate) from first-class cricket. Among other aspects, it seems that Kent had not solicited the views of the Cricketers' Association, whose opinion, as a thoroughly responsible body, should have been sought.

It subsequently transpired that David Clark and Jack Bailey had, prior to the meeting, gone to the United States to hear the WSC proposals for an amicable solution, both parties being particularly anxious that the meeting should be a matter of great secrecy. These proposals, given in detail below, are so ludicrous, as to evoke intense speculation as to what WSC hoped to achieve by them. Was it that Packer had no wish for an agreement, and was confident of his own future without any need to placate anyone in cricket? If he was looking for a middle-of-the-road settlement, then these absurd proposals would generate contempt rather than stimulate a mood of reconciliation and lead to sensible discussion. The Packer package was as follows.

> WSC ask for fully representative teams (to be selected by WSC) to be available for WSC matches on the following basis:
>
> A – October-November: India, New Zealand and Pakistan to play a preliminary knockout competition in one of these countries to provide a winner to participate in the one-day internationals and "super Test" series in Australia later in the season.
>
> B – December 22-January 24: Australia, England, West Indies and Pakistan (or whoever may be the winners of the preliminary competition) and a World XI to play in a series of one-day internationals, avoiding actual dates of official Test matches in Australia.
>
> C – February 2-March 12: Australia, England, West Indies and Pakistan (or whoever may be the winners of the preliminary competition) to play in a WSC "super Test" series. These teams, plus a World XI, would also play further one-day internationals.
>
> D – Assuming Australia were the winners, for approximately three weeks in March-April, May-June, September-October and October-November, the winners of the WSC "super Test" series to play in West Indies, England, India and Pakistan respectively.

The ICC gave their reason for finding these proposals totally unacceptable, though elaboration was hardly necessary. This was the dignified reply.

> 1 – Any official tour to Australia would be disrupted by having to release some or all players for a number of days in December and January. The leading Australian players would also be unavailable for their domestic cricket in this period.
>
> 2 – No official tours allowing free selection of teams could be arranged between member countries between mid-December and mid-March (the prime period in most countries) because of the necessity for national teams to remain intact while touring other countries.
>
> 3 – It would be virtually impossible to arrange any worthwile official tours prior to mid-December, bearing in mind the proposed WSC commitments of India, New Zealand and Pakistan and the "super Test" tour to Pakistan.

4 – Official tours after mid-March are not feasible other than in West Indies (until late April) and in England (May until August). The WSC programme would involve the "super Test" champions visiting West Indies in March and April, and England in May and June.

Despite the two sides being poles apart, it was agreed that the dialogue should be continued, and that WSC be asked to reconsider their proposals. A sub-committee was to be set up to monitor all future developments. It had, in any case, been understood by both parties that no alteration to tours already arranged for the coming winter was possible. Andrew Caro, managing director of WSC, gave his version of events as showing the first real chink of light (some chink, and some light, a few would say!) and followed at a Press conference by calling the WSC proposals a working document and giving a few nebulous alternative ideas.

Just what sort of a hand was WSC playing? Did they hold all the honours or not? If they were contemptuous of organised cricket, and in no need of it, why bother to submit proposals? The plot deepens. One feasible explanation could be that Packer, like a good union official or shop steward, must put on a good front on behalf of his players and be seen to give them confidence in the future. Clearly, such terms as those outlined above would create the impression of negotiating from strength, while, at the same time, playing for time. Packer would obviously want to know how WSC matches fare in Australia with an official Australia v England series going on. That would give him some guide as to the depth of his roots.

It was said in the early days that Packer resented the use of the word "Circus" in relation to his cricket, which was to be serious stuff at the highest level. Hardly the highest level in September when his stars went to New York and, as "World All Stars", met an "American All Stars" XI for a rather undistinguished trophy given by a Brooklyn sporting goods shop – and lost! Mr Greig announced that he would be back in a year's time – and win. Perhaps with players like Greig, Sobers, Hookes, Majid Khan and Fredericks in the Packer contingent, it was better mileage to lose, so creating a big story. Who knows?

In the meantime, Pakistan, smarting from the very poor showing of their side in England, turned back to their Packer players. General K. M. Azhar, responsible for cricket in Pakistan, said: "We do not have the schedule of the Packer series, but if there is no clash of fixtures and nothing in their [the Packer players'] contracts to stand in the way, then we should welcome them." Five Pakistani players were then under contract to Packer – Imran Kahn, Majid Khan, Mushtaq Mohammad, Zaheer Abbas and Asif Iqbal.

It had already been rumoured that Richard Hadlee, who had improved his reputation in England in the summer of 1978, was now on the Packer list of potentials. It was said that Hadlee's involvement would be limited to a series of professional matches to be staged in New Zealand between November 2 and November 16; before WSC opened their second Australian season. There was also talk that Geoff Howarth, the other New Zealander to play well against England, was a candidate. With Richard Hadlee's father, Walter Hadlee, chairman of the New Zealand Board, it was a ticklish situation for him, and one he would almost inevitably want to leave to the other members of his Board, hoping they could reach agreement without needing the chairman's casting vote.

In England, at the end of the summer, attention was focused on two players at the opposite ends of the earth; Dennis Amiss in Warwickshire and Jeff Thomson in Australia. Amiss was told by Warwickshire that, as a Packer player, he would not be retained by the county in 1979. Thomson, despite being under contract to the official Australian Cricket Board, signed a three-year contract with World Series Cricket. It was announced that the Board would be seeking legal advice.

To take Warwickshire first. The announcement that Amiss would not be retained caused a furore amongst Warwickshire members. Their view was: Why should Warwickshire deplete their ranks when Kent, who had just won the Championship, were retaining their Packer men, as were a few other counties. It seemed that Warwickshire cricket was split right down the middle, and it was no great surprise when a Special

General Meeting was convened for Tuesday, September 26. The surprise was that at the request of Amiss himself, the meeting was called off. Why? There is a ready answer. It appears, almost for the first time since the Packer saga began, that the Cricketers' Association was able to play a substantial part in striving for peace.

They apparently advised Amiss that if, during the winter, talks between WSC and the ICC could establish some sort of peace, Warwickshire would obviously be happy to retain a player who had scored over 2,000 runs for them in the summer; especially as the player himself wanted to stay. If nothing was achieved, then Amiss could re-think the situation. In any event, the Cricketers' Association had one or two crucial resolutions to deal with at their next meeting, and they felt that these would be better kept on ice until the outcome of any talks during the winter.

It seemed that both the Cricketers' Association and some of the Packer players were anxious for WSC and the ICC to get together as soon as possible, to see if the framework of an agreement could be worked out. Warwickshire were alone in standing on principles, but their supporters' view that what is good for the goose is good for the gander is readily understandable. Dennis Amiss, at this point, emerged from the furore with honour, as did the Cricketers' Association.

Thomson's move, however, represented yet another twist in his topsyturvy relationship with Packer. First he signed; then he withdrew on the advice of his agent, who was taken to court by Packer. Now, on the eve of an Ashes series, he has defected again in breach of another contract. The Australian Board are particularly unfortunate, because obviously Thomson was Australia's principal drawing-card in the series against England. Packer knew this well, and countered with a contract and a cheque book; in 1978, the two together seem to be a passport to anywhere.

Swiftly on the heels of Thomson's defection, the Australian Cricket Board issued the following statement:

> "It was announced last Friday, September 29 that World Series Cricket had entered into a three-year contract with Mr Jeff Thomson despite its awareness that Mr Thomson had agreed to play only in matches controlled by the Board and state associations during the 1978-79 Australian season, and despite the publicity given to the fact that the Board had refused Mr Thomson's request that he be released from his contractual obligations to the Board.
>
> The Board would naturally have preferred to resolve this matter without resort to the courts and, in order that Mr Thomson's contractual obligations to the Board should be respected, the Board sought an assurance from World Series Cricket that it would not select Mr Thomson to play cricket in any of its teams until after the conclusion of the Australian cricket season on March 31, 1979. World Series Cricket has declined to give such an assurance."

In the subsequent court action, Mr Justice Kearney decided, after a twelve-day hearing, that Thomson, who has said he will never play test cricket for Australia again, was bound by a contract he signed with the Australian Cricket Board earlier in the year. He could not, therefore, play for Packer until April. Judge Kearney said that some of Thomson's evidence before the court had been quite unreliable. He awarded costs against Thomson and World Series Cricket. Thomson replied by saying that he would probably spend the summer as a professional fisherman off the Queensland coast rather than play grade cricket; in the words of the famous Bing Crosby song – "Gone Fishin'".

Meantime, it was rumoured that the WSC organisation was busy recruiting Indian players who were at that time on tour in Pakistan. Bedi, the captain, in particular was mentioned, as was Gavaskar, the opening bastman. It was also said that a prominent Pakistan cricketer close to the organisation was acting as the recruiting officer. No official confirmation was issued either way at the time.

So, amidst litigation, rumour, resignations and Press conferences, this long-drawn-out saga rolls relentlessly on, first in one direction, then another, as apparently it will continue to do for a long time to come.

The documentation of the Packer case, which began in the 1978 Wisden, *is continued here, from the point it reached in last year's edition with the decision in an Australian court by Mr Justice Kearney that J. R. Thomson, the Australian fast bowler, was bound by a contract he signed with the Australian Cricket Board and could not therefore play for Packer until April. Costs were awarded against Thomson and World Series Cricket.*

The supreme test for Packer's brand of jet-age razzamatazz cricket was to come in the winter of 1978-79 when an official Ashes series would take place in Australia at the same time. To seasoned and ardent followers of the game, Packer's offering was almost a masquerade of the game of cricket; to young Australians, however, especially when it was staged at night with the right sort of refreshment available, WSC was certainly having appeal. To them, whether or not it conformed to the accepted standards of the game of cricket was immaterial, as long as it provided dramatic entertainment. So it seemed likely that as well as two separate series being played, they would be watched by two quite diverse species of Australian life.

Tony Lewis, reporting from Sydney, in January 1979, had this to say of the World Series Cricket game in a feature in the *Sunday Telegraph*:

"The most dangerous act in the entertainment business these days is not balancing on the high wire nor even putting a head in the lion's mouth. It is, without doubt, batting in Kerry Packer's Flying Circus. Fast bowling and repeated bouncers are destroying some of the best batsmen we have ever seen. I have never seen so many bouncers bowled in a session as by the World team against the West Indies in a one-day game last week."

Tony Greig, in the *Sun Herald*, gave the true flavour of WSC cricket when he wrote:

"The competition in WSC is so intense, teams can no longer afford to allow the opposition tailenders to hang around. Consequently the pace bowlers are dishing out an unprecedented amount of bouncers to the 'rabbits'. So it is pleasing to see that cricketers like Dennis Lillee and Garth le Roux have got the message, swallowed their pride, and are wearing helmets."

Are these cricketers, or mercenaries risking their skin for a sizeable bag of gold? *The Australian* reported the conclusion of one game as follows:

"Last night's game ended dramatically when number 11 batsman, Joel Garner, playing with a broken left middle finger from an accident only nine days previously, was struck on the finger by a short ball from World XI all-rounder Clive Rice. Garner was in considerable pain and walked from the field, giving the World XI a win by 35 runs."

While the circus moved from place to place for one-day stands, the Ashes series was taking the course the Australian Cricket Board had reason to fear most. Their team, without the cream of its talent who had defected to Packer, were no match for a competent England side, except for a little splutter in the middle of the series when Australia won the third Test at Melbourne by 103 runs. England won the series by five tests to that solitary one. The Australian public (and who can blame them?) have little stomach for the second best in sport, and this, to a measurable degree, was reflected in attendances. On the other hand, Packer gave the public free parking at Sydney, free transport out to the Waverley ground in Melbourne, and played his matches when spectators have time to watch – at night, and with a white ball which they can see better. In addition, with his television network, he promoted his stars as Hollywood used to theirs in the thirties. They became household names, and faces. It was all a personality cult.

There had been many estimates as to how much the Packer organisation had lost in its first season of WSC cricket. But much of the enormous outlay of capital expenditure would not apply a second time round. Although the figures were not available until March 1979, the Group's figures up to December 23, for the half-year, suggested that Packer cricket would open its account in the coming months of 1979 as follows.

"The holding company and operators of TCN channel 9, Publishing and Broadcasting Holdings Ltd., yesterday confirmed the improvement with a solid 26 per cent profit rise from $A6,657,000 to $A8,407,000 in the half-year to December 23. While no figures for WSC are published in the interim report, if the rising attendances and substantially lower costs are any criteria, Mr Packer would have been laughing at the end of the six-month period.

After losing at least $A3.5 million in its first season WSC would now be close to breaking even and may even chalk up a maiden profit for the full year to June 30. But this depends largely on the financial success of the current WSC Australian tour of the West Indies.

During the 1978-79 Australian season, WSC is said to have drawn about 730,000 people through the gates over 85 days of cricket. An estimated 580,000 people went through the turnstiles up to the end of Publishing and Broadcasting's interim period – December 23 – although it is not known how many of these were paying customers. But it is known that WSC costs that season were substantially lower than the start-up costs of the previous year. Publishing and Broadcasting would also have benefited from better advertising response during the cricket coverage on Channel 9 and inter-state stations."

So, at this stage, Packer seemed to have the edge over the Australian Cricket Board on the question of balancing budgets. The official Test series, in what was once the greatest of sporting series – the Fight for The Ashes – had done financially worse than any series before it; much worse.

As far as Packer's next move was concerned, the spotlight switched to England, where there was considerable conjecture as to what might happen at the next Cricketers' Association meeting. Would the players in English domestic cricket, especially those who constituted the present England team, vote for a ban on Packer players? If they did, Packer had always threatened to bring his circus to England, and no-one ever doubted that Packer meant what he said. When Ian Davis, a bank employee, was refused leave to join Packer's tour to the West Indies, Packer sharpened his teeth and promptly withdrew two very substantial accounts.

From the start, there had always been a strong feeling in cricket's higher echelon that Packer would never be able to find suitable grounds in Britain. But there was an equally strong body of confident opinion that he would. A great number of cricket grounds are not owned by the county which plays on them. Take, as an example, St Helen's, Swansea, which belongs to the City Corporation. Could they possibly refuse a glittering cash guarantee from Packer if he wanted to play there? Glamorgan could reply by refusing to play there again if the Corporation sold out to Packer, but would that matter as much to the Corporation as it might to Glamorgan.

Packer had always claimed that his first season of WSC was a disappointment, mainly because, to quote him, "People had been so heavily indoctrinated against the idea". The reprisal this time was to indoctrinate people in favour of the idea in preference to orthodox cricket. Almost every Australian newspaper had a former player who was on the Packer payroll banging the drum, and Packer's own television network remorselessly did the same. Still, not everyone was taken in. In a letter to an Australian newspaper, D. M. Elliston of Tasmania wrote: "Are these posturing gum-chewing yahoos who participate in that rather poor standard television production called or perhaps mis-called World Series Cricket members of actors equity? With sadness I remember back to the days when some of them were cricketers."

Packer admitted that he was fading himself into the background. "I spent a disproportionate amount of time on cricket at first – it's only three of five per cent of the business." He told Alan Lee in an interview in February that, if he had been asked "Would you do it all over again?" he would probably have said "No". He was "still prepared to compromise for the good of cricket, but the longer it goes on the less eager I shall be". Alan Lee, writing of this interview in the *Sunday Telegraph*, concluded: "World Series Cricket has grown beyond being a temporary intrusion on the game, and its threat to

England adds completely new pressures to every county player at their crucial April meeting. Packer is awaiting their decision with something more than indifference."

It was reported, however, that a group of England players who toured Australia were stepping up their campaign against players affiliated to World Series Cricket. They were proposing to the annual meeting of the Cricketers' Association in April 1979 that no county should be allowed to sign a player dismissed by another county because of his links with Kerry Packer. Additionally, they said that no county should recruit any further players on the WSC payroll, or known to be about to sign for the organisation. They would reserve the right to refuse to play against them.

Some England players, however, were hoping for an encouraging statement before the Association's meeting from the International Cricket Conference about talks held with Packer representatives in Australia. If these gave some hint of compromise, then their proposals could be dropped. But there were still proposals on the table which could seriously affect the coming Prudential World Cup, calling, as they did, for English players to refuse to play with or against any of the Packer men. Certainly, West Indies and Pakistan would select their Packer players, so confrontation and disruption of the World Cup was, at that stage, a serious possibility.

Packer, in the meantime, was turning his attention to the West Indies. It will be remembered that the half-year financial report had suggested that a possible profit on the cricket operation depended largely on the financial success of the current WSC Australian tour of the West Indies. There must be considerable sympathy for the West Indies Board who, by the nature of events in the Caribbean, operate within the framework of the most slender financial resources at the best of times. Their position had worsened considerably since the arrival of Packer. The 1977-78 series against Bobby Simpson's Australians, virtually a second team, was diluted still further when Clive Lloyd and his Packer players withdrew from the Test in Georgetown. The series, having become totally unrepresentative, resulted in heavy financial loss.

For season 1978-79, with the absence of the Packer men – a team and a half of them – and with West Indies committed to sending a team to India and Sri Lanka, there was not a single first-class match in any of the territories until the end of March. Then within a few weeks, because a large number of their players would be due back in England, the Shell Shield matches – once the backbone of cricket in the West Indies – would have to be rushed through. Meanwhile, the Packer circus was on the road in the Caribbean; and as it contained all the top players of both countries, the attraction was inevitable and immediate.

In the desperate necessity to stay afloat financially, the West Indies Board had only one option – to seek some stability, regardless of where it came from. Of course, it came from Packer. E. W. Swanton wrote:

> "There is, however, one consolation at the moment for West Indies cricket. The various territories are getting from WSC both rentals for grounds and a portion of the gate over an agreed figure; also – let us give the devil his due – the Board itself is to receive an ex-gratia payment which will at least do something to compensate for the inevitable diminution of interest in its own Shell Shield and the absence of opportunity of discovering new talent until the tail-end of the season."

Mr Swanton went on:

> "So, although the International Cricket Conference has done all possible from the start to accommodate any reasonable proposals put forward by the opposition – and I gather, by the way, that the January talks at Sydney, between the ICC representatives and Kerry Packer, were decorously conducted – the Boards of individual countries can only proceed on the basis that, in the foreseeable future, the two systems may co-exist."

With Packer in the West Indies, the cricket world had by now accepted unconditionally that his influence on the game was likely to be of a permanent nature. It was not a pie in the sky that would go as it came, simply because of the established business principle that he could now negotiate from strength.

Packer's tour of the West Indies will be remembered, not for its cricket but for violent crowd scenes almost unprecedented in an area where crowd disturbances have become almost routine. Tony Cozier, writing in *The Cricketer* of the fourth Supertest in Georgetown, gave this dramatic account of the proceedings:

> "After a sunny Saturday, Guyana's lone Sunday newspaper quoted a WSC official as giving the assurance that play would commence on time on Sunday provided no more rain fell. Far from there being rain, the weather remained fine and a capacity crowd of 13,000 packed the tiny ground from as early as 7.00 a.m. to watch the much-heralded superstars in action.
>
> Gradually it became clear to everyone that the optimistic predictions of a prompt start were unfounded. The public-address system announced that the umpires had inspected and would inspect again at 12 noon. In the interim, players, dressed in civvies, appeared on the ground, prodding it dubiously with much shrugging of shoulders. The noon inspection led to a further announcement of a 2.00 p.m. inspection. As the alcohol flowed and the temperature became less bearable, spectators' patience became shorter and shorter. A good forty minutes after the 2.00 p.m. survey by the umpires it was announced that play would commence at 3.30 p.m.
>
> Too late. The hurricane was already blowing and could not now be curbed. By the time it was over, the ground was in shambles, fences torn down, benches and chairs hurled on to the outfield, broken bottles all over the place. The pavilion had been stormed and ransacked and the two teams trapped in their dressing-rooms where they remained huddled in corners, most using their helmets as protection against drink bottles, not cricket balls. Two West Indies were slightly cut but the riot police, with their tear gas, arrive before the rampant mob could do any further damage. The prior disturbances in Barbados and Trinidad were minor by comparison. Apart from the embarrassment of the various disturbances, WSC also had its image tarnished by an incident involving Ian Chappell who was charged, convicted and fined $G150 in a Georgetown magistrate's court for assaulting a local WSC official and using indecent language."

Financially, however, WSC reported favourably. There were excellent crowds and substantial in-put by sponsors, the Board was a beneficiary, and a coaching programme by former West Indies Test cricketers was apparently highly successful. Whether the product is good, bad or indifferent, much of its success or failure lies in marketing techniques, and in this respect Packer has clearly shown the way to success. The West Indies Board, having seen the size and nature of the sponsorships, would obviously be looking at this source of revenue for their own future advantage.

When the much-heralded Cricketers' Association meeting took place at Edgbaston on April 5, all the anticipted heat was taken out of it by news that something was in the wind. In the words of their president, John Arlott: "We have been asked not to rock the boat. We have been given assurances, but not facts, that close negotiations are going on between the two sides and that a settlement is hoped for in weeks rather than months." The Australian Board was due to meet on April 23 and 24 to make what was expected to be their final decision on their television contract, the root of all the turmoil in the first place.

It was agreed at the Edgbaston meeting that, should there be no settlement, another meeting of the Association would be held on July 5 when the much tougher proposals laid down a year previously would certainly be debated with a fair chance of being carried. By then, however, the Prudential World Cup would have been completed. The representatives were also assured that traditional cricket would not be the loser from any settlement made. It was felt that this did, at least, open up the way for Warwickshire and Amiss to be reunited, for when Warwickshire made their decision the previous September not to renew Amiss's contract, they did say it could be changed if agreement between

ICC and WSC was reached or thought to be imminent. This proved to be the case, and an agreement between Warwickshire and Amiss followed closely on the heels of this meeting.

Towards the end of April there came the Australian Cricket Board's long-expected granting to Kerry Packer's Channel 9 of exclusive television rights for Test and other matches in Australia. What Packer had tried to achieve in 1976 he had achieved in 1979, at a damaging cost all round. It will be remembered that the Board had said throughout that they would put this contract out to tender when the time came for its renewal.

Opinion at this latest news was cautious, to say the least. Much more detail was needed, but the agreement apparently was for three years and the Board would benefit by an estimated £600,000. As to the future of World Series Cricket, it was reported that this would be disbanded from January 31, 1980. It need never have started had Packer accepted that the Australian Cricket Board was bound by a contract to the Australian Broadcasting Commission until 1979, and that his money was likely to win the prize he so dearly sought when the time came.

This news of Packer winning the television contract was largely expected, and was nothing like the bombshell which exploded upon the cricket world a month later when, from the outside, it appeared that from being arch-enemies with no compromise possible in any set of circumstances, the two parties had wed and were now hand in hand for, as they said, the future good of cricket. Whether the rest of the world thought so was quite another matter. The feeling in many quarters was that when the Australian Board first found Packer at their throats, the rest of the cricket world had supported them to the hilt; even to the extent of highly expensive court cases which cricket could ill afford. Now, when it suited Australia, they had brushed their friends aside to meet their own ends. Let us, first of all, look at the full text of the statement made by the chairman of the Australian Cricket Board, Bob Parish.

"I am pleased to announce that the agreement between the Australian Cricket Board and PBL Sports Pty Ltd has been signed and will be lodged with the Trade Practices Commissioner.

Under the agreement the Board has granted PBL Sports Pty Ltd the exclusive right, for a term of ten years, to promote the programme of cricket organised by the Board and to arrange the televising and merchandising in respect of that programme. For the first three years of the agreement the Board has agreed that PBL Sports Pty Ltd may arrange a contract for the televising of the programme with the Channel 9 network.

World Series Cricket Pty Ltd will cease to promote cricket matches in Australia or elsewhere during the term of the agreement. However, under the programme the World Series logo will continue to be worn in international one-day matches by Australian players.

The Australian Board will have the exclusive responsibility for the selection of Australian teams and has agreed that no player will be excluded from selection by reason only of that player having participated prior to the commencement of the 1979-80 cricket season in any match not authorised by the Board. There will be no change in Board policy that Australian teams will be selected only from those players who participate in Sheffield Shield cricket.

It is envisaged that the programme each season will comprise five or six Test matches and an international one-day series, to be known as the Benson and Hedges World Series Cup, of fifteen matches plus a final which will be the best of five matches. These international matches will involve two overseas teams and the Australian team. The programme will also include the Sheffield Shield competition and a one-day series of nine matches between the states.

Playing conditions of all matches will be under the control of the Board and the Board has agreed to consider favourably the introduction of the 30-yard circle in limited-overs matches, day/night matches and, on an experimental basis, the use of coloured clothing in Benson and Hedges World Series one-day limited-overs international matches.

The programme for the 1979-80 season will not be finally determined for some weeks. England and India have accepted invitations to come to Australia in 1979-80. The Board has agreed to ask the Indian board to defer their visit until next season, 1980-81, and will invite the West Indian Board to send an official team to participate in the 1979-80 programme.

A basic programme of matches has been prepared by the Board programme committee. All matches will be played on venues as determined by the Board.

The following prize-money will be provided: for each test – $A10,000 comprising $A6,000 to the winner, $A3,000 to the loser, $A1,000 to the player of the match. For each one-day match – $A5,000 comprising $A3,000 to the winner, $A1,500 to the loser, $A500 to the player of the match. For the one-day final – $A50,000 comprising $A32,000 to the winner, $A16,000 to the loser, $A2,000 to the player of the match.

The Board is pleased to advise that the Benson and Hedges company will continue to be the sole and official sponsor of international cricket in Australia, of the Sheffield Shield competition and the Australian team.

Finally, although the Board's cricket sub-committee, first established in September 1976, and which comprises three Board representatives and an elected player representative of each of the six states' practice squads, will continue to meet regularly, the Board has agreed that the Australian captain, for the time being, and/or a players' representative elected by the six state representatives, may attend board meetings on request or by invitation to discuss any matters they may wish to discuss or that the Board may wish to discuss with them. The Board will also endeavour to arrange that the captain of a state team and/or the elected players' representative may similarly attend state association meetings.

The Board is unanimously of the opinion that its decision to accept the proposal from PBL is in the best interests of Australian and international cricket."

India, of course, had more reason than most to be unhappy, because their scheduled tour of Australia was to be deferred. New Zealand, too, must have wondered what might happen to them as one of the lesser crowd-pulling cricketing countries. Would the new deal mean that the weak would go under because they would have too little television appeal? Throughout the debate, the sixty-four thousand dollar question was "Why has the Australian Board done this?", and the sixty-four thousand dollar answer can be succinctly given in one word – "Money". For the first time in the history of the Ashes, an Australia v England series had lost money. Faced with nothing in the kitty, and a tour by India – and this was bound to lose money – the Australian Board could see the spectre of bankruptcy close round the corner. It was left with precious little bargaining power.

Packer had all the cards in his hand. It could be said that, in the circumstances, Australia had come out of it pretty well. Financially, of course, they may have, but time alone will tell whether the Australian Board – a very small dog, with Packer as a very large tail – will find that the tail wags the dog on any issue of divided opinion. It easily could.

Knowing the dilemma the Australian Board was in after losing an estimated £445,000 in the two-year dispute, it was not too surprising that the International Cricket Conference, at its annual meeting at Lord's in 1979, approved the Australian Board's agreement with Kerry Packer's PBL Pty Ltd, a subsidiary of Consolidated Press. They were satisfied that PBL will not be involved in promoting cricket in Australia or elsewhere, and that PBL Pty Ltd would be the agent of the Board, not its master.

The ICC announced that it was likely that England and West Indies would go to Australia in the coming winter, India and New Zealand in 1980–81, and West Indies and Pakistan in 1981-82, so for all countries honour was satisfied. India accepted a year's postponement with good grace on the assurance that, in the three-year programme of international cricket currently being worked out, they will have an equitable share of Test series, home and away.

The Australian Board's agreement with PBL was for ten years, but there is no commitment to have two tours every Australian season, and England's next visit after the coming winter should be for a full season.

Although some say that this will have little affect on established cricket in England, this view might have to be taken with a pinch of salt. It is practically impossible for one of the major components of a small unit – the countries involved in international cricket – to commit itself to such far-reaching proposals as these without some of the implications rubbing off elsewhere. A glut of one-day cricket could be one example, as could the development of a new breed of cricketer who seeks the quick pickings of easy money in preference to the long hard road of becoming thoroughly accomplished. Will the watcher lose all sense of the aesthetic qualities of cricket because, in a one-day game, snicks through an unguarded slip area count for as much as the beauty of the supreme cover-drive?

The Test and County Cricket Board swiftly put some uneasy minds at rest when they announced that, although they reluctantly agreed to compete in the ICC-approved one-day competition involving Australia and West Indies, they have told the Australians they want the next tour in 1982-83 to revert to the traditional format of five or six Tests. The TCCB added: "The Australian Board have agreed to a significant reduction in one-day international cricket from their original programme. England are strongly of the opinion that there are still too many of these matches as opposed to Tests than is desirable."

The TCCB also insisted that "no abnormal conditions" be imposed for the limited-overs series. This obviously meant that England would refuse to play in coloured clothing and suffer any of the other intolerable gimmicks of WSC television presentation. Furthermore, they had their way over the position of the Ashes in the three-Test series, and these were not at stake.

One immediate example of the new "all money" attitude by the Australian Board was the length of time it took for the TCCB to negotiate terms for the recent winter tour, which, in the first instance, were unacceptable. In fact, whether or not the tour was on was touch and go for some time. Agreement was finally reached for an announcement to be made on October 4, and even then an estimated £30,000 to be divided among the counties seemed paltry reward for a tour which was not really wanted, and was purely a gesture to help Australia – and Packer, too. The illogicality of it all had surely reached its peak.

LANCASHIRE v AUSTRALIANS

Played at Manchester, August 16, 17, 18, 1980

Drawn. A superb century by Chappell dominated the first day on a green but easy paced pitch. However, the touring captain made few friends when he walked away from the wicket without a word of explanation or apology to the opposition immediately he reached three figures. He retired to allow other batsmen to practise and Laird, with a stubborn 55 spread over 165 minutes, and Marsh, with a more aggressive half-century in an hour, enabled the Australians to declare at 296 for five. Lancashire made a good start with Lloyd and Kennedy putting on 49 in the last hour of the opening day. Major honours on the Sunday went to Hayes, whose first century in two years included three 6s. A declaration with Lancashire 44 runs behind was of no avail when rain prevented the match being continued on the last day.

Australians

B. M. Laird run out	55	– not out 0
J. Dyson c Simmons b Hogg	3	– not out 0
G. M. Wood c Fowler b Simmons	28	
*G. S. Chappell retired	101	
K. J. Hughes c Fowler b Hughes	14	
G. N. Yallop not out	26	
†R. W. Marsh not out	50	
B 12, l-b 2, n-b 5	19	
1/12 2/71 3/124 4/189 5/220	(5 wkts dec.) 296	(no wkt) 0

R. J. Bright, A. A. Mallett, G. Dymock and L. S. Pascoe did not bat.

Bowling: *First Innings*—Hogg 16–3–56–1; Malone 14.1–4–26–0; Allott 6–0–21–0; Simmons 24–4–78–1; Hughes 27–5–76–1; O'Shaughnessy 9–1–20–0. *Second Innings*—Hogg 0.5–0–0–0.

Lancashire

A. Kennedy c Marsh b Pascoe	40
D. Lloyd c Marsh b Pascoe	38
*F. C. Hayes not out	102
B. W. Reidy b Dymock	18
S. J. O'Shaughnessy lbw b Pascoe	1
J. Simmons c Chappell b Bright	7
†G. Fowler c Laird b Bright	6
D. P. Hughes c Wood b Bright	22
P. J. W. Allott not out	4
L-b 5, n-b 9	14
1/74 2/87 3/148 4/150 5/157 6/201 7/236	(7 wkts dec.) 252

M. F. Malone and W. Hogg did not bat.

Bowling: *First Innings*—Pascoe 21–2–52–3; Dymock 14–4–35–1; Mallett 24–6–74–0; Bright 22.1–10–77–3.

Umpires: H. D. Bird and D. G. L. Evans.

OLD ENGLAND v OLD AUSTRALIA

Played at The Oval, August 27, 1980

Australia's former Test cricketers maintained their country's statistical advantage over England when they defeated Old England by seven wickets in a 50-over match. The home team was the more experienced, boasting 724 England caps to 401 Australian, but Old Australia had youth on their side, being an aggregate of 96 years the junior. The match, played at the scene of the first Test match between the two countries in England, was a feature of the Centenary celebrations to commemorate 100 years of Test cricket in England.

Old England

J. H. Edrich c Redpath b Simpson	61
P. E. Richardson b Corling	6
*M. C. Cowdrey st Taber b Gleeson	44
K. F. Barrington c Harvey b Corling	45
M. J. K. Smith b Simpson	3
B. L. D'Oliveira not out	56
†J. M. Parks not out	5
L-b 6, w 3, n-b 1	10
1/12 2/87 3/119 4/127 5/197	(5 wkts, 50 overs) 230

F. J. Titmus, F. S. Trueman, G. A. R. Lock, F. H. Tyson and †T. G. Evans did not bat.

Bowling: Connolly 10–2–37–0; Misson 2–0–3–0; Corling 9–1–29–2; Gleeson 10–0–42–1; Veivers 5–0–35–0; Simpson 5–0–22–2; Cowper 5–0–31–0; Stackpole 4–0–21–0.

Old Australia

*R. B. Simpson st Evans b Titmus	75
I. R. Redpath st Evans b Titmus	27
R. M. Cowper st Parks b Lock	35
K. R. Stackpole not out	57
R. N. Harvey not out	29
B 1, l-b 7	8
1/79 2/124 3/158 (3 wkts, 39.2 overs)	231

†B. N. Jarman, G. E. Corling, T. R. Veivers, A. N. Connolly, J. W. Gleeson, F. M. Misson and †H. B. Taber did not bat.

Bowling: *First Innings*—Trueman 6–0–24–0; Tyson 5–0–31–0; Lock 10–0–66–1; Titmus 5–0–29–2; Barrington 7–0–41–0; D'Oliveira 6.2–0–32–0.

Umpires: C. S. Elliott and J. G. Langridge.

ENGLAND v AUSTRALIA

Cornhill Centenary Test

Played at Lord's, August 28, 29, 30, September 1, 2, 1980

Drawn. It had been hoped that England's Centenary Test, to mark the centenary of the first Test played in England – at The Oval in 1880 – might be played in late summer sunshine with many a nostalgic reunion, some splendid fighting cricket and a finish to savour.

Over 200 former England and Australian players assembled from all over the world; it was impossible to move anywhere at Lord's without meeting the heroes of yesteryear. The welcoming parties, the dinners and the take-over by Cornhill Insurance of a London theatre for a night were all hugely successful. Sadly, however, the party in the middle was markedly less so.

After almost ten hours had been lost to rain in the first three days, the match ended in a tepid draw, with many people disappointed that England did not make a bolder bid to meet Australia's final challenge to score 370 in 350 minutes. With Boycott 128 not out and Gatting 51 not out they had reached only 244 for three at the finish.

As much as for the cricket, though, the game will be remembered for a regrettable incident, seen by millions on television on the Saturday afternoon, in which angry MCC members were involved in a momentary scuffle with umpire Constant as the umpires and captains moved into the Long Room after their fifth pitch inspection of the day. Ian Botham, the England captain, and Greg Chappell, his Australian counterpart, saw to it that matters got not worse. When play finally started at 3.45 p.m., police escorted the umpires through the Long Room and on to the field.

Two MCC members, identified by Chappell, were questioned by the Secretary, Mr J. A. Bailey, after the incident on Saturday afternoon. This was followed, on the Monday, by the following statement:

"Enquiries instituted today into the behaviour of certain MCC members towards the umpires and captains on Saturday leave no doubt that their conduct was inexcusable in any circumstances. Investigations are continuing and will be rigorously pursued with a view to identifying and disciplining the culprits. Meanwhile the club is sending to the umpires and to the captains of both sides their profound apologies that such an unhappy incident should have occurred at the headquarters of the game and on an occasion of such importance."

Fifty minutes had been lost to rain on the first day and all but an hour and a quarter on the second. On the third, the Saturday, ninety minutes' rain in the early morning left a soft area around two old uncovered pitches on the Tavern side of the ground. The ground staff, however, thought play could have started by lunch, as did a crowd of some 20,000 who were growing increasingly impatient in sunshine and breeze. Umpires Bird and Constant were the sole judges of when play should start, with one captain noticeably keener to play than the other; Australia being in the stronger position, Chappell was the more eager of the two. They conducted inspection after inspection, seemingly insensitive to the crowd's rising anger and the need for flexibility on such a special occasion. By the time the President of MCC, Mr S. C. Griffith, exerted pressure on the umpires to get the game started, the pavilion fracas had occurred. Although the authorities decided, when play did resume, that it could continue until eight o'clock that Saturday evening, it was fairly certain the light, by then, would not have been fit for play. In the event it soon rained again. An extra hour was also added to each of the last two days of the match.

On the field Australia were much the more convincing side, making a nonsense of the pre-match odds of seven to one against an Australian victory. After Chappell had won the toss Australia batted well through repeated interruptions before declaring on the Saturday evening at 385 for five. Wood contributed a battling 112, before being brilliantly stumped by Bairstow off Emburey, and Hughes graced the occasion with a highly talented and spirited 117 in which he hit three 6s and fourteen 4s, every stroke being played according to the fighting intentions of his side. Against such aggression England's bowling, with the exception of Old, looked very ordinary.

Lillee and Pascoe, with faster and more skilful bowling than their opponents', routed England for 205 on the Monday with enough time left that evening for Australia to score 106 for two, taking their lead to 286. In England's first innings Boycott, Gower and Old were the only batsmen to pass 20. Lillee, superbly controlled, removed the first four batsmen, and Pascoe finished the innings with a spell of five for 15 in 32 balls. Both bowlers took all their wickets at the Nursery End, once so infamous for its ridge. Chappell insisted that the ridge was still plainly visible and very much in play although the pitch had been shifted some four or five feet away from the Pavilion End in an effort to escape its influence.

England's first innings collapse, in which they lost their last seven wickets for 68 runs, had left Australia in a potentially winning position when the last day began. They hammered a further 83 runs in under an hour before Chappell's second declaration left England to score for almost six hours at over a run a minute. In Australia's second innings Chappell made a sound 59 and Hughes a brilliant 84. Moving into his shots with zest and certainty Hughes played the most spectacular stroke of the match when he danced down the pitch to hit the lively Old on to the top deck of the pavilion.

England did not attempt to meet Chappell's challenge. When Lillee trapped Gooch lbw for 16 and Pascoe removed Athey, to a bat-pad catch, for 1, survival became the priority. The in-form Boycott dropped anchor and Gower curbed his attacking instincts as they consolidated. When the score had reached 112 for two by three o'clock, with play possible until seven o'clock, many felt it would have been fitting if Botham had come in himself and had a fling. But the highest total England have ever made in a fourth innings to beat Australia in England is 269 for nine, at The Oval in 1902, and now they looked upon their first innings collapse as good enough reason for not risking another. Amid more boos than cheers they moved unhurriedly towards a draw. During the match the insatiable Boycott passed the Test aggregates of both Sir Leonard Hutton (6,971) and Sir Donald Bradman (6,996) and took his own Test aggregate to 7,115 runs. Boycott's second innings hundred was his sixth against Australia and his nineteenth in Tests.

The Cornhill Trophy and cheque for £500 as Man of the Match went to Hughes, and the prize-money of £4,500 was split between the sides. The official attendance was 84,938; takings were £360,850.50.

Australia

G. M. Wood st Bairstow b Emburey	112	(2) lbw b Old	8
B. M. Laird c Bairstow b Old	24	(1) c Bairstow b Old	6
*G. S. Chappell c Gatting b Old	47	b Old	59
K. J. Hughes c Athey b Old	117	lbw b Botham	84
G. N. Yallop lbw b Hendrick	2		
A. R. Border not out	56	(5) not out	21
†R. W. Marsh not out	16		
B 1, l-b 8, n-b 2	11	B 1, l-b 8, n-b 2	11
1/64 2/150 3/260 4/267 5/320	(5 wkts dec.) 385	1/15 2/28 3/139 4/189	(4 wkts dec.) 189

D. K. Lillee, A. A. Mallett, R. J. Bright and L. S. Pascoe did not bat.

Bowling: *First Innings*—Old 35–9–91–3; Hendrick 30–6–67–1; Botham 22–2–89–0; Emburey 38–9–104–1; Gooch 8–3–16–0; Willey 1–0–7–0. *Second Innings*—Old 20–6–47–3; Hendrick 15–4–53–0; Emburey 9–2–35–0; Botham 9.2–1–43–1.

England

G. A. Gooch c Bright b Lillee	8	lbw b Lillee	16
G. Boycott c Marsh b Lillee	62	not out	128
C. W. J. Athey b Lillee	9	c Laird b Pascoe	1
D. I. Gower b Lillee	45	b Mallett	35
M. W. Gatting lbw b Pascoe	12	not out	51
*I. T. Botham c Wood b Pascoe	0		
P. Willey lbw b Pascoe	5		
†D. L. Bairstow lbw b Pascoe	6		
J. E. Emburey lbw b Pascoe	3		
C. M. Old not out	24		
M. Hendrick c Border b Mallett	5		
B 6, l-b 8, n-b 12	26	B 3, l-b 2, n-b 8	13
1/10 2/41 3/137 4/151 5/158 6/163 7/164 8/173 9/200	205	1/19 2/43 3/124	(3 wkts) 244

Bowling: *First Innings*—Lillee 15–4–43–4; Pascoe 18–5–59–5; Chappell 2–0–2–0; Bright 21–6–50–0; Mallett 7.2–3–25–1. *Second Innings*—Lillee 19–5–53–1; Pascoe 17–1–73–1; Bright 25–9–44–0; Mallett 21–2–61–1.

H. D. Bird and D. J. Constant.

NOTES BY THE EDITOR, 1981

THE CENTENARY FRACAS

This great jamboree, arranged to celebrate 100 years of Test cricket between England and Australia in England, had been eagerly awaited. Its counterpart, at Melbourne in 1977, had been a wonderful success. As will be clear from the account of it elsewhere in this Almanack, last summer's match was ill-fated from the start. Some would say that the hours from eleven o'clock until six o'clock on the Saturday were like a nightmare. So incensed were certain members of MCC by the middle of the afternoon that play was not in progress, owing, as they thought, to the obstinacy of the umpires, that a scuffle took place on the steps of the pavilion, in which the umpires, one or two members, and the captains were involved. As a result of it, the umpires were shaken, the reputation of MCC was damaged and the occasion impaired.

Two and a half months later, following what MCC described as a "thorough inquiry" – which included taking the evidence of the umpires, the captains and a number of members, and studying a BBC film recording of the incident – Peter May, President of MCC, wrote in a letter to all members of the club that "appropriate disciplinary action" had been taken. He made the point, too, that it was no more fitting for members of a club publicly to question the decision of the umpires, let alone abuse them, than for players to do so on the field. If good is to come from a sorry affair, it will be to see that efforts are redoubled to provide the best possible covering on all first-class grounds, especially those where Test matches are staged. As many have said, it seems laughable to be able to land a man on the moon yet to have discovered no adequate way of protecting the square at Lord's.

FIFTY YEARS ON

By G. O. Allen

The Test match against Australia at Lord's in 1930 was my first. Now, 50 years later, presumably because I am, sadly, the only surviving member of that England team, I have been asked to record my impressions of, and draw some comparisons between, that match and the Centenary Test match against Australia at Lord's last summer.

That the former was one of the great games in cricket history and the latter was not was due partly to chance. For one thing, the weather in 1930 was perfect. So, though on the slow side, was the pitch, which had been specially prepared, this being the first ever four-day Test match at Lord's. In 1890 it rained often enough and hard enough on the first three days to have confounded even the 1930 sides from providing as much entertainment and fine cricket as I believe they did half a century ago. To that extent, Chappell and Botham and their two sides were up against it from the start. On the other hand, I am sure that in 1930, in conditions similar to those on the Saturday of the Centenary Test match, play would have started much earlier than it did. In fact, looking back to the thirties, when pitches were uncovered and there was much less covering generally, I think that play was often started too soon; but surely the pendulum has now swung too far in the opposite direction.

It must seem incredible to many who play and watch the game today that England could have made 425 in the first innings of a four-day match, as they did at Lord's in 1930, and yet have lost. In reply, Australia scored 729 for six declared. In the last two hours forty minutes on the second day, Australia went from 162 for one to 404 for two – 255 runs, that is, in 160 minutes, of which Bradman made 155. At the start of the last day England, in their second innings, were 98 for two, still 206 behind with Hobbs and Woolley out, and it needed a great innings of 121 in two and half hours by Chapman to save his side from an innings defeat. In the end Australia, losing three wickets (including that of Bradman) for 22 runs, had a minor crisis to surmount before winning with an hour to spare.

But this was the age of the batsman, the age before the lbw law was changed, and this was a batsman's match throughout. The pitch, for the reason I have mentioned, was easy-paced, and the bowlers, the leg-spinners and White excepted, were perhaps slightly below standard, Tate by then being a little over the top.

For England the outstanding innings were those of Chapman and Duleepsinhji, though Woolley's 41 in very quick time on the first morning was a gem. Duleepsinhji's 173 in his first Test match against Australia was one of the most graceful exhibitions of batting I have ever seen: he was a superb player of spinners as he proved on this occasion. Chapman's was a fine effort, particularly the second half of it, though he played and missed many times in his first fifty. I can vouch for this as I was in with him, and he should have been out before scoring. I can see it now: he failed to spot Grimmett's googly and hit a skier on the off side. Woodfull, Richardson and Ponsford all could have caught it easily, but at the last moment, no one having called, each left it to the other. Amidst much laughter and some apologies all Grimmett said was "Never mind, I'll get him out next over". When watching the Centenary match with Ponsford, I mentioned the incident to him. He remembered it well, but to our mutual enjoyment he was disinclined to admit to more than a minor share of the guilt.

For Australia, the first four, Woodfull, Ponsford, Bradman and Kippax, all played fine innings, each in his own rather different style: Woodfull with his short backlift, very sure but always looking for runs; Ponsford mainly on the back foot or up the wicket to the spinners and a superb timer of the ball; Kippax a very elegant stroke-player on both sides of the wicket – and then, of course, Bradman. The best comment on Bradman's innings is probably his own. When asked which was the best innings he ever played, he is on record as saying: "My 254 at Lord's in 1930 because I never hit a ball anywhere than I intended and I never lifted one off the ground until the stroke from which I was out." Some believe he was unorthodox. Well, perhaps he was when he was really on the rampage, but in defence and when necessary, none was more correct. It was his early judgment of length, his quickness of foot and his ruthless concentration which made him the undoubted genius he was.

The Centenary Test match is a different story. As I have already said, conditions were unfavourable from the start. Even had MCC acquired an additional cover, and before the match the captains and umpires had been requested by the authorities to be rather less stern in their judgment as to fitness for play, I doubt if it would have helped greatly as it is always difficult to make a game flow once it has been subject to frequent interruptions.

I hate saying it, but I do not think either looked a very good side. There were, of course, several high-class batsmen amongst them, and in Lillee certainly the best fast bowler in either match. Although perhaps not quite as fast as he was, his rhythm, his ability to move the ball and vary his pace, and his unbounded determination were a feature of the match.

For Australia, Wood played a sound first innings and Chappell two good though for him rather subdued innings. In form, with all his strokes going, Chappell must rank high amongst batsmen of our time. But in this match it was Hughes who caught the eye, at least mine. Of course he took some chances and had his moments of luck, particularly in the second innings, but he was reluctant to be dictated to, moved his feet well, and with a wholesome backlift was able and prepared to play all the strokes. After 50 years one's memory is hazy, but of one thing I am sure – his straight six off Old was unquestionably the best hit in either match, indeed possibly the most remarkable straight hit I have seen. To take two paces up the wicket to a fast-medium bowler of Old's class and hit a flat "skimmer" on to the top of the Pavilion at Lord's takes some beating. Goodness only knows where it might have gone had he, to use a golfing term, taken a slightly more lofted club.

For England, the batting, with two exceptions, was below Test match standard, even after making allowances for the excellent fast attack of Lillee and Pascoe and the fact that the match took place late in the season after a difficult series against some relentless West Indian fast bowling. Boycott showed his undoubted class in two typically determined innings. Technically he is head and shoulders ahead of any other batsman in England, indeed his technique is so good it is surprising he does not tear the attack apart more often. Gower twice played some fine strokes and was beginning to look the batsman all Englishmen hope and believe he will be, only to get out to two bad shots. Unfortunately Gooch, who is now an extremely good opener and a powerful striker of the ball, failed in both innings.

So much for my impressions of the two matches: now for some comparisons. My first and foremost must be regarding the pace at which they were played, and the Centenary match is a fair example of how the game has slowed down over the span of years. I may have some regrets about the present-day game, but this is my one real criticism of it. Statistics are often boring and can be unjust, but in this instance I think they are interesting and revealing in that they provide some indication as to how much and why this state of affairs has come about.

In the 1930 match 1,601 runs were scored in 23 hours 10 minutes, that is at an average of 69 runs per hour, whereas in the Centenary match 1,023 were scored in 21 hours 7 minutes, an average of 48.4, per hour. A difference of 20 runs an hour is disturbing, to say the least; yet if one looks at the runs per 100 balls one finds very little between them, there being 53 runs in 1930 and 51.2 in 1980. If one then takes into account the importance nowadays attached by captains to containment and the present high standard of fielding, it is clear the batsmen must be exonerated.

And so, inevitably, to the over rate. In 1930, 260 overs of pace and 245 of spin were bowled at an average of 21.50 an hour: in 1980, 210 overs of pace and 122 of spin were bowled at an average of 15.82 an hour. These figures for pace and spin suggest to me that it is not solely the predominance of fast bowling that is responsible for the loss of 5.68 overs an hour. The endless discussions between bowlers and captains, the frequent changes in field-placing – and the waiting for new batsmen to reach the crease before making some of them – waste part of the time. But it is the absurdly long run-ups of many of the fast bowlers, and even of some of the medium-paced bowlers, often coupled with a funeral walk back to their marks, that are the real cause of the trouble. For those who saw little or no cricket before World War Two, I can assure them one could count on the fingers of one hand the number of fast bowlers who ran more than 25 yards: nowadays one can count on the fingers of one hand those who do not – and some run 40 or 45 yards. Of course a few of these long-runners are a fine sight coming in, but please let us be spared their country strolls.

One last statistic, a sombre thought. In a 30-hour Test match, the loss of 5.68 overs and 20 runs an hour could mean the loss of as many as 170 overs and 600 runs. Put another way, the debit, in terms of the modern rate as compared with the old, is roughly two whole days' play.

The comparison between the number of paying customers and the takings for the two matches is illuminating: in 1930, 110,000 people paid £14,500 to watch the four-day match; in 1980, 84,938 over the five-day match paid £360,850 and had the weather been kinder that figure must have been in excess of £400,000. At the moment the situation is clearly very satisfactory, but might not the crunch come if the tempo is not increased, especially when the opposition is less glamorous?

As regards the fielding there can be no argument. In the 1930 match it was moderate. For England Hammond and Duleepsinhji were two fine "slippers"; I still maintain that the former was the best I have ever seen. Chapman, who made magnificent catches to dismiss Bradman in both innings, was excellent anywhere, as was Robins. Hobbs, Hendren and Woolley, who had all been of the highest class, were by then getting on in years. For Australia only Bradman and Richardson really stood out. In the Centenary match the general standard was far superior, the ground fielding and throwing being superb. The catching was not put to the test, but knowing something of both sides I am certain it, too, would have been of the highest order. The "sliding tackle" is a spectacular innovation. In the thirties, even if I had thought of it, I could barely have afforded the additional cleaning bills.

In addition to the tempo there was another fundamental difference between the two matches, namely the approach and tactics of the sides in the field. In 1930, with both teams relying heavily on a leg-spinner and slow left-armer, the theme was always likely to be attack. In the modern game, though rather less in evidence in the Centenary match, defensive field placing, containment, call it what you will, plays an important rôle. Hence the attraction for the crowds lies more in the brilliance of the fielding and perhaps a fiercer sense of conflict engendered by the menace of the fast bowling. It is not surprising that defensive tactics have crept into cricket – they are common to most sports today. No doubt more or earlier use of them might have been advantageous in the thirties, but strange, even crazy, as it may seen now, I simply do not think that was the way either captains or players wanted to play their cricket.

I said earlier that I might have some regrets about the present-day game. Well, I do have one or two. I particularly regret the lack of variety, once one of the charms of cricket, and for much of this I blame, each in its own way, the change in the lbw law introduced way back in 1935 and the lack of pace in many of the pitches. The change in the lbw law was designed to prevent "padding-up"; it was also argued that it would help all types of bowlers equally and increase off-side play. In the event, apart from reducing the use of the pads to some extent, it has, in my opinion, done more harm than good. As it has helped disproportionally bowlers who bring the ball into the batsman, it has swung the game more towards the leg-side and has contributed in no small degree to the demise of both the leg-spinner and the slow left-armer. Then, with pitches getting slower and slower, containment was bound to become the order of the day. I, for one, do not blame the players, I simply pray for more variety. But how to restore it is the baffling question.

I regret, too, the predominance of the "forward prod" to balls short of a length: that can certainly be blamed on the lbw law. It is safer forward. But excessive forward play must restrict the batsman's range, there being so many attractive and lucrative strokes to be found off the back foot.

And my last lament: I find the incessant noise on many big-match days thoroughly irksome. I welcome the enthusiasm, the cheering and the clapping, but the banging of cans and the endless alcoholic shouting is not for me.

But I have no wish to end these thoughts on a critical note. The game has undoubtedly changed in some respects, mainly in the last 25 years, but in saying this I am not suggesting that it is not in a healthy state: it is. Sadly, circumstances conspired against the Centenary match; yet it was a happy, nostalgic occasion, wherein old rivalries were recalled and old friendships renewed. There is, after all, nothing in cricket to compare with England v Australia, the oldest of all Test match fixtures.

DERBYSHIRE v AUSTRALIANS

Played at Derby, June 10, 11, 12, 1981

Drawn. A high-class innings by Wright, in which he became the first to hit a century against the 1981 touring side, was the highest-ever by a Derbyshire batsman against the Australians. Eighth out at 207, having reached his century out of 144, the New Zealander hit nineteen 4s in five and a quarter hours. No other batsman could come to terms with a disappointingly slow pitch and the Australians made predictably erratic progress on the second day, when Anderson's off-spin earned him career-best figures. The match was notable for the presence of two players who had received birthday honours, both Lillee and Taylor having been awarded the MBE.

Derbyshire

J. G. Wright b Alderman	144	– c Hughes b Alderman	3
B. Wood c Rixon b Lillee	2	– b Bright	25
P. N. Kirsten c Bright b Beard	1	– c Hughes b Border	41
D. S. Steele c Alderman b Bright	20	– not out	46
K. J. Barnett c Rixon b Alderman	2	– run out	28
A. Hill lbw b Alderman	4	– lbw b Alderman	0
I. S. Anderson c Rixon b Lillee	4	– not out	0
*G. Miller lbw b Alderman	14		
†R. W. Taylor not out	5		
C. J. Tunnicliffe c Border b Bright	7		
L-b 5, w 2, n-b 8	15	B 11, l-b 5, w 1, n-b 3	20
1/11 2/15 3/86 4/112 5/116 6/143 7/201 8/207 9/218	(9 wkts dec.) 218	1/9 2/62 3/93 4/147 5/156	(5 wkts dec.) 163

P. G. Newman did not bat.

Bowling: *First Innings*—Lillee 24–9–53–2; Alderman 21–5–38–4; Beard 17–5–38–1; Bright 24.3–10–43–2; Border 5–0–13–0; Chappell 4–1–18–0. *Second Innings*—Lillee 19–8–38–0; Alderman 13–8–18–2; Bright 25–9–55–1; Border 9–5–12–1; Beard 9–4–15–0; Hughes 3–2–3–0; Dyson 1–0–2–0.

Australians

J. Dyson b Anderson	61
T. M. Chappell run out	14
M. F. Kent b Wood	2
*K. J. Hughes c Miller b Anderson	19
A. R. Border c Kirsten b Anderson	5
D. M. Wellham not out	47
†S. J. Rixon c Hill b Anderson	24
R. J. Bright lbw b Kirsten	0
G. R. Beard c Anderson b Newman	2
B 4, l-b 5, n-b 7	16
1/25 2/37 3/91 4/101 5/126 6/170 7/171 8/190 (8 wkts dec.)	190

D. K. Lillee and T. M. Alderman did not bat.

Bowling: Newman 14.2–4–28–1; Tunnicliffe 13–3–27–0; Wood 18–3–41–1; Steele 9–6–4–0; Miller 10–2–23–0; Anderson 18–7–35–4; Kirsten 6–1–16–1.

Umpires: D. G. L. Evans and D. O. Oslear.

ENGLAND v AUSTRALIA

Third Cornhill Test

Played at Leeds, July 16, 17, 18, 20, 21, 1981

England won by 18 runs. A match which had initially produced all the wet and tedious traits of recent Leeds Tests finally ended in a way to stretch the bounds of logic and belief. England's victory, achieved under the gaze of a spellbound nation, was the first this century by a team following on, and only the second such result in the history of Test cricket.

The transformation occurred in less than 24 hours, after England had appeared likely to suffer their second four-day defeat of the series. Wherever one looked, there were personal dramas: Brearley, returning as captain like England's saviour: Botham, who was named Man of the Match, brilliant once more in his first game back in the ranks; Willis, whose career has so often heard the distant drums, producing the most staggering bowling of his life when his place again seemed threatened.

Others, too, had good reason to remember this game. It was the first time in nineteen Tests that Willey had been a member of a victorious side, there were wicket-keeping records for both Taylor (all first-class cricket) and Marsh (Tests), Dyson made his maiden century for Australia, and Lillee moved further up the list of bowling immortals. But if the statisticians revelled in such facts, they were, for most of us, submerged in the tension of a climax as near to miraculous as a Test ever can have been.

None of this had seemed remotely likely on the opening day when the familiar slate-grey clouds engulfed the chimneys which stretch away from the Kirkstall Lane End. Australia, one up in the series, were unchanged; England made two changes, Woolmer standing down for Brearley and Old returning on his home ground at the expense of Emburey.

England thus went in with four seamers and only Willey to provide a measure of spin. It was a selectorial policy which caused considerable discussion. Brearley later confessed he lost sleep on the first night for fear that it had been a mistake. As things transpired, however, it was largely irrelevant.

Australia, having chosen to bat, ended the first day in fine health at 203 for three, the extra hour having reduced lost time to only fifty minutes. Dyson batted diligently for his century, playing chiefly off the back foot, and survived one chance to Botham in the gully, when 57. Chappell, who supported Dyson staunchly in a stand of 94 for the second wicket, was twice reprieved – by Gower and Botham again – so England, not for the first time this summer, suffered for their ineptitude in the field. The other talking-point of the day concerned Headingley's new electronic scoreboard, which had a mixed reception, being difficult to see from most parts of the ground when the sun began to sink.

It will come as a surprise when, in future years, people look back on a Test of such apparently outrageous drama, to know that the second day was pedestrian in the extreme. Botham, to some degree, salvaged English pride by taking five more wickets, all of them in an after-tea spell costing 35 runs, and finishing with six for 95. Naturally, the assumption was drawn that he is a more effective player without leadership duties. Despite his efforts, Australia extended their score to 401 for nine, thanks to half-centuries from Hughes and Yallop. It was another day of patchy weather and patchy cricket, completed when Gooch and Boycott saw out an over apiece from Lillee and Alderman without mishap.

At this stage, the odds seemed in favour of a draw. An England win was on offer generously, though by no means as extravagantly as 24 hours later when Ladbrokes, from their tent on the ground, posted it at 500 to 1. The reason for their estimate was a truncated day on which England were dismissed for 174 and, following on 227 behind, lost Gooch without addition. Australia's seamers had shown what could be done by bowling straighter and to a fuller length than their counterparts. Other than Botham, who opted for all-out aggression and profited by a swift 50, England at no stage commanded and were occasionally undone by deliveries performing contortions at speed. Botham fell victim to just such a ball from Lillee and the catch by Marsh was his 264th in Tests, beating Knott's record.

The third day ended with unhappy scenes similar to those seen at Lord's, when spectators hurled cushions and abuse at the umpires. On this occasion, Messrs Meyer and Evans had walked to the middle, wearing blazers, at five to six, after a lengthy stoppage for poor light. They consulted their meters and summoned the covers, abandoning play just before the hour. With cruel irony, the light improved instantly, the sun was soon breaking through and the large crowd was incited to wrathful demands for explanations as to why they were not watching the prescribed extra hour. Once more, it seems, confusion in interpretation of the playing regulations was the cause of the ill feeling: they stated only that conditions must be fit for play at the scheduled time of finish and not, as the umpires thought, that play must actually be in motion. Whether it was, in fact, fit at six o'clock is open to doubt, but the TCCB soon adjusted the ruling so that play in future Tests in the series could restart at any stage of the extra hour.

This heated diversion seemed likely to achieve nothing more than a stay of sentence for England, a view which appeared amply confirmed by late afternoon on the Monday. England were then 135 for seven, still 92 behind, and the distant objective of avoiding an innings defeat surely their only available prize. Lillee and Alderman had continued where Saturday's disturbances had forced them to leave off, and for all Boycott's skilful resistance, the cause seemed lost. Boycott, who batted three and a half hours, was sixth out to an lbw decision he seemed not to relish, and when Taylor followed quickly, the England players' decision to check out of their hotel seemed a sound move. Three hours later, the registration desks around Leeds were coping with a flood of re-bookings, Botham having destroyed the game's apparently set course with an astonishing, unbeaten 145, ably and forcefully aided by Dilley. Together they added 117 in 80 minutes for the eighth wicket, only 7 short of an England record against Australia. Both struck the ball so cleanly and vigorously that Hughes's men were temporarily in disarray; when Dilley departed after scoring 56 precious runs. Old arrived to add 67 more with Botham, who still had Willis as a partner at the close, with England 124 ahead.

Botham advanced his unforgettable innings to 149 not out before losing Willis the next morning, but Australia, needing 130, still remained clear favourites. Then, at 56 for one, Willis, having changed ends to bowl with the wind, dismissed Chappell with a rearing delivery and the staggering turnabout was under way. Willis bowled as if inspired. It is not uncommon to see him perform for England as if his very life depended on it, but this was something unique. In all, he took eight wickets for 43, the best of his career, as Australia's last nine wickets tumbled for 55 runs despite a stand of 35 in four overs between Bright and Lillee. Old bowled straight and aggressively and England rose to the need to produce an outstanding show in the field. Yet this was Willis's hour, watched or listened to by a vast invisible audience. At the end, the crowd gathered to wave their Union Jacks and chant patriotically, eight days in advance of the Royal Wedding.

Takings were £206,500 and the attendance 52,566.

Australia

J. Dyson b Dilley	102	– (2) c Taylor b Willis	34
G. M. Wood lbw b Botham	34	– (1) c Taylor b Botham	10
T. M. Chappell c Taylor b Willey	27	– c Taylor b Willis	8
*K. J. Hughes c and b Botham	89	– c Botham b Willis	0
R. J. Bright b Dilley	7	– (8) b Willis	19
G. N. Yallop c Taylor b Botham	58	– (5) c Gatting b Willis	0
A. R. Border lbw b Botham	8	– (6) b Old	0
†R. W. Marsh b Botham	28	– (7) c Dilley b Willis	4
G. F. Lawson c Taylor b Botham	13	– c Taylor b Willis	1
D. K. Lillee not out	3	– c Gatting b Willis	17
T. M. Alderman not out	0	– not out	0
B 4, l-b 13, w 3, n-b 12	32	L-b 3, w 1, n-b 14	18
1/55 2/149 3/196 4/220 5/332 6/354 7/357 8/396 9/401	(9 wkts dec.) 401	1/13 2/56 3/58 4/58 5/65 6/68 7/74 8/75 9/110	111

Bowling: *First Innings*—Willis 30–8–72–0; Old 43–14–91–0; Dilley 27–4–78–2; Botham 39.2–11–95–6; Willey 13–2–31–1; Boycott 3–2–2–0. *Second Innings*—Botham 7–3–14–1; Dilley 2–0–11–0; Willis 15.1–3–43–8; Old 9–1–21–1; Willey 3–1–4–0.

England

G. A. Gooch lbw b Alderman	2	– c Alderman b Lillee	0
G. Boycott b Lawson	12	– lbw b Alderman	46
*J. M. Brearley c Marsh b Alderman	10	– c Alderman b Lillee	14
D. I. Gower c Marsh b Lawson	24	– c Border b Alderman	9
M. W. Gatting lbw b Lillee	15	– lbw b Alderman	1
P. Willey b Lawson	8	– c Dyson b Lillee	33
I. T. Botham c Marsh b Lillee	50	– not out	149
†R. W. Taylor c March b Lillee	5	– c Bright b Alderman	1
G. R. Dilley c and b Lillee	13	– b Alderman	56
C. M. Old c Border b Alderman	0	– b Lawson	29
R. G. D. Willis not out	1	– c Border b Alderman	2
B 6, l-b 11, w 6, n-b 11	34	B 5, l-b 3, w 3, n-b 5	16
1/12 2/40 3/42 4/84 5/87 6/112 7/148 8/166 9/167	174	1/0 2/18 3/37 4/41 5/105 6/133 7/135 8/252 9/319	356

Bowling: *First Innings*—Lillee 18.5–7–49–4; Alderman 19–4–59–3; Lawson 13–3–32–3. *Second Innings*—Lillee 25–6–94–3; Alderman 35.3–6–135–6; Lawson 23–4–96–1; Bright 4–0–15–0.

Umpires: B. J. Meyer and D. G. L. Evans.

ENGLAND v AUSTRALIA

Fourth Cornhill Test

Played at Birmingham, July 30, 31, August 1, 2, 1981

England won by 29 runs. A startling spell of bowling by Botham, from the Pressbox End, which brought him five wickets for 1 run in 28 deliveries, ended an extraordinary Test match at 4.30 p.m. on a glorious Sunday afternoon. And so, for a second successive Test, England contrived to win after appearing badly beaten. As at Leeds, a large crowd helped give the match an exciting and emotional finish and once again critics, commentators and writers were left looking foolish, a fact that the players of both teams were quick to point out afterwards.

For a third time in the series, after Trent Bridge and Headingley, the pitch was the centre of controversy, though when Brearley elected to bat on a fine sunny morning on what is traditionally regarded as one of the finest surfaces in England, it looked in superb condition. Hughes was reported to have said that it looked good for 800 runs. The outfield was fast and the temperature acceptable to Melbourne. Certainly no-one at Edgbaston could have dreamt that this would be the first Test since 1934, anywhere in the world, in which no batsman made a fifty.

Boycott and Brearley opened, a change in the order that had caused misgivings, and had reached 29 in forty-five minutes when Alderman's late swing defeated Boycott and then, two overs later, provoked Gower, a reluctant number three, to try, unsuccessfully, to hit over mid-on. Alderman had figures then of 7–4–4–2, and although Brearley denied himself a run for an hour, surviving a vehement appeal for a slip catch by Wood, he and Gooch saw Alderman and Lillee retire. It was Bright, making the spinner's now customary appearance just before the interval, who tempted Gooch into a rash pull that cost a third wicket at 60.

The afternoon was an English disaster. Bright, from the Pavilion End, used the rough outside the leg stump while Alderman, with Lillee in the unusual rôle of deputy, and Hogg were straight and swift from the other. By 5.30 p.m. England had been dismissed for 189, of which Brearley had made 48 in just under four hours, four boundaries off Lillee promoting his innings from one of mere resistance. Alderman had taken five for 42 before Old, from that same Pressbox End, then rattled the teaspoons in the Australian dressing-room by removing Dyson and Border, in five overs, for 19 runs by the close.

The pitch, declared England's players the following day, after they had been roasted overnight by the media, was untrustworthy. It was too dry, the surface was less than firm, the occasional ball kept low, and there was turn for the spinner. Shoulder to shoulder, Australia's batsmen were later to demonstrate their solidarity with their English colleagues.

Friday was cool and grey and England did well to restrict the Australian lead to 69. Brearley was at his best, constantly varying pressure on each batsman by his bowling and fielding changes, never losing the initiative, while his men responded admirably, running out Wood and Hogg and causing enough apprehension to deter Australia from attempting up to a dozen further singles. Hughes, batting well through a stormy spell by Willis, whose five bouncers in two overs caused the umpires to confer, was unlucky to be leg-before to a low bounce. Although Brearley fell to Lillee on a gloomy evening, England had narrowed the margin to 20 runs.

Blue sky and Satuday sunshine attracted 15,000 spectators, whose holiday mood was not jollied along by Boycott, who spent three hours three minutes raising his score to 29 – 7 short of Cowdrey's Test aggregate record for an Englishman – before falling to Bright. So, too, did Gower, Gooch and Willey, and when Botham was caught behind off Lillee, England's lead was no more than 46, with four wickets standing. Fortunately for England their tail-end batsmen, urged on by the combative Gatting, batted bravely. Emburey, 37 not out, demonstrated that Bright's line allowed him to be swept profitably, while Old hit straight and hard before taking the ball to dismiss Wood in the evening haze. Yet Australia needed only another 142 to win, with two days to play. Miracles, wrote a distinguished correspondent, like lightning, do not strike twice.

Willis, bowling again as if the devil were at his heels, removed Dyson and Hughes in the first forty minutes on the fourth morning (Sunday), but Border was his resolute self and at 105 for four, with only 46 more needed, Australia seemed to have the match won. However, Border was then desperately unlucky to be caught off his gloves, a ball from Emburey suddenly lifting prodigiously. Brearley, who had ordered Willey to loosen up with the idea of using spin at both ends, in a last gamble, changed his mind and called on a reluctant Botham.

Somerset's giant bowled quicker than for some time, was straight and pitched the ball up, and one after another five Australian batsmen walked into the point of the lance. The crowd, dotted with green and gold, were beside themselves with agony and ecstasy as, only twelve days after Headingley, history amazingly repeated itself.

Botham was again named Man of the Match, though Emburey would have been the choice of many. Takings for the match amounted to £183,000 from a total attendance of 55,750.

England

G. Boycott c Marsh b Alderman	13	– c Marsh b Bright	29
*J. M. Brearley c Border b Lillee	48	– lbw b Lillee	13
D. I. Gower c Hogg b Alderman	0	– c Border b Bright	23
G. A. Gooch c Marsh b Bright	21	– b Bright	21
M. W. Gatting c Alderman b Lillee	21	– b Bright	39
P. Willey b Bright	16	– b Bright	5
I. T. Botham b Alderman	26	– c Marsh b Lillee	3
J. E. Emburey b Hogg	3	– (9) not out	37
†R. W. Taylor b Alderman	0	– (10) lbw b Alderman	8
C. M. Old not out	11	– (8) c Marsh b Alderman	23
R. G. D. Willis c Marsh b Alderman	13	– c Marsh b Alderman	2
B 1, l-b 5, w 1, n-b 10	17	L-b 6, w 1, n-b 9	16
1/29 2/29 3/60 4/101 5/126 6/145 7/161 8/161 9/165	189	1/18 2/52 3/89 4/98 5/110 6/115 7/154 8/167 9/217	219

Bowling: *First Innings*—Lillee 18–4–61–2; Alderman 23.1–8–42–5; Hogg 16–3–49–1; Bright 12–4–20–2. *Second Innings*—Lillee 26–9–51–2; Alderman 22–5–65–3; Hogg 10–3–19–0; Bright 34–17–68–5.

Australia

G. M. Wood run out	38	– (2) lbw b Old	2
J. Dyson b Old	1	– (1) lbw b Willis	13
A. R. Border c Taylor b Old	2	– c Gatting b Emburey	40
R. J. Bright lbw b Botham	27	– (8) lbw b Botham	0
*K. J. Hughes lbw b Old	47	– (4) c Emburey b Willis	5
G. N. Yallop b Emburey	30	– (5) c Botham b Emburey	30
M. F. Kent c Willis b Emburey	46	– (6) b Botham	10
†R. W. Marsh b Emburey	2	– (7) b Botham	4
D. K. Lillee b Emburey	18	– c Taylor b Botham	3
R. M. Hogg run out	0	– not out	0
T. M. Alderman not out	3	– b Botham	0
B 4, l-b 19, n-b 21	44	B 1, l-b 2, n-b 11	14
1/5 2/14 3/62 4/115 5/166 6/203 7/220 8/253 9/253	258	1/2 2/19 3/29 4/87 5/105 6/114 7/114 8/120 9/121	121

Bowling: *First Innings*—Willis 19–3–63–0; Old 21–8–44–3; Emburey 26.5–12–43–4; Botham 20–1–64–1. *Second Innings*—Willis 20–6–37–2; Old 11–4–19–1; Emburey 22–10–40–2; Botham 14–9–11–5.

H. D. Bird and D. O. Oslear.

ESSEX v AUSTRALIANS

Played at Chelmsford, August 8, 9, 10, 1981

Drawn. Although the fifth Test was less than a week away, the game was played in a friendly vein, with Rixon, Marsh and Yallop each keeping wicket – and bowling. Gooch, with four 6s and eight 4s, provided the fun on the opening day after overnight rain had delayed the start until half an hour after lunch. Consistent rather than spectacular batting enabled the Australians to declare 24 runs ahead, after which Essex took advantage of gentle bowling to hurry to a declaration. Lilley (two 6s and eight 4s) shared in a stand of 101 with Leiper, a nineteen-year-old left-hander making his first-class début. McEwan raced to 50 in only 33 minutes (one 6 and eight 4s) and Phillip also scored freely. The Australians, chasing 247 in three hours, suffered the loss of Kent and Wellham in Phillip's second over, but they never gave up the chase as Ray East, skippering the side in the absence of the injured Fletcher, kept the game open. However, despite a partnership of 94 in 75 minutes between Wood and Yallop, the touring side finished 10 runs short with two wickets left.

Essex

G. A. Gooch st Rixon b Yallop	86	– (7) c Bright b Beard	7
A. W. Lilley c and b Bright	21	– (1) st Marsh b Beard	64
R. J. Leiper c Kent b Beard	1	– c Wood b Lawson	49
K. S. McEwan c Wood b Yallop	39	– (6) c Lawson b Beard	50
B. R. Hardie c Lawson b Yallop	6	– (2) c Rixon b Beard	0
D. R. Pringle lbw b Marsh	28	– (9) not out	6
N. Phillip b Yallop	31	– (5) c Yallop b Hogg	45
†D. E. East not out	0	– c Rixon b Wellham	11
S. Turner (did not bat)		– (4) c Rixon b Yallop	14
*R. E. East (did not bat)		– not out	9
B 2, n-b 2	4	B 5, l-b 8, w 2	15
1/49 2/77 3/138 4/153 5/161 6/216 7/216 (7 wkts dec.)	216	1/0 2/101 3/126 4/147 5/226 6/238 7/246 8/259 (8 wkts dec.)	270

D. L. Acfield did not bat.

Bowling: *First Innings*—Lawson 6–1–25–0; Hogg 5–1–14–0; Bright 22–9–49–1; Beard 17–5–61–1; Yallop 19–6–63–4; Marsh 0.2–0–0–1. *Second Innings*—Yallop 17–2–80–1; Beard 23–2–92–4; Bright 8–4–17–0; Lawson 7–1–24–1; Rixon 2–0–19–0; Hogg 8–1–12–1; Wellham 2–0–11–1.

Australians

G. M. Wood b Turner	45	– (6) c Turner b R. E. East	60
M. F. Kent c D. E. East b Pringle	17	– c Lilley b Phillip	0
G. N. Yallop lbw b Pringle	49	– (7) not out	59
T. M. Chappell c Phillip b R. E. East	46	– (10) not out	3
D. M. Wellham not out	37	– (3) b Phillip	0
*R. W. Marsh c Gooch b R. E. East	28	– (4) c Lilley b Turner	38
†S. J. Rixon not out	6	– (1) c D. E. East b Gooch	40
R. J. Bright (did not bat)		– (5) c Acfield b Turner	20
G. R. Beard (did not bat)		– (8) c Pringle b Acfield	9
G. F. Lawson (did not bat)		– (9) b Acfield	3
L-b 3, w 1, n-b 8	12	B 1, n-b 4	5
1/36 2/84 3/152 4/189 5/230 (5 wkts dec.)	240	1/7 2/7 3/64 4/86 5/109 6/203 7/225 8/230 (8 wkts)	237

R. M. Hogg did not bat.

Bowling: *First Innings*—Phillip 4–0–11–0; Pringle 15–2–49–2; Acfield 20–4–61–0; Turner 12–3–54–1; R. E. East 18–3–53–2. *Second Innings*—Phillip 6–1–31–2; Pringle 5–0–16–0; Turner 13–2–41–2; Gooch 2–0–10–1; Acfield 20.5–2–87–2; R. E. East 9–0–47–1.

Umpires: A. Jepson and P. J. Eele.

ENGLAND v AUSTRALIA

Fifth Cornhill Test

Played at Manchester, August 13, 14, 15, 16, 17, 1981

England won by 103 runs, retaining the Ashes by going three-one up in the series. Like its two predecessors, the fifth test was a game of extraordinary fluctuations and drama, made wholly unforgettable by yet another *tour de force* by Man of the Match Botham, who, with the pendulum starting to swing Australia's way in England's second innings, launched an attack on Lillee and Alderman which, for its ferocious yet effortless power and dazzling cleanness of stroke, can surely never have been bettered in a Test match, even by the legendary Jessop.

Striding in to join Tavaré in front of 20,000 spectators on the Saturday afternoon when England, 101 ahead on first innings, had surrendered the initiative so totally that in 69 overs they had collapsed to 104 for five, Botham plundered 118 in 123 minutes. His innings included six 6s – a record for Anglo-Australian Tests – and thirteen 4s, all but one of which, an inside edge that narrowly missed the off stump on its way to fine leg, exploded off as near the middle of the bat as makes no odds. Of the 102 balls he faced (86 to reach the hundred), 53 were used up in reconnaissance in his first 28 runs (70 minutes). Then Alderman and Lillee took the second new ball and Botham erupted, smashing 66 off eight overs by tea with three 6s off Lillee, all hooked, and one off Alderman, a huge pull far back in the crowd to the left of the pavilion. He completed his hundred with his fifth 6, a sweep, added the sixth with an immense and perfectly struck blow over the sight-screen, also off Bright, and was caught at the wicket a few moments later off 22-year-old Mike Whitney. The brisk left-armer, after only six first-class games (four for New South Wales, two for Gloucestershire), had been plucked out of obscurity on the eve of the match when Australia learned that neither Hogg nor Lawson was fit to play.

Unkindly, it was to the greenhorn Whitney, running back from deep mid-off, that Botham, at 32, offered the first of two chances – nearer "quarter" than "half" – a high, swirling mishit over Alderman's head. The other came at 91 when Dyson, sprinting off the third-man boundary, then sliding forward on his knees and elbows, made a heroic effort to get his hands underneath a sliced square-cut off Lillee.

Of the 149 Botham and Tavaré added for the sixth wicket – after a morning in which England had lost three for 29 off 28 overs – Tavaré's share was 28. But his seven-hour 78, embodying the third-slowest 50 in Test cricket (304 minutes) was the rock on which Knott and Emburey sustained the recovery as the last four wickets added 151.

With the pitch growing steadily easier throughout the match, the full value of Tavaré's survival was seen on the fourth and fifth days when, thanks to Yallop's artistic 114 (three hours) and a fighting 123 not out in six and threequarter hours by Border, batting with a broken finger, Australia more than once seemed to be within reach of scoring 506 to win. Border's hundred, taking 373 minutes, was the slowest by an Australian in any Test, beating by four minutes Hughes's time for his hundred against England in 1978-79.

Had Australia managed to win, it would have been in keeping with a bizarre series; but with Lillee buoyantly supporting Border for the eighth wicket, Brearley threw a smokescreen over proceedings by allowing both batsmen singles – and the Australians, suspecting some sinister motive, lost impetus and purpose. The end came with 85 minutes left for play, when Whitney was caught by Gatting at short leg.

Except that after Headingley and Edgbaston one was forewarned that the impossible was likely to become commonplace, there was no indication on the first day that the match would produce such captivating theatre. Paul Allott, who was to play a vital rôle, was one of three England changes from the fourth Test, winning his first cap on his home ground in place of the injured Old, while Tavaré came in for Willey and Knott for Taylor. Underwood, in the original twelve on the assumption that the pitch would start bone dry and later crumble, was left out in favour of a fourth seamer when moisture was found beneath the surface following a storm the week before.

It was a toss Brearley would not have minded losing. But with Australia's fourth innings collapses in mind, he chose to bat. On a slowish, seaming pitch and in often gloomy light, Lillee and Alderman, with help from Whitney, reduced England to 175 for nine by close of play, with forty minutes lost to rain. Boycott passed Colin Cowdrey's record of 7,624 runs for England, but the only innings of note was Tavaré's stoic 69 in four and threequarter hours – the first half-century in twelve Tests by an England number three.

Next morning Hughes unaccountably used Whitney as Lillee's partner rather than Alderman, his most prolific bowler, and Allott and Willis added a priceless 56. Allott, displaying a technique and calmness well above his station, mingled some good strokes through the covers with a few lucky inside edges to make 52 not out, his highest score in first-class cricket.

Wood began with three hooked 4s and a 6 off Willis and Allott, like a man working off an insult. But just as suddenly Australia were 24 for four and *en route* to their shortest innings since 1902, when Rhodes (seven for 17) and Hirst (three for 15) bundled them out for 36 in 23 overs after rain. But on this occasion they had no such excuses to fall back on; indeed, they batted with a manic desperation wholly at odds with their need to win the match. The collapse began with three fine deliveries from Willis and one from Allott in the space of seven balls, a combination of disasters to shake the most confident of side. In Willis's third over, Dyson and Yallop could not keep down rapid, rising balls, while Hughes was trapped lbw by a breakback; and the first ball of the next over, by Allott, came back to have Wood lbw. Kent counter-attacked strongly with 52 in 70 minutes, but the loss of Border, to a stupendous overhead catch by Gower at fourth slip, and Marsh, when he could not pull his bat away in time to avoid another lifting ball from Willis, wrecked Australia's chances of recovery.

Just under a day later, when England had slumped to 104 for five, Australia may have entertained the hope that their 130 would not be terminal. But then came Botham . . . and it was.

Attendance was 80,000 and receipts were £295,000.

England

G. A. Gooch lbw b Lillee	10	– b Alderman	5
G. Boycott c Marsh b Alderman	10	– lbw b Alderman	37
C. J. Tavaré c Alderman b Whitney	69	– c Kent b Alderman	78
D. I. Gower c Yallop b Whitney	23	– c Bright b Lillee	1
*J. M. Brearley lbw b Alderman	2	– (6) c Marsh b Alderman	3
M. W. Gatting c Border b Lillee	32	– (5) lbw b Alderman	11
I. T. Botham c Bright b Lillee	0	– c Marsh b Whitney	118
†A. P. E. Knott c Border b Alderman	13	– c Dyson b Lillee	59
J. E. Emburey c Border b Alderman	1	– c Kent b Whitney	57
P. J. W. Allott not out	52	– c Hughes b Bright	14
R. G. D. Willis c Hughes b Lillee	11	– not out	5
L-b 6, w 2	8	B 1, l-b 12, n-b 3	16
1/19 2/25 3/57 4/62 5/109 6/109 7/131 8/137 9/175	231	1/7 2/79 3/80 4/98 5/104 6/253 7/282 8/356 9/396	404

Bowling: *First Innings*—Lillee 24.1–8–55–4; Alderman 29–5–88–4; Whitney 17–3–50–2; Bright 16–6–30–0. *Second Innings*—Lillee 46–13–137–2; Alderman 52–19–109–5; Whitney 27–6–74–2; Bright 26.4–12–68–1.

Australia

G. M. Wood lbw b Allott	19	– (2) c Knott b Allott	6
J. Dyson c Botham b Willis	0	– (1) run out	5
*K. J. Hughes lbw b Willis	4	– lbw b Botham	43
G. N. Yallop c Botham b Willis	0	– b Emburey	114
M. F. Kent c Knott b Emburey	52	– (6) c Brearley b Emburey	2
A. R. Border c Gower b Botham	11	– (5) not out	123
†R. W. Marsh c Botham b Willis	1	– c Knott b Willis	47
R. J. Bright c Knott b Botham	22	– c Knott b Willis	5
D. K. Lillee c Gooch b Botham	13	– c Botham b Allott	28
M. R. Whitney b Allott	0	– (11) c Gatting b Willis	0
T. M. Alderman not out	2	– (10) lbw b Botham	0
N-b 6	6	L-b 9, w 2, n-b 18	29
1/20 2/24 3/24 4/24 5/58 6/59 7/104 8/125 9/126	130	1/7 2/24 3/119 4/198 5/206 6/296 7/322 8/373 9/378	402

Bowling: *First Innings*—Willis 14–0–63–4; Allott 6–1–17–2; Botham 6.2–1–28–3; Emburey 4–0–16–1. *Second Innings*—Willis 30.5–2–96–3; Allott 17–3–71–2; Botham 36–16–86–2; Emburey 49–9–107–2; Gatting 3–1–13–0.

Umpires: D. J. Constant and K. E. Palmer.

NOTES BY THE EDITOR, 1982

In two unforgettable months, English cricket emerged in 1981 from a period of much gloom to a well-being that was reflected even in the enthusiasm with which ordinary men and women set about their labours. After several weeks of dreadful weather (not a single ball was bowled in any of Gloucestershire's three Championship matches in May), culminating in the loss by England of the first Test match, the sun got the better of the rain and England gained two of the more dramatic victories in the history of the game. A third, soon afterwards, meant that the Ashes were retained.

The change in England's fortunes coincided with Michael Brearley's return as captain. This not only lifted the spirits of the side, it improved its direction and freed Ian Botham of a burden which was threatening to ruin his cricket. Botham's record speaks for itself. In his twelve matches as England's captain, between June 1980 and July 1981, he scored 276 runs at an average of 13.80 (top score 57) and his 35 wickets cost 32 runs apiece. Yet by the end of last season he had made eight Test hundreds and taken five wickets in an innings seventeen times – always when without the cares of captaincy.

The seventh of these hundreds, in the third Test at Headingley, snatched victory from the jaws of defeat; the eighth won the fifth Test at Old Trafford. With some wonderful hitting Botham reached three figures in 87 balls at Headingley and in 86 at Old Trafford. At Edgbaston, between giving the Australian bowlers two such unmerciful poundings, he finished off the fourth Test by taking five wickets for 1 run when Australia needed only a handful of runs to win. Botham's catching, too, was back to its prehensile best. Small wonder that Australia's captain, Kim Hughes, said when the series was over that the difference between the two sides was represented by one man and one man only.

LIKE JESSOP, LIKE BOTHAM

No-one, I believe, can ever have played a finer Test innings *of its type* than Botham's at Old Trafford. I have been told that Australia's attack was by no means one of their strongest, and that by the time Botham came in the best of their bowlers, Lillee and Alderman, were on their last legs. To which I will say only that you would never have known it from the way they were bowling. At Headingley and Old Trafford we witnessed the reincarnation of Gilbert Jessop. Those who saw Willis take eight for 43 at Headingley or watched Brearley's cool handling of each succeeding crisis also have a great story to tell – one to last them a lifetime.

Australia came so near to winning three of the first four Test matches, depsite losing two of them, that if they felt frustrated when they left for home they had good reason to. Alderman and Border, two of their younger players, made a considerable impression; another, Wellham, became the first Australian this century to score a hundred in England in his maiden Test; Lillee made up in virtuosity what he had lost in pace. Not even collectively, though, could such benefits compensate for the collapses, at vital times, which their batting suffered.

SOUTH AFRICANS IN ENGLAND

DERBYSHIRE v SOUTH AFRICANS

Played at Chesterfield, June 26, 28, 29, 1965

Derbyshire won by seven wickets. It was the county's only victory over a South African team since they first met in 1901 and their first over any official touring side since 1937 when they beat the New Zealanders. The match itself was more notable for the no-balling of Rhodes by Buller for throwing in the South Africans' second innings, yet despite his withdrawal from the attack, Derbyshire dismissed them for 119. As Derbyshire had already played for two months, whereas this was the South Africans' first match in strange and difficult conditions for batsmen, the county began with a big advantage. On the first day when van der Merwe won the toss, a strong cross wind, a softish pitch and slow outfield favoured the bowlers and Rhodes, Jackson and Smith carried all before them; only Barlow, R. G. Pollock and Bland reached double figures. Before the day ended, J. R. Eyre and Hall saw the Derbyshire total to 75 without being parted. On Monday, with the pitch drier and the weather sunny and warm, the South Africans excelled in the field and, though without P. M. Pollock, gained a lead of six runs. Lack of practice was the main reason for the South Africans failing a second time with the bat and Derbyshire, left to make 126, won comfortably, thanks to a stylish display by Johnson who appropriately made the winning hit.

South Africans

E. J. Barlow run out	50	– c T. J. P. Eyre b Buxton	23
†D. Gamsy b Rhodes	5	– c Buxton b Jackson	10
A. Bacher b Rhodes	5	– c and b Buxton	5
R. G. Pollock b Jackson	37	– c Hall b Smith	5
K. C. Bland b Smith	29	– c Taylor b Buxton	12
*P. L. van der Merwe lbw b Rhodes	0	– c Taylor b Smith	26
J. D. Lindsay b Jackson	1	– b Morgan	13
R. Dumbrill c Morgan b Rhodes	7	– run out	3
J. T. Botten lbw b Smith	1	– b Jackson	7
M. J. Macaulay run out	4	– b Jackson	7
H. D. Bromfield not out	1	– not out	0
B 2, l-b 3, w 1, n-b 3	9	B 4, l-b 3, n-b 1	8
1/11 2/25 3/95 4/125 5/130 6/134 7/134 8/141 9/148	149	1/21 2/38 3/41 4/64 5/94 6/100 7/100 8/112 9/115	119

Bowling: *First Innings*—Jackson 19–6–32–2; Rhodes 15.3–5–35–4; Morgan 6–2–16–0; Buxton 6–2–8–0; Smith 23–10–43–2; T. J. P. Eyre 2–0–6–0. *Second Innings*—Jackson 18–5–35–3; Rhodes 1–0–3–0; Morgan 13–4–19–1; Buxton 14–7–16–3; Smith 19.4–11–29–2; T. J. P. Eyre 5–1–9–0.

Derbyshire

J. R. Eyre run out	36	– b Botten	8
I. W. Hall b Botten	36	– lbw b Barlow	23
M. H. Page b Dumbrill	12	– c and b Barlow	27
H. L. Johnson c Gamsy b Bromfield	26	– not out	44
I. R. Buxton c Gamsy b Bromfield	0	– not out	19
*D. C. Morgan b Macaulay	4		
T. J. P. Eyre c Macaulay b Botten	4		
E. Smith c Barlow b Botten	0		
†R. W. Taylor not out	14		
H. J. Rhodes c Barlow b Dumbrill	0		
A. B. Jackson c Gamsy b Dumbrill	1		
B 1, l-b 7, n-b 2	10	L-b 3, n-b 2	5
1/75 2/83 3/115 4/116 5/122 6/128 7/128 8/128 9/131	143	1/20 2/57 3/69	(3 wkts) 126

Bowling: *First Innings*—Macaulay 17–9–12–1; Botten 29–8–55–3; Barlow 13–5–23–0; Dumbrill 23–11–32–4; Bromfield 8–4–11–1. *Second Innings*—Macaulay 7–2–14–0; Botten 14–2–29–1; Barlow 8–4–9–2; Dumbrill 10–3–26–0; Bromfield 20.3–11–43–0.

Umpires: J. S. Buller and J. F. Crapp.

ENGLAND v SOUTH AFRICA

First Test Match

Played at Lord's, July 22, 23, 24, 26, 27, 1965

Drawn. The 100th Test Match between the countries was thrilling from start to finish. It aroused plenty of interest throughout the country and assured the South Africans of financial success. The wonderful fielding of Bland, in particular, captured the imagination and so did the finish, with both sides going close to victory. The repeated swings in the fortunes of the game with neither team able to force an advantage kept the crowd, which totalled about 100,000 in a state of continuous tension.

Boycott replaced Parfitt for England and Brown, who gained his first cap, came in for Illingworth (twelfth man). South Africa won the toss and on a good cricket pitch made a shaky start. Fine catches by Barber, at short fine leg, Brown, a return catch ankle high and Titmus, full length in the gulley, accounted for the first three wickets which fell for 75, but Graeme Pollock and Bland brought a recovery with a stand of 80 in ninety-five minutes. Then came another breakdown and at 178 for seven South Africa looked in trouble. The last three wickets added 102.

Rain restricted the second day's play to just under two and a half hours. Cricket did not start until after lunch. At the close England were 26 without loss in reply to South Africa's 280. A crowd of 26,000 saw a fine innings by Barrington on the Saturday. Boycott and Barber began with a stand of 82, but both were out as well as Edrich for the addition of six. Barrington hit one 6 and eleven 4s while scoring 91 in three hours. Smith helped him add 96 before Bland made the first of his two thrilling run outs, hitting Barrington's stumps direct after running from mid-wicket towards mid-on and having barely more than one stump to aim at. Parks was another victim of the accuracy of Bland. Titmus played a useful innings and England led by 58.

Barlow began South Africa's second innings aggressively and Lance, first out, made only nine of the 55 scored. At 120 for four South Africa were in real danger, but Bland, well supported by Bacher and van der Merwe, brought recovery.

England needed 191 to win in five minutes under four hours, but the time was cut considerably by the slow over rate. Edrich, hit on the side of the head by a ball from Peter Pollock, had to retire and the innings never really got going. England steadily fell behind the clock and in the end had to struggle to save the game.

South Africa

E. J. Barlow c Barber b Rumsey	1	c Parks b Brown	52
H. Lance c and b Brown	28	c Titmus b Brown	9
†J. D. Lindsay c Titmus b Rumsey	40	c Parks b Larter	22
R. G. Pollock c Barrington b Titmus	56	b Brown	5
K. C. Bland b Brown	39	c Edrich b Barber	70
A. Bacher lbw b Titmus	4	b Titmus	37
*P. L. van der Merwe c Barrington b Rumsey	17	c Barrington b Rumsey	31
R. Dumbrill b Barber	3	c Cowdrey b Rumsey	2
J. T. Botten b Brown	33	b Rumsey	0
P. M. Pollock st Parks b Barber	34	not out	14
H. D. Bromfield not out	9	run out	0
L-b 14, n-b 2	16	B 4, l-b 2	6
1/1 2/60 3/75 4/155 5/170 6/170 7/178 8/212 9/247	280	1/55 2/62 3/68 4/120 5/170 6/216 7/230 8/230 9/247	248

Bowling: *First Innings*—Larter 26–10–47–0; Rumsey 30–9–84–3; Brown 24–9–44–3; Titmus 29–10–59–2; Barber 10.3–3–30–2. *Second Innings*—Larter 17–2–67–1; Rumsey 21–8–49–3; Brown 21–11–30–3; Titmus 26–13–36–1; Barber 25–5–60–1.

England

G. Boycott c Barlow b Botten	31	c and b Dumbrill	28
R. W. Barber b Bromfield	56	c Lindsay b P. M. Pollock	12
J. H. Edrich lbw b P. M. Pollock	0	retired hurt	7
K. F. Barrington run out	91	lbw b Dumbrill	18
M. C. Cowdrey b Dumbrill	29	lbw b P. M. Pollock	37
*M. J. K. Smith c Lindsay b Botten	26	c Lindsay b Dumbrill	13
†J. M. Parks run out	32	c van der Merwe b Dumbrill	7
F. J. Titmus c P. M. Pollock b Bromfield	59	not out	9
D. J. Brown c Bromfield b Dumbrill	1	c Barlow b R. G. Pollock	5
F. E. Rumsey b Dumbrill	3	not out	0
J. D. F. Larter not out	0		
B 1, l-b 4, w 1, n-b 4	10	L-b 7, w 1, n-b 1	9
1/82 2/88 3/88 4/144 5/240 6/240 7/294 8/314 9/338	338	1/23 2/70 3/79 4/113 5/121 6/135 7/140	(7 wkts) 145

Bowling: *First Innings*—P. M. Pollock 39–12–91–1; Botten 33–11–65–2; Barlow 19–6–31–0; Bromfield 25.2–5–71–2; Dumbrill 24–11–31–3; Lance 5–0–18–0; R. G. Pollock 5–1–21–0. *Second Innings*—P. M. Pollock 20–6–52–2; Botten 12–6–25–0; Dumbrill 18–8–30–4; Barlow 9–1–25–0; Bromfield 5–4–4–0; R. G. Pollock 4–4–0–1.

Umpires: J. S. Buller and A. E. Rhodes.

KENT v SOUTH AFRICANS

At Canterbury, July 28, 29, 1965

South Africans won by an innings and 147 runs with a day to spare. A wonderful double century by Graeme Pollock reminded many of the elderly spectators of the grace and charm of their old favourite, Frank Woolley, whose style the young South African left-hander so much resembled. Seldom lost for a punishing stroke and excelling with the drive, Pollock completed his first hundred of the tour in three hours and doubled it in the next hour. He hit five 6s and twenty-eight 4s and also received one five. After Bacher had helped to put on 137, Bland (eight 4s) stayed while an unbroken stand yielded 188 in one hour, fifty minutes. With Peter Richardson unable to bat through a bout of influenza, Kent cut a very sorry figure against the speed of Peter Pollock who took five wickets for 28. When the county followed on 291 behind, Dixon and Fillary defied the spin bowlers before Macaulay put an abrupt end to the proceedings by performing the hat-trick. He bowled Dixon, had Brown caught at the wicket and Underwood, last man, taken by his captain at backward short leg.

South Africans

E. J. Barlow b Dixon	13	K. C. Bland not out	61
H. Lance c Knott b Underwood	24	B 3, l-b 4	7
A. Bacher run out	57		——
R. G. Pollock not out	203	1/40 2/40 3/177 (3 wkts dec.)	365

*P. L. Van der Merwe, †D. Gamsy, N. S. Crookes, P. M. Pollock, M. J. Macaulay and A. H. McKinnon did not bat.

Bowling: Brown 23–4–92–0; Dixon 38–12–125–1; Underwood 21–4–87–1; Fillary 11–1–54–0.

Kent

M. H. Denness c Macaulay b Lance	30	– b P. M. Pollock	2
B. W. Luckhurst b Macaulay	7	– b Macaulay	22
R. C. Wilson b P. M. Pollock	2	– b Crookes	25
*M. C. Cowdrey lbw b P. M. Pollock	2	– c R. G. Pollock b P. M. Pollock	1
S. E. Leary c Gamsy b Macaulay	8	– c Gamsy b Crookes	9
E. W. J. Fillary lbw b Crookes	3	– not out	27
†A. P. E. Knott lbw b P. M. Pollock	14	– st Gamsy b Crookes	0
A. L. Dixon c Lance b P. M. Pollock	8	– b Macaulay	53
A. Brown not out	0	– c Gamsy b Macaulay	0
D. L. Underwood b P. M. Pollock	0	– c van der Merwe b Macaulay	0
P. E. Richardson absent ill	0	– absent ill	0
	——		——
1/17 2/30 3/32 4/49 5/49 6/66 7/70 8/74 9/74	74	1/2 2/35 3/38 4/60 5/63 6/63 7/144 8/144 9/144	144

Bowling: *First Innings*—P. M. Pollock 12.4–5–28–5; Macaulay 15–6–20–2; Lance 8–3–16–1; Crookes 8–4–8–1; McKinnon 4–3–2–0. *Second Innings*—P. M. Pollock 11–2–23–2; Macaulay 9–2–22–4; Lance 4–2–5–0; Crookes 16–5–38–3; McKinnon 13–5–33–0; R. G. Pollock 3–0–18–0.

Umpires: C. S. Elliott and F. Jakeman.

ENGLAND v SOUTH AFRICA

Second Test Match

Played at Nottingham, August 5, 6, 7, 9, 1965

South Africa won by 94 runs with a day to spare. It was their first Test victory in England for ten years and a personal triumph for the brothers Graeme and Peter Pollock. Their fraternal effort has no parallel in Test cricket. Graeme, the batsman, made 184 runs, held a fine slip catch and took a vital wicket on the last day. Peter, the bowler, with five wickets in each England innings, finished with an analysis of 10 wickets for 87 runs in 48 overs.

This was another grand game, quite as exciting as the previous one at Lord's. South Africa certainly deserved their success but once again much of the England batting was pathetic until Parks and Parfitt made a belated flourish.

Injury compelled D. Brown to withdraw from England's original twelve whereupon Snow was called up. Then Rumsey became doubtful and the selectors sent for I. J. Jones. On the first morning, both left-arm bowlers, Rumsey and Jones (twelfth man), were omitted.

In view of the overcast weather England included Cartwright for his only Test of the season and on van der Merwe winning the toss Cartwright soon gave England the initiative. They took the first five South African wickets for 80 and at the end of the innings Cartwright's figures were six for 94. Unfortunately for England he broke his right thumb when stopping a hot return and he did not bowl again in the match.

That South Africa finished with a total of 269 was entirely due to their brilliant 21-year-old left-hander, Graeme Pollock. At the crease for no more than two hours and twenty minutes, he scored 125 out of 160 and hit twenty-one 4s. This was one of the finest Test displays of all time. It was divided into two parts. In seventy minutes before lunch, Pollock felt his way tentatively while making 34 and seeing the total to 76 for four. Afterwards he reigned supreme for seventy more minutes while he lashed the bowling for 92 out of 102. For the most part Pollock made his strokes cleanly and he offered no chance until Cowdrey smartly held him at slip.

England had to bat for thirty-five minutes before the close and Peter Pollock delivered two shattering blows by removing Boycott and Barrington for 16 runs. Titmus, night-watchman helped Barber to put on 55 but Cowdrey alone really mastered the bowling. He received valuable help from Smith and England recovered well until after tea when, taking the new ball in the 86th over at 220, Peter Pollock and Botten cleaned up the tail, the last five wickets falling for 20 more runs. Hitting his 17th Test century in his 78th match, Cowdrey showed himself the true artist. He batted just over three hours and hit eleven 4s.

South Africa held a narrow lead of 29 and they promptly lost Lance, but Barlow, who had not fielded owing to a bruised toe, served them well on the third day in a desperate struggle for runs. Boycott, in the absence of Cartwright, kept the pavilion end tight in two long spells in which his analysis read: 19–10–25–0. Fourth to leave at 193, Barlow spent three hours, ten minutes for his 76 but South Africa had reached 219 for the loss of only four wickets when Snow and Larter took the second new ball.

Both England fast bowlers rose to the occasion and the remaining six wickets added only 70 more runs. Graeme Pollock, sixth out, again hit freely in getting 59 and Smith could be congratulated on managing his depleted attack so skilfully. He reserved his pace men for the new ball and Larter finished with five for 68, probably his best performance to date for his country.

England wanted 319 to win and again they had to bat for thirty-five minutes, and again they lost two wickets, those of Barber and Titmus. England certainly came in for much adverse criticism for preferring night-watchmen to the regular batsmen. It meant that Snow also went to the crease late on Saturday so that Parks, one of the most punishing batsmen at their disposal, was relegated to number nine.

When Snow left first thing on Monday morning without addition to the score, three wickets were down for 10 and South Africa had clearly taken control. Peter Pollock soon trapped Barrington who fell hooking a bouncer. Instead of showing initiative Boycott made only six in an hour. In fact, he occupied two hours and twenty minutes over 16, a dreadful effort when courage was needed.

Parfitt was little better at this stage. Bad light and rain caused a break of fifty-five minutes, including the tea interval when England were 127 for seven and still requiring 192. Parfitt had made 40 in two hours, forty minutes and Parks 5 in half an hour.

Now, when all seemed lost, Parfitt and Parks flayed the bowling. Parks began the onslaught with 10 in an over from Dumbrill. Even the new ball at 165 did not deter them. They helped themselves to 27 from the first three overs. In an hour they added 80, their stand altogether producing 93 before Parfitt hitting across, was bowled so that Parks was left to take out his bat. It was England's first defeat in 15 matches under M. J. K. Smith's captaincy.

South Africa richly earned this success. They possessed an inspiring captain in Peter van der Merwe who shared the fielding honours with Bland. Throughout the four days large crowds were present, the full attendance approaching 75,000.

South Africa

E. J. Barlow c Cowdrey b Cartwright	19	– b Titmus	76
H. Lance lbw b Cartwright	7	– c Barber b Snow	0
†J. D. Lindsay c Parks b Cartwright	0	– c Cowdrey b Larter	9
R. G. Pollock c Cowdrey b Cartwright	125	– c Titmus b Larter	59
K. C. Bland st Parks b Titmus	1	– b Snow	10
A. Bacher b Snow	12	– lbw b Larter	67
*P. L. van der Merwe run out	38	– c Parfitt b Larter	4
R. Drumbrill c Parfitt c Cartwright	30	– b Snow	13
J. T. Botten c Parks b Larter	10	– b Larter	18
P. M. Pollock c Larter b Cartwright	15	– not out	12
A. H. McKinnon not out	8	– b Titmus	9
L-b 4	4	B 4, l-b 5, n-b 3	12
1/16 2/16 3/42 4/43 5/80 6/178 7/221 8/242 9/252	269	1/2 2/35 3/134 4/193 5/228 6/232 7/243 8/265 9/269	289

Bowling: *First Innings*—Larter 17–6–25–1; Snow 22–6–63–1; Cartwright 31.3–9–94–6; Titmus 22–8–44–1; Barber 9–3–39–0. *Second Innings*—Larter 29–7–68–5; Snow 33–6–83–3; Titmus 19.4–5–46–2; Boycott 26–10–60–0; Barber 3–0–20–0.

England

G. Boycott c Lance b P. M. Pollock	0	– b McKinnon	16
R. W. Barber c Bacher b Dumbrill	41	– c Lindsay b P. M. Pollock	1
K. F. Barrington b P. M. Pollock	1	– c Lindsay b P. M. Pollock	1
F. J. Titmus c R. G. Pollock b McKinnon	20	– c Lindsay b McKinnon	4
M. C. Cowdrey c Lindsay b Botten	105	– st Lindsay b McKinnon	20
P. H. Parfitt c Dumbrill b P. M. Pollock	18	– b P. M. Pollock	86
*M. J. K. Smith b P. M. Pollock	32	– lbw b R. G. Pollock	24
†J. M. Parks c and b Botten	6	– not out	44
J. A. Snow run out	3	– b Botten	0
J. D. F. Larter b P. M. Pollock	2	– c van der Merwe b P. M. Pollock	10
T. W. Cartwright not out	1	– lbw b P. M. Pollock	0
B 1, l-b 3, w 1, n-b 6	11	L-b 5, w 2, n-b 11	18
1/0 2/8 3/63 4/67 5/133 6/225 7/229 8/236 9/238	240	1/1 2/10 3/10 4/13 5/41 6/59 7/114 8/207 9/207	224

Bowling: *First Innings*—P. M. Pollock 23.5–8–53–5; Botten 23–5–60–2; McKinnon 28–11–54–1; Dumbrill 18–3–60–1; R. G. Pollock 1–0–2–0. *Second Innings*—P. M. Pollock 24–15–34–5; Botten 19–5–58–1; McKinnon 27–12–50–3; Dumbrill 16–4–40–0; Barlow 11–1–20–0; R. G. Pollock 5–2–4–1.

Umpires: C. S. Elliott and J. F. Crapp.

THE D'OLIVEIRA CASE

CANCELLATION OF SOUTH AFRICAN TOUR [1969]

By Michael Melford

The bitterness engendered by the sequence of events leading up to the cancellation of MCC's proposed tour of South Africa only six weeks before the scheduled starting date made a sad end to the 1968 English season. Almost from the moment that England walked off the field at The Oval with a rare victory over Australia to their credit, English cricket was caught up in a whirlpool of acrimony and political argument such as it can seldom have known before. The culmination, on September 17, was the refusal by the South African Prime Minister, Mr John Vorster, to accept Basil D'Oliveira, a Cape Coloured, as a member of the MCC team, and the MCC Committee's consequent cancellation of the tour.

Since D'Oliveira came successfully into English cricket, and even before he first played for England in 1966, it had been evident that a delicate situation might arise if he were selected for this tour of his native country. However, what appeared to be a relatively simple problem of whether he was acceptable or not had been greatly complicated when the time came, especially by his original omission from the team and the outcry which greeted it.

When the New Zealand Rugby Board were refused permission to bring their Maoris to South Africa in 1967 by Mr Vorster's predecessor, Dr Verwoerd, they cancelled the tour with so little rancour that it was soon being replanned for 1970 with the ban removed. Cricket, however, ever more exposed to publicity, had to endure charges and recriminations of a passion which resounded far outside the sporting world. Not until December, when, at a special general meeting of MCC the Committee defeated three resolutions put forward by dissident members, was relief in sight from a period of unpleasantness which must have been a nightmare to the ordinary sensitive lover of cricket.

By a coincidence, M. J. K. Smith's MCC side, managed by the secretary, S. C. Griffith, was in New Zealand in March 1966 when the New Zealand Rugby authorities were about to cancel their tour of South Africa. Mr Griffith was asked what action he thought his committee would take in similar circumstances and he replied unequivocally that no other course but cancellation was conceivable.

In the following winter Mr Griffith visited South Africa at the invitation of the South African Cricket Association. With one other cricket correspondent, Louis Duffus of the Johannesburg *Star*, I interviewed Mr Griffith and the then President of the SACA, Mr Boon Wallace, in Cape Town at the end of the visit. Asked if the case of D'Oliveira had been discussed with the SACA, Mr Griffith said that naturally it had in principle and he had made MCC's position abundantly clear. They had considered the broader question of non-European cricketers in general as members of MCC sides. In view of the number of cricketers of West Indian descent likely to be playing in English domestic cricket in the future, the discussions had not concerned only one player.

Later in January 1967 a reporter of the Johannesburg *Sunday Express* put a similar question by telephone to Mr P. Le Roux, the Minister of the Interior, one Saturday night. The reply, as given in next day's paper, stated the law as it existed at the time and the inference was drawn that D'Oliveira would not be acceptable. Though to most people in South Africa at the time this seemed far from an inspired statement and to be running against the tide of the Prime Minister's policy, it excited public criticism in Britain and the West Indies. In one quarter it induced questions in the House of Commons and in the other the withdrawal of an invitation to three South Africans, the Pollock brothers and Colin Bland, to play in Barbados.

After a week Mr Denis Howell, the Minister with special responsibility for sport, in a statement in the House, scotched suggestions that MCC might give way. "MCC has informed the Government that the team to tour South Africa will be chosen on merit.... If any player chosen were to be rejected by the host country, then ... the projected tour would be abandoned." This was what Mr Griffith had told the New Zealand Rugby Board a year before.

On April 11, 1967, Mr Vorster, speaking in the House of Assembly in Cape Town, clarified the position of coloured sportsmen in teams visiting South Africa. Visiting teams of mixed race would be able to tour the country if they were teams from countries with which South Africa had "traditional sporting ties" and "if no political capital was made out of the situation".

Superficially this appeared to make the way clear for any non-European to visit South Africa with an MCC team, but D'Oliveira, as a native of South Africa, might be considered likely to be the focus of political influences where others would not. MCC therefore wrote to the SACA in January 1968 asking for an assurance that no pre-conditions would be laid on their choice of players. At about the same time Sir Alec Douglas-Home, the previous year's President of MCC, talked to Mr Vorster in Cape Town during a tour which he made as Opposition spokesman on foreign affairs.

MCC had received no firm answer to their question by late March and had then to decide whether to cancel the tour or to go ahead as planned, leaving the matter of a player's non-acceptability until it happened. On Sir Alec Douglas-Home's advice they decided to go ahead and for much of the summer the issue seemed unlikely to arise.

D'Oliveira had toured West Indies with Colin Cowdrey's team but without success. He had played in the First Test against Australia at Old Trafford in June and had made 87 not out in the second innings, but he had been left out at Lord's in favour of a third fast bowler. England almost won at Lord's and as their fortunes improved without him, D'Oliveira lost form for Worcestershire with the bat. Though he took plenty of wickets later in the season, they were mostly on imperfect pitches and were not obvious recommendations for a Test place.

However, after the team for the Fifth Test had been chosen on August 18, R. M. Prideaux, one of the opening batsmen in the prolonged absence through injury of G. Boycott, dropped out through bronchitis. He was replaced by D'Oliveira, an unexpected choice, made partly to help the side's balance and partly, perhaps, on a hunch.

The hunch came off. D'Oliveira, though little used as a bowler, made 158. England won and that night, August 27, the selectors sat down to pick the team for South Africa. When it was announced next day that this did not include D'Oliveira, the chairman of the selectors, D. J. Insole, explained that the selectors regarded him "from an overseas tour point of view as a batsman rather than an all-rounder. We put him beside the seven batsmen that we had, along with Colin Milburn whom we also had to leave out with regret." This explanation of a selection was no new departure and followed the selectors' practice over the last fifteen years.

To the non-cricketing public, however, D'Oliveira's omission immediately after his innings at The Oval was largely incomprehensible. It was easy for many to assume political motives behind it and a bowing to South Africa's racial policies. More knowledgeable cricketers were split between those who agreed that on technical grounds D'Oliveira was far from an automatic choice and who were doubtful if he would be any more effective in South Africa than he had been in West Indies, and those who thought that after his successful comeback to Test cricket, it was "inhuman" not to pick him.

Some holding the latter opinion were also ready to see non-cricketing reasons for the omission, refusing to believe Mr Insole and Mr Griffith, who publicly stated that none existed. Much was said which was regretted later – four out of nineteen members of MCC who resigned in protest applied for reinstatement within a few days – and Lord Fisher of Lambeth, the former Archbishop of Canterbury, was prompted to write to the *Daily Telegraph* condemning a leader "which appeared to cast doubt on the word of the selectors". A group of twenty MCC members, the number required to call a special meeting of the club, asserted this right, co-opting the Rev. D. S. Sheppard as their main spokesman. For three weeks the affair simmered like an angry volcano.

During this period the *News of the World* announced that it had engaged D'Oliveira to report the tour in South Africa. This did much to antagonise Government opinion in South Africa, as had several events unrelated to the team's selection. One of these was MCC's refusal in June to include Rhodesia in their itinerary. Two others, outside MCC's province, were the rejection of a mixed South African Olympic team and the turning-back of Colin Bland at London Airport in August because he had a Rhodesian passport.

Though the *News of the World* emphasised that D'Oliveira would only be reporting the cricket and though there were precedents (Wardle in 1958 and Close in 1967) for players left out of MCC teams being sent by newspapers, suspicion of English motives and of political intrigue was undoubtedly increased in South Africa. When so many voices in England were discussing the political side of the affair, it was hard for any one at a distance who did not know them to believe that D. J. Insole, A. V. Bedser, P. B. H. May and D. Kenyon, augmented by G. O. Allen and A. E. R. Gilligan and the captain, M. C. Cowdrey, were impervious to political influences and were picking a side purely on cricketing qualifications.

It was harder still after the final readjustment of the team on September 16. Cartwright had been unfit when picked originally but the assurances given by specialists of his imminent recovery had been provisionally accepted and he had bowled ten overs for Warwickshire on September 14 without apparent discomfort. However, the subsequent medical report ruled him out and D'Oliveira was chosen to replace him.

In view of Mr Insole's previous statement that D'Oliveira had been considered only as a batsman, his substitution now for a bowler must have been the final proof to the South African Government that political influences were at work. Mr Insole's explanation that the balance of the side had had to be entirely reviewed made little impact. No replacement of Cartwright's type or experience did in fact exist in England in the unavailability, for different reasons of B. R. Knight, R. Illingworth and others.

On the following evening, Mr Vorster said that South Africa was not prepared to receive a team which had been forced upon her by people "with certain political aims". It was one of many unhappy chances that he should be speaking in Bloemfontein where cricket has probably a less enthusiastic following than anywhere else in a country where it is generally booming. A dignified speech of regret might have done something to heal the wounds but Mr Vorster broke the eighty-year-old links between English and South African cricket in a speech for internal political consumption – in "crude and boorish words", as the *Daily Mail* leader put it – and with a harshness which can have won him little sympathy outside his own party.

It only remained for the MCC Committee to make the formal cancellation of the tour, which they did on September 24. At the meeting, the Committee discussed future cricket relations between the two countries with two members of the South African Board, A. H. Coy and J. E. Cheetham, who had flown overnight from Johannesburg.

The special general meeting of MCC was fixed for December 5 at Church House, Westminster, with the President, Mr R. Aird, in the chair. A vote was asked for on the following resolutions:

1. That the Members of MCC regret their Committee's mishandling of affairs leading up to the selection of the team for the intended tour of South Africa in 1968-69.
2. That no further tours to or from South Africa be undertaken until evidence can be given of actual progress by South Africa towards non-racial cricket.
3. That a Special Committee be set up to examine such proposals by the SACA towards non-racial cricket; the MCC to report on progress to the Annual General Meeting of the Club; and to the Governing Body for Cricket – the MCC Council.

The meeting, which lasted nearly four hours, was attended by over 1,000 members and, through a special decision of the Committee, by the Press. The main speakers for the resolutions were the Rev. David Sheppard and J. M. Brearley and for the Committee, D. R. W. Silk and A. M. Crawley.

Those putting the case for the resolutions said that their main concern was to debate future policy rather than to analyse past events, but they maintained that the Committee had acted weakly and irresponsibly and should have insisted on a definite answer from the SACA in the spring to the question "Would D'Oliveira be acceptable as an MCC tourist without conditions?". Had the answer been a public "Yes", the selectors' disinterestedness in choosing the team in August could not have been challenged. Had the answer been "No", or continued equivocation, then, reluctantly, the tour should have been called off. Those who protest, they said, are frequently charged with bringing politics into cricket. "It is, of course, South Africa which organises its sport on political grounds and intrudes its politics upon all teams which visit the country."

The Committee said that they were motivated by a continuing desire to foster cricket wherever it is played. Over the years MCC had never thought it the collective function of its Committee to act as inquisitor-general into the domestic attitudes towards race-relations, immigration, political orientation or anything else of the governments or governing bodies of their respective opponents. They had accepted Sir Alec Douglas-Home's opinion that to confront the South African Government with individual possible selections was wrong and would undoubtedly result in a refusal to answer hypothetical questions. To have pressed for an immediate answer to their letter would have appeared to be not only hypothetical, but politically inspired. The England captain, Colin Cowdrey, stated that the selectors had never been put in an "intolerable position", as was suggested. "We were quite free to pick the best team on cricketing merit," he said.

The first resolution was defeated by 4,357 to 1,570, the bulk of the votes having been recorded by post. The Committee had a 386 to 314 majority in the hall. The second resolution was lost by 4,664 to 1,214 and the third by 4,508 to 1,352. The voting in the hall on these two resolutions was 516 to 137 and 474 to 155 respectively.

After the meeting, Mr Sheppard said that the vote made clear that a large proportion of the MCC membership cared about the issue. "What is more important than votes, however, is that ideas have been ventilated. Nothing will be quite the same in English cricket after the debate."

Mr Aird, the President, said that he was pleased that most members of the Club still saw cricket as a game to be played wherever and whenever possible. "We shall strive for the welfare of all cricketers both in South Africa and wherever the game is played." Mr Aird also paid tribute to the "great dignity which Basil D'Oliveira has maintained throughout the whole business".

THE SOUTH AFRICAN TOUR DISPUTE [1971]

A RECORD OF CONFLICT, 1970

By Irving Rosenwater

"To my mind sportsmanship and the colour bar are incompatible. Sport is supposed to teach all those virtues that the colour bar destroys. Sport is supposed to teach people to know and respect one another, and to want to see fair play for all. Sport is supposed to teach us to admire the prowess of others, not to want to restrict it."

—Alan Paton *at inaugural conference of the South African Sports Association, Durban, January, 1959.*

Cricket as a way of life has been a feature of British society ever since the game emerged in its present recognisable form something like two hundred years ago. Poets have sung its praises, and its charm and influence and its appeal to the emotions have been invoked in aid of all that is good in life and play. Cricket is a liberal education in itself, said Andrew Lang, and did not Professor Trevelyan once surmise that if the French *noblesse* had been capable of playing cricket with their peasants, their *châteaux* would never have been burnt?

Whether cricket is an art, an exercise, an interest, a cult or a philosophy, it was never meant to do a mischief, let alone cause strife. But the bitter, emotional – sometimes hysterical – aura that hung over English cricket in 1970 divided the nation, cricket lovers or not, into impassioned camps, each clinging firmly to its principles: the one anxious, for a variety of reasons, to welcome the South African Cricket Association side to England; the other as anxious, indeed desperately so, not to welcome it.

Sport has given rise to conflict before. Ill-will may stem from a mere lapse of amiability – or be a positive expression of ideology, and cricket of course had its moments of passion before 1970. Personal rivalries on the field have sometimes (but fortunately only rarely) grown into feuds. There have been allegations about bowlers with doubtful actions. The 1932-33 tour of Australia strained Anglo-Australian relations in quarters far beyond those of cricket. But all these disputes were *technical* ones – and even Larwood in the course of time was forgiven by a once hostile and outraged Australian populace.

The bitterness of 1970 was not technical at all. It was moral, political, personal, ideological. Confusion and hate were brought into cricket together with prejudices of race, creed and colour – brought into the very sport which had shown perhaps the greatest tolerance of all sports in the passage of history, and where friendly, civilised competition had for so long been paramount. The overtones and undertones were such that most men found it terribly difficult to be dispassionate. The summer of a General Election did not help to cool matters, either. How thankful must have been the village, club and school sides of England who happily played their cricket last year with their traditional blend of innocence, zest and good fellowship.

Before the distaste and disquiet of last year can be properly understood, it is necessary to consider briefly something of the history preceding it. The South African government's attitude towards mixed sport within South Africa was dealt with at length by the Prime Minister, Mr B. J. Vorster, in the House of Assembly in Cape Town on April 11, 1967, when he said unambiguously that the policy inside the country was that there would not be mixed sporting events, no matter how good were the participants. "In respect of this principle we are not prepared to compromise, we are not prepared to negotiate, and we are not prepared to make any concessions." Fundamentally it was this uncompromising – and in some ways curiously obtuse – defence of apartheid put up by Mr Vorster that led directly to the events of last year. Political attitudes struck thousands of miles away in England were, arguably, unhelpful in the struggle against injustice; and, anyway, Mr Vorster's views by no means religiously reflected the moral heart-searching among his more thoughtful supporter and among many of South Africa's leading cricketers. But while opportunities for white and non-white cricketers were unequal, and while they could not take part together in trials and other matches to test their respective abilities, a case against South Africa's sporting system existed.

Mr Vorster at the same time made one other relevant statement, not frequently quoted: "The demand has been put to us that our Springbok team would not be welcomed unless it includes members of all race groups. If that demand is made a condition of the continuation of sports relations, I say we are not prepared to meet it because it is our affair and ours alone." The tone brooked no argument, but it was noted in many parts of the world. So far as cricket teams visiting South Africa were concerned – as well as any other sporting side from a country having "traditional ties" with South Africa – Mr Vorster made it clear that mixed teams would be acceptable provided politicians did not interfere to harm relations between countries or between groups inside South Africa.

How Mr Vorster in September 1968 rejected an MCC side that included Basil D'Oliveira is well enough known, and the seething discontent that arose from that episode never subsided until May of last year, having by then reached a dangerous boiling point such as sport in this country had never known.

Without fuss or heroics the South Africans' programme for their English tour was released in September 1969 – a full season's fixture-list from May 2 to September 8, including five Tests and matches against all the counties. The news at first went almost unnoticed – until Mr Denis Howell, the then Minister with responsibility for Sport, declared on television on October 19 that the South African team "should stay away from Britain". The same night Mr Jack Cheetham, president of the SACA, at once rejoined by saying that South Africa had no intention of withdrawing from the 1970 tour. The battle was on. Mr S. C. Griffith, Secretary of MCC said, not for the last time, that "the Cricket Council have stated, and still feel, that more good is achieved by maintaining sporting links with South Africa than by cutting them off altogether". It was this policy of "open bridges" that was in due course to be attacked so vehemently by the tour opponents.

With a South African Rugby Union tour of Britain about to start on November 5, the seeds of controversy were dangerously apparent. People were beginning to take sides: it was easy to forecast that passions could be aroused to split the nation.

Meanwhile a new name had entered the lists – that of Peter Hain, a 19-year-old white South African and first-year engineering student at Imperial College, London. From a liberal Pretoria family and with opinions formed during his youth, he had been in England only three and a half years when he organised and launched the Stop the Seventy Tour Committee in September 1969, and was its chairman throughout. During the summer of 1969 he had taken part in demonstrations against Wilfred Isaacs' South African touring side. His committee – much to Hain's surprise – began to make an increasingly strong impact. He was committed to non-violent protest, from which platform he doubtless derived the support he obtained.

In South Africa talks got under way between the white and non-white cricket bodies in the hope of improving relations, but they quickly broke down in a flurry of charge and countercharge of "insincerity". In these exchanges it was important for the observer to remember that SACA officials could only go as far as their government would allow. But matters were not helped when Mr Arthur Coy, convenor of the SACA selectors, announced there was no question of non-white players being included in a South African team.

The rigorous police control necessary at the South African Rugby matches – troubles and nasty incidents were encountered in England, Wales, Scotland and Ireland: by mid-December alone 68 policeman had been injured – began to convince cricket officials of the impossibility of protecting cricket grounds in 1970 without counties facing enormous bills. The ease with which play could be disrupted by determined demonstrators was not underestimated. The South African Rugby players themselves were suffering considerable distress from the intensity of the demonstrators' actions. In this atmosphere Messrs Cheetham and Coy flew into England in November for talks at Lord's to finalise the tour arrangements. (When the South African Rugby team left England, their manager, Mr Corrie Bornman, said: "The last three months have been an ordeal to which I would never again subject young sportsmen. . . . The players were really fed up. . . . Mercifully, no one was hurt, but the violence we have seen leaves me in no doubt that any future South African team in Britain will be in danger.")

The decision confirming the continuance of the cricket tour was taken by the Cricket Council at Lord's on November 27, and a confidential letter was sent to all county clubs asking them to consult police and other authorities to assess the security arrangements for the South African games. Lord's officials were also in touch for the first time with the Home Office about arrangements. Figures of between £7,000 and £10,000 (and even – later – £18,000) were being quoted to protect a three-day match, and the size and strength of the continued Rugby demonstrations were no comfort for those who cherished the hope that anti-South Africa activity would diminish before the cricketers arrived. The actual cost at a South African Rugby match at Manchester in November 1969, when 2,300 police were on duty – 29 of them were injured and there were 93 arrests – was £8,985.

Such a bill would have wiped out completely the anticipated profit of £7,000 each county could have expected from the tour. Security arrangements for the South Africans' two scheduled visits to Birmingham were expected to total about £250,000, mostly to be borne by ratepayers. The newly-consecrated Bishop of Woolwich, the Right Rev David

Sheppard (who had refused to play against the South Africans in 1960), while unwaveringly opposing the tour, warned demonstrators against disruption and violence, which could "destroy the whole cause of anti-apartheid". The trade unions were also beginning to agitate, and more than 100 Liberal and Labour MPs signed a letter to MCC saying they had every intention of joining the protestors if the South African team came to England.

The TCCB had plenty on its plate for its two-day meeting at Lord's on December 10-11, 1969. Jack Cheetham, in Johannesburg, "pinned all hopes" on the tour proceeding, and the Lord's meeting issued the following statement:

> The Test and County Cricket Board, comprising representatives from all first-class counties and the minor counties, have confirmed unanimously their recommendation that the South African tour will take place.
>
> In re-affirming this decision, they repeat their aversion to racial discrimination of any kind. They also respect the rights of those who wish to demonstrate peacefully.
>
> Equally, they are unanimous in their resolve to uphold the rights of individuals in this country to take part in lawful pursuits, particularly where these pursuits have the support of the majority.
>
> A sub-committee has been appointed to deal with all matters relevant to the tour and to report to the TCCB.

Four days later Jack Cheetham, in Cape Town, announced that future South African sides would be selected "on merit" alone, "irrespective of colour considerations" – which drew the immediate riposte of "empty words" from Mr Hassan Howa, president-designate of the non-white South African Cricket Board of Control. Mr Cheetham's announcement and the TCCB's decision pleased as many people as it angered others, and thenceforth there was little peace in the land on the vexed and emotional tour issue. On the one hand the TCCB had made a representative and honourable decision; on the other a tragic and irresponsible one.

The sequence of events thereafter became so crowded, with individuals and organisations in England and abroad voicing impassioned pleas for both factions, that even the salient happenings came thick and fast. The East African sections of MCC's proposed tour there and to the Far East early in 1970 fell an early victim after Uganda accused the Cricket Council of having "double standards" by playing both all-white South Africa and coloured teams; a referendum by the Cricketers' Association in January showed that just over 81 per cent of English first-class players were in favour of the South African tour; on the night of January 19-20 co-ordinated action saw anti-apartheid attacks directed at a dozen county grounds; an eight-man delegation from Lord's conferred with Mr Callaghan and Mr Howell at the Home Office; Messrs Cheetham and Coy flew in for further confidential talks; a shortened tour of 12 matches (on fairly "defensible" grounds) was announced by the Cricket Council; South Africa duly announced their 14-man side under Ali Bacher – all white – to tour England; and the Prime Minister, Mr Harold Wilson, in a hotly-criticised television interview on April 16, considered that MCC had made "a big mistake" in inviting the South African team – "a very ill-judged decision". He said, with the proviso that any protests must not be violent: "Everyone should be free to demonstrate against apartheid – I hope people will feel free to do so."

Money – and lots of it – seemed one way of saving the tour, though the true cost of protecting grounds was absolutely unpredictable. On April 23 "The 1970 Cricket Fund", with a minimum target of £200,000 and with the approval of the Cricket Council, was launched at Lord's under the chairmanship of Lt Col Charles Newman, VC, and with a distinguished list of patrons who included the Duke of Norfolk, the Duke of Beaufort, Viscount Portal, Lord Wakefield, Judge Sir Carl Aarvold, Sir Peter Studd, M. J. C. Allom, Alec Bedser, Brian Close and Colin Cowdrey. Money for financing the tour had been arriving well before this date, but the chairman made it clear that no donations would be accepted from South Africa. But on the very day the fund was launched the Supreme Council for Sport in Africa (which includes 36 countries in its membership) threatened the withdrawal of 13 African countries from the British Commonweath Games in Edinburgh scheduled for July: all depended on whether or not the tour was called off, and this Commonweath Games issue became yet another major factor in the saga.

The Fair Cricket Campaign also came into being in April, with its first objective to stop the tour. It made no secret of its intention to organise "a massive and peaceful march of conscience past Lord's on Saturday, June 20" – the Saturday of the Lord's Test. The Bishop of Woolwich was chairman, and his vice-chairmen were Sir Edward Boyle, MP (now Lord Boyle of Handsworth) and Mr Reginald Prentice, MP. The Bishop of Woolwich and Sir Edward Boyle were major speakers urging cancellation at the MCC Annual General Meeting last year, when the potential danger to race relations and to international sport was also ventilated. The great majority of MCC members, however, were in favour of the tour proceeding, and the AGM in fact had no real influence on the situation at all. The TCCB meanwhile took the precaution of writing to players to say that those English cricketers appearing in the five Tests and for the Southern and Northern Counties sides would have their lives insured for £15,000. Lancashire's two overseas players, Clive Lloyd and Farokh Engineer, had previously been threatened with violence (and their families too) if they did not withdraw from the county's proposed match against the tourists.

A rare event in British life – a House of Commons emergency debate on a sporting topic – took place, at the instance of Mr Philip Noel-Baker, on May 14, when for three hours the tour issue was passiontely thrashed out. (No vote was to be taken.) Mr Denis Howell declared that never in his experience had he had to deal with a question "where the issues were as deep, as emotional and as involved as in this one".

Mr Howell said that the proposed tour raised deep feelings, and four questions of great public importance had to be considered by the Government and by the Cricket Council. First, the effect of the proposed tour upon racial harmony; secondly, questions of law and order; thirdly, the implications for the Commonwealth Games; fourthly, the long term interests of sport.

Mr Howell dealt with the points in turn and announced the latest resolution of the Sports Council for Great Britain (of which he was chairman) which "strongly urged" the Cricket Council to withdraw the 1970 tour invitation "because it believes the consequences of the tour taking place will have harmful repercussions on sport, especially multi-racial sport, extending far beyond cricket itself."

Mr Reginald Maudling, then Deputy Leader of the Opposition, argued that:

> It is a positive gain to encourage people to come here and play games with us so that they are able to see the freedom and tolerance in this country. Let them learn from our system, a system that is based on merit. Let them play with teams here who are always chosen on the basis of merit and not on grounds of race, creed, religion or politics.
>
> . . . I believe our basic principle must be that any man is entitled to do what is lawful and to expect that the State will protect him from unlawful interference. This must be the first duty of government. . . .
>
> Once a man is denied the right to do what is lawful because other people at home or overseas may disagree with his views, it would be striking at the roots of freedom under the law. Once we admit the right of people to enforce their views by violent means with impunity – and there are many examples in the world today – democracy is at risk.

Sir Edward Boyle explained to the House why he had agreed to become a vice-chairman of the Fair Cricket Campaign:

> I did so because, as someone who utterly deplores and opposes violence and disorder, I had come reluctantly to the view that the South African cricket tour was likely to be bad for community relations in this country, bad for the future of cricket, bad for the future of sport generally, bad for the Commonwealth, and bad for law and order in Britain.
>
> . . . Many hon. Members believe that this summer will be unpleasant but that, somehow, we will get through and that international sport within the Commonwealth will then go on as before. I hope they are right, but I ask the House to seriously consider the possibility that it may not prove so simple as that. It would be tragic if one wrong decision now were to undo all the fine work which the MCC has done over the years to promote integration in sport.

... This is an apt moment to pay tribute to the work of the MCC, whose members are justly proud of what they have achieved. I also take this opportunity to thank personally the members of the MCC and the Cricket Council for all the courtesy that has been shown by them to me and to other visitors who have discussed this matter with them recently.

The Home Secretary, Mr James Callaghan, referred to the "unparalleled crescendo of opposition" to the tour, and went on:

When I hear the list of organisations who oppose the tour, when I consider the possible damage that could be done.... I repeat to the Cricket Council that it is for it to consider ... whether its judgement to proceed with this tour is right.

What I fear is that there will be damage done to racial relations and other matters. But I have to weigh that, in the discharge of my duties, against imposing my judgment that the damage to be done is so grave that I should interfere with the traditional rights of people to carry on a lawful pursuit, even though it is an unpopular pursuit. So far, I have reached the conclusion it would not be right to do that....

I believe that that is correct and that it is not unfair to throw the responsibility upon the Cricket Council. It invited the South Africans; it can uninvite them if it chooses to do so. If it does, I promise the Council this: no one will construe it, because he will not be correct, to mean that the Council will be bowing to the forces of lawlessness or disorder, or the demonstrators in this country.

It seemed at the time that if there were to be a watershed at all before the scheduled arrival of the tourists on June 1, then it would be the Commons debate. Up to that point the Cricket Council insisted, come hell or high water, that the tour was on. On the evening of May 14 they had parliamentary pleas on which to pause and ponder. If there was any chink of dissension discernible within the Cricket Council, it had come only via whispered rumours: the public face of the Council was carefully presented as solid and unified. But in all conscience there was a vast and simmering edifice of responsible opinion, building itself into a more powerful and insistent structure each day, that was hammering on the portals of the Council. The gathering momentum of the demonstrators was now joined by a corpus of opposition to the tour that took as its common theme an appeal to the Cricket Council "to demonstrate their sense of responsibility as citizens, and at the same time their concern for the future of international cricket" by cancelling the tour invitation.

This was the text of a letter in *The Times* on May 6 signed by seventeen prominent persons, among them the Bishop of Woolwich, Lord Constantine, Fr Trevor Huddleston, Jeremy Thorpe and Sir Edward Boyle. Whether it was letters such as this, Mr Callaghan's words, the more responsible elements of the press, the Commonwealth Games issue, the potential antagonism of some ICC countries, the attitude of the Church, of the Sports Council or the Race Relations Board, or even the apparently lukewarm response to the 1970 Tour Fund, the Council had food for thought (and much of it unpalatable) from every quarter. It is as well to record that the anti-tour movement attracted a fanatical fringe as well as a large body of ordinary, sincere people. Its more militant allies had motives that were probably as questionable as their tactics were reprehensible, but as the campaign progressed these voices became less audible than those of other elements carrying more weight.

Hot on the heels of the Commons debate came the shattering news for South Africa of her formal expulsion from the Olympic movement – the first nation ever so expelled since the Olympic movement was revived in 1894: in a secret ballot in Amsterdam the International Olympic Committee – with the names of Basil D'Oliveira and Arthur Ashe well in their minds, it is said – made perhaps the most momentous decision in sporting history. "*It will be noted*", said a spokesman at Lord's. The expulsion made a much stronger impact on most people than the many resolutions against apartheid dutifully passed at the United Nations. On the same day the Royal Commonwealth Society, with its impeccable record of good sense and responsibility, expressed "great concern at the harm that would be done by the tour to multi-racial sport and good relations within the Commonwealth". In Cape Town, Jack Cheetham made a last desperate plea to keep the tour alive. The Fair Cricket Campaign (with new recruits in Sir William Robson Brown, MP and Mr Nicholas Scott, MP) stepped up its activities by sending out 20,000 invitations to organisations and individuals to stop the tour. The Archbishop of Canterbury and the Chief Rabbi added their voices to the wave of opposition. It was even made public that, according to unofficial sources, the Queen, in her personal capacity, was opposed to the tour. It seemed that the mightiest and the humblest in the land, and all those in between, were committed one way or the other. (An announcement from Buckingham Palace, by the way, said that the South African cricketers would not be received there; nor was there to have been a Royal visit to Lord's for the Test match – as there had likewise not been to Twickenham for the England–South Africa rugger match the previous December.)

What a great section of the public – both pro and anti the tour – considered would be an eleventh-hour reappraisal came at Lord's at a special and secret meeting of the Cricket Council on the evening of Monday, May 18. The meeting was a long one, deep into the night, and what agonies of conscience were experienced will only be known by those who were there. It did not transpire until the following day that the meeting had taken place – a critical meeting, to be sure, and held, incidentally, on the same day that the Prime Minister announced that the General Election would be held on June 18. (This date was the scheduled start of the Lord's Test, and visions of race riots on polling day could not have been a welcome thought to any political party.)

In Barbados, a statement from the West Indies Board of Control set out its positive opposition to the tour, adding that "irreparable harm" would come from it. P. D. B. Short, the Board secretary, said that the Board fervently hoped that the direct representations that had been made would result in cancellation. The West Indies Board had also been asked that the forthcoming tour of England by the West Indies Young Cricketers (in July–August 1970) be called off if the South Africans toured. Mr Mark Bonham Carter, chairman of the Race Relations Board, who had spoken eloquently at the MCC AGM, expressed his further concern in a private letter to Mr G. O. Allen, vice-chairman of the Cricket Council. The council of the 14,000-strong Inner London Teachers' Association deplored the prospect of the tour and the "inevitable repercussions" in schools. And a last-minute petition to halt the tour was presented to MCC on behalf of several hundred people living near Lord's.

It was against this background – and there were many more pressures too numerous to enumerate – that the Cricket Council came to their decision on May 18. At 7 p.m. the following evening, after a day of somewhat wild speculation, and while protest groups with banners paraded outside the Grace Gates, a crowded Press Conference in the Long Room at Lord's received the following statement from Mr Griffith:

At a meeting held yesterday the Cricket Council – representing all grades of cricket in the United Kingdom – were given a full report by the Executive Committee on all matters relating to the South African tour which had arisen since the Council's last meeting on April 23. The Council weighed carefully the strength of opinion both for and against the tour. This full statement of the Council's deliberations is indicative of their concern and of their awareness of the responsibilities with which they were faced.

The Council have decided by a substantial majority, that this tour should proceed as arranged. It has always believed that cricket in South Africa should be given the longest possible time to bring about conditions in which all cricketers in their own country, regardless of their origin, are able to play and be selected on equal terms. The South African Cricket Association have taken the first step by announcing tht all future touring teams will be selected on merit. The Council have confirmed the present tour in the hope and belief that this intention will be capable of fulfilment in the future. It is for this reason that the Council, while confirming finally their invitation to the South African Cricket Association to tour this summer, wish to make clear their position regarding the future.

They have informed the South African Cricket Association that no further Test tours between South Africa and this country will take place until South African cricket is played and teams are selected on a multi-racial basis in South Africa.

In this increasingly complicated issue the Council felt that they should first reassess their responsibilities. These they confirmed as being contained in the following broad headings:

1. To cricket and cricketers both in the United Kingdom and throughout the world;
2. To other sports and sportsmen.

It should be stressed that the Council have taken into account other matters of a public and political nature, but they consider these matters to be the responsibility of the Government who are best equipped to judge and act upon them.

In reviewing their original decision to confirm the invitation to the South African Cricket Association, the Council had to consider whether the desirability – so often repeated – of maintaining contact with South Africa had in any way changed. It was agreed that in the long term this policy was in the best interests of cricket, and cricketers of all races in South Africa.

The Council had also to consider its responsibilities to cricket and cricketers throughout the world, taking into account the opposition to the tour from certain quarters and the effect on other cricket-playing countries if the tour proceeded. The Council sympathised with those Boards of Control who had themselves been put under considerable pressure in regard to this tour but felt that the long term effects upon cricket could be disastrous if they were to succumb to similar pressure.

The Council also had to consider whether cricket would be a practical proposition if played amidst all the stresses and strains which have been threatened and predicted. The Council were under no illusions as to the risks of disruption at the matches to be played. They had also to consider the recent statement of the Home Secretary in the House of Commons on May 14 that "there need be no fear in anybody's mind that the police are incapable of handling this kind of demonstration". They also noted his assurance that it would be the duty of the police to prevent a breach of the peace and bring them (the offenders) before the courts.

The Council discussed the question of the Commonwealth Games in Scotland and deeply regretted the attitude of those countries who had threatened to withdraw if the cricket tour took place. The Council acknowledged a degree of responsibility to other sports and recognised the problems with which the organising bodies are faced. They hope, in view of their statement as to the future, that these countries will reconsider their attitude.

Two other issues which have already been mentioned should perhaps be further elaborated.

First, the question of community relations. The Council recognise that there has been a growing concern in the United Kingdom with the unacceptable apartheid policies of the present South African Government. The Council share this concern, but wish to re-emphasise that cricket has made an outstanding and widely acknowledged contribution to the maintenance of good relations between all people among whom the game has been played.

Secondly, the question of freedom under the law in this country. The Council do not consider it the duty or responsibility of cricket to campaign for freedom under the law at the expense of the game itself. But the Council and its constituent members are aware of the dangers of a minority group being allowed to take the law into their own hands by direct action. However distasteful to this minority group, the South African tour this summer is not only a lawful event, but as shown by the outcome of recent opinion polls, it is clearly the wish of the majority that the tour should take place.

Thus the 1970 tour was still "on". And so was the hubbub against it.

Meanwhile, what was the attitude in South Africa of the SACA? South Africa's cricket future was in jeopardy, and rightly or wrongly the SACA believed that cancellation of the tour – for which they had been preparing since the original invitation was extended by MCC in July 1966 – would mean the isolation of South African cricket for a very long time ahead. The reluctance of the SACA to take any step in cancelling the tour was bolstered, too, by the fact that the 1968-69 MCC tour of their country was cancelled as a result of interference by the South African government. The ordeal likely to face their players in Britain was never minimised, but they expressed much faith in what they trusted would be the "good sense and fair play" of the British public. In the midst of the furore Jack Cheetham declared: "I have said it before, and I say it again, that the British public will, as ever, stand by visitors to their country. I place my confidence in this."

While these protestations of faith were being sent across the world, objectionable tactics to disrupt the twelve tour matches were being carefully hatched, estimates were being bandied about of between 10,000 and 50,000 demonstrators who would converge on Lord's on June 6, and barbed wire and artificial pitches (if the natural pitch were maliciously damaged) were being laid at cricket grounds to withstand the expected intrusion. But by the third week-end in May, with a feeling of shock and disappointment in South Africa over the Olympic decision, and the Sports Minister, Mr Frank Waring, lamenting that "politics have triumphed over sport", many realists in the Republic believed the cricket tour to be impossible. This was despite a South African poll which showed that only one-fifth of those questioned were against the tour taking place. South African newspapers showed dramatic pictures of Springbok wives depicted as "the women who wait and pray". The influential *Rand Daily Mail*, a persistent supporter of the tour, said that even if Bacher's side did make the journey to Britain, it was "difficult to see them getting very far with the business of playing cricket". The paper added that only "a clear, unambiguous statement by our cricket authorities on the principle of non-racialism in sport" could help the tour. Those who recognised this as South Africa's own problem had long awaited such a statement. It had not been forthcoming, and it was not forthcoming now.

An unequivocal statement against sports segregation by either the captain, Ali Bacher, or the tour manager, Jack Plimsoll, would have been welcomed in the absence of one from the SACA itself. But presumably they regarded apartheid as the national policy and not the responsibility of sportsmen (so far as public pronouncements went, at any rate). It is true that neither of them was completely silent, but – before the cancellation, at least – their words were very guarded. Bacher, a doctor working in a hospital for non-Europeans near Johannesburg, soon after his appointment as captain for the English tour, said he would welcome multi-racial cricket in South Africa "as soon as the Government finds it practical". He was at all times behind his governing body in supporting the tour, and consulted Dawie de Villiers, the rugger captain, to find out what his team might expect to encounter in England. "I would always speak to a demonstrator," said Bacher, "provided he was polite." But he was firm in urging that demonstrators must not be allowed to break up the tour, lest there be "dire consequences" for world sport. "We are not politicians." he said early in May. "We are going to England to play cricket."

Bacher and the other 13 members of his team – not one of whom, incidentally, ever considered withdrawing because of the potential threats – had come under attack from the Stop the Seventy Tour Committee for not declaring themselves against apartheid sport and thus seeming to condone it. Bacher and Peter Pollock were quick to reject this: the reticence of cricketers on the issue of apartheid did not of course mean that they were necessarily in favour of it. Bacher, indeed, publicly recognised the right to stage demonstrations, provided they were peaceful and did not disrupt a match – precisely the view held, though they were on opposing sides, by both S. C. Griffith and David Sheppard, and expressed by them in October 1969.

As the tour drama was reaching its climax Jack Plimsoll, up to then silent about the controversy, said in an interview that he was not against mixed sport in South Africa. "There are a lot of non-white cricketers who, in better company, would improve with increased competition and could force their way into a Springbok side," he said. But this did not amount to a plea for the breaking down of the barriers.

Exactly two weeks before the South Africans were due to land in England, the SACA Board of Control, after a week-end meeting in Johannesburg, unanimously reaffirmed that it was proceeding with its plans for the team's practices in Durban and subsequent departure for England. The announcement came as world-wide controversy seemed to be reaching a peak, and amidst fresh criticism from even within South Africa, where Kevin Craig in the Johannesburg *Sunday Times* warned the SACA that unless they called off the tour they would "expose our cricketers to physical danger and maybe death". In South Africa, as in Britain, there had been speculation whether the government might not step in and call off the tour. At a political rally at Uitenhage on April 11, Mr B. J. Schoeman, the Minister of Transport and number two in the South African cabinet, said that if he had his way he would not send the side to Britain. "Why should we allow our boys to be insulted by those long-haired louts?" he asked. He stressed this was a personal view, but at no time – so far as one can ascertain from governmental and SACA sources – was there any approach from the South African government to SACA to reconsider the tour.

After the Cricket Council's statement of May 19, events moved swiftly to their climax. Outrage and determination to increase demonstrations was the reaction of the anti-tour groups, but those who cared about liberty and law and order felt greatly in debt to the

Cricket Council. There was relief in South Africa, even though the Council had admitted there was something grossly wrong with cricket selection there.

Almost at once Mr Callaghan invited the Cricket Council to meet him at the Home Office on May 21. The chairman, Mr M. J. C. Allom, and the secretary, Mr S. C. Griffith, attended a three-hour meeting at which the Home Secretary requested that the tour be cancelled "on the grounds of broad public policy".

The Home Secretary's letter to the Chairman of the Cricket Council read:

When you and Mr Griffith came to see me this morning, we discussed the statement issued on behalf of the Cricket Council on May 19 about the South African tour.

You explained that the Council had come to their conclusion that the tour should go on after reassessing their own responsibilities, which were limited to the impact of the decision on cricket and cricketers, both in the United Kingdom and throughout the world, and on other sports and sportsmen. You emphasized however that although the Council were naturally concerned with various other matters of a public and political nature which had been brought to their notice and had taken them into account, at the same time they felt that these matters fell outside their own responsibilities and that it was beyond their competence to judge what significance to attach to them. This, they felt, was the responsibility of the Government, who were equipped to judge and act upon them.

I accepted this distinction.

The Government have therefore been very carefully considering the implications of the tour, if it were to take place, in the light of the many representations that have been received from a wide variety of interests and persons. We have had particularly in mind the possible impact on relations with other Commonwealth countries, race relations in this country and the divisive effect on the community. Another matter for concern is the effect on the Commonwealth Games. I have taken into account too the position of the police; there is not doubt as to their ability to cope with any situation which might arise, but a tour of this nature would mean diverting police resources on a large scale from their essential ordinary duties.

The Government have come to the conclusion, after reviewing all these considerations, that on grounds of broad public policy they must request the Cricket Council to withdraw their invitation to the South African Cricket Association, and I should be grateful if you would put this request before the Council.

This amounted to a government directive, and faced with a formal request of this kind, the Cricket Council had little choice but to agree. They bowed to *force majeure*. Not even a vote was taken.

The cancellation came on May 22. The final statement on behalf of the Cricket Council read thus:

At a meeting held this afternoon at Lord's, the Cricket Council considered the formal request from Her Majesty's Government to withdraw the invitation to the South African touring team this summer.

With deep regret the Council were of the opinion that they had no alterntive but to accede to this request and they are informing the South African Cricket Association accordingly.

The Council are grateful for the overwhelming support of cricketers, cricket lovers and many others, and share their disappointment at the cancellation of the tour. At the same time they regret the discourtesy to the South African Cricket Association and the inconvenience caused to so many people.

The Council see no reason to repeat the arguments, to which they still adhere, which led them to sustain the invitation to the South African cricketers issued four years ago. They do, however, deplore the activities of those who by the intimidation of individual cricketers and threats of violent disruption have inflamed the whole issue.

Thus the sorry saga – apart from the inevitable series of reactions both in England and abroad – was at an end. It had been distressing and distasteful. Cricket, and especially Mr Griffith at Lord's had been subjected to pressures never experienced in the game before. Let us hope that cricket will never know such conflict again.

SOUTH AFRICA'S CHOSEN FOURTEEN

For the sake of the record here are the names of the fourteen players the South African selectors chose in the middle of March, 1970 for the proposed tour of England:

Dr Ali Bacher (Transvaal) captain, E. J. Barlow (Western Province) vice-captain, B. A. Richards (Natal), R. G. Pollock (Eastern Province), B. L. Irvine (Transvaal), D. Lindsay (N.E. Transvaal), H. R. Lance (Transvaal), M. J. Procter (Western Province), P. M. Pollock (Eastern Province), P. H. J. Trimborn (Natal), A. J. Traicos (Rhodesia), A. M. Short (Natal), G. L. G. Watson (Transvaal), G. A. Chevalier (Western Province).

Manager – J. B. Plimsoll.

WEST INDIANS IN ENGLAND

GLOUCESTERSHIRE v WEST INDIES

Played at Bristol, May 4, 6, 7, 1963

West Indies won by 65 runs. Griffith, Sobers, Smith and Young were outstanding performers in an entertaining game enjoyed by 7000 spectators on the Saturday. Griffith, fast and deadly accurate, gained a remarkable match analysis of thirteen wickets for 58, and Smith, who swung and moved the ball disconcertingly, took eleven for 92. Sobers excelled in bowling and fielding, and Young, with a fine innings of 127, just failed to turn the tide of success in favour of his county. Gloucestershire's bowlers, backed by smart fielding and handled capably by Graveney, their new captain, made the most on the first day of a pitch from which the ball rose unevenly. Milton held four slip catches in succession; Meyer also took four catches, and the tourists were out in just over two and a half hours.

Gloucestershire fared worse against Griffith and were dismissed in two and a quarter hours. Griffith, using the yorker effectively, sent back the first five men for 10 runs out of 31 and finished with eight for 23.

On the second day Smith added to his laurels with more fine bowling – he knocked down the middle stump in beating Nurse and Sobers and bowled Worrell leg-stump – but Solomon and Rodriguez by sound stroke-play helped to set the county to make 280 to win. They were 88 for three at the close, but despite the confident driving, pulling and cutting of Young – first in and ninth out at 212 – West Indies won just before lunch.

West Indies

C. C. Hunte c Brown b Smith	3	– c Meyer b Brown	13
M. C. Carew lbw b Smith	0	– b Smith	19
S. M. Nurse c Milton b Allen	16	– b Smith	23
G. S. Sobers c Meyer b Smith	3	– b Smith	11
J. S. Solomon c Milton b A'Court	19	– c Brown b Smith	56
*F. M. Worrell c Milton b A'Court	7	– b Smith	39
W. V. Rodriguez c Milton b Allen	4	– b Smith	44
†D. L. Murray c Meyer b A'Court	0	– b Brown	3
L. R. Gibbs c Mayer b Smith	1	– b Brown	6
C. C. Griffith c Meyer b Smith	22	– not out	5
L. A. King not out	9	– b A'Court	10
B 4, l-b 1	5	B 12, l-b 9	21
1/3 2/4 3/11 4/41 5/41 6/50 7/52 8/53 9/58	89	1/21 2/64 3/75 4/80 5/146 6/215 7/228 8/234 9/235	250

Bowling: *First Innings*—Smith 17.5–9–25–5; Brown 10–4–16–0; Graveney 1–1–0–0; Allen 14–5–28–2; A'Court 7–2–15–3. *Second Innings*—Smith 32–3–67–6; Brown 27–4–71–3; A'Court 18.5–5–43–1; Graveney 6–1–19–0; Mortimore 18–4–29–0.

Gloucestershire

D. M. Young c Murray b Griffith	13	– c Sobers b Griffith	127
R. B. Nicholls b Griffith	0	– c Nurse b Griffith	0
C. A. Milton lbw b Griffith	2	– lbw b Griffith	8
D. Carpenter lbw b Griffith	6	– b Sobers	12
J. B. Mortimore b Griffith	2	– c Murray b Sobers	26
D. A. Allen c Murray b Griffith	12	– c Worrell b Sobers	0
A. S. Brown b King	9	– b Sobers	8
*J. K. Graveney b King	1	– b Griffith	3
†B. J. Meyer b Griffith	4	– b Gibbs	13
D. R. Smith not out	4	– c Sobers b Griffith	0
D. G. A'Court b Griffith	0	– not out	3
B 1, l-b 5, n-b 1	7	B 7, l-b 4, w 2, n-b 1	14
1/5 2/7 3/25 4/26 5/31 6/46 7/50 8/55 9/60	60	1/3 2/25 3/61 4/142 5/142 6/158 7/187 8/211 9/212	214

Bowling: *First Innings*—Griffith 17.3–4–23–8; King 17–4–30–2. *Second Innings*—Griffith 15.4–2–35–5; King 10–1–23–0; Sobers 37–8–75–4; Gibbs 25–10–37–1; Rodriguez 8–1–30–0.

Umpires: J. S. Buller and J. Arnold.

YORKSHIRE v WEST INDIES

Played at Middlesbrough, May 15, 16, 17, 1963

Yorkshire won by 111 runs. The West Indies' first defeat of the tour was brought about largely by the play of Trueman. He had a match analysis of ten for 81, scored 75 for once out and also held two catches – a splendid performance. On a pitch from which the ball went through at varying heights, Yorkshire lost six wickets for less than 100 aginst the accurate and sustained pace of Griffith and King. Hampshire, knocked out by a rising ball from Griffith, pluckily returned to complete his innings. A seventh wicket partnership between Stott and Trueman of 78 in an hour, which Worrell, the West Indies captain, later said was the decisive feature of the match, pulled the county round. Stott batted an hour and fifty minutes and hit nine 4s. Trueman stayed for an hour and three quarters and hit two 6s and six 4s. None of the touring team mastered the alien pitch, which Trueman and Taylor exploited to full advantage. Yorkshire suffered an early blow when they batted a second time. Padgett was deceived by Griffith's pace and sustained a painful hit in the face. Worrell did not use his spinners this time and Yorkshire were always struggling before Close declared and set the West Indies to score 263 in four hours, forty minutes. To their credit they accepted the challenge and went boldly for their strokes. Sobers and Nurse added 46 at almost two a minute and Butcher included one 6 and six 4s in his not out 46. Despite this brave front, Yorkshire, and especially Trueman, called the tune.

Yorkshire

D. E. V. Padgett c Allan b King	5	– retired hurt	2
J. H. Hampshire b King	19	– c Solomon b Worrell	25
P. J. Sharpe lbw b Griffith	20	– lbw b King	10
*D. B. Close b Griffith	23	– lbw b Worrell	23
K. Taylor lbw b Griffith	10	– c Allan b Worrell	13
W. B. Stott c Kanhai b Valentine	65	– b Griffith	8
R. Illingworth c Allan b King	1	– c King b Worrell	28
F. S. Trueman c Allan b Griffith	55	– not out	20
D. Wilson b Sobers	4		
†J. G. Binks b Griffith	14	– not out	13
M. Ryan not out	5		
L-b 5	5	L-b 2, w 1	3
1/13 2/50 3/61 4/66 5/85 6/95 7/173 8/187 9/219	226	1/32 2/50 3/72 4/77 5/105 6/119	(6 wkts dec.) 145

Bowling: *First Innings*—Griffith 22.2–7–37–5; King 22–4–67–3; Worrell 9–1–19–0; Sobers 17–3–48–1; Valentine 8–1–50–1. *Second Innings*—Griffith 19–9–33–1; King 20–3–47–1; Worrell 20–3–62–4.

West Indies

*F. M. Worrell c Close b Ryan	22	– b Trueman	18
M. C. Carew c Taylor b Ryan	8	– c Illingworth b Ryan	3
R. B. Kanhai b Trueman	19	– b Trueman	9
S. M. Nurse c Binks b Trueman	7	– b Illingworth	26
G. S. Sobers c Trueman b Taylor	17	– b Taylor	29
B. F. Butcher c Binks b Taylor	13	– not out	46
J. S. Solomon c Sharpe b Taylor	4	– c Hampshire b Trueman	12
†D. W. Allan not out	16	– c Trueman b Ryan	0
C. C. Griffith hit wicket b Trueman	2	– c Binks b Trueman	4
L. A. King c Taylor b Trueman	0	– b Trueman	4
A. L. Valentine c Close b Trueman	0	– absent hurt	0
L-b 1	1		
1/29 2/37 3/56 4/57 5/75 6/99 7/100 8/103 9/103	109	1/1 2/6 3/8 4/25 5/71 6/71 7/110 8/147 9/151	151

Bowling: *First Innings*—Trueman 20–5–38–5; Ryan 25–11–32–2; Taylor 26–12–33–3; Illingworth 2–1–4–0; Close 1–0–1–0. *Second Innings*—Trueman 13.3–5–43–5; Ryan 14–3–52–2; Illingworth 12–4–42–1; Taylor 11–5–14–1.

Umpires: N. Oldfield and H. Yarnold.

MCC v WEST INDIES

Played at Lord's, May 18, 20, 21, 1963

West Indies won by 93 runs with half an hour to spare after a contrived finish on the last day. A crowd of 20,000 saw West Indies bat brightly on the Saturday. Hunte and Butcher put on 108 in ninety-five minutes, and Kanhai hit 34 in half an hour, but the last seven wickets fell for 97. Bad light ended play thirty-five minutes early, and on the second day when the weather was dull and cold two hours were lost. MCC batted cautiously and slowly, reaching 120 for five. On the last morning Cowdrey declared first thing and Hunte, acting captain because of injury to Worrell, did not enforce the follow on although 186 ahead. When he declared MCC needed 266 in four and a quarter hours. Edrich and Atkinson gave them a good start, but after tea eight wickets fell for 53, no attempt being made to save the game. Substitutes were required for Worrell, Allan and Gibbs. Gibbs was prevented from bowling for a time when he returned to the field and Hunte wanted to put him on immediately. The umpires considered this came under "fair and unfair play", as he came "warm" from the pavilion and all the other players were "cold". When he bowled half an hour later he soon finished the innings.

West Indies

C. C. Hunte c Sharpe b Titmus	91	– c Murray b White	3
E. D. McMorris c Sharpe b Titmus	24	– not out	26
R. B. Kanhai b Titmus	34		
B. F. Butcher lbw b Cotton	70		
G. S. Sobers c Murray b Cotton	4		
J. S. Solomon lbw b Cotton	24	– not out	44
*F. M. Worrell b Milburn	19		
†D. W. Allan c Murray b Milburn	14		
W. W. Hall b Cotton	1		
L. R. Gibbs b Milburn	10		
C. C. Griffith not out	5		
L-b 10	10	B 5, l-b 1	6
1/55 2/101 3/209 4/213 5/246 6/264 7/283 8/288 9/294	306	1/4 (1 wkt dec.)	79

Bowling: *First Innings*—White 16–3–34–0; Cotton 17–2–49–4; Milburn 6.5–0–26–3; Barber 23–5–91–0; Titmus 26–10–52–3; Gifford 11–2–44–0. *Second Innings*—White 6–1–7–1; Cotton 7–0–22–0; Titmus 11–5–22–0; Gifford 8–1–22–0.

MCC

J. H. Edrich b Griffith	65	– c sub b Griffith	39
G. Atkinson lbw b Sobers	2	– c Hunte b Solomon	63
R. W. Barber c Butcher b Sobers	16	– c Sobers b Gibbs	9
P. J. Sharpe b Sobers	0	– run out	19
*M. C. Cowdrey not out	24	– lbw b Hall	5
C. Milburn b Hall	6	– c Hunte b Gibbs	6
F. J. Titmus not out	0	– lbw b Gibbs	7
†J. T. Murray (did not bat)		– b Gibbs	3
D. W. White (did not bat)		– c sub b Sobers	8
J. Cotton (did not bat)		– st sub b Sobers	1
N. Gifford (did not bat)		– not out	0
B 1, l-b 1, n-b 5	7	B 7, l-b 4, n-b 1	12
1/2 2/53 3/53 4/110 5/120 (5 wkts dec.)	120	1/69 2/111 3/120 4/140 5/145 6/151 7/156 8/171 9/171	172

Bowling: *First Innings*—Hall 21–9–35–1; Sobers 20–1–48–3; Griffith 21–9–30–1; Gibbs 1–1–0–0. *Second Innings*—Hall 16–3–38–1; Griffith 11–4–32–1; Sobers 20.1–7–36–2; Solomon 8–1–34–1; Gibbs 19–9–20–4.

Umpires: J. S. Buller and John Langridge.

ENGLAND v WEST INDIES

Second Test Match

Played at Lord's, June 20, 21, 22, 24, 25, 1963

Drawn. One of the most dramatic Test matches ever to be played in England attracted large crowds and aroused tremendous interest throughout the country. All through the cricket had been keen and thrilling, but the climax was remarkable, Cowdrey having to go in with a broken bone in his arm. About 300 people rushed the ground at the end of the match seeking souvenirs and patting the players on the back. The West Indies supporters called for Worrell and Hall, who appeared on the balcony, sending them home happy.

When the final over arrived any one of four results could have occurred – a win for

England, victory for West Indies, a tie or a draw. The match was drawn with England six runs short of success and West Indies needing one more wicket. Most people felt happy about the result, for it would have been a pity if either side had lost after playing so well.

The England selectors sprang a surprise by recalling Shackleton, aged thirty-eight, after a gap of more than eleven years. His form at the time plus the fact that he had a fine record at Lord's, influenced them. He replaced Statham, and to strengthen the batting Parks came in for Andrew as wicket-keeper. West Indies preferred McMorris as opening batsman to Carew.

Worrell won the toss for West Indies, and after rain had delayed the start for twenty-three minutes the game began on a high note with Hunte taking 4s off the first three balls of the match, bowled by Trueman. Shackleton frequently worried Hunte, who offered two sharp chances off him. The scoring dropped right back, and at lunch the total was only 47. The first wicket fell at 51 and the next at 64. Then Sobers and Kanhai, in an entertaining stand lasting sixty-five minutes, added 63. A fifth wicket partnership of 74 between Kanhai and Solomon put West Indies in a useful position, but with Worrell failing to score England were well in the picture. At the close West Indies were 245 for six, and they carried the total to 301.

Shackleton failed to take a wicket on the first day, but he terminated the innings with three in four balls, dismissing Solomon, Griffith and Gibbs. Trueman bowled well for long spells and claimed six for 100.

Edrich fell to the first ball he received, and with Stewart also going early England were 20 for two at lunch. Afterwards Dexter gave a thrilling display of powerful driving, hooking and cutting. He took only forty-eight minutes to reach 52, and when leg-before he had made 70 in eighty-one minutes off 73 balls received. His hits included ten 4s, and the way he stood up and punished the fiery fast bowling of Hall and Griffith was exciting to see. Barrington played a minor role in helping Dexter add 82 in sixty-two minutes but later took over command.

Cowdrey again disappointed, but Parks shared a sixth wicket partnership of 55 in an hour. Barrington, still searching for his first Test century in England, drove a catch to cover after batting three hours, ten minutes for 80. England finished with 244 for seven. On the Saturday, when the gates were closed ten minutes before the start, Titmus played a sound innings and England finished within four of the West Indies total. Griffith took five for 91, always being awkward to play.

When West Indies lost their opening pair for 15 the issue was wide open. Cowdrey, at slip, held his third successive catch to dismiss Kanhai, and with Sobers and Solomon going cheaply, West Indies were 104 for five with England apparently on top. Then came a complete swing, Butcher, showing excellent form and hitting the bad ball hard, checked the slide and with Worrell carried the score to 214 for five by the close. West Indies then led by 218 and were well placed only to lose ground again in a remarkable twenty-five minutes on Monday morning when the last five wickets went for 15 in six overs.

Butcher, ninth out for 133 (two 6s and seventeen 4s) batted splendidly for nearly four and a half hours. He and Worrell put on 110. Trueman, with five for 52, claimed eleven for 152 in the match, one of his best performances for England. Shackleton supported him well with seven for 165 in the two innings.

So England went in to get 234 to win. Their hopes sank when Edrich, Stewart and Dexter were out for 31, but Barrington again rose to the occasion. He and Cowdrey had to withstand some fierce bowling from Hall, who often pitched short and struck the batsmen on the body and fingers. Eventually Cowdrey received such a blow that a bone just above the left wrist was broken and he had to retire, having shown his best form of the series and helping to carry the score to 72. Close took his place and the England fight back continued, Barrington hitting Gibbs over mid-wicket for two 6s in an over. Bad light handicapped the batsmen, and there were two stoppages before the game was given up for the day at 4.45 p.m. with England 116 for three, needing another 118.

To add to the tenseness of the situation, rain and poor light delayed the resumption next day until 2.20 p.m. Hall and Griffith, bowling at their best on a pitch which had remained lively throughout the match, made the batsmen fight desperately for every run. Barrington added only five in fifty-five minutes, and the first hour brought no more than 18 runs.

Close and Parks took the score to 158, and Titmus also fought well. At tea, it was still anyone's game with England 171 for five, Cowdrey injured and 63 needed in eighty-five minutes. With West Indies averaging only 14 overs an hour, this was a harder task than it looked on paper. The game moved back in West Indies favour when Titmus and Trueman fell to successive balls. Close, who had defended with rare courage despite being hit often on the body and finishing with a mass of bruises, decided the time had come to change his methods. He began moving down the pitch to Hall and Griffith to upset their length. He succeeded for a time, but eventually he just touched the ball when trying a big swing and was caught at the wicket. Worrell said afterwards that while not wishing to detract from a very fine innings, he thought Close's changed tactics were wrong. Others paid high tribute to what they termed a magnificent and courageous innings which lasted three hours, fifty minutes. He made 70, easily his highest score for England.

Shackleton joined Allen with nineteen minutes left and 15 runs required. They fell further behind the clock and when Hall began his last dramatic over eight were needed. Singles came off the second and third balls, but Shackleton was run out off the fourth when Worrell raced from short-leg with the ball and beat the batsman to the bowler's end. That meant Cowdrey had to come in with two balls left and six wanted. He did not have to face a ball, Allen playing out the last two. If he had to shape up, Cowdrey intended to turn round and bat left-handed to protect his left arm.

Hall, in particular, and Griffith, showed remarkable stamina. Hall bowled throughout the three hours, twenty minutes play was in progress on the last day, never losing his speed and always being menacing. He took four for 93 off forty overs in the innings. Griffith bowled all but five overs on the last day.

The game which attracted 110,287 paying spectators and approximately £25,000 all told, gave cricket a fine boost which was reflected immediately in improved bookings for the third Test at Edgbaston. The receipts were £56,300, not far short of the record for any match. Those who saw it, and the millions who followed the game's progress over television and radio, were kept in a constant state of excitement. It was a game to remember.

West Indies

C. C. Hunte c Close b Trueman	44	– c Cowdrey b Shackleton	7
E. D. McMorris lbw b Trueman	16	– c Cowdrey b Trueman	8
G. S. Sobers c Cowdrey b Allen	42	– c Parks b Trueman	8
R. B. Kanhai c Edrich b Trueman	73	– c Cowdrey b Shackleton	21
B. F. Butcher c Barrington b Trueman	14	– lbw b Shackleton	133
J. S. Solomon lbw b Shackleton	56	– c Stewart b Allen	5
*F. M. Worrell b Trueman	0	– c Stewart b Trueman	33
†D. L. Murray c Cowdrey b Trueman	20	– c Parks b Trueman	2
W. W. Hall not out	25	– c Parks b Trueman	2
C. C. Griffith c Cowdrey b Shackleton	0	– b Shackleton	1
L. R. Gibbs c Stewart b Shackleton	0	– not out	1
B 10, l-b 1	11	B 5, l-b 2, n-b 1	8
1/51 2/64 3/127 4/145 5/219 6/219 7/263 8/297 9/297	301	1/15 2/15 3/64 4/84 5/104 6/214 7/224 8/226 9/228	229

Bowling: *First Innings*—Trueman 44–16–100–6; Shackleton 50.2–22–93–3; Dexter 20–6–41–0; Close 9–3–21–0; Allen 10–3–35–1. *Second Innings*—Trueman 26–9–52–5; Shackleton 34–14–72–4; Titmus 17–3–47–0; Allen 21–7–50–1.

England

M. J. Stewart c Kanhai b Griffith	2	– c Solomon b Hall	17
J. H. Edrich c Murray b Griffith	0	– c Murray b Hall	8
*E. R. Dexter lbw b Sobers	70	– b Gibbs	2
K. F. Barrington c Sobers b Worrell	80	– c Murray b Griffith	60
M. C. Cowdrey b Gibbs	4	– not out	19
D. B. Close c Murray b Griffith	9	– c Murray b Griffith	70
†J. M. Parks b Worrell	35	– lbw b Griffith	17
F. J. Titmus not out	52	– c McMorris b Hall	11
F. S. Trueman b Hall	10	– c Murray b Hall	0
D. A. Allen lbw b Griffith	2	– not out	4
D. Shackleton b Griffith	8	– run out	4
B 8, l-b 8, n-b 9	25	B 5, l-b 8, n-b 3	16
1/2 2/20 3/102 4/115 5/151 6/206 7/235 8/271 9/274	297	1/15 2/27 3/31 4/130 5/158 6/203 7/203 8/219 9/228	(9 wkts) 228

Bowling: *First Innings*—Hall 18–2–65–1; Griffith 26–6–91–5; Sobers 18–4–45–1; Gibbs 27–9–59–1; Worrell 13–6–12–2. *Second Innings*—Hall 40–9–93–4; Griffith 30–7–59–3; Gibbs 17–7–56–1; Sobers 4–1–4–0.

Umpires: J. S. Buller and W. E. Phillipson.

ENGLAND v WEST INDIES

Third Test Match

Played at Birmingham, July 4, 5, 6, 8, 9, 1963

England won by 217 runs and maintained their unbeaten Test record at the Edgbaston ground. They had to thank Trueman for another splendid bowling performance. In the previous Test at Lord's he took eleven wickets for 152 runs and now he finished with twelve for 119, the best Test analysis of his whole career. It was a wonderful effort for a man of 32, an age when many fast bowlers are getting over the hill, but Trueman proved the value of experience.

That the match went into the last afternoon was due almost entirely to the time lost through rain. The West Indies rarely do themselves justice in the absence of sunshine and England seized the chance to avenge their defeat at Old Trafford and level the series. The team showed three changes from Lord's, Richardson, Sharpe and Lock coming in for Edrich, Cowdrey and Allen. West Indies preferred McMorris to Carew.

A deluge drenched the ground on the eve of the match, neither team being able to practice, but the covered pitch, if rather lifeless at times, never suffered any damage and, in fact, was fast and true when West Indies collapsed for 91 in the fourth innings.

The cricket on the first day after Dexter had won the toss gave no indication of England's eventual success. When a downpour prevented play after tea West Indies had captured five wickets in just under four hours for 157 runs. The conditions did not suit Hall and Griffith although Hall knocked over Richardson's leg stump in his second over.

Sobers carried much more danger for the batsmen, bowling left arm over the wicket at a lively pace through the air. Close again served England splendidly and Dexter drove well. Sharpe survived some early difficulties, but generally the batting was disappointing.

The second day was almost completely spoiled by rain which restricted play to one hour and fifty minutes during which time the last five England wickets fell for 59 more runs. With Sobers achieving his best Test bowling performance in taking five wickets for 60 runs, the West Indies could claim the better of the argument at that stage. Sobers bowled through the seventy minutes cricket that was in progress before lunch and Worrell gave him the new ball in preference to Hall. Close and Parks exercised care against the varied swing of Sobers and the spin of Gibbs. The Yorkshire left-hander batted seven minutes short of three hours for his 55 which included five 4s.

There was a delay of over three hours after lunch before England resumed batting for the last forty minutes. Then Worrell relied on Hall and Griffith who proceeded to finish the innings.

On the third day, Saturday, the gates were closed with 28,000 present, but the cricket was limited to two hours and forty minutes during which West Indies replied with a score of 110 for four wickets. Play did not start until ten minutes to one and not a ball could be bowled after tea. With no hard pitch to encourage him, Trueman reduced his run up and his pace to cut the ball either way. He maintained his attack for two hours and ten minutes, his only break being during the lunch interval.

Hunte faced the full brunt of Trueman while the tall left-handed Carew generally had more of Shackleton. Hunte lost his off stump when he played back to a half volley, but Carew hooked to good purpose until he gave a soft return off the splice to Trueman. Dexter bowled splendidly for seventy-five minutes, but the third wicket went to Shackleton when Kanhai, after staying eight-five minutes, was smartly taken low by Lock at short fine leg. In the next over, Solomon offered no stroke and was leg before having kneed the ball away from the off stump.

The fourth day, Monday, yielded the first full-day's play of the match and a crowd of 17,500 saw some splendid cricket during which 14 wickets went down for 302 runs. England soon gained the upper hand by taking the remaining six West Indies wickets in eighty minutes for 76, the only resistance coming from Murray and Hall.

England's heroes were Dexter, Trueman and Sharpe. Dexter excelled in an all-round capacity for in taking four wickets for 38 he shared the bowling honours with Trueman and on top of this he gave a glimpse of his most attractive batting in scoring 57.

Again the pitch proved too slow for Hall, but Griffith and Sobers caused England to lose their first four wickets for 69. Stewart served England spendidly by staying one and three-quarter hours while the bowling was most difficult. When he left Sharpe began a most valuable partnership with Dexter. At first both concentrated on defence. One hour passed before Dexter struck his first boundary, but after tea the England captain launched a fearful attack on the bowling. He hooked and drove his rival captain, Worrell, for five 4s.

England were 200 ahead and virtually out of danger when Dexter was smartly stumped by Murray and though Parks, Titmus and Trueman accomplished little, Lock joined Sharpe in a final half hour to complete this triumphal day for England. He presented a straight bat in defence and excelled with his favourite cover drive while making 23 out of the last 37 runs scored that day. Sharpe, 69 not out, drove splendidly, getting his runs in two and three-quarter hours and so England's total reached 226 for eight, a lead of 256.

Even the new ball did not trouble Sharpe and Lock on the last morning. The Yorkshireman, defiant to a degree, was outshone by his tail-end partner and they carried their stand to 89, the best for the ninth witcket for England against West Indies. Lock claimed his first fifty in Test cricket. He hit seven 4s and Sharpe, not out for 85 in just under four hours, could look back on a memorable Test début. His was the highest individual score and he held two vital catches at first slip.

The stage seemed set for an exciting finish when shortly after mid-day Dexter declared and set West Indies to make 309 in four hours forty minutes, a rate of 67 an hour. This challenge was not beyond their power but England struck early, seizing the initiative which they never relinquished. Trueman began the bowling from the pavilion end, assisted by a high cross wind. Shackleton drew first blood with his third ball which trapped Carew leg-before. Next over, Trueman claimed his first victim, Hunte falling to a fine catch by Barrington at second slip.

The loss of the two opening batsmen for 10 runs proved a tragedy for West Indies. When Trueman rested after his first spell of fifty minutes the total stood at 38 for two and his figures were: 7–0–24–1. Dexter relieved Trueman and with his second ball knocked back Butcher's off stump. By lunch England were in sight of victory with West Indies 55 for three.

Kanhai and Sobers resumed in a punishing mood, but with Trueman sharing the attack with Shackleton the rest of the side suddenly collapsed. England needed only fifty-five more minutes to polish them off for the last seven wickets added only 36 to the interval total. Trueman's final onslaught gave him the last six wickets in 24 balls during which the only scoring stroke was a late cut for 4 by Gibbs, the last man. With a crowd of 11,000 on the last day the full match attendance was 86,500 with recepts of £36,349.

England

P. E. Richardson b Hall	2	– c Murray b Griffith	14
M. J. Stewart lbw b Sobers	39	– c Murray b Griffith	27
*E. R. Dexter b Sobers	29	– st Murray b Gibbs	57
K. F. Barrington b Sobers	9	– b Sobers	1
D. B. Close lbw b Sobers	55	– c Sobers b Griffith	13
P. J. Sharpe c Kanhai b Gibbs	23	– not out	85
†J. M. Parks c Murray b Sobers	12	– c Sobers b Gibbs	5
F. J. Titmus c Griffith b Hall	27	– b Gibbs	0
F. S. Trueman b Griffith	4	– c Gibbs b Sobers	1
G. A. R. Lock b Griffith	1	– b Gibbs	56
D. Shackleton not out	6		
L-b 6, n-b 3	9	B 9, l-b 9, n-b 1	19
1/2 2/50 3/72 4/89 5/129 6/172 7/187 8/194 9/200	216	1/30 2/31 3/60 4/69 5/170 6/184 7/184 8/189 9/278 (9 wkts dec.)	278

Bowling: *First Innings*—Hall 16.4–2–56–2; Griffith 21–5–48–2; Sobers 31–10–60–5; Worrell 14–5–15–0; Gibbs 16–7–28–1. *Second Innings*—Hall 16–1–47–0; Griffith 28–7–55–3; Worrell 8–3–28–0; Sobers 27–4–80–2; Gibbs 26.2–4–49–4.

West Indies

C. C. Hunte b Trueman	18	– c Barrington b Trueman	5
M. C. Carew c and b Trueman	40	– lbw b Shackleton	1
R. B. Kanhai c Lock b Shackleton	32	– c Lock b Trueman	38
B. F. Butcher lbw b Dexter	15	– b Dexter	14
J. S. Solomon lbw b Dexter	0	– c Parks b Trueman	14
G. S. Sobers b Trueman	19	– c Sharpe b Shackleton	9
*F. M. Worrell b Dexter	1	– c Parks b Trueman	0
†D. L. Murray not out	20	– c Parks b Trueman	3
W. W. Hall c Sharpe b Dexter	28	– b Trueman	0
C. C. Griffith lbw b Trueman	5	– lbw b Trueman	0
L. R. Gibbs b Trueman	0	– not out	4
L-b 7, w 1	8	L-b-2 w 1	3
1/42 2/79 3/108 4/109 5/128 6/130 7/130 8/178 9/186	186	1/2 2/10 3/38 4/64 5/78 6/80 7/86 8/86 9/86	91

Bowling: *First Innings*—Trueman 26–5–75–5; Shackleton 21–9–60–1; Lock 2–1–5–0; Dexter 20–5–38–4. *Second Innings*—Trueman 14.3–2–44–7; Shackleton 17–4–37–2; Dexter 3–1–7–1.

Umpires: C. S. Elliott and L. H. Gray.

ENGLAND v WEST INDIES

Fifth Test Match

Played at The Oval, August 22, 23, 24, 26, 1963

West Indies won by eight wickets with a day to spare and therefore carried off the rubber and the Wisden Trophy by a margin of three victories to one. There was no question that they were the superior side in all phases given decent weather and a firm pitch, but at the end of three days in this match honours were even. Indeed, England held a first innings lead of 29 and West Indies, batting last, found themselves wanting 253 to win on Saturday evening when they knocked off five without loss. Trueman was England's key man. His three first innings wickets had given him 34 for the series, a new record for a bowler in an England-West Indies rubber, but he damaged his left ankle on Saturday morning. The injury, diagnosed as a bruised bone, did not respond to treatment over the week-end and as Trueman sent down only one over in the West Indies second innings they found little to trouble them and coasted home comfortably to the delight of hordes of exuberant supporters who filled The Oval all four days.

Those who were present will never forget the fantastic final scene. Early in the day the gates had been closed with 25,350 present. About two-thirds of the attendance were West Indies people now resident in London. They were jubilant, excited and well-behaved, but as Hunte and Butcher got nearer to the target so those in the front crept nearer to the boundary. Then on the stroke of twenty-five minutes past five, Butcher made the winning hit off Statham – an on drive – and the ball was never seen again as the hundreds of coloured supporters invaded the field running towards the pavilion. There they stayed for some time cheering their heroes as each appeared on the balcony.

When Dexter won the toss for the second time in the series, the West Indies players were despondent. They feared their chance had gone. England, who had to call in Edrich to replace Stewart who went down with gastro-enteritis, rather surprisingly left out Titmus, but judging from the lack of success which attended Gibbs the selectors were proved right. West Indies preferred Rodriguez as the opening partner for Hunte and so the other ten played in all five Tests, a rare happening.

The match was a great triumph for Hunte, the West Indies vice-captain, who played two grand innings of 80 and 108 not out, and also for Griffith, who took nine wickets. Kanhai and Sobers, too, shone with the bat and Murray, the wicket-keeper, by taking three catches in each innings finished with 24 victims in the series, a record for an official Test rubber.

Worrell, by his calm and astute leadership, held his men together and inspired them to give of their best. The game was also memorable for the action of Buller, the umpire, in taking a firm stand over the problem of dangerous and short pitch intimidatory bouncers delivered by Hall and Griffith.

Early on the first day after Edrich had been struck by Hall, and the same bowler, in his sixth over, sent down two successive bouncers at Bolus, Buller walked over to Worrell and said, "We don't want this sort of bowling to get out of hand otherwise I will have to speak to the bowler."

Later, just before the close of play, Buller warned Griffith direct about his short pitched bowling in accordance with the procedure laid down in Law 46 (Fair and Unfair Play) and he also told Worrell that he had spoken to the bowler, saying "Look this can't go on. You will have to stop it skipper." Griffith then remarked, "I am allowed two every over" and Buller replied, "No, You are not allowed any." Happily, Worrell abided with Buller's action and after play he closed the incident, saying: "As far as I am concerned the umpires are the sole judges of fair and unfair play."

England's opening pair, Bolus and Edrich, showed great courage in withstanding the initial assault by Hall and Griffith. They stayed together for an hour and a half before Bolus, trying to drive Sobers, was taken by Murray. Edrich went almost the same way in Sober's next over, and with Dexter and Barrington failing to take charge West Indies captured the first four wickets for 115 runs. Then came a fighting stand of 101 by the two

Yorkshiremen, Close and Sharpe, so that England seemed to have recovered at five o'clock when their total reached 216 for 4. Then Griffith took the new ball and in nine overs went clean through the rest of the side. This spell gave him five wickets for 27 and in the innings he took six for 71, following his success in the previous Test at Headingley where his match figures were nine for 81.

West Indies began their reply next day and though Rodriguez failed England seemed to be in dire straits shortly after tea when the total stood at 184 for three wickets. Then in quick succession two of the West Indies best batsmen, Butcher and Sobers, were run out and the score changed to 198 for five. Butcher was extremely unlucky. He was backing up when Sobers produced a magnificent straight drive, Lock, the bowler, stuck out a hand, touching the ball which hit the stumps with Butcher out of his ground. A superb return by Close from deep backward point which broke the wicket accounted for Sobers when he was taking a sharp single for a cut by Solomon.

Thereupon Trueman and Statham took the new ball and proceeded to remove Worrell, Murray and Hall. Consequently, West Indies finished the day still wanting 45 for the lead with two wickets left. Hunte, who was third to leave at 152, when he tried to cut, played steadily for his 80, which included seven 4s. He batted three and a quarter hours. During the morning session Close kept wicket most efficiently as Parks was lame from a blow on the left foot by a yorker from Hall the previous evening. An X-ray revealed no serious trouble.

On the third morning (Saturday) Trueman in the gully held Solomon, who had occupied ninety-eight minutes for 16, and then removed Gibbs' leg stump so that England claimed a slight advantage at the half-way stage.

The fortunes of the two teams continued to hang on a slender shred. The well-prepared pitch showed no traces of wear and another exciting day's cricket ensued. The exuberant West Indies supporters who thronged the terraces danced with joy, twirled their coloured parasols and flung their cushions high in the air every time an England wicket fell.

England, in keeping with the uncertainty they had shown throughout the summer, again lost their first four wickets cheaply before recovering when Sharpe took part in two stands of 52 with Dexter and Parks.

Sharpe could be criticised for not moving his feet to get to the pitch of the ball but unlike several of his colleagues he did keep his bat straight and again he was top scorer for England being last out when he touched a bouncer. He drove splendidly during his stay of three and a quarter hours and hit ten 4s.

Barrington enjoyed one glorious over immediately after lunch when he hooked the short stuff from Griffith for 15, but Worrell tendered some fatherly advice to Griffith who then concentrated on a fuller length; no-one could complain in this innings of an excessive barrage of bumpers.

The bowling honours really went to Sobers. He entered the attack with only 18 scored and maintained his left-arm medium fast attack almost through the day. He rarely delivered a bad ball and sent down 33 overs at a cost of only 77 runs for three wickets. Moreover, he suffered from missed catches; otherwise he would have established a unique Test double of 4,000 runs and 100 wickets. He still wants two wickets. Dexter had a life off him when only 6, Murray intercepting a ball which was going first to Gibbs at slip and Rodriguez at second slip failed to hold an easy chance when Sharpe was 32 and the total 130.

After the tense struggle of the first three days, the complete mastery of the West Indies in the final innings came as a surprise, but with Trueman unable to bowl they were able to pursue a steady course, avoiding unnecessary risks.

Rodriguez helped Hunte to give the innings a solid foundation by seeing the opening stand to 78 and then came the dashing Kanhai. He gave the crowd the type of cricket they wanted and in seventy minutes scored 77 out of a very fine partnership of 113 with Hunte. Finally Butcher contributed 31 to the last unbroken stand of 64. Hunte was the hero. He took out his bat for 108, having defied England for five hours. The full attendance for the four days came to 97,350 and the receipts amounted to £42,688.

England

J. B. Bolus c Murray b Sobers	33	– c Gibbs b Sobers	15
J. H. Edrich c Murray b Sobers	25	– c Murray b Griffith	12
*E. R. Dexter c and b Griffith	29	– c Murray b Sobers	27
K. F. Barrington c Sobers b Gibbs	16	– b Griffith	28
D. B. Close b Griffith	46	– lbw b Sobers	4
P. J. Sharpe c Murray b Griffith	63	– c Murray b Hall	83
†J. M. Parks c Kanhai b Griffith	19	– lbw b Griffith	23
F. S. Trueman b Griffith	19	– c Sobers b Hall	5
G. A. R. Lock hit wkt b Griffith	4	– b Hall	0
J. B. Statham b Hall	8	– b Hall	14
D. Shackleton not out	0	– not out	0
B 4, l-b 2, n-b 7	13	B 5, l-b 3, n-b 4	12
1/59 2/64 3/103 4/115 5/216 6/224 7/252 8/258 9/275	275	1/29 2/31 3/64 4/69 5/121 6/173 7/196 8/196 9/218	223

Bowling: *First Innings*—Hall 22.2–2–71–1; Griffith 27–3–71–6; Sobers 21–4–44–2; Gibbs 27–7–50–1; Worrell 5–0–26–0. *Second Innings*—Hall 16–3–39–4; Griffith 23–7–66–3; Sobers 33–6–77–3; Gibbs 9–1–29–0.

West Indies

C. C. Hunte c Parks b Shackleton	80	– not out	108
W. C. Rodriguez c Lock b Statham	5	– c Lock b Dexter	28
R. B. Kanhai b Lock	30	– c Bolus b Lock	77
B. F. Butcher run out	53	– not out	31
G. S. Sobers run out	26		
J. S. Solomon c Trueman b Statham	16		
*F. M. Worrell b Statham	9		
†D. L. Murray c Lock b Trueman	5		
W. W. Hall b Trueman	2		
C. C. Griffith not out	13		
L. R. Gibbs b Trueman	4		
L-b 3	3	B 4, l-b 7	11
1/10 2/72 3/152 4/185 5/198 6/214 7/221 8/225 9/233	246	1/78 2/191	(2 wkts) 255

Bowling: *First Innings*—Trueman 26.1–2–65–3; Statham 22–2–68–3; Shackleton 21–5–37–1; Lock 29–6–65–1; Dexter 6–1–8–0. *Second Innings*—Statham 22–2–54–0; Shackleton 32–7–68–0; Trueman 1–1–0–0; Lock 25–8–52–1; Dexter 9–1–34–1; Close 6–0–36–0.

Umpires: J. S. Buller and A. E. Rhodes.

ENGLAND v WEST INDIES

First Test Match

Played at Manchester, June 2, 3, 4, 1966

West Indies won by an innings and 40 runs with two days to spare. It was the first time England had lost in three days since they went down to Australia at Leeds in 1938 and it was the first time they had been beaten so soon in a five-day Test. No doubt, West Indies were fortunate to win the toss and bat on a newly prepared pitch before it turned in favour of spin. Only thirty wickets went down in the match and of these 24 fell to the slow bowlers. Titmus and Allen took seven for England, but easily the most deadly artist in this important phase of the game was Gibbs, who with five wickets in each innings, finished with a full analysis of ten for 106. Holford, in his first Test, and Sobers gave sound support and between them claimed seven victims with varied leg spin.

The match was favoured with three days of really hot weather. The England selectors made B. D'Oliveira twelfth man and committed the side to carrying an excessively long tail, which proved a great mistake. The play followed very much the pattern of the 1963 match on the same ground. Then West Indies batting first scored 501 for six declared, with Hunte 182, and they won by ten wickets, Gibbs's figures being eleven for 157.

Now Hunte dominated the cricket for five hours and made 135 (nineteen 4s) of the first day's total of 343 for five wickets, he being fifth out to the new ball at 283 when he fell to a grand catch at short fine leg. The cavalier treatment of the England bowlers began with the very first ball which Jones pitched short and Hunte square cut for four with a handsome stroke. Yet in Jones's second over Hunte, when seven and the total 10, was dropped by Higgs on the leg boundary; Higgs appeared to sight the ball very late against the distant background of dark coated spectators.

At times, Jones, Brown and Higgs made the ball fly awkwardly but the West Indies batsmen were adept in punishing anything a shade loose. England began well when Higgs disposed of McMorris and Kanhai (yorked middle stump) in six deliveries but Butcher, Nurse and Sobers helped Hunte in stands of 74, 99 and 68.

In the last two hours Sobers set the seal on the day's play with a devastating exhibition during which he helped himself to 83 while the score rose by 128. Holford arrived for the last hour while Sobers, his elder cousin, collared the bowling, Holford's share of an unbroken stand of 60 amounting to 6.

Fielding blunders cost England dearly. Sobers, for all his brilliance, was let off four times: the first when 63, Brown misjudging a high catch from Higgs at long-on. Next morning the West Indies captain offered three more chances when in the "nineties" and altogether he stayed four hours and eight minutes for his 161, which contained one 6 and twenty-six 4s, being ninth out at 482 just before the innings, which lasted eight hours and ten minutes, closed for 484.

The respect Titmus commanded and the spin he acquired in taking five for 83 in thirty-five overs helped to undermine the confidence of the England batsmen who realized the pitch had already turned in favour of the spin bowling.

England began their reply at half past two on Friday and at once disaster overtook them, Milburn, on his first Test appearance, being run out for a duck. He pushed Hall straight to Gibbs at cover, went for a single, only to be sent back by Russell, but Gibbs had time to sprint across and break the wicket. Although Russell stayed for ninety minutes, England never recovered from that early reverse and when Smith was fifth to leave Gibbs had already cast his net, his figures reading 9–6–3–3. Parks and Allen batted sensibly for an hour while adding 58, but the end of the second day found England 163 for eight, needing 122 to save the follow on.

Consequently, just before noon on Saturday, England faced the task of getting 317 to avoid an innings defeat, a feat they did not achieve though they put up a better show at the second attempt.

The two big boys, Milburn and Cowdrey, were the mainstays. Milburn redeemed his duck with a powerful display of big hitting. Dropped three times, he enjoyed plenty of good luck on this sporting pitch and moreover he provided plenty of entertainment for the big crowd. This time Sobers, against the wind, opened the bowling while Griffith and Hall attacked in turn from the Stretford end. Milburn hooked Hall for 6 and he reached 94 when he hooked Gibbs for 6. Then he slashed across the line of the ball and was bowled, having made his runs out of 166 in two and a half hours. He also hit twelve 4s.

Thereafter, Cowdrey alone proved equal to dealing with Sobers, Gibbs and Holford who were able to make the ball lift and turn in disconcerting fashion. By watchful defence and clean hitting, Cowdrey (nine 4s), stayed for two hours and ten minutes. When heavy clouds threatened rain, Brown remained an hour, making 6 in a stand of 50 with Cowdrey.

With the light indifferent, Sobers stuck to his spinners, who finished the match by a quarter to six. Sobers was the central figure in his side's success. He followed his 161 with skilful leadership, and long spells of bowling in three different forms which earned his three wickets, and he held five catches, four of them in the leg trap.

During the match Griffith was no-balled nine times for overstepping the crease. In turn, each umpire scrutinized his action from square leg, sometimes crossing to point. Hall, with a run of 35 yards, which he covered in 17 paces, was erratic in length and direction, most of his deliveries going down the leg side.

The total attendance for the three days was 61,127; receipts £26,500.

West Indies

C. C. Hunte c Smith b Higgs	135
E. D. McMorris c Russell b Higgs	11
R. B. Kanhai b Higgs	0
B. F. Butcher c Parks b Titmus	44
S. M. Nurse b Titmus	49
*G. S. Sobers c Cowdrey b Titmus	161
D. A. J. Holford c Smith b Allen	32
†D. W. Allan lbw b Titmus	1
C. C. Griffith lbw b Titmus	30
W. W. Hall b Allen	1
L. R. Gibbs not out	1
B 8, l-b 10, n-b 1	19
1/38 2/42 3/116 4/215 5/283 6/410 7/411 8/471 9/482	484

Bowling: Jones 28–6–100–0; Brown 28–4–84–0; Higgs 31–5–94–3; Allen 31.1–8–104–2; Titmus 35–10–83–5.

England

C. Milburn run out	0	– b Gibbs	94
W. E. Russell c Sobers b Gibbs	26	– b Griffith	20
K. F. Barrington c and b Griffith	5	– c Nurse b Holford	30
M. C. Cowdrey c and b Gibbs	12	– c Butcher b Sobers	69
*M. J. K. Smith c Butcher b Gibbs	5	– b Gibbs	6
†J. M. Parks c Nurse b Holford	43	– c and b Sobers	11
F. J. Titmus b Holford	15	– c Butcher b Sobers	12
D. A. Allen c Sobers b Gibbs	37	– c Allan b Gibbs	1
D. J. Brown b Gibbs	14	– c Sobers b Gibbs	10
K. Higgs c Sobers b Holford	1	– st Allan b Gibbs	5
I. J. Jones not out	0	– not out	0
B 1, l-b 4, n-b 4	9	B 11, l-b 1, n-b 7	19
1/11 2/24 3/42 4/48 5/65 6/85 7/143 8/153 9/163	167	1/53 2/142 3/166 4/184 5/203 6/217 7/218 8/268 9/276	277

Bowling: *First Innings*—Hall 14–6–43–0; Griffith 10–3–28–1; Sobers 7–1–16–0; Gibbs 28.1–13–37–5; Holford 15–4–34–3. *Second Innings*—Sobers 42–11–87–3; Hall 5–0–28–0; Griffith 6–1–25–1; Gibbs 41–16–69–5; Holford 14–2–49–1.

Umpires: J. S. Buller and C. S. Elliott.

GLOUCESTERSHIRE v WEST INDIES

Played at Bristol, June 8, 9, 10, 1966

Drawn with the scores level. Gloucestershire punished an indifferent attack and their 332 for nine declared was the highest at that stage by any county against the West Indies. Nicholls gave one of his best displays and hit his 108, which included fourteen 4s, in three and a half hours. His innings came to a close through one of Kanhai's five catches which assisted Brancker to take six wickets for 101. The tourists failed badly against the seamers of Windows, whose inspired bowling earned him his best analysis, eight for 78. Hunte, 68, alone held the innings together. Gloucestershire led by 181 but did not enforce the follow-on. They set West Indies 285 to win in four hours and five minutes. The county attack was mastered by Carew. He hit his first century of the tour, an attractive innings which included twelve 4s and came in two and three-quarter hours. In the last over West Indies with five wickets in hand needed 12 to win. They obtained 11 and then required a single off the last ball. Holford made a mighty swing but was bowled, leaving the scores level.

Gloucestershire

R. B. Nicholls c Kanhai b Brancker	108	– c Carew b Cohen	13
C. A. Milton lbw b Cohen	19	– c Hunte b Hall	0
H. Jarman c Kanhai b Brancker	28	– c Hunte b Hall	1
S. E. Russell c Kanhai b Brancker	3	– c Holford b Cohen	29
D. Shepherd c Kanhai b Brancker	29	– b Cohen	2
D. A. Allen c Allan b Cohen	34	– c Allan b Lashley	17
*J. B. Mortimore c Kanhai b Brancker	64	– b Lashley	12
A. S. Brown b Cohen	8	– c Brancker b Carew	10
A. R. Windows c Cohen b Brancker	25	– c Brancker b Lashley	11
M. D. Mence not out	2	– not out	2
L-b 6, n-b 3, w 3	12	B 1, l-b 5	6
1/45 2/128 3/154 4/188 5/204 6/260 7/274 8/320 9/332	(9 wkts dec.) 332	1/9 2/17 3/30 4/41 5/58 6/79 7/80 8/96 9/103	(9 wkts dec.) 103

†B. J. Meyer did not bat.

Bowling: *First Innings*—Hall 16–4–45–0; Cohen 21–3–59–3; Holford 26–6–68–0; Lashley 13–2–36–0; Brancker 37.3–11–101–6; Carew 9–3–11–0. *Second Innings*—Hall 19–5–39–2; Cohen 18–6–35–3; Lashley 5–1–15–3; Carew 4.5–2–8–1.

West Indies

M. C. Carew lbw b Brown	7	– b Brown	132
E. D. McMorris c Milton b Windows	2	– c Mortimore b Brown	1
R. B. Kanhai b Windows	4	– c Mortimore b Mence	13
*C. C. Hunte lbw b Windows	68	– run out	43
P. D. Lashley c Mortimore b Windows	3		
J. S. Solomon c Milton b Windows	11	– c Windows b Brown	39
R. C. Brancker lbw b Windows	28		
D. A. J. Holford c Meyer b Windows	22	– b Brown	27
†D. W. Allan b Windows	0		
W. W. Hall b Brown	3	– not out	13
R. A. Cohen not out	1		
B 1, l-b 1	2	B 5, l-b 9, n-b 2	16
1/6 2/14 3/14 4/17 5/47 6/119 7/132 8/138 9/141	151	1/11 2/112 3/150 4/222 5/267 6/284	(6 wkts) 294

Bowling: *First Innings*—Brown 23–5–52–2; Windows 24.1–8–78–8; Mence 5–0–15–0; Mortimore 1–0–4–0. *Second Innings*—Brown 11–0–61–4; Windows 16–1–63–0; Allen 19–4–46–0; Mence 23–5–77–1; Mortimore 11–3–21–0.

Umpires: W. E. Phillipson and J. F. Crapp.

SUSSEX v WEST INDIES

Played at Hove, June 11, 13, 1966

Sussex won by nine wickets. The West Indies, asked to bat first, were visibly shaken out of their stride by a "green" Hove pitch and an atmosphere helping swing, so that they played unimpressive cricket in losing for the first time on the tour. They were beaten with an hour and half of the second day, not to mention all the third, to spare. Their first innings lasted three and a quarter hours and they were out for 67 in two and a quarter hours at the second attempt.

This was the second lowest total ever recorded by a West Indies team in England, being nine more than the 58 of R. K. Nunes's side against Yorkshire in 1928, a year when Sussex also beat them, by an innings and 87 runs. The only stand of any consequence in the West Indies second innings was of 34 by Solomon and Lashley. No other batsman got into double figures. Three West Indians managed it in the first innings, Carew with 56, Nurse 24 and Butcher 12. Even then, Carew had a charmed life and the kindest comment on his knock was to say that he did not let the good fortune affect him. He played each ball on merit.

Snow, bowling up the hill, took seven for 29 in the initial collapse of the touring team, tearing out the heart of their innings in his second spell with six for 14. He also returned the same figures as his fellow seamer Buss on the Monday, four for 18, and finished with match figures of eleven for 47. Parks took seven catches behind the wicket, which perhaps reflected the lack of resolution in the batting.

Sussex had their worries, too, when facing Cohen and Griffith, but they were steered into a first-innings lead of 62 by Graves in only his second game of the summer. This 20-year-old left-hander showed a more sensible approach than older colleagues and opponents. Finally, Sussex needed only six to win but even this produced something out of the ordinary. Sobers gave the opening over to Griffith, whose first ball rose and struck Suttle on the jaw. He went to hospital for an X-ray, which showed nothing more serious than bruising.

West Indies

M. C. Carew lbw b Snow	56	– c Pataudi b Buss	3
E. D. McMorris c Pataudi b Snow	1	– c Pataudi b Buss	0
S. M. Nurse b Bates	24	– c Foreman b Buss	8
B. F. Butcher lbw b Suttle	12	– lbw b Snow	0
*G. S. Sobers c Parks b Bates	0	– b Buss	8
J. S. Solomon c Parks b Snow	6	– c Parks b Snow	17
P. D. Lashley b Snow	6	– c Parks b Snow	14
C. C. Griffith c Parks b Snow	1	– c Parks b Bates	1
†J. L. Hendriks c Lenham b Snow	8	– b Snow	3
L. R. Gibbs b Snow	5	– c Parks b Bates	7
R. A. Cohen not out	1	– not out	2
L-b 3	3	L-b 1, n-b 1	2
1/14 2/45 3/60 4/61 5/77 6/97 7/108 8/109 9/118	123	1/2 2/7 3/12 4/16 5/20 6/54 7/55 8/55 9/63	67

Bowling: *First Innings*—Snow 16.5–5–29–7; Buss 15–5–27–0; Suttle 6–1–18–1; Bates 17–1–46–2. *Second Innings*—Snow 11.3–4–18–4; Buss 11–6–18–4; Bates 10–3–19–2; Suttle 4–1–8–0.

Sussex

K. G. Suttle b Griffith	0	– retired hurt	0
L. J. Lenham b Cohen	0	– not out	4
*Nawab of Pataudi c Hendriks b Cohen	32		
†J. M. Parks c Hendriks b Cohen	3	– not out	1
M. G. Griffith c Hendriks b Cohen	0		
D. J. Foreman c Lashley b Griffith	2		
P. J. Graves c Solomon b Griffith	64	– lbw b Griffith	0
A. S. M. Oakman c Lashley b Cohen	31		
A. Buss c Sobers b Griffith	21		
J. A. Snow b Cohen	5		
D. L. Bates not out	10		
L-b 8, n-b 8, w 1	17	N-b 1	1
1/0 2/2 3/16 4/18 5/38 6/40 7/99 8/131 9/158	185	1/1 (1 wkt)	6

Bowling: *First Innings*—Griffith 17.4–6–43–4; Cohen 17–3–71–6; Sobers 14–5–36–0; Gibbs 5–1–18–0. *Second Innings*—Griffith 1–1–0–1; Solomon 2–1–4–0; Lashley 1.2–1–1–0.

Umpires: J. Langridge and L. H. Gray.

ENGLAND v WEST INDIES

Second Test Match

Played at Lord's, June 16, 17, 18, 20, 21, 1966

Drawn. Despite losing the toss again, England, who had a different captain in Cowdrey, gave a much better account of themselves than in the first Test. In fact, this match was splendidly contested throughout, interest being sustained right to the end.

Again Sobers was a key figure for West Indies and he thwarted England on the fourth day when victory seemed just round the corner for the old country. Having gained a lead of 86, England took the first five West Indies second-innings wickets for 95 and looked to be romping home. Then Sobers was joined by his young cousin, Holford, and they remained together for five hours and twenty minutes until Sobers declared at ten minutes to one on Tuesday. This unbroken stand of 274 was a record for the fifth wicket for West Indies against England. Sobers, who batted ten minutes longer, hit thirteen 4s in his excellent 163 and Holford showed six boundaries in his 105.

Holford gained the distinction of hitting his maiden Test century on only his second appearance and later in the day Milburn, three 6s and seventeen 4s, wound up this grand struggle by emulating Holford's feat and taking out his bat for 126, made in three hours.

Over the five days, four hours and fifty minutes' play was lost through rain, there being only two and three-quarter hours' cricket on the first day when West Indies reached 155 for four wickets. Personal honours went to Higgs who prised through the early West Indies batsmen, taking three wickets for 14 runs in his first nine overs. He kept a splendid length and moved the ball slightly each way.

The next morning Nurse and Sobers lasted an hour together while they carried their stand to 86 and the total to 205 before D'Oliveira, playing in his first Test, deceived Nurse with a fine ball from the Nursery end which turned up the slope and took his leg stump.

Nurse did not offer a stroke, nor did Sobers when he covered up and was lbw to Knight so that at lunch time on Friday West Indies were 247 for six. Higgs and Jones took the new ball directly after the interval and the remaining four wickets were captured for 22 more runs. Higgs, with three for 11 in five overs, finished with six for 91, a grand effort, and Parks claimed Gibbs as his 100th Test victim.

The return of Graveney to Test cricket after an interval of three years during which England played 38 Tests proved a wise move by the selectors. Milburn went cheaply on Friday but Boycott and Graveney progressed steadily in a stand of 115 and at nightfall England were 145 for two; Graveney 65, Barrington 8.

Next day, only D'Oliveira and Parks rose to the occasion against some much improved bowling. There was no excuse for the poor displays of Barrington, Cowdrey, Knight and Titmus. Sobers attacked persistently and Hall and Griffith kept more in line with the stumps, yet Graveney batted almost without blemish for four hours and twenty minutes. He wanted only four for his hundred when he cut at a rising ball from Hall and was taken by the wicket-keeper. He hit eleven 4s.

Even the new ball did not disturb Parks and D'Oliveira and their partnership of 48 was in full sail when Parks drove back so fast that the ball went off D'Oliveira's heel and bounced back from the broken wicket. Hall, with commendable presence of mind, swept up the ball and pulled up the stump with both hands without the South African making any attempt to recover his ground.

It was left to the left-handed Higgs to keep up his end while Parks hit freely so that the ninth stand yielded 59, but altogether England occupied eight and a quarter hours for their total of 355.

A fine leg slip catch by Knight disposed of Carew on Saturday evening when West Indies finished the third day 18 for one. The pitch sweated under the covers during the week-end when more rain soaked the outfield and by ten minutes to one on Monday, following a prompt start, four more wickets had gone and West Indies faced a hopeless position. At least, so it seemed, but there followed that wonderful partnership between Sobers and Holford which meant that England were set to get 284 to win in four hours.

Rain reduced the time by an hour, but at first West Indies made a brave attempt to achieve success. Griffith disposed of Boycott and Barrington for 43 and at 67 Sobers switched Hall to the nursery end where he removed Cowdrey and Parks with his first two deliveries.

It had not been intended that Graveney should bat owing to a badly bruised right thumb, but he came to the rescue, averted a hat-trick, and stayed with Milburn for the last hour and fifty minutes while they added 130 in England's highest fifth-wicket stand against West Indies. Graveney batted almost one handed, continually drawing away the other, but while he defended, Milburn followed up his 94 at Manchester with another amazing display of powerful hitting. This was a much better effort. He hoisted Holford, Gibbs and Hall in turn for 6 and made very few false strokes.

England, who did not claim the extra half hour, fell 87 short of their target. The receipts of £58,000 were a record for a cricket match in any part of the world. The full attendance was estimated to be 125,500, of whom 104,000 paid the six shillings outer gate admission fee.

West Indies

C. C. Hunte c Parks b Higgs	18	– c Milburn b Knight	13
M. C. Carew c Parks b Higgs	2	– c Knight b Higgs	0
R. B. Kanhai c Titmus b Higgs	25	– c Parks b Knight	40
B. F. Butcher c Milburn b Knight	49	– lbw b Higgs	3
S. M. Nurse b D'Oliveira	64	– c Parks b D'Oliveira	35
*G. S. Sobers lbw b Knight	46	– not out	163
D. A. J. Holford b Jones	26	– not out	105
†D. W. Allan c Titmus b Higgs	13		
C. C. Grifith lbw b Higgs	5		
W. W. Hall not out	8		
L. R. Gibbs c Parks b Higgs	4		
B 2, l-b 7	9	L-b 8, n-b 2	10
1/8 2/42 3/53 4/119 5/205 6/213 7/252 8/252 9/261	269	1/2 2/22 3/25 4/91 5/95	(5 wkts dec.) 369

Bowling: *First Innings*—Jones 21–3–64–1; Higgs 33–9–91–6; Knight 21–0–63–2; Titmus 5–0–18–0; D'Oliveira 14–5–24–1. *Second Innings*—Jones 25–2–95–0; Higgs 34–5–82–2; Knight 30–3–106–2; D'Oliveira 25–7–46–1; Titmus 19–3–30–0.

England

G. Boycott c Griffith b Gibbs	60	– c Allan b Griffith	25
C. Milburn lbw b Hall	6	– not out	126
T. W. Graveney c Allan b Hall	96	– not out	30
K. F. Barrington b Sobers	19	– b Griffith	5
*M. C. Cowdrey c Gibbs b Hall	9	– c Allan b Hall	5
†J. M. Parks lbw b Carew	91	– b Hall	0
B. D'Oliveira run out	27		
B. R. Knight b Griffith	6		
F. J. Titmus c Allan b Hall	6		
K. Higgs c Holford b Gibbs	13		
I. J. Jones not out	0		
B 7, l-b 10, n-b 5	22	B 4, l-b 2	6
1/8 2/123 3/164 4/198 5/203 6/251 7/266 8/296 9/355	355	1/37 2/43 3/67 4/67	(4 wkts) 197

Bowling: *First Innings*—Sobers 39–12–89–1; Hall 36–2–106–4; Griffith 28–4–79–1; Gibbs 37.3–18–48–2; Carew 3–0–11–1. *Second Innings*—Hall 14–1–65–2; Griffith 11–2–43–2; Gibbs 13–4–40–0; Sobers 8–4–8–0; Holford 9–1–35–0.

Umpires: J. S. Buller and W. F. Price.

ENGLAND v WEST INDIES
Third Test Match

Played at Trent Bridge, June 30, July 1, 2, 4, 5, 1966

West Indies won by 139 runs. Again they proved the superior side and extricated themselves from an inferior position. They fell 90 behind on the first innings and then lost two wickets for 65, yet were able to declare with only five men out and set England the reasonable task of scoring 393 in six and a half hours, a rate of exactly 60 an hour.

England caused much surprise just before the match began by omitting Barrington on the grounds that he was suffering from physical and nervous strain through playing too much cricket in the past six years. They also left out Knight (twelfth man) and introduced Underwood to Test cricket, there being altogether four changes compared with the Lord's Test. Lashley and Hendriks made their first Test appearances in England for the West Indies.

For the third time in the series Sobers won the toss and again the West Indies captain played a notable part. Besides hitting 94 in just over two hours when it was necessary to press for runs, Sobers took five wickets, including that of Boycott with the second ball in England's first innings, and he held five catches, besides handling his bowlers and setting his field with marked skill. Nurse and Butcher both played profitable innings.

England were indebted to Graveney for a fine century, his third in successive Test appearances at Trent Bridge and to Cowdrey who helped the Worcestershire player to a valuable stand of 169 after the first three wickets had gone for 13. D'Oliveira hit splendidly in both innings and like Higgs, bowled well, but England were guilty once again of poor fielding. They dropped Butcher five times and Boycott, at cover, alone stood out in a favourable light.

The Nottinghamshire groundsman must be congratulated on preparing a fast true pitch which encouraged the pace bowlers, especially in the early stages of the match. They enjoyed a notable first day when thirteen wickets went down for 268 runs. Snow and Higgs were lively and aggressive for England, but Lashley, with a short back lift and receiving at least one life, proved stubborn while staying over three hours for 49. Time and again the batsmen were saved by their pads; even Nurse had his anxious moments. Still, his was a fine display for he made 93, including eleven 4s, in two and three-quarter hours, but fell as soon as Snow took the second new ball.

When England batted for the last fifty minutes it was the same tale of the previous year on this ground against South Africa who twice captured cheap wickets by night fall. This time, Boycott, Milburn and Russell all failed so that Graveney and Cowdrey had to play through the final half hour. They took the score to 33 for three.

Next day, in heavy cloudy weather, the England fourth pair had to use all their skill and resource to combat the menacing attack of Hall, Sobers, Griffith, Gibbs and Holford. Only 36 runs came in the first hour, but by lunch, when the total was 128, each had reached his fifty and Graveney had pulled Gibbs for 6. Subsequently, a barrage of bumpers increased the batsmen's problems, Cowdrey suffering painful blows under the heart from Hall. There were two stoppages for bad light and it was after tea, at 4.40, that Graveney went to a brilliant left-handed catch in the gully, having scored 109, out of 172 in three hours fifty minutes. In addition to his 6, he hit eleven 4s.

Cowdrey saw England go ahead and then at 238, having batted over five hours for 96 and hit only six 4s he was taken at the wicket. As Illingworth failed England were 254 for seven at the close.

The ground was full on Saturday when in warm sunshine England consolidated their position, thanks to Underwood keeping up his end for eighty-five minutes with D'Oliveira while 65 runs were added, a record for England's last wicket against West Indies, D'Oliveira hit ten 4s in his excellent 76. Next, he disposed of Hunte and Lashley, the latter taking one and three-quarter hours for 23.

Butcher joined Kanhai at 3.45 p.m. and with their side in a precarious position they added only 73 runs in the remaining two and a half hours before the close. Underwood, left arm medium over the wicket, who bowled unchanged from 3.30 p.m. till 6 o'clock had these figures 22–13–17–0 but he failed to take his first wicket in Test cricket, D'Oliveira missing a slip catch from Kanhai, who was then 36.

On Monday, the West Indies wasted no time in piling on 334 runs in five and a quarter hours. The hero was Butcher. Severely criticised for his stonewalling on Saturday, he went on to punish England for 209 not out in seven and three-quarter hours and he hit twenty-two 4s. His double century had only been bettered for West Indies in England by F. M. Worrell – 261 at Trent Bridge, 1950. Moreover, Butcher had the rare distinction of taking part in three successive three-figure stands, with Kanhai, Nurse and Sobers. His partnership with Sobers of 173 in two hours was a whirlwind affair.

England had a poor day in the field. Higgs alone of the five bowlers maintained his best form. Snow found the pitch lifeless and his attempts to produce bouncers presented no difficulties.

England began their second innings with half an hour left on Monday and this time Boycott and Milburn survived. Milburn hooked Hall for 6, but was fortunate in the final over to be missed off the same bowler by Lashley at third slip. So on the last morning England resumed at 30 without loss, but the fifth ball of the first over accounted for Milburn who mishooked Hall to mid-on. Boycott faced the situation with rare skill, his defence being superb, but Russell never appeared confident and West Indies, in the two and a half hours session before lunch, gained absolute control, taking five wickets for the addition of 112 runs. Boycott pulled Sobers for 6 and also hit six 4s in his 71, made in two and a half hours.

Griffith delivered some vicious bouncers, one only just missing Cowdrey's head. Again D'Oliveira hit freely and he was particularly aggressive on being joined by Higgs. There were ten 4s in his 54. Snow withstood the bowling for half an hour and, when Underwood again resisted, Griffith brought forth wholesale condemnation by producing another of his bouncers which struck the Kent bowler in the mouth.

In the end, West Indies won with eighty-five minutes to spare. The weather remained fine and a crowd of 105,000 produced receipts of £36,396, a record for a Trent Bridge Test.

West Indies

C. C. Hunte lbw b Higgs	9	– c Graveney b D'Oliveira	12
P. D. Lashley c Parks b Snow	49	– lbw b D'Oliveira	23
R. B. Kanhai c Underwood b Higgs	32	– c Cowdrey b Higgs	63
B. F. Butcher b Snow	5	– not out	209
S. M. Nurse c Illingworth b Snow	93	– lbw b Higgs	53
*G. S. Sobers c Parks b Snow	3	– c Underwood b Higgs	94
D. A. J. Holford lbw b D'Oliveira	11	– not out	17
†J. L. Hendriks b D'Oliveira	2		
C. C. Griffith c Cowdrey b Higgs	14		
W. W. Hall b Higgs	12		
L. R. Gibbs not out	0		
B 3, l-b 2	5	L-b 6, w 5	11
1/19 2/68 3/80 4/140 5/144 6/180 7/190 8/215 9/228	235	1/29 2/265 3/175 4/282 5/455 (5 wkts dec.)	482

Bowling: *First Innings*—Snow 25–7–82–4; Higgs 25.4–3–71–4; D'Oliveira 30–14–51–2; Underwood 2–1–5–0; Illingworth 8–1–21–0. *Second Innings*—Snow 38–10–117–0; Higgs 38–6–109–3; D'Oliveira 34–8–77–2; Underwood 43–15–86–0; Illingworth 25–7–82–0.

England

G. Boycott lbw b Sobers	0	– c Sobers b Griffith	71
C. Milburn c Sobers b Hall	7	– c Griffith b Hall	12
W. E. Russell b Hall	4	– c Sobers c Gibbs	11
T. W. Graveney c Holford b Sobers	109	– c Hendricks b Griffith	32
*M. C. Cowdrey c Hendriks b Griffith	96	– c Sobers b Gibbs	32
†J. M. Parks c Butcher b Sobers	11	– c Lashley b Hall	7
B. D'Oliveira b Hall	76	– lbw b Griffith	54
R. Illingworth c Lashley b Griffith	0	– c Lashley b Sobers	4
K. Higgs c Lashley b Sobers	5	– c Sobers b Gibbs	4
J. A. Snow b Hall	0	– b Griffith	3
D. L. Underwood not out	12	– not out	10
L-b 2, n-b 3	5	B 8, l-b 2, n-b 3	13
1/0 2/10 3/13 4/182 5/221 6/238 7/247 8/255 9/260	325	1/32 2/71 3/125 4/132 5/142 6/176 7/181 8/222 9/240	253

Bowling: *First Innings*—Sobers 49–12–90–4; Hall 34.3–8–105–4; Griffith 20–5–62–2; Gibbs 23–9–40–0; Holford 8–2–23–0. *Second Innings*—Sobers 31–6–71–1; Hall 16–3–52–2; Griffith 13.3–3–34–4; Gibbs 48–16–83–3.

Umpires: C. S. Elliott and A. Jepson.

KENT v WEST INDIES

Played at Canterbury, July 9, 11, 12, 1966

West Indies won by an innings and 56 runs. They outplayed Kent who on a fast dry pitch gave two woeful displays of batting, apart from Luckhurst. McMorris defended stoutly for for a long time but finished with four 6s and nine 4s in his 116 which was notable for his powerful driving. Kent were baffled by spin bowling. Luckhurst alone showed ability to deal with Brancker's flighted left-arm slows and he hit his fourth hundred (eleven 4s) in nine innings during a stay of three hours ten minutes. When Kent followed on 180 behind, Sobers soon dismissed Denness at his fast pace, two wickets being down for 19 at the close. Next day he finished the innings three-quarters of an hour before lunch by taking the eight remaining wickets for 39 runs. Sobers' full analysis read 19.4–6–49–9 and he became the first West Indies cricketer to take nine wickets in an innings in England. On that last morning Sobers adopted his unorthodox left-arm spin and the Kent players fell victims one after the other to the "chinaman".

West Indies

E. D. McMorris c Sayer b Dixon	116
P. D. Lashley lbw b Dixon	27
R. C. Brancker lbw b Sayer	26
D. A. J. Holford c Ealham b Luckhurst	55
*G. S. Sobers c Leary b Dixon	5
J. S. Solomon c Denness b Dixon	42
M. C. Carew b Sayer	20
S. M. Nurse lbw b Dixon	1
†J. L. Hendriks c Knott b Underwood	28
W. W. Hall b Dye	5
R. A. Cohen not out	32
B 10, l-b 12, w 2, n-b 1	25
1/45 2/94 3/235 4/244 5/247 6/297 7/298 8/308 9/320	382

Bowling: Sayer 23–6–51–2; Dye 25–5–76–1; Dixon 43–15–138–5; Underwood 19.2–3–54–1; Luckhurst 12–3–30–1; Leary 1–0–8–0.

Kent

M. H. Denness c Hendriks b Carew	20	– c Brancker b Sobers	22
B. W. Luckhurst c and b Brancker	104	– c Hendriks b Sobers	5
D. Nicholls b Carew	0	– lbw b Holford	0
*M. C. Cowdrey c Holford b Brancker	19	– c Hendriks b Sobers	1
S. E. Leary st Hendriks b Brancker	7	– c Nurse b Sobers	38
A. Ealham c Carew b Brancker	24	– c Carew b Sobers	13
†A. Knott lbw b Brancker	0	– st Hendriks b Sobers	15
A. L. Dixon c Brancker b Holford	7	– c Hall b Sobers	5
D. L. Underwood c and b Brancker	10	– c Hall b Sobers	10
D. M. Sayer b Brancker	7	– b Sobers	1
J. C. Dye not out	2	– not out	1
W 1, n-b 1	2	B 9, l-b 4	13
1/40 2/42 3/79 4/91 5/147 6/147 7/164 8/184 9/193	202	1/15 2/18 3/27 4/37 5/38 6/60 7/78 8/100 9/118	124

Bowling: *First Innings*—Hall 3–1–3–0; Cohen 6–0–26–0; Sobers 2–0–7–0; Carew 20–9–32–2; Brancker 31.3–8–78–7; Holford 18–0–54–1. *Second Innings*—Cohen 4–2–8–0; Sobers 19.4–6–49–9; Carew 1–1–0–0; Brancker 10–5–17–0; Holford 10–2–37–1.

Umpires: G. H. Pope and P. A. Gibb.

ENGLAND v WEST INDIES
Fourth Test Match

Played at Leeds, August 4, 5, 6, 8, 1966

West Indies won by an innings and 55 runs just after three o'clock on the fourth day with a day to spare. So they completed three wonderful years in which they twice won the rubber convincingly in England – and twice carried off the Wisden trophy – and for the first time beat Australia in a series. They achieved their ambition like World Champions and, while they excelled as a team, standing high above the rest of them was their captain, Sobers, who in this match made the top score, 174, and took eight wickets for 80 runs, besides directing his men with masterly skill. In the four Tests Sobers had then scored 641 runs, average 128.20 and taken 17 wickets, as well as holding ten catches close to the bat.

As for England, this was a sorry performance and one felt at the end of the match that the selectors would have to take drastic action. This they did. They dropped Cowdrey, Milburn, Parks, Titmus, Underwood, and Snow, although Snow played at The Oval owing to the withdrawal of Price, the Middlesex fast bowler.

For this Leeds match, England played Barber for the first time since his triumphs in Australia and recalled Titmus, leaving out Russell and Illingworth. West Indies relied on the eleven which played at Trent Bridge and at once Sobers gained a big advantage for his side by winning the toss for the fourth time and batting on an excellent pitch that lasted well and never offered bowlers undue help.

On a restricted first day when rain and bad light limited the cricket to three and a quarter hours England fared pretty well in dismissing Lashley, Kanhai and Hunte for 137. Another success came early the next morning when Butcher was out off the second ball of the day that he received from Higgs, the fourth wicket falling at 154.

Thereupon, Sobers and Nurse took charge and for four hours the England bowlers toiled in vain while Sobers hit his seventeenth Test century, his seventh against England and his third of the series. Moreover, he never offered a chance while making 174 out of 265, the highest West Indies stand for the fifth wicket against England. Sobers struck twenty-four 4s and he had the rare experience of hitting a hundred between lunch and tea. During the course of his great display, in which he square cut, hooked, pulled and drove as he pleased, he became the first cricketer to attain a Test aggregate of 5,000 runs and also 100 wickets. In addition, in this, his eighteenth innings of the tour, he completed his 1,000 for the summer.

The fact that Nurse hit his first hundred against England passed almost unnoticed, yet he played a most valuable innings of 137 out of 367, which covered five and three-quarter hours and contained two 6s and fourteen 4s.

The England bowlers simply could not penetrate the defences of these two fine players. Cowdrey tried to unsettle them by ringing his bowling changes. Perhaps he should have used Barber earlier, for West Indies had made 324 before the wrist-spinner was introduced. Barber certainly puzzled Nurse and he bowled Sobers, but by then the West Indies captain was a tired man. Sobers declared at 500, West Indies' highest total of the tour, and Barber and Boycott scored four from the four overs delivered by Hall and Griffith before the end of the day.

An opening spell of eighty minutes by Hall at his fastest and best destroyed England on Saturday when he sent back Boycott, Cowdrey and Graveney. Sheer speed led each batsman into error and Milburn also suffered through not offering a stroke to a ball that struck him such a painful blow on the left elbow that he had to retire. When Milburn returned three and a half hours later he could only defend as he lacked power in that arm to hit with his usual freedom.

When the England total stood at 18 for two, just before mid-day, Griffith was cautioned against throwing by umpire Elliott after he had delivered a vicious bouncer to Graveney. Both umpires conferred and later Elliott said: "I told Syd Buller that in my opinion that delivery was illegal. We agreed that I should speak to Griffith about it. I then said to him: 'You can bowl, Charlie. Any more like that and I will have to call you. That delivery to Graveney was illegal.'" Following the incident, much of Griffith's pace disappeared and he took only one more wicket in the match when D'Oliveira skied a loose ball to cover.

Sobers eventually relieved Hall and adopting his quick pace soon removed Parks (with his first ball) and Titmus so that six wickets were down for 83 and England's fate was a foregone conclusion.

At last, D'Oliveira and Higgs made a stand, putting on 96 together. The South African played his third consecutive Test innings of over fifty. He hit four 6s, one a magnificent straight drive from Hall, of all people, and eight 4s; Higgs also hit two 6s and played his longest and highest innings in first-class cricket, two and a quarter hours for 49 while the total rose by 155.

Sobers finally put in two spells of mixed spin and picked up the last three wickets in four balls so that England followed on 260 behind. They batted for fifty minutes before bad light caused over an hour to be lost at the end of Saturday and during that time, Lashley, with his first spell in Test cricket, trapped Boycott with this third delivery, Hendriks holding a smart catch wide and low of the off-stump.

Only Barber and Milburn really troubled the West Indies bowlers on Monday when the remaining nine second-innings wickets went down for 165 runs. Barber, top scorer, defended soundly and drove and hit to leg confidently. Milburn, batting number seven – D'Oliveira went in at three – hit Holford for five 4s and hooked Gibbs over the square-leg pavilion for 6, he and Titmus adding 51 in twenty-five minutes. That was England's final fling against slow bowlers prepared to buy their wickets.

Gibbs bowled splendidly, sometimes with plenty of pace and skilful variation of flight rather than prodigious spin. He took six for 39, England's last five wickets falling in under an hour for 77.

West Indies

C. C. Hunte lbw b Snow	48
P. D. Lashley b Higgs	9
R. B. Kanhai c Graveney b Underwood	45
B. F. Butcher c Parks b Higgs	38
S. M. Nurse c Titmus b Snow	137
*G. S. Sobers b Barber	174
D. A. J. Holford b Higgs	24
C. C. Griffith b Higgs	0
J. L. Hendriks not out	9
W. W. Hall b Snow	1
L. R. Gibbs not out	2
B 1, l-b 12	13
(9 wkts dec.)	500

1/37 2/102 3/128 4/154 5/419 6/467 7/467 8/489 9/491

Bowling: Snow 42–6–146–3; Higgs 43–11–94–4; D'Oliveira 19–3–52–0; Titmus 22–7–59–0; Underwood 24–9–81–1; Barber 14–2–55–1.

England

R. W. Barber c Hendriks b Griffith	6	– b Sobers	55
G. Boycott c Holford b Hall	12	– c Hendriks b Lashley	14
C. Milburn not out	29	– b Gibbs	42
T. W. Graveney b Hall	8	– b Gibbs	19
*M. C. Cowdrey b Hall	17	– lbw b Gibbs	12
B. D'Oliveira c Hall b Griffith	88	– c Butcher b Sobers	7
†J. M. Parks lbw b Sobers	2	– c Nurse b Gibbs	16
F. J. Titmus c Hendriks b Sobers	6	– b Gibbs	22
K. Higgs c Nurse b Sobers	49	– c Hunte b Sobers	7
D. L. Underwood c Gibbs b Sobers	0	– c Kanhai b Gibbs	0
J. A. Snow c Holford b Sobers	0	– not out	0
B 12, l-b 11	23	B 8, l-b 1, n-b 2	11
1/10 2/18 3/42 4/49 5/63 6/83 7/179 8/238 9/240	240	1/28 2/70 3/84 4/109 5/128 6/133 7/184 8/205 9/205	205

Bowling: *First Innings*—Hall 17–5–47–3; Griffith 12–2–37–2; Sobers 19.3–4–41–5; Gibbs 20–5–49–0; Holford 10–3–43–0. *Second Innings*—Sobers 20.1–5–39–3; Griffith 12–0–52–0; Lashley 3–2–1–1; Hall 8–2–24–0; Gibbs 19–6–39–6; Holford 9–0–39–0.

Umpires: J. S. Buller and C. S. Elliott.

ENGLAND v WEST INDIES

Fifth Test Match

Played at The Oval, August 18, 19, 20, 22, 1966

England won by an innings and 34 runs fifteen minutes after lunch on Monday with nearly ten hours to spare. It was a great triumph after so many humiliations during the summer and proved that England was not so poverty stricken in talent as previous performances suggested. Personal honours went to Brian Close, captain of his country for the first time and one of the six changes the selectors made after the rubber was lost in the fourth Test at Headingley. Close set his men a splendid example at short leg and silly mid-off and he used his bowlers shrewdly, not being afraid to introduce Barber with his wrist spin early in the proceedings. Moreover, Barber took five wickets.

Sharing the honours with Close were Graveney, Murray, Higgs and Snow, all of whom batted magnificently after England, facing a total of 268, lost their first seven wickets for 166. At that stage everything pointed to another run-away win for West Indies, but once again the glorious uncertainty of cricket was demonstrated by these heroes who caused 361 runs to be added for the last three wickets so that West Indies, batting a second time, faced a deficit of 259.

Never before in Test cricket had the last three wickets produced 361 runs, nor had the last three men scored one hundred and two fifties. Murray, moreover, became only the third number nine to make a Test hundred. In 1931 at Lord's, G. O. Allen scored 122 and with L. E. G. Ames (137) added 246 for the eighth wicket against New Zealand and in

1946-47 at Melbourne R. R. Lindwall hit 100 out of 185 against England in under two hours.

The match was favoured with fine weather, the first three days cricket being played in a heat wave with the ground crowded to capacity. In spite of Sobers winning the toss for the fifth time, England took the initiative by dismissing Hunte, McMorris, Butcher and Nurse before lunch for 83. There followed a fine stand for West Indies with Kanhai hitting his first Test century in England. He batted for three and three-quarter hours and many of his fourteen 4s came from drives past cover and mid-off. Sobers, never in difficulty, drove, cut and pulled freely until he mis-hit a short ball, giving mid-off an easy catch. The partnership yielded 122 and then only the last pair offered real opposition, the innings being completed in five hours and ten minutes, but before the end of the day England lost Boycott for 20.

Sobers, bowling his unorthodox left-handed spin, caused England trouble first thing on Friday. His third ball, a googly, accounted for Barber, and though Edrich and Amiss batted stubbornly, by the lunch interval five wickets had fallen and worse followed before Graveney at last found a reliable partner in Murray, whose neat and efficient wicket-keeping earlier had done so much towards bringing the fielding up to Test standard. Graveney shouldered the early burden of keeping his end intact amid numerous failures. He showed the determination to build a long innings and when Murray settled down both men drove gracefully and hit to leg with power. When stumps were drawn on Friday, this pair had seen England take the lead; the total reached 330 with Graveney 132 and Murray 81. The form of Murray, who incidentally hit a century in May against the West Indies for MCC, was a revelation. He looked every bit as good as Graveney.

On Saturday the same batsmen continued serenely until Gibbs smartly ran out Graveney, who had spent six hours hitting his 165, which included nineteen 4s. Murray went on to 112, more than double his previous best Test score, before he was leg before to Sobers at 399. He batted four and a half hours and hit thirteen 4s.

The West Indies bowlers must have looked forward to an early rest, but the England opening bowlers, Higgs and Snow, displayed their talent for batting in a highly diverting partnership of 128 in two hours, defying all the pace and spin the West Indies could offer and the new ball. Before Higgs left to a return catch this plucky pair came within two runs of the world Test record last wicket stand, 130 by R. E. Foster and W. Rhodes for England against Australia at Sydney in 1903-4. Neither Higgs nor Snow had previously completed fifty in first-class cricket.

Snow, who kept his place in the England team only at the last minute owing to an injury to Price, further distinguished himself in conjunction with Murray by disposing of McMorris and Hunte for 12 to be followed by D'Oliveira who upset Kanhai's wicket. Butcher hit spiritedly with nine 4s in his 60 in under an hour and a half before slamming a full toss into the hands of Barber at mid-wicket so that on Saturday evening, with West Indies 135 for four and still 124 behind, England were in sight of victory provided they could contain Sobers on the two remaining days.

This they did. In fact, England captured the remaining six wickets on Monday in two and a quarter hours. After a maiden over by Higgs to Nurse, the third and fourth deliveries of the day from Snow ruined any prospect West Indies entertained of saving the match. Holford unwisely went for a third run when Illingworth at third man was returning the ball on top of the stumps to Murray. Sobers, next in, went first ball, Close, waiting square in the leg trap, having directed Snow to try a bouncer. Sobers tried to hook this gift, only to give his rival captain a simple catch.

Nurse alone of the class batsmen remained. He pierced the closely set field with splendid drives and strong strokes to leg until Close recalled Barber at 164. Nurse pulled the first ball to the boundary (his fourteenth 4) and swept the next but it went high to Edrich deep behind the square leg umpire and the fielder held it at the second attempt. Nurse had stayed two hours, ten minutes for his 70 before being eighth to leave at 168. Griffith and Hall defended dourly for fifty minutes and finally Gibbs gave a return catch to Barber, West Indies being all out for 225, their lowest total of the series.

During the four days the attendance reached 90,000 and the receipts £45,494.

West Indies

C. C. Hunte b Higgs	1	– c Murray b Snow	7
E. D. McMorris b Snow	14	– c Murray b Snow	1
R. B. Kanhai c Graveney b Illingworth	104	– b D'Oliveira	15
B. F. Butcher c Illingworth b Close	12	– c Barber b Illingworth	60
S. M. Nurse c Graveney b D'Oliveira	0	– c Edrich b Barber	70
*G. S. Sobers c Graveney b Barber	81	– c Close b Snow	0
D. A. J. Holford c D'Oliveira b Illingworth	5	– run out	7
†J. L. Hendriks b Barber	0	– b Higgs	0
C. C. Griffith b Higgs b Barber	4	– not out	29
W. W. Hall not out	30	– c D'Oliveira b Illingworth	17
L. R. Gibbs c Murray b Snow	12	– c and b Barber	3
B 1, l-b 3, n-b 1	5	B 1, l-b 14, n-b 1	16
1/1 2/56 3/73 4/74 5/196 6/218 7/218 8/223 9/223	268	1/5 2/12 3/50 4/107 5/137 6/137 7/142 8/168 9/204	225

Bowling: *First Innings:*—Snow 20.5–1–66–2; Higgs 17–4–52–1; D'Oliveira 21–7–35–1; Close 9–2–21–1; Barber 15–3–49–3; Illingworth 15–7–40–2. *Second Innings*—Snow 13–5–40–3; Higgs 15–6–18–1; D'Oliveira 17–4–44–1; Illingworth 15–9–22–2; Barber 22.1–2–78–2; Close 3–1–7–0.

England

R. W. Barber c Nurse b Sobers	36
G. Boycott b Hall	4
J. H. Edrich c Hendriks b Sobers	35
T. W. Graveney run out	165
D. L. Amiss lbw b Hall	17
B. D'Oliveira b Hall	4
*D. B. Close run out	4
R. Illingworth c Hendriks b Griffith	3
†J. T. Murray lbw b Sobers	112
K. Higgs c and b Holford	63
J. A. Snow not out	59
B 8, l-b 14, n-b 3	25
1/6 2/72 3/85 4/126 5/130 6/150 7/166 8/383 9/399	527

Bowling: Hall 31–8–85–3; Griffith 32–7–78–1; Sobers 54–23–104–3; Holford 25.5–1–79–1; Gibbs 44–16–115–0; Hunte 13–2–41–0.

Umpires: J. S. Buller and C. S. Elliott.

SOBERS – THE LION OF CRICKET

By Sir Neville Cardus

Garfield St Aubrun Sobers, thirty years old in July 1966 – the most renowned name of any cricketer since Bradman's high noon. He is, in fact, even more famous than Bradman ever was; for he is accomplished in every department of the game, and has exhibited his genius in all climes and conditions. Test matches everywhere, West Indies, India, Pakistan, Australia, New Zealand, England; in Lancashire League and Sheffield Shield cricket. We can safely agree that no player has proven versatility of skill as convincingly as Sobers has done, effortlessly, and after the manner born.

He is a stylish, prolific batsman; two bowlers in one, fastish left-arm, seaming the new ball, and slow to medium back-of-the-hand spinner with the old ball; a swift, accurate, slip fieldsman in the class of Hammond and Simpson, and generally an astute captain. Statistics concerning him speak volumes.

Sobers holds a unique Test double, over 5,500 runs, and close on 150 wickets. Four years ago he set up an Australian record when playing for South Australia by scoring 1,000 runs and taking 50 wickets in the same season. To emphasize this remarkable feat he repeated it the following summer out there.

Only last January he established in India a record for consecutive Test apperances, surpassing J. R. Reid's 58 for New Zealand. He is also amongst the select nine who have hit a century and taken five or more wickets in one Test, joining J. H. Sinclair, G. A. Faulkner, C. E. Kelleway, J. M. Gregory, V. Mankad, K. R. Miller, P. R. Umrigar and B. R. Taylor.

Is Sobers the greatest all-round cricketer in history? Once upon a time there was W. G. Grace, who in his career scored 54,896 runs and took 2,876 wickets, many of which *must* really have been out; also W.G. was a household name, an eminent Victorian, permanent in the National gallery of representative Englishmen. Aubrey Faulkner, South African, a "googly" bowler too, scored 1,754 runs in Test matches, average 40.79, and took 82 wickets, average 26.58. In 1906, George Hirst achieved the marvellous double performance of 2,385 runs and 208 wickets. When asked if he thought anybody would ever equal this feat he replied, "Well, whoever does it will be tired." But Hirst's record in Test matches was insignificant compared with Sobers', over a period. (All the same, shouldn't we estimate a man by his finest hour?)

There was Wilfred Rhodes, let us not forget. In his career he amassed no fewer than 39,802 runs, average 30.83, and his wickets amounted to 4,187, average 16.71. In first for England with Jack Hobbs at Melbourne in 1912, and colleague in the record first-wicket stand against Australia of 323; and in last for England in 1903, partner of R. E. Foster in a last-wicket stand of 130. Again, what of Frank Woolley, 39,802 runs in Tests, 83 wickets?

It is, of course, vain to measure ability in one age with ability in another. Material circumstances, the environment which moulds technique, are different. Only providence, timeless and all-seeing, is qualified to weigh in the balance the arts and personality of a Hammond and a Sobers. It is enough that the deeds of Sobers are appreciated in our own time, as we have witnessed them. He has, as I have pointed out, boxed the compass of the world of present-day cricket, revealing his gifts easefully, abundantly. And here we touch on his secret: power of relaxation and the gift of holding himself in reserve. Nobody has seen Sobers obviously in labour. He makes a stroke with moments to spare. His fastest ball – and it can be very fast – is bowled as though he could, with physical pressure, have bowled it a shade faster. He can, in the slips catch the lightning snick with the grace and nonchalance of Hammond himself. The sure sign of mastery, of genius of any order, is absence of strain, natural freedom of rhythm.

In the Test matches in England last summer, 1966, his prowess exceeded all precedents: 722 runs, average 103.14, twenty wickets, average 27.25, and ten catches. In the first game, at Manchester, 161 and three wickets for 103; in the second, at Lord's, 46 and 163 not out and one wicket for 97; in the third, at Nottingham, 3 and 94, five wickets for 161; in the fourth, at Leeds, 174 and eight wickets for 80; in the fifth, at The Oval, 81 and 0, with three wickets for 104. A writer of highly-coloured boys' school stories wouldn't dare to presume that the hero could go on like this, staggering credulity match after match. I am not sure that his most impressive assertion of his quality was not seen in the Lord's Test. Assertion is too strenuous a word to apply to the 163 not out scored then; for it was done entirely free of apparent exertion, even though at one stage of the proceedings the West Indies seemed beaten beyond salvage. When the fifth second-innings wicket fell, the West Indies were leading by nine runs only. Nothing reliable to come in the way of batsmanship, nobody likely to stay with Sobers, excepting Holford. As everybody concerned with cricket knows, Sobers and his cousin added, undefeated, 274. It is easy to argue that Cowdrey, England's captain, did not surround Sobers with a close field. Sobers hinted of no technical flaw, no mental or temperamental anxiety. If he slashed a ball when 93, to Cowdrey's hands, Cowdrey merely let us know that he was mortal when he missed a blistering chance. Bradman has expressed his opinion that few batsmen of his acquaintance hits with the velocity and strength of Sobers. And a sliced shot can travel at murderous pace.

At his best, Sobers scores as easily as any left-handed batsman I have seen since Frank Woolley. He is not classical in his grammar of batsmanship as, say, Martin Donnelly was. To describe Sobers' method I would use the term lyrical. His immense power is concealed, or lightened, to the spectator's eye, by a rhythm which has in it as little obvious propulsion as a movement of music by Mozart (who could be as dramatically strong as Wagner!). A drive through the covers by Sobers sometimes appears to be quite lazy, until we see an offside fieldsman nursing bruised palms, or hear the impact of ball striking the fence. His hook is almost as majestic as MacLaren's, though he hasn't MacLaren's serenity of poise as he makes it. I have actually seen Sobers carried round, off foot balance, while making a hook; it is his only visibly violent stroke – an assault. MacLaren, as I have written many times before, dismissed the ball from his presence. The only flaw in Sobers' technique of batsmanship, as far as I and better judges have been able so far to discern, is a tendency to play at a dangerously swinging away off-side ball "with his arms" – that is to say, with his bat a shade (and more) too far from his body. I fancy Sydney F. Barnes would have concentrated on this chink in the generally shining armour.

He is a natural product of the West Indies' physical and climatic environment, and of the condition of the game in the West Indies, historical and material, in which he was nurtured. He grew up at a time when the first impulses of West Indies' cricket were becoming rationalised; experience was being added to the original instinctive creative urge, which established the general style and pattern – a creative urge inspired largely by Constantine, after George Challenor had laid a second organised basis of batting technique. Sobers, indeed, flowered as West Indies' cricket was "coming of age". As a youth he could look at Worrell, at Weekes, at Walcott, at Ramadhin, at Valentine. The amazing thing is that he learned from all these superb and definitely formative, constructive West Indies cricketers; for each of them made vintage of the sowings of Challenor, George Headley, Constantine, Austin, Nunes, Roach, and Browne – to name but a few pioneers. Sobers began at the age of ten to bowl orthodox slow left-arm; he had no systematic coaching. (Much the same could safely be said of most truly gifted and individual cricketers.) Practising in the spare time given to him from his first job as a clerk in a shipping house, he developed his spin far enough to win a place, 16 years old now, in a Barbados team against an Indian touring side; moreover, he contrived to get seven wickets in the match for 142.

In the West Indies season of 1953-54, Sobers, now 17, received his Test match baptism at Sabina Park, Kingston. Valentine dropped out of the West Indies XI because of physical disability and Sobers was given his chance – as a bowler, in the Fifth game of the rubber. His order in the batting was ninth but he bowled 28 overs, 5 balls for 75 runs, 4 wickets, when England piled-up 414, Hutton 215. In two innings he made 14 not out, and 26. Henceforward he advanced as a predestined master, opening up fresh aspects of his rich endowment of gifts. He began to concentrate on batsmanship, so much so that in 1955, against Australia in the West Indies, he actually shared the opening of an innings, with J. K. Holt, in the fourth Test. Facing Lindwall and Miller, after Australia had scored 668, he assaulted the greatest fast bowlers of the period to the tune of 43 in a quarter of an hour. Then he suffered the temporary set-back which the fates, in their wisdom, inflict on every budding talent, to prove strength of character. On a tour to New Zealand, the young man, now rising twenty, was one of a West Indies contingent. His Test match record there was modest enough – 81 runs in five innings and two wickets for 49.

He first played for the West Indies in England in 1957, and his form could scarcely have given compensation to his disappointed compatriots when the rubber was lost by three victories to none. His all-round record then was 10 innings, 320 runs, with five wickets costing 70.10 each. Next he became a professional for Radcliffe in the Central Lancashire League, where, as a bowler, he relied on speed and swing. In 1958/9 he was one of the West Indies team in India and Pakistan; and now talent burgeoned prodigiously. On the hard wickets he cultivated his left-arm "googlies", and this new study did not in the least hinder the maturing of his batsmanship. Against India he scored 557, average 92.83 and took ten for 292. Against Pakistan he scored 160, averge 32.0 and failed to get anybody out for 78.

The course of his primrose procession since then has been constantly spectacular, rising to a climax of personal glory in Australia in 1960-1961. He had staggered cricketers everywhere by his 365 not out v Pakistan in 1958; as a batsman he has gone on and on, threatening to debase the Bradman currency, all the time swinging round a crucial match the West Indies' way by removing an important opposing batsman, or by taking a catch of wondrous rapidity. He has betrodden hemispheres of cricket, become a national symbol of his own islands, the representative image on a postage stamp. Best of all, he has generally maintained the *art* of cricket at a time which day by day – especially in England – threatens to change the game into (a) real industry or (b) a sort of out-of-door "Bingo" cup jousting. He has demonstrated, probably unaware of what he has been doing, the worth of trust in natural-born ability, a lesson wasted on most players here. If he has once or twice lost concentration at the pinch – as he did at Kennington Oval in the Fifth test last year – well, it is human to err, occasionally, even if the gods have lavished on you a share of grace and skill not given to ordinary mortals. The greatest ever? – certainly the greatest all-rounder today, and for decades. And all the more precious is he now, considering the general nakedness of the land.

D. H. ROBINS' XI v WEST INDIES

Played at Eastbourne, April 30, May 1, 2, 1969

Drawn. The Pakistan and Northamptonshire all-rounder, Mushtaq Mohammad, accomplished an exceptional performance by hitting a century in each innings and bowling 47 overs for seven wickets. Butcher and Fredericks hit fine hundreds for the touring team on a pitch made for batting. There was a splendid third-day's cricket. Robins' side, set to make 345 to win in four hours, fifty minutes, fell only eight runs short with their last pair together.

West Indies

R. C. Fredericks c and b Walker	41	– c Milburn b Walker	116
G. S. Camacho st Murray b Slade	33	– b Walker	47
M. L. C. Foster lbw b Walker	0	– b Mushtaq	61
B. F. Butcher c Smith b Slade	113	– b Mushtaq	6
C. A. Davis c Murray b Walker	18	– not out	53
*G. S. Sobers b Mushtaq	24		
J. N. Shepherd b Slade	22	– lbw b Mushtaq	4
†T. M. Findlay b Mushtaq	20	– lbw b Mushtaq	4
V. A. Holder b Slade	3	– not out	4
P. Roberts b Slade	1	– c Walker b Mushtaq	13
P. D. Blair not out	4		
B 2, l-b 6	8	L-b 11	11
1/62 2/63 3/80 4/150 5/193 6/239 7/262 8/271 9/283	287	1/100 2/209 3/255 4/267 5/271 6/305 7/313 (7 wkts dec.)	319

Bowling: *First Innings*—Price 11–0–50–0; Spencer 12–2–40–0; Walker 20–7–55–3; Slade 17.1–5–45–5; Mushtaq 15–1–89–2. *Second Innings*—Price 8–2–16–0; Spencer 6–3–8–0; Slade 35–9–82–0; Mushtaq 32–6–121–5; Walker 20–3–81–2.

D. H. Robins' XI

C. Milburn b Blair	0 – lbw b Holder	23
R. M. Prideaux b Blair	0 – b Blair	17
M. H. Denness c Findlay b Davis	43 – c Findlay b Sobers	30
M. J. K. Smith b Blair	17 – b Holder	1
Mushtaq Mohammad not out	128 – c Sobers b Shepherd	123
†J. T. Murray b Holder	7 – c and b Shepherd	75
P. M. Walker c Sobers b Shepherd	10 – lbw b Sobers	23
D. N. F. Slade b Foster	3 – lbw b Shepherd	0
J. S. E. Price not out	53 – not out	17
C. T. Spencer (did not bat)	– c Davis b Sobers	9
*D. H. Robins (did not bat)	– not out	13
N-b	1 L-b 5, n-b 1	6
1/0 2/5 3/40 4/74 5/111 6/122 7/139 (7 wkts dec.)	262 1/23 2/49 3/54 4/82 5/248 6/287 7/298 8/308 9/309 (9 wkts)	337

Bowling: *First Innings*—Blair 11–1–59–3; Holder 9–1–25–1; Davis 7–0–27–1; Roberts 18–6–53–0; Shepherd 13–4–37–1; Foster 8–3–28–1; Sobers 9–2–32–0. *Second Innings*—Blair 7–0–62–1; Holder 18–3–55–2; Shepherd 24–3–95–3; Sobers 18–3–49–3; Roberts 8–2–41–0; Foster 5–1–29–0.

Umpires: J. S. Buller and C. S. Elliott.

ENGLAND v WEST INDIES

Second Test Match

Played at Lord's, June 26, 27, 28, 30, July 1, 1969

Drawn. This Test took two days to get properly moving, but the cricket was always keen and the last three days found the teams locked in a tremendous struggle for supremacy. The sun shone gloriously all the time and altogether 100,500 people attended, the receipts of £67,700 falling only £5,000 short of the world record in the corresponding match of 1968. Batsmen generally held sway, except when England broke down at the beginning of their first innings. The match brought distinction to John Hampshire, who became the first Englishman to hit a century on his Test début at Lord's. Back in 1893, H. Graham did likewise for Australia. As Illingworth and Boycott also reached three figures, we had three Yorkshiremen making centuries in the same Test.

On Monday, when 19,000 people were present, The Queen, accompanied by Prince Philip and Prince Charles, met the officials and players of both teams who were presented to her in front of the pavilion after lunch. The Royal party stayed for two hours watching the cricket with the committee and players.

Not for the first time, the England selectors decided to enter the match with an unbalanced attack—of all people they left out Underwood, hoping that the pitch would prove ideal for fast and medium paced bowling, but the first session revealed that a series of bouncers held no terrors for the West Indies and afterwards a fuller length earned more respect and kept down the runs.

West Indies showed three changes compared with Old Trafford; they brought in Camacho, Findlay and Shillingford for Carew, Hendriks and Foster. A total of 246 for four on the first day was not so slow as it seemed, for England sent down only 99 overs. Early, Snow was twice warned by Buller for running down the pitch, whereupon he moved back his mark and avoided further trouble.

West Indies began soundly, Fredericks hooking to good purpose, and their opening stand of 106 assured a substantial total unless they lost their heads. Fredericks, first to leave, struck the ball against his pads for Hampshire to make a smart catch at leg slip. It was the highest first-wicket partnership by West Indies in England, compiled in two and a half hours; Camacho stayed seventy-five more minutes and meanwhile Davis settled down to a sound display, but Butcher went cheaply. The West Indies looked to Sobers to make the most of their promising start. Sobers soon established his authority in a stand of 50, but there was a misunderstanding over taking a leg-bye when the ball bounded forward off Sobers' legs and Boycott from square-leg ran to the wicket, whipping off the bails with the West Indies' captain half-way down the pitch.

The next day Davis made such slow progress that he batted six and a quarter hours for his 103 and could show only six boundaries, though he had the satisfaction of scoring his maiden Test hundred. The real value of his concentrated effort was seen when the first England five wickets were shared by Sobers, Holder and Shepherd for merely 61 runs. At the close on Friday England were 46 for four and Sobers, who had bowled at his quickest, had the analysis: 11–8–9–2.

On Saturday came the transformation. The gates were closed with 27,000 spectators inside the ground. Sharpe soon played on and then followed a wonderful stand by Hampshire and Knott that wrested the initiative from the opposition. It seemed strange that until that day Hampshire, in eight years of first-class cricket, had hit only ten hundreds. He had shown no decent form even this season and only got his place in the absence of Cowdrey, Barrington, Milburn, Graveney and Dexter—all of whom played against Australia the previous year. Now Hampshire produced the courage and ability to match the occasion which most Yorkshiremen knew that he possessed. For once his concentration did not falter. He excelled in forcing the ball off his legs and driving straight and to the off-side off his back foot. Knott, short and perky, was quick on his feet to get to the pitch of the ball and both men were sure in defence.

To the West Indies' delight Shillingford claimed his first Test wicket by yorking Knott when the stand had put on 128, but England were still 191 behind. By now Sobers was lame and after tea Gibbs took over the captaincy. It was only the second time Sobers had required a substitute in his 75 Tests. Twice Hampshire, who hit fifteen 4s, was struck on the left arm by bouncers from Holder, but he went on nobly to his hundred before Shepherd dismissed him leg-before. Hampshire saw the score rise from 37 for four to 249 for seven during a stay of four hours, ten minutes and he hit fifteen 4s.

Knight and Brown failed but with Illingworth adept in gaining the strike and Snow defending manfully they saw the total to 321 for nine by the close. Illingworth claimed 69 out of 72 in this unbroken stand and needing only three to complete his hundred he made no mistake on Monday morning. In his previous 31 Tests Illingworth's highest score had been 40. His was a grand innings, full of bold strokes and notable for forward play. It lasted three and a half hours and contained twelve 4s.

So West Indies led by no more than 36. Fredericks played another fine innings for his third successive Test sixty but the sweep cost several wickets. Lloyd, in dazzling mood, struck D'Oliveira twice for 6 and also hit eight 4s while scoring 70 in one hundred minutes. Sobers had Camacho as runner and on Tuesday morning the touring team added 48 while losing three more wickets before Sobers declared.

It was a sporting challenge; England wanted 332 in five hours, and 20 overs, if necessary, had to be bowled after the fourth hour. Sobers caused some surprise by bowling 29 overs considering his absence from the field and his batting with a runner, but apparently Illingworth did not object. It seemed that England went into their final task determined not to lose. Boycott occupied two and a half hours for his first 50 and Parfitt two hours for 39, while Sobers was banking on spin bowling on a still perfect pitch. The West Indies reeled off their overs at 21 an hour. Gibbs was their saviour, for he delivered 40 successive overs from the pavilion end for 87 runs.

Sharpe changed England's tune and with Boycott accelerating they put on 126 in ninety minutes, but England had left their bid for victory too late. The downfall of Boycott (sixteen 4s) and Sharpe in the space of a few minutes meant that 61 runs were needed from the last 10 overs and in the end England fell 37 runs short of their objective.

West Indies

Batsman	First innings		Second innings	
G. S. Camacho	c Sharpe b Snow	67	b D'Oliveira	45
R. C. Fredericks	c Hampshire b Knight	63	c Hampshire b Illingworth	60
C. A. Davis	c Knott b Brown	103	c Illingworth b D'Oliveira	0
B. F. Butcher	c Hampshire b Brown	9	b Illingworth	24
*G. S. Sobers	run out	29	not out	50
C. H. Lloyd	c Illingworth b Brown	18	c Knott b Snow	70
J. N. Shepherd	c Edrich b Snow	32	c Sharpe b Illingworth	11
†T. M. Findlay	b Snow	23	c Sharpe b Knight	11
V. A. Holder	lbw b Snow	6	run out	7
L. R. Gibbs	not out	18	b Knight	5
G. C. Shillingford	c Knott b Snow	3		
	B 5, l-b 4	9	B 4, l-b 7, n-b 1	12
	1/106 2/151 3/167 4/217 5/247 6/234 7/336 8/343 9/376	380	1/73 2/73 3/128 4/135 5/191 6/232 7/263 8/280 9/295 (9 wkts dec.)	295

Bowling: *First Innings*—Snow 39–5–114–5; Brown 38–8–99–3; Knight 38–11–65–1; D'Oliveira 26–10–46–0; Illingworth 16–4–39–0; Parfitt 1–0–8–0. *Second Innings*—Snow 22–4–69–1; Brown 9–3–25–0; Knight 27.5–6–78–2; D'Oliveira 15–2–45–2; Illingworth 27–9–66–3.

England

Batsman	First innings		Second innings	
G. Boycott	c Findlay b Shepherd	23	c Butcher b Shillingford	106
J. H. Edrich	c Fredericks b Holder	7	c Camacho b Holder	1
P. H. Parfitt	c Davis b Sobers	4	c Findlay b Shepherd	39
B. L. D'Oliveira	c Shepherd b Sobers	0	c Fredricks b Gibbs	18
P. J. Sharpe	b Holder	11	c Davis b Sobers	86
J. H. Hampshire	lbw b Shepherd	107	run out	5
†A. P. E. Knott	b Shillingford	53	b Shillingford	11
*R. Illingworth	c and b Gibbs	113	not out	9
B. R. Knight	lbw b Shillingford	0	not out	1
D. J. Brown	c Findlay b Shepherd	1		
J. A. Snow	not out	0		
	B 1, l-b 5, n-b 10	16	B 9, l-b 5, n-b 5	19
	1/19 2/37 3/37 4/37 5/61 6/189 7/249 8/250 9/261	344	1/1 2/94 3/137 4/263 5/271 6/272 7/292 (7 wkts)	295

Bowling: *First Innings*—Sobers 26–12–57–2; Holder 38–16–83–2; Shillingford 19–4–53–2; Shepherd 43–14–74–3; Gibbs 27.4–9–53–1; Davis 1–0–2–0; Butcher 3–1–6–0. *Second Innings*—Sobers 29–8–72–1; Holder 11–4–36–1; Shillingford 13–4–30–2; Shepherd 12–3–45–1; Gibbs 41–14–93–1.

Umpires: J. S. Buller and A. E. Fagg.

IRELAND v WEST INDIES

Played at Sion Mills, Londonderry, July 2, 1969

Ireland won by nine wickets. In some ways this one-day match provided the sensation of the 1969 season. The West Indies, with six of the team who had escaped on the previous day from defeat in the Lord's Test, were skittled for 25 in this tiny Ulster town on a damp and definitely emerald green pitch. The conditions were all in favour of the bowlers, but the West Indies batsmen fell in the main to careless strokes and smart catching. Goodwin, the Irish captain, took five wickets for 6 runs and O'Riordan four for 18. Both bowled medium pace at a reasonable length and the pitch did the rest. It was not a first-class match, but Ireland's performance deserves a permanent record and therefore we give the full score.

West Indies

G. S. Camacho c Dineen b Goodwin	1	– c Dineen b Goodwin	1
M. C. Carew c Hughes b O'Riordan	0	– c Pigot b Duffy	25
M. L. C. Foster run out	2	– c Pigot b Goodwin	0
*B. F. Butcher c Duffy b O'Riordan	2	– c Waters b Duffy	50
C. H. Lloyd c Waters b Goodwin	1	– not out	0
C. L. Walcott c Anderson b O'Riordan	6	– not out	0
J. N. Shepherd c Duffy b Goodwin	0		
†T. M. Findlay c Waters b Goodwin	0		
G. C. Shillingford not out	9		
P. Roberts c Colhoun b O'Riordan	0		
P. D. Blair b Goodwin	3		
B 1	1	L-b 2	2
1/1 2/1 3/3 4/6 5/6 6/8 7/12 8/12 9/12	25	1/1 2/2 3/73 4/78 (4 wkts)	78

Bowling: *First Innings*—O'Riordan 13–8–18–4; Goodwin 12.3–8–6–5. *Second Innings*—O'Riordan 6–1–21–0; Goodwin 2–1–1–2; Hughes 7–4–10–0; Duffy 12–8–2–2; Anderson 7–1–32–0.

Ireland

R. H. C. Waters c Findlay b Blair	2
D. M. Pigot c Camacho b Shillingford	37
M. Reith lbw b Shepherd	10
J. Harrison lbw b Shepherd	0
I. Anderson c Shepherd b Roberts	7
P. J. Dineen b Shepherd	0
A. J. O'Riordan c and b Carew	35
G. A. Duffy not out	15
L. F. Hughes c sub b Carew	13
L-b 2, n-b 4	6
1/19 2/30 3/34 4/51 5/55 6/69 7/103 8/125 (8 wkts dec.)	125

*D. E. Goodwin and †O. D. Colhoun did not bat.

Bowling: Blair 8–4–14–1; Shillingford 7–2–19–1; Shepherd 13–4–20–3; Roberts 16–3–43–1; Carew 3.2–0–23–2.

Umpires: M. Stott and A. Trickett.

GLAMORGAN v WEST INDIES

Played at Swansea, July 5, 6, 7, 1969

Drawn. Although the loss of play through rain on Sunday caused much reduced receipts, the game produced some remarkable cricket. Lloyd and Butcher figured in a record-breaking stand of 335 for the fifth wicket after the tourists had lost four wickets for 63 before lunch on the opening day. Lloyd hit eight 6s and twenty-one 4s in his 201 not out and Butcher hit two 6s and twenty-three 4s in his 151. All the glory did not belong to the West Indies. In Glamorgan's first innings the Pakistani Test player, Majid, produced a superb 147 in two and a half hours. It was majestic batting and had power as well as elegance, including five 6s and nineteen 4s. The rest of the cricket was an anti-climax and two meaningless declarations seemed just a formality.

West Indies

*B. F. Butcher c Majid b Walker	151		
R. C. Fredericks c E. Jones b Nash	12	– not out	40
G. S. Camacho c E. Jones b Nash	22	– c E. Jones b D. H. Lewis	2
M. C. Carew c Cordle b Wheatley	17	– c Lyons b Wheatley	67
C. A. Davis c Majid b Nash	7	– not out	7
C. H. Lloyd not out	201		
J. N. Shepherd not out	4		
B 1, l-b 3, n-b 1	5	B 8	8
1/13 2/45 3/59 4/63 5/398 (5 wkts dec.)	419	1/11 2/113 (2 wkts dec.)	124

†T. M. Findlay, V. A. Holder, P. Roberts and G. C. Shillingford did not bat.

Bowling: *First Innings*—Wheatley 28–6–93–1; Nash 32–9–104–3; Cordle 21–5–73–0; D. H. Lewis 14–1–82–0; Walker 12.3–0–62–1. *Second Innings*—Wheatley 4–1–13–1; Cordle 1–1–0–0; D. H. Lewis 13–3–58–1; Walker 6–1–10–0; Davis 9–0–35–0.

Glamorgan

B. A. Davis c Lloyd b Holder	0	– c Findlay b Holder	11
A. Jones c Butcher b Shillingford	10	– c Carew b Camacho	17
K. Lyons c Shepherd b Holder	6	– not out	12
*A. R. Lewis b Shillingford	1	– not out	3
Majid Jahangir c Fredericks b Shillingford	147		
P. M. Walker c Findlay b Carew	58		
†E. Jones not out	23		
M. A. Nash (did not bat)		– retired hurt	0
W 1, n-b 2	3	N-b 1	1
1/7 2/17 3/17 4/19 5/172 6/248 (6 wkts dec.)	248	1/18 2/41 (2 wkts)	44

A. E. Cordle, D. H. Lewis and O. S. Wheatley did not bat.

Bowling: *First Innings*—Holder 14–2–60–2; Shillingford 13.5–3–62–3; Shepherd 6–0–21–0; Roberts 9–1–38–0; Davis 3–0–11–0; Carew 7–0–44–1; Fredericks 1–0–9–0. *Second Innings*—Lloyd 6–3–7–0; Camacho 2–0–2–1; Holder 5–0–17–1; Shillingford 5–1–10–0; Fredericks 3–0–7–0.

Umpires: W. E. Alley and J. G. Langridge.

LEICESTERSHIRE v WEST INDIES

Played at Leicester, July 16, 17, 18, 1969

Drawn. With the Test series over, West Indies batted in uninhibited style, and lost only four wickets in the match. The two left-handers, Carew and Fredericks, put on 324 for the second wicket in four and a half hours in the first innings, and were still together when Gibbs declared. Fredericks hit thirty-one 4s and Carew twenty-two 4s, but both were helped by missed chances. Leicestershire responded in kind, Dudleston being the mainstay in one of the best innings of his career. Inman also batted fluently until having to retire with a pulled side muscle. Although the last five county wickets fell cheaply, West Indies were restricted to a lead of 51. They added to this briskly, Fredericks, Butcher and Lloyd all showing a wide range of strokes. The second declaration, however, set Leicestershire too stiff a task, 301 in ten minutes under three hours, and they did not attempt to get the runs.

West Indies

G. S. Camacho c McKenzie b Birkenshaw	38	– c and b Birkenshaw	13
M. C. Carew not out	172		
R. C. Fredericks not out	168	– run out	84
M. L. C. Foster (did not bat)		– lbw b Birkenshaw	11
B. F. Butcher (did not bat)		– not out	76
C. H. Lloyd (did not bat)		– not out	63
L-b 3, n-b 4	7	B 1, n-b 1	2
1/61	(1 wkt dec.) 385	1/41 2/69 3/131	(3 wkts dec.) 249

†J. L. Hendriks, P. Roberts, V. A. Holder, *L. R. Gibbs and G. C. Shillingford did not bat.

Bowling: *First Innings*—McKenzie 10–0–57–0; Spencer 13–2–57–0; Cotton 15–0–84–0; Birkenshaw 19–7–52–1; Illingworth 17–6–34–0; Marner 11–0–56–0; Booth 6–0–38–0. *Second Innings*—McKenzie 10–2–32–0; Cotton 8–2–25–0; Birkenshaw 19–2–84–2; Illingworth 9–1–27–0; Spencer 8–0–28–0; Booth 3–0–25–0; Dudleston 3–0–26–0.

Leicestershire

M. E. Norman c and b Roberts	17	– not out	40
B. Dudleston lbw b Butcher	122	– b Butcher	23
P. T. Marner c Carew b Roberts	15	– c Fredericks b Butcher	6
B. J. Booth c Camacho b Gibbs	28	– b Carew	6
C. C. Inman retired hurt	68		
*R. Illingworth b Butcher	17		
J. Birkenshaw c Gibbs b Holder	13		
†R. W. Tolchard b Butcher	0	– not out	20
G. D. McKenzie c Gibbs b Shillingford	17		
C. T. Spencer b Lloyd	21		
J. Cotton not out	10		
B 1, l-b 2, n-b 3	6	B 5, n-b 1	6
1/34 2/64 3/143 4/239 5/273 6/273 7/283 8/305 9/334	334	1/46 2/52 3/66	(3 wkts) 101

Bowling: *First Innings*—Holder 16–3–63–1; Shillingford 8–0–29–1; Roberts 22–6–64–2; Gibbs 16–3–42–1; Butcher 16–2–58–3; Foster 22–10–44–0; Carew 10–2–25–0; Lloyd 1.5–0–3–1. *Second Innings*—Holder 2–1–1–0; Shillingford 2–0–4–0; Gibbs 12–6–30–0; Roberts 9–5–8–0; Foster 8–4–7–0; Butcher 3–1–6–2; Camacho 11–2–29–0; Carew 3–2–1–1; Lloyd 1–0–9–0.

Umpires: W. E. Phillipson and G. H. Pope.

NOTES BY THE EDITOR, 1974

THE FAGG INCIDENT

While on the subject of captaincy, it was regrettable that Kanhai showed such open dissent on the field at Edgbaston when umpire Fagg turned down an appeal against Boycott for a catch at the wicket. Fagg threatened to quit the match and indeed it took a lot of persuasion behind the scenes before he agreed to resume next morning after missing the first over. The reaction of Fagg while at boiling point met with much criticism, and it would certainly have been better had he grappled with the situation through the Test and County Cricket Board representative who was on hand for just such an occurrence rather than in the Press, but at least it brought the matter to a head. For too long, and not only in this country, players from junior to senior standing have been reflecting their dislike at umpire's decisions almost with disdain. Now the TCCB have taken a firm stand by declaring at their December meeting that umpires will receive full support in reporting, as is their duty, any pressurising on the field. I am afraid Kanhai lost his way, of all places, on the ground where for years he has proved such a popular figure. Maybe he did so in his anxiety not to let slip any chance of capitalizing on his team's victory in the first of the three Tests, but that cannot excuse his behaviour. Captains more than hold the key to clearing up a bad habit which has no place in the game of cricket.

ENGLAND v WEST INDIES

Third Test Match

Played at Lord's, August 23, 24, 25, 27, 1973

West Indies won by an innings and 226 runs. This match will assuredly be known in cricket history as "The Bomb Scare Test". There was drama on the Saturday afternoon when 28,000 people were ordered to leave the ground following a telephone warning that a bomb had been planted. The call proved to be a hoax but no chances could be taken with the safety of players and spectators because an IRA bomb campaign was in full swing in London at the time.

The incident caused the loss of eighty-five minutes playing time and it was agreed that half an hour would be added to the day's play and further extra time provided for on Monday and Tuesday. But the triumphant West Indies had no need of it and they won with a day and a half to spare. They swept aside a demoralized England side whose margin of defeat had been exceeded once only at Brisbane on the 1946-47 tour of Australia.

As Illingworth said afterwards "We were outbatted, outbowled and outfielded. There are no excuses." It was a sad end to the Illingworth era, for England's cricketers, with a few doughty exceptions, played without spirit or fight on a pitch of pace and bounce which was a credit to the Lord's groundsman, Jim Fairbrother. Kanhai, Sobers and the exuberant Julien played major innings for West Indies, whose total was their highest in England, while the pace bowlers again provided the sustained aggression which proved too much for the majority of the English batsmen.

The crowd behaviour was once more unsatisfactory. Despite the lessons of The Oval the ground authorities decided to allow spectators to sit on the grass. As West Indies gained the upper hand the unruly elements became more and more uncontrollable and when Boycott was leaving the field on the Saturday evening he was buffeted by a group of them. As a result the crowd were confined to the stands on the Monday, a Bank Holiday, when soon after lunch thousands of West Indians were dancing around the outfield to celebrate victory after a match that was embarrassingly one-sided.

England's hopes of squaring the series had all but disappeared by the end of the first day, which was dominated by Kanhai in magnificent form and ended with the tourists at 335 for four. England brought in Willis for Old and the young fast bowler who performed with great heart and enthusiasm proved one of the few successes.

West Indies made over 100 runs in each session after Fredericks, the "slow coach" of Edgbaston, had sent them away with a rapid, no-nonsense innings of 51. Kanhai, who passed 6,000 runs in Test cricket during his knock, engaged in a partnership of 138 in even time with Lloyd and reached his fifth century against England in three and a half hours. At the end of the day he and Sobers belaboured the attack for 79 and Kanhai, who was 156 not out after batting five and a half hours, received a standing ovation.

He was soon disposed of next morning, and there was a quiet period while Sobers played within himself and Foster struggled against some accurate fast bowling. But England's relief was short-lived for on Foster's dismissal young Julien came in to confirm his high promise by making his maiden century in a Test Match. His first two scoring strokes went to the boundary before he was missed on the long-leg boundary by Fletcher off Greig. Thereafter Julien gave the bowlers little encouragement, striking the ball cleanly, powerfully and in mainly orthodox fashion to all parts of the ground in a thrilling display. In the last fifty-three minutes before lunch he and Sobers added 81, Julien's share being 47.

Sobers moved gracefully to his twenty-sixth Test hundred for his country and the partnership was worth 155 in under two hours, a seventh wicket record for West Indies against England before a stomach upset caused Sobers to retire temporarily.

Julien went on at a fine pace reaching his hundred in two and a half hours from 127 balls. At this point some spectators could restrain themselves no longer and the first serious pitch invasion of the match took place. Sobers returned to take his score to 150 including nineteen 4s in four and three-quarter hours before Kanhai called off the onslaught of the weary England bowlers.

England were soon in trouble. Boycott, trying to hook a rising ball outside the off-stump, was caught at first slip and although Amiss and Fletcher frequently pierced the attacking field in the closing overs England finished in the unhappy position of having three wickets down for 88.

On a fine Saturday the ground was packed to capacity. Although Amiss was soon accounted for, England made a useful recovery as the confident Fletcher and a rather fortunate Greig added 79 for the fifth wicket. The loss of Fletcher and Illingworth to successive balls just before lunch sent the innings into its final decline. The successful bowler, Gibbs had them both smartly taken by Sobers crouched at close backward short-leg, the two best of his six catches in the match which equalled the Test record for a fieldsman.

Half an hour after the interval, as Willis came out to join Arnold, the secretary of MCC announced over the loudspeakers that the ground would have to be cleared. For some time the players stayed in the middle surrounded by curious spectators. Eventually the West Indies went back to their hotel in Maida Vale and the England players to a tent behind the pavilion while police searched the empty stands. Thousands stayed on the playing area, refusing to leave.

When play resumed at 4.30 only a few thousand spectators had failed to return to watch cricket in an unreal atmosphere. The England innings closed at 233 and they followed-on 419 behind. Eighty-five minutes remained when Boycott and Amiss went out and with the West Indies fast bowlers showing reaction from their earlier efforts the batsmen did well enough for sixty-five minutes. Then Boyce, called upon for a final burst from the pavilion end, removed most remaining doubts about the eventual outcome by taking three wickets for six runs in 3.5 overs. His victims were Amiss, Knott and Boycott.

The Yorkshireman fell into an obvious trap in the final over by hooking a short ball direct to Kallicharran on the square leg boundary. It was a stroke of remarkably ill judgement by a player of such class and experience, but it emphasized the depths to which the England batting had sunk during the series.

A fine innings in a lost cause by Fletcher kept the game going until shortly before three o'clock on Monday. As in his first innings he showed how to deal with the fast, short-pitched ball and played well enough to deserve a century. Underwood, his last partner, stayed while 47 were added but Fletcher was still 14 short of three figures when Gibbs ended the match by bowling Underwood.

The Prudential-Wisden awards of £150 went to G. S. Sobers and R. G. D. Willis. Special prizes of £100 for the series went to C. H. Lloyd and K. W. R. Fletcher and the £300 award for the "Player of the Series" was won by K. D. Boyce. Attendance: 95,530. Receipts: £87,304.

West Indies

R. C. Fredericks c Underwood b Willis	51
†D. L. Murray b Willis	4
*R. B. Kanhai c Greig b Willis	157
C. H. Lloyd c and b Willis	63
A. I. Kallicharran c Arnold b Illingworth	14
G. S. Sobers not out	150
M. L. C. Foster c Willis b Greig	9
B. D. Julien c and b Greig	121
K. D. Boyce c Amiss b Greig	36
V. A. Holder not out	23
B 1, l-b 14, w 1, n-b 8	24
1/8 2/87 3/225 4/256 5/339 6/373 7/604 8/610 (8 wkts dec.)	652

L. R. Gibbs did not bat.

Bowling: Arnold 35–6–111–0; Willis 35–3–118–4; Greig 33–2–180–3; Underwood 34–6–105–0; Illingworth 31.4–3–114–1.

England

G. Boycott c Kanhai b Holder	4	– c Kallicharran b Boyce	15
D. L. Amiss c Sobers b Holder	35	– c Sobers b Boyce	10
B. W. Luckhurst c Murray b Boyce	1	– c Sobers b Julien	12
F. C. Hayes c Fredericks b Holder	8	– c Holder b Boyce	0
K. W. R. Fletcher c Sobers b Gibbs	68	– not out	86
A. W. Greig c Sobers b Boyce	44	– lbw b Julien	13
*R. Illingworth c Sobers b Gibbs	0	– c Kanhai b Gibbs	13
†A. P. E. Knott c Murray b Boyce	21	– c Murray b Boyce	5
G. G. Arnold c Murray b Boyce	5	– c Fredericks b Gibbs	1
R. G. D. Willis not out	5	– c Fredericks b Julien	0
D. L. Underwood c Gibbs b Holder	12	– b Gibbs	14
B 6, l-b 4, w 3, n-b 17	30	B 9, w 1, n-b 14	24
1/5 2/7 3/29 4/97 5/176 6/176 7/178 8/205 9/213	233	1/2 2/38 3/42 4/49 5/63 6/87 7/132 8/143 9/146	193

Bowling: *First Innings*—Holder 15–3–56–4; Boyce 20–7–50–4; Julien 11–4–26–0; Gibbs 18–3–39–2; Sobers 8–0–30–0; Foster 1–0–2–0. *Second Innings*—Holder 14–4–18–0; Boyce 16–5–49–4; Julien 18–2–69–3; Gibbs 13.3–3–26–3; Sobers 4–1–7–0.

Umpires: H. D. Bird and C. S. Elliott.

SIR GARFIELD SOBERS

CRICKET'S MOST VERSATILE PERFORMER

By John Arlott

Sir Garfield Sobers, the finest all-round player in the history of cricket, has announced his retirement from full time county cricket at the age of thirty-eight. Circumstances seem to suggest he will not be seen again in Test Matches. He was not with West Indies on their recent tour of India and Pakistan; and they have no other international commitment until 1976, when their full length tour of England might well prove too physically trying for a forty-year old Sobers, most deservedly given a Knighthood in the [1975] New Year Honours.

So it is likely that international cricket has seen the last of its most versatile performer. For twenty years – plus, to be precise, seven days – he served and graced West Indian cricket in almost every capacity. To review his career compels so many statistics as might mask the splendidly exciting quality of his play. Nevertheless, since many of his figures are, quite literally, unequalled, they must be quoted. Between March 30 1954 and April 5 1974, for West Indies, he appeared in 93 Tests – more than any other overseas cricketer; he played the highest Test innings – 365 not out against Pakistan at Kingston in 1958; scored the highest individual aggregate of runs in Test matches; and captained his country a record 39 times. His 110 catches and – except for a left hander – his 235 wickets are not unique: but his talents in those directions alone justified a Test place. I quote his West Indies figures.

Garfield Sobers was seventeen when he first played for West Indies – primarily as an orthodox slow left arm bowler (four for 81), though he scored 40 runs for once out in a losing side. His batting developed more rapidly than his bowling and, in the 1957-58 series with Pakistan in West Indies, he played six consecutive innings of over fifty – the last three of them centuries. Through the sixties he developed left-arm wrist-spin, turning the ball sharply and concealing his googly well. Outstandingly, however, at the need of his perceptive captain, Sir Frank Worrell, he made himself a Test-class fast medium bowler. Out of his instinctive athleticism he evolved an ideally economic action, coupling life from the pitch with late movement through the air and, frequently, off the seam. Nothing in all his cricket was more impressive than his ability to switch from one bowling style to another with instant control.

He was always capable of bowling orthodox left arm accurately, with a surprising faster ball and as much turn as the pitch would allow a finger spinner. He had, through, an innate urge to attack, which was his fundamental reason for taking up the less economical but often more penetrative "chinaman", and the pace bowling which enabled him to make such hostile use of the new ball.

As a fieldsman he is remembered chiefly for his work at slip – where he made catching look absurdly simple – or at short leg where he splendidly reinforced the off-spin of Lance Gibbs. Few recall that as a young man he was extremely fast – and had a fine "arm" – in the deep, and that he could look like a specialist at cover point.

Everything he did was marked by a natural grace, apparent at first sight. As he walked out to bat, six feet tall, lithe but with adequately wide shoulders, he moved with long strides, which, even when he was hurrying, had an air of laziness, the hip joints rippling like those of a great cat. He was, it seems, born with basic orthodoxy in batting; the fundamental reason for his high scoring lay in the correctness of his defence. Once he was established (and he did not always settle in quickly), his sharp eye, early assessment, and inborn gift of timing, enabled him to play almost any stroke. Neither a back foot not a front foot player, he was either as the ball and conditions demanded. When he stepped out and drove it was with a full flow of the bat and a complete follow through, in the classical manner. When he could not get to the pitch of the ball, he would go back, wait – as it sometimes seemed, impossibly long – until he identified it and then, at the slightest opportunity, with an explosive whip of the wrists, he hit it with immense power. His quick reactions and natural ability linked with his attacking instinct made him a brilliant improviser of strokes. When he was on the kill it was all but impossible to bowl to him – and he was one of the most thrilling of all batsmen to watch.

Crucially, Garfield Sobers was not merely extremely gifted, but a highly combative player. That was apparent on his first tour of England, under John Goddard in 1957. Too many members of that team lost appetite for the fight as England took the five-match rubber by three to none. Sobers, however, remained resistant to the end. He was a junior member of the side – his twenty-first birthday fell during the tour – but he batted with immense concentration an determination. He was only twice out cheaply in Tests: in two Worrell took him in to open the batting and, convincingly, in the rout at The Oval, he was top scorer in each West Indies innings. He was third in the Test batting averages of that series which marked his accession to technical and temperamental maturity.

The classic example of his competitive quality was the Lord's Test of 1966 when West Indies, with five second innings wickets left, were only nine in front and Holford – a raw cricketer but their last remaining batting hope – came in to join his cousin Sobers. From the edge of defeat, they set a new West Indies Test record of 274 for the sixth wicket and, so far from losing, made a strong attempt to win the match.

Again, at Kingston in 1967-68, West Indies followed on against England and, with five second innings wickets down, still needed 29 to avoid an innings defeat. Sobers – who fell for a duck in the first innings – was left with only tail-enders for support yet, on an unreliable pitch, he made 113 – the highest score of the match – and then, taking the first two English wickets for no runs, almost carried West Indies to a win.

For many years, despite the presence of some other handsome stroke-makers in the side, West Indies placed heavy reliance on his batting, especially when a game was running against them. Against England 1959-60 and Australia 1964-65, West Indies lost the one Test in each series when Sobers failed. His effectiveness can be measured by the fact that in his 93 Tests for West Indies he scored 26 centuries, and fifties in 30 other innings; four times – twice against England – averaged over one hundred for a complete series; and had an overall average of 57.78. There is a case, too, that he played a crucial part as a bowler in winning at least a dozen Tests.

To add captaincy to his batting, different styles of bowling and close fielding may have been the final burden that brought his Test career to an early end. He was a generally sound, if orthodox, tactician but after thirty-nine matches as skipper, the strain undoubtedly proved wearing. In everyday life he enjoys gambling and, as a Test captain, he is still remembered for taking a chance which failed. It occurred in the 1967-68 series against England, when he made more runs at a higher average – and bowled more overs than anyone else except Gibbs – on either side. After high scores by England, the first three Tests were drawn, but in the fourth, after Butcher surprisingly had bowled out England in their first innings with leg spin, Sobers made a challenging declaration. Butcher could not repeat his performance and Boycott and Cowdrey skilfully paced England to a win. Thereupon the very critics who constantly bemoaned the fact that Test match captains were afraid to take a chance castigated Sobers for doing so – and losing. The epilogue to that "failure" was memorable. With characteristic confidence in his own ability, he set out to win the fifth Test and square the rubber. He scored 152 and 95 not out, took three for 72 in the first England innings and three for 53 in the second – only to fall short of winning by one wicket with a hundred runs in hand.

Students of sporting psychology will long ponder the causes of Sobers' retirement. Why did this admirably equipped, well rewarded and single-minded cricketer limp out of the top level game which had brought him such eminence and success? He was only thirty-eight: some great players of the past continued appreciably longer. Simply enough, mentally and physically tired, he had lost his zest for the sport which had been his life – and was still his only observable means of earning a living. Ostensibly he had a damaged knee; in truth he was the victim of his unique range of talents – and the jet age. Because he was capable of doing so much, he was asked to do it too frequently. He did more than any other cricketer, and did it more concentratedly because high speed aircraft enabled him to travel half across the world in a day or two. Perhaps the long sea voyages between seasons of old had a restorative effect.

In a historically sapping career, Sobers has played for Barbados for twenty-one seasons; in English league cricket for eight, for South Australia in the Sheffield Shield for three, and Nottinghamshire for seven; he turned out regularly for the Cavaliers on Sundays for several years before there was a Sunday League in England; made nine tours for West Indies, two with Rest of the World sides and several in lesser teams; 89 of his 93 Tests for the West Indies were consecutive and he averaged more than four a year for twenty years. There is no doubt, also, that his car accident in which Collie Smith was killed affected him more profoundly and for longer than most people realized.

The wonder was not that the spark grew dim but that it endured so bright for so long. Though it happened so frequently and for so many years, it was always thrilling even to see Sobers come to the wicket. As lately as 1968 he hit six sixes from a six ball over. In 1974 on his "farewell" circuit of England he still, from time to time, recaptured his former glory, playing a lordly stroke or making the ball leave the pitch faster than the batsman believed possible. As he walked away afterwards, though, his step dragged. He was a weary man – as his unparalleled results do not merely justify, but demand. Anyone who ever matches Garfield Sobers' performances will have to be an extremely strong man – and he, too, will be weary.

An amazing man, he still insists, "As long as I am fit and the West Indies need me, I will be willing to play for them". Only time will tell if we shall see him in the Test arena again. In October last he joined the executive staff of National Continental Corporation to promote the company's products in the Caribbean and United Kingdom.

And now he has joined his lamented compatriots Sir Learie Constantine and Sir Frank Worrell with the title Sir Garfield Sobers.

WELCOME WEST INDIES

HOW THEY ROSE TO FAME

By Henry Blofeld

The West Indies may not have made much of an impact on Test cricket until after the Second War, but their cricket and their cricketers have always been as full of character and individuality as any in the world. The West Indians are a people with volatile temperaments and they have always tended to play their cricket in the same way that they live their lives. Because they are by nature gay, excitable and flamboyant, their approach to cricket has captured the imagination in a way which the cricket of no other country has done.

There is about the development of West Indies cricket a curious paradox, however, which is perhaps worth stating at the start of an article which is, incidentally, being written just a week before I fly out to Australia to watch them play six Test Matches against the West Indies, the result of which may possibly temporarily invalidate one or two of the comments made in following paragraphs.

RAMADHIN AND VALENTINE

In spite of all their exciting and compelling characteristics, the West Indies did not become a major cricketing power until their best players had learned to discipline themselves to the demands of Test cricket. This moment arrived in 1950 when Ramadhin and Valentine spun England to defeat, but by then a generation of West Indian cricketers had grown up who understood what was required to win a Test Match against top class opponents. Quick fifties and sixties may be breathtakingly memorable, but it is seldom that they have a lasting impact on a Test Match. [Hence their recent collapses in Australia. – Ed.]

Rae, Stollmeyer, Weekes, Walcott and Worrell knew this and in 1950, after their spin bowlers had disposed of England's batsmen, began to build up big enough totals in an uncharacteristically consistent way, and the last three being the batsmen they were, in a glamorous way at that. At last their batting was reliable and if Rae and Stollmeyer were less than typically flamboyant for West Indian batsmen, the value of their batting was immense. So often the three wonderful strokemakers who followed came in with a solid foundation laid which meant that they could concentrate all their efforts on scoring runs from the start. I think that the importance of Hunte's batting is sometimes underestimated in the later success of Worrell's side when Sobers and Kanhai batted so enthrallingly. Hunte seldom failed to give his side a solid start which made it easier for those who followed.

GREAT FUN

To be fully understood and appreciated West Indian cricket ought really to be seen in its own indigenous surroundings in the Caribbean. There, the game and the crowd are one and indivisible and there is total participation not only by the players and the spectators, but also by the entire population of each island or territory. When West Indies teams have played abroad in recent years, particularly in England, the expatriate West Indians have done their best to recreate the atmosphere which is found at, say, the Queen's Park Oval in Port of Spain. Great fun it has been too, but West Indian gaiety and frivolity and exuberance do not always lie easily on the more staid and unbending atmospheres of Lord's or The Oval. An impromptu calypso is splendid, but it is not the same as an impromptu calypso under a palm tree on the popular side of a West Indian ground. How could it be?

Although the success which has followed West Indies cricket since that tour of England in 1950 is relatively new, their essential tradition of cricket is anything but new and it embraces many characters who were just as colourful as any produced in the last two decades, but who, because they never had the chance or at any rate, a slender chance at Test level, remain unknown to all save the most ardent followers of the game. It was these rich characters who handed down to the present generation the West Indies way of playing cricket, which has given the game so much in recent years.

EARLY DAYS

Cricket in the West Indies as everywhere else was originally played by the English colonists. At the start of 1897 two English teams, one captained by Lord Hawke and the other by Mr Arthur Priestley, toured the West Indies and both found that cricket in that part of the world had considerably improved. It was still predominantly a white man's game and black men were not allowed to play in the Inter-Colonial Cup Competition. In their matches against the two English sides neither Barbados nor Demerara (Guyana) included black men, but Trinidad did and they were, according to P. F. Warner's account of Lord Hawke's tour in the 1898 edition of *Wisden*, the strongest side of all.

It is an account which does not tell us much about the individual players they encountered, but Mr Warner states his opposition to the policy pursued by Barbados and Demerara in respect of coloured players. He goes on to say, "These black men add considerably to the strength of a side, while their inclusion makes the game more popular locally and tends to instil a great and universal enthusiasm among all classes of the population." These guarded words form probably the first written acknowledgement of the spectator participation which is so much a part of the tradition of West Indies cricket.

TWO BLACK BOWLERS

Lord Hawke's side lost both their matches against Trinidad as did Mr Priestley's side later on in February 1897. Mr Warner says of their performance, "The chief credit of the victory rested with the two black bowlers, Woods and Cumberbatch, who between them took thirty-nine wickets in the two matches. Woods bowls very fast with a somewhat low and swinging action. He is very straight and every now and then breaks back considerably. Cumberbatch, who is perhaps the better bowler of the two, is a medium pace right-hander. He breaks a little both ways and varies his pace with much judgement. The fielding of the Trinidad team was splendid. The black men are especially fine fielders; they throw very well and seldom miss a catch." He tells us that Trinidad also had excellent batsmen in D'Ade and L. Constantine, Senior, who played in all the matches against both touring sides and came to England with some West Indian cricketers in 1900.

Mr Warner ends his piece by saying, "The hospitality of the people is unbounded. We had numerous picnics, dinners, dances, etc. A trip up the Essequibo river in British Guiana stands out very prominently. The visit of a West Indian team to England is by no means improbable and there can be little doubt that a capital side could be got together from the different islands and British Guiana if the black men were included. Without them it would be absurd to attempt to play the first-class counties."

All of this was written about West Indies cricket in its very early days and yet even in this rather dated description of Lord Hawke's tour one can sense something of the same atmosphere which is today so much a part of the West Indies and the cricket which is played there. Indeed, the first three sentences might have been written by one of Denness's MCC sides in 1974. West Indians have their own way of appreciating cricket just as much as they have their own way of playing it and the one can be as much fun as the other.

FIRST TOUR TO WEST INDIES

The first-ever tour of the West Indies had been undertaken in 1894 by a side captained by R. Slade Lucas and as there were few first-class cricketers among them, they were made to struggle. Although this was the first time that West Indian cricketers had played against the English, inter-colonial cricket had been going on in the Caribbean for more than thirty years and there had been tours with Canada and the United States of America and so they were well prepared for this first English side.

After these early tours, minor tours between players from England and the West Indies happened fairly regularly. A party of West Indians came to England in 1900 and indirectly produced the original forerunner of all the West Indians engaged in county cricket today. C. A. Ollivierre from Jamaica played some brilliant innings and later qualified to play for Derbyshire. All the time the standard of the West Indies side improved and when H. B. G. Austin, the captain of Barbados, brought a team to England in 1923, they won twelve matches and George Challenor, also from Barbados, hit eight hundreds and scored almost 2,000 runs.

LEARIE CONSTANTINE ARRIVES

Each time an English side went to the West Indies the party was stronger and in 1926 the Hon. F. S. G. Calthorpe's team included Walter Hammond, who made 238 not out in the first representative match. At last, in 1928 the West Indies were awarded three Test Matches on their tour of England, but under the captaincy of Karl Nunes from Jamaica they lost all three matches by an innings. It was during this tour that the young Learie Constantine first made a name for himself with his fast bowling, his furious hitting and his amazing fielding. Against Middlesex at Lord's in 1928 he made 86 out of 107 after the West Indies had been 79 for five and then took seven for 57 before taking his side to victory by scoring 103 out of 133 in an hour – Sobers in excelsis.

Constantine was a cricketer whose value could not be seen in terms of statistics, indeed from his statistics it seems surprising that he acquired the reputation he did. Yet, Constantine epitomised West Indies cricket. He was never consistent, he was always exciting, sometimes incredibly so, he was gloriously and extravagantly unorthodox and a wonderful entertainer.

In the last fifteen years West Indies cricket has had many brilliant moments. There has been the bowling of Hall and Roberts and Sobers the batting of Sobers and Kanhai, and Lloyd and Kallicharran, the fielding of Sobers and Boyce and Richards and the most incredible moment of all when late in the day on an almost empty ground at Brisbane in early December 1960 off the second last ball of the match, little Joe Solomon picked up the ball at cover about twelve yards from the bat and with one stump to aim at, knocked it over with Meckiff still a couple of yards short of his crease and Australia and the West Indies had shared the first and only tie in the history of Test cricket. Somehow all these great West Indian moments seem to have their origin in Constantine. Learie Constantine is a legendary figure, but one who has not the figures to rival any of the later players, and yet one cannot help but feel that their explosive powers, their most brilliant moments and their attitude to the game of cricket has been handed down at least in part from Constantaine.

Such is the power of legend and those who saw the West Indies sides before the war will be able to point to others who played with the same uncomplicated whole-heartedness, but Constantine's was a voice in the wilderness in that he was the first composite West Indian cricketer and not just a Trinidadian cricketer.

Inter-island rivalries and jealousies have so often worked to the detriment of West Indies cricket and maybe at times still do in the matter of team selection. Frank Worrell may have been the first man successfully to overcome this, but Constantine saw that if West Indies cricket was to become a major force in the world it could only be on a composite basis. He was an Old Testament prophet rather than a Messiah, but he had a clear vision of the future of West Indies cricket and no one derived greater pleasure from seeing his hopes become fact.

GEORGE HEADLEY TRULY GREAT

When the Hon. F. S. G. Calthorpe took his second side out to the West Indies in 1930 they could only halve the series although of course he did not have a full-strength MCC party. In that series George Headley appeared against England for the first time and made a tremendous impact. In the four Tests he scored four hundreds including two in the match at Georgetown and 223 in the last at Kingston after Sandham had made 325 for England. Headley was undoubtedly the best of the pre-war West Indies batsmen and his runs for the West Indies are made to seem even more remarkable when one remembers that he was given such slender support by his colleagues at the other end. Headley made 2,190 runs in 22 Test Matches and has an average of 60.83, which is higher than Sobers, Kanhai, Weekes, Worrell, Walcott or any other West Indian.

When the West Indies came to England in 1933 they again disappointed, but the two exceptions were Headley who was from Jamaica and scored over 2,300 runs and Manny Martindale from Barbados, a fast bowler, who took 103 wickets on the tour. Two years later R. E. S. Wyatt took another MCC team to the West Indies and this time the West Indies won their first series against England, 2-1. England lost the last Test at Kingston by an innings and Headley made 270 not out. Then, in the final series before the war, in 1939, England won, 1-0. Up to that point the West Indies had justified their rise to Test Match status on their own pitches against MCC teams which missed a few of the best English players, but they had been less successful in England, although they had improved on each succeeding tour.

THE THREE W's

Although the war put an end to Test cricket, the domestic competition continued in the West Indies and by the time it had ended three young Barbadians, Frank Worrell, Clyde Walcott and Everton Weekes, were carrying all before them. Worrell and Walcott put on 574 without being dismissed for Barbados against Trinidad in 1945-46 which is still the second highest partnership ever recorded in first-class cricket. The future of West Indies cricket looked assured. When G. O. Allen brought a slightly makeshift England side to the West Indies in 1947-48 they were well beaten, although in fairness it must be said that they were plagued by injuries.

For all that, the new West Indies side which was being built up under the leadership of the Barbados captain, John Goddard, had a greater depth of batting, a more dependable bowling line-up and in general more consistency than perhaps any of its pre-war predecessors. They were scheduled to come to England in 1950, a fine batting side, but short of top class bowling. Before the touring party was chosen they staged some trial matches, however, and two young spin bowlers, neither of whom had played in a first-class match before, were chosen for these games. A nineteen year-old called Sonny Ramadhin from Trinidad who was able to bowl a mixture of leg breaks and off breaks which were difficult to distinguish at slow medium, took twelve wickets and was chosen to tour England. More surprisingly perhaps, Alfred Valentine, who was also nineteen and came from Jamaica, played in these matches as a slow orthodox left arm spinner and after taking only two wickets was selected to go to England.

THE INSCRUTABLE PAIR

These two formed an inscrutable combination, Ramadhin short, shirt sleeves buttoned at the wrists, bowling in his cap with a bustling action, and Valentine on the tall side, slim, lugubrious looking with a slow precise action. Between them, Ramadhin and Valentine gave Goddard's West Indies side the key which turned a very good side into a winning one. England were beaten by three matches to one in the four match series. Valentine took 33 wickets and Ramadhin 26. Of course, the five main batsmen all played very important parts, but it must be doubtful if without their two spinners the West Indies would have had the bowling to beat England. In their eleven years of Test cricket up to the outbreak of the Second War, the West Indies had struggled, at times painfully, to hold their own at the highest level of the game. Now, four years after the war had ended, they had convincingly beaten England in England and their place in the top company was assured as of right.

The two who had made it possible were both rather different from the idea of the typical West Indian cricketer to which Constantine had given birth, but both were in keeping with the part of the world which had produced them. Valentine kept on bowling seemingly for ever, so much so that when he went to Australia with the West Indies in 1951-52 he was known as 'Young Man River' for he just kept bowling along. He pushed the ball through, usually found some turn and gave the batsman no rest.

Ramadhin, who was of Indian extraction, was a more highly strung, temperamentally unpredictable character and was more the conjuror. At that time no one could tell for sure which way the ball was going to turn, he varied his pace cleverly and then there was the one which floated late across the batsman's body from leg to off. Like so many of the great West Indies cricketers they were remarkable in terms of their ability, their sheer virtuosity and as their careers went on, unpredictability. They complemented one another perfectly, but although they were only twenty when they achieved their finest performance, in England in 1950, for some reason they never quite found this devastating form again.

ELEGANT WORRELL

While their 59 wickets – an astonishing achievement – in just four Test Matches destroyed England, the unhurried elegance of Frank Worrell, the almost mechanical beauty of Everton Weekes' strokeplay and the murderous power of Clyde Walcott especially off the back foot were other abiding memories from that tour. So too were the efficient if less glamorous opening partnerships of Rae and Stollmeyer. The first three combined everything that is good about West Indies batsmanship and together showed for the first time that instinct, although supreme, could be effectively disciplined to bring victory. Before the war George Challoner, one of the most correct batsmen the West Indies has produced, and George Headley had both shown that it could be done, but they were without support. Now Rae and Stollmeyer were another indication that the West Indies understood Test cricket and its requirements more fully.

In 1950 it seemed that the West Indies were unbeatable, but eighteen months later they lost 4-1 in Australia. They were unlucky with injuries to Weekes and Walcott, and Ramadhin and Valentine found the pitches less responsive than they had done in England. Another factor probably was that although they had shown in England that they could come to terms with the extravagant demands of their West Indian temperaments, they had not got the upper hand completely.

West Indies sides have always been temperamentally suspect. When they are good they are very, very good, but when things go badly they tend to go really badly. They lost again to Australia 3-0 in the Caribbean in 1954-55. Then, in England in 1957 with Goddard again captain, Ramadhin and Valentine were thwarted by May and Cowdrey in their fourth wicket stand of 411 in the first Test at Birmingham after they had bowled England out for 186 in the first innings and made 475 themselves. The side never recovered from this stand.

SOBERS AND KANHAI IN ENGLAND

This tour was the start of a period of rebuilding for the West Indies. Weekes and Walcott were no longer quite the batsmen they had been, Ramadhin and Valentine were less effective and Sobers and Kanhai made their first tours of England. In the next three years the marvellous side which Worrell took to Australia in 1960-61 and to England in 1963 appeared. First, Gerry Alexander of Jamaica succeeded Goddard as captain while Wes Hall and Lance Gibbs and Seymour Nurse and Cammie Smith and Conrad Hunte filled the main places in the side. This was the nucleus of the side which tied with Australia at Brisbane in the First Test in 1960-61. In that side Hall, Sobers, Kanhai, Smith were all the direct descendants from the spirit of Constantine while Worrell himself, Hunte and Alexander who had such a wonderful series with the bat, and at times the others too, had added the extra dimension of discipline to this same spirit without detracting one wit from the entertainment value of the side at the same time as increasing enormously the success potential although the series was eventually lost.

EXPLOSIVE GRIFFITH

By 1963 the explosive qualities of Charlie Griffith and the dapper precise batting methods of Basil Butcher had been added to the above side. But most important of all, Worrell, the captain, had managed to weld his team together in a way which almost completely conquered the West Indian temperament. Nothing was left to chance any more. This was to be Worrell's last Test series, however, and within four years he was dead, a tragic victim of leukaemia.

Sobers was his natural successor and in 1966 almost the same side again beat England convincingly, but then once more age began to take its toll. It is at times like these that the minute-to-minute tactical considerations of a good captain are so important to a side and which enable it to keep together. When Sobers took over Worrell's side it captained itself to a large extent, but when the West Indies reached Australia in 1968-69 they were past their best. After winning the first Test they lost the second at Melbourne and then fell apart in a remarkable way, losing the series 3-1. Sobers did not have the same authority over his side as Worrell and on a short tour of England the following summer the West Indies lost two of the three Test Matches and they entered another period of rebuilding.

EVERGREEN GIBBS

The vast reservoirs of natural talent in the Caribbean islands seem to be unending and soon successors for Worrell's old side were being found. It was not quite such an easy transition as that of the late 1950s though, and the West Indies had to suffer the humiliation of losing a series to India in the West Indies and then, in the following year at home, of failing to beat New Zealand in any of the five Test Matches on their first ever tour of the West Indies. After that tour Sobers was replaced by Kanhai as captain and by now Clive Lloyd, Vanburn Holder, Keith Boyce, Bernard Julien, Alvin Kallicharran, Roy Fredericks and Lawrence Rowe were taking over from the previous generation, although Gibbs bowled his off breaks as well as ever and remained a link between the old and the new.

The next winter Australia won by two matches to nil in the Caribbean, but by then it was obvious that the new West Indies side was about to break through and become probably as good as its predecessors. But the first victory proved elusive and after losing a splendid game of cricket to Australia in the fourth Test at Port of Spain, the innate weakness of temperament showed itself again and they were beaten unnecessarily badly in the last Test Match at Georgetown.

ANOTHER FORMIDABLE SIDE

In 1973 they were back in England again and now at last everything came right for them. They won two Tests out of three against England and were a formidable side. Again it was all based on the spirit of Constantine. Fredericks and Kanhai and Lloyd and Kallicharran played thrilling innings and Boyce, Julien and Holder bowled England out. But now it was left to Sobers with an impressive innings of 150 and occasionally Kanhai and some of the others to provide the stabilising element when it was required. They were checked very surprisingly the following winter by Denness's England side which, although completely outplayed for the first three Test Matches managed to win the last at Port of Spain and to draw the series. This was Sobers' last series and also Kanhai's. He was replaced by Clive Lloyd as captain and by now three more exciting players, Andy Roberts, their fastest bowler since Hall, Vivian Richards and Gordon Greenidge had come into the side. The first two came from Antigua, which was an indication of the improvement shown by the smaller islands in the West Indies.

"WORLD CHAMPIONS"

After winning an exciting series in India by the odd Test Match in five, Lloyd brought his side to England last summer where they won the Prudential Cup for the first-ever one-day world championship, beating Australia narrowly in a thrilling finish to a wonderfully successful competition. It was therefore as "World Champions" that the West Indies went to Australia at the start of an arduous twelve months' cricket. On their return from Australia they were due to play four Tests against India before undertaking a full tour of England in 1976 which will mean playing fifteen Test Matches in ten months.

ENGLAND v WEST INDIES

First Test Match

Played at Nottingham, June 3, 4, 5, 7, 8, 1976

Drawn. A marvellous innings of 232 by the 24-year-old Vivian Richards overshadowed everything else in this match. England had to struggle to save the follow-on but thanks to Steele, who hit his first Test century, and steady work also by Woolmer, Edrich and Close the West Indies were held at bay. They entered the match without a spinner of any class and their ill-balanced attack of four seam bowlers failed to dismiss England twice in the last three days. The match was patronized by good sized crowds who altogether paid £65,000.

If little went right for England during the first two days after Lloyd won the toss, it was the policy of attempting to contain the West Indies batsmen with a run-saving field that proved a failure. Not until a quarter to six when the total was 235 did Greig call on Underwood and so the West Indies made 274 on the opening day for the loss of only their opening pair, Fredericks and Greenidge.

Hendrick, who so often breaks down through strains, bowled throughout the two-hour first session and he performed magnificently, but he was not fit to take part in the next Test at Lord's.

Although there were moments when Richards played and missed, his display was more notable for brilliant strokes all round the wicket and particularly his stylish and powerful driving off the front foot. Kallicharran concentrated more on defence and at the close on Thursday Richards (143) had completed his ninth hundred since January; Kallicharran was 52.

Next day, the pair remained together until 2.30 p.m., their stand producing 303, of which Kallicharran's share was 97. Richards finished in a blaze of glory, for he hit 36 runs off the last thirteen balls he received before Greig on the long off boundary held a steepling catch. Richards batted seven hours twenty-five minutes and struck four 6s and thirty-one 4s. When Kallicharran was held at backward point he had batted six hours.

Following their departure the bowlers came into their own with the West Indies bent on pushing the score along. England, after spending eleven hours in the field, were thankful that bad light caused a delay of nearly an hour so there was time for only one over at the end of the day, which was safely negotiated by Edrich who played a maiden to Roberts.

On the third morning Brearley, in his first Test, and Close, recalled to the Test scene after an interval of nine years, both failed. Edrich stayed three hours, taking the score to 98 with Steele against some hostile bowling by Roberts, Holder and Daniel. Julien, too, commanded respect with his varied movement. Daniel, of great pace, was erratic at first and warned for running on the pitch, but he found a better length as the day advanced. At the close when Steele was 105 and Woolmer 52, England had reached 221 for three and looked comparatively safe, but after the rest on Sunday West Indies regained the upper hand.

Now Daniel had the new ball instead of Julien. He sent down two wides and received a final warning from umpire Bird for running on the pitch. Then in his second over he induced Steele to hook a short ball to Roberts at long leg. He batted over six hours. Thereupon Greig and Knott went cheaply, and with Woolmer, who had stayed four and a half hours, leg before playing back to Julien, it was questionable whether England could make the opposition bat again.

Worse followed when Old had to go to hospital after being struck on the wrist by Roberts, but Snow lasted nearly two hours and so West Indies had to be content with a ead of 162.

As if inspired by his batting, Snow bowled splendidly, as did Underwood when West ndies needed to score quickly. England objected when Greenidge was limping and King not playing in the match) appeared as his runner; he was replaced by Gomes. Next, the atsmen protested that Old distracted them with a white bandage on his damaged left orearm; so the Yorkshireman rolled down both sleeves to please them. Richards was gain in fine form, and West Indies were 124 for three at the close of the fourth day.

Julien fell to the first ball of the final day but Kallicharran hit freely. In seven overs hared by Snow and Old, West Indies put on 52 in thirty-five minutes and then Lloyd, at is own dismissal, declared, setting England to get 339 to win in five and a quarter hours, a ask that was never entertained.

For once, Steele failed, but Brearley stayed fifty minutes. After the fall of the second vicket at 55, the two left-handers, Edrich and Close, assumed command. West Indies elaxed and four batsmen took over from the regular bowlers on a dry pitch that had lost ts pace.

From England's point of view it had been a disappointing performance.

West Indies

R. C. Fredericks c Hendrick b Greig	42	– b Snow	15
C. G. Greenidge c Edrich b Hendrick	22	– c and b Old	23
. V. A. Richards c Greig b Underwood	232	– lbw b Snow	63
A. I. Kallicharran c Steele b Underwood	97	– not out	29
C. H. Lloyd c Hendrick b Underwood	16	– c Brearley b Snow	21
B. D. Julien c Knott b Old	21	– c Hendrick b Snow	13
H. A. Gomes c Close b Underwood	0		
D. L. Murray c Close b Snow	19		
V. A. Holder not out	19		
A. M. E. Roberts b Old	1		
W. W. Daniel c Knott b Old	4		
L-b 12, w 1, n-b 8	21	L-b 6, w 2, n-b 4	12
/36 2/105 3/408 4/423 /432 6/432 7/458 8/481 9/488	494	1/33 2/77 3/109 4/124 5/176	(5 wkts dec.) 176

Bowling: *First Innings*—Snow 31–5–123–1; Hendrick 24–7–59–1; Old 34.3–7–80–3; Greig 27–4–82–1; Woolmer 10–2–47–0; Underwood 27–8–82–4; *Second Innings*—Hendrick –2–22–0; Snow 11–2–53–4; Underwood 7–3–9–0; Old 10–0–64–1; Greig 1–0–16–0.

England

. H. Edrich c Murray b Daniel	37	– not out	76
. M. Brearley c Richards b Julien	0	– c Murray b Holder	17
D. S. Steele c Roberts b Daniel	106	– c Julien b Roberts	6
D. B. Close c Murray b Daniel	2	– not out	36
. A. Woolmer lbw b Julien	82		
A. W. Greig b Roberts	0		
A. P. E. Knott c sub b Holder	9		
C. M. Old b Daniel	33		
. A. Snow not out	20		
D. L. Underwood c Murray b Holder	0		
M. Hendrick c Daniel b Fredericks	5		
B 5, l-b 1, w 3, n-b 29	38	B 9, w 2, n-b 10	21
/0 2/98 3/105 4/226 /229 6/255 7/278 8/278 9/318	332	1/38 2/55	(2 wkts) 156

Bowling: *First Innings*—Roberts 34–15–53–1; Julien 34–9–75–2; Holder 25–5–66–2; Dani 23–8–53–4; Fredericks 8.4–2–24–1; Richards 3–1–8–0; Gomes 4–1–8–0; Lloyd 3–1–7–0. *Secon Innings*—Roberts 9–3–20–1; Julien 16–8–19–0; Daniel 10–2–20–0; Holder 12–6–12– Fredericks 9–1–21–0; Richards 3–1–7–0; Gomes 9–1–18–0; Kallicharran 10–3–18–0.

Umpires: T. W. Spencer and H. D. Bird.

MIDDLESEX v WEST INDIES

Played at Lord's, July 31, August 2, 3, 1976

Middlesex won by four wickets, inflicting on West Indies the first defeat of their tour. Th badly under-strength Middlesex team performed wonders to hustle West Indies ou cheaply. All the batsmen attacked, but only Greenidge, in a cascade of unstoppable dazzling strokes, succeeded. He hit one 6 and twenty 4s in two and a quarter hours Middlesex were 160 for three at the close of the first day, Smith having played some crisp decisive strokes. Edmonds hit powerfully on the second morning and Clark, making hi first appearance for the county since 1968, provided a glimpse of past glories. Robert broke their stand, but Padmore returned his best tour figures to that date in working hi way through the rest.

The West Indies batsmen again surged away with fierce, reckless stroke-play, 14 coming in the opening 25 overs. Richards played more calmly than most and Murray an Roberts had to stabilize matters, Roberts eventually driving Titmus for two vast 6s Middlesex wanted 274 and had almost all the last day to make them. Smith and Brearle recorded their third century partnership in the last four innings and they were half-wa there before a wicket fell. Butcher followed the openers' methodical example, but Smith' departure at 240 introduced an abrupt collapse as Middlesex stuttered at the gates o victory. When it came, it was their first over a touring team since the 1936 Indians. A strange feature of the match was that five wicket-keepers were used, Brearley and ther Butcher replacing the injured Kinkead-Weekes and Findlay relieving Murray.

West Indies

R. C. Fredericks lbw b Selvey	4	– b Titmus	4
C. G. Greenidge c Emburey b Titmus	123	– c Featherstone b Emburey	6
I. V. A. Richards b Selvey	4	– b Titmus	5
H. A. Gomes b Emburey	28	– b Emburey	
B. D. Julien b Titmus	9	– c and b Featherstone	1
C. L. King lbw b Selvey	13	– c Emburey b Featherstone	
*D. L. Murray b Selvey	1	– c and b Emburey	3
†T. M. Findlay lbw b Titmus	9	– c Emburey b Featherstone	1
A. M. E. Roberts not out	8	– not out	5
A. L. Padmore b Titmus	0	– c sub b Featherstone	
R. R. Jumadeen b Titmus	1	– c Emburey b Selvey	
B 12, l-b 6, w 1, n-b 3	22	B 16, l-b 2, n-b 2	2
1/4 2/17 3/85 4/144 5/174 6/198 7/200 8/214 9/214	222	1/89 2/146 3/151 4/174 5/176 6/204 7/227 8/285 9/302	30

Bowling: *First Innings*—Selvey 18–3–58–4; Lamb 8–1–43–0; Emburey 8–0–28–1; Butche 2–0–30–0; Titmus 11.3–2–41–5. *Second Innings*—Selvey 10.5–1–35–1; Lamb 9–0–63–0 Emburey 26–4–86–3; Titmus 19–6–54–2; Featherstone 22–7–50–4.

Лiddlesex

1. J. Smith lbw b Padmore	95 – c Greenidge b Julien	108
J. M. Brearley c Findlay b Padmore	39 – c Julien b Padmore	62
.. O. Butcher c Richards b Padmore	2 – lbw b Padmore	45
I. G. Featherstone c Fredericks b Padmore	20 – c Fredericks b King	21
. M. Lamb b Padmore	9 – c Richards b Padmore	0
. H. Edmonds c Findlay b Roberts	53 – c Greenidge b Padmore	20
'. A. Clark c Richards b King	26 – not out	6
E. Emburey b Padmore	2 – not out	4
'. J. Titmus b King	0	
1. W. W. Selvey not out	0	
R. C. Kinkead-Weekes absent hurt	0	
B 1, l-b 7, n-b 3	11	L-b 3, n-b 6 9
	257	(6 wkts) 275

/101 2/113 3/155 4/163 — 1/131 2/208
/189 6/238 7/252 8/256 9/257 — 3/240 4/265 5/265 6/266

Bowling: *First Innings*—Roberts 13–1–51–1; King 15–3–44–2; Gomes 6–2–21–0; Padmore 9–9–69–6; Jumadeen 24–6–61–0. *Second Innings*—Roberts 12–0–40–0; King 15–5–27–1; ;omes 5–2–13–0; Padmore 32.3–6–78–4; Jumadeen 25–7–54–0; Julien 12–2–54–1.

Umpires: H. Horton and J. G. Langridge.

GLAMORGAN v WEST INDIES

Played at Swansea, August 7, 9, 10, 1976

Vest Indies won by an innings and 141 runs. After failing by only four minutes to score ıe fastest century of the season, Clive Lloyd launched a merciless assault on the ;lamorgan bowlers and sent the West Indies total soaring to 554 for four off 84 overs. .loyd reached his hundred in eighty minutes and his second hundred took only forty ıinutes. It was the fastest double century since Gilbert Jessop's days in 1903. Chief ıilestones of West Indies' marathon innings were: Greenidge's seventh century of the tour ı two hours, eighteen minutes; it included three 6s and twenty 4s. Richards' hundred took n minutes longer and included two 6s and twenty-one 4s. Their third wicket partnership ealized 224 and the fourth wicket partnership between Lloyd and Rowe produced 287 in wo hours four minutes, a West Indies record for that wicket in Britain. Lloyd hit seven 6s nd twenty-eight 4s.

;lamorgan

A. Jones c Daniel b Julien	42 – lbw b Julien	26
'. L. Powell b Daniel	0 – b Holding	0
). A. Francis c Lloyd b Gomes	36 – b Julien	53
Лajid J. Khan c Julien b Padmore	22 – b Holding	21
. A. Hopkins c Lloyd b Padmore	27 – b Julien	2
l. C. Ontong lbw b Holding	34 – lbw b Julien	0
Л. A. Nash c Richards b Padmore	64 – b Julien	1
E. W. Jones b Holding	13 – b Holding	13
. J. Lloyd c Julien b Padmore	3 – not out	13
. E. Cordle not out	8 – c Findlay b Julien	4
. W. Allin b Padmore	4 – st Findlay b Padmore	5
L-b 4, n-b 9	13	B 5, l-b 2, w 1, n-b 1 9
	266	147

/4 2/56 3/95 4/137 — 1/37 2/73 3/75 4/79
/137 6/233 7/239 8/254 9/256 — 5/85 6/119 7/125 8/125 9/130

Bowling: *First Innings*—Holding 16–6–67–2; Daniel 6–2–15–1; Julien 17–4–50–1; Lloy 7–4–13–0; Padmore 20.4–6–84–5; Gomes 8–3–24–1. *Second Innings*—Holding 10–4–21– Daniel 4–0–30–0; Julien 17–5–54–6; Padmore 14.4–5–30–1; Fredericks 3–1–3–0.

West Indies

R. C. Fredericks lbw b Cordle	2	*C. H. Lloyd not out	2(
C. G. Greenidge b Lloyd	130	B 4, l-b 6, n-b 2	
I. V. A. Richards c Nash b Allin	121		—
L. G. Rowe c Ontong b Allin	88	1/3 2/227 3/267 4/554	(4 wkts) 5

H. A. Gomes, B. D. Julien, †T. M. Findlay, M. A. Holding, W. W. Daniel and A. L. Padmore d not bat.

Bowling: Nash 12–0–77–0; Cordle 16–1–83–1; Ontong 13–0–92–0; Allin 19.3–1–128– Lloyd 23–0–162–1.

Umpires: A. Jepson and A. G. T. Whitehead.

ENGLAND v WEST INDIES

Fifth Test Match

Played at The Oval, August 12, 13, 14, 16, 17, 1976

West Indies won by 231 runs and retained the Wisden Trophy by winning the series 3- The previous time England went down by a similar margin in a home series was in 194 against Bradman's Australia side. West Indies, moreover, recorded their fifth victory in th last eight Tests in England, and many by wide margins.

This contest produced many splendid personal performances. Holding achieved tw bowling records for West Indies by taking eight first innings wickets for 92 and with six fc 57 on the fifth day his full analysis was fourteen for 149 – a great triumph for one of th world's fastest bowlers of all time.

After Lloyd had won the toss for the fourth time in the five Tests, Richards gave ye another glorious display with the bat. Making 291 out of 519, he hit thirty-eight 4s in stay of eight minutes short of eight hours.

For England, Amiss made a memorable return to the Test Match scene. He looked th only class batsman in the side as he held the England first innings together by scoring 20 out of 342 before being seventh to leave, bowled behind his legs. He played nobly for fiv hours, twenty minutes and struck twenty-eight 4s.

While West Indies retained the eleven which won the previous Test at Headingle England showed three changes. Amiss was preferred to Hayes, and with Snow and War unfit Selvey returned and Miller received his first cap after Edmonds had withdrawn fro the original selection because of a sore spinning finger. Miller had an excellent match a an off-spinner and stylish bat.

Willis struck early for England when he removed Greenidge leg-before, but Richard soon took charge and with Fredericks and Rowe providing sound assistance West Indie reached 373 for three by the end of the first day. Greig caused a surprise when, after Will had dismissed Greenidge with the last ball of his second over, he put on Underwood. superb right hand catch by Balderstone who dived to his right at cover dismisse Fredericks and at six o'clock Knott stumped Rowe for his 220th victim in Tests agains other countries and beat Godfrey Evans's record.

Richards, 200 overnight, continued his majestic exhibition and he and Lloyd put on 14 in the 32 overs England sent down on the second day before lunch, Richards getting 83 t Lloyd's 48. So Richards passed Sir Frank Worrell's 261 at Trent Bridge in 1950, th previous best for West Indies in England. One imagined that he would challenge Sir Gary Sobers' 365, the highest for all Tests, but having driven Greig high towards the Vauxhall End he went to repeat the stroke next ball only to touch it into his stumps.

During this period Greig bowled his off spin with much skill and he accounted for Lloyd at 547, but the runs still flowed until shortly before half past five, Lloyd declared, setting England the task of making 488 to prevent the follow on. West Indies' total of 687 was their highest in England, beating their 552 at Lord's three years earlier.

With the pitch slow and dusty, the West Indies decision to rely on the pacemen to the exclusion of any recognized spinner caused a good deal of comment, but Holding's speed through the air provided the answer, particularly as his side had so many runs on the board.

Amiss and Woolmer safely negotiated the 12 overs they faced at the end of the second day when some classic strokes by Amiss (22) helped the score to 34 without loss. Next morning, Holding began his devastating work by getting Woolmer leg before to a ball that kept low. Then Steele defended steadily while putting on 100 with Amiss before also being plainly leg-before. As Holding promptly removed Balderstone, England were in sore straits, but Willey resolutely kept up his end in a stand of 128 and all the while Amiss imbued confidence by the way he faced the bouncers, taking two quick steps back with a very open stance.

Greig raised hopes of a long stay with two grand cover drives off Holding, but trying again he was bowled off his pads. A disgraceful scene followed. A huge section of the crowd, mainly West Indians, swept over the ground and trampled on the pitch with the departure of the England captain. The umpires led the players off the field at about 6.10 p.m. When peace was restored Amiss and Underwood played out the last seven minutes, England's total at the week-end being 304 for five with Amiss 178.

Amiss again played well on Monday morning, but Underwood soon became another Holding victim. There was spirited late resistance by Knott and Miller but West Indies finished the half way stage with a lead of 252.

With Daniel injured and Holding needing a rest, Lloyd preferred to bat again and leave England to face the last innings. This time, the two West Indies openers enjoyed themselves at the England bowlers' expense and in two hours, twenty minutes took their unbroken partnership to 182, Greenidge hitting twelve 4s and Fredericks nine.

So Lloyd left England six hours, twenty minutes to get the runs or save the match and although Woolmer and Amiss hit freely on the fourth evening for 43, the first hour of the fifth day left England without a ghost of a chance. Half the wickets crashed for 78 and although Knott made his second fifty and Miller was again in form the West Indies sailed home with eighty minutes to spare.

The total attendance for the match was 70,000 with receipts £58,395. The full attendance for the series came to 383,000 and the gross receipts £465,000.

West Indies

R. C. Fredericks c Balderstone b Miller	71	– not out	86
C. G. Greenidge lbw b Willis	0	– not out	85
I. V. A. Richards b Greig	291		
L. G. Rowe st Knott b Underwood	70		
*C. H. Lloyd c Knott b Greig	84		
C. L. King c Selvey b Balderstone	63		
†D. L. Murray c and b Underwood	36		
V. A. Holder not out	13		
M. A. Holding b Underwood	32		
B 1, l-b 17, n-b 9	27	B 4, l-b 1, w 1, n-b 5	11
1/5 2/159 3/350 4/524 5/547 6/640 7/642 8/687	(8 wkts dec.) 687		(no wkt dec.) 182

A. M. E. Roberts and W. W. Daniel did not bat.

Bowling: *First Innings:*—Willis 15–3–71–1; Selvey 15–0–67–0; Underwood 60.5–15–165–3 Woolmer 9–0–44–0; Miller 27–4–106–1; Balderstone 16–0–80–1; Greig 34–5–96–2; Willey 3–0–11–0; Steele 3–0–18–0. *Second Innings*—Willis 7–0–48–0; Selvey 9–1–44–0; Underwood 9–2–38–0; Woolmer 5–0–30–0; Greig 2–0–11–0.

England

D. L. Amiss b Holding	203	– c Greenidge b Holding	1
R. A. Woolmer lbw b Holding	8	– c Murray b Holding	3
D. S. Steele lbw b Holding	44	– c Murray b Holder	4
J. C. Balderstone b Holding	0	– b Holding	
P. Willey c Fredericks b King	33	– c Greenidge b Holder	1
*A. W. Greig b Holding	12	– b Holding	1
D. L. Underwood b Holding	4	– c Lloyd b Roberts	2
†A. P. E. Knott b Holding	50	– b Holding	5
G. Miller c sub b Holder	36	– b Richards	24
M. W. W. Selvey b Holding	0	– not out	4
R. G. D. Willis not out	5	– lbw b Holding	
B 8, l-b 11, n-b 21	40	B 15, l-b 3, w 8	2
1/47 2/147 3/151 4/279 5/303 6/323 7/342 8/411 9/411	435	1/49 2/54 3/64 4/77 5/78 6/148 7/196 8/196 9/202	20

Bowling: *First Innings*—Roberts 27–4–102–0; Holding 33–9–92–8; Holder 27.5–7–75–1 Daniel 10–1–30–0; Fredericks 11–2–36–0; Richards 14–4–30–0; King 7–3–30–1. *Second Innings*—Roberts 13–4–37–1; Holding 20.4–6–57–6; Holder 14–5–29–2; Fredericks 12–5–33–0 Richards 11–6–11–1; King 6–2–9–0; Lloyd 2–1–1–0.

Umpires: W. E. Alley and H. D. Bird.

WARWICKSHIRE v WEST INDIANS

Played at Birmingham, August 2, 3, 4, 1980

Drawn. Warwickshire, without Amiss, became only the fourth county to avoid defeat by the touring team, after declining to go for a target of 320 in 255 minutes. Play ended fifty minutes early on the first day with the county at 11 without loss in reply to the West Indians' 315, of which Kallicharran and Richards added 125 for the fifth wicket. Warwickshire began shakily on the Sunday, losing three early wickets before Humpage and Oliver punished an under-strength attack in a robust stand of 118 off nineteen overs. Ferreira added 30, but the early momentum was not maintained and the innings closed 92 behind. The West Indians had increased their lead to 158 at the start of the last day and Richards made a spectacular 41 which included three 6s and five 4s; in seven consecutive balls from Clifford he hit 4-6-6-4-4-6-4. Smith later countered with a solid 86, hitting one 6 and twelve 4s.

West Indians

D. L. Haynes c Smith b Oliver . . . . 62 – lbw b Ferreira 20
S. F. A. Bacchus c Humpage b Small . . . . 25 – b Small 1
Timur Mohamed c Willis b Ferreira . . . . 2 – c Humpage b Small 45
C. L. King b Ferreira . . . . 4 – c Lloyd b Willis 3
A. I. Kallicharran c Humpage b Ferreira . . . . 75 – (6) lbw b Doshi 38
*I. V. A. Richards c Oliver b Small . . . . 62 – (7) st Humpage b Doshi 41
†D. L. Murray lbw b Willis . . . . 30 – (9) not out 10
D. A. Murray c and b Doshi . . . . 3 – (5) b Clifford 49
D. R. Parry run out . . . . 9 – (8) not out 5
M. D. Marshall not out 32
A. M. E. Roberts lbw b Willis 0
B 1, l-b 5, w 1, n-b 4 11   B 3, l-b 6, w 1, n-b 5 15

1/43 2/64 3/93 4/105 5/230 6/241 7/247 8/264 9/315 — 315   1/8 2/42 3/66 4/105 5/171 6/171 7/214 — (7 wkts dec.) 227

Bowling: *First Innings*—Willis 11–4–37–2; Small 13–3–55–2; Ferreira 18–6–50–3; Oliver 5–0–24–1; Clifford 22–6–60–0; Doshi 31–9–78–1. *Second Innings*—Willis 9–1–25–1; Small 14–5–36–2; Ferreira 9–1–42–1; Doshi 19–4–65–2; Clifford 11–2–44–1.

Warwickshire

K. D. Smith b King . . . . 25 – c D. A. Murray b Richards 86
T. A. Lloyd b Roberts . . . . 2 – retired hurt 24
J. A. Claughton retired hurt 9
†G. W. Humpage c D. A. Murray b Roberts . . . . 62 – (3) c D. L. Murray b Marshall 0
J. Whitehouse lbw b Marshall . . . . 4 – (4) c sub b Parry 3
P. R. Oliver b Parry . . . . 57 – (5) not out 35
A. M. Ferreira lbw b Marshall . . . . 30 – (6) not out 25
G. C. Small c D. A. Murray b Parry 1
*R. G. D. Willis b Marshall 5
D. R. Doshi st D. L. Murray b Parry 3
C. C. Clifford not out 0
B 6, l-b 7, w 4, n-b 8 25   B 1, l-b 1, w 1, n-b 4 7

1/13 2/42 3/51 4/184 5/190 6/211 7/216 8/221 9/223 — 223   1/43 2/67 3/133 — (3 wkts) 180

Bowling: *First Innings*—Roberts 16–5–45–2; Marshall 16–5–29–3; King 15–4–59–1; Parry 17.2–5–54–3; Richards 3–1–11–0. *Second Innings*—Roberts 4–3–4–0; Marshall 11–5–19–1; King 11–1–34–0; Parry 29–8–70–1; Richards 14–3–37–1; D. A. Murray 1–0–1–0; Bacchus 1–0–8–0.

Umpires: D. J. Halfyard and A. Jepson.

NEW ZEALANDERS IN ENGLAND

ENGLAND v NEW ZEALAND

Third Test Match

Played at Leeds, July 8, 9, 10, 12, 13, 1965

England won by an innings and 187 runs. This match was a triumph for Surrey in th persons of John Edrich and Barrington. Both men made a glorious return to the Englan team. The left-handed Edrich, after hitting a century on his dèbut against Australia a Lord's the previous summer, was left out of the Oval Test and by MCC for the tour t South Africa. Barrington reappeared after being dropped for his negative attitude durin the first Test with New Zealand a month earlier.

Edrich, 310 not out, gained the distinction of being only the eighth batsman in th history of Test cricket to score a triple century. Sir Donald Bradman stands alone. H performed the feat twice on this very ground, 334 and 304. The other six are G. S. Sober 365 not out; Sir Leonard Hutton, 364; Hanif Mohammad 337; W. R. Hammond, 336 nc out; A. Sandham, 325 and R. B. Simpson 311.

Edrich's 310 was also the highest by an Englishman in Test or County cricket a Headingley and the England total, 546 for four declared, the highest in England agains New Zealand.

Batting for eight minutes short of nine hours, Edrich hit five 6s and fifty-two 4s. H scored more runs in boundaries than any other Test player. For instance, Sobers' 36 not out for West Indies against Pakistan at Kingston in March, 1958 contained thirty eight 4s.

The partnership of 369 in five hours, thirty-nine minutes was the best in Tests betwee England and New Zealand and fell only 13 runs behind England's highest second-wick stand against all countries of 382 by Hutton and Leyland against Australia at The Oval i 1938. It was also only 42 short of England's highest for any wicket, 411 by P. B. H. Ma and M. C. Cowdrey against West Indies at Edgbaston in 1957.

With such a feast of runs the feat of F. J. Titmus on the fourth day when he took fou wickets in six balls scarcely received the acclaim it deserved.

Apart from a bitterly cold north wind, the conditions were perfect for the batsmen After Smith won the toss Barber soon revealed the fast pace on the outfield when he cu the fourth ball, from Motz, to the boundary. Barber did not last long, being taken behin the stumps by Ward, making his first appearance against England.

So Barrington joined Edrich at five minutes to twelve and they remained together unti noon the next day. Edrich, having spent half an hour before scoring, took his cue fron Barrington who needed only fifteen scoring strokes, cuts, pulls, and drives, to complete 5 out of 89. Motz always bowled splendidly and quietened Barrington with two maide overs.

The tempo increased after lunch when all trace of greenness disappeared from the pitch Edrich became the dominant partner and he overtook Barrington when he straight drov Yuile for 6, which took him to 93. Still, Barrington was first to his century, in under thre hours. Edrich excelled with the cover drive which he placed with perfect precision and h celebrated his 150 by driving Pollard for his second 6 and soon came his third, also fron Pollard – a mighty on-drive into the corner of the cricket-football stand.

Two breaks for rain gave New Zealand no respite and the close of the first day found England 366 for one wicket; Edrich 194, Barrington 152. Strangely, it was a moot point whether either of this pair would have played in the match, but for mishaps to Boycott and Dexter.

Next day, Motz took the new ball in the one hundredth over with England still 366, following two maiden overs. Barrington added only 11, including two 4s from Motz, when he touched a rising ball to Ward. He hit twenty-six 4s and an overthrow credited him with a 7. Edrich was 199 when he lost Barrington, and he remained the centre of interest. Parfitt hit only two 4s but he helped to add 109 in ninety-seven minutes.

Whether concentrating on defence or making progress with the cover and straight drive besides the cut, Edrich rarely looked like getting out. He offered difficult slip chances when 40 and 287 and he had his quiet periods. Then he would let fly again.

Not for Edrich the stolen single to reach a coveted landmark. It was a superb off drive from Motz which whistled past the field that took Edrich to 300 and he added two more boundaries before Smith called halt to the onslaught.

New Zealand never wilted in the field. The three pace bowlers, Motz, Collinge and Taylor, shouldered the main burden and their final figures scarcely did justice to their hours of honest toil.

New Zealand's performance with the bat provided an anti-climax. Not for the first time the innings disintegrated. Four wickets went for 61, but as at Edgbaston and Lord's, Pollard played the bowling confidently and this time Reid sealed the opposite end. The New Zealand captain drove cleanly and pulled Illingworth for 6, besides hitting nine 4s when almost on the stroke of time he played back to the Yorkshireman's medium pace and was leg before.

New Zealand resumed on Saturday with their total 100 for five, but when it seemed doubtful if they could survive the week-end rain held up cricket. The tail made a noble response in raising the total to 193, but they followed on 353 behind. Larter and Illingworth, both playing for the first time for England this season, shared the bowling honours with four wickets each.

New Zealand virtually began their second innings, in bright sunshine, on Monday – seven balls were bowled without a run on Saturday – and this time Dowling batted well for one hundred minutes before being yorked by Rumsey. At lunch the total reached 86 for three, but the weather turned dull and rain caused two delays.

Pollard again shaped soundly and Yuile lasted an hour in seeing the total to 158 for five before Titmus removed Yuile, Taylor, Motz and Collinge in the course of six deliveries and yet was denied a hat-trick: W.WW.W. His full analysis read 24–17–16–5 and he did not receive the slightest help from the pitch.

As rain prevented any play during the last seventy minutes, New Zealand still had one wicket left. Next morning Ward and Pollard lasted fifteen minutes before Cowdrey held Pollard at slip; it was only just in time. As the players left the field the rain returned and soon the ground was waterlogged. Edrich had the unusual experience of being on the field throughout the match.

England

R. W. Barber c Ward b Taylor	13	*M. J. K. Smith not out	2
J. H. Edrich not out	310	B 4, l-b 8, n-b 1	13
K. F. Barrington c Ward b Motz	163		
M. C. Cowdrey b Taylor	13	1/13 2/382 3/407	(4 wkts dec.) 546
P. H. Parfitt b Collinge	32	4/516	

†J. M. Parks, R. Illingworth, F. J. Titmus, F. E. Rumsey and J. D. F. Larter did not bat.

Bowling: Motz 41–8–140–1; Taylor 40–8–140–2; Collinge 32–7–87–1; Yuile 17–5–80–0; Morgan 6–0–28–0; Pollard 11–2–46–0; Congdon 4–0–12–0.

New Zealand

G. T. Dowling c Parks b Larter	5	– b Rumsey	41
B. E. Congdon c Parks b Rumsey	13	– b Rumsey	1
B. W. Sinclair c Smith b Larter	13	– lbw b Larter	29
*J. R. Reid lbw b Illingworth	54	– c Barrington b Rumsey	5
R. W. Morgan b Illingworth	1	– b Titmus	21
V. Pollard run out	33	– c Cowdrey b Larter	53
B. W. Yuile b Larter	46	– c Cowdrey b Titmus	12
B. R. Taylor c Parks b Illingworth	9	– c and b Titmus	0
R. C. Motz c Barber b Illingworth	3	– c Barrington b Titmus	0
†J. T. Ward not out	0	– not out	2
R. O. Collinge b Larter	8	– b Titmus	0
B 5, l-b 1, w 2	8	N-b 2	2
1/15 2/19 3/53 4/61 5/100 6/153 7/165 8/173 9/181	193	1/4 2/67 3/75 4/86 5/111 6/158 7/158 8/158 9/158	166

Bowling: *First Innings*—Rumsey 24–6–59–1; Larter 28.1–6–66–4; Illingworth 28–14–42–4; Titmus 6–2–16–0; Barber 2–0–2–0. *Second Innings*—Rumsey 15–5–49–3; Larter 22–10–54–2; Illingworth 7–0–28–0; Titmus 26–17–19–5; Barber 14–7–14–0.

Umpires: C. S. Elliott and J. F. Crapp.

HAMPSHIRE v NEW ZEALANDERS

Played at Southampton, August 13, 14, 15, 1969

Drawn. Rain ruined this match, restricting the second day to two hours, forty minutes, and washing out the third completely. The first day, which lost the last hour to bad light, provided superb entertainment, thanks to an exhilarating innings by Richards after the New Zealanders had sent Hampshire in. Richards made them suffer for this decision on another excellent batting strip at Southampton. He scored his third hundred of the season with a full range of strokes, coupled with fine defensive technique, that brought him twenty-six 4s in a stay of three and a quarter hours. Gilliat, too, was in good form before hooking Collinge to long-leg when one short of 100. Hampshire's makeshift attack, which included Worrell, a regular soldier and a distant relative of the late Sir Frank Worrell, could make little headway against Dowling and Murray, who put on 94 before being parted by Holder, who bowled his off-spin steadily. The rain brought an untimely end to what had promised to be a grand contest.

Hampshire

B. A. Richards c sub b Cunis	132
R. V. Lewis c Hastings b Cunis	20
D. R. Turner c Collinge b Yuile	21
*R. M. C. Gilliat c Yuile b Collinge	99
P. J. Sainsbury not out	45
K. J. Wheatley not out	0
B 7, l-b 5, n-b 1	13
1/35 2/77 3/214 4/330	(4 wkts dec.) 330

T. E. Jesty, L. R. Worrell, †G. R. Stephenson, J. W. Holder and W. D. Buck did not bat.

Bowling: Collinge 15.3–4–42–1; Taylor 24–5–65–0; Cunis 21–3–84–2; Yuile 19–4–81–1; Pollard 11–3–23–0; Burgess 6–1–22–0.

New Zealanders

*G. T. Dowling b Holder	48
B. A. G. Murray c Stephenson b Holder	55
B. F. Hastings not out	7
M. G. Burgess not out	8
B 1	1
1/94 2/107	(2 wkts) 119

V. Pollard, B. W. Yuile, B. R. Taylor, K. J. Wadsworth, R. S. Cunis, R. O. Collinge and †B. D. Milburn did not bat.

Bowling: Holder 12–4–38–2; Buck 14–4–25–0; Jesty 9–3–21–0; Worrell 11–4–25–0; Sainsbury 4–2–9–0.

Umpires: G. H. Pope and H. Mellows.

GLENN TURNER JOINS THE ELITE

1,000 RUNS BY THE END OF MAY

By Basil Easterbrook

Glenn Maitland Turner was born in Dunedin, most appropriately in the month of May. Between April 24 and May 31, 1973, in eleven matches for the seventh official touring side of New Zealand to England he scored 1,018 runs, a feat which had not been accomplished for thirty-five years. In doing so he confounded a great many people.

It had been done only seven times between 1895 and 1938. Of the men who might have been expected to do it there are some notable absentees – Hobbs, Woolley, Hendren, Mead, Sutcliffe, Sandham, Compton, Graveney, Hutton, Washbrook, Cowdrey and May to list a dozen.

It is the host of great batsmen who never got there that gives the true glory to the seven who have done – Bradman who performed it twice just to underline his place in cricket as a man apart, and predictably Wally Hammond and W. G. Grace. Tom Hayward, the prototype of professional batsmen at the turn of the century is there, so is that wonderful little fighter Bill Edrich and, slightly different in such company perhaps, the solitary left-hander Charles Hallows of Lancashire. And now Turner has scaled this improbable Parnassus and given cricket in New Zealand an immeasurable lift.

To make any comparisons between members of the game's most exclusive body must be odious in the extreme. Hammond scored 1,042 runs in 22 days in 1927 and Grace 1,016 in the same number of days. Bradman, being Bradman, did it twice, but Turner's effort cannot be dismissed as being in the least degree inferior to any of them. Only one of his eleven matches, the first, suffered no interference from the weather. In all fifty-five and a half hours playing time was lost through rain and bad light in the next ten matches. To reach four figures Turner made eighteen visits to the crease and batted thirty-five hours, forty-two minutes. He compiled four centuries, hitting seven 6s and 120 4s but in eight of his innings he was dismissed for 30 or under. If further proof is needed that Turner was as human and therefore as fallible as any other batsman, only one of his four centuries, his 153 not out against MCC at Lord's, was chanceless. In his 151 not out against Robins' XI at Eastbourne he gave a hard return chance to Graham of Kent when 84. At Worcester, when he made 143 off his own county, he was missed by Ormrod when 74 off an attempted drive. And at Northampton where his 111 finally earned him cricket immortality he was dropped in the slips by Dye when 16.

His failures included two runs against Derbyshire, three in the second innings against MCC, seven against Kent at Canterbury, eight and 17 against Gloucestershire, 13 against Somerset in the second innings and 30 and 10 against Leicestershire.

Bert Sutcliffe, one of the finest batsmen New Zealand has produced, coached Turner at school and predicted a future for him and to be sure Billy Ibadulla, for several winters coach to Otago, told Turner he would make the grade in county cricket in England. As a youth he was learning the insurance business, but in pursuit of an ambition that most people warned him was an improbable dream he threw up his career and the security it promised and for thirteen months he worked at night in a bakery. Almost every penny of the £22 a week he earned from this new work, he set aside towards his passage money to England. When he made his first-class debut for Otago at 17 the New Zealand Press saw in him anything but the prodigy who was to earn world fame less than a decade away. He was severely criticised for slow scoring and his general stodgy approach to cricket.

He was 19 when he received a letter from Warwickshire, the county who had promised him a chance on Ibadulla's recommendation, to say they had completed their permitted ration of overseas players. M. J. K. Smith said Warwickshire would give him a trial if he still wanted to come and if they thought he was any good they would do their best to fix him up with another county. On this faint hope Turner arrived at Edgbaston. When he went out for a net practice at Birmingham he was staking his past, his present and his future. In my opinion that was the morning he earned greatness rather than the day at Northampton last May when he gave the lie to the 35 years that had gone before.

W. G. GRACE

To go back 78 years in time to the occasion the feat was first performed. It was undoubtedly the most remarkable of all the "1,000 Runs in May". In 1895 Dr William Gilbert Grace, was two months off 47 years of age when he became the first of the few. He did not play in a first class match until as late as May 9 – the latest start for the 1,000 in the season's first month. On that date he presented himself at Lord's to play for MCC against Sussex. MCC won the toss and batted first and Grace's maiden first-class innings of the season could not have been less of a pointer to what was to follow in the next three weeks. On the evening of May 31 Grace had played ten innings, had scored 1,016 runs and had an average of 112.8 but on this Thursday morning of May 9 he had scored only 13 when he was caught by a young Indian nobleman making his debut for Sussex – a certain K. S. Ranjitsinhji. By the close MCC after making a very respectable 293 had five Sussex wickets down for 124 and although Ranji was not out for 77, the county were all out for 219 on the Friday and Grace now played the first of nine innings which were to bring him 1,003 runs in 21 days. He had just completed his first century of the season when at 103 he gave a catch off Ranji to become one of the Indian's six victims in the 32 overs he bowled in the club's second innings. Sussex, left 405 to win, lost their first four for 42 but the unknown Ranji made the match his own with his maiden first class hundred.

Grace remained at Lord's for the match with Yorkshire and failed twice. He was caught at the wicket off Peel for 18 by David Hunter and gave a return catch to F. W. Milligan for 25. He then returned to Bristol and Gloucestershire's local derby with Somerset. May was half over and he had a modest 159 runs to his name. That season Gloucestershire played only 18 matches in the County Championship and this game was their only appearance at their Ashley Down headquarters before mid-July but what a match it was!

Somerset batted first and Fowler and Lionel Palairet scored 205 for the first wicket. Grace broke the stand and went on to finish with five for 87 in 45 overs, Somerset being all out 303. He then began the Gloucestershire reply. Five hours twenty minutes later when he was ninth out, caught off a towering hit off Sammy Woods, he had scored 288 – his 100th century in first class cricket and the first man to reach batting's supreme milestone. He hit 38 4s, ran 11 3s, 29 2s and 45 singles. Gloucestershire's lead was 171 and Grace said "I think we have them now". He is then reported to have said to one of his fellow amateurs "I don't feel like bowling for the moment, Townsend, but I can safely leave it to you and Murch", and Murch returned eight for 68, Townsend got the remaining two and Somerset were all out for 189, Grace sending in his tail-enders to score the 19 required for victory. The county having no match the following three days, Grace went to Cambridge to play for the Gentlemen of England against the University. In his only innings he made 52 and travelled to Gravesend where, on the famous Bat and Ball ground, there took place another incredible match which no man in the modern game can begin to visualise if he is honest.

Kent batted first, made 470 – and lost the match by nine wickets! Gloucestershire in reply batted until lunch on the third day when they were finally all out for 443. Grace, first in, was last out with 257. In the afternoon Kent were demolished for 76. Gloucestershire were left 106 to win in little more than an hour and Grace swept his side to triumph with 73 not out and minutes to spare. The Old Man, who was in his 30th season of first-class cricket, had scored 330 for once out and was on the field for every ball of the match!

Gloucestershire were not due to be in action again until May 30 when they came up to Lord's to meet Middlesex but Grace made the short journey from Gravesend to The Oval where he played for England against Surrey in W. W. Read's Testimonial Match. England won easily by an innings and 75 but Grace showed he was indeed a mortal man being bowled by Tom Richardson for 18. Perhaps he was just a little weary for at nearly 47 he could not throw his cricket gear and overnight bag into the boot of a Jaguar or Rover 2000. All the travelling was by train and horse-drawn carriage.

He arrived once more at Lord's on the morning of Thursday, May 30, 1895 with 847 runs. When he made out the batting order he observed to the dressing room in general "I see we are very much below full strength so I had better win the toss and make a few". This incredible person did more than that. He won the toss and scored a chanceless 169 before being bowled by Dr Thornton. He had reached the 1,000 runs in May for the first time with a day to spare and less than a fortnight after becoming the first man to make 100 centuries.

In 1880 in the Oval Test Grace made 152 for England and W. L. Murdoch made 153 for Australia. The Australians started a discussion as to who was the greatest player. Bannerman, the man they called the little stonewaller, was a real Aussie. He was also accepted as being a very fine judge of the game. He listened for a time and then ended all further argument with an expressive noise followed by the remark – "W.G. has forgotten more about batting than Billy ever knew".

TOM HAYWARD

Now I pass on to Tom Hayward. When he went out to bat against London County at The Oval on Easter Monday, 1900, he was less than three weeks past his twenty-ninth birthday. Slim, upright, moustached, Hayward was the ideal prototype of the successful professional cricketer of his time. A dedicated cricketer, he spent ten days intensive practice at Cambridge before this match and in dull, showery weather he showed form no other batsman could approach. Going in number five he took out his bat for 120. The strength of the opposition can perhaps be judged by the first six – W. G. Grace (manager and captain), C. B. Fry, L. C. Braund, C. L. Townsend, G. L. Jessop and A. E. Trott. Surrey won by an innings and 34 in two days notwithstanding, and a return match was played at the old Crystal Palace ground beginning on May 3. This time a magnificent pitch had been prepared and three innings produced over 1100 runs. Hayward had made 55 in the first of these when his partner drove a ball straight back which was deflected by Lockwood, the bowler, into the stumps. Hayward backing up was run out but in his second innings, which was described as "quite exceptional in quality", he scored 108. *Wisden*'s account reminds us that the country was at war, the last sentence reading: "On the third day Sir George White, recently back in England after the siege of Ladysmith, drove on to the ground with Lady White and had an enthusiastic reception."

Surrey next played a draw with Warwickshire in which Hayward again took out his bat, this time for 131 made in three hours. Then Surrey beat Hampshire by an innings and 78, Hayward making 55 before giving a return catch.

Hayward's first appearance in the provinces saw Surrey gain another crushing innings success with 149 runs to spare. Surrey made exactly 500 with Hayward's contribution

193 in three and three-quarter hours, including two 6s, one 5 and seventeen 4s. So up to Derbyshire and another Surrey victory, by ten wickets. In his only visit to the crease Hayward made 120 and when the team returned to London for four successive matches at The Oval, starting on May 21, he had an average of better than 156. He had scored 782 runs in seven innings, been twice not out, had made five centuries and two scores of 55.

Now the bad patch which comes to all batsmen hit Hayward. In a rain-ruined game with Worcestershire, in which Surrey made 495 for five declared all on the first day, Tom had his castle knocked over for 5. Against Essex Hayward fell twice to Mead, bowled for 6 and leg before for 3, which helped Mead achieve a match analysis of twelve for 98 and victory for Essex – their first ever at The Oval – by five runs.

The weather turned for the visit of Sussex on May 28 and Hayward regained form with 40, followed by his sixth hundred of the season in the second innings on the last afternoon of what clearly would be a drawn game. The interest and excitement were never so intense as Hayward went on towards his thousand. 950, 960, 970, 980, 982. The runs clocked up easily, the bat the complete master of the ball. Then with 18 still wanted, Hayward on 146 popped the simplest of catches into the hands of Bland at mid-on off a ball from A. E. Relf.

Well, even Homer nodded, but the question now on all lips was – could he get those 18 runs on the following day, Thursday, May 31? Gloucestershire, last of the visiting quartet, won the toss and batted but Lockwood, seven for 94, and Richardson, three for 99, dismissed them for 212 and Jephson, the Surrey captain, sent in Hayward to open with Abel. There was never any question about his getting those 18 runs. He and Abel helped themselves to 201 in just over two hours for the first wicket, Hayward failing to record his seventh century of the season by only eight runs. Hayward ended May with 1,074 runs and an average of 97.6.

Tom Hayward's father, Dan, was groundsman of Parker's Piece, that fine public sports field at Cambridge. It was on this very Parker's Piece that the son of another Cambridge Groundsman, John Berry Hobbs, first displayed his talent and enthusiasm for cricket and had these brought to the attention of Tom Hayward and through him Surrey by Mr Hayward senior. So does destiny shape the lives of men.

WALTER HAMMOND

The world was a different place when Wally Hammond became the third man to make 1,000 runs before June 1. He was twenty-four when he scored his 1,000 in 22 days and he did not get a match until Gloucestershire opened their county championship programme against Yorkshire at the Wagon Works Ground, Gloucester, on May 7. During Hammond's tour of the West Indies in 1926 he had contracted an illness which caused him to miss the whole of the English season of 1926, so on the morning of May 7, 1927, he felt himself to be nearly back to 1923 when he had been an unknown of 20, very much on trial with Gloucestershire. After making 27, he gave Maurice Leyland a catch off the bowling of Abe Waddington. And then incredibly came three hundreds in four days. Missed at 11, Hammond made 135 in the second innings to hold up Yorkshire for close on four hours on their way to an innings victory.

At The Oval, Hammond made 108 but Gloucestershire, despite a total of 406, had to follow on, Surrey having scored 577 for seven declared. Going in again when both openers had gone for 2, he made 128. Once, shortly before he retired as Surrey's scorer, I asked Andy Sandham about Hammond's form in that match. "Two good 'uns he played. Percy Fender got him the first time and it was the first bad stroke he had made. Second time he and Reg Sinfield put on 195 in two hours and the only shot Wally lifted off the ground was a drive over mid-off's head for 4." 195 in two hours? Surely the veteran's memory was sadly adrift. I dug up *Wisden*'s for 1928 and he was only ten minutes out.

Hammond's third match was the return with Yorkshire at Dewsbury, a venue the White Rose no longer use. In a rain affected match he failed twice. Just how justified Wilfred

Rhodes was in continuing to play in his fiftieth year was proved when he got Hammond both times. First he drew him forward for Dolphin to stump him for 17 and then Rhodes clean bowled him for 11.

Against the odds the northern weather changed suddenly and at Manchester in bright sunshine Hammond, broad-shouldered but lithe as a leopard, outshone the dazzling May weather. Gloucestershire were 11 for three when Hammond got cracking with 50 in seventy minutes. As McDonald, one of the greatest fast bowlers of all time, cut away his partners at the other end, Hammond fought for sheer survival. Then, at 99, he touched one from McDonald to the wicket-keeper. The western county were all out for 235; Lancashire gained a lead of over 100, and on the third day the Lancashire bowlers thought they could get the match over quickly, and taxis were ordered to stand by to drive the home team to Manchester races, for Lancashire's next game was also at Old Trafford on the Saturday.

Writing fourteen years ago of this never-to-be-forgotten Friday at Old Trafford, Sir Neville Cardus showed his memory to be still as matchless as his prose: "I can see the scene vividly; McDonald opened his attack from the Stretford end, running silently on the grass. The arm wheeled over, the wrist curved, and the ball was released at killing velocity. Hammond drove it to the off, from the back foot. And McDonald's next four balls were also summarily dismissed – to the boundary. Five fours from five balls, the first of the day from the greatest living fast bowler set upon getting to the racecourse in time to have his money on a good thing at a good starting price. Moreover, the sixth ball of this same over would also have gone for four if Jack Iddon, fielding at the sight screen behind McDonald's arm, had not been there, on the edge of the field, to stop a terrific drive withering the grass. A man in the crowd saw visions and became exalted. 'Marvellous,' he said in good Lancastrian accent, ''opes 'e gets couple hundred.' 'What about Lancashire?' I asked him. 'Lancashire be buggered!' he replied."

McDonald and his mates never got to the races, for Gloucestershire batted out the match, their last wicket falling on the stroke of time.

From Manchester, Gloucestershire went to Hinckley and another away fixture against Leicestershire. Perhaps this homely little ground at the back of the local bus garage was no fitting stage for Hammond's virtuosity. He gave George Geary a return catch after scoring 4 and Alec Skelding bowled him for 30.

In his first appearance that season at Bristol Hammond made 83 out of 120 in one hundred minutes before being superbly stumped by Fred Price and in a second innings collapse against Middlesex Hammond fell once more to a caught and bowled, this time by Durston after scoring only 7.

On the morning of Saturday, May 28, Gloucestershire took the field at Southampton, in their last match of the month, with Hammond having scored 836 runs in twelve completed innings. Hammond did not have to wait long before he was taking guard for his thirteenth knock of the season. But he batted with a lighthearted devil-may-care approach which showed how lightly he regarded his 800-odd runs.

Before he died in 1959 I spent an afternoon in the company of Alec Kennedy, the great Hampshire bowler. Talking of this match he said, "You would have thought Wally was playing at Scarborough in September. He reached 100 in eighty-five minutes and made 192 out of 227 and from the time he walked out of the pavilion until he unbuckled his pads in the dressing room not more than two and a half hours could have passed. Mind you, we had only ourselves to blame. We missed him five times."

What a sight it must have been! Five catches put down and Hammond hitting twenty-seven 4s and clearing the boundary on six occasions. It was Kennedy who finally caught him off George Brown but Hammond was already 28 runs past the 1,000 mark in twenty-two days to equal the 32 years record of Grace when that happened. On the Monday, the last day of May, in an atmosphere of anti-climax, Hammond scored 14 before losing his wicket to Boyes, to bring his haul for the month to 1,042 runs at an average of over 74. He had scored five centuries and a 99 in seven matches – and his county did not win a match until June 20!

CHARLIE HALLOWS

Charles Hallows was born in 1895 just one month before W. G. Grace made history. At the start of the 1928 season the Lancashire opening batsman was thus already past his thirty-third birthday. Like Hammond, the year before, he played in only seven matches, but whereas Hammond played 14 completed innings, Hallows played only 11 innings and on three occasions was not out. His average was thus 125. He compiled a further four centuries to end the season with ten hundreds but was not considered for the 1928-29 tour of Australia under Percy Chapman which England won by four Tests to one! Lancashire opened their championship programme in 1928 by beating Northamptonshire by an innings at Old Trafford and in his one innings Hallows made exactly 100 before he gave Matthews a catch off the bowling of Jupp. Glamorgan were the next visitors to Manchester and Hallows went one better, reaching 101 before being caught by Bates off Dai Davies. Lancashire were left to score over 100 to win and Hallows added another 50 not out as he and Frank Watson ran them home by ten wickets. In the space of six days this pair made opening stands of 200, 202 and 107, unbroken.

Lancashire moved down to Edgbaston. Only 25 wickets fell in three days but Hallows put his seal on the hopeless draw by making a century in each innings – 123 and 101 not out. At Lord's against Middlesex, Lancashire ran into bad weather for the first time and Hallows after ten days of tremendous scoring made a modest 22. The county headed back north for the return with Warwickshire at Seedhill, the Nelson ground where Learie Constantine became a well loved figure. Hallows again proved a scourge to the Midland county's attack and hit 74 and 104. When he was bowled by Wyatt Lancashire declared and Warwickshire, asked to score 313, were mowed down by McDonald for 136. Hallows made that 104 in under two hours on a suspect pitch against seven bowlers. It was champion cricket. In a drawn Roses match at Sheffield, Hallows made 58 before being bowled by Rhodes and 34 not out.

So Lancashire came back to Old Trafford to meet Sussex, a fixture which began on May 30. Lancashire won the toss but no one that morning thought in terms of Hallows emulating Hammond's feat of the previous season. He had made a wonderful beginning to the campaign with five centuries in ten innings but his aggregate, with little more than 12 hours cricket in the month left, was 768. The pitch was a beauty and Hallows batted throughout that long glorious day to reach 190 by stumps, his one heart stopping moment a chance when he was 175 which was not accepted. Suddenly it was realised that Hallows wanted only 42 on the Thursday to reach four figures on the last day of the month.

Some years ago when Charles Hallows was coach to Worcestershire, I came across him one night taking dinner in "The Crown", that ancient hostelry just up the street from the County ground which was closed for rebuilding in 1973. Our conversation got round to that morning of May 31, 1928.

"When I woke up I scarcely dared look out of the window. I mean, to expect two fine days in succession in Manchester.

"Well, I got those 42 runs but when I saw 232 come up on the scoreboard under my number and I heard the crowd and saw the Sussex chaps applauding, I felt it was all a dream. I saw Arthur Gilligan coming in to bowl the next ball but I couldn't grasp that he was bowling at me. I made a vague pass of the bat and the next thing I see is Jim Parks throwing the ball up. I was out."

Yes, Hallows was out and the most memorable innings of his life extended over seven hours ten minutes. His Test career consisted of one appearance against Australia in 1921 and one against West Indies in 1928. From then until the end of his playing days Hallows fulfilled his true function – a backbone county professional of the first rank, maker of 55 centuries.

DONALD GEORGE BRADMAN

And now we come inescapably to Bradman. Any writer atempting to give Bradman his true place in cricket to the receptive minds of a new generation should say just that

Bradman played in 52 Tests, scored virtually 7,000 runs, hit 29 centuries and retired with an average of 99.94 – damn it, 100. In 1930 he burst upon the English scene with the effect of all the fireworks at a Brock's Benefit night being set off at the same time. A glorious driver, a perfect placer of the ball, he could cut, hook or turn the ball to leg with nearly the same certainty. To display all his glittering array Bradman had an eye which was uncanny in its power to gauge the length of a ball and his footwork was as nimble as Nureyev's. Add to all that a quiet but supreme confidence in himself and an iron determination with which men on the short side are often equipped and you had the greatest killer of bowling the world so far has seen.

The Australian tour of 1930 began on a chilly day at Worcester to mark the end of April. Not out 75 at close of play on May Day, Bradman carried his first innings on English soil to 236 in just over four hours, his one chance a hard return catch at 215. At Leicester in the tourists' second match, Bradman had his first encounter with slow, rain-affected English turf. He spent over two hours reaching 50 but by the end of the second day when his side were 365 for five, Bradman was still there with 185 runs to his name.

The following day was washed out but the name "Bradman" with all its magic qualities which live unimpaired to this very day was already on all lips. He was given a rest in the match against Essex, but at Bramall Lane, Sheffield, alas now a football stadium only with, in my opinion, all the makings of a white elephant, Bradman made 78 out of 107 in one hundred minutes before being caught and bowled by Macaulay. Then over to Liverpool to meet Lancashire at Aigburth. Caught on a drying pitch by a team on their way to their fourth championship in five years, the Australians were struggling for the first time. Bradman was bowled by McDonald, a fellow Australian, for 9 – his first failure in England. The game had to be abandoned on the Friday and the following day Lord's saw Bradman for the first time. Again rain interfered to create a draw but Bradman was second top scorer in the Australian first innings with 66 when he was bowled by Allom. G. T. S. Stevens got him lbw for 4 in the second. At Queen's Park, Chesterfield, Bradman, in his only chance to bat, made 44 before being caught at the wicket off Worthington.

The season was already showing signs of developing into a typical wet English summer and the Australians' game with Surrey was reduced to a single day, not a ball being bowled on the Monday and Tuesday. But the Saturday was something a few old men still talk about at The Oval. This was the first time Bradman, the compact little assassin, had worked out under the shadow of the gigantic gasholder, going in first wicket down at 11. He was not out 252 at the close in a total of 379 for five. Bradman described his maiden appearance at one of the world's most famous cricket arenas as "satisfactory". 252 not out on a soft, slow pitch – yes, there might be some justification in calling that satisfactory.

Normally Bradman was due for another three days off at Oxford, but he had reached 922 runs after his Oval epic and no Australian had ever achieved the feat of 1,000 runs before June 1. There were, too, only four days of May left. So Bradman played and Woodfull won the toss, the day was fine and Oxford's attack was weak. The Australians declared at 406 for two – but one of those wickets was Bradman's and he had scored only 32 of the 78 he needed. He had batted carefully for nearly an hour when he went on to the back foot, from where he was so devastating, to a ball from Garland-Wells. It was well up to him and was through him into the stumps, making him look positively mortal.

The thirtieth of May slipped by in enforced idleness, Oxford having been beaten in two days and on Saturday, May 31, the Australians' next opponents, Hampshire, won the toss and batted. Bradman's chances of making the 46 runs he still needed appeared slim, but Grimmett took seven for 39 and Hampshire were all out 151. The threat as always through the May of 1930 was the weather. Rain was obviously on the way and Woodfull knew there was only one thing to do. He dropped himself down to five in the order and sent Bradman in to open with Jackson.

Hampshire attacked with Kennedy, Newman, Herman and Boyes, a formidable quartet, and young "Lofty" Herman removed Jackson before he had scored. But

Bradman was Bradman. He got those 46 runs, the ground rose to him, the players clapped, the deed was done. He scored one more run – and the heavens opened, no more play being possible until Monday. When play was resumed Bradman was last out, caught by Mead for 191 off a big hit, trying to reach 200 before his last partner departed. But that and how he scored 131 in the first Test at Trent Bridge, 254 at Lord's in the second, 334 at Leeds in the third, and 232 at The Oval in the fifth has nothing to do with the theme of this article.

The late R. C. Robertson-Glasgow, writing on Bradman a quarter of a century ago, just after his farewell to the game as a player, said: "Above all he was a business cricketer. About his batting there was to be no style for style's sake. If there was to be any charm, that was for the spectator to find or miss. It was not Bradman's concern. His aim was the making of runs, and he made them in staggering profusion."

BRADMAN AGAIN IN 1938

When Bradman scored 1,056 runs in 32 days in 1938 on his third visit to England and his first as captain, it had the least impact of any of the 1,000 in May feats. Already a legend in his own lifetime, it was half expected he would do it a second time. Worcester once again and again on the last day of April. By the close of play Bradman was already over a quarter of the way and May had not started. Out of an Australian total of 474 for six, Bradman made 258 and the catch he gave off Howorth was his first and only chance. When Bradman was lbw for 58 in the next match, one evening paper actually produced a headline "Bradman fails at Oxford"! Has there ever been a better unwitting tribute?

Bradman rested himself for the match against Leicestershire, came back at Fenner's and out of a total of 708 for five contributed a lighthearted 137 including twenty boundaries. Ah, said the grudging ones, it's all very well to help himself to cheap runs off the undergraduates, but wait until he comes up against the MCC at Lord's. That was on the Friday. By lunchtime on Monday Bradman's aggregate was an incredible 731 and he had a full fortnight ahead of him to score a further 269 and so become the only man in history to perform the feat twice. The gates were closed by three o'clock on the Saturday with 32,000 inside and Bradman rewarded them with his brightest innings of the tour. In six hours of flawless mastery in which he made no detectable mistake the Australian phenomenon took 278 off the representative MCC attack. He hit one 6 and thirty-five 4s and was not dismissed until he attempted to square cut a bad ball from Jim Smith and was magnificently caught at cover by Walter Robins. At Northampton he fell to the fast medium of Partridge for 2 but back in town for the second Saturday running he took 143 off Surrey at The Oval.

When the Australians played Hampshire at Southampton on May 25, 26, 27, 1938, Bradman batted in the fashion which caused Crusoe to dub him "a business cricketer". This time there was no play at all on the first day and as in 1930 the Australians lost the toss. Hampshire, bedevilled by the wrist spin of O'Reilly, who took six for 65, were all out for 157 but shortly after Bradman began to bat there was another long hold-up for rain. On the third day with no chance of a finish, Bradman handled the six-man Hampshire attack with cold, calculating care. On the rain-affected turf he was not completely sure against the spin of Boyes and Hill but he picked his way to his fifth century in seven innings and when he notched his 124th run he had done what he set out to do. He was and is still the only man in something like 200 years of organised cricket to score 1,000 runs before the end of May, not once, but twice. For the third time Southampton had been the appointed place.

BILL EDRICH

The story does not end there, for three days of cricket remained in May in which the Australians were back at Lord's to meet Middlesex. Bradman's feats in this game were unexceptional and unimportant to the terms of reference of this article. After continuous rain on Saturday and Sunday, the Australians did not show to advantage in the prevailing conditions. There was no question of them being beaten, but for Bill Edrich the game looked like being a personal tragedy when O'Reilly bowled him for 9 in the first innings which left him with 990 runs. His innings included 104 for MCC v Yorkshire, 115 for MCC v Surrey, 182 for Middlesex v Gloucestershire and 245 v Nottinghamshire.

With less than half an hour to play out the formalities of a hopelessly drawn game Bradman proved his humanity by declaring and saying to Edrich: "See if you can get those 10, Bill." There was just time for half a dozen quick overs shared by McCabe and Waite and Edrich got those 10 and helped himself to 10 more for luck. He had made 1,010 runs by May 31 with an average of over 84 and there was one unique factor about this particular achievement. Every one of those runs was made at Lord's. There is no need to dwell further on Edrich, for I wrote about him at some length in last year's *Wisden* [1973].

The chronicle is done and even before the memory of Glenn Turner has faded the voices can be heard to the effect it will not be done again. This time I shall not join them. The 1,000 runs in May may remain inviolate for another 35 years or even longer but the time will surely come when another Turner will force his way through and confound everyone by achieving the improbable for the ninth time.

ENGLAND v NEW ZEALAND

Second Test Match

Played at Lord's, June 21, 22, 23, 25, 26, 1973

Drawn. New Zealand have never been closer to beating England than they were on the final afternoon of this match in which Illingworth's side were outplayed almost throughout. Only a mature, dedicated second innings of 178 by Fletcher enabled England to escape. Fletcher, after a long series of disappointments in home Tests, except against the Rest of the World in 1970 when he scored 340 runs, average 48.57, rose to the occasion and denied New Zealand what would have been a well-deserved triumph.

It was a close-run thing for when the number ten, Arnold, came to join Fletcher two hours remained for play and England were no more than 70 runs ahead. Arnold snicked the third ball he received from Pollard, but Wadsworth could not grasp the ankle high chance. Had that catch been accepted England would almost certainly have gone down. Congdon had every reason to be disappointed for he had played another fine innings of 175 and was supported by two other century makers, Burgess and Pollard, as New Zealand ran up their biggest total against England.

England were put in on a humid first morning, a move foiled to some extent by Boycott who batted in skilled fashion until trying for his third six he hit a catch to square leg. England had reached 148 for two just before tea and then five wickets went for 47 runs to the bowling of Dayle Hadlee and Howarth. Only some lusty hitting by Greig, who was missed early on, carried the innings into the second day.

The final wicket soon went down on the second morning of a day of slow scoring and slow over rate as New Zealand consolidated their advantage. Turner and Parker were both dismissed by the time the score had reached double figures, but Congdon and Hastings defied the bowlers in a partnership not broken until five minutes from the close. Congdon became the first New Zealander to make three centuries against England and Hastings, badly missed by Fletcher off Illingworth when 21, supported him admirably in a stand of 190, a new third wicket record for New Zealand against England, surpassing their own effort at Nottingham in 1969.

England could take only three wickets on the Saturday when a crowd of 25,000 saw the New Zealand batsmen gain complete command. In the morning 70 runs were scored for the loss of the nightwatchman Howarth. In the afternoon, when Congdon finally fell after a stay of eight hours thirty-five minutes, 92 runs were made while a further 130 came in the closing session of under two hours. Burgess's second century against England included many fine drives and cuts. Old missed him off a difficult caught and bowled chance before he had scored but thereafter he was rarely in difficulty. His partnership of 117 with Pollard was a sixth wicket record. Pollard, after a slow start, played some amazing strokes against the new ball, running up the pitch to Arnold and Snow.

On Monday, New Zealand batted for a further eighty minutes, Pollard becoming the third century maker in three hours fifty minutes. Old, who had replaced the unfit Lewis in the England side, took five for 113 on his first Test appearance at Lord's. Illingworth alone of the main bowlers did not concede over 100 runs.

To their credit England did not overdo their caution in trying to avoid defeat and this was unnecessary because the pitch played well until the end. Boycott and Amiss gave them a fine start with a sprightly partnership of 112 in two hours. Boycott again played stylishly and effectively until, like Amiss before him, he hit a full toss from Howarth back to the bowler.

So England began the final day, 224 for two, still 74 behind. Roope stayed to make his second patient 50 of the match, but thereafter Fletcher carried the main burden and he responded coolly and with authority, realising that runs were as important as time. Howarth purveyed his left-arm slows steadily and when he dismissed Illingworth, after a sixth wicket partnership had lasted nearly two hours, there was a batting breakdown which left England perilously placed. Following Arnold's escape Fletcher hit out, taking 16 off an over from Pollard. The new ball failed to effect a breach and finally, as at Trent Bridge, New Zealand took the honours but no victory. By the time the gallant Fletcher was caught on the boundary five mintues from the close he had gained new status as a Test player while batting for six hours and a quarter and hitting two 6s and twenty-one 4s. Attendance 75,000. Receipts £59,495.

England

G. Boycott c Parker b Collinge	61	– c and b Howarth	92
D. L. Amiss c Howarth b Hadlee	9	– c and b Howarth	53
G. R. J. Roope lbw b Howarth	56	– c Parker b Taylor	51
K. W. R. Fletcher c Hastings b Howarth	25	– c Taylor b Collinge	178
A. W. Greig c Howarth b Collinge	63	– c Wadsworth b Hadlee	12
*R. Illingworth c Collinge b Hadlee	3	– c Turner b Howarth	22
†A. P. E. Knott b Hadlee	0	– c Congdon b Howarth	0
C. M. Old b Howarth	7	– c Congdon b Pollard	7
J. A. Snow b Taylor	2	– c Hastings b Pollard	0
G. G. Arnold not out	8	– not out	23
N. Gifford c Wadsworth b Collinge	8	– not out	2
L-b 1, w 1, n-b 9	11	B 8, l-b 3, n-b 12	23
1/24 2/116 3/148 4/165 5/171 6/175 7/195 8/217 9/237	253	1/112 2/185 3/250 4/274 5/335 6/339 7/352 8/368 9/460	(9 wkts) 463

Bowling: *First Innings*—Collinge 31–8–69–3; Taylor 19–1–54–1; Hadlee 26–4–70–3; Congdon 5–2–7–0; Howarth 25–6–42–3. *Second Innings*—Collinge 19–4–41–1; Taylor 34–10–90–1; Hadlee 25–2–79–1; Congdon 8–3–22–0; Howarth 70–24–144–4; Pollard 39–11–61–2; Hastings 1–0–3–0.

New Zealand

G. M. Turner c Greig b Arnold	4
J. M. Parker c Knott b Snow	3
*B. E. Congdon c Knott b Old	175
B. F. Hastings lbw b Snow	86
H. J. Howarth hit wkt b Old	17
M. G. Burgess b Snow	105
V. Pollard not out	105
†K. J. Wadsworth c Knott b Old	27
B. R. Taylor b Old	11
D. R. Hadlee c Fletcher b Old	6
L-b 5, n-b 7	12
1/5 2/10 3/200 4/249 5/330 6/447 7/523 8/535 9/551	(9 wkts dec.) 551

R. O. Collinge did not bat.

Bowling: Snow 38–4–109–3; Arnold 41–6–108–1; Old 41.5–7–113–5; Roope 6–1–15–0; Gifford 39–6–107–0; Illingworth 39–12–87–0.

Umpires: A. E. Fagg and T. W. Spencer.

GLOUCESTERSHIRE v NEW ZEALANDERS

Played at Bristol, June 28, 29, 30, 1978

Drawn. The touring side just failed in a run-chase on the final day, finishing three short of victory at the end of the last twenty overs. They might have got there had not the innings been held up for a few minutes while a sponsor's hot air balloon was removed from the field. Burgess had opened up the match by declaring 48 behind and his enterprise was rewarded by another declaration from Shepherd.

Zaheer alone made much of the New Zealand bowling on the first day, when the spin of Boock troubled all the batsmen. Play on the second day could not start until 2.00, and although Brain bowled effectively New Zealand passed 150 with only two men out before the pace bowler effected a breakthrough. Zaheer, who reached his 1,000 runs during the course of his second innings century, joined with Shephered in a fruitful fourth-wicket partnership of 147 before lunch on the final day. New Zealand made a brave attempt to get the runs, although Wright and Howarth were far from fit. Anderson accelerated briskly and looked to be winning the day before he was caught behind off Davey for 122, one short of his highest score.

Gloucestershire

A. W. Stovold lbw b Cairns	33	– b Bracewell	0
A. Tait c Edgar b Bracewell	4	– c Edwards b Bracewell	6
Zaheer Abbas c Bracewell b Boock	83	– not out	121
*D. R. Shepherd lbw b Thomson	5	– not out	53
S. Williams b Thomson	0		
D. A. Graveney c Howarth b Boock	36		
I. C. Crawford c Edwards b Boock	14		
†A. J. Brassington lbw b Boock	5	– b Bracewell	15
J. H. Shackleton c and b Cairns	1		
J. Davey not out	15		
B. M. Brain c Bracewell b Cairns	12		
B 6, l-b 6, n-b 7	19	B 4, l-b 5, n-b 3	12
1/18 2/74 3/89 4/89 5/161 6/193 7/196 8/199 9/205	227	1/0 2/16 3/60 (3 wkts dec.)	207

Bowling: *First Innings*—Bracewell 16–2–60–1; Thomson 22–9–50–2; Cairns 25–5–63–3; Boock 22–9–35–4. *Second Innings*—Bracewell 12–1–38–3; Thomson 21–2–74–0; Cairns 7–1–26–0; Boock 11–2–57–0.

New Zealanders

J. G. Wright retired hurt	7	– not out	3
R. W. Anderson c Brassington b Brain	4	– c Brassington b Davey	122
B. A. Edgar b Brain	12	– run out	50
G. P. Howarth lbw b Brain	69	– b Davey	5
*M. G. Burgess c Tait b Graveney	56	– c Zaheer b Shackleton	14
B. E. Congdon lbw b Brain	0	– not out	43
†G. N. Edwards not out	9	– b Brain	0
B. L. Cairns c and b Brain	13	– c Shepherd b Brain	3
B 5, l-b 1, w 1, n-b 2	9	B 2, l-b 11	13
1/13 2/40 3/154 4/154 5/156 6/179 (6 wkts dec.)	179	1/81 2/154 3/211 4/216 5/233 6/242 (6 wkts)	253

B. P. Bracewell, G. B. Thomson and S. E. Boock did not bat.

Bowling: *First Innings*—Brain 16.4–1–48–5; Davey 13–5–17–0; Shackleton 10–1–32–0; Graveney 12–2–47–1; Crawford 5–1–26–0. *Second Innings*—Brain 19–2–68–2; Davey 18–3–68–2; Shackleton 15–3–72–1; Graveney 9–4–32–0.

Umpires: J. G. Langridge and J. van Geloven.

ENGLAND v NEW ZEALAND

Second Cornhill Test

Played at Nottingham, August 10, 11, 12, 14, 1978

England won by an innings and 119 runs with a day to spare, despite three hours being lost on Saturday. While everything seemed to go right for the victors, ill luck dogged the losers, particularly on the third morning when, after only two balls had been bowled by Botham, the umpires stopped play for bad light. Play thus having begun that day, the pitch remained exposed to the elements.

Although personal honours among the England team went to Botham, the 22-year-old Somerset all-rounder taking six for 34 and three for 59, a match aggregate of nine for 93, Boycott, after missing four Tests, returned to the scene of his triumph against Australia the previous year and hit another century. It was only his second against New Zealand, but his sixteenth in Tests. With Gooch, Radley, and Brearley each passing fifty and Gower getting 46, England built a mammoth total of 429.

Rain had fallen on nine successive days immediately prior to the match, yet the groundsman, Ron Allsopp, prepared a very good, if slow, pitch for the batsmen; he borrowed the Wimbledon green covers which did such good work in the previous Test at The Oval to protect the rest of the square. Apart from the bad light and the drizzle of Saturday, the weather remained fine with the sun shining brilliantly on Friday when the ground was almost filled to capacity.

Brearley's luck was in from the start. He won the toss, and with Boycott present and Gooch in impressive form, England received easily their best beginning of the summer with an opening stand of 111. With Radley as solid as ever, a stand of 129 followed this, and Gower was with Boycott when 300 appeared with only two wickets down.

For New Zealand, Hadlee, on his home county ground and inspired by his local admirers, maintained a hostile pace, sending down 44 overs for four wickets at a cost of 94 runs. At times the ball swung awkwardly and Boycott, when on 2, should have gone in Hadlee's second over. He gave an easy chance to Howarth at third slip, the same spot where McCosker missed him the previous year. Twice Hadlee rapped Boycott on the pads, his appeals for lbw being turned down by umpire Spencer, and Boycott took three hours twenty minutes to reach his fifty. England were 252 for two at the end of the first day with Boycott 108 in six hours. He returned on Friday morning bent on a second hundred, but Hadlee bowled him two short balls. The first he hooked for his tenth boundary, and repeating the stroke next ball skied it back to the bowler, having spent six hours, fifty five minutes for 131.

Now came Brearley, having demoted himself to number five after scores of 38, 2, and 0 against Pakistan and 2 and 11 at The Oval against New Zealand. He was really on trial and he took a long time to settle down. He saw Gower carelessly loft a ball to Cairns at mid-on, after which none of his partners except Taylor offered much resistance. Still, Brearley produced some well-timed cover drives and pulls until, having reached 50 in three hours, he was held off the youthful and enthusiastic Bracewell by Parker at first slip.

In the absence of Wright, laid low by a throat infection, the 21-year-old left-hander Edgar, in only his second Test, opened the New Zealand innings with Anderson. Ninety minutes remained of the second day, and all went well for an hour for New Zealand until Botham entered the attack with the score at 17. He soon had Edgar taken behind the wicket by Taylor and then removed Anderson, leg-before. Worse followed when Howarth, having made 7, ducked, turned his head, and was struck by a Botham bouncer that caused him to retire. Next, Parker fell to a brilliant catch by Taylor wide of the off stump and New Zealand were reduced to 35 for three by the close.

The third day began with those controversial two balls, after which play was held up until 3.15; and as the delay lasted more than one hour, cricket continued until 7.30. Now, Botham slightly reduced his pace and caused the ball to swing either way. Howarth, although a bit dizzy, returned and played exceedingly well, but Botham was irresistible, except when Congdon batted resolutely with Howarth and the pair put on 50 for the sixth wicket. Before falling to a superb low left-handed catch by Hendrick at second slip, Congdon had the satisfaction of passing John Reid's 3,431 which stood as the highest Test aggregate for New Zealand. The tail then folded up, leaving Howarth to take out his bat, and New Zealand followed on, wanting 309 to avert an innings defeat. There was time for one maiden over from Botham which Edgar played.

On Monday, two stupid run outs illustrated New Zealand's continuous misfortune. First, Anderson attempted a single to mid-off and Gower swept across from cover, his under-arm throw hitting the only stump he could see. Later, at 127, Parker was third out when he slipped after being sent back by Edgar from the first ball after a brief stoppage for rain.

For four hours the upright Edgar defied England, and was well supported by Howarth and Parker. Then Botham enjoyed a successful spell and the last seven wickets crashed for 63 runs. Edmonds, four for 44, bowled his left-arm slows admirably.

Throughout the match England fielded magnificently. Not a catch was dropped and Taylor, with six victims, gave another fine display of wicket-keeping. Praise must also be given to Boock, the tall New Zealand left-arm spinner, who conceded only 29 runs from 28 overs for two wickets.

England

G. Boycott c and b Hadlee	131
G. A. Gooch c Burgess b Bracewell	55
C. T. Radley lbw b Hadlee	59
D. I. Gower c Cairns b Boock	46
*J. M. Brearley c Parker b Bracewell	50
P. H. Edmonds b Cairns	6
G. Miller c Howarth b Hadlee	4
I. T. Botham c Hadlee b Boock	8
†R. W. Taylor b Hadlee	22
R. G. D. Willis not out	1
M. Hendrick c Edwards b Bracewell	7
B 16, l-b 12, w 1, n-b 11	40
1/111 2/240 3/301 4/342 5/350 6/364 7/374 8/419 9/427	429

Bowling: Hadlee 42–11–94–4; Bracewell 33.5–2–110–3; Cairns 38–7–85–1; Congdon 39–15–71–0; Boock 28–18–29–2.

New Zealand

B. A. Edgar c Taylor b Botham	6	c Botham b Edmonds	60
R. W. Anderson lbw b Botham	19	run out	0
G. P. Howarth not out	31	c Botham b Hendrick	34
S. L. Boock c Taylor b Willis	8	b Edmonds	2
J. M. Parker c Taylor b Hendrick	0	run out	38
*M. G. Burgess c Taylor b Botham	5	c Brearley b Edmonds	7
B. E. Congdon c Hendrick b Botham	27	c Brearley b Botham	4
†G. N. Edwards c Taylor b Botham	0	c and b Edmonds	18
B. L. Cairns b Edmonds	9	lbw b Botham	0
R. J. Hadlee c Gooch b Botham	4	c Taylor b Botham	11
B. P. Bracewell b Edmonds	0	not out	0
L-b 1, w 1, n-b 9	11	L-b 6, w 1, n-b 9	16
1/22 2/27 3/35 4/47 5/49 6/99 7/99 8/110 9/115	120	1/5 2/63 3/127 4/148 5/152 6/164 7/168 8/180 9/190	190

Bowling: *First Innings*—Willis 12–5–22–1; Hendrick 15–9–18–1; Botham 21–9–34–6; Edmonds 15.4–5–21–2; Miller 6–1–14–0. *Second Innings*—Willis 9–0–31–0; Hendrick 20–7–30–1; Botham 24–7–59–3; Edmonds 33.1–15–44–4; Miller 6–3–10–0.

Umpires: D. J. Constant and T. W. Spencer.

INDIANS IN ENGLAND

ENGLAND v INDIA

First Test Match

Played at Headingley, Leeds, June 8, 9, 10, 12, 13, 1967

England won by six wickets with two and three-quarter hours to spare. India, hit by the weather in May with little chance of accustoming themselves to English conditions, entered the match without a victory to their credit and their reputations so sullied that only small crowds attended, the best being on Saturday when 12,000 were present. Happily, the sun shone continuously and, inspired by the fine batting of their captain, The Nawab of Pataudi, the touring team covered themselves with glory after two dismal days when they appeared to be reeling to swift defeat.

They might well have been demoralized when on the first day two key bowlers, Surti and Bedi, were laid low by injuries. Ten minutes after the lunch interval, Surti, fielding at short fine leg, was struck below the left knee and an hour and a half later Bedi went off with severe leg strain. Neither fielded again and could only hobble to the wicket to bat with a runner.

Yet, despite all their misfortunes the gallant Indians struggled bravely, Pataudi batted magnificently for 64 and 148 and Engineer, in both innings, Wadekar and Hanumant showed excellent form. Indeed, India, 386 behind on the first innings, accomplished the rare feat of passing 500 in the follow on. Test cricket provides only two previous instances; England made 551 against South Africa at Trent Bridge in 1947 after being 325 behind, Pakistan, at Bridgetown in 1958, having made only 106 in reply to West Indies' 579 followed with 657 for eight, of which Hanif Mohammad scored 337 in sixteen hours, thirty-nine minutes, the longest innings in first-class cricket.

The Headingley groundsman had prepared an excellent pitch but later watering left it damp at the pavilion end on the first day, when after Close won the toss England for a long time struggled for runs. But they reached 281 for three by the time stumps were drawn with Boycott, 106 not out, Barrington (one 6 and eight 4s) and Graveney (one 6 and nine 4s), providing the best entertainment.

On Friday, England treated the depleted Indian attack mercilessly and in three and a half hours put on 269 before Close declared. Boycott finished with 246 not out, the highest individual innings for any Test between England and India, as well as his own highest in first-class cricket. He hit one 6 and twenty-nine 4s and did not make a false stroke, but his lack of enterprise met with much disapproval and the selectors dropped him for the next Test. D'Oliveira (thirteen 4s) hit his first Test century and his stand of 252 with Boycott was the second highest in the series, falling only 14 behind that by W. R. Hammond and T. S. Worthington at The Oval in 1936.

In the absence of Surti, Saxena opened the India innings with Engineer and they saw the total to 28 at tea. Afterwards, the batting broke down and although the Nawab proved defiant for the last fifty minutes, six wickets fell in an hour and a half for 86; the match looked as good as over.

Boycott, who had trodden on the ball, did not field again until the fifth day. India, despite their seemingly hopeless position, fought back nobly after Snow had removed Guha's off stump at 92. Surti limped to the wicket with Wadekar as his runner and he stayed ninety-six minutes, helping Pataudi to put on 59. Hobbs held a return catch by Surti from a full toss for his first wicket in a Test, and he finished the innings by taking the last three in ten balls. Pataudi, last out, batted splendidly for just over three hours. He drove Illingworth for 6 and also hit seven 4s.

When India followed on shortly after lunch on Saturday, Surti, with the twelfth man Venkataraghavan as his runner, went in first with Engineer, but soon edged Snow to the wicket-keeper. Then the England bowlers sampled the brilliant form Indian batsmen often display on their own sun drenched grounds. In a scintillating record second-wicket stand of 168 for India against England in two and a half hours, Engineer and Wadekar struck boundary after boundary. Engineer, hit fourteen 4s and after he left, Wadekar turned to defence, playing out the remaining three-quarters of an hour with Borde, so that the total reached 198 for two at the week-end, with Wadekar 84 not out.

India continued their grand fight on the fourth day and for the second time in the match the Nawab set his men a splendid example. Wadekar was taken at leg side for 91 after half an hour. He had hit sixteen 4s and made his runs in three and three-quarter hours. Half an hour later Borde hooked across the spin and was bowled, whereupon Hanumant and Pataudi proceeded to clear off the remainder of the first innings deficit. They were together for three hours, adding 134, and before the end of the day Pataudi had completed his sixth Test century; his third against England. Prasanna, who had bowled so spiritedly for hour after hour, stayed with his captain while the seventh wicket put on 60. Next Higgs gained his first wicket of the match when he knocked over Guha's middle stump and India were 475 at the close, Pataudi having made 129 not out in five hours.

The captain batted for fifty more minutes on Tuesday, altogether hitting one 6 and fifteen 4s and finally Bedi was held in the deep when the innings had lasted ten and a half hours. India's total of 510 was their highest against England.

England wanted only 125 to win and with Barrington, who opened the innings with Edrich, hitting freely for 46, it proved a light task, despite some fine bowling by Chandrasekhar and Prasanna.

England

G. Boycott not out	246		
J. H. Edrich c Engineer b Surti	1	– c Wadekar b Chandrasekhar	22
K. F. Barrington run out	93	– c Engineer b Chandrasekhar	46
T. W. Graveney c sub b Chandresekhar	59	– b Chandrasekhar	14
*B. L. D'Oliveira c sub b Chandrasekhar	109	– not out	24
*D. B. Close not out	22		
†J. T. Murray (did not bat)		– c sub b Prasanna	4
R. Illingworth (did not bat)		– not out	12
B 8, l-b 12	20	B 3, l-b 1	4
1/17 2/146 3/253 4/505	(4 wkts dec.) 550	1/58 2/78 3/87 4/92	(4 wkts) 126

K. Higgs, J. A. Snow and R. N. S. Hobbs did not bat.

Bowling: *First Innings*—Guha 43–10–105–0; Surti 11–2–25–1; Chandrasekhar 45–9–121–2; Bedi 15–8–32–0; Prasanna 59–8–187–0; Pataudi 4–1–13–0; Wadekar 1–0–9–0; Hanumant 3–0–27–0; Saxena 2–0–11–0. *Second Innings*—Guhu 5–0–10–0; Wadekar 2–0–8–0; Prasanna 21.3–5–54–1; Chandrasekhar 19–8–50–3.

India

†F. M. Engineer c and b Illingworth	42	– c and b Close	87
R. Saxena b D'Oliveira	9	– b Snow	16
A. L. Wadekar run out	0	– c Close b Illingworth	91
C. G. Borde b Snow	8	– b Illingworth	33
Hanumant Singh c D'Oliveira b Illingworth	9	– c D'Oliveira b Illingworth	73
*Nawab of Pataudi c Barrington b Hobbs	64	– b Illingworth	148
E. A. S. Prasanna c Murray b Illingworth	0	– lbw b Close	19
S. Guhu b Snow	4	– b Higgs	1
R. F. Surti c and b Hobbs	22	– c Murray b Snow	5
B. S. Bedi lbw b Hobbs	0	– c Snow b Hobbs	14
B. S. Chandrasekhar not out	0	– not out	0
L-b 6	6	B 10, l-b 13	23
1/39 2/40 3/59 4/59 5/81 6/81 7/92 8/151 9/151	164	1/5 2/173 3/217 4/228 5/362 6/388 7/448 8/469 9/506	510

Bowling: *First Innings*—Snow 17–7–34–2; Higgs 14–8–19–0; D'Oliveira 9–4–29–1; Hobbs 22.2–9–45–3; Illingworth 22–11–31–3; Close 3–3–0–0. *Second Innings*—Snow 41–10–108–2; Higgs 24–3–71–1; D'Oliveira 11–5–22–0; Illingworth 58–26–100–4; Hobbs 45.2–13–100–1; Barrington 9–1–38–0; Close 21–5–48–2.

Umpires: C. S. Elliott and H. Yarnold.

ENGLAND v INDIA

Second Test Match

Played at Lord's, June 22, 23, 24, 26, 1967

England won by an innings and 124 runs, with a day and a half to spare. India, dismissed for 152 and 110, failed with the bat after Pataudi won the toss and took first innings on a hard, fast pitch. Injuries kept out Hanumant and their two fastest bowlers, Guha and Mohol. Compared with Leeds, England included Amiss and Brown for Boycott and Higgs. Engineer, after taking two 4s in Brown's first over, edged an intended drive in the fourth over of the match. Much more serious was the loss of Sardesai in the ninth over when a ball from Snow struck his right hand and broke a bone. Although he returned later before an x-ray revealed the fracture, Sardesai took no further part in the tour.

The pace of Snow and Brown on a murky day brought about India's downfall and only the stylish, left-handed, Wadekar proved equal to the situation; he hit nine boundaries during his stay of two and a quarter hours.

The first day's cricket provided a triumph for Murray, who by holding six catches equalled the world's Test wicket-keeping record held by Grout (Australia) and Lindsay (South Africa).

England soon lost Edrich, but Barrington (54 not out) and Amiss placed them in a strong position. They finished the first day only 45 behind, with eight wickets in hand. The batsmen proceeded with the utmost care during the three hours in which cricket was possible on the second day. A crowd of 12,000 watched almost silently while Barrington, Graveney and D'Oliveira treated Chandrasekhar and the two left-arm bowlers, Surti and Bedi, with such respect that only 145 runs were added for the loss of Barrington. Chandrasekhar upset the latter's off stump as soon as he returned for his second spell. So Barrington, 93 at Headingley and this time 97, again departed when in sight of a hundred. He had spent just over four hours for his runs, which included ten 4s and in fourteen Test innings at Lord's he had yet to reach three figures.

Graveney, elegant as ever, placed his forcing strokes so skilfully that he hooked Bedi for 6 and also hit ten 4s while reaching 74 not out before rain intervened shortly after three o'clock.

The early cricket on Saturday belonged almost entirely to Graveney. Fifteen years previously he had hit his first Test hundred against India in Bombay and now he progressed towards his ninth in Tests and the 113th of his career. While D'Oliveira struggled to find his form – he added only six in an hour – Graveney never looked in the slightest trouble and when stumped off the third ball after lunch he was sixth out, having hit two 6s and twenty 4s in his superb 151 made in five hours. England, in an impregnable position, offered no further resistance. In fact, the last five wickets went down in three-quarters of an hour after lunch for the addition of 27 runs to the interval total. Despite India's poor catching and ground fielding, Chandrasekhar mixing his pacey googlies with the occasional leg break, bowled untiringly for long spells.

India wanted 234 to compel England to bat again, but could not begin the task until Monday owing to more rain. Apart from Kunderan, who opened the innings in place of Sardesai, India gave another inept display with the bat on a damp pitch which helped the pace bowlers to acquire lift and the spinners to turn the ball. Nevertheless, the pitch was not spiteful and Kunderan hit six 4s, staying two and three-quarter hours until he was eighth out. Illingworth came on at 18 and except for changing ends bowled till the match was completed. In two hours before lunch, India made 75 for three, but during the interval a sharp shower livened the pitch and the remaining six wickets went down in less than an hour for 35 runs, Illingworth taking five for 12 in 10 overs.

Although the match went into the fourth day, England won in two and a half days' playing time. Victory came so soon after lunch on Monday that play had finished half an hour before the Queen and the Duke of Edinburgh arrived. The teams and officials were presented on the field by Sir Alec Douglas-Home, the President of the MCC.

India

D. N. Sardesai c Murray b Illingworth	28	– absent hurt	0
†F. M. Engineer c Murray b Brown	8	– c Amiss b Snow	8
A. L. Wadekar c Illingworth b D'Oliveira	57	– b Illingworth	19
C. G. Borde b Snow	0	– c Snow b Close	1
*Nawab of Pataudi c Murray b Brown	5	– c Graveney b Close	5
R. F. Surti c Murray b D'Oliveira	6	– c D'Oliveira b Illingworth	0
V. Subramanya c Murray b Brown	0	– c Edrich b Illingworth	1
B. K. Kunderan c Murray b Snow	20	– lbw b Illingworth	47
E. A. S. Prasanna run out	17	– c D'Oliveira b Illingworth	0
B. S. Bedi c Amiss b Snow	5	– b Illingworth	11
B. S. Chandrasekhar not out	2	– not out	3
B 2, l-b 2	4	B 11, l-b 4	15
1/12 2/24 3/29 4/45 5/58 6/102 7/112 8/144 9/145	152	1/8 2/60 3/67 4/79 5/80 6/86 7/90 8/101 9/110	110

Bowling: *First Innings*—Snow 20.4–5–49–3; Brown 18–3–61–3; D'Oliveira 15–6–38–2; Illingworth 2–2–0–1. *Second Innings*—Snow 8–4–12–1; Brown 5–2–10–0; Illingworth 22.3–12–29–6; Hobbs 6–1–16–0; Close 15–5–28–2.

England

J. H. Edrich c and b Surti	12
K. F. Barrington b Chandrasekhar	97
D. L. Amiss b Chandrasekhar	29
T. W. Graveney st Engineer b Bedi	151
B. L. d'Oliveira c and b Chandrasekhar	33
*D. B. Close c Borde b Prasanna	7
†J. T. Murray b Chandrasekhar	7
R. Illingworth lbw b Chandrasekhar	4
R. N. S. Hobbs b Bedi	7
D. J. Brown c Pataudi b Bedi	5
J. A. Snow not out	8
B 5, l-b 18, w 1, n-b 2	26
1/46 2/107 3/185 4/307 5/334 6/359 7/365 8/372 9/372	386

Bowling: Surti 31–10–67–1; Subramanya 7–1–20–0; Chandrasekhar 53–9–127–5; Bedi 31.2–13–68–3; Prasanna 32–5–78–1.

Umpires: J. S. Buller and A. Jepson.

LEICESTERSHIRE v INDIA

Played at Leicester, July 8, 9, 10, 1967

Leicestershire won by seven wickets. India found no answer to good seam bowling on a quickish pitch, and were defeated early in the afternoon of the third day. Their batting in the first innings was dominated by Hanumant Singh and Subramanya in a sixth-wicket partnership of 109 which Saxena followed with his first fifty of the tour. Leicestershire also leaned heavily on their sixth pair, Knight and Tolchard, who put on 92. Bedi, slow left arm, and Prasanna, off spin, were India's main bowlers, though the pitch offered no help.

The dramatic cricket was reserved for the third innings, when Cotton, with nine for 29, utterly demolished the tourists' batting in just over two hours. India's 63 was their lowest total of the tour, and the county gained their first victory over a touring side since 1906.

India

†B. K. Kunderan hit wkt b Cotton	17	– c Tolchard b Cotton	0
R. F. Surti c Marner b Spencer	13	– c Spencer b Cotton	15
A. L. Wadekar c Tolchard b Knight	31	– c and b Cotton	0
C. G. Borde b Knight	4	– b Knight	24
*Nawab of Pataudi b Knight	10	– c Tolchard b Cotton	3
Hanumant Singh c Matthews b Marner	40	– c Tolchard b Cotton	2
V. Subramanya b Birkenshaw	64	– b Cotton	2
R. Saxena not out	53	– c Booth b Cotton	1
S. Venkataraghavan b Marner	0	– b Cotton	2
B. S. Bedi lbw b Lock	12	– c Tolchard b Cotton	8
E. A. S. Prasanna c Booth b Matthews	25	– not out	2
L-b 6, n-b 6	12	L-b 4	4
1/16 2/46 3/56 4/77 5/78 6/187 7/188 8/195 9/236	281	1/0 2/0 3/34 4/42 5/44 6/46 7/46 8/47 9/60	63

Bowling: *First Innings*—Cotton 21–5–79–1; Spencer 13–2–41–1; Knight 20–3–51–3; Birkenshaw 10–1–33–1; Marner 10–0–35–2; Lock 7–1–22–1; Matthews 1.4–0–8–1. *Second Innings*—Cotton 14–4–29–9; Spencer 5–0–11–0; Knight 11–4–19–1.

Leicestershire

B. J. Booth b Bedi	54	– lbw b Bedi	32
B. Dudleston lbw b Surti	13	– c Wadekar b Prasanna	37
J. Birkenshaw c Kunderan b Bedi	5	– not out	12
C. C. Inman c Wadekar b Bedi	15	– c Subramanya b Prasanna	9
P. T. Marner b Bedi	3	– not out	9
B. R. Knight c Subramanya b Prasanna	47		
†R. W. Tolchard st Kunderan b Prasanna	54		
A. Matthews c Wadekar b Prasanna	0		
*G. A. R. Lock b Prasanna	20		
C. T. Spencer lbw b Bedi	19		
J. Cotton not out	0		
B 9, l-b 3, n-b 3	15	L-b 1	1
1/47 2/58 3/93 4/97 5/106 6/198 7/199 8/212 9/243	245	1/67 2/71 3/85	(3 wkts) 100

Bowling: *First Innings*—Surti 13–2–45–1; Subramanya 7–2–16–0; Bedi 40–13–69–5; Venkataraghavan 14–2–26–0; Prasanna 18.4–2–74–4. *Second Innings*—Surti 6–0–14–0; Subramanya 4–0–11–0; Venkataraghavan 1–0–4–0; Prasanna 15–4–36–2; Bedi 13–1–32–1; Pataudi 0.2–0–2–0.

Umpires: T. W. Spencer and J. F. Crapp.

WARWICKSHIRE v INDIA

Played at Birmingham, July 10, 12, 13, 1971

India won by an innings and three runs. Jameson thrashed the Indian bowling in an exhilarating innings of 231 in four hours and twenty-three minutes. Brutal leg-side hits earned him four 6s and the majority of his thirty-three 4s. He made his highest score and completely overshadowed Whitehouse and M. J. K. Smith in partnerships for the first and third wickets. The Indian team as a unit found the pitch to their liking and scored their highest total in England although they failed really to dominate a below-strength attack. Sardesai's 120 occupied four and a quarter hours and Wadekar's 77 took three hours. Well flighted spin bowling by Bedi and Prasanna, assisted by bad strokes, earned the tourists an unexpected victory on a pitch still in excellent condition.

Warwickshire

J. Whitehouse st Krishnamurthy b Bedi	52	– c Krishnamurthy b Bedi	25
J. A. Jameson lbw b Bedi	231	– c Bedi b Abid Ali	11
R. B. Kanhai c Abid Ali b Bedi	4	– c and b Bedi	59
M. J. K. Smith not out	72	– c and b Bedi	38
E. E. Hemmings (did not bat)		– lbw b Prasanna	9
K. Ibadulla (did not bat)		– not out	13
W. Blenkiron (did not bat)		– c Prasanna b Bedi	1
*†A. C. Smith (did not bat)		– c Gavaskar b Prasanna	3
P. J. Lewington (did not bat)		– lbw b Prasanna	10
P. R. Dunkels (did not bat)		– c Gavaskar b Bedi	0
W. N. Tidy (did not bat)		– c sub b Prasanna	0
B 7, l-b 10, n-b 1	18	B 5, l-b 6, n-b 2	13
1/132 2/136 3/377 (3 wkts dec.)	377	1/28 2/64 3/132 4/149 5/151 6/152 7/160 8/178 9/179	182

Bowling: *First Innings*—Govindraj 12–2–50–0; Abid Ali 15–2–74–0; Solkar 5–0–33–0; Bedi 22–3–106–3; Prasanna 26–3–96–0. *Second Innings*—Govindraj 3–0–21–0; Abid Ali 10–1–20–1; Bedi 37–13–64–5; Prasanna 30.2–9–57–4; Gavaskar 1–0–7–0.

India

S. M. Gavaskar c Jameson b Blenkiron	25	D. Govindraj b Blenkiron	7
A. A. Baig c Jameson b Blenkiron	32	E. A. S. Prasanna lbw b Ibadulla	10
*A. L. Wadekar c Jameson b Lewington	77	B. S. Bedi not out	6
D. N. Sardesai b Ibadulla	120		
G. R. Viswanath c and b Jameson	90	B 12, l-b 6, n-b 17	35
E. D. Solkar c Hemmings b Jameson	35		
S. Abid Ali b Blenkiron	93	1/50 2/70 3/214 4/332 5/388 6/421 7/525 8/537 9/553	562
†P. Krishnamurthy c Jameson b Blenkiron	32		

Bowling: Blenkiron 30.1–4–100–5; Dunkels 25–2–91–0; Hemmings 25–5–67–0; Tidy 32–4–124–0; Lewington 16–5–34–1; Ibadulla 15–6–23–2; Jameson 19–2–76–2; A. C. Smith 2–0–12–0.

Umpires: J. G. Langridge and D. L. Evans.

HAMPSHIRE v INDIA

Played at Bournemouth, July 17, 19, 20, 1971

India won by five wickets. Mankad, Viswanath and Venkataraghavan all played major roles in this comfortable success by the tourists, while Hampshire were able to applaud the performance of O'Sullivan a slow left-arm bowler from New Zealand, making his début. Hampshire did not bat well enough on the first day, when Gilliat, the captain, showed good form before inexplicably going for a run to short-leg, and the Indians never allowed the initiative to be wrested from them. Their progress was at times pedestrian, but Mankad and Viswanath scored centuries and the long period of consolidation was the foundation of a first-innings lead of 166. Hampshire were without Cottam and most of the bowling fell on O'Sullivan and Worrell, both of whom did well considering their inexperience. Hampshire batted bravely in the second innings, but Venkataraghavan achieved the best bowling analysis of the summer to open the door to victory for his side, who surprisingly lost five wickets in making 106.

Hampshire

B. A. Richards c and b Solkar	10	– st Krishnamurthy b Venkataraghavan.	45
R. V. Lewis c Krishnamurthy b Prasanna	28	– c Krishnamurthy b Venkataraghavan.	71
D. R. Turner lbw b Govindraj	0	– c Solkar b Venkataraghavan	11
*R. M. C. Gilliat run out	50	– st Krishnamurthy b Vankataraghavan.	79
D. A. Livingstone c Viswanath b Prasanna	44	– c Gavaskar b Venkataraghavan	9
T. E. Jesty b Venkataraghavan	5	– not out	11
†G. R. Stephenson c Sardesai b Gavaskar	27	– c Solkar b Venkataraghavan	15
J. K. Holder c Sardesai b Prasanna	5	– c Gavaskar b Venkataraghavan	0
D. R. O'Sullivan not out	25	– lbw b Venkataraghavan	4
L. R. Worrell c and b Govindraj	2	– b Solkar	16
D. W. White lbw b Gavaskar	1	– c Baig b Venkataraghavan	0
L-b 1	1	B 7, l-b 3	10
1/13 2/22 3/59 4/101 5/114 6/144 7/161 8/188 9/195	198	1/73 2/113 3/173 4/195 5/225 6/231 7/231 8/252 9/270	271

Bowling: *First Innings*—Govindraj 10–2–43–2; Solkar 13–4–33–1; Prasanna 27–9–37–3; Venkataraghavan 22–5–76–1; Gavaskar 1.3–0–8–2. *Second Innings*—Govindraj 6–1–15–0; Solkar 17–4–47–1; Prasanna 33–6–81–0; Venkataraghavan 36.3–13–93–9; Gavaskar 3–0–25–0; Wadekar 1–1–0–0.

India

S. M. Gavaskar c Livingstone b O'Sullivan	53	– c Richards b O'Sullivan	25
A. A. Baig c O'Sullivan b White	4	– b Holder	2
A. V. Mankad c Gilliat b Worrell	109		
D. N. Sardesai c Holder b O'Sullivan	12	– c and b O'Sullivan	4
G. R. Viswanath st Stephenson b O'Sullivan	122		
*A. L. Wadekar b Worrell	20	– c Worrell b O'Sullivan	27
E. D. Solkar c Richards b Worrell	5	– not out	7
S. Venkataraghavan st Stephenson b O'Sullivan	7	– c and b Worrell	19
†P. Krisnamurthy c and b O'Sullivan	2		
D. Govindraj c Gilliat b Worrell	6	– not out	15
E. A. S. Prasanna not out	7		
B 2, l-b 4, w 1, n-b 10	17	L-b 3, n-b 4	7
1/13 2/97 3/125 4/268 5/304 6/342 7/342 8/345 9/352	364	1/4 2/54 3/63 4/72 5/94	(5 wkts) 106

Bowling: *First Innings*—White 21–10–46–1; Holder 23–5–57–0; Worrell 49–18–102–4; O'Sullivan 34.4–18–116–5; Richards 5–2–8–0; Turner 5–1–18–0. *Second Innings*—White 5–1–13–0; Holder 6–1–13–1; Worrell 12–1–47–1; O'Sullivan 10–1–27–3.

Umpires: A. E. Fagg and H. Yarnold.

WORCESTERSHIRE v INDIA

Played at Worcester, September 1, 2, 3, 1971

Drawn. Worcestershire put down two chances from Gavaskar before he had scored and their punishment was a second-wicket partnership of 327 between the opener and his captain, Wadekar. In compiling the season's highest stand, Gavaskar batted throughout the first day, hitting twenty-eight 4s, and his left-handed partner hit two 6s and sixteen 4s in nearly five and a half hours. The injury-weakened county lost half their side for 92, but John Parker, a 20-year-old right-hand batsman from New Zealand, marked his first-class début with a mature innings of 91, which enabled Worcestershire to avoid the follow-on by 14 runs. Wilkinson helped Parker put on 100. A pleasant fifty by Viswanath was the highlight of the Indians' progress to a declaration challenging the county to make 286 in three and a half hours. The early loss of the openers looked ominous for Worcestershire, but the left-handed Yardley reached a competent maiden century in under three hours and his partnership with Ormrod, playing his highest innings of the season, brought 139 at a brisk rate. Worcestershire needed 121 from the last twenty overs and might have achieved the target but for an understandably cautions start by Imran Khan, the Pakistani, who was making his first county appearance. Holder quickened the pace at the end, but Worcestershire fell 36 short.

India

K. Jayantilal b Carter	2	– c Parker b Carter	4
S. N. Gavaskar c Yardley b Wilkinson	194	– c Headley b Carter	6
*A. L. Wadekar c Parker b Wilkinson	150		
G. R. Viswanath not out	22	– c Yardley b Wilkinson	53
D. N. Sardesai not out	0	– st Wilcock b Griffith	13
E. D. Solkar (did not bat)		– c sub b Wilkinson	14
S. Abid Ali (did not bat)		– c Carter b Griffith	23
S. Venkataraghavan (did not bat)		– b Wilkinson	12
†S. M. H. Kirmani (did not bat)		– not out	3
B. S. Bedi (did not bat)		– c Stimpson b Griffith	7
B. S. Chandrasekhar (did not bat)		– not out	4
B 1, l-b 6, n-b 8	15	L-b 6, w 2, n-b 3	11
1/2 2/329 3/373 (3 wkts dec.)	383	1/9 2/14 3/40 4/57 5/106 6/121 7/134 8/145 (8 wkts dec.)	150

Bowling: *First Innings*—Holder 18–2–64–0; Carter 23–2–81–1; Wilkinson 30–6–84–2; Imran Khan 16–0–73–0; Griffith 25–5–66–0. *Second Innings*—Carter 8–1–18–2; Wilkinson 17–3–48–3; Imran Khan 5–1–15–0; Griffith 14–3–58–3.

Worcestershire

*R. G. A. Headley c Venkataraghavan b Chandrasekhar	25	– c and b Solkar	13
P. J. Stimpson lbw b Bedi	24	– c Wadekar b Abid Ali	5
J. A. Ormrod c Chandrasekhar b Bedi	16	– b Abid Ali	76
T. J. Yardley b Venkataraghavan	18	– not out	104
J. M. Parker c Gavaskar b Abid Ali	91		
Imran Khan run out	0	– b Abid Ali	15
K. Wilkinson c Solkar b Venkataraghavan	48		
K. Griffith b Venkataraghavan	1		
†H. G. Wilcock b Venkataraghavan	0		
V. A. Holder c Abid Ali b Solkar	9	– b Solkar	27
R. G. M. Carter not out	0		
B 8, l-b 5, n-b 3	16	B 3, l-b 6, n-b 1	10
1/53 2/53 3/90 4/92 5/92 6/192 7/208 8/208 9/246	248	1/18 2/26 3/165 4/202 5/250 (5 wkts)	250

Bowling: *First Innings*—Abid Ali 7.4–1–26–1; Solkar 10–2–24–1; Bedi 27–9–50–2; Venkataraghavan 34–11–60–4; Chandrasekhar 27–8–66–1; Gavaskar 2–1–6–0. *Second Innings*—Abid Ali 21–2–64–3; Solkar 20.5–2–85–2; Bedi 10–0–41–0; Venkataraghavan 9–1–31–0; Chandrasekhar 3–0–19–0.

Umpires: C. Cook and D. L. Evans.

T. N. PEARCE'S XI v INDIA

Played at Scarborough, September 4, 6, 7, 1971

India won by five wickets with three-quarters of an hour to spare and so concluded their tour on a satisfactory note. They played real Festival cricket. Indeed, all the batsmen showed the right approach, which reflected considerable merit on the leg-break bowling of Hobbs, the only successful bowler. He took nine for 158 in the match. Otherwise, the batsmen made merry, with hundreds by Virgin and Bolus for Pearce's XI and Mankad and Gavaskar for India. Virgin set the pattern on the opening afternoon when he plundered the bowling for eight 6s and three 4s in scoring 73 in one period of twenty minutes. Mankad stayed five hours to make sure that India's reply was adequate carrying his bat for 154 (nineteen 4s) and Bolus (one 6, fifteen 4s) batted swiftly enough to allow Lewis to set a task, which at 251 in four hours proved over generous. As far as one could see through a dense sea fret, Gavaskar had no difficulty in steering India home; he hit four 6s and thirteen 4s.

T. N. Pearce's XI

R. T. Virgin st Krishnamurthy b Solkar	176	– lbw b Chandrasekhar	22
J. B. Bolus run out	75	– not out	106
P. H. Parfitt c Mankad b Chandrasekhar	4	– b Bedi	63
K. W. R. Fletcher not out	67		
*A. R. Lewis not out	21	– not out	1
D. B. Close (did not bat)		– c Govindraj b Bedi	1
B 12, l-b 1, w 1	14	B 6	6
1/155 2/164 3/308	(3 wkts dec.) 357	1/47 2/190 3/194	(3 wkts dec.) 199

P. M. Walker, †B. Taylor, K. D. Boyce, R. N. S. Hobbs and J. S. E. Price did not bat.

Bowling: *First Innings*—Govindraj 10–2–39–0; Solkar 12–1–37–1; Gavaskar 3–0–9–0; Venkataraghavan 17–1–94–0; Chandrasekhar 16–3–59–1; Bedi 16–3–77–0; Mankad 5–1–28–0. *Second Innings*—Govindraj 9–2–37–0; Solkar 9–2–15–0; Venkataraghavan 15–3–53–0; Chandrasekhar 15–3–44–1; Bedi 10–0–44–2.

India

A. V. Mankad not out	154	– c Parfitt b Close	30
K. Jayantilal b Parfitt	8		
S. M. Gavaskar c Lewis b Hobbs	2	– b Hobbs	128
G. R. Viswanath c Walker b Parfitt	3	– c sub b Hobbs	21
A. A. Baig c Close b Hobbs	22	– b Hobbs	33
E. D. Solkar c Virgin b Walker	79	– not out	7
*S. Venkataraghavan c Price b Hobbs	5	– c sub b Hobbs	16
D. Govindraj c Price b Hobbs	12	– not out	8
†P. Krishnamurthy st Taylor b Hobbs	5		
B. S. Bedi c Hobbs b Boyce	4		
B. S. Chandrasekhar b Boyce	0		
B 1, l-b 3, n-b 8	12	B 2, l-b 3, n-b 4	9
1/35 2/38 3/45 4/91 5/214 6/244 7/276 8/289 9/306	306	1/68 2/185 3/211 4/222 5/240	(5 wkts) 252

Bowling: *First Innings*—Price 14–2–44–0; Boyce 13.4–3–33–2; Parfitt 22–8–59–2; Hobbs 32–4–94–5; Walker 16–2–64–1. *Second Innings*—Price 6–0–13–0; Boyce 8–0–39–0; Parfitt 13–2–53–0; Hobbs 17.5–3–64–4; Walker 10–0–38–0; Close 7–2–36–1.

Umpires: R. Aspinall and T. W. Spencer.

ENGLAND v INDIA

First Cornhill Test

Played at Birmingham, July 12, 13, 14, 16, 1979

England won by an innings and 83 runs with a day to spare. Favoured by fine sunny weather and a perfect pitch for run-making. England made the most of Brearley's good fortune in winning the toss. Though overwhelmed in the end, India's batsmen put up a most gallant display. However, apart from Kapil Dev, who took all five England wickets with his lively pace, and Venkataraghavan's modest off-spin, much of the bowling was second-rate and off the target.

England again owed much to Boycott, whose solid resistance for more than seven and a half hours (he hit twelve 4s in his 155) led to the mammoth total of 633 for five. Boycott himself was fourth to leave at 426. Only twice had England exceeded that score at home – both times against Australia in 1938.

The talented, fair-haired Gower deservedly received the Man of the Match award of £300 for his not out 200, his highest first-class innings. If less aggressive than usual, he paid due respect to the bowling, but for six hours he stroked the ball with effortless ease past cover, and hooked and pulled anything short. Altogether he hit one 6 and 24 4s.

After a staid opening stand by Boycott and Brearley of 66, including 24 extras, Gooch arrived just before lunch following the dismissal of Randall. At last the runs began to flow as the tall Essex player struck one 6 and thirteen 4s in his brilliant 83 in two hours. By the end of the first day England had reached 318 for three, with Boycott 113 and Gower 43. All three wickets had been snapped up by Reddy, the Indian wicket-keeper, on his Test début.

On the second day England put on 315 runs in four and half hours. The day belonged to the left-handed Gower, whose stand with Boycott ran to 191, and whose unbroken partnership of 165 with Miller was the best for the sixth wicket for England against India. Miller took toll of weary bowlers for nearly two and a half hours. For once, Chandrasekhar did not do himself justice. On the eve of the match he was declared unfit to play because of Achilles' tendon trouble in his left ankle, but he did play and bowled extremely well early in the match until unable to stand the strain. Amarnath also went lame, with the result that a tremendous amount of work fell on the willing opening pair, Kapil Dev and left-armer Ghavri.

After their long spell in the field India had to bat for seventy-five minutes at the end of the second day. Almost immediately Botham struck; in his second over Chauhan could not avoid a lifting ball and went to a fine low catch by Gooch at third slip. Gavaskar and the tall Vengsarkar settled down well against an attacking field, and all went smoothly until the last ball of the day when Vengsarkar, with India on 59, fell to another smart catch by Gooch, this time at silly point.

Not until thirty-five minutes before tea did any England bowler meet with success on Saturday, when a large crowd admired the superb backs-to-the-wall efforts of Gavaskar and his brother-in-law, Viswanath. For one hundred minutes they defied all that Brearley could offer, and then came a tragic run out. Gavaskar turned Willis towards mid-wicket where Randall, tearing in from mid-on, swooped on the ball. Viswanath sent back Gavaskar, but Taylor, who had been standing well back, sprinted up and broke the wicket with Gavaskar still far from home. For three hours Gavaskar had looked safe and sound in his white sun hat, giving the impression that he was bound for his twentieth Test century. He hit three 4s.

Viswanath still resisted manfully, altogether for three and a half hours. He hit nine 4s before Edmonds induced a bat and pad catch at point. Gaekwad stayed for two hours and Amarnath withstood much short stuff from Botham, but England were well on top. They fielded brilliantly and Brearley varied his attack skilfully. India had to follow on 336 behind and stood seven without loss over the week-end.

Botham stole the honours on the fourth day with another of his amazing spells of bowling when England took the second new ball at 227 for four. Up to that point India had defended nobly on a perfect pitch which had given no encouragement to the bowlers. Then in forty minutes they collapsed dramatically with the last six wickets falling in 10.1 overs for 26 runs. Botham claimed four for 10 runs in five overs and took his record in eighteen Tests to 94 wickets. This time he reduced his pace, and, concentrating on line and length, regained his ability to swing the ball in alarming fashion for the unfortunate Indians. For once, Taylor was not at his best behind the stumps and he missed stumping Viswanath and Amarnath off Edmonds. Earlier Gavaskar and Chauhan had played through the pre-lunch session and raised their opening partnership to 124 before Randall picked up Chauhan at shortish cover.

Botham finished with five for 70 and he had an able assistant in Hendrick, who took four for 45. It was a surprise lifting ball from Hendrick which deceived Gavaskar and provided a catch at third slip for Gooch, who later began the Indian collapse when he dived low to his left, again at third slip, and held a slice from Gaekwad. Long before Willis had retired with a tiresome pain in his ribs.

England

*J. M. Brearley c Reddy b Kapil Dev	24
G. Boycott lbw b Kapil Dev	155
D. W. Randall c Reddy b Kapil Dev	15
G. A. Gooch c Reddy b Kapil Dev	83
D. I. Gower not out	200
I. T. Botham b Kapil Dev	33
G. Miller not out	63
B 4, l-b 27, w 11, n-b 18	60
1/66 2/90 3/235 4/426 5/468	(5 wkts dec.) 633

P. H. Edmonds, †R. W. Taylor, R. G. D. Willis and M. Hendrick did not bat.

Bowling: Kapil Dev 48–15–146–5; Ghavri 38–5–129–0; Amarnath 13.2–2–47–0; Chandrasekhar 29–1–113–0; Venkataraghavan 31–4–107–0; Gaekwad 3–0–12–0; Chauhan 3–0–19–0.

India

S. M. Gavaskar run out	61	– c Gooch b Hendrick	68
C. P. S. Chauhan c Gooch b Botham	4	– c Randall b Willis	56
D. B. Vengsarkar c Gooch b Edmonds	22	– c Edmonds b Hendrick	7
G. R. Viswanath c Botham b Edmonds	78	– c Taylor b Botham	51
A. D. Gaekwad c Botham b Willis	25	– c Gooch b Botham	15
M. Amarnath b Willis	31	– lbw b Botham	10
Kapil Dev lbw b Botham	1	– c Hendrick b Botham	21
K. D. Ghavri c Brearley b Willis	6	– c Randall b Hendrick	4
†B. Reddy b Hendrick	21	– lbw b Hendrick	0
*S. Venkataraghavan c Botham b Hendrick	28	– lbw b Botham	0
B. S. Chandrasekhar not out	0	– not out	0
B 1, l-b 4, w 3, n-b 12	20	B 7, l-b 12, n-b 2	21
1/15 2/59 3/129 4/205 5/209 6/210 7/229 8/251 9/294	297	1/124 2/136 3/136 4/182 5/227 6/240 7/249 8/250 9/251	253

Bowling: *First Innings*—Willis 24–9–69–3; Botham 26–4–86–2; Hendrick 24.1–9–36–2; Edmonds 26–11–60–2; Boycott 5–1–8–0; Miller 11–3–18–0. *Second Innings*—Willis 14–3–45–1; Botham 29–8–70–5; Hendrick 20.4–8–45–4; Edmonds 17–6–37–0; Miller 9–1–27–0; Gooch 6–3–8–0.

Umpires: D. J. Constant and B. J. Meyer.

ENGLAND v INDIA

Fourth Cornhill Test

Played at The Oval, August 30, 31, September 1, 3, 4, 1979

Drawn, after the most gripping closing overs in a home Test since the draw at Lord's against West Indies in 1963, a match it closely resembled as all four results were possible with three balls left. Gavaskar's inspiring and technically flawless 221 earned him the Man of the Match award and brought that rarity in recent Tests in England – a final day charged with interest. Botham played the major part in preventing an Indian victory and confirmed his status as Man of the Series. As the teams fought each other to a standstill, there were many Englishmen in the crowd who would not have displayed their customary dejection at a Test defeat.

Gavaskar's innings was the highest by an Indian against England, overtaking the unbeaten 203 by the younger Nawab of Pataudi at Delhi in 1964, and his stand of 213 with Chauhan surpassed the previous best opening partnership for his country against England – 203 by Mushtaq Ali and Merchant at Manchester in 1936. India's 429 for eight – they were set 438 in 500 minutes – was the fourth-highest score in the fourth innings of a Test. To reach their target they would have needed to set a new mark for a side batting fourth and winning, but this generation of Indian batsmen have some notable performances in that department and the job did not frighten them.

England gave first caps to Butcher and Bairstow, omitting Randall and Taylor, while Willey returned after a gap of three years for Miller. Yajurvindra Singh replaced the injured Amarnath for India.

The game, played in virtually unbroken sunshine, began prosaically as Butcher and Boycott dug in without attempting to dominate. Butcher's disappointing innings ended in the over before lunch and Kapil Dev, as at Leeds, extended the breakthrough by taking two quick wickets. He slanted one into Boycott, and three balls later made one straighten at Gower, whom he had also claimed lbw for a duck at Headingley. Willey and Gooch repaired the damage, Willey playing the strokes of the day by hooking and cover-driving with immense power. Botham achieved the 3 runs he needed to reach the landmark of 1,000 runs and 100 wickets in his 21st Test, beating the 23 Tests required by Mankad for this double. But Gooch's first Test century still eluded him; he fell in the first over of the second day.

Botham, as bowler and fielder, sent India sliding into trouble, taking two wickets and holding two catches, and India had subsided to 137 for five when bad light halted the game forty minutes early. Botham's second catch was remarkable. Bairstow could only parry the ball when Vengsarkar edged Willis. The ball struck Brearley on the boot, flew upwards, and as Bairstow came across to retrieve it, Botham grabbed it one-handed at second slip. Viswanath had played exquisitely for almost three hours.

England were batting again by lunch on Saturday. The regular fall of wickets, caused by much batting below Test class from both sides, had driven the match along swifter than the normal sedate progress of a Test, and this was, of course, an important factor in allowing the marvellous finish.

Butcher was unable to improve significantly on his first innings form. Gooch drove one vast 6, but when Gower failed again, Willey and Boycott decided on rather pedestrian consolidation over the last seventy-five minutes. Later events proved their caution justified. Boycott toiled with the handicap of back trouble on the Monday in the last three hours of his seven-hour effort. Botham was run out, neglecting to ascertain Boycott's intentions as he charged up the pitch, and so England were indebted to a crisp knock from Bairstow as they moved to their declaration.

At 76 for no wicket on the fifth morning, India wanted roughly a run a minute. Their rate was never brisk – 48 in the first hour, 45 in the second, and 44 in the third. Hendrick, allowing only 11 runs in six overs, did most to peg India's progress and, in mid-afternoon, Willey conceded only 2 runs in eight grudging overs. However, Hendrick disappeared for good with shoulder trouble after his spell, and Brearley's capacity for restriction was limited.

England were despairing of wickets when, after five and a quarter hours, Chauhan edged Willis. The despair soon returned as Vengsarkar joined Gavaskar in an accelerating stand which produced 153 at better than a run a minute. Gevaskar masterminded the show, doing all the thinking and playing most of the shots. Tea came at 304 for one and, after a mere six overs between the interval and five o'clock – England ruthlessly slowed down the game – the last twenty overs began at 328 for one with 110 wanted, and India favourites.

At 365 Botham uncharacteristically dropped Vengsarkar on the boundary – an error for which he swiftly compensated by transforming the match with three wickets, a catch and a run-out in the remaining twelve overs. He collected a simple catch off Vengsarkar at 366 and Willey swept aside the promoted Kapil Dev. Yashpal Sharma and Gavaskar rattled the score along to 389 when Botham returned with eight overs left. It was a gamble by Brearley, for Botham had looked innocuous during the day. But he struck with the key wicket, Gavaskar drilling a catch to mid-on shortly after England had taken a drinks break – a rare move, tactically based, with the end so near. Gavaskar's memorable innings lasted eight hours, nine minutes and he hit twenty-one 4s, most of them coming from firm clips past mid-wicket and his unexpectedly powerful cover-drive. However, his cool control of the developing crisis was missed by India as much as his runs.

Viswanath unerringly found one of the widely spaced fielders, as had Vengsarkar and Gavaskar. Then Botham firmly ended India's hopes by having Yajurvindra Singh and Yashpal Sharma lbw in successive overs and, in between, making a slick stop to run out Venkataraghavan. Botham's final four overs brought him an absolutely crucial three for seventeen. A target of 15 from the last over was too much, and the climax came with fielders encircling the bat.

England

G. Boycott lbw b Kapil Dev	35	– b Ghavri	125
A. R. Butcher c Yajurvindra b Venkataraghavan	14	– c Venkataraghavan b Ghavri	20
G. A. Gooch c Viswanath b Ghavri	79	– lbw b Kapil Dev	31
D. I. Gower lbw b Kapil Dev	0	– c Reddy b Bedi	7
P. Willey c Yajurvindra b Bedi	52	– c Reddy b Ghavri	31
I. T. Botham st Reddy b Venkataraghavan	38	– run out	0
*J. M. Brearley b Ghavri	34	– b Venkataraghavan	11
†D. L. Bairstow c Reddy b Kapil Dev	9	– c Gavaskar b Kapil Dev	59
P. H. Edmonds c Kapil Dev b Venkataraghavan	16	– not out	27
R. G. D. Willis not out	10		
M. Hendrick c Gavaskar b Bedi	0		
L-b 9, w 4, n-b 5	18	L-b 14, w 2, n-b 7	23
1/45 2/51 3/51 4/148 5/203 6/245 7/272 8/275 9/304	305	1/43 2/107 3/125 4/192 5/194 6/215 7/291 8/334 (8 wkts dec.)	334

Bowling: *First Innings*—Kapil Dev 32–12–83–3; Ghavri 26–8–61–2; Bedi 29.5–4–69–2; Yajurvindra 8–2–15–0; Venkataraghavan 29–9–59–3. *Second Innings*—Kapil Dev 28.5–4–89–2; Ghavri 34–11–76–3; Venkataraghavan 26–4–75–1; Bedi 26–4–67–1; Yajurvindra 2–0–4–0.

India

S. M. Gavaskar c Bairstow b Botham	13	– c Gower b Botham	221
C. P. S. Chauhan c Botham b Willis	6	– c Botham b Willis	80
D. B. Vengsarkar c Botham b Willis	0	– c Botham b Edmonds	52
G. R. Viswanath c Brearley b Botham	62	– c Brearley b Willey	15
Yashpal Sharma lbw b Willis	27	– lbw b Botham	19
Yajurvindra Singh not out	43	– lbw b Botham	1
Kapil Dev b Hendrick	16	– c Gooch b Willey	0
K. D. Ghavri c Bairstow b Botham	7	– not out	3
†B. Reddy c Bairstow b Botham	12	– not out	5
*S. Venkataraghavan c and b Hendrick	2	– run out	6
B. S. Bedi c Brearley b Hendrick	1		
B 2, l-b 3, w 5, n-b 3	13	B 11, l-b 15, w 1	27
1/9 2/9 3/47 4/91 5/130 6/161 7/172 8/192 9/200	202	1/213 2/366 3/367 4/389 5/410 6/411 7/419 8/423	(8 wkts) 429

Bowling: *First Innings*—Willis 18–2–53–3; Botham 28–7–65–4; Hendrick 22.3–7–38–3; Willey 4–1–10–0; Gooch 2–0–6–0; Edmonds 5–1–17–0. *Second Innings*—Willis 28–4–89–1; Botham 29–5–97–3; Hendrick 8–2–15–0; Edmonds 38–11–87–1; Willey 43.5–15–96–2; Gooch 2–0–9–0; Butcher 2–0–9–0.

Umpires: D. J. Constant and K. E. Palmer.

NOTES BY THE EDITOR, 1980

BOTHAM'S FASTEST TEST DOUBLE

In the past two years the Somerset all-rounder, Ian Botham, has stamped his name on the Test and county scene. Now he has reached the Test double of 1,000 runs and 100 wickets in only 21 Tests at the age of 23. It is the fastest double in Test history, for he accomplished it in two fewer matches than Vinoo Mankad, the Indian all-rounder whose Test career began late owing to World War Two. Botham captured his 100th wicket in the second Test against India at Lord's, when he had Gavaskar caught in the second innings by Brearley, and his 1,000th run came in the first innings of the fourth Test at The Oval. He required only 3 runs after his magnificent 137 at Leeds in the previous Test.

Among English cricketers, Maurice Tate previously held the record in 33 appearances. Among other great all-rounders, Sir Garfield Sobers took 48 Tests for his double. Botham is the first to admit that much of his success with the ball has been due to England's wonderful catching. Soon England will be looking for someone to succeed Mike Brearley as captain. It was significant that, on the latest tour to Australia, Botham became one of the team selectors and he might well get the England captaincy. It is argued that he lacks experience of leadership, but I remember Sir Leonard Hutton (Yorkshire) and Peter May (Surrey) playing under N. W. D. Yardley and Stuart Surridge respectively. In fact, Hutton was never officially captain of Yorkshire.

PAKISTANIS IN ENGLAND

MIDDLESEX v PAKISTAN

Played at Lord's, July 5, 6, 7, 1967

Drawn. Pakistan gave a most uneven display in their first innings. Burki, Saeed and Aizazuddin could not assert themselves, but Majid, whose 51 occupied sixty-eight minutes, Abbas and Asif responded to Latchman's long spell of leg-breaks with more entertaining batting. Latchman, in achieving the best figures of his career, spun and flighted like an experienced craftsman. The Middlesex opening batsmen, Russell and Harris, took advantage of one of the most perfect pitches produced at Lord's for many seasons to accumulate at an ever-accelerating rate until they passed the record for the county's first wicket, the 310 scored by J. D. Robertson and S. M. Brown against Nottinghamshire at Lord's in 1947. Their partnership was also the highest for any wicket against the Pakistan team in England, the previous best being the unfinished 267 by R. E. Marshall and D. A. Livingstone (Hampshire) at Bournemouth in 1962. Similar in style, both profited from off-drives and the glance. Harris achieved the highest score of his career, batting five and a half hours and hitting eighteen 4s. During his innings he passed 1,000 runs for the season and after it he was awarded his county cap. Russell struck sixteen 4s in his stay of four hours, fifty-five minutes. Parfitt and Murray then proceeded to score off almost every ball, Murray reaching 50 in thirty-three minutes. Pakistan experienced no difficulty in making the game safe on the last day. Burki played himself into form for four hours, and Majid saw the bad ball very early in his three-hour effort.

Pakistan

Mohammad Ilyas c Russell b Latchman	40	– c and b Latchman	34
Javed Burki b Stewart	6	– b Bick	114
*Saeed Ahmed c Parfitt b Latchman	19	– c Parfitt b Titmus	7
Majid Jahangir lbw b Latchman	51	– not out	107
Fakir Aizazuddin c Radley b Latchman	5	– c Titmus b Russell	9
Ghulam Abbas b Latchman	55	– not out	21
Asif Iqbal b Stewart	30		
Salahuddin c and b Parfitt	14		
†Wasim Bari b Latchman	5		
Arif Butt b Latchman	3		
Pervez Sajjad not out	3		
L-b 6	6	B 4, l-b 5	9
1/23 2/59 3/74 4/123 5/128 6/190 7/215 8/225 9/229	237	1/88 2/109 3/222 4/242	(4 wkts) 301

Bowling: *First Innings*—Price 7–0–14–0; Stewart 26–7–48–2; Hooker 7–4–8–0; Titmus 10–3–24–0; Latchman 39–11–91–7; Bick 14–6–31–0; Russell 4–1–13–0; Parfitt 3.4–2–2–1. *Second Innings*—Stewart 16–2–39–0; Titmus 28–15–42–1; Latchman 31–10–100–1; Bick 27–11–45–1; Russell 5–3–6–1; Parfitt 8–2–29–0; Harris 9–0–31–0.

Middlesex

W. E. Russell c and b Majid	167	*F. J. Titmus not out	11
M. J. Harris c and b Saeed	160	B 5, l-b 9, n-b 2	16
P. H. Parfitt not out	45		
†J. T. Murray b Arif	53	1/312 2/350 3/433	(3 wkts dec.) 452

C. T. Radley, R. W. Hooker, D. A. Bick, H. C. Latchman, J. S. E. Price and R. W. Stewart did not bat.

Bowling: Asif Iqbal 18–1–73–0; Majid Jahangir 13–1–30–1; Arif Butt 26–7–80–1; Pervez Sajjad 26–5–109–0; Saeed Ahmed 18–1–78–1; Salahuddin 12–2–39–0; Mohammad Ilyas 4–0–27–0.

Umpires: W. F. Price and C. S. Elliott.

YORKSHIRE v PAKISTAN

Played at Headingley, August 2, 3, 4, 1967

Drawn. Pakistan showed to little advantage in a match eventually abandoned in heavy rain on the third afternoon. Their bowlers were so ineffective in the easy batting conditions of the first day that Yorkshire were able to score 368 for the loss of only one wicket, Boycott hitting eighteen 4s in the opening partnership of 210, made in three hours and forty minutes. Continuing into the second day, Sharpe shared a second-wicket partnership of 192 with Padgett and in six and a half hours he hit twenty-three 4s. Except for Majid, Pakistan maintained a defensive approach to batting and they allowed Yorkshire to take and hold the initiative until rain ended the match.

Yorkshire

G. Boycott b Intikhab	128	R. Illingworth not out	2
P. J. Sharpe b Arif	197	B 6, l-b 5, n-b 2	13
D. E. V. Padgett lbw b Nasim	70		—
J. H. Hampshire not out	4	1/210 2/402 3/412 (3 wkts dec.)	414

*D. B. Close, R. A. Hutton, †J. G. Binks, F. S. Trueman, D. Wilson and A. G. Nicholson did not bat.

Bowling: Arif 36.4–5–104–1; Nasim 32–6–96–1; Burki 4–1–20–0; Intikhab 29–4–75–1; Salahuddin 25–3–75–0; Hanif 4–0–22–0; Waqar 1–0–9–0.

Pakistan

Javed Burki b Wilson	20	– not out	38
Fakir Aizazuddin c Close b Nicholson	5	– not out	0
Nasim-ul-Ghani c Boycott b Hutton	14		
Majid Jahangir b Illingworth	42		
Ghulam Abbas c Hampshire b Hutton	43		
*Hanif Mohammad b Illingworth	1		
Waqar Ahmed c Padgett b Illingworth	2		
Salahuddin lbw b Close	1		
Intikhab Alam lbw b Illingworth	0		
†Wasim Bari b Nicholson	9		
Arif Butt not out	0		
B 1, l-b 7, n-b 5	13		
	—		—
1/16 2/36 3/62 4/100 5/110 6/112 7/113 8/120 9/150	150	(no wkt)	38

Bowling: *First Innings*—Trueman 13–9–13–0; Nicholson 14–5–37–2; Hutton 10.2–4–21–2; Close 16–9–21–1; Illingworth 24–12–34–4; Wilson 8–6–11–1. *Second Innings*—Nicholson 5–1–15–0; Hutton 6–3–19–0; Close 4–4–0–0; Illingworth 1–0–4–0.

Umpires: J. Arnold and A. E. Rhodes.

GLAMORGAN v PAKISTAN

Played at Swansea, August 5, 7, 8, 1967

Drawn. Majid Jahangir went near to making cricket history with a display of big hitting in the Pakistan second innings. In a score of 147 which took only eighty-nine minutes he hit no fewer than thirteen 6s, a record for a first-class match in this country. Five of the 6s came in one over by R. Davis, a young off-spin bowler. Majid also scored the fastest century of the season, in sixty-one minutes. Saeed Ahmed, his partner in a fourth-wicket stand of 215 in eighty-five minutes seemed slow in comparison. Yet his 50 took only fifty minutes. All this spectacular batting, however, was in vain. Pakistan delayed their declaration until they led by 323 runs, and only two hours, fifty minutes remained for play. Lewis decided that such a task was impossible and when rain brought play to a premature close the game had become a formality. The feature of the earlier cricket was a century by Lewis, his first of the season, after repeated failures. He batted three and a quarter hours for 128 not out, which included three 6s and eleven 4s.

Pakistan

Mohammad Ilyas lbw b I. J. Jones	0	– b Davis	63
Fakir Aizazuddin lbw b Cordle	0	– retired hurt	9
*Saeed Ahmed c I. J. Jones b Shepherd	26	– not out	72
Ghulam Abbas c E. Jones b Cordle	10	– c and b Davis	0
Majid Jahangir c E. Jones b Shepherd	37	– not out	147
Waqar Ahmed not out	79		
Asif Iqbal lbw b Cordle	75		
Salahuddin c Nash b Cordle	2		
†Fasihuddin c Davis b Cordle	0	– c Lewis b Davis	18
Niaz Ahmed c Davis b I. J. Jones	1		
Pervez Sajjad not out	3		
L-b 8, n-b 8	16	B 4, l-b 2, n-b 9	15
1/0 2/1 3/30 4/61 5/88 6/224 7/233 8/235 9/236 (9 wkts dec.)	249	1/98 2/102 3/109 (3 wkts dec.)	324

Bowling: *First Innings*—I. J. Jones 27–7–53–2; Cordle 22–10–29–5; Nash 23–7–48–0; Jarrett 8–2–37–0; Davis 14–6–24–0; Shepherd 23–7–42–2. *Second Innings*—I. J. Jones 12–3–32–0; Cordle 10–1–26–0; Nash 9–0–65–0; Shepherd 16–4–49–0; Davis 18–4–98–3; Jarrett 4–0–39–0.

Glamorgan

A. Jones c Fasihuddin b Asif	3	– not out	37
R. Davis lbw b Niaz	21	– b Niaz	1
A. Rees c Fasihuddin b Niaz	3	– c sub b Niaz	11
*A. R. Lewis not out	128		
K. Lyons c Abbas b Saeed	51		
K. S. Jarrett lbw b Pervez	9	– not out	18
†E. Jones not out	15		
B 4, l-b 13, n-b 3	20	B 4, n-b 1	5
1/28 2/28 3/35 4/156 5/196 (5 wkts dec.)	250	1/3 2/37 (2 wkts)	72

A. E. Cordle, M. Nash, D. J. Shepherd and I. J. Jones did not bat.

Bowling: *First Innings*—Asif 14–7–27–1; Niaz 21–6–69–2; Pervez 22.2–5–74–1; Saeed 21–5–54–1; Salahuddin 4–1–6–0. *Second Innings*—Asif 4–1–13–0; Niaz 10–6–12–2; Pervez 11–3–32–0; Saeed 4–0–10–0.

Umpires: T. W. Spencer and H. Yarnold.

ENGLAND v PAKISTAN

Third Test Match

Played at The Oval, August 24, 25, 26, 28, 1967

England won by eight wickets. Everything else in this match was dwarfed by a wonderful innings of 146 from Asif Iqbal but it did not save Pakistan from defeat. Still, it provided a rare treat for the Bank Holiday crowd. When Asif arrived at the crease Pakistan had slumped to 53 for seven wickets and the match seemed bound to finish before lunch as they still needed 167 to make England bat again. He found a staunch ally in Intikhab and they indulged in a partnership of 190, a new record for the ninth wicket in Test cricket. Asif's 146 was the highest score by a number nine Test batsman. Indeed, only three men going in so late in that position can boast a hundred in Test matches: John Murray, 112, on this very ground the previous year against West Indies; R. R. Lindwall, 100, against England at Melbourne in 1946-47 and G. O. Allen, 122, against New Zealand at Lord's in 1931.

Hitting boldly, Asif excelled with the drive and hook. He raced to 50 out of 56 and Higgs, Arnold and Underwood, so supreme at one stage, all suffered during his drastic punishment. Intikhab's share when the stand reached three figures was 28. A sparkling off-drive from Higgs gave Asif his fourteenth 4 and took him to his first Test century in two hours, nineteen minutes. An amazing scene followed. Hundreds of Pakistanis raced to the wicket and hoisted Asif shoulder high. The game was held up for five minutes and when a squad of police rescued him, the poor fellow was bruised and battered.

The team manager revived him with a drink and he celebrated his great day by striking Higgs for five more boundaries in two overs. Close had kept a fairly tight field, always expecting Asif to make a fatal mistake. Finally, Close entered the attack for the first time during the innings and with his fifth ball, a short off break from round the wicket, lured Asif far out of his ground for Knott to stump him. Asif spent three hours, ten minutes for his 146 out of 202 and he hit two 6s and twenty-one 4s. Intikhab, last out, followed in the next over, bowled by Titmus for a noble 51 which included six 4s.

A throat infection laid Boycott low on the morning of the match and Close, who won the toss and decided to put in Pakistan to bat in a heavy misty atmosphere, announced that he would open the innings with Cowdrey and that Amiss would be included at number five. Arnold, five for 58, and Higgs, three for 61, soon made a breach in the Pakistan innings and only some stout-hearted batting by Mushtaq prevented a complete rout. Mushtaq began with a glorious hook for 6 off Higgs; he based his defence on playing forward with a straight bat. He looked much safer than in his previous Test innings at Lord's and Trent Bridge where he preferred to play back with disastrous consequences.

Barrington held the stage on the second day when he made his first Test century at The Oval; his third in successive Tests against Pakistan and his nineteenth in seventy-four Tests. Moreover he became the only cricketer to reach three figures for England on each of the six home Test Match centres. This was a vastly different display from his seven-hour marathon in the second Test a fortnight earlier. For two and a half hours in the middle of the day the crowd, basking in the sunshine, saw cricket at its best while Barrington and Graveney put on 141. Graveney, who hit ten 4s, gave an artistic display. Barrington placed his off drives with marked skill and he hooked strongly, England finishing with a total of 257 for three at the close, Barrington 129.

Dull batting by England followed on Saturday when in four hours before tea only 160 runs were added while the Pakistan bowlers were content to average sixteen overs an hour. Barrington added only 13 in just under the first hour so that altogether his chanceless 142 occupied five and three-quarter hours. He hit one 5 and fourteen 4s. Later Arnold batted splendidly for his highest score in England; his 59 in one hour fifty minutes included two 6s and six 4s and in the end Pakistan needed 224 to avoid an innings defeat.

They went in again at five minutes past five and Higgs in his first three overs, all maidens, dismissed Ilyas, Saeed and Majid. Wasim Bari, sent in first, defended solidly for eighty minutes but at the close, Pakistan, 26 for four, were in a hopeless position.

The story of their partial recovery on Monday has already been told, but they left England only 32 to win, and before the finish Asif crowned a great personal triumph by disposing of the two England opening batsmen, Close and Cowdrey, so that Barrington was left to make the winning hit, a cover drive for 4 from Hanif, the match being completed by ten minutes past five with a day to spare.

Pakistan

*Hanif Mohammad b Higgs	3	– c Knott b Higgs	18
Mohammad Ilyas b Arnold	2	– c Cowdrey b Higgs	1
Saeed Ahmed b Arnold	38	– c Knott b Higgs	0
Majid Jahangir c Knott b Arnold	6	– b Higgs	0
Mushtaq Mohammad lbw b Higgs	66	– c D'Oliveira b Underwood	17
Javed Burki c D'Oliveira b Titmus	27	– b Underwood	7
Ghulam Abbas c Underwood b Titmus	12	– c Knott b Higgs	0
Asif Iqbal c Close b Arnold	26	– st Knott b Close	146
Intikhab Alam b Higgs	20	– b Titmus	51
†Wasim Bari c Knott b Arnold	1	– b Titmus	12
Salim Altaf not out	7	– not out	0
B 5, l-b 2, n-b 1	8	B 1, l-b 1, n-b 1	3
1/3 2/5 3/17 4/74 5/138 6/155 7/182 8/188 9/194	216	1/1 2/5 3/5 4/26 5/26 6/41 7/53 8/65 9/255	255

Bowling: *First Innings*—Arnold 29–9–58–5; Higgs 29–10–61–3; D'Oliveira 17–6–41–0; Close 5–1–15–0; Titmus 13–6–21–2; Underwood 9–5–12–0. *Second Innings*—Arnold 17–5–49–0; Higgs 20–7–58–5; Titmus 29.1–8–64–2; Underwood 26–12–48–2; Barrington 8–2–29–0; Close 1–0–4–1.

England

M. C. Cowdrey c Mushtaq b Majid	16	– c Intikhab b Asif	9
*D. B. Close c Wasim b Asif	6	– b Asif	8
K. F. Barrington c Wasim b Salim	142	– not out	13
T. W. Graveney c Majid b Intikhab	77		
D. L. Amiss c Saeed b Asif	26	– not out	3
B. L. D'Oliveira c Mushtaq b Asif	3		
F. J. Titmus c sub b Mushtaq	65		
†A. Knott c Ilyas b Mushtaq	28		
G. Arnold c Majid b Mustaq	59		
K. Higgs b Mushtaq	7		
D. L. Underwood not out	2		
L-b 4, n-b 5	9	N-b 1	1
1/16 2/35 3/176 4/270 5/276 6/276 7/323 8/416 9/437	440	1/17 2/20 (2 wkts)	34

Bowling: *First Innings*—Salim 40–14–94–1; Asif 42–19–66–3; Majid 10–0–29–1; Mushtaq 26.4–7–80–4; Saeed 21–5–69–0; Intikhab 28–3–93–1. *Second Innings*—Salim 2–1–8–0; Asif 4–1–14–2; Saeed 2–0–7–0; Hanif 0.2–0–4–0.

Umpires: W. F. Price and H. Yarnold.

ENGLAND v PAKISTAN

First Test Match

Played at Birmingham, June 3, 4, 5, 7, 8, 1971

Drawn. Pakistan took all the honours. They had a wonderful chance of winning when rain intervened on the last day. After making 608 for seven they dismissed England for 353, enforced the follow-on and by the close of the fourth day had their opponents 184 for three in their second innings. Then came the rain. Play was not possible on the fifth day until just after 5 p.m. and then after 14.5 overs bad light sent the players off with England still 26 behind with only five wickets left.

On an easy paced pitch five centuries were made and the most remarkable was that by Zaheer Abbas, whose 274 was the highest individual score made by a Pakistan batsman against England. It fell only four short of D. C. S. Compton's 278, the highest for England against Pakistan, at Trent Bridge in 1954. Zaheer and Mushtaq Mohammad enjoyed a record second-wicket stand of 291 while Asif Iqbal with 104 not out emphasized Pakistan's immense batting strength. England would have been in a sorry state but for Knott's attacking 116 in the first innings and Luckhurst's defiant 108 not out in the second.

After returning home from Australia with the Ashes, England entered the match in understandably confident mood, Amiss of Warwickshire being the only member of the team not to have been in the tour party. Both Boycott and Snow were unfit.

Pakistan gave a first Test cap to their eighteen-year-old all-rounder, Imran Khan, because of the illness of Salim Altaf. They must have been surprised at the ease with which runs came after winning the toss. Ward's third delivery struck Aftab on the head and he had to retire to have the wound stitched. This brought in Zaheer and one soon appreciated that he was a batsmen out of the ordinary. He was particularly strong on the leg side, piercing the field with ease. Sadiq's was the only wicket England took on the first day when Pakistan finished at 270 for one, Zaheer 159; Mustaq 72. The pair scored 82 in an hour after tea.

Next morning Mushtaq was out after batting nine minutes short of six hours but Zaheer stayed for nine hours ten minutes, hitting thirty-eight 4s before a sweep at Illingworth brought his downfall. When he reached 261, Zaheer became the first batsman to complete 1,000 runs in the English season. He said afterwards that he had not felt too tired and was thinking in terms of the world Test record just before he was dismissed.

Asif Iqbal punished the dispirited bowlers on Zaheer's departure and Intikhab allowed the innings to run into the third morning when Iqbal completed his century which came in just over three hours.

England began disastrously against Asif Masood, who dismissed Edrich, Cowdrey and Amiss in his first 8.1 overs at a cost of 25 runs. A vicious break back was his most effective ball. Luckhurst fought hard and D'Oliveira hit back with 73 in two and a quarter hours but when he was out six men had gone for 148.

Knott decided to attack the spinners and succeeded brilliantly. With Lever a sturdy partner 159 were added for the seventh wicket. The England wicket-keeper raced to his century in three minutes over two hours. It included twenty-one 4s and a feast of audacious footwork. He was soon out on the Monday morning and before lunch England followed on for the first time against Pakistan.

Asif Masood, although stricken with stomach trouble and a strained thigh, again caused England to struggle, dismissing Edrich at 34, before he had to leave the field. Luckhurst and Cowdrey made a determined effort to pull the game round, but when Asif Masood came back he claimed Cowdrey with his first delivery. Amiss fell to a bouncer before the close when England were 184 for three and the new ball only nine overs away.

Then the rain came to England's aid. But Luckhurst was unbeaten at the end having completed 1,000 runs for his country in less than a year and scored a century on his first appearance against Pakistan. Asif Masood finished with nine wickets for 160 in the match and had Salim been there to give him support even the rain might not have saved England. Much of the match was played in dull, cool weather and the total attendance was no more than 25,000.

Pakistan

Aftab Gul b D'Oliveira	28	*Intikhab Alam c Underwood b D'Oliveira	9
Sadiq Mohammad c and b Lever	17	Imran Khan run out	5
Zaheer Abbas c Luckhurst b Illingworth	274	†Wasim Bari not out	4
Mushtaq Mohammad c Cowdrey b Illingworth	100	B 6, l-b 14, n-b 12	32
Majid J. Khan c Lever b Illingworth	35	1/68 2/359 3/441 4/456 5/469 6/567 7/581	(7 wkts dec.) 608
Asif Iqbal not out	104		

Asif Masood and Pervez Sajjad did not bat.

Bowling: Ward 29–3–115–0; Lever 38–7–126–1; Shuttleworth 23–2–83–0; D'Oliveira 38–17–78–2; Underwood 41–13–102–0; Illingworth 26–5–72–3.

England

J. H. Edrich c Zaheer b Asif Masood	0	c Wasim b Asif Masood	15
B. W. Luckhurst c Sadiq b Pervez	35	not out	108
M. C. Cowdrey b Asif Masood	16	b Asif Masood	34
D. L. Amiss b Asif Masood	4	c Pervez b Asif Masood	22
B. L. D'Oliveira c Mushtaq b Intikhab	73	c Mushtaq b Asif Iqbal	22
*R. Illingworth b Intikhab	1	c Wasim b Asif Masood	1
†A. P. E. Knott b Asif Masood	116	not out	4
P. Lever c Pervez b Asif Masood	47		
K. Shuttleworth c Imran b Pervez	21		
D. L. Underwood not out	9		
A. Ward c Mushtaq b Pervez	0		
B 16, l-b 6, w 3, n-b 6	31	B 4, l-b 5, w 6, n-b 8	23
1/0 2/29 3/46 4/112 5/127 6/148 7/307 8/324 9/351	353	1/34 2/114 3/169 4/218 5/221	(5 wkts) 229

Bowling: *First Innings*—Asif Masood 34–6–111–5; Imran 23–9–36–0; Khan 4–1–8–0; Intikhab 31–13–82–2; Pervez 15.5–6–46–3; Mushtaq 13–3–39–0. *Second Innings*—Asif Masood 23.5–7–49–4; Asif Iqbal 20–6–36–1; Imran 5–0–19–0; Intikhab 20–8–52–0; Pervez 14–4–27–0; Mushtaq 8–2–23–0.

Umpires: C. S. Elliott and T. W. Spencer.

YORKSHIRE v PAKISTAN

Played at Bradford, June 9, 10, 11, 1971

Drawn. Rain delayed the start until 2.35 p.m. on the first day and washed out the whole of the third day. The miserable conditions saw a crowd of 1,000 only on the first day with 311 paying £89 and 2,000 on the second day with 887 paying £219. In a press interview just before the game the Pakistan manager said, most unfortunately, "It was a game treated as nothing more than a practice match." Nevertheless, the first day's play was keenly contested. The Pakistan captain, Intikhab, expected Boycott to declare early on the second day. When he did not do so, Intikhab allowed the game to drift, tossed the ball into the air, and saw Yorkshire reach 302 for eight wickets by lunchtime, Hutton completing a good century. When Boycott still did not declare Intikhab put on his two opening batsmen to bowl, neither fieldsmen nor bowlers made an effort, and in an hour of the afternoon Yorkshire added another 120 runs, Hutton taking his score to 189 before he was caught and Yorkshire declared. Boycott might have vindicated his policy by claiming a follow-on on the third day, but rain ended play on the second day.

Yorkshire

*G. Boycott b Intikhab	24
J. D. Woodford c Naushad b Salim	17
D. E. V. Padgett c Intikhab b Sadiq	61
J. H. Hampshire c Nazir b Intikhab	15
B. Leadbeater b Imran	41
R. A. Hutton b Nazir	189
C. M. Old b Intikhab	12
†D. L. Bairstow lbw b Intikhab	0
D. Wilson c Sadiq b Intikhab	2
G. A. Cope not out	30
B 8, l-b 16, n-b 7	31
1/44 2/46 3/68 4/159 5/208 6/227 7/227 8/243 9/422	(9 wkts dec) 422

A. G. Nicholson did not bat.

Bowling: Salim 22–6–40–1; Imran 18–4–50–1; Intikhab 39–8–97–5; Pervez 18–7–53–0; Nazir 15.4–5–39–1; Sadiq 11–1–53–1; Zaheer 10–0–45–0; Talat 4–0–14–0.

Pakistan

Asmat Rana c Hampshire b Wilson	36
Talat Ali b Hutton	32
Zaheer Abbas c Bairstow b Cope	34
Aftab Gul c Old b Wilson	11
†Naushad Ali c Leadbeater b Wilson	8
Sadiq Mohammad not out	1
*Intikhab Alam not out	6
B 6, l-b 4, n-b 2	12
1/58 2/111 3/117 4/126 5/133	(5 wkts) 140

Imran Khan, Salim Altaf, Mohammad Nazir and Pervez Sajjad did not bat.

Bowling: Old 6–0–9–0; Nicholson 11–1–30–0; Hutton 11–2–34–1; Cope 20–8–32–1; Wilson 12–6–12–3; Hampshire 3–0–11–0.

Umpires: R. Aspinall and W. E. Alley.

MIDDLESEX v PAKISTAN

Played at Lord's, June 29, July 1, 2, 1974

Pakistan won by six wickets. The Pakistan team continued their sweeping early successes with an impressive display which made the complete loss of the first day irrelevant. With the most handsome, fluently produced strokes, Majid and Asif Iqbal balanced the innings' three noughts. Asif Masood performed the hat-trick in his eighth and ninth overs, dismissing Smith, Featherstone and Ross. His next eight balls brought two more wickets, giving him five in a span of eleven balls, and Middlesex were all out for 77 in just over two hours. Intikhab rounded off the innings with two wickets in two balls. Smith earned a call-up to the Birmingham Test against India as possible substitute for Edrich with a chanceless hundred which seemed likely to save Middlesex. The final wickets, though, were casually thrown away, giving Mushtaq his best figures in England. Pakistan needed 112 in sixteen overs. Intikhab, undeterred by drizzle, bad light and the loss of two wickets in the first two overs, promoted himself and won the match by driving with immense force. He received only thirty-eight balls and hit nine 4s. He left with 19 wanted from four overs and a 6 by Mushtaq took his side to a great victory with seven balls to spare.

Pakistan

Aftab Gul lbw b Selvey	0	– c Radley b Selvey	4
Majid J. Khan not out	105	– run out	1
Zaheer Abbas lbw b Jones	17		
Mushtaq Mohammad b Selvey	0	– not out	30
Asif Iqbal b Edmonds	64	– b Vernon	10
Aftab Baloch c Brearley b Edmonds	0		
Wasim Raja c Vernon b Jones	18	– not out	2
*Intikhab Alam not out	1	– c Featherstone b Jones	61
B 2, l-b 1	3	L-b 4, n-b 1	5
1/4 2/42 3/43 4/156 5/156 6/199 (6 wkts dec.)	208	1/4 2/6 3/23 4/93 (4 wkts)	113

†Wasim Bari, Sarfraz Nawaz and Asif Masood did not bat.

Bowling: *First Innings*—Selvey 18–5–56–2; Vernon 6–0–38–0; Jones 13–3–40–2; Titmus 6–1–14–0; Edmonds 19–3–57–2. *Second Innings*—Selvey 5–0–33–1; Vernon 6–0–43–1; Jones 1.5–0–13–1; Edmonds 2–0–19–0.

Middlesex

M. J. Smith c Raja b Masood	27	– c Iqbal b Mushtaq	101
G. D. Barlow lbw b Sarfraz	9	– c Majid b Masood	2
*J. M. Brearley c Iqbal b Sarfraz	0	– c Bari b Intikhab	32
C. T. Radley c Raja b Masood	7	– c Bari b Mushtaq	36
N. G. Featherstone lbw b Masood	0	– not out	37
†N. P. D. Ross b Masood	0	– b Mushtaq	11
P. H. Edmonds lbw b Masood	2	– lbw b Mushtaq	0
K. V. Jones lbw b Intikhab	14	– c Iqbal b Mushtaq	7
F. J. Titmus c Zaheer b Iqbal	4	– st Bari b Mushtaq	10
M. J. Vernon not out	2	– b Intikhab	0
M. W. W. Selvey lbw b Intikhab	0	– b Mushtaq	0
B 4, l-b 4, w 2, n-b 2	12	B 4, n-b 2	6
1/24 2/24 3/44 4/44 5/44 6/46 7/47 8/61 9/77	77	1/11 2/89 3/168 4/180 5/204 6/204 7/221 8/241 9/241	242

Bowling: *First Innings*—Asif Masood 11–1–35–5; Sarfraz 14–6–24–2; Asif Iqbal 4–1–6–1; Intikhab 1–1–0–2. *Second Innings*—Asif Masood 13–3–30–1; Sarfraz 16–1–45–0; Asif Iqbal 3–1–10–0; Intikhab 21.2–5–54–2; Mushtaq 27–9–59–7; Wasim Raja 14–2–38–0.

Umpires: C. Cook and C. S. Elliott.

ENGLAND v PAKISTAN

Second Test Match

Played at Lord's, August 8, 9, 10, 12, 13, 1974

Drawn. Rain and leaky covers spoilt this match, but when cricket was possible Underwood excelled in exploiting damp patches. Taking five wickets for 20 and eight for 51, he finished with thirteen for 71. He was the first Englishman to capture eight wickets in an innings in a Lord's Test since 1934, when following a storm on the Saturday night and sunshine throughout Sunday Hedley Verity – the pitch was never wholly covered in those days – took fifteen Australian wickets on the Monday.

If England were unfortunate that no play took place on the last day when they wanted only 60 to win with all their wickets intact, at least justice was done considering that previously all the bad luck had fallen on Pakistan. On the first, third and fourth days with rain interfering, play was extended one hour until 7.30 p.m.

Pakistan were extremely happy on the sunny first morning when Intikhab won the toss and looked for a total of about 500. During the first hour Sadiq and Majid responded so handsomely that 51 runs were taken off the England seam bowlers and a mammoth score was in the offing, but the weather changed and no more cricket was possible for five hours. Yet with the extra hour allowed, three more hours were available that day.

With the sun shining with full warmth, everyone realised that in Underwood, England possessed the ideal left-arm slow to medium bowler for the occasion. Denness brought him on immediately, but half an hour passed before he was able to make the ball turn and lift at varying speed and height. Hendrick, although wayward in control, broke the opening stand at 71 by getting Sadiq leg before. Soon Greig was operating at the pavilion end and in his first over he induced Majid to lift a half-volley to Old at square leg, whereupon Underwood, with the pitch becoming more spiteful, carried all before him.

The young left-handed Wasin Raja hit straight to good purpose until he was last out to a mighty drive, but Greig fielding in the deep, ran across the sight screen and, leaping in the air, brought off a remarkable left-handed acrobatic catch. With fifty minutes possible to test the England batsmen, Intikhab declared and his enterprise was rewarded. Amiss falling to a fine close catch by Sadiq following a lifter from Masood. Then Lloyd and Edrich confidently saw England to 42 for one at the close.

Pakistan fought back splendidly on the second day, being very well served by their pace bowlers, Asif Masood, Sarfraz and Imran, while Intikhab, at a vital point, removed Edrich with a sharp off break that the Surrey captain turned to short leg. Brilliant fielding at cover by Asif, who threw down the wicket at the bowler's end, ran out Greig and reduced England to 118 for six. Yet the last four wickets put on 152 more runs, thanks mainly to Knott, who found capable assistants. The best was Old, for he was unafraid to hit straight and was the dominant partner in a stand of 69. On his departure, Knott shaped more freely until he was last out, having seen England to a valuable lead of 140.

Showers caused much interference on Saturday when again the fortunes of both sides fluctuated. The faster England bowlers made little impression and Sadiq again batted splendidly, but he saw Majid and Zaheer fall to Underwood who now had no help from the pitch, but always commanded respect with his accurate length and varied pace.

The loss of three men for 77 with so little to spare was serious for Pakistan, but Mushtaq and Wasim Raja overcame the crisis with two masterly displays, the experienced Mushtaq exercising a steadying influence on his exuberant young partner. They took Pakistan to 173 for three at the week-end with two days remaining.

Much rain fell on Sunday and on Monday morning, and again the covering did not contain the water down the slope which soaked the pitch. The Pakistan manager, Omar Kureishi, accused MCC, in an official protest of "*an appalling show of negligence and incompetence in not covering the wicket adequately*".

MCC replied through their secretary, Jack Bailey: "*It is deeply regretted that the covering did on this occasion prove inadequate. Even more comprehensive precautions than those which had previously kept the pitch and surrounds dry throughout three days and nights of heavy intermittent rain were taken, but the deluge overnight and this morning meant that some water escaped on to the wicket.*

"*MCC have experimented continuously, and have spent many thousands of pounds over the past few years in trying to devise a means of overcoming a covering problem which is made extremely difficult by the slope at Lord's, and by the necessity of having at the same time, to allow air to circulate under those covers which are on the pitch. I am certain that the head groundsman and his staff have done everything that could humanly be asked of them in order to provide a good wicket and keep it that way.*"

Not until 5.15 was the match resumed on Monday and while the pitch at the nursery end was unaffected Underwood again found the surface at the pavilion end ideal for his turn and lift. For half an hour, Mushtaq and Wasim Raja, who had put on 96 on Saturday, survived before a smart left handed catch by Lloyd at short leg removed Wasim and from that point Underwood became virtually unplayable. Within the next hour Pakistan were all out for 34 more runs. Underwood having taken six wickets for nine runs in 11.5 overs. Mushtaq resisted England for four and a quarter hours and hit nine 4s and the gallant Waja (three 4's) batted three and three-quarter hours.

The match marked the retirement from the Test Match scene of Charlie Elliott. This was his 44th Test as umpire and only Frank Chester stood more times, his Tests numbering 48. Elliott was a model sportsman excelling as a player at football (Derby County) and cricket (Derbyshire) and finally as a first-class umpire who always carried out his duties in a dignified manner. Full attendance 65,373; receipts £50,445.

Pakistan

Sadiq Mohammad lbw b Hendrick	49	– lbw b Arnold	43
Majid Khan c Old b Greig	48	– lbw b Underwood	19
Zaheer Abbas c Hendrick b Underwood	1	– c Greig b Underwood	1
Mushtaq Mohammad c Greig b Underwood	0	– c Denness b Greig	76
Wasim Raja c Greig b Underwood	24	– c Lloyd b Underwood	53
Asif Iqbal c Amiss b Underwood	2	– c Greig b Underwood	0
*Intikhab Alam b Underwood	5	– b Underwood	0
Imran Khan c Hendrick b Greig	4	– c Lloyd b Underwood	0
†Wasim Bari lbw b Greig	4	– lbw b Underwood	1
Sarfraz Nawaz not out	0	– c Lloyd b Underwood	1
Asif Masood (did not bat)		– not out	17
N-b 2	2	B 8, n-b 7	15
1/71 2/91 3/91 4/91 5/103 6/111 7/116 8/130 9/130	(9 wkts dec.) 130	1/55 2/61 3/77 4/192 5/192 6/200 7/200 8/206 9/208	226

Bowling: *First Innings*—Arnold 8–1–32–0; Old 5–0–17–0; Hendrick 9–2–36–1; Underwood 14–8–20–5; Greig 8.5–4–23–3. *Second Innings*—Arnold 15–3–37–1; Old 14–1–39–0; Hendrick 15–4–29–0; Underwood 34.5–17–51–8; Greig 19–6–55–1.

England

D. Lloyd c Zaheer b Sarfraz	23	– not out	12
D. L. Amiss c Sadiq b Masood	2	– not out	14
J. H. Edrich c Sadiq b Intikhab	40		
*M. H. Denness b Imran	20		
K. W. R. Fletcher lbw b Imran	8		
A. W. Greig run out	9		
†A. P. E. Knott c Bari b Masood	83		
C. M. Old c Bari b Mushtaq	41		
G. G. Arnold c Bari b Masood	10		
D. L. Underwood not out	12		
M. Hendrick c Imran b Intikhab	6		
L-b 14, w 1, n-b 1	16	N-b 1	1
1/2 2/52 3/90 4/94 5/100 6/118 7/187 8/231 9-254	270	(no wkt)	27

Bowling: *First Innings*—Masood 25–10–47–3; Sarfraz 22–8–42–1; Intikhab 26–4–80–2; Raja 2–0–8–0; Mushtaq 7–3–16–1; Imran 18–2–48–2; Iqbal 5–0–13–0. *Second Innings*—Sarfraz 3–0–7–0; Majid 2–0–10–0; Masood 4–0–9–0; Intikhab 1–1–0–0.

Umpires: D. J. Constant and C. S. Elliott.

ENGLAND v PAKISTAN

Third Test Match

Played at The Oval, August 22, 23, 24, 26, 27, 1974

Drawn. Hopes that this encounter would provide a worthy finale to the series were dashed by a pitch so slow in pace that bowlers were reduced to impotence. There was some fine batting, with memorable innings from Majid and Zaheer for Pakistan, and Amiss for England, but a draw always looked the likely outcome.

England, in fact, had nothing else to play for once Pakistan occupied nearly two days amassing 600 for seven wickets after Intikhab had won the toss for the third time. Before Amiss retired hurt with 178 to his name they did so attractively enough but thereafter Fletcher was so painstaking that he took seven hours forty minutes to reach three figures, the slowest first class hundred made in England. Only Peter Richardson, who batted eight hours eight minutes for his century in Johannesburg in 1956, made a slower hundred for England.

England made one change, Willis for Hendrick, and the Warwickshire bowler was an early sufferer at the hands of Majid who launched the Pakistan innings in thrilling fashion. Willis's first four overs cost 25 as Majid drove and pulled with effortless timing in a display of controlled aggression that was delightful to watch. When Sadiq fell to a boundary catch in the 17th over there were already 66 runs on the board. Majid did not play a crude or unworthy stroke until he reached 98. Then, immediately following the afternoon break for drinks, he employed an ugly sweep against Underwood in search of his fourteenth 4 and was bowled.

Underwood was easily the best of England's bowlers, operating as an orthodox spinner in intelligent fashion, but he could not separate Zaheer and Mushtaq.

By the close of the first day Pakistan had taken the score to 317 for two, with Zaheer already past his hundred, having been missed at slip by Fletcher off Lloyd from the last ball before tea, when he was 74. Strangely it was Zaheer's first Test century since his 274 on début against England at Edgbaston in 1971. He went on to reach 240, being sixth out with the score at 550. England managed one quick wicket with the new ball at the start of the second day, Arnold knocking out Mushtaq's middle stump to end a record third wicket stand of 172.

Zaheer and Asif Iqbal made 74 in the hour before lunch with a string of brilliant strokes, allied to fleet-footed running. With all the ground in use and the outfield lush there were numerous all run fours.

Greig's dismissal of Asif in the first over after the interval slowed the scoring but Zaheer accumulated steadily and when he was finally dismissed after a stay of nine hours ten minutes, Intikhab led a final onslaught, twice hitting Old for huge sixes.

In thirty-five minutes batting before the close England lost Lloyd, taken at short leg, but on the Saturday the nightwatchman Underwood showed just how hard was the bowlers' task by staying for three hours before he was second out at 143. Amiss played with calm authority from the start as England moved steadily towards the 401 needed to avoid the follow on. Underwood was not restricted entirely to defence. He produced some good attacking shots and it was not until Pakistan used their sixth bowler, Wasim Raja, that he was finally tempted into error.

Amiss gave the bowlers no hope at all. He reached his eighth Test match hundred – the third against Pakistan – in just over four hours. He had one narrow escape just before tea when an 80-yard throw from the twelfth man Aftab Baloch had him diving desperately for his crease after slipping at the start of a third run.

Amiss was 168 not out at the close when England had reached 293 for four, Intikhab having winkled out Edrich, and Denness having fallen to a running boundary catch by Imran Khan after hooking a bouncer from Asif Masood using the new ball.

Another bouncer halted Amiss on Monday when the crowd was over 10,000 even though the resumption was delayed until 2.15 following heavy rain. Amiss had added 10 runs when he mistimed a hook against Sarfraz and was hit on the right cheekbone. An X-ray revealed no serious damage but he had retired hurt leaving Fletcher to inch England towards safety. It was a grim business. In five hours cricket 145 runs came from 72 overs, but play was not without incident. Pakistan frustration showed in the final over before tea. Sarfraz, his run-up interrupted by movement among pavilion spectators, threw the ball to the ground. His next ball was a fast full toss to Fletcher, who took a single. The following ball, a beamer, flew past Greig's head without bouncing. The two glared at each other but umpire Bird moved quickly to restrain the bowler, who was advised to "calm down".

England saved the follow-on after batting for 163.3 overs whereas Pakistan had made 600 in two overs more. When Intikhab bowled Knott he became the first Pakistan player to complete the Test double of 100 wickets and 1,000 runs for his country. With England 438 for six at the start, the final day seemed doomed to be a drab formality and so it proved. The two and a half hours before lunch were unutterably dreary. Pakistan, relying completely on pace bowling, delivered only 32 overs. England, in the persons of Fletcher and Old, added 82 runs. It was hard to tell whether the batting or the bowling was the more defensive. When Fletcher was finally run out for 122 he had laboured eight hours and thirty-eight minutes.

Old passed 50 for the first time in Test cricket before the Pakistan leg spinners rounded up the tail. Amiss returned at the fall of the ninth wicket and added five more before he was caught off Intikhab, who finished with 5 for 116.

In the last two hours four Pakistan batsmen fell to lighthearted strokes, leaving the moribund pitch the only winner, but in a summer of so many downpours a really hard surface could not be expected. Attendance 49,780; receipts £37,725.

Pakistan

Sadiq Mohammad c Old b Willis	21	– c and b Arnold	4
Majid Khan b Underwood	98	– c Denness b Old	18
Zaheer Abbas b Underwood	240	– c Knott b Arnold	15
Mushtaq Mohammad b Arnold	76	– b Underwood	8
Asif Iqbal c and b Greig	29		
Wasim Raja c Denness b Greig	28	– not out	30
Imran Khan c Knott b Willis	24	– not out	10
*Intikhab Alam not out	32		
Sarfraz Nawaz not out	14		
B 6, l-b 18, n-b 14	38	B 5, n-b 4	9
1/66 2/166 3/338 4/431 5/503 6/550 7/550 (7 wkts dec.)	600	1/8 2/33 3/41 4/68 (4 wkts)	94

†Wasim Bari and Asif Masood did not bat.

Bowling: *First Innings*—Arnold 37–5–106–1; Willis 28–3–102–2; Old 29.3–3–143–0; Underwood 44–14–106–2; Greig 25–5–92–2; Lloyd 2–0–13–0. *Second Innings*—Arnold 6–0–22–2; Willis 7–1–27–0; Old 2–0–6–1; Underwood 8–2–15–1; Greig 7–1–15–0.

England

D. L. Amiss c Majid b Intikhab	183
D. Lloyd c Sadiq b Sarfraz	4
D. L. Underwood lbw b Wasim Raja	43
J. H. Edrich c Wasim Bari b Intikhab	25
*M. H. Denness c Imran b Asif Masood	18
K. W. R. Fletcher run out	122
A. W. Greig b Intikhab	32
†A. P. E. Knott b Intikhab	9
C. M. Old lbw b Intikhab	65
G. G. Arnold c Bari b Mushtaq	2
R. G. D. Willis not out	1
B 8, l-b 13, n-b 20	41
1/14 2/143 3/209 4/244 5/383 6/401 7/531 8/539 9/539	545

Bowling: Asif Masood 40–13–66–1; Sarfraz 38–8–103–1; Intikhab 51.4–14–116–5; Imran 44–16–100–0; Mushtaq 29–12–51–1; Wasim Raja 23–6–68–1.

Umpires: W. E. Alley and H. D. Bird.

ENGLAND v PAKISTAN

First Cornhill Test

Played at Birmingham, June 1, 2, 3, 5, 1978

England won by an innings and 57 runs. This convincing victory was accomplished in only twenty hours, four minutes playing time, and contained notable displays from Old, Radley, Gower, and Botham. Old performed the extremely rare feat of taking four wickets in five balls, and the three batsmen – all of whom were uncapped a year earlier – played ideal innings to suit England's situation. Radley and Botham made centuries in contrasting moods and, in between, Gower's 58 was one of the most auspicious beginnings in recent years. The satisfaction at these achievements was overshadowed, though, by a distressing incident on the fourth and last morning.

Pakistan had used Iqbal Qasim as a nightwatchman on Saturday evening after following on, and when play resumed on the Monday, Willis, with a stiff breeze behind him, gave Qasim at least three lifting balls, including one in his first over which flew narrowly over the batsman's head. These failed to unsettle the defiant left-hander and, at 12.10, Willis went round the wicket. From this new angle he immediately hurled in another bumper which leapt from the pitch, forced its way between Qasim's hands, and struck him in the mouth. Fortunately he was not severely hurt, but he was led from the pitch bleeding freely and needed two stitches in his lip. The ramifications of this ball continued into the second Test.

Brearley, who had had to withdraw from the winter tour after breaking his arm in Pakistan, returned to lead England, but Boycott withdrew the day before the match, having failed to recover from the thumb injury received in the Prudential game the previous week. Wood replaced him. Hendrick was twelfth man for the three Tests, having filled a similar role in the Prudential matches.

Boycott's absence meant that England fielded an unusually inexperienced batting line-up, but the newer players were enabled to succeed without being confronted by Pakistan's spearhead, Sarfraz Nawaz, who strained his ribs while batting and bowled only six undemanding overs. The margin between the sides was emphasized by shifts in the weather pattern. Pakistan twice batted in overcast conditions – clouds arriving just before Old's historic spell – while England's batsmen operated in sunshine.

The match began encouragingly for Pakistan. Their openers played their shots and the game ran for them until Botham's second ball. Sadiq was caught on the boundary hooking Old and they lunched at 81 for two. Mohsin had played some exquisite shots, but became the victim of an exceptionally hostile spell from Willis which put Pakistan on the downward path. Willis had softened up Pakistan – he was warned by umpire Bird for excessive bumpers and for running on the pitch – when Old struck. He had been bowling for seventy-five minutes since lunch before devastating the later batsmen in his nineteenth over. During this over Pakistan went from 125 for five to 126 for nine in five balls. Old was twice on a hat-trick, being denied this prize first by a no-ball and then by Liaqat's straight bat. Wasim Raja and Qasim, the first and third victims, were caught behind. Qasim giving Taylor a low chance that the wicket-keeper plucked off the turf at full stretch. Wasim Bari, the second wicket, played inside an off-cutter, and the fourth man, Sikander, who must have been taking his leisure a few moments before bustling out, edged low to second slip. The over, which read "0 w w nb w w 1" in the book, was a supreme example of straight bowling with the ball being moved just enough to find uncertain edges. M. J. C. Allom, in 1930 at Christchurch, and K. Cranston, against South Africa at Leeds in 1947, also took four wickets in an over, Allom's including a hat-trick.

Sarfraz watched all this from Old's end before ending the excitement. He lifted Pakistan to 161 for nine when bad light halted the game, virtually for the day, just before tea. Old quickly wrapped up the innings on the second morning, recording his best Test figures.

England passed 100 for the loss of only Wood. Radley and Brearley batted capably until, in a moment of aberration, Brearley went for a second to long-leg and failed. The quality of the batting was immediately raised when Gower nonchalantly pulled his first ball in Tests – a long-hop from Liaqat – for four. Though badly missed when 15 by Liaqat at mid-on off Mudassar, Gower played with the assurance of a Test veteran, hitting the ball off his legs and past cover with cultured, firm strokes for the bulk of his nine 4s. He caught Radley in the fifties, having given him a start of one hundred minutes, but then surrendered to an uncharacteristic, wild swing.

Radley chugged steadfastly on and completed his second consecutive Test century at the start of Saturday's play before being the first victim of a useful spell from Sikander. He batted five hours ten minutes, hitting eleven 4s. Sikander's two wickets merely cleared the way for Botham, who hit the ball with immense force, turning the screw firmly on an attack that toiled bravely but lacked menace. Botham's hundred came in three hours ten minutes and contained eleven 4s; his stand with the reliable Miller added 122.

England declared at tea 287 runs ahead, and the Pakistan openers batted with commendable freedom for almost two hours until Mudassar was bowled in the penultimate over of the day, bringing in Qasim.

Following Qasim's retirement on Monday, Sadiq, clearly unsettled by the injury, was lbw in the next over. Still Pakistan fought, with Mohsin, for the second time in the game, and Javed Miandad each playing some flowing strokes. Yet there was no real suggestion of permanence, even though they reached 176 for two just before lunch. Miandad was then caught sweeping and, after a break when it rained, Haroon and Wasim Raja were both bowled by balls that came into them. The later batsmen were unable to combat Edmonds and Miller on a pitch now taking spin freely, and the new ball after tea ended the match.

After the game, Pakistan's manager, Mahmood Hussain, described Willis's tactics when bowling at Qasim as "unfair", adding: "The umpires should not have allowed him to bowl like that. Brearley is well aware that the man who was hit is a lower-order batsman and it was a clear infringement of the Playing Conditions." These state: "Captains must instruct their players that the fast, short-pitched ball should at no time be directed at non-recognised batsmen."

Brearley defended his policy by observing: "Anyone who takes a bat in his hand accepts a certain amount of risk and a nightwatchman expects to be treated like a batsman. Qasim looked a competent defensive player to us and I know that he has batted for a long time in various parts of the world. There are difficulties in distinguishing between bumpers and ordinary short balls that lift, and I would not accept that Willis bowled that many bumpers, and the line dividing batsmen from non-recognised batsmen is also difficult to gauge".

Between the first two Tests the controversy was debated at all levels of cricket. The TCCB issued two statements, the core of which was that they "bitterly regretted" the incident, reminded Brearley of his responsibilities, and encouraged the captains to exchange lists of nonrecognised batsmen.

Though there was some justice in Brearley's view that Qasim was blunting England's attack, it did seem that he was interpreting the Playing Conditions too loosely. The early bumpers were as potentially dangerous as the one that injured Qasim, and the whole performance was unnecessarily ruthless, especially as England were so dominant and there were two days left.

Before the week-end there had been a milder issue, when Wasim Bari complained that England's middle-order batsmen had run up and down the pitch and that the umpires had warned the batsmen several times each.

Old was the sponsor's Man of the Match; the receipts were £38,250 from an attendance of 28,500.

Pakistan

Mudassar Nazar c and b Botham	14 – b Edmonds	30
Sadiq Mohammad c Radley b Old	23 – b Old	79
Mohsin Khan b Willis	35 – c Old b Miller	38
Javed Miandad c Taylor b Old	15 – c Brearley b Edmonds	39
Haroon Rashid c Roope b Willis	3 – b Willis	4
Wasim Raja c Taylor b Old	17 – b Edmonds	9
Sarfraz Nawaz not out	32 – not out	6
*†Wasim Bari b Old	0 – c Miller b Edmonds	3
Iqbal Qasim c Taylor b Old	0 – retired hurt	5
Sikander Bakht c Roope b Old	0 – c Roope b Miller	2
Liaqat Ali c Brearley b Old	9 – b Willis	3
L-b 3, n-b 13	16 B 4, l-b 4, w 1, n-b 4	13
1/20 2/56 3/91 4/94 5/103 6/125 7/125 8/126 9/126	164 1/94 2/123 3/176 4/193 5/214 6/220 7/224 8/227 9/231	231

Bowling: *First Innings*—Willis 16–2–42–2; Old 22.4–6–50–7; Botham 15–4–52–1; Wood 3–2–2–0; Edmonds 4–2–2–0. *Second Innings*—Willis 23.4–3–70–2; Old 25–12–38–1; Botham 17–3–47–0; Edmonds 26–10–44–4; Miller 12–4–19–2.

England

*J. M. Brearley run out	38
B. Wood lbw b Sikander	14
C. T. Radley lbw b Sikander	106
D. I. Gower c Miandad b Sikander	58
G. R. H. Roope b Sikander	32
G. Miller c Bari b Mudassar	48
I. T. Botham c Qasim b Liaqat	100
C. M. Old c Mudassar b Qasim	5
P. H. Edmonds not out	4
L-b 26, w 5, n-b 16	46
1/36 2/101 3/190 4/275 5/276 6/399 7/447 8/452	(8 wkts dec.) 452

†R. W. Taylor and R. G. D. Willis did not bat.

Bowling: Sarfraz 6–1–12–0; Liaqat 42–9–114–1; Mudassar 27–7–59–1; Qasim 14–2–56–1; Sikander 45–13–132–4; Raja 10–1–32–0.

Umpires: H. D. Bird and K. E. Palmer.

THE COUNTY MATCHES

DERBYSHIRE

DERBYSHIRE v HAMPSHIRE

Played at Chesterfield, August 24, 26, 27, 1963

Derbyshire won by 144 runs. They batted indifferently on a good pitch against the pace of White and Cottam, but Morgan shaped soundly and found a good partner in Taylor for the eighth wicket, which added 77. The Hampshire first innings followed a different course. Brisk batting by Marshall and sound play by Horton gave them a good start, but lively bowling by Rhodes and Brian Jackson brought about a collapse and the last five wickets fell for 18 runs. Derbyshire batted consistently in the second innings and Lee set Hampshire to score 277 in just under four hours. Rhodes soon put this out of the question, taking four wickets for nine runs, so that half the side was out for 33. Keith resisted for three hours, but Derbyshire won with ten minutes to spare.

Derbyshire

*C. Lee c Livingstone b Wassell	17	– lbw b Cottam	16
J. Harvey c Barnard b White	3	– c Timms b Cottam	73
I. R. Buxton b Gray	10	– c Marshall b Gray	46
D. Millner c Wassell b Cottam	17	– lbw b Wassell	1
I. W. Hall c Cottam	15	– lbw b Cottam	4
D. C. Morgan c Livingstone b Cottam	82	– not out	36
E. Smith lbw b White	3	– not out	35
H. J. Rhodes c Timms b Wassell	1		
†R. W. Taylor b White	31		
A. B. Jackson b Cottam	1		
H. L. Jackson not out	1		
B 6, l-b 3, w 1, n-b 8	18	L-b 5, n-b 4	9
1/11 2/34 3/36 4/67 5/86 6/98 7/113 8/190 9/197	199	1/28 2/110 3/121 4/136 5/161	(5 wkts dec.) 220

Bowling: *First Innings*—White 21.1–3–67–3; Cottam 24–7–50–4; Wassell 38–23–40–2; Gray 15–3–24–1. *Second Innings*—White 20–5–53–0; Cottam 25–4–74–3; Wassell 35–11–59–1; Gray 10–3–25–1.

Hampshire

*R. E. Marshall c Taylor b A. Jackson	50	– b Rhodes	0
J. R. Gray c Taylor b Rhodes	0	– c Taylor b Rhodes	8
H. Horton b Rhodes	60	– c Taylor b Rhodes	4
D. A. Livingstone c Millner b Buxton	4	– c Buxton b Rhodes	11
P. J. Sainsbury c Taylor b Buxton	0	– c Taylor b Buxton	28
H. M. Barnard run out	10	– lbw b A. Jackson	1
G. L. Keith c Taylor b A. Jackson	8	– not out	44
†B. S. V. Timms lbw b Rhodes	4	– b A. Jackson	3
A. Wassell b Rhodes	1	– c Taylor b H. Jackson	5
D. W. White not out	2	– c Taylor b Rhodes	11
R. M. H. Cottam c Taylor b A. Jackson	0	– c Buxton b A. Jackson	5
L-b 1, n-b 3	4	B 1, l-b 5, w 1, n-b 5	12
1/2 2/75 3/88 4/94 5/125 6/126 7/131 8/137 9/143	143	1/8 2/9 3/23 4/33 5/33 6/83 7/93 8/106 9/117	132

Bowling: *First Innings*—H. Jackson 17–4–29–0; Rhodes 28–8–58–4; A. Jackson 14.4–4–29–3; Buxton 11–8–12–2; Smith 8–4–11–0. *Second Innings*—H. Jackson 20–8–26–1; Rhodes 20–5–41–5; A. Jackson 14.2–4–24–3; Buxton 7–3–16–1; Smith 10–4–13–0.

Umpires: P. A. Gibb and F. Jakeman.

DERBYSHIRE v WORCESTERSHIRE

Played at Chesterfield, July 31, August 2, 3, 1965

Worcestershire won by an innings and 31 runs. Twice the Derbyshire batting broke down against the powerful, varied attack of the champions. On the opening day skilful bowling by Coldwell and D'Oliveira was too much for the home county, and by the close Headley and Graveney, in a sound third-wicket partnership, had given Worcestershire a lead which eventually amounted to 99. Rain interfered seriously with play on the second day, and in drying conditions on the third day Derbyshire lost their last seven wickets in thirty-five minutes while eight runs were added. Gifford, with left-arm slows, performed the hat-trick and achieved the best figures of his career, seven for 23.

Derbyshire

J. R. Eyre run out	15	– c Booth b Coldwell	7
I. W. Hall c Ormrod b D'Oliveira	17	– c Booth b Gifford	14
H. L. Johnson c and b D'Oliveira	4	– c Flavell b Gifford	5
M. H. Page c Ormrod b Coldwell	3	– c D'Oliveira b Coldwell	20
I. R. Buxton not out	29	– c D'Oliveira b Gifford	14
J. F. Harvey c Booth b Coldwell	1	– c Gifford b Coldwell	1
†R. W. Taylor b Coldwell	0	– b Gifford	0
E. Smith run out	3	– st Booth b Gifford	4
*G. W. Richardson lbw b D'Oliveira	1	– not out	2
H. J. Rhodes c Coldwell b D'Oliveira	0	– b Gifford	0
A. B. Jackson c Booth b Coldwell	0	– c Headley b Gifford	1
B 5, l-b 2	7	L-b 1	1
1/26 2/36 3/37 4/61 5/69 6/69 7/73 8/79 9/79	80	1/10 2/26 3/27 4/60 5/62 6/62 7/66 8/68 9/68	68

Bowling: *First Innings*—Coldwell 20.5–12–18–4; Flavell 13–3–25–0; D'Oliveira 19–8–26–4; Gifford 7–4–4–0. *Second Innings*—Flavell 7–0–13–0; Coldwell 16–8–16–3; Gifford 21.5–15–23–7; Slade 7–6–4–0; D'Oliveira 7–4–4–0; Horton 8–2–7–0.

Worcestershire

*D. Kenyon c Johnson b Rhodes	8	†R. Booth b Jackson	11
M. J. Horton b Jackson	6	L. J. Coldwell b Jackson	17
R. G. A. Headley b Rhodes	40	J. A. Flavell c Taylor b Jackson	8
T. W. Graveney c Taylor b Rhodes	49		
D. N. F. Slade c Taylor b Rhodes	0	B 3	3
N. Gifford c Taylor b Jackson	1		
B. D'Oliveira b Richardson	8	1/13 2/19 3/97 4/101 5/106	179
J. A. Ormrod not out	28	6/108 7/124 8/139 9/165	

Bowling: Jackson 29.5–9–71–5; Rhodes 24–6–43–4; Buxton 10–4–13–0; Smith 15–8–18–0; Richardson 14–1–31–1.

DERBYSHIRE v GLOUCESTERSHIRE

Played at Derby, August 3, 4, 5, 1966

Gloucestershire won by 60 runs. Because of rain only three hours' play was possible on the first two days. Gloucestershire, who struggled for runs after winning the toss, declared their first innings on the last morning and, after Derbyshire had declared 47 runs behind, eventually set the home county a target of 119 to win in ninety-five minutes. Although the pitch was slow and moist at one end, the odds seemed in favour of the batting side, but they collapsed in startling fashion against the spin of Allen and the left-arm Bissex. These two did not enter the attack until Derbyshire had passed 20 for the loss of one wicket, yet the innings lasted only one hour. Five wickets fell while the score moved from 51 to 52, Allen taking three in one over without cost. The ball turned, but many batsmen fell to poor strokes.

Gloucestershire

C. A. Milton c Taylor b Jackson	11	– not out	30
M. Bissex c J. R. Eyre b Buxton	13	– lbw b Jackson	0
D. Brown c Harvey b Buxton	38	– b Buxton	0
D. Shepherd b Jackson	0	– c sub b Morgan	34
R. B. Nicholls c Hall b Buxton	21	– not out	7
M. D. Mence b Jackson	5		
*J. B. Mortimore not out	2		
L-b 9	9		
1/26 2/31 3/37 4/85 5/97 6/99	(6 wkts dec.) 99	1/0 2/1 3/56	(3 wkts dec.) 71

D. A. Allen, A. S. Brown, †B. J. Meyer and D. R. Smith did not bat.

Bowling: *First Innings*—Jackson 21–10–18–3; Rhodes 9–3–7–0; Buxton 24–11–36–3; Morgan 11–6–14–0; Page 5–1–15–0. *Second Innings*—Jackson 5–4–3–1; Buxton 8–2–16–1; Morgan 9–2–33–1; Page 3–0–19–0.

Derbyshire

I. W. Hall c Meyer b Smith	1	– b A. S. Brown	1
J. R. Eyre not out	37	– c Nicholls b Bissex	18
M. H. Page not out	12	– b Allen	15
J. F. Harvey (did not bat)		– c A. S. Brown b Allen	4
M. Hill (did not bat)		– c D. Brown b A. S. Brown	4
I. R. Buxton (did not bat)		– c Mortimore b Bissex	8
*D. C. Morgan (did not bat)		– c A. S. Brown b Allen	0
T. J. P. Eyre (did not bat)		– c Nicholls b Allen	0
†R. W. Taylor (did not bat)		– lbw b Allen	0
A. B. Jackson (did not bat)		– not out	5
H. J. Rhodes (did not bat)		– c Nicholls b Bissex	1
L-b 2	2	L-b 2	2
1/4	(1 wkt dec.) 52	1/5 2/26 3/32 4/37 5/51 6/52 7/52 8/52 9/52	58

Bowling: *First Innings*—Brown 5–2–15–0; Smith 8–2–17–1; Mortimore 3–1–18–0. *Second Innings*—Smith 3–0–14–0; A. S. Brown 6–0–17–2; Allen 7–0–25–5; Bissex 3.3–3–0–3.

Umpires: T. W. Spencer and W. F. Simpson.

DERBYSHIRE v GLAMORGAN

Played at Derby, August 20, 22, 23, 1966

65 overs. Glamorgan won by 78 runs. A sound innings by Rees formed the backbone of Glamorgan's total, but Derbyshire led by 12 on first innings after some brisk scoring by Morgan and Taylor. Glamorgan took advantage of a good wicket to build up a solid second innings, during which Taylor, the Derbyshire wicket-keeper, held seven catches, breaking the county's record and equalling the best for championship cricket. Once again, batting last proved an ordeal for Derbyshire's suspect batting and the Glamorgan bowlers, helped by some good close catching, took their side to victory.

Glamorgan

A. Jones, c J. R. Eyre b Russell	27	– c Taylor b Russell	48
W. Slade b Jackson	1	– c Taylor b T. J. P. Eyre	14
P. M. Walker b T. J. P. Eyre	7	– c Russell b Jackson	31
A. R. Lewis c T. J. P. Eyre b Smith	29	– c T. J. P. Eyre b Russell	39
A. Rees not out	53	– c Taylor b Jackson	0
R. Davis not out	2	– c Harvey b T. J. P. Eyre	52
†D. L. Evans b Jackson	7	– c Taylor b Jackson	16
A. E. Cordle run out	18	– c Taylor b T. J. P. Eyre	10
D. J. Shepherd c Morgan b T. J. P. Eyre	0	– c Taylor b Jackson	0
*O. S. Wheatley (did not bat)		– c Taylor b Jackson	9
I. J. Jones (did not bat)		– not out	13
B 1, l-b 8	9	B 6, l-b 5	11
1/1 2/12 3/42 4/98 5/130 6/147 7/148	(7 wkts, 65 overs) 153	1/32 2/101 3/103 4/105 5/177 6/208 7/221 8/221 9/224	243

Bowling: *First Innings*—Jackson 15–2–33–2; T. J. P. Eyre 15–2–29–2; Russell 18–6–40–1; Morgan 4–1–7–0; Smith 13–4–35–1. *Second Innings*—Jackson 32–8–68–5; T. J. P. Eyre 35–13–66–3; Russell 24–6–41–2; Morgan 14–6–25–0; Smith 24–12–32–0.

Derbyshire

J. R. Eyre b Shepherd	11	– c Walker b I. J. Jones	4
P. J. K. Gibbs b Cordle	43	– c Walker b Shepherd	29
J. F. Harvey c Walker b Cordle	0	– b Wheatley	26
M. Hill c Evans b Cordle	1	– c A. Jones b Shepherd	5
H. L. Johnson run out	1	– b Wheatley	4
P. E. Russell b I. J. Jones	14	– c Rees b Shepherd	28
*D. C. Morgan not out	46	– run out	15
T. J. P. Eyre c I. J. Jones b Wheatley	15	– c I. J. Jones b Shepherd	11
†R. W. Taylor not out	31	– b Cordle	16
E. Smith (did not bat)		– c Walker b Cordle	4
A. B. Jackson (did not bat)		– not out	0
N-b 3	3	B 4, w 4, n-b 3	11
1/3 2/40 3/46 4/49 5/63 6/87 7/119	(7 wkts, 65 overs) 165	1/25 2/66 3/66 4/71 5/81 6/111 7/129 8/146 9/152	153

Bowling: *First Innings*—I. J. Jones 13–4–35–1; Wheatley 18–4–50–1; Cordle 16–3–34–3; Shepherd 18–7–43–1. *Second Innings*—I. J. Jones 8–2–16–1; Wheatley 10–3–16–2; Cordle 18.2–3–44–2; Shepherd 27–13–48–4; Walker 6–0–18–0.

Umpires: W. F. Price and L. H. Gray.

DERBYSHIRE v WORCESTERSHIRE

Played at Derby, June 19, 20, 1968

Derbyshire won by an innings and 110 runs. After winning the toss, Derbyshire did well to make 305 on a greenish wicket, a total which would have been much smaller if the Worcestershire attack had made better use of the conditions. Gibbs and Harvey played particularly well. Overnight rain freshened the wicket and Worcestershire, without Graveney and D'Oliveira, were bowled out twice in two days, Buxton taking 11 wickets, on the same day, for 33 runs, with six for 25, the best figures of his career, in the second innings, when Ormrod fought an almost solitary battle to save his side.

Derbyshire

P. J. K. Gibbs c Griffith b Brain	70	†R. W. Taylor c Ormrod b Holder	5
D. H. K. Smith c Hemsley b Coldwell	55	*E. Smith not out	41
M. H. Page c Booth b Brain	8	L-b 3, n-b 8	11
I. R. Buxton b Gifford	4		——
J. F. Harvey not out	74	1/125 2/140 3/140 (6 wkts dec.)	305
T. J. P. Eyre c Gifford b Griffith	37	4/158 5/207 6/240	

P. E. Russell, H. J. Rhodes and A. B. Jackson did not bat.

Bowling: Coldwell 19–5–42–1; Holder 17–2–73–1; Brain 29–3–86–2; Griffith 13–2–41–1; Gifford 21–9–47–1; Hemsley 1–0–5–0.

Worcestershire

R. G. A. Headley c Taylor b Jackson	20	– c Page b Jackson	7
C. D. Fearnley c Taylor b Jackson	12	– retired hurt	11
N. Gifford b Jackson	4	– c Page b E. Smith	4
J. A. Ormrod c Gibbs b Eyre	2	– c Gibbs b Buxton	58
G. M. Turner c Taylor b Jackson	1	– b Buxton	7
E. J. O. Hemsley b Buxton	34	– c D. H. K. Smith b Buxton	0
*†R. Booth b Buxton	11	– c Taylor b Buxton	1
K. Griffith st Taylor b Buxton	0	– st Taylor b Buxton	0
V. A. Holder b Buxton	0	– st Taylor b Buxton	1
B. M. Brain not out	1	– run out	0
L. J. Coldwell b Buxton	0	– not out	2
B 1, l-b 2, n-b 1	4	B 12, l-b 1, n-b 2	15
	——		——
1/25 2/33 3/39 4/39 5/42	89	1/14 2/40 3/40 4/46 5/52	106
6/73 7/77 8/79 9/89		6/80 7/97 8/99 9/106	

Bowling: *First Innings*—Jackson 19–5–27–4; Rhodes 9–2–23–0; E. Smith 3–1–2–0; Eyre 10–3–16–1; Russell 2–0–9–0; Buxton 7.5–3–8–5. *Second Innings*—Jackson 10–4–8–1; Rhodes 9–2–9–0; E. Smith 17–10–13–1; Eyre 12–1–25–0; Buxton 23.4–15–25–6.

Umpires: J. F. Crapp and J. G. Langridge.

DERBYSHIRE v SURREY

Played at Ilkeston, July 24, 25, 26, 1968

Surrey won by three wickets. Derbyshire ended their first-ever Ilkeston cricket week by losing for the second time, a fate which seemed unlikely when they made 302 in the first innings on a slow-paced pitch, largely due to Page and Eyre. With the pitch taking spin, Surrey fell 90 behind on first innings, struggling against Smith and Rhodes after a good opening stand by W. A. Smith and Edwards. Derbyshire collapsed in startling fashion against the left-arm spin of Harman, whose eight for 16 included the hat-trick and was at the time the season's best bowling performance. Rhodes achieved a dubious distinction by being the hat-trick victim and collecting a "King Pair". Another good innings by Edwards enabled Surrey to win. The Derbyshire bowlers did not extract the most from the conditions.

Derbyshire

P. J. K. Gibbs c Edwards b Pocock	19	– st Long b Harman	22
D. H. K. Smith lbw b Jackman	36	– run out	22
M. H. Page lbw b Harman	91	– c and b Harman	5
I. R. Buxton c and b Harman	5	– c Edwards b Harman	16
*D. C. Morgan c Stewart b Harman	12	– c Stewart b Harman	4
E. Smith b Harman	26	– c Storey b Harman	7
J. F. Harvey c Younis b Pocock	22	– c Edwards b Harman	11
T. J. P. Eyre not out	63	– c Storey b Harman	0
†R. W. Taylor c Hooper b Pocock	5	– b Pocock	0
H. J. Rhodes c Younis b Harman	0	– b Harman	0
A. B. Jackson c and b Harman	10	– not out	2
B 1, l-b 6, n-b 6	13	N-b 1	1
1/49 2/72 3/81 4/100 5/143 6/180 7/251 8/270 9/276	302	1/41 2/41 3/47 4/54 5/68 6/72 7/81 8/81 9/81	90

Bowling: *First Innings*—Jackman 21–2–49–1; Roope 15–4–32–0; Storey 21–5–37–0; Pocock 32–12–74–3; Harman 36–9–97–6. *Second Innings*—Jackman 4–0–15–0; Roope 2–0–18–0; Storey 6–2–13–0; Pocock 11–3–27–1; Harman 8.5–3–16–8.

Surrey

M. J. Edwards c D. H. K. Smith b E. Smith	48	– b Morgan	70
W. A. Smith st Taylor b E. Smith	50	– c Taylor b Rhodes	33
G. R. J. Roope c D. H. K. Smith b E. Smith	9	– c Buxton b Rhodes	0
*M. J. Stewart c Taylor b Rhodes	34	– c Morgan b Rhodes	3
Younis Ahmed c Harvey b E. Smith	33	– c Morgan b E. Smith	40
S. J. Storey lbw b Rhodes	0	– c Page b Morgan	11
J. M. M. Hooper c Buxton b Rhodes	7	– not out	6
†A. Long c Eyre b Jackson	1	– not out	14
P. I. Pocock c Rhodes b Morgan	16	– lbw b Morgan	0
R. Harman b E. Smith	5		
R. D. Jackman not out	2		
B 2, l-b 3, n-b 2	7	B 1, n-b 3	4
1/79 2/100 3/119 4/154 5/155 6/181 7/186 8/203 9/203	212	1/54 2/54 3/37 4/142 5/157 6/162 7/162	(7 wkts) 181

Bowling: *First Innings*—Jackson 15–4–38–1; Rhodes 20–6–34–3; E. Smith 38.1–14–70–5; Morgan 31–15–54–1; Buxton 4–2–9–0. *Second Innings*—Jackson 6–4–3–0; Rhodes 22–4–40–3; E. Smith 29–7–76–1; Morgan 20.3–7–49–3; Gibbs 3–1–9–0.

Umpires: H. Mellows and F. Jakeman.

DERBYSHIRE v OXFORD UNIVERSITY

Played at Derby, June 14, 15, 16, 1969

Drawn. Buxton, leading Derbyshire for the first time in the absence of Morgan, invited the University to bat and then accomplished his best bowling performance with his medium-paced inswing of seven for 33, including his first hat-trick. The Derbyshire opening pair, Smith and Gibbs, had no difficulty in passing the University's total together, and they reached their highest partnership of the season before Heard broke the stand. Morgan, deputising as wicket-keeper for Westley, caught all four Derbyshire batsmen who lost their wickets, but the University were struggling to save the match when rain ended play on the third afternoon.

Oxford University

*F. S. Goldstein lbw b Rhodes	4	– c Swarbrook b Hendrick	13
A. Campbell c Taylor b Buxton	33	– not out	13
P. R. B. Wilson c and b Buxton	0		
R. L. Burchnall run out	13	– not out	0
J. W. O. Allerton c Taylor b Buxton	28		
A. J. Khan st Taylor b Buxton	5		
†A. H. Morgan b Hendrick	5		
J. R. Kilbee not out	4		
M. St. J. Burton c Hall b Buxton	9		
H. Heard c Russell b Buxton	0		
R. A. Niven b Buxton	0		
L-b 2, n-b 7	9	L-b 1, w 2, n-b 2	5
1/6 2/30 3/51 4/82 5/82 6/96 7/96 8/110 9/110	110	1/28 (1 wkt)	31

Bowling: *First Innings*—Rhodes 10–5–16–1; Hendrick 12–3–38–1; Russell 9–3–14–0; Buxton 14.5–6–33–7. *Second Innings*—Rhodes 8–4–11–0; Hendrick 5.4–2–11–1; Russell 1–1–0–0; Buxton 3–3–0–0; Swarbrook 2–1–4–0.

Derbyshire

P. J. K. Gibbs c Morgan b Heard	86	C. P. Marks not out	0
D. H. K. Smith c Morgan b Heard	87		
I. W. Hall c Morgan b Heard	54	B 4, l-b 2, n-b 3	9
*I. R. Buxton c Morgan b Burton	12		
J. F. Harvey not out	55	1/177 2/182 3/216 4/216 (4 wkts dec.)	303

†R. W. Taylor, P. E. Russell, F. W. Swarbrook, M. Hendrick and H. J. Rhodes did not bat.

Bowling: Niven 25–6–58–0; Kilbee 13–2–54–0; Burton 18–6–64–1; Khan 21–6–42–0; Heard 20–3–76–3.

Umpires: C. Petrie and G. H. Pope.

DERBYSHIRE v WARWICKSHIRE

Played at Derby, May 23, 25, 26, 1970

Drawn. On a good wicket, Derbyshire faltered after a brisk start, but Hall and Taylor took them to respectability. A brilliant display by Kanhai, with good support from Ibadulla and Mike Smith, put Warwickshire in control, although Ward was unlucky to have no reward for some fine bowling. Deciding to bat on, Warwickshire extended their lead to 188 but were unable to bowl Derbyshire out a second time, despite the efforts of

Brown and Blenkiron. Page sustained a hairline fracture of the thumb in a fielding accident. A. C. Smith took six catches behind the wicket in Derbyshire's first innings.

Derbyshire

P. J. K. Gibbs c Kanhai b Blenkiron	62 – c Kanhai b Brown	12
C. P. Wilkins c A. C. Smith b Brown	29 – c A. C. Smith b Blenkiron	12
M. H. Page c A. C. Smith b Ibadulla	17	
D. H. K. Smith lbw b Ibadulla	10 – not out	55
I. W. Hall run out	47 – c Ibadulla b Brown	0
*I. R. Buxton c A. C. Smith b Blenkiron	9 – c Kanhai b Blenkiron	26
†R. W. Taylor c A. C. Smith b Blenkiron	56 – not out	48
P. E. Russell c A. C. Smith b Gibbs	5	
F. W. Swarbrook c A. C. Smith b Gibbs	8	
E. Smith not out	19	
A. Ward c Warner b Brown	9	
L-b 7, n-b 2	9 B 1, l-b 8, n-b 2	11
1/57 2/93 3/111 4/132 5/154 6/205 7/218 8/252 9/252	280 1/16 2/26 3/27 4/86	(4 wkts) 164

Bowling: *First Innings*—Brown 17.3–1–60–2; Blenkiron 24–4–65–3; McVicker 20–3–53–0; Ibadulla 18–1–72–2; Gibbs 15–5–21–2. *Second Innings*—Brown 16–7–27–2; Blenkiron 18–10–37–2; McVicker 11–1–42–0; Ibadulla 5–3–8–0; Gibbs 18–11–33–0; Jameson 3–1–6–0.

Warwickshire

J. A. Jameson c Wilkins b Russell	25
K. Ibadulla c Wilkins b Swarbrook	53
R. B. Kanhai c Page b Wilkins	165
M. J. K. Smith run out	61
D. L. Amiss c Gibbs b Russell	48
G. S. Warner not out	37
D. J. Brown b Russell	16
*†A. C. Smith c Wilkins b Russell	0
W. Blenkiron not out	47
B 7, l-b 7, w 1, n-b 1	16
1/38 2/159 3/282 4/348 5/372 6/396 7/396	(7 wkts dec.) 468

N. M. McVicker and L. R. Gibbs did not bat.

Bowling: Ward 35–15–63–0; Russell 34–11–109–4; Buxton 14–1–57–0; Wilkins 15–2–51–1; E. Smith 35–6–115–0; Swarbrook 13–1–57–1.

Umpires: G. H. Pope and A. G. T. Whitehead.

DERBYSHIRE v HAMPSHIRE

Played at Chesterfield, June 13, 15, 16, 1970

Drawn. After winning the toss, Derbyshire batted without much distinction, Wilkins and Gibbs apart. Hampshire built up a substantial first-innings lead, thanks to a magnificent display by Richards who scored a hundred before lunch on the second day. This was not without controversy for the South African survived a confident appeal for a catch at the wicket off the first ball of the innings, bowled by Ward. Derbyshire batted more substantially in the second innings, but rain prevented what promised to be an interesting finish.

Derbyshire

P. J. K. Gibbs b Castell	35	– b White	15
D. H. K. Smith c Stephenson b Castell	28	– b Sainsbury	17
*I. R. Buxton lbw b Cottam	2	– c Sainsbury b Castell	25
C. P. Wilkins lbw b Jesty	59	– b Cottam	43
I. W. Hall c Stephenson b Jesty	18	– c Stephenson b Jesty	10
J. F. Harvey b Jesty	0	– b White	80
†R. W. Taylor b White	12	– lbw b Cottam	50
F. W. Swarbrook c Richards b White	9	– not out	16
E. Smith b Castell	0	– b White	6
A. Ward lbw b Castell	10	– not out	4
M. Hendrick not out	1		
B 1, l-b 1, w 1, n-b 3	6	L-b 8, w 1, n-b 6	15
1/58 2/63 3/73 4/140 5/147 6/148 7/167 8/168 9/168	180	1/24 2/62 3/83 4/108 5/125 6/242 7/254 8/269	281

Bowling: *First Innings*—White 20–7–36–2; Cottam 10–2–29–1; Castell 20.2–7–46–4; Jesty 17–5–39–3; Sainsbury 14–9–24–0. *Second Innings*—White 24–4–76–3; Cottam 32–11–69–2; Castell 23–7–67–1; Jesty 11–4–17–1; Sainsbury 14–4–30–1; Richards 5–2–7–0.

Hampshire

B. A. Richards b Buxton	153
B. L. Reed b E. Smith	47
D. R. Turner c Buxton b E. Smith	10
*R. E. Marshall b Ward	6
D. A. Livingstone run out	45
T. E. Jesty c sub b E. Smith	32
P. J. Sainsbury not out	4
†G. R. Stephenson not out	2
B 2, l-b 1	3
1/80 2/206 3/212 4/232 5/286 6/298	(6 wkts dec.) 302

A. T. Castell, R. M. H. Cottam and D. W. White did not bat.

Bowling: Ward 15–1–69–1; Hendrick 11–1–40–0; Buxton 14–5–31–1; E. Smith 23–7–74–3; Wilkins 15–3–45–0; Swarbrook 10–1–40–0.

Umpires: R. Aspinall and W. L. Budd.

DERBYSHIRE v OXFORD UNIVERSITY

Played at Burton, June 23, 24, 25, 1971

Oxford University won by two wickets. Ashley Harvey-Walker, a 26-year-old right-hand batsman, made Derbyshire history by becoming the first player to score a century on his first appearance for the county. He batted less than three hours and hit one 6 and eighteen 4s to beat the previous highest débūt innings, 74 by John Kelly in 1950. (Earlier in the season, Borrington's 70 against Essex was the highest score by a Derbyshire batsman in his first innings for the county.) Derbyshire set the University 270 to win in four and three-quarter hours, a task which seemed beyond them when the first four wickets went cheaply. Ward and May, however, both played extremely well and by the time the Oxford captain's innings of three and a half hours ended it became clear that Derbyshire were to pay the penalty for some modest and unambitious out-cricket. It was the first time Oxford had fielded the team that was to represent them at Lord's and when Corlett made the winning hit off the second ball of the 20th over of the final hour, it was their first first-class win for two seasons.

Derbyshire

P. J. K. Gibbs b May b Burton	40	– c May b Burton	31
A. J. Borrington st Robinson b Corlett	34	– lbw b Wingfield-Digby	0
A. Harvey-Walker c P. C. H. Jones b Wingfield-Digby	16	– not out	110
C. P. Wilkins lbw b Burton	10	– c Burton b P. C. H. Jones	34
J. F. Harvey c A. K. C. Jones b Wingfield-Digby	94	– not out	25
†R. W. Taylor lbw b P. C. H. Jones	53		
P. E. Russell c Hamblin b Burton	5		
F. W. Swarbrook not out	22		
T. J. P. Eyre not out	1		
L-b 9	9	L-b 2	2
1/79 2/83 3/96 4/112 5/222 6/243 7/277	(7 wkts dec.) 284	1/0 2/85 3/131	(3 wkts dec.) 202

*E. Smith and D. Wilde did not bat.

Bowling: *First Innings*—Wingfield-Digby 23–5–55–2; Hamblin 22–2–71–0; Burton 39–17–75–3; Corlett 10–4–30–1; P. C. H. Jones 15–2–44–1. *Second Innings*—Wingfield-Digby 13–1–42–1; Hamblin 19–5–57–0; Burton 15–5–51–1; Corlett 6–0–31–0; P. C. H. Jones 3–0–19–1.

Oxford University

A. K. C. Jones b Swarbrook	23	– lbw b Smith	17
†G. A. Robinson run out	44	– c Taylor b Swarbrook	24
R. L. Burchnall b Wilde	24	– c Taylor b Smith	9
*B. May b Eyre	15	– b Swarbrook	77
P. R. Carroll c Wilkins b Smith	45	– b Smith	18
J. M. Ward c and b Smith	31	– b Swarbrook	49
M. St J. Burton c Russell b Wilkins	22	– b Swarbrook	24
P. C. H. Jones c Harvey-Walker b Smith	0	– b Smith	26
S. C. Corlett st Taylor b Smith	0	– not out	18
A. R. Wingfield-Digby c Eyre b Wilkins	4	– not out	2
C. B. Hamblin not out	0		
B 4, l-b 1, n-b 4	9	L-b 7, n-b 1	8
1/74 2/75 3/104 4/124 5/182 6/193 7/193 8/213 9/217	217	1/37 2/45 3/64 4/69 5/146 6/192 7/249 8/263	(8 wkts) 272

Bowling: *First Innings*—Wilde 16–7–47–1; Eyre 16–4–42–1; Smith 14.3–4–32–4; Swarbrook 21–7–41–1; Russell 21–13–38–0; Wilkins 1–0–8–2. *Second Innings*—Wilde 5–2–9–0; Eyre 16–2–50–0; Smith 23–6–71–4; Swarbrook 30.2–9–91–4; Russell 18–7–30–0; Wilkins 3–0–13–0.

Umpires: F. Jakeman and T. W. Spencer.

DERBYSHIRE v YORKSHIRE

Played at Chesterfield, July 12, 14, 15, 1975

Drawn. After putting Yorkshire in on a damp green pitch, Taylor, the Derbyshire captain, took seven catches to equal the English record for an innings, which he also achieved against Glamorgan in 1966. Only a late revival enabled Yorkshire to reach three figures after some effective bowling by Hendrick. The second day was lost to rain and on the third Derbyshire took their lead to 80, though they might have effectively declared earlier. As it was Yorkshire lost seven wickets in clearing the arrears and at the start of the last hour were only three ahead with two wickets left. One of them, however, was Lumb who defied a bruised thumb and helped to save the match for his side.

Yorkshire

R. G. Lumb not out	3 – not out	9
G. A. Cope b Hendrick	9 – c Venkat b Hendrick	12
J. D. Love c Taylor b Hendrick	0 – b Stevenson	4
*J. H. Hampshire c Taylor b Hendrick	5 – lbw b Hendrick	7
P. J. Squires c Taylor b Hendrick	10 – c Taylor b Stevenson	2
A. Sidebottom c Taylor b Russell	8 – c Taylor b Russell	11
A. W. Hampshire c Taylor b Stevenson	17 – c Sharpe b Hendrick	1
†D. L. Bairstow b Russell	6 – b Hendrick	5
P. Carrick c Taylor b Venkat	46 – c Bolus b Stevenson	19
H. P. Cooper lbw b Hendrick	1 – not out	11
A. L. Robinson c Taylor b Hendrick	22	
B 4, l-b 6, n-b 9	19 L-b 4, n-b 14	18
1/12 2/21 3/24 4/42 5/46 6/63 7/75 8/76 9/146	146 1/6 2/9 3/29 4/39 5/43 6/51 7/63 8/83 (8 wkts)	99

Bowling: *First Innings*—Hendrick 21–10–36–6; Stevenson 19–4–48–1; Venkataraghavan 8.1–0–22–1; Russell 13–5–21–2. *Second Innings*—Hendrick 19–8–21–4; Stevenson 10–1–23–3; Venkataraghavan 7–3–7–0; Russell 16–7–28–1; Swarbrook 5–4–2–0.

Derbyshire

P. J. Sharpe b Cooper	6
J. B. Bolus lbw b Sidebottom	27
M. H. Page lbw b Robinson	41
A. Morris c Bairstow b Sidebottom	12
J. M. Ward st Bairstow b Carrick	37
F. W. Swarbrook c A. W. Hampshire b Cope	36
*†R. W. Taylor c J. H. Hampshire b Carrick	4
S. Venkataraghavan c Cooper b Carrick	33
P. E. Russell c J. H. Hampshire b Sidebottom	12
K. Stevenson not out	0
M. Hendrick c Bairstow b Sidebottom	0
L-b 6, w 2, n-b 10	18
1/7 2/64 3/94 4/94 5/153 6/166 7/199 8/223 9/226	226

Bowling: Cooper 25–7–54–1; Robinson 21–7–43–1; Sidebottom 26–8–47–4; Cope 8–2–28–1; Carrick 10–2–36–3.

Umpires: R. Aspinall and R. E. Barnard.

DERBYSHIRE v SURREY

Played at Ilkeston, July 28, 29, 30, 1976

Derbyshire won by four wickets. This win represented a remarkable recovery by Derbyshire from the disasters of the previous game and it was made possible by the virtuoso batting of Barlow, whose 217 was his highest score in first-class cricket and a remarkable display which clearly lifted the entire team. On the first day Surrey laboured, though Roope played well for his not out century. They were not helped by an over rate of 16 an hour and if Edrich had not declared, Derbyshire would not have batted on the first day. The second day belonged exclusively to Barlow, who batted four hours, twenty-four minutes without offering a chance. Barlow took two hours to make his first 50, having once gone 11 overs without scoring, but after that his assault on the Surrey attack was breathtaking to watch. His next 50 arrived in sixty-three minutes, the third in even time and the fourth in only twenty-six minutes. He made 138 between lunch and tea and had hit six 6s and twenty-five 4s when he was finally caught on the boundary. On the last day Surrey lost their last seven wickets in 20 overs to the spin of Miller and Swarbrook and Derbyshire in turn had some uneasy moments before moving to their first win over these opponents for ten years.

Surrey

*J. H. Edrich lbw b Barlow	35	– b Swarbrook	36
A. R. Butcher b Hendrick	11	– c Hendrick b Miller	43
G. P. Howarth c Taylor b Barlow	23	– c Swarbrook b Miller	47
T. M. G. Hansell b Barlow	17	– b Swarbrook	11
G. R. J. Roope not out	100	– lbw b Swarbrook	7
D. M. Smith lbw b Barlow	27	– c Cartwright b Miller	0
†L. E. Skinner c and b Miller	2	– c Miller b Swarbrook	7
Intikhab Alam c Taylor b Hendrick	6	– b Swarbrook	14
R. D. Jackman c and b Hendrick	15	– c Barlow b Miller	8
G. G. Arnold not out	0	– c Borrington b Miller	12
P. I. Pocock (did not bat)		– not out	4
L-b 9, n-b 8	17	B 4, l-b 5, w 2, n-b 1	12
1/33 2/67 3/84 4/93 5/173 6/188 7/227 8/248	(8 wkts dec.) 253	1/58 2/96 3/132 4/152 5/156 6/156 7/175 8/178 9/190	201

Bowling: *First Innings*—Hendrick 19–6–47–3; Ward 19.4–2–56–0; Stevenson 10–2–24–0; Barlow 22–6–53–4; Swarbrook 15–6–21–0; Miller 14–4–35–1. *Second Innings*—Hendrick 12–2–27–0; Ward 5–1–22–0; Swarbrook 37–11–66–5; Miller 27.1–9–74–5.

Derbyshire

A. Hill lbw b Intikhab	35	– b Arnold	6
P. J. Sharpe lbw b Arnold	7	– c Skinner b Arnold	0
*E. J. Barlow c Roope b Pocock	217	– b Pocock	30
A. J. Borrington b Pocock	25	– c Roope b Intikhab	4
G. Miller lbw b Jackman	6	– c Skinner b Pocock	38
H. Cartwright b Arnold	20	– c Jackman b Pocock	0
†R. W. Taylor c Arnold b Pocock	15	– not out	11
F. W. Swarbrook not out	10	– not out	14
K. Stevenson not out	1		
B 5, l-b 7, w 1, n-b 3	16	L-b 2	2
1/22 2/85 3/169 4/196 5/286 6/328 7/343	(7 wkts) 352	1/0 2/13 3/21 4/66 5/70 6/85	(6 wkts) 105

A. Ward and M. Hendrick did not bat.

Bowling: *First Innings*—Arnold 15–2–41–2; Jackman 19–3–81–1; Pocock 30–10–91–3; Roope 9–2–30–0; Intikhab 24–8–80–1; Smith 3–0–13–0. *Second Innings*—Arnold 8–3–10–2; Jackman 4–1–7–0; Pocock 14–1–41–3; Intikhab 13–1–45–1.

Umpires: J. F. Crapp and D. Oslear.

DERBYSHIRE v GLAMORGAN

Played at Chesterfield, June 10, 12, 1978

Derbyshire won by an innings and 20 runs. History was made just before the end of this game when Russell, fielding at short leg, was struck by a fierce blow from Nash, the ball temporarily lodging in the visor of his protective helmet. Despite this protection, Russell suffered a fractured cheekbone. The umpires had to decide whether a catch had technically been made. In the event, they ruled "dead ball", a decision subsequently approved by the TCCB. Derbyshire totally overwhelmed their opponents, Kirsten hitting a dazzling not out double century, with five 6s and twenty-one 4s, the first by a Derbyshire batsman on this ground since 1935. On an excellent pitch, with bounce and pace, Glamorgan succumbed to the bowling of Hendrick and Tunnicliffe and, following on, were beaten well inside two days.

Derbyshire

A. Hill c Hopkins b Wilkins	13
A. J. Borrington b Wilkins	5
P. N. Kirsten not out	206
*E. J. Barlow c E. W. Jones b Lloyd	42
G. Miller b Lloyd	22
H. Cartwright c Wilkins b Lloyd	28
J. M. H. Graham-Brown c Ontong b Nash	11
†R. W. Taylor not out	0
B 4, l-b 7, w 1, n-b 2	14
1/10 2/33 3/128 4/209 5/290 6/340	(6 wkts) 341

C. J. Tunnicliffe, P. E. Russell and M. Hendrick did not bat.

Bowling: Nash 22–6–65–1; Wilkins 26–4–88–2; Ontong 16–3–39–0; Swart 7–1–26–0; Lloyd 25–7–77–3; Richards 4–0–32–0.

Glamorgan

*A. Jones c Taylor b Tunnicliffe	4	b Miller	22
J. A. Hopkins c Russell b Tunnicliffe	1	c Cartwright b Miller	29
P. G. Crowther c Cartwright b Tunnicliffe	4	c Russell b Hendrick	0
M. J. Llewellyn c Barlow b Tunnicliffe	21	c Barlow b Hendrick	0
R. C. Ontong c Cartwright b Hendrick	5	c Taylor b Barlow	10
B. J. Lloyd c Taylor b Hendrick	5	not out	15
P. D. Swart c Miller b Barlow	34	c Hill b Miller	38
G. Richards c Miller b Hendrick	18	b Miller	23
†E. W. Jones c Kirsten b Hendrick	2	c Taylor b Hendrick	2
M. A. Nash c Taylor b Russell	41	c Graham-Brown b Tunnicliffe	21
A. H. Wilkins not out	4	c Taylor b Kirsten	1
L-b 1	1	B 9, l-b 10, w 1	20
1/2 2/7 3/10 4/21 5/41 6/41 7/70 8/72 9/126	140	1/50 2/51 3/61 4/61 5/90 6/130 7/133 8/143 9/171	181

Bowling: *First Innings*—Hendrick 15–5–29–4; Tunnicliffe 14–2–67–4; Barlow 5.3–2–18–1; Russell 5–0–24–1. *Second Innings*—Hendrick 19–8–43–3; Tunnicliffe 20–9–44–1; Graham-Brown 7–3–10–0; Barlow 8–1–21–1; Miller 30–18–40–4; Kirsten 2.4–2–0–1; Russell 4–1–3–0.

Umpires: H. D. Bird and W. E. Phillipson.

NOTES BY THE EDITOR, 1979

THE UGLY HELMET

The 1978 season will go into cricket history as the one when the ugly helmet was used by many players to protect themselves from injury, not only when batting but also when fielding in the suicide positions. I remember that Patsy Hendren first used one, made by his wife, in the early 1930s when facing Larwood and Voce and the West Indies contingent, but that was an isolated case. Now, when batsmen have been laid low by the spate of bouncers that captains and umpires have tolerated, how could I, as an observer in a safe and comfortable seat, blame the players for wearing something to protect themselves from serious injury. Dennis Amiss, the only batsman to score 2,000 runs, wore one regularly. It was made of fibre-glass in Birmingham and retailed at £29; more than 100 went to the counties.

Whether a fielder should be allowed to wear a helmet is a different matter. When Philip Russell (Derbyshire) was struck in the face at short leg by a shot from Malcom Nash (Glamorgan) at Chesterfield in June, the ball lodged in the visor of his helmet. He suffered a fractured cheekbone, but the injury might have been much more serious. It was no catch because umpire Harold Bird promptly called "dead ball"; and that is now the official ruling from Lord's in the event of similar incidents. Nor is the batsman out if the ball bounces off a helmet and without touching the ground is held by a fielder. The TCCB have ruled that the wearing of a helmet gives the fielder an unfair advantage, and if the ball rebounds from a helmet the umpire must call "dead ball". However, a catch may be taken if a batsman snicks the ball on to his own helmet.

DERBYSHIRE v KENT

Played at Chesterfield, July 21, 23, 24, 1979

Kent won by eight wickets. The final stages of this match saw one of the most embarrassing displays ever produced by Derbyshire as Kent, needing 95 to win, made them from only 10.3 overs against bowling and fielding of poor quality. Earlier, Underwood had exploited a drying pitch with typical efficiency to take six for 36, although Derbyshire's resistance had taken the game into the last hour. Woolmer made a century before lunch in Kent's first innings.

Derbyshire

A. Hill c Jarvis b Underwood	34	– c Tavaré b Jarvis	2
J. G. Wright c Downton b Shepherd	34	– c Rowe b Dilley	39
P. N. Kirsten c Rowe b Jarvis	31	– b Dilley	19
D. S. Steele c Woolmer b Jarvis	20	– c Dilley b Johnson	58
K. J. Barnett c Underwood b Jarvis	62	– b Underwood	20
*G. Miller c Downton b Dilley	28	– c Downton b Underwood	1
J. W. Lister c Jarvis b Dilley	7	– b Underwood	3
J. Walters not out	2	– c Tavaré b Underwood	1
†R. W. Taylor b Dilley	0	– c Tavaré b Underwood	19
R. C. Wincer not out	13	– c Dilley b Underwood	26
A. J. Mellor (did not bat)		– not out	1
L-b 14, w 2, n-b 5	21	B 8, l-b 8, w 7, n-b 11	34
1/77 2/81 3/135 4/135 5/216 6/232 7/236 8/237	(8 wkts) 252	1/13 2/46 3/72 4/150 5/157 6/157 7/160 8/163 9/212	223

Bowling: *First Innings*—Jarvis 25–8–72–3; Shepherd 25–11–31–1; Dilley 17–3–54–3; Underwood 24–12–38–1; Johnson 4–1–17–0; Woolmer 5–0–19–0. *Second Innings*—Jarvis 13–5–24–1; Shepherd 14–3–42–0; Dilley 12–3–37–2; Underwood 40.5–27–36–6; Johnson 32–18–26–1; Woolmer 6–0–24–0.

Kent

R. A. Woolmer c Miller b Steele	117	– c Kirsten b Walters	9
C. J. C. Rowe c and b Mellor	1	– b Walters	7
C. J. Tavaré c Miller b Wincer	43	– not out	42
C. S. Cowdrey lbw b Miller	83	– not out	33
*A. G. E. Ealham c Barnett b Steele	8		
J. N. Shepherd c Miller b Wincer	38		
G. W. Johnson not out	47		
†P. R. Downton c Miller b Walters	8		
D. L. Underwood run out	1		
G. R. Dilley c Wright b Steele	4		
B 8, l-b 5, w 2, n-b 16	31	L-b 3, n-b 1	4
1/38 2/161 3/187 4/209 5/307 6/319 7/346 8/351 9/381	(9 wkts dec.) 381	1/13 2/22	(2 wkts) 95

K. B. S. Jarvis did not bat.

Bowling: *First Innings*—Wincer 21–3–78–2; Walters 12–4–42–1; Mellor 11–1–27–1; Miller 20–4–68–1; Kirsten 8–1–29–0; Steele 21.5–4–93–3; Barnett 3–0–13–0. *Second Innings*—Wincer 1–0–12–0; Walters 2–0–14–2; Kirsten 2–0–20–0. Miller 3–0–22–0; Steele 2.3–0–23–0.

Umpires: T. W. Spencer and W. L. Budd.

DERBYSHIRE v WORCESTERSHIRE

Played at Derby, August 18, 20, 21, 1979

Drawn. This game ended on an unfortunate and probably unique note of controversy. Worcestershire started their second innings at 5.50 p.m. on the last day under the impression that they had four overs in which to make 25 to win. According to the Worcestershire captain, Gifford, this information had been imparted to them by the umpires, but as the innings started a telephone call to Lord's established that the officials had apparently misinterpreted the regulations. The game was left drawn, and so Worcestershire missed the opportunity to stay in the Championship race by acquiring an extra twelve points. Gifford himself protested to Lord's and asked that the final ten minutes be replayed, a request that was turned down. The ending marred an excellent day's cricket, which featured good batting from Neale and Patel, after which Derbyshire fell to the spin of Patel and Gifford.

Derbyshire

A. Hill c Turner b Inchmore	1	– c Humphries b Gifford	28
J. G. Wright c Humphries b Inchmore	0	– c Ormrod b Gifford	10
*P. N. Kirsten st Humphries b Gifford	33	– c Humphries b Inchmore	2
D. S. Steele b Gifford	34	– c Patel b Holder	56
K. J. Barnett c Humphries b Inchmore	45	– c Ormrod b Patel	35
A. J. Borrington b Inchmore	11	– c Humphries b Gifford	0
J. Walters c Humphries b Inchmore	1	– c Gifford b Patel	2
C. J. Tunnicliffe b Gifford	42	– c Inchmore b Patel	7
†A. J. McLellan c Humphries b Inchmore	2	– c Hemsley b Patel	2
A. J. Mellor lbw b Gifford	0	– not out	3
R. C. Wincer not out	0	– c Patel b Gifford	0
L-b 7, n-b 18	25	B 2, l-b 3, n-b 8	13
1/0 2/17 3/66 4/89 5/119 6/121 7/192 8/194 9/194	194	1/27 2/30 3/73 4/122 5/132 6/143 7/144 8/154 9/155	158

Bowling: *First Innings*—Holder 21–5–58–0; Inchmore 19.1–6–46–6; Gifford 29–10–49–4; Cumbes 2–0–8–0; Patel 4–2–8–0. *Second Innings*—Holder 16–2–39–1; Inchmore 10–4–16–1; Gifford 39–15–52–4; Patel 20–10–38–4.

Worcestershire

G. M. Turner c Steele b Walters	15	– c Kirsten b Walters	2
J. A. Ormrod c Steele b Walters	12		
P. A. Neale c Steele b Mellor	111		
E. J. O. Hemsley c Steele b Walters	6	– not out	2
Younis Ahmed b Tunnicliffe	76	– not out	13
D. N. Patel c Mellor b Steele	48		
†D. J. Humphries b Walters	29		
J. D. Inchmore c Borrington b Steele	1		
V. A. Holder not out	3		
*N. Gifford c Borrington b Steele	1		
B 2, l-b 5, w 3, n-b 16	26		
1/21 2/60 3/68 4/216 5/250 6/302 7/303 8/324 9/328 (9 wkts dec.)	328	1/6 (1 wkt)	17

J. Cumbes did not bat.

Bowling: *First Innings*—Tunnicliffe 27–4–76–1; Walters 38–8–100–4; Steele 19.4–6–57–3; Mellor 10–1–54–1; Kirsten 3–0–15–0. *Second Innings*—Tunnicliffe 1–0–6–0; Walters 1–0–11–1.

Umpires: D. J. Halfyard and T. W. Spencer.

DERBYSHIRE v GLAMORGAN

Played at Derby, June 7, 9, 10, 1980

Drawn. In a remarkable display of attacking batsmanship, Kirsten made his second double century in successive months and became the first Derbyshire player ever to make three. His first was also made against Glamorgan, in 1978. Hitting thirty-two 4s and five 6s in two hundred and thirty-one minutes, Kirsten devastated an unpretentious attack in an innings of only 68 overs. He made a century between lunch and tea, then added his final 105 runs out of 127 in eighteen overs, making 63 from the last seven overs of the innings. For Glamorgan, Alan Jones hit the 49th century of his career, but the visitors were still 85 behind. After rain on the last day, they were asked to make 227 in 150 minutes, and had reached 177 for three with eight overs left when Steele cut short their challenge by dismissing Nash, Featherstone and Holmes to achieve the hat-trick for the first time.

Derbyshire

B. Wood c A. Jones b Ontong	43	– b Lloyd	22
J. G. Wright run out	94	– not out	75
P. N. Kirsten not out	213	– c E. W. Jones b Nash	39
D. S. Steele c Hopkins b Holmes	16	– not out	1
K. J. Barnett c Nash b Holmes	3		
J. Walters not out	20		
B 4, l-b 6, n-b 3	13	L-b 3, n-b 1	4
1/83 2/191 3/259 4/275	(4 wkts) 402	1/67 2/138	(2 wkts dec.) 141

*G. Miller, I. S. Anderson, †R. W. Taylor, C. J. Tunnicliffe and S. Oldham did not bat.

Bowling: *First Innings*—Nash 23–4–80–0; A. A. Jones 21–2–90–0; Ontong 17–3–57–1; Lloyd 15–3–64–0; Hobbs 11–2–44–0; Holmes 13–3–54–2. *Second Innings*—A. A. Jones 7–1–44–0; Nash 15.3–7–51–1; Ontong 8–2–30–0; Lloyd 4–1–11–1; Hobbs 2–1–1–0; Featherstone 1–1–0–0.

Glamorgan

A. Jones c Steele b Wood	119	– c Taylor b Miller	44
J. A. Hopkins b Miller	61	– c sub b Steele	39
R. C. Ontong c Kirsten b Steele	52	– run out	20
Javed Miandad st Taylor b Steele	28	– not out	44
N. G. Featherstone st Taylor b Steele	2	– (6) c Wood b Steele	0
G. C. Holmes not out	11	– (7) c and b Steele	0
†E. W. Jones c Walters b Steele	2	– (8) c Oldham b Steele	5
*M. A. Nash b Oldham	13	– (5) c and b Steele	35
B. J. Lloyd not out	14	– not out	0
L-b 5, n-b 10	15	L-b 3, n-b 8	11
1/152 2/228 3/266 4/271 5/275 6/278 7/296	(7 wkts) 317	1/79 2/102 3/117 4/177 5/177 6/177 7/193	(7 wkts) 198

R. N. S. Hobbs and A. A. Jones did not bat.

Bowling: *First Innings*—Oldham 23–6–63–1; Tunnicliffe 11–3–33–0; Steele 28–6–94–4; Wood 15–1–61–1; Miller 17–6–25–1; Barnett 2–1–4–0; Anderson 4–0–22–0. *Second Innings*—Oldham 5–0–25–0; Wood 3–1–4–0; Miller 21–3–84–1; Steele 20–4–74–5.

Umpires: H. D. Bird and D. J. Dennis.

DERBYSHIRE v WARWICKSHIRE

Played at Derby, June 6, 8, 9, 1981

Drawn. When rain ended the game in the first over of the last hour, Derbyshire were halfway to their target of 218, having encountered more problems with the rate of Warwickshire's bowling than with its quality. On a slow pitch, Wright's 75 was the cornerstone of their first innings, but the batting highlight came from Amiss, Warwickshire's acting-captain, who was injured after an hour of his first innings and yet completed two centures in the match, batting each time with a runner.

Warwickshire

*D. L. Amiss c Newman b Wood	109	– st Taylor b Steele	127
K. D. Smith c Taylor b Tunnicliffe	16	– b Newman	4
T. A. Lloyd run out	0	– run out	42
A. I. Kallicharran b Miller	30	– c Taylor b Steele	12
Asif Din c Wood b Newman	15	– c Miller b Steele	43
†C. Maynard c Taylor b Newman	22	– c sub b Steele	0
S. J. Rouse c Miller b Newman	1	– c Hill b Barnett	10
G. C. Small c Wright b Oldham	19	– lbw b Barnett	0
S. P. Perryman c Miller b Oldham	1	– st Taylor b Steele	2
W. Hogg b Tunnicliffe	16	– c Kirsten b Steele	7
D. R. Doshi not out	0	– not out	1
L-b 4, n-b 14	18	L-b 5, n-b 17	22
1/23 2/24 3/84 4/117 5/169 6/177 7/218 8/230 9/247	247	1/7 2/148 3/194 4/205 5/205 6/240 7/246 8/259 9/267	270

Bowling: *First Innings*—Tunnicliffe 25–11–49–2; Oldham 16.3–2–54–2; Newman 20–9–36–3; Steele 21–10–31–0; Miller 14–3–40–1; Wood 5–0–19–1. *Second Innings*—Newman 8–4–24–1; Tunnicliffe 8–1–12–0; Oldham 3–1–16–0; Steele 21.4–6–77–6; Barnett 24–5–86–2; Kirsten 5–0–33–0.

Derbyshire

B. Wood b Perryman	29	– st Maynard b Doshi	37
J. G. Wright c Asif Din b Perryman	75	– not out	54
P. N. Kirsten c Maynard b Doshi	45	– not out	8
D. S. Steele c Lloyd b Perryman	12		
K. J. Barnett c Lloyd b Perryman	2		
A. Hill not out	56		
*G. Miller not out	51		
B 2, l-b 10, w 1, n-b 17	30	L-b 6, w 2, n-b 2	10
1/70 2/162 3/164 4/167 5/189	(5 wkts dec.) 300	1/79	(1 wkt) 109

†R. W. Taylor, C. J. Tunnicliffe, P. G. Newman and S. Oldham did not bat.

Bowling: *First Innings*—Hogg 19–4–46–0; Rouse 14–1–59–0; Small 13.2–2–51–0; Perryman 24–8–64–4; Doshi 26–7–53–1; Lloyd 1–0–1–0. *Second Innings*—Hogg 6–2–12–0; Rouse 1–0–11–0; Perryman 5–0–28–0; Small 4.2–0–26–0; Doshi 4–0–22–1.

Umpires: C. Cook and R. S. Herman.

DERBYSHIRE v NORTHAMPTONSHIRE

Played at Derby, June 20, 22, 23, 1981

Northamptonshire won by nine wickets. A match which produced 1,022 runs was won by an exhilarating display of strokes from Larkins, who hit a century out of 158 in under two hours and shared in an opening partnership of 239 with Cook. Northamptonshire, required to score 276 at almost 90 an hour, made them off only 53 overs after a whirlwind start which produced 37 off the first four. Earlier Derbyshire's overseas players, Wright and Kirsten, had also made centuries and Allan Lamb had hit a high-class 91 before the visitors collapsed in their first innings. Taylor's five catches took his total number of victims for Derbyshire to a record 1,184.

Derbyshire

J. G. Wright c Cook b Griffiths	110		
B. Wood b Carter	40	– (1) lbw b Griffiths	10
P. N. Kirsten not out	59	– c Cook b Williams	114
D. S. Steele not out	30	– b Larkins	28
A. Hill (did not bat)		– (2) b Williams	74
*G. Miller (did not bat)		– (5) not out	12
C. J. Tunnicliffe (did not bat)		– (6) c Sharp b Larkins	0
K. J. Barnett (did not bat)		– (7) not out	7
L-b 5, w 3, n-b 5	13	L-b 1, n-b 11	12
1/138 2/191	(2 wkts dec.) 252	1/21 2/189 3/232 4/242 5/242	(5 wkts dec.) 257

†R. W. Taylor, P. G. Newman and S. Oldham did not bat.

Bowling: *First Innings*—Griffiths 24–5–70–1; T. M. Lamb 23–6–54–0; Williams 19.4–4–60–0; Booden 3–0–19–0; Carter 12–2–36–1. *Second Innings*—Griffiths 12–4–20–1; Booden 15–4–37–0; Carter 10–1–51–0; T. M. Lamb 14–1–35–0; Williams 22–2–57–2; Tindall 6–1–23–0; Larkins 6–1–22–2.

Northamptonshire

*G. Cook c Tunnicliffe b Steele	32	– not out	120
W. Larkins c Taylor b Tunnicliffe	0	– c Hill b Miller	126
R. G. Williams run out	22		
A. J. Lamb c Taylor b Miller	91	– (3) not out	17
T. J. Yardley c Taylor b Miller	27		
R. M. Tindall c Taylor b Newman	7		
R. M. Carter b Tunnicliffe	0		
†G. Sharp c Hill b Newman	24		
T. M. Lamb c Taylor b Tunnicliffe	2		
C. D. Booden not out	4		
B 1, l-b 7, w 2, n-b 15	25	B 2, l-b 7, n-b 7	16
1/11 2/47 3/137 4/182 5/200 6/202 7/206 8/218 9/234	(9 wkts dec.) 234	1/239	(1 wkt) 279

B. J. Griffiths did not bat.

Bowling: *First Innings*—Newman 13.1–2–39–2; Tunnicliffe 11–0–59–3; Oldham 6–1–23–0; Wood 4–2–11–0; Miller 21–8–43–2; Steele 9–2–34–1. *Second Innings*—Newman 6–2–27–0; Tunnicliffe 5–0–43–0; Oldham 8–0–36–0; Steele 13–1–52–0; Miller 15–2–65–1; Wood 5.5–0–40–0.

Umpires: B. J. Meyer and P. J. Eele.

DERBYSHIRE v GLOUCESTERSHIRE

Played at Derby, July 29, 30, 1981

Derbyshire won by an innings and 26 runs. On a remarkable first morning, Stovold made 50 out of 58, suggesting that he could reach a century before lunch, whereupon Gloucestershire lost all ten wickets for only 27 runs in exactly an hour. Maher, making his first appearance as wicket-keeper, took five catches. Derbyshire, beginning strongly, relinquished the initiative when Miller was run out, losing their last six wickets for 19 runs. Childs took five for 4 in eight overs. However, a lead of 176 was still too much for Gloucestershire, who were bowled out for a second time before tea on the second day.

Gloucestershire

B. C. Broad c Maher b Tunnicliffe	16	– lbw b Oldham	12
A. W. Stovold c Maher b Newman	50	– c sub b Oldham	19
Sadiq Mohammad c Wood b Newman	4	– c Miller b Tunnicliffe	7
Zaheer Abbas lbw b Tunnicliffe	0	– c Wood b Newman	17
A. J. Hignell c Maher b Newman	9	– c sub b Steele	45
P. Bainbridge c Miller b Tunnicliffe	0	– lbw b Newman	7
*D. A. Graveney lbw b Newman	0	– c Tunnicliffe b Miller	23
A. H. Wilkins c Miller b Tunnicliffe	2	– st Maher b Steele	2
†A. J. Brassington c Maher b Oldham	0	– (11) absent hurt	0
J. H. Childs c Maher b Tunnicliffe	2	– (9) c Miller b Steele	3
D. Surridge not out	0	– (10) not out	0
L-b 3, w 3, n-b 2	8	B 2, l-b 8, n-b 5	15
1/64 2/69 3/71 4/83 5/84 6/84 7/85 8/89 9/89	91	1/33 2/34 3/61 4/63 5/92 6/132 7/142 8/150 9/150	150

Bowling: *First Innings*—Oldham 9–3–20–1; Tunnicliffe 11.1–2–40–5; Wood 4–1–12–0; Newman 7–4–11–4. *Second Innings*—Oldham 13–1–47–2; Tunnicliffe 10–3–29–1; Miller 7–2–6–1; Newman 8–0–39–2; Steele 13.5–9–14–3.

Derbyshire

*B. Wood lbw b Bainbridge	54
J. G. Wright b Surridge	38
P. N. Kirsten lbw b Wilkins	8
D. S. Steele b Childs	58
G. Miller run out	62
A. Hill c Sadiq b Graveney	5
I. S. Anderson c Hignell b Childs	0
C. J. Tunnicliffe c Zaheer b Childs	6
P. G. Newman b Childs	3
S. Oldham c Hignell b Childs	3
†B. J. M. Maher not out	4
B 8, l-b 7, w 7, n-b 4	26
1/92 2/106 3/116 4/226 5/248 6/248 7/249 8/260 9/260	267

Bowling: Wilkins 23–3–79–1; Surridge 18–2–62–1; Bainbridge 16–5–42–1; Childs 22–9–43–5; Graveney 12–4–15–1.

Umpires: J. van Geloven and A. Jepson

ESSEX

ESSEX v SUSSEX

Played at Clacton, July 22, 23, 24, 1964

Sussex won by nine wickets on a pitch generally helpful to seam bowlers. A restrained innings of three hours ten minutes by Barker, missed when 14, stood Essex in good stead, but though he and Bear put on 65, only Bailey afterwards gave much trouble and the last six wickets fell for 49. Griffith behind the wicket held six catches. Despite a partnership of 60 between Suttle and Cooper, Sussex lost half the side for 140. Then Ledden played the highest innings for Sussex and Pountain batted carefully, the last five wickets realising 133. Hilton bowled 19 no-balls during the innings. Eight Essex wickets went down before 52 of arrears of 85 were cleared and though Taylor (one 6, seven 4s) hooked splendidly and he and Hobbs added 74, Sussex required only 46 to win.

Essex

M. J. Bear c Griffith b Pountain	29	– b Snow	14
G. J. Smith c Griffith b Thomson	7	– c Oakman b Snow	7
G. E. Barker c Oakman b Snow	68	– c Griffith b Thomson	0
K. Fletcher c Langridge b Bates	22	– c Oakman b Snow	1
*T. E. Bailey c Griffith b Snow	38	– c Ledden b Thomson	8
B. R. Knight c Griffith b Bates	5	– c Oakman b Thomson	4
†B. Taylor c Griffith b Pountain	0	– b Bates	50
B. Edmeades c Oakman b Suttle	5	– b Snow	5
P. J. Phelan c Griffith b Suttle	0	– b Thomson	4
R. Hobbs b Bates	0	– not out	26
C. Hilton not out	0	– c Oakman b Bates	0
B 4, l-b 2, n-b 8	14	L-b 2, w 4, n-b 5	11
1/7 2/72 3/107 4/139 5/147 6/150 7/165 8/173 9/176	188	1/16 2/32 3/33 4/34 5/34 6/44 7/47 8/52 9/126	130

Bowling: *First Innings*—Snow 15.5–8–20–2; Thomson 18–5–37–1; Bates 24–9–46–3; Pountain 24–5–61–2; Suttle 8–4–10–2. *Second Innings*—Snow 20–6–57–4; Thomson 22–8–45–4; Bates 3–0–17–2.

Sussex

K. G. Suttle c Fletcher b Edmeades	51	– not out	20
R. J. Langridge c Taylor b Bailey	7	– c Smith b Phelan	26
G. C. Cooper c Edmeades b Knight	24	– not out	0
*A. S. M. Oakman lbw b Bailey	10		
F. R. Pountain lbw b Edmeades	47		
†M. G. Griffith c Taylor b Knight	18		
P. J. Ledden c Taylor b Bailey	76		
J. A. Snow run out	12		
N. I. Thomson b Bailey	7		
R. V. Bell lbw b Knight	2		
D. L. Bates not out	6		
B 2, l-b 2, n-b 9	13		
1/20 2/80 3/89 4/99 5/140 6/178 7/213 8/246 9/253	273	1/42 (1 wkt)	46

Bowling: *First Innings*—Knight 36–8–81–3; Hilton 22–3–94–0; Bailey 32.3–11–49–4; Edmeades 18–7–23–2; Phelan 3–1–13–0. *Second Innings*—Knight 5–1–15–0; Bailey 5–0–12–0; Phelan 4–1–7–1; Hobbs 3.5–1–12–0.

Umpires: R. Aspinall and R. S. Lay.

ESSEX v WORCESTERSHIRE

Played at Brentwood, May 12, 13, 14, 1965

Essex won by 48 runs. A brave 163 (one 6, twenty-three 4s) in three hours twenty minutes by D'Oliveira could not save the champions from defeat when set to score 338 at a run a minute. Essex owed much to a seventh-wicket stand of 139 between Bailey and Wilcox, and then Worcestershire struggled with three men out for five runs. Headley checked the collapse, but though Essex gained a lead of 167, they did not enforce the follow-on. Fletcher hit four 6s and shared with Knight a third-wicket stand of 75 before Coldwell, dismissing Fletcher, Taylor and Smith, performed the first hat-trick of the season.

Essex

G. E. Barker c Elliott b Flavell	15	– b Gifford	28
M. J. Bear c Headley b D'Oliveira	22	– c Slade b Gifford	36
K. Fletcher b Gifford	12	– b Coldwell	40
B. R. Knight run out	15	– not out	53
*T. E. Bailey b Slade	74		
G. J. Smith c D'Oliveira b Slade	49	– lbw b Coldwell	0
†B. Taylor b Horton	24	– c Graveney b Coldwell	0
J. Wilcox c Kenyon b Slade	87	– b Flavell	7
R. N. S. Hobbs b Slade	0		
B. Edmeades lbw b Slade	0		
P. J. Phelan not out	2		
B 2	2	B 1, l-b 5	6
1/26 2/48 3/54 4/65 5/118 6/154 7/293 8/295 9/295	302	1/66 2/74 3/149 4/149 5/149 6/170	(6 wkts dec.) 170

Bowling: *First Innings*—Flavell 14–2–45–1; Coldwell 15–3–27–0; D'Oliveira 24–7–52–1; Gifford 29–15–71–1; Slade 31.2–10–68–5; Horton 11–3–37–1. *Second Innings*—Coldwell 12–3–34–3; Flavell 8.1–1–28–1; Gifford 10–5–23–2; Slade 5–2–20–0; Horton 6–3–8–0; D'Oliveira 13–3–51–0.

Worcestershire

*D. Kenyon lbw b Knight	2	– c Bailey b Knight	9
M. J. Horton b Hobbs	0	– c Fletcher b Phelan	47
D. N. F. Slade c Knight b Hobbs	3	– c Edmeades b Phelan	6
N. Gifford run out	11	– c Taylor b Phelan	14
R. G. A. Headley c Fletcher b Hobbs	74	– lbw b Phelan	14
T. W. Graveney c Taylor b Phelan	1	– c Smith b Phelan	0
B. D'Oliveira c Wilcox b Hobbs	19	– lbw b Knight	163
D. W. Richardson c Fletcher b Phelan	1	– c and b Phelan	5
†J. W. Elliott lbw b Phelan	4	– c Fletcher b Phelan	4
L. J. Coldwell not out	11	– b Bailey	4
J. A. Flavell b Hobbs	3	– not out	4
B 5, n-b 1	6	B 13, l-b 5, n-b 1	19
1/2 2/2 3/5 4/61 5/66 6/102 7/108 8/114 9/122	135	1/14 2/51 3/51 4/88 5/118 6/146 7/226 8/248 9/285	289

Bowling: *First Innings*—Knight 7–3–5–1; Hobbs 25–11–46–5; Edmeades 6–2–15–0; Bailey 5–2–12–0; Phelan 24–8–51–3. *Second Innings*—Knight 10–2–20–2; Edmeades 8–1–27–0; Hobbs 37–14–95–0; Phelan 35–11–80–7; Bailey 9.2–3–23–1; Smith 8–1–25–0.

Umpires: N. Oldfield and F. Jakeman.

ESSEX v WARWICKSHIRE

Played at Clacton, August 4, 5, 6, 1965

Drawn, the last pair of Essex batsmen surviving the closing quarter of an hour. Restrained batting by Stewart saved Warwickshire from first-innings failure against Knight and Bailey. Essex lost seven wickets for 77, mostly to the pace of Bannister, but the left-handed Wrightson, after two "lives", held out for over four hours. Amiss took honours when Warwickshire batted again and in the end Essex needed 203 in three hours fifty-five minutes. With Webster unable to bowl, A. C. Smith, the wicket-keeper, joined the attack and he performed the hat-trick at the expense of Barker, G. Smith and Fletcher. When disposing of Bailey, Smith had taken four wickets in 34 deliveries without cost, but grim defence saved Essex.

Warwickshire

K. Ibadulla c Taylor b Knight	26	– c Fletcher b Bailey	17
B. A. Richardson c Taylor b Knight	4	– c Turner b Smith	30
D. L. Amiss lbw b Turner	12	– c Wrightson b Bailey	54
J. A. Jameson c Turner b Bailey	26	– c Taylor b Turner	8
W. J. Stewart lbw b Knight	54	– c Fletcher b Bailey	20
D. R. Oakes lbw b Bailey	3	– c Taylor b Knight	0
*†A. C. Smith lbw b Turner	8	– c Bailey b Knight	11
R. Miller c and b Knight	3	– lbw b Hobbs	29
R. B. Edmonds lbw b Knight	19	– lbw b Knight	1
R. V. Webster not out	2	– c Steward b Hobbs	27
J. D. Bannister c Hobbs b Bailey	0	– not out	2
B 1, l-b 2	3	B 4, l-b 1, w 1	6
1/5 2/38 3/52 4/83 5/89 6/102 7/111 8/156 9/157	160	1/22 2/86 3/98 4/114 5/115 6/140 7/150 8/155 9/202	205

Bowling: *First Innings*—Knight 25–7–38–5; Bailey 29.2–6–47–3; Edmeades 21–6–29–0; Turner 17–5–28–2; Hobbs 6–2–13–0; Smith 1–0–2–0. *Second Innings*—Knight 26–5–38–3; Bailey 27–6–65–3; Edmeades 8–0–26–0; Turner 12–0–33–1; Hobbs 7.1–2–20–2; Smith 5–0–17–1.

Essex

G. E. Barker b Bannister	4	– c Edmonds b Smith	12
G. J. Smith lbw b Webster	1	– c Oakes b Smith	15
E. A. Steward lbw b Bannister	0	– c Stewart b Miller	3
K. Fletcher c Smith b Bannister	2	– c Oakes b Smith	0
†B. Taylor c Smith b Webster	19	– c Oakes b Bannister	3
R. W. Wrightson c and b Edmonds	84	– lbw b Miller	18
B. Edmeades c Amiss b Bannister	5	– not out	24
*T. E. Bailey c Oakes b Webster	4	– c Amiss b Smith	1
B. R. Knight c Stewart b Bannister	19	– lbw b Miller	44
S. Turner lbw b Edmonds	12	– c Ibadulla b Miller	13
R. N. S. Hobbs not out	12	– not out	4
L-b 1	1	B 1, l-b 3	4
1/5 2/5 3/7 4/7 5/39 6/58 7/77 8/111 9/142	163	1/28 2/28 3/28 4/29 5/51 6/60 7/87 8/112 9/136	(9 wkts) 141

Bowling: *First Innings*—Bannister 27–10–47–5; Webster 25–6–78–3; Ibadulla 12–2–24–0; Edmonds 7.1–2–13–2. *Second Innings*—Bannister 17–7–28–1; Ibadulla 7–3–12–0; Smith 21–10–36–4; Edmonds 13–10–6–0; Miller 23–9–55–4.

Umpires: A. E. Rhodes and C. Cook

ESSEX v CAMBRIDGE UNIVERSITY

Played at Brentwood, June 11, 13, 14, 1966

Essex won by 188 runs a match rendered notable by the performance of Boyce who, on his début for the county, took nine wickets for 61 runs in the University first innings. His pace proved too much for all but the experienced Murray. Taylor hit eight boundaries in 33; Cass (one 6, eleven 4s) and Bailey put on 101 and Hobbs enlivened the later stages of the county first innings with free scoring. Though leading by 157, Essex did not enforce the follow-on and hard driving by Bear (one 6, ten 4s) and Taylor (ten 4s) led to a declaration which left Cambridge to get 396 to win. Six men were out for 62, but Palfreman followed good bowling with an excellent innings and he and Cottrell delayed the end with a stand of 110.

Essex

M. J. Bear c Acfield b Palfreman	13	– c Murray b Palfreman	79
G. J. Saville c Murray b Palfreman	23	– c Cosh b Palfreman	15
*B. Taylor b Cottrell	33	– c Palfreman b Acfield	59
K. W. R. Fletcher c Malalasekera b Acfield	37	– c Murray b Roopnaraine	8
G. R. Cass c Malalasekera b Acfield	65	– not out	39
K. D. Boyce c Murray b Cottrell	0	– c Chambers b Palfreman	6
*T. E. Bailey c Chambers b Acfield	39		
B. Edmeades c Chambers b Acfield	18	– c Russell b Palfreman	10
R. N. S Hobbs c Chambers b Acfield	40	– c Hays b Palfreman	21
A. M. Jordan not out	7		
R. East lbw b Acfield	0		
B 5, l-b 1, w 1, n-b 2	9	N-b 1	1
1/19 2/50 3/86 4/117 5/117 6/211 7/223 8/246 9/284	284	1/40 2/60 3/88 4/168 5/172 6/183 7/238	(7 wkts dec.) 238

Bowling: *First Innings*—Russell 21–4–77–0; Palfreman 15–3–53–2; Cottrell 11–6–29–2; Acfield 29.3–14–69–6; Roopnaraine 19–8–47–0. *Second Innings*—Russell 5–0–28–0; Palfreman 26.1 –7–63–5; Roopnaraine 12–2–50–1; Acfield 24–4–68–1; Cottrell 4–1–28–0.

Cambridge University

K. P. W. J. McAdam c Bailey b Boyce	15	– c East b Boyce	22
R. E. J. Chambers b Boyce	18	– c Cass b Boyce	10
D. L. Hays b Boyce	6	– c Taylor b Hobbs	7
V. P. Malalasekera c Fletcher b Boyce	4	– b Hobbs	2
*†D. L. Murray not out	58	– b Boyce	12
N. J. Cosh b Boyce	4	– c Taylor b Boyce	0
G. A. Cottrell c Fletcher b Boyce	6	– c Edmeades b East	44
A. E. Palfreman b Edmeades	1	– lbw b East	67
R. Roopnaraine c Taylor b Boyce	9	– c Cass b Hobbs	20
D. L. Acfield b Boyce	0	– not out	3
S. G. Russell b Boyce	5	– st Taylor b Hobbs	11
L-b 1	1	L-b 1, n-b 8	9
1/33 2/34 3/40 4/45 5/55 6/81 7/90 8/121 9/121	127	1/29 2/38 3/44 4/45 5/53 6/62 7/172 8/179 9/195	207

Bowling: *First Innings*—Jorden 7–0–34–0; Boyce 18.5–4–61–9; Hobbs 6–1–13–0; Edmeades 6–1–18–1. *Second Innings*—Jorden 4–1–23–0; Boyce 18–1–47–4; Hobbs 18.2–2–71–4; East 20–7–57–2.

Umpires: J. Arnold and T. W. Spencer.

ESSEX v KENT

Played at Westcliff, July 13, 14, 1966

Kent won by eight wickets. So pronounced was the mastery of the bowlers on a pitch dusty from the start that 32 wickets fell for an aggregate of 292 runs and the match ended before lunch on the second day. Underwood in the second Essex innings proved so effective with left-arm deliveries of medium pace that in 20 overs he dismissed nine batsmen at a cost of 37 runs – the best analysis of the season – bringing his match-record to 13 wickets for 57 runs. Leary, whose bold methods brought Kent a lead of 42, and Barker, defending stoutly during the whole of the two hours ten minutes the Essex second innings lasted were the only batsmen to achieve anything of note.

Essex

*G. E. Barker b Dixon	15	– not out	36
M. J. Bear c Knott b Dye	2	– b Underwood	2
G. J. Saville c Cowdrey b Sayer	0	– c Leary b Underwood	0
K. W. R. Fletcher c Cowdrey b Sayer	4	– st Knott b Underwood	12
†B. Taylor b Underwood	7	– b Underwood	0
G. R. Cass c Prodger b Underwood	10	– c Ealham b Underwood	0
B. Edmeades c Cowdrey b Underwood	19	– c Luckhurst b Underwood	7
R. N. S. Hobbs c Luckhurst b Underwood	0	– c Knott b Underwood	6
A. M. Jorden c Leary b Dixon	1	– c Cowdrey b Underwood	7
R. East b Dixon	2	– b Dixon	6
D. L. Acfield not out	0	– c Luckhurst b Underwood	0
B 4	4	L-b 4	4
1/4 2/11 3/17 4/32 5/32 6/61 7/61 8/62 9/64	64	1/10 2/10 3/24 4/24 5/26 6/38 7/52 8/70 9/79	80

Bowling: *First Innings*—Sayer 9–2–14–2; Dye 9–4–9–1; Underwood 11.3–5–20–4; Dixon 6–1–17–3. *Second Innings*—Sayer 3–0–6–0; Dye 2–1–4–0; Underwood 20–5–37–9; Dixon 19–3–29–1.

Kent

M. H. Denness lbw b Edmeades	4	– not out	18
B. W. Luckhurst c Hobbs b Edmeades	3	– c Fletcher b Jorden	10
J. M. Prodger c Taylor b Jorden	0		
*M. C. Cowdrey c Hobbs b Edmeades	7		
S. E. Leary c Taylor b Edmeades	35	– not out	6
A. Ealham c Fletcher b Edmeades	8		
†A. Knott b Jorden	11		
A. L. Dixon st Taylor b East	14	– b Jorden	6
D. L. Underwood b Jorden	5		
D. M. Sayer b Jorden	12		
J. C. Dye not out	4		
B 2, l-b 1	3	B 1, l-b 1	2
1/7 2/8 3/8 4/29 5/48 6/63 7/83 8/88 9/89	106	1/16 2/30 (2 wkts)	42

Bowling: *First Innings*—Jorden 13.2–3–34–4; Edmeades 15–4–58–5; Hobbs 2–0–10–0; East 1–0–1–1. *Second Innings*—Jorden 7.1–0–20–2; Edmeades 3–0–8–0; East 5–0–12–0.

Umpires: J. S. Buller and W. F. Price.

ESSEX v NORTHAMPTONSHIRE

Played at Clacton, August 17, 18, 19, 1966

Northamptonshire won by seven wickets. The feature of the match was undoubtedly the batting of Milburn. Omitted from the England team for the final Test, he drove, hooked and hit to leg with such power that he registered four 6s and twenty-two 4s while scoring 203 – the highest innings of his career – in a partnership of 293 in four hours ten minutes with Prideaux (eighteen 4s). This stand beat a forty-years-old record for the Northamptonshire first wicket. Against the off-spin of Sully, Essex rarely looked like saving the follow-on and though Bear drove strongly for eighty minutes and Fletcher brought off some hard strokes, Northamptonshire required no more than 55 to win. Despite the loss of Milburn and Prideaux without a run on the board, the result was never in doubt.

Northamptonshire

C. Milburn c Bear b Acfield	203	– c and b Knight	0
R. M. Prideaux not out	153	– c Knight b Jorden	0
B. L. Reynolds c Fletcher b Hobbs	4	– c Knight b Barker	18
Mushtaq Mohammad not out	42	– not out	31
D. S. Steele (did not bat)		– not out	4
L-b 10, n-b 1	11	L-b 2, n-b 1	3
1/293 2/308 (2 wkts dec.)	413	1/0 2/0 3/48 (3 wkts)	56

P. J. Watts, B. Crump, *†K. V. Andrew, M. E. Scott, H. Sully and A. J. Durose did not bat.

Bowling: *First Innings*—Knight 25–4–69–0; Jorden 11–1–62–0; Edmeades 19–1–77–0; Hobbs 30–3–94–1; Acfield 23–3–99–1; Barker 1–0–1–0. *Second Innings*—Knight 5–2–12–1; Jorden 8–0–35–1; Hobbs 2–0–6–0; Barker 1–1–0–1.

Essex

G. J. Saville c Andrew b Durose	29	– c Watts b Mushtaq	22
M. J. Bear c Watts b Durose	3	– c Steele b Sully	65
*G. E. Barker c Milburn b Sully	34	– lbw b Scott	23
K. W. R. Fletcher c Watts b Sully	24	– c Watts b Scott	41
†B. Taylor lbw b Sully	43	– c Steele b Scott	20
B. R. Knight c Andrew b Sully	2	– c Sully b Scott	22
G. R. Cass c Watts b Sully	29	– c Reynolds b Scott	4
B. Edmeades lbw b Sully	47	– c Watts b Durose	8
R. N. S. Hobbs b Crump	4	– b Crump	16
A. M. Jorden c Andrew b Sully	4	– not out	7
D. L. Acfield not out	0	– lbw b Crump	0
B 6, l-b 4, n-b 5	15	B 2, l-b 1, w 1, n-b 1	5
1/5 2/68 3/68 4/112 5/136 6/149 7/203 8/215 9/220	234	1/42 2/86 3/122 4/122 5/157 6/190 7/207 8/222 9/223	233

Bowling: *First Innings*—Crump 29–8–47–1; Durose 11–1–36–2; Watts 10–4–26–0; Sully 36–12–69–7; Mushtaq 8–2–15–0; Scott 17–6–26–0. *Second Innings*—Durose 8–2–14–1; Crump 9.4–1–28–2; Mushtaq 10–4–20–1; Scott 33–9–69–5; Sully 16–2–69–1; Steele 8–1–27–0.

Umpires: H. Yarnold and A. Jepson.

ESSEX v WARWICKSHIRE

Played at Leyton, August 10, 11, 12, 1968

Warwickshire won by 49 runs. Rain, which prevented cricket on the opening day, left the pitch so helpful to bowlers that forty wickets went down for an aggregate of 343 runs. East, with left-arm spin, achieved the best analysis of his career in the Warwickshire second innings, taking eight wickets for 63 runs, and he came out with match figures of fifteen for 115. He was chiefly responsible for the first innings breakdown, in which the last nine batsmen were dismissed for 54 runs. Essex collapsed completely in face of the pace of Brown and the off-breaks of Gibbs and Warwickshire gained a surprisingly substantial lead of 51. Abberley, twice missed, held the Warwickshire second innings together and Essex needed 150 to win. Blenkiron then began a breakdown which Gibbs continued and though Irvine hit two 6s and six 4s in a bold innings, the issue was in no doubt.

Warwickshire

W. J. Stewart c East b Lever	21	– c Fletcher b East	1
K. Ibadulla c Lever b East	22	– c Barker b Lever	9
D. L. Amiss c Taylor b East	4	– c Fletcher b East	11
R. B. Kanhai c Barker b East	0	– c Fletcher b East	10
J. A. Jameson c Irvine b Lever	25	– c Jorden b East	0
R. N. Abberley c Taylor b East	1	– c Irvine b East	35
*†A. C. Smith b Boyce	7	– c Barker b Lever	8
D. J. Brown not out	16	– lbw b East	2
W. Blenkiron b East	0	– c Irvine b East	0
L. R. Gibbs c Jorden b East	0	– not out	17
J. D. Bannister c Jorden b East	0	– c Ward b East	0
N-b 2	2	B 4, l-b 1	5
1/44 2/48 3/48 4/48 5/49 6/58 7/96 8/96 9/98	98	1/10 2/12 3/26 4/26 5/31 6/42 7/59 8/59 9/95	98

Bowling: *First Innings*—Boyce 10–2–21–1; Lever 19–9–23–2; East 24.5–8–52–7. *Second Innings*—Lever 21–6–28–2; East 22–5–63–8; Hobbs 1–0–2–0.

Essex

B. Ward c Gibbs b Bannister	0	– b Blenkiron	19
B. E. Edmeades lbw b Brown	1	– lbw b Gibbs	7
G. Barker c Amiss b Gibbs	18	– c Brown b Blenkiron	13
K. W. R. Fletcher c Amiss b Gibbs	8	– b Blenkiron	4
J. K. Lever c Abberley b Gibbs	1	– not out	3
B. L. Irvine lbw b Brown	3	– lbw b Gibbs	41
K. D. Boyce lbw b Brown	3	– lbw b Blenkiron	0
*†B. Taylor c Jameson b Brown	0	– c Smith b Gibbs	0
A. M. Jorden c Ibadulla b Brown	6	– c Abberley b Brown	5
R. N. S. Hobbs c Stewart b Gibbs	0	– c Amiss b Gibbs	0
R. E. East not out	0	– b Gibbs	0
L-b 7	7	B 2, l-b 4, n-b 2	8
1/1 2/3 3/28 4/35 5/38 6/38 7/38 8/44 9/47	47	1/20 2/35 3/46 4/51 5/51 6/52 7/92 8/92 9/96	100

Bowling: *First Innings*—Brown 10.3–5–21–5; Bannister 9–4–9–1; Gibbs 11–5–10–4. *Second Innings*—Brown 10–4–23–1; Blenkiron 14–6–34–4; Gibbs 19–9–35–5.

Umpires: O. W. Herman and J. G. Langridge.

ESSEX v KENT

Played at Brentwood, May 21, 22, 1969

Kent won by seven wickets. Hot sunshine followed heavy morning rain on the opening day, and the pitch favoured bowlers so strongly that 27 wickets fell for an aggregate of 242 runs. By skilful play, Barker and Fletcher, who scored all but 45 of the runs which came from the bat, averted complete disaster in the Essex first innings in face of Underwood's spin. Despite stubborn work by the middle-order batsmen, Kent broke down against the spin of Acfield and East and Essex led on the first innings by 50. There followed such a collapse before the pace of Graham, who made the ball lift awkwardly and returned the best analysis of his career, that seven Essex men were out for 30 runs by the close of play and the innings swiftly ended next morning. Any doubts about the result were dispelled by good driving on the part of Denness and the 85 runs required by Kent for victory were hit off without serious difficulty.

Essex

B. Ward b Graham	8	– c Luckhurst b Underwood	3
B. E. Edmeades c Leary b Asif	18	– c Hooper b Underwood	5
G. Barker run out	40	– lbw b Graham	2
K. W. R. Fletcher c Woolmer b Underwood	41	– c Luckhurst b Graham	5
B. L. Irvine c Denness b Underwood	0	– c Knott b Graham	2
K. D. Boyce c Leary b Underwood	0	– c Knott b Graham	2
*†B. Taylor b Underwood	8	– b Graham	12
S. Turner c Woolmer b Underwood	0	– c Leary b Graham	0
R. E. East st Knott b Hooper	1	– b Graham	2
R. N. S. Hobbs b Underwood	9	– not out	0
D. L. Acfield not out	1	– c Nicholls b Graham	0
B 4, l-b 1	5	B 1	1
1/16 2/36 3/76 4/84 5/86 6/94 7/94 8/103 9/129	131	1/6 2/10 3/10 4/16 5/18 6/30 7/30 8/31 9/34	34

Bowling: *First Innings*—Graham 12–4–29–1; Asif 8–2–19–1; Underwood 18–4–45–6; Woolmer 6–1–11–0; Hooper 5–2–22–1. *Second Innings*—Graham 10–3–20–8; Asif 1–0–4–0; Underwood 8–3–9–2.

Kent

*M. H. Denness b Acfield	16	– not out	48
B. W. Luckhurst c East b Turner	4	– b Turner	12
D. Nicholls c Taylor b Acfield	0	– c East b Turner	6
†A. P. E. Knott b East	1	– c Boyce b East	5
Asif Iqbal c Hobbs b Acfield	13	– not out	7
S. E. Leary lbw b East	17		
A. Ealham b Acfield	17		
R. Woolmer c Irvine b East	0		
D. L. Underwood c Hobbs b East	9		
A. J. Hooper b Acfield	0		
J. N. Graham not out	0		
L-b 2, w 1, n-b 1	4	L-b 3, n-b 5	8
1/6 2/7 3/12 4/34 5/55 6/55 7/65 8/77 9/81	81	1/39 2/57 3/62 (3 wkts)	86

Bowling: *First Innings*—Boyce 2–1–4–0; Turner 6–3–10–1; Acfield 16–6–39–5; East 16.1–8–24–4. *Second Innings*—Boyce 4–2–5–0; Turner 14–2–38–2; East 13–3–27–1; Acfield 4–1–8–0.

Umpires: P. B. Wight and W. L. Budd.

ESSEX v YORKSHIRE

Played at Colchester, July 25, 27, 28, 1970

Yorkshire won by an innings and 101 runs. Two players, Boycott, who played his highest ever innings, and Cope, whose off-spin bowling brought him the best analysis of his career, contributed most to Yorkshire's victory. Batting for seven hours without serious error and hitting twenty-seven 4s, Boycott shared partnerships of 144 with Sharpe and 212 with Hampshire (eleven 4s). Essex began well enough, Edmeades and Ward making 122 for the first wicket, but a collapse followed the last nine wickets falling for 102. Following on 224 behind, Essex fared disastrously against Cope. On helpful turf and ably served by the members of his leg-trap, Cope performed the hat-trick in dismissing Saville, Fletcher and Barker and in that spell he took five wickets in eight deliveries without cost. His match record was ten wickets for 80 runs.

Yorkshire

G. Boycott not out	260	R. A. Hutton not out	10
J. D. Woodford c Boyce b Turner	16	B 9, l-b 6, w 2, n-b 5	22
*D. B. Close b Turner	4		
P. J. Sharpe c Taylor b Acfield	58	1/39 2/61 3/205 (4 wkts dec.)	450
J. H. Hampshire c Ward b Turner	80	4/417	

†D. L. Bairstow, D. Wilson, G. A. Cope, C. M. Old and A. G. Nicholson did not bat.

Bowling: Boyce 32–2–132–0; Edmeades 6–2–7–0; Turner 32–7–85–3; Hobbs 25.3–3–85–0; Acfield 15–2–60–1; East 20–4–59–0.

Essex

B. E. Edmeades c Sharpe b Cope	78	– c Close b Cope	0
B. Ward c Hampshire b Wilson	44	– c Hampshire b Cope	39
G. J. Saville c Hutton b Nicholson	31	– c Hampshire b Cope	0
K. W. R. Fletcher b Cope	4	– c Close b Cope	0
G. Barker c Boycott b Hutton	7	– c Hampshire b Cope	0
K. D. Boyce c Cope b Hutton	13	– hit wkt b Wilson	28
*†B. Taylor c Bairstow b Old	22	– not out	13
S. Turner c Wilson b Hutton	22	– c Sharpe b Wilson	0
R. N. S. Hobbs b Cope	2	– c Hutton b Wilson	0
R. E. East not out	0	– c Hutton b Cope	18
D. L. Acfield c Sharpe b Hutton	0	– b Cope	24
B 1, l-b 1, n-b 1	3	L-b 1	1
1/122 2/130 3/143 4/152 5/168 6/200 7/206 8/226 9/226	226	1/49 2/49 3/53 4/53 5/53 6/70 7/94 8/94 9/96	123

Bowling: *First Innings*—Old 7–4–12–1; Nicholson 16–4–50–1; Hutton 15.4–1–60–4; Wilson 19–4–57–1; Cope 21–8–44–3. *Second Innings*—Hutton 8–2–20–0; Old 5–0–16–0; Nicholson 3–1–7–0; Cope 18.1–8–36–7; Wilson 11–2–43–3.

Umpires: J. S. Buller and F. Jakeman.

ESSEX v LEICESTERSHIRE

Played at Leyton, August 7, 9, 10, 1971

Drawn. The loss of the first day through rain ruled out a definite result despite two declarations. A century by Dudleston in four hours ten minutes averted a collapse in the

Leicestershire first innings. Mainly by drives, he hit one 6 and eleven 4s. Inman helped him to add 64, but East began a breakdown in which the last five wickets fell for 56. Francis, in fine form, shared in partnerships of 55 with Edmeades and 91 with Saville and on the last day Taylor declared 32 behind. After a moderate start, Tolchard also closed the Leicestershire innings, but with insufficient time remaining, Essex did not attempt to get 194 to win.

Leicestershire

B. Dudleston not out	101	– c Turner b Boyce	18
J. F. Steele b Boyce	4	– b Acfield	14
M. E. Norman c Taylor b Boyce	1	– b Ward	46
C. Inman c Turner b East	26	– st Taylor b East	32
B. F. Davison c Hobbs b Acfield	15	– c Ward b Saville	21
B. J. Booth c Saville b East	5	– not out	15
J. Birkenshaw c Saville b East	1		
*†R. W. Tolchard c Turner b East	0		
P. M. Stringer c Lever b East	10	– b Acfield	9
G. D. McKenzie run out	3		
R. Matthews c Ward b East	1		
L-b 5, n-b 6	11	L-b 2, n-b 4	6
1/15 2/17 3/71 4/97 5/122 6/130 7/134 8/156 9/160	178	1/26 2/43 3/54 4/96 5/131 6/161	(6 wkts dec.) 161

Bowling: *First Innings*—Boyce 9–1–29–2; Lever 6–3–15–0; Acfield 27–6–65–1; Turner 7–3–8–0; East 28.2–9–50–6. *Second Innings*—Boyce 5–0–15–1; Lever 4–1–13–0; East 14–3–40–1; Acfield 13–3–42–2; Saville 5–0–26–1; Ward 4.2–0–19–1.

Essex

B. E. A. Edmeades b Steele	19		
B. C. Francis not out	89		
G. J. Saville not out	35		
R. N. S. Hobbs (did not bat)		– c Dudleston b Steele	17
*†B. Taylor (did not bat)		– c Stringer b McKenzie	8
S. Turner (did not bat)		– not out	13
B. Ward (did not bat)		– not out	5
L-b 2, n-b 1	3	L-b 2	2
1/55	(1 wkt dec.) 146	1/27 2/29	(2 wkts) 45

K. D. Boyce, R. E. East, J. K. Lever and D. L. Acfield did not bat.

Bowling: *First Innings*—McKenzie 10–1–32–0; Matthews 5–2–17–0; Stringer 6–3–13–0; Birkenshaw 20–6–51–0; Steele 11–5–30–1. *Second Innings*—McKenzie 4–0–14–1; Matthews 4–1–13–0; Steele 6–1–10–1; Birkenshaw 6–4–6–0.

Umpires: H. D. Bird and C. G. Pepper.

ESSEX v NOTTINGHAMSHIRE

Played at Chelmsford, August 28, 30, 31, 1971

Drawn. Recovering from an uncertain start, Essex batted solidly. Francis, Fletcher, Boyce and East all did well and Pont, an 18-year-old newcomer, showed distinct promise. Missed when 42, Harris overshadowed all the other Nottinghamshire batsmen, but the leg-breaks of Hobbs paved the way to a lead of 50. In the Essex second innings Francis, sharing an opening stand of 111 with Edmeades, reached the highest score of his career and enabled

Taylor to declare. Though Nottinghamshire did not seriously attempt to get the 279 required to win, Harris enjoyed the distinction of hitting two centuries in a match for the second time during the season and he also completed 2,000 runs.

Essex

B. E. A. Edmeades lbw b Stead	6	– c Sobers b White	36
B. C. Francis c Bolus b Stead	51	– b Plummer	140
B. Ward lbw b Stead	51	– c Bolus b White	3
K. W. R. Fletcher c Frost b Taylor	97	– c Sobers b White	5
K. R. Pont c and b Taylor	25	– not out	35
K. D. Boyce c Harris b White	55	– c White b Plummer	6
*†B. Taylor c Taylor b White	24	– c Harris b Plummer	0
R. N. S. Hobbs c and b White	4		
R. E. East not out	41		
J. K. Lever b White	19		
D. L. Acfield run out	6		
B 4, l-b 5	9	L-b 3	3
1/6 2/10 3/85 4/166 5/217 6/258 7/270 8/275 9/306	339	1/111 2/119 3/131 4/220 5/228 6/228	(6 wkts dec.) 228

Bowling: *First Innings*—Stead 20.1–3–56–3; Sobers 12–1–41–0; White 23–4–94–4; Taylor 19–3–51–2; Plummer 8–0–35–0; Harris 8–0–53–0. *Second Innings*—Stead 12–2–25–0; Taylor 8–1–34–0; White 29–11–76–3; Plummer 9.5–0–39–3; Sobers 13–2–51–0.

Nottinghamshire

M. J. Harris c Taylor b Boyce	107	– not out	131
G. Frost lbw b Acfield	10	– lbw b Lever	22
M. J. Smedley lbw b Boyce	11	– b Lever	2
J. B. Bolus c Boyce b Acfield	27	– st Taylor b Hobbs	21
B. Hassan b Hobbs	37	– b Fletcher	5
*G. S. Sobers lbw b Hobbs	9	– c Pont b Hobbs	1
R. A. White c Fletcher b Boyce	42	– c and b Hobbs	9
M. N. S. Taylor b Hobbs	13	– not out	2
P. J. Plummer c Lever b Hobbs	4		
†D. A. Pullan c Ward b Hobbs	13		
B. Stead not out	0		
B 1, l-b 13, n-b 2	16	B 6, l-b 2, w 1, n-b 1	10
1/30 2/46 3/112 4/206 5/210 6/215 7/243 8/253 9/289	289	1/33 2/38 3/114 4/118 5/127 6/168	(6 wkts) 203

Bowling: *First Innings*—Boyce 24–1–78–3; Lever 13–2–32–0; Acfield 20–6–44–2; East 22–6–52–0; Hobbs 19–5–67–5. *Second Innings*—Boyce 6–2–19–0; Lever 10–2–31–2; East 8–3–30–0; Acfield 12–5–34–0; Hobbs 16–5–36–3; Fletcher 10–0–42–1; Taylor 1–0–1–0.

Umpires: J. F. Crapp and G. H. Pope.

ESSEX v GLOUCESTERSHIRE

Played at Westcliff, July 15, 17, 18, 1972

Gloucestershire won by 107 runs. Nearly all the honours of the match went to Procter for a fine all-round feat. Twice he rescued Gloucestershire from impending danger, scoring an aggregate of 153 runs, and he took eight wickets for 73 runs. Most excitement came on the last day when Essex went in to get 245 to win. Any hope they may have possessed disappeared when Procter, bowling round the wicket at a great pace, dismissed the first four batsmen in 27 balls for eight runs. He performed the hat-trick when disposing of Edmeades, Ward and Boyce. Making the ball rear from the hard pitch, Procter caused the temporary retirement through injury of Taylor and Turner. Fletcher alone played him with any assurance. After a rest, Procter did not present the same menace, but the damage had been done.

Gloucestershire

R. B. Nicholls c Taylor b Lever	8	– lbw b Boyce	9
J. C. Foat c Turner b Boyce	0	– c Saville b Acfield	6
R. D. V. Knight c Turner b Lever	16	– run out	10
M. J. Procter c Taylor b Turner	51	– c Edmeades b Turner	102
Sadiq Mohammad c Taylor b Lever	2	– hit wkt b Lever	48
D. R. Shepherd c Saville b Turner	59	– lbw b Acfield	4
M. Bissex lbw b Turner	0	– c Taylor b Acfield	9
*A. S. Brown b Boyce	5	– c Saville b Boyce	4
†R. Swetman c Taylor b Lever	10	– not out	14
J. B. Mortimore not out	22	– c East b Turner	12
J. Davey b Turner	4	– b Lever	0
B 1, l-b 3, n-b 3	7	B 5, l-b 5, w 1, n-b 9	20
1/3 2/17 3/28 4/42 5/98 6/98 7/113 8/139 9/174	184	1/9 2/55 3/94 4/109 5/135 6/171 7/192 8/216 9/236	238

Bowling: *First Innings*—Boyce 21–3–59–2; Lever 16–3–39–4; Turner 21.3–4–67–4; Hobbs 4–1–12–0. *Second Innings*—Boyce 27–8–59–2; Lever 17.4–2–60–2; Turner 23–5–45–2; Acfield 15–2–54–3.

Essex

B. E. A. Edmeades c Procter b Brown	72	– lbw b Procter	8
G. J. Saville c Swetman b Procter	1	– lbw b Procter	1
K. W. R. Fletcher c Swetman b Davey	20	– c Bissex b Davey	40
B. Ward run out	13	– lbw b Procter	0
K. D. Boyce c Foat b Brown	14	– lbw b Procter	0
*†B. Taylor c Knight b Procter	15	– b Brown	37
S. Turner c Shepherd b Brown	17	– c Swetman b Knight	11
R. N. S. Hobbs b Procter	4	– b Procter	12
R. E. East c Knight b Brown	1	– lbw b Brown	19
J. K. Lever not out	9	– c Nicholls b Sadiq	1
D. L. Acfield run out	0	– not out	0
B 3, l-b 2, n-b 7	12	B 1, w 5, n-b 2	8
1/16 2/57 3/81 4/97 5/123 6/163 7/164 8/168 9/177	178	1/10 2/17 3/17 4/17 5/51 6/80 7/89 8/128 9/137	137

Bowling: *First Innings*—Procter 15.4–4–43–3; Davey 15–2–70–1; Brown 22–6–53–4. *Second Innings*—Procter 16–4–30–5; Davey 11–0–38–1; Brown 16.2–6–36–2; Knight 6–2–14–1; Mortimore 1–0–5–0; Sadiq 3–2–6–1.

Umpires: A. G. T. Whitehead and W. L. Budd.

ESSEX v LEICESTERSHIRE

Played at Chelmsford, May 7, 8, 9, 1975

Drawn. This match will long be remembered for the remarkable all-round ability of Boyce. For after scoring a whirlwind century in only fifty-eight minutes – the fastest championship hundred for 38 years – he then took twelve wickets for 73. In all, Boyce scored 113 and his innings was all the more sensational from the fact that it was played on a wicket helpful to spin. The West Indian Test star's knock included eight 6s and seven 4s and he scored all his runs during a partnership of 122 with Fletcher for the fourth wicket. Faced with a total of 300, Leicestershire lost their first six wickets for 15, but Illingworth, with a fighting 33, saved them from complete humiliation as Boyce finished with six for 25. Thanks to a resolute and disciplined innings of 101 by Balderstone, Leicestershire managed to force a draw when they followed on. Balderstone eventually fell to Boyce, who finished with six second innings wickets for 48.

Essex

B. R. Hardie c Steele b Illingworth	51	†N. Smith not out	20
K. S. McEwan c Balderstone b Illingworth	38	R. N. S. Hobbs run out	5
*K. W. R. Fletcher b Steele	31	J. K. Lever b Steele	3
G. A. Gooch st Tolchard b Balderstone	7		
K. D. Boyce lbw b Higgs	113	B 4, l-b 2, n-b 1	7
S. Turner c sub b Balderstone	5		
K. R. Pont b Steele	20	1/85 2/94 3/107 4/229 5/238	300
R. E. East c Higgs b Steele	0	6/250 7/250 8/287 9/292	

Bowling: McKenzie 12–3–44–0; Higgs 16–6–34–1; McVicker 8–2–17–0; Steele 11.5–1–42–4; Illingworth 27–9–77–2; Balderstone 25–9–79–2.

Leicestershire

M. E. Norman c and b Boyce	0	– c Smith b Turner	11
J. F. Steele c Boyce b East	0	– lbw b Boyce	9
J. C. Balderstone c Pont b Boyce	0	– lbw b Boyce	101
B. F. Davison b Boyce	1	– c East b Boyce	25
†R. W. Tolchard lbw b Boyce	9	– b Boyce	0
N. M. McVicker c Boyce b East	1	– b Boyce	9
*R. Illingworth b East	33	– c Hardie b Pont	29
G. D. McKenzie c East B Boyce	4	– not out	0
B. Dudleston lbw b East	2	– not out	6
K. Higgs b Boyce	3		
J. Birkenshaw not out	3	– c Hardie b Boyce	4
B 1, l-b 2, w 1	4	L-b 5, w 1, n-b 7	13
1/0 2/0 3/2 4/8 5/13 6/15 7/20 8/31 9/56	60	1/13 2/28 3/88 4/88 5/159 6/188 7/197 8/207	(8 wkts) 207

Bowling: *First Innings*—Boyce 13.1–6–25–6; Lever 12–8–7–0; East 20–10–24–4; Hobbs 1–1–0–0. *Second Innings*—Boyce 30–9–48–6; Lever 19–6–29–0; Turner 24–7–40–1; East 24–9–32–0; Hobbs 22–9–39–0; Pont 4–3–6–1.

Umpires: W. E. Alley and W. L. Budd.

ESSEX v SUSSEX

Played at Chelmsford June 25, 27, 28, 1977

Drawn. The brilliance of McEwan overshadowed everything else. Treating the bowling with utmost contempt, he struck the Sussex attack to all parts of the ground during a thrilling exhibition of stroke play. After Essex had found themselves precariously placed at 12 for three shortly after the start of the second day. McEwan raced to his century before lunch and went on to hit two 6s and thirty-six 4s in the first double century of his career. He so dominated a fourth wicket stand with Fletcher, that he scored 180 of the 258 which it produced. By comparison, the opening day was a dour affair, despite an aggressive not out 43 by Spencer. Knight batted soundly in making his first championship fifty of the summer and following it up on the final day with a resolute 81 in three-and-half hours. Greig also batted with great determination in the second innings as Sussex easily batted on for a draw on a pitch of friendly nature.

Sussex

J. R. T. Barclay c Smith b Turner	35	– st Smith b Acfield	24
K. C. Wessels lbw b Lever	0	– c Smith b Lever	39
R. D. V. Knight b East	52	– c Hardie b East	81
Javed Miandad c Hardie b East	33	– c McEwan b East	9
P. J. Graves b Turner	23	– lbw b Acfield	16
*A. W. Greig c Hardie b East	30	– c Hardie b Pont	88
M. A. Buss run out	2	– lbw b Gooch	8
J. A. Snow b East	7	– b Gooch	4
†A. Long c Pont b Acfield	17	– not out	8
J. Spencer not out	43	– not out	8
C. E. Waller b Acfield	1		
L-b 12, n-b 8	20	B 3, l-b 2, n-b 7	12
1/1 2/71 3/125 4/140 5/189 6/193 7/194 8/200 9/243	263	1/47 2/124 3/139 4/173 5/216 6/276 7/280 8/293	(8 wkts) 297

Bowling: *First Innings*—Lever 25–5–71–1; Turner 31–7–73–2; Gooch 6–1–21–0; East 30–8–63–4; Acfield 7.5–3–15–2. *Second Innings*—Lever 22–6–60–1; Turner 19–3–42–0; Gooch 5–2–14–2; Acfield 36–10–67–2; East 35–12–61–2; Pont 6–2–32–1; McEwan 2–1–7–0; Hardie 1–0–2–0.

Essex

B. R. Hardie c Long b Snow	7
M. H. Denness b Spencer	1
R. E. East b Long b Spencer	3
K. S. McEwan c Javed b Greig	218
*K. W. R. Fletcher c and b Greig	70
G. A. Gooch b Spencer b Buss	16
K. R. Pont b Greig	22
S. Turner not out	18
†N. Smith c Greig b Snow	7
L-b 1, w 5, n-b 3	9
1/2 2/12 3/12 4/270 5/315 6/325 7/356 8/371	(8 wkts dec.) 371

J. K. Lever and D. L. Acfield did not bat.

Bowling: Snow 20.4–4–64–2; Spencer 12–5–29–2; Greig 17–0–95–3; Buss 29–12–65–1; Javed 8–1–34–0; Waller 12–2–75–0.

Umpires: H. D. Bird and T. F. Brooks.

ESSEX v GLOUCESTERSHIRE

Played at Southend, July 6, 7, 8, 1977

Gloucestershire won by five wickets. A hat-trick by Procter, his second against Essex in five years, paved the way for the visitors' victory. Going in a second time 39 behind, Essex had advanced to 23 when Procter dismissed Hardie, McEwan and Gooch with the first three balls of his fifth over. Despite a gallant effort by Fletcher, last man out for 67, Essex never recovered as Procter went on to finish with seven for 45, his best figures in England. Gloucestershire achieved victory without too much alarm shortly after lunch on the final day. The opening day belonged to McEwan, whose century was his fourth in consecutive innings. Fosh, down from Cambridge and making his championship début, also batted elegantly for 56 and shared a century opening stand with the resolute Hardie. Zaheer (82) and Sadiq (56) shared a second wicket stand of 131 for Gloucestershire and Shepherd, after a cautious start, dealt some competent blows to help to extract maximum batting points against an attack weakened by the absence of Boyce and Lever.

Essex

B. R. Hardie c Sadiq b Childs	56	– b Procter	14
M. K. Fosh c Sadiq b Childs	56	– c Hignell b Shackleton	15
K. S. McEwan not out	106	– lbw b Procter	0
*K. W. R. Fletcher c Partridge b Shackleton	27	– b Procter	67
G. A. Gooch b Procter	30	– lbw b Procter	0
K. R. Pont c Zaheer b Brain	11	– lbw b Procter	0
S. Turner not out	3	– c Shackleton b Brain	7
M. H. Denness (did not bat)		– lbw b Procter	16
R. E. East (did not bat)		– c Procter b Brain	2
†N. Smith (did not bat)		– b Procter	20
D. L. Ackfield (did not bat)		– not out	0
B 2, l-b 3	5	B 4, l-b 2	6
1/101 2/132 3/215 4/265 5/286	(5 wkts) 294	1/23 2/23 3/23 4/47 5/78 6/78 7/92 8/108 9/136	147

Bowling: *First Innings:*—Procter 35–10–94–1; Brain 17–4–42–1; Shackleton 17–6–72–1; Childs 31–6–81–2. *Second Innings*—Procter 17.1–6–45–7; Brain 20–2–49–2; Shackleton 11–5–25–1; Childs 5–1–22–0.

Gloucestershire

Sadiq Mohammad c Smith b Acfield	56	– c Fletcher b Pont	9
†A. W. Stovold b East	22	– c Smith b Pont	22
Zaheer Abbas c Gooch b Turner	82	– lbw b Acfield	27
*M. J. Procter c Smith b Gooch	35	– c Gooch b East	5
D. R. Shepherd c East b Pont	68	– not out	15
A. J. Hignell not out	44	– c Fletcher b East	17
J. C. Foat b Acfield	0	– not out	9
D. M. Partridge not out	6		
B 4, l-b 7, n-b 9	20	B 1, l-b 3, n-b 1	5
1/34 2/165 3/181 4/235 5/317 6/319	(6 wkts) 333	1/28 2/36 3/60 4/68 5/90	(5 wkts) 109

J. H. Shackleton, B. M. Brain and J. H. Childs did not bat.

Bowling: *First Innings*—Turner 25–4–93–1; Pont 18–2–61–1; East 18–6–50–1; Acfield 33–9–90–2; Gooch 6–1–19–1. *Second Innings*—Turner 3–0–15–0; Pont 6–0–30–2; Acfield 19.1–8–25–1; East 16–7–34–2.

ESSEX v NORTHAMPTONSHIRE

Played at Ilford, June 3, 5, 6, 1978

Essex won by an innings and 39 runs. Highlight of this match was a record 321 second-wicket stand between McEwan and Gooch. The county's previous best was that of 294 by Avery and Gibb in 1952 when Northamptonshire were also on the receiving end. The majestic McEwan hit twenty-six 4s and one 6 during his four-hour stay for 186, while Gooch confirmed his talent with his second successive Championship hundred, his 129 including thirteen 4s. Their record-breaking feat came on the second day after Willey, displaying discipline and punishing drives, had held the visitors together with a superb 112 out of a total of 195. The match also proved a personal triumph for Lever. The left-arm fast bowler continued his spell of form with seven for 56 in the first innings and six for 89 in the second. Only Cook, Willey, and Watts offered any sort of resistance as Northamptonshire failed in their attempt to stave off defeat.

Northamptonshire

G. Cook c Hardie b Lever	0	– c Lever b Turner	55
W. Larkins c Gooch b Lever	9	– b Lever	16
D. S. Steele lbw b Phillip	2	– lbw b Lever	2
R. G. Williams b Lever	12	– lbw b Turner	18
P. Willey c Smith b Phillip	112	– c East b Turner	42
T. J. Yardley b Lever	22	– c Smith b Lever	15
*P. J. Watts c Gooch b Lever	1	– c Smith b Lever	30
†G. Sharp b Lever	0	– c Smith b Turner	8
T. M. Lamb c Smith b East	16	– c Smith b Lever	6
A. Hodgson c Gooch b Lever	10	– b Lever	1
B. J. Griffiths not out	0	– not out	5
L-b 4, w 1, n-b 6	11	B 4, l-b 4, w 3, n-b 14	25
1/0 2/12 3/12 4/40 5/89 6/92 7/92 8/162 9/183	195	1/44 2/49 3/82 4/111 5/144 6/171 7/188 8/213 9/216	223

Bowling: *First Innings*—Lever 24–6–56–7; Phillip 23.3–3–57–2; Turner 18–2–39–0; East 16–6–32–1. *Second Innings*—Lever 29.5–3–89–6; Phillip 14–1–52–0; Turner 25–10–48–4; East 4–1–9–0.

Essex

M. H. Denness c Sharp b Hodgson	16
G. A. Gooch lbw b Watts	129
K. S. McEwan c Sharp b Griffiths	186
*K. W. R. Fletcher c Steele b Hodgson	31
B. R. Hardie not out	73
S. Turner lbw b Griffiths	3
N. Phillip not out	8
L-b 8, n-b 3	11
1/18 2/339 3/339 4/416 5/439 (5 wkts dec.)	457

R. E. East, †N. Smith, J. K. Lever and D. L. Acfield did not bat.

Bowling: Hodgson 20–1–113–2; Griffiths 30–5–92–2; Lamb 28–5–98–0; Willey 12–3–52–0; Larkins 4–0–20–0; Steel 7–0–40–0; Watts 11–3–31–1.

Umpires: J. van Geloven and D. O. Oslear.

ESSEX v WARWICKSHIRE

Played at Colchester, July 15, 17, 18, 1978

Essex won by 45 runs. Warwickshire, thanks to a magnificent effort from Amiss, carried the match into the final 20 overs before admitting defeat. Left a victory target of 319, Warwickshire were in desperate straits at 29 for four; Phillip and Turner caused the wreckage. Amiss went on to carry his bat for 122, receiving stout support from Humpage, Rouse and Hemmings before East polished off the tail. Amiss also batted well for 40 in the first innings, during which East took five for 54. The Warwickshire attack suffered at the hands of Denness, whose knock of 71 in the first innings was followed by one of 125 in the second, the opener's first Championship hundred of the season. Hardie and McEvoy, standing in for England's Graham Gooch, gave him admirable support.

Essex

M. H. Denness c Kallicharran b Rouse	71	– c Amiss b Hemmings	126
M. S. A. McEvoy lbw b Perryman	25	– c Hemmings b Clifford	51
K. S. McEwan c Abberley b Brown	2	– c Clifford b Perryman	34
*K. W. R. Fletcher c Kallicharran b Brown	12		
B. R. Hardie c Humpage b Perryman	61		
K. R. Pont b Clifford	19	– not out	20
N. Phillip b Perryman	5	– c Amiss b Brown	6
S. Turner c Hemmings b Clifford	32		
R. E. East b Clifford	19		
D. R. Pringle c Whitehouse b Clifford	4		
†N. Smith not out	1	– not out	8
L-b 11, n-b 9	20	B 4, l-b 4, w 3, n-b 2	13
1/67 2/86 3/113 4/170 5/201 6/207 7/221 8/251 9/270	271	1/153 2/222 3/230 4/242	(4 wkts dec.) 258

Bowling: *First Innings*—Brown 18–1–63–2; Rouse 16–3–67–1; Perryman 36–12–74–3; Clifford 19–8–47–4. *Second Innings*—Brown 12–2–35–1; Rouse 2–0–23–0; Perryman 23–10–62–1; Clifford 23–7–50–1; Hemmings 17–3–75–1.

Warwickshire

D. L. Amiss lbw b Phillip	50	– not out	122
K. D. Smith run out	27	– lbw b Phillip	2
R. N. Abberley b Phillip	0	– c and b Phillip	3
*J. Whitehouse c Turner b Phillip	4	– c Hardie b Turner	0
A. I. Kallicharran b Pont	51	– c Fletcher b Phillip	0
†G. W. Humpage c McEvoy b East	41	– b Pont	25
S. J. Rouse lbw b East	1	– lbw b Phillip	33
E. E. Hemmings c Smith b East	0	– b East	51
D. J. Brown not out	10	– c and b East	4
S. P. Perryman c Hardie b East	0	– c Fletcher b East	1
C. Clifford c Hardie b East	7	– c Pont b East	12
L-b 9, n-b 11	20	B 1, l-b 10, n-b 9	20
1/71 2/71 3/108 4/114 5/184 6/189 7/191 8/195 9/201	211	1/21 2/28 3/28 4/29 5/86 6/136 7/228 8/241 9/249	273

Bowling: *First Innings*—Phillip 20–4–58–3; Turner 19–4–42–0; East 23.5–7–54–5; Pringle 4–1–9–0; Pont 14–4–28–1. *Second Innings*—Phillip 27–3–61–4; Turner 15–2–50–1; East 34.3–9–94–4; Pont 9–1–48–1.

Umpires: R. A. Aspinall and R. T. Wilson.

ESSEX v KENT

Played at Chelmsford, May 2, 3, 4, 1979

Drawn. Most of the drama came late in the third day. Batting a second time with a first innings lead of 55 and with only one hour and fifty minutes remaining, Essex capitulated to 26 for eight inside an hour. A drying wicket and irresponsible stroke-play led to the collapse before Lever and Phillip resisted long enough to end Kent's hopes of pulling off the "impossible". In a match marred by stoppages for rain, Turner drove and pulled magnificently during the Essex first innings for his century, reaching three figures in only 113 minutes with five 6s and nine 4s. In contrast, Rowe took just over six hours for his hundred as Kent struggled in the face of an accurate attack. Off-spinner Johnson was mainly responsible for Essex's late scare, finishing with five for 12 in 6.1 overs.

Essex

M. H. Denness b Hills	37	– c Knott b Jarvis	0
G. A. Gooch b Jarvis	13	– lbw b Underwood	11
K. S. McEwan c Johnson b Shepherd	20	– c Knott b Jarvis	0
*K. W. R. Fletcher c Tavaré b Hills	41	– c Hills b Johnson	4
B. R. Hardie c Tavaré b Hills	15	– c Shepherd b Johnson	4
K. R. Pont c Woolmer b Shepherd	33	– c Cowdrey b Underwood	0
S. Turner c Hills b Shepherd	102	– c Ealham b Johnson	6
N. Phillip not out	39	– not out	3
†N. Smith not out	0	– c Shepherd b Johnson	0
J. K. Lever (did not bat)		– c Knott b Johnson	12
L-b 3, n-b 2	5	L-b 1, n-b 2	3
1/17 2/55 3/86 4/128 5/129 6/204 7/304	(7 wkts dec.) 305	1/0 2/0 3/15 4/15 5/19 6/19 7/26 8/26 9/43	(9 wkts) 43

D. L. Acfield did not bat.

Bowling: *First Innings*—Jarvis 16–2–77–1; Shepherd 28–4–81–3; Hills 23–6–59–3; Underwood 20–7–45–0; Johnson 3–0–38–0. *Second Innings*—Jarvis 5–4–4–2; Shepherd 6–2–11–0; Underwood 8–4–13–2; Johnson 6.1–3–12–5.

Kent

R. A. Woolmer c Hardie b Phillip	29
C. J. C. Rowe not out	108
C. J. Tavaré c Smith b Pont	34
C. S. Cowdrey c Turner b Phillip	19
*A. G. E. Ealham c Lever b Phillip	15
J. N. Shepherd c Smith b Pont	19
G. W. Johnson c Smith b Pont	0
†A. P. E. Knott lbw b Acfield	1
R. W. Hills b Acfield	0
D. L. Underwood not out	9
L-b 10, w 1, n-b 6	17
1/63 2/122 3/160 4/176 5/220 6/220 7/224 8/230	(8 wkts) 250

K. B. S. Jarvis did not bat.

Bowling: Lever 20–6–36–0; Phillip 24–12–37–3; Turner 32–11–79–0; Acfield 9–2–28–2; Pont 20–6–44–3; Gooch 5–2–9–0.

Umpires: A. Jepson and D. J. Dennis.

ESSEX v DERBYSHIRE

Played at Chelmsford, June 20, 21, 22, 1979

Essex won by an innings and 40 runs. After Derbyshire were in dire straits at 53 for six, Swarbrook, Tunnicliffe and Walters hit fifties to pick up three unexpected bonus points. Lever continued his excellent form with a five-wicket haul and received fine support from Phillip. The Essex innings was dominated by McEwan who, after reaching his century in only eighty-five minutes, went on to make 185 with the aid of three 6s and twenty-nine 4s. He so dominated the third-wicket stand with Denness that he scored 109 of the 131 it produced. Pont also batted with authority for his 77 as Essex ran up a massive 435 for nine before declaring. Derbyshire never looked like staving off defeat as Lever and Phillip speeded Essex to victory an hour or so after lunch on the final day.

Derbyshire

A. Hill lbw b Lever	10	– b Lever	19
I. S. Anderson b Phillip	2	– lbw b Lever	0
*D. S. Steele lbw b Phillip	4	– c Hardie b Phillip	5
P. N. Kirsten b Lever	11	– c Denness b Turner	3
A. J. Borrington c Smith b Phillip	12	– lbw b East	34
K. J. Barnett c Smith b Lever	0	– c Smith b Lever	21
F. W. Swarbrook c Smith b Turner	52	– b Phillip	5
J. Walters c Pont b Lever	54	– c East b Lever	9
C. J. Tunnicliffe b Phillip	57	– not out	18
R. C. Wincer lbw b Lever	3	– b Phillip	3
†A. J. McLellan not out	8	– c Smith b Phillip	0
B 5, l-b 24, w 3, n-b 13	45	B 4, l-b 5, w 2, n-b 9	20
1/4 2/14 3/28 4/29 5/43 6/53 7/138 8/208 9/215	258	1/1 2/18 3/28 4/36 5/95 6/95 7/109 8/126 9/131	137

Bowling: *First Innings*—Lever 30–5–72–5; Phillip 26.4–11–59–4; Turner 27–6–51–1; Pont 11–2–29–0; East 3–1–2–0. *Second Innings*—Lever 18–4–45–4; Phillip 10–0–28–4; Turner 15–7–27–1; East 15–2–17–1.

Essex

M. H. Denness c Steele b Walters	35
A. W. Lilley c Barnett b Tunnicliffe	0
R. E. East c McLellan b Wincer	19
K. S. McEwan c Steele b Kirsten	185
*K. W. R. Fletcher c Steele b Wincer	15
B. R. Hardie c McLellan b Kirsten	7
K. R. Pont c McLellan b Kirsten	77
N. Phillip c Barnett b Tunnicliffe	6
S. Turner b Walters	43
†N. Smith not out	16
B 3, l-b 15, n-b 14	32
1/0 2/39 3/170 4/232 5/278 6/280 7/293 8/375 9/435	(9 wkts dec.) 435

J. K. Lever did not bat.

Bowling: Wincer 20–3–84–2; Tunnicliffe 19–6–74–2; Walters 33–6–120–2; Steele 6–0–39–0; Swarbrook 3–0–28–0; Kirsten 18.2–3–58–3.

Umpires: H. D. Bird and B. J. Meyer.

ESSEX v MIDDLESEX

Played at Ilford, June 17, 18, 19, 1981

Essex won by 95 runs. Chasing a target of 259 in 223 minutes, the champions might have anticipated victory as they passed 100 with only two wickets down. But then spinners Acfield and East got to work on a pitch giving encouragement and won the match for Essex with seventeen overs remaining. Lilley, making his first Championship appearance of the season, and Pont dominated the Essex first innings after Fletcher had retired with a damaged thumb – sustained while facing Selvey. The visitors' first innings was held together by Brearley, whose third century in five innings took five and a quarter hours and included ten 4s. Hardie was the mainstay of the home side's second innings before falling to slow left-arm bowler Monteith, who returned career-best Championship figures. At a later date, it was ruled that Middlesex should lose their 7 bonus points for fielding a non-registered player, C. R. V. Taylor.

Essex

B. R. Hardie lbw b Daniel	21	– c Butcher b Monteith	70
M. S. A. McEvoy b Daniel	21	– c Taylor b Selvey	14
*K. W. R. Fletcher retired hurt	8		
A. W. Lilley b Edmonds	90	– (3) lbw b Edmonds	0
K. R. Pont c Taylor b Thomson	87	– (4) c Brearley b Monteith	7
N. Phillip lbw b Monteith	13	– c Taylor b Edmonds	17
S. Turner c and b Edmonds	25	– c Butcher b Monteith	36
R. E. East c Butcher b Monteith	15	– (5) c Thomson b Monteith	12
†N. Smith c Taylor b Daniel	1	– (8) c Butcher b Monteith	27
J. K. Lever not out	2	– (9) b Edmonds	1
D. L. Acfield b Thomson	0	– (10) not out	7
L-b 18, w 1, n-b 1	20	B 13, l-b 13, w 1	27
1/38 2/49 3/202 4/229 5/264 6/297 7/298 8/302 9/303	303	1/40 2/53 3/74 4/98 5/132 6/138 7/210 8/210 9/218	(9 wkts dec.) 218

Bowling: *First Innings*—Thomson 14.3–4–36–2; Selvey 12–4–36–0; Daniel 19–1–71–3; Edmonds 20–2–70–2; Monteith 23–6–70–2. *Second Innings*—Thomson 6–1–34–0; Daniel 4–0–17–0; Selvey 8–2–24–1; Edmonds 29.3–5–56–3; Monteith 20–4–60–5

Middlesex

*J. M. Brearley b Turner	113	– c McEvoy b Acfield	45
W. N. Slack lbw b Phillip	1	– c Hardie b Turner	14
C. T. Radley c McEvoy b Lever	8	– c Pont b East	54
R. O. Butcher b Turner	48	– c Fletcher b Acfield	8
K. P. Tomlins lbw b Turner	3	– (6) c Fletcher b Acfield	4
P. H. Edmonds c Lever b Acfield	15	– (5) c and b Acfield	6
M. W. W. Selvey c Smith b Lever	57	– b East	2
J. R. Thomson b Turner	3	– not out	1
J. D. Monteith b Lever	1	– b East	8
W. W. Daniel not out	7	– st Smith b Acfield	4
†C. R. V. Taylor c Smith b Lever	1	– lbw b East	5
L-b 5, n-b 1	6	B 3, l-b 9	12
1/10 2/39 3/107 4/116 5/149 6/248 7/254 8/254 9/261	263	1/28 2/87 3/101 4/129 5/141 6/141 7/145 8/153 9/158	163

Bowling: *First Innings*—Lever 22.4–4–75–4; Phillip 14–4–28–1; East 33–9–65–0; Acfield 15–2–45–1; Turner 22–8–44–4. *Second Innings*—Lever 6–0–16–0; Phillip 3–0–9–0; Turner 4–0–12–1; East 21.4–2–56–4; Acfield 20–3–58–5.

Umpires: H. D. Bird and Shakoor Rana.

ESSEX v GLAMORGAN

Played at Colchester, August 29, 31, September 1, 1981

Essex won by 13 runs. A memorable match ended with Essex clinching victory in the thirteenth of the final twenty overs. The brilliance of Miandad was responsible for setting up such a thrilling finish, for after the Welsh county had been set 325 in 323 minutes, he hit a magnificent, unbeaten 200 (twenty-two 4s) in five and a quarter hours, equalling Gilbert Parkhouse's record, set in 1950, of seven first-class hundreds in a season for Glamorgan. His effort ended when Lever removed his partners, shortly after taking the new ball. Miandad had earlier displayed his class in Glamorgan's first innings as, with

Featherstone, he earned his side a useful lead, despite the excellent bowling of Acfield. However, Essex made light of the 87 runs' deficit, clearing it in only 48 minutes before Gooch, in just under an hour and a half, completed his third century in eight days, hitting one 6 and twenty 4s. Lilley later underlined his potential with 88 in 72 minutes (two 6s and thirteen 4s), while Hardie, content to accumulate runs in his methodical way, was undefeated on 114 in four and a half hours when Fletcher declared. Hobbs bowled well against his former county, fully deserving his five wickets in their second innings.

Essex

G. A. Gooch lbw b Nash	16	– c A. L. Jones b Lloyd	113
B. R. Hardie c Daniels b Ontong	37	– not out	114
*K. W. R. Fletcher lbw b Daniels	6	– b Ontong	6
K. S. McEwan, c E. W. Jones b Daniels	0	– c Miandad b Ontong	2
A. W. Lilley c Featherstone b Ontong	14	– c E. W. Jones b Hobbs	88
N. Phillip c Miandad b Daniels	21	– lbw b Hobbs	4
S. Turner lbw b Nash	36	– c Daniels b Ontong	31
R. E. East c Daniels b Ontong	19	– (9) c and b Hobbs	4
†D. E. East c Featherstone b Nash	5	– (8) st E. W. Jones b Hobbs	4
J. K. Lever not out	14	– st E. W. Jones b Hobbs	9
D. L. Acfield c Miandad b Ontong	0		
B 4, l-b 6, w 6, n-b 3	19	B 16, l-b 15, w 4, n-b 1	36
1/20 2/29 3/29 4/69 5/93 6/132 7/152 8/167 9/174	187	1/169 2/186 3/188 4/332 5/341 6/388 7/398 8/402 9/411 (9 wkts dec.)	411

Bowling: *First Innings*—Nash 19–4–76–3; Daniels 11–3–33–3; Ontong 13.4–2–37–4; Lloyd 6–0–22–0. *Second Innings*—Nash 6–0–33–0; Daniels 7–0–45–0; Ontong 21–3–102–3; Lloyd 31–4–110–1; Hobbs 21.5–3–85–5.

Glamorgan

A. Jones b Lever	31	– c D. E. East b Lever	0
J. A. Hopkins c Gooch b Lever	46	– c Fletcher b Lever	16
R. C. Ontong lbw b Turner	5	– c R. E. East b Turner	4
Javed Miandad st D. E. East b Acfield	81	– not out	200
N. G. Featherstone st D. E. East b R. E. East	59	– c Fletcher b Lever	0
A. L. Jones c Gooch b Acfield	15	– lbw b Acfield	36
†E. W. Jones c Fletcher b Acfield	1	– st D. E. East b R. E. East	24
*M. A. Nash c Lever b Acfield	10	– (10) c Turner b Lever	1
B. J. Lloyd lbw b Acfield	4	– (8) b Acfield	0
S. A. B. Daniels c Fletcher b Acfield	2	– (11) lbw b Lever	8
R. N. S. Hobbs not out	6	– (9) c Fletcher b Acfield	0
B 2, l-b 10, w 1, n-b 1	14	B 12, l-b 8, n-b 2	22
1/56 2/61 3/99 4/229 5/229 6/232 7/245 8/262 9/265	274	1/0 2/7 3/44 4/44 5/155 6/224 7/227 8/270 9/291	311

Bowling: *First Innings*—Lever 19–3–59–2; Phillip 15–1–51–0; Turner 9–1–30–1; R. E. East 28–7–56–1; Acfield 24.5–8–64–6. *Second Innings*—Lever 17–2–62–5; Turner 8–0–34–1; Acfield 33–7–84–3; R. E. East 30–8–97–1; Phillip 3–0–12–0.

Umpires: D. G. L. Evans and K. E. Palmer.

GLAMORGAN

GLAMORGAN v DERBYSHIRE

Played at Llanelly, May 6, 7, 8, 1964

Drawn. Not even three declarations on the last day could produce a definite result after rain had washed out the first day and all but an hour and forty minutes of the second. After Derbyshire declared at their overnight total on the third day, Wheatley closed the Glamorgan first innings after one ball. When Derbyshire batted a second time, they were tied down by Walker, Wheatley and Shepherd on a difficult pitch and had lost eight wickets when Lee set Glamorgan the task of scoring 135 runs in two hours, twenty-five minutes. In the end it was left to Pressdee to play out time after poor running between the wickets and accurate spin bowling by Allen had dashed Glamorgan's hopes.

Derbyshire

I. W. Hall not out	19	– c Evans b Walker	13
J. F. Harvey not out	26	– c A. Jones b Walker	12
I. R. Buxton (did not bat)		– c Wheatley b Shepherd	4
*C. Lee (did not bat)		– b Wheatley	22
D. C. Morgan (did not bat)		– c Rees b Wheatley	16
†H. L. Johnson (did not bat)		– c Evans b Shepherd	6
W. F. Oates (did not bat)		– c Wheatley b Shepherd	5
E. Smith (did not bat)		– c Evans b Wheatley	6
H. J. Rhodes (did not bat)		– not out	2
		L-b 4	4
(No wkt dec.)	45	1/23 2/32 3/36 4/64 5/73 6/77 7/87 8/90 (8 wkts dec.)	90

M. H. J. Allen and A. B. Jackson did not bat.

Bowling: *First Innings*—I. Jones 5–3–2–0; Wheatley 7–5–4–0; Walker 3–2–8–0; Shepherd 13–7–14–0; Pressdee 8–3–17–0. *Second Innings*—I. Jones 3–2–5–0; Wheatley 11–2–34–3; Walker 12–5–21–2; Shepherd 17–5–26–3.

Glamorgan

D. J. Shepherd not out	1	– run out	1
I. J. Jones not out	0		
W. G. A. Parkhouse (did not bat)		– b Jackson	11
A. Jones (did not bat)		– run out	7
A. R. Lewis (did not bat)		– c Johnson b Allen	20
B. Hedges (did not bat)		– c Hall b Oates	11
P. M. Walker (did not bat)		– c Lee b Allen	5
J. Pressdee (did not bat)		– not out	22
A. Rees (did not bat)		– c Rhodes b Allen	9
†D. L. Evans (did not bat)		– not out	2
		L-b 1, n-b 1	2
(No wkt dec.)	1	1/16 2/21 3/51 4/51 5/56 6/67 7/78 (7 wkts)	90

*O. S. Wheatley did not bat.

Bowling: *First Innings*—Morgan 0.1–0–1–0. *Second Innings*—Rhodes 11–6–12–0; Jackson 10–4–10–1; Morgan 6–2–9–0; Buxton 2–2–0–0; Smith 6–1–7–0; Allen 11–4–25–3; Oates 6–1–25–1.

Umpires: H. Yarnold and N. Oldfield.

GLAMORGAN v WORCESTERSHIRE

Played at Cardiff, June 6, 8, 9, 1964

Worcestershire won by nine wickets. No play was possible on the first day because of rain. On a damaged pitch, Worcestershire, without their Test bowlers Coldwell and Flavell, possessed a capable deputy in Standen, whose deceptive change of pace puzzled the batsmen. Gifford bowled with remarkable accuracy and conceded only one scoring stroke in twelve overs. Worcestershire also found batting hazardous against Wheatley and Shepherd, but Glamorgan fared a little better when they batted a second time though only Hedges and Pressdee appeared likely to stay long. Worcestershire adopted bold tactics when they needed 109 in one hundred minutes for victory. Kenyon led the way with three 6s and four 4s.

Glamorgan

A. Jones b Standen	14	– c Headley b Standen	16
B. Hedges c Headley b Standen	18	– b Gifford	34
A. R. Lewis c Booth b Standen	0	– st Booth b Slade	19
A. Rees c and b Standen	5	– b Gifford	1
J. Pressdee run out	5	– c Booth b Gifford	25
P. M. Walker c Fearnley b Carter	6	– c Richardson b Slade	0
G. Hughes c Booth b Standen	6	– b Carter	0
†D. L. Evans c Graveney b Carter	4	– run out	0
D. J. Shepherd c Booth b Standen	0	– c and b Carter	2
*O. S. Wheatley b Standen	8	– c and b Standen	12
I. J. Jones not out	4	– not out	6
L-b 1	1	B 2, l-b 1	3
1/27 2/27 3/34 4/37 5/48 6/50 7/59 8/59 9/65	71	1/45 2/53 3/61 4/71 5/71 6/74 7/78 8/84 9/108	118

Bowling: *First Innings*—Carter 14–3–31–2; Standen 26–12–35–7; Gifford 12–11–4–0. *Second Innings*—Carter 23–8–44–2; Standen 14.5–6–24–2; Gifford 17–8–35–3; Slade 17–12–12–2.

Worcestershire

*D. Kenyon b I. Jones	5	– c Hughes b Wheatley	49
M. J. Horton c and b Wheatley	18	– not out	35
R. G. A. Headley c A. Jones b Shepherd	25	– not out	24
T. W. Graveney c Walker b Shepherd	2		
D. W. Richardson lbw b Wheatley	3		
C. D. Fearnley lbw b Wheatley	0		
†R. Booth b Shepherd	4		
D. N. F. Slade b Wheatley	10		
J. Standen c Walker b Shepherd	0		
N. Gifford c A. Jones b Shepherd	4		
R. G. M. Carter not out	0		
B 4, l-b 6	10	L-b 1	1
1/10 2/39 3/43 4/50 5/50 6/67 7/67 8/67 9/81	81	1/69	(1 wkt) 109

Bowling: *First Innings*—I. Jones 8–1–22–1; Wheatley 21.1–8–29–4; Shepherd 15–7–20–5. *Second Innings*—Wheatley 7–0–30–1; I. Jones 5–1–19–0; Shepherd 5.4–0–25–0; Pressdee 2–0–20–0; Walker 3–0–14–0.

Umpires: T. Drinkwater and R. Aspinall.

GLAMORGAN v NORTHAMPTONSHIRE

Played at Swansea, June, 10, 11, 12, 1964

Glamorgan won by seven wickets. Only Milburn, who scored his fifty (one 6, six 4s) in just over an hour, offered any real resistance to Shepherd and Pressdee on a helpful pitch. Glamorgan got away to a flying start when Jones and Hedges equalled their rivals' total. Jones hit one 6 and eleven 4s in his innings of eighty minutes. Splendid bowling by P. J. Watts prevented Glamorgan gaining a large lead. A hat-trick by Shepherd – the first of his career – hastened the end of Northamptonshire's second innings after determined defence by Reynolds, Lightfoot and Steele. Norman, the Northamptonshire opening batsman, had the unenviable distinction of being dismissed with the first ball of each innings on Wednesday when twenty-three wickets went down.

Northamptonshire

M. Norman c Walker b Wheatley	0	– c Pressdee b Wheatley	0
B. L. Reynolds c A. Jones b Shepherd	4	– lbw b Wheatley	36
C. Milburn b Shepherd	50	– c Rees b Pressdee	12
R. M. Prideaux st Evans b Pressdee	7	– c Hughes b Pressdee	4
A. Lightfoot c E. Lewis b Pressdee	2	– c Walker b Shepherd	39
P. J. Watts c and b Pressdee	0	– c Evans b Wheatley	23
D. S. Steele hit wkt b Pressdee	5	– c Pressdee b E. Lewis	30
M. E. Scott c Walker b Shepherd	5	– c Evans b Shepherd	0
B. Crump st Evans b Shepherd	16	– c Walker b Shepherd	0
P. D. Watts not out	5	– c Walker b Pressdee	7
*†K. V. Andrew c A. Jones b Shepherd	0	– not out	1
L-b 4	4	B 4, l-b 5	9
1/0 2/11 3/51 4/63 5/63 6/63 7/69 8/77 9/98	98	1/0 2/13 3/27 4/66 5/114 6/132 7/132 8/132 9/155	161

Bowling: *First Innings*—Wheatley 6–2–14–1; Walker 5–2–10–0; Shepherd 17.4–5–41–5; Pressdee 12–5–29–4. *Second Innings*—Wheatley 33–16–37–3; Walker 8–2–30–0; Shepherd 46–25–55–3; Pressdee 14–5–26–3; E. Lewis 3.1–2–4–1.

Glamorgan

A. Jones lbw b Crump	61	– not out	15
B. Hedges c P. D. Watts b P. J. Watts	45	– c Milburn b P. J. Watts	11
E. Lewis c Andrew b P. J. Watts	4	– b Scott	33
A. R. Lewis c Norman b Scott	29	– not out	0
A. Rees c Andrew b P. J. Watts	0		
J. Pressdee c P. D. Watts b Scott	6		
P. M. Walker run out	9		
G. Hughes c Andrew b P. J. Watts	0		
†D. L. Evans c Milburn b P. J. Watts	0		
D. J. Shepherd not out	22	– c Andrew b Scott	13
*O. S. Wheatley c P. J. Watts b Scott	1		
B 4, l-b 1	5	B 1, l-b 5	6
1/98 2/108 3/115 4/127 5/149 6/150 7/159 8/159 9/163	182	1/50 2/59 3/70	78

Bowling: *First Innings*—Crump 12–4–22–1; Scott 26–12–69–3; Steele 5–1–19–0; P. D. Watts 8–0–39–0; P. J. Watts 17–5–28–5. *Second Innings*—Crump 5–0–9–0; P. J. Watts 11–3–28–1; Scott 6.3–1–35–2.

Umpires: T. Drinkwater and R. Aspinall.

GLAMORGAN v YORKSHIRE

Played at Swansea, June 9, 10, 1965

Glamorgan won by 31 runs after their two leading spin bowlers, Shepherd and Pressdee, each captured nine wickets in an innings. The pitch took spin from the start and Rees and E. Lewis were the only Glamorgan batsmen to defy Close for long. Pressdee routed Yorkshire in their first innings and Boycott, who batted for two hours, alone stayed for any period. Wilson, with five wickets, was Yorkshire's most successful bowler when Glamorgan batted a second time. Yorkshire, left to score 166, appeared well set after a second-wicket partnership of 64 between Boycott and Padgett. When they were dismissed, only Hampshire, with two 6s and five 4s, offered more than token resistance against Shepherd's off-spin.

Glamorgan

A. Jones run out	19	– c Wilson b Illingworth	7
B. Hedges b Close	11	– c Sharpe b Wilson	28
A. R. Lewis lbw b Close	19	– c Hampshire b Wilson	20
A. Rees b Illingworth	34	– c Trueman b Illingworth	0
J. Pressdee lbw b Illingworth	0	– lbw b Wilson	5
P. M. Walker b Illingworth	1	– c Taylor b Wilson	0
E. Lewis c and b Close	30	– not out	29
W. Slade c Taylor b Close	12	– b Close	4
†D. L. Evans not out	11	– b Illingworth	1
D. J. Shepherd c Boycott b Close	0	– c Sharpe b Wilson	16
*O. S. Wheatley c Taylor b Close	1	– c Hampshire b Close	11
L-b 2	2		
1/17 2/42 3/71 4/72 5/74 6/107 7/119 8/130 9/130	140	1/23 2/28 3/57 4/58 5/63 6/64 7/69 8/72 9/93	121

Bowling: *First Innings*—Trueman 3–0–4–0; Nicholson 5–3–2–0; Close 22.5–8–52–6; Illingworth 24–6–68–3; Wilson 4–2–12–0. Second Innings—Illingworth 24–5–59–3; Close 10.3–3–25–2; Wilson 13–3–37–5.

Yorkshire

G. Boycott c A. R. Lewis b Pressdee	18	– c Walker b Pressdee	21
K. Taylor c Wheatley b Pressdee	21	– b Shepherd	4
D. E. V. Padgett c Slade b Pressdee	1	– c Pressdee b Shepherd	46
P. J. Sharpe c Shepherd b Pressdee	4	– b Shepherd	9
*D. B. Close c Shepherd b Pressdee	23	– lbw b Shepherd	0
J. H. Hampshire run out	4	– b Shepherd	41
R. Illingworth c Slade b Pressdee	4	– c Slade b Shepherd	0
†J. G. Binks c Wheatley b Pressdee	20	– lbw b Shepherd	1
F. S. Trueman c Evans b Pressdee	0	– c Rees b Shepherd	0
D. Wilson c E. Lewis b Pressdee	0	– st Evans b Shepherd	8
A. G. Nicholson not out	1	– not out	0
		B 1, l-b 3	4
1/31 2/33 3/37 4/63 5/68 6/73 7/76 8/84 9/84	96	1/4 2/68 3/72 4/72 5/74 6/119 7/119 8/124 9/129	134

Bowling: *First Innings*—Wheatley 2–0–6–0; Walker 2–0–14–0; Pressdee 23.3–12–43–9; Shepherd 23–12–33–0. *Second Innings*—Wheatley 4–1–3–0; Shepherd 27.5–12–48–9; Pressdee 26–8–73–1; E. Lewis 10–5–6–0.

Umpires: C. Cook and C. G. Pepper.

GLAMORGAN v LEICESTERSHIRE

Played at Ebbw Vale, July 28, 29, 30, 1965

Glamorgan won by 115 runs. A. Jones and Walker did their best to make up almost six hours lost through rain on the first two days and shared a second-wicket partnership of 173 in three hours, forty minutes. Jones was the dominant partner and his 108 included four 6s and ten 4s. Leicestershire began badly but Hallam and Inman guided them to the lead. When they batted a second time, Glamorgan sacrificed wickets for quick runs and were well served by A. R. Lewis and Walker, who added 83 in an hour for the second wicket. Left to score 149 in an hour and fifty minutes, Leicestershire were routed in eighty minutes for 33 – the lowest total against Glamorgan in their 44 years in the Championship. Shepherd gained the remarkable figures of 10–8–2–5.

Glamorgan

A. Jones c Hallam b Savage	108	– c Hallam b Savage	8
A. R. Lewis b Lock	1	– c Inman b Barratt	44
P. M. Walker not out	79	– c Inman b Barratt	55
A. Rees not out	1	– not out	23
J. Pressdee (did not bat)		– c van Geloven b Lock	4
H. Miller (did not bat)		– lbw b Lock	1
E. Lewis (did not bat)		– c Savage b Barratt	1
D. J. Shepherd (did not bat)		– b Barratt	2
†D. L. Evans (did not bat)		– run out	0
I. J. Jones (did not bat)		– c van Geloven b Lock	6
B 4, l-b 3, w 4, n-b 5	16	B 7, l-b 1	8
1/15 2/188 (2 wkts dec.)	205	1/17 2/98 3/116 4/117 5/118 6/119 7/129 8/141 9/152 (9 wkts dec.)	152

*O. S. Wheatley did not bat.

Bowling: *First Innings*—van Geloven 19–6–45–0; Marner 9–2–30–0; Lock 20–1–58–1; Savage 21–9–41–1; Barratt 9–3–15–0. *Second Innings*—van Geloven 8–3–14–0; Marner 4–1–11–0; Savage 7–0–25–1; Lock 15.3–1–56–3; Barratt 12–2–38–4.

Leicestershire

*M. R. Hallam not out	95	– c A. R. Lewis b Wheatley	6
B. J. Booth lbw b I. J. Jones	1	– b I. J. Jones	3
J. Birkenshaw c A. Jones b Pressdee	11	– c D. L. Evans b E. Lewis	11
S. Jayasinghe run out	2	– c D. L. Evans b Shepherd	5
C. C. Inman b Rees	74	– lbw b Pressdee	2
P. Marner not out	16	– c I. J. Jones b Shepherd	5
J. van Geloven (did not bat)		– c Pressdee b Shepherd	0
G. A. R. Lock (did not bat)		– b Shepherd	1
†R. Julian (did not bat)		– b E. Lewis	0
R. J. Barratt (did not bat)		– not out	0
J. S. Savage (did not bat)		– c Pressdee b Shepherd	0
B 4, l-b 6	10		
1/7 2/31 3/34 4/170 (4 wkts)	209	1/7 2/13 3/17 4/19 5/21 6/23 7/32 8/33 9/33	33

Bowling: *First Innings*—A. R. Lewis 2–0–10–0; I. J. Jones 12–6–18–1; Wheatley 10–5–19–0; Shepherd 19–9–36–0; E. Lewis 12–4–35–0; Pressdee 13–3–30–1; Miller 4–2–9–0; A. Jones 4–2–13–0; Rees 4.3–0–29–1. *Second Innings*—I. J. Jones 4–1–12–1; Wheatley 3–1–5–1; Shepherd 10–8–2–5; Pressdee 4–1–7–1; E. Lewis 5–3–7–2.

Umpires: John Langridge and P. A. Gibb.

GLAMORGAN v HAMPSHIRE

Played at Cardiff, May 28, 30, 31, 1966

65 overs. Glamorgan won by 46 runs. A remarkable spell of bowling by Shepherd was responsible for the rout of Hampshire in their second innings, when they wanted only 122 to win. In his first four overs Shepherd snapped up three wickets without conceding a run and when Hampshire were skittled out for 75 his analysis read seven for seven. Yet during the previous two days Hampshire appeared to be in command. They gained a first-innings lead of 24 runs and in the Glamorgan second innings only the sound batting of Alan Jones prevented Hampshire from consolidating their position. Seventh to leave at 135, Jones had held out against Hampshire's array of seam bowlers almost single handed for three and three-quarter hours for his 78, which included nine 4s.

Glamorgan

B. Hedges b Shackleton	0	– b Shackleton	0
A. Jones c Reed b White	4	– lbw b Cottam	78
E. Lewis lbw b White	10	– lbw b Shackleton	7
A. R. Lewis c Barnard b White	43	– b Wheatley	21
A. Rees st Timms b Shackleton	26	– c Sainsbury b Wheatley	1
I. Morris c Livingstone b White	38	– lbw b Wheatley	6
F. J. Davis c Cottam b Shackleton	9	– lbw b Shackleton	1
D. J. Shepherd c Reed b Cottam	10	– not out	6
†D. L. Evans b Cottam	1	– b Cottam	12
I. J. Jones run out	8	– b Cottam	0
*O. S. Wheatley not out	0	– b White	0
B 4, l-b 7, w 1, n-b 6	18	3 B 6, l-b 5, n-b 2	13
1/11 2/16 3/27 4/74 5/115 6/143 7/146 8/151 9/167	167	1/2 2/33 3/68 4/70 5/90 6/103 7/135 8/144 9/144	145

Bowling: *First Innings*—Shackleton 23–9–56–3; White 20–6–46–4; Cottam 14–2–32–2; Sainsbury 8–3–15–0. *Second Innings*—Shackleton 20–9–32–3; White 11.5–0–30–1; Cottam 17–3–26–3; Wheatley 18–8–30–3; Sainsbury 8–3–14–0.

Hampshire

*R. E. Marshall c and b Wheatley	5	– c Evans b I. J. Jones	3
B. L. Reed c Evans b I. J. Jones	41	– lbw b I. J. Jones	28
H. Horton c Rees b I. J. Jones	47	– c Rees b I. J. Jones	17
D. A. Livingstone c A. R. Lewis b I. J. Jones	55	– c Davis b Shepherd	2
H. M. Barnard c Evans b Wheatley	18	– c A. R. Lewis b Shepherd	1
D. W. White not out	7	– b Shepherd	0
P. J. Sainsbury not out	5	– c Morris b Shepherd	8
†B. S. V. Timms (did not bat)		– lbw b Shepherd	0
K. J. Wheatley (did not bat)		– not out	13
D. Shackleton (did not bat)		– c Morris b Shepherd	0
R. M. Cottam (did not bat)		– c and b Shepherd	0
L-b 13	13	B 2, n-b 1	3
1/13 2/81 3/120 4/179 5/185	(5 wkts, 60 overs) 191	1/4 2/32 3/47 4/49 5/49 6/61 7/67 8/67 9/67	75

Bowling: *First Innings*—I. J. Jones 24–7–64–3; Wheatley 22–6–62–2; Shepherd 12–2–26–0; E. Lewis 4–1–13–0; Davis 3–1–13–0. *Second Innings*—I. J. Jones 12–3–41–3; Wheatley 8–0–24–0; Shepherd 9.1–6–7–7.

Umpires: C. G. Pepper and L. H. Gray.

GLAMORGAN v YORKSHIRE

Played at Swansea, June 10, 12, 13, 1967

Yorkshire won by ten wickets. In striking contrast to the sinister pitch at Cardiff Glamorgan met Yorkshire on what was described as the best wicket ever prepared a Swansea. Glamorgan did not make the best use of it, and were dismissed for th disappointing total of 141. Playing for the first time this season, Old, of Middlesbrough snapped up the first three wickets, while another young bowler, Cope, took the last thre wickets for three runs. Methodically and relentlessly Yorkshire built up a commandin first-innings lead with Sharpe acting as the anchor man. He batted five and a quarter hour for 93, which included fourteen 4s. Glamorgan, 248 behind, were in grave danger of a innings defeat, but they showed more fight when they batted a second time, mainl through a spirited partnership between A. Jones and A. R. Lewis, who added 119 in tw hours. Jones was unlucky to miss his first century of the season by only a single. He batte four hours, forty minutes and hit sixteen 4s. Eventually Yorkshire had half an hour to ge the 26 runs they needed to win.

Glamorgan

A. Jones b Old	6	– c Binks b Trueman	9
B. Hedges c and b Old	21	– c Sharpe b Nicholson	
A. Rees run out	17	– c Binks b Nicholson	1
P. M. Walker c Sharpe b Old	14	– c Sharpe b Nicholson	
*A. R. Lewis c Sharpe b Nicholson	14	– c Trueman b Cope	6
M. Nash c Binks b Nicholson	2	– b Trueman	2
A. E. Cordle b Cope	30	– run out	
B. Lewis b Nicholson	6	– b Cope	
†D. L. Evans lbw b Cope	9	– not out	1
D. J. Shepherd not out	11	– b Old	
I. J. Jones b Cope	0	– run out	1
B 5, l-b 3, n-b 3	11	B 8, l-b 4, n-b 9	2
1/15 2/34 3/53 4/76 5/82 6/82 7/93 8/130 9/141	141	1/19 2/38 3/38 4/157 5/213 6/227 7/234 8/259 9/262	27

Bowling: *First Innings*—Trueman 16–5–27–0; Nicholson 23–6–30–3; Old 14–4–34–3; Taylo 5–0–11–0; Wilson 8–1–25–0; Cope 2.5–1–3–3. *Second Innings*—Trueman 15–6–31–2; Nichol son 27–11–61–3; Old 10.3–2–19–1; Wilson 9–3–14–0; Cope 32–15–60–2; Hampshir 17–3–67–0.

Yorkshire

P. J. Sharpe c Evans b I. J. Jones	93	– not out	1
K. Taylor c Evans b Cordle	19	– not out	4
D. E. V. Padgett c Evans b Cordle	0		
J. H. Hampshire c Evans b I. J. Jones	94		
B. Leadbeater c B. Lewis b Shepherd	3		
C. Old b Shepherd	45		
D. Wilson b Cordle	36		
†J. G. Binks c Evans b I. J. Jones	55		
*F. S. Trueman c Evans b I. J. Jones	10		
A. G. Nicholson b I. J. Jones	14		
G. Cope not out	3		
L-b 10, n-b 7	17	L-b 4	4
1/35 2/35 3/181 4/188 5/239 6/301 7/339 8/355 9/371	389	(no wkt)	27

Bowling: *First Innings*—I. J. Jones 36.4–11–76–5; Cordle 33–9–108–3; Walker 9–3–34–0; Shepherd 26–5–70–2; Nash 19–4–49–0; B. Lewis 7–1–35–0. *Second Innings*—I. J. Jones 2.2–0–9–0; Cordle 2–0–14–0.

Umpires: H. Mellows and A. E. Rhodes.

GLAMORGAN v WARWICKSHIRE

Played at Swansea, August 9, 10, 11, 1967

Warwickshire won by seven wickets. Magnificent seam bowling by Cartwright enabled Warwickshire to hold the initiative throughout this low-scoring match, but when a storm flooded the ground on the third day it looked as if Warwickshire would be deprived of the full points they so richly deserved. Although needing only 49 runs with eight wickets in hand, they had to wait nearly all day before the umpires decided that the pitch was fit for play when only forty-nine minutes remained. Cartwright wrecked Glamorgan's first innings in one short deadly spell when in five balls he captured three wickets without conceding a run. He finished with eight for 50 and again in the Glamorgan second innings he was the complete master, and by taking seven for 39 had a match analysis of fifteen for 89, easily his best performance in big cricket.

Glamorgan

A. Jones c Jameson b Cartwright	24	– c Richardson b Bannister	4
R. Davis c Jameson b Cartwright	22	– c Cartwright b Bannister	26
A. Rees c Abberley b Cartwright	0	– c Richardson b Bannister	1
*A. R. Lewis b Cartwright	0	– lbw b Cartwright	6
P. M. Walker lbw b Cartwright	26	– c A. C. Smith b Cartwright	8
K. Lyons c Bannister b Cartwright	18	– c Gordon b Cartwright	15
A. E. Cordle c Gordon b Allan	10	– b Cartwright	16
†D. L. Evans c Bannister b Cartwright	5	– c Barber b Cartwright	2
M. Nash b Cartwright	0	– b Cartwright	10
†D. J. Shepherd c Barber b Allan	17	– not out	1
I. J. Jones not out	3	– c Barber b Cartwright	1
L-b 2	2	N-b 1	1
1/44 2/44 3/44 4/59 5/89 6/92 7/98 8/98 9/108	127	1/6 2/14 3/29 4/37 5/47 6/69 7/78 8/83 9/88	91

Bowling: *First Innings*—Bannister 7–2–12–0; Blenkiron 7–2–16–0; Cartwright 29–12–50–8; Allan 28.2–16–47–2. *Second Innings*—Bannister 17–5–40–3; Blenkiron 7–1–11–0; Cartwright 17.3–4–39–7.

Warwickshire

R. W. Barber st Evans b Walker	35	– lbw b I. J. Jones	0
R. N. Abberley c and b Cordle	4	– run out	37
*M. J. K. Smith c Walker b Nash	30	– not out	25
J. A. Jameson c Walker b I. J. Jones	12	– not out	1
B. A. Richardson c Davis b I. J. Jones	7		
A. Gordon c Evans b. I. J. Jones	0		
†A. C. Smith c Davis b I. J. Jones	10		
T. W. Cartwright b I. J. Jones	12		
J. M. Allan c Walker b Shepherd	1	– c Shepherd b I. J. Jones	13
W. Blenkiron c A. Jones b Shepherd	4		
J. D. Bannister not out	9		
B 4, n-b 3	7	B 1, l-b 4, w 4 n-b 34	12
1/6 2/69 3/81 4/94 5/94	131	1/38 2/38 3/85 (3 wkts)	88

Bowling: *First Innings*—I. J. Jones 21–5–34–5; Cordle 9–1–31–1; Nash 9–2–23–1; Shepherd 15–6–30–2; Walker 6–3–6–1. *Second Innings*—I. J. Jones 13.3–4–34–2; Cordle 10–4–23–0; Nash 3–0–19–0.

Umpires: H. Yarnold and T. W. Spencer

GLAMORGAN v HAMPSHIRE

Played at Cardiff, June 8, 9, 10, 1968

Glamorgan won by an innings and 16 runs. This was the first county championship match to be played in Wales on a Sunday and it turned out to be "a big hit". The attendance of 5,000 and receipts of £500 were well above the average. The big crowd saw some fine batting by Majid and Tony Lewis in Glamorgan's first innings after Hampshire had been dismissed on the opening day for 145. Majid and Lewis added 109 for the third wicket, the partnership being dominated by the Pakistani. He batted two and three-quarter hours for 91 and hit eleven 4s. Hampshire, 68 behind on the first innings, were then tumbled out for 52 to give Glamorgan the double. The Hampshire collapse was started by Cordle, who took four wickets for 24. Then Walker, going on when Hampshire had lost half their wickets for 40, took three wickets in five balls and finished with five for nine.

Hampshire

B. A. Richards c E. Jones b Cordle	7	– b Cordle	4
B. L. Reed c Majid b Cordle	59	– c Walker b Nash	4
P. J. Sainsbury c Cordle b Walker	24	– c E. Jones b Cordle	0
*R. E. Marshall c Morris b Cordle	19	– c A. Jones b Walker	14
D. R. Turner c E. Jones b Cordle	2	– lbw b Cordle	4
R. M. C. Gilliat c Nash b Cordle	9	– c E. Jones b Walker	6
K. J. Wheatley c Morris b Nash	8	– c Cordle b Walker	2
†B. S. V. Timms b Cordle	7	– lbw b Cordle	8
D. Shackleton c and b Nash	5	– c E. Jones b Walker	0
D. W. White b Cordle	0	– c E. Jones b Walker	5
R. M. H. Cottam not out	1	– not out	1
B 2, l-b 2	4	B 1, l-b 3	4
1/24 2/70 3/110 4/112 5/117 6/132 7/132 8/141 9/141	145	1/4 2/4 3/16 4/16 5/34 6/40 7/44 8/44 9/51	52

Bowling: *First Innings*—Cordle 20–3–43–7; Nash 23.3–7–51–2; Walker 11–2–31–1; Shepherd 7–2–16–0. *Second Innings*—Cordle 13–7–24–4; Nash 9–4–15–1; Walker 3.4–0–9–5.

Glamorgan

A. Jones c Richards b Cottam	20
I. Morris b White	17
Majid Jahangir b Shackleton	91
*A. R. Lewis b Cottam	53
A. Rees c Richards b Cottam	5
P. M. Walker c Sainsbury b Shackleton	3
†E. Jones c Timms b Cottam	6
A. E. Cordle b Cottam	12
M. A. Nash c Richards b Cottam	0
D. Lewis not out	1
L-b 2, n-b 3	5
1/32 2/63 3/172 4/190 5/190 6/194 7/208 9/213 (9 wkts dec.)	213

D. J. Shepherd did not bat.

Bowling: Shackleton 32–16–53–2; White 21–2–55–1; Cottam 19.3–4–54–6; Sainsbury 9–0–46–0.

Umpires: P. B. Wight and J. F. Crapp.

GLAMORGAN v SOMERSET

Played at Swansea, July 17, 18, 19, 1968

Glamorgan won by nine wickets. Somerset must have wondered how they lost this game. They were leading by 133 runs on the first innings, but a magnificent spell of swing bowling by the 23-year-old Nash completely transformed the picture late on the second day when Somerset, batting a second time, were tumbled out for 40. Nash had the following remarkable analysis – 13.3 overs, 7 maidens, 15 runs, 7 wickets. This, on the same pitch on which Somerset scored 337 in their first innings, was incredible. Kitchen, Chappell and Palmer had batted so soundly that Somerset's subsequent collapse was inexplicable. The pitch had not deteriorated in any way and this was emphasized when Glamorgan, needing 174 to win, got their runs for the loss of only one wicket. Alan Jones was the pace maker with his first century of the season. It was his fifth century against Somerset in five seasons.

Somerset

R. Virgin c E. Jones b Cordle	29	– b Nash	2
M. Kitchen c Walker b B. Lewis	82	– lbw b Cordle	7
G. S. Chappell c Majid b Cordle	81	– b Cordle	4
L. M. L. Barnwell c Walker b B. Lewis	0	– c Davis b Nash	9
W. E. Alley run out	29	– b Nash	1
K. E. Palmer c E. Jones b Majid	59	– b Cordle	1
*R. C. Kerslake b Nash	1	– c Cordle b Nash	5
G. Burgess c E. Jones b Majid	32	– c Majid b Nash	3
P. J. Robinson b Nash	8	– c Walker b Nash	1
B. A. Langford c B. Lewis b Nash	4	– not out	1
†R. A. Brooks not out	0	– c E. Jones b Nash	0
L-b 12	12	L-b 6	6
1/59 2/132 3/144 4/185 5/251 6/252 7/310 8/327 9/331	337	1/11 2/16 3/22 4/29 5/29 6/29 7/33 8/39 9/40	40

Bowling: *First Innings*—Cordle 24–3–66–2; Nash 26–6–67–3; Majid 12.5–3–41–2; Shepherd 20–8–27–0; B. Lewis 22–2–88–2; Walker 20–7–36–0. *Second Innings*—Cordle 9–4–14–3; Nash 13.3–7–15–7; Majid 3–1–2–0; Shepherd 2–1–3–0.

Glamorgan

A. Jones c Kitchen b Palmer	9	– not out	102
R. Davis lbw b Alley	52	– lbw b Palmer	6
*A. R. Lewis b Robinson b Alley	34	– not out	60
†E. Jones c Kerslake b Langford	0		
Majid Jahangir c Alley b Langford	39		
A. Rees c Virgin b Langford	7		
P. M. Walker b Langford	21		
A. E. Cordle c Chappell b Robinson	20		
B. Lewis b Langford	0		
M. A. Nash not out	12		
D. J. Shepherd b Langford	7		
B 1, l-b 1, n-b 1	3	B 4, l-b 2	6
1/19 2/92 3/193 4/103 5/139 6/150 7/182 8/183 9/196	204	1/10	(1 wkt) 174

Bowling: *First Innings*—Burgess 15–4–29–0; Palmer 17–2–60–1; Langford 38.2–14–58–6; Alley 16–6–34–2; Robinson 9–5–20–1. *Second Innings*—Burgess 11–3–27–0; Palmer 4–0–15–1; Langford 9–2–39–0; Alley 6–2–7–0; Robinson 7–1–37–0; Chappell 6–0–31–0; Kerslake 3.3–0–12–0.

Umpires: J. S. Buller and R. Aspinall.

GLAMORGAN v SUSSEX

Played at Ebbw Vale, July 27, 28, 29, 1968

Glamorgan won by an innings and seven runs. After obtaining a substantial first-innings lead of 117 through another sound century by Alan Jones, Glamorgan never relaxed their grip on the game, and an innings victory was assured by the magnificent bowling of Wheatley when Sussex batted a second time. He took the first seven wickets that fell at a personal cost of 33 runs and, claiming the extra half hour, Glamorgan tried to win in two days. Lewis and Bates, however, held out, although on the final morning Wheatley soon captured the remaining wickets to finish with nine for 60 – his best analysis in first-class cricket. Since joining the side in an emergency owing to the injury to Jeff Jones, Wheatley's record was 43 wickets in eight matches, and his bowling was a big factor in Glamorgan's revival which brought them their fourth successive victory.

In Glamorgan's innings Alan Jones' second century of the season occupied two hours and forty minutes. He hit two 6s and fourteen 4s, and with Majid and Nash also hitting out breezily Glamorgan gained five bonus points and twenty for the match.

Sussex

L. J. Lenham lbw b Shepherd	17	– c E. Jones b Wheatley	0
T. B. Racionzer c E. Jones b Wheatley	4	– lbw b Wheatley	33
K. G. Suttle lbw b Wheatley	19	– c Davis b Wheatley	6
A. W. Greig b Cordle	12	– c A. Lewis b Wheatley	4
†J. M. Parks c Nash b Shepherd	57	– c E. Jones b Wheatley	9
*M. G. Griffith c Walker b Cordle	0	– b Wheatley	6
G. C. Cooper c E. Jones b Shepherd	11	– c Davis b B. Lewis	16
A. Buss c Davis b Cordle	21	– c A. Lewis b Wheatley	2
E. Lewis c E. Jones b B. Lewis	24	– not out	22
D. J. Bates not out	4	– lbw b Wheatley	9
A. A. Jones c Wheatley b Shepherd	3	– c A. Jones b Wheatley	0
N-b 1	1	L-b 4	4
1/7 2/31 3/52 4/54 5/55 6/76 7/110 8/166 9/166	173	1/0 2/20 3/24 4/51 5/56 6/65 7/67 8/80 9/111	111

Bowling: *First Innings*—Wheatley 19–3–55–2; Nash 12–3–30–0; Cordle 16–3–29–3; Shepherd 18.3–4–39–4; B. Lewis 5–0–19–1. *Second Innings*—Wheatley 31.3–12–60–9; Nash 7–1–12–0; Cordle 14–5–20–0; Shepherd 2–0–6–0; B. Lewis 8–3–9–1.

Glamorgan

A. Jones c Griffith b Lewis	110
R. Davis c Suttle b Lewis	30
*A. R. Lewis c Suttle b Lewis	13
P. M. Walker c Parks b Bates	9
A. Rees c Greig b Bates	1
†E. Jones c Suttle b Lewis	8
A. E. Cordle b Bates	9
B. Lewis c Lewis b Jones	31
M. A. Nash c Buss b Jones	43
D. J. Shepherd not out	18
O. S. Wheatley b Jones	5
B 10, l-b 3, w 1	14
1/87 2/103 3/126 4/126 5/174 6/179 7/187 8/263 9/267	291

Bowling: Buss 9–1–26–0; Jones 8.3–0–37–3; Greig 11–1–48–0; Bates 30–10–66–3; Lewis 28–10–100–4.

Umpires: O. W. Herman and J. Arnold.

GLAMORGAN v NOTTINGHAMSHIRE

Played at Swansea, August 31, September 1, 2, 1968

Nottinghamshire won by 166 runs. This was the history-making match in which the incredible Garfield Sobers created a new world record by hitting six 6s in a six-ball over. Somehow one sensed that something extraordinary was going to happen when Sobers sauntered to the wicket. With over 300 runs on the board for the loss of only five wickets, he had the right sort of platform from which to launch a spectacular assault, and the manner in which he immediately settled down to score at a fast rate was ominous.

Then came the history-making over by the 23-year-old Malcolm Nash. First crouched like a black panther eager to pounce, Sobers with lightning footwork got into position for a vicious straight drive or pull. As Tony Lewis, Glamorgan's captain said afterwards, "It was not sheer slogging through strength, but scientific hitting with every movement working in harmony." Twice the ball was slashed out of the ground, and when the last six landed in the street outside it was not recovered until the next day. Then it was presented to Sobers and will have a permanent place in the Trent Bridge Cricket Museum.

All other events were overshadowed by Sobers' achievement, but the rest of the cricket was not without distinction. In the Nottinghamshire first innings Bolus hit a magnificent century in three hours, fifty minutes, including six 6s and fifteen 4s. Glamorgan could not match such boldness although Walker batted steadily for his second century of the season in two hours, forty minutes.

With a first-innings lead of 140 Nottinghamshire then lost half their wickets for 70, but again Sobers accomplished the inevitable, scoring 72 out of 94 in nine minutes under two hours. Eventually Glamorgan had to get 280 to win in four hours, but good bowling by Taylor, who made the most of a damp pitch caused by overnight rain, resulted in them being dismissed for 113.

Nottinghamshire

J. B. Bolus c sub b Nash	140	– run out	3
R. A. White c Wheatley b B. Lewis	73	– b Cordle	1
G. Frost c A. R. Lewis b Nash	50	– b Nash	2
M. J. Smedley c A. R. Lewis b Nash	27	– c Majid b Cordle	24
†D. L. Murray b Nash	0	– c Cordle b Shepherd	13
J. M. Parkin not out	15	– not out	9
*G. S. Sobers not out	76	– b Shepherd	72
S. R. Bielby (did not bat)		– not out	13
B 4, l-b 7, n-b 2	13	B 1, n-b 1	2
1/126 2/258 3/289 4/289 5/308 (5 wkts dec.)	394	1/2 2/7 3/7 4/30 5/70 6/124 (6 wkts dec.)	139

M. N. Taylor, D. J. Halfyard and B. Stead did not bat.

Bowling: *First Innings*—Wheatley 5–0–22–0; Nash 21–3–100–4; Cordle 3–1–24–0; Walker 32–4–109–0; Shepherd 25–5–82–0; B. Lewis 13–1–44–1. *Second Innings*—Nash 17–4–53–1; Cordle 16–4–41–2; Shepherd 25–10–43–2.

Glamorgan

A. Jones c Murray b Taylor	25	– c Parkin b Taylor	1
R. Davis c Taylor b Stead	0	– b Stead	18
Majid Jahangir c Taylor b Halfyard	41	– c Bolus b Taylor	4
*A. R. Lewis c Bielby b Taylor	0	– c Bielby b White	52
P. M. Walker not out	104	– c Sobers b White	16
†E. Jones lbw b Sobers	29	– c Stead b Taylor	3
A. E. Cordle lbw b Halfyard	4	– c Smedley b Taylor	4
M. A. Nash b Sobers	8	– b White	5
B. Lewis run out	38	– b Taylor	4
D. J. Shepherd c Sobers b Halfyard	0	– b White	4
O. S. Wheatley b White	1	– not out	0
L-b 3, w 1	4	L-b 2	2
1/0 2/46 3/56 4/78 5/137 6/142 7/179 8/252 9/253	254	1/40 2/45 3/49 4/85 5/96 6/100 7/100 8/105 9/113	113

Bowling: *First Innings*—Sobers 20–6–63–2; Stead 9–3–27–1; Taylor 9–2–23–2; Halfyard 31–8–71–3; White 23.2–5–66–1. *Second Innings*—Stead 9–1–26–1; Taylor 16–6–47–5; Halfyard 7–1–29–0; White 8–5–9–4.

Umpires: J. G. Langridge and W. E. Phillipson.

GLAMORGAN v LEICESTERSHIRE

Played at Colwyn Bay, June 21, 23, 24, 1969

Drawn. In Leicestershire's first innings Cordle took nine wickets for 49. He was not brought into the attack until 84 runs had been scored without loss and was the seventh bowler to be tried. Then he dismissed both opening batsmen in his first three overs for nine runs and proceeded to bowl for two and a half hours. Glamorgan gained a narrow lead of 22 runs and appeared to hold the initiative when Leicestershire, batting a second time, lost seven wickets for 149. Then Birkenshaw and Tolchard added 51. Glamorgan's opening batsmen scored 58 in forty minutes, but after these wickets had fallen they abandoned all hope of chasing the 190 runs which they needed.

Leicestershire

M. R. Hallam c Walker b Cordle	33	– b Cordle	46
M. E. Norman b Cordle	50	– b Walker	13
B. J. Booth c E. Jones b Cordle	41	– run out	7
C. C. Inman c Walker b Cordle	18	– lbw b Cordle	51
P. T. Marner c and b Cordle	19	– c Walker b Cordle	4
*R. Illingworth b Cordle	4	– b Williams	6
B. R. Knight c E. W. Jones b Cordle	16	– c E. W. Jones b Cordle	13
J. Birkenshaw c R. C. Davis b Wheatley	0	– c Lewis b Shepherd	32
†R. W. Tolchard lbw b Cordle	0	– not out	30
G. D. McKenzie lbw b Cordle	9	– not out	1
R. J. Barratt not out	2		
L-b 3, w 1, n-b 7	1	L-b 3, w 1, n-b 4	8
1/86 2/95 3/125 4/153 5/169 6/178 7/179 8/180 9/194	203	1/23 2/41 3/104 4/110 5/131 6/136 7/149 8/200 (8 wkts dec.)	211

Bowling: *First Innings*—Wheatley 17–5–38–1; Williams 15–5–31–0; Shepherd 18–5–33–0; Walker 9–2–17–0; R. C. Davis 5–1–8–0; Majid 5–1–8–0; Cordle 24.4–4–49–9. *Second Innings*—Wheatley 2–1–4–0; Williams 10–2–22–1; Shepherd 26–12–55–1; Walker 13–5–39–1; R. C. Davis 5–0–22–0; Corlde 18–3–61–4.

Glamorgan

B. A. Davis c and b Barratt	47	– lbw b Barratt	33
A. Jones lbw b Barratt	43	– b Barratt	19
R. C. Davis b Barratt	4	– not out	24
*A. R. Lewis b McKenzie	45	– c Norman b Birkenshaw	28
Majid Jahangir b Birkenshaw	2	– c and b Knight	0
P. M. Walker b McKenzie	41	– not out	6
†E. W. Jones not out	31		
A. E. Cordle c Booth b Knight	1		
D. L. Williams run out	0		
D. J. Shepherd b McKenzie	1		
O. S. Wheatley c Norman b Barratt	1		
B 2, l-b 2, n-b 5	9	B 4, w 1, n-b 1	6
1/74 2/80 3/104 4/113 5/167 6/213 7/214 8/217 9/220	225	1/56 2/59 3/66 4/87	(4 wkts) 116

Bowling: *First Innings*—McKenzie 17–5–28–3; Knight 13–5–23–1; Birkenshaw 28–8–87–1; Illingworth 8–3–16–0; Barratt 27.5–6–54–4; Marner 4–0–8–0. *Second Innings*—McKenzie 5–1–21–0; Knight 8–2–12–1; Birkenshaw 10–2–33–1; Barratt 15–3–44–2.

Umpires: C. Petrie and H. Mellows.

GLAMORGAN v DERBYSHIRE

Played at Cardiff, August 9, 11, 12, 1969

Drawn. Rain and Derbyshire's sturdy but passive resistance combined to deprive Glamorgan of the winning points they needed to strengthen their Championship challenge. Glamorgan gained a first-innings lead of 77 mainly through a fine bowling spell by Williams, who in one burst of eight deliveries took three wickets for 3 runs. Rain curtailed play on the second day and again delayed the resumption on the final day until after lunch. So Glamorgan had only two hours in which to bowl out Derbyshire, who had scored 34 without loss the previous evening. Smith and Gibbs stayed for seventy-five minutes before being separted, and it looked as if Derbyshire would easily hold out, but suddenly they lost five wickets for 11 runs. Yet there was just not enough time for Glamorgan's bowlers to complete their task. The grimness of the batting can be judged from Walker's bowling figures. In 90 deliveries he conceded only four runs.

Derbyshire

D. H. K. Smith c R. C. Davis b Williams	8	– c Cordle b R. C. Davis	12
P. J. K. Gibbs lbw b Nash	1	– c B. A. Davis b Walker	28
M. H. Page lbw b Williams	4	– c Majid b Walker	0
I. W. Hall c Majid b Shepherd	22	– lbw b Shepherd	0
I. R. Buxton b Williams	2	– c E. W. Jones b Walker	3
*D. C. Morgan c E. W. Jones b Shepherd	25	– b Shepherd	4
†R. W. Taylor c and b Walker	22	– not out	1
F. W. Swarbrook c E. W. Jones b Nash	7	– c R. C. Davis b Shepherd	1
T. J. P. Eyre b Williams	13	– not out	0
E. Smith run out	9		
M. Hendrick not out	9		
B 4, l-b 2, n-b 2, w 2	10	B 4, l-b 1, n-b 2	7
1/1 2/13 3/14 4/16 5/55 6/71 7/98 8/98 9/117	132	1/43 2/43 3/46 4/50 5/54 6/54 7/56	(7 wkts) 56

Bowling: *First Innings*—Williams 17–5–31–4; Nash 13–5–17–2; Cordle 7–3–17–0; Walker 16–6–27–1; Shepherd 19–7–30–2. *Second Innings*—Williams 6–2–8–0; Nash 8–2–7–0; Cordle 5–1–6–0; Walker 15–14–4–3; Shepherd 20–11–17–3; R. C. Davis 9–4–7–1.

Glamorgan

A. Jones c D. H. K. Smith b Swarbrook	41	M. A. Nash c Taylor b Eyre	24
R. C. Davis c Gibbs b Morgan	14	D. L. Williams c Gibbs b Eyre	9
Majid Jahangir c Buxton b E. Smith	12	D. J. Shepherd not out	9
*A. R. Lewis c Taylor b Hendrick	17		
B. A. Davis lbw b E. Smith	6	B 4, l-b 12, w 3, n-b 7	26
P. M. Walker c Morgan b Swarbrook	16		——
†E. W. Jones c Hendrick b Swarbrook	27	1/28 2/53 3/94 4/95 5/105	209
A. E. Cordle c and b Swarbrook	8	6/154 7/157 8/166 9/194	

Bowling: Hendrick 17–5–27–1; Eyre 13.1–1–38–2; Morgan 16–6–31–1; E. Smith 23–9–49–2; Swarbrook 20–8–38–4.

Umpires: J. S. Buller and P. B. Wight.

GLAMORGAN v DERBYSHIRE

Played at Swansea, August 29, 31, September 1, 1970

Glamorgan won by four wickets. Although Derbyshire made a fighting recovery after following on 174 runs behind Glamorgan eventually triumphed. They needed only 136 to win, but lost half their wickets for 109. In the Derbyshire second innings Glamorgan had their worst attack of Championship jitters. At least three simple catches were dropped as Page and Russell helped to build up a total of 309. The match turned out to be a personal triumph for Russell, who in addition to achieving his best bowling performance, in the Glamorgan first innings (six for 61) also recorded his highest score – 72 in seventy minutes after being dropped at 18, 26 and 30. The Swansea wicket was always taking spin, which made Derbyshire's recovery all the more remarkable. The gate receipts of £736 were the highest in the County Championship matches during the season.

Glamorgan

B. A. Davis c Hall b Russell	91	– b Russell	23
G. P. Ellis c D. H. K. Smith b Russell	28	– c Page b Russell	11
Majid J. Khan c Hall b Russell	1	– c Taylor b Swarbrook	12
*A. R. Lewis c Swarbrook b E. Smith	7	– c Taylor b Swarbrook	21
P. M. Walker b Russell	57	– b E. Smith	7
R. C. Davis c Ward b Russell	2	– c D. H. K. Smith b Swarbrook	25
†E. W. Jones c D. H. K. Smith b E. Smith	9	– not out	4
A. E. Cordle b Ward	17	– not out	20
M. A. Nash c Taylor b Ward	2		
D. J. Shepherd not out	36		
D. L. Williams c D. H. K. Smith b Russell	0		
B 4, l-b 4, n-b 3	11	B 2, l-b 10, n-b 1	13
	——		——
1/80 2/89 3/127 4/139 5/143	261	1/28 2/47 3/61	(6 wkts) 136
6/168 7/201 8/203 9/249		4/71 5/109 6/127	

Bowling: *First Innings*—Ward 19–0–66–2; Buxton 8–1–23–0; E. Smith 27–7–74–2; Russell 32.3–11–61–6; Swarbrook 7–1–26–0. *Second Innings*—Ward 4–0–21–0; Buxton 4–1–13–0; E. Smith 5–2–22–1; Russell 24.2–11–32–2; Swarbrook 18–9–35–3.

Derbyshire

I. W. Hall c Majid b Shepherd	13	– c Walker b Shepherd	17
D H. K. Smith c Nash b Walker	4	– c B. A. Davis b Walker	32
M. H. Page c R. C. Davis b Shepherd	4	– c Walker b R. C. Davis	71
F. W. Swarbrook b Walker	7	– c R. C. Davis b Nash	0
P. E. Russell c Walker b Shepherd	12	– c Walker b Shepherd	72
C. P. Wilkins c R. C. Davis b Shepherd	12	– c Walker b Shepherd	19
J. F. Harvey c Shepherd b Walker	7	– c E. W. Jones b Cordle	19
*I. R. Buxton c Walker b Shepherd	0	– c Walker b Shepherd	10
†R. W. Taylor c Walker b Shepherd	3	– c E. W. Jones b Shepherd	15
E. Smith c Cordle b Walker	21	– lbw b Shepherd	5
A. Ward not out	0	– not out	0
L-b 4	4	B 31, l-b 12, n-b 6	49
1/18 2/22 3/23 4/41 5/45 6/54 7/58 8/60 9/87	87	1/25 2/109 3/134 4/172 5/192 6/209 7/265 8/304 9/305	309

Bowling: *First Innings*—Nash 6–4–6–0; Williams 3–1–2–0; Shepherd 19–7–33–6; Walker 16.5–4–42–4. *Second Innings*—Nash 13–4–23–1; Williams 1–0–2–0; Shepherd 57.4–26–106–6; Walker 46–12–92–1; R. C. Davis 12–1–24–1; Majid 8–3–11–0; Cordle 4–2–2–1.

Umpires: F. Jakeman and A. G. T. Whitehead.

GLAMORGAN v NORTHAMPTONSHIRE

Played at Swansea, August 26, 28, 29, 1972

Northamptonshire won by 29 runs. After setting up a record partnership for any wicket and batting brilliantly for most of the match, Glamorgan lost as the result of a sensational late collapse; they lost seven wickets for seven runs when they needed only 42 to win in ten overs. It was in their first innings that Jones and Fredericks figured in their record-breaking opening stand. It realised 330 in four and three-quarter hours. Fredericks' 228 was also his highest. Altogether he was batting just over five hours and hit three 6s and thirty-two 4s. Jones was not so fluent but played the part of anchor man. Northamptonshire, 46 behind in the first innings, were put into a position to declare through an unbroken stand of 83 by Steele and Watts for the fifth wicket in forty-five minutes. Needing 248 to win in two hours, twenty-five minutes, Glamorgan made an exhilarating start and the first 50 runs came off 43 balls. Khan and Lewis carried on the fine work and their third-wicket partnership added 113 in 20 overs to place Glamorgan within sight of a brilliant win. Then came that pathetic collapse before the pace of Cottam and the spin of Bedi.

Northamptonshire

G. Cook c E. W. Jones b Cordle	29	– lbw b Davis	63
P. Willey c E. W. Jones b Nash	51	– c Davis b Walker	7
D. S. Steele c Walker b Davis	42	– not out	73
Mushtaq Mohammad c Khan b Davis	59	– c A. Jones b Davis	47
W. Larkins lbw b Davis	2		
*P. J. Watts not out	75	– not out	51
D. Breakwell c Khan b Davis	1		
†G. Sharp st E. W. Jones b Davis	17	– c Davis b Walker	39
R. M. H. Cottam c and b Williams	9		
B. S. Bedi b Cordle	4		
J. C. Dye c Khan b Cordle	0		
B 5, l-b 2, n-b 4	11	B 9, l-b 3, n-b 1	13
1/73 2/93 3/160 4/168 5/196 6/201 7/249 8/291 9/300	300	1/33 2/109 3/125 4/210 (4 wkts dec.)	293

Bowling: *First Innings*—Nash 23–5–75–1; Williams 19–2–65–1; Cordle 17–4–47–3; Khan 16–5–38–0; Davis 19–3–55–5; Walker 1–0–9–0. *Second Innings*—Nash 8–1–28–0; Williams 12–4–34–0; Davis 36–5–92–2; Walker 29–8–109–2; Llewllyn 4–0–17–0.

Glamorgan

A. Jones b Steele	105	– c Bedi b Mushtaq	23
R. C. Fredericks not out	228	– b Mushtaq	35
Majid J. Khan lbw b Dye	5	– b Cottam	66
*A. R. Lewis not out	4	– c Steele b Cottam	60
M. J. Llewellyn (did not bat)		– b Bedi	20
R. C. Davis (did not bat)		– c Dye b Bedi	0
P. M. Walker (did not bat)		– not out	3
M. A. Nash (did not bat)		– b Cottam	1
†E. W. Jones (did not bat)		– c Bedi b Cottam	1
A. E. Cordle (did not bat)		– lbw b Cottam	1
D. J. Williams (did not bat)		– c Cook b Bedi	0
B 1, n-b 3	4	L-b 3, w 4, n-b 1	8
1/330 2/335	(2 wkts dec.) 346	1/62 2/69 3/182 4/211 5/212 6/212 7/213 8/215 9/217	218

Bowling: *First Innings*—Cottam 19–4–59–0; Dye 16–3–64–1; Bedi 19–1–83–0; Willey 9–1–43–0; Mushtaq 18–3–62–0; Steele 12–1–31–1. *Second Innings*—Cottam 11–1–52–5; Dye 4–0–26–0; Bedi 15.4–1–57–3; Mushtaq 6–1–43–2; Steele 5–0–32–0.

Umpires: W. L. Budd and C. Cook.

GLAMORGAN v GLOUCESTERSHIRE

Played at Swansea, August 18, 19, 20, 1973

Drawn. In a high scoring match batting honours went to Procter and Knight for Gloucestershire and Eifion Jones and Nash for Glamorgan. By scoring 152 in two hours, twenty minutes (six 6s and seventeen 4s) Procter registered his fourth century in eleven days. His third wicket partnership with Knight added 224. Glamorgan made a spirited response with Nash and E. W. Jones adding 142 for the seventh wicket. Nash hit nine 6s in his 89 in ninety-eight minutes. The prolific scoring was maintained to the end and Glamorgan only just failed to score the 295 runs they wanted to win in three hours. They were well within their target of five runs per over due to a fine century by Alan Jones when Brown, the Gloucestershire captain, transformed the game by completing a hat trick. He dismissed Richards and Cordle with the last two balls of one over and had Jones caught at cover with the first ball of his next over.

Gloucestershire

Sadiq Mohammad c E. W. Jones b Solanky	21	– b Nash	4
†A. W. Stovold b Nash	0	– lbw b Nash	12
R. D. V. Knight c E. W. Jones b Ellis	101	– lbw b Solanky	67
M. J. Procter c Khan b Ellis	152	– c Solanky b Ellis	66
Zaheer Abbas c Cordle b Nash	40	– run out	18
D. R. Shepherd c A. Jones b Nash	86		
M. S. T. Dunstan not out	16	– not out	31
*A. S. Brown c Richards b Nash	10	– c A. Jones b Solanky	15
J. C. Foat (did not bat)		– c Khan b Solanky	0
D. A. Graveney (did not bat)		– not out	7
B 2, l-b 12, n-b 4	18	B 1, l-b 2, n-b 2	5
1/6 2/53 3/277 4/289 5/394 6/422 7/444	(7 wkts dec.) 444	1/13 2/28 3/137 4/161 5/161 6/172 7/201	(7 wkts dec.) 225

J. B. Mortimore did not bat.

Bowling: *First Innings*—Cordle 17–2–79–0; Nash 25.5–3–134–4; Williams 22–4–73–0; Solanky 19–7–44–1; Lloyd 5–1–24–0; Davis 7–0–37–0; Ellis 11–1–35–2. *Second Innings*—Cordle 11–2–41–0; Nash 12–3–38–2; Williams 12–3–35–0; Solanky 20–4–65–3; Ellis 14–4–41–1.

Glamorgan

A. Jones b Brown	42	– c Graveney b Brown	109
R. C. Davis lbw b Graveney	48	– c Mortimore b Knight	41
G. P. Ellis c Foat b Mortimore	15	– b Knight	57
*Majid J. Khan c Procter b Graveney	0		
G. Richards b Mortimore	52	– b Brown	36
J. W. Solanky run out	2	– not out	3
†E. W. Jones not out	96		
M. A. Nash c Stovold b Knight	89	– not out	4
A. E. Cordle not out	20	– lbw b Brown	0
B 8, l-b 2, n-b 1	11	B 1, l-b 8, n-b 1	10
1/83 2/95 3/95 4/123 5/151 6/179 7/321 (7 wkts dec.)	375	1/111 2/193 3/250 4/250 5/253 (5 wkts)	260

B. J. Lloyd and D. L. Williams did not bat.

Bowling: *First Innings*—Procter 13–1–61–0; Knight 10–1–34–1; Brown 20–4–56–1; Mortimore 25–6–87–2; Sadiq 16–4–55–0; Graveney 25–5–71–2. *Second Innings.*—Procter 11–1–36–0; Knight 17–1–66–2; Brown 10–0–42–3; Mortimore 3–0–25–0; Graveney 15–1–81–0.

Umpires: W. L. Budd and C. G. Pepper.

GLAMORGAN v NORTHAMPTONSHIRE

Played at Swansea, June 15, 17, 18, 1974

Drawn. After leading by 88 runs on the first innings Glamorgan had to be content with a draw because of a magnificent innings by Watts, who unluckily missed the distinction of scoring two centuries in a match for the first time in his career. The Northamptonshire captain scored 104 not out in the first innings and was 96 in the second when Majid Khan, Glamorgan's captain, conceded that he could not take the last four wickets in the four remaining overs and led his team off the field. Khan, himself, had scored a magnificent century in Glamorgan's first innings although he rose from a sick bed only the day before. He batted four and three-quarter hours for 164 which included two 6s and twenty-one 4s. Still, Watts was the man of the match, and in the closing stages he alone held up Glamorgan. Northamptonshire had to get 293 to win in four hours and when they lost their first four wickets for 46 they concentrated on saving the game, and they succeeded through a long vigil by their captain.

Glamorgan

A. Jones c Virgin b Hodgson	26	– b Hodgson	1
R. C. Davis lbw b Griffiths	19	– c and b Hodgson	12
*Majid J. Kahn c Cook b Hodgson	164	– lbw b Dye	0
M. J. Llewellyn b Willey	38	– c Griffiths b Dye	43
A. R. Lewis lbw b Dye	4	– b Hodgson	27
G. Richards b Steele	15	– c and b Steele	61
L. W. Hill not out	56	– c Cook b Steele	33
M. A. Nash c Sharp b Hodgson	20	– c Cook b Willey	8
J. W. Solanky not out	0	– not out	13
B 5, l-b 1, n-b 2	8	L-b 4, n-b 2	6
1/37 2/59 3/124 4/133 5/197 6/325 7/349	(7 wkts) 350	1/3 2/4 3/20 4/75 5/98 6/165 7/184 8/204	(8 wkts dec.) 204

†E. W. Jones and D. L. Williams did not bat.

Bowling: *First Innings*—Dye 27–5–96–1; Hodgson 27–4–73–3; Griffiths 9–2–32–1; Milburn 9–0–38–0; Willey 16–2–69–1; Steele 12–3–34–1. *Second Innings*—Dye 20–6–34–2; Hodgson 18–5–46–3; Griffiths 13–1–40–0; Milburn 4–0–15–0; Willey 3.1–2–5–1; Steele 15–4–58–2.

Northamptonshire

R. T. Virgin b Nash	5	– b Solanky	49
C. Milburn b Nash	2	– b Nash	7
D. S. Steele b Williams	16	– c Davis b Nash	5
G. Cook c Khan b Solanky	67	– b Williams	4
P. Willey lbw b Solanky	37	– c Khan b Nash	6
*P. J. Watts not out	104	– not out	96
W. Larkins c Lewis b Davis	5	– lbw b Nash	6
†G. Sharp c Llewellyn b Davis	4	– not out	19
A. Hodgson c E. W. Jones b Williams	1		
J. C. Dye not out	6		
B 5, l-b 3, n-b 7	15	L-b 2, n-b 1	3
1/4 2/9 3/32 4/87 5/173 6/214 7/225 8/238	(8 wkts) 262	1/7 2/21 3/30 4/46 5/92 6/121	(6 wkts) 195

J. Griffiths did not bat.

Bowling: *First Innings*—Nash 20–4–49–2; Williams 23–3–70–2; Solanky 27–4–86–2; Davis 30–9–42–2. *Second Innings*—Nash 24–9–52–4; Williams 15–4–46–1; Solanky 19–2–52–1; Davis 17–4–42–0.

Umpires: B. J. Meyer and H. D. Bird.

GLAMORGAN v HAMPSHIRE

Played at Cardiff, August 17, 19, 20, 1974

Glamorgan won by five wickets. After appearing to have the game well in hand, Hampshire suffered an unexpected defeat which, as it turned out, had a vital affect on the championship. Glamorgan only just saved the follow on as the result of a devastating spell of fast bowling by Roberts, who took his first seven wickets for 17 runs including a burst of four wickets in five balls. Roberts also became the first bowler in the country to complete his hundred wickets for the season. Then, although leading by 144 runs on the first innings, Hampshire surprisingly lost their grip through slack batting in their second innings which realised only 137, of which Richards scored 60 after reaching 50 out of 76 in one hundred minutes. Glamorgan needed 282 to win with ample time at their disposal. Wisely they put their heads down, took no risks and waited for the runs to come. The winning factor was a disciplined fourth wicket partnership between Hill and Eifion Jones which realised 106. Hill batted five and three-quarter hours for 90. It was the right type of innings in the circumstances.

Hampshire

B. A. Richards b Nash	42	– b Lloyd	60
C. G. Greenidge lbw b Nash	15	– c and b Nash	1
D. R. Turner b Nash	13	– lbw b Nash	5
*R. M. C. Gilliat c A. Jones b Davis	65	– lbw b Cordle	11
T. E. Jesty b Nash	8	– b Cordle	3
P. J. Sainsbury lbw b Solanky	9	– c Richards b Lloyd	6
N. G. Cowley c and b Solanky	6	– b Lloyd	6
M. N. S. Taylor c Lloyd b Nash	23	– c Cordle b Davis	8
†G. R. Stephenson not out	32	– c Hill b Nash	19
R. S. Herman b Davis	0	– c Lloyd b Nash	10
A. M. E. Roberts b Cordle	12	– not out	2
L-b 4, n-b 5	9	L-b 3, n-b 3	6
1/43 2/60 3/81 4/100 5/129 6/165 7/166 8/216 9/218	234	1/7 2/20 3/41 4/45 5/89 6/90 7/101 8/107 9/135	137

Bowling: *First Innings*—Nash 29–5–73–5; Williams 11–4–35–0; Davis 26–6–35–2; Lloyd 2–0–12–0; Cordle 11.1–1–24–1; Solanky 19–6–45–2. *Second Innings*—Nash 11.5–4–35–4; Williams 5–0–11–0; Davis 16–6–24–1; Lloyd 14–7–26–3; Cordle 11–2–23–2; Solanky 3–0–12–0.

Glamorgan

*A. Jones c Richards b Roberts	15	– run out	33
G. P. Ellis c Sainsbury b Roberts	8	– c Gilliat b Cowley	11
R. C. Davis not out	33	– not out	32
L. W. Hill lbw b Roberts	1	– c Greenidge b Cowley	90
J. W. Solanky b Roberts	0		
G. Richards b Roberts	0	– lbw b Roberts	10
†E. W. Jones lbw b Roberts	0	– c Herman b Sainsbury	67
A. E. Cordle c Richards b Roberts	16	– not out	28
B. J. Lloyd c Stephenson b Roberts	0		
M. A. Nash c and b Sainsbury	2		
D. L. Williams run out	3		
B 2, l-b 4, w 3, n-b 3	12	B 3, l-b 9, n-b 1	13
1/16 2/29 3/39 4/41 5/41 6/41 7/41 8/63 9/72	90	1/19 2/60 3/118 4/224 5/248	(5 wkts) 284

Bowling: *First Innings*—Roberts 22–6–47–8; Herman 7–2–21–0; Taylor 5–2–4–0; Sainsbury 10.2–7–6–1; Cowley 1–1–0–0. *Second Innings*—Roberts 31–4–91–1; Herman 15–2–29–0; Taylor 5–2–7–0; Sainsbury 63–38–73–1; Cowley 21.1–7–43–2; Richards 12–5–25–0; Jesty 5–4–3–0.

Umpires: D. J. Constant and D. L. Evans.

GLAMORGAN v WORCESTERSHIRE

Played at Swansea, June 29, 30, July 1, 1977

Drawn. This will go down as Turner's match. He scored 141 out of Worcestershire's total of 169. No other batsman reached double figures. In fact, the other ten batsmen contributed only 14 scoring shots between them. The next highest scorer was Gifford with

7 and he stayed with Turner for fifty minutes during which 57 were added for the ninth wicket. This not only enabled Turner to complete a century, but also saved Worcestershire from following on. The only blemish came when he was 93, Ontong missing a slip catch. A feature of Glamorgan's batting which gave them a first innings lead of 140 was an unbroken fifth wicket partnership between Llewellyn and Richards of 161. But rain on the third day denied Glamorgan the opportunity of turning their advantage into a win.

Glamorgan

*A. Jones lbw b Gifford	48	– b Holder	7
J. A. Hopkins lbw b Pridgeon	28	– c Neale b D'Oliveira	45
R. C. Ontong st Humphries b Gifford	21	– b Cumbes	56
C. L. King c D'Oliveira b Gifford	25	– c D'Oliveira b Holder	2
M. J. Llewellyn not out	91	– b Holder	12
G. Richards not out	74	– lbw b Cumbes	0
†E. W. Jones (did not bat)		– b Cumbes	4
M. A. Nash (did not bat)		– not out	5
A. E. Cordle (did not bat)		– not out	4
B 4, l-b 6, n-b 12	22	B 5, n-b 2	7
1/57 2/98 3/117 4/148	(4 wkts) 309	1/17 2/23 3/82 4/119 5/124 6/132 7/137	(7 wkts) 142

B. J. Lloyd and A. H. Wilkins did not bat.

Bowling: *First Innings*—Holder 19–1–54–0; Cumbes 19–3–54–0; Pridgeon 14–1–45–1; Gifford 30–8–91–3; D'Oliveira 18–8–43–0. *Second Innings*—Holder 9.3–6–48–3; Cumbes 14–4–30–3; Gifford 12–6–25–0; D'Oliveira 17–4–32–1.

Worcestershire

G. M. Turner not out	141
B. J. R. Jones lbw b Nash	1
P. A. Neale c E. W. Jones b Wilkins	3
E. J. O. Hemsley b Cordle	3
B. L. D'Oliveira c E. W. Jones b Cordle	0
D. N. Patel c E. W. Jones b Nash	4
†D. J. Humphries c Llewellyn b Cordle	0
V. A. Holder lbw b Cordle	4
*N. Gifford c Llewellyn b Lloyd	7
J. Cumbes lbw b Nash	5
A. P. Pridgeon lbw b Cordle	0
L-b 1	1
1/18 2/35 3/68 4/71 5/71 6/82 7/87 8/93 9/150	169

Bowling: Nash 31–14–51–3; Cordle 24–9–53–5; Wilkins 7–0–33–1; Ontong 3–0–20–0; Lloyd 3–1–11–1.

Umpires: W. E. Alley and R. Julian.

GLAMORGAN v LANCASHIRE

Played at Swansea, August 27, 29, 30, 1977

Drawn. Rain robbed Lancashire of a win which their all-round superior cricket warranted. It will always be remembered because of the hurricane hitting of Hayes who only narrowly missed equalling the world record of scoring 36 runs in a six ball over. His sequence of shots was 6, 4, 6, 6, 6, 6, and ironically it was against Nash, the left-arm seam bowler, whom Sobers hammered for six 6s on the same ground in 1968. Hayes took two hours ten minutes to score his first 50 runs, but raced from 50 to 100 in only twenty minutes.

Altogether he hit seven 6s and thirteen 4s. Wood provided the platform. He stood firm for just over six hours to carry out his bat for 155, which included eighteen boundaries. The third wicket partnership between Wood and Hayes realised 202.

Glamorgan

*A. Jones c and b Arrowsmith	26	– st Scott b Simmons	20
J. A. Hopkins b Lee	30	– lbw b Arrowsmith	24
R. C. Ontong c Abrahams b Simmons	12	– st Scott b Arrowsmith	13
D. A. Francis c Pilling b Arrowsmith	25	– not out	7
M. J. Llewellyn lbw b Simmons	19		
G. Richards c Hayes b Simmons	20	– not out	30
†E. W. Jones c Lee b Simmons	35		
M. A. Nash b Simmons	12		
A. E. Cordle lbw b Simmons	19		
T. W. Cartwright c Simmons b Arrowsmith	4		
A. H. Wilkins not out	0		
B 6, l-b 5, n-b 4	15	B 8, w 1, n-b 2	11
1/45 2/76 3/78 4/110 5/126 6/152 7/170 8/210 9/217	217	1/38 2/56 3/69	(3 wkts) 105

Bowling: *First Innings*—Lee 10–1–19–1; Hogg 6–2–17–0; Simmons 39–14–74–6; Arrowsmith 25.2–9–79–3; Lloyd 4–0–13–0. *Second Innings*—Lee 6–0–19–0; Hogg 2–0–14–0; Simmons 12–2–32–1; Arrowsmith 9–4–29–2.

Lancashire

B. Wood not out	155	J. Simmons not out	2
*D. Lloyd b Wilkins	32	B 7, l-b 12, n-b 3	22
H. Pilling st E. W. Jones b Wilkins	32		
F. C. Hayes b Wilkins	119	1/54 2/155 3/357	(3 wkts) 362

J. Abrahams, B. W. Reidy, R. Arrowsmith, †C. Scott, W. Hogg and P. G. Lee did not bat.

Bowling: Nash 15–5–71–0; Cordle 18–4–70–0; Richards 30–9–81–0; Ontong 6–1–30–0; Wilkins 25–7–56–3; Cartwright 21–10–32–0.

Umpires: C. Cook and A. Jepson.

GLAMORGAN v HAMPSHIRE

Played at Swansea, May 27, 29, 30, 1978

Drawn. Two centuries by A. Jones, the Glamorgan captain, made this fixture notable. It was the third time he had accomplished the feat in a match and the first occasion anyone had achieved that distinction on the St Helen's ground. He scored 147 in the first innings and then, with the pitch taking spin slowly, had to battle for almost five hours against the superbly directed slow bowling of Cowley and Southern to reach 100 in the second. Greenidge, attempting to reach his century with a six, was caught on the boundary for 95. Gilliat came out as last man with a chipped finger bone to score the five runs Hampshire needed for a fourth batting point.

Glamorgan

*A. Jones run out	147	– c sub b Cowley	100
J. A. Hopkins c Greenidge b Southern	80	– b Cowley	20
R. C. Ontong b Stevenson	5		
M. J. Llewellyn not out	57	– b Cowley	5
P. D. Swart run out	0	– b Cowley	51
D. A. Francis c Stephenson b Roberts	4	– lbw b Southern	11
G. Richards not out	4	– run out	38
†E. W. Jones (did not bat)		– not out	8
M. A. Nash (did not bat)		– c Rock b Southern	10
A. E. Cordle (did not bat)		– not out	13
L-b 4, w 2, n-b 3	10	B 4, l-b 9, n-b 1	14
1/193 2/224 3/255 4/255 5/276	(5 wkts) 307	1/47 2/70 3/76 4/164 5/234 6/235 7/249	(7 wkts dec.) 270

B. J. Lloyd did not bat.

Bowling: *First Innings*—Roberts 20–2–70–1; Stevenson 22–4–70–1; Taylor 10–2–28–0; Jesty 9–0–22–0; Cowley 20–6–59–0; Southern 19–6–48–1. *Second Innings*—Roberts 15–3–33–0; Stevenson 6–0–20–0; Taylor 10–1–19–0; Cowley 47.2–21–95–4; Southern 33–12–89–2.

Hampshire

D. J. Rock c E. W. Jones b Nash	0	– c Swart b Cordle	0
C. G. Greenidge c Llewellyn b Swart	95	– c E. W. Jones b Nash	8
D. R. Turner c E. W. Jones b Richards	92	– b Lloyd	21
T. E. Jesty b Lloyd	3	– c Francis b Swart	36
N. G. Cowley run out	13	– c Francis b Richards	28
†G. R. Stephenson c Francis b Lloyd	0	– not out	18
A. M. E. Roberts c Cordle b Lloyd	17		
K. Stevenson c E. W. Jones b Richards	19		
J. W. Southern c A. Jones b Richards	13		
M. N. S. Taylor not out	24	– not out	54
*R. M. C. Gilliat not out	5		
B 8, l-b 9, w 1, n-b 1	19	N-b 1	1
1/24 2/144 3/147 4/187 5/188 6/230 7/238 8/251 9/295	(9 wkts dec.) 300	1/4 2/8 3/65 4/67 5/122	(5 wkts) 166

Bowling: *First Innings*—Nash 25–3–97–1; Cordle 15–4–48–0; Richards 16.4–4–46–3; Swart 10–0–33–1; Lloyd 25–9–57–3. *Second Innings*—Nash 12–2–64–1. Cordle 6–1–19–1; Richards 12–3–41–1; Swart 6–0–11–1; Lloyd 14–5–30–1.

Umpires: A. Jepson and K. E. Palmer.

GLAMORGAN v NORTHAMPTONSHIRE

Played at Cardiff, May 31, June 2, 3, 1980

Drawn. In a rain-ruined match, there was no play on the first day and only eighty minutes on the second, when Northamptonshire scored 63 for two. On the third day they declared at this total and Glamorgan forfeited their first innings in an attempt to achieve a result. Thus no bonus points were earned by either side. In their second innings the visitors declared at 193 for two after a splendid innings by Larkins who hit two 6s and ten 4s. Glamorgan went for the runs at first but, at 121 for six, defeat seemed imminent until Holmes and Nash steered them to safety.

Northamptonshire

G. Cook lbw b Nash	0	– lbw b Moseley	28
W. Larkins c E. W. Jones b Nash	32	– not out	103
R. G. Williams not out	19	– c Featherstone b Lloyd	37
A. J. Lamb not out	11	– not out	12
N-b 1	1	B 1, l-b 5, n-b 7	13
1/29 2/40 (2 wkts dec.)	63	1/64 2/165 (2 wkts dec.)	193

P. Willey, T. J. Yardley, †G. Sharp, *P. J. Watts, T. M. Lamb, B. J. Griffiths and Sarfraz Nawaz did not bat.

Bowling: *First Innings*—Nash 10–4–17–2; A. A. Jones 6–2–31–0; Lloyd 5–2–12–0; Moseley 2–1–2–0. *Second Innings*—Nash 2–0–14–0; A. A. Jones 10–1–28–0; Moseley 10–2–26–1; Lloyd 18.1–3–83–1; Holmes 8–1–29–0.

Glamorgan

A. Jones (did not bat)	– c A. J. Lamb b Sarfraz	22
J. A. Hopkins (did not bat)	– c Sharp b Sarfraz	10
N. G. Featherstone (did not bat)	– b Sarfraz	16
Javed Miandad (did not bat)	– c Sharp b Willey	34
M. J. Llewellyn (did not bat)	– lbw b T. M. Lamb	5
G. C. Holmes (did not bat)	– not out	39
†E. W. Jones (did not bat)	– c Sarfaz b Willey	3
*M. A. Nash (did not bat)	– not out	49
	L-b 6, w 1, n-b 17	24
	1/38 2/44 3/74 4/104 5/106 6/121 (6 wkts)	202

B. J. Lloyd, E. A. Moseley and A. A. Jones did not bat.

Bowling: Sarfraz 15–4–56–3; Griffiths 9–1–40–0; T. M. Lamb 10–4–24–1; Willey 8–1–31–2; Williams 6–0–27–0.

Glamorgan forfeited their first innings.

Umpires: C. Cook and P. S. G. Stevens.

GLAMORGAN v SUSSEX

Played at Swansea, July 9, 10, 1980

Sussex won by an innings and 189 runs. Glamorgan suffered their heaviest defeat in 31 years in a match that was completed in two days. They were dismissed for 135 in 45.5 overs before Sussex replied with 283 for three in 50 overs. Imran Khan was supreme, taking four Glamorgan wickets for 25 and then hitting an undefeated 89. On the second day Sussex proved even more formidable as Imran (five 6s and thirteen 4s) moved on to 124 and Wells scored his maiden century with four 6s and nineteen 4s, in a partnership of 256. The visitors declared at 440 for eight, setting Glamorgan a target of 306 to avoid an innings defeat. However, they managed only 116, with Imran taking four for 8 in nine overs and le Roux five for 49.

Glamorgan

A. Jones c Waller b Imran	2	– c Arnold b le Roux	1
J. A. Hopkins c Long b Imran	25	– c Mendis b Imran	6
G. C. Holmes lbw b Imran	2	– absent hurt	0
Javed Miandad c Phillipson b Imran	20	– (3) lbw b le Roux	42
N. G. Featherstone c Greig b Arnold	0	– (4) b Imran	4
M. J. Llewellyn lbw b Arnold	4	– (5) c Barclay b Imran	0
†E. W. Jones c Barclay b le Roux	36	– (6) c Barclay b le Roux	36
*B. J. Lloyd c le Roux b Arnold	16	– (7) not out	6
E. A. Moseley not out	0	– (8) c Phillipson b le Roux	6
R. N. S. Hobbs b le Roux	0	– (9) lbw b Imran	2
A. A. Jones c Greig b le Roux	12	– (10) c Phillipson b le Roux	0
L-b 6, w 1, n-b 11	18	L-b 3, w 6, n-b 2	11
1/4 2/7 3/55 4/57 5/57 6/65 7/119 8/123 9/123	135	1/13 2/14 3/38 4/45 5/95 6/102 7/108 8/115 9/116	116

Bowling: *First Innings*—Imran 10–5–25–4; le Roux 16.5–7–43–3; Arnold 17–7–35–3; Greig 2–0–14–0. *Second Innings*—Imran 9–3–8–4; le Roux 12.3–3–49–5; Arnold 4–2–21–0; Waller 9–3–27–0.

Sussex

G. D. Mendis c Llewellyn b A. A. Jones	53
J. R. T. Barclay c Miandad b Moseley	23
P. W. G. Parker c A. A. Jones b Moseley	15
Imran Khan c Llewellyn b A. A. Jones	124
C. M. Wells c A. Jones b A. A. Jones	135
C. P. Phillipson c E. W. Jones b A. A. Jones	0
I. A. Greig c E. W. Jones b Lloyd	6
G. S. le Roux st E. W. Jones b Hobbs	46
*†A. Long not out	8
B 10, l-b 4, w 10, n-b 6	30
1/71 2/97 3/111 4/367 5/367 6/384 7/384 8/440 (8 wkts dec.)	440

G. G. Arnold and C. E. Waller did not bat.

Bowling: A. A. Jones 23–2–102–4; Moseley 23–4–111–2; Lloyd 18–4–79–1; Holmes 12–2–63–0; Hobbs 5.4–0–37–1; Featherstone 3–0–18–0.

Umpires: B. J. Meyer and P. S. G. Stevens.

GLAMORGAN v SOMERSET

Played at Swansea, June 27, 29, 30, 1981

Drawn. With Garner threatening to wreck Glamorgan's first innings, Miandad came to their rescue with a brilliant hundred, sharing in a saving fourth-wicket century stand with Featherstone. Glamorgan, having obtained maximum bonus points, declared on the second day, only to suffer Botham's first century in thirteen months, an undefeated 123 (three 6s and eighteen 4s) in 137 minutes which took Somerset ahead before their declaration. Glamorgan finished the day at 63 for one and on Tuesday Miandad completed his second century of the match (twelve 4s and two 6s) and his third in succession for Glamorgan, a feat performed only twice before by Glamorgan players – Dai Davies (1928) and Gilbert Parkhouse (1950).

Glamorgan

A. Jones c Taylor b Garner	36	– lbw b Garner	14
J. A. Hopkins c Olive b Garner	13	– c Roebuck b Moseley	45
A. L. Jones c Marks b Garner	10	– c Taylor b Garner	12
Javed Miandad not out	137	– c Botham b Richards	106
N. G. Featherstone run out	63	– c Marks b Breakwell	6
G. C. Holmes not out	28	– not out	50
E. A. Moseley (did not bat)		– not out	7
B 1, l-b 7, n-b 6	14	B 3, l-b 2, n-b 2	7
1/38 2/60 3/67 4/210 (4 wkts dec.)	301	1/40 2/70 3/78 4/109 5/226 (5 wkts dec.)	247

*M. A. Nash, †E. W. Jones, B. J. Lloyd and R. N. S. Hobbs did not bat.

Bowling: *First Innings*—Garner 23.3–5–64–3; Botham 16–0–81–0; Moseley 18–2–60–0; Marks 24–6–63–0; Breakwell 6–0–19–0. *Second Innings*—Garner 14–5–22–2; Botham 15–3–61–0; Marks 22–5–51–0; Moseley 9–1–22–1; Breakwell 17–2–66–1; Richards 9.4–2–18–1.

Somerset

*B. C. Rose b Lloyd	40	– lbw b Holmes	18
M. Olive c Holmes b Nash	3	– lbw b Nash	5
I. V. A. Richards lbw b Moseley	2	– not out	15
P. M. Roebuck c and b Moseley	51	– not out	6
P. W. Denning st E. W. Jones b Lloyd	4		
I. T. Botham not out	123		
V. J. Marks c E. W. Jones b Moseley	0		
D. Breakwell c E. W. Jones b Nash	10		
†D. J. S. Taylor c Lloyd b Nash	5		
J. Garner run out	18		
H. R. Moseley not out	9		
B 6, l-b 22, w 3, n-b 7	38	W 2	2
1/18 2/23 3/102 4/106 5/175 6/176 7/237 8/245 9/272 (9 wkts dec.)	303	1/20 2/24 (2 wkts)	46

Bowling: *First Innings*—Nash 20–3–75–3; Moseley 13–4–55–3; Holmes 2–0–10–0; Lloyd 19–5–56–2; Hobbs 19.3–4–69–0. *Second Innings*—Nash 10–3–30–1; Moseley 4–1–4–0; Holmes 6–2–8–1; Lloyd 3–2–2–0; Featherstone 2–2–0–0.

Umpires: C. Cook and C. T. Spencer.

GLOUCESTERSHIRE

GLOUCESTERSHIRE v YORKSHIRE

Played at Bristol, September 2, 3, 1964

Yorkshire won by an innings and 294 runs. They outplayed Gloucestershire at all points scoring 425 for seven on the first day and twice dismissing the home county for an aggregate of 131 in three and three-quarter hours on the second. Boycott, with a wide variety of powerful strokes featuring fine drives, led Yorkshire's scoring revel. In a stay of five hours and fifty minutes for 177, he hit one 6 and twenty-three 4s and with Close, who often danced out audaciously, shared a stand of 151 for the fourth wicket. Close and Illingworth each hit ten 4s. Next day, on turf enlivened by morning rain Gloucestershire were twice routed. Allen alone reached double figures in the first innings in which Trueman took four of the first five wickets for eight runs. Illingworth sent back four of the last five men for 20. Following on 378 behind, Gloucestershire lost two men in Trueman's first over, and Hutton, at brisk pace, helped to bring about a second collapse. Trueman's match figures were seven for 36.

Yorkshire

G. Boycott c Allen b Graveney	177
P. J. Sharpe b Brown	45
D. E. V. Padgett c Meyer b Brown	1
J. H. Hampshire b Mortimore	17
*D. B. Close c Allen b Smith	82
R. Illingworth not out	70
R. A. Hutton st Meyer b Cook	3
D. Wilson c Young b Cook	0
†J. G. Binks not out	13
B 12, l-b 1, n-b 4	17
1/108 2/112 3/153 4/304 5/384 6/391 7/393	(7 wkts dec.) 425

F. S. Trueman and M. Ryan did not bat.

Bowling: Smith 14–2–40–1; Brown 24–6–71–2; Cook 24–8–65–2; Allen 22–3–78–0; Mortimore 32–2–106–1; Graveney 20–3–48–1.

Gloucestershire

D. M. Young b Trueman	2	– b Trueman	8
R. B. Nicholls c sub b Illingworth	7	– c Binks b Hutton	0
R. C. White b Trueman	0	– c Close b Trueman	0
A. S. Brown c and b Trueman	2	– c Close b Hutton	1
J. B. Mortimore lbw b Ryan	0	– b Hutton	19
M. Bissex b Trueman	1	– c Binks b Hutton	17
D. A. Allen lbw b Illingworth	20	– c Close b Ryan	2
†B. J. Meyer c Hutton b Wilson	5	– not out	12
*J. K. Graveney c Hampshire b Illingworth	3	– c Padgett b Wilson	19
D. R. Smith not out	0	– b Trueman	0
C. Cook c and b Illingworth	1	– st Binks b Wilson	3
L-b 2, w 1, n-b 3	6	B 1, n-b 2	3
1/6 2/6 3/8 4/10 5/11 6/32 7/42 8/46 9/46	47	1/8 2/8 3/9 4/12 5/46 6/49 7/51 8/73 9/77	84

Bowling: *First Innings*—Trueman 8–4–8–4; Hutton 3–2–5–0; Ryan 3–1–2–1; Illingworth 10.1–2–20–4; Wilson 9–6–6–1. *Second Innings*—Trueman 7–0–28–3; Hutton 10–3–24–4; Ryan 4–1–14–1; Wilson 2.2–0–15–2.

Umpires: C. G. Pepper and A. E. D. Smith.

GLOUCESTERSHIRE v WORCESTERSHIRE

Played at Cheltenham, August 12, 14, 15, 1967

Worcestershire won by ten wickets. Gloucestershire never recovered from losing their first six wickets for 43 on a damp pitch to the devastating opening attack of Carter and Flavell. The last four wickets more than doubled the score, but Headley completed brilliant fielding at short leg to make his fifth catch and end the innings at 123. Mainly due to a third-wicket stand of 104 by Fearnley and Ormrod, followed by a sound innings by Slade, who hit six 4s, Worcestershire gained a commanding first-innings lead of 124. In their second venture Gloucestershire started to fight back and when rain made play impossible on the final day until after lunch, they were 72 for one. They carried their score to 101 for three and looked safe from defeat, but they collapsed against Gifford, who captured the last four wickets for 2 runs and his final five for 53 included two 6s by Shepherd in one over. Worcestershire soon hit the 32 for victory without loss with twelve minutes of normal time remaining.

Gloucestershire

R. B. Nicholls c Headley b Carter	1	– c Gifford b Coldwell	58
C. A. Milton c Headley b Flavell	6	– run out	24
S. E. Russell c Booth b Flavell	3	– c Hemsley b Flavell	18
D. Brown c Hemsley b Carter	11	– c Ormrod b Gifford	6
M. Bissex run out	16	– lbw b Slade	10
D. Shepherd c Headley b Carter	5	– b Gifford	23
A. S. Brown b Flavell	25	– c Hemsley b Gifford	2
*J. B. Mortimore c Carter b Gifford	13	– b Flavell	4
D. A. Allen c Headley b Coldwell	18	– c Fearnley b Gifford	0
†B. J. Meyer not out	21	– not out	0
J. Davey c Headley b Carter	0	– c Slade b Gifford	0
L-b 3, n-b 1	4	B 7, l-b 3	10
1/1 2/7 3/12 4/35 5/37 6/43 7/83 8/83 9/108	123	1/54 2/88 3/101 4/120 5/130 6/150 7/153 8/155 9/155	155

Bowling: *First Innings*—Flavell 17–3–39–3; Carter 12.3–3–31–4; Coldwell 13–4–28–1; Gifford 15–7–21–1. *Second Innings*—Flavell 21–6–32–2; Carter 11–3–24–0; Coldwell 12–6–19–1; Gifford 34–23–53–5; Slade 14–5–17–1.

Worcestershire

*D. Kenyon c Meyer b Davey	1	– not out	7
R. G. A. Headley b Davey	24	– not out	27
C. D. Fearnley lbw b Allen	63		
J. A. Ormrod c and b Allen	46		
E. J. O. Hemsley c Davey b Mortimore	0		
D. N. F. Slade c Bissex b Allen	49		
†R. Booth c Milton b Allen	16		
N. Gifford b Allen	26		
L. J. Coldwell b Davey	7		
J. A. Flavell run out	4		
R. G. M. Carter not out	1		
B 7, l-b 3	10	W 1	1
1/8 2/35 3/139 4/142 5/142 6/168 7/222 8/242 9/242	247	(no wkt)	35

Bowling: *First Innings*—Davey 24.2–4–48–3; A. S. Brown 14–2–38–0; Mortimore 27–4–52–1; Allen 36–13–75–5; Bissex 9–3–24–0. *Second Innings*—Davey 4–1–15–0; A. S. Brown 3.5–0–19–0.

Umpires: A. Jepson and D. J. Halfyard.

GLOUCESTERSHIRE v DERBYSHIRE

Played at Bristol, September 1, 2, 3, 1976

Derbyshire won by five wickets. Pursuing their slender hopes of winning the Championship, Gloucestershire finally faltered when they failed to take full bowling points from Derby. They had been given an excellent start by Sadiq Mohammad with his second century in two days. On a very damp wicket he batted from first to last staying five and a half hours for his 163 not out. There was every advantage in batting first and Gloucestershire reached 308 for seven before Brown declared in the 98th over. Sharpe and Hill laid the foundations of Derbyshire's eventual win by going along with utmost patience. At one point Hill spent half an hour on 31, but he had got the measure of the home bowling, as he proved with a century in the second innings which brought Gloucestershire's very good run to an abrupt halt. In Gloucestershire's second innings Sadiq had scored yet another century.

Gloucestershire

Sadiq Mohammad not out	163	– c sub b Swarbrook	150
A. W. Stovold c Taylor b Stevenson	4	– b Swarbrook	12
Zaheer Abbas c Hendrick b Swarbrook	43	– c and b Barlow	26
A. J. Hignell b Barlow	65	– c Hill b Hendrick	17
M. J. Procter c Taylor b Barlow	4	– b Swarbrook	9
D. R. Shepherd c Cartwright b Stevenson	6	– c Taylor b Hendrick	0
D. A. Graveney st Taylor b Swarbrook	2	– not out	25
*A. S. Brown c and b Swarbrook	15	– not out	16
B. M. Brain not out	3		
B 1, l-b 6, w 1, n-b 5	13	B 2, l-b 4	6
1/5 2/88 3/106 4/201 5/230 6/259 7/310	(7 wkts dec.) 318	1/52 2/101 3/141 4/161 5/164 6/232	(6 wkts dec.) 261

†A. J. Brassington and J. H. Childs did not bat.

Bowling: *First Innings*—Hendrick 17–6–48–0; Stevenson 12–1–65–2; Russell 18–3–53–0; Miller 8–3–30–0; Swarbrook 32.5–5–85–3; Barlow 10–1–24–2. *Second Innings*—Hendrick 19–2–62–2; Stevenson 6–1–25–0; Russell 8–0–39–0; Swarbrook 27–2–105–3; Barlow 6–0–24–1.

Derbyshire

A. Hill c Brassington b Brown	61	– c Brown b Stovold	126
P. J. Sharpe lbw b Brown	85	– c Hignell b Graveney	31
*E. J. Barlow c sub b Sadiq	54	– st Brassington b Brown	58
A. Morris lbw b Graveney	1	– not out	0
H. Cartwright c and b Sadiq	41	– b Childs	37
†R. W. Taylor c Brassington b Sadiq	0		
F. W. Swarbrook not out	30	– not out	4
P. E. Russell b Graveney	5		
G. Miller not out	2	– b Brain	10
B 5, l-b 19, n-b 2	26	B 3, l-b 6, n-b 2	11
1/153 2/172 3/188 4/243 5/244 6/273 7/298	(7 wkts dec.) 305	1/64 2/163 3/191 4/273 5/273	(5 wkts) 277

K. Stevenson and M. Hendrick did not bat.

Bowling: *First Innings*—Procter 16–4–50–0; Brain 10–2–36–0; Graveney 29–7–75–2; Childs 15–5–35–0; Sadiq 18–5–49–3; Brown 14–3–34–2. *Second Innings*—Procter 19–4–56–0; Brain 9–1–44–1; Graveney 20–3–59–1; Childs 11.5–0–43–1; Sadiq 8–0–34–0; Brown 5–0–30–1; Stovold 1–1–0–1.

Umpires: W. E. Alley and W. L. Budd.

GLOUCESTERSHIRE v SOMERSET

Played at Bristol, June 4, 6, 7, 1977

Drawn. With a double century Richards became the first player to reach 1,000 as he rescued Somerset from their first innings collapse before the pace attack of Brain and Procter. Somerset had settled for a draw but Richards made it a memorable one, his graceful range of shots producing four 6s and thirty-two 4s as he reached his highest county score of 241. It was the first double century at Bristol for thirteen years and it came out of 293 in a remarkable innings which lasted four hours, forty-nine minutes. The only possible chance he gave was at 110 when a rising ball struck the shoulder of his bat and hovered close to the wicket-keeper. A casual shot and a good catch at slip had ended his first innings almost before it began as Somerset were put out for 133. After rain had held up play Zaheer and Procter put on 119. Zaheer's second century inside a week included one 6 and fifteen 4s while Procter hit fourteen boundaries in his 73. The other big innings, by Stovold, who reached 96, included fourteen 4s.

Somerset

B. C. Rose lbw b Brain	16	– c Graveney b Brain	20
P. W. Denning c Shepherd b Procter	2	– b Procter	0
I. V. A. Richards c Zaheer b Brain	5	– not out	241
M. J. Kitchen c Graveney b Brain	9	– c Sadiq b Procter	4
P. A. Slocombe c Brassington b Procter	37	– c Sadiq b Procter	51
*D. B. Close lbw b Brain	3	– b Childs	1
G. I. Burgess c Zaheer b Brain	11	– not out	11
D. Breakwell b Graveney	27	– st Brassington b Graveney	51
C. H. Dredge c Brassington b Procter	9		
†T. Gard c Brassington b Procter	3		
H. R. Moseley not out	6		
B 1, l-b 2, n-b 2	5	L-b 3, n-b 3	6
1/5 2/10 3/22 4/37 5/55 6/83 7/95 8/115 9/123	133	1/3 2/61 3/76 4/257 5/262 6/358	(6 wkts) 385

Bowling: *First Innings*—Procter 24–7–51–4; Brain 20–6–52–5; Graveney 8–1–17–1; Shackleton 9–7–4–0; Childs 1–0–4–0. *Second Innings*—Procter 22–3–76–3; Brain 15–4–55–1; Graveney 27–6–107–1; Childs 25–6–77–1; Sadiq 10–1–49–1; Zaheer 5–2–6–0; Stovold 2–0–9–0.

Gloucestershire

Sadiq Mohammad c Richards b Breakwell	39
A. W. Stovold b Moseley	96
Zaheer Abbas c and b Dredge	105
J. C. Foat lbw b Breakwell	1
*M. J. Procter not out	73
B 4, l-b 8, n-b 3	15
1/95 2/199 3/210 4/329	(4 wkts dec.) 329

D. R. Shepherd, D. A. Graveney, J. H. Shackleton, †A. J. Brassington, B. M. Brain and J. H. Childs did not bat.

Bowling: Moseley 29–5–85–1; Dredge 23–2–88–1; Burgess 2.4–0–5–0; Breakwell 33–15–62–2; Richards 13–1–63–0; Rose 2–0–11–0.

Umpires: C. G. Pepper and P. Rochford.

GLOUCESTERSHIRE v WORCESTERSHIRE

Played at Cheltenham, July 27, 28, 29, 1977

Gloucestershire won by an innings and 35 runs. A fine all round performance by Procter enabled Gloucestershire to win comfortably. He achieved one of his best performances of the season to take seven for 35 as Worcestershire were bundled out for 167, only Neale and Hemsley producing any substantial scores. Gloucestershire lost their first three wickets for 43 runs before solid batting by Zaheer, Hignell and Shepherd helped them to recover and a first century of the season by Procter finally saw them to a respectable total of 338. Holder took seven wickets for 117. In their second innings Worcestershire lost their first six wickets for only 40 runs, despite some stubborn batting by Ormrod. Again Procter did the damage, finishing with six for 38 for a match analysis of thirteen for 73.

Worcestershire

G. M. Turner c Zaheer b Procter	9	c Procter b Childs	16
J. A. Ormrod c Stovold b Brain	19	c Hignell b Graveney	44
P. A. Neale b Procter	38	lbw b Procter	1
E. J. O. Hemsley c Childs b Procter	56	b Procter	10
B. L. D'Oliveira c Stovold b Procter	0	c Graveney b Procter	23
S. P. Henderson c Stovold b Procter	2	b Procter	6
C. N. Boyns lbw b Procter	0	lbw b Procter	1
†D. J. Humphries lbw b Brain	12	lbw b Shackleton	0
V. A. Holder run out	8	lbw b Procter	12
*N. Gifford c Stovold b Procter	9	b Graveney	8
J. Cumbes not out	0	not out	2
L-b 8, n-b 6	14	B 9, n-b 4	13
1/16 2/61 3/83 4/84 5/87 6/87 7/114 8/151 9/163	167	1/2 2/10 3/24 4/30 5/31 6/40 7/104 8/114 9/131	136

Bowling: *First Innings*—Brain 22–5–56–2; Procter 18.5–5–35–7; Shackleton 11–1–27–0; Graveney 8–6–10–0; Childs 13–4–25–0. *Second Innings*—Procter 20–6–38–6; Shackleton 6–1–6–1; Graveney 11.4–5–19–2; Childs 17–9–24–1; Sadiq 11–4–36–0.

Gloucestershire

Sadiq Mohammad c Turner b Holder	8
†A. W. Stovold b Boyns b Holder	0
Zaheer Abbas c Humphries b Holder	23
A. J. Hignell b Boyns	64
D. R. Shepherd c Humphries b Holder	38
J. H. Shackleton c Turner b Holder	0
*M. J. Procter c sub b Cumbes	108
P. Bainbridge c Humphries b Holder	40
D. A. Graveney b Holder	32
B. M. Brain b Cumbes	6
J. H. Childs not out	0
B 2, l-b 7, n-b 10	19
1/1 2/19 3/43 4/108 5/112 6/204 7/259 8/331 9/338	338

Bowling: Holder 35.5–7–117–7; Cumbes 23–4–72–2; Gifford 27–9–59–0; Boyns 18–2–61–1; Hemsley 3–0–10–0.

Umpires: W. L. Budd and W. E. Phillipson.

GLOUCESTERSHIRE v SUSSEX

Played at Cheltenham, July 30, August 1, 2, 1977

Gloucestershire won by eight wickets. Everything else in this match was dwarfed by the batting of Zaheer, who set a world record when he became the first player to score a double and a single century for the third time. Remarkably his other two performances, against Kent and Surrey in 1976, finished not out like those in this game. For his 205 he batted five hours, twenty minutes, his chief hits being one 5 and twenty-two 4s and he did not offer a chance, although he lofted the ball more than usual. His 108, notable for superb cover drives, contained one 6 and seventeen 4s and came in three and a quarter hours when Gloucestershire needed 219 to win in just under four hours.

Sussex

J. R. T. Barclay st Stovold b Childs	105	– c Bainbridge b Procter	11
*P. J. Graves c Stovold b Procter	56	– b Graveney	11
R. D. V. Knight b Graveney	18	– c and b Graveney	21
Javed Miandad c Procter b Graveney	48	– c Stovold b Graveney	30
Imran Khan b Graveney	1	– run out	39
P. W. G. Parker c Zaheer b Graveney	32	– c Hignell b Graveney	2
M. A. Buss st Stovold b Childs	9	– lbw b Procter	30
†A. Long not out	11	– b Procter	20
J. A. Snow not out	8	– b Childs	56
J. Spencer (did not bat)		– not out	9
R. G. L. Cheatle (did not bat)		– c Shackleton b Childs	8
B 4, l-b 14, w 1, n-b 2	21	B 17, l-b 2, n-b 6	25
1/119 2/144 3/222 4/224 5/266 6/284 7/291	(7 wkts) 309	1/12 2/47 3/51 4/93 5/99 6/144 7/174 8/214 9/248	262

Bowling: *First Innings*—Procter 25–7–51–1; Vernon 7–1–37–0; Shackleton 12–1–38–0; Childs 23–4–72–2; Graveney 33–5–90–4. *Second Innings*—Procter 29–5–91–3; Vernon 2–0–13–0; Shackleton 3–0–22–0; Childs 13.4–7–25–2; Graveney 35–10–84–4; Sadiq 1–0–2–0.

Gloucestershire

Sadiq Mohammad c Barclay b Imran	0	– c Barclay b Javed	33
†A. W. Stovold c and b Buss	61	– c Long b Imran	30
Zaheer Abbas not out	205	– not out	108
A. J. Hignell c Long b Cheatle	8	– not out	33
*M. J. Procter b Imran	17		
D. R. Shepherd c Knight b Spencer	32		
P. Bainbridge c Javed b Buss	7		
D. A. Graveney c Long b Snow	16		
J. H. Shackleton not out	1		
L-b 2, w 1, n-b 3	6	B5, l-b 4, w 3, n-b 3	15
1/2 2/146 3/169 4/200 5/300 6/319 7/349	(7 wkts) 353	1/47 2/106	(2 wkts) 219

M. J. Vernon and J. H. Childs did not bat.

Bowling: *First Innings*—Imran 17–5–52–2; Snow 18–3–68–1; Spencer 16–2–58–1; Buss 24–5–53–2; Cheatle 18–3–79–1; Barclay 2–1–3–0; Javed 1–0–12–0; Knight 4–0–22–0. *Second Innings*—Imran 7–3–15–1; Snow 3–0–11–0; Buss 4–0–16–0; Cheatle 18–3–71–0; Barclay 10–1–45–0; Javed 7.4–0–44–1; Long 1–0–2–0.

Umpires: W. L. Budd and D. Oslear.

GLOUCESTERSHIRE v ESSEX

Played at Gloucestershire, June 10, 12, 13, 1978

Essex won by two wickets. A magnificent match, containing two memorable innings, finished in favour of Essex with just two balls remaining. Procter's double century on the first day was generally regarded as the best innings seen on the ground since Hammond's heyday. In rescuing his side from 70 for three the Gloucestershire captain, with characteristic timing and power, hit 203 in two and three-quarter hours with four 6s and twenty-six 4s. Foat, although never idle, contributed a mere 31 to their fifth-wicket partnership of 219 as the majestic Procter gave a glorious exhibition. Essex batted consistently with Denness, McEwan, Fletcher, and Hardie all taking toll of the bowling. On the final day, Procter left Essex to make 313 in 200 minutes. He tried to buy wickets with some friendly spin from Childs and Graveney, but the match looked a certain draw when the final twenty overs began at 185 for four. But Phillip had other ideas. The West Indian, who had never previously made a century, now hit about him in furious fashion as the excitement mounted. He reached three figures in 112 minutes. A target of 58 from the last seven overs proved no obstacle as Phillip went on boldly. He hit seven 6s and twelve 4s and by the time he fell to Procter, with three balls remaining, Essex wanted only two runs for a famous victory.

Gloucestershire

A. W. Stovold c and b Lever	26	– c Smith b Lever	18
A. Tait c Fletcher b Lever	4	– c Denness b East	36
Zaheer Abbas lbw b Lever	23	– c Hardie b Acfield	49
D. R. Shepherd c East b Acfield	11	– run out	16
*M. J. Procter b Lever	203	– c McEwan b Acfield	43
J. C. Foat st Smith b East	56	– not out	53
M. D. Partridge not out	5	– c Smith b Phillip	1
D. A. Graveney not out	1	– not out	34
L-b 14, n-b 7	21	B 2, l-b 7, w 2, n-b 6	17
1/7 2/45 3/70 4/100 5/319 6/347	(6 wkts) 350	1/27 2/93 3/118 4/144 5/180 6/191	(6 wkts dec.) 267

†A. J. Brassington, B. M. Brain and J. H. Childs did not bat.

Bowling: *First Innings*—Lever 23–5–79–4; Phillip 23–4–69–0; Turner 24–8–76–0; East 20–9–55–1; Acfield 10–3–50–1. *Second Innings*—Lever 18–2–66–1; Phillip 16–3–48–1; Turner 7–1–18–0; East 25–11–33–1; Acfield 31–1–85–2.

Essex

M. H. Denness c and b Graveney	81	– lbw b Procter	8
G. A. Gooch b Brain	7	– run out	50
K. S. McEwan c and b Graveney	73	– b Childs	38
*K. W. Fletcher not out	73	– st Stovold b Childs	14
B. R. Hardie not out	52	– b Procter	29
N. Phillip (did not bat)		– c and b Procter	134
S. Turner (did not bat)		– b Brain	9
†N. Smith (did not bat)		– b Brain	0
R. East (did not bat)		– not out	20
J. K. Lever (did not bat)		– not out	2
L-b 10, n-b 9	19	B 4, l-b 5	9
1/13 2/162 3/169	(3 wkts) 305	1/13 2/84 3/104 4/120 5/226 6/255 7/255 8/311	(8 wkts) 313

D. L. Acfield did not bat.

Bowling: *First Innings*—Brain 19–5–51–1; Procter 15–1–50–0; Childs 27–5–76–0; Partridge 9–1–37–0; Graveney 30–8–72–2. *Second Innings*—Brain 11–1–40–2; Procter 12.4–4–38–3; Childs 20–0–134–2; Graveney 20–7–92–0.

Umpires: A. G. T. Whitehead and T. G. Wilson.

GLOUCESTERSHIRE v GLAMORGAN

Played at Bristol, June 30, July 2, 3, 1979

Drawn. Although Sadiq scored a century in each innings, the hero of this match was 20-year-old Geoff Holmes, a former Lord's groundstaff boy. Coming in when Glamorgan's first innings was in tatters at 59 for five, for the next five hours he quietly and composedly wore down the attack. His innings was interrupted for twenty minutes by a swarm of bees and reflections from a window overlooking the ground. Nor did Procter spare the bouncer against him, and when 66 he wrenched a shoulder so badly that he played on in obvious pain. But with one 5 and twelve 4s as his chief hits he went steadily to a remarkable maiden hundred. Even though Sadiq scored 171 on the Saturday, Gloucestershire failed by a single run to earn the fourth batting point against accurate medium-pace bowling. His second century enabled Procter to declare, leaving Glamorgan to score 261 in two and three-quarter hours. But with Holmes fit to bat only in an emergency they showed no interest in the target.

Gloucestershire

A. W. Stovold c Lloyd b Swart	29	– c Hopkins b Cordle	20
Sadiq Mohammad c Holmes b Swart	171	– c Richards b Hobbs	103
Zaheer Abbas c A. Jones b Swart	9	– c and b Lloyd	46
J. C. Foat c E. W. Jones b Ontong	15	– not out	39
*M. J. Procter c A. Jones b Swart	3	– c Hopkins b Hobbs	22
A. J. Hignell c E. W. Jones b Nash	23	– not out	47
M. D. Partridge not out	29		
D. A. Graveney c E. W. Jones b Cordle	1		
†A. J. Brassington c E. W. Jones b Cordle	1		
B. M. Brain b Cordle	3		
J. H. Childs run out	7		
L-b 8	8	B 6, l-b 2, w 2, n-b 1	11
1/55 2/67 3/108 4/111 5/188 6/272 7/277 8/281 9/291	299	1/37 2/176 3/176 4/203	(4 wkts dec.) 288

Bowling: *First Innings*—Nash 22–6–63–1; Cordle 20–4–62–3; Swart 19–4–61–4; Ontong 15–5–29–1; Lloyd 17–3–53–0; Hobbs 7–1–23–0. *Second Innings*—Nash 15–3–37–0; Cordle 13–2–52–1; Hobbs 26–7–66–2; Swart 8–1–39–0; Ontong 3–0–15–0; Lloyd 15–3–68–1.

Glamorgan

A. Jones b Brain	10	– b Partridge	23
J. A. Hopkins lbw b Procter	1	– c Stovold b Partridge	48
R. C. Ontong b Procter	0	– c Sadiq b Stovold	50
P. D. Swart c Stovold b Childs	75	– not out	4
B. J. Lloyd lbw b Procter	12		
G. Richards b Procter	0		
G. C. Holmes not out	100		
†E. W. Jones c Zaheer b Brain	9	– not out	0
M. A. Nash c Hignell b Brain	41		
A. E. Cordle b Childs	22		
*R. N. S. Hobbs c Foat b Graveney	26		
B 6, l-b 7, w 1, n-b 17	31	L-b 1, w 1, n-b 7	9
1/6 2/6 3/18 4/39 5/59 6/144 7/159 8/234 9/282	327	1/29 2/116 3/134	(3 wkts) 134

Bowling: *First Innings*—Brain 29–10–73–3; Procter 31–4–112–4; Partridge 9–3–34–0; Childs 21–8–60–2; Graveney 3–1–17–1. *Second Innings*—Brain 3–1–13–0; Procter 2–1–2–0; Childs 20–3–60–0; Partridge 8–2–16–2; Graveney 11–3–30–0; Stovold 1–0–4–1.

Umpires: K. E. Palmer and D. L. Evans.

GLOUCESTERSHIRE v LEICESTERSHIRE

Played at Bristol, August 1, 2, 3, 1979

Gloucestershire won by eight wickets. Procter's marvellous all-round skills proved decisive as Gloucestershire gained their first Championship victory at the county ground for nearly three years. He not only hit a century before lunch but also achieved the hat-trick – a formidable double even by his exalted standards. Yet Leicestershire ended the first day in a position of dominance, having taken maximum batting points for the loss of four wickets and then removing three Gloucestershire batsmen for 25 thanks to a burst by Higgs with the new ball. Bainbridge went early on the second morning, but this exposed Leicestershire to Procter, who made 122 in 104 minutes with two 6s and nineteen 4s. Leicestershire lost two wickets clearing the arrears of 74 and were fewer than 50 ahead with six wickets left when a heavy shower caused an interruption. Thereafter Procter was lethal on the rain-affected pitch. Balderstone, Clift and Shuttleworth went to successive deliveries in a spell in which he picked up five wickets in sixteen balls for 1 run.

Leicestershire

B. Dudleston lbw b Bainbridge	78	– c Childs b Bainbridge	12
J. F. Steele b Brain	4	– b Procter	7
J. C. Balderstone c Stovold b Graveney	95	– c Hignell b Procter	56
B. F. Davison c Brassington b Childs	41	– lbw b Procter	35
N. E. Briers not out	66	– b Brain	3
†R. W. Tolchard not out	21	– not out	9
N. G. B. Cook (did not bat)		– c Sadiq b Brain	8
P. B. Clift (did not bat)		– lbw b Procter	0
K. Shuttleworth (did not bat)		– lbw b Procter	0
G. J. Parsons (did not bat)		– c Hignell b Procter	0
*K. Higgs (did not bat)		– c Brassington b Procter	1
L-b 3, n-b 6	9	L-b 1, w 1, n-b 1	3
1/7 2/160 3/202 4/231	(4 wkts) 314	1/8 2/25 3/95 4/113 5/123 6/124 7/124 8/124 9/132	134

Bowling: *First Innings*—Brain 17–3–55–1; Procter 8–2–32–0; Partridge 14–4–44–0; Childs 24–5–97–1; Graveney 27–13–55–1; Bainbridge 10–5–22–1. *Second Innings*—Brain 15–4–33–2; Procter 17.5–5–26–7; Partridge 4–0–13–0; Bainbridge 5–4–3–1; Graveney 7–1–17–0; Childs 5–0–23–0; Sadiq 6–1–16–0.

Gloucestershire

A. W. Stovold b Higgs	4	– b Cook	25
Sadiq Mohammad c and b Steele	137	– not out	28
Zaheer Abbas c Tolchard b Higgs	8	– run out	8
A. J. Hignell lbw b Higgs	0	– not out	0
P. Bainbridge c Briers b Cook	14		
*M. J. Procter c Tolchard b Parsons	122		
M. D. Partridge not out	74		
D. A. Graveney c and b Steele	1		
B. M. Brain b Parsons	9		
†A. J. Brassington not out	7		
B 7, l-b 3, n-b 2	12		
1/15 2/25 3/25 4/64 5/231 6/330 7/336 8/354	(8 wkts) 388	1/37 2/60	(2 wkts) 61

J. H. Childs did not bat.

Bowling: *First Innings*—Parsons 14–3–77–2; Higgs 19–4–58–3; Shuttleworth 16–3–56–0; Cook 24–8–59–1; Steele 11–2–48–2; Clift 14–3–62–0; Balderstone 2–1–16–0. *Second Innings*—Higgs 3–2–9–0; Shuttleworth 4–2–7– 0; Clift 7–1–23–0; Cook 8–2–15–1; Steele 2.4–0–7–0.

Umpires: R. Julian and R. Palmer.

GLOUCESTERSHIRE v YORKSHIRE

Played at Cheltenham, August 11, 13, 14, 1979

Drawn. Though ruined by rain, this match was nevertheless full of incident. Yorkshire made a splendid recovery after Procter had shocked them on the Saturday by claiming the second all-lbw hat-trick of his career and his second in successive games. Bowling round the wicket, he sent back Lumb, Athey and Hampshire, beating them with speed and in-swing under overcast skies. Yorkshire were 42 for four at the close and declined further to 52 for five early on Monday, all wickets falling to the Gloucestershire captain. Only Boycott remained immovable, and by the time rain stopped play in early afternoon he and Carrick had the innings on a firmer footing. Play was not possible again until after lunch on Tuesday. The pitch dried too slowly for the spinners, and although Childs hurried one through to get Boycott lbw for 95, Carrick proceeded to enjoy himself. He hit his way to his highest effort – 128 not out, including three 6s and eighteen 4s. The feature of the Gloucestershire innings was a first Championship century for Hignell, who when 7 played a ball from Cope into his stumps without dislodging a bail.

Gloucestershire

A. W. Stovold c Lumb b Sidebottom 62
Sadiq Mohammad c Hampshire b Stevenson. 4
Zaheer Abbas b Sidebottom 29
M. W. Stovold c Bairstow b Carrick. 2
*M. J. Procter b Athey b Carrick 17
A. J. Hignell b Old .102
M. D. Partridge c Athey b Cope. 10
D. A. Graveney not out 30
B. M. Brain c Lumb b Old 17
B 1, l-b 4, n-b 10 15

1/8 2/63 3/67 4/102 5/150 6/209 7/258 8/288 (8 wkts) 288

†A. J. Brassington and J. H. Childs did not bat.

Bowling: Old 17–5–53–2; Stevenson 14–3–37–1; Sidebottom 15–4–39–2; Carrick 30–11–76–2; Cope 23–6–64–1; Athey 1–0–4–0.

Yorkshire

G. Boycott lbw b Childs 95
R. G. Lumb lbw b Procter 11
C. W. J. Athey lbw b Procter 0
*J. H. Hampshire lbw b Procter 0
K. Sharp c Zaheer b Procter. 0
†D. L. Bairstow b Procter. 7
P. Carrick not out 128
A. Sidebottom b Procter 16
G. B. Stevenson c M. W. Stovold b Childs . . 10
C. M. Old not out 18
B 7, l-b 4, w 1, n-b 6 18

1/18 2/18 3/18 4/24 5/54 6/189 7/237 8/252 (8 wkts dec.) 303

G. A. Cope did not bat.

Bowling: Brain 20–6–42–0; Procter 36–11–107–6; Childs 23–3–84–2; Graveney 12–2–44–0; Partridge 1–0–8–0.

Umpires: K. E. Palmer and R. Julian.

GLOUCESTERSHIRE v WORCESTERSHIRE

Played at Cheltenham, August 6, 7, 8, 1980

Gloucestershire won by 96 runs. After a relatively quiet season Procter exploded into life with a vengeance, taking fourteen wickets to record the best Championship bowling performance of the season. He was not idle with the bat either; his powerfully hit 73 took Gloucestershire to a respectable total after they had been put in. No-one else could cope with the bowling of Inchmore and Pridgeon, ably assisted by wicket-keeper Fisher, who took five catches on his début following his move from Middlesex. Worcestershire ended the first day at 84 for one but totalled only 111 after Procter's spell of seven wickets for 9 runs the following morning. It was a mixture of pace and off-spin which brought him his second innings haul of seven for 60 as Worcestershire were defeated, despite a defiant half-century from Ormrod.

Gloucestershire

B. C. Broad c Fisher b Holder	9	– c and b Inchmore	5
Sadiq Mohammad c Fisher b Inchmore	5	– c Younis b Holder	12
Zaheer Abbas c Younis b Inchmore	0	– c Fisher b Pridgeon	34
A. W. Stovold c Fisher b Inchmore	32	– c Fisher b Pridgeon	7
*M. J. Procter c Fisher b Inchmore	73	– c Neale b Pridgeon	35
P. Bainbridge c Younis b Inchmore	2	– c Turner b Gifford	18
D. A. Graveney c Fisher b Pridgeon	15	– c Holder b Inchmore	42
A. H. Wilkins c Gifford b Pridgeon	3	– c Turner b Gifford	0
†A. J. Brassington c Gifford b Pridgeon	2	– b Inchmore	2
B. M. Brain c Gifford b Pridgeon	23	– c Henderson b Inchmore	0
J. H. Childs not out	1	– not out	6
L-b 6, w 3, n-b 4	13	L-b 2, w 5, n-b 9	16
1/8 2/8 3/27 4/111 5/121 6/134 7/137 8/143 9/172	178	1/21 2/23 3/41 4/86 5/110 6/126 7/126 8/134 9/134	177

Bowling: *First Innings*—Holder 13–3–52–1; Inchmore 20–3–62–5; Gifford 2–0–5–0; Pridgeon 16.2–3–46–4. *Second Innings*—Holder 16–2–41–1; Inchmore 17.5–4–59–4; Pridgeon 12–1–42–3; Gifford 15–7–19–2.

Worcestershire

G. M. Turner c Sadiq b Procter	57	– c Brassington b Procter	0
J. A. Ormrod c Sadiq b Bainbridge	26	– c Sadiq b Childs	53
P. A. Neale c Brassington b Procter	0	– c Childs b Procter	1
Younis Ahmed b Wilkins	9	– c Brain b Procter	15
B. J. R. Jones c Brassington b Procter	1	– c Graveney b Procter	0
S. P. Henderson c and b Procter	7	– c Brassington b Procter	38
†P. B. Fisher c Sadiq b Wilkins	0	– c Bainbridge b Procter	2
J. D. Inchmore b Procter	4	– st Brassington b Childs	9
V. A. Holder not out	5	– c Brassington b Childs	1
*N. Gifford c Sadiq b Procter	0	– not out	13
A. P. Pridgeon b Procter	0	– c Wilkins b Procter	10
L-b 2	2	B 3, l-b 1, w 1, n-b 1	6
1/72 2/84 3/85 4/93 5/97 6/97 7/102 8/111 9/111	111	1/1 2/9 3/29 4/29 5/105 6/111 7/111 8/112 9/137	148

Bowling: *First Innings*—Brain 10–2–29–0; Procter 15.5–7–16–7; Wilkins 19–4–52–2; Bainbridge 2–0–12–1. *Second Innings*—Procter 27.3–9–60–7; Wilkins 9–1–35–0; Graveney 10–2–19–0; Childs 13–4–28–3.

Umpires: J. G. Langridge and D. J. Dennis.

GLOUCESTERSHIRE v MIDDLESEX

Played at Cheltenham, August 9, 11, 12, 1980

Gloucestershire won by six wickets. The champions elect had a grip on this match until the final afternnoon, when a remarkable innings by Procter won the match for Gloucestershire, who had narrowly averted the follow on. Middlesex were put in on a damp pitch and did well to reach 220. At the close, van der Bijl, fully exploiting the conditions, had reduced Gloucestershire to 37 for five. However, Broad stood firm and, with Graveney and Wilkins making valuable contributions, Middlesex's lead was restricted to 111. Stoppages for rain reduced Middlesex's second innings batting time but Brearley's declaration, leaving the opposition 270 in 285 minutes, looked reasonable. Zaheer hit briskly for a while yet, with three down for 65, Gloucestershire looked a beaten side. Then entered Procter to play one of his finest innings, making the formidable Middlesex attack look almost ordinary. He gave one chance, at 58 when Brearley missed him at second slip of Daniel, but otherwise it was a virtuoso display, full of cultured drives and cuts. Sadiq and Bainbridge played the supporting rôles as Procter finished the match with more than an hour to spare, scoring his only century of the season but one of the best ever seen on the College ground.

Middlesex

*J. M. Brearley lbw b Brain	5	– lbw b Wilkins	54
†P. R. Downton c Bainbridge b Procter	44	– lbw b Graveney	16
C. T. Radley c Bainbridge b Brain	17	– (4) not out	21
R. O. Butcher st Brassington b Childs	35	– (5) c Broad b Wilkins	15
G. D. Barlow c Wilkins b Brain	47	– (3) c Bainbridge b Wilkins	18
K. P. Tomlins c Sadiq b Brain	34	– not out	20
V. A. P. van der Bijl c Procter b Childs	3		
M. W. W. Selvey lbw b Wilkins	21		
R. Maru c Sadiq b Brain	1		
F. J. Titmus lbw b Procter	4		
W. W. Daniel not out	0		
L-b 8, n-b 1	9	B 4, l-b 7, n-b 3	14
1/11 2/33 3/92 4/111 5/189 6/190 7/192 8/199 9/220	220	1/44 2/86 3/99 4/121	(4 wkts dec.) 158

Bowling: *First Innings*—Brain 18–6–46–5; Procter 16.1–5–40–2; Wilkins 10–4–22–1; Bainbridge 2–0–6–0; Graveney 22–12–36–0; Childs 23–10–61–2. *Second Innings*—Brain 12–0–55–0; Procter 4–1–12–0; Wilkins 8–2–31–3; Graveney 12–5–19–1; Childs 11–4–27–0.

Gloucestershire

B. C. Broad c Downton b Titmus	36	– c Maru b Titmus	11
Sadiq Mohammad c Titmus b van der Bijl	6	– (3) b Daniel	37
Zaheer Abbas c Radley b Daniel	1	– (4) c Radley b Daniel	37
A. W. Stovold b van der Bijl	1	– (2) c Radley b van der Bijl	10
*M. J. Procter b van der Bijl	4	– not out	134
†A. J. Brassington lbw b van der Bijl	2		
P. Bainbridge c Downton b Daniel	1	– (6) not out	32
D. A. Graveney c Downton b Daniel	18		
A. H. Wilkins b Daniel	23		
B. M. Brain not out	8		
J. H. Childs c Downton b Daniel	4		
L-b 2, w 1, n-b 2	5	L-b 2, w 1, n-b 7	10
1/12 2/13 3/16 4/30 5/36 6/41 7/63 8/96 9/101	109	1/15 2/24 3/65 4/172	(4 wkts) 271

Bowling: *First Innings*—van der Bijl 19–1–45–4; Daniel 15.4–5–32–5; Titmus 12–3–25–1 Maru 1–0–2–0. *Second Innings*—van der Bijl 16–1–70–1; Daniel 16–3–61–2; Titmus 14–2–43–1 Maru 2–0–22–0; Selvey 9–0–36–0; Tomlins 2–0–21–0; Brearley 0.4–0–8–0.

Umpires: D. G. L. Evans and R. Palmer.

GLOUCESTERSHIRE v SOMERSET

Played at Bristol, August 23, 25, 26 1980

Drawn. Somerset took six extra points as the team batting last in a match in which th scores finished level. Championship regulations and The Laws of Cricket were require reading at the end. Roebuck, needing a single off the last ball, attempted a run with th bails off and the ball in Brassington's gloves. But umpire Palmer had already called "over" to finish the match after rejecting Gloucestershire's appeals for lbw. This was one of th best West Country derby games for many years. Gloucestershire struggled agains Dredge but still reached a substantial total. However, Somerset took control thanks to third-wicket partnership of 239 in 51 overs between Roebuck and Richards, who hit thre 6s – all off Graveney – and twenty-six 4s. With Stovold and Sadiq adding 138 and Procte attempting the season's fastest century (84 in 48 minutes), Gloucestershire looked lik saving the game with ease. But the later batsmen were swept aside by Marks, an Somerset needed 201 in 38 overs. When Richards, unwell, was caught first ball they wer in trouble at 140 for six before Roebuck and Popplewell took them to the brink of victory.

Gloucestershire

A. W. Stovold b Popplewell	37	– c and b Lloyds	8
B. C. Broad run out	0	– c Popplewell b Gore	
Sadiq Mohammad b Dredge	43	– c Popplewell b Lloyds	9
Zaheer Abbas c Popplewell b Dredge	5	– absent hurt	
*M. J. Procter c Botham b Dredge	57	– (4) st Gard b Marks	8
M. D. Partridge c Olive b Botham	48	– (5) c Olive b Marks	1
D. A. Graveney c Richards b Dredge	55	– (6) c Botham b Marks	1
A. H. Wilkins c Botham b Popplewell	32	– (7) b Marks	1
†A. J. Brassington b Popplewell	12	– (8) b Marks	
B. M. Brain c Gard b Dredge	4	– (9) b Lloyds	
J. H. Childs not out	1	– (10) not out	
B 1, l-b 8, w 1, n-b 5	15	B 4, l-b 6, n-b 7	1
1/6 2/69 3/74 4/112 5/161 6/224 7/274 8/290 9/299	309	1/14 2/152 3/272 4/276 5/300 6/313 7/316 8/317 9/317	31

Bowling: *First Innings*—Gore 12–3–34–0; Dredge 32–6–95–5; Popplewell 23.5–5–54–3 Richards 6–0–24–0; Botham 14–5–55–1; Marks 9–2–32–0. *Second Innings*—Gore 13–2–48–1 Dredge 10–0–47–0; Marks 30–11–77–5; Lloyds 29.2–11–77–3; Popplewell 8–1–51–0.

Somerset

M. Olive c Brassington b Brain	1	– c Sadiq b Childs	21
J. W. Lloyds c Brassington b Brain	33	– c Childs b Graveney	64
I. V. A. Richards c Brain b Childs	170	– (7) c sub b Graveney	0
P. M. Roebuck st Brassington b Childs	101	– (6) not out	37
P. W. Denning c Procter b Wilkins	4	– (4) run out	1
*I. T. Botham c Childs b Wilkins	18	– (5) c sub b Graveney	13
V. J. Marks c Brassington b Childs	29	– (3) st Brassington b Graveney	32
N. F. M. Popplewell st Brassington b Childs	19	– b Brain	25
†T. Gard b Procter	22		
C. H. Dredge not out	13	– (9) not out	1
H. I. E. Gore b Procter	4		
B 9, n-b 3	12	L-b 6	6
1/4 2/61 3/300 4/311 5/333 6/342 7/371 8/390 9/419	426	1/70 2/96 3/104 4/119 5/140 6/140 7/197	(7 wkts) 200

Bowling: *First Innings*—Brain 20–1–91–2; Wilkins 24–5–94–2; Procter 2.5–0–13–2; Partridge 6–0–43–0; Graveney 23–2–103–0; Childs 25–6–70–4. *Second Innings*—Brain 8–2–32–1; Wilkins 4–0–24–0; Childs 15–0–73–1; Procter 2–0–12–0; Graveney 9–0–53–4.

Umpires: K. E. Palmer and C. T. Spencer.

GLOUCESTERSHIRE v WARWICKSHIRE

Played at Gloucester, June 27, 29, 30, 1981

Drawn. There were two outstanding personal achievements in a match that featured three challenging declarations. Zaheer became the first to 1,000 runs when he reached 35 in his second innings, all his runs having come in June. Only Grace and Hammond among Gloucestershire batsmen have previously achieved the feat during a calendar month – May in their case. Humpage followed a career-best 146 with a second innings century to avert a threatened collapse and so become one of those few wicket-keepers who have made two hundreds in the same match. Willis's second declaration left Gloucestershire a reasonable target of 282 in about four hours and with Zaheer and Procter together at tea at 115 for four, an interesting struggle was in prospect. However, both fell soon afterwards to Ferreira, leaving Bainbridge and Graveney to see the match through to a draw.

Warwickshire

D. L. Amiss c Wilkins b Bainbridge	22	– c Procter b Bainbridge	18
G. P. Thomas b Childs	43	– lbw b Procter	6
T. A. Lloyd c Zaheer b Surridge	78	– c Stovold b Procter	0
†G. W. Humpage c Childs b Wilkins	146	– b Wilkins	110
Asif Din lbw b Wilkins	5	– c Graveney b Wilkins	43
S. H. Wootton c Sadiq b Procter	16	– not out	26
A. M. Ferreira not out	3	– c Hignell b Zaheer	19
G. C. Small (did not bat)		– c Childs b Zaheer	0
*R. G. D. Willis (did not bat)		– c Surridge b Zaheer	6
W. Hogg (did not bat)		– not out	11
B 3, l-b 6, w 1, n-b 2	12	B 9, l-b 9	18
1/70 2/70 3/299 4/299 5/312 6/325	(6 wkts dec.) 325	1/11 2/11 3/66 4/186 5/197 6/225 7/225 8/241	(8 wkts dec.) 257

D. R. Doshi did not bat.

Bowling: *First Innings*——Procter 11–2–40–1; Surridge 16–2–65–1; Wilkins 16–3–60–2; Bainbridge 11–2–27–1; Childs 31–5–84–1; Graveney 11–0–37–0. *Second Innings*—Procter 16–6–30–2; Surridge 10–4–21–0; Bainbridge 8–2–17–1; Wilkins 18–6–44–2; Childs 23–8–57–0; Graveney 15–5–27–0; Zaheer 5–0–32–3; Sadiq 4–1–11–0.

Gloucestershire

B. C. Broad c Amiss b Hogg	16	– (2) c Lloyd b Willis	10
Sadiq Mohammad lbw b Hogg	3	– (1) c Wootton b Small	25
†A. W. Stovold c Humpage b Willis	37	– b Willis	1
Zaheer Abbas lbw b Small	100	– c Amiss b Ferreira	51
A. J. Hignell lbw b Doshi	39	– b Small	14
*M. J. Procter c Thomas b Small	31	– c Thomas b Ferreira	1
P. Bainbridge c Humpage b Small	3	– not out	43
D. A. Graveney not out	28	– not out	37
A. H. Wilkins c Humpage b Small	1		
J. H. Childs not out	19		
B 5, l-b 7, w 2, n-b 10	24	B 8, l-b 1, w 3, n-b 4	16
1/19 2/22 3/109 4/183 5/231 6/248 7/248 8/250	(8 wkts dec.) 301	1/36 2/39 3/49 4/92 5/116 6/119	(6 wkts) 198

D. Surridge did not bat.

Bowling: *First Innings*—Small 20–4–70–4; Hogg 14–4–50–2; Willis 13.2–2–40–1; Doshi 25–5–74–1; Ferreira 8–0–43–0. *Second Innings*—Willis 14–3–32–2; Hogg 8–1–22–0; Doshi 17–8–34–0; Small 9–0–47–2; Ferreira 10–1–31–2; Asif Din 4–1–9–0; Wootton 1–0–7–0.

Umpires: A. G. T. Whitehead and R. S. Herman.

GLOUCESTERSHIRE v SOMERSET

Played at Bristol, August 29, 31, September 1, 1981

Somerset won by 58 runs. Bowlers of all types enjoyed this West Country derby in which twenty wickets fell on the first day. Eighteen-year old Ollis, on his first-class début, was one of only three Somerset batsmen to reach 20, while Doughty, a twenty-year-old Yorkshire-born fast bowler from the Lord's groundstaff and also making his début, dismissed both Rose and Marks. Garner and Dredge then swept through the Gloucestershire batting with only Bainbridge delaying them. When, on Monday, Lloyds and Ollis put together an opening partnership of 99 to increase a first innings lead of 71, Gloucestershire looked well beaten, but now it was the turn of Childs, with his left-arm spin, to bemuse the batsmen. His return of nine for 56 was the season's best in first-class cricket, and any thoughts that the pitch had become a slow turner were soon discarded as Garner and Dredge removed the early Gloucestershire batting. However, Zaheer and Hignell settled in to produce the best batting of the match, their partnership carrying the socre, on the third day, to 128 before the fourth wicket fell. Dredge, following a career-best six for 37 in the first innings, removed them both and Garner proved too much for the later batsmen although none of them surrendered tamely.

Somerset

J. W. Lloyds b Wilkins	6	– c A. W. Stovold b Childs	75
R. L. Ollis lbw b Wilkins	20	– c Broad b Childs	18
N. F. M. Popplewell c Wilkins b Bainbridge	21	– b Graveney	8
P. M. Roebuck b Bainbridge	18	– lbw b Childs	2
P. W. Denning c M. W. Stovold b Bainbridge	9	– c Sadiq b Childs	23
*B. C. Rose c M. W. Stovold b Doughty	13	– c and b Childs	6
V. J. Marks c Broad b Doughty	0	– c Zaheer b Childs	18
†D. J. S. Taylor c Zaheer b Wilkins	19	– c Sadiq b Childs	1
J. Garner c Hignell b Wilkins	20	– c Broad b Childs	7
H. R. Moseley b Bainbridge	2	– (11) c and b Childs	1
C. H. Dredge not out	0	– (10) not out	6
B 5, l-b 9, w 4, n-b 1	19	B 7, l-b 3, w 5	15
1/12 2/40 3/76 4/84 5/103 6/103 7/108 8/139 9/147	147	1/99 2/104 3/110 4/110 5/125 6/149 7/153 8/165 9/178	180

Bowling: *First Innings*—Wilkins 18.3–5–62–4; Doughty 19–9–28–2; Bainbridge 18–2–38–4. *Second Innings*—11–3–32–0; Doughty 8–1–27–0; Childs 32.3–13–56–9; Graveney 30–15–50–1.

Gloucestershire

B. C. Broad c Roebuck b Garner	6	– (2) c Roebuck b Dredge	0
Sadiq Mohammad b Garner	6	– (1) c Lloyds b Garner	8
P. Bainbridge c Popplewell b Garner	29	– c Rose b Garner	13
Zaheer Abbas lbw b Dredge	7	– b Dredge	72
A. J. Hignell c Taylor b Dredge	1	– lbw b Dredge	38
†A. W. Stovold b Dredge	0	– c Roebuck b Garner	7
M. W. Stovold c Taylor b Dredge	0	– b Garner	3
*D. A. Graveney c Lloyds b Garner	2	– (9) not out	11
R. J. Doughty b Dredge	7	– (8) b Garner	10
J. H. Childs not out	4	– c Moseley b Marks	6
A. H. Wilkins b Dredge	5	– b Garner	10
B 4, l-b 3, w 2	9	B 5, l-b 4, w 1, n-b 5	15
1/11 2/16 3/45 4/49 5/55 6/55 7/57 8/66 9/66	76	1/4 2/12 3/30 4/128 5/145 6/145 7/154 8/163 9/179	193

Bowling: *First Innings*—Garner 17–5–24–4; Moseley 6–3–6–0; Dredge 10.4–3–37–6. *Second Innings*—Garner 26.4–7–56–6; Dredge 25–6–63–3; Marks 18–7–46–1; Lloyds 1–0–2–0; Moseley 8–3–11–0.

Umpires: Mahboob Shah and P. B. Wight.

HAMPSHIRE

HAMPSHIRE v LEICESTERSHIRE

Played at Portsmouth, June 27, 29, 30, 1964

Leicestershire won by five wickets. On a pitch which remained true throughout the match bowlers never really gained the upper hand. Livingstone laid the foundation of the Hampshire first innings total of 327, his 124 including one 6 and seventeen 4s. Leicestershire lost six wickets for 96, but Inman and Burch demonstrated the easy nature of the turf by adding 135 for the seventh wicket. Inman reached his century after four and a half hours. Leicestershire were left to score 237 to win in two and a quarter hours and Inman completed a fine match by hitting the winning run with five minutes left. Timms dismissed six batsmen from behind the stumps during the Leicestershire first innings, a record for Hampshire.

Hampshire

R. E. Marshall c Hallam b Spencer	21		
G. L. Keith c Pratt b Cross	0	– c Burch b Spencer	2
J. R. Gray b Cross	55	– b Pratt	54
D. A. Livingstone c Booth b Savage	124	– c Jayasinghe b Savage	28
R. G. Caple c Jayasinghe b Smith	33	– not out	29
P. J. Sainsbury c Burch b Cross	19		
*A. C. D. Ingleby-Mackenzie c Burch b Cross	43	– run out	18
†B. S. V. Timms lbw b Pratt	22		
D. Shackleton c Cross b Pratt	5		
D. W. White run out	0	– not out	25
R. M. H. Cottam not out	1		
B 2, l-b 2	4	B 4, l-b 2, n-b 1	7
1/0 2/30 3/141 4/223 5/237 6/275 7/310 8/322 9/322	327	1/72 2/84 3/132 4/133 (4 wkts dec.)	186

Bowling: *First Innings*—Spencer 19–4–65–1; Cross 24–3–76–4; Pratt 6.1–2–17–2; Savage 19–4–56–1; Smith 22–5–69–1; Birkenshaw 9–2–26–0; Jayasinghe 4–1–14–0. *Second Innings*—Spencer 18–5–34–1; Cross 13–3–37–0; Booth 2–1–5–0; Pratt 17–6–58–1; Savage 14–4–45–1.

Leicestershire

*M. R. Hallam b Cottam	11	– c sub b Sainsbury	33
B. J. Booth b Cottam	7	– b White	3
G. Cross c Timms b Shackleton	4	– st Timms b Sainsbury	78
C. C. Inman c Sainsbury b Shackleton	106	– not out	43
S. Jayasinghe c Timms b Gray	20	– c Timms b Sainsbury	34
J. Birkenshaw st Timms b Gray	20	– not out	9
R. L. Pratt st Timms b Gray	0		
†G. W. Burch c Timms b Shackleton	59		
R. C. Smith c Timms b Shackleton	0		
C. T. Spencer b Shackleton	40	– b White	32
J. S. Savage not out	5		
N-b 5	5	L-b 4, n-b 1	5
1/15 2/20 3/46 4/72 5/94 6/96 7/231 8/231 9/246	277	1/6 2/85 3/151 4/154 5/214 (5 wkts)	237

Bowling: *First Innings*—Shackleton 30.3–15–56–5; White 28–6–76–0; Cottam 16–4–47–2; Gray 6–0–28–3; Caple 5–0–20–0; Sainsbury 16–5–35–0; Keith 4–1–10–0. *Second Innings*—Shackleton 22–4–52–0; White 10.5–2–42–2; Cottam 5–0–21–0; Sainsbury 18–4–78–3; Gray 8–1–39–0.

Umpires: N. Oldfield and J. F. Crapp.

HAMPSHIRE v WORCESTERSHIRE

Played at Bournemouth, August 25, 26, 27, 1965

Worcestershire won by 115 runs. Victory for them was essential to keep alive their chance of retaining the Championship. The fact that there were three declarations, Hampshire closing their first innings 146 behind, caused a great deal of controversy, but this was the pattern of many other matches during the wet season. Kenyon reacted promptly to Ingleby-Mackenzie's closure on the last day by declaring after the Hampshire captain himself had opened the bowling and delivered only one ball. Rain on the second day had cut the playing time by half and when Hampshire, struggling to save the follow on, had made 76 on Friday morning while losing only two wickets there seemed no reason to expect that their batting would collapse when they were left to get 147 to win in two hours, forty minutes. Suddenly, powerful sunshine turned the wet pitch into a batsman's nightmare after lunch and Hampshire were shot out in sixty-five minutes for 31. Flavell took five for nine and Coldwell five for 22.

Worcestershire

*D. Kenyon c Sainsbury b White	12		
R. G. A. Headley c Reed b Sainsbury	123	– not out	0
J. A. Ormrod c Shackleton b Sainsbury	17		
T. W. Graveney c Keith b Shackleton	104		
B. D'Oliveira lbw b Shackleton	44		
D. Richardson c Wassell b Shackleton	9		
†R. Booth b White	25	– not out	0
D. N. F. Slade c Reed b White	7		
N. Gifford b Shackleton	12		
L. J. Coldwell not out	0		
B 6, l-b 4	10		
1/18 2/71 3/247 4/274 5/290 6/327 7/349 8/352 9/363 (9 wkts dec.)	363	(no wkt dec.)	0

J. A. Flavell did not bat.

Bowling: *First Innings*—Shackleton 34.4–14–66–4; White 27–7–86–3; Sainsbury 24–9–72–2; Wassell 19–4–81–0; Caple 7–0–35–0; Keith 3–0–13–0. *Second Innings*—Ingleby-Mackenzie 0.1–0–0–0.

Hampshire

R. E. Marshall c Headley b Coldwell	12 – c Headley b Flavell	5
B. L. Reed b Coldwell	55 – c Flavell b Coldwell	8
A. Wassell c D'Oliveira b Coldwell	6 – c Graveney b Coldwell	0
H. Horton c Richardson b D'Oliveira	10 – c Slade b Coldwell	5
R. G. Caple c Booth b Coldwell	61 – c Kenyon b Flavell	0
G. L. Keith c Headley b Flavell	12 – c Booth b Flavell	0
P. J. Sainsbury not out	31 – b Flavell	0
†B. S. V. Timms not out	25 – not out	1
*A. C. D. Ingleby-Mackenzie (did not bat)	– c Booth b Coldwell	4
D. Shackleton (did not bat)	– c Graveney b Coldwell	4
D. W. White (did not bat)	– b Flavell	2
B 4, l-b 1	5	
1/19 2/37 3/68 4/118 5/150 6/170	(6 wkts dec.) 217 1/6 2/15 3/18 4/18 5/18 6/22 7/24 8/24 9/28	31

Bowling: *First Innings*—Flavell 36–13–74–1; Coldwell 33–10–61–4; Gifford 20–13–24–0; Slade 7–4–4–0; D'Oliveira 26–14–29–1; Ormrod 2–0–5–0; Kenyon 1–0–3–0; Richardson 1–0–12–0. *Second Innings*—Flavell 8.3–4–9–5; Coldwell 8–2–22–5.

Umpires: J. F. Crapp and H. Yarnold.

NOTES BY THE EDITOR, 1966

CONTROVERSIAL DECLARATIONS

Manufactured finishes to County matches have become common in the last ten years, due to the negative attitude most counties adopt towards run-getting on the first two days. The matter blew up at the end of the season when Worcestershire snatched a valuable victory over Hampshire at Bournemouth after A. C. D. Ingleby-Mackenzie closed his first innings at lunch-time. In any case, the sun had transformed the pitch and no doubt Worcestershire would have needed only a few overs to dispose of the tail. The general grievance was that Worcestershire were given a chance to get ten points when their main rivals, Northamptonshire, had completed their programme. Northamptonshire did not complain. They remembered they received similar generosity at Clacton when T. E. Bailey, the Essex captain, declared 145 behind with only six wickets down, and that K. V. Andrew promptly declared his second innings when only one ball had been bowled. Then they shot out Essex for 88.

HAMPSHIRE v LEICESTERSHIRE

Played at Portsmouth, May 6, 7, 8, 1967

Leicestershire won by eight wickets. Leicestershire's captain Lock had a big share in his side's victory. He put Hampshire in on a wet wicket, took four wickets for 35, and was top scorer with 46 in his side's first innings. Hampshire started badly, losing Marshall and Reed, the openers, for only five runs. Horton and Livingstone improved matters, but the innings closed for 122. Leicestershire were ahead (133 for seven) by the close and the next day – the first time Hampshire had played on Sunday in home games – took their total to 206 in spite of the efforts of White, who took five wickets for 49. In their second innings Hampshire had no answer to the pace of Spencer and Cotton, though a sixth-wicket stand of 83 by Sainsbury and Timms checked Leicestershire. Hampshire were out for 183 and Leicestershire, on a drying wicket had plenty of time to get the 100 runs needed for victory. White raised Hampshire's hopes by dismissing the first two batsmen for eight runs, but Hallam and Inman saw Leicestershire to victory. Lock claimed the first Sunday hat-trick by bowling Livingstone after dismissing White and Cottam the previous day.

Hampshire

*R. E. Marshall c Marner b Cotton	3	– b Spencer	7
B. L. Reed c Tolchard b Spencer	0	– c Tolchard b Cotton	1
H. Horton c Constant b Birkenshaw	24	– b Spencer	23
D. A. Livingstone c Hallam b Birkenshaw	44	– b Lock	9
K. J. Wheatley c Hallam b Lock	1	– c Constant b Spencer	19
P. J. Sainsbury c Hallam b Birkenshaw	17	– c Tolchard b Cotton	48
†B. S. V. Timms lbw b Lock	12	– b Cotton	34
A. T. Castell b Birkenshaw	4	– not out	6
D. Shackleton not out	2	– lbw b Cotton	2
D. W. White c Spencer b Lock	11	– b Spencer	2
R. M. H. Cottam b Lock	0	– c and b Cotton	13
L-b 4	4	B 9	9
1/3 2/5 3/67 4/68 5/78 6/95 7/105 8/109 9/122	122	1/4 2/10 3/23 4/58 5/65 6/148 7/151 8/153 9/166	183

Bowling: *First Innings*—Spencer 4–1–7–1; Cotton 5–1–13–1; Lock 21.4–9–37–4; Birkenshaw 20–3–57–4; Marner 1–0–4–0. *Second Innings*—Spencer 27–8–48–4; Cotton 19.3–4–42–5; Lock 27–9–52–1; Birkenshaw 16–4–32–0.

Leicestershire

M. R. Hallam b White	1	– not out	26
B. J. Booth run out	20	– b White	3
M. E. Norman run out	30	– lbw b White	0
C. C. Inman c Livingstone b Castell	2	– not out	65
P. Marner c Wheatley b Sainsbury	27		
D. Constant b White	22		
J. Birkenshaw c Timms b White	28		
†R. W. Tolchard b White	0		
*G. A. R. Lock c Castell b White	46		
C. T. Spencer c Wheatley b Cottam	13		
J. Cotton not out	4		
B 6, l-b 6, n-b 2	13	B 4, l-b 1, n-b 1	6
1/1 2/49 3/52 4/74 5/90 6/131 7/133 8/160 9/182	206	1/8 2/8	(2 wkts) 100

Bowling: *First Innings*—Shackleton 16–9–23–0; White 19.4–7–49–5; Cottam 19–4–51–1; Castell 15–4–31–1; Sainsbury 22–10–39–1. *Second Innings*—Shackleton 13–8–14–0; White 9–3–19–2; Cottam 9–2–21–0; Castell 8–1–23–0; Sainsbury 2–1–5–0; Wheatley 1.5–0–12–0.

Umpires: J. S. Buller and A. E. Alderman.

HAMPSHIRE v KENT

Played at Bournemouth, July 9, 10, 11, 1969

Hampshire won by ten wickets. Hampshire won with ease to increase their challenge in the County Championship after Kent had laboured on a slow but true wicket. In reaching a first-innings total of 96, Kent scored 22 in 20 overs and 79 in 59 overs and only Luckhurst, who carried his bat for 46, showed any degree of comfort. Although Graham troubled Hampshire, they built a lead of 125 thanks mainly to Marshall, but it was not without cost for the Hampshire captain broke a thumb when hit by a ball from Graham. Against the pace of White and the off-spin of Richards, Kent fared only a little better when they batted again. Asif and Dixon offered resistance, but on the final day the last four wickets fell for 12 runs and Hampshire were left with a simple task.

Kent

B. W. Luckhurst not out	46	– b White	3
*M. H. Denness b Cottam	11	– c Castell b Sainsbury	17
†D. Nicholls c Richards b Castell	7	– c sub b Richards	13
Asif Iqbal c and b Cottam	8	– st Stephenson b Richards	29
S. E. Leary run out	15	– not out	15
A. Ealham c Gilliat b Sainsbury	1	– b Richards	6
R. A. Woolmer lbw b Cottam	1	– c Lewis b Sainsbury	13
A. L. Dixon c Lewis b Sainsbury	5	– c Stephenson b White	25
A. J. Hooper b Sainsbury	0	– c Lewis b White	0
J. N. Graham run out	1	– c sub b White	8
J. C. Dye c Lewis b Sainsbury	0	– b White	4
L-b 1	1	L-b 2, w 2, n-b 1	5
1/20 2/32 3/54 4/69 5/71 6/76 7/87 8/89 9/90	96	1/8 2/25 3/64 4/67 5/75 6/101 7/126 8/126 9/134	138

Bowling: *First Innings*—White 4–0–11–0; Cottam 30–14–30–3; Sainsbury 31.1–17–38–4; Castell 5–1–16–1. *Second Innings*—White 20.4–10–24–5; Cottam 18–8–32–0; Sainsbury 22–10–47–2; Castell 5–2–9–0; Richards 11–5–21–3.

Hampshire

B. A. Richards lbw b Dixon	32		
B. L. Reed b Graham	20	– not out	0
R. M. C. Gilliat c Ealham b Hooper	32		
*R. E. Marshall c Nicholls b Graham	67		
P. J. Sainsbury c Denness b Graham	4		
D. A. Livingstone b Dixon	18		
R. V. Lewis c Nicholls b Dixon	17	– not out	12
†G. R. Stephenson lbw b Graham	5		
A. T. Castell not out	2		
R. M. H. Cottam b Graham	4		
D. W. White c Nicholls b Graham	0		
B 12, l-b 1, n-b 7	20	L-b 4	4
1/43 2/77 3/115 4/135 5/175 6/205 7/213 8/215 9/221	221		(no wkt) 16

Bowling: *First Innings*—Graham 39.3–14–57–6; Dye 4–1–12–0; Dixon 25–6–65–3; Hooper 22–7–67–1. *Second Innings*—Graham 2–2–0–0; Dye 1.2–0–12–0.

Umpires: L. H. Gray and A. S. M. Oakman.

HAMPSHIRE v NORTHAMPTONSHIRE

Played at Bournemouth, August 27, 28, 29, 1969

Northamptonshire won by 139 runs. Having lost two early wickets, Northamptonshire had to thank Mushtaq for leading a magnificent recovery and forcing Hampshire to spend a frustrating day in the field. Adding to Hampshire's difficulties was the loss of Marshall, the captain, who trod on the ball and had to be carried from the field with a damaged ankle which prevented him from taking any further part in the match. Hampshire's reply was entirely a one-man affair, for Richards hit his fifth century of the summer and carried his bat. McIlwaine, a young bowler playing his first Championship match, stayed with him while the follow-on was averted. Finally Northamptonshire left Hampshire to score 283 in four and a half hours, but Richards had been hit on the head and only Gilliat batted with real assurance against Mushtaq and Breakwell.

Northamptonshire

F. S. Goldstein lbw b White	7	– lbw b White	20
H. M. Ackerman b White	54	– b Jesty	34
A. Lightfoot c Stephenson b Cottam	9	– b White	41
Mushtaq Mohammad not out	154	– c Gilliat b McIlwaine	2
*R. M. Prideaux c Livingstone b White	30	– b Cottam	7
P. Willey c Stephenson b Cottam	48	– run out	12
†L. A. Johnson not out	0	– b White	0
D. S. Steele (did not bat)		– not out	16
M. K. Kettle (did not bat)		– c Cottam b White	3
D. Breakwell (did not bat)		– not out	3
B 11, l-b 9, w 1, n-b 2	23	B 4, l-b 3, n-b 4	11
1/10 2/33 3/111 4/201 5/325	(5 wkts dec.) 325	1/25 2/70 3/87 4/113 5/113 6/120 7/138 8/144	(8 wkts dec.) 149

P. Lee did not bat.

Bowling: *First Innings*—White 27–6–89–3; Cottam 33–10–78–2; Jesty 25–6–69–0; McIlwaine 23–7–58–0; Wheatley 2–1–8–0. *Second Innings*—White 17–4–45–4; Cottam 18–2–44–1; Jesty 9–1–37–1; McIlwaine 8–3–12–1.

Hampshire

B. A. Richards not out	127	– c Kettle b Mushtaq	19
D. R. Turner lbw b Lee	4	– c Steele b Willey	2
R. M. C. Gilliat c Mushtaq b Lee	0	– lbw b Breakwell	54
D. A. Livingstone c Lightfoot b Breakwell	17	– c Goldstein b Mushtaq	28
K. J. Wheatley c Willey b Breakwell	0	– c Lee b Breakwell	4
T. E. Jesty b Breakwell	0	– c Kettle b Breakwell	0
†G. R. Stephenson lbw b Lee	15	– lbw b Breakwell	23
R. M. H. Cottam b Mushtaq	4	– st Johnson b Mushtaq	4
D. W. White st Johnson b Mushtaq	4	– b Breakwell	1
R. McIlwaine st Johnson b Mushtaq	17	– not out	2
*R. E. Marshall absent hurt	0	– absent hurt	0
L-b 1, n-b 3	4	L-b 2, n-b 4	6
1/19 2/19 3/95 4/97 5/97 6/127 7/146 8/156 9/192	192	1/2 2/82 3/94 5/94 6/121 7/125 8/134 9/143	143

Bowling: *First Innings*—Lee 14–7–24–3; Willey 5–3–5–0; Kettle 12–4–28–0; Mushtaq 24.2–5–79–3; Breakwell 17–5–52–3. *Second Innings*—Lee 8–2–16–0; Willey 7–1–12–1; Kettle 9–1–28–0; Mushtaq 17–3–55–3; Breakwell 12.2–5–26–5.

Umpires: C. S. Elliott and C. Petrie.

HAMPSHIRE v KENT

Played at Portsmouth, June 10, 11, 12, 1970

Drawn. Hampshire, already without Gilliat and Castell through injury, had their troubles increased when White broke down with a pulled muscle after only four overs, but Sainsbury bowled accurately and Kent were restricted to 195 for seven at tea. Then followed a fine display of controlled aggression by Shepherd, who hit one 6 and fifteen 4s in scoring a century in two hours off 128 deliveries. The Kent first-innings total was boosted considerably by 40 extras, to which Holder was the major contributor with 12 wides and 19 no balls. He bowled one over of 12 balls, which, incredibly, was a maiden. Although Marshall and Turner shared a third-wicket partnership of 153 in 130 minutes, Hampshire did not bat confidently afterwards and they declared 33 behind. Cottam joined White on the injured list, but the Kent batting lacked conviction on the third day before Cowdrey set Hampshire a target of 210 in two and a quarter hours. The challenge was not accepted and the extra half-hour was not claimed.

Kent

B. W. Luckhurst c Richards b Holder	13	– lbw b Holder	18
M. H. Denness b Sainsbury	64	– c Wheatley b Jesty	0
G. W. Johnson c Sainsbury b Jesty	14	– c sub b Jesty	22
*M. C. Cowdrey lbw b Jesty	10	– not out	32
Asif Iqbal c Stephenson b Holder	26	– c Turner b Sainsbury	12
†A. P. E. Knott c Stephenson b Sainsbury	13	– c Richards b Sainsbury	0
J. N. Shepherd c sub b Sainsbury	105	– not out	49
S. E. Leary c Holder b Sainsbury	2		
A. Brown b Cottam	11		
D. L. Underwood by Sainsbury	12	– c and b Jesty	32
J. N. Graham not out	0		
L-b 6, w 14, n-b 20	40	L-b 4, w 4, n-b 3	11
1/43 2/96 3/116 4/124 5/161 6/161 7/177 8/253 9/304	310	1/0 2/38 3/76 4/82 5/103 (6 wkts dec.)	176

Bowling: *First Innings*—White 4–2–16–0; Cottam 25–7–68–1; Holder 21–5–56–2; Jesty 26–4–72–2; Sainsbury 31.5–14–58–5. *Second Innings*—Holder 16–3–48–1; Jesty 24–9–63–3; Sainsbury 22–11–54–2.

Hampshire

B. A. Richards c and b Shepherd	43	– not out	60
P. J. Sainsbury c Johnson b Shepherd	22	– not out	8
D. R. Turner c Shepherd b Brown	84		
*R. E. Marshall c Asif b Graham	77		
D. A. Livingstone c Asif b Graham	10		
K. J. Wheatley c Luckhurst b Brown	8		
T. E. Jesty c Leary b Graham	0		
†G. R. Stephenson not out	19		
R. M. H. Cottam not out	3		
J. W. Holder c Denness b Graham	3		
B 2, l-b 3, w 1, n-b 2	8	L-b 4, n-b 2	6
1/59 2/71 3/224 4/234 5/248 6/252 7/252 8/262 (8 wkts dec.)	277	(No wkt)	74

D. W. White did not bat.

Bowling: *First Innings*—Brown 24–9–46–2; Graham 41–13–95–4; Underwood 19–2–59–0; Shepherd 28–6–69–2. *Second Innings*—Brown 8–5–10–0; Graham 4–3–3–0; Underwood 12–4–30–0; Shepherd 8–2–25–0.

Umpires: J. S. Buller and A. G. T. Whitehead.

HAMPSHIRE v SUSSEX

Played at Southampton, May 9, 10, 11, 1973

Hampshire won by seven wickets. Sixteen wickets fell on a cold and grey first day with batsmen suspicious of a pitch which offered some assistance to the spinners and on which the ball "stopped" at times. Sainsbury was the chief destroyer of Sussex with the excellent figures of six for 29 in 29.2 overs, while Joshi posed problems when Hampshire went in. Taylor, supported splendidly by Herman, played with good sense and judgment to see a lead of 38 gained. Taylor then showed good form with the ball and Sussex were soon in trouble in their second innings, but in Geoffrey Greenidge they possessed a man of ideal temperament and technique for the situation. He carried his bat for exactly 100 before Joshi was out after a last-wicket stand worth 58 in one hundred minutes. Hampshire had plenty of time in which to score 143 for victory and the target was reached off the last ball before tea.

Sussex

M. A. Buss lbw b Herman	8	– lbw b Herman	0
G. A. Greenidge c Richards b Sainsbury	23	– not out	100
R. M. Prideaux run out	20	– c Richards b Taylor	13
P. J. Graves c Richards b Sainsbury	6	– c Richards b Sainsbury	0
*A. W. Greig c Stephenson b Sainsbury	5	– lbw b Sainsbury	6
M. G. Griffith c Taylor b Sainsbury	0	– c Gilliat b O'Sullivan	10
†A. Mansell b Sainsbury	0	– b Taylor	9
J. R. T. Barclay c Stephenson b Sainsbury	14	– c O'Sullivan b Taylor	1
A. Buss b O'Sullivan	2	– c Turner b Sainsbury	2
J. Spencer c Gilliat b Herman	25	– b Taylor	5
U. C. Joshi not out	12	– c Richards b Jesty	21
L-b 7, n-b 2	9	L-b 8, n-b 5	13
1/15 2/45 3/57 4/63 5/63 6/63 7/66 8/73 9/105	124	1/0 2/22 3/32 4/40 5/65 6/90 7/96 8/107 9/122	180

Bowling: *First Innings*—Herman 15–4–23–2; Taylor 5–1–8–0; O'Sullivan 32–15–46–1; Jesty 3–0–9–0; Sainsbury 29.2–20–29–6. *Second Innings*—Herman 12–1–23–1; Taylor 32–12–39–4; O'Sullivan 46–26–56–1; Jesty 2–0–4–1; Sainsbury 48–28–45–3.

Hampshire

B. A. Richards c and b Greig	15	– c Graves b Joshi	39
C. G. Greenidge c Spencer b Greig	5	– lbw b Greig	14
D. R. Turner b Barclay	18	– lbw b Spencer	44
*R. M. C. Gilliat c Prideaux b Joshi	14	– not out	15
R. V. Lewis b Joshi	2	– not out	18
T. E. Jesty c Barclay b Joshi	9		
P. J. Sainsbury c Prideaux b Greig	17		
M. N. S. Taylor not out	33		
†G. R. Stephenson c Mansell b Joshi	11		
D. R. O'Sullivan c Graves b M. A. Buss	2		
R. S. Herman b Greig	20		
B 12, l-b 2, n-b 2	16	B 4, l-b 3, n-b 6	13
1/6 2/30 3/52 4/60 5/60 6/84 7/99 8/119 9/130	162	1/22 2/94 3/112	(3 wkts) 143

Bowling: *First Innings*—Greig 21.5–10–44–4; Spencer 5–1–15–0; Joshi 29–11–43–4; Barclay 8–3–26–1; M. A. Buss 8–3–16–1; Greenidge 1–0–2–0. *Second Innings*—Greig 6–1–27–1; Spencer 10–2–26–1; Joshi 19–8–31–1; M. A. Buss 3–0–16–0; Greenidge 1–0–12–0; A. Buss 10–1–18–0.

Umpires: J. F. Crapp and H. Yarnold.

HAMPSHIRE v SURREY

Played at Portsmouth, June 9, 11, 12, 1973

Drawn. A good-sized crowd were disappointed by Surrey's failure to score briskly, but took heart from Hampshire's performance in the field. Although Richards uncharacteristically dropped three catches, Hampshire dismissed their opponents for 204, Herman enjoying one fine spell of 11 overs in which he took three wickets for seven runs. The Hampshire batting was in complete contrast and Richards and Greenidge took them to lunch on the second day at 203 for no wicket, 183 having been added to the Saturday score in two hours. Richards made 97 in ninety minutes, but was out to the second ball after the break and then Greenidge was out for 99. Hampshire led by 163, but they were unable to press home their advantage as Surrey batted through the last day.

Surrey

*J. H. Edrich c Stephenson b Herman	72	– lbw b Jesty	59
R. M. Lewis c Taylor b Herman	6	– st Stephenson b Sainsbury	70
G. P. Howarth b Taylor	43	– run out	15
Younis Ahmed c Richards b Herman	13	– c Stephenson b Jesty	52
D. R. Owen-Thomas run out	10	– lbw b Taylor	10
S. J. Storey lbw b Herman	0	– not out	22
Intikhab Alam c Gilliat b Jesty	14	– not out	46
†A. Long c Turner b Mottram	23		
R. D. Jackman c Stephenson b Mottram	1		
C. E. Waller b Mottram	13		
R. P. Baker not out	1		
L-b 3, n-b 5	8	B 2, l-b 2, w 1, n-b 2	7
1/10 2/109 3/134 4/149 5/149 6/156 7/166 8/167 9/197	204	1/99 2/140 3/164 4/183 5/216	(5 wkts) 281

Bowling: *First Innings*—Herman 27–8–41–4; Mottram 17.4–4–48–3; Taylor 15–3–44–1; Jesty 17–3–43–1; Sainsbury 14–6–20–0. *Second Innings*—Herman 21–7–58–0; Mottram 19–3–51–0; Taylor 17–7–35–1; Jesty 17–8–23–2; Sainsbury 25–9–45–1; Richards 4–0–23–0; Turner 6–1–16–0; Lewis 4–0–23–0.

Hampshire

B. A. Richards c Long b Jackman	116
C. G. Greenidge c Baker b Storey	99
D. R. Turner c Long b Intikhab	35
*R. M. C. Gilliat c Younis b Storey	7
R. V. Lewis lbw b Waller	18
T. E. Jesty b Intikhab	0
P. J. Sainsbury lbw b Jackman	34
M. N. S. Taylor c Lewis b Baker	20
†G. R. Stephenson b Jackman	6
R. S. Herman b Baker	13
T. J. Mottram not out	1
B 2, l-b 9, n-b 7	18
1/207 2/253 3/270 4/270 5/275 6/309 7/347 8/351 9/365	367

Bowling: Jackman 27–4–81–3; Baker 19.3–1–91–2; Storey 17–2–54–2; Intikhab 29–5–86–2; Waller 21–9–37–1.

Umpires: A. Jepson and H. D. Bird.

HAMPSHIRE v KENT

Played at Southampton, September 8, 10, 11, 1973

Drawn. Hampshire just failed to finish a glorious season with victory, but they did remain the only unbeaten side in the County Championship. This final game produced some excellent cricket in superb September weather. Kent, who won the toss, lost three wickets for 14, but were rescued majestically by Asif, who, missed off a sharp chance to gully when 17, scored a hundred before lunch. Kent's attractive batting earned them eight bonus points, but Hampshire went at an even greater pace, despite an injury to Richards. The South African and Greenidge shared an opening stand of 241 – just eight short of the Hampshire record – before Richards was hit in the face when hooking Elms and retired hurt with a depressed fracture of the right cheekbone. Greenidge went on to his fifth championship century of the season and the score was 334 when the first wicket fell. Hampshire declared at their highest total of the season and O'Sullivan soon had Kent in trouble as he took five of the first seven wickets. At 107 for seven, Kent were still 42 behind, but Knott batted well for the second time in the match and his stands with Woolmer and Underwood foiled Hampshire. There was just time for Hampshire to bowl Kent out a second time and, appropriately, Gilliat, the captain, took the final wicket of the season.

Kent

B. W. Luckhurst c Stephenson b Mottram	3	– c Gilliat b O'Sullivan	13
G. W. Johnson c Greenidge b Herman	10	– c Stephenson b Herman	11
*M. H. Denness lbw b Mottram	0	– lbw b Sainsbury	9
Asif Iqbal c Turner b Herman	120	– st Stephenson b O'Sullivan	4
M. C. Cowdrey lbw b Taylor	10	– c Gilliat b O'Sullivan	34
A. G. E. Ealham b Herman	35	– c Jesty b O'Sullivan	16
J. N. Shepherd lbw b O'Sullivan	40	– c Jesty b O'Sullivan	4
†A. P. E. Knott c Richards b Sainsbury	58	– not out	84
R. A. Woolmer not out	32	– c Stephenson b Herman	43
R. B. Elms run out	0	– b Mottram	0
D. L. Underwood b Sainsbury	1	– c Greenidge b Gilliat	8
B 2, l-b 1, n-b 10	13	L-b 4, n-b 5	9
1/14 2/14 3/14 4/71 5/154 6/191 7/254 8/313 9/313	322	1/19 2/37 3/41 4/45 5/88 6/92 7/107 8/165 9/174	235

Bowling: *First Innings*—Herman 15–3–42–3; Mottram 16–1–73–2; Jesty 11–2–47–0; Taylor 12–0–59–1; O'Sullivan 23–5–68–1; Sainsbury 6.5–0–20–2. *Second Innings*—Herman 27–15–32–2. Mottram 17–5–50–1; Taylor 2–0–7–0; O'Sullivan 40–17–93–5; Sainsbury 30–17–35–1; Greenidge 1–0–6–0; Turner 1–1–0–0; Gilliat 1–0–3–1.

Hampshire

B. A. Richards retired hurt	143
C. G. Greenidge c Cowdrey b Elms	118
D. R. Turner c Ealham b Shepherd	64
*R. M. C. Gilliat lbw b Woolmer	54
T. E. Jesty c Knott b Shepherd	7
P. J. Sainsbury c Woolmer b Shepherd	26
M. N. S. Taylor lbw b Shepherd	7
D. R. O'Sullivan c Knott b Woolmer	5
†G. R. Stephenson not out	5
R. S. Herman c Asif b Woolmer	7
B 9, l-b 12, w 3, n-b 11	35
1/334 2/409 3/413 4/423 5/433 6/454 7/462 8/471 (8 wkts dec.)	471

T. J. Mottram did not bat.

Bowling: Elms 28–4–112–1; Shepherd 29–6–108–4; Underwood 25–6–75–0; Johnson 8–1–48–0; Woolmer 27.2–4–93–3.

Umpires: D. J. Constant and D. L. Evans.

HAMPSHIRE v SUSSEX

Played at Southampton, August 30, September 1, 2, 1975

Drawn. Despite their defeats at Bournemouth earlier in the month, Hampshire went into this match still in a position to challenge for the Championship, but they badly missed

Roberts, who broke down with a shin injury during his practice run-up, and they neither bowled nor caught well enough. Yet their batting escaped all criticism as they amassed the highest total since the 100-over first innings was introduced.

Without Snow and Greig, playing for England, the Sussex bowlers carried no threat on an easy paced wicket and Greenidge led the slaughter with the highest individual innings of the summer and the highest by a Hampshire batsman since the war. Greenidge reached his 50, 100, 150 and 200 with sixes and his 250 with a four and his major hits in a stay at the crease over five hours were thirteen 6s and twenty-four 4s. His thirteen 6s set a record for a Championship innings, beating the eleven hit by C. J. Barnett for Gloucestershire against Somerset at Bath in 1934.

The Hampshire bowling lacked penetration in Roberts' absence and, although following on 242 behind, Sussex made a splendid job of saving the match, principally through Faber's sensible and well-judged batting. But at the end of the day, when even Stephenson, the wicket-keeper, bowled, there were easy runs to be collected and Spencer was on target for the fastest hundred of the season when he was out for 79 made in just twenty-five minutes.

Hampshire

B. A. Richards c Spencer b Buss	49
C. G. Greenidge c Groome b Barclay	259
D. R. Turner c Mansell b Phillipson	62
T. E. Jesty lbw b Spencer	34
*R. M. C. Gilliat lbw b Barclay	61
M. N. S. Taylor not out	10
B 12, l-b 11, w 1, n-b 2	26
1/88 2/253 3/344 4/465 5/501	(5 wkts dec.) 501

P. J. Sainsbury, J. M. Rice, †G. R. Stephenson, A. M. E. Roberts and J. W. Southern did not bat.

Bowling: Spencer 19–1–85–1; Phillipson 29–5–126–1; Buss 19–3–93–1; Waller 19–1–84–0; Barclay 12.5–0–65–2; Hoadley 1–0–22–0.

Sussex

J. R. T. Barclay c Jesty b Rice	12	– b Jesty 21
J. J. Groome c Greenidge b Richards	38	– c Greenidge b Sainsbury 70
A. E. W. Parsons c Turner b Southern	65	– lbw b Jesty 0
*P. J. Graves c Stephenson b Taylor	35	– c Richards b Sainsbury 26
M. J. J. Faber c Greenidge b Sainsbury	9	– st Stephenson b Greenidge 176
M. A. Buss run out	36	– c Sainsbury b Richards 7
S. J. Hoadley b Southern	6	– c Sainsbury b Greenidge 58
†A. W. Mansell c Greenidge b Sainsbury	23	– c Turner b Greenidge 79
J. Spencer not out	21	– c Turner b Greenidge 79
C. E. Waller not out	4	– run out 0
C. P. Phillipson (did not bat)		– st Jesty b Gilliat 16
L-b 3, w 1, n-b 6	10	B 5, l-b 3, w 8, n-b 4 20
1/50 2/70 3/126 4/153 5/180 6/207 7/215 8/248	(8 wkts) 259	1/36 2/36 3/86 4/215 5/256 6/345 7/410 8/502 9/504 524

Bowling: *First Innings*—Jesty 10–2–18–0; Rice 21–4–45–1; Southern 32–13–78–2; Taylor 12–3–41–1; Richards 7–1–42–1; Sainsbury 18–6–25–2. *Second Innings*—Jesty 15–2–44–2; Rice 19–5–55–0; Southern 56–27–114–0; Taylor 12–5–18–0; Richards 19–8–49–1; Sainsbury 40–22–49–2; Greenidge 16–3–84–3; Turner 3–0–12–0; Stephenson 5–1–28–0; Gilliat 4.3–0–51–1.

Umpires: K. E. Palmer and D. L. Evans.

NOTES BY THE EDITOR, 1976

GREENIDGE'S RECORD 259

While on the subject of high and fast scoring, it was no mean feat by Gordon Greenidge at Southampton at the end of August to hit 259 against Sussex, even if they were without Snow and Greig. Hampshire's total of 501 was the highest for a limited 100 overs innings, and Greenidge's 259 was the best for Hampshire since the war. Also his thirteen 6s set a record for a Championship innings as it surpassed C. J. Barnett's eleven 6s for Gloucestershire against Somerset at Bath in 1934.

HAMPSHIRE v KENT

Played at Southampton, May 29, 31, June 1, 1976

Drawn. A high-scoring match was dominated by Richards, who ended a lean spell with two centuries. In the first innings, the timing of his drives and delicacy of cuts brought him two 6s and twenty-six 4s as he completed the 71st hundred of his career. Hampshire looked in a strong position when they dismissed Luckhurst, Asif and Woolmer for 56, but Clinton and Shepherd launched a recovery which Ealham and Nicholls continued. Then Richards ruled again. He raced to his second century in just eighty-three minutes (twenty-one 4s) and with Lewis shared an opening stand of 140. Turner and Gilliat added 102 in only fifty-five minutes before Kent were set the task of scoring 299 in three and three-quarter hours. The early loss of Clinton and Asif did not help their cause and they never really took up the challenge.

Hampshire

B. A. Richards b Hills	159	– b Underwood	108
R. V. Lewis c Nicholls b Shepherd	6	– c Rowe b Underwood	30
D. R. Turner lbw b Woolmer	37	– not out	82
T. E. Jesty c Shepherd b Woolmer	3	– b Jarvis	10
*R. M. C. Gilliat c Asif b Shepherd	24	– c Rowe b Underwood	50
P. J. Sainsbury b Hills	7	– c Nicholls b Underwood	1
J. M. Rice c Hills b Underwood	15	– c Shepherd b Woolmer	2
M. N. S. Taylor c Shepherd b Underwood	5	– not out	5
†M. J. Hill not out	2		
R. S. Herman c Asif b Jarvis	14		
J. W. Southern b Underwood	6		
B 5, l-b 10, w 11, n-b 3	29	B 6, l-b 3, w 1, n-b 2	12
1/16 2/152 3/157 4/240 5/251 6/253 7/277 8/284 9/300	307	1/140 2/141 3/163 4/265 5/268 6/277	(6 wkts dec.) 300

Bowling: *First Innings*—Jarvis 15–3–61–1; Shepherd 15–3–49–2; Hills 16–3–52–2; Underwood 17.5–7–53–3; Woolmer 20–3–59–2; Rowe 2–1–4–0. *Second Innings*—Jarvis 14–4–43–1; Shepherd 5–0–23–0; Hills 8–0–42–0; Underwood 24–8–78–4; Woolmer 13–0–64–1; Rowe 6–1–38–0.

Kent

*B. W. Luckhurst c Rice b Herman	1	– c Sainsbury b Rice	69
G. S. Clinton b Taylor	47	– c Gilliat b Taylor	13
Asif Iqbal c Hill b Rice	22	– c Jesty b Southern	6
R. A. Woolmer c Sainsbury b Rice	9	– c Rice b Sainsbury	48
J. N. Shepherd c Rice b Southern	73	– c Hill b Rice	4
†D. Nicholls c Taylor b Southern	50		
A. G. E. Ealham c Jesty b Sainsbury	51	– not out	37
C. J. C. Rowe c Hill b Taylor	1	– not out	30
R. W. Hills c Taylor b Sainsbury	14		
D. L. Underwood b Sainsbury	0		
K. B. S. Jarvis not out	0		
B 5, l-b 13, w 12, n-b 11	41	B 4, l-b 11, n-b 7	22
1/5 2/43 3/56 4/165 5/186 6/195 7/283 8/309 9/309	309	1/48 2/64 3/140 4/146 5/155	(5 wkts) 229

Bowling: *First Innings*—Herman 16–1–57–1; Rice 18–2–62–2; Jesty 10–2–27–0; Southern 18–10–32–2; Taylor 19–5–58–2; Sainsbury 12.3–4–32–3. *Second Innings*—Herman 8–3–22–0; Rice 13–3–40–2; Jesty 3–0–17–0; Southern 21–7–50–1; Taylor 10–2–26–1; Sainsbury 14–4–48–1; Richards 2–1–4–0.

Umpires: P. B. Wight and P. Rochford.

HAMPSHIRE v GLAMORGAN

Played at Bournemouth, July 10, 12, 1976

Hampshire won by an innings and 119 runs with a day to spare. Richards, Turner and Gilliat were all in sparkling form and scored centuries. Richards completed his hundred before lunch, his runs coming off 88 balls in ninety minutes; Gilliat took only three minutes longer to reach three figures. This was the first time since 1950 that three Hampshire batsmen had scored centuries in the same innings. Turner shared partnerships of 122 with Richards and 181 with Gilliat, and Cowley and Sainsbury made useful contributions. Glamorgan finished the first day deep in trouble with five men out for 97 and they lost 15 wickets on the second day. They were never comfortable on a pitch which took slow turn, Majid followed his first innings of 58 with another hard-hit fifty, which included twelve boundaries.

Hampshire

B. A. Richards c Francis b Williams	111
R. V. Lewis c Llewellyn b Nash	6
D. R. Turner c A. Jones b Richards	127
T. E. Jesty c Llewellyn b Nash	7
*R. M. C. Gilliat c E. W. Jones b Llewellyn	101
N. G. Cowley b Richards	47
P. J. Sainsbury c Nash b Richards	55
M. N. S. Taylor not out	9
J. M. Rice c E. W. Jones b Richards	13
†G. R. Stephenson b Nash	6
J. W. Southern b Nash	2
B 4, l-b 6, n-b 1	11
1/29 2/151 3/179 4/360 5/362 6/454 7/477 8/484 9/490	495

Bowling: Nash 30.3–2–146–4; Cordle 14–3–61–0; Solanky 9–1–59–0; Williams 10–0–57–1; Richards 22–0–103–4; Ellis 7–0–41–0; Llewellyn 7–1–17–1.

Glamorgan

A. Jones c Stephenson b Jesty	7	– c Richards b Jesty	3
G. P. Ellis c Sainsbury b Rice	6	– c Richards b Sainsbury	9
*Majid J. Khan c Rice b Southern	58	– c Taylor b Southern	53
G. Richards c Rice b Jesty	0	– lbw b Cowley	34
M. J. Llewellyn c Richards b Southern	13	– c Stephenson b Cowley	5
D. A. Francis b Rice	17	– lbw b Taylor	7
M. A. Nash c Jesty b Southern	48	– c Jesty b Southern	43
J. W. Solanky c Taylor b Sainsbury	9	– st Stephenson b Cowley	26
†E. W. Jones c Richards b Sainsbury	1	– c Richards b Southern	5
A. E. Cordle c Lewis b Southern	6	– not out	17
D. L. Williams not out	0	– c Turner b Cowley	4
L-b 1	1	L-b 2, n-b 2	4
1/9 2/15 3/15 4/76 5/93 6/131 7/151 8/160 9/166	166	1/5 2/67 3/67 4/106 5/108 6/156 7/165 8/187 9/192	210

Bowling: *First Innings*—Rice 17–2–55–2; Jesty 8–2–26–2; Southern 30–13–47–4; Sainsbury 18.1–7–37–2. *Second Innings*—Rice 9–2–34–0; Jesty 8–5–14–1; Southern 23–13–42–3; Sainsbury 27–16–29–1; Cowley 16.5–6–43–4; Taylor 6–0–36–1; Richards 4–3–8–0.

Umpires: D. L. Evans and P. B. Wight.

HAMPSHIRE v WARWICKSHIRE

Played at Bournemouth, August 25, 26, 27, 1976

Warwickshire won by 18 runs. Although Hampshire suffered their eighth successive defeat, the game produced some highly entertaining cricket and a good finish. Jameson and Smith shared an opening partnership of 221 from which Warwickshire reached 414 for six in their 100 overs. Jameson punished a depleted Hampshire attack with a century before lunch and in all batted two and three-quarter hours, hitting four 6s and twenty-one 4s. The fast scoring was continued by Richards. The South African was in scintillating form and reached his hundred in ninety minutes, the second fifty taking twenty-one minutes. Turner was in good form, too, before, when four short of a century, he was bowled without offering a stroke. Warwickshire's first innings lead of 24 grew thanks largely to a fifth wicket stand of 178 between Abberley and Rouse, whose highest score of 93 included five 6s. Hampshire needed 287 in under four hours and made a bold attempt, but there was insufficient support for Turner, who was not out with 130. Hemmings, helped by some poor strokes, took seven for 92.

Warwickshire

J. A. Jameson c and b Rice	144	– c Gilliat b Taylor	8
K. D. Smith c Turner b Southern	84	– c Rice b Taylor	16
J. Whitehouse b Rice	9	– lbw b Taylor	34
R. B. Kanhai b Rice	6	– c Richards b Murtagh	10
R. N. Abberley c Turner b Murtagh	25	– lbw b Murtagh	92
G. W. Humpage run out	86	– not out	0
W. A. Bourne not out	38		
E. E. Hemmings not out	17		
S. J. Rouse (did not bat)		– c Southern b Taylor	93
B 1, l-b 2, n-b 2	5	B 5, l-b 3, n-b 1	9
1/221 2/230 3/240 4/246 5/322 6/381	(6 wkts) 414	1/21 2/27 3/41 4/84 5/262 6/262	(6 wkts dec.) 262

R. le Q. Savage and *D. J. Brown did not bat.

Bowling: *First Innings*—Rice 20–5–64–3; Taylor 17–2–54–0; Pocock 4–2–21–0; Southern 29–7–126–1; Murtagh 16–2–86–1; Cowley 14–3–58–0. *Second Innings*—Rice 19–4–29–0; Taylor 19.2–2–64–4; Southern 13–1–50–0; Murtagh 11–0–46–2; Cowley 11–2–31–0; Richards 10–1–33–0.

Hampshire

B. A. Richards b Brown	101	– b Hemmings	49
J. M. Rice c and b Hemmings	28	– c Brown b Hemmings	25
D. R. Turner b Hemmings	96	– not out	130
T. E. Jesty b Brown	9	– c Brown b Savage	0
N. E. J. Pocock c Whitehouse b Hemmings	25	– c Rouse b Hemmings	5
A. J. Murtagh c Bourne b Hemmings	4	– c Rouse b Hemmings	9
*R. M. C. Gilliat c Smith b Hemmings	45	– lbw b Savage	4
M. N. S. Taylor not out	41	– c Smith b Hemmings	3
N. G. Cowley c Brown b Hemmings	2	– c Brown b Hemmings	13
†G. R. Stephenson c Humpage b Bourne	5	– c Abberley b Savage	11
J. W. Southern run out	9	– lbw b Hemmings	0
B 7, l-b 11, n-b 7	25	B 10, l-b 4, n-b 5	19
1/34 2/138 3/174 4/237 5/245 6/296 7/327 8/346 9/346	390	1/67 2/106 3/107 4/117 5/136 6/157 7/212 8/247 9/266	268

Bowling: *First Innings*—Rouse 11–2–59–0; Bourne 16–1–43–1; Brown 17–3–53–2; Hemmings 34–5–145–6; Savage 11–2–26–0; Jameson 8–1–39–0. *Second Innings*—Rouse 4–0–22–0; Bourne 6–0–33–0; Brown 6–1–21–0; Hemmings 27.3–3–92–7; Savage 24–3–81–3.

Umpires: R. Aspinall and P. Rochford.

HAMPSHIRE v DERBYSHIRE

Played at Bournemouth, May 18, 19, 20, 1977

Drawn. Richards, who scored a century before lunch, and Gilliat were the principal contributors to Hampshire's first innings. Richards began quietly and made his first fifty in ninety minutes, but his second, scored out of 67, came in thirty-five minutes. Derbyshire's first innings also produced a century-maker in Wright, a New Zealander, who shared an opening partnership of 199 with Hill. There was little success for the Hampshire bowlers, but Hendrick rocked Hampshire at the start of their second innings by dismissing Richards and Turner with successive balls. Indeed, with six men out for 96, Hampshire were in danger of defeat, but Rice batted with determination and was supported well by Stephenson. Derbyshire needed 202 to win, but wickets fell regularly and only two remained midway through the final hour. Then Taylor and Hendrick thwarted Hampshire's bid for victory.

Hampshire

C. G. Greenidge b Hendrick	22	– c Barlow b Miller	19
B. A. Richards b Miller	115	– c Barlow b Hendrick	2
D. R. Turner lbw b Miller	5	– b Hendrick	0
T. E. Jesty b Hendrick	28	– c Wright b Miller	19
*R. M. C. Gilliat c Tunnicliffe b Swarbrook	90	– c Miller b Swarbrook	11
J. M. Rice c Miller b Barlow	15	– c Barlow b Tunnicliffe	71
N. G. Cowley c Graham-Brown b Barlow	4	– c Barlow b Swarbrook	13
M. N. S. Taylor run out	3	– c Wright b Hendrick	0
†G. R. Stephenson not out	13	– c Tunnicliffe b Swarbrook	25
A. M. E. Roberts c Tunnicliffe b Swarbrook	5	– b Tunnicliffe	11
J. W. Southern run out	1	– not out	1
L-b 5, n-b 8	13	L-b 16, n-b 1	17
1/34 2/65 3/166 4/180	314	1/9 2/9 3/34 4/47	189
5/235 6/248 7/279 8/295 9/311		5/70 6/96 7/97 8/158 9/184	

Bowling: *First Innings*—Hendrick 21–5–49–2; Tunnicliffe 17–2–62–0; Barlow 13–1–49–2; Miller 28–7–83–2; Swarbrook 21–5–58–2. *Second Innings*—Hendrick 19–9–29–3; Tunnicliffe 19.4–9–32–2; Barlow 9–1–20–0; Miller 26–12–54–2; Swarbrook 39–24–37–3.

Derbyshire

A. Hill run out	90	– c Stephenson b Roberts	0
J. G. Wright b Rice	151	– b Taylor	27
G. Miller c and b Southern	2	– c Richards b Southern	45
*E. J. Barlow c Greenidge b Rice	33	– c Stephenson b Taylor	11
A. J. Borrington not out	9	– b Southern	1
H. Cartwright not out	5	– c Gilliat b Cowley	19
F. W. Swarbrook (did not bat)		– b Roberts	8
J. M. H. Graham-Brown (did not bat)		– c Jesty b Southern	0
†R. W. Taylor (did not bat)		– not out	12
M. Hendrick (did not bat)		– not out	6
B 2, l-b 7, n-b 3	12	L-b 2, n-b 2	4
1/199 2/218	(4 wkts) 302	1/6 2/39 3/71	(8 wkts) 133
3/287 4/290		4/72 5/105 6/107 7/107 8/119	

C. J. Tunnicliffe did not bat.

Bowling: *First Innings*—Roberts 15–2–50–0; Rice 18–7–37–2; Jesty 8–3–12–0; Southern 28–7–82–1; Cowley 15–3–43–0; Richards 4–1–17–0; Taylor 12–2–49–0. *Second Innings*—Roberts 13–5–21–2; Rice 9–3–20–0; Southern 18–6–47–3; Cowley 7.5–2–17–1; Taylor 7–2–24–2.

Umpires: D. L. Evans and A. Jepson.

HAMPSHIRE v SOMERSET

Played at Southampton, May 28, 30, 31, 1977

Drawn. Somerset slumped after Vivian Richards, batting with characteristic fluency, and Kitchen had shared a third wicket partnership of 117. Then, throughout a collapse, Kitchen, uncertain himself early on, batted with determination and thoroughly deserved his century, which included one 6 and sixteen 4s. Hampshire, with plenty of overs, established a lead of 148, Jesty, who drove most handsomely, scoring 136, and Rice giving further evidence of his development as a batsman with an enterprising and responsible innings. Roberts' pace had earned him five wickets in the first innings but when Somerset went in again the Hampshire bowling lacked penetration. Denning took advantage of the good wicket to become the third century-maker before Close set Hampshire to score 195 to win in an hour and three-quarters. Hampshire declined this stiff challenge and Greenidge and Richards used the time for practice.

Somerset

B. C. Rose c Stephenson b Roberts	2	– c Elms b Taylor	24
P. W. Denning c Jesty b Roberts	13	– b Jesty	109
I. V. A. Richards b Southern	76	– c Rice b Southern	41
M. J. Kitchen c Richards b Taylor	105	– c Stephenson b Southern	49
I. T. Botham c Gilliat b Southern	0	– c Richards b Southern	9
*D. B. Close c Elms b Taylor	0	– b Southern	47
G. I. Burgess c Stephenson b Roberts	5	– c Rice b Southern	4
†D. J. S. Taylor lbw b Roberts	0	– c Richards b Southern	1
D. Breakwell b Roberts	2	– c Stephenson b Elms	21
C. H. Dredge c Rice b Taylor	11	– not out	16
H. R. Moseley not out	2	– not out	6
B 2, l-b 5, n-b 1	8	B 5, l-b 8, w 1, n-b 1	15
1/2 2/29 3/146 4/148 5/148 6/154 7/158 8/176 9/219	224	1/71 2/139 3/225 4/237 5/257 7/281 7/287 8/298 9/320	(9 wkts dec.) 342

Bowling: *First Innings*—Roberts 15–5–40–5; Elms 11–0–65–0; Taylor 12.5–2–42–3; Rice 13–2–66–0; Southern 3–2–3–2. *Second Innings*—Roberts 21–4–82–0; Elms 19–4–33–1; Taylor 18–4–65–1; Rice 2.2–1–12–0; Southern 39–12–84–6; Jesty 15–5–30–1; Richards 6–2–21–0.

Hampshire

C. G. Greenidge c Taylor b Moseley	8	– not out	38
B. A. Richards b Dredge	42	– not out	28
D. R. Turner c Taylor b Botham	34		
T. E. Jesty b Richards	136		
*R. M. C. Gilliat c Taylor b Moseley	28		
J. M. Rice b Breakwell	78		
M. N. S. Taylor c Close b Botham	11		
†G. R. Stephenson b Moseley	6		
R. B. Elms c Botham b Breakwell	13		
A. M. E. Roberts c Kitchen b Breakwell	5		
J. W. Southern not out	0		
B 4, l-b 6, w 1	11	L-b 5	5
1/34 2/57 3/118 4/201 5/28 6/315 7/328 8/364 9/371	372		(No wkt) 71

Bowling: *First Innings*—Moseley 37–8–96–3; Botham 34–7–95–2; Dredge 14–1–47–1; Burgess 21–1–78–0; Breakwell 18.5–6–38–3; Richards 5–1–7–1. *Second Innings*—Moseley 4–2–4–0; Botham 3–0–4–0; Dredge 4–1–14–0; Burgess 6–1–16–0; Breakwell 5–2–8–0; Rose 5–1–20–0.

Umpires: D. J. Constant and D. J. Halfyard.

HAMPSHIRE v KENT

Played at Bournemouth, August 26, 28, 29, 1978

Hampshire won by seven wickets. Kent, who went into the match needing 18 points to make sure of the title, were denied by the brilliant batting of Greenidge, who scored two centuries. It all started well for Kent with Asif reaching his century in just over two hours. Johnson and Tavaré contributed splendidly to a good first innings total. Hampshire, in reply, owed much to Greenidge, whose hundred contained three 6s and sixteen 4s, but when he was fourth out at 189 Hampshire collapsed, the last six wickets adding only 47. Kent soon built on their lead of 93 and they batted for one over on the final day before declaring and setting Hampshire a target of 312 in 348 minutes. Hampshire, in fact, made light of the task, racing to victory with two hours to spare. Greenidge reached his second century of the match in ninety-one minutes to equal the season's fastest – set by Clive Lloyd (Lancashire) against Glamorgan at Liverpool in June – and Jesty also reached a hundred. He finished the match by hitting his twentieth 4.

Kent

C. J. C. Rowe c and b Taylor	19	– c Rice b Southern	25
G. W. Johnson b Cowley	95	– lbw b Cowley	65
C. J. Tavaré c Greenidge b Cowley	69	– not out	45
Asif Iqbal not out	115	– c Rock b Cowley	42
*A. G. E. Ealham run out	4	– c Gilliat b Cowley	1
J. N. Shepherd not out	19	– not out	33
B 2, l-b 3, n-b 3	8	B 3, l-b 4	7
1/53 2/149 3/258 4/273	(4 wkts) 329	1/93 2/93 3/152 4/157	(4 wkts dec.) 218

C. S. Cowdrey, R. W. Hills, †P. R. Downton, D. L. Underwood and K. B. S. Jarvis did not bat.

Bowling: *First Innings*—Stevenson 16–3–56–0; Jesty 6–3–8–0; Rice 17–2–59–0; Taylor 13–1–51–1; Southern 21–2–58–0; Cowley 27–5–89–2. *Second Innings*—Stevenson 7–1–27–0; Jesty 12–3–40–0; Taylor 5–2–15–0; Cowley 21–2–65–3; Southern 20–2–64–1.

Hampshire

C. G. Greenidge st Downton b Underwood	136	– st Downton b Underwood	120
D. J. Rock c Downton b Jarvis	8	– b Underwood	30
D. R. Turner c Downton b Shepherd	9	– c Asif b Johnson	10
T. E. Jesty c Johnson b Shepherd	30	– not out	106
N. G. Cowley c Ealham b Underwood	24	– not out	31
*R. M. C. Gilliat c Shepherd b Underwood	1		
M. N. S. Taylor b Underwood	18		
J. M. Rice c Tavaré b Hills	0		
†G. R. Stephenson c Ealham b Underwood	1		
K. Stevenson not out	2		
J. W. Southern lbw b Hills	0		
L-b 5, w 1, n-b 1	7	B 4, l-b 5, n-b 7	16
1/35 2/84 3/142 4/189 5/197 6/232 7/233 8/233 9/236	236	1/116 2/169 3/173	(3 wkts) 313

Bowling: *First Innings*—Jarvis 12–4–47–1; Shepherd 20–6–56–2; Underwood 17–6–52–5; Johnson 13–2–29–0; Hills 12.1–2–45–2. *Second Innings*—Jarvis 8–2–42–0; Shepherd 9–1–44–0; Hills 8–0–47–0; Underwood 26–5–97–2; Johnson 23–9–63–1; Ealham 0.2–0–4–0.

Umpires: D. J. Halfyard and J. F. Crapp.

HAMPSHIRE v NOTTINGHAMSHIRE

Played at Bournemouth, July 4, 6, 1981

Hampshire won by nine wickets. Hampshire moved to the top of the Championship table with victory in two days. Nottinghamshire, put in, were dismissed for 143, with Rice alone able to master the movement extracted by Hampshire's bowlers and scoring a remarkable unbeaten 105 (one 6 and sixteen 4s), Robinson's 10 being the next highest score. By the close on the first day, Hampshire had established a lead of 3 runs, but they lost their remaining six wickets for 44 in an hour and a quarter as the pitch continued to assist seamers. Nottinghamshire were again dismissed cheaply, Marshall and Stevenson taking five wickets apiece, and only Hadlee showing much resistance with one 6 and six 4s in a lusty knock, leaving Hampshire to score 53. Nicholas made the winning hit with a 6 over long-on off Hemmings.

Nottinghamshire

P. A. Todd lbw b Stevenson	1	– lbw b Stevenson	6
R. T. Robinson c Parks b Jesty	10	– (11) not out	4
B. Hassan lbw b Stevenson	8	– (2) lbw b Stevenson	12
*C. E. B. Rice not out	105	– (5) c Nicholas b Marshall	9
R. E. Dexter c Parks b Marshall	4	– (3) c Smith b Marshall	4
J. D. Birch c Parks b Marshall	4	– (4) lbw b Stevenson	6
R. J. Hadlee c and b Marshall	2	– (6) c Jesty b Stevenson	40
E. E. Hemmings c Parks b Stevenson	0	– (7) lbw b Stevenson	2
K. E. Cooper b Stevenson	0	– (8) b Marshall	1
†C. Scott c Bailey b Marshall	6	– (9) c Turner b Marshall	8
M. K. Bore c Bailey b Jesty	0	– (10) c Pocock b Marshall	4
L-b 3	3	L-b 3	3
1/1 2/19 3/27 4/56 5/62 6/80 7/89 8/89 9/142	143	1/13 2/18 3/30 4/30 5/57 6/60 7/77 8/83 9/88	99

Bowling: *First Innings*—Marshall 20–9–32–4; Stevenson 19–3–86–4; Jesty 10–2–22–2. *Second Innings*—Marshall 16.2–2–64–5; Stevenson 16–7–32–5.

Hampshire

C. L. Smith c Scott b Cooper	34	– not out	18
T. M. Tremlett c Rice b Hadlee	23	– c sub b Hemmings	8
M. C. J. Nicholas b Cooper	1	– not out	22
T. E. Jesty c Rice b Hadlee	15		
D. R. Turner c Scott b Rice	42		
*N. E. J. Pocock c Hadlee b Rice	25		
N. G. Cowley c Hemmings b Rice	4		
†R. J. Parks b Hadlee	15		
M. D. Marshall b Rice	8		
M. J. Bailey lbw b Hadlee	6		
K. Stevenson not out	1		
B 3, l-b 8, w 1, n-b 4	16	L-b 4, n-b 1	5
1/47 2/50 3/78 4/97 5/147 6/157 7/174 8/176 9/188	190	1/23	(1 wkt) 53

Bowling: *First Innings*—Hadlee 28.3–9–59–4; Rice 19–6–50–4; Bore 6–2–11–0; Cooper 18–7–42–2; Hemmings 6–0–12–0. *Second Innings*—Hadlee 3–0–11–0; Rice 5–1–9–0; Hemmings 6.3–5–8–1; Bore 4–0–20–0.

Umpires: B. J. Meyer and Shakoor Rana.

HAMPSHIRE v DERBYSHIRE

Played at Portsmouth, July 15, 16, 17, 1981

Hampshire won by an innings and 32 runs. Derbyshire's decision to bat first on a greenish pitch seemed ill-advised when they were reduced to 53 for five by lunch with Tremlett taking four for 11. They never recovered, and the willing Stevenson would have achieved the first hat-trick of his career had Nicholas not dropped Hendrick at first slip. Hampshire made batting a much easier exercise and by the close they were 20 ahead. Greenidge, given excellent support by Turner, played a highly responsible innings with five 6s and nine 4s, his century coming in four and a half hours. Hampshire declared with a lead of 241, and Marshall, full of hostility, Stevenson and Jesty bowled them to victory. The match was a personal triumph for Parks, Hampshire's 22-year-old wicket-keeper; his six catches in Derbyshire's first innings set a Hampshire record and, with ten in the match, he bettered Walter Livsey's nine (4 ct, 5 st) against Warwickshire at Southampton in 1914.

Derbyshire

B. Wood c Parks b Stevenson	14	– lbw b Stevenson	38
J. G. Wright c Greenidge b Tremlett	6	– c Parks b Marshall	3
P. N. Kirsten c Parks b Tremlett	12	– c Parks b Marshall	36
D. S. Steele c Jesty b Tremlett	7	– c Parks b Jesty	55
*G. Miller c Parks b Tremlett	2	– (9) c Parks b Stevenson	10
A Hill not out	33	– (5) c Greenidge b Marshall	3
I. S. Anderson c Parks b Stevenson	3	– (6) b Jesty	22
†M. J. Deakin c Greenidge b Stevenson	9	– (7) c Bailey b Jesty	3
C. J. Tunnicliffe lbw b Stevenson	0	– (8) c Stevenson b Bailey	1
M. Hendrick c Parks b Marshall	1	– b Stevenson	21
S. Oldham c Parks b Stevenson	5	– not out	3
B 1, l-b 4, w 7	12	B 1, l-b 11, w 1, n-b 1	14
1/20 2/26 3/44 4/46 5/51 6/63 7/92 8/92 9/93	104	1/12 2/84 3/86 4/99 5/164 6/168 7/175 8/175 9/206	209

Bowling: *First Innings*—Marshall 21–10–27–1; Stevenson 23.1–8–49–5; Tremlett 13–8–11–4; Jesty 4–2–5–0; Bailey 1–1–0–0. *Second Innings*—Stevenson 20.4–3–54–3; Marshall 30–14–59–3; Jesty 24–10–43–3; Tremlett 8–3–17–0; Bailey 7–0–21–1; Cowley 3–2–1–0.

Hampshire

C. G. Greenidge c Kirsten b Wood	109
T. M. Tremlett c Deakin b Oldham	0
M. C. J. Nicholas c Kirsten b Wood	30
*T. E. Jesty b Hendrick	25
D. R. Turner b Tunnicliffe	48
V. P. Terry b Oldham	14
N. G. Cowley c Tunnicliffe b Hendrick	19
†R. J. Parks c sub b Anderson	21
M. D. Marshall not out	40
M. J. Bailey not out	4
B 6, l-b 9, n-b 20	35
1/4 2/63 3/138 4/223 5/245 6/262 7/272 8/336	(8 wkts dec.) 345

K. Stevenson did not bat.

Bowling: Hendrick 26–6–63–2; Oldham 28–8–80–2; Tunnicliffe 24–6–74–1; Wood 20–3–67–2; Steele 6–2–9–0; Anderson 3–0–17–1.

Umpires: D. J. Halfyard and K. E. Palmer.

HAMPSHIRE v SURREY

Played at Portsmouth, July 18, 20, 21, 1981

Surrey won by 130 runs. After putting Surrey in, Hampshire gave Butcher three lives before Stevenson removed both openers in one over and, with Jesty taking four for 24 in a nine-over spell, Surrey slipped to 154 for eight before Richards and Jackman added 48 for the ninth wicket. Hampshire were quickly in trouble as Clarke removed Tremlett and Nicholas in three balls, and at the close they were 71 for four. On Monday, Greenidge was needlessly run out, Pocock suffered a fracture to his right hand from a lifting delivery by

Clarke, and the innings ended 40 behind. Surrey soon slumped to 34 for four, but the middle- and late-order batsmen scored consistently and the innings ended off the day's last ball, leaving the home side a target of 222. Achieving it looked remote when they lost three wickets, including that of Greenidge, for 6 runs and, although Jesty and Turner put on 74 for the fourth wicket, the last six went for 11 runs, Jackman taking four for 0 in eight balls as Hampshire crashed to their first defeat of the season.

Surrey

A. R. Butcher lbw b Stevenson	26	– c sub b Marshall	15
G. S. Clinton c Greenidge b Stevenson	21	– lbw b Stevenson	10
*R. D. V. Knight c Parks b Marshall	48	– c Tremlett b Stevenson	6
D. M. Smith b Marshall	3	– c Greenidge b Marshall	0
M. A. Lynch c Parks b Jesty	17	– lbw b Jesty	19
G. R. J. Roope c Parks b Jesty	19	– b Jesty	25
†C. J. Richards b Tremlett	25	– (8) b Marshall	36
I. R. Payne lbw b Jesty	1	– (7) c sub b Tremlett	14
S. T. Clarke b Jesty	3	– (10) c Bailey b Marshall	26
R. D. Jackman not out	20	– (9) c Jesty b Marshall	6
P. I. Pocock c Greenidge b Marshall	0	– not out	2
B 1, l-b 18, w 2	21	B 8, l-b 9, w 4, n-b 1	22
1/54 2/55 3/64 4/111 5/143 6/143 7/151 8/154 9/202	204	1/28 2/30 3/30 4/34 5/73 6/100 7/113 8/150 9/155	181

Bowling: *First Innings*—Marshall 22.4–4–68–3; Stevenson 25–4–72–2; Tremlett 11–8–5–1; Jesty 13–2–38–4. *Second Innings*—Marshall 15.5–4–60–5; Stevenson 10–2–33–2; Jesty 13–3–32–2; Tremlett 18–8–34–1.

Hampshire

C. G. Greenidge run out	43	– c Smith b Clarke	3
T. M. Tremlett b Clarke	1	– b Clarke	0
M. C. J. Nicholas b Clarke	0	– c Richards b Jackman	1
T. E. Jesty c Richards b Jackman	9	– c Payne b Pocock	28
D. R. Turner b Jackman	13	– not out	38
*N. E. J. Pocock not out	8	– (11) absent injured	0
N. G. Cowley b Clarke	1	– (6) c Roope b Pocock	5
†R. J. Parks c Clinton b Payne	19	– (7) c Roope b Jackman	0
M. D. Marshall c Clarke b Payne	7	– (8) c Smith b Jackman	0
M. J. Bailey c Roope b Clarke	14	– (9) lbw b Jackman	0
K. Stevenson b Clarke	31	– (10) c Payne b Jackman	0
B 3, l-b 3, w 2, n-b 10	18	B 5, l-b 7, w 2, n-b 2	16
1/8 2/8 3/22 4/37 5/81 6/81 7/102 8/117 9/161	164	1/5 2/6 3/6 4/80 5/88 6/91 7/91 8/91 9/91	91

Bowling: *First Innings*—Clarke 21.2–10–41–5; Jackman 19–4–52–2; Payne 11–4–28–2; Pocock 7–0–19–0; Knight 6–3–6–0. *Second Innings*—Clarke 10–1–25–2; Jackman 16–6–30–5; Payne 6–2–17–0; Knight 6–4–2–0; Pocock 6–5–1–2.

Umpires: D. J. Halfyard and K. E. Palmer.

KENT

KENT v MIDDLESEX

Played at Tunbridge Wells, June 15, 17, 18, 1963

Drawn. The late arrival on Monday morning of nine of the Middlesex team, including Drybrough, the captain, provided a situation without parallel in the history of first-class cricket. At the close on Saturday, Middlesex, having dismissed Kent for 150, were 121 for three wickets with White 43 not out, Hooker 13 not out. The team had stayed at a local hotel on Friday night and arranged to do the same on Monday night, but they returned to their London homes at the week-end.

Three players arrived at the ground with plenty of time to spare. They were White and S. E. Russell, who had already been dismissed, and Clark, the twelfth man. White put on his pads and gloves and waited on the boundary, hoping his partner would be in time while the umpires and the Kent players went to the middle. After a wait of a liberal two minutes, the umpires led the players off the field and it was officially stated that the umpires had closed the Middlesex innings.

It was decided that Kent should begin their second innings within ten minutes and Cowdrey agreed that Clark could keep wicket while if necessary White and S. E. Russell shared the bowling, Kent providing sufficient substitute fielders to make up eleven in the field for Middlesex. Actually, Underwood, Catt, Prodger, Brown and Dye assisted their opponents, but within three overs the whole Middlesex side were present and fielding. Thus, Kent recovered from a desperate situation and thanks to bold hitting by Richardson they were able to set Middlesex to get 371 to win in six and a half hours. An unsatisfactory match was completely spoiled on the last day when rain permitted very little cricket. MCC ruled that the umpires ordered Middlesex to close their first innings.

Kent

P. E. Richardson b Hooker	35	– c Murray b Titmus	95
B. W. Luckhurst c Murray b Hooker	26	– c sub b Bennett	4
D. Nicholls c Parfitt b Titmus	15	– lbw b Bennett	16
*M. C. Cowdrey c and b Hooker	8	– c Hooker b Moss	23
S. E. Leary c Moss b Hooker	6	– not out	92
J. Prodger c Hooker b Titmus	30	– c Drybrough b Hooker	74
†A. W. Catt c Moss b Titmus	19	– c Hooker b Price	25
A. L. Dixon c Titmus b Drybrough	0	– c Moss b Price	5
D. Underwood not out	4	– not out	6
A. Brown b Drybrough	0		
J. Dye lbw b Titmus	1		
B 4, l-b 2	6	B 1	1
1/53 2/70 3/79 4/90 5/91 6/144 7/145 8/148 9/145	150	1/5 2/75 3/120 4/150 5/270 6/307 7/317	(7 wkts dec.) 341

Bowling: *First Innings*—Moss 8–2–12–0; Price 6–1–25–0; Hooker 21–6–57–4; Titmus 29.1–14–39–4; Drybrough 10–4–11–2. *Second Innings*—Bennett 9–1–48–2; Price 11–0–81–2; Moss 22–7–48–1; Titmus 28–6–82–1; Drybrough 19–7–50–0; Hooker 8–0–31–1.

Middlesex

W. E. Russell b Dixon	4	– lbw b Dixon	4
S. E. Russell c Cowdrey b Brown	3	– c Leary b Dixon	28
P. H. Parfitt run out	54	– c Prodger b Brown	27
R. A. White not out	43	– not out	19
R. W. Hooker not out	13	– not out	2
L-b 4	4	N-b 2	2
1/5 2/9 3/106 (3 wkts dec.)	121	1/5 2/51 3/73 (3 wkts)	82

F. J. Titmus, D. Bennett, †J. T. Murray, *C. D. Drybrough, J. S. E. Price, A. E. Moss, did not bat.

Bowling: *First Innings*—Brown 16–2–34–1; Dixon 18–7–26–1; Dye 2–0–10–0; Underwood 9–3–33–0; Leary 7–2–14–0. *Second Innings*—Brown 11–3–33–1; Dixon 8–4–15–2; Underwood 3.3–1–21–0; Dye 2–0–11–0.

Umpires: O. W. Herman and A. E. Rhodes.

KENT v SURREY

Played at Blackheath, July 27, 28, 29, 1963

Kent won by four wickets. They had an unexpected shock, however, when they were within nine runs of victory. Harman achieved the hat-trick for Surrey when he caught and bowled Luckhurst and Denness with the last two balls of one over and bowled Leary with the first delivery of his next. Kent eventually won with nearly an hour to spare. Underwood was the most successful Kent bowler, following his first innings four for 25 with six for 88 and another of the younger members – Luckhurst – was instrumental in taking Kent to a first innings lead of 193, scoring his maiden century in Championship cricket. Kent were asked to score 102 to win in two and a quarter hours and Richardson, Nicholls and Wilson put them on the right road before Harman produced his late surprise.

Surrey

J. H. Edrich c Catt b Dye	10	– c Richardson b Underwood	74
W. A. Smith c Leary b Underwood	21	– b Dye	2
A. B. D. Parsons lbw b Leary	21	– lbw b Leary	30
R. A. E. Tindall run out	48	– c Luckhurst b Underwood	12
S. J. Storey c Luckhurst b Underwood	0	– c Richardson b Underwood	7
*B. Constable c Catt b Brown	17	– b Brown	63
D. Gibson c Luckhurst b Underwood	4	– not out	48
R. Harman c Dye b Underwood	4	– lbw b Underwood	13
†O. D. Kember not out	17	– c Richardson b Underwood	0
D. A. D. Sydenham c Denness b Leary	6	– b Brown	5
P. J. Loader c Underwood b Leary	5	– c Luckhurst b Underwood	6
B 1, l-b 6, n-b 6	13	B 19, l-b 11, n-b 4	34
1/19 2/42 3/60 4/76 5/122 6/123 7/127 8/134 9/149	166	1/12 2/69 3/74 4/98 5/112 6/185 7/257 8/278 9/282	294

Bowling: *First Innings*—Brown 19–11–25–1; Dye 17–5–35–1; Underwood 29–20–25–4; Leary 15–2–61–3; Fillary 2–0–7–0. *Second Innings*—Brown 19–8– 46–2; Dye 12–4–37–1; Underwood 34.3–12–88–6; Leary 26–8–60–1; Fillary 7–4–14–0; Luckhurst 7–3–15–0.

Kent

*P. E. Richardson run out	49	– lbw b Tindall	35
D. Nicholls lbw b Loader	10	– b Tindall	26
R. C. Wilson c Kember b Sydenham	2	– b Harman	23
S. E. Leary c Tindall b Gibson	55	– b Harman	6
B. W. Luckhurst not out	126	– c and b Harman	0
M. H. Denness c and b Harman	53	– c and b Harman	0
E. W. J. Fillary c Sydenham b Harman	0	– not out	4
†A. W. Catt c Tindall b Gibson	35	– not out	1
A. Brown b Sydenham	1		
D. Underwood b Sydenham	1		
J. Dye b Sydenham	3		
B 12, l-b 8, w 1, n-b 3	24	B 2, l-b 4, n-b 1	7
1/23 2/26 3/87 4/149 5/258 6/270 7/338 8/340 9/354	359	1/50 2/67 3/91 4/93 5/93 6/96	(6 wkts) 102

Bowling: *First Innings*—Loader 14–3–48–1; Sydenham 18–1–45–4; Gibson 19–5–57–2; Harman 29–10–98–2; Tindall 27–6–66–0; Storey 5–0–21–0. *Second Innings*—Sydenham 2–0–7–0; Gibson 2–0–10–0; Harman 12.3–1–54–4; Tindall 12–4–24–2.

Umpires: H. E. Hammond and O. W. Herman.

KENT v GLAMORGAN

Played at Maidstone, July 15, 16, 17, 1964

Drawn. The match was memorable for a fine not out innings of 137 by Leary who rescued Kent from a poor start, a hat-trick by Sayer who ended the Glamorgan first innings, and an unbroken stand of 206 between Pressdee and Rees who baulked Kent's chance of victory. Leary batted five hours and hit one 6 and twelve 4s, being assisted in entertaining partnerships by Wilson, Prodger and Luckhurst. Pressdee and Rees also batted well in the Glamorgan first innings, but, although both passed fifty, Kent were able to enforce the follow-on with a lead of 154. Sayer, who finished with six for 55, bowled Evans and Wheatley with the last two deliveries of one over and had I. J. Jones caught from the first ball of his next to achieve the second hat-trick of his career. Rees joined Pressdee when 18 runs were needed to avoid an innings defeat and his maiden century which took three hours included fourteen boundaries.

Kent

P. E. Richardson c A. Jones b Wheatley	1
M. H. Denness lbw b Walker	13
R. C. Wilson run out	56
*M. C. Cowdrey b Wheatley	4
S. E. Leary not out	137
J. M. Prodger c Evans b I. J. Jones	57
B. W. Luckhurst not out	52
B 11, l-b 12, n-b 3	26
1/3 2/26 3/33 4/122 5/235	(5 wkts dec.) 346

A. L. Dixon, †A. W. Catt, D. Underwood, D. M. Sayer did not bat.

Bowling: I. J. Jones 28–4–87–1; Wheatley 33–9–69–2; Walker 22–4–71–1; Hedges 3–1–6–0; Shepherd 14–2–36–0; Pressdee 12–0–51–0.

Glamorgan

A. Jones b Dixon	12	– b Dixon	8
B. Hedges c Catt b Sayer	26	– c Luckhurst b Underwood	18
A. R. Lewis c Cowdrey b Underwood	28	– c and b Leary	58
P. M. Walker c Catt b Sayer	0	– lbw b Dixon	33
J. Pressdee c Catt b Dixon	58	– not out	97
A. Harris b Sayer	5	– lbw b Sayer	1
A. Rees lbw b Dixon	50	– not out	106
†D. L. Evans b Sayer	5		
D. J. Shepherd not out	0		
*O. S. Wheatley b Sayer	0		
I. J. Jones c Leary b Sayer	0		
B 5, l-b 2, w 1	8	B 11, l-b 8, w 2	21
1/33 2/39 3/40 4/94 5/107 6/167 7/192 8/192 9/192	192	1/11 2/50 3/128 4/132 5/136	(5 wkts) 342

Bowling: *First Innings*—Sayer 25.1–6–55–6; Dixon 25–10–51–3; Underwood 26–17–27–1; Leary 17–7–37–0; Luckhurst 5–1–14–0. *Second Innings*—Sayer 21–9–39–1; Dixon 43–14–115–2; Luckhurst 14–3–23–0. Leary 36–10–115–1; Underwood 20–12–29–1.

Umpires: T. Drinkwater and C. G. Pepper.

KENT v HAMPSHIRE

(R. C. Wilson's Benefit)

Played at Canterbury, August 1, 3, 4, 1964

Drawn. In a match dominated by batsmen Livingstone scored a century in each innings, Cowdrey failed by one run to do likewise, Richardson hit 103 not out before lunch on the first day and Wilson, the beneficiary, made 130. Shackleton, when he dismissed Wilson, became the first bowler to take 100 wickets in the season. Richardson (twenty-one 4s) and Wilson (fifteen 4s), put on 147 in just over two hours and Cowdrey hit fourteen boundaries before the declaration. Livingstone, who scored seventeen 4s in four and a quarter hours, and Horton, steered Hampshire out of trouble on the second day and Ingleby-Mackenzie declared 66 behind. Cowdrey took only two hours thirty-five minutes for his century but Hampshire, set to make 244 in two hours, fifty minutes lost their chance when Marshall and Livingstone were parted at 130.

Kent

P. E. Richardson c and b Wassell	124	– retired hurt	11
M. H. Denness b White	15	– c Livingstone b Shackleton	15
R. C. Wilson c Wassell b Shackleton	130	– c Sainsbury b Shackleton	15
*M. C. Cowdrey c Timms b Shackleton	99	– not out	100
S. E. Leary not out	15	– c Timms b Shackleton	6
†A. W. Catt lbw b Shackleton	2	– c Barnard b Sainsbury	0
B. W. Luckhurst (did not bat)		– b Wassell	23
A. L. Dixon (did not bat)		– st Timms b Gray	1
D. Underwood (did not bat)		– not out	0
L-b 1, n-b 2	3	B 3, l-b 2, n-b 1	6
1/38 2/185 3/352 4/384 5/388	(5 wkts dec.) 388	1/28 2/61 3/71 4/123 5/134 6/154	(6 wkts dec.) 177

D. M. Sayer and J. Dye did not bat.

Bowling: *First Innings*—Shackleton 30.1–5–113–3; White 22–3–99–1; Gray 9–0–30–0; Wassell 23–4–90–1; Sainsbury 15–1–53–0. *Second Innings*—Shackleton 18–6–38–3; White 15.1–2–61–0; Gray 10–0–32–1; Wassell 10–2–31–1; Sainsbury 2–0–9–1.

Hampshire

R. E. Marshall c Underwood b Dye	3	– c Denness b Underwood	75
H. M. Barnard b Dye	13	– c Denness b Sayer	10
H. Horton c and b Luckhurst	79	– c sub b Luckhurst	0
D. A. Livingstone c Denness b Luckhurst	117	– not out	105
J. R. Gray c Richardson b Luckhurst	0	– c and b Dixon	8
P. J. Sainsbury b Underwood	61	– b Dixon	8
*A. C. D. Ingleby-Mackenzie c Wilson b Underwood	17	– b Dixon	5
†B. S. V. Timms c Catt b Sayer	3	– not out	0
A. Wassell b Dye	1		
D. Shackleton not out	23	– c Wilson b Underwood	0
D. W. White (did not bat)		– c sub b Dixon	4
B 1, l-b 2, n-b 2	5	B 4, l-b 5	9
1/3 2/16 3/200 4/206 5/231 6/272 7/275 8/280 9/322	(9 wkts dec.) 322	1/19 2/130 3/164 4/172 5/176 6/197 7/198 8/212	(8 wkts) 224

Bowling: *First Innings*—Dye 24–9–41–3; Sayer 19–3–53–1; Dixon 28–7–87–0; Underwood 22.3–8–48–2; Leary 16–2–35–0; Luckhurst 10–0–53–3. *Second Innings*—Dye 8–1–24–0; Sayer 10–1–32–1; Underwood 14–1–64–2; Dixon 13–0–74–4; Leary 2–1–8–0; Luckhurst 3–2–1–1; Cowdrey 2–0–12–0.

Umpires: J. S. Buller and W. F. Price.

KENT v DERBYSHIRE

Played at Folkestone, July 3, 5, 6, 1965

Drawn. Hall struck sixteen 4s in Derbyshire's first century of the season, sharing a second-wicket stand of 146 with Page, but from 176 for two Derbyshire slumped to 264 all out, Sayer celebrating his return to the side with four for 67. Denness, with a career best of 174, was instrumental in establishing first-innings supremacy for Kent. Wilson and Cowdrey assisted the Scot in attractive partnerships. Kent, leading by 107, looked well placed when Derbyshire lost three second-innings wickets for 40, but Hall killed any hopes of victory with his second century, which also included sixteen boundaries.

Derbyshire

J. R. Eyre c Prodger b Dixon	21	– c Sayer b Brown	14
I. W. Hall c Knott b Sayer	101	– b Underwood	101
M. H. Page c Leary b Dixon	57	– c Knott b Sayer	19
H. L. Johnson c Cowdrey b Brown	30	– c Cowdrey b Sayer	23
I. R. Buxton c Prodger b Brown	0	– c Cowdrey b Dixon	23
J. F. Harvey c Knott b Brown	5	– not out	4
*D. C. Morgan c Knott b Sayer	17	– not out	11
E. Smith c Cowdrey b Brown	16		
†R. W. Taylor not out	8	– b Brown	23
M. H. J. Allen c Luckhurst b Sayer	1	– c Cowdrey b Brown	0
A. B. Jackson b Sayer	3		
B 1, l-b 4	5	B 4, l-b 3, n-b 2	9
1/30 2/176 3/190 4/192 5/198 6/219 7/252 8/255 9/260	264	1/5 2/30 3/40 4/72 5/144 6/212 7/212	(7 wkts) 227

Bowling: *First Innings*—Brown 26–3–72–4; Dixon 31–12–74–2; Sayer 24.1–7–67–4; Underwood 26–12–46–0. *Second Innings*—Brown 13–5–23–3; Sayer 25–5–50–2; Dixon 37–18–58–1; Underwood 36–22–47–1; Luckhurst 8–1–40–0.

Kent

M. H. Denness c Taylor b Allen	174	D. L. Underwood run out	0
B. W. Luckhurst c Page b Buxton	2	A. Brown c Smith b Jackson	6
R. C. Wilson c Morgan b Jackson	58	D. M. Sayer not out	1
*M. C. Cowdrey lbw b Smith	57		
S. E. Leary c Page b Buxton	12	B 3, l-b 7, n-b 1	11
J. M. Prodger c Page b Jackson	9		—
†A. Knott c Morgan b Jackson	32	1/6 2/140 3/329 4/265 5/274	371
A. L. Dixon c Taylor b Allen	9	6/337 7/349 8/355 9/366	

Bowling: Jackson 26.2–8–75–4; Buxton 25–4–68–2; Morgan 31–6–83–0; Smith 21–4–58–1; Allen 19–2–76–2.

Umpires: W. F. Price and J. Langridge.

KENT v NOTTINGHAMSHIRE

Played at Dover, August 21, 23, 24, 1965

Drawn. This was a notable match for Taylor, the Nottinghamshire 22-year-old all-rounder who performed the hat-trick while taking five wickets for the first time. No play was possible on Saturday and, when Wilson and Cowdrey were putting the Kent innings back on its feet following a bad start, Taylor struck, sending back Wilson, Cowdrey and Leary with successive balls. Nottinghamshire got to within one run of Kent's 76 for the loss of half their wickets and then Taylor showed his batting ability with a top-score 28, giving his side a lead of 67. Brown, three for 44, completed 100 wickets in a season for the first time. Denness and Luckhurst put on 116 for the first wicket when Kent batted again but at 206 for four, rain washed out hopes of a good finish.

Kent

M. H. Denness b Corran	3	– b Corran	59
B. W. Luckhurst c Johnson b Davison	5	– c Davison b Taylor	84
R. C. Wilson b Taylor	9	– b Davison	6
*M. C. Cowdrey c Hill b Taylor	18	– not out	24
J. M. Prodger not out	21	– not out	0
S. E. Leary c Hill b Taylor	0		
†A. Knott c Johnson b Taylor	4		
A. L. Dixon b Corran	0	– b Taylor	14
A. Brown b Corran	6		
D. M. Sayer b Taylor	4		
J. C. Dye run out	0		
B 5, l-b 1	6	B 11, l-b 7, n-b 1	19
	—		—
1/4 2/14 3/35 4/36 5/36 6/40 7/43 8/53 9/64	76	1/116 2/135 3/167 4/206	(4 wkts) 206

Bowling: *First Innings*—Corran 18–6–27–3; Davison 8–4–6–1; Johnson 5–1–14–0; Taylor 10.2–1–23–5. *Second Innings*—Corran 20–9–53–1; Davison 14–4–26–1; Johnson 13–2–52–0; Taylor 16.4–1–56–2.

Nottinghamshire

N. Hill c Cowdrey b Dye	22
J. B. Bolus lbw b Dye	11
B. Whittingham c Knott b Sayer	3
I. Moore b Brown	11
M. J. Smedley c Prodger b Brown	9
M. Taylor c Knott b Sayer	28
*†G. Millman b Brown	13
K. Gillhouley b Sayer	11
A. Johnson b Dixon	15
A. J. Corran c Knott b Sayer	3
J. Davison not out	4
L-b 13	13
1/36 2/41 3/41 4/58 5/75 6/89 7/113 8/134 9/136	143

Bowling: Brown 15–1–44–3; Sayer 13.2–5–41–4; Dye 14–2–30–2; Dixon 5–1–15–1.

Umpires: A. E. Rhodes and C. Cook.

KENT v MIDDLESEX

Played at Gravesend, May 14, 16, 17, 1966

Drawn. A match which produced many highlights on the first two days, ended on the third in a not unfamiliar manner with Middlesex running out of time in which to bowl out their opponents who, in turn, were short of the target. A best performance by the Middlesex forcing right-hand batsman, Clark, who featured in a third-wicket stand of 162 in two and a half hours with Parfitt, enabled Middlesex to build up an impressive total. Clark proved that aggression paid handsomely on this perfect batting wicket which Kent, in their first innings, apart from Wilson, failed to appreciate until their last pair came together. Then the fast bowlers, Brown and Sayer, hit a whirlwind 94 in exactly an hour, with the former recording his highest score. It was a thrilling last-wicket stand which, in his forty years' experience of Kent cricket, secretary-manager Leslie Ames did not think had been bettered for Kent by batsmen numbers ten and eleven. During the Middlesex first innings, the young Kent wicket-keeper Knott equalled the Kent wicket-keeping record by dismissing six batsmen – four of them caught and two stumped.

Middlesex

M. J. Harris c Knott b Brown	28	– c Luckhurst b Underwood	56
C. T. Radley c Knott b Sayer	1	– c Knott b Underwood	57
P. H. Parfitt c Knott b Sayer	85	– c Knott b Brown	1
E. A. Clark lbw b Dixon	149	– c Brown b Dixon	24
*F. J. Titmus c Underwood b Sayer	32	– lbw b Dixon	25
R. W. Hooker c Knott b Underwood	27	– run out	21
M. J. Smith st Knott b Underwood	10	– not out	17
D. A. Bick c Luckhurst b Dixon	0	– not out	11
H. C. Latchman not out	1		
†E. G. Clifton st Knott b Dixon	0		
R. W. Stewart b Dixon	1		
L-b 2, w 1	3	B 5, l-b 4, n-b 1	10
1/1 2/39 3/201 4/283 5/316 6/324 7/333 8/334 9/335	337	1/113 2/114 3/114 4/159 5/186 6/206 (6 wkts dec.)	222

Bowling: *First Innings*—Brown 20–1–94–1; Sayer 22–4–62–3; Dixon 32–9–90–4; Underwood 23–5–80–2; Fillary 4–0–8–0. *Second Innings*—Brown 20–7–38–1; Sayer 11–0–39–0; Dixon 21–5–64–2; Underwood 30–11–71–2.

Kent

E. W. J. Fillary c Parfitt b Latchman	1	– c Parfitt b Latchman	7
B. W. Luckhurst c Clifton b Stewart	20	– c Titmus b Stewart	10
D. Nicholls c Parfitt b Titmus	1	– lbw b Hooker	23
R. C. Wilson c Hooker b Titmus	74	– c Stewart b Titmus	53
S. E. Leary b Latchman	18	– lbw b Bick	46
J. M. Prodger c Radley b Bick	5	– b Bick	21
†A. Knott run out	4	– lbw b Titmus	36
*A. L. Dixon c Titmus b Bick	30	– not out	44
D. L. Underwood lbw b Stewart	0	– c Clifton b Bick	5
A. Brown not out	52	– not out	0
D. M. Sayer b Clark	39		
B 1, l-b 11, n-b 1	13	B 9, l-b 12, w 1	22
1/11 2/18 3/33 4/78 5/110 6/125 7/132 8/133 9/163	257	1/31 2/35 3/118 4/156 5/164 6/194 7/216 8/235	(8 wkts) 267

Bowling: *First Innings*—Stewart 25–10–36–2; Hooker 17–5–53–0; Latchman 17–4–57–2; Titmus 29–8–50–2; Bick 16–5–45–2; Clark 2.2–1–3–1. *Second Innings*—Stewart 9–2–27–1; Hooker 13–0–41–1; Latchman 8–3–21–1; Titmus 27–7–76–2; Bick 21–6–69–3; Smith 2–0–11–0.

Umpires: A. E. Alderman and R. S. Lay.

KENT v SURREY

Played at Blackheath, July 2, 4, 5, 1966

Drawn. Both sides defied the reputation of the Blackheath pitch to cause batsmen discomfort by running up big scores on the first two days. Then when the wicket really was awkward on the third day, an interesting finish was denied by the intervention of the weather after Graham and Dixon had caused Surrey to collapse in their second innings. On the opening day Edrich and Edwards figured in a century partnership. Edrich went on to score 132, hitting two 6s and sixteen 4s in a stay of five hours and Stewart helped himself to fourteen boundaries in an innings of just over two hours. When Kent lost half their side for 156 runs on the second day it appeared that the pitch had already helped the bowlers to gain the upper hand but Luckhurst with 183, his highest innings on the ground when he scored his first century in County cricket, enabled Kent to recover. Luckhurst hit twenty-nine 4s in a stay of just over five hours and thanks to good support from Knott and Dixon plus a thrilling last-wicket stand, Kent won an exciting struggle for first-innings lead. For Surrey, Storey bowled splendidly in taking six wickets for 100.

Surrey

J. H. Edrich c Luckhurst b Dixon	132	– c Nicholls b Dixon	28
M. J. Edwards run out	65	– lbw b Dixon	15
M. D. Willett c Knott b Dixon	10	– c Ealham b Graham	1
R. A. E. Tindall lbw b Graham	12	– c Sayer b Graham	8
*M. J. Stewart run out	77	– c Denness b Dixon	9
S. J. Storey c Dixon b Sayer	0	– lbw b Dixon	6
G. R. J. Roope not out	31	– b Graham	0
R. I. Jefferson c Ealham b Graham	12	– c Luckhurst b Graham	0
*A. Long not out	0	– c Knott b Dixon	0
P. I. Pocock (did not bat)		– not out	0
R. Harman (did not bat)		– not out	1
B 9, l-b 10, w 1, n-b 1	21	B 6, l-b 2	8
1/125 2/156 3/199 4/283 5/283 6/334 7/356	(7 wkts dec.) 360	1/30 2/33 3/51 4/61 5/67 6/69 7/69 8/73 9/75	(9 wkts) 76

Bowling: *First Innings*—Sayer 18–3–63–1; Dye 18–6–42–0; Graham 28–6–54–2; Dixon 47–11–147–2; Luckhurst 13–2–33–0. *Second Innings*—Sayer 6–3–14–0; Dye 2–1–1–0; Graham 14–4–20–4; Dixon 17–10–35–5.

Kent

M. H. Denness c Edwards b Harman	28
B. W. Luckhurst c Tindall b Storey	183
D. Nicholls c Edwards b Storey	21
S. E. Leary b Storey	4
J. M. Prodger c Edwards b Storey	2
A. Ealham c Edwards b Jefferson	4
†A. Knott c Stewart b Pocock	46
*A. L. Dixon lbw b Pocock	41
D. M. Sayer lbw b Storey	3
J. N. Graham b Storey	12
J. C. Dye not out	6
B 8, l-b 5	12
1/50 2/139 3/143 4/147 5/156 6/236 7/308 8/343 9/348	362

Bowling: Jefferson 30–8–75–1; Storey 37.4–8–100–6; Harman 29–3–77–1; Pocock 17–3–64–2; Tindall 5–1–20–0; Roope 5–0–14–0.

Umpires: P. B. Wright and C. G. Pepper.

KENT v GLOUCESTERSHIRE

Played at Folkestone, July 6, 7, 8, 1966

65 overs. Kent won by 173 runs. A spell of three wickets for one run in six balls by Mortimore, the Gloucestershire captain, had Kent struggling in their first innings, but Ealham and Knott launched a recovery and Ealham was later responsible for Gloucestershire being in even worse trouble when they batted. He took five catches in the same place in the deep, all off Underwood, whose figures of six for 52 completed Gloucestershire's first-innings downfall. A fine century by Luckhurst was a feature of the Kent second innings which ensured that Gloucestershire were left a formidable target. Milton defied the Kent attack for two and a half hours but the only other real resistance came from Mence and Kent eventually pulled off a convincing victory.

Kent

M. H. Denness lbw b Allen	28	– lbw b Allen	39
B. W. Luckhurst c and b Mortimore	33	– c Meyer b Mence	133
D. Nicholls c Milton b Mortimore	0	– c Milton b Mence	53
S. E. Leary lbw b Mortimore	22		
*M. C. Cowdrey c D. Brown b Mortimore	0		
A. Ealham c Meyer b A. S. Brown	4	– not out	28
†A. Knott c D. Brown b A. S. Brown	47	– c Russell b A. S. Brown	11
A. L. Dixon st Meyer b Windows	20	– not out	26
D. L. Underwood run out	1		
D. M. Sayer not out	0		
B 2, l-b 7, n-b 1	10	B 1, l-b 5	6
1/64 2/67 3/68 4/68 5/107 6/167 7/202 8/205 9/205 (9 wkts, 65 overs)	205	1/71 2/199 3/224 4/246 (4 wkts dec.)	296

J. C. Dye did not bat.

Bowling: *First Innings*—A. S. Brown 12–1–46–2; Windows 15–1–59–1; Allen 21–6–53–1; Mortimore 17–5–37–4. *Second Innings*—A. S. Brown 17–0–84–1; Windows 20–2–70–0; Allen 14–3–56–1; Mortimore 7–4–8–0; Mence 21–4–72–2.

Gloucestershire

R. B. Nicholls b Sayer	29 – c Denness b Sayer	2
C. A. Milton c Sayer b Underwood	27 – hit wkt b Underwood	43
D. Brown c Ealham b Underwood	8 – b Dye	12
S. E. Russell c Ealham b Underwood	6 – c Leary b Underwood	7
D. Shepherd b Dye	4 – c Cowdrey b Sayer	12
M. D. Mence c Ealham b Underwood	0 – c Luckhurst b Dye	55
*J. B. Mortimore c Ealham b Underwood	10 – c Cowdrey b Leary	20
A. S. Brown b Sayer	13 – lbw b Sayer	24
A. R. Windows c Ealham b Underwood	16 – lbw b Sayer	0
D. A. Allen not out	10 – hit wkt b Leary	16
†B. J. Meyer not out	6 – not out	0
L-b 2	2 B 4, l-b 2	6
1/56 2/56 3/63 4/71 5/74 6/74 7/90 8/101 9/115	(9 wkts, 65 overs) 131	197
	1/10 2/37 4/66 5/84 6/117 7/143 8/197 9/197	

Bowling: *First Innings*—Sayer 22–8–45–2; Dixon 6–0–19–0; Underwood 26–10–52–6; Dye 11–6–13–1. *Second Innings*—Sayer 16–2–32–4; Dixon 18–8–44–0; Underwood 21–16–21–2; Dye 16.2–6–31–2; Leary 18–1–63–2.

Umpires: P. B. Wight and C. G. Pepper.

KENT v NORTHAMPTONSHIRE

Played at Maidstone, July 16, 18, 19, 1966

Drawn. Rain ruined this match after Kent had played themselves into a sound position. Northampton made a shocking start, losing three wickets for 20 runs and half the side was dismissed for 72. The left-handed Wills, who the previous season had twice defied the Kent attack to get him out, defended soundly and was last out, having batted nearly five and a half hours for his highest first-class score, 82. Knott, for the second time in the summer, equalled the Kent wicket-keeping record by dismissing six batsmen in an innings. Kent were given a wonderful start by Denness and the left-handed Wilson, whose second-wicket partnership realised 154. On the third day rain prevented any play and Kent had to be content with two points.

Northamptonshire

C. Milburn c Ealham b Sayer	0
R. Wills c Knott b Dye	82
D. S. Steele c Knott b Dixon	0
B. L. Reynolds c Knott b Dye	5
Mushtaq Mohammad st Knott b Underwood	13
P. J. Watts c and b Dixon	12
A. Lightfoot b Dye	19
B. Crump c Knott b Sayer	10
H. Sully c Knott b Dye	1
*†K. V. Andrew lbw b Sayer	21
A. Durose not out	16
L-b 5, n-b 6	11
1/6 2/7 3/20 4/48 5/72 6/122 7/138 8/139 9/168	180

Bowling: Sayer 29–10–40–3; Dixon 27–10–46–2; Dye 24.5–4–41–4; Underwood 27–14–42–1.

Kent

M. H. Denness c Steele b Lightfoot	96
B. W. Luckhurst b Crump	15
R. C. Wilson st Andrew b Sully	88
*M. C. Cowdrey not out	41
A. L. Dixon c Steele b Sully	19
†A. Knott not out	17
L-b 5	5
1/35 2/189 3/203 4/237	(4 wkts) 281

S. E. Leary, A. Ealham, D. L. Underwood, D. M. Sayer and J. C. Dye did not bat.

Bowling: Crump 22–3–80–1; Durose 19–4–48–0; Lightfoot 22–4–52–1; Sully 17–5–52–2; Mushtaq 3–0–12–0; Watts 12–2–32–0.

Umpires: A. E. Alderman and J. F. Crapp.

KENT v SUSSEX

Played at Tunbridge Wells, June 17, 19, 20, 1967

Kent won by 208 runs. Kent began a wonderful week for them and for their pace bowler, Graham, with an overwhelming victory over Sussex. After slumping to 96 for six, Kent were indebted to fighting innings by Luckhurst and Dixon which eventually enabled them to reach a very respectable total. Then Graham made the ball rear up and with fine support from Sayer, Sussex were bowled out for 141, most resistance coming from Greig who found his height a very useful asset. With a lead of 112, Kent made another bad start, but Shepherd batted well and an unbroken ninth-wicket stand between Underwood and Sayer enabled them to declare and present Sussex with a mammoth task. They collapsed dramatically. Graham performed with great accuracy on a worn pitch and was at times virtually unplayable. He took twelve wickets for 77 runs.

Kent

M. H. Denness c Lewis b A. Buss	3	– c Parks b Snow	29
B. W. Luckhurst not out	126	– c Lewis b A. Buss	12
S. E. Leary c Parks b Bates	2	– c Lewis b A. Buss	3
*M. C. Cowdrey c M. A. Buss b Bates	9	– lbw b Greig	26
†A. Knott lbw b Snow	1	– c M. A. Buss b A. Buss	0
A. Ealham c Foreman b Snow	6	– c Foreman b Suttle	10
J. Shepherd b A. Buss	28	– c Parks b Greig	60
A. L. Dixon b A. Buss	64	– c Parks b Bates	3
D. L. Underwood b A. Buss	4	– not out	27
D. M. Sayer run out	0	– not out	35
J. N. Graham b Snow	0		
L-b 9, n-b 1	10	L-b 2, n-b 3	5
1/13 2/25 3/45 4/46 5/58 6/96 7/242 8/252 9/253	253	1/40 2/42 3/53 4/53 5/72 6/96 8/159	(8 wkts dec.) 210

Bowling: *First Innings*—Snow 25–10–45–3; A. Buss 22.5–4–63–4; Bates 23–6–62–2; Greig 9–3–29–0; Suttle 8–2–16–0; Lewis 6–0–28–0. *Second Innings*—Snow 18–3–68–1; A. Buss 21–5–49–3; Bates 11–3–33–1; Greig 13–2–51–2; Suttle 1–0–4–1.

Sussex

M. A. Buss c Knott b Sayer	4	– c Denness b Graham	1
D. J. Foreman c Knott b Sayer	3	– c Underwood b Sayer	21
K. G. Suttle c Leary b Graham	21	– c Cowdrey b Graham	0
G. C. Cooper c Knott b Graham	24	– lbw b Sayer	4
A. Buss c Cowdrey b Graham	4	– c Cowdrey b Graham	17
*†J. M. Parks c Luckhurst b Graham	0	– c Denness b Dixon	23
A. W. Greig b Sayer	56	– c Underwood b Graham	14
M. G. Griffith c Knott b Graham	0	– b Graham	6
E. Lewis c Cowdrey b Sayer	0	– c Underwood b Dixon	0
J. A. Snow not out	24	– c Underwood b Dixon	24
D. L. Bates c Luckhurst b Graham	1	– not out	0
L-b 3, w 1	4	L-b 4	4
1/5 2/22 3/38 4/42 5/42 6/79 7/79 8/86 9/129	141	1/7 2/15 3/33 4/37 5/66 6/84 7/84 8/97 9/106	114

Bowling: *First Innings*—Graham 22.4–3–48–6; Sayer 19–4–60–4; Dixon 4–2–4–0; Shepherd 7–1–25–0. *Second Innings*—Graham 18.4–9–29–6; Sayer 12–2–40–2; Dixon 8–2–35–2; Shepherd 3–1–6–0.

Umpires: C. G. Pepper and R. S. Lay.

KENT v LANCASHIRE

Played at Folkestone, July 8, 9, 10, 1967

Kent won by ten wickets. A second-wicket partnership by Atkinson and Pilling paved the way for Lancashire to build a big total, but their later batsmen failed against Graham, Sayer and Dixon who swept up the first innings in which the last eight wickets fell for 75 runs. Knott was in fine form and for the third time equalled a Kent wicket-keeping record of six dismissals in an innings, this being the first occasion on which all six had been caught. Kent made a good start and their promise of building a large score materialised with most of the recognised batsmen in the right mood. Lancashire then lost three wickets for 46 runs and although Atkinson stayed, Underwood reaped six for 28 in 29 overs and Kent were left with a simple task.

Lancashire

G. Atkinson lbw b Dixon	75	– c Denness b Underwood	53
B. Wood c Knott b Graham	18	– b Sayer	6
H. Pilling c Knott b Dixon	48	– c Cowdrey b Underwood	5
G. Pullar c Knott b Dixon	0	– c Knott b Dixon	12
*J. D. Bond c Denness b Dixon	16	– c Sayer b Dixon	8
J. Sullivan c Knott b Sayer	7	– c Cowdrey b Underwood	32
P. Lever b Graham	2	– c Denness b Underwood	0
K. Higgs lbw b Sayer	10	– c Shepherd b Underwood	0
K. Shuttleworth c Knott b Graham	14	– b Sayer	25
†K. Goodwin not out	1	– c Luckhurst b Underwood	0
J. S. Savage c Knott b Sayer	0	– not out	16
L-b 6	6	B 6	6
1/30 2/122 3/122 4/152 5/170 6/172 7/172 8/190 9/196	197	1/14 2/24 3/46 4/108 5/117 6/117 7/117 8/117 9/134	163

Bowling: *First Innings*—Graham 24–11–39–3; Sayer 16.5–4–38–3; Dixon 18–4–45–4; Shepherd 9–1–27–0; Underwood 23–9–42–0. *Second Innings*—Graham 12–4–25–0; Sayer 6.2–2–12–2; Dixon 34–11–73–2; Underwood 29–20–28–6; Leary 6–1–19–0.

Kent

M. H. Denness lbw b Higgs	29	– not out	11
B. W. Luckhurst c Goodwin b Savage	65	– not out	18
J. M. Prodger b Shuttleworth	1		
*M. C. Cowdrey c Wood b Higgs	46		
†A. Knott c Wood b Higgs	65		
S. E. Leary c Goodwin b Savage	34		
J. Shepherd c Higgs b Shuttleworth	47		
A. L. Dixon b Higgs	7		
D. L. Underwood b Shuttleworth	25		
D. M. Sayer c Wood b Higgs	1		
J. N. Graham not out	0		
B 5, l-b 10	15		
1/67 2/74 3/134 4/153 5/192 6/279 7/297 8/311 9/328	335	(no wkt)	29

Bowling: *First Innings*—Higgs 40–11–98–5; Shuttleworth 26.3–6–81–3; Lever 20–1–63–0; Savage 23–8–62–2; Wood 6–2–16–0. *Second Innings*—Savage 3–0–7–0; Wood 4–1–12–0; Sullivan 0.4–0–10–0.

Umpires: W. F. Price and R. Aspinall.

KENT v HAMPSHIRE

Played at Maidstone, July 22, 23, 1967

Kent won by an innings and 170 runs. A fine innings by Shepherd who hit two 6s and ten 4s paved the way for a Kent recovery after a dubious start. The good work was continued by Leary. On the second day came one of the most dramatic turns of the season as Hampshire were bowled out twice to an innings defeat. The pitch had gone at one end and Underwood was the man to exploit it. The first five Hampshire wickets crashed for 39 runs before the only resistance of the day came from Sainsbury and Turner. Hampshire were dismissed for 95 and fared even worse on their second encounter. No one reached double figures and the innings and the match were over in another seventy-six minutes with the last six wickets falling at the same total. Underwood finished with the remarkable match figures of twelve for 50.

Kent

M. H. Denness c Turner b Cottam	16
B. W. Luckhurst c Livingstone b Shackleton	24
J. Shepherd c Turner b Cottam	72
*M. C. Cowdrey b White	38
S. E. Leary c Marshall b White	82
†A. Knott c Timms b Cottam	10
A. Ealham c Timms b Shackleton	2
A. L. Dixon b Shackleton	0
D. L. Underwood c Castell b White	24
A. Brown c Livingstone b Shackleton	19
J. C. Dye not out	0
L-b 5, n-b 4	9
1/39 2/47 3/131 4/158 5/182 6/189 7/189 8/260 9/285	296

Bowling: Shackleton 31–9–77–4; White 20–3–50–3; Cottam 25–7–78–3; Castell 12–1–46–0; Sainsbury 9–2–36–0.

Hampshire

*R. E. Marshall c Luckhurst b Underwood	6	– c Ealham b Underwood	1
B. L. Reed c Shepherd b Brown	10	– c Knott b Underwood	8
R. M. C. Gilliat b Underwood	19	– c Luckhurst b Dixon	4
D. A. Livingstone b Underwood	0	– c Knott b Dye	8
P. J. Sainsbury c Leary b Dye	26	– c Ealham b Underwood	3
D. R. Turner c Leary b Dixon	15	– b Dixon	3
†B. S. V. Timms c Ealham b Underwood	4	– c Ealham b Underwood	0
A. T. Castell not out	3	– b Underwood	0
D. Shackleton b Underwood	5	– c Shepherd b Dixon	0
D. W. White c sub b Underwood	0	– c Knott b Dixon	0
R. M. H. Cottam c Luckhurst b Underwood	1	– not out	0
B 1, l-b 5	6	B 4	4
1/14 2/18 3/26 4/26 5/39 6/79 7/87 8/92 9/92	95	1/1 2/13 3/13 4/20 5/31 6/31 7/31 8/31 9/31	31

Bowling: *First Innings*—Dye 7–3–13–1; Brown 9–3–28–1; Underwood 18.4–8–35–7; Dixon 6–1–13–1. *Second Innings*—Dye 2–2–0–1; Brown 2–0–2–0; Underwood 9–5–15–5; Dixon 7.2–2–10–4.

Umpires: H. Yarnold and G. H. Pope.

KENT v HAMPSHIRE

Played at Gillingham, July 6, 7, 8, 1968

Kent won by 120 runs. Once again the Gillingham pitch, adversely reported upon to MCC in 1967, really only lasted one day and Kent, batting first, were no doubt well pleased with their eventual total, especially as they had lost their first four wickets for 39 runs. Fortunately, Luckhurst batted extremely well and eventually found useful support forthcoming from Leary and Knott. He hit fourteen 4s in a stay of five hours twenty minutes and paved the way for victory. Hampshire, once the openers were separated, struggled and lost their last four wickets for three runs on a pitch which always helped the bowlers, the ball lifting and turning awkwardly. Kent, batting again, went for quick runs and lost their wickets also quickly to Shackleton and Cottam. Then Underwood, wonderfully suited to the conditions, made Hampshire's final innings a nightmare. He finished with eleven for 64.

Kent

M. H. Denness run out	5	– lbw b Shackleton	3
B. W. Luckhurst c Timms b Cottam	111	– c Richards b Cottam	5
Asif Iqbal b White	3	– c Timms b Cottam	21
*M. C. Cowdrey c Castell b White	0	– c Lewis b Shackleton	8
J. N. Shepherd c Livingstone b Shackleton	12	– c Lewis b Cottam	1
S. E. Leary c and b Cottam	34	– run out	19
†A. P. E. Knott c Timms b White	37	– c Castell b Shackleton	8
A. J. Dixon b Shackleton	6	– c Turner b Cottam	8
A. Brown b White	0	– not out	10
D. L. Underwood c Timms b White	1		
J. N. Graham not out	1	– c Timms b Shackleton	1
B 4, n-b 9	13	B 2, l-b 1, n-b 4	7
1/16 2/23 3/23 4/39 5/113 6/198 7/212 8/213 9/215	223	1/7 2/19 3/32 4/33 5/41 6/53 7/72 8/81 9/91 (9 wkts dec.)	91

Bowling: *First Innings*—Shackleton 30–7–71–2; White 22–3–52–5; Cottam 17.1–3–37–2; Castell 7–0–44–0; Sainsbury 7–4–6–0. *Second Innings*—Shackleton 20.3–8–32–4; White 1–0–2–0; Cottam 20–6–50–4.

Hampshire

B. A. Richards c Denness b Underwood	29	– b Graham	1
B. L. Reed c Cowdrey b Underwood	29	– c Leary b Underwood	17
R. V. Lewis lbw b Underwood	0	– c Luckhurst b Underwood	7
D. A. Livingstone c Knott b Graham	10	– b Dixon	8
*P. J. Sainsbury c Denness b Underwood	6	– c Luckhurst b Underwood	3
D. R. Turner c Denness b Dixon	19	– not out	14
†B. S. V. Timms not out	19	– lbw b Underwood	4
A. T. Castell b Dixon	5	– c Cowdrey b Underwood	1
D. Shackleton lbw b Graham	0	– st Knott b Underwood	0
R. M. H. Cottam c and b Graham	0	– st Knott b Dixon	1
D. W. White run out	0	– b Underwood	0
B 8, l-b 9, w 1, n-b 1	19	L-b 2	2
1/47 2/58 3/59 4/72 5/98 6/116 7/133 8/135 9/135	136	1/2 2/26 3/34 4/34 5/37 6/41 7/43 8/43 9/43	58

Bowling: *First Innings*—Brown 7–3–11–0; Graham 28–12–33–3; Underwood 33–17–47–4; Dixon 10–3–17–2; Shepherd 4–2–9–0. *Second Innings*—Brown 2–1–1–0; Graham 5–1–11–1; Underwood 12–8–17–7; Dixon 9.2–4–27–2.

Umpires: L. H. Gray and O. W. Herman.

KENT v YORKSHIRE

Played at Canterbury, July 31, August 1, 2, 1968

Drawn. With nine hours lost to the weather, not a ball being bowled on Thursday, there was little chance of a definite result to this important match, for Kent were pressing in second place to the Champions. The sun never shone but 12,000 people were present on Wednesday when the pace bowlers were in complete command. They swung the ball in the heavy atmosphere and a hard fast pitch gave them bounce, Nicholson taking eight wickets for 22 in one of his best efforts for Yorkshire. Dye and Shepherd proved just as awkward for Kent and Yorkshire finished the first day at 84 for eight. They batted for forty-five minutes on Friday, but Kent could not get the fifth bonus point and the rest of the proceedings were merely formal. On Thursday, the Duke of Kent, Patron of Kent, paid his first visit to the St. Lawrence ground, accompanied by his wife, the Duchess, Patron of Yorkshire. On this notable day, Sir Robert Menzies, the former Australian Prime Minister, consented to become President of Kent in 1969.

Kent

M. H. Denness c Sharpe b Nicholson	18	– b Nicholson	15
B. W. Luckhurst c Close b Nicholson	2	– c Illingworth b Close	42
G. W. Johnson c Binks b Trueman	2	– not out	7
Asif Iqbal lbw b Nicholson	30	– b Nicholson	1
S. E. Leary st Binks b Nicholson	4	– c Taylor b Wilson	13
J. N. Shepherd b Nicholson	3	– not out	18
†A. P. E. Knott st Binks b Nicholson	1	– c Hampshire b Wilson	29
*A. L. Dixon b Trueman	3		
D. L. Underwood lbw b Nicholson	10		
D. M. Sayer not out	3		
J. C. Dye lbw b Nicholson	1		
L-b 1, n-b 3	4	L-b 10, n-b 1	11
1/2 2/5 3/40 4/48 5/61 6/62 7/65 8/74 9/79	81	1/23 2/87 3/88 4/102 5/113 (5 wkts dec.)	136

Bowling: *First Innings*—Trueman 8–1–25–2; Nicholson 12–4–22–8; Hutton 7–1–30–0. *Second Innings*—Trueman 7–2–18–0; Nicholson 17–9–33–2; Hutton 14–3–36–0; Illingworth 2–0–10–0; Wilson 8–3–21–2; Close 3–0–7–1.

Yorkshire

P. J. Sharpe lbw b Dye	11	– not out	2
K. Taylor c Knott b Dye	1	– not out	0
D. E. V. Padgett c Knott b Dye	7		
J. H. Hampshire lbw b Shepherd	28		
*D. B. Close c Knott b Shepherd	1		
R. Illingworth c Luckhurst b Sayer	0		
†J. G. Binks b Shepherd	3		
R. A. Hutton not out	31		
F. S. Trueman b Shepherd	0		
D. Wilson lbw b Dye	6		
A. G. Nicholson not out	3		
L-b 2	2		
1/7 2/16 3/29 4/47 5/48 6/43 7/63 8/63 9/86 (9 wkts dec.)	93	(No wkt)	2

Bowling: *First Innings*—Dye 22–9–42–4; Sayer 6–1–10–1; Shepherd 23–16–29–4; Dixon 3–1–10–0; Underwood 1–1–0–0. *Second Innings*—Shepherd 2–1–2–0; Underwood 1–1–0–0.

Umpires: L. H. Gray and C. S. Elliott.

KENT v NOTTINGHAMSHIRE

Played at Dover, August 3, 4, 5, 1968

Nottinghamshire won by seven wickets. Not even the most ardent Kent supporter would deny that this was Sobers' match. After Denness (who batted two and a half hours and hit twelve 4s) and Knott had added 113 for the third wicket, Sobers, with left-arm pace worried the rest of the Kent batsmen and he recorded his best bowling performance of the season to date. Moore made his highest score of the season so far and Nottinghamshire declared seven runs behind with 85 overs completed. When Kent batted again, Denness once more did well and Shepherd hit 56 in seventy-eight minutes, including eleven 4s, but Sobers, now bowling spinners, finally was set a target of 186 to win in two and a quarter hours. He came in when his side lost their first wicket and proceeded to annihilate the Kent bowling. He drove, hooked and cut with equal ferocity and raced to 51 out of 71 in forty minutes and with two 6s and eighteen 4s tore to the fastest century of the season in seventy-seven thrilling minutes. So his side won with five overs to spare and Kent were left with the final "Sobering" thought of what might happen next time they meet the West Indies captain. Last time – at Canterbury, in 1966, when playing for his country, he took nine for 49 – the best bowling performance of his career.

Kent

M. H. Denness lbw b Forbes	85	– st Murray b Sobers	49
B. W. Luckhurst lbw b Sobers	7	– c Hill be Forbes	13
D. Nicholls b Sobers	6	– c Bielby b Taylor	1
†A. P. E. Knott c Halfyard b Forbes	54	– c Frost b Taylor	11
S. E. Leary c Murray b Sobers	21	– lbw b Taylor	3
J. N. Shepherd lbw b Sobers	19	– c Forbes b Sobers	56
G. W. Johnson c Murray b Halfyard	18	– lbw b Forbes	10
*A. L. Dixon b Sobers	13	– c Hill b Sobers	5
D. L. Underwood b Sobers	0	– not out	16
D. M. Sayer c Taylor b Sobers	6	– c Murray b Sobers	9
J. C. Dye not out	1	– b Forbes	1
L-b 3, n-b 2	5	L-b 3, n-b 1	4
1/18 2/37 3/150 4/157 5/195 6/198 7/228 8/228 9/228	235	1/24 2/31 3/47 4/64 5/96 6/123 7/140 8/153 9/177	178

Bowling: *First Innings*—Sobers 22.3–3–69–7; Forbes 16–3–53–2; Taylor 13–2–43–0; Halfyard 21–7–65–1. *Second Innings*—Sobers 26–3–87–4; Forbes 21.2–6–39–3; Taylor 17–8–48–3.

Nottinghamshire

J. B. Bolus lbw b Underwood	49	– c Luckhurst b Underwood	20
N. Hill b Dye	0	– c sub b Underwood	26
G. Frost b Sayer	3		
M. J. Smedley c Knott b Sayer	36	– c Shepherd b Dixon	29
H. I. Moore c Knott b Underwood	74	– not out	5
†D. L. Murray c Knott b Dixon	12		
*G. S. Sobers c Sayer b Shepherd	17	– not out	105
S. R. Bielby not out	22		
M. N. Taylor not out	11		
L-b 1, w 1, n-b 2	4	L-b 1	1
1/0 2/5 3/83 4/91 5/131 6/169 7/200	(7 wkts dec.) 228	1/38 2/84 3/164	(3 wkts) 186

C. Forbes and D. J. Halfyard did not bat.

Bowling: *First Innings*—Dye 3–1–6–1; Sayer 14–2–35–2; Shepherd 35–13–84–1; Dixon 8–1–32–1; Underwood 25–6–67–2. *Second Innings*—Shepherd 17–3–68–0; Sayer 4–0–20–0; Underwood 13.2–2–65–2; Dixon 6–0–32–1.

Umpires: O. W. Herman and J. G. Langridge.

KENT v REST OF THE WORLD XI

Played at Canterbury, August 24, 26, 27, 1968

Rest of the World XI won by five wickets. This match provided a feast of runs and Luckhurst was the dominating factor in the Kent first innings. He figured in a second-wicket stand of 115 with Nicholls and batted for three hours fifty minutes hitting one six and thirteen 4s. Shepherd hit ten boundaries and added 104 with Ealham. The Rest's bowlers were obviously lacking in match practice and their batting faltered before a third-wicket stand of 136 by Hanif and Butcher. The West Indian played some splendid shots and later Ramnarace struck two 6s and four 4s in a short but entertaining stay. When Kent batted again, Luckhurst hit his second century of the match. He and Denness put on 190 for the first wicket and as soon as Luckhurst completed his century, in three hours with one 6, one 5 and eight 4s, Kent declared. The World XI accepted the challenge of getting 253 to win in three and a half hours. Barlow, opening with Richards, his possible South African Test partner, raced to 50 in sixty-seven minutes, 100 in one and three-quarter hours, and was first out, having scored 153 out of 225 with one 6 and twenty-two 4s in only two hours, twenty-five minutes. The result was never really in doubt and victory was achieved with ten overs to spare.

Kent

M. H. Denness b Ramnarace	29	– b Saeed	95
B. W. Luckhurst c Richards b Pollock	113	– not out	100
†D. Nicholls st Lindsay b Barlow	39	– not out	3
J. N. Shepherd c Hanif b Ramnarace	56		
S. E. Leary c Lindsay b Pollock	0		
A. Ealham not out	58		
R. Woolmer not out	32		
L-b 5, w 1, n-b 6	12	L-b 1, w 1, n-b 1	3
1/57 2/172 3/194 4/194 5/298	(5 wkts, dec.) 339	1/190	(1 wkt, dec.) 201

G. W. Johnson, *A. L. Dixon, A. Brown and D. M. Sayer did not bat.

Bowling: *First Innings*—Hall 19–1–62–0; Pollock 15–1–67–2; Ramnarace 25–5–58–2; Barlow 10–1–53–1; Saeed 12–2–35–0; Butcher 7–1–23–0; Richards 3–0–29–0. *Second Innings*—Hall 7–0–34–0; Pollock 10–1–45–0; Ramnarace 12–2–30–0; Barlow 12–1–48–0; Saeed 10–1–31–1; Richards 7–3–10–0.

Rest of the World XI

*Hanif Mohammad b Dixon	79		
E. J. Barlow run out	0	– st Nicholls b Leary	153
S. M. Nurse c Ealham b Brown	14	– not out	0
B. F. Butcher c Johnson b Sayer	70	– not out	5
Saeed Ahmed lbw b Shepherd	11	– c Nicholls b Leary	2
B. A. Richards b Shepherd	0	– c Sayer b Leary	81
†J. D. Lindsay c Brown b Johnson	20		
R. E. Marshall b Johnson	24	– c Shepherd b Leary	5
P. M. Pollock not out	16		
R. Ramnarace c Brown b Leary	41	– lbw b Dixon	0
W. W. Hall not out	5		
B 2, l-b 1, n-b 5	8	B 5, l-b 3, n-b 1	9
1/4 2/25 3/161 4/175 5/176 6/183 7/218 8/229 9/274	(9 wkts, dec.) 288	1/225 2/231 3/246 4/248 5/250	(5 wkts) 255

Bowling: *First Innings*—Brown 19–5–52–1; Sayer 14–5–25–1; Shepherd 20–3–74–2; Dixon 15–5–53–1; Woolmer 2–0–9–0; Johnson 11–1–24–2; Leary 8–1–43–1. *Second Innings*—Brown 10–0–28–0; Sayer 7–2–29–0; Shepherd 13–0–69–0; Dixon 13–3–46–1; Johnson 7–0–40–0; Leary 6–1–13–4; Luckhurst 3–0–21–0.

Umpires: J. Bean and J. G. Langridge.

M. C. COWDREY – CENTURION AND CAPTAIN COURTEOUS [1969]

By John Arlott

When England met Australia on June 12, 1968, at Edgbaston, Colin Cowdrey become the first man to play in one hundred Test Matches. He was captain of England in that match and, appropriately enough, he scored a century. Characteristically, too, he reached 95 overnight and appeared much less anxious than his friends while he made the next five runs on the following morning.

One by one the records have gone down before him. As this tribute is written he has scored more runs in Test cricket than any other batsman except Hammond. By the time it is printed he will almost certainly have passed that figure: and half a dozen years of play at the highest level should still lie ahead of him. Among the batsmen we have seen, only Sobers, who is four years younger, can be expected to pass his ultimate total in representative play, while Graveney alone among cricketers still active has scored more runs in all first-class cricket. His once promising leg-spin bowling is no longer regarded seriously but he is arguably the finest slip fieldsman in the world at present.

At the end of the 1968 season he had captained England in nineteen Test matches, Oxford University for one season and Kent for a dozen: under him the county won the Gillette Cup in 1967 and were runners-up in the Championships of 1967 and 1968.

Colin Cowdrey's cricket and his behaviour are both characterised by unrufflable rectitude. His batting is correct, splendid in its controlled rhythms but never in unorthodoxy or violence. Similarly, his bearing in face of treatment which has often been at least tactless, and which would have roused most normally quiet men to indignation, has been impeccably courteous.

For more than twenty years – ever since he was thirteen years old – he has been subjected to the uncharitable scrutiny of publicity: in that entire time he has never said a word out of place. Yet it would miss his quality completely to think him insensitive: his almost boyish jump of glee in the field when an important wicket falls or his gaily quick recognition of a joke are those of a responsive and lively-witted person. His family life is ample indication of the depth and warmth of his feelings. His entire upbringing, however, conspired to make him self-contained, a man who thinks before he speaks – and then, often, does not speak.

His father, the cricket enthusiast (top scorer for the Europeans against Arthur Gilligan's 1926-27 touring team in India) who christened his son Michael Colin Cowdrey to give him the initials of the unique cricket club, was a tea-planter in India. His only child was born in Bangalore and, at the age of five, was sent to England, a boarding school education and the homes of different relatives during vacations. After 1938 Colin Cowdrey did not see his parents until 1945 and subsequently only during their four-yearly leave periods until 1954.

He believes that his cricket was decisively shaped by the headmaster of his preparatory school – Homefield at Sutton in Surrey – Charles Walford, a capable games-player who, as teacher and man, adhered strictly to Victorian public school tenets. Across a gap of almost sixty years he saw no need to congratulate the young cricketer of outstanding promise, only to give him ample practice under a sternly critical eye and infallibly to correct his errors.

So faithfully did he maintain this attitude that Colin Cowdrey left Homefield at the age of thirteen quite unaware that he was probably the finest child cricketer ever produced in England. At the suggestion of his headmaster he would have gone on to Uppingham or Marlborough if either school could have taken him before his father returned from his leave in September 1945. Because Tonbridge had an earlier vacancy he went there almost by chance, as he was later to join Kent rather than Leicestershire.

Before his first cricket term he went for coaching to Gover's School where the experienced professionals were so impressed by his talent that Alf Gover wrote to Ewart Astill, then coach at Tonbridge, and told him to expect a thirteen-year-old good enough to play for the first team. That judgement was confirmed as soon as he went into the Tonbridge nets. But the propriety of playing him in the XI was debated under the concerned attention of the headmaster. It was decided that he might be accepted on a kind of probation. The problem was put to him: he was good enough for the XI: but if he played it meant that he went from fagging perhaps to bowl out the school captain in the nets, and then to return and become a fag again: could he do so without violating protocol? It was a savage dilemma for a thirteen-year-old under scrutiny. There is no more conclusive evidence of Colin Cowdrey's sense of purpose than the fact that he resolved it; but it is not surprising that it made him an undemonstrative cricketer.

He was originally chosen for Tonbridge as a leg-break bowler but when he went to the match with Clifton two months later, he was also batting first wicket down. The outcome would seem a storybook fantasy if it were not to be read in *Wisden*. The youngest player ever to take part in a Public Schools match at Lord's, he scored 75 – more than half the runs scored from the bat – in the first innings of 156, and 44 out of 175 in the second. In the first Clifton innings he took three wickets for 58 and in their second, when they looked likely to win, he put out their last five batsmen for 33 to win the match by two runs.

He continued, as batsman and bowler, the major figure of Tonbridge cricket for four years, until 1950, when as captain of the Public Schools XI he scored a century against the Combined Services at Lord's and went on to play his first match for Kent. A full season with Kent and two centuries, three years an Oxford Blue took him to the end of the 1954 season.

The father who was so delighted by his success, whom he had missed, and whom he so much desired to please, had retired and returned to England at the beginning of that summer. Sadly enough he watched his son as captain of Oxford have a relatively indifferent playing season on a series of wet pitches so that it was for his unmistakable ability rather than current form that he was chosen for Hutton's 1954-55 team to Australia. While he was on the voyage out, his father died. Once more Colin Cowdrey contained his emotions and went on to the success that was, we may suspect, his tribute to the father he had so briefly known.

He batted capably in the first two Tests and then at Melbourne, with the rubber even and England reduced by Miller to 41 for four, he made his first Test century and tilted the match which turned the series.

From that innings he has remained one of the world's outstanding batsmen. He was dropped from the team against Australia in 1964 and West Indies in 1966 by selectors torn by the old tug between class and current form. Over the last six years, too, the England captaincy has been given to him and taken from him in a fashion which, if it happened in a school or club would have been regarded as pettifogging. Always, however, he has continued without apparent pique and now is captain and major batsman of his country, as he and his father wished him to be.

He has gradually found his feet in captaincy and his handling of Kent, particularly in knock-out matches of the Gillette Cup, has become enterprising, intuitive and successful. His lasting reputation will be based upon his batting. The mark of greatness is clear in the air of time to spare about his stroke-making. He never appears to have to hurry and he is remarkably sure of the ball. The nicety of his timing and assessment of line and length are such that, with perhaps the exception of Garfield Sobers, he middles the ball more consistently than any other batsman of this time.

Because, in his early training, Charles Walford compelled him to concentrate, and because of his own studious bent, he has constantly enhanced his technique. Until he reached county standard his natural powers were such that he could play effectively with minimal foot-movement. In his first season with Kent, between school and University, however, he was puzzled that he frequently founded an innings only to be out to the faster bowlers. Arthur Fagg, with characteristic terseness, told him "You aren't moving early enough" and left him to follow the thought. He became more mobile and on Australian wickets in 1954-55 under the influence of Len Hutton, for whom he retains immense admiration, he became predominantly a forward player in defence against pace. This led to a series of injuries on faster pitches in England during 1955 so that afterwards, in the manner of the true masters, he became completely adaptable, a back foot player in some circumstances, front foot in others.

From the first his eye was such that he was untroubled by the speed of bowling. He showed his mastery of spin against the West Indies at Edgbaston in the first Test of 1957 when he and Peter May, by their partnership of 411, changed an apparent losing position, broke Ramadhin's domination, and set England upon a winning course in the rubber. In dealing with Ramadhin primarily as an off-spinner Cowdrey evolved the technique of playing forward with the bat close to the left leg and behind the pad which has since proved remarkably effective and dispiriting against off-break bowlers.

Partly because he is tall, broad, reposeful and commanding in style, Cowdrey has been likened to Walter Hammond. He has, too, Hammond's power and control in cover strokes. He is, however, fundamentally different in method because, as he himself regrets, he is an instinctive off-side player born into a leg-side age. He has become adept in gathering runs to the on but he is at his happiest when he drives anywhere between point and straight. In recent years, too, he has refined his cover play so that by adjusting the point and angle of impact or by the turn of his wrists, he can direct the off-side ball along almost any line between third man and mid-off. His stroke-making is all but perfect. Once in a charity match – true it was no more, and the bowler co-operated – he hit every ball of an over exactly over the centre of the sight screen for six: and the bat moved as gently as if he were patting a tennis ball back to a child.

For more than a dozen years he has been a target for the most intimidating bowling at the command of the Test captains of the world. In the West Indies in 1959-60 he took a heavy battering and at Lord's in 1963 his arm was cruelly fractured. Yet in 1968 he was playing with all his old assurance. He is less acquisitive, less run-hungry and less combative than some of his contemporaries but he seems to relish, almost as an intellectual exercise, the problem of a difficult pitch or bowler.

If he has come gradually to his fullest maturity as a batsman, his advance as a captain has been rapid in recent years. His modesty and his deep Christian conviction have always combined to make him less aggressive than some in his approach to cricket. But in 1968, perhaps because he had the reassurance of the rubber won in the West Indies, he handled the English team after Old Trafford with a firm sense of purpose. He had already worked to create a basis of communal feeling within a cadre of players and he built steadily on it until, at the end of the series, his players, rather than those of the touring side, had made the greater advance in team power.

His natural ability at ball-games made him a useful Rugby and soccer player while, in 1953, he surprised some mature opponents by advancing through the English Rackets Championship until he was defeated by Geoffrey Atkins, the World Champion, in the final. He is still a capable performer at squash, rackets, tennis and, increasingly, golf. Cricket, however, remains his main interest outside his family and he still approaches it with an impressive blend of enthusiasm, respect and modesty. The chronic congenital weakness in his feet – *hallux rigidus* – which caused him to be invalided out of the RAF will, he fears, eventually end his cricket career. Until that happens there is no doubt that the first man to appear in a hundred Test matches will continue to play cricket in the classic style with goodwill and dignity.

KENT v SURREY

Played at Canterbury, May 19, 20, 21, 1971

Kent won by four wickets. A splendid innings by Edrich held the Surrey innings together and Storey, Long and Willis helped to add 97 runs for the last four wickets. Kent soon lost two wickets, but Cowdrey, in good stands with Luckhurst and Ealham, put them on the path to recovery. At the end of the second day Surrey lost three wickets in moving 30 runs ahead. Again Edrich rescued them with a century in three and three-quarter hours, hitting fourteen 4s. Kent were left 207 to win in roughly two and a half hours. Denness and Luckhurst started with a century stand and Ealham really punished the Surrey attack. Off the last 10 overs 58 runs were needed and Kent appeared to be coasting home when Jackman did the hat-trick. In the end Kent won with seven balls to spare.

Surrey

J. H. Edrich c Woolmer b Underwood	73	– c Luckhurst b Julien	111
M. J. Edwards c Knott b Shepherd	12	– b Julien	22
*M. J. Stewart c Knott b Woolmer	11	– c Denness b Underwood	4
Younis Ahmed c Knott b Woolmer	22	– c and b Woolmer	27
G. R. J. Roope c Denness b Underwood	8	– lbw b Shepherd	3
S. J. Storey b Underwood	45	– c Julien b Shepherd	6
†A. Long c Underwood b Shepherd	38	– c Denness b Shepherd	0
P. I. Pocock b Underwood	12	– c Knott b Julien	5
R. D. Jackman lbw b Julien	5	– c Knott b Julien	7
C. E. Waller not out	8	– b Shepherd	15
R. G. D. Willis c Julien b Shepherd	33	– not out	13
B 9, l-b 9, n-b 7	25	B 8, l-b 5, w 2, n-b 2	17
1/27 2/43 3/77 4/97 5/156 6/195 7/220 8/240 9/252	292	1/30 2/42 3/54 4/104 5/113 6/127 7/138 8/161 9/192	230

Bowling: *First Innings*—Dye 16–2–51–0; Julien 14–1–47–1; Shepherd 29.1–5–76–3; Woolmer 20–4–57–2; Underwood 19–8–35–4; Leary 1–0–1–0. *Second Innings*—Dye 5–0–24–0; Julien 19.2–6–46–4; Shepherd 31–7–68–4; Woolmer 13–1–41–1; Underwood 17–6–34–1.

Kent

M. H. Denness c Stewart b Willis	10	– b Storey	49
B. W. Luckhurst c Storey b Waller	54	– c Storey b Jackman	85
D. L. Underwood c Edrich b Willis	3		
*M. C. Cowdrey c Long b Roope	82	– c Long b Waller	11
A. G. E. Ealham c Younis b Waller	63	– c and b Jackman	45
†A. P. E. Knott not out	38	– not out	8
B. D. Julien c Roope b Waller	10	– b Jackman	0
J. N. Shepherd c Long b Waller	4	– b Roope	1
R. A. Woolmer not out	35	– not out	1
B 1, l-b 9, w 1, n-b 6	17	L-b 6, n-b 2	8
1/14 2/26 3/119 4/204 5/228 6/246 7/255	(7 wkts dec.) 316	1/100 2/121 3/196 4/196 5/196 6/203	(6 wkts) 208

S. E. Leary and J. C. Dye did not bat.

Bowling: *First Innings*—Jackman 15–1–45–0; Willis 19–3–56–2; Storey 7–1–18–0; Pocock 23–2–82–0; Waller 24–4–62–4; Roope 10–0–36–1. *Second Innings*—Jackman 10–3–29–3; Willis 7–1–47–0; Storey 12–1–44–1; Pocock 7–0–38–0; Waller 3–0–21–1; Roope 4.5–0–21–1.

Umpires: D. J. Constant and J. G. Langridge.

KENT v SURREY

Played at Maidstone, May 27, 29, 30, 1972

Drawn. Batsmen were generally on top and none more so than Knott who hit a century in each innings for the first time in his career. His first innings, which included one 6 and fourteen 4s in a stay of three hours, forty minutes, rescued Kent from disaster. He and Woolmer added 120 for the seventh wicket in ninety minutes off 32 overs. Edrich took the stage for five hours with one 6 and twenty 4s as he dominated Surrey's reply and Kent, batting again, soon lost three wickets before the close of the second day. Then Knott again rescued them. He hit 108 out of 165 added in two hours, ten minutes, with Luckhurst and in all hit one 6 and fifteen 4s. Surrey, left 222 to win in two and a half hours, were never in the hunt as they lost half their side for 86. They needed 136 to win off the last 20 overs and Kent called off a fruitless quest for further wickets with eight overs left.

Kent

B. W. Luckhurst c Long b Jackman	39	– c Storey b Roope	68
D. Nicholls c Edrich b Jackman	25	– c Roope b Arnold	0
M. C. Cowdrey c Roope b Arnold	7	– lbw b Arnold	1
*M. H. Denness c Storey b Arnold	0	– c Long b Arnold	5
Asif Iqbal c Waller b Arnold	3	– c Long b Jackman	17
†A. P. E. Knott not out	127	– not out	118
J. N. Shepherd c Stewart b Storey	19	– not out	3
R. A. Woolmer c Edrich b Waller	57		
B. D. Julien lbw b Jackman	9		
D. L. Underwood lbw b Storey	10		
J. N. Graham st Long b Storey	0		
L-b 6	6	L-b 2. n-b 2	4
1/44 2/51 3/53 4/59 5/75 6/98 7/218 8/244 9/302	301	1/3 2/10 3/18 4/38 5/203	(5 wkts dec.) 216

Bowling—*First Innings*—Arnold 27–4–79–3; Jackman 27–5–82–3; Storey 17–3–58–3; Roope 7–2–21–0; Pocock 6–0–25–0; Waller 4–0–31–1. *Second Innings*—Arnold 14–1–32–3; Jackman 15–1–46–1; Storey 10–1–27–0; Roope 2–0–15–1; Pocock 11–2–57–0; Waller 7–0–35–0.

Surrey

J. H. Edrich c Knott b Julien	168	– c Luckhurst b Graham	9
M. J. Edwards c Julien b Underwood	41	– b Julien	4
*M. J. Stewart b Woolmer	12	– c Julien b Underwood	12
Younis Ahmed b Luckhurst b Woolmer	6	– run out	35
G. R. J. Roope b Underwood	17	– c Shepherd b Luckhurst	15
S. J. Storey c Cowdrey b Graham	1	– not out	37
†A. Long not out	24	– not out	15
P. I. Pocock c Knott b Graham	1		
G. G. Arnold not out	1		
B 4, l-b 16, w 1, n-b 5	26	L-b 1	1
1/108 2/157 3/172 4/233 5/247 6/281 7/296	(7 wkts dec.) 297	1/14 2/14 3/44 4/62 5/86	(5 wkts) 128

R. D. Jackman and C. E. Waller did not bat.

Bowling: *First Innings*—Graham 22–5–62–2; Julien 16–3–47–1; Shepherd 11–0–45–0; Underwood 32–9–80–2; Woolmer 16–5–37–2. *Second Innings*—Graham 11–5–27–1; Julien 10–2–31–1; Underwood 8–2–22–1; Woolmer 3–0–20–0; Luckhurst 6–2–27–1.

Umpires: J. Arnold and A. E. G. Rhodes.

KENT v SOMERSET

Played at Maidstone, June 30, July 2, 3, 1973

Drawn. Put in to bat, Somerset fared badly. Only Close and Parks offered real resistance against the pace and seam of Graham, Shepherd and Woolmer. Johnson with one 6 and seven 4s in his 53 in ninety minutes began a Kent run riot which continued into the second day. Denness reached his highest score in first-class cricket, batting nearly six hours with twenty-five 4s. He added 241 with Cowdrey, whose 99th century came in four and three-quarter hours with fourteen 4s. When Somerset slipped to 79 for three Kent hopes were high. Parks shattered them with a fine display of attacking shots. He hit twenty-four 4s, adding 163 with Burgess. Cartwright was seventh out at 276 in the second of the last 20 overs, but that was Kent's final success and they called off their bid for victory with five overs to go and Somerset 15 ahead.

Somerset

S. G. Wilkinson c Woolmer b Shepherd	0	– b Shepherd	9
P. J. Robinson c Johnson b Graham	9	– c Johnson b Shepherd	8
*D. B. Close lbw b Woolmer	41	– b Underwood	19
J. M. Parks lbw b Shepherd	41	– c Woolmer b Shepherd	155
G. I. Burgess c Knott b Woolmer	2	– c Cowdrey b Graham	59
P. W. Denning c Knott b Johnson	6	– c Underwood b Shepherd	2
T. W. Cartwright c Ealham b Shepherd	9	– lbw b Graham	4
D. Breakwell c Knott b Shepherd	16	– not out	31
†D. J. S. Taylor b Graham	9	– not out	13
H. R. Moseley not out	16		
A. A. Jones b Graham	0		
L-b 10, n-b 4	14	B 1, l-b 8	9
1/2 2/28 3/72 4/78 5/87 6/114 7/120 8/143 9/146	163	1/17 2/20 3/79 4/242 5/246 6/266 7/276	(7 wkts) 309

Bowling: *First Innings*—Graham 14.5–5–23–3; Shepherd 23–4–66–4; Johnson 10–3–20–1; Woolmer 19–5–40–2. *Second Innings*—Graham 25–13–50–2; Shepherd 27–8–78–4; Johnson 19–4–58–0; Woolmer 11–2–44–0; Underwood 29–12–55–1; Luckhurst 1–0–1–0; Cowdrey 5–1–14–0.

Kent

B. W. Luckhurst lbw b Cartwright	25	†A. P. E. Knott not out	19
G. W. Johnson c Parks b Burgess	53		
*M. H. Denness c Moseley b Breakwell	178	B 4, l-b 7, n-b 7	18
Asif Iqbal c Taylor b Jones	41		——
A. G. E. Ealham b Jones	0	1/36 2/106 3/174	(5 wkts dec.) 457
M. C. Cowdrey not out	123	4/174 5/415	

J. N. Shepherd, R. A. Woolmer, D. L. Underwood and J. N. Graham did not bat.

Bowling: Jones 22–4–105–2; Moseley 25–4–78–0; Cartwright 31–7–89–1; Burgess 24–4–86–1; Close 8–1–40–0; Breakwell 13–3–41–1.

Umpires: J. F. Crapp and C. G. Pepper.

KENT v SUSSEX

Played at Maidstone, June 14, 16, 17, 1975

Kent won by an innings and 10 runs. This was the first visit by Sussex to Mote Park since 1937. A magnificent all-round performance by Shepherd was the keynote of Kent's comfortable victory. In marathon spells, bowling throughout both Sussex innings, apart from a change of ends in the second, his match analysis was fifteen for 147, the first Kent bowler to achieve 15 victims in a match for the county since Halfyard, on the same ground against Worcestershire, in 1959. Johnson with fourteen 4s in his 89 in three hours gave Kent a good start but half the side were out only 13 runs behind the Sussex total. Then Shepherd who hit eight 4s, and the left-handed Nicholls, (ten 4s) added 122 for the sixth wicket. Shepherd, well supported by Hills, soon had Sussex in trouble again and only Graves stopped Kent winning in the extra half-hour of the second day. Victory was completed in six minutes on the third morning.

Sussex

J. R. T. Barclay c Johnson b Graham	15	– c Topley b Shepherd	13
G. A. Greenidge c Cowdrey b Shepherd	25	– c Cowdrey b Shepherd	0
M. J. J. Faber c Rowe b Shepherd	5	– c Nicholls b Shepherd	24
*P. J. Graves c Jarvis b Shepherd	33	– c Cowdrey b Shepherd	35
A. E. W. Parsons lbw b Shepherd	34	– c Nicholls b Hills	25
J. J. Groome lbw b Shepherd	2	– c Nicholls b Hills	5
†A. W. Mansell c Topley b Shepherd	11	– c Topley b Shepherd	4
C. E. Waller c Johnson b Jarvis	1	– b Shepherd	0
C. P. Phillipson lbw b Shepherd	0	– c Nicholls b Hills	5
R. P. T. Marshall c Johnson b Shepherd	32	– b Shepherd	3
J. Spencer not out	16	– not out	6
B 2, l-b 6, w 1, n-b 1	10	B 9, l-b 5, n-b 1	15
	——		——
1/26 2/35 3/80 4/91 5/101	184	1/0 2/37 3/38 4/71 5/101	135
6/127 7/128 8/132 9/137		6/110 7/110 8/116 9/129	

Bowling: *First Innings*—Shepherd 32.5–6–93–8; Graham 20–3–56–1; Jarvis 12–3–25–1. *Second Innings*—Shepherd 39–11–54–7; Jarvis 10–4–26–0; Hills 19.5–4–40–3.

Kent

*B. W. Luckhurst c Mansell b Spencer	26
G. W. Johnson lbw b Spencer	89
M. C. Cowdrey c Waller b Marshall	10
P. A. Topley c Mansell b Spencer	19
A. G. E. Ealham run out	25
†D. Nicholls c Mansell b Phillipson	68
J. N. Shepherd c Graves b Barclay	52
C. J. C. Rowe c Phillipson b Barclay	25
R. W. Hills c Faber b Barclay	4
K. B. S. Jarvis lbw b Spencer	0
J. N. Graham not out	0
B 5, l-b 5, w 1	11
1/79 2/107 3/139 4/160 5/171 6/293 7/305 8/329 9/329	329

Bowling: Spencer 37–5–99–4; Marshall 30–8–94–1; Waller 23–8–46–0; Phillipson 25–7–58–1; Barclay 12.2–7–21–3.

Umpires: W. E. Phillipson and P. Rochford.

KENT v MIDDLESEX

Played at Canterbury, August 2, 4, 5, 1975

Middlesex won by 156 runs. Middlesex won the toss and enjoyed the advantage of a perfect batting wicket, Smith and Brearley putting on 169 in 46 overs. Smith reached his hundred out of 166 in under two and a quarter hours before lunch with thirteen 4s. Radley and Featherstone added 122, Featherstone playing splendidly. His not out 127 took only two hours, thirty-five minutes and he hit one 6 and fifteen 4s. He and Barlow in fact added 94 in 16 overs before Brearley declared. Kent began badly, losing three wickets before the close and never recovered on the second day against the pace of Price and the spin of Titmus and Edmonds. Middlesex did not enforce the follow on and this gave Featherstone the chance to reach his second century of the match in well under two hours with one 6 and eleven 4s. Kent were left to score 432 to win but when they had lost half their wickets for 114, they were obviously out of the hunt. It was left to Shepherd to make his only century of the season and he was last out, having batted two hours and hit three 6s and eleven 4s.

Middlesex

M. J. Smith run out	107	– c Nicholls b Jarvis	1
*J. M. Brearley b Rowe	57	– c Luckhurst b Hills	30
C. T. Radley c Nicholls b Jarvis	63	– b Jarvis	8
N. G. Featherstone not out	127	– not out	100
H. A. Gomes c Denness b Jarvis	6	– not out	29
G. D. Barlow not out	42		
B 13, l-b 13, n-b 2	28	B 6, l-b 5, n-b 1	12
1/69 2/180 3/302 4/336 (4 wkts)	430	1/2 2/16 3/71 (3 wkts dec.)	180

†J. T. Murray, P. H. Edmonds, F. J. Titmus, M. W. W. Selvey and J. S. E. Price did not bat.

Bowling: *First Innings*—Jarvis 21–3–56–2; Asif 12–1–55–0; Shepherd 17–0–83–0; Hills 17–0–69–0; Rowe 23–3–81–1; Topley 8–1–39–0; Luckhurst 2–0–19–0. *Second Innings*—Jarvis 14–1–54–2; Shepherd 12–2–41–0; Hills 11–1–29–1; Rowe 2–0–20–0; Topley 2.5–0–24–0.

Kent

*M. H. Denness c Murray b Price	5	– b Price	10
B. W. Luckhurst lbw b Titmus	26	– run out	32
Asif Iqbal c Edmonds b Selvey	22	– run out	18
P. A. Topley c Murray b Titmus	0	– b Titmus	7
M. C. Cowdrey c Murray b Price	5	– c Murray b Edmonds	0
J. N. Shepherd lbw b Price	46	– st Murray b Edmonds	116
†D. Nicholls c Featherstone b Edmonds	24	– c Murray b Titmus	42
A. G. E. Ealham b Edmonds	9	– b Price	0
C. J. C. Rowe b Titmus	21	– lbw b Selvey	24
R. W. Hills not out	7	– c sub b Titmus	6
K. B. S. Jarvis b Titmus	1	– not out	4
B 6, l-b 7	13	B 10, l-b 5, n-b 1	16
1/13 2/38 3/50 4/62 5/62 6/126 7/141 8/167 9/167	179	1/72 2/79 3/114 4/114 5/114 6/121 7/182 8/195 9/245	275

Bowling: *First Innings*—Price 16–4–38–3; Selvey 13–3–39–1; Gomes 10–3–26–0; Titmus 11.4–6–15–4; Edmonds 22–7–48–2. *Second Innings*—Price 12–4–44–2; Selvey 15–2–37–1; Titmus 31–4–100–3; Edmonds 27.3–9–78–2.

Umpires: R. Aspinall and A. E. Fagg.

KENT v HAMPSHIRE

Played at Maidstone, July 3, 5, 6, 1976

Hampshire won by 29 runs. Richards dominated this game with a magnificent innings on the first day. He cruised to 52 out of 82 and reached 101 out of 172, and he had hit three 6s and twenty 4s when fifth out, having scored 179 out of 264. Underwood had a spell of three for 0 in seven overs, as Hampshire lost five wickets for 28 runs. Kent recovered from a dreadful start thanks to Johnson and Denness. Later, Knott, well supported by Elms, moved to 50 in seventy-five minutes with one 6 and eight 4s. Denness declared 60 behind and after Richards had been dismissed, Shepherd put Kent back in the game, taking five for 60 in his first fourteen overs. Again, Kent began badly on a turning wicket and apart from Denness and Knott, who reached another fifty, there was little resistance to the spin of Sainsbury and Southern, although Elms, as in the first innings, offered Knott determined support.

Hampshire

B. A. Richards c Woolmer b Shepherd	179	– c Underwood b Shepherd	43
R. V. Lewis b Jarvis	3	– c Denness b Underwood	28
D. R. Turner b Underwood	19	– b Shepherd	8
T. E. Jesty c Knott b Shepherd	4	– c Denness b Shepherd	0
*R. M. C. Gilliat c Woolmer b Underwood	29	– c Knott b Shepherd	24
P. J. Sainsbury b Underwood	19	– b Underwood	22
J. M. Rice b Underwood	7	– c Asif b Shepherd	13
M. N. S. Taylor lbw b Jarvis	9	– c Nicholls b Underwood	1
†G. R. Stephenson c Knott b Underwood	0	– c Shepherd b Johnson	16
R. S. Herman b Shepherd	19	– c sub b Johnson	0
J. W. Southern not out	4	– not out	0
B 9, l-b 7, w 2, n-b 5	23	B 6, l-b 10, n-b 3	19
1/4 2/71 3/86 4/159 5/264 6/274 7/288 8/288 9/292	315	1/62 2/70 3/70 4/102 5/113 6/135 7/138 8/160 9/160	174

Bowling—*First Innings*—Jarvis 10–1–41–2; Elms 14–2–54–0; Shepherd 23–5–60–3; Underwood 33–15–83–5; Johnson 15–2–54–0. *Second Innings*—Jarvis 6–0–22–0; Elms 3–0–19–0; Shepherd 19–0–69–5; Underwood 24.1–13–44–3; Johnson 6–5–1–2.

Kent

G. W. Johnson b Sainsbury	40	– c Rice b Sainsbury	17
R. A. Woolmer run out	6	– b Southern	14
Asif Iqbal b Jesty	0	– c Gilliat b Sainsbury	5
*M. H. Denness c Turner b Sainsbury	51	– b Sainsbury	34
A. G. E. Ealham b Sainsbury	30	– c Richards b Southern	7
J. N. Shepherd c Herman b Southern	8	– c Taylor b Southern	8
†A. P. E. Knott c Gilliat b Southern	68	– c Richards b Sainsbury	54
D. Nicholls b Southern	19	– c Richards b Sainsbury	20
R. B. Elms c Gilliat b Rice	14	– b Sainsbury	17
D. L. Underwood not out	6	– b Sainsbury	11
K. B. S. Jarvis not out	0	– not out	6
L-b 7, w 2, n-b 4	13	B 4, l-b 5, w 2, n-b 1	12
1/8 2/8 3/74 4/125 5/134 6/140 7/174 8/248 9/251	(9 wkts dec.) 255	1/33 2/39 3/39 4/67 5/98 6/109 7/123 8/166 9/186	205

Bowling: *First Innings*—Herman 4–2–3–0; Jesty 7–2–20–1; Rice 11–5–13–1; Southern 43–20–93–3; Sainsbury 26–11–90–3; Richards 3–2–8–0; Taylor 6–1–15–0. *Second Innings*—Herman 2–0–3–0; Jesty 4–0–14–0; Rice 3–1–5–0; Southern 43–17–91–3; Sainsbury 41–16–60–7; Taylor 8–3–20–0.

Umpires: J. G. Langridge and T. W. Spencer.

KENT v GLOUCESTERSHIRE

(A. P. E. Knott's Benefit Match)

Played at Canterbury, August 7, 9, 10, 1976

Gloucestershire won by seven wickets. Shepherd, who hit one 6 and eight 4s in his fifty in sixty-seven minutes, rescued Kent and then Tavaré (thirteen 4s) and Jarvis added 53 for the last wicket. But this was Zaheer's match. He and Sadiq added 229, Zaheer hitting thirty-seven 4s in his not out 230 in six hours, eleven minutes. Asif hit 50 in as many minutes and on the final day Knott hit fourteen 4s in forty-nine minutes during which 111 were added with Ealham. It was all a prelude to another remarkable innings by Zaheer, against the clock. Stovold helped him to add 107 in an hour and Gloucestershire's steep target of 132 off the last 20 overs was reduced to 60 off 10 and 18 off five. Zaheer reached his century with his twelfth 4 in ninety-eight minutes to level the scores and hit four off the next ball to win this wonderful match with 3.1 overs to spare.

Kent

G. W. Johnson b Brain	13	– b Brain	4
R. A. Woolmer c and b Davey	39	– b Childs	54
Asif Iqbal b Davey	2	– c and b Brown	58
*M. H. Denness b Brown	18	– b Childs	29
A. G. E. Ealham b Brown	22	– b Brain	64
J. N. Shepherd c Childs b Brown	52	– st Stovold b Childs	28
†A. P. E. Knott st Stovold b Graveney	18	– lbw b Brain	67
C. J. Tavaré not out	67	– c and b Sadiq	15
R. W. Hills lbw b Graveney	4	– c Procter b Graveney	21
D. L. Underwood c Shepherd b Graveney	4	– c Stovold b Sadiq	12
K. B. S. Jarvis c sub b Graveney	2	– not out	0
B 2, l-b 4, n-b 4	10	B 8, l-b 4, n-b 5	17
1/28 2/33 3/59 4/84 5/107 6/170 7/170 8/182 9/198	251	1/15 2/104 3/143 4/148 5/182 6/293 7/324 8/346 9/346	369

Bowling: *First Innings*—Brain 13–0–52–1; Davey 17–1–77–2; Brown 18–3–47–3; Childs 15–5–44–0; Graveney 16.3–8–16–4; Sadiq 3–1–5–0. *Second Innings*—Brain 15–1–74–3; Davey 3–0–10–0; Brown 4–0–25–1; Childs 26–9–77–3; Graveney 26–8–79–1; Sadiq 8.3–4–17–2; Procter 14–1–70–0.

Gloucestershire

Sadiq Mohammad c Jarvis b Hills	71	– c Tavaré b Asif	36
†A. W. Stovold b Jarvis	2	– c Jarvis b Underwood	66
Zaheer Abbas not out	230	– not out	104
A. J. Hignell c Woolmer b Hills	0	– not out	8
M. J. Procter run out	29	– b Jarvis	16
D. R. Shepherd c Underwood b Jarvis	11		
D. A. Graveney c Shepherd b Asif	14		
*A. S. Brown c and b Asif	4		
B 1, l-b 4, n-b 8	13	L-b 18, n-b 2	20
1/3 2/232 3/236 4/299 5/330 6/369	(7 wkts dec.) 374	1/68 2/175 3/128	(3 wkts) 250

B. M. Brain, J. Davey and J. H. Childs did not bat.

Bowling: *First Innings*—Jarvis 20–1–67–2; Shepherd 29–6–87–0; Hills 28–2–91–2; Underwood 27–11–62–0; Johnson 9–1–46–0; Asif 3–0–8–2. *Second Innings*—Jarvis 11–1–56–1; Shepherd 10.5–1–45–0; Hills 4–0–26–0; Underwood 14–1–78–1; Asif 6–1–25–1.

Umpires: W. L. Budd and W. E. Phillipson.

KENT v LEICESTERSHIRE

Played at Maidstone, July 2, 4, 5, 1977

Kent won by an innings and two runs. Although Rowe reached 53 out of 85 in ninety minutes, Kent struggled until Asif and Knott launched an exciting counter-attack with a fifth wicket stand of 193. Knott raced to 100 out of 166 in under two hours with one 6 and ten 4s. Asif hit ten 4s in his century made in three hours. Leicestershire began badly and although Balderstone resisted for four hours, they followed on and lost half the side for 65 – their batsmen never comfortable against the pace and seam. Tolchard reached 50, but Kent cruised to a comfortable victory. Knott had nine victims in a match for the first time in his career.

Kent

R. A. Woolmer c and b Clift	30
G. S. Clinton c Illingworth b Shuttleworth	2
C. J. C. Rowe b Clift	53
*Asif Iqbal c and b Balderstone	116
A. G. E. Ealham c Tolchard b Shuttleworth	0
†A. P. E. Knott c Briers b Higgs	109
B. D. Julien c Balderstone b Clift	48
J. N. Shepherd b Balderstone	7
R. W. Hills b Higgs	18
D. L. Underwood not out	1
B 4, l-b 5, w 1, n-b 5	15
1/2, 2/80 3/89 4/94 5/287 6/333 7/349 8/398 9/399	(9 wkts dec.) 399

K. B. S. Jarvis did not bat.

Bowling: Higgs 22.4–6–51–2; Shuttleworth 17–0–50–2; Clift 21–2–82–3; Steele 10–2–40–0; Birkenshaw 8–0–63–0; Illingworth 8–2–35–0; Balderstone 13–0–63–2.

Leicestershire

J. F. Steele c Knott b Julien	8	– lbw b Julien	35
N. E. Briers lbw b Jarvis	8	– c and b Julien	1
J. C. Balderstone c Knott b Julien	68	– c Knott b Shepherd	5
B. F. Davison c Knott b Shepherd	38	– c Asif b Jarvis	3
D. I. Gower c Knott b Shepherd	0	– c Woolmer b Jarvis	2
†R. W. Tolchard c Knott b Jarvis	0	– c Shepherd b Woolmer	68
*R. Illingworth c Woolmer b Julien	20	– c Knott b Woolmer	33
J. Birkenshaw c Asif b Julien	30	– not out	10
P. B. Clift c Julien b Underwood	18	– c Knott b Woolmer	0
K. Shuttleworth c Jarvis b Woolmer	29	– b Shepherd	3
K. Higgs not out	1	– c Knott b Shepherd	0
L-b 1, n-b 9	10	L-b 2, w 2, n-b 3	7
1/13 2/17 3/80 4/80 5/91 6/125 7/180 8/181 9/217	230	1/10 2/20 3/29 4/32 5/65 6/152 7/154 8/154 9/156	167

Bowling: *First Innings*—Jarvis 27–8–88–2; Julien 23–10–43–4; Shepherd 24–9–57–2; Underwood 7–2–13–1; Woolmer 7.1–3–19–1. *Second Innings*—Jarvis 15–4–54–2; Julien 15–5–38–2; Shepherd 18.1–4–55–3; Underwood 1–1–0–0; Woolmer 8–5–7–3; Asif 1–0–1–0; Hills 3–0–5–0.

Umpires: R. Aspinall and A. G. T. Whitehead.

KENT v ESSEX

Played at Folkestone, August 16, 18, 1980

Essex won by 50 runs. On a wicket which saw the ball lift and turn, 40 wickets crashed, mainly to the spinners, for 362 runs in just over nine hours of play. Top score for the match was Turner's 35, out of 41, in Essex's first innings when Underwood swept to his best figures of the season. Acfield performed even more economically, bowling Essex to a lead of 42 runs as Kent's last six wickets tumbled for 14 runs in seven overs, and on the second day Underwood, again well supported by Shepherd, bettered his first innings figures to return a match analysis of twelve for 99. Yet there was no stopping Essex and, after the medium pace of Turner and Pringle had done early damage, Acfield and East spun Kent to defeat. The wicket was reported to Lord's by the umpires, and a new wicket hurriedly prepared further down the square for the Gloucestershire match.

Essex

G. A. Gooch c Knott b Shepherd	0	– b Shepherd	0
M. S. A. McEvoy c Johnson b Underwood	19	– c Taylor b Shepherd	3
K. S. McEwan c Tavaré b Underwood	15	– b Underwood	30
*K. W. R. Fletcher c Johnson b Underwood	30	– c Taylor b Shepherd	18
B. R. Hardie b Shepherd	1	– b Underwood	6
D. R. Pringle lbw b Shepherd	2	– c Cowdrey b Underwood	0
S. Turner lbw b Underwood	35	– lbw b Underwood	9
R. E. East lbw b Johnson	17	– run out	0
†N. Smith c Hills b Underwood	5	– c Kemp b Underwood	1
J. K. Lever not out	1	– b Underwood	4
D. L. Acfield b Underwood	1	– not out	3
B 1, l-b 2, n-b 1	4	L-b 1, w 1	2
1/0 2/17 3/56 4/57 5/59 6/100 7/113 8/127 9/127	130	1/4 2/5 3/41 4/55 5/55 6/58 7/58 8/59 9/69	76

Bowling: *First Innings*—Shepherd 14–4–30–3; Underwood 24.1–7–71–6; Johnson 11–0–25–1. *Second Innings*—Shepherd 11–2–31–3; Underwood 7.2–1–28–6; Kemp 4–0–15–0.

Kent

G. W. Johnson lbw b Lever	0	– c Fletcher b Turner	10
N. R. Taylor c Acfield	10	– c Hardie b Pringle	0
C. J. Tavaré c Gooch b East	33	– b Turner	4
Asif Iqbal b Pringle	11	– (5) c Smith b East	15
*A. G. E. Ealham lbw b Acfield	2	– (6) c Smith b East	11
C. S. Cowdrey lbw b Acfield	9	– (4) c McEvoy b Acfield	8
†A. P. E. Knott lbw b Acfield	2	– lbw b East	0
J. N. Shepherd c McEwan b East	2	– c McEwan b East	0
R. W. Hills c Fletcher b Acfield	2	– not out	5
N. J. Kemp b Acfield	6	– b Acfield	1
D. L. Underwood not out	1	– lbw b Acfield	0
B 7, l-b 1, n-b 2	10	B 5, l-b 7, n-b 2	14
1/0 2/14 3/33 4/42 5/74 6/76 7/76 8/80 9/81	88	1/7 2/14 3/20 4/32 5/55 6/57 7/62 8/63 9/68	68

Bowling: *First Innings*—Lever 5–3–4–1; Pringle 11–2–26–1; Acfield 18.4–4–37–6; East 9–5–11–2. *Second Innings*—Pringle 5–2–3–1; Turner 14–5–16–2; Acfield 14.3–6–23–3; East 7–3–12–4.

Umpires: C. Cook and P. B. Wight.

KENT v LANCASHIRE

Played at Maidstone, July 4, 6, 7, 1981

Drawn. Lancashire, asked to bat, found runs difficult against a pace and seam attack in which Baptiste returned his best-ever first-class figures. But for O'Shaughnessy's valuable late innings, Kent would have been batting sooner, although when they did Allott quickly had them in trouble. Asif provided the much-needed rescue operation, reaching 102 (one 6 and ten 4s) out of 174 in three hours. Lancashire's second innings owed much to Hughes, who hit seven 4s in his 175-minute half-century, and when he was seventh out, with Lancashire 156 ahead, Kent, bowling for a declaration, were savaged by Abrahams and Simmons in a stand of 115 in 85 minutes. Left 272 to win in two hours ten minutes, Kent were immediately in disarray with Tavaré dismissed and two batsmen retiring hurt with only 1 run scored. However, Ealham blasted them out of trouble, and with seven of the last twenty overs still to be bowled the match ended in a draw. For Knott, the match produced a personal milestone with Allott providing him with his 1,000th catch in first-class cricket.

Lancashire

A. Kennedy c Knott b Jarvis	18	– c Tavaré b Jarvis	8
†G. Fowler c Knott b Shepherd	14	– st Knott b Underwood	41
D. Lloyd c Knott b Baptiste	12	– (7) lbw b Johnson	32
*C. H. Lloyd c Benson b Baptiste	30	– c Johnson b Underwood	38
D. P. Hughes c Knott b Jarvis	29	– c Knott b Jarvis	54
I. Cockbain c Knott b Baptiste	15	– (3) lbw b Shepherd	4
J. Abrahams b Baptiste	10	– (8) not out	59
J. Simmons c Asif b Shepherd	5	– (9) not out	65
S. J. O'Shaughnessy b Baptiste	35		
N. V. Radford b Underwood	15		
P. J. W. Allott not out	5	– (6) c Knott b Shepherd	6
L-b 7, w 2, n-b 6	15	L-b 6, n-b 5	11
1/28 2/36 3/58 4/101 5/116 6/133 7/142 8/146 9/176	203	1/17 2/34 3/79 4/104 5/128 6/176 7/203	(7 wkts dec.) 318

Bowling: *First Innings*—Jarvis 25–10–57–2; Shepherd 27–5–72–2; Baptiste 20.4–7–37–5; Johnson 4–1–22–0; Underwood 4–4–0–1. *Second Innings*—Jarvis 21–7–62–2; Shepherd 27–9–58–2; Baptiste 10–1–39–0; Underwood 31–12–44–2; Johnson 21–6–49–1; Asif 4–0–32–0; Taylor 4–0–23–0.

Kent

M. R. Benson c Fowler b Allott	5	(2) retired hurt	0
N. R. Taylor lbw b Radford	32	(1) retired hurt	1
C. J. Tavaré c Fowler b Allott	11	b Radford	0
*Asif Iqbal c C. H. Lloyd b Hughes	112		
A. G. E. Ealham c D. Lloyd b Kennedy	22	c Hughes b O'Shaughnessy	48
†A. P. E. Knott lbw b Allott	6		
G. W. Johnson c Fowler b Hughes	30	not out	12
J. N. Shepherd c Simmons b Hughes	6	(4) c Fowler b O'Shaughnessy	17
E. A. Baptiste not out	10	(6) not out	37
D. L. Underwood not out	10		
L-b 1, w 3, n-b 2	6	B 4, l-b 2, n-b 2	8
1/6 2/22 3/105 4/142 5/155 6/209 7/219 8/237	(8 wkts dec.) 250	1/1 2/65 3/78	(3 wkts) 123

K. B. S. Jarvis did not bat.

Bowling: *First Innings*—Allott 25–5–62–3; Radford 13–3–60–1; O'Shaughnessy 5–0–26–0; Kennedy 10–2–26–1; Hughes 14–2–34–3; Simmons 15–1–36–0. *Second Innings*—Allott 8–2–30–0; Radford 4–0–34–1; O'Shaughnessy 3.2–0–12–2; D. Lloyd 8–1–23–0; Abrahams 7–1–16–0.

Umpires: P. J. Eele and P. B. Wight.

LANCASHIRE

LANCASHIRE v WORCESTERSHIRE

Played at Manchester, May 29, 30, 31, 1963

Drawn. In a high-scoring match, Worcestershire failed by 11 runs to achieve the task of making 227 in two hours, twenty minutes, following three declarations. Booth, who hit one 6 and fifteen 4s, and Tebay set the pattern for the match with an opening stand for Lancashire of 170, and the total passed 300 for three wickets before Flavell achieved a hat-trick with lbw decisions by umpire Gardner, only the second time this has been done in the history of first-class cricket. He dismissed Pilling and Dyson with the last two balls of one over and Lever with the first of his next. In 1932, at Sheffield, H. Fisher, of Yorkshire, dismissed N. S. Mitchell-Innes, W. H. Andrews and W. T. Luckes of Somerset, in similar fashion, the umpire on that occasion being A. Skelding. In both these matches the batsmen concerned upheld the umpires as correct.

Worcestershire scored even more freely, with Kenyon and Headley making hard-hit hundreds before Kenyon declared 23 runs ahead. Booth and Tebay again shared a century partnership before the second Lancashire declaration.

Lancashire

B. Booth c Devereux b Slade	118	– c Graveney b Slade	65
K. Tebay c Ormrod b Devereux	87	– c Graveney b Richardson	60
*K. J. Grieves b Flavell	55	– not out	4
P. Marner not out	47	– not out	26
H. Pilling lbw b Flavell	8	– b Richardson	31
J. Dyson lbw b Flavell	0	– c Richardson b Ormrod	58
†G. Clayton lbw b Devereux	0		
P. Lever lbw b Flavell	1		
J. B. Stathan not out	1		
B 4, n-b 5	9	L-b 4, n-b 1	5
1/170 2/243 3/289 4/312 5/312 6/315 7/320 (7 wkts dec.)	326	1/103 2/142 3/177 4/244 (4 wkts dec.)	249

T. Greenhough and K. Higgs did not bat.

Bowling: *First Innings*—Flavell 32–4–99–4; Coldwell 10–2–32–0; Slade 31–7–69–1; Devereux 26–4–77–2; Horton 14–3–40–0. *Second Innings*—Flavell 9–2–21–0; Devereux 10–2–34–0; Horton 7–2–14–0; Slade 11–2–35–1; Graveney 7–1–17–0; Ormrod 16–2–58–1; Richardson 7–2–11–2; Kenyon 9–0–54–0.

Worcestershire

*D. Kenyon c Booth b Lever	166	– b Lever	63
M. J. Horton c Lever b Statham	0	– c Clayton b Higgs	44
D. N. F. Slade b Dyson	33	– not out	0
R. G. A. Headley c Clayton b Greenhough	108	– not out	65
T. W. Graveney not out	28	– b Higgs	2
D. W. Richardson not out	4	– c Higgs b Lever	12
†R. Booth (did not bat)		– c Lever b Statham	18
R. J. Devereux (did not bat)		– b Higgs	3
B 1, l-b 4, n-b 5	10	L-b 8, n-b 1	9
1/5 2/109 3/272 4/338 (4 wkts dec.)	349	1/104 2/2110 3/135 4/140 5/197 6/216 (6 wkts)	216

A. Ormrod, L. J. Coldwell and J. A. Flavell did not bat.

Bowling: *First Innings*—Statham 24–7–69–1; Higgs 21–0–55–0; Lever 23–2–76–1; Greenhough 21–5–60–1; Dyson 23–4–79–1. *Second Innings*—Statham 10–6–58–1; Lever 16–0–93–2; Higgs 11–1–56–3.

Umpires: T. W. Spencer and F. C. Gardner.

LANCASHIRE v DERBYSHIRE

Played at Liverpool, June 15, 17, 18, 1963

Drawn. On a pitch helpful to bowlers, the controlled pace of Statham and varied spin of Greenhough sadly troubled the Derbyshire batsmen, of whom only Johnson and Millner resisted for long. Lancashire owed their first innings points almost entirely to Booth, who became the first batsman of his county to carry his bat throughout an innings for thirteen years. He batted for four hours. Howard forfeited his innings on Monday morning when, as a not out batsman, he arrived late. Statham, this time with Lever as his main partner, again bowled splendidly when Derbyshire batted a second time, but rain set in after tea on the second day and prevented further play in the match.

Derbyshire

I. W. Hall c Clayton b Howard	15	– c Clayton b Lever	1
H. L. Johnson c Clayton b Statham	32	– c Greenhough b Statham	2
W. F. Oates c Greenhough b Statham	18	– b Statham	16
D. Millner b Greenhough	29	– b Statham	5
D. C. Morgan c Clayton b Statham	0	– b Lever	33
I. R. Buxton lbw b Greenhough	1	– not out	41
E. Smith c Marner b Statham	1	– b Statham	7
†R. W. Taylor c and b Greenhough	0	– b Statham	9
H. J. Rhodes run out	1	– c Clayton b Lever	5
A. B. Jackson c Lever b Greenhough	16	– not out	0
*H. L. Jackson not out	1		
L-b 1, n-b 1	2	L-b 7, w 1, n-b 1	9
1/26 2/66 3/67 4/67 5/68 6/69 7/76 8/77 9/113	116	1/6 2/8 3/31 4/32 5/74 6/94 7/110 8/128	(8 wkts) 128

Bowling: *First Innings*—Statham 21–7–40–4; Lever 5–0–9–0; Howard 15–9–17–1; Greenhough 24.3–5–48–4. *Second Innings*—Statham 21–5–45–5; Lever 18.4–6–30–3; Greenhough 21–7–36–0; Howard 12–8–8–0.

Lancashire

B. Booth not out	62
R. Bennett b A. B. Jackson	10
R. Entwistle lbw b Morgan	1
*K. J. Grieves c Taylor b Rhodes	38
K. Howard retired out	1
P. Marner c Buxton b H. L. Jackson	5
H. Pilling b A. B. Jackson	11
†G. Clayton b A. B. Jackson	2
P. Lever run out	0
J. B. Statham b Morgan	0
T. Greenhough run out	0
B 4, l-b 4, n-b 2	10
1/28 2/33 3/102 4/103 5/111 6/130 7/136 8/136 9/136	140

Bowling: H. L. Jackson 17–5–30–1; Rhodes 17–3–32–1; Morgan 20–10–28–2; A. B. Jackson 14.5–4–28–3; Smith 7–4–12–0.

Umpires: T. W. Spencer and F. Jakeman.

NEVILLE CARDUS [1964]

By John Arlott

The Birthday Honours List of 1964 included the award of the CBE to Mr Neville Cardus "for services to music and cricket". It was the first – and, some may feel, belated – official recognition of the modest man who, for almost fifty years, has written with sympathy and integrity about the two chief interests – indeed, enthusiasms – of his life. Throughout that time his work has never become jaded, but has unfailingly reflected the happiness of one who always felt privileged, even grateful, to earn his living from his pleasures.

The honour was acclaimed in the two spheres where he has long been accorded affection as a man, and respect as a writer. It would be short-sighted for cricketers to overlook Mr Cardus's work on music. Few are qualified to compare his writings on the two subjects: in any case, the comparison would be pointless. It may be said, however, that while his standing in the world of music is high, in the field of cricket it is unique.

The form of musical criticism had already been shaped, by such men as Shaw, Newman, Langford, Hanslick and Professor Dent, before Mr Cardus came to it. On the other hand, by innovation and influence, he virtually created modern cricket-writing. In doing so, he led thousands of people to greater enjoyment of the game.

Today he may be regarded as just one of a number of imaginative cricket-writers; but he appears so only to those who do not recall the immense novelty and impact of his writing when it first reached the public in the nineteen-twenties. Before then there had been much competent cricket-reporting, informed, sound in judgement, pleasant in manner. But the Cardus of the years shortly after the First World War first brought to it the qualities of personalization, literary allusion and imagery. By such methods as presenting the contest between bowler and batsman as a clash not only of skills but of characters, he created something near to a mythology of the game. His early writing has been described, not always with complimentary intent, as romantic. That is the essence of his appeal. To the enthusiast, cricket *is* romantic: and in Mr Cardus's reports, the ordinary spectator saw his romantic and heroic feelings put into words for the first time.

Every modern cricket-writer with any pretension to style owes half that he is to Neville Cardus, if only in the stern realism of making such an approach accepable to editors. The consciously literary method can lead to lush and imprecise writing and, in the cases of some of Mr Cardus's imitators, that has happened. His own work, however, always has a ballast of practicality, humanity and humour.

There was no cricket at his Board School, but on strips of waste land near his childhood home in the Rusholme suburb of Manchester, he learnt enough of the game to become assistant coach at Shrewsbury School. Though he does not labour technical points, he never loses sight of the basic principles. He is, too, sufficiently self-critical to relish the reaction to one of his high-flown passages of that earthy Lancashire cricketer and character, Richard Tyldesley: "Ah'd like to bowl at bugger soom da-ay". Thus, his unerring touch constantly saved him from the pitfall of extravagance, by balancing rich imagery with the earthiness of the genuine common tongue.

No cricketer of whom he ever wrote trod a more remarkable path from a humble upbringing to success than this man who achieved more than he would have dared to regard as ambition, but which must have seemed to him so remote as to be beyond dreams.

Nothing in his wide-ranging and relishable *Autobiography* is more vivid than the description of his childhood in the house of his grandfather who retired from the police force as a result of a series of blows – the bumps from which gleamed ever afterwards on his scalp – from the jemmy of no less a celebrity than Charles Peace. The grandmother took in washing: her three buxom daughters, one of them Neville Cardus's mother, laundered and ironed: the grandfather delivered the wash by pony-cart, except in the case of "rush orders", which the young Cardus took in a perambulator.

Once, as music critic of *The Manchester Guardian*, he was given dinner by the Chairman of the Hallé Concerts Society and, as he leant back and drew on one of his host's cigars, he could think: "What a world! I have delivered his washing."

He was ten years old when he earned his first money – as a pavement artist. He left school at thirteen with little more education than the ability to read and write: but he had discovered Dickens – and the urge to read. "I went alone on Saturday evenings to the Free Library, not in the spirit of a good boy stirred upward and on by visions of an improving kind: I revelled in it all."

By the time he was fourteen he had sold newspapers, pushed a builder's hand-cart, boiled type in a printing works and sold chocolate (and avidly watched the performance) in a Manchester theatre. But already Cardus the writer was beginning to take shape. He had been to Old Trafford and seen A. C. MacLaren and R. H. Spooner, two of the players from whom he gained so much pleasure, and whom he repaid with a measure of immortality in his writing. In his own words: "I spent sixteen years of my youth mainly in books and music and in the sixpenny galleries of theatres. The men on the cricket field were mixed up with the heroes of books and plays." This is why a Cardus quotation is always unforced: it springs from a mind not stocked by formal education but by enthusiastic reading.

He settled as a clerk in an insurance office, living in a lodging house, reading voraciously and attending free lectures at the University, until he reached the age of twenty-one and a salary of a pound a week. In 1912 he applied for a post at Shrewsbury School ("Shastbury" of some of his most charming essays) as assistant to the cricket professional, Attewell ("William" of *The Summer Game*). To his surprise he was engaged. He bowled just well enough – once, in desperation, *just* fast enough – to keep his job until the day the headmaster, Dr C. A. Alington, finding his unlikely-looking young cricket pro reading *Euripides*, made him his secretary. During this time Cardus's first musical criticism was published – in the old *Daily Citizen*. When Alington left Shrewsbury, Cardus went back to Manchester – his poor eyesight alone precluded him from war service – and wrote, with slight hope, to ask for work as a clerk in *The Guardian* office. That remarkable man and editor, C. P. Scott, saw the letter and took Cardus as his secretary. A year later he was put on the staff of the paper as a reporter and, by 1917, had worked his way up to edit the Miscellany and to be number two to C. E. Montague, the paper's dramatic critic.

By yet another odd circumstance, he fell ill in 1919; and afterwards the News Editor, W. P. Crozier, suggested he might be amused to combine convalescence with cricket reporting at Old Trafford. The outcome was instantly successful. By the beginning of the next season he was *The Manchester Guardian*'s cricket correspondent, under the pen-name "Cricketer", which, during the next twenty years, he made increasingly famous.

To his added delight he was also made assistant, and eventually successor, to Samuel Langford, the paper's music critic. *The Guardian*'s circulation and payment rates were small by comparison with those of the London papers. There was no doubt, however, that Neville Cardus was one of the rare cricket writers who positively *sold* newspapers: and he might have multiplied both his salary and his circulation considerably if he had accepted any of the offers to join a larger paper. He refused them for the reason which distinguished him both as man and writer – he was completely happy with his work and with the traditions and atmosphere of *The Guardian*: and, granted the variety afforded by a summer touring the cricket grounds, happy with Manchester, too.

He could not help but realise the impact of his work: he observed the opportunity to publish in book form and he knew the book world well enough to approach, quite astutely, Grant Richards, whose open-minded attitude to fresh types of writing made him one of the most successful publishers of new work and rising writers of the period. Yet Cardus's letters to him were so deferential as to suggest a complete lack of self-confidence in his own work.

Richards, however, was enthusiastic. The result was *A Cricketer's Book*, published in 1922. It began with "The Greatest Test Match" an account of the last day of

England-Australia at The Oval in 1882, still the most vivid reconstruction of a cricket match ever written. There followed a series of those evocative essays in which great players were presented larger, but credibly so, than life, and closed with accounts of the Test series of 1921 and some thoughts on Australian cricket. This book was a landmark in cricket-writing.

Over the next eight years he published *Days in the Sun*, *The Summer Game* and *Cricket*, in the "English Heritage" series, and established his reputation widely and firmly. The last of these is slight in size but it is wide – almost majestic – in scope, and posterity could yet esteem it as the finest of his cricket books. It completed his reputation as the most widely accepted writer the game had known. His achievement could be defined as giving cricket the first sustained writing it had known of the type usually described as "appreciation".

By now he had many imitators but no peer, if only for the reason that, driven by the urge that possesses every worthwhile writer, he never stood still. He broke fresh ground with *Australian Summer*, a book-length account of the 1936-37 MCC tour of Australia. Then, in 1940, he left *The Guardian* for Australia, attracted by a fresh challenge, to deliver an hour-long broadcast each week on music, which he did for the remarkable period of seven years. He also covered music for *The Sydney Morning Herald* and addressed himself to writing his autobiography by hand. This was one more successful departure: the *Autobiography* is expansive, richly human, poignant and humorous: but for the fact that its cricket content was not acceptable to the American reading public, it would have been a world best-seller.

A selection of his work was made by Rupert Hart-Davis under the title *The Essential Neville Cardus* in a series which, with Hemingway, Mary Webb, Joyce and Jefferies, reached a literary level never before attained by a cricket writer.

Although he had contentedly devoted himself to music for some years, the sailing of the Australian side for England in 1948 proved irresistible. He returned to report that tour and to become *The Guardian*'s London music critic. Meanwhile he wrote for *The Sunday Times* for a year, over a considerable period for *World Sports* and, from May, 1960, he has written a monthly essay for *The Playfair Cricket Magazine*. Still, too, usually on the occasion of the death of one of the players of earlier days, he contributes on cricket to *The Guardian*.

Of recent years, too, he has written regulary in *Wisden* – with mellow and dignified nostalgia about old comrades like George Gunn, Charlie Macartney and Hubert Preston: with genuine appreciation of what is for him the younger generation in Sir Leonard Hutton, Godfrey Evans, Cyril Washbrook; of current influences; and, with genuine historic sweep, of Lancashire cricket and "Six Giants of the Wisden Century".

In the post-war period he produced a series of books on music – *Ten Composers*, *Talking of Music*, studies of Sir Thomas Beecham and Mahler, and edited a book about Kathleen Ferrier.

Nowadays, rising seventy-seven, he covers chosen events in European music and watches cricket for pleasure. Though his last collection of cricket essays, *The Playfair Cardus*, revealed fresh facets of style, he probably is content to be judged on his already published work.

Some critics, though amiably disposed, have, nevertheless, done him the injustice of failing to observe his development. There are times when he blushes for what he regards as the excesses of his youth. His essential qualities, as a man, observer and recorder are, of course, constant: but his genuine artistic sensibility, if only that, dictated change in his style. The later Cardus is not to be categorised as better or worse than the early Cardus: but it does him less than justice not to recognise it as different.

Let us take two examples of the change: thirty years ago, in *Good Days*, which some critics regard as his best book, he concluded a study of A. C. MacLaren with this paragraph: "He was the noblest Roman of them all. The last impression in my memory of him is the best. I saw him batting in a match just before the (1914) war; he was coming to the end of his sway as a great batsman. And on a bad wicket he was knocked about by a vile fast bowler, hit all over the body. Yet every now and then one of the old imperious strokes shot grandeur over the field. There he stood, a fallible MacLaren, riddled through and through, but glorious still. I thought of Turner's 'The Fighting Temaraire' as MacLaren batted a scarred innings that day, and at last returned to the pavilion with the sky of his career red with a sun that was going down."

Lately his essay on Sir Leonard Hutton in *The Playfair Cardus* contained: "Technically his batsmanship was as soundly based and studied as any since Jack Hobbs. He played very close to the line of the ball, so much over it that he sometimes suggested, by the slope of his shoulders, the concentration of the student. Even in his beautiful cover drives – and none have been more beautifully poised than his – his head and eyes were inclined downward, and the bat's swing seldom went beyond the front leg before the ball was struck. Like every master he played 'late', so late that he could check the movement of any stroke at the last split second, if the ball suddenly 'did' something contrary to the eyes' and instinct's first promptings."

Comparisons would be pointless: not better, nor worse, but different – with the difference that thirty years make in any man's mind. There was a period when he felt his writings on music were more important than those on cricket. Perhaps he was temporarily, if understandably, disenchanted. Mozart and Beethoven do not change: cricket does. Few cricket-followers past middle age have ever been content that the players they watch then are so good as those of thirty years earlier. Perhaps indeed, Mr Cardus was right: perhaps cricket is not what it was in 1930, or 1920 or 1900. But he has written as felicitously of Denis Compton, Richie Benaud, Neil Harvey, Sir Leonard Hutton and Keith Miller as he once did of Frank Woolley, Ted McDonald, Archie MacLaren or Reggie Spooner – or nearly so.

Moreover, without professional compulsion, he has returned to watching cricket. Much of his erstwhile diffidence has evaporated: indeed he has developed into a conversationalist and a salty raconteur, irresistible on such of his old theme characters as George Gunn, Walter Brearley, Harry Makepeace and Maurice Tate. He may be found taking coffee and talk at Lord's or The Oval half an hour or so before play begins: and he occasionally holds modest court on the little triangle of grass behind the Warner Stand.

He has many friends and still not a few imitators. He is courteous to them all: and, apparently effortlessly, he can observe a cricket match and turn a phrase with any of them. He has made a contribution to cricket which no one can ever duplicate. It may be true that cricket was always an art, but no one until Neville Cardus presented it as an art with all an artist's perception. Because of him, thousands of people enjoy watching the game more than they would have done if he had not lived and written. He has said that his recipe was laid down by C. E. Montague: "To bring to the day's diet of sights and sounds the wine of your own temperament."

LANCASHIRE v HAMPSHIRE

Played at Manchester, June 9, 10, 11, 1965

Hampshire won by 13 runs. They batted very slowly on the opening day against keen bowling, particularly by Statham and Higgs. Lancashire batted much more brightly, especially Green, who drove with power, but their last eight wickets tumbled in astonishing fashion to Cottam who made full use of a treacherous pitch. Higgs and Statham found the conditions just as much to their liking when Hampshire went in again, and Lancashire were set to make 126. They started splendidly, thanks to more aggressive hitting by Green, but Shackleton and White caused another collapse. At the end of an exciting second day in which 27 wickets fell for 252 runs, Lancashire needed 17 runs with two wickets left, but they made only three singles before the match ended early on the final day.

Hampshire

R. E. Marshall c Knox b Higgs	3	– c Statham b Higgs	7
H. M. Barnard c Knox b Higgs	15	– b Statham	30
H. Horton b Statham	30	– b Higgs	11
D. A. Livingstone c Goodwin b Statham	27	– c Howard b Higgs	0
P. J. Sainsbury c Goodwin b Higgs	11	– c Beddow b Statham	2
*A. C. D. Ingleby-Mackenzie b Howard	22	– b Higgs	0
†G. L. Keith c Pullar b Statham	41	– not out	13
B. S. V. Timms run out	8	– lbw b Statham	6
D. Shackleton not out	8	– lbw b Higgs	0
D. W. White c Beddow b Statham	0	– b Statham	8
R. M. Cottam lbw b Statham	0	– lbw b Higgs	0
L-b 3	3		
1/10 2/23 3/75 4/76 5/108 6/110 7/158 8/172 9/174	174	1/11 2/40 3/40 4/43 5/54 6/62 7/62 8/63 9/76	77

Bowling: *First Innings*—Statham 24.1–5–41–5; Higgs 27–9–49–3; Howard 24–5–48–1; Greenhough 21–8–33–0. *Second Innings*—Statham 16–4–41–4; Higgs 15.3–4–33–6; Howard 1–0–3–0.

Lancashire

D. M. Green b Cottam	61	– c Marshall b Shackleton	53
G. K. Knox c Ingleby-Mackenzie b Shackleton	10	– c Barnard b Shackleton	25
G. Pullar c Livingstone b Cottam	37	– lbw b White	0
J. D. Bond c Cottam	4	– lbw b White	1
J. Sullivan c Sainsbury b Cottam	2	– c Livingstone b White	0
A. M. Beddow c Sainsbury b Cottam	3	– c Timms b Shackleton	1
K. Howard hit wkt b Cottam	11	– c Ingleby-Mackenzie b Shackleton	4
K. Higgs c Keith b Cottam	0	– c Shackleton b White	12
*J. B. Statham c Timms b Cottam	0	– c Livingstone b White	1
T. Greenhough c Timms b Cottam	4	– not out	1
†K. Goodwin not out	1	– b White	1
L-b 1, n-b 2	3	L-b 2, n-b 1	3
1/34 2/102 3/115 4/116 5/117 6/125 7/125 8/125 9/133	136	1/67 2/67 3/69 4/69 5/72 6/83 7/87 8/91 9/99	102

Bowling: *First Innings*—Shackleton 16–6–38–1; White 15–3–70–0; Cottam 11.1–4–25–9. *Second Innings*—White 22.3–2–48–6; Shackleton 12–8–15–4; Cottam 13–4–36–0.

Umpires: J. S. Buller and W. H. Copson.

LANCASHIRE v KENT

Played at Blackpool, August 17, 18, 19, 1966

65 overs. Kent won by an innings and 30 runs. Winning the toss presented problems for Green, the acting Lancashire captain, for the pitch was of doubtful lasting qualities, though its state alone could not excuse two feeble batting displays. The left arm spin of Underwood completely undermined Lancashire in the first innings but when the early moisture disappeared the pitch played easily. Capturing six wickets for only nine runs, Underwood was the entire master yet Kent scored 251 for eight before their 65 overs were completed. The first five batsmen all showed good form with Cowdrey leading the way. Lancashire fought back admirably in their second innings with Worsley hitting spendidly for 76 without being able to save the game for his side or extend it into the third day. Again Underwood was Kent's most successful bowler and his full haul of ten wickets for 68 runs was a masterly piece of bowling.

ancashire

I. Pilling c Knott b Underwood	13	– c Cowdrey b Graham	0
D. M. Green c Denness b Sayer	0	– c Wilson b Sayer	2
. D. Bond c Knott b Sayer	1	– c Luckhurst b Underwood	17
). R. Worsley c Luckhurst b Underwood	14	– run out	76
. Wood c Leary b Underwood	1	– c Knott b Graham	31
. Sullivan c Underwood b Dixon	2	– b Underwood	15
. Lever c Dixon b Underwood	0	– c Luckhurst b Underwood	0
). Lloyd c Ealham b Underwood	6	– c Wilson b Dixon	0
. Shuttleworth c and b Underwood	11	– b Dixon	6
K. Goodwin b Sayer	13	– c Cowdrey b Underwood	4
. Cumbes not out	0	– not out	0
L-b 1	1	B 2, l-b 4, w 1, n-b 1	8
/4 2/6 3/21 4/29 5/30 /32 7/35 8/38 9/62	62	1/3 2/3 3/48 4/112 5/136 6/137 7/137 8/148 9/155	159

Bowling—*First Innings*—Sayer 12–6–13–3; Graham 11–6–17–0; Underwood 10.1–7–9–6;)ixon 7–2–22–1. *Second Innings*—Sayer 5–1–17–1; Graham 6–2–15–2; Underwood 3–15–59–4; Dixon 36.4–17–56–2; Luckhurst 3–2–4–0.

ent

. W. Luckhurst b Cumbes	40
M. H. Denness c Worsley b Cumbes	45
. C. Wilson c Worsley b Green	47
M. C. Cowdrey c Goodwin b Green	56
. E. Leary lbw b Lever	22
. Ealham c Shuttleworth b Cumbes	21
A. Knott c Goodwin b Cumbes	1
A. L. Dixon c Goodwin b Lever	3
D. L. Underwood not out	7
D. M. Sayer not out	1
L-b 5, n-b 3	8
1/84 2/87 3/175 4/212 5/239 6/239 7/242 8/244 (8 wkts, 65 overs)	251

. N. Graham did not bat.

Bowling: Lever 15–1–61–2; Shuttleworth 11–1–40–0; Worsley 12–1–42–0; Cumbes 7–4–42–4; Lloyd 5–0–26–0; Green 5–0–32–2.

Umpires: R. Aspinall and T. W. Spencer.

LANCASHIRE v SURREY

Played at Manchester, July 5, 6, 7, 1967

Drawn. Good seam bowling by Arnold and Storey left Lancashire struggling for runs on an easy-paced pitch and Pilling alone really mastered the Surrey attack. Facing an awkward half hour before close of play, Surrey lost Edrich and Edwards for 33 runs, but Barrington and Younis batted soundly on the second morning. Higgs accounted for Barrington, and Lever dismissed Storey to place Surrey in trouble at 101 for six, but Younis and Arnold joined forces and added 64 for the eighth wicket before Surrey gained a lead of 15. Better batting, with Atkinson hitting a century, saw Lancashire reach 266 for four before declaring in their second innings but Bond, batting on for one over and one run after lunch, did not make his challenge attractive enough and Surrey slowly batted out time for a dull draw.

Lancashire

G. Atkinson c Long b Pocock	32	– b Storey	11
B. Wood c Long b Arnold	13	– c Edwards b Storey	5
H. Pilling c Harman b Storey	77	– not out	7
D. R. Worsley c Long b Storey	35	– c Pocock b Storey	
*J. D. Bond c Long b Harman	0	– b Storey	1
J. Sullivan b Storey	5	– not out	
P. Lever c Edrich b Jackman	18		
K. Higgs c Long b Arnold	0		
K. Shuttleworth c Long b Arnold	2		
†K. Goodwin not out	0		
J. S. Savage b Arnold	1		
B 2	2	N-b 3	
1/19 2/65 3/146 4/151 5/157 6/176 7/180 8/182 9/184	185	1/127 2/215 3/220 4/259 (4 wkts dec.)	26

Bowling: *First Innings*—Arnold 22.1–6–39–4; Jackman 19–3–43–1; Storey 25–9–39–3 Pocock 18–4–47–1; Harman 8–2–15–1. *Second Innings*—Arnold 20–8–45–0; Jackma 17–5–53–0; Storey 26–5–59–4; Pocock 6–1–18–0; Harman 28–7–73–0; Barrington 5–0–14–0 Edrich 1–0–1–0.

Surrey

J. H. Edrich c Goodwin b Shuttleworth	0	– c Wood b Higgs	
M. J. Edwards c and b Shuttleworth	19	– b Savage	3
W. A. Smith c Atkinson b Higgs	7	– not out	
*K. F. Barrington c Goodwin b Higgs	20	– not out	3
Mohammad Younis b Savage	57	– c Higgs b Savage	2
S. J. Storey c Bond b Lever	19		
†A. Long lbw b Shuttleworth	12		
P. I. Pocock lbw b Lever	0		
G. Arnold c Sullivan b Savage	48		
R. D. Jackman lbw b Savage	9		
R. Harman not out	4		
B 3, l-b 1, n-b 1	5	L-b 4, n-b 1	
1/0 2/21 3/33 4/34 5/58 6/58 7/101 8/165 9/189	200	1/16 2/44 3/92 (3 wkts)	9

Bowling: *First Innings*—Shuttleworth 22–3–65–3; Higgs 28–6–67–2; Lever 13–1–50–2; Savag 10.5–6–13–3. *Second Innings*—Shuttleworth 5–2–5–0; Higgs 5–1–8–1; Savage 20–8–28–2 Wood 9–5–18–0; Worsley 5–2–8–0; Sullivan 6–1–24–0.

Umpires: P. B. Wright and W. H. Copson.

LANCASHIRE v HAMPSHIRE

Played at Blackpool, August 9, 10, 1967

Lancashire won by an innings and 10 runs. On a pitch of unpredictable pace and bounce Lancashire batted steadily to reach 197 with Atkinson, Snellgrove and Shuttleworth playing well in face of the ever-accurate swing of Shackleton. He captured six wickets for 42 runs in masterly manner. Hampshire lost Marshall and Reed cheaply before close of play on the first day and with rain during the night saturating the pitch there was some sensational cricket on the second day when Savage proved unplayable; his off-spinners brought him five wickets for only one run in six deadly overs. All out for 39, Hampshire put up a much better show when following on, but the steady Lancashire attack finally clinched the issue in extra time despite a patient innings from Sainsbury and some dogged late resistance from Timms and Shackleton.

Lancashire

G. Atkinson lbw b Shackleton	43
B. Wood b White	5
H. Pilling b White	1
K. Snellgrove b Shackleton	57
J. D. Bond b Shackleton	0
D. Lloyd c Timms b Shackleton	15
P. Lever b Sainsbury	5
K. Shuttleworth c Gilliat b Shackleton	40
†K. Goodwin c Timms b Cottam	7
*J. B Statham c Timms b Shackleton	1
J. S. Savage not out	0
B 9, l-b 9, n-b 5	23
1/15 2/22 3/108 4/108 5/125 6/138 7/161 8/196 9/196	197

Bowling: Shackleton 29.3–15–42–6; White 18–6–60–2; Cottam 14–4–27–1; Castell 7–1–16–0; Sainsbury 16–7–29–1.

Hampshire

*R. E. Marshall c Lloyd b Shuttleworth	3	– c sub b Lever	12
B. L. Reed c Atkinson b Shuttleworth	3	– b Savage	11
R. M. C. Gilliat c Wood b Savage	12	– c Shuttleworth b Lever	0
D. A. Livingstone c Wood b Statham	0	– c Wood b Savage	1
P. J. Sainsbury c Wood b Savage	3	– c Lever b Shuttleworth	42
R. G. Caple b Lever	0	– c Lloyd b Savage	0
†B. S. V. Timms c Goodwin b Lever	0	– c Goodwin b Shuttleworth	35
A. T. Castell not out	1	– c Pilling b Statham	10
D. Shackleton st Goodwin b Savage	1	– not out	29
D. W. White st Goodwin b Savage	0	– b Statham	0
R. M. H. Cottam b Savage	0	– b Lever	1
L-b 13, b 3	16	B 6, n-b 1	7
1/3 2/12 3/21 4/26 5/30 6/30 7/33 8/33 9/33	39	1/15 2/15 3/20 4/37 5/57 6/93 7/110 8/136 9/136	148

Bowling: *First Innings*—Statham 10–3–14–1; Shuttleworth 9–5–6–2; Lever 6–4–2–2; Savage 5.4–5–1–5. *Second Innings*—Statham 16–4–34–2; Shuttleworth 16–6–30–2; Lever 15.4–8–14–3; Savage 37–20–34–3; Lloyd 15–7–29–0.

Umpires: C. S. Elliott and J. F. Crapp.

J. B. STATHAM – GENTLEMAN GEORGE [1969]

SOMETIMES HE BOWLED TOO SUPERBLY

By Sir Neville Cardus

Lancashire County Cricket has enjoyed a long an sequential lineage of fast bowlers, though one or two of those in the succession were, so to say, born under a *bar sinister* – in other words, two of them, Crossland and Mold, blotted the escutcheon because they were throwers or "chuckers" of the ball. Two Lancastrian fast bowlers satisfied the severest tests of breeding and deportment, Brearley and Brian Statham; but only one fast bowler playing for my native county could stand comparison, in point of classic poise and action, against Brian Statham, and he was an Australian, none other than E. A. McDonald.

I make a great compliment both to Statham and to the ghost of Ted McDonald by coupling their names. McDonald's action was as easy and as rhythmical as music, and so was Statham's. Purist critics, during Statham's first seasons, suggested that as his right arm swung over, the batsman was able to see too much of his chest; the left shoulder didn't point the way of the flight down the wicket.

The truth about Statham's action is that it was so elastic and balanced (and double-jointed) that there was no forward shoulder rigidity possible; his movement, from the beginning of his run to deliver, to the final accumulated propulsion, had not an awkward angle in it at all. The whole man of him, from his first swinging steps of approach to the launching of the ball from the right foot, was the effortless and natural dynamo and life-force of his attack. He wasn't called "The Whippet" for nothing.

Fast bowlers, as a rule, are aggressive by nature, rough-hewn and physically overbearing. Statham, like McDonald, was unruffled of temper, almost deceptively pacific. I have seen McDonald lose control and let fly a fusillade of unbeautiful "bouncers", wasting fuel, or petrol, like a perfectly engineered car back-firing going up hill. Never have I seen the equanimity of Statham's temperament or technique rendered out of harmony for a minute.

Again, resembling McDonald, he found, in Test cricket, his ideal foils and contrasts. McDonald came to the front when J. M. Gregory was his collaborator in pace; he was the piercing lance to the bludgeon of Gregory. Likewise Statham was the flash of lightning to the thunder of Trueman or the typhoon of Tyson.

Did Statham ever send down a "wide"? He was marvellously accurate in direction; not even Larwood equalled Statham's persistent certainty of length and direction. To describe him as a "seamer" is libellous. He could bring the ball back viciously – and the Press Box would tell us that he "did it off the seam", which is a phrase that is meaningless; moreover, it is a phrase which would have us believe that a bowler can, while achieving rare velocity of flight, drop the ball's seam exactly where he would like it to drop.

I imagine that Statham's break-back was, like Tom Richardson's, caused by body-swing, with the right arm sweeping across the ball's direction at the last split-second of release. I have been told by more than one batsman – in two hemispheres – that Statham has cleaned bowled them, middle or leg stump, by balls pitching outside the off – *and during flight tending to swing away* to the slips. There is no answer to this trick, as the South Africans were obliged to admit at Lord's in the Test match of 1955; Statham on this occasion bowled 56 overs: two for 49 first innings, seven for 39 second, relieved by a two-hour weather break.

At the age of twenty, Statham provoked some sensation in the Lancashire v Yorkshire match at Old Trafford, 1950, by taking five wickets for 52, in the ancient enemy's first innings. On the strength, maybe, of this performance he was flown out, with Tattersall, as reinforcements for F. R. Brown's gallant team in Australia, 1950-51.

These two Lancashire lads arrived in what must have seemed to them then a truly foreign climate; for they had been rushed out of an English winter, still unnourished in a post-rationed environment, to a land of plenty. They came to Sydney looking as though each had escaped from a Lowry canvas, lean and hungry. Statham did not play in a Test match during this rubber; in fact he found the Australian air rather a strain on his breathing apparatus. Nonetheless, he took eleven wickets at 20 runs each against State and Country XI's and in New Zealand.

Back in England he began to foretell the quality soon to come; he had 90 Championship wickets for Lancashire, average 14.65; and in two Test matches v South Africa his contribution as a bowler was four wickets for 78. Invited to play for England in India and Pakistan, in 1951-52, his record was merely modest, eight wickets costing 36.62 runs each in the important engagements. Though in 1952 he harvested 100 wickets for Lancashire at 17.99 runs each, he was not asked to play for England v India; and next summer he was chosen only once for England v Australia – at Lord's – where he took one for 48, and one for 40, though he came sixth in the season's bowling averages, with 101 wickets at 16.33 each; easily the best figures of any English fast bowler that year.

His time was at hand; his place in an England XI became almost a permanency after the Test matches in the West Indies of 1953-54. Now he headed the England bowling averages, 16 wickets for 460 runs.

He was a fairly certain selection for Sir Leonard Hutton's conquering contingent which won the rubber in Australia, 1954-55. This was the rubber in which Frank Tyson achieved a hair-raising speed, so fast that Arthur Morris told me that Tyson was "through you almost before you had picked up your bat". Tyson stole all the limelight, but he was ndebted for much of his blinding efficiency to Statham. And most generously has he acknowledged this indebtedness, in print, for he has written: "The glamour of success was undoubtedly mine. When in the second innings of the Sydney Test I captured six for 85, few spared a thought for Statham, who on that day bowled unremittingly for two hours nto a stiff breeze and took three for 45."

Tyson adds that he "owed much to desperation injected into the batsmen's methods by Statham's relentless pursuit. To me it felt like having Menuhin playing second fiddle to my ead".

This is the most generous tribute paid by one cricketer to another since MacLaren maintained in a conversation with me, "Talk about class and style? Well, I was supposed to be a batsman of some majesty but, believe me, compared to Victor Trumper I was like a cab-horse side by side with a thoroughbred Derby winner."

The Statham-Trueman collaboration of speed is recent history. Trueman in Test matches took 307 wickets, average 21.57. Statham in Tests took 252, average 24.84. It is useless to measure one against the other. As well we might try to assess Wagner and Mozart on the same level. Trueman, on occasion, nearly lost a big match by loss of technical (and temperamental) control; Statham never.

I particularly like Frank Tyson's story of the West Indies bowler who hit Laker over the eye. When subsequently the West Indies "bouncer" came in to bat and reluctantly took guard, somebody asked Statham to retaliate in kind and explosive "kick". "No", said Statham, "I think I'll just bowl him out".

Here, in a phrase, is the essence of Statham's character. Gentleman "George".* Sometimes he bowled too superbly to tail-end batsmen, they were not good enough to get into touch. It is rare for a fast bowler to play all round the world for nearly twenty years and not suffer animosity or verbal abuse from the opposition.

In his first-class seasons of the game, Statham overthrew no fewer than 2,259 batsmen, and each of them were glad to call him a friend. What is more, he could use a bat himself (left-handed) on occasion. At Sydney, in December of 1954, Statham, in number 11, scored 25 at the moment of high crisis and, with Appleyard, added 46 for England's last wicket. And England won the match by only 38 runs.

At the game's end Statham waved aside congratulations. "When I bat and miss I'm usually out. When I bowl and they miss, well – *they* are usually out." He has been an adornment to the game, as a fast bowler of the classic mould, and as a man and character of the rarest breed and likeableness. Also he is amongst the select company of fast bowlers who could field and catch. Cricket will for long have a gap without him.

His benefit of 1961 against the Australians at Old Trafford realised £13,047 and is second only to that of Cyril Washbrook who received £14,000 in 1948. Lancashire in further appreciation of this "model example for all to copy", as they put it, "modest, unassuming, ever-willing to shoulder the burden of the attack or to 'rest' in the outfield where speed of foot and unerring accuracy of throw made him a man to be feared", have organised a Testimonial for him this year. I feel sure that again the response will be generous from his legion of admirers.

LANCASHIRE v NOTTINGHAMSHIRE

Played at Manchester, May 10, 12, 13, 1969

Drawn. Rain prevented play on the first day and on the second Lancashire, winning the toss, put Nottinghamshire in and bowled them out for 152. The highlight of the innings was a hat-trick by Lever. He dismissed Harris lbw at 38 and next ball had Smedley caught at slip. From the first delivery of his next over, Murray was caught at short leg. Not until Taylor and Forbes came together with the score at 67 for seven did the visitors really attack the bowling with any degree of confidence. Halfyard used the long handle to good

* To his friends he has been "George" through his cricketing career.

effect and Nottinghamshire finally achieved semi-respectability in spite of some steady spin bowling by Hughes late in the innings. Lloyd and Atkinson put together an opening partnership of 44 before Pilling provided a neat display. He lost Atkinson in the last over of the day. The last day was a complete wash-out, rain falling relentlessly, and the match was abandoned half an hour before the time for resumption.

Nottinghamshire

M. J. Harris lbw b Lever	11
S. B. Hassan b Higgs	19
*J. B. Bolus b Hughes	17
M. J. Smedley c Higgs b Lever	0
†D. L. Murray c Lloyd b Lever	0
H. I. Moore run out	6
R. A. White c Bond b Simmons	5
M. N. Taylor c Higgs b Shuttleworth	40
C. Forbes lbw b Hughes	26
D. J. Halfyard b Shuttleworth	15
B. Stead not out	1
B 5, l-b 4, n-b 3	12
1/31 2/38 3/38 4/40 5/51 6/65 7/67 8/122 9/150	152

Bowling: Higgs 16–3–33–1; Shuttleworth 10–0–36–2; Lever 12–1–29–3; Simmons 13–6–15–1; Hughes 13–7–27–2.

Lancashire

D. Lloyd c Harris b Halfyard	26
G. Atkinson c Murray b Halfyard	49
H. Pilling not out	45
J. Simmons not out	0
L-b 1	1
1/44 2/120 (2 wkts)	121

D. Bailey, *J. D. Bond, †F. M. Engineer, D. Hughes, K. Shuttleworth, P. Lever and K. Higgs did not bat.

Bowling: Stead 12–3–38–0; Forbes 6–3–13–0; Taylor 7–3–11–0; Halfyard 17–7–27–2; White 9–1–31–0.

Umpires: J. S. Buller and C. G. Pepper.

LANCASHIRE v NORTHAMPTONSHIRE

Played at Liverpool, May 16, 18, 19, 1970

Lancashire won by nine wickets. Splendid bowling by Shuttleworth and Lever enabled Lancashire to restrict Northamptonshire to 156 with no visiting batsman really mastering a pair of pace bowlers who got lift off the pitch and movement through the air throughout the innings. Engineer took six catches. Wood and Pilling were dismissed cheaply when Lancashire replied but the two Lloyds put on 162 for the third wicket, with David Lloyd topping his previous highest in Championship cricket in reaching 108. Clive Lloyd's 89 included one 6 and fifteen 4s against his colleague's one 6 and fourteen 4s. Lancashire declared with a lead of 212. Although Prideaux and Ackerman opened with a partnership of 68 and Mushtaq made 53, Northamptonshire were eventually dismissed for 257, leaving Lancashire to hit 46 from the last 13 overs after rain had held up the start for one hundred and ten minutes on the last day.

Northamptonshire

*R. M. Prideaux b Shuttleworth	31	– b Shuttleworth	60
H. M. Ackerman c Engineer b Lever	2	– c Engineer b Lever	41
P. Willey c Engineer b Lever	0	– b Shuttleworth	0
Mushtaq Mohammad c Engineer b Shuttleworth	32	– c C. H. Lloyd b Hughes	53
P. J. Watts c Engineer b Shuttleworth	22	– c Engineer b Shuttleworth	21
D. S. Steele c Engineer b Shuttleworth	6	– b Shuttleworth	23
B. S. Crump c Engineer b Lever	28	– b Lever	29
D. Breakwell b Hughes	19	– b Shuttleworth	4
M. K. Kettle b Hughes	1	– c and b Lever	4
†L. A. Johnson c D. Lloyd b Shuttleworth	0	– c Hughes b Shuttleworth	4
Sarfraz Nawaz not out	0	– not out	14
B 8, l-b 5, n-b 2	15	B 1, l-b 2, w 1	4
1/9 2/11 3/49 4/90 5/102 6/105 7/148 8/152 9/156	156	1/68 2/69 3/144 4/165 5/181 6/225 7/231 8/236 9/248	257

Bowling: *First Innings*—Lever 18–5–34–3; Shuttleworth 19.2–3–54–5; C. H. Lloyd 13–4–24–0; Wood 5–0–16–0; Hughes 8–3–13–2. *Second Innings*—Lever 30–9–87–3; Shuttleworth 30.1–3–121–6; C. H. Lloyd 2–1–9–0; Hughes 11–3–21–1; D. Lloyd 1–1–0–0; Simmons 8–1–15–0.

Lancashire

D. Lloyd c Sarfraz b Mushtaq	108	– not out	19
B. Wood c Willey b Sarfraz	2		
H. Pilling lbw b Watts	12	– not out	5
C. H. Lloyd lbw b Mushtaq	89		
†F. M. Engineer lbw b Sarfraz	19	– c Watts b Sarfraz	21
*J. D. Bond st Johnson b Mushtaq	28		
J. Sullivan b Sarfraz	57		
D. Hughes not out	33		
J. Simmons c Mushtaq b Crump	7		
K. Shuttleworth not out	1		
L-b 7, n-b 5	12	L-b 2, w 1, n-b 1	4
1/6 2/50 3/212 4/225 5/275 6/324 7/330 8/350	(8 wkts dec.) 368	1/36	(1 wkt) 49

P. Lever did not bat.

Bowling: *First Innings*—Sarfraz 33–11–79–3; Crump 19–4–56–1; Kettle 12–1–58–0; Watts 9–1–45–1; Mushtaq 17–0–96–3; Willey 9–5–13–0; Breakwell 3–0–9–0. *Second Innings*—Sarfraz 4.2–0–27–1; Crump 4–0–18–0.

Umpires: F. Jakeman and W. E. Phillipson.

LANCASHIRE v WARWICKSHIRE

Played at Manchester, June 10, 11, 12, 1970

On a pitch that had little to offer bowlers, Lancashire batted somewhat laboriously on the first day. Ibadulla claimed four wickets and Pilling hit his second century in successive matches. Bond declared first thing on Thursday and Warwickshire owed most to Jameson, whose 158 included four 6s and twenty-two 4s before A. C. Smith also declared, 59 behind. Pilling became the first Lancashire batsman to hit centuries in each innings of a match since Place and Washbrook did so in 1947 but his not-out 104 lost some of its value considering Warwickshire employed ten bowlers in an attempt to force a third declaration. When it came and the visitors were asked to make 278 in one hundred minutes the game was doomed.

Lancashire

D. Lloyd c Kanhai b Brown	39	– run out	0
B. Wood lbw b Ibadulla	28	– c Brown b Blenkiron	12
H. Pilling not out	119	– not out	104
C. H. Lloyd c Abberley b Ibadulla	58	– c Kanhai b Jameson	73
†F. M. Engineer c Amiss b Ibadulla	0		
J. Sullivan c Abberley b Ibadulla	0	– c J. K. Smith b Amiss	5
*J. D. Bond not out	53		
D. P. Hughes (did not bat)		– not out	20
L-b 10, w 1, n-b 2	13	B 4	4
1/62 2/90 3/185 4/187 5/187 (5 wkts dec.)	310	1/0 2/19 3/150 4/169 (4 wkts dec.)	218

J. Simmons, P. Lever and K. Shuttleworth did not bat.

Bowling: *First Innings*—Brown 22–2–79–1; Blenkiron 19–3–63–0; Gibbs 28–9–65–0; Ibadulla 18–4–34–4; Tidy 20–3–56–0. *Second Innings*—Blenkiron 9–4–17–1; Brown 2–0–5–0; Gibbs 16–8–31–0; Tidy 12–0–54–0; Jameson 7–1–46–1; Abberley 5–0–14–0; M. J. K. Smith 2–0–4–0; A. C. Smith 4–0–26–0; Amiss 4–2–8–1; Kanhai 1–0–9–0.

Warwickshire

J. A. Jameson not out	158	– c and b C. H. Lloyd	0
R. N. Abberley c Engineer b C. H. Lloyd	14	– not out	15
R. B. Kanhai c Engineer b C. H. Lloyd	2		
M. J. K. Smith c Engineer b C. H. Lloyd	0	– not out	8
D. L. Amiss b Hughes	27		
K. Ibadulla c C. H. Lloyd b Hughes	17		
D. J. Brown not out	27		
B 4, l-b 1, n-b 1	6		
1/44 2/48 3/48 4/117 5/147 (5 wkts dec.)	251	1/4 (1 wkt)	23

*†A. C. Smith, W. Blenkiron, L. R. Gibbs and W. N. Tidy did not bat.

Bowling: *First Innings*—Lever 16–2–51–0; Shuttleworth 9.4–1–37–0; Wood 7–1–13–0; C. H. Lloyd 17–3–44–3; Hughes 21–5–86–2; Simmons 9–4–14–0. *Second Innings*—C. H. Lloyd 4–2–3–1; Wood 3–0–9–0; Hughes 10–8–3–0; Simmons 9–5–8–0.

Umpires: W. L. Budd and O. W. Herman.

LANCASHIRE v YORKSHIRE

Played at Manchester, May 29, 31, June 1, 1971

Drawn. With the weather uncertain and the pitch freshened by showers from time to time, the batsmen were always struggling for runs and Engineer with an aggressive 49 was the main scorer in a Lancashire total of 168. In reply Yorkshire began slowly with only 43 from 22 overs after tea on the first day and, trapped on a drying wicket on the Monday, were all out for 79 in face of excellent bowling by Lever and Hughes. It was Lancashire's turn to struggle on the last morning after a storm had ended play early on the Monday. Hutton followed up his first innings six for 36 with five for 24 and Lancashire were dismissed for 75. Yorkshire were left with roughly three hours to make 165 for victory on a much easier pitch, but with Boycott absent ill they made no attempt to get the runs.

Lancashire

D. Lloyd lbw b Hutton	7	– c Nicholson b Hutton	8
B. Wood c Bairstow b Old	7	– c Bairstow b Hutton	2
H. Pilling c Bairstow b Hutton	0	– c and b Wilson	14
C. H. Lloyd c Bairstow b Hutton	15	– c Padgett b Cope	9
K. L. Snellgrove c Bairstow b Old	37	– b Hutton	0
†F. M. Engineer c Old b Wilson	49	– b Hutton	8
*J. D. Bond c Padgett b Hutton	16	– c Bairstow b Cope	0
J. Simmons lbw b Cope	19	– run out	20
D. P. Hughes c Bairstow b Hutton	5	– c Old b Hutton	0
P. Lever c Bairstow b Hutton	1	– c Bairstow b Wilson	6
K. Shuttleworth not out	6	– not out	0
L-b 3, w 1, n-b 2	6	B 2, l-b 2, w 1, n-b 3	8
1/15 2/15 3/21 4/47 5/104 6/121 7/149 8/153 9/161	168	1/3 2/26 3/34 4/35 5/35 6/36 7/55 8/60 9/70	75

Bowling: *First Innings*—Old 19–6–56–2; Nicholson 13–3–35–0; Hutton 19.2–5–38–6; Wilson 10–4–20–1; Cope 5–2–13–1. *Second Innings*—Old 5–1–16–0; Hutton 14–4–24–5; Wilson 8.2–3–21–2; Cope 4–2–6–2.

Yorkshire

*G. Boycott run out	9		
J. D. Woodford c D. Lloyd b Simmons	16	– c Wood b Simmons	32
D. E. V. Padgett c Simmons b Lever	15	– c Engineer b Shuttleworth	1
J. H. Hampshire b Hughes	10	– c Wood b Simmons	44
B. Leadbeater lbw b Lever	8	– b Lever	1
R. A. Hutton b Lever	0	– lbw b Lever	2
C. M. Old b Hughes	0	– not out	11
†D. L. Bairstow c Wood b Hughes	2	– not out	0
D. Wilson b Lever	0		
G. A. Cope not out	13	– c Engineer b Shuttleworth	2
A. G. Nicholson c Simmons b Lever	2		
L-b 1, n-b 3	4	B 6, l-b 2, w 1, n-b 1	10
1/9 2/43 3/43 4/61 5/61 6/61 7/63 8/64 9/64	79	1/2 2/59 3/62 4/66 5/94 6/101	(6 wkts) 103

Bowling—*First Innings*—Lever 24.3–11–27–5; Shuttleworth 13–6–24–0; Wood 10–5–10–0; C. H. Lloyd 2–0–2–0; Hughes 8–3–10–3; Simmons 1–0–2–1. *Second Innings*—Lever 12–1–29–2; Shuttleworth 11–6–22–2; Hughes 14–7–13–0; Simmons 14–5–29–2.

Umpires: A. Jepson and A. E. G. Rhodes.

LANCASHIRE v NOTTINGHAMSHIRE

Played at Manchester, July 3, 5, 6, 1971

Lancashire won by six wickets. This was a match dominated by batsmen. Smedley excelled for Nottinghamshire with a century in each innings against a Lancashire attack lacking Lever, who was injured. Winning the toss, Nottinghamshire totalled 257. Smedley played stylishly for 109 and Wood was the only effective bowler. Lancashire replied with 285 for 7 before declaring after Pilling and the two Lloyds had shown sound form. Nottinghamshire were again indebted to Smedley for a fine 119 before Sobers declared, leaving Lancashire to make 253 in two hours thirty-five minutes. Accepting the challenge, Lancashire raced to victory with three overs to spare. Clive Lloyd led the way with a brilliant 62, supported by Snellgrove with a well-judged 59 before Engineer finished the task.

Nottinghamshire

M. J. Harris b Wood	18	– c Engineer b Shuttleworth	6
J. B. Bolus c Simmons b Shuttleworth	6	– b Cumbes	21
M. J. Smedley b C. H. Lloyd	109	– st Engineer b Hughes	119
*G. S. Sobers b Wood	19	– c Simmons b D. Lloyd	42
B. Hassan b Hughes	36	– c Engineer b Hughes	61
R. A. White c Engineer b Cumbes	6	– c Hughes b Simmons	12
S. R. Bielby run out	22	– not out	9
M. N. S. Taylor c Bond b Wood	25		
†D. A. Pullan lbw b Simmons	5		
B. Stead c Cumbes b Simmons	9		
W. Taylor not out	0		
B 1, n-b 1	2	B 2, l-b 7, n-b 1	10
1/23 2/25 3/51 4/137 5/162 6/206 7/239 8/248 9/257	257	1/9 2/54 3/148 4/217 5/246 6/280	(6 wkts dec.) 280

Bowling: *First Innings*—Shuttleworth 18–3–53–1; Cumbes 15–4–41–1; Wood 26–7–51–3; Hughes 16–6–55–1; Simmons 21–5–51–2; C. H. Lloyd 5–2–4–1. *Second Innings*—Shuttleworth 10–3–15–1; Cumbes 8–2–15–1; Wood 5–1–7–0; Hughes 20.3–7–76–2; Simmons 29–9–70–1; D. Lloyd 20–4–87–1.

Lancashire

D. Lloyd c Sobers b White	58	– c Hassan b M. N. S. Taylor	37
B. Wood c Pullan b Stead	21	– b W. Taylor	39
H. Pilling c Hassan b W. Taylor	84	– not out	12
C. H. Lloyd c Smedley b M. N. S. Taylor	63	– c W. Taylor b Stead	62
K. L. Snellgrove c Pullan b M. N. S. Taylor	20	– c Pullan b Sobers	59
†F. M. Engineer run out	3	– not out	39
*J. D. Bond c Pullan b M. N. S. Taylor	2		
J. Simmons not out	12		
D. P. Hughes not out	6		
B 10, l-b 6	16	B 2, n-b 3	5
1/30 2/122 3/242 4/242 5/246 6/251 7/274	(7 wkts dec.) 285	1/61 2/93 3/185 4/220	(4 wkts) 253

K. Shuttleworth and J. Cumbes did not bat.

Bowling—*First Innings*—Stead 16–4–60–1; W. Taylor 16–1–44–1; M. N. S. Taylor 19–3–61–3; Sobers 14–3–28–0; Harris 6–1–32–0; White 14–5–44–1. *Second Innings*—Stead 11–0–65–1; W. Taylor 11–0–67–1; M. N. S. Taylor 14–1–83–1; Sobers 6–0–33–1.

Umpires: E. J. Rowe and H. Yarnold.

LANCASHIRE v NORTHAMPTONSHIRE

Played at Manchester, April 28, 29, 30, 1976

Northamptonshire won by 116 runs. On a pitch that was never constant in pace or bounce Northamptonshire totalled 216 on winning the toss, Steele hitting twelve 4s and reaching 93. He had a runner because of a groin strain. Without Lever, also injured, Lancashire gave Good his chance and the youngster took five wickets for 62 despite being freely punished with the new ball. Lancashire found Cottam's seam bowling a barrier to progress and were dismissed for 150. Lloyd was struck on the head when he mistimed a hook against Cottam. Batting a second time, Northamptonshire were dismissed for 175 as Ratcliffe took four for 52, but a target of 242 runs in five and a quarter hours was always beyond Lancashire's reach, Cottam again being in great form. His match figures were thirteen for 104. It was Lancashire's first championship defeat at Old Trafford since 1972.

Northamptonshire

R. T. Virgin b Good	35	– c Engineer b Lee	36
G. Cook lbw b Ratcliffe	11	– c Engineer b Ratcliffe	18
D. S. Steele not out	93	– c Kennedy b Good	18
*Mushtaq Mohammad c Engineer b Good	0	– lbw b Wood	23
W. Larkins b Good	10	– c Engineer b Ratcliffe	10
T. J. Yardley b Good	4	– c Simmons b Ratcliffe	0
P. Willey c Simmons b Good	14	– c Simmons b Good	27
†G. Sharp lbw b Lee	32	– c Simmons b Lee	10
Sarfraz Nawaz c Simmons b Lee	2	– not out	17
R. M. H. Cottam b Lee	5	– c Hayes b Ratcliffe	4
J. C. J. Dye c Simmons b Lee	1	– b Lee	0
L-b 2, n-b 7	9	B 1, l-b 2, n-b 9	12
1/38 2/55 3/55 4/67 5/75 6/117 7/173 8/175 9/191	216	1/32 2/70 3/82 4/102 5/108 6/114 7/144 8/165 9/170	175

Bowling: *First Innings*—Lee 30.3–9–65–4; Good 17–3–62–5; Ratcliffe 28–12–52–1; Wood 4–1–16–0; Hughes 7–2–12–0. *Second Innings*—Lee 33.5–12–48–3; Good 19–5–52–2; Ratcliffe 26–9–52–4; Wood 5–1–11–1.

Lancashire

B. Wood c Sharp b Cottam	14	– lbw b Sarfraz	16
A. Kennedy c Yardley b Dye	15	– c Cook b Cottam	29
H. Pilling not out	59	– b Cottam	27
F. C. Hayes c Sharp b Cottam	21	– c Virgin b Cottam	2
*D. Lloyd hit wkt b Cottam	2	– absent hurt	0
†F. M. Engineer b Cottam	23	– c Cook b Dye	26
D. P. Hughes c Sharp b Cottam	1	– c Cook b Cottam	0
J. Simmons c Sharp b Sarfraz	5	– not out	12
R. M. Ratcliffe b Dye	3	– c Sharp b Cottam	6
A. J. Good lbw b Cottam	0	– c Cook b Cottam	0
P. G. Lee c Sharp b Dye	0	– c Virgin b Cottam	1
L-b 5, w 1, n-b 1	7	L-b 3, n-b 3	6
1/28 2/42 3/79 4/83 5/111 6/121 7/126 8/142 9/140	150	1/26 2/56 3/62 4/100 5/100 6/104 7/119 8/119 9/125	125

Bowling: *First Innings*—Sarfraz 22–6–31–1; Dye 15.2–5–31–3; Cottam 21–2–65–6; Mushtaq 2–0–16–0. *Second Innings*—Sarfraz 15–6–34–1; Dye 13–0–46–1; Cottam 17.1–5–39–7.

Umpires: C. G. Pepper and W. E. Phillipson.

LANCASHIRE v ESSEX

Played at Southport, July 29, 31, August 1, 1978

Essex won by an innings and 115 runs. A century before lunch by McEwan, who hit four 6s and fifteen 4s, after Essex had won the toss enabled his side to pick up maximum batting points with a total of 379. Then they made serious inroads into the early Lancashire batting as four wickets went for a mere 8 runs in face of hostile new ball bowling by Lever and Phillip. Resuming on the Monday morning Lancashire were all out for 70 with Lever taking five for 23 and Phillip four for 37. Essex forced Lancashire to follow on 309 runs behind and they had the home batsmen struggling a second time. Five wickets went down for 81 before Simmons and Reidy fought back with a partnership of 76 which ended when East dismissed Simmons for 43. When the spinner also accounted for

Reidy for 40, defeat for Lancashire was inevitable. They managed to take the game into the first five minutes of the extra half hour on the second day before Acfield bowled Croft to close the innings at 194 on a pitch that always helped the bowlers.

Essex

M. H. Denness c D. Lloyd b Sutcliffe	10
M. S. A. McEvoy c Reidy b Croft	0
K. S. McEwan c Abrahams b Reidy	128
*K. W. R. Fletcher c Lyon b Arrowsmith	68
B. R. Hardie lbw b Simmons	39
N. Phillip c C. H. Lloyd b Arrowsmith	20
S. Turner c Simmons b Croft	24
R. E. East c Arrowsmith b Simmons	40
†N. Smith c Simmons b Arrowsmith	1
J. K. Lever c D. Lloyd b Simmons	3
D. A. Acfield not out	12
B 20, l-b 7, w 3, n-b 4	34
1/3 2/21 3/192 4/244 5/267 6/308 7/308 8/316 9/342	379

Bowling: Croft 22–3–61–2; Sutcliffe 12–3–37–1; Reidy 13–1–63–1; Arrowsmith 30–5–103–3; Simmons 22.5–3–81–3.

Lancashire

A. Kennedy b Phillip	4	– c Lever b Phillip	9
D. Lloyd c Denness b Lever	2	– c Turner b Lever	17
J. Abrahams c Fletcher b Phillip	0	– c Smith b Lever	22
C. H. Lloyd c McEwan b Phillip	0	– c Hardie b East	4
H. Pilling lbw b Lever	4	– b Turner	22
B. W. Reidy b Lever	16	– c Phillip b East	40
*J. Simmons b Lever	2	– c Denness b East	43
†J. Lyon c Smith b Lever	4	– lbw b East	8
R. Arrowsmith b Phillip	1	– c East b Acfield	0
C. E. H. Croft lbw b East	19	– b Acfield	4
R. Sutcliffe not out	10	– not out	0
L-b 5, w 1, n-b 2	8	B 8, l-b 11, n-b 6	25
1/6 2/7 3/7 4/8 5/28 6/33 7/38 8/39 9/41	70	1/23 2/31 3/70 4/77 5/81 6/157 7/174 8/175 9/185	194

Bowling—*First Innings*—Lever 14–4–23–5; Phillip 14–5–37–4; East 2–0–2–1. *Second Innings*—Lever 11–0–30–2; Phillip 9–3–16–1; East 35–10–86–4; Acfield 19.1–11–25–2; Turner 7–2–12–1.

Umpires: A. Jepson and P. B. Wight.

LANCASHIRE v WORCESTERSHIRE

Played at Southport, June 30, July 1, 2, 1979

Lancashire won by eight wickets. Winning the toss in unsettled weather and batting first on an easy-paced pitch, Worcestershire were always scoring briskly. Turner scored an admirable century after failing by just 1 run to reach three figures before lunch. His 109 and a well-hit 63 from Hemsley helped Worcestershire total 342 for nine, to which Lancashire replied adequately after David Lloyd had batted soundly for 116 and Abrahams had put together a stylish 73. With the pitch showing some signs of wear on Monday afternoon, Worcestershire batted disappointingly. Allott returned his best figures of five for 39 with some excellent pace bowling backed up by good catching in the slips. Set to hit 188 on the last day, Lancashire lost Trim and Abrahams cheaply but the two Lloyds added 119 spectacular runs in little more than an hour to win the match shortly after lunch. David Lloyd, unbeaten for his second century of the match, achieved a feat not accomplished for Lancashire since Pilling did the "double" against Warwickshire in 1970.

Worcestershire

G. M. Turner c and b Ratcliffe	109	– c Simmons b Allott	6
J. A. Ormrod c Hughes b Lee	15	– c D. Lloyd b Simmons	29
P. A. Neale c Trim b Simmons	18	– c Allott b Simmons	23
E. J. O. Hemsley c Abrahams b Hughes	63	– c Lyon b Hughes	19
Younis Ahmed c Ratcliffe b Simmons	50	– lbw b Allott	19
B. J. R. Jones b Hughes	17	– c Lyon b Allott	0
†D. J. Humphries b Hughes	16	– c C. H. Lloyd b Simmons	22
J. D. Inchmore c Trim b Hughes	16	– c Hughes b Ratcliffe	9
G. G. Watson c sub b Simmons	10	– c Ratcliffe b Allott	4
*N. Gifford not out	6	– c Abrahams b Allott	1
J. Cumbes not out	6	– not out	0
B 1, l-b 7, n-b 8	16	B 8, l-b 4, n-b 4	16
1/70 2/137 3/170 4/263 5/272 6/301 7/313 8/330 9/331	(9 wkts) 342	1/10 2/49 3/67 4/94 5/94 6/118 7/127 8/142 9/148	148

Bowling: *First Innings*—Lee 12–4–33–1; Allott 14–2–54–0; Ratcliffe 17–2–71–1; Hughes 27–4–77–4; Simmons 30–5–91–3. *Second Innings*—Allott 21.2–5–39–5; Ratcliffe 12–5–32–1; Hughes 18–8–33–1; Simmons 17–5–23–3; D. Lloyd 1–0–5–0.

Lancashire

G. E. Trim lbw b Watson	0	– c Humphries b Inchmore	17
D. Lloyd c Humphries b Watson	116	– not out	104
J. Abrahams c Turner b Gifford	73	– c and b Gifford	2
C. H. Lloyd c Neale b Cumbes	43	– not out	57
B. W. Reidy b Watson	21		
*J. Simmons not out	26		
D. P. Hughes c Inchmore b Gifford	3		
R. M. Ratcliffe b Watson	7		
†J. Lyon not out	2		
L-b 10, w 1, n-b 1	12	B 4, l-b 3, n-b 4	11
1/7 2/156 3/231 4/256 5/269 6/278 7/298	(7 wkts) 303	1/56 2/72	(2 wkts) 191

P. J. W. Allott and P. G. Lee did not bat.

Bowling: *First Innings*—Watson 17–3–49–4; Inchmore 7–3–19–0; Younis 3–0–13–0; Cumbes 33–4–100–1; Gifford 40–9–110–2. *Second Innings*—Inchmore 8–1–26–1; Watson 10–0–30–0; Younis 1.5–0–14–0; Cumbes 9–0–39–0; Gifford 15–1–46–1; Ormrod 1–0–14–0; Hemsley 5–2–11–0.

Umpires: J. G. Langridge and R. Aspinall.

LEICESTERSHIRE

FOLLOWING LEICESTERSHIRE [1964]

By Brian Chapman

My first recollection of Leicestershire cricket still remains one of the most vivid, far back though it is. One morning in the summer of 1911, my father took me to the Aylestone Road ground to watch the County play against Yorkshire – even to a boy of nine renowned as paladins of the game.

We arrived just before lunch to meet the crowd streaming away. The match was over, Yorkshire beaten by an innings and 20 runs. Jack King, with his awesome black moustache the very paragon of an Edwardian professional, had ensnared Yorkshire with his left-arm spinners (ah, bliss of uncovered wickets!), finishing them off with a spell of seven for none.

Much, much later, only half a dozen seasons ago, I sat with Wilfred Rhodes during a Leicestershire–Yorkshire game at Grace Road, he sightlessly "reading" events in the middle, I an entranced listener.

I asked the great man if he remembered that distant day. Not only did he remember, but he filled in details with fascinating clarity. Then he chuckled: "I said to Jack King, 'I'll give you some stick next time.' And I did!" I checked that claim later. Rhodes indeed scored 92 at Bradford and King took 0 for 50.

Is this touch of personal reminiscence out of place in the present brief sketch – a sporting print, as it were – of Leicestershire's history? One hopes not, for if the joy of cricket is not shared intimacy it is a vain thing. To the writer growing up at the time, first-class cricket is impressionably the names of Geary and Astill, those pillars of the temple between two wars. It is sentimentally the delicate tracery of well-loved Aylestone Road pavilion, seen through the sunny haze of youth, with sandwiches and tea in a medicine bottle, the whole washed down with "giant" cherry ciders.

If you scan tables, or your fancy is to browse upon title-winning statistics, the County whose badge is the golden running fox may not detain you long. Yet it is surely not entirely a rose-coloured view that bestows on them a special quality. They were always a County of character and *characters*. Their ups and downs match the rolling landscape of the Quorn, with perhaps more downs than ups.

About one of the stalwarts, "Sammy" Coe, a left-hander like King and still holder of the County record with 252 against Northants in 1914, Neville Cardus has written: "See an innings by Coe, of Leicestershire, and you ought not to be long guessing from the smack of rotund nature about it that he has passed the main portion of his days in the sun on a field with rustic benches running intimately round."

Another boyhood hero, Albert Knight, of the flashing square drive, the punitive throw-in and the unforgettably blue eyes, seemed somehow remote from other men, yet one of the "originals" of the game. So, later, was Alex Skelding, whose salty music-hall pronouncements, both as player and umpire, have passed into the folklore of cricket. Once at Lord's, Alex thought a fast bowler was making overmuch fuss in the placing of pyramids of sawdust. At last, after much delay, the bowler was ready for action. Skelding dramatically halted him three parts through his run, walked solemnly to the farthest mound of sawdust, picked up a *PINCH* of it between finger and thumb, minced back to the stumps and deposited it to form his own mock foothold. Then he gravely announced: "Play!" Knight wrote a sadly neglected masterpiece called "The Complete Cricketer" which can still be – and ought to be – savoured. The Izaac Walton of cricket writing!

More recently, one of the County's shrewdest captains, C. H. Palmer – he led them briefly to the top – revived the lost art of the donkey drop with results embarrassing for batsmen as distinguished as Worrell and Kanhai. Who could capture, with seeming amiability glinting through rimless spectacles, 8 for 0 against the Surrey Champions and, with Laker's world record of 8 for 2 at his mercy, ignore the frantic advice of the crowd: "Take yourself off, Charlie!" The queerest quirk was that Palmer intended only one over, to change his bowlers round. But he sent Peter May packing – and persevered!

What is the rarest and maybe least known "double"? Well, in 1888, Leicestershire won the Second Class Championship and beat Australia. There's unexpected glory for you! It was with much quiet pride that local enthusiasts noted in last year's Centenary *Wisden* that they shared with Northamptonshire (among Counties now rated first-class) the honour of first forming a "county organisation" in 1820. Much earlier Leicestershire was stirring and bustling with interest. Sides like Melton Mowbray, Barrow-on-Soar, Mountsorrel and Barwell (where George Geary "first saw the light") bristled with challenge.

In his admirable *History of Leicestershire* (to which all chroniclers are deeply indebted) Mr E. E. Snow places 1744 as the earliest Midland mention – lines recited in praise of the game as "desired by the Gentlemen of Barrow". By May 1780, ardent spirits met "to give gentlemen an opportunity of becoming members of a Cricket Club in Leicester founded upon eligible principles". Three months later comes the first recorded match, Loughborough beating Leicester by more than 50 notches on St. Margaret's Pasture, that "most kindly nurse" of the County's growth. Right until 1825 most of the big matches were played there.

Those were vigorous masculine times, not less disputatious than some today. Leicester's first encounter with Nottingham in 1781 was a no-decision affair, the umpires (not entirely unprejudiced) falling out on a point of law and calling the whole thing off.

And what a set-to with Coventry, staged half-way between the two towns at Hinckley in 1787. The neutrality of the scene failed to calm passions (there were one hundred guineas at stake). The victorious Leicester players, quaffing and regaling, fell foul of defeated supporters. "The Hinchley shopkeepers having shut their windows, a scene of bloodshed ensued, scarcely to be credited" (what had become of those gentlemanly "eligible principles"?).

Leicestershire's fame, and that of neighbouring Rutland, spread abroad, attracting representative sides within their borders. Playing for All-England against Hampshire at Burley-on-the-Hill, near Oakham (one thousand guineas the stake) Silver Billy Beldham collected a "pair". After the turn of the century, cricket's hold was established so firmly that public and players looked about for better accommodation. Things started to be organised; the modern era could be dimly decried. "Leicester New Club" had the temerity to humble Leicestershire Gentlemen in 1820 with scores of 65 and 72 against 61 and 30. In 1825, a new ground was taken over in Wharf Street. It has long since been submerged by repeated waves of builders and "developers". Then it was hailed as "more extensive than any except Lord's".

Among visiting celebrities was 18-stone Alfred Mynn, who, listed as Number Ten for South against North, managed to hit 21 and 125, both not out. The finish was unhappy. "Mr. A. Mynn strained his leg (*no wonder*!) and being unable to endure the agony longer, begged Lord Beauclerk to accompany him to one of the marquees, there showing his leg to his Lordship. Lord Frederick instantly sent for a fly to convey him to the stage coach, upon which he proceeded to London."

That was 1836. As the years rolled past, the cricketing fox found new coverts and hunting grounds. Derbyshire Gentlemen, Birmingham, Manchester, Stamford and Rugby appear in fixture lists. Wharf Street passed under the hammer in 1860. Nobly, its final game drew Daft, Caesar and George Parr. Nobly, 22 of Leicestershire humbled these immortals of All England by an innings. One can imagine the blow dealt by this loss of the centre and being of local cricket, and indeed enthusiasm languished for some time. It was six or seven years before a "square" (as the moderns say) was levelled in the centre of the old racecourse on windswept Victoria Park (later a turmoil of interlaced club matches on Thursdays and Saturdays, where one club reporter somehow "covered" eleven games in the afternoon). As it proved, this was a makeshift arrangement and the next major move was to Aylestone (now Grace Road) in 1878.

What a send-off to be sure! Leicestershire (not yet officially such) went the whole financial hog, being the only club to guarantee Murdoch's Australians a lump sum. They were rewarded with a crowd of 13,000 paying spectators on the second day, which stood as a single day record until Bradman's all-conquering farewell 60 years later.

Bannerman's batting and Spofforth's bowling proved decisive, but a fast left round-armer, Bobby Rylott (somehow that name always calls to mind Sherlock Holmes' grim adversary Dr Roylott), later to do great deeds, proved that home-bred talent was not so homespun. Imagine the spur such crowded scenes afforded to those at the head of affairs in town and county! It must have been a jam of horse brakes hired for family outings, smart dog-carts of the gentry, and the cloth caps of the stockingers mixing with Corinthian bowlers and tie-pinned cravats round embroiled entrance gates.

Little time was wasted. On February 25, 1879, a meeting at the Bulls Head Inn (a recent pious pilgrimage found it, alas! silent and shuttered) was sponsored by the Leicester Cricket Club Company. Preliminaries cleared out of the way, a fully-fledged meeting "with full powers" took place in Friar Lane. There the Leicestershire County Cricket Club officially came into being. The sixth Earl of Lanesborough, a cricketer in his own not inconsiderable right, was elected President. All officials had one welcome quality in common. They, too, were cricketers, not "guinea pig" names. Among the committee were W. H. Hay, already a member of county sides; R. W. Gillespie-Stainton, of the Harrow XI; and Canon E. H. L. Willes, of Oxford University, Hampshire and Kent, then vicar at Ashby-de-la-Zouch, on whose rural ground, conjuring up the jousting spirits of "Ivanhoe", the County still enters the lists each season.

It cost one guinea to join and the first match was an Easter friendly against 22 Colts. Wisely guided, the County found favouring winds. They beat Northamptonshire twice by an innings and Sussex twice, Rylott adding to his growing reputation. Stronger opponents were sought and the young County was certainly not discouraged by achieving two draws with Yorkshire in 1883 and beating Surrey by 7 runs. Leaner seasons were in store (as too often in the future), brightened by the emergence of one of the outstanding names in Leicestershire history. This was A. D. (Dick) Pougher, known to more than Midland fame by his amazing 5 wickets for 0 for MCC against Australia in 1896, when a side boasting S. E. Gregory, Hill, Trumble and Darling was dismissed for 18.

Contemporary pictures suggest a lean, tall figure and a somewhat withdrawn manner (which perhaps explained absent-minded failings in the field). His best ball was a medium pace off break of high action rising sharply to the bat's shoulder, but he could move the ball from leg as well. Pougher was good enough to trouble the best, no mopper-up of "nine, ten, jack". Bobby Abel esteemed him the most difficult of all bowlers, an opinion reinforced when he and Rylott, bowling unchanged throughout, skittled Surrey for 26 and 83. Six times Pougher took 13 or 14 wickets. He died at the cricket ground hotel, Grace Road, in 1926 – the year in which his most notable successor, George Geary, was helping England to regain the Ashes and long-lost national pride. ("Woodfull, caught Geary b Larwood 0, Macartney, caught Geary b Larwood 16," we read gloatingly in the stop press from The Oval. Sheer poetry! The best words in the best order!)

Just over the horizon was that wonder year of 1888. Though mauled by Yorkshire, Leicestershire skittled Australia for 62 and 87 on a bad wicket to win by 20 runs. With 10 for 71 in the match, Pougher began his habit of treating Australians almost contemptuously as his "rabbits" – if that term can be applied to victims like Bannerman (twice), that mighty hitter Bonnor, Turner, Blackham (then opening with Bannerman) and McDonnell.

Leicestershire had to wait seven more years before they were elected to first-class status. They were piloted to promotion chiefly by the inspiring leadership of C. E. de Trafford, who bestrode their fortunes as captain for 16 years from 1890 onwards. Without troubling about the niceties of getting to the ball with his feet, de Trafford certainly got to it with his hands. A huge and unhesitating hitter, he seldom bothered about gloves and once struck a four off his knuckles. Another feat was to break the committee room window at Lord's (what more uncompromising way of "attracting the attention of the selectors"?). It can be conjectured that Leicestershire did not lack the sort of aggression and vigour that Mr R. W. V. Robins would heartily applaud. He was fortunate in bringing on men with big reputations to build. Men like Arthur Woodcock (a bowler of almost scaring pace) like King and Knight, and rising batsmen of the class of Coe (firmest of off drivers) and, especially, C. J. B. Wood.

Like Pougher, Woodcock rather fancied himself against Australia and in 1902 dismissed Duff, Hill and Gregory for one run. Still, cricket in the top class was a battle rather than a primrose path and the County usually finished well down in the Championship table.

The new century bought migration to Aylestone Road ("too far for the horse trams" was the verdict on Grace Road) and there Leicestershire remained until 1939. Topping over 2,000 in 1901, Cecil Wood gave a foretaste of the triumphs he was to achieve as possibly the most determined, consistent opening bat in England. He was not exactly graceful to watch, but defence was often enforced in his sheet-anchor role. We boys found him a figure of fun as a bowler, mimicking an unclassic style with whoops of delight. But he took wickets!

For a dozen years or more, he drove bowlers to near-despair. Proof of his watchful and indestructible technique is that seventeen times he "carried his bat". More astonishing – and unlikely ever to be equalled – he brought off this feat twice in one match against Yorkshire – curiously, the occasion of Rhodes' personal tit-for-tat against King. The score card read: Wood not out 107, Wood not out 117. The bowlers? A few trifling tyros, name of Hirst, Booth, Haigh, Rhodes, Bayes. No wonder Hirst, even though he claimed nine wickets all told, exclaimed in exasperation: "Next time, Maister Wood, we'll SHOOT you out with a gun."

Not until 1904 did Leicestershire really challenge in the Championship race. That season, they stood fourth half-way, but could not quite keep it up and finished seventh. Next year was still better – fifth in the list, a position they were to wait many a long summer to better. Wood was "in good nick", as they say nowadays, with 1765 runs, average 43. With their knack for unearthing fast bowlers, the county found still another top performer, Thomas Jayes, born at Ratby, a notable nursery. Jayes would now be compared, in smooth run-up and action, with E. A. McDonald or R. R. Lindwall. Lung weakness ended his career just short of the heights. Veterans who remember him will not hear of Jayes being rated below England class, but the only time he was picked – against Australia at Lord's – he was the one to be omitted on the eve of the Test.

Unfortunately, the County's high hopes of better things were not sustained and in the nine years until the First World War they never rose above tenth. Standing out like a peak above much that was inclined to be featureless was their record 701 for 4 against Worcestershire in 1906 (Wood 225, Harry Whitehead 174, Knight 97, V. F. S. Crawford 102). Yet they still produced "characters" like Bill Shipman, swarthy, strong-built fast bowler – again a Ratby man.

Once at The Oval, Bill was handed a telegram as he went out to field. It announced that he was the proud father of a bouncing boy. He proceeded to clean bowl Hayward, Hobbs and Hayes and capture the first nine Surrey wickets. A stripling called Astill, possibly feeling that parental pride could be carried too far, nippled in with the tenth.

Then there was "Pecker" Mounteney, mighty if un-Spoonerish hitter. Meeting the powerful Kent team he decided it was impossible to hit the fabled Colin Blythe off his length. But you could, with luck, hit the person of Blythe. He did just that. A slogging straight drive struck Blythe on the thigh, the ball cannoned to MID-OFF, who made the catch! Relating the incident with a raconteur's zest, Aubrey Sharp told me: "So old Pecker was out, caught Humphreys, bowled Blythe. But so was Blythe. They retired to the pavilion together. If you don't believe me, it's all in *Wisden*" (It is!). See *Wisden* 1913, page 301. But Blythe took 15 for 45 in that very match.

Sharp himself was in the dozen best amateur batsmen of his day and is, besides, in the

C. B. Fry class as a demonstrator and critic over coffee and cigars. A solicitor-soldier, he got a summons to join the colours in August, 1914, when Leicestershire were playing at Northampton. "We only wanted 90 to win so I left it to them," he recalls. "Actually we lost by 4 runs. The point is I left my boots and bat behind. They were handed to me when we went back to Northampton in 1919."

Now Sharp takes as much pride in following (or presiding over) the fortunes of his village team at Scraptoft as he ever did in leading Leicestershire or hitting 216 against Derbyshire.

One glimmer – perhaps even a dawn – was vouchsafed of fame to come. I still treasure a faded cricket annual that first mentions the names of Astill and Geary. "William Ewart Astill (so a brief entry runs). There is a Gladstonian ring about his name that alone should spell success." How true was that prophet in his green covers and yellowed pages! Already, in 1914, Geary captured 117 wickets at 20 and a bit. Fulfilment was postponed; it was not ultimately denied.

From 1919 the County almost WAS Astill and Geary, and Geary and Astill were Leicestershire. Bradman has described the surprise, almost shock, of encountering Geary's leg cutter, then unfamiliar to him, though he later came to think that Alec Bedser's was more deadly. No doubt, it was Geary's most potent ball, but he was armed with all the weapons of medium-fast attack – zip off the pitch, concealed change of pace, perfect and unwearying control. He won England honours both at home and on tour. For his County he took over 100 wickets eleven times, with 10 for 18 against Glamorgan in 1929 his personal best. He was, besides, a very present help when runs were needed, a slip little below the Hammond class, and a willing encourager of young players which Charterhouse – and Peter May – found of inestimable value later on.

Seventy in *Wisden*'s centenary year, George was until recently turning his arm over in the winter nets. "He can still make 'em fizz a bit," the new generation had to acknowledge.

Astill, of the handsome aristocratic looks, possessed an easy, almost lazy approach to the wicket that concealed off spin wicked on a helpful wicket. Almost, he cajoled batsmen to their downfall. "Somehow, he wheel's 'em up and wheels 'em out," said one old pro. There was nothing plebeian about his batting; Astill did everything with an air. Yes, "the lad with the delicate air", the touch that made him superb at billiards. He was Leicestershire's supreme all-rounder. Nine times he accomplished the double, in consecutive seasons from 1921 save for 1927. News of his death, which reached an MCC side touring the West Indies in 1948, came as a real sense of loss.

It was still pretty hard pounding in the Championship. A meritorious ninth in 1919 was followed by uneven standards leading to lowly positions. Tommy Sidwell, a little prince of wicket-keepers in the Strudwick mould and worthy of that comparison, gave stout-hearted support to the two *non-pareils*. Alec Skelding kept up the fast bowling tradition. For half a dozen overs his glasses flashed lightning.

Charles Bray, doyen of cricketer-journalists, recalls opening at Aylestone Road for Essex in his first match. His partner, A. C. Russell, turned to him with words of ghostly advice:

"Mr Bray, there are two bowlers you are just going to face. One runs a mile and bowls medium. The other takes six strides and let's her go. That's Skelding and he's almighty quick."

A break-through to seventh enlivened 1927. The attack was varied and E. W. Dawson (a Cambridge acquisition to the batting) and Geary and Astill were all picked to tour South Africa. All three enjoyed repeat performances in 1929 – Dawson 1909 runs, Geary 152 wickets at 19.6 each, Astill 121 wickets at 20.9.

Another prolific batsman, L. G. Berry, advanced to the front with 232 against Sussex in 1930. "Jinks" Berry, a dedicated cricketer and footballer (he kept goal for Sheffield Wednesday, Bristol Rovers and Swindon Town) claimed a distinguished record both for his County and the RAF. For Leicestershire he scored more runs in a season than any other player – 2,446; more centuries – 45; more thousands in a season – 18 times; and highest career aggregate – 30,106.

Perhaps the achievement that gave him most pleasure was batting through the innings against Nottinghamshire at Ashby in 1932 with Larwood and Voce in full flight and winning the match in a last-wicket stand with wicket-keeper, Corrall.

Team-wise, old faults crept in and the final indignity – bottom place for the first time – chastened spirits in 1933. It needed the bold step of promoting Astill as first professional captain to send Leicestershire riding high. Under him the side did not lack authority and maturity. That season of 1935 they shot up to sixth, with a record number of 11 matches won.

That season also stands out as the début of C. S. ("Stewie") Dempster, forming with Willie Watson (imported later from Yorkshire) the only couple of genuine world-class batsmen who have won the County's green blazer. Even the New Zealander's accomplished batting (a rippling century at Hove springs delightfully to mind) failed to check a renewed decline which sank Leicestershire to bottom in 1939.

War, and the ugly encroachment of industry, spelt the end of Aylestone Road. The story is told of George Headley affecting to believe that falling smuts were black snow! A return was made to Grace Road, thenceforward the County's headquarters. The fame – and burdens – of Geary and Astill now rested on the broad Australian shoulders of Jack Walsh and Vic Jackson. Berry took over the captaincy and, says *Wisden*, "his leadership and experience proved of immense value to the younger members of the team".

In 1947, Berry, a hard-hitting opener of unruffled temperament, scored over 1,000 runs for the fifteenth time and Walsh had a magnificent season, taking 152 wickets with his unorthodox left-arm bag of tricks. Better still, this immensely popular player raised the bidding next season to 174. I remember Bill O'Reilly, sitting in the Press box behind Walsh's arm, nominating the wong 'un with expert infallibility. The batsmen were not always so successful.

Sadly, slipshot fielding and other weaknesses crept in and it was a case of rock bottom again in 1949, a gap of 16 points below the next worse county. So it was a heavy responsibility that Charles Palmer assumed as captain. Playing many good knocks with the fluent Maurice Tompkin, he just managed to lift the side "out of the cellar". That was the rearguard action. They went two better next time, climbed to sixth in 1952. That was the battle course.

They really went "over the top" in the fine summer of 1953, which suited both the batting and bowling. Leicestershire, in their best-ever season, finished equal third with Lancashire. One splendid week-end in August they led the field, a fact which won Page One prominence in a national newspaper! Palmer gained his place as player-manager of Hutton's tour to the West Indies. Tompkin's cultured driving, beautiful to watch, brought him close on 2,000 runs. But, again to quote *Wisden*, "excellent team work under Palmer's leadership, which showed itself in many fighting recoveries, was the main factor in the county's success rather than outstanding individual brilliance".

Dismal weather induced a relapse to sixteenth, but Palmer led his keen side back to sixth the following year. The batting was spiced by the free-scoring style of Maurice Hallam, a fine slip catcher and an opener destined to spread delight across many English fields. Palmer's out-to-win policy led to a spate of close finishes. He and Tompkin each hit a century on opposite sides in the Gentlemen v Players fixture at Lord's. Palmer, mischievously put on to bowl when his professional colleague was in the nineties, found himself faced with divided loyalties, which he contrived to resolve satisfactorily!

The skipper capped a captivating year with that eight for 7 against Surrey, whose players, notably May, wryly remember Palmer popping his face round their dressing-room door and exclaiming with a cherubic grin, "Sorry, gentlemen!"

Leicestershire were decidedly no team of "wet bobs" and dismal summers plummetted them twice to the foot of the chart. Tompkin was pursued by ill health that showed its first symptoms when touring Pakistan for MCC and died, a deeply lamented cavalier of the game, gay as a player, a model of quiet charm as a companion, a perfect ambassador for his country.

With Palmer retiring, and desperate to find extra strength, the Committee called in

Watson as captain. His broad, punishing bat provided stiffening urgently needed; too often, however, he received feeble support. Collapses were liable to happen even on good wickets. Leicestershire supporters watching at Lord's in 1960 were exhilarated to see Watson and Hallam put on 196 for the first wicket against Middlesex. Rejoicings were wiped out by a final 214 all out. Nothing more dramatically exposed fatal limitations, and last place was not unexpected or undeserved.

Unremitting search for extra solidity brought Alan Wharton from Lancashire and the attack, getting reasonable targets to bowl at, took heart of grace. The fast men, Brian Boshier (108 wickets at 17.8 each), Terry Spencer (123 at 19.5) and off spinner John Savage, were all grouped near the top of the national averages and consequently Leicestershire rose half-way up the table.

Next season's descent to the depths was hardly deserved. Watson was often away as Test selector and although Jack van Geloven achieved his double "on the post" luck was unkind. As consolation Leicestershire enjoyed much the better of a last-match draw against Yorkshire, avid for points to clinch the Championship. One Yorkshire player, a trifle shaken, commented: "Yon lads must be best wooden spooners in ruddy history."

Now Leicestershire fight under an able and likeable leader in Hallam, one who (perhaps as well) bears adversity stoically and who cannot avoid cheerfulness breaking in. His label, "the best opener who never played for England", is currently popular and there is some logic in it. His chance seemed to have arrived when he struck tremendous early form in 1959. Had a certain selector prolonged a visit to Grace Road the story might have been different. Hallam went on to hit two quick-time double hundreds. But his eminent audience had departed.

Leicestershire's energetic secretary, Mr Michael Turner, and assiduous committee keep up the search for new talent. Two newcomers from Ceylon, Stan Jayasinghe and Clive Inman, have already made their marks. If determination – and Hallam – cannot command success it will at least be richly deserved. The County that pioneered Saturday starts and pilot-schemed the Knock-out Cup must, surely, be "in the hunt". HARK FORRARD is the cry!

LEICESTERSHIRE v DERBYSHIRE

Played at Loughborough, June 16, 17, 18, 1965

Derbyshire won by 66 runs. Leicestershire went down fighting in their first Championship defeat of the season. In a rain ravaged match Rhodes, the Derbyshire fast bowler, caused Leicestershire most trouble, earning match figures of ten for 50. To all intents doomed after being shot out for 36 in their first innings by Rhodes (six wickets for nine runs), Leicestershire offered stiffer resistance when left to make 219 in three and a quarter hours and, not until the verge of extra time, did Derbyshire finally emerge victorious.

Derbyshire

J. R. Eyre b Marner	3	– c Marner b Lock	13
I. W. Hall lbw b Marner	3	– lbw b Marner	9
M. H. Page c and b Marner	9	– c Jayasinghe b Lock	6
H. L. Johnson c Hallam b Marner	22	– c Jayasinghe b Lock	0
I. R. Buxton c Birkenshaw b Lock	70	– not out	43
*D. C. Morgan c Marner b Savage	10	– c Marner b Lock	8
E. Smith c Cross b Lock	1	– c Cross b Lock	3
†R. W. Taylor b Spencer	37	– c Inman b Savage	1
M. H. J. Allen c Jayasinghe b Lock	1		
H. J. Rhodes not out	0		
A. B. Jackson c Jayasinghe b Savage	0		
B 7, l-b 5	12	B 1, l-b 2	3
1/4 2/15 3/34 4/41 5/62 6/75 7/164 8/165 9/168	168	1/18 2/28 3/28 4/51 5/59 6/66 7/86 (7 wkts dec.)	86

Bowling: *First Innings*—Spencer 11–2–17–1; Marner 21–3–46–4; Lock 36–18–41–3; Savage 22.1–8–52–2. *Second Innings*—Spencer 8–1–23–0; Marner 6–0–15–1; Lock 13.1–10–8–5; Savage 9–1–37–1.

Leicestershire

*M. R. Hallam c Johnson b Rhodes	0	– b Allen	48
B. J. Booth st Taylor b Jackson	12	– c Hall b Rhodes	27
P. Marner c Allen b Rhodes	1	– b Rhodes	17
S. Jayasinghe c Allen b Rhodes	0	– c Taylor b Allen	17
C. C. Inman c Smith b Jackson	2	– c Rhodes b Smith	14
G. Cross run out	0	– c Jackson b Allen	5
J. Birkenshaw b Rhodes	10	– c Johnson b Smith	0
G. A. R. Lock c Taylor b Jackson	0	– c and b Smith	10
C. T. Spencer c Eyre b Rhodes	1	– c Page b Rhodes	8
†R. Julian not out	5	– b Rhodes	0
J. S. Savage b Rhodes	2	– not out	4
L-b 3	3	B 1, n-b 1	2
1/3 2/5 3/5 4/12 5/12 6/22 7/22 8/23 9/34	36	1/70 2/90 3/97 4/121 5/133 6/140 7/140 8/148 9/148	152

Bowling: *First Innings*—Rhodes 14.1–6–9–6; Jackson 14–5–21–3; Smith 1–0–3–0. *Second Innings*—Jackson 7–1–26–0; Rhodes 13–0–41–4; Allen 19–1–55–3; Smith 13.4–3–28–3.

Umpires: T. Drinkwater and R. Aspinall.

LEICESTERSHIRE v WORCESTERSHIRE

Played at Leicester, June 30, July 1, 2, 1965

Drawn. Although Leicestershire failed to gain any points they had the satisfaction of a century in each innings by their captain, Hallam, his first three figures scores against the Champions. Hallam and Booth gave Leicestershire a fine start with an opening partnership of 143 but loss of play through rain brought an early declaration. Worcestershire later declared after going ahead, but expectations of a close fight on the last innings were ruled out when Leicestershire batted until after lunch, before asking their opponents to score 235 under two and a half hours. Hallam, who reached a first-innings century in four hours (nine 4s), followed with 149 not out (one 6, seventeen 4s). This was the third time in his career that he scored two centuries in a match. He was on the field for the entire three days.

Leicestershire

*M. R. Hallam not out	107	– not out	149
B. J. Booth c Graveney b Carter	64	– st Booth b Gifford	83
J. Birkenshaw c Brain b Horton	20	– not out	2
S. Jayasinghe run out	4		
C. C. Inman not out	16		
L-b 3	3	B 1, l-b 2	3
1/143 2/174 3/178	(3 wkts dec.) 214	1/204	(1 wkt dec.) 237

P. Marner, G. A. R. Lock, †R. Julian, C. T. Spencer, J. S. Savage and J. Cotton did not bat.

Bowling: *First Innings*—Flavell 10–2–36–0; Brain 8–0–26–0; Carter 22–7–54–1; Gifford 12–4–30–0; Horton 20–5–50–1; D'Oliveira 6–1–15–0. *Second Innings*—Flavell 11–2–36–0; Brain 12–1–51–0; Carter 5–3–5–0; Horton 13–2–49–0; Gifford 14–4–39–1; Kenyon 10–0–50–0; Richardson 1–0–4–0.

Worcestershire

M. J. Horton c Julian b Marner	24	– c Jayasinghe b Spencer	0
D. W. Richardson c Savage b Marner	33	– c Julian b Spencer	12
R. G. A. Headley not out	81	– c Jayasinghe b Birkenshaw	14
T. W. Graveney retired hurt	36	– b Birkenshaw	6
B. D'Oliveira c Lock b Birkenshaw	39	– not out	35
*D. Kenyon not out	3	– c Lock b Birkenshaw	11
†R. Booth (did not bat)		– not out	18
N-b 1	1	L-b 4	4
1/47 2/62 3/207	(3 wkts dec.) 217	1/3 2/12 3/36 4/43 5/51	(5 wkts) 100

N. Gifford, B. M. Brain, J. A. Flavell and R. G. M. Carter did not bat.

Bowling: *First Innings*—Spencer 8–3–10–0; Cotton 10–1–27–0; Lock 32–10–80–0; Marner 17–2–37–2; Savage 25.3–8–45–0; Birkenshaw 8–4–17–1. *Second Innings*—Cotton 3–1–6–0; Spencer 4–1–12–2; Lock 16–5–38–0; Birkenshaw 15–3–38–3; Savage 8–6–2–0.

Umpires: J. S. Buller and W. E. Phillipson.

NOTES BY THE EDITOR, 1966

FARCE OF THE FASTEST FIFTY

A player from Ceylon, C. C. Inman, the Leicestershire left-hander, set up new world records for the fastest fifty which he completed in eight minutes with eleven scoring strokes against Nottinghamshire at Trent Bridge. This was another case of farcical third-day county cricket when the fielding side, through N. Hill, who served up slow full tosses, gave away runs to persuade the opposition to make a declaration that would provide a chance of a definite result. Not surprisingly, umpire J. S. Buller sent a report to MCC.

LEICESTERSHIRE v SOMERSET

Played at Leicester, June 17, 18, 19, 1967

Leicestershire won by two wickets. This fine match mounted to a magnificent finish, Lock hitting the winning four off the fifth ball of the last over on Monday evening. For Somerset, who won the toss, Kitchen's 141 was his highest score in first-class cricket, made in four hours, with one 6 and twenty 4s. Atkinson supported him in a second-wicket stand of 76, and Somerset ended the first day at 328 for six. The next morning Atkinson declared at 402 for eight, and retired from the match with a strained groin. Leicestershire lost half their wickets to the spinners, Langford and Robinson, for 84, but Inman and Birkenshaw put on 64 quickly and Cotton, the last man, hit two 6s to avoid the follow-on. Somerset, using Clarkson as an emergency opener, declared again, leaving Leicestershire to make 296 in four hours. With 150 needed in the last ninety minutes, the outlook seemed hopeless but, with 98 still wanted, and forty-five minutes left, Birkenshaw and Tolchard, in a fine seventh-wicket stand, raised 89 in forty minutes. Tension was unbearable when Lock faced the last over from Rumsey, with two needed. Lock drove the fifth ball of the over square to the boundary, tossing his bat aloft in triumph.

Somerset

R. Virgin b Birkenshaw	23	– c Dudleston b Lock	34
*C. R. M. Atkinson c Cotton b Lock	63	– absent hurt	0
M. Kitchen b Cotton	141	– c and b Lock	18
G. Burgess c and b Cotton	10	– c Tolchard b Lock	8
W. E. Alley lbw b Birkenshaw	52	– c and b Lock	18
A. Clarkson b Lock	2	– c Spencer b Birkenshaw	45
K. E. Palmer c Tolchard b Lock	22	– c Norman b Lock	18
†G. Clayton not out	33	– not out	4
P. J. Robinson c Tolchard b Spencer	28	– st Tolchard b Lock	7
B. A. Langford not out	7		
B 7, l-b 7, w 1, n-b 6	21	B 2, l-b 2	4
1/61 2/137 3/171 4/285 5/285 6/300 7/344 8/393	(8 wkts dec.) 402	1/53 2/80 3/90 4/118 5/144 6/146 7/156	(7 wkts dec.) 156

F. E. Rumsey did not bat.

Bowling: *First Innings*—Spencer 21.2–3–87–1; Cotton 32–4–110–2; Marner 10–1–44–0; Birkenshaw 40–10–71–2; Lock 33–11–69–3. *Second Innings*—Spencer 7–1–18–0; Cotton 6–2–11–0; Birkenshaw 17–2–78–1; Lock 18–4–45–6.

Leicestershire

M. R. Hallam c Alley b Robinson	16	– c Kitchen b Robinson	38
M. E. Norman b Palmer	10	– c Rumsey b Robinson	70
B. J. Booth c and b Robinson	14	– b Robinson	3
C. C. Inman b Langford	76	– c Kitchen b Langford	14
P. T. Marner c Burgess b Robinson	6	– c Alley b Langford	8
J. Birkenshaw not out	73	– c Robinson b Alley	42
B. Dudleston c Robinson b Langford	0	– st Clayton b Langford	51
†R. W. Tolchard c Alley b Robinson	7	– lbw b Alley	43
*G. A. R. Lock c and b Robinson	27	– not out	9
C. T. Spencer st Robinson b Langford	0	– not out	0
J. Cotton c sub b Langford	24		
B 2, l-b 4, w 1, n-b 3	10	B 1, l-b 15, w 1, n-b 3	20
1/22 2/35 3/70 4/84 5/84 6/148 7/168 8/202 9/211	263	1/59 2/67 3/100 4/109 5/190 6/200 7/289 8/292	(8 wkts) 298

Bowling: *First Innings*—Rumsey 4–0–14–0; Palmer 5–0–12–1; Langford 27.5–4–99–4; Robinson 24–5–128–5. *Second Innings*—Rumsey 7.5–3–34–0; Palmer 4–0–13–0; Langford 30–5–78–3; Robinson 30–9–123–3; Clarkson 4–0–19–0; Alley 2–0–11–2.

Umpires: T. W. Spencer and G. H. Pope.

LEICESTERSHIRE v CAMBRIDGE UNIVERSITY

Played at Leicester, June 21, 22, 1967

Leicestershire won by an innings and 21 runs. Beaten in two days, the University were no match for a team with the sharper approach. One exception was the Ceylon batsman, Ponniah, who scored 98 not out in the first innings and 50 in the second. He batted with excellent judgement on a wicket helpful to the spin bowlers, being partnered by Knight in a second-wicket stand of 60, and by Acfield, in raising 80 for the eighth wicket. Leicestershire brought in Knight and Matthews, and retained Dudleston. Norman gave the University reason to remember him for, having batted six hours against them for his highest score, 221 not out, a fortnight earlier, he endured for four hours, twenty minutes, in making 116. Cambridge trials were extended by Booth, who spent almost the same time for 125, and the pair added 169. Acfield bowled his off spinners patiently and was Ponniah's most competent lieutenant in the Cambridge first innings, a distinction that went to Cottrell in the second innings. Malalasekera jarred a shoulder by a heavy fall in the field, and new opening partners for Ponniah were Norris and Knight.

Leicestershire

M. E. Norman c sub b Acfield	116
B. Dudleston c Norris b Cottrell	44
B. J. Booth b Aers b Acfield	125
P. T. Marner c Cosh b Russell	7
*M. R. Hallam not out	27
D. J. Constant c Ponniah b Acfield	31
B. R. Knight c Norris b Russell	6
J. Birkenshaw c Cottrell b Acfield	1
†R. W. Tolchard not out	1
L-b 11, n-b 3	14
1/80 2/249 3/258 4/272 5/332 6/368 7/370	(7 wkts dec.) 372

A. Matthews and C. T. Spencer did not bat.

Bowling: *First Innings*—Palfreman 19–1–77–0; Russell 29–7–86–2; Cottrell 18–5–47–1; Acfield 31–8–89–4; Aers 19–4–44–0; Knight 7–1–15–0.

Cambridge University

C. E. M. Ponniah not out	98	– c Dudleston b Birkenshaw	50
†D. W. Norris c Hallam b Knight	1	– c Norman b Booth	0
R. D. V. Knight b Birkenshaw	34	– lbw b Knight	7
N. J. Cosh b Birkenshaw	2	– c Constant b Booth	6
C. P. Pyemont c Constant b Matthews	1	– c Matthews b Birkenshaw	11
G. A. Cottrell c Tolchard b Matthews	5	– c Matthews b Birkenshaw	43
D. R. Aers c Marner b Birkenshaw	1	– c Dudleston b Birkenshaw	0
A. B. Palfreman c Knight b Matthews	9	– not out	6
D. L. Acfield c and b Booth	42	– c Hallam b Booth	9
*S. G. Russell c Knight b Matthews	2	– b Booth	7
V. P. Malalasekera c Marner b Birkenshaw	0	– absent hurt	0
B 11	11	B 1, l-b 4, w 1	6
1/7 2/67 3/69 4/74 5/80 6/96 7/105 8/185 9/206	206	1/12 2/37 3/50 4/105 5/113 6/118 7/128 8/130 9/145	145

Bowling: *First Innings*—Knight 12–4–32–1; Spencer 8–0–24–0; Matthews 25–3–87–4; Birkenshaw 19.3–4–41–4; Marner 1–1–0–0; Booth 3–0–11–1. *Second Innings*—Knight 4–0–8–1; Spencer 5–1–6–0; Matthews 7–2–25–0; Birkenshaw 19–7–44–4; Booth 21.2–3–56–4.

Umpires: T. W. Spencer and G. H. Pope.

LEICESTERSHIRE v NORTHAMPTONSHIRE

Played at Leicester, August 30, 31, September 1, 1967

Leicestershire won by 163 runs. A remarkable week for the Leicestershire captain, Lock, closed with another big haul, thirteen wickets for 118 runs, bringing his tally for the two matches to twenty-three wickets. The pitch for the last match was a fiery instrument in Lock's hands, many deliveries lifting as well as turning. Indeed, the Northamptonshire captain, Prideaux, complained that the pitch was unsatisfactory for first-class cricket. Leicestershire registered their third successive victory, to attain the highest final position in their history, being joint leaders with Kent, each having 176 points. But Yorkshire, still with a match in hand of both, eventually leapfrogged over them. The match was followed by enthusiastic scenes outside the pavilion. Mushtaq bore the burden of attack for Northamptonshire, taking seven of the first eight wickets, but he could not suppress Norman and Hallam during an opening stand of 185. Hallam's first century of the season came in three hours, fifty minutes, with eleven 4s. Inman followed with a volatile 58 and Booth, sharing a third-wicket stand of 82, helped to underline the failure of the other Northamptonshire bowlers on a responsive pitch. Milburn, striking thirteen 4s in his 87 in two and three-quarter hours served Northamptonshire admirably, the Leicestershire lead being kept down to 129. Lock left his rivals 277 to get in reasonable time, a target they never looked like reaching against Lock, who was aided efficiently by Birkenshaw. This was Leicestershire's tenth win, their best since 1955.

Leicestershire

M. R. Hallam lbw b Mushtaq	103	– c Willey b Crump	3
M. E. Norman c Kettle b Mushtaq	90	– c Johnson b Kettle	37
B. J. Booth c Lightfoot b Mushtaq	37	– st Johnson b Steele	36
C. C. Inman lbw b Mushtaq	58	– c Willey b Kettle	26
P. T. Marner not out	2	– c Kettle b Crump	2
B. Dudleston b Kettle	33	– c Steele b Kettle	8
J. Birkenshaw c Johnson b Mushtaq	2	– not out	18
†R. W. Tolchard c Johnson b Mushtaq	4	– not out	15
*G. A. R. Lock c Sully b Kettle	2		
C. T. Spencer c Johnson b Kettle	0		
J. Cotton b Mushtaq	0		
B 3, l-b 2, n-b 4	9	L-b 2	2
1/185 2/200 3/282 4/301 5/327 6/335 7/338 8/338 9/340	340	1/8 2/77 3/81 4/86 5/112 6/115	(6 wkts dec.) 147

Bowling: *First Innings*—Crump 17–3–46–0; Kettle 25.3–4–74–3; Sully 26–6–75–0; Willey 3–0–11–0; Mushtaq 36–10–75–7; Steele 21–5–50–0. *Second Innings*—Crump 17–4–48–2; Kettle 13–3–41–3; Sully 3–0–14–0; Mushtaq 5–0–26–0; Steele 4–1–16–1.

Northamptonshire

*R. M. Prideaux c Tolchard b Lock	15	– c Lock b Birkenshaw	24
C. Milburn c Inman b Lock	87	– c Lock b Birkenshaw	26
B. L. Reynolds c Norman b Lock	6	– c Tolchard b Birkenshaw	0
Mushtaq Mohammad c Dudleston b Lock	6	– c Marner b Lock	2
A. Lightfoot c Cotton b Birkenshaw	47	– c Marner b Lock	4
D. S. Steele c Hallam b Lock	15	– lbw b Lock	12
B. Crump c Booth b Birkenshaw	6	– c Spencer b Lock	8
P. Willey c Lock b Birkenshaw	5	– st Tolchard b Lock	8
M. K. Kettle c Marner b Lock	2	– not out	11
†L. A. Johnson c Spencer b Lock	0	– c Tolchard b Lock	12
H. Sully not out	5	– c Spencer b Birkenshaw	0
B 8, l-b 8, n-b 1	17	B 5, n-b 1	6
1/33 2/49 3/94 4/140 5/175 6/192 7/197 8/202 9/202	211	1/50 2/50 3/53 4/57 5/63 6/80 7/84 8/91 9/111	113

Bowling: *First Innings*—Cotton 6–2–7–0; Spencer 7–0–27–0; Lock 28.2–16–75–7; Marner 4–0–25–0; Birkenshaw 32–9–60–3. *Second Innings*—Cotton 3–0–11–0; Spencer 3–0–12–0; Lock 20–8–43–6; Birkenshaw 19.1–6–41–4.

Umpires: A. Gaskell and P. B. Wight.

LEICESTERSHIRE v ESSEX

Played at Leicester, July 31, August 1, 2, 1968

Drawn. Again losing the toss, Hallam was much relieved to see his bowlers dismiss Essex so cheaply. Rain lopped off ninety minutes and forty-five minutes were lost at the end of the first day owing to bad light. Playing against his old county for the first time, Knight infused enough fire into his seam bowling to undermine the Essex batting, Tolchard holding four catches at the wicket. Before close of play, Leicestershire replied with an unfinished opening stand of 60, which was increased to 88 on the second day. Then followed a continuation of Marner's compelling form, with a magnificent 90, fifteen 4s, including six off an over from Lever. Essex became the first county to concede seven batting bonus points, but they confirmed the friendliness of the pitch to batsmen by making 61 without loss before easily avoiding an innings defeat, thanks largely to a century by Edmeades in four and a half hours, with one 6 and nine 4s.

Essex

B. Ward b Knight	6	– b Booth	46
B. E. Edmeades c Tolchard b Knight	0	– c and b Birkenshaw	107
*†B. Taylor lbw b Cotton	35	– c Birkenshaw b Marner	0
K. W. R. Fletcher lbw b Spencer	1	– c Norman b Knight	24
B. L. Irvine c Booth b Marner	36	– not out	44
K. D. Boyce c Tolchard b Marner	8	– c Booth b Spencer	31
S. Turner c Marner b Cotton	3		
A. M. Jorden c Tolchard b Knight	7	– not out	8
R. N. S. Hobbs c Hallam b Knight	33		
R. E. East c Tolchard b Knight	16		
J. K. Lever not out	4		
B 4, l-b 4	8	B 2, l-b 5, n-b 3	10
1/0 2/23 3/24 4/80 5/87 6/89 7/128 8/131 9/133	157	1/108 2/115 3/153 4/193 5/255	(5 wkts) 270

Bowling: *First Innings*—Cotton 16–3–48–2; Knight 13.4–3–49–5; Spencer 6–1–24–1; Marner 8–0–28–2. *Second Innings*—Cotton 17–3–54–0; Knight 17–4–36–1; Spencer 20–6–44–1; Marner 14–2–44–1; Birkenshaw 20–11–45–1; Booth 11–3–37–1; Dudleston 1–1–0–0.

Leicestershire

*M. R. Hallam b Boyce	39
M. E. Norman b Boyce	40
B. J. Booth c Taylor b Jorden	29
C. C. Inman c Hobbs b Jorden	56
P. T. Marner b Jorden	90
B. R. Knight c Boyce b Lever	17
J. Birkenshaw c Jorden b Lever	10
B. Dudleston b East	37
†R. W. Tolchard not out	33
J. Cotton c and b Hobbs	25
C. T. Spencer not out	9
L-b 10, n-b 16	26
1/88 2/95 3/175 4/184 5/246 6/263 7/318 8/369 9/398	(9 wkts dec.) 411

Bowling: Boyce 29–5–89–2; Lever 23–5–85–2; Jorden 24–5–91–3; East 23–4–77–1; Hobbs 14–2–43–1.

Umpires: J. S. Buller and H. Yarnold.

LEICESTERSHIRE v NOTTINGHAMSHIRE

Played at Leicester, May 12, 13, 14, 1971

Drawn. Good batting marked this draw. Harris, the Nottinghamshire opener, scored a century in both innings and Booth, making his first hundred for three seasons, helped Leicestershire to seven batting points. Harris dominated Nottinghamshire's first innings, although he took second place to Sobers in a third-wicket partnership of 128. A third-wicket stand of 120 between Booth and Inman, during which three bonus points were earned, was the feature of the Leicestershire first innings but the most exciting moment was Pember's six off M. N. S. Taylor which earned the county their seventh point. There was a less positive approach when Leicestershire wanted 211 in two hours, twenty minutes and they were forced to fight for a draw after W. Taylor took three wickets for 15, including Davison and Illingworth in four balls.

Nottinghamshire

J. B. Bolus c Birkenshaw b Mackenzie	13	– c Tolchard b Pember	0
M. J. Harris c and b Pember	118	– c Pember b Dudleston	123
S. B. Hassan c Tolchard b Davison	25	– run out	2
M. J. Smedley lbw b Pember	2	– c and b Steele	50
*G. S. Sobers c Birkenshaw b McKenzie	81	– c Steele b Dudleston	5
R. A. White b McKenzie	9	– c Birkenshaw b Dudleston	30
S. R. Bielby not out	28	– not out	28
M. N. S. Taylor b Steele	14	– not out	12
B 2, l-b 4, w 3, n-b 3	12	B 5, l-b 1, n-b 1	7
1/57 2/110 3/117 4/245 5/253 6/264 7/302 (7 wkts dec.)	302	1/0 2/24 3/158 4/167 5/200 6/217 (6 wkts dec.)	257

†D. A. Pullan, B. Stead and W. Taylor did not bat.

Bowling: *First Innings*—McKenzie 20–3–59–3; Stringer 13–4–41–0; Pember 26–5–80–2; Birkenshaw 10–4–24–0; Davison 24–9–52–1; Steele 9.1–2–25–1; Booth 2–0–9–0. *Second Innings*—McKenzie 10–4–19–0; Pember 7–1–20–1; Birkenshaw 27–12–48–0; Illingworth 8–4–12–0; Booth 6–0–28–0; Steele 21–7–41–1; Dudleston 20–4–75–3; Inman 1–0–7–0.

Leicestershire

B. Dudleston c Pullan b White	33	– lbw b Sobers	15
J. F. Steele lbw b Stead	43		
B. J. Booth c Sobers b M. N. S. Taylor	138	– b W. Taylor	23
C. Inman c Beilby b White	57	– not out	62
B. F. Davison lbw b White	19	– c Sobers b W. Taylor	5
G. D. McKenzie c Pullan b W. Taylor	22		
J. D. D. Pember not out	20		
†R. W. Tolchard (did not bat)		– lbw b Sobers	7
*R. Illingworth (did not bat)		– c Pullan b W. Taylor	0
J. Birkenshaw (did not bat)		– not out	12
B 11, l-b 5, n-b 1	17	B 8, l-b 2, n-b 1	11
1/45 2/123 3/243 4/301 5/307 6/349 (6 wkts dec.)	349	1/39 2/45 3/51 4/64 5/64 (5 wkts)	135

P. M. Stringer did not bat.

Bowling: *First Innings*—Stead 15–5–44–1; M. N. S. Taylor 14–2–53–1; W. Taylor 15.2–1–65–1; White 28–5–99–3; Sobers 16–1–55–0; Harris 4–0–16–0. *Second Innings*—Sobers 12–2–43–2; Stead 4–0–17–0; W. Taylor 9–2–15–3; White 4–1–13–0; Harris 10–2–36–0; Bielby 1–1–0–0.

Umpires: A. Jepson and A. G. T. Whitehead.

LEICESTERSHIRE v SURREY

Played at Leicester, July 24, 26, 27, 1971

Drawn. A valiant attempt by Birkenshaw and McKenzie to try an impossible second run off the last ball of the match ended with a run out, producing the situation of levelled scores with Leicestershire collecting an extra five points as the side still batting in the fourth innings. It was a thrilling climax to a game full of good cricket. Surrey, in trouble at 45 for three in their first innings, were saved by a stand of 226 by Younis and Roope, each driving delightfully to their individual centuries. Leicestershire, too, were indebted to a large stand after their first five wickets had tumbled for 95. Roger Tolchard and Booth put on 237 unfinished, which was only 25 short of the county's record for the sixth wicket, dispelling all thoughts of a follow-on and enabling Leicestershire to declare with the scores level. On the final day Roope completed his second century of the match, a prelude to the excitement which followed. Leicestershire needed two runs off the last ball. McKenzie drove Arnold into the covers but the second run was really impossible and Birkenshaw was run out.

Surrey

*M. J. Stewart c Dudleston b Spencer	16	– c Tolchard b McKenzie	0
M. J. Edwards run out	21	– c Davison b Matthews	15
D. R. Owen-Thomas c Davison b Matthews	1	– c Davison b McKenzie	11
Younis Ahmed not out	138	– c Dudleston b Matthews	6
G. R. J. Roope c Tolchard b Matthews	109	– not out	103
S. J. Storey c Tolchard b Matthews	0	– c Tolchard b Birkenshaw	16
Intikhab Alam c Inman b Birkenshaw	1	– c Norman b Birkenshaw	26
†A. Long lbw b Matthews	5	– c Spencer b Birkenshaw	4
P. I. Pocock not out	29	– c and b Steele	5
G. G. Arnold (did not bat)		– b Birkenshaw	1
R. D. Jackman (did not bat)		– not out	7
B 1, l-b 2, n-b 9	12	N-b 4	4
1/36 2/37 3/45 4/271 5/273 6/274 7/292	(7 wkts dec.) 332	1/0 2/26 3/26 4/32 5/79 6/143 7/151 8/178 9/181	(9 wkts dec.) 198

Bowling: *First Innings*—McKenzie 26–3–74–0; Matthews 19–3–55–4; Spencer 21–1–79–1; Birkenshaw 13–0–55–1; Davison 12–4–41–0; Steele 6–2–16–0. *Second Innings*—McKenzie 14–4–27–2; Spencer 3–0–6–0; Matthews 11–2–37–2; Birkenshaw 26.2–9–60–4; Steele 22–4–64–1.

Leicestershire

B. Dudleston b Intikhab	46	– c Jackman b Pocock	32
J. F. Steele lbw b Intikhab	30	– c and b Arnold	0
M. E. Norman c Long b Arnold	8	– b Intikhab	44
C. Inman c Owen-Thomas b Intikhab	3	– b Intikhab	42
B. F. Davison c Stewart b Intikhab	0	– c Long b Arnold	35
*†R. W. Tolchard not out	105	– c Younis b Arnold	16
B. J. Booth not out	130	– c Pocock b Arnold	22
J. Birkenshaw (did not bat)		– run out	3
G. D. McKenzie (did not bat)		– not out	3
B 3, l-b 3, n-b 4	10	W 1	1
1/70 2/87 3/91 4/91 5/95	(5 wkts dec.) 332	1/5 2/62 3/107 4/148 5/154 6/189 7/194 8/198	(8 wkts) 198

C. T. Spencer and R. Matthews did not bat.

Bowling: *First Innings*—Arnold 25–3–81–1; Jackman 13–1–68–0; Pocock 16–2–59–0; Storey 13–4–18–0; Intikhab 27–2–91–4. *Second Innings*—Arnold 13–0–53–4; Jackman 4–0–18–0; Intikhab 16–1–80–2; Pocock 8–0–46–1.

Umpires: E. J. Rowe and R. Aspinall.

LEICESTERSHIRE v GLAMORGAN

Played at Leicester, August 18, 19, 1971

Leicestershire won by an innings and 119 runs. This was McKenzie's match without doubt. He scored 53 not out before producing an amazing bowling performance which sent Glamorgan crashing to the lowest total of the season. This helped Leicestershire to record their second successive two-day victory. McKenzie took seven for eight and was almost unplayable. He moved the ball in the air and off the seam and finished with match figures of eleven for 37. Glamorgan were virtually dismissed twice in one day. They began the second day in an unenviable position, having lost three wickets for six runs the previous evening and in the first hour lost the remaining seven, six to McKenzie, for 18. Their second innings progressed little better, although Fredericks defended stubbornly for 22 in just over two hours. Hadley, the Cambridge Blue was the only Glamorgan player to emerge with credit, marking his Championship début by taking five Leicestershire wickets for 32.

Leicestershire

B. Dudleston b Nash	0	J. Birkenshaw c E. W. Jones b Hadley	5
J. F. Steele b Khan	13	P. M. Stringer c Khan b Shepherd	10
M. E. Norman lbw b Hadley	11	G. D. McKenzie not out	53
C. Inman c A. Jones b Hadley	31	B 5, l-b 3, n-b 3	11
B. F. Davison b Hadley	34		
B. J. Booth c Khan b Hadley	4	1/0 2/26 3/28 4/97 (8 wkts dec.)	209
*†R. W. Tolchard not out	37	5/97 6/102 7/110 8/123	

C. T. Spencer did not bat.

Bowling: Cordle 10–2–37–0; Nash 26–8–62–1; Shepherd 19.1–7–26–1; Hadley 18–6–32–5; Khan 20–6–38–1; Davis 2–0–3–0.

Glamorgan

R. C. Fredericks c Stringer b Spencer	2	– c David b Birkenshaw	22
A. Jones c Tolchard b McKenzie	1	– c Tolchard b Stringer	4
A. E. Cordle run out	2	– b Birkenshaw	1
†E. W. Jones c Dudleston b McKenzie	3	– b McKenzie	10
Majid J. Khan b Spencer	0	– b McKenzie	9
*A. R. Lewis c Spencer b McKenzie	0	– c Booth b Birkenshaw	7
P. M. Walker b McKenzie	10	– c Stringer b Birkenshaw	0
R. C. Davis c Tolchard b McKenzie	0	– c Stringer b McKenzie	7
M. A. Nash c Birkenshaw b McKenzie	0	– st Tolchard b Birkenshaw	1
D. J. Shepherd not out	2	– b McKenzie	0
R. H. Hadley b McKenzie	0	– not out	4
L-b 4	4	B 1	1
1/3 2/5 3/6 4/6 5/8 6/9 7/9 8/11 9/24	24	1/15 2/33 3/42 4/42 5/43 6/56 7/61 8/61 9/62	66

Bowling: *First Innings*—McKenzie 11.4–6–8–7; Spencer 11–6–12–2. *Second Innings*—McKenzie 14–3–29–4; Spencer 3–2–9–0; Stringer 2–0–4–1; Birkenshaw 10.2–3–23–5.

Umpires: E. J. Rowe and O. W. Herman.

LEICESTERSHIRE v MIDDLESEX

Played at Leicester, July 7, 9, 10, 1973

Drawn. Leicestershire had to thank Birkenshaw and their 20-year-old student, Peter Booth, playing in his first championship game, that they finished in a respectable position after the first day. Seven wickets fell for 137 before they came together and, despite numerous bowling changes, put on 61. The Middlesex reply began in tremendous fashion with a century opening stand, but spin won out. Birkenshaw, in particular, and Balderstone turned the ball, and from 135 for no wicket Middlesex finished only five runs ahead on the first innings. In the end Middlesex owed much to their opener, Smith. His innings lasted two hours and against some wayward fast bowling he hit one 6 and fifteen 4s. A splendid 50 by Davison enabled Leicestershire to set a target of 235 in nearly three hours but the challenge was rejected. Smith, again, was in excellent form, but after 50 had come in fifty-five minutes he adopted the anchor role when the effort was called off following the fall of the fourth wicket at 79.

Leicestershire

B. Dudleston lbw b Jones	19	– lbw b Selvey	2
J. F. Steele run out	15	– b Emburey	23
J. C. Balderstone b Selvey	24	– b Latchman	23
B. F. Davison c Murray b Jones	47	– b Titmus	50
*†R. W. Tolchard c Radley b Titmus	3	– c Selvey b Latchman	29
J. G. Tolchard lbw b Jones	7	– c Emburey b Latchman	46
P. R. Hayward c Emburey b Titmus	11	– c Murray b Emburey	11
J. Birkenshaw b Emburey	47	– c Radley b Emburey	4
P. Booth c Gomes b Emburey	21	– run out	9
K. Higgs not out	22	– not out	22
R. B. Matthews b Latchman	5	– c Featherstone b Titmus	10
B 7, l-b 4	11	B 5, l-b 5	10
1/28 2/43 3/89 4/98 5/116 6/117 7/137 8/198 9/211	232	1/2 2/49 3/57 4/61 5/128 6/158 7/186 8/200 9/218	239

Bowling: *First Innings*—Selvey 30–7–58–1; Jones 24–7–47–3; Titmus 42–17–61–2; Emburey 17–3–50–2; Latchman 4.1–2–5–1. *Second Innings*—Selvey 10–3–28–1; Jones 4–1–5–0; Titmus 41–13–60–2; Emburey 24–6–74–3; Latchman 21–4–62–3.

Middlesex

M. J. Smith c Haywood b Balderstone	100	– not out	60
N. G. Featherstone c Davison b Birkenshaw	29	– lbw b Booth	0
*J. M. Brearley c Steele b Birkenshaw	18	– c R. W. Tolchard b Booth	8
C. T. Radley lbw b Balderstone	9	– c Balderstone b Birkenshaw	20
L. A. Gomes c Birkenshaw b Steele	47	– b Dudleston	6
†J. T. Murray c Higgs b Birkenshaw	6	– not out	1
F. J. Titmus c Balderstone b Birkenshaw	0		
K. V. Jones c Birkenshaw b Steele	17		
H. C. Latchman c Balderstone b Birkenshaw	0		
M. W. W. Selvey c Booth b Birkenshaw	0		
J. E. Emburey not out	0		
B 4, l-b 3, n-b 4	11	B 3, l-b 3, w 1	7
1/135 2/137 3/163 4/171 5/197 6/197 7/230 8/231 9/237	237	1/0 2/27 3/70 4/79	(4 wkts) 102

Bowling: *First Innings*—Higgs 9–3–22–0; Booth 8–0–46–0. Matthews 6–0–34–0; Birkenshaw 37–12–71–6; Steele 7–4–9–2; Balderstone 24–11–44–2. *Second Innings*—Higgs 7–2–20–0; Booth 7–1–18–2; Birkenshaw 19–6–37–1; Steele 8–3–11–0; Dudleston 3–0–7–1; Balderstone 5–3–2–0.

Umpires: A. Jepson and C. G. Pepper.

LEICESTERSHIRE v SOMERSET

Played at Leicester, July 14, 16, 17, 1979

Drawn. From a position of 32 for four, Leicestershire recovered to claim maximum batting points, thanks to a record fifth-wicket partnership between Tolchard and Briers. They put on 233, beating the previous best of 226 for the county set 78 years previously. Briers completed his century in four and a half hours with fifteen boundaries while Tolchard, dismissed for the same score, took half an hour less and hit eleven boundaries. Richards dominated Somerset's first innings with a century, and with only two wickets down for 275 a huge lead looked likely. Once Richards was out in the 82nd over, however, only 25 runs came off the next thirteen overs and Somerset eventually finished with a lead of 13. The pitch continued to play true, and Dudleston's first century in four years enabled Leicestershire to set Somerset 291 in three hours. Although Rose raced to 50 in seventy-five minutes, the tempo was not maintained and the game was concluded half an hour early.

Leicestershire

B. Dudleston c Marks b Dredge	8	– c Roebuck b Marks	142
J. F. Steele c Roebuck b Garner	12	– c Richards b Garner	14
J. C. Balderstone c Richards b Garner	0	– c Jennings b Marks	51
N. E. Briers b Dredge	109	– lbw b Richards	15
B. F. Davison c Denning b Garner	7	– c Marks b Breakwell	8
*†R. W. Tolchard b Garner	109	– not out	23
P. Booth b Garner	6	– not out	4
P. B. Clift not out	30	– c Dredge b Richards	27
K. Shuttleworth not out	3		
B 2, l-b 5, w 1, n-b 15	23	B 7, l-b 11, n-b 1	19
1/20 2/20 3/32 4/32 5/265 6/267 7/279	(7 wkts) 307	1/27 2/136 3/175 4/241 5/245 6/292	(6 wkts dec.) 303

N. G. B. Cook and L. B. Taylor did not bat.

Bowling: *First Innings*—Garner 23–7–62–5; Dredge 17–4–58–2; Jennings 16–3–64–0; Breakwell 22–7–50–0; Marks 21–4–45–0; Richards 1–0–5–0. *Second Innings*—Garner 8–4–8–1; Dredge 7–2–26–0; Breakwell 32–9–89–1; Jennings 7–3–13–0; Marks 31–9–96–2; Richards 9–0–47–2; Roebuck 2–0–5–0.

Somerset

*B. C. Rose lbw b Shuttleworth	49	– not out	72
P. A. Slocombe b Clift	66	– b Shuttleworth	4
I. V. A. Richards b Steele	106	– b Booth	26
P. M. Roebuck c Dudleston b Cook	45	– c Steele b Cook	11
P. W. Denning c Dudleston b Cook	11	– not out	20
V. J. Marks c Davison b Cook	0		
†D. J. S. Taylor lbw b Clift	7		
D. Breakwell not out	10		
C. H. Dredge not out	14		
B 1, l-b 7, n-b 4	12	B 2, l-b 2, w 1, n-b 1	6
1/84 2/155 3/275 4/281 5/281 6/296 7/296	(7 wkts) 320	1/26 2/74 3/96	(3 wkts) 139

K. F. Jennings and J. Garner did not bat.

Bowling: *First Innings*—Taylor 12–1–36–0; Shuttleworth 21–6–58–1; Balderstone 6–1–17–0; Clift 21–11–40–2; Booth 8–0–42–0; Steele 16–2–60–1; Cook 16–3–55–3. *Second Innings*—Shuttleworth 6–0–33–1; Booth 8–1–35–1; Clift 11–3–21–0; Cook 14–6–25–1; Balderstone 6–2–10–0; Steele 3–0–8–0; Briers 3–2–1–0.

Umpires: W. E. Alley and K. E. Palmer.

LEICESTERSHIRE v MIDDLESEX

Played at Leicester, July 25, 26, 27, 1979

Middlesex won by 2 runs. Middlesex, bowled out for under 100 in their first innings, staged a remarkable recovery. Brearley held the first innings together, but even so Middlesex were dismissed by lunch-time. Some sensible batting, particularly from Balderstone, put Leicestershire in a strong position at the end of the first day and Gower added to this superiority with an innings that ended 2 short of a century. It still failed to gain Leicestershire maximum batting points, but in the end they had a lead of 206. Middlesex again began badly as Taylor, having taken two successive wickets to end their first innings, completed his hat-trick by dismissing Smith first ball. A century in ninety-two minutes by Butcher rallied the side, and with Radley he put on 162 for the fourth wicket. The final target of 112 hardly seemed a stiff challenge for Leicestershire, but Daniel bowled extremely fast to remove the first three in the order. Tolchard provided stiff resistance after the first seven wickets had gone for 50, and the last three wickets put on 59. Then, in mounting excitement, Tolchard fell with just 3 runs needed for victory, playing on to Emburey.

Middlesex

*J. M. Brearley c Tolchard b Clift	42	– c Tolchard b Shuttleworth	16
M. J. Smith c Balderstone b Taylor	7	– c Tolchard b Taylor	0
C. T. Radley c Higgs b Shuttleworth	7	– c Higgs b Taylor	81
G. D. Barlow lbw b Clift	11	– c Gower b Balderstone	19
R. O. Butcher c Tolchard b Shuttleworth	1	– c Tolchard b Taylor	106
†I. J. Gould lbw b Shuttleworth	0	– c Tolchard b Shuttleworth	35
P. H. Edmonds c Shuttleworth b Taylor	11	– c Briers b Balderstone	1
J. E. Emburey lbw b Higgs	8	– b Shuttleworth	20
M. W. W. Selvey c Tolchard b Higgs	0	– c Higgs b Balderstone	19
W. W. Daniel not out	0	– b Shuttleworth	0
W. G. Merry c Tolchard b Taylor	0	– not out	4
B 1, l-b 7, n-b 2	10	B 5, l-b 7, w 2, n-b 2	16
1/14 2/46 3/70 4/71 5/71 6/73 7/95 8/97 9/97	97	1/0 2/31 3/58 4/220 5/239 6/241 7/280 8/311 9/311	317

Bowling: *First Innings*—Taylor 11.2–2–29–3. Higgs 13–5–20–2; Shuttleworth 11–4–19–3; Clift 9–2–19–2. *Second Innings*—Taylor 23–4–55–3; Higgs 15–5–35–0; Shuttleworth 18–4–60–4; Steele 13–5–53–0; Balderstone 23.2–3–81–3; Dudleston 3–0–17–0.

Leicestershire

B. Dudleston lbw b Selvey	10	– b Daniel	5
J. F. Steele c and b Edmonds	33	– lbw b Daniel	8
J. C. Balderstone lbw b Daniel	56	– b Daniel	6
B. F. Davison c Edmonds b Daniel	13	– c and b Emburey	14
D. I. Gower c Selvey b Emburey	98	– c Radley b Edmonds	1
N. E. Briers c Radley b Emburey	16	– c Radley b Daniel	0
†R. W. Tolchard c Emburey b Edmonds	20	– b Emburey	40
K. Shuttleworth run out	7	– c Butcher b Emburey	12
*K. Higgs c Gould b Selvey	9	– b Edmonds	4
P. B. Clift b Emburey	1	– c Radley b Edmonds	1
L. B. Taylor not out	9	– not out	2
L-b 15, w 2, n-b 14	31	B 1, l-b 9, n-b 6	16
1/15 2/71 3/92 4/142 5/219 6/262 7/278 8/285 9/286	303	1/13 2/19 3/27 4/32 5/38 5/38 6/45 7/50 8/74 9/93	109

Bowling: *First Innings*—Daniel 22–4–73–2; Selvey 15.2–5–36–2; Merry 9–1–19–0; Edmonds 39–9–102–2; Emburey 22–9–42–3. *Second Innings*—Daniel 14–1–42–4; Selvey 2–0–2–0; Edmonds 17–5–29–3; Emburey 16.1–4–20–3.

Umpires: J. V. C. Griffiths and T. W. Spencer.

LEICESTERSHIRE v DERBYSHIRE

Played at Leicester, August 15, 16, 17, 1979

Drawn. Dudleston and Steele dominated the whole of the first day, setting up a new first wicket record for Leicestershire with 390, beating the previous best set in 1906 by 10 runs. Dudleston's 202 was his highest career score and contained twenty-eight 4s, while Steele's 187 included one 6 and twenty-one 4s. Derbyshire's attack, without England Test players Hendrick and Miller, suffered accordingly, but even so, little could be taken from the Leicestershire openers, who made full use of a perfect batting pitch to display their wide range of strokes. Derbyshire were undaunted, and centuries by Wright and Kirsten, whose not out 135 took only 65 overs and contained three 6s and nine 4s, left the match interestingly placed until rain brought an early end to the second day's play and completely washed out the third.

Leicestershire

B. Dudleston c Tunnicliffe b Wincer	202
J. F. Steele c McLellan b Tunnicliffe	187
B. F. Davison lbw b Tunnicliffe	3
J. C. Balderstone run out	16
P. B. Clift not out	23
B 4, l-b 5, n-b 14	23
1/390 2/400 3/425 4/454	(4 wkts dec.) 454

†R. W. Tolchard, J. Birkenshaw, P. Booth, K. Shuttleworth, N. G. B. Cook and *K. Higgs did not bat.

Bowling: Tunnicliffe 23.4–3–108–2; Wincer 26–2–117–1; Walters 22–2–80–0; Steele 5–2–16–0; Mellor 18–2–78–0; Kirsten 2–0–13–0; Barnett 3–0–19–0.

Derbyshire

A. Hill b Cook	44
J. G. Wright c Higgs b Birkenshaw	105
*P. N. Kirsten not out	135
D. S. Steele c Booth b Birkenshaw	5
K. J. Barnett run out	5
A. J. Borrington lbw b Cook	5
C. J. Tunnicliffe not out	9
B 4, l-b 3	7
1/96 2/238 3/260 4/282 5/304	(5 wkts) 315

J. Walters, †A. J. McLellan, R. C. Wincer and A. J. Mellor did not bat.

Bowling: Higgs 4–3–1–0; Booth 3–1–14–0; Birkenshaw 33–5–98–2; Cook 35–8–99–2; Clift 5–1–22–0; Shuttleworth 9–1–42–0; Balderstone 5–1–22–0; Steele 6–4–10–0.

Umpires: R. Aspinall and A. Jepson.

LEICESTERSHIRE v NORTHAMPTONSHIRE

Played at Leicester, August 25, 27, 28, 1979

Drawn. Allan Lamb ruled the Northamptonshire first innings with a career best 178, which included one 6 and twenty-nine 4s. Leicestershire made a positive reply and scored freely in their 104 overs. An opening stand of 119 provided a good foundation, and Dudleston and Gower made solid contributions. Northamptonshire, with a lead of 9 runs, did not make many friends among the Bank Holiday crowd by batting tediously in their second innings, taking almost six hours over their 250. Although Gower was promoted up the order, Leicestershire always looked unlikely to make the 260 required in two and a quarter hours and the match finished tamely.

Northamptonshire

G. Cook lbw b Shuttleworth	18	– b Cook	16
P. Willey b Taylor	67	– c Higgs b Cook	69
R. G. Williams c Dudleston b Shuttleworth	9	– run out	11
A. J. Lamb b Clift	178	– b Cook	12
T. J. Yardley c Gower b Clift	18	– c Gower b Shuttleworth	57
R. M. Carter lbw b Clift	0	– c Davison b Birkenshaw	9
†G. Sharp b Steele	35	– b Cook	32
*P. J. Watts st Dudleston b Birkenshaw	9	– c Steele b Cook	13
A. Hodgson c Shuttleworth b Birkenshaw	0	– c Davison b Cook	5
T. M. Lamb run out	0	– not out	6
B. J. Griffiths not out	1	– b Clift	5
B 14, l-b 16, n-b 1	31	B 5, l-b 10	15
1/56 2/80 3/144 4/193 5/193 6/315 7/350 8/352 9/364	366	1/52 2/89 3/105 4/122 5/142 6/194 7/224 8/230 9/241	250

Bowling: *First Innings*—Taylor 14–2–50–1; Higgs 14–2–48–0; Shuttleworth 8–0–40–2; Clift 23.5–8–68–3; Cook 10–1–38–0; Balderstone 9–1–39–0; Birkenshaw 10–2–29–2; Steele 6–0–23–1. *Second Innings*—Taylor 1–1–0–0. Higgs 4–0–17–0; Clift 4.2–1–12–1; Shuttleworth 11–2–19–1; Cook 43–17–72–6; Balderstone 31–10–50–0; Birkenshaw 22–3–47–1; Steele 11–6–18–0.

Leicestershire

†B. Dudleston lbw b Williams	93	– b Griffiths	11
J. F. Steele c Cook b T. M. Lamb	46	– not out	4
J. C. Balderstone c Willey b Griffiths	34	– c Watts b Griffiths	1
B. F. Davison c A. J. Lamb b Griffiths	35	– lbw b Willey	25
D. I. Gower not out	84	– c Watts b Hodgson	17
P. B. Clift c Watts b Hodgson	29		
J. Birkenshaw not out	17	– not out	23
B 6, l-b 10, n-b 3	19	B 4, l-b 1, n-b 1	6
1/119 2/172 3/196 4/264 5/318	(5 wkts) 357	1/20 2/31 3/31 4/70	(4 wkts) 87

K. Shuttleworth, N. G. B. Cook, *K. Higgs and L. B. Taylor did not bat.

Bowling: *First Innings*—Griffiths 22–4–60–2; Hodgson 17–2–83–1; Willey 25–4–73–0; T. M. Lamb 18–4–67–1; Williams 22–5–55–1. *Second Innings*—Griffiths 8–2–25–2; Hodgson 6–2–14–1; Willey 12–6–12–1; Williams 10–2–30–0.

Umpires: D. J. Dennis and A. G. T. Whitehead.

LEICESTERSHIRE v SOMERSET

Played at Leicester, July 4, 6, 7, 1981

Somerset won by ten wickets. West Indies Test players Richards and Garner won this match with outstanding performances. Garner's height and lift proved too much for Leicestershire's inexperienced batsmen, his pace in the first innings producing three bowled victims out of the seven he claimed in seventeen overs. Popplewell highlighted some excellent close-to-the-bat fielding by taking three catches at short leg. In Leicestershire's second innings Garner, not receiving the same generous bounce, was kept in the field longer, particularly by an obstinate Balderstone, but eventually he proved to be master again and Somerset, requiring only 51, achieved victory with more than an hour and a half to spare. Richards completely dominated both Somerset's first innings and the tiring Leicestershire bowlers, hitting two 6s and twenty-six 4s. He offered two chances once he reached 150 and was out finally only 4 short of a double-century, deflecting a delivery from Agnew into his stumps after offering no stroke.

Leicestershire

R. A. Cobb c Taylor b Moseley	4	– (2) b Garner	37
*J. C. Balderstone c Popplewell b Garner	10	– (1) lbw b Garner	71
T. J. Boon b Garner	18	– c Popplewell b Garner	44
B. F. Davison b Garner	8	– c Taylor b Moseley	29
N. E. Briers c Taylor b Garner	23	– c Taylor b Popplewell	23
†M. A. Garnham c Popplewell b Garner	1	– b Dredge	13
J. F. Steele c Taylor b Dredge	0	– c Denning b Marks	19
P. Booth c Lloyds b Moseley	30	– run out	21
J. P. Agnew c Popplewell b Garner	9	– b Garner	7
G. J. Parsons b Garner	0	– b Garner	0
N. G. B. Cook not out	6	– not out	0
B 1, n-b 6	7	B 11, l-b 6, w 1, n-b 8	26
1/14 2/28 3/41 4/56 5/59 6/70 7/71 8/86 9/89	116	1/49 2/157 3/198 4/200 5/235 6/235 7/280 8/282 9/289	290

Bowling: *First Innings*—Garner 17–6–41–7; Moseley 12–5–28–2; Dredge 10–1–40–1; Marks 1–1–0–0. *Second Innings*—Garner 28–7–65–5; Moseley 24–11–49–1; Popplewell 21–8–34–1; Dredge 20–8–38–1; Richards 29–7–44–0; Marks 27–15–26–1; Lloyds 4–2–8–0.

Somerset

J. W. Lloyds lbw b Parsons	73	– not out	43
P. A. Slocombe c Steele b Parsons	6	– not out	5
*I. V. A. Richards b Agnew	196		
P. M. Roebuck b Parsons	0		
P. W. Denning c Balderstone b Agnew	9		
N. F. M. Popplewell c Agnew b Booth	17		
V. J. Marks c Davison b Steele	2		
†D. J. S. Taylor c Parsons b Cook	13		
J. Garner lbw b Agnew	18		
H. R. Moseley b Parsons	10		
C. H. Dredge not out	0		
B 7, l-b 1, w 1, n-b 3	12	B 4, w 1	5
1/27 2/34 3/59 4/119 5/138 6/168 7/217 8/334 9/356	356	(no wkt)	53

Bowling: *First Innings*—Agnew 25–5–76–3; Parsons 24.3–2–115–4; Steele 14–0–37–1; Booth 17–3–58–1; Cook 15–1–58–1. *Second Innings*—Agnew 3–1–15–0; Parsons 2–1–6–0; Cook 4–4–0–0; Briers 4.2–0–27–0.

Umpires: H. D. Bird and D. J. Constant.

MIDDLESEX

A MIDDLESEX CENTURY [1964]

By I. A. R. Peebles

On December 15, 1863, a number of gentlemen met in the London Tavern, Bishopsgate, to consider a momentous project. This was the formation of a Middlesex County Cricket Club, and the proceedings were conducted with admirable energy and decision.

Indeed, so assured is the report of the meeting, immediately released to the London newspapers, that it has some resemblance to the announcements following more recent and very much less pleasant events. It opens with a sweeping and surely debatable assumption. "Sir" it says "Middlesex being the only cricketing county in England that has no County Club". It proceeds to say that a provisional committee had been formed, and that a general meeting would be held in the London Tavern in February of the following year.

As a result of this benevolent coup d'état events rushed forward. At the promised meeting the secretary, Mr C. Hillyard, recorded the names of a fair nucleus of members, a regular committee of 16 was appointed, a ground hired in Islington, and four bowlers engaged. The staff was completed by the arrival of a groundsman, happily named George Hearne, and an umpire. A president, in the person of Viscount Enfield, followed soon afterwards.

The Middlesex team burst into action in 1865, with matches against Sussex, Bucks, Hants and MCC, with several lesser fixtures. Challenges from the established and powerful counties of Surrey and Lancashire were shrewdly side-stepped for the time being.

Such a dynamic start was not to be maintained. By 1869 Middlesex lost the use of Islington ground, and could not then afford to accept the MCC terms to play at Lord's. A melancholy two years on the rough Amateur Athletic Association Ground at Lillie Bridge was followed by another abortive tenancy of Prince's ground, near Hyde Park Barracks, which never gave much promise of permanency. At a meeting in 1877 is was decided to take the major step of playing at Lord's, starting the following year with four matches. From this time onwards the fortunes of Middlesex were inevitably bound up with those of MCC, yet the tenants have always maintained a sturdy independence in the conduct of their affairs, a state of affairs which exists to this day. From the formation of this partnership starts the real progress of Middlesex as a County Cricket Club.

Many enthusiastic members, players, and administrators had seen the Club through these early vicissitudes. It is not possible to mention many of these deserving names but that of Walker has ever been immortal in Middlesex. "The Walkers of Southgate" was a brotherly triumvirate whose initials R.D., V.E. and I.D. are still fresh and familiar in the annals of the Club. All were competent administrators as well as being fine cricketers and so contributed to every aspect of the Club's establishment and progress.

The County Championship Birth and Residential qualifications had been introduced in 1873 and Middlesex had competed from that year with varying, but seldom more than modest success except in 1878 when they led the Counties. The start of the new tenancy marked no spectacular advances in these fortunes but very soon some very famous names came to support and perpetuate the foundations laid by the Walkers. In 1876 C. I. Thornton made his first appearance and was soon recognised as a hitter of unprecedented power. A. J. Webbe's active association with the Club began in 1875 and was to last until 1937, as player, captain and President. Webbe played for England but once and his interests were almost entirely focused on Middlesex. In light of this undivided devotion he may justly be described as the greatest figure in the County's hundred years of history. Aided by two Lytteltons and three Studds and, a little later, by Sir Timothy O'Brien, and the great A. E. Stoddart, Middlesex scored more attractively than ever in the eighties but, despite G. Burton's consistent slows, were a somewhat ineffective bowling side.

The names of Stoddard and O'Brien were linked as those in later years of Hearne and Hendren, and Compton and Edrich. Stoddart is still regarded by many competent judges as the greatest amateur batsman ever to represent Middlesex. In the course of an outstanding county career he went four times to Australia, twice as captain. His average of 35.57 for 30 innings against Australia was remarkable for the figures of his time. His record on the Rugby football field was no less illustrious.

It was in 1888 that J. T. Hearne made his first appearance, to reach his full powers in 1892, when he took 163 wickets. On the fast side of medium pace he had a beautiful wheeling action, spun the ball sharply from the off, and soon made his mark as the finest bowler of his type in the country. Through the next decade he was the mainstay of the attack with the support of J. T. Rawlin, a serviceable fast bowler. It was not until 1897 that Albert Trott had qualified to spin his leg-breaks from a prodigious hand. (In passing it may be said that this was regarded as the largest hand in cricket until lost in the enveloping grip of A. D. Nourse.)

In the first half of the nineties Middlesex with a wealth of amateur batting, and the unflagging talents of J. T. Hearne, kept well to the fore, being third in the table in 1893 and 1894. The names of the amateur batsmen were nigh legion but collectively they had a certain mercurial quality to thwart that consistency which makes for champion counties. Thus, although thrice third and twice runner's-up in the nineties Middlesex were bested in the first half by neighbouring Surrey and, latterly, by Yorkshire and Lancashire. Surrey were at one time almost invincible with the irresistible force or Richardson and W. H. Lockwood to exploit the performances of a dependable batting order.

Middlesex entered the twentieth century well established as one of the major powers in the County Championship. In the North, Yorkshire always had a slight ascendancy in the struggle for power with their Lancashire neighbours. Nottinghamshire ruled the Midlands. In the South, Middlesex and Surrey dominated the scene. Through the nineties Surrey had a great deal the better of the argument but, by the turn of the century, the relative strengths of the rivals had altered so that Yorkshire succeeded as champions in 1900 and 1902 and Middlesex were top in 1903.

Although Middlesex did not again head the table before the outbreak of war, the county prospered greatly under the enlightened captaincy of P. F. Warner who, after a spell during which G. MacGregor led, had succeeded Webbe. In fact, as deputy captain Warner had handled the side frequently during MacGregor's tenure. Warner was very much greater in the international scene than Webbe, but Middlesex was still his first and greatest love. During his term of office he became one of the greatest all-round amateur batsmen in the country if not quite in the same category as C. B. Fry, K. S. Ranjitsinhji and F. S. Jackson. An indomitable defence was allied to sound orthodox scoring strokes, especially to the on, and the whole technique was applied with great intelligence and concentration. Warner brought the same qualities to his captaincy and had, at all times, an observant eye for every detail of the play. He used the extraordinary and occasionally erratic talents of A. E. Trott to best advantage. These consisted of a commendably aggressive attitude to batting, and a great power of leg-spin allied to a remarkably fast and accurate yorker. Many thought the first attribute unduly exaggerated by Trott's determination, on every occasion, to repeat his monumental straight drive which cleared the Lord's Pavilion. All players found it instructive and enormously pleasant to be a member of Warner's side.

The start of the century was quite promising but 1902, a wet season, brought almost unprecedented disaster. Only two matches were won by a Middlesex side which, for one reason or another was seldom fully represented. It was a surprise to all, including the winners, when Middlesex went to the top of the table in the following year. Warner was now at the height of his powers as a batsman and was well supported by the normal Middlesex reservoir of amateur talent. Trott and Hearne were a formidable pair in this wettest of seasons and had the support of B. J. T. Bosanquet whose "googlies" had a considerable impact on the game as a whole. Bosanquet, like some other pioneers, never mastered his invention to the extent achieved by many successors but the novelty was too much for many batsmen as the Australians found at Sydney and Trent Bridge. He was in addition a fine batsman with a short pick up but plenty of power.

In 1908 Warner became the official captain of Middlesex. By this time he had wide and varied experience of his craft and got the best out of his side for the next nine playing seasons, culminating in the glorious win of 1920.

Trott's career came to an end in 1909 but F. A. Tarrant had now developed into a splendid all-rounder. A sound and dependable batsman, his left-hand spinners were regarded as being equal to those of Wilfred Rhodes and Colin Blythe in all but accuracy. Further to enhance the County's prospects, J. W. Hearne and E. (Patsy) Hendren had just embarked. Hendren was to take some time to come to full bloom but Hearne's progress was so rapid that within a couple of years he was thought of in the same context as Rhodes and G. H. Hirst. He was a neat, precise batsman who preferred the back foot as a general base of operation. His leg-breaks he spun more than any Englishman within memory, and was only outspun on the arrival of A. A. Mailey. His googly was at least serviceable in an era as yet not wholly familiar with this form of deception. H. R. Murrell, a man of great personality, who was to play a lasting part in Middlesex affairs, kept wicket and batted with great spirit when the occasion demanded.

In an era when County cricket flourished and opposition from the North, Midlands and South bank of the Thames was formidable, Middlesex were always in the first six of the Championship. In 1910 and 1911 they were third and in 1914 ran into second place. With Warner, Tarrant and Hearne at the height of their powers, and Hendren verging on his potential greatness, Middlesex might well have gone further but for the untimely interruption. There were many young men whose names were to become prominent in the twenties, F. T. Mann, N. E. Haig, C. N. Bruce, R. H. Twining, S. H. Saville and G. E. V. Crutchley, to name a few, who brought a fine youthful zeal to support the professional skill.

The year of 1919 was an uneasy one for English cricket which, like many other institutions, was striving to re-organise a wholly disrupted institution. The experiment of three two-day matches a week was found to be a strenuous and unsatisfactory arrangement. The most pleasing development at Lord's was the batting of Hendren whose form far outstripped any hope based on pre-war performances.

In the following year P. F. Warner ended his long and brilliant career by leading his side to the top of the Championship table. His unsurpassed qualities as a captain and tactician made full use of a very talented side. Hendren and Hearne were the foundation of a very good batting side. G. T. S. Stevens, largely a protégé of the perspicacious Warner, was a great amateur addition to the professional core of batsmen, and bowled a dangerous mixture of leg-breaks and googlies. It was not, however, until late in the season that the Middlesex challenge became apparent, and not until the closing moments of the last match of the season that the prize was finally grasped. Middlesex won a very important toss but were headed by 73 runs on the first innings. Centuries by H. W. Lee and C. H. L. Skeet got Middlesex well on the way to a good second innings but time ordained that Warner should set Surrey, a strong, aggressive batting side, 244 to make in three hours. At one point Surrey seemed to be well on the way to victory but, appropriately, a typically shrewd move from Warner turned the day. Seeing Fender on the balcony give the signal to the batsmen for "general chase" he removed Hendren from short leg to deep long-on. Very soon Shepherd was caught in that position, and the spin of Hearne and Stevens saw Surrey defeated by 55 runs with only ten minutes to spare.

Warner, departing gloriously, handed over to F. T. Mann, who for eight years led the County with a firm but happy touch which gained him the lasting affection and admiration of all who played for or against Middlesex. His reign opened auspiciously when, in 1921, Middlesex again won the Championship. With T. J. Durston and Haig to open, the bowling was now a very fair complement to the plentiful batting. Without ever repeating this success Middlesex were well amongst the leaders for the remainder of the twenties. The flow of amateur batting was undiminished with Twining, Bruce, Crutchley, H. J.

Enthoven and H. L. Dales all available for reasonable periods. Haig, Stevens and G. O. Allen were a tower of all round strength and Mann was ever liable to dominate the game with his explosive hitting powers.

During the season 1929 Mann, although still officially captain, was prevented by matters of business from playing more than occasional matches. In his absence Haig took over, and proved himself another most able captain. The season, with Hearne and Hendren still fine cricketers, despite the latter's lean patch early on, was brightened by the splendid all-round cricket and dazzling fielding of R. W. V. Robins. His leg breaks, bowled at medium pace, were occasionally erratic, but had a most devastating power of spin and were coupled to a well concealed googly. Middlesex seemed on the threshold of another splendid decade but, in the early thirties, fortunes declined to a low ebb. As occasionally happens, to any side, the powers of several important members suffered a sudden decrease, and others were removed by business calls. It was not until Robins took over in 1935 that once again things got under way.

The side was now largely reconstituted. C. I. J. ("Big Jim") Smith, imported from Wiltshire, had found his best form with the new ball and, employing one basic stroke, hit the ball higher and further than anyone before or since. Soon the great batting partnership of D. C. S. Compton and W. J. Edrich was to take shape while J. D. Robertson had developed into a most polished Number One. H. G. O. Owen-Smith and J. H. Human played the same dynamic cricket as their captain and Joe Hulme continued to fly round the deep. J. M. Sims developed into a medium-pace leg-spinner. Only a superb Yorkshire side stood between Middlesex and the Championship. This they succeeded in doing until the war, with Derbyshire at the top in 1936. The season of 1939 saw the retirement of Robins but the momentum he had generated carried the team to second place in the table on the eve of the war, a position they had occupied in the previous three seasons. This was a fine period in Middlesex play, for Robins made the most positive use of the young and energetic talent at his command.

In 1946 Robins returned to the helm and immediately set about reorganising affairs. After a season's effort and experiment Middlesex were poised for the triumph of 1947. The summer was a fine one and the Middlesex batting calculated to make the most of good wickets and bowling which had not yet regained pre-war standards. Robertson and S. M. Brown regularly opened and both scored over 2,000 runs. They were followed by the truly devastating power of Compton and Edrich, both of whom topped the three thousand. This mass of runs was acquired with a speed which gave a good attack, led by L. H. Gray and sustained by J. A. Young, ample time to despatch the opposition. Having won the Championship, Robins retired and F. G. Mann took over. In 1948 the presence of the Australians robbed him of his best players for long periods but, in 1949, he was better served, and Middlesex shared first place with Yorkshire. At this Mann, the only son to succeed a Championship winning father, retired and Middlesex fortunes flagged.

Robins returned for the third time as captain for 1950, before a joint captaincy, shared by Compton and Edrich, fared no better for two years than such compromises incline to do. Edrich took over for five years, but the form of the great fluctuated and little glory came to Lord's.

Compton and Edrich retired in 1957 but J. J. Warr brought a strong reviving influence to bear in 1958, and Middlesex again pushed forward. F. J. Titmus was now a splendid all-rounder and A. E. Moss, who had done so well for almost a decade, still had a fair head of steam to call on. A promising crop of young batsmen including R. A. Gale, W. E. Russell and P. H. Parfitt helped Middlesex to reach third place in 1960 and when P. I. Bedford succeeded Warr in 1961 he achieved the same success. He, in 1963, gave way to C. D. Drybrough and, whilst the record has been moderate, the prospects are indeed bright at the moment of writing.

Titmus will captain a side which, with himself, includes five of the party that toured South Africa. In addition, Russell has advanced to be a most promising batsman.

After one hundred years of continued existence most institutions, and certainly County Cricket Clubs, take on a distinct character. That of Middlesex is pre-eminently of cheerfulness and enjoyment. These qualities permeate from the players to all associated with the club. Perhaps the best testimony to this spirit was the fact that, after ninety years of harmonious life, it was accidentally discovered that, as the original rules had been lost, the club had operated withouth any written code for almost its entire existence to that date.

Those who have played for Middlesex have known the very best that cricket can offer. It is meet that in so many cases their personal association with the club remains unbroken in the form of service and support. In a comparatively brief survey it has not been possible to pay tribute to more than a few individuals but, in the spirit of the club, those not mentioned would not consider themselves omitted.

The Duke of Edinburgh and the Prime Minister, Sir Alec Douglas-Home, who as Lord Dunglass played a few games for Middlesex, attended the One Hundred Years Celebration dinner at Grosvenor House, Park Lane, on July 20 at which the Middlesex Centenary Youth Campaign was launched. I take this opportunity to extract from the Campaign brochure the full list of:

MIDDLESEX TEST PLAYERS FOR ENGLAND

1878-84	Lucas, A. P.	1898-12	Warner, P. F.	1935-37	Sims J. M.
1878-79	Webbe, A. J.	1903-05	Bosanquet, B. J. T.	1937-56	Compton, D. C. S.
1880-84	Lyttelton, Hon. A.	1905-06	Moon, L. J.	1938-55	Edrich, W. J.
1882-83	Leslie, C. F. H.	1911-26	Hearne, J. W.	1938	Price, W. F.
1882-83	Studd, C. T.	1920-35	Hendren, E.	1947-52	Robertson, J. D.
1882-83	Studd, G. B.	1921	Durston, T. J.	1947-49	Young, J. A.
1882-83	Vernon, G. F.	1921-30	Haig, N. E.	1948-51	Dewes, J. G.
1884-96	O'Brien, Sir T. C.	1922-23	Mann, F. T.	1948-49	Mann, F. G.
1887-98	Stoddart, A. E.	1922-30	Stevens, G. T. S.	1950-51	Warr, J. J.
1890-93	MacGregor, G.	1927-31	Peebles, I. A. R.	1953-60	Moss, A. E.
1891-99	Hearne, J. T.	1929	Killick, Rev. E. T.	1955	Titmus, F. J.
1891-95	Philipson, H.	1929-37	Robins, R. W. V.	1961	Murray, J. T.
1894-95	Ford, F. G. T.	1930-48	Allen, G. O.	1961	Parfitt, P. H.
1895-98	Davenport, H. R. Bromley	1930-31	Lee, H. W.	1961	Russell, W. E.
1898-99	Trott, A. E.	1934-37	Smith, C. I. J.	1964	Price, J. S. E.

MIDDLESEX v SUSSEX

Played at Lord's, May 16, 18, 19, 1964

Drawn. The Sussex batsmen found more trouble contending with a slow pitch than the Middlesex bowlers on the first day. With the ball rarely coming on to the bat at any pace, they spent five and a half hours scoring 239. Oakman, the backbone of the Sussex innings, spent three and a half hours for his 89. Hooker alone of the Middlesex bowlers gained any help from the turf and took six for 68. Clark dominated the Middlesex innings. His century contained 64 in boundaries, including two 6s. Sussex, 82 behind, lost three wickets clearing the arrears, but Dexter dispelled any hopes of an early victory for Middlesex. He hit ten 4s in 64 not out before rain, setting in during lunch, brought an end to the game. Lawrence, the Middlesex seam bowler, was called twice for throwing by Umpire Aspinall on the first day and did not bowl again in the match.

Sussex

R. J. Langridge c Titmus b Hooker	18	– lbw b Titmus	13
K. G. Suttle lbw b Hooker	32	– st Murray b Titmus	14
*E. R. Dexter c Murray b Price	4	– not out	64
L. J. Lenham c Murray b Hooker	20	– lbw b Hooker	7
†J. M. Parks c Hooker b Bennett	9	– lbw b Hooker	14
A. S. M. Oakman c Clark b Hooker	89	– not out	6
G. C. Cooper lbw b Bennett	6		
N. I. Thomson run out	33		
A. Buss c Bennett b Hooker	15		
R. V. Bell not out	0		
J. A. Snow b Hooker	0		
B 5, l-b 6, n-b 2	13	B 8, l-b 1	9
1/42 2/48 3/60 4/85 5/89 6/106 7/173 8/238 9/239	239	1/23 2/44 3/67 4/111	(4 wkts) 127

Bowling: *First Innings*—Price 19–4–37–1; Bennett 23–3–59–2; Lawrence 3–0–3–0; Hooker 27.5–2–68–6; Titmus 25–7–45–0; Drybrough 10–3–14–0. *Second Innings*—Price 9–2–20–0; Bennett 4–1–14–0; Hooker 21–8–49–2; Titmus 16–6–35–2.

Middlesex

S. E. Russell c Snow b Thomson	36
W. E. Russell c Dexter b Thomson	21
R. A. White lbw b Thomson	4
R. W. Hooker st Parks b Bell	60
E. A. Clark c Parks b Suttle	105
F. J. Titmus b Buss	31
†J. T. Murray b Buss	9
D. Bennett c Langridge b Buss	21
*C. D. Drybrough not out	16
J. S. E. Price b Snow	13
P. Lawrence run out	2
L-b 2, n-b 1	3
1/31 2/47 3/90 4/156 5/254 6/266 7/271 8/290 9/318	321

Bowling: Buss 27.5–3–91–3; Snow 21–0–65–1; Thomson 23–6–49–3; Suttle 5–0–14–1; Oakman 12–4–32–0; Bell 20–6–67–1.

Umpires: R. Aspinall and A. E. Rhodes.

MIDDLESEX v LEICESTERSHIRE

Played at Lord's, August 14, 16, 17, 1965

Middlesex won by seven wickets a game which yielded 1,100 runs for the loss of 18 wickets. Booth could consider himself unfortunate to be on the losing side after hitting two separate centuries in a match for the first time. He shared stands of 139 with Marner and 105 with Jayasinghe in the first innings. Titmus (one 6, fifteen 4s) hit freely for Middlesex, putting on 130 with Radley, who also helped Clark add 68. An opening partnership of 143 between Hallam and Booth and another good innings by Marner led to a second Leicestershire declaration. Middlesex needed 253 in three hours and Russell (eighteen 4s), batting splendidly for two hours thirty-five minutes, bore the leading part in stands of 113 with Brearley and 90 with Clark.

Leicestershire

*M. R. Hallam c Radley b Herman	1	– c Murray b Parfitt	68
B. J. Booth st Murray b Bick	109	– c Bick b Hooker	104
P. Marner b Hooker	76	– c Herman b Parfitt	60
S. Jayasinghe c Murray b Titmus	50	– not out	12
C. C. Inman not out	24		
D. Constant b Titmus	0		
C. T. Spencer b Titmus	7		
†R. Julian b Titmus	1		
R. Barratt not out	13		
B 6, l-b 7, w 1, n-b 1	15	B 2, l-b 6, n-b 1	9
1/3 2/142 3/247 4/247 5/247 6/261 7/279	(7 wkts dec.) 296	1/143 2/208 3/253	(3 wkts dec.) 253

J. S. Savage and J. Cotton did not bat.

Bowling: *First Innings*—Hooker 19–5–36–1; Herman 15–3–54–1; Bennett 10–0–50–0; Clarke 5–1–18–0; Titmus 31–10–56–4; Bick 26–4–67–1. *Second Innings*—Herman 11–1–49–0; Hooker 17–3–66–1; Titmus 7–1–10–0; Bennett 3–0–29–0; Bick 12–1–44–0; Parfitt 10.5–1–46–2.

Middlesex

W. E. Russell c Jayasinghe b Barratt	37	– not out	134
J. M. Brearley c Julian b Cotton	0	– b Cotton	39
P. H. Parfitt c Jayasinghe b Marner	31	– st Julian b Barratt	18
E. A. Clark b Cotton	63	– c and b Jayasinghe	51
†J. T. Murray c Inman b Barratt	14	– not out	5
C. T. Radley not out	54		
*F. J. Titmus not out	89		
B 4, l-b 2, n-b 3	9	B 4, l-b 2, n-b 1	7
1/10 2/69 3/73 4/99 5/167	(5 wkts dec.) 297	1/113 2/153 3/243	(3 wkts) 254

R. W. Hooker, D. Bennett, D. A. Bick and R. S. Herman did not bat.

Bowling: *First Innings*—Cotton 13.2–4–43–2; Spencer 15–1–53–0; Marner 23–6–66–1; Savage 17–5–55–0; Barratt 19–4–71–2. *Second Innings*—Spencer 9–0–47–0; Cotton 7–1–33–1; Savage 10–0–49–0; Marner 4–0–25–0; Barratt 12–0–71–1; Jayasinghe 2.1–0–10–1; Booth 2–0–12–0.

Umpires: C. Cook and A. Jepson.

MIDDLESEX v WORCESTERSHIRE

Played at Lord's, September 4, 5, 6, 1968

Middlesex won by nine wickets. The match was played on a rain-affected pitch which afforded all types of bowlers some assistance. Less than three hours cricket took place on the first day. Booth, playing his final match for Worcestershire, and the young Griffith rescued Worcestershire with a defiant stand. On the second day Carter dislocated the Middlesex innings. It was saved by Radley, who hit with impressive selection. Spin troubled all the Worcestershire batsmen at their second attempt after Price had made early inroads, and Middlesex, with almost all the final day to get 69, were encouraged by the threat of rain to hurry to their target in an hour.

Worcestershire

R. G A. Headley c Smith b Herman	9	– c Murray b Price	11
A. R. Barker c Murray b Price	8	– c Murray b Price	0
J. A. Ormrod c Murray b Price	6	– lbw b Titmus	13
B. L. D'Oliveira c Parfitt b Herman	9	– lbw b Titmus	25
T. J. Yardley c Smith b Hooker	4	– c Hooker b Latchman	6
K. Griffith c Parfitt b Latchman	24	– lbw b Titmus	3
*†R. Booth not out	27	– c Parfitt b Latchman	0
N. Gifford c Smith b Titmus	1	– c Brearley b Titmus	18
B. M. Brain not out	0	– c Latchman b Titmus	2
L. J. Coldwell (did not bat)		– not out	0
R. G. M. Carter (did not bat)		– c Radley b Price	0
B 4, n-b 2	6	B 1, l-b 5, n-b 1	7
1/13 2/22 3/23 4/28 5/38 6/82 7/87 (7 wkts dec.)	94	1/3 2/14 3/44 4/54 5/60 6/61 7/65 8/84 9/85	85

Bowling: *First Innings*—Price 13–4–28–2; Herman 7–3–19–2; Hooker 15–5–29–1; Titmus 9–4–5–1; Latchman 6–1–7–1. *Second Innings*—Price 9–0–35–3; Herman 3–2–8–0; Titmus 18.4–12–11–5; Latchman 13–7–24–2; Parfitt 2–2–0–0.

Middlesex

W. E. Russell c Ormrod b Brain	18	– c and b Carter	41
M. J. Smith b Coldwell	0	– not out	21
*P. H. Parfitt c Ormrod b Carter	0	– not out	4
J. M. Brearley c Gifford b Carter	0		
†J. T. Murray b Coldwell	6		
C. T. Radley b Coldwell	46		
F. J. Titmus b Carter	10		
R. W. Hooker c Yardley b Carter	18		
H. C. Latchman b Carter	3		
R. S. Herman c Griffith b Carter	8		
J. S. E. Price not out	1		
L-b 1	1	B 3	3
1/1 2/10 3/10 4/20 5/63 6/72 7/85 8/95 9/108	111	1/61 (1 wkt)	69

Bowling: *First Innings*—Coldwell 12–3–29–3; Carter 12.5–5–20–6; Brain 12–1–52–1; D'Oliveira 4–1–9–0. *Second Innings*—Coldwell 2–1–3–0; Carter 3–0–15–1; Brain 3.5–0–10–0; D'Oliveira 3–0–16–0; Gifford 5–0–22–0.

Umpires: A. E. Alderman and J. G. Langridge.

MIDDLESEX v YORKSHIRE

Played at Lord's, July 3, 5, 6, 1971

Drawn. In the middle of his prolific run, Boycott inevitably produced a huge score, carrying his bat throughout the day and the Yorkshire innings for his sixth hundred of the season. Titmus tested him and mastered most of the other batsmen. Bore, in his slower style, reduced Middlesex's hopes of batting points. Smith drove powerfully, but there was little freedom until Radley's effort near the declaration. Boycott's rearranged batting order failed against the hostility of Price and varied spin, Boycott, at number seven, being in the middle of the slump. Nicholson joined Hampshire twenty minutes before lunch and remarkably they remained throughout the last afternoon, defending dourly on the excellent pitch. Both went in the over after tea, but by then the match was virtually saved.

Yorkshire

*G. Boycott not out	182	– b Titmus	6
P. J. Sharpe b Titmus	36	– c Featherstone b Price	0
D. E. V. Padgett b Titmus	8	– c Murray b Price	0
J. H. Hampshire lbw b Titmus	11	– c Smith b Latchman	74
B. Leadbeater run out	0	– c Jones b Price	10
J. D. Woodford b Parfitt	23	– lbw b Titmus	14
R. A. Hutton c and b Titmus	8	– b Parfitt	1
†D. L. Bairstow c Featherstone b Titmus	21	– c Brearley b Jones	6
A. G. Nicholson b Jones	6	– c Parfitt b Latchman	33
G. A. Cope b Parfitt	4	– not out	2
M. K. Bore lbw b Titmus	10	– c Parfitt b Smith	0
B 7, l-b 1, w 1, n-b 2	11	L-b 2, n-b 9	11
1/53 2/73 3/117 4/121 5/178 6/201 7/247 8/265 9/289	320	1/1 2/16 3/17 4/18 5/56 6/72 7/79 8/153 9/154	157

Bowling: *First Innings*—Price 23–6–67–0; Jones 25–3–70–1; Titmus 42.5–12–92–6; Latchman 6–0–34–0; Parfitt 14–4–34–2; Russell 2–0–12–0. *Second Innings*—Price 18–8–33–3; Jones 20–10–32–1; Titmus 27–11–23–2; Latchman 9–4–18–2; Parfitt 18–6–30–1; Featherstone 2–0–10–0; Smith 1.2–1–0–1.

Middlesex

W. E. Russell b Bore	35		
M. J. Smith c Bairstow b Bore	106	– not out	4
P. H. Parfitt c and b Bore	48		
*J. M. Brearley c Hampshire b Bore	20		
C. T. Radley not out	47		
†J. T. Murray b Hutton	24		
N. G. Featherstone not out	7	– b Bore	9
K. V. Jones (did not bat)		– not out	9
B 6, l-b 10, n-b 1	17		
1/61 2/193 3/211 4/226 5/284	(5 wkts dec.) 304	1/14	(1 wkt) 22

H. C. Latchman, F. J. Titmus and J. S. E. Price did not bat.

Bowling: *First Innings*—Nicholson 26–3–67–0; Hutton 18–3–59–1; Cope 29–5–85–0; Bore 31–4–76–4. *Second Innings*—Nicholson 2–0–10–0; Hutton 5–1–11–0; Bore 3–2–1–1.

Umpires: J. Arnold and C. Cook.

MIDDLESEX v HAMPSHIRE

Played at Lord's, Jun 26, 28, 29, 1976

Hampshire won by six wickets. Middlesex gave an uneven batting display, the best coming from Radley and Brearley, who added 145, but there were some poor strokes later. Only Gilliat and Jesty faced the spinners with any assurance, both mingling belligerent strokes with watchful defence. Middlesex attacked briskly on the second evening, making 135 for two at better than a run a minute. On the last day Middlesex lost wickets too freely to declare and it was as well that Brearley batted throughout. Taylor took the last five wickets for 24 in 9.2 overs and Stephenson equalled the Hampshire wicket-keeping record of six victims. Hampshire wanted 248 in three and a half hours. Dropped catches enabled them to remain in a challenging position all through, but it needed Richards, who had been ill earlier, to come in at number six and help Turner to clinch the victory with three balls to spare.

Middlesex

M. J. Smith c Gilliat b Mottram	2	– c Stephenson b Herman	27
*J. M. Brearley c Lewis b Southern	79	– not out	128
C. T. Radley c Southern b Sainsbury	66	– c Stephenson b Southern	22
G. D. Barlow lbw b Jesty	8	– c Stephenson b Jesty	44
N. G. Featherstone c Taylor b Southern	21	– c Gilliat b Sainsbury	10
M. W. Gatting b Sainsbury	27	– st Stephenson b Southern	17
†I. J. Gould b Jesty	4	– c Stephenson b Taylor	2
P. H. Edmonds c sub b Southern	19	– c Turner b Taylor	2
F. J. Titmus c Gilliat b Southern	1	– c Gilliat b Taylor	6
M. W. W. Selvey not out	3	– c Stephenson b Taylor	0
A. A. Jones c Stephenson b Sainsbury	0	– b Taylor	3
L-b 2, n-b 5	7	B 3, l-b 8, w 1, n-b 2	14
1/4 2/149 3/153 4/173 5/187 6/192 7/229 8/233 9/237	237	1/38 2/86 3/180 4/199 5/241 6/254 7/256 8/269 9/269	275

Bowling: *First Innings*—Herman 14–2–48–0; Mottram 3.2–1–4–1; Jesty 22–8–26–2; Taylor 7.4–0–34–0; Sainsbury 24.2–5–69–3; Southern 26–12–49–4. *Second Innings*—Herman 19–5–71–1; Jesty 17–3–51–1; Taylor 9.2–2–24–5; Sainsbury 18–6–61–1; Southern 18–4–54–2.

Hampshire

B. A. Richards c Featherstone b Selvey	8	– not out	12
R. V. Lewis c Selvey b Edmonds	41	– c and b Edmonds	59
D. R. Turner c Gould b Selvey	8	– not out	116
T. E. Jesty c Edmonds b Titmus	50	– c Featherstone b Titmus	29
*R. M. C. Gilliat c Barlow b Titmus	65	– b Edmonds	13
P. J. Sainsbury c Featherstone b Edmonds	15		
J. W. Southern lbw b Titmus	5		
M. N. S Taylor b Titmus	20	– run out	13
†G. R. Stephenson c Titmus b Edmonds	17		
R. S. Herman c Gatting b Edmonds	18		
T. J. Mottram not out	0		
B 10, l-b 7, w 1	18	L-b 4, w 1, n-b 1	6
1/18 2/30 3/115 4/127 5/177 6/215 7/232 8/256 9/265	265	1/114 2/169 3/194 4/214	(4 wkts) 248

Bowling: *First Innings*—Jones 17–4–31–0; Selvey 17–3–69–2; Titmus 34–9–82–4; Edmonds 33.1–11–65–4. *Second Innings*—Jones 10–2–40–0; Selvey 9.3–0–37–0; Titmus 20–0–76–1; Edmonds 23–3–74–2; Featherstone 3–1–15–0.

Umpires: R. Julian and A. G. T. Whitehead.

MIDDLESEX v GLOUCESTERSHIRE

Played at Lord's, July 20, 21, 22, 1977

Drawn. An extraordinary match with two distinct halves reached a controversial, tense climax after seeming all over on the second afternoon. Brearley batted all the first day for his 145 and both he and Gatting were missed twice. After tumbling from 48 for no wicket to 80 all out Gloucestershire came back strongly with an unbroken opening stand of 145 on the second day. The second innings could hardly have provided a greater contrast, for every batsman fought tenaciously after the first three had fallen in the opening hour of the last day. While Edmonds and Emburey toiled through a vast number of overs – Edmonds' 77 has rarely been surpassed in the championship – their colleagues gradually showed the strain and substitutes were needed, including their coach Don Bennett, for Brearley, Smith, Featherstone and Selvey. The last wicket fell at 5.12, but umpire Alley allowed Middlesex only 12 overs to make 75 (as five had already been bowled since 5.00), seeming to ignore the regulation that when a new innings starts inside the last hour it should contain one over for every three minutes. 38 minutes should have meant 13 overs, but a note from Brearley to the umpires as Middlesex vainly tackled their task proved fruitless. Against Procter at his fastest Middlesex sacrificed wickets recklessly, but finished 12 short.

Middlesex

M. J. Smith c Stovold b Brain	1	– c Vernon b Brain	22
*J. M. Brearley b Procter	145	– run out	0
G. D. Barlow b Childs	55	– c Shepherd b Brain	0
C. T. Radley c Stovold b Childs	28	– b Brain	10
M. W. Gatting c Stovold b Brain	79	– not out	21
N. G. Featherstone c Vernon b Procter	7		
P. H. Edmonds not out	0	– c and b Procter	1
†I. J. Gould (did not bat)		– run out	1
J. E. Emburey (did not bat)		– not out	0
M. W. W Selvey (did not bat)		– b Brain	0
B 11, l-b 8, w 2, n-b 7	28	B 3, l-b 4, n-b 1	8
1/4 2/146 3/211 4/310 5/332 6/343	(6 wkts dec.) 343	1/18 2/22 3/53 4/57 5/59 6/59 7/63	(7 wkts) 63

W. W. Daniel did not bat.

Bowling: *First Innings*—Procter 32–4–85–2; Brain 22.5–4–85–2; Vernon 17–2–58–0; Childs 28–3–87–2. *Second Innings*—Procter 6–0–28–1; Brain 5.5–0–27–4.

Gloucestershire

Sadiq Mohammad c Radley b Emburey	32	– c Emburey b Edmonds	82
†A. W. Stovold c and b Edmonds	19	– c Emburey b Edmonds	81
Zaheer Abbas b Edmonds	0	– b Emburey	6
A. J. Hignell c Gatting b Emburey	1	– b Edmonds	26
*M. J. Procter lbw b Edmonds	0	– c Radley b Edmonds	38
D. R. Shepherd lbw b Edmonds	5	– c Gatting b Edmonds	22
J. C. Foat lbw b Emburey	0	– c Smith b Edmonds	17
J. H. Shackleton st Gould b Edmonds	5	– c Gatting b Emburey	28
M. J. Vernon c Radley b Emburey	2	– lbw b Edmonds	3
B. M. Brain not out	2	– c Gatting b Edmonds	0
J. H. Childs b Edmonds	0	– not out	0
B 6, l-b 6, n-b 2	14	B 19, l-b 5, n-b 10	34
1/48 2/48 3/49 4/52 5/58 6/59 7/76 8/76 9/79	80	1/155 2/168 3/186 4/241 5/270 6/277 7/316 8/326 9/335	337

Bowling: *First Innings*—Daniel 4–0–12–0; Selvey 5–0–24–0; Edmonds 16–6–18–6; Emburey 13–6–12–4. *Second Innings*—Daniel 13–4–27–0; Selvey 4–2–5–0; Edmonds 77–13–132–8; Emburey 66.4–26–91–2; Gatting 5–2–17–0; Featherstone 12–3–29–0; Smith 2–0–2–0.

Umpires: W. E. Alley and J. van Geloven.

MIDDLESEX v SURREY

Played at Lord's, August 6, 8, 9, 1977

Middlesex won by nine wickets. There was no play on the first day and only five overs on the second, when Surrey lost Butcher, so the stage was set for a remarkable last day. On a rain-damaged pitch the Surrey batsmen lacked both technique and resolution and the innings folded by 12.15, but they were back twenty minutes later, Brearley having declared after one ball. This master-stroke brought Middlesex the chance of 12 extra points – the best they could have realistically hoped for by orthodox means would have been two batting points – but both batsmen and bowlers had to produce supreme efforts to bring in the prize. One advantage of the declaration was that Surrey again batted on a damp pitch, and again the pace bowlers proved masters, the unfortunate Lynch recording a pair before lunch. Butcher existed for two hours and it was only when Richards and Arnold were joined that Surrey recognised the need for runs. Middlesex, wanting 139 in eighty-eight minutes, received a start of 47 in the first seven overs – Arnold was unable to bowl – and the task of 92 in the last 20 overs proved to be easy, victory coming with eleven balls to spare, for the loss of only one wicket.

Surrey

A. R. Butcher c Gould b Daniel	1	– b Daniel	10
G. P. Howarth c Edmonds b Selvey	9	– c Gould b Selvey	8
M. A. Lynch c Gould b Daniel	0	– b Selvey	0
Younis Ahmed c Featherstone b Daniel	4	– c Gould b Daniel	14
D. M. Smith lbw b Selvey	0	– c Radley b Emburey	10
Intikhab Alam b Daniel	15	– c Barlow b Daniel	2
*R. D. Jackman b Daniel	0	– c Brearley b Selvey	1
I. R. Payne lbw b Selvey	6	– c Smith b Daniel	5
G. G. Arnold not out	8	– not out	19
†C. J. Richards c Edmonds b Gatting	1	– c Emburey b Gatting	6
P. J. Pocock b Gatting	3	– c Edmonds b Gatting	0
W 1, n-b 1	2	B 3, l-b 8, w 1, n-b 2	14
1/7 2/8 3/12 4/12 5/26 6/31 7/32 8/38 9/45	49	1/14 2/14 3/31 4/46 5/48 6/53 7/58 8/59 9/83	89

Bowling: *First Innings*—Daniel 9–5–16–5; Selvey 11–2–29–3; Gatting 2.5–2–2–2. *Second Innings*—Daniel 15–8–23–4; Selvey 19–6–31–3; Gatting 1.3–1–1–2; Emburey 9–4–17–1; Edmonds 6–4–3–0.

Middlesex

J. E. Emburey not out	0		
†I. T. Gould not out	0		
M. J. Smith (did not bat)		– st Richards b Pocock	51
*J. M. Brearley (did not bat)		– not out	66
C. T. Radley (did not bat)		– not out	21
		L-b 3, n-b 1	4
(No wkt dec.)	0	1/101 (1 wkt)	142

M. W. Gatting, G. D. Barlow, N. G. Featherstone, P. H. Edmonds, M. W. W. Selvey and W. W. Daniel did not bat.

Bowling: *First Innings*—Jackman 0.1–0–0–0. *Second Innings*—Jackman 12.1–0–61–0; Payne 2–0–19–0; Butcher 2–0–11–0; Intikhab 3–0–20–0; Pocock 6–0–27–1.

Umpires: W. E. Phillipson and J. van Geloven.

MIDDLESEX v SOMERSET

Played at Chelmsford, August 31, September 1, 2, 1977

Drawn. This match was postponed from its original date one week before to allow the weather-hit Gillette Cup semi-final between the same counties to be fitted in and was moved from Lord's so that preparations for the final would not be interrupted. This was the first time that Middlesex had played away from Lord's since 1959, when they went to

Hornsey, and the first time out of Middlesex since 1939, when they played one "home" game at The Oval. The seven points they won were an absolute bonus for Middlesex, since play would not have proved possible on the scheduled date and even on the first day rain would have prevented a start at Lord's. A weakened Somerset side batted capably, Marks leading an aggressive display by the middle order. Radley shared two big stands on the second afternoon, a sedate one with Brearley and one featuring fierce hitting with Gatting, who drove Marks for three 6s and pulled Jennings for another. Burgess slowed Middlesex's progress with a spell of four for ten and rain on the last day halted them altogether.

Somerset

B. C. Rose b Edmonds	33	C. H. Dredge b Selvey	13
P. W. Denning c Brearley b Daniel	16	K. F. Jennings c Radley b Selvey	0
P. A. Slocombe c Radley b Daniel	22	†T. Gard lbw b Selvey	0
P. M. Roebuck b Daniel	0		
*D. B. Close st Gould b Edmonds	23	L-b 3, n-b 9	12
V. J. Marks c Emburey b Edmonds	53		
G. I. Burgess b Gatting	20	1/22 2/72 3/78 4/88	220
D. Breakwell not out	28	5/129 6/179 7/181 8/216 9/216	

Bowling: Daniel 14–5–27–3; Selvey 27.3–9–55–3; Emburey 21–7–46–0; Gatting 10–1–40–1; Edmonds 16–6–29–3; Featherstone 4–1–11–0.

Middlesex

M. J. Smith c Marks b Jennings	1	†I. J. Gould c Gard b Burgess	0
*J. M. Brearley b Marks	49	J. E. Emburey c Jennings b Marks	16
C. T. Radley c Slocombe b Dredge	85	M. W. W. Selvey not out	1
M. W. Gatting c and b Burgess	54	L-b 7, n-b 5, w 4	16
G. D. Barlow not out	26		
N. G. Featherstone c Gard b Burgess	2	1/21 2/102 3/197	(8 wkts) 258
P. H. Edmonds c and b Burgess	8	4/197 5/207 6/217 7/225 8/257	

W. W. Daniel did not bat.

Bowling: Burgess 31–8–82–4; Dredge 12–3–30–1; Jennings 19–6–49–1; Marks 13–1–54–2; Breakwell 10–1–27–0.

Umpires: P. B. Wight and A. Jepson.

MIDDLESEX v SOMERSET

Played at Lord's, June 6, 8, 9, 1981

Drawn. Richards once more showed his liking for Lord's with an innings, typically rich in thunderous strokes, that featured a crushing assault on Thomson and lasted two and a half hours. Somerset made 132 during the 35 overs that he was in and Denning batted breezily, but Roebuck toiled for nearly five hours, preventing Somerset from earning full batting points. Barlow's dismissal introduced a period of caution for Middlesex, who took 45 overs to reach 100; Butcher then cut loose and the next 100 came in 22 overs. Thomson, fearsomely fast, picked up two wickets after Middlesex had declared 59 behind and forced Rose to retire overnight. Following an hour's delay at the start of the third day, Middlesex were further encouraged when Daniel had Richards caught at slip with his first ball, but more rain in the afternoon killed the match.

Somerset

*B. C. Rose c Butcher b Thomson	23	– retired hurt 6
J. W. Lloyds b Selvey	12	– c Slack b Thomson 8
I. V. A. Richards c Downton b Selvey	92	– (4) c Butcher b Daniel 3
P. M. Roebuck c Barlow b Daniel	68	– (5) c Slack b Merry 33
P. W. Denning b Merry	63	– (6) not out 75
V. J. Marks b Merry	0	– (7) not out 26
†D. J. S. Taylor c Edmonds b Thomson	6	
D. Breakwell c Downton b Thomson	12	– (3) c Downton b Thomson 7
J. Garner c Downton b Selvey	29	
H. R. Moseley not out	2	
B 3, l-b 6, n-b 8	17	L-b 3, n-b 5 8
1/35 2/64 3/167 4/263 5/264 6/274 7/287 8/297 9/324	(9 wkts dec.) 324	1/13 2/21 3/24 4/106 (4 wkts dec.) 166

C. H. Dredge did not bat.

Bowling: *First Innings*—Daniel 23–4–58–1; Selvey 33.3–11–78–3; Thomson 18–2–59–3; Merry 15–1–58–2; Edmonds 18–4–54–0. *Second Innings*—Thomson 9–1–31–2; Daniel 9–3–26–1; Merry 12–0–43–1; Edmonds 5–1–12–0; Selvey 5–1–18–0; Slack 8–1–28–0.

Middlesex

*J. M. Brearley c Taylor b Moseley	2
G. D. Barlow lbw b Marks	32
C. T. Radley lbw b Moseley	87
R. O. Butcher not out	106
W. N. Slack lbw b Garner	17
P. H. Edmonds not out	11
L-b 7, n-b 3	10
1/7 2/59 3/205 4/236	(4 wkts dec.) 265

†P. R. Downton, M. W. W. Selvey, J. R. Thomson, W. G. Merry and W. W. Daniel did not bat.

Bowling: Garner 18–1–52–1; Moseley 20–3–55–2; Dredge 15–1–50–0; Marks 18–5–38–1; Lloyds 4–0–25–0; Breakwell 9–0–35–0.

Umpires: W. L. Budd and P. S. G. Stevens.

MIDDLESEX v KENT

Played at Lord's, July 15, 16, 17, 1981

Drawn. Batting became so much easier during the match that Middlesex's first innings toils were transformed into a record first-wicket partnership for the county. Barlow (four 6s and sixteen 4s) and Slack, whose maiden century included three 6s and twenty 4s, exceeded by 55 runs the previous record of Eric Russell and Mike Harris – 312 against the Pakistanis in 1967. The previous Championship best was 310 scored by Jack Robertson and Sid Brown against Nottinghamshire in 1947. Conditions favoured swing and cut on the first morning when Shepherd added to his long list of damaging performances against Middlesex, although Slack gave a foretaste of future events and Downton fought tenaciously. From 99 for four at the close, Kent batted consistently to achieve a substantial first innings lead. Middlesex started the last day on 97 and Kent had chances of splitting the partnership when Slack was 50 and again when Barlow was 107, both off Rowe. As Kent offered easy runs to force a declaration, the batsmen added 194 from 24 overs in a 70-minute spell spanning lunch, and the eventual target was 251 in 172 minutes. When rain caused a delay of more than an hour after one over, however, the chase become meaningless.

Middlesex

G. D. Barlow c Woolmer b Jarvis	7	– not out 174
W. N. Slack b Underwood	56	– not out 181
C. T. Radley c Knott b Jarvis	0	
R. O. Butcher c Knott b Shepherd	2	
K. P. Tomlins c Johnson b Shepherd	7	
*P. H. Edmonds b Shepherd	26	
†P. R. Downton c and b Jarvis	44	
M. W. W. Selvey c sub b Underwood	11	
J. D. Monteith b Shepherd	5	
W. W. Daniel b Shepherd	0	
W. G. Merry not out	7	
B 1, n-b 1	2	B 1, l-b 8, w 3 12
1/10 2/12 3/15 4/33 5/95 6/99 7/126 8/137 9/141	167	(no wkt dec.) 367

Bowling: *First Innings*—Jarvis 23.2–7–53–3; Shepherd 31–12–61–5; Cowdrey 5–1–21–0; Asif 4–2–12–0; Underwood 10–4–18–2. *Second Innings*—Jarvis 9–2–26–0; Shepherd 14–4–31–0; Cowdrey 2–0–9–0; Underwood 20–4–54–0; Johnson 15–2–56–0; Rowe 14–2–60–0; Tavaré 9–1–91–0; Benson 4–0–28–0.

Kent

R. A. Woolmer c Downton b Daniel	39	– c Butcher b Selvey 18
C. J. C. Rowe c Barlow b Daniel	4	– c Butcher b Selvey 0
C. J. Tavaré lbw b Selvey	11	– not out 26
M. R. Benson c Monteith b Edmonds	33	– not out 21
*Asif Iqbal c Downton b Selvey	55	
D. L. Underwood c Monteith b Selvey	12	
C. S. Cowdrey c Downton b Monteith	60	
†A. P. E. Knott b Daniel	24	
G. W. Johnson b Daniel	28	
J. N. Shepherd not out	13	
K. B. S. Jarvis run out	0	
L-b 2, w 1, n-b 2	5	L-b 1, n-b 1 2
1/7 2/22 3/89 4/91 5/106 6/196 7/226 8/269 9/272	284	1/8 2/23 (2 wkts) 67

Bowling: *First Innings*—Daniel 22–0–74–4; Selvey 29–10–90–3; Merry 19–3–54–0; Edmonds 14–2–37–1; Monteith 12–3–24–1. *Second Innings*—Daniel 6–0–31–0; Selvey 4–1–7–2; Monteith 7–2–10–0; Edmonds 6–1–16–0; Radley 1–0–1–0.

Umpires: Mahboob Shah and A. G. T. Whitehead.

MIDDLESEX v SURREY

Played at Uxbridge, September 9, 10, 11, 1981

Middlesex won by six wickets. This was a marvellously entertaining match, packed with incident and containing a sharp transformation in Middlesex's fortunes. Although Alan Butcher, who gave three chances, hit two 6s and eight 4s in his cavalier knock, and Lynch flicked two 6s over mid-wicket in one over from Emburey, the Surrey lynch-pin was Clinton, who used the areas behind the wicket to collect seventeen 4s. Gatting's thrilling innings then turned the match as, hitting the ball with immense force and treating the bowling with arrogance, he struck nine 6s – five off Intikhab – and eighteen 4s. Radley, sensibly, merely watched such carnage, contributing only 10 to their century stand and 44 to the partnership of 197 in 111 minutes which ended when Gatting, having batted for 138 minutes and made the highest score of his career, carelessly ran himself out off a no ball. After Middlesex had declared 19 behind Daniel, very fast, ripped out two wickets, Emburey weaved through three more, and Surrey were 90 for six on the second evening. Lynch went third ball on the last day, ensuring Middlesex of an inviting target, and fearing rain they sprinted home in a furious assault after lunch, collecting the final 146 runs in an hour and a half.

Surrey

A. R. Butcher c Downton b Emburey	75	– c and b Emburey	20
G. S. Clinton b Edmonds	114	– c Gatting b Daniel	2
D. B. Pauline st Downton b Emburey	5	– c Downton b Daniel	0
*R. D. V. Knight c Downton b Hughes	31	– c Butcher b Emburey	34
D. M. Smith b Edmonds	5	– c Radley b Emburey	0
M. A. Lynch c Butcher b Emburey	58	– lbw b Daniel	23
Intikhab Alam b Edmonds	21	– run out	0
†C. J. Richards c Edmonds b Emburey	40	– st Downton b Emburey	33
R. D. Jackman c Downton b Edmonds	0	– c sub b Emburey	19
G. Monkhouse not out	28	– c Slack b Edmonds	0
P. I. Pocock c Daniel b Emburey	8	– not out	6
B 9, l-b 6, w 5, n-b 6	26	B 4, l-b 3, n-b 1	8
1/122 2/132 3/182 4/201 5/274 6/316 7/326 8/326 9/397	411	1/12 2/12 3/24 4/26 5/78 6/78 7/91 8/123 9/124	145

Bowling: *First Innings*—Daniel 16–0–78–0; Hughes 17–2–52–1; Edmonds 37–5–121–4; Emburey 41–8–134–5. *Second Innings*—Daniel 13–3–40–3; Hughes 4–0–28–0; Edmonds 18–4–32–1; Emburey 16.1–6–37–5.

Middlesex

*J. M. Brearley run out	21	– c Butcher b Pocock	31
W. N. Slack c Butcher b Intikhab	60	– lbw b Pocock	10
G. D. Barlow c Richards b Intikhab	35	– (6) not out	17
M. W. Gatting run out	169	– c Butcher b Intikhab	38
C. T. Radley c Butcher b Intikhab	44	– (3) not out	56
R. O. Butcher c Richards b Pocock	10	– (5) c Monkhouse b Intikhab	7
P. H. Edmonds c Lynch b Intikhab	11		
J. E. Emburey b Pocock	2		
†P. R. Downton not out	14		
W. W. Daniel not out	0		
B 10, l-b 11, n-b 5	26	B 4, l-b 2	6
1/32 2/107 3/146 4/343 5/343 6/359 7/365 8/391	(8 wkts dec.) 392	1/19 2/56 3/118 4/128	(4 wkts) 165

S. P. Hughes did not bat.

Bowling: *First Innings*—Intikhab 28–4–133–4; Pocock 28.1–15–117–2; Jackman 12–4–48–0; Monkhouse 8–1–21–0; Butcher 8–1–33–0; Pauline 2–0–14–0. *Second Innings*—Jackman 3–0–6–0; Monkhouse 2–0–7–0; Intikhab 12–2–68–2; Pocock 14.4–3–62–2; Butcher 3–0–16–0.

Umpires: D. J. Constant and B. J. Meyer.

NORTHAMPTONSHIRE

NORTHAMPTONSHIRE v MIDDLESEX

Played at Northampton, August 12, 13, 14, 1964

Northamptonshire won by ten wickets thanks to two left-arm slow bowlers, Steele and Scott, operating effectively when the pitch began to take spin on the last day. Previously the bat had been on top with 740 runs hit in the first two innings. Middlesex began well with a partnershp of 174 between Russell and Brearley for the first wicket and Russell went on to hit 138 (one 6 and seventeen 4s) in four hours, forty minutes. Afterwards, Smith prevented a complete collapse when Bailey, in only his second match, took five for 25 in an excellent spell of pace bowling. Northamptonshire also started well, with Milburn and Reynolds hitting 188 in two and a half hours of exhilarating batting, and they scored readily well down the order despite a hat-trick by Drybrough. Scott, Crum pand Larter fell to Drybrough in three balls and he took seven for 94 altogether with his left-arm slows.

Middlesex

W. E. Russell b Bailey	138	– run out	3
J. M. Brearley c Steele b P. D. Watts	75	– c Andrew b Scott	38
R. A. White lbw b P. D. Watts	7	– c Milburn b Bailey	0
E. A. Clark lbw b P. D. Watts	0	– lbw b Scott	7
†J. T. Murray c Milburn b Steele	2	– c Milburn b Steele	42
M. J. Smith not out	64	– c Steele b Larter	14
R. Pearman b Bailey	0	– c P. D. Watts b Scott	0
D. Bennett b Bailey	0	– c Larter b Steele	30
*C. D. Drybrough c Andrew b Bailey	0	– c Bailey b Steele	14
D. A. Bick b Bailey	12	– c Milburn b Steele	1
A. C Waite b Crump	4	– not out	3
L-b 1, w 1, n-b 1	3	L-b 4, n-b 4	8
1/174 2/185 3/195 4/203 5/241 6/247 7/251 8/251 9/281	305	1/1 2/53 3/57 4/61 5/66 6/66 7/131 8/153 9/155	160

Bowling: *First Innings*—Larter 11–2–31–0; Crump 24.4–3–73–1; Bailey 29–7–72–5; Scott 18–5–53–0; Steele 14–5–25–1; P. D. Watts 14–2–48–3. *Second Innings*—Bailey 8–2–22–1; Crump 7–2–13–0; Scott 23–12–39–3; P. D. Watts 2–0–11–0; Larter 16–3–38–1; Steele 17.1–8–29–4.

Northamptonshire

B. L. Reynolds c sub b Bennett	81	– not out	16
C. Milburn c Pearman b Bick	104	– not out	18
R. M. Prideaux b Drybrough	93		
M. Norman c Clark b Drybrough	34		
D. S. Steele b Drybrough	41		
P. D. Watts st Murray b Bick	26		
B. Crump c White b Drybrough	21		
M. E. Scott c Bennett b Drybrough	18		
R. Bailey st Murray b Drybrough	0		
J. D. F. Larter lbw b Drybrough	0		
*†K. V. Andrew not out	1		
B 3, l-b 10, w 3	16		
1/188 2/194 3/248 4/341 5/389 6/395 7/434 8/434 9/434	435	(No wkt)	34

Bowling—*First Innings*—Bennett 17–0–71–1; Waite 21–3–80–0; Bick 40–11–109–2; Drybrough 29–7–94–7; Clark 15–1–61–0; Smith 1–0–4–0. *Second Innings*—Drybrough 3–0–13–0; Bick 3–0–16–0; Smith 0.4–0–5–0.

Umpires: H. Yarnold and O. W. Herman.

NORTHAMPTONSHIRE v LANCASHIRE

Played at Wellingborough, August 12, 13, 14, 1967

Lancashire won by five wickets with three minutes to spare. Although Prideaux and Reynolds hit valuable fifties, Shuttleworth bowled well after tea on the first day. Lancashire fell for 86 against effective off-spin by Sully, aided by Steele and Durose. Prideaux declared early in the second innings and left Lancashire three hours, twenty minutes to score 162 and this proved to be just too generous. Pilling ensured that Lancashire reached their target. In a brave innings of 77, he batted just over two hours, hitting one 6 and ten 4s. Sully achieved the hat-trick when he dismissed Atkinson with his first ball in the second innings.

Northamptonshire

*R. M. Prideaux c Lloyd b Lever	50	– not out	10
C. Milburn c Goodwin b Statham	15	– lbw b Statham	17
B. L. Reynolds c Wood b Shuttleworth	61	– not out	1
A. Lightfoot c Lever b Savage	19		
D. S. Steele c Wood b Shuttleworth	18		
B. Crump b Shuttleworth	4		
P. Willey c Goodwin b Shuttleworth	4		
M. K. Kettle b Statham	9		
†L. A. Johnson b Shuttleworth	1		
H. Sully not out	16		
A. J. Durose b Lever	1		
B 5, l-b 12, n-b 1	18	B 1, n-b 2	3
1/40 2/83 3/114 4/160 5/180 6/185 7/188 8/194 9/203	216	1/22 (1 wkt dec.)	31

Bowling: *First Innings*—Statham 22–6–52–2; Shuttleworth 25–7–42–5; Savage 25–6–59–1; Lever 17.5–5–29–2; Wood 10–3–16–0. *Second Innings*—Statham 5.4–1–12–1; Lever 5–2–16–0.

Lancashire

G. Atkinson c Reynolds b Sully	12	– c Kettle b Sully	6
B. Wood c Johnson b Durose	0	– c Kettle b Steele	24
H. Pilling lbw b Durose	2	– lbw b Crump	77
G. Pullar lbw b Sully	32	– b Durose	17
K. Snellgrove c Reynolds b Steele	0	– c Johnson b Durose	3
D. Lloyd b Steele	7	– not out	10
P. Lever b Sully	4		
K. Shuttleworth b Crump	11	– not out	19
†K. Goodwin c Crump b Sully	11		
*J. B. Statham c Reynolds b Sully	5		
J. S. Savage not out	0		
L-b 2	2	L-b 4, n-b 3	7
1/2 2/4 3/43 4/43 5/53 6/53 7/60 8/74 9/86	86	1/18 2/54 3/107 4/119 5/141 (5 wkts)	163

Bowling: *First Innings*—Crump 18–11–17–1; Durose 9–4–15–2; Sully 19.4–7–39–5; Steele 11–5–13–2. *Second Innings*—Crump 20–0–64–1; Durose 16–7–22–2; Sully 14–4–42–1; Steel 7–2–20–1; Kettle 4–2–8–0.

Umpires: A. E. Alderman and G. H. Pope.

NORTHAMPTONSHIRE v HAMPSHIRE

Played at Northampton, May 29, 30, 31, 1968

Drawn. Hampshire took advantage of a fine wicket after Prideaux put them into bat. They gained five batting bonus points, thanks mainly to an opening stand of 182 by Richards and Reed. Richards enjoyed a triumphant game with a century in each innings. His 130 came in three and three-quarter hours with two 6s and seventeen 4s. This he followed with 104 not out in just over three hours, with seventeen 4s. Northamptonshire collapsed in their first innings, despite a determined 74 by Milburn. Then Crump, aided by three capable partners, saw the last three wickets put on 126. Finally, Hampshire set a target of 240 runs in two hours, forty minutes, which Northamptonshire found too high after losing early wickets.

Hampshire

B. A. Richards c Kettle b Durose	130	– not out	104
B. L. Reed c Ackerman b Willey	70	– c Milburn b Durose	9
R. M. C. Gilliat c Ackerman b Durose	50		
*R. E. Marshall b Durose	10		
P. J. Sainsbury run out	41	– not out	33
D. R. Turner b Kettle	4		
K. J. Wheatley c Milburn b Kettle	5		
†B. S. V. Timms b Crump	9		
D. Shackleton not out	4		
B 4, l-b 2, n-b 7	13	L-b 1, n-b 7	8
1/182 2/238 3/260 4/274 5/288 6/306 7/331 8/336	(8 wkts dec.) 336	1/34	(1 wkt dec.) 154

D. W. White and R. M. H. Cottam did not bat.

Bowling: *First Innings*—Crump 25–6–58–1; Kettle 23–5–55–2; Scott 20–5–65–0; Durose 13.4–1–61–3; Mushtaq 10–0–39–0; Willey 11–1–45–1. *Second Innings*—Crump 14–4–15–0; Kettle 14–5–33–0; Scott 8–1–30–0; Durose 18–4–41–1; Willey 4–0–26–0; Ackerman 1–0–1–0.

Northamptonshire

*R. M. Prideaux c Turner b White	0	– b White	3
C. Milburn b Sainsbury	74	– c Turner b White	24
P. Willey b White	15	– not out	4
H. M. Ackerman lbw b Shackleton	11	– not out	39
Mushtaq Mohammad c Richards b Cottam	0	– c and b Cottam	14
D. S. Steele lbw b Sainsbury	11	– c Wheatley b Cottam	0
B. Crump c Turner b Shackleton	74		
M. E. Scott c Richards b White	0		
M. K. Kettle c Timms b White	21		
†L. A. Johnson lbw b Cottam	22		
A. J. Durose not out	13		
L-b 2, n-b 8	10	B 5, l-b 1, n-b 2	8
1/0 2/27 3/53 4/56 5/102 6/124 7/125 8/187 9/231	251	1/27 2/32 3/61 4/85	(4 wkts) 92

Bowling: *First Innings*—Shackleton 32–14–66–2; White 30–8–82–4; Cottam 25.4–3–60–2; Sainsbury 19–13–21–2; Wheatley 5–1–12–0. *Second Innings*—Shackleton 10–2–31–0; White 10–2–23–2; Cottam 7–5–5–2; Sainsbury 3–2–1–0; Wheatley 5–2–24–0.

Umpires: G. H. Pope and H. Mellows.

NORTHAMPTONSHIRE v LEICESTERSHIRE

Played at Peterborough, July 13, 14, 15, 1968

Northamptonshire won by nine wickets. The Leicestershire captain, Hallam, must have regretted his decision to put Northamptonshire in to bat on a pitch that was affected by heavy rain. The home team found the best batting conditions and Prideaux, Lightfoot and Steele gained a winning position. Marner bowled well to dismiss the later men. Then Durose produced his best bowling performance as Leicestershire collapsed for 43, and had to follow-on. Sully, Crump and Durose bowled well in the second innings and only a fine display by Inman averted an innings defeat. Needing 16 in the last nine minutes of extra time on the second day, Northamptonshire lost Steele off the last ball with the scores level. The two teams had to turn out on the third morning for the one run that was required.

Northamptonshire

*R. M. Prideaux lbw b Marner	54	– not out	14
D. S. Steele b Marner	47	– lbw b Marner	4
A. Lightfoot c and b Marner	52	– not out	0
Mushtaq Mohammad c Barratt b Birkenshaw	0		
H. M. Ackerman run out	8		
B. L. Reynolds c Dudleston b Marner	9		
P. Willey c and b Birkenshaw	1		
B. S. Crump b Marner	9		
†L. A. Johnson c Tolchard b Marner	9		
A. J. Durose b Birkenshaw	4		
H. Sully not out	4		
B 6, l-b 5	11	L-b 1	1
1/73 2/146 3/147 4/171 5/175 6/181 7/181 8/192 9/196	208	1/15 (1 wkt)	19

Bowling—*First Innings*—Spencer 10–3–18–0; Pember 7–5–9–0; Birkenshaw 35–9–79–3; Barratt 11–5–18–0; Marner 30.2–5–73–6. *Second Innings*—Spencer 1–0–6–0; Marner 2–0–8–1; Norman 0.1–0–4–0.

Leicestershire

M. E. Norman c Mushtaq b Crump	6	– c Crump b Durose	8
B. J. Booth c Mushtaq b Crump	0	– hit wkt b Durose	2
*M. R. Hallam b Durose	4	– c Steele b Durose	20
C. C. Inman c Johnson b Durose	0	– st Johnson b Sully	79
J. Birkenshaw c Mushtaq b Durose	2	– b Crump	1
B. Dudleston b Durose	0	– c Steele b Sully	1
P. T. Marner c Willey b Crump	10	– c Mushtaq b Sully	24
†R. W. Tolchard c Mushtaq b Durose	0	– not out	14
J. D. D. Pember c Johnson b Durose	4	– b Sully	0
R. Barratt c Mushtaq b Durose	5	– b Mushtaq	23
C. T. Spencer not out	4	– c and b Crump	4
L-b 8	8	B 2, n-b 2	4
1/13 2/13 3/14 4/15 5/16 6/17 7/19 8/23 9/35	43	1/9 2/11 3/53 4/106 5/121 6/122 7/139 8/141 9/172	180

Bowling: *First Innings*—Crump 13.1–7–12–3; Durose 13–5–23–7. *Second Innings*—Crump 16.1–5–36–2; Durose 18–1–78–3; Lightfoot 1–0–2–0; Sully 16–5–55–4; Mushtaq 3–1–5–1.

Umpires: J. Arnold and J. G. Langridge.

NORTHAMPTONSHIRE v KENT

Played at Wellingborough, August 7, 9, 10, 1971

Drawn. Heavy rain washed out the last day's play when Kent, with nine wickets left, needed another 204 runs to win. Northamptonshire's first innings was dominated by a fine effort from their captain, Watts, with useful help from Cook and Ackerman. Graham began with three cheap wickets, and was helped by Julien and Shepherd. The Kent captain, Denness, carried his bat when Mushtaq caused a collapse with his leg-breaks. Northamptonshire led by 47, and were further boosted by a second wicket stand of 92 by Ackerman and Steele. But later the innings crumbled against the effective bowling of Underwood.

Northamptonshire

A. Tait c Shepherd b Graham	14	– run out	0
H. M. Ackerman c Julien b Underwood	25	– c and b Shepherd	48
D. S. Steele c Leary b Graham	9	– c Nicholls b Shepherd	34
Mushtaq Mohammad c Leary b Graham	1	– b Dye	13
G. Cook b Julien	37	– lbw b Dye	12
*P. J. Watts c Ealham b Dye	74	– run out	0
B . S. Crump c Asif b Shepherd	0	– c Asif b Underwood	9
Sarfraz Nawaz b Julien	10	– c Denness b Underwood	7
J. W Swinburne c Nicholls b Shepherd	2	– b Underwood	2
†L. A. Johnson lbw b Dye	1	– not out	12
P. Lee not out	2	– c Nicholls b Underwood	4
L-b 6, n-b 2	8	B 15, l-b 10, n-b 2	27
1/25 2/37 3/39 4/70 5/121 6/122 7/140 8/157 9/170	183	1/0 2/92 3/103 4/126 5/130 6/130 7/137 8/139 9/156	168

Bowling: *First Innings*—Dye 13.2–2–37–2; Graham 14–2–47–3; Underwood 20–7–35–1; Johnson 3–2–6–0; Shepherd 30–5–33–2; Julien 9–4–17–2. *Second Innings*—Dye 19–6–35–2; Graham 4–2–12–0; Underwood 27.4–12–41–4; Shepherd 15–3–30–2; Julien 6–0–23–0.

Kent

*M. H. Denness not out	69	– c and b Crump	0
†D. Nicholls c Swinburne b Crump	4	– not out	10
G. W. Johnson b Lee	2	– not out	1
A. G. E. Ealham c Ackerman b Lee	8		
Asif Iqbal c Steele b Crump	25		
J. N. Shepherd c Crump b Mushtaq	19		
S. E. Leary b Lee	3		
B. D. Julien c Steele b Mushtaq	1		
D. L. Underwood b Mushtaq	0		
J. C. Dye c Johnson b Mushtaq	0		
J. N. Graham b Mushtaq	4		
N-b 1	1	L-b 1	1
1/8 2/15 3/37 4/77 5/107 6/117 7/118 8/120 9/128	136	1/5 (1 wkt)	12

Bowling: *First Innings*—Lee 24–6–62–3; Crump 15–2–45–2; Swinburne 4–0–11–0; Sarfraz 3–1–5–0; Mushtaq 7.4–4–12–5. *Second Innings*—Lee 7–5–5–0; Crump 5–3–2–1; Swinburne 1–0–4–0.

Umpires: G. H. Pope and C. S. Elliott.

NORTHAMPTONSHIRE v SURREY

Played at Kettering, August 21, 23, 1971

Surrey won by an innings and six runs. Surrey finished the game on the second afternoon when devastating bowling by Arnold had the home batsmen in trouble. Willis began the collapse by bowling Cook and Steele in his first over. Ackerman carried his bat through the innings for 39. Jackman also bowled well. This trio, together with Pocock, had also dismissed Northamptonshire for a moderate first-innings score. In the Surrey innings Stewart hit a valuable 81 with help from Roope, Younis, Storey and Long.

Northamptonshire

H. M. Ackerman c Storey b Willis	20	– not out	39
G. Cook c Roope b Willis	22	– b Willis	0
D. S. Steele c Long b Jackman	7	– b Willis	0
Mushtaq Mohammad c Long b Arnold	20	– b Arnold	4
*P. J. Watts c Owen-Thomas b Pocock	24	– b Arnold	3
B. S. Crump c Long b Arnold	0	– c Long b Arnold	0
D. Breakwell c Lewis b Arnold	30	– lbw b Arnold	4
Sarfraz Nawaz c Long b Pocock	2	– b Arnold	11
†L. A. Johnson b Willis	19	– b Jackman	1
J. W. Swinburne c Long b Jackman	7	– lbw b Jackman	0
P. Lee not out	0	– b Arnold	4
L-b 10, w 1, n-b 12	23	B 4, l-b 5, n-b 2	11
1/42 2/53 3/57 4/90 5/91 6/139 7/142 8/153 9/174	174	1/2 2/2 3/27 4/31 5/51 6/51 7/65 8/68 9/68	77

Bowling: *First Innings*—Arnold 24–6–41–3; Willis 16.1–1–32–3; Jackman 21–6–50–2; Storey 10–4–12–0; Pocock 11–4–16–2. *Second Innings*—Arnold 14.1–3–31–6; Willis 4–1–12–2; Jackman 10–3–23–2.

Surrey

*M. J. Stewart lbw b Mushtaq	81
R. M. Lewis b Sarfraz	8
D. R. Owen-Thomas c Ackerman b Sarfraz	0
Younis Ahmed b Mushtaq	36
G. R. J. Roope c Lee b Breakwell	49
S. J. Storey c Watts b Breakwell	23
†A. Long run out	20
P. I. Pocock b Crump	14
R. G. D. Willis b Crump	4
R. D. Jackman b Crump	9
G. G. Arnold not out	0
B 1, l-b 4, w 1, n-b 7	13
1/21 2/21 3/99 4/159 5/199 6/218 7/240 8/244 9/256	257

Bowling: Lee 14–3–41–0; Crump 22.2–7–59–3; Sarfraz 19–3–48–2; Mushtaq 16–4–56–2; Breakwell 11–1–40–2.

Umpires: J. G. Langridge and F. Jakeman.

NORTHAMPTONSHIRE v SOMERSET

Played at Northampton, June 26, 28, 29, 1976

Northamptonshire won by an innings and 86 runs. The outstanding feature of this game was a Northamptonshire record fourth wicket stand of 370 in six and a half hours by Willey and Virgin, the former Somerset batsman. Willey hit his highest score, 227, including thirty-seven 4s, before he was unluckily run out as his partner, Larkins, refused a quick single. Virgin also batted well for 145 with twenty-four 4s, while Larkins gathered a brisk not out 54. Somerset ran into trouble on the first day against the pace of Sarfraz and Larkins, only Close and Botham showing much resistance. Then Bedi had them struggling with his spin in the second innings although Close again showed fight. Finally, the last man, Moseley, hit five 6s off five successive balls from Willey, the last three balls of one over and the first two from Willey's next.

Somerset

B. C. Rose c Sharp b Sarfraz	19	– c Hodgson b Sarfraz	8
†D. J. S. Taylor lbw b Sarfraz	5	– c Sharp b Bedi	20
P. W. Denning b Sarfraz	6	– c Sharp b Bedi	38
*D. B. Close c Sharp b Larkins	31	– c Sharp b Willey	34
M. J. Kitchen c Hodgson b Larkins	23	– c Virgin b Willey	23
I. T. Botham b Willey	34	– c and b Mushtaq	17
G. I. Burgess c Mushtaq b Larkins	0	– c Cook and Bedi	21
D. Breakwell c Virgin b Sarfraz	9	– c Sharp b Bedi	8
K. F. Jennings c Sharp b Bedi	17	– c and b Bedi	2
C. Dredge not out	16	– not out	1
H . R. Moseley c Cook b Willey	4	– b Bedi	40
B 8, l-b 5, w 1	14	B 4, l-b 2	6
1/7 2/23 3/35 4/96 5/97 6/103 7/134 8/145 9/169	178	1/14 2/56 3/74 4/99 5/114 6/121 7/159 8/169 9/177	218

Bowling: *First Innings*—Sarfraz 18–2–48–4; Hodgson 12–2–31–0; Larkins 11–3–34–3; Bedi 14–3–43–1; Willey 3.4–2–8–2. *Second Innings*—Sarfraz 15–7–29–1; Hodgson 5–0–24–0; Bedi 37.4–17–71–6; Willey 24–6–74–2; Mushtaq 8–3–14–1.

Northamptonshire

R. T. Virgin b Moseley	145
G. Cook c Botham b Moseley	6
D. S. Steele c Taylor b Botham	0
*Mushtaq Mohammad b Moseley	10
P. Willey run out	227
W. Larkins not out	54
R. G. Williams lbw b Moseley	0
†G. Sharp not out	4
B 6, l-b 12, w 7, n-b 11	36
1/11 2/12 3/27 4/397 5/417 6/417	(6 wkts) 482

Sarfraz Nawaz, A. Hodgson and B. S. Bedi did not bat.

Bowling: Moseley 25–8–76–4; Botham 26–2–109–1; Jennings 13–2–61–0; Dredge 18–3–63–0; Burgess 15–4–52–0; Breakwell 23–3–77–0; Close 3–1–8–0.

Umpires: W. E. Phillipson and G. H. Pope.

NORTHAMPTONSHIRE v LANCASHIRE

Played at Northampton, August 10, 11, 12, 1977

Drawn. Lancashire made an amazing recovery. They were dismissed for 33 on the first morning by the pace of Sarfraz, Hodgson and Griffiths on a lively wicket. Sarfraz was unplayable. Then Northamptonshire built an overwhelming lead of 350. Virgin hit a fine century in three hours ten minutes with sixteen 4s, and Steele and Mushtaq each reached fifty. But from a hopeless position Lancashire hit back to make 501. Hayes scored a splendid 135 in four hours, thirty-five minutes including eighteen 4s. Wood was only two short of a century and Abrahams, Pilling and Reidy all played excellent innings.

Lancashire

B. Wood b Hodgson	1	– b Sarfraz	98
J. Abrahams c Sharp b Sarfraz	4	– c Sharp b Bedi	71
*H. Pilling c Steele b Sarfraz	0	– lbw b Griffiths	45
F. C. Hayes b Hodgson	0	– c Cook b Bedi	135
B. W. Reidy c Steele b Hodgson	0	– c Cook b Bedi	78
D. P. Hughes c Virgin b Sarfraz	11	– c Cook b Mushtaq	6
J. Simmons b Sarfraz	0	– lbw b Bedi	31
†J. Lyons lbw b Griffiths	5	– c Steele b Bedi	11
C. Croft not out	8	– c Hodgson b Steele	3
R. Arrowsmith b Sarfraz	0	– lbw b Bedi	0
P. G. Lee b Sarfraz	0	– not out	0
L-b 1, w 1, n-b 2	4	B 7, l-b 9, n-b 7	23
1/6 2/6 3/6 4/6 5/6 6/7 7/24 8/24 9/29	33	1/175 2/177 3/267 4/439 5/444 6/450 7/475 8/501 9/501	501

Bowling: *First Innings*—Sarfraz 13.2–9–8–6; Hodgson 9–6–17–3; Griffiths 4–3–4–1. *Second Innings*—Sarfraz 24–5–64–1; Hodgson 20–3–62–0; Griffiths 25–6–57–1; Bedi 48–19–98–6; Mushtaq 38–8–140–1; Willey 29–10–57–0; Steele 1–1–0–1.

Northamptonshire

R. T. Virgin c Lyon b Croft	106		
G. Cook c and b Arrowsmith	39	– not out	6
D. S Steele run out	56		
*Mushtaq Mohammad b Simmons	53	– not out	1
W. Larkins c Wood b Simmons	0		
P. Willey c Wood b Arrowsmith	0	– c Simmons b Croft	19
Sarfraz Nawaz run out	19		
†G. Sharp lbw b Hughes	37		
A. Hodgson b Simmons	40		
B. S. Bedi c and b Simmons	9		
B. J. Griffiths not out	1		
B 9, l-b 4, n-b 10	23	L-b 1, n-b 1	2
1/112 2/170 3/246 4/246 5/251 6/278 7/296 8/366 9/374	383	1/23 (1 wkt)	28

Bowling: *First Innings*—Croft 22–5–55–1; Lee 19–3–64–0; Wood 12–5–27–0; Arrowsmith 36–8–131–2; Simmons 28.4–11–68–4; Hughes 5–0–15–1. *Second Innings*—Croft 3–0–16–1; Lee 2–0–10–0.

Umpires: D. J. Constant and J. G. Langridge.

NORTHAMPTONSHIRE v WARWICKSHIRE

Played at Northampton, July 7, 9, 10, 1979

This was a match notable for high scoring and some fine individual performances. Williams, the 21-year-old Northamptonshire player, scored a century in each innings and was awarded his county cap. His unbeaten 151 was his third century in successive innings and his fourth in four games. In the first innings he batted just over two and half hours for his 109 and hit nineteen 4s; in the second he reached his best score in four and a half hours with one 6 and twenty-one 4s and clearly established himself as a young batsman of class. On the opening day Williams was splendidly assisted by Cook and Allan Lamb in a free-scoring effort, and Lamb again batted brilliantly in the second innings, narrowly missing a century. Warwickshire's first innings was dominated by Kallicharran, whose not out 170 was his highest score in England. He hit twenty-four 4s in an innings of five and a half hours. In contrast, Whitehouse took nearly as long for his 98, but this pair put on 282 in 91 overs for the third wicket. After so many runs in the first three innings, the home captain, Watts, played safe and set Warwickshire a final target of 348 in three hours. Sarfraz caused a scare with four cheap wickets before Lloyd and Oliver played out time.

Northamptonshire

G. Cook c Ferreira b Clifford	90	– c Smith b Willis	1
I. M. Richards c Lloyd b Perryman	42	– c Ammis b Ferreira	0
R. G. Williams c Humpage b Oliver	109	– not out	151
A. J. Lamb not out	72	– st Humpage b Oliver	93
P. Willey not out	36	– c Perryman b Clifford	9
*P. J. Watts (did not bat)		– not out	29
B 1, l-b 2, w 1, n-b 3	7	B 7, l-b 10, n-b 2	19
1/81 2/241 3/247	(3 wkts) 356	1/0 2/4 3/175 4/228	(4 wkts dec.) 302

†G. Sharp, Sarfraz Nawaz, T. M. Lamb, B. J. Griffiths and L. McFarlane did not bat.

Bowling: *First Innings*—Willis 21–6–70–0; Ferreira 25–4–97–0; Perryman 23–5–72–1; Clifford 18–4–66–1; Oliver 13–2–44–1. *Second Innings*—Willis 15–7–28–1; Ferreira 4–0–10–1; Perryman 21–4–72–0; Oliver 22–4–72–1; Clifford 28–11–60–1; Kallicharran 4–0–18–0; Lloyd 2–0–19–0; Whitehouse 1–0–4–0.

Warwickshire

D. L. Amiss c Sharp c Griffiths	4	– b Sarfraz	7
K. D. Smith c Sharp b Sarfraz	1	– lbw b Sarfraz	2
*J. Whitehouse c Watts b Griffiths	98	– lbw b Griffiths	0
A. I. Kallicharran not out	170	– c A. J. Lamb b Sarfraz	5
T. A. Lloyd not out	7	– not out	41
†G. W. Humpage (did not bat)		– b Sarfraz	3
P. R. Oliver (did not bat)		– not out	22
L-b 12, n-b 19	31	L-b 2, w 1, n-b 3	6
1/6 2/7 3/289	(3 wkts) 311	1/9 2/11 3/16 4/28 5/37	(5 wkts) 86

A. M. Ferreira, R. G. D. Willis, C. C. Clifford and S. P. Perryman did not bat.

Bowling: *First Innings*—Sarfraz 24–10–50–1; Griffiths 24–7–67–2; McFarlane 18–3–60–0; Willey 12–3–28–0; T. M. Lamb 15–5–48–0; Williams 7–1–27–0. *Second Innings*—Sarfraz 15–1–45–4; Griffiths 12–4–11–1; Willey 10–2–10–0; Williams 8–6–4–0; McFarlane 3–1–10–0.

Umpires: A. G. T. Whitehead and D. J. Dennis.

NORTHAMPTONSHIRE v GLOUCESTERSHIRE

Played at Northampton, July 1, 2, 3, 1981

Drawn. Two overseas batsmen of the highest class dominated a high-scoring game which neither side looked like winning. Zaheer, after scoring 1,000 runs in June, began July with a century in each innings for the fifth time in his career, while for Northamptonshire Allan Lamb batted brilliantly for 162 (one 6 and twenty-seven 4s) in 222 minutes and 79. Zaheer's 135 on the second day took 161 minutes and included a 6 and twenty 4s. Gloucestershire declared soon after securing maximum batting points, and with Cook, Williams and Lamb all scoring rapidly in the second innings, Northamptonshire were able to set Gloucestershire a target of 356 in 248 minutes. This Gloucestershire found too much after losing early wickets, but with Zaheer masterly and Bainbridge solid Northamptonshire were denied the possibility of a breakthrough.

Northamptonshire

*G. Cook c Childs b Brain	10	(2) b Childs	84
R. M. Carter lbw b Wilkins	17	(1) c Broad b Brain	0
R. G. Williams c Wilkins b Procter	29	b Childs	80
A. J. Lamb lbw b Graveney	162	c Brain b Bainbridge	79
T. J. Yardley c Bainbridge b Brain	18	lbw b Childs	1
R. M. Tindall b Wilkins	21	b Bainbridge	9
Kapil Dev lbw b Graveney	18	lbw b Brain	43
†G. Sharp st Stovold b Graveney	14	not out	23
D. J. Wild not out	4	not out	12
T. M. Lamb st Stovold b Graveney	0		
B. J. Griffiths b Graveney	8		
B 2, l-b 6, n-b 3	11	B 2, l-b 10, n-b 1	13
1/19 2/42 3/101 4/130 5/178 6/221 7/293 8/300 9/304	312	1/1 2/161 3/180 4/188 5/235 6/307 7/307 (7 wkts dec.)	344

Bowling: *First Innings*—Brain 18–2–74–2; Wilkins 15–4–67–2; Bainbridge 12–2–56–0; Procter 9–3–18–1; Childs 16–4–42–0; Graveney 12.2–5–44–5. *Second Innings*—Brain 14–2–53–2; Wilkins 17–3–58–0; Bainbridge 17–2–47–2; Broad 5–0–32–0; Graveney 21–5–56–0; Childs 21–7–72–3; Procter 1–0–13–0.

Gloucestershire

B. C. Broad c A. J. Lamb b Griffiths	9	lbw b T. M. Lamb	13
Sadiq Mohammad lbw b Kapil Dev	25	lbw b Griffiths	6
†A. W. Stovold b T. M. Lamb	26	b Griffiths	0
Zaheer Abbas not out	135	b Cook	128
A. H. Wilkins c Cook b Kapil Dev	0		
A. J. Hignell lbw b Williams	72	(5) lbw b T. M. Lamb	9
*M. J. Procter c Kapil Dev b T. M. Lamb	10		
P. Bainbridge not out	14	(6) not out	53
L-b 3, n-b 7	10	B 3, l-b 7, n-b 5	15
1/13 2/61 3/67 4/69 5/228 6/265 (6 wkts dec.)	301	1/10 2/11 3/58 4/87 5/224 (5 wkts)	224

D. A. Graveney, B. M. Brain and J. H. Childs did not bat.

Bowling: *First Innings*—Kapil Dev 21–9–81–2; Griffiths 16.3–4–63–1; T. M. Lamb 19–1–68–2; Williams 11–3–43–1; Wild 5–0–36–0. *Second Innings*—Kapil Dev 13–6–39–0; Griffiths 17–6–41–2; T. M. Lamb 13–3–37–2; Williams 11–2–43–0; Carter 2–0–15–0; Wild 5–0–27–0; Cook 1.4–0–7–1.

Umpires: R. S. Herman and B. Leadbeater.

NOTTINGHAMSHIRE

NOTTINGHAMSHIRE v SOMERSET

Played at Nottingham, May 8, 9, 10, 1963

Drawn. Some of the most amazing cricket seen at Trent Bridge for many seasons was crowded into the play on the first morning. After Palmer conceded 23 runs in his first two overs, he returned to the attack when Nottingham were 59 for no wicket and dismissed eight batsmen for 28 runs in 11.5 overs. Bolus again batted well, being top scorer. Somerset went ahead for the loss of four wickets and declared 182 runs on. During the final day Nottinghamshire were saved by a stubborn innings of 72 not out from Winfield and the weather, rain causing five delays. Somerset, deserving more, thus gained only two points.

Nottinghamshire

J. B. Bolus b Palmer	47	– lbw b Alley	10
A. Gill c C. R. M. Atkinson b Palmer	16	– lbw b Rumsey	5
H. M. Winfield c G. Atkinson b Palmer	0	– not out	72
B. Whittingham b Palmer	19	– b Palmer	19
M. Hill c Greetham b Palmer	6	– c Palmer b Greetham	16
C. Forbes b Palmer	0	– b Greetham	13
*†G. Millman b Palmer	25	– c Wight b Greetham	20
K. Gillhouley c Stephenson b Palmer	2	– lbw b Palmer	1
J. Davison c Rumsey b Palmer	18	– b Rumsey	0
J. Cotton not out	12	– not out	4
B. D. Wells c Stephenson b Rumsey	4		
L-b 3, n-b 1	4	B 12, l-b 11, w 1, n-b 3	27
1/59 2/ 59 3/66 4/76 5/88 6/89 7/93 8/125 9/148	153	1/19 2/22 3/82 4/114 5/140 6/166 7/171 8/177	(8 wkts) 187

Bowling: *First Innings*—Rumsey 13.5–2–45–1; Palmer 19–3–57–9; Alley 13–1–47–0. *Second Innings*—Rumsey 23–4–41–2; Palmer 33.3–14–55–2; Alley 26–10–41–1; Greetham 15–5–23–3.

Somerset

G. Atkinson run out	46	K. E. Palmer c and b Forbes	12
B. Roe b Forbes	44	*†H. W. Stephenson c Wells b Forbes	17
R Virgin b Davison	2	L-b 3, n-b 3	6
W. E. Alley c Millman b Wells	39		
P. B. Wight c Gillhouley b Forbes	94	1/82 2/85 3/121 4/153 5/256 6/295 7/335	(7 wkts dec.) 335
C. Greetham not out	75		

C. R. M. Atkinson, B. Langford, F. Rumsey did not bat.

Bowling: Cotton 16–2–51–0; Davison 23–2–82–1; Forbes 27–5–110–4; Wells 13–2–31–1; Gillhouley 14–5–55–0.

Umpires: C. S. Elliott and W. E. Phillipson.

NOTTINGHAMSHIRE v LEICESTERSHIRE

Played at Nottingham, August 18, 19, 20, 1965

Drawn. Inman, the 29-year-old Leicestershire batsman from Colombo, established a world record on the final day by scoring 51 runs in eight minutes, 50 of these in two overs from Hill. Beginning his innings at 199 for three when Nottinghamshire were giving away cheap runs in the hope of a declaration, he took a single off the last ball of an over from Bolus and then hit 18 – 4, 4, 6, 4 – and 32 – 4, 6, 6, 6, 6, 4 – off successive overs from Hill. They were slow inviting deliveries which Inman pulled to, or over, the mid-wicket boundary. The previous record was by Jim Smith of Middlesex who scored fifty in eleven minutes against Gloucestershire at Bristol in 1938. Marner's first innings century for Leicestershire included fourteen 4s before Nottinghamshire won an exciting tussle for the lead thanks to a maiden century by Whittingham which contained ten 4s and took three hours forty minutes. Nottinghamshire were left to make 258 in two and a half hours, a task that proved beyond them, despite good batting by Bolus, Whittingham and Smedley.

Leicestershire

*M. R. Hallam c Millman b Davison	54	– b Corran	22
B. J. Booth c Millman b Corran	20	– b Davison	6
P. Marner c Smedley b Taylor	109	– not out	71
S. Jayasinghe c Millman b Forbes	25	– b Bolus	99
C. C. Inman b Forbes	8	– not out	57
D. Constant not out	45		
J. van Geloven c Hill b Taylor	3		
†R. Julian b Forbes	3		
R. J. Barratt c and b Corran	1		
J. S. Savage not out	9		
L-b 7, w 1, n-b 3	11	L-b 3	3
1/54 2/113 3/172 4/206 5/231 6/244 7/263 8/264	(8 wkts dec.) 288	1/28 2/28 3/199	(3 wkts dec.) 258

J. Cotton did not bat.

Bowling: *First Innings*—Corran 20–4–61–2; Forbes 26–4–79–3; Davison 17–3–40–1; Taylor 21–7–56–2; Gillhouley 17–3–41–0. *Second Innings*—Corran 8–1–28–1; Davison 8–3–26–1; Taylor 6–1–18–0; Gillhouley 5–0–18–0; Whittingham 10–0–44–0; Moore 10–0–44–0; Bolus 8–3–27–1; Hill 2–0–50–0.

Nottinghamshire

N. Hill c and b Cotton	10	– c Julian b Cotton	6
J. B. Bolus c Constant b Barratt	39	– b van Geloven	46
B. Whittingham c Julian b Cotton	126	– c Booth b van Geloven	43
I. Moore c Jayasinghe b Savage	10	– not out	7
M. J. Smedley c Julian b Marner	58	– not out	55
M. Taylor c Jayasinghe b van Geloven	13		
*†G. Millman b Marner	6		
K. Gillhouley not out	9		
A. J. Corran lbw b van Geloven	7		
I. Davison not out	0		
L-b 5, w 2, n-b 4	11	B 3, l-b 4, n-b 2	9
1/14 2/95 3/123 4/249 5/261 6/272 7/274 8/287	(8 wkts dec.) 289	1/14 2/100 3/126	(3 wkts) 166

C. Forbes did not bat.

Bowling: *First Innings*—Cotton 24–2–62–2; Marner 29–6–86–2; van Geloven 24–6–45–2; Savage 21–7–40–1; Barratt 16–1–45–1. *Second Innings*—Cotton 6–0–23–1; Marner 3–0–6–0; van Geloven 10–1–47–2; Savage 12–1–58–0; Barratt 7–1–23–0.

Umpires: J. S. Buller and W. H. Copson.

NOTTINGHAMSHIRE v SOMERSET

Played at Nottingham, May 25, 26, 27, 1966

65 overs. Somerset won by 178 runs. Somerset won the toss but began disastrously losing their first two wickets for 3 runs and a third at 24. G. Atkinson, however, played a sound innings of 59 and Alley, the veteran Australian, provided the sparkle with a dashing innings of 36. His captain, C. R. M. Atkinson, also batted well. Nottinghamshire's early batsmen were not too convincing, half the side being out for 75; Then Swetman and Taylor came together in a useful seventh-wicket partnership of 88. Despite this Nottinghamshire finished 21 runs behind when their allotted overs ran out. Alley was in even more devastating form in the Somerset second innings for having been missed when one, he ran up 115. This, and a useful 54 not out from Palmer, enabled the visitors to declare at 219 for seven. Hill and Bolus put on 37 for Nottinghamshire's opening stand in the second innings but the slow left-arm bowler, Robinson, created havoc by fine bowling on a pitch which was still good and his final figures of seven for 10, the best of his career, resulted in Nottinghamshire collapsing for 62.

Somerset

R. Virgin c Swetman b Johnson	3	– c Swetman b Forbes	26
A. Clarkson c Hill b Davison	0	– c Swetman b Davison	0
M. Kitchen c Swetman b Johnson	7	– lbw b Davison	0
G. Atkinson b Davison	59	– c White b Johnson	1
W. E. Alley c Bolus b Taylor	36	– c Bolus b White	115
*C. R. M. Atkinson c Swetman b Forbes	36	– c Hill b Forbes	0
K. E. Palmer b Davison	6	– not out	54
†G. Clayton c Swetman b Forbes	17	– c White b Gillhouley	0
P. J. Robinson not out	11		
B. A. Langford c Johnson b Forbes	1		
F. E. Rumsey not out	1		
L-b 6, w 1, n-b 5	12	B 9, l-b 7, w 1, n-b 6	23
1/3 2/3 3/24 (9 wkts, 65 overs)	189	1/0 2/0 3/4 (7 wkts dec.)	219
4/68 5/145 6/153 7/175 8/181 9/184		4/75 5/75 6/218 7/219	

Bowling: *First Innings*—Davison 19–4–48–3; Johnson 15–3–50–2; Forbes 19–3–47–3; Taylor 12–6–32–1. *Second Innings*—Davison 12–1–37–2; Johnson 11–2–31–1; Forbes 11–3–36–2; Gillhouley 14.3–1–58–1; Taylor 5–0–15–0; White 5–0–19–1.

Nottinghamshire

*N. Hill c Robinson b Rumsey	12	– c C. R. M. Atkinson b Robinson	22
J. B. Bolus c G. Atkinson b Alley	22	– c Palmer b Langford	18
B. Whittingham c Clayton b Palmer	16	– b Robinson	0
R. A. White lbw b Rumsey	12	– c and b Robinson	4
M. J. Smedley c Alley b Rumsey	5	– c Langford b Robinson	0
†R. Swetman not out	41	– b Robinson	1
M. Taylor c Clayton b Rumsey	48	– b Robinson	1
A. Johnson run out	1	– run out	0
K. Gillhouley not out	0	– c Kitchen b Rumsey	10
C. Forbes (did not bat)		– lbw b Robinson	3
I. Davison (did not bat)		– not out	0
L-b 6, n-b 5	11	B 1, w 1, n-b 2	4
1/30 2/42 3/64 4/69 5/75 6/163 7/167	(7 wkts, 65 overs) 168	1/37 2/41 3/47 4/47 5/47 6/47 7/59 8/59 9/62	62

Bowling: *First Innings*—Rumsey 21–3–44–4; Palmer 18–5–61–1; Alley 26–7–52–1. *Second Innings*—Rumsey 11–3–18–1; Palmer 5–0–19–0; Langford 12–5–11–1; Robinson 17.2–14–10–7.

Umpires: F. Jakeman and W. F. Simpson.

NOTTINGHAMSHIRE v HAMPSHIRE

Played at Nottingham, June 4, 5, 6, 1966

65 overs. Drawn. Nottinghamshire's first county game ever to include Sunday play proved a memorable one, with Hampshire gaining seven points, two for first innings lead and five because the scores finished level with the visitors having five wickets in hand. It was fully half an hour after the game had ended before the result was known because of some doubt about the legitimacy of the run off the last ball which levelled the scores. Horton played the ball a short way along the pitch and then as the bowler went to collect it the batsman in the excitement kicked the ball away and he and Wheatley completed the vital run. It appeared a clear case of obstruction but Bolus, the acting Nottinghamshire captain, later said no appeal had been made against Horton although it appeared as though Swetman, the wicket-keeper, had given a shout. At the time of the incident Nottinghamshire committee members were meeting and their deliberations were suspended until the result had been sorted out.

The fight for first innings lead was also close. The Hampshire last pair were together with the scores level when Shackleton was missed by Parkin at first slip. The unlucky bowler was Davison who in this innings finished with five wickets for 71. In the Nottinghamshire second innings the left-handed Whittingham reached his best score, 133. He batted five hours fifty minutes and hit sixteen 4s. On the Sunday, with admission free, 1/- each was charged for scorecards and with other fund raising activities £178 was taken.

Nottinghamshire

*J. B. Bolus c Reed b White	42	– c Marshall b Cottam	1
B. Whittingham c Livingstone b Shackleton	25	– c Livingstone b Shackleton	13
R. A. White b Shackleton	42	– c White b Wheatley	1
H. I. Moore run out	22	– b Cottam	
M. J. Smedley c Livingstone b Shackleton	5	– c Livingstone b Sainsbury	2
†R. Swetman not out	22	– b Shackleton	
J. Parkin run out	8	– c Marshall b Shackleton	2
M. Taylor c Timms b Cottam	11	– b Sainsbury	
C. Forbes b Cottam	0	– c Timms b Shackleton	
I. Davison (did not bat)		– c Barnard b White	
B. Stead (did not bat)		– not out	
L-b 7, n-b 1	8	B 4, l-b 5	
1/46 2/83 3/128 4/140 5/147 6/159 7/185 8/185	(8 wkts, 65 overs) 185	1/27 2/64 3/77 4/100 5/103 6/162 7/234 8/240 9/240	25

Bowling: *First Innings*—Shackleton 32–7–77–3; White 20–4–54–1; Cottam 13–1–46– *Second Innings*—Shackleton 40–21–52–4; White 19–1–62–1; Cottam 24–7–50–2; Wheatle 24–7–47–1; Sainsbury 25–12–32–2.

Hampshire

*R. E. Marshall c Swetman b Davison	51	– c Bolus b Forbes	2
B. L. Reed c Parkin b Davison	6	– c Taylor b Stead	7
H. Horton c Swetman b Forbes	46	– not out	6
D. A. Livingstone c Taylor b Davison	0	– b Davison	2
H. M. Barnard b Taylor	5	– c Davison b Stead	1
P. J. Sainsbury c Swetman b Forbes	18		
†B. S. V. Timms c Forbes b Davison	19		
K. J. Wheatley c Stead b Forbes	12	– not out	
D. Shackleton not out	14		
D. W. White c Taylor b Davison	10	– c Bolus b Taylor	1
R. M. Cottam not out	8		
L-b 3, n-b 8	11	L-b 3, w 1, n-b 4	
1/19 2/89 3/90 4/112 5/120 6/142 7/166 8/167 9/179	(9 wkts, 65 overs) 200	1/64 2/114 3/163 4/188 5/225	(5 wkts) 23

Bowling: *First Innings*—Davison 23–3–71–5; Stead 11–0–39–0; Taylor 6–1–26–1; Forbe 25–9–53–3. *Second Innings*—Davison 14–1–74–1; Forbes 15–1–65–1; Stead 11–1–60–2; Taylo 7–0–30–1.

Umpires: W. H. Copson and C. G. Pepper.

NOTTINGHAMSHIRE v NORTHAMPTONSHIRE

Played at Nottingham, June 8, 9, 10, 1966

65 overs. Northamptonshire won by 245 runs, Northamptonshire dominated the gam throughout after winning the toss. From the start Milburn attacked the bowling and it too him eighty-two minutes and just seventy-seven deliveries to hit the season's fastest centur to date. He scored 113 of an opening partnership of 157 in thirty-eight scoring strokes, hi major hits being three 6s and eighteen 4s. Prideaux, too, made a century in just unde three hours (one 6, thirteen 4s). At the end of sixty-five overs free hitting Northampton shire had amassed 355 for seven, the highest then achieved in a limited overs game. Moor hit a compact 81 and Smedley 89 not out but at the end of Nottinghamshire's ove allotment they had made 220 for four and were well behind. Prideaux completed a centur for the second time in the match in three hours twenty minutes (eleven 4s) to become th first Northamptonshire player to do so since D. Brookes in 1946, and only the third i their history. After Northamptonshire declared, the accurate left-arm bowling of Scott (five for 30) and the spin of Mushtaq (four for 16) proved too much for Nottinghamshire, who collapsed badly on a pitch still in good order.

Northamptonshire

C. Milburn c Swetman b Davison	113	– b Davison	6
*R. M. Prideaux c Smedley b Taylor	106	– c Bolus b White	100
B. L. Reynolds c Whittingham b Davison	60	– c Swetman b Forbes	67
Mushtaq Mohammad c Smedley b Forbes	29	– c Davison b White	22
P. J. Watts c Swetman b Davison	22	– not out	1
D. S. Steele b Forbes	2	– not out	23
B. Crump not out	9		
H. Sully b Davison	1		
L-b 9, n-b 4	13	B 1, l-b 7, n-b 3	11
1/157 2/262 3/301 4/341 5/342 6/350 7/355 (7 wkts, 65 overs)	355	1/8 2/166 3/192 4/223 (4 wkts dec.)	230

M. E. Scott, †L. A. Johnson and R. Bailey did not bat.

Bowling: *First Innings*—Davison 19–2–96–4; Forbes 21–4–89–2; Stead 11–1–61–0; Taylor 11–0–72–1; White 3–0–24–0. *Second Innings*—Davison 15–2–31–1; Forbes 17–5–42–1; Taylor 24–0–88–0; Stead 11–0–40–0; White 5–0–18–2.

Nottinghamshire

*J. B. Bolus c Johnson b Crump	1	– c Mushtaq b Watts	13
B. Whittingham c Scott b Crump	0	– lbw b Scott	45
R. A. White b Scott	41	– b Scott	16
H. I. Moore c Crump b Bailey	81	– st Johnson b Mushtaq	10
M. J. Smedley not out	89	– c Reynolds b Scott	5
†R. Swetman not out	7	– c Mushtaq b Scott	4
J. Parkin (did not bat)		– c and b Mushtaq	0
M. Taylor (did not bat)		– not out	19
C. Forbes (did not bat)		– b Mushtaq	2
I. Davison (did not bat)		– c Prideaux b Scott	0
B. Stead (did not bat)		– c Milburn b Mushtaq	2
W 1	1	B 2, l-b 2	4
1/1 2/9 3/85 4/169 (4 wkts, 65 overs)	220	1/29 2/70 3/77 4/91 5/95 6/95 7/95 8/98 9/99	120

Bowling: *First Innings*—Crump 18–3–51–2; Bailey 13–0–48–1; Watts 12–0–50–0; Sully 8–0–23–0; Scott 12–3–31–1; Mushtaq 2–0–16–0. *Second Innings*—Crump 13–5–23–0; Bailey 2–0–3–0; Watts 9–1–30–1; Sully 14–4–15–0; Scott 24–13–30–5; Mushtaq 13.4–7–16–4.

NOTTINGHAMSHIRE v GLOUCESTERSHIRE

Played at Nottingham, July 23, 25, 26, 1966

Nottinghamshire won by 88 runs. After winning the toss Nottinghamshire batted so soundly that they were able to declare at 363 for nine wickets, their highest total of the season. Hill and Bolus paved the way with an opening partnership of 115 scored at a fast rate. Both batsmen topped the half century as did Smedley and White later. The fastest scoring of an exhilarating opening day came in the last half hour when White and Forbes added 62 runs. Gloucestershire made a brave reply reaching 294, helped by Milton's 121 in just over four hours. In this innings Nottinghamshire's left-arm slow bowler Gillhouley was taken off after a long consultation between the square-leg umpire Herman and Hill, the Nottinghamshire captain. Bowlers came more into their own in the second innings.

Allen claimed five for 51 with his off-spin and Nottinghamshire were tumbled out for 123, but Gloucestershire fared even worse on the rain-affected pitch and with Forbes taking seven for 31 were routed for 104. A. S. Brown equalled a fielding record by taking seven catches in the Nottinghamshire second innings.

Nottinghamshire

*N. Hill b Smith	50	– c Meyer b Smith	2
J. B. Bolus c Milton b Mortimore	79	– c and b A. S. Brown	15
M. Taylor c Allen b Smith	12	– c A. S. Brown b Allen	10
H. I. Moore c Allen b Smith	0	– c A. S. Brown b Smith	13
M. J. Smedley c D. Brown b Smith	71	– c A. S. Brown b Bissex	38
D. L. Murray c Meyer b Mortimore	30	– c A. S. Brown b Allen	1
R. A. White not out	55	– c A. S. Brown b Allen	9
†R. Swetman c Nicholls b Smith	20	– lbw b Mortimore	0
K. Gillhouley b A. S. Brown	3	– c A. S. Brown b Allen	10
C. Forbes b Windows	33	– not out	10
B. Stead (did not bat)		– lbw b Allen	0
L-b 8, n-b 2	10	B 9, l-b 5, w 1	15
1/115 2/138 3/144 4/145 5/201 6/252 7/296 8/301 9/363	(9 wkts dec.) 363	1/11 2/23 3/39 4/43 5/54 6/86 7/87 8/98 9/116	123

Bowling: *First Innings*—A. S. Brown 23–2–102–1; Smith 27–7–74–5; Windows 22.5–5–91–1; Mortimore 22–8–45–2; Allen 28–13–41–0. *Second Innings*—A. S. Brown 12–2–18–1; Windows 1–0–2–0; Smith 14 –3–22–2; Allen 23–6–51–5; Mortimore 9–2–15–1; Bissex 1–1–0–1.

Gloucestershire

C. A. Milton c Smedley b Taylor	121	– c Taylor b Forbes	0
M. Bissex b Gillhouley	53	– c and b Stead	10
D. Brown c and b Gillhouley	55	– c Taylor b Forbes	4
D. Shepherd c White b Stead	1	– b White	39
R. B. Nicholls lbw b Stead	8	– c Hill b Forbes	2
A. R. Windows b Forbes	19	– c Bolus b Forbes	2
D. A. Allen lbw b Stead	1	– b Forbes	0
*J. B. Mortimore run out	9	– c Gillhouley b White	24
A. S. Brown b Stead	5	– not out	5
†B. J. Meyer lbw b Forbes	8	– c Moore b Forbes	2
D. R. Smith not out	10	– c Murray b Forbes	12
L-b 3, n-b 1	4	B 4	4
1/118 2/225 3/233 4/233 5/244 6/252 7/268 8/272 9/278	294	1/5 2/9 3/17 4/22 5/36 6/36 7/79 8/85 9/88	104

Bowling: *First Innings*—Forbes 34.1–11–63–2; Stead 29–5–79–4; Taylor 21–6–58–1; Gillhouley 16–3–52–2; White 11–3–30–0; Murray 1–0–8–0. *Second Innings*—Forbes 20.2–10–31–7; Stead 4–1–6–1; Taylor 4–1–16–0; White 12–2–47–2.

Umpires: O. W. Herman and H. Mellows.

NOTTINGHAMSHIRE v YORKSHIRE

Played at Worksop, July 27, 28, 29, 1966

Yorkshire won by ten wickets. Yorkshire won the toss and put Nottinghamshire in to bat. Close's gamble looked like succeeding when half the Nottinghamshire wickets fell for 57, but late resistance came from White and Swetman. The Nottinghamshire attack held little terror for Yorkshire as Close was in particularly good form. He reached his third century of the season in three hours ten minutes. When he declared Yorkshire held a first-innings lead of 128 and he was 115 not out. Nottinghamshire began their second innings more confidently, Hill and Bolus putting on 56, but when they were separated the visitors made swift strides towards victory. The left-arm slow bowler Wilson claimed the second hat-trick of his career in dismissing Swetman, Forbes and White. The first time he achieved the feat was also against Nottinghamshire, at Middlesbrough in 1959. On the turning pitch Wilson finished with five wickets for 46 and Illingworth took five for 54.

Nottinghamshire

*N. Hill c Binks b Nicholson	0	– c Sharpe b Illingworth	22
J. B. Bolus b Nicholson	10	– c Nicholson b Wilson	53
M. Taylor lbw b Nicholson	15	– c Close b Illingworth	0
H. I. Moore b Wilson	23	– b Illingworth	1
M. J. Smedley c Close b Wilson	2	– lbw b Illingworth	1
D. L. Murray c Close b Wilson	26	– c Hampshire b Wilson	0
R. A. White c Close b Wilson	48	– c Taylor b Wilson	13
†R. Swetman c Wilson b Trueman	52	– c Nicholson b Wilson	23
C. Forbes b Illingworth	7	– c Close b Wilson	0
B. Stead b Nicholson	4	– not out	1
I. Davison not out	0	– c Taylor b Illingworth	13
B 4, l-b 9, n-b 4	17	B 4, l-b 1, n-b 2	7
1/6 2/19 3/35 4/52 5/57 6/100 7/162 8/194 9/202	204	1/56 2/56 3/61 4/77 5/79 6/79 7/118 8/118 9/119	134

Bowling: *First Innings*—Trueman 16.3–3–33–1; Nicholson 18–7–36–4; Close 3–0–11–0; Wilson 26–8–66–4; Illingworth 25–10–41–1. *Second Innings*—Trueman 4–1–5–0; Nicholson 3–2–5–0; Illingworth 20.4–5–54–5; Wilson 14–4–46–5; Close 7–2–17–0.

Yorkshire

G. Boycott c Swetman b Forbes	25		
K. Taylor c Swetman b Forbes	29	– not out	7
D. E. V. Padgett b Forbes	25		
J. H. Hampshire c Bolus b Davison	6		
*D. B. Close not out	115		
P. J. Sharpe c Smedley b Davison	48		
R. Illingworth lbw b Forbes	9		
F. S. Trueman c Stead b Davison	24		
D. Wilson c Bolus b Davison	29		
†J. G. Binks not out	0	– not out	1
B 5, l-b 9, n-b 8	22	W 1	1
1/58 2/61 3/70 4/111 5/230 6/254 7/285 8/329	(8 wkts dec.) 332		(for no wkt) 9

A. G. Nicholson did not bat.

Bowling: *First Innings*—Davison 31–6–109–4; Stead 11–1–69–0; Forbes 28–11–68–4; Taylor 13–2–37–0; White 13–3–27–0. *Second Innings*—Swetman 2–0–4–0; Bolus 1.3–1–4–0.

Umpires: P. B. Wight and W. F. Price.

NOTTINGHAMSHIRE v GLAMORGAN

Played at Nottingham, July 12, 13, 14, 1967

Drawn. In a tedious game on a good pitch it took the counties fifteen and a half hours to resolve the issue of first-innings lead, which Glamorgan just achieved. Nottinghamshire, batting first, scored a modest total of 288 for five in the six-hour day, despite an attractive stand of 151 between Moore and Murray. Moore, in reaching his second century in seven days, batted four and a half hours for his 115 and hit fourteen 4s. Nottinghamshire altogether batted just over seven and a quarter hours. Glamorgan spent even longer over their runs – just under eight and a quarter hours and Alan Jones carried his bat throughout the innings for the first time in his career, his 166 not out containing twenty-eight 4s. Taylor claimed seven for 106 with his medium-paced deliveries, the best performance of his career. Ironically, in the short time remaining, Hasann hit the season's fastest century at this date in ninety-eight minutes and it included eighteen 4s.

Nottinghamshire

*N. Hill lbw b Wheatley	24		
J. B. Bolus run out	30	– c Evans b Slade	34
H. I. Moore c Slade b I. J. Jones	115	– not out	10
M. J. Smedley b Slade	20		
D. L. Murray c Evans b I. J. Jones	75		
†R. Swetman not out	19		
M. Taylor c Evans b I. J. Jones	0		
S. B. Hassan c Lewis b I. J. Jones	6	– not out	107
P. D. Watts not out	50		
B 6, l-b 6, n-b 6	18	B 4, n-b 1	5
1/49 2/55 3/123 4/274 5/283 6/288 7/297	(7 wkts dec.) 357	1/83	(1 wkt) 156

C. Forbes and B. Stead did not bat.

Bowling: *First Innings*—Wheatley 20–6–47–1; I. J. Jones 22–4–75–4; Walker 22–4–56–0; Cordle 27–7–70–0; Shepherd 30–12–69–0; Slade 7–1–22–1. *Second Innings*—I. J. Jones 5–1–15–0; Walker 2–0–13–0; Cordle 6–1–13–0; Shepherd 1–0–1–0; Slade 7–2–22–1; Hill 2–0–17–0; Rees 4–0–17–0; Lewis 4–0–36–0; A. Jones 2–0–17–0.

Glamorgan

A. Jones not out	166
W. D. Slade c and b Taylor	21
A. Rees b Taylor	12
*A. R. Lewis b Taylor	6
P. M. Walker c Hill b Forbes	81
L. W. Hill c Watts b Taylor	14
A. F. Cordle lbw b Taylor	28
†D. L. Evans c Watts b Taylor	0
D. J. Shepherd b Forbes	3
I. J. Jones c Moore b Taylor	2
O. S. Wheatley b Watts	5
B 9, l-b 13, w 1, n-b 3	26
1/49 2/79 3/90 4/234 5/257 6/319 7/319 8/324 9/359	364

Bowling: Forbes 35–12–114–2; Stead 31–10–57–0; Taylor 50–16–106–7; Watts 21.5–9–46–1; Hassan 6–2–15–0.

Umpires: J. Arnold and L. H. Gray.

NOTES BY THE EDITOR, 1968

SOBERS SIGNS FOR NOTTINGHAMSHIRE

County cricket has taken its biggest step forward in recent years by opening the door to Overseas players through the process of immediate registration. This bold move could be the salvation of the three-day County Championship and I am only surprised that the plunge was not taken sooner. The numerous provisos safeguard the welfare of

English-born players and the very fact that a heavy responsibility will now rest upon the star cricketer should help the promising youngster to take his place in first-class company without the worry that any temporary failure will weigh heavily against his side.

HEADING FOR A TRANSFER SYSTEM?

No county will be allowed to engage a second star within three years of taking on the first and at no time will more than two overseas players be specially registered for the same county, though after five years, under a previous arrangement, a player from another country enters the same category as a home-born man. Hence, the fears that cricket may be heading for a transfer system similar to professional football can be regarded as groundless. Yet when one takes into account all the publicity and the interest that League football gains from the exchange of players is the time so very far distant when cricket will be conducted in similar fashion?

While Yorkshire with their broad acres and vast resources must be admired for their adherence to local talent, the imported player from outside the county border and from overseas is no stranger among the other sixteen counties. Did not Warwickshire win the Championship in 1951 with only C. W. Grove and F. C. Gardner of the regular side born within the county? When Nottinghamshire met Leicestershire at Newark last season half the players who took part in the match were former players of other counties.

One of the reasons why the Advisory Committee retained the two-year qualification rule for so long was because our Test opponents, and Australia in particular, feared the draining of their resources if there was a steady flow of leading stars to the United Kingdom. That state of affairs no longer exists because now a man who is qualifying by residence may at any time play for the country of his birth. Hence, Lance Gibbs, who will assist Warwickshire this summer, was able to play for West Indies in the recent Test series against England.

THE BIG PRIZE

As soon as the way was made clear for the immediate entry of Overseas players in County Cricket the destination of Gary Sobers, the West Indies captain, became the great talking point. Seven counties made inquiries and after a fortnight of speculation Nottinghamshire announced on December 14 their capture of cricket's greatest prize, and that he would captain the side. For the first time in their history Nottinghamshire did not win a match last season and now they look to Sobers to bring back the crowds to Trent Bridge and revive their fortunes. They remember how the Australian all-rounder, Bruce Dooland, rescued them in the early 1950's. They finished sixteenth in 1952, the season before he joined them, and in five seasons in English first-class cricket Dooland scored 5,245 runs and took 805 wickets, twice performing the double. Nottinghamshire soon shot up the Championship table, but on his departure another slump occurred.

SOBERS'S SHEFFIELD SHIELD FEATS

Sobers says that he prefers the challenge of first-class cricket, even though he has enjoyed League cricket with Norton, and he looks forward to putting Nottinghamshire on their feet again. A few years ago Sobers made his presence felt in Australia when he helped South Australia to win the Sheffield Shield for only the second time in twenty-five years. For three years Sobers played for South Australia and in two he achieved the double of 1,000 runs and 50 wickets, adding another record to his name. The financial details of Sobers's contract with Nottinghamshire were not disclosed. It will run for three years and could be worth £7,000 a year, including a flat and a car. One may ask where is the money coming from to pay these expensive stars with county cricket in its present parlous financial state?

NOTTINGHAMSHIRE v WARWICKSHIRE

Played at Nottingham, June 1, 3, 4, 1968

Drawn. This was an astonishing match. Nottinghamshire, on winning the toss, put in the opposition, and on a pitch giving some early assistance to seam bowlers dismissed them for 93, Taylor, medium pace, claiming six wickets for 42 runs. Nottinghamshire, with their West Indians, Murray and Sobers, batting well, built up a lead of 189. Warwickshire began their second innings by losing three wickets for six runs and were in imminent danger of defeat. Kanhai and Ibadulla then came together. Both enjoyed immediate escapes but survived to establish a fourth-wicket partnership of 402 in six and three-quarter hours. This created a new Warwickshire record for any wicket and it was also a record stand for any wicket against Nottinghamshire. Kanhai's massive innings of 253 contained one 6 and thirty-six 4s. Ibadulla hit sixteen 4s in his 147 not out. Warwickshire declared and left Nottinghamshire to get 247 in just under two hours – an impossible task.

Warwickshire

R. W. Barber c Smedley b Taylor	22	– c Frost b Sobers	0
W. J. Stewart c Sobers b Forbes	19	– c Taylor b Forbes	3
D. L. Amiss c Murray b Taylor	10	– lbw b Forbes	1
R. B. Kanhai lbw b Taylor	8	– c Murray b Taylor	253
K. Ibadulla c Sobers b Taylor	8	– not out	147
J. A. Jameson c Hill b Halfyard	2	– not out	12
T. W. Cartwright c Murray b Taylor	3		
*†A. C. Smith c Murray b Halfyard	4		
D. J. Brown c Frost b Taylor	16		
J. D. Bannister c Taylor b Halfyard	0		
L. R. Gibbs not out	0		
N-b 1	1	B 5, l-b 6, n-b 8	19
1/37 2/51 3/58 4/63 5/70 6/70 7/73 8/85 9/93	93	1/0 2/4 3/6 4/408 (4 wkts dec.)	435

Bowling—*First Innings*—Sobers 7–0–11–0; Forbes 11–1–19–1; Taylor 19–7–42–6; Halfyard 14.2–6–20–3. *Second Innings*—Sobers 32–9–87–1; Forbes 29–6–76–2; Taylor 33–10–95–1; Halfyard 32–9–106–0; White 20–7–52–0.

Nottinghamshire

N. Hill c Jameson b Cartwright	13	– not out	53
J. B. Bolus c Gibbs b Brown	23	– c Gibbs b Cartwright	56
H. I. Moore c Smith b Cartwright	1	– c Jameson b Smith	9
M. J. Smedley c Ibadulla b Cartwright	13	– not out	3
*G. S. Sobers c and b Barber	54		
†D. L. Murray c Smith b Cartwright	92		
G. Frost b Barber	4		
M. Taylor c Smith b Gibbs	25		
R. A. White c Barber b Bannister	28		
C. Forbes c Kanhai b Bannister	11		
D. J. Halfyard	10		
B 4, l-b 1, n-b 2, w 1	8	L-b 1, n-b 1	2
1/19 2/27 3/43 4/76 5/130 6/142 7/215 8/233 9/267	282	1/107 2/120 (2 wkts)	123

Bowling: *First Innings*—Brown 18–2–75–1; Bannister 16–7–39–2; Cartwright 35–14–86–4; Gibbs 18–5–42–1; Barber 12–3–32–2. *Second Innings*—Brown 6–1–22–0; Bannister 5–0–25–0; Cartwright 10–0–33–1; Gibbs 10–2–34–0; Amiss 1–0–2–0; Smith 2–0–5–1.

Umpires: A. Jepson and A. Gaskell.

NOTTINGHAMSHIRE v HAMPSHIRE

Played at Nottingham, May 25, 27, 1974

Hampshire won by an innings and 101 runs. Taylor, allowed to depart at the end of the 1972 season by Nottinghamshire, had sweet revenge in this game. The home county, for whom Latchman's 23 not out was the largest contribution, were all out for 98 and the medium-paced Taylor had the remarkable figures of five wickets for 29 runs. Hampshire's reply was based on Richards in his finest vein. He carried his bat during a five-hour stay and his 225 not out contained 140 runs in boundary strokes. Hampshire's total of 344 gave them a lead of 246 and in the most prolific partnership of the innings, 202 for the seventh wicket, Taylor collected 68 and demonstrated his all-round value. Smedley, with 46, enabled Nottinghamshire to fare slightly better in the second innings but Hampshire achieved their overwhelming victory inside two days.

Nottinghamshire

P. A. Todd b Herman	7	– c Jesty b Roberts	14
R. A. White lbw b Roberts	3	– c Stephenson b Herman	14
D. W. Randall lbw b Taylor	9	– c Roberts b Sainsbury	29
G. S. Sobers b Taylor	11	– c Sainsbury b Herman	2
M. J. Smedley lbw b Roberts	9	– b Sainsbury	46
S. B. Hassan c Gilliat b Taylor	18	– b Herman	21
*J. D. Bond c Stephenson b Taylor	1	– c Stephenson b Herman	0
H. C. Latchman not out	23	– lbw b Taylor	4
B. Stead b Roberts	2	– c Gilliat b Taylor	3
P. A. Wilkinson b Taylor	9	– not out	0
†D. A. Pullan b Herman	1	– b Sainsbury	6
L-b 2, n-b 3	5	B 1, w 2, n-b 3	6
1/10 2/10 3/30 4/33 5/46 6/49 7/70 8/78 9/91	98	1/27 2/31 3/37 4/66 5/109 6/109 7/125 8/137 9/139	145

Bowling: *First Innings*—Herman 19–10–22–2; Roberts 18–5–36–3; Taylor 15–4–29–5; Jesty 5–1–6–0; Sainsbury 1–1–0–0. *Second Innings*—Herman 19–7–34–4; Roberts 15–6–39–1; Taylor 11–0–33–2; Jesty 4–2–4–0; Sainsbury 11–6–15–3; Richards 3–0–14–0.

Hampshire

B. A. Richards not out	225
C. G. Greenidge run out	14
D. R. Turner lbw b Sobers	7
*R. M. C. Gilliat lbw b Wilkinson	3
T. E. Jesty c Pullan b Wilkinson	0
R. V. Lewis c Pullan b White	7
P. J. Sainsbury b White	1
M. N. S. Taylor c and b White	68
†G. R. Stephenson c Sobers b White	4
R. S. Herman b Stead	8
A. M. E. Roberts b White	1
B 1, l-b 4, n-b 1	6
1/49 2/74 3/77 4/77 5/105 6/113 7/315 8/319 9/329	344

Bowling: Stead 25.4–5–106–1; Wilkinson 23–8–68–2; Sobers 22–5–55–1; White 17–1–82–5; Latchman 6–0–27–0.

Umpires: C. S. Elliott and D. L. Evans.

NOTTINGHAMSHIRE v SOMERSET

Played at Nottingham, August 7, 8, 9, 1974

Drawn. An interesting game ended in controversy, Nottinghamshire's acting captain Smedley criticising the umpires for reducing the home county's bid to get 17 runs to win to two overs. Despite a valiant effort they fell three runs short of their objective. When the last Somerset second innings wicket fell, three overs of the last 20 remained, but a slight drizzle prevented the umpires from going out immediately and they ruled that only two overs could be bowled. Smedley maintained that the weather was no different than when Somerset were batting. Nottinghamshire, with Harris hitting 96 and Sobers 108, held the upper hand throughout. White, with twelve wickets for 101 in the match, and Sobers, six for 85 dominated Somerset throughout on a rain-affected pitch.

Nottinghamshire

†M. J. Harris b Burgess	96		
P. A. Todd c Kitchen b Moseley	2		
S. B. Hassan c Burgess b Botham	27	– not out	4
G. S. Sobers c Burgess b Jones	108		
*M. J. Smedley lbw b Moseley	17		
D. W. Randall st Taylor b Burgess	28	– not out	7
R. A. White b Burgess	5		
J. D. Birch c Taylor b Moseley	0		
H. C. Latchman not out	8		
B. Stead b Botham	13		
W. Taylor b Botham	0		
B 3, l-b 7, w 1, n-b 7	18	B 2, l-b 1	3
1/4 2/46 3/226 4/257 5/278 6/284 7/285 8/304 9/322	322	(no wkt)	14

Bowling: *First Innings*—Jones 21–6–66–1; Moseley 22–3–59–3; Burgess 26–6–86–3; Botham 19.5–4–61–3; Langford 6–2–32–0. *Second Innings*—Jones 1–0–4–0; Moseley 1–0–7–0.

Somerset

M. J. Kitchen c Latchman b White	56	– b White	9
†D. J. S. Taylor lbw b Stead	43	– b White	14
P. W. Denning c Todd b White	13	– c Birch b White	42
I. V. A. Richards c Randall b White	10	– b Latchman	31
*D. B. Close not out	31	– b Sobers	27
J. M. Parks c Latchman b White	0	– c Sobers b White	17
G. I. Burgess c Latchman b Sobers	0	– c Hassan b White	10
I. T. Botham c Birch b White	0	– c Smedley b Sobers	14
B. A. Langford c Harris b Sobers	0	– c Birch b Sobers	2
H. R. Moseley b Sobers	0	– b White	0
A. A. Jones c Randall b White	6	– not out	0
B 1, l-b 4, n-b 1	6	B 2, l-b 4, n-b 1	7
1/97 2/103 3/116 4/138 5/138 6/143 7/144 8/144 9/144	165	1/42 2/44 3/97 4/137 5/137 6/146 7/171 8/171 9/173	173

Bowling: *First Innings*—Stead 17–4–41–1; Taylor 8–1–21–0; Birch 8–1–30–0; White 30.5–14–41–6; Sobers 19–7–26–3. *Second Innings*—Stead 5–1–6–0; Taylor 4–2–4–0; White 22.2–9–60–6; Sobers 25–8–59–3; Latchman 8–0–37–1.

Umpires: B. J. Meyer and A. G. T. Whitehead.

NOTTINGHAMSHIRE v DERBYSHIRE

Played at Nottingham, August 24, 26, 27, 1974

Drawn. Nottinghamshire lost their opening batsman, Harris, cheaply but the remainder performed solidly. Hassan and Sobers shared a useful partnership and later Smedley and Tunnicliffe took toll of the bowling. Tunnicliffe's 87 was the highest of his first-class career. Rain restricted the second day's play to thirty-eight minutes and although

Derbyshire struggled on a pitch helpful to the slow bowlers a draw always seemed inevitable. White claimed four victims before Derbyshire declared 82 runs behind with two wickets still standing. Nottinghamshire were shocked by losing four second innings wickets for 27 but Smedley took command and when time ran out he was 98 not out. During the lunch interval Sobers, playing his last County Championship game at Trent Bridge, was presented with a silver tankard by the Nottinghamshire president, Frank Gregory. It was inscribed "To Gary Sobers – a great player and a gentleman."

Nottinghamshire

†M. J. Harris c Rowe b Hendrick	14	– c Venkat b Hendrick	9
S. B. Hassan c Rowe b Hendrick	53	– c Cartwright b Hendrick	5
G. S. Sobers c Taylor b Miller	37	– c Swarbrook b Miller	1
*M. J. Smedley c Hendrick b Venkat	55	– not out	98
H. T. Tunnicliffe b Swarbrook	87	– run out	18
R. A. White c Taylor b Miller	22	– c Swarbrook b Rowe	15
J. D. Birch not out	17	– b Miller	3
P. A. Todd not out	5	– c Page b Hendrick	5
H. C. Latchman (did not bat)		– not out	5
L-b 3, n-b 11	14	N-b 8	8
1/36 2/92 3/136 4/193 5/264 6/292	(6 wkts) 304	1/14 2/21 3/24 4/27 5/93 6/125 7/138	(7 wkts) 167

B. Stead and W. Taylor did not bat.

Bowling: *First Innings*—Hendrick 14–4–36–2; Ward 11–2–47–0; Miller 27–9–52–2; Venkataraghavan 28–2–93–1; Swarbrook 20–6–62–1. *Second Innings*—Hendrick 8–0–14–3; Ward 4–0–12–0; Miller 16–5–40–2; Venkataraghavan 13–3–44–0; Swarbrook 9–1–27–0; Rowe 9–3–22–1.

Derbyshire

M. H. Page c Hassan b Latchman	91
F. W. Swarbrook b Stead	1
L. G. Rowe c Harris b Stead	5
H. Cartwright b White	16
*J. B. Bolus c Latchman b White	18
J. M. Ward c Birch b Latchman	5
G. Miller c Latchman b White	12
†R. W. Taylor not out	32
S. Venkataraghavan c Smedley b White	31
L-b 7, w 1, n-b 3	11
1/18 2/30 3/57 4/112 5/121 6/139 7/167	(8 wkts dec.) 222

A. Ward and M. Hendrick did not bat.

Bowling: Stead 16–5–20–2; Taylor 16–4–27–0; Birch 3–1–8–0; White 26.3–9–68–4; Sobers 17–3–51–0; Latchman 14–4–37–2.

Umpires: J. F. Crapp and D. L. Evans.

NOTTINGHAMSHIRE v SOMERSET

Played at Nottingham, July 31, August 2, 3, 1976

Somerset won by six wickets. A high scoring game ended with Somerset meeting the challenge of getting 301 to win in three hours fifty minutes and, indeed, due to the sparkle of Botham, they had 7.1 overs to spare. The Nottinghamshire first innings was dominated by Randall, whose 204 not out was the first double century of his career. His off-driving was immaculate and brought many boundaries. It was the highest championship score by a Nottinghamshire player for 24 years and he figured in century partnerships with Rice, Nanan and Smedley. Somerset battled resolutely in reply and Slocombe with a patient 90 and Botham with a sparkling 80 contributed largely to their total of 304. Harris and

Hassan shone in the Nottinghamshire second innings and when Smedley declared the visitors faced the formidable task of getting 301 to win. Botham responded with a magnificent maiden century and his 167 not out contained six 6s and twenty 4s. Nottinghamshire paid a high price for dropping Botham at slip when he had made 26, for he and Burgess took full toll of a depleted attack to put on 206 together.

Nottinghamshire

S. B. Hassan b Botham	10	– c Taylor b Moseley	48
P. A. Todd c Rose b Gurr	11	– lbw b Gurr	7
D. W. Randall not out	204	– c Taylor b Gurr	0
C. E. B. Rice c Marks b Gurr	50	– c Marks b Botham	13
N. Nanan lbw b Marks	46	– b Gurr	21
*M. J. Smedley not out	30	– c Roebuck b Breakwell	31
†M. J. Harris (did not bat)		– c Taylor b Breakwell	79
R. A. White (did not bat)		– c Roebuck b Close	22
J. D. Birch (did not bat)		– not out	1
P. A. Wilkinson (did not bat)		– c Roebuck b Close	0
B 2, l-b 9, n-b 2	13	B 6, l-b 3, w 4, n-b 5	18
1/14 2/34 3/135 4/261	(4 wkts) 364	1/21 2/21 3/56 4/79 5/107 6/175 7/239 8/239 9/240	(9 wkts dec.) 240

K. Cooper did not bat.

Bowling: *First Innings*—Moseley 19–6–49–0; Gurr 14–2–81–2; Burgess 22–9–76–0; Botham 14–2–59–1; Close 1–0–8–0; Breakwell 20–4–52–0; Marks 10–4–26–1. *Second Innings*—Moseley 18–3–53–1; Gurr 17–3–65–3; Burgess 8–1–29–0; Botham 13–4–16–1; Close 5.1–0–31–2; Breakwell 10–5–28–2.

Somerset

B. C. Rose retired hurt	20		
P. M. Roebuck c Rice b Wilkinson	15	– b Wilkinson	8
P. A. Slocombe c Todd b Wilkinson	90	– c Nanan b Cooper	0
†D. J. S Taylor c Harris b Cooper	6	– not out	3
*D. B. Close c Smedley b Hassan	26	– lbw b Wilkinson	35
I. T. Botham c Nanan b White	80	– not out	167
G. I. Burgess c Rice b Cooper	12	– c sub b White	78
V. J. Marks c Harris b Wilkinson	24		
D. Breakwell c Harris b Wilkinson	0		
H. R. Moseley not out	7		
D. R. Gurr not out	6		
B 4, l-b 12, n-b 2	18	B 1, l-b 8, n-b 2	11
1/19 2/59 3/110 4/234 5/262 6/279 7/281 8/295	(8 wkts) 304	1/2 2/40 3/51 4/257	(4 wkts) 302

Bowling: *First Innings*—Wilkinson 29–8–58–4; Cooper 22–0–74–2; Birch 15–4–61–0; Hassan 8–3–22–1; White 24–5–66–1; Nanan 2–1–5–0. *Second Innings*—Wilkinson 15–2–46–2; Cooper 15–1–82–1; Birch 8–1–41–0; Hassan 8–0–28–0; White 18.5–2–94–1.

Umpires: W. L. Budd and J. F. Crapp.

NOTTINGHAMSHIRE v ESSEX

Played at Nottingham, September 6, 7, 8, 1978

Essex won by nine wickets. Despite the serious inroads of rain, enterprising leadership by both captains produced a decisive result. For Essex, Lilley hit his maiden century on his first-class début. It was late on the first day before a start was possible. Nottinghamshire, helped by an inspiring second-wicket partnership of 138 by Todd and Randall, began well.

The latter, celebrating his selection for Australia, hit a fine 86. After his departure a slump set in, and with eighteen overs of the innings still available Smedley declared at 200 for eight. Essex made their contribution to keeping the game alive by closing their innings 78 behind. In the end Smedley set Essex to chase 222 runs in two and a half hours. Gooch and young Lilley rose to the challenge, putting on 159, and when Gooch was caught behind he was three runs short of his century. Lilley, who scored 43 of the last 63 runs wanted, reached his 100 with four 6s and nine 4s and Essex won with 5.1 overs to spare.

Nottinghamshire

R. E. Dexter lbw b Lever	1	– c Fletcher b East	9
P. A. Todd c Hardie b East	59	– b Acfield	33
D. W. Randall c Gooch b East	86	– b East	0
C. E. B. Rice c Hardie b Acfield	13	– c McEwan b Acfield	3
*M. J. Smedley c Fletcher b East	1	– not out	48
†B. N. French c and b Acfield	1	– c and b East	30
K. S. Mackintosh not out	23	– not out	13
P. J. Hacker c Gooch b East	0		
K. Cooper c Fletcher b Acfield	1		
M. E. Allbrook not out	1		
L-b 7, w 1, n-b 6	14	B 2, l-b 3, n-b 2	7
1/2 2/140 3/167 4/172 5/173 6/177 7/178 8/179	(8 wkts dec.) 200	1/38 2/41 3/43 4/60 5/118	(5 wkts dec.) 143

D. R. Doshi did not bat.

Bowling: *First Innings*—Lever 20–4–50–1; Turner 21–5–52–0; East 24–7–51–4; Acfield 17–6–33–3. *Second Innings*—Lever 7–1–19–0; Turner 6–1–11–0; Acfield 19–3–43–2; East 18.2–3–63–3.

Essex

G. A. Gooch c Todd b Cooper	0	– c French b Mackintosh	97
A. W. Lilley c Rice b Doshi	22	– not out	100
K. S. McEwan c Cooper b Doshi	28	– not out	18
R. E. East c and b Cooper	13		
*K. W. R. Fletcher not out	11		
B. R. Hardie c Smedley b Doshi	6		
K. R. Pont c Rice b Doshi	0		
S. Turner c Smedley b Cooper	3		
†N. Smith not out	32		
B 4, l-b 3	7	B 2, l-b 4, w 1	7
1/0 2/50 3/54 4/65 5/72 6/72 7/75	(7 wkts dec.) 122	1/159	(1 wkt) 222

J. K. Lever and D. L. Acfield did not bat.

Bowling: *First Innings*—Cooper 10–2–55–3; Doshi 15–6–28–4; Allbrook 7–1–18–0; Hacker 1–0–14–0. *Second Innings*—Cooper 6–1–22–0; Hacker 5–0–37–0; Doshi 12–1–67–0; Allbrook 5–1–42–0; Mackintosh 6.5–0–47–1.

Umpires: K. E. Palmer and D. O. Oslear.

NOTTINGHAMSHIRE v LEICESTERSHIRE

Played at Nottingham, May 16, 17, 18, 1979

Drawn. A brilliant century by Randall before lunch on the final day was the highlight of a match punctuated by rain showers. After a useful start to their first innings, in which Todd again looked impressive, Nottinghamshire were bowled out for a modest 184. Although

Davison took the challenge to the Nottinghamshire bowlers, the Hadlee–Rice combination gave the home side a first innings lead of 31, which Randall's century and Harris's supporting 62 swelled. Smedley invited Leicestershire to score 247 in the fourth innings and, although Hadlee took two cheap wickets, the game ended quietly.

Nottinghamshire

P. A. Todd c Tolchard b Clift	45	– lbw b Taylor	0
M. J. Harris c Balderstone b Clift	24	– lbw b Clift	62
D. W. Randall run out	15	– c Tolchard b Agnew	121
C. E. B. Rice c Balderstone b Taylor	25	– c Balderstone b Agnew	8
*M. J. Smedley c and b Taylor	1	– c Tolchard b Taylor	7
H. T. Tunnicliffe lbw b Agnew	23	– c Steele b Clift	3
E. E. Hemmings c Tolchard b Taylor	20	– not out	6
R. J. Hadlee c Balderstone b Agnew	2	– not out	3
†B. N. French not out	11		
M. K. Bore b Clift	6		
K. Cooper b Booth	5		
L-b 5, w 1, n-b 1	7	L-b 4, n-b 1	5
1/52 2/89 3/90 4/91 5/130 6/143 7/153 8/162 9/177	184	1/1 2/174 3/192 4/194 5/202 6/202	(6 wkts dec.) 215

Bowling: *First Innings*—Taylor 20–3–36–3; Agnew 16–5–33–2; Booth 19.3–5–54–1; Clift 28–8–44–3; Birkenshaw 2–0–10–0. *Second Innings*—Taylor 16–4–45–2; Agnew 15–3–54–2; Balderstone 9–0–37–0; Clift 17–4–46–2; Booth 5–0–28–0.

Leicestershire

N. E. Briers c Tunnicliffe b Cooper	5	– c Todd b Hadlee	1
J. F. Steele b Cooper	21	– b Hadlee	13
J. C. Balderstone b Hemmings	14	– not out	14
B. F. Davison b Hadlee	44	– c Hemmings b Tunnicliffe	32
D. I. Gower c and b Hadlee	13	– not out	6
*†R. W. Tolchard c Tunnicliffe b Hadlee	5		
P. B. Clift c French b Rice	16		
J. Birkenshaw lbw b Hemmings	3		
P. Booth c Smedley b Rice	20		
J. P. Agnew c French b Rice	9		
L. B. Taylor not out	1		
B 2	2	L-b 2	2
1/26 2/27 3/84 4/84 5/102 6/102 7/121 8/131 9/150	153	1/1 2/14 3/58	(3 wkts) 68

Bowling: *First Innings*—Hadlee 15–3–53–3; Rice 16.4–6–33–3; Cooper 9–0–30–2; Hemmings 23–10–30–2; Bore 4–2–5–0. *Second Innings*—Hadlee 11–8–12–2; Rice 6–1–13–0; Cooper 3–0–6–0; Hemmings 9–2–26–0; Tunnicliffe 5–3–9–1.

Umpires: H. D. Bird and D. Shackleton.

NOTTINGHAMSHIRE v NORTHAMPTONSHIRE

Played at Nottingham, June 20, 21, 22, 1979

Nottinghamshire won by seven wickets. In a match of four centuries, Harris's twin efforts for Nottinghamshire gave them their second successive Championship victory. Williams' maiden century for Northamptonshire – he shared in a stand of 171 with Lamb – was followed by a painstaking 133 not out by Harris, who batted all through the second day as Nottinghamshire finished 41 behind on the first innings. On a placid wicket which continued to encourage stroke-making. Lamb's 118 not out enabled Watts to declare, leaving Nottinghamshire to score 256 in two and a half hours. Harris – scoring two centuries in a match for the third time in his career – took up the challenge along with Todd and Rice. Although 13 were still needed off the last two overs. Birch hit a straight 6 and followed up with another boundary as Nottinghamshire got home with three balls to spare.

Northamptonshire

G. Cook c Birch b Tunnicliffe	16	– b Bore	77
I. M. Richards c French b Tunnicliffe	25	– b Cooper	6
R. G. Williams not out	103	– b Watson	2
A. J. Lamb b Hemmings	94	– not out	118
P. Willey c Tunnicliffe b Hemmings	31	– not out	7
T. J. Yardley b Bore	4		
*P. J. Watts b Bore	3		
R. M. Carter b Bore	0		
†G. Sharp b Bore	2		
B 4, l-b 8, w 2, n-b 4	18	L-b 3, n-b 1	4
1/46 2/52 3/223 4/279 5/284 6/294 7/296 8/296	(8 wkts) 296	1/16 2/21 3/184	(3 wkts dec.) 214

A. Hodgson and L. McFarlane did not bat.

Bowling: *First Innings*—Rice 9–2–26–0; Watson 12–2–46–0; Cooper 9–2–44–0; Tunnicliffe 11–4–37–2; Hemmings 33–12–68–2; Bore 26–6–57–4. *Second Innings*—Rice 6–2–20–0; Watson 6–2–13–1; Cooper 4.4–1–14–1; Tunnicliffe 3–1–12–0; Bore 22–4–78–1; Hemmings 21–3–73–0.

Nottinghamshire

M. J. Harris not out	133	– b Watts	132
P. A. Todd c Sharp b Hodgson	10	– c Yardley b Williams	51
*M. J. Smedley c Sharp b Carter	5		
C. E. B. Rice b Williams	63	– c Cook b Watts	53
J. D. Birch c Willey b Williams	8	– not out	10
H. T. Tunnicliffe c and b McFarlane	10	– not out	2
E. E. Hemmings c Watts b Hodgson	4		
†B. N. French not out	16		
L-b 2, w 4	6	B 1, l-b 6, w 2, n-b 1	10
1/25 2/38 3/162 4/178 5/204 6/209	(6 wkts) 255	1/121 2/245 3/246	(3 wkts) 258

W. K. Watson, M. K. Bore and K. Cooper did not bat.

Bowling: *First Innings*—McFarlane 19–2–62–1; Hodgson 23–5–60–2; Willey 23–6–47–0; Carter 9–5–18–1; Watts 6–1–23–0; Williams 20–7–39–2. *Second Innings*—Hodgson 6.3–0–45–0; McFarlane 10–2–41–0; Willey 15–1–75–0; Carter 4–0–23–0; Williams 9–0–54–1; Watts 2–0–10–2.

Umpires: C. T. Spencer and J. van Geloven.

NOTTINGHAMSHIRE v WORCESTERSHIRE

Played at Nottingham, July 7, 9, 10, 1979

Worcestershire won by 49 runs. Put in to bat by Smedley, the visitors were in control from the first day. Highlight of Worcestershire's first innings was a career-best 221 not out by Younis, who, with Ormrod, added 281 and broke a 48-year-old record for the county's fourth wicket. On a wicket that never really assisted the bowlers Nottinghamshire were left to chase 327 for victory in four and a half hours after Gifford declared. With Rice,

Randall and Tunnicliffe keeping Nottinghamshire in touch with the asking-rate, the game was delicately balanced before Gifford and Patel broke through at crucial stages to secure victory for Worcestershire.

Worcestershire

G. M. Turner c Smedley b Hadlee	0	– c sub b Bore	60
J. A. Ormrod c Randall b Hadlee	107	– c and b Hemmings	71
P. A. Neale lbw b Rice	2	– c Curzon b Bore	2
E. J. O. Hemsley c Smedley b Hacker	3	– c Harris b Bore	35
Younis Ahmed not out	221	– not out	39
D. N. Patel b Hemmings	5	– not out	5
†D. J. Humphries c sub b Hemmings	10	– st Curzon b Hemmings	3
G. G. Watson not out	18		
B 5, l-b 4, w 9, n-b 2	20	B 6, l-b 2, w 4	12
1/8 2/28 3/41 4/322 5/332 6/354	(6 wkts) 386	1/136 2/143 3/145 4/209 5/213	(5 wkts dec.) 227

J. D. Inchmore, *N. Gifford and J. Cumbes did not bat.

Bowling: *First Innings*—Hadlee 19–5–47–2; Rice 14–5–36–1; Hacker 11–1–54–1; Bore 28–3–119–0. Tunnicliffe 8–0–45–0; Hemmings 20–4–65–2. *Second Innings*—Hadlee 6–0–20–0; Rice 4–1–11–0; Bore 32–5–102–3; Hemmings 31–2–82–2.

Nottinghamshire

M. J. Harris c Turner b Patel	94	– c Younis b Gifford	25
*M. J. Smedley c Humphries b Watson	15	– c sub b Watson	10
D. W. Randall c Humphries b Gifford	42	– c Hemsley b Patel	75
C. E. B. Rice run out	59	– c Hemsley b Gifford	78
H. T. Tunnicliffe not out	26	– run out	39
E. E. Hemmings c Hemsley b Gifford	26	– b Patel	13
R. J. Hadlee c Patel b Gifford	9	– c Turner b Gifford	15
†C. C. Curzon not out	1	– c Hemsley b Patel	7
P. A. Todd (did not bat)		– c Neale b Gifford	6
P. J. Hacker (did not bat)		– not out	0
M. K. Bore (did not bat)		– lbw b Patel	0
B 1, l-b 10, n-b 4	15	B 3, l-b 6	9
1/25 2/128 3/222 4/222 5/266 6/281	(6 wkts) 287	1/27 2/49 3/139 4/222 5/246 6/248 7/258 8/277 9/277	277

Bowling: *First Innings*—Watson 21–3–47–1; Cumbes 24–2–74–0; Patel 17–3–58–1; Gifford 38–12–93–3. *Second Innings*—Watson 9–2–26–1; Cumbes 24–2–77–0; Gifford 39–6–94–4; Patel 20.2–3–71–4.

Umpires: B. J. Meyer and C. T. Spencer.

NOTTINGHAMSHIRE v YORKSHIRE

Played at Worksop, July 25, 26, 27, 1979

Nottinghamshire won by eight wickets. Not even six hours of Boycott defiance could stop Nottinghamshire completing another victory and so moving into second place on the Championship table. Nottinghamshire, led by Rice for the first time, dominated the first day with some aggressive stroke-play, particularly from Birch who hit his best score, 94. His innings included five 6s – three of them off the hapless Cope on his return to the Yorkshire side. Yorkshire lost their first four wickets for 6 runs against an attack spearheaded by Watson, and although the middle-order effected a recovery they were forced to follow-on 212 runs behind. It was a situation really made for Boycott, who batted four and a quarter hours for his third century in successive matches. He carried his bat for the first time for a magnificent 175 that left Nottinghamshire to get 149 for victory. Randall's not out 53 made sure there were no slips.

Nottinghamshire

M. J. Harris c Old b Stevenson	64	– b Cope	27
P. A. Todd lbw b Old	73	– lbw b Old	22
D. W. Randall c Bairstow b Stevenson	27	– not out	53
*C. E. B. Rice c Hampshire b Old	30		
H. T. Tunnicliffe c Sharp b Stevenson	62	– not out	35
J. D. Birch not out	94		
E. E. Hemmings b Stevenson	3		
L-b 7, w 1, n-b 10	18	L-b 8, w 1, n-b 3	12
1/102 2/163 3/200 4/216 5/365 6/371	(6 wkts dec.) 371	1/36 2/77	(2 wkts) 149

†B. N. French, W. K. Watson, P. J. Hacker and M. K. Bore did not bat.

Bowling: *First Innings*—Old 26–4–84–2; Stevenson 25.5–2–98–4; Oldham 18–3–51–0; Carrick 7–0–43–0; Cope 23–5–77–0. *Second Innings*—Old 9–2–31–1; Stevenson 6–0–23–0; Carrick 19.3–6–37–0; Cope 14–1–46–1.

Yorkshire

R. G. Lumb b Watson	1	– run out	10
G. Boycott c Harris b Watson	2	– not out	175
G. A. Cope c Randall b Rice	0	– lbw b Rice	0
C. W. J. Athey c and b Watson	1	– c French b Hemmings	4
*J. H. Hampshire c Todd b Watson	35	– c and b Bore	29
K. Sharp lbw b Rice	5	– lbw b Rice	33
†D. L. Bairstow c Tunnicliffe b Hemmings	36	– b Tunnicliffe	61
P. Carrick c Tunnicliffe b Hemmings	38	– c Randall b Hemmings	0
G. B. Stevenson b Rice	16	– c Watson b Hemmings	12
C. M. Old not out	14	– c French b Watson	20
S. Oldham c and b Hemmings	2	– c Birch b Watson	0
B 4, l-b 2, n-b 3	9	B 7, l-b 1, w 2, n-b 6	16
1/2 2/5 3/5 4/6 5/26 6/66 7/105 8/138 9/138	159	1/47 2/57 3/90 4/159 5/159 6/303 7/304 8/323 9/360	360

Bowling: *First Innings*—Rice 16–7–42–3; Watson 13–5–31–4; Hacker 4–0–30–0; Tunnicliffe 5–2–15–0; Hemmings 15.1–7–18–3; Bore 3–0–14–0. *Second Innings*—Rice 22–12–37–2; Watson 17.5–5–73–2; Hacker 6–0–54–0; Tunnicliffe 14–5–25–1; Hemmings 36–11–119–3; Bore 12–3–36–1.

Umpires: R. Palmer and H. D. Bird.

NOTTINGHAMSHIRE v MIDDLESEX

Played at Nottingham, September 5, 6, 7, 1979

Drawn. Although the game ended early in bad light on the final day, enough cricket was played during the three days for Randall to stamp an historic mark on the proceedings. In what had been a fairly moderate season for him, he signed off with a double century and a century – the first time the feat had ever been achieved at Trent Bridge, and Randall became only the seventeenth player of all time to accomplish it. He scored 209, including thirty boundaries, in five and a half hours in the first innings, and only commendable bowling by Selvey could restrict him. After Barlow had completed a fluent century – his first Championship hundred of the season – for Middlesex, Randall's 146 took Nottinghamshire towards their declaration. Although Middlesex lost both openers, there was never really any chance of them getting 294 to win in two and three-quarter hours.

Nottinghamshire

M. J. Harris c Fisher b Selvey	0	not out	58
D. W. Randall c Tomlins b Edmonds	209	st Fisher b Emburey	146
H. T. Tunnicliffe lbw b Selvey	26	not out	24
*C. E. B. Rice lbw b Selvey	0		
J. D. Birch b Emburey	42		
R. T. Robinson run out	28	c Edmonds b Jones	40
†B. N. French c Fisher b Selvey	3		
E. E. Hemmings c Gatting b Selvey	29		
W. K. Watson not out	5		
K. Cooper not out	11		
B 4, l-b 7, n-b 12	23	B 4, l-b 6, w 1	11
1/0 2/70 3/70 4/198 5/272 6/294 7/356 8/359	(8 wkts) 376	1/107 2/249	(2 wkts dec.) 279

M. K. Bore did not bat.

Bowling: *First Innings:*—Selvey 28–3–109–5; Jones 13.2–2–50–0; Gatting 7.4–0–42–0; Edmonds 30–7–85–1; Tomlins 2–0–13–0; Emburey 19–4–54–1. *Second Innings*—Selvey 22–7–52–0; Jones 30–4–93–1; Emburey 23–6–65–1; Edmonds 14–4–49–0; Smith 1–0–9–0.

Middlesex

M. J. Smith lbw b Rice	18	c Tunnicliffe b Watson	0
W. N. Slack c French b Watson	66	c and b Hemmings	28
*C. T. Radley c French b Watson	5	not out	1
G. D. Barlow c Cooper b Bore	133	not out	60
M. W. Gatting c Rice b Bore	56		
K. P. Tomlins c Cooper b Bore	4		
P. H. Edmonds not out	41		
J. E. Emburey b Rice	24		
L-b 10, w 1, n-b 4	15	B 4, l-b 6, w 1, n-b 1	12
1/26 2/35 3/204 4/252 5/269 6/321 7/362	(7 wkts dec) 362	1/0 2/68	(2 wkts) 101

M. W. W. Selvey, †P. B. Fisher and A. A. Jones did not bat.

Bowling: *First Innings*—Rice 22.4–4–85–2; Watson 27–12–57–2; Cooper 9–2–36–0; Bore 19–1–74–3; Hemmings 18–3–80–0; Tunnicliffe 4–0–15–0. *Second Innings*—Watson 7–1–26–1; Rice 9–5–14–0; Bore 6–1–17–0; Hemmings 5–1–12–1; Cooper 4–1–20–0.

Umpires: D. O. Oslear and R. Aspinall.

NOTTINGHAMSHIRE v SOMERSET

Played at Nottingham, July 9, 10, 11, 1980

Drawn. Both sides were considerably weakened – Somerset by Test calls and Nottinghamshire by injuries – but, although the game ended disappointingly, it produced some intriguing cricket. Nottinghamshire captain Rice made the most of the amiable pitch, hitting two centuries, and the dashing stroke-play of Randall as well as the calm assurance of Robinson, who hit a career-best 92, were other pleasing features of the home county's batting. Somerset's outstanding performer was Denning (three 6s and eighteen 4s) who, with his side in some trouble, produced a superb career-best 184 in four hours seven minutes to give the visitors a first innings lead. When Nottinghamshire set Somerset a target of 266 in eighty minutes plus the statutory twenty overs, a draw was inevitable.

Nottinghamshire

B. Hassan c Taylor b Dredge	4	– c Taylor b Moseley	0
R. T. Robinson c Dredge b Moseley	35	– c Roebuck b Marks	92
D. W. Randall b Moseley	63	– c Gavaskar b Breakwell	86
*C. E. B. Rice not out	131	– not out	114
J. D. Birch lbw b Dredge	4	– not out	15
M. J. Harris c Roebuck b Breakwell	19		
†B. N. French b Moseley	0		
E. E. Hemmings lbw b Moseley	15		
W. K. Watson lbw b Dredge	6		
P. J. Hacker not out	7		
B 2, l-b 20, w 1, n-b 5	28	B 1, l-b 4, n-b 3	8
1/5 2/92 3/127 4/141 5/216 6/219 7/247 8/274	(8 wkts dec.) 312	1/0 2/129 3/267	(3 wkts dec.) 315

M. K. Bore did not bat.

Bowling: *First Innings*—Moseley 30–6–65–4; Dredge 26–3–83–3; Popplewell 30–6–78–0; Marks 5–0–23–0; Breakwell 8–1–35–1. *Second Innings*—Moseley 12–2–29–1; Dredge 8–3–30–0; Popplewell 3–0–14–0; Marks 28–7–98–1; Breakwell 28–4–106–1; Gavaskar 4–0–19–0; Roebuck 1–0–5–0; Slocombe 1–0–6–0.

Somerset

S. M. Gavaskar c French b Watson	3	– c Randall b Hacker	0
M. Olive c Robinson b Bore	6		
P. M. Roebuck c French b Hacker	2	– not out	34
P. W. Denning c Hassan b Hemmings	184	– (2) c Hemmings b Hacker	34
P. A. Slocombe c Harris b Watson	4	– not out	3
*V. J. Marks c Robinson b Watson	82	– (4) c Hemmings b Hacker	11
†D. J. S. Taylor not out	57		
N. F. M. Popplewell not out	18		
L-b 3, n-b 3	6	L-b 2	2
1/3 2/7 3/62 4/67 5/232 6/319	(6 wkts dec.) 362	1/0 2/61 3/79	(3 wkts) 84

D. Breakwell, C. H. Dredge and H. R. Moseley did not bat.

Bowling: *First Innings*—Hacker 20–2–88–1; Watson 21–3–86–3; Bore 27–7–73–1; Hemmings 25.3–5–109–1. *Second Innings*—Hacker 9.3–1–33–3; Watson 5–0–40–0; Bore 4–0–9–0.

Umpires: R. Julian and T. W. Spencer.

NOTTINGHAMSHIRE v DERBYSHIRE

Played at Nottingham, August 29, 31, September 1, 1981

Nottinghamshire won by nine wickets. Career-best match figures of thirteen for 129 by Hemmings spun Nottinghamshire to victory after Derbyshire had held their own for the first two days. After being put in, Derbyshire looked set for prosperity at 117 for one, Hill going on to 79 after being dropped when 0, but the innings folded once Hemmings found some turn. Tunnicliffe and Steele shared nine wickets to curb Nottinghamshire's run-making, but an unbeaten 62 by Birch brought a third batting point and a lead of 57, which was wiped out by Wood and Hill before the close of the second day. However, from 67 without loss, Derbyshire capitulated again to Hemmings, only Steele offering any real application and Tunnicliffe any aggression once Wood had departed. Left to get 90 for victory, Nottinghamshire did so for the loss of Todd, the irrepressible Randall and Robinson knocking off the winning runs with the innings only fifty-nine minutes old.

Derbyshire

*B. Wood b Rice	34	– (2) c Birch b Hemmings	43
A. Hill c and b Hemmings	79	– (1) c Hassan b Hemmings	17
P. N. Kirsten c Robinson b Bore	36	– c French b Rice	3
D. S. Steele b Hemmings	10	– c Hassan b Hemmings	27
G. Miller c Robinson b Hemmings	6	– c French b Cooper	3
K. J. Barnett c Randall b Hadlee	18	– c Rice b Hemmings	1
I. S. Anderson c French b Hemmings	0	– c French b Hemmings	6
†R. W. Taylor b Hemmings	2	– lbw b Hemmings	13
C. J. Tunnicliffe b Hemmings	0	– (10) not out	17
P. G. Newman b Hemmings	5	– (11) c Hassan b Rice	3
D. G. Moir not out	6	– (9) c Birch b Rice	4
B 4, l-b 3, w 1, n-b 4	12	B 4, l-b 2, w 1, n-b 2	9
1/55 2/117 3/139 4/169 5/179 6/183 7/197 8/197 9/198	208	1/67 2/70 3/70 4/88 5/95 6/105 7/118 8/123 9/141	146

Bowling: *First Innings*—Hadlee 31–11–57–1; Rice 14–3–33–1; Cooper 10–2–21–0; Hemmings 34.4–16–59–7; Bore 14–6–26–1. *Second Innings*—Hadlee 10–2–21–0; Rice 20–11–22–3; Hemmings 36–10–70–6; Bore 9–5–14–0; Cooper 6–2–10–1.

Nottinghamshire

P. A. Todd c Taylor b Steele	1	– c Tunnicliffe b Moir	11
R. T. Robinson b Newman	38	– not out	30
†B. N. French lbw b Steele	24		
D. W. Randall b Tunnicliffe	42	– (3) not out	47
B. Hassan b Steele	29		
*C. E. B. Rice lbw b Tunnicliffe	8		
J. D. Birch not out	62		
R. J. Hadlee c Taylor b Tunnicliffe	12		
E. E. Hemmings c Taylor b Steele	4		
K. E. Cooper c Steele b Tunnicliffe	20		
M. K. Bore c Anderson b Tunnicliffe	5		
B 11, n-b 9	20	L-b 1, n-b 1	2
1/4 2/52 3/104 4/117 5/125 6/165 7/188 8/206 9/256	265	1/20 (1 wkt)	90

Bowling: *First Innings*—Tunnicliffe 21.3–2–75–5; Newman 23–5–59–1; Steele 18–5–37–4; Wood 8–2–15–0; Moir 11–3–34–0; Miller 9–1–25–0. *Second Innings*—Tunnicliffe 1–0–10–0; Newman 1–0–5–0; Steele 7–1–33–0; Moir 6.2–1–20–1; Miller 3–0–20–0.

Umpires: P. J. Eele and R. Palmer.

SOMERSET

SOMERSET v WORCESTERSHIRE

Played at Yeovil, August 20, 22, 23, 1966

Worcestershire won by eight wickets. A notable all-round performance by Horton, who made 84 and 55 not out, as well as taking five wickets for 74 in 42 overs followed a decisive first-innings spell of six for 28 by Gifford which gave the champions an easy victory with ninety-five minutes to spare. The pitch was never entirely reliable. Horton, third out at 160, hit eleven 4s, while putting his side on the way to a large score. Langford, however, with a remarkable spell of six for 8 in 57 deliveries restricted the first-innings lead to 83. Next an opening partnership of 53 between Virgin and G. Atkinson, suggested that Somerset would make a fight but Horton took four wickets and altered things again. Clayton, Palmer and Robinson fought sternly to pose a task of 121 in nearly four hours. Fearnley was out immediately, but Kenyon and Ormrod provided excellent assistance for Horton, who hit seven boundaries in his 55 not out which occupied two and a quarter hours.

Somerset

G. Atkinson c Booth b Gifford	19	– c Headley b Horton	16
R. Virgin c Ormrod b Coldwell	13	– lbw b Gifford	40
M. Kitchen run out	23	– c Ormrod b Horton	16
G. Burgess c Ormrod b Gifford	12	– c and b Horton	10
W. E. Alley b Gifford	0	– st Booth b Horton	24
*C. R. M. Atkinson b Horton	11	– c and b Gifford	8
K. E. Palmer c Ormrod b Gifford	5	– c Booth b Brain	33
†G. Clayton c Horton b Gifford	0	– c Headley b Coldwell	28
P. J. Robinson not out	13	– b Coldwell	18
B. A. Langford lbw b Gifford	6	– b Brain	0
F. E. Rumsey b Brain	5	– not out	1
B 1, l-b 2	3	B 4, l-b 4, n-b 1	9
1/25 2/40 3/66 4/66 5/70 6/83 7/85 8/85 9/103	110	1/53 2/77 3/77 4/100 5/111 6/125 7/167 8/195 9/197	203

Bowling: *First Innings*—Coldwell 11–7–10–1; Brain 11–3–21–1; Carter 7–1–25–0; Gifford 25–13–28–6; Horton 18–7–23–1. *Second Innings*—Coldwell 24.5–11–41–2; Brain 13–4–27–2; Carter 5–0–6–0; Gifford 33–15–69–2; Horton 24–10–51–4.

Worcestershire

M. J. Horton b Alley	84	– not out	55
C. D. Fearnley b Rumsey	32	– c Kitchen b Palmer	2
*D. Kenyon b Rumsey	24	– c Virgin b Alley	29
J. A. Ormrod c Kitchen b Langford	23	– not out	24
R. G. A. Headley c Virgin b Langford	9		
D. W. Richardson c Virgin b Langford	0		
†R. Booth c Burgess b Langford	12		
N. Gifford lbw b Langford	1		
L. J. Coldwell not out	1		
B. M. Brain b Alley	0		
R. G. M. Carter b Langford	0		
L-b 6, n-b 1	7	B 4, l-b 4, n-b 4	12
1/75 2/114 3/160 4/174 5/174 6/177 7/187 8/192 9/192	193	1/2 2/61	(2 wkts) 122

Bowling: *First Innings*—Rumsey 21–3–49–2; Palmer 11–3–33–0; Alley 21–7–27–2; Langford 27.4–13–43–6; Robinson 12–2–34–0. *Second Innings*—Rumsey 10–2–20–0; Palmer 8–0–36–1; Alley 6–2–8–1; Langford 11–2–32–0; Robinson 4–3–1–0; Burgess 2.4–0–13–0.

Umpires: J. Arnold and A. E. Fagg.

SOMERSET v NORTHAMPTONSHIRE

Played at Taunton, May 19, 20, 21, 1968

Somerset won by four wickets with one over left. Prideaux, with 174 runs in the match, and Kitchen, who carried his bat in the first innings and compiled 207 for once out, were the batting heroes as the match fluctuated vividly on a good pitch. Kitchen's 161 not out rescued Somerset from complete collapse at 31 for five. Kettle, swinging the ball late on a cloudy Monday morning, took four wickets for five runs in fifteen deliveries. Altogether Kitchen batted five and a half hours and hit twenty-seven 4s as Somerset led by 83 runs. Willey, going in first, gave Northamptonshire a brisk start in their second innings, and once again Prideaux was very confident until brilliantly caught. Ackerman's first Championship 50 included four 6s and seven 4s, while Mushtaq's 82 not out occupied only two hours. Somerset, set to get 208 in two and a quarter hours, began well and their progress was maintained. Somerset needed 119 runs from the last 20 overs and when Palmer and Alley came together 40 was required off eight overs. Each hit one 6, and amid great excitement, Palmer struck Durose for 4 over the covers for the winning hit. The final day brought twelve wickets, 459 runs and ten 6s.

Northamptonshire

*R. M. Prideaux run out	95	– c Robinson b Langford	79
B. L. Reynolds lbw b Rumsey	5	– c and b Robinson	24
D. S. Steele b Palmer	7	– c and b Robinson	0
H. M. Ackerman lbw b Palmer	18	– c Brooks b Robinson	67
Mushtaq Mohammad c Brooks b Palmer	2	– not out	82
P. Willey run out	42	– c Brooks b Chappell	26
M. K. Kettle c Burgess b Robinson	11	– c Burgess b Robinson	1
M. E. Scott not out	5	– c Chappell b Langford	4
†L. A. Johnson lbw b Rumsey	7	– not out	4
A. J. Durose b Rumsey	0		
H. Sully lbw b Langford	7		
L-b 5	5	L-b 2, n-b 1	3
1/37 2/49 3/73 4/75 5/159 6/184 7/187 8/197 9/197	204	1/42 2/102 3/154 4/238 5/246 6/250 7/260	(7 wkts dec.) 290

Bowling: *First Innings*—Rumsey 15–0–58–3; Palmer 18–3–53–3; Alley 19–8–37–0; Langford 15–8–16–1; Chappell 5–0–28–0; Robinson 4–1–7–1. *Second Innings*—Rumsey 6–2–17–0; Palmer 11–5–37–0; Alley 2–1–1–0; Langford 36–14–84–2; Chappell 9–1–33–1; Robinson 27–6–79–4; Burgess 10–1–36–0.

Somerset

R. Virgin c Johnson b Durose	5	– lbw b Durose	18
M. Kitchen not out	161	– c Durose b Sully	46
G. Burgess b Kettle	0	– run out	49
T. I. Barwell c Johnson b Kettle	4	– st Johnson b Steele	32
G. S. Chappell b Kettle	0	– c Johnson b Durose	7
W. E. Alley b Kettle	0	– not out	23
P. J. Robinson lbw b Mushtaq	29		
R. Palmer lbw b Scott	32	– not out	20
*B. A. Langford c Steele b Durose	1	– b Steele	0
†R. A. Brooks c Durose b Scott	37		
F. E. Rumsey b Steele	0		
B 1, l-b 8, n-b 9	18	B 2, l-b 9, w 1, n-b 4	16
1/5 2/23 3/31 4/31 5/31 6/111 7/170 8/177 9/285	287	1/38 2/81 3/128 4/128 5/164 6/168	(6 wkts) 211

Bowling: *First Innings*—Kettle 24–3–67–4; Durose 20–6–60–2; Willey 6–3–6–0; Mushtaq 21–4–68–1; Sully 22–11–48–0; Scott 9–4–18–2; Steele 1.3–0–2–1. *Second Innings*—Kettle 6–0–29–0; Durose 11–2–32–2; Mushtaq 1–0–16–0; Sully 8–2–46–1; Scott 11–1–32–0; Steele 6–0–40–2.

Umpires: G. H. Pope and P. B. Wight.

SOMERSET v LANCASHIRE

Played at Weston-super-Mare, July 31, August 1, 2, 1968

Lancashire won by 11 runs. In a tense finish, the match ended with the last ball before lunch of the final day. On Wednesday the Somerset opening bowlers failed to make use of a dry, lively pitch, Wood playing finely for three hours. Engineer hit well and the tail established a good position. Rumsey and Alley were not fit to bowl during the latter stages, but Alley, on a difficult pitch against tight bowling and admirable fielding, made 66 in two and three-quarter hours, being the main agent in restricting the lead to 35 runs. Only Pilling had any answer to the spinners Langford and Robinson. Somerset were left a target of 123 in ten minutes and the whole of the last day. Kitchen survived for an hour and Chappell applied himself excellently, but Hughes achieved his best bowling performance, six for 61, which gave Lancashire their fourth successive win in the Championship.

Lancashire

D. Lloyd c Brooks b Palmer	4	– c Chappell b Burgess	3
B. Wood c Robinson b Langford	62	– b Langford	18
H. Pilling c Robinson b Burgess	24	– c Kerslake b Langford	37
K. Snellgrove c Robinson b Burgess	0	– c Langford b Robinson	7
*J. D. Bond b Robinson	22	– c Kerslake b Langford	0
†F. M. Engineer c Brooks b Burgess	34	– b Robinson	10
D. Hughes c Virgin b Robinson	11	– c Kerslake b Robinson	4
K. Shuttleworth c Robinson b Langford	20	– c Virgin b Robinson	0
P. Lever c Alley b Robinson	19	– c Robinson b Langford	5
K. Higgs c Robinson b Langford	18	– not out	0
J. S. Savage not out	0	– c Kerslake b Langford	0
L-b 8, n-b 11	19	L-b 1, n-b 2	3
1/8 2/47 3/54 4/104 5/142 6/163 7/189 8/189 9/233	233	1/9 2/33 3/57 4/57 5/72 6/78 7/78 8/86 9/87	87

Bowling: *First Innings*—Rumsey 9–6–21–0; Palmer 16–3–40–1; Burgess 21–6–48–3; Chappell 2–0–12–0; Langford 25–12–50–3; Robinson 13.2–4–43–3. *Second Innings*—Palmer 5–1–7–0; Burgess 7–0–20–1; Langford 15.4–8–23–5; Robinson 17–6–34–4.

Somerset

R. Virgin lbw b Lever	17	– c Wood b Hughes	13
M. Kitchen lbw b Savage	36	– c Pilling b Savage	22
P. J. Robinson c Engineer b Higgs	1	– c Higgs b Savage	3
G. S. Chappell c Hughes b Shuttleworth	20	– c Lloyd b Hughes	22
W. E. Alley c Wood b Savage	66	– c Engineer b Hughes	4
*R. C. Kerslake c Wood b Hughes	2	– b Hughes	0
G. Burgess st Engineer b Hughes	26	– c Higgs b Hughes	15
R. Palmer b Hughes	0	– c Lloyd b Hughes	10
B. A. Langford lbw b Higgs	17	– not out	11
†R. A. Brooks c Hughes b Shuttleworth	8	– c Wood b Higgs	4
F. E. Rumsey not out	0	– c Savage b Shuttleworth	0
B 2, l-b 1, n-b 2	5	B 4, l-b 2, n-b 1	7
1/41 2/43 3/72 4/100 5/119 6/168 7/170 8/177 9/194	198	1/28 2/32 3/39 4/52 5/52 6/81 7/90 8/101 9/110	111

Bowling: *First Innings*—Shuttleworth 18.1–1–46–2; Higgs 16–2–32–2; Savage 24–9–51–2; Lever 17–6–33–1; Hughes 15–5–31–3. *Second Innings*—Shuttleworth 3–1–4–1; Higgs 9–1–12–1; Savage 20–11–27–2; Hughes 22–7–61–6.

Umpires: P. B. Wight and J. Arnold.

SOMERSET v. GLAMORGAN

Played at Taunton, August 24, 25, 26, 1968

Glamorgan won by 53 runs. Majid's brilliant stroke play which brought him 123 out of 155 in two hours, thirty-five minutes, supported by 96 by Walker made in widely varying tempo gave Glamorgan their early advantage, which Wheatley underlined. Although Robinson and Kitchen added 98 for the third wicket, Wheatley finished the innings with his first hat-trick, taking six for 46. Consequently, Somerset only narrowly avoided the follow-on. Another fine contribution by Majid allowed Glamorgan to set a task of 299 to win in four hours, ten minutes. When the enterprise of Clarkson and Virgin enabled them to begin with a stand of 151 in two hours, victory for Somerset seemed assured. However, Walker's remarkable steadiness held them in check and, after Virgin was run out, the last nine wickets fell for 94 runs. Five overs remained for play when the game concluded, Walker having taken five for 66.

Glamorgan

A. Jones b Rumsey	6	– c Alley b Palmer	21
R. Davis lbw b Burgess	15	– c and b Palmer	42
Majid Jahangir c Virgin b Palmer	123	– not out	61
P. M. Walker b Palmer	96	– not out	17
*A. R. Lewis c Carter b Palmer	1		
†E. Jones c Carter b Rumsey	51		
A. E. Cordle not out	35		
M. A. Nash not out	14		
B 5, l-b 8, w 2, n-b 6	21	L-b 8, n-b 5	13
1/10 2/63 3/165 4/171 5/299 6/309	(6 wkts dec.) 362	1/67 2/74	(2 wkts dec.) 154

B. Lewis, D. J. Shepherd and O. S. Wheatley did not bat.

Bowling: *First Innings*—Rumsey 20–4–80–2; Palmer 17–3–70–3; Burgess 24–3–85–1; Alley 15–6–41–0; Langford 15–4–41–0; Robinson 10–3–24–0. *Second Innings*—Rumsey 8.4–2–27–0; Palmer 11–0–50–2; Burgess 6–0–29–0; Langford 13–2–35–0.

Somerset

R. Virgin b Shepherd	24	– run out	67
A. Clarkson c E. Jones b B. Lewis	20	– c Davis b Walker	82
P. J. Robinson b Wheatley	65	– c Majid b Walker	10
M. Kitchen b Walker	45	– lbw b Shepherd	17
W. E. Alley c E. Jones b Wheatley	18	– c E. Jones b Shepherd	5
*R. C. Kerslake c Nash b Shepherd	24	– lbw b Walker	22
G. Burgess c B. Lewis b Wheatley	2	– c and b Walker	16
R. Palmer not out	9	– c Shepherd b Walker	1
B. A. Langford c Walker b Wheatley	1	– not out	7
†C. E. P. Carter b Wheatley	0	– c Walker b B. Lewis	0
F. E. Rumsey b Wheatley	0	– c Davis b Wheatley	5
B 1, l-b 5, n-b 4	10	B 8, l-b 4, w 1	13
1/38 2/53 3/151 4/174 5/183 6/185 7/217 8/218 9/218	218	1/151 2/160 3/182 4/184 5/188 6/220 7/228 8/231 9/232	245

Bowling: *First Innings*—Wheatley 27.3–10–46–6; Nash 12–3–28–0; Shepherd 14–4–37–2; B. Lewis 15–6–40–1; Cordle 11–2–30–0; Walker 13–6–27–1. *Second Innings*—Wheatley 15–5–32–1; Nash 5–0–17–0; Shepherd 23–3–73–2; B. Lewis 4–0–28–1; Cordle 5–1–16–0; Walker 30–12–66–5.

Umpires: H. Yarnold and H. Mellows.

SOMERSET v GLOUCESTERSHIRE

Played at Taunton, May 29, 31, June 1, 1976

Gloucestershire won by eight runs. This remarkably contradictory match had an astonishing conclusion, the victory being achieved after a follow-on 254 behind. On a green pitch, Somerset, led by Rose who made a splendid century, prospered while, after the early heavy cloud, the evening was fine. Gloucestershire collapsed before Botham. He and Clapp continued their devastation on a dull, chilly Monday, but by now Somerset had two bowling casualties. Burgess, sweeping at Graveney on Saturday, had a badly cut eyebrow, and Clapp strained his side. Zaheer played superbly and hit twenty-three 4s while batting only two and three-quarter hours. Botham achieved his best bowling figures, eleven for 150. Somerset needed only 119 in nearly four and a half hours. Rose and Slocombe put on 43 in good time and then Brown swept away three good wickets before Procter, now bowling a mixture of off-breaks and very sharp pace, often in the same over, had a final match-winning spell of six for 13.

Somerset

B. C. Rose c Brassington b Graveney	104	– c Shepherd b Procter	48
P. A. Slocombe lbw b Brown	36	– lbw b Brown	17
P. W. Denning b Brown	41	– c Sadiq b Brown	4
*D. B. Close b Brown	0	– c Shackleton b Brown	10
M. J. Kitchen c Davey b Graveney	69	– c Shackleton b Procter	10
†D. J. S. Taylor not out	41	– c Sadiq b Procter	0
G. I. Burgess retired hurt	10	– not out	1
I. T. Botham b Graveney	13	– b Procter	3
D. Breakwell b Davey	0	– c Shepherd b Graveney	0
K. F. Jennings not out	3	– c Stovold b Procter	6
R. J. Clapp (did not bat)		– c Sadiq b Procter	1
B 5, l-b 9. n-b 2	16	B 4, l-b 5, n-b 1	10
1/58 2/138 3/138 4/237 5/290 6/326 7/327	(7 wkts) 333	1/43 2/47 3/73 4/97 5/97 6/100 7/101 8/108 9/108	110

Bowling: *First Innings*—Davey 20–2–82–1; Shackleton 10–1–34–0; Procter 16–5–32–0; Brown 28–8–64–3; Graveney 24–4–94–3; Sadiq 2–0–11–0. *Second Innings*—Procter 14.3–4–35–6; Davey 5–0–20–0; Brown 9–2–27–3; Graveney 14–9–18–1.

Gloucestershire

Sadiq Mohammad c Breakwell b Botham	2	– c and b Jennings	8
N. H. C. Cooper b Botham	1	– b Botham	38
Zaheer Abbas b Clapp	5	– b Close	141
M. J. Procter c Taylor b Botham	7	– c Breakwell b Close	32
†A. W. Stovold c Close b Botham	18	– b Botham	58
D. R. Shepherd b Clapp	27	– lbw b Jennings	30
*A. S. Brown lbw b Botham	0	– b Botham	4
D. A. Graveney lbw b Jennings	2	– b Botham	0
J. H. Shackleton c Close b Clapp	0	– st Taylor b Breakwell	30
†A. J. Brassington not out	4	– not out	15
J. Davey b Botham	1	– b Botham	0
B 4, l-b 2, w 5, n-b 1	12	B 8, l-b 7, n-b 1	16
1/3 2/9 3/9 4/29 5/52 6/52 7/61 8/68 9/74	79	1/11 2/126 3/209 4/236 5/319 6/325 7/325 8/327 9/371	372

Bowling: *First Innings*—Clapp 13–6–18–3; Botham 16.1–6–25–6; Jennings 8–1–24–1; Close 1–1–0–0; Kitchen 1–1–0–0. *Second Innings*—Botham 37.1–6–125–5; Jennings 25–6–71–2; Close 27–9–90–2; Kitchen 3–0–21–0; Rose 4–0–9–0; Breakwell 24–12–40–1.

Note: Brassington kept wicket in the first innings, Stovold in the second.

Umpires: H. Horton and A. E. Fagg.

SOMERSET v SURREY

Played at Weston-super-Mare, August 10, 11, 12, 1977

Somerset won by 158 runs with nearly two hours to spare. A memorable display by Richards, who hit five 6s and thirty-five 4s in just over three and a quarter hours, as he reached 2,000 runs for the season, dominated the first day. Roebuck hit his first century for Somerset in accomplished style with sixteen 4s. He helped Richards to a new Somerset record of 251 for the fourth wicket. After an opening partnership of 93, Surrey faltered badly against Burgess and Marks as the pitch gave slightly varied bounce and slow turn; only Younis and Howarth kept the deficit to 235. Richards struck 48 in twenty-seven minutes and extended Surrey's task to 372 in six and half hours. After an opening spell of three for 16 in 9 overs by Burgess had reduced them to 63 for five there was much defiance. Howarth led the way, keeping the strike well, although badly dropped when 94. Jackman supported him doggedly to add 95, but Burgess broke through again before Richards took two wickets with slow full pitches and tidied up the match. Howarth's magnificent not out century contained eighteen 4s.

Somerset

G. I. Burgess c Intikhab b Mack	11	
P. W. Denning b Jackman	17	– not out 37
I. V. A. Richards c Pocock b Jackman	204	– b Jackman 48
M. J. Kitchen c Rochards b Jackman	11	– c Richards b Jackman 23
P. M. Roebuck c Younis b Pocock	112	– not out 5
*D. B. Close c Smith b Needham	5	
V. J. Marks st Richards b Pocock	69	
J. Garner c Richards b Pocock	37	
†D. J. S. Taylor not out	4	
C. H. Dredge not out	2	
K. F. Jennings (did not bat)		– c Richards b Jackman 0
B 4, l-b 11, w 1, n-b 4	20	B 14, l-b 4, w 1, n-b 4 23
1/25 2/36 3/79 4/330 5/340 6/426 7/469 8/488	(8 wkts) 492	1/54 2/112 3/112 (3 wkts dec.) 136

Bowling: *First Innings*—Jackman 26–3–119–3; Mack 11–1–86–1; Smith 6–1–20–0; Pocock 29–8–118–3; Intikhab 19–2–101–0; Needham 9–3–28–1. *Second Innings*—Jackman 14–0–65–3; Mack 3–0–19–0; Butcher 3–0–25–0; Pocock 7–4–4–0.

Surrey

A. R. Butcher b Garner	48	– c Burgess b Dredge 1
M. A. Lynch b Burgess	44	– c Roebuck b Marks 24
D. M. Smith c Close b Burgess	0	– lbw b Burgess 13
G. P. Howarth lbw b Marks	28	– not out 110
Younis Ahmed c and b Jennings	53	– st Taylor b Burgess 0
Intikhab Alam c Close b Burgess	16	– c Roebuck b Burgess 0
*R. D. Jackman c Garner b Marks	0	– c Garner b Burgess 21
†C. J. Richards c Jennings b Marks	14	– b Richards 11
A. Needham not out	15	– c and b Richards 2
P. I. Pocock c Kitchen b Marks	8	– c Dredge b Richards 4
A. J. Mack b Marks	16	– st Taylor b Roebuck 5
B 4, l-b 3, n-b 8	15	B 14, l-b 4, w 2, n-b 2 22
1/93 2/97 3/115 4/145 5/175 6/184 7/211 8/217 9/227	257	1/2 2/38 3/51 4/60 5/63 6/158 7/196 8/198 9/208 213

Bowling: *First Innings:*—Garner 21–3–51–1; Dredge 12–3–41–0; Burgess 28–9–67–3; Jennings 12–3–25–1; Marks 15.1–4–50–5; Roebuck 1–0–8–0. *Second Innings*—Garner 19–7–31–0; Dredge 14–7–29–1; Burgess 18–11–31–4; Marks 20–6–59–1; Jennings 4–2–8–0; Roebuck 12.5–8–18–1; Richards 8–3–15–3.

Umpires: T. W. Spencer and T. F. Brooks.

SOMERSET v GLOUCESTERSHIRE

Played at Taunton, August 27, 29, 30, 1977

Somerset won by five wickets with eleven balls to spare. In good conditions for swing bowling Somerset's depleted attack did well on the first day, only Sadiq, dropped three times (the first at 56) and Bainbridge excelling. A typical 70 in sixty-five minutes by Richards on Saturday, a splendid 122 by Denning and useful support all through gave Somerset a lead of 113. As Sadiq equalled his first innings 88, and Stovold and Procter hit freely, Gloucestershire soon adjusted the situation but the bowlers struck back and on Tuesday morning Gloucestershire were in some peril when only 104 ahead with four wickets left. Shepherd, however, with a beautifully controlled innings and Graveney, defending stoutly, added 151 and Somerset were set to get 272 in three hours. Richards had cracked a finger bone and batted, unwisely it seemed, at the fall of the third wicket. Denning, with his second memorable century of the match received fine support. Kitchen helped him to add 93 in an hour of gloomy light and occasional rain, and Close in his final home match for Somerset, did magnificently. Hitting one 6 and thirteen 4s, he and Denning added 144 in ninety minutes and virtually decided an enthralling contest.

Gloucestershire

Sadiq Mohammad st Taylor b Burgess	88	– c Denning b Richards	88
†A. V. Stovold b Dredge	6	– st Taylor b Jennings	40
Zaheer Abbas c Taylor b Dredge	7	– lbw b Burgess	0
A. J. Hignell b Burgess	15	– c Close b Breakwell	18
*M. J. Procter c Burgess b Dredge	25	– c Robinson b Burgess	46
D. R. Shepherd c Taylor b Burgess	4	– not out	142
P. Bainbridge lbw b Robinson	39	– lbw b Burgess	0
D. A. Graveney c Kitchen b Marks	11	– c Jennings b Robinson	28
J. H. Shackleton not out	18	– not out	10
B. M. Brain b Robinson	0		
J. H. Childs c Jennings b Marks	6		
L-b 12, n-b 5	17	L-b 7, n-b 5	12
1/11 2/29 3/88 4/144 5/149 6/163 7/197 8/214 9/214	236	1/51 2/52 3/108 4/179 5/183 6/215 7/366	(7 wkts dec.) 384

Bowling: *First Innings*—Burgess 31–10–67–3; Dredge 24–5–63–3; Jennings 16–7–31–0; Breakwell 13–7–28–0; Marks 11.2–7–23–2; Robinson 3–0–7–2. *Second Innings*—Burgess 29–7–87–3; Dredge 16–1–71–0; Jennings 16–2–64–1; Marks 26–8–68–0; Breakwell 18–8–39–1; Richards 6–1–10–1; Robinson 10–3–25–1; Close 0.2–0–8–0.

Somerset

P. W. Denning b Graveney	122	– b Childs	107
G. I. Burgess c Stovold b Procter	4	– c Stovold b Brain	9
I. V. A. Richards c Stovold b Childs	70	– b Childs	3
C. H. Dredge c Shackleton b Childs	1		
M. J. Kitchen b Brain	32	– c Stovold b Graveney	36
*D. B. Close b Shackleton	23	– c Zaheer b Brain	87
V. J. Marks b Procter	19	– not out	11
†D. J. S. Taylor c Shackleton b Procter	40	– not out	3
D. Breakwell c Zaheer b Procter	16		
K. F. Jennings c Hignell b Graveney	0		
P. J. Robinson not out	0		
B 5, l-b 7, n-b 10	22	B 7, l-b 3, n-b 6	16
1/4 2/101 3/103 4/146 5/189 6/240 7/315 8/336 9/349	349	1/13 2/106 3/250 4/253 5/255	(5 wkts) 272

Bowling: *First Innings*—Procter 21.1–0–100–4; Brain 21–4–83–1; Shackleton 10–1–51–1; Childs 12–2–38–2; Graveney 13–2–55–2. *Second Innings*—Procter 17.1–3–83–0; Brain 15–2–79–2; Graveney 15–5–49–1; Childs 12–1–45–2.

Umpires: W. E. Phillipson and R. Julian.

SOMERSET v LANCASHIRE

Played at Bath, June 10, 12, 13, 1978

Somerset won by four wickets. On an awkward dry pitch, only Abrahams and Simmons solved the problem of the Somerset seamers. Then a fighting, dedicated 93 not out by

Slocombe in five and a half hours, plus useful assistance from Richards and Roebuck gave Somerset a lead of 74. Not since 1975 had a Somerset batsmen carried his bat through an innings. The pitch slowed appreciably but showed some wear when Lancashire batted again. They owed much to a beautifully composed innings of three hours forty minutes by Abrahams, and to two other vital partnerships – Lyon and Ratcliffe put on 80, and the last pair, Croft and Hogg, added a further 39. Somerset were set to get 231 in two and three-quarter hours and, in spite of an over rate in the first one and three-quarter hours of barely fourteen an hour, got them brilliantly. Richards hit one 6 and twelve 4s in seventeen overs, and Denning, with six 4s, added a dazzling 89 in eleven overs. Well-fashioned innings by Roebuck (eight 4s) and Burgess, who ended the match with a six with nineteen balls to spare, steered Somerset back to the top of the table.

Lancashire

B. Wood c Taylor b Botham	5	– b Jennings	18
A. Kennedy lbw b Moseley	0	– b Botham	21
J. Abrahams lbw b Burgess	32	– b Moseley	61
C. H. Lloyd lbw b Moseley	1	– c Botham b Moseley	27
*F. C. Hayes lbw b Botham	17	– c Richards b Botham	4
D. P. Hughes c Richards b Botham	15	– b Moseley	1
J. Simmons not out	40	– b Jennings	15
†J. Lyon c Jennings b Burgess	10	– c Roebuck b Botham	45
R. M. Ratcliffe c Taylor b Moseley	0	– c Taylor b Moseley	40
C. E. H. Croft b Moseley	0	– not out	19
W. Hogg st Taylor b Burgess	2	– not out	16
L-b 9, w 2, n-b 3	14	B 11, l-b 14, w 6, n-b 6	37
1/0 2/12 3/13 4/54 5/74 6/98 7/114 8/115 9/119	136	1/28 2/66 3/118 4/123 5/126 6/158 7/181 8/261 9/265	(9 wkts dec.) 304

Bowling: *First Innings*—Botham 15–5–29–3; Moseley 20–9–28–4; Burgess 14.2–4–45–3; Jennings 9–4–20–0. *Second Innings*—Botham 35–9–86–3; Moseley 35–10–84–4; Burgess 16–1–42–0; Jennings 27–14–33–2; Roebuck 5–0–22–0; Richards 1–1–0–0.

Somerset

P. W. Denning b Croft	0	– c Abrahams b Ratcliffe	40
P. A. Slocombe not out	93	– c Hayes b Croft	0
I. V. A. Richards c Hayes b Hogg	26	– c Lyon b Hogg	71
M. J. Kitchen run out	9	– c Lloyd b Ratcliffe	20
I. T. Botham b Ratcliffe	14	– c Simmons b Croft	0
P. M. Roebuck c Wood b Croft	37	– not out	50
*B. C. Rose c Abrahams b Hughes	0	– c and b Ratcliffe	6
G. I. Burgess c Lyon b Croft	0	– not out	33
†D. J. S. Taylor c Lyon b Ratcliffe	4		
K. F. Jennings c Lyon b Hogg	7		
H. R. Moseley b Hogg	4		
B 1, l-b 7, n-b 8	16	W 1, n-b 13	14
1/0 2/40 3/53 4/78 5/159 6/161 7/162 8/176 9/194	210	1/2 2/91 3/131 4/132 5/159 6/172	(6 wkts) 234

Bowling: *First Innings*—Croft 25–11–61–3; Hogg 24.2–7–57–3; Ratcliffe 19–4–42–2; Simmons 5–3–5–0; Hughes 16–6–29–1. *Second Innings*—Croft 12–1–63–2; Hogg 11–1–79–1; Ratcliffe 10–2–54–3; Simmons 3–1–5–0; Hughes 2.5–0–19–0.

Umpires: D. G. L. Evans and R. Aspinall.

SOMERSET v. MIDDLESEX

Played at Taunton, August 19, 21, 22, 1978

Middlesex won by eight wickets with four and threequarter hours to spare. A sound, attractive batting display led by Radley, who hit two 6s and ten 4s in 49 overs, and a lively 89 in 87 balls from Featherstone (eighteen 4s) gave Middlesex a firm base. Then, under evening cloud, Selvey and Daniel reduced Somerset to 42 for five on the Saturday. Although Slocombe carried his bat for the second time this season, and Moseley enjoyed a cheerful half-hour, Somerset followed on 210 behind. Rose struck fifteen boundaries in a delightful innings, being aided by Slocombe and Richards. They took Somerset to 163 before an inspired spell of five for 19 in eleven overs by Selvey, who ended with match figures of nine for 92, turned the tide. Burgess and Taylor added 45 for the seventh wicket but went quickly on the last morning. Middlesex needed only 57 to win. A hostile, fiery opening by Botham soon reduced them to 10 for two but Radley, escaping a desperately difficult wicket-keeper's chance off a Botham bouncer when 2, responded forcefully and in company with a determined Gatting saw his side home.

Middlesex

*J. M. Brearley lbw b Botham	44	– b Botham	1
M. J. Smith c Taylor b Dredge	5	– lbw b Botham	4
C. T. Radley b Dredge	80	– not out	25
M. W. Gatting lbw b Marks	42	– not out	17
G. D. Barlow c Botham b Marks	19		
N. G. Featherstone c Richards b Moseley	89		
†I. J. Gould c Slocombe b Moseley	21		
P. H. Edmonds c Roebuck b Moseley	0		
J. E. Emburey c Richards b Dredge	2		
M. W. W. Selvey c Richards b Botham	9		
W. W. Daniel not out	0		
L-b 9, n-b 8	17	B 5, l-b 1, w 1, n-b 4	11
1/23 2/98 3/173 4/185 5/203 6/246 7/258 8/297 9/328	328	1/5 2/10 (2 wkts)	58

Bowling: *First Innings*—Botham 19–1–79–2; Dredge 22–4–57–3; Moseley 16.3–4–34–3; Gurr 13–3–41–0; Marks 19–3–82–2; Richards 2–0–18–0. *Second Innings*—Botham 7–0–36–2; Gurr 5–3–9–0; Marks 1.1–0–2–0.

Somerset

*B. C. Rose b Selvey	4	– c Radley b Selvey	99
P. A. Slocombe not out	35	– st Gould b Edmonds	29
I. V. A. Richards b Daniel	4	– lbw b Selvey	39
P. M. Roebuck c Gould b Selvey	0	– c Barlow b Selvey	7
V. J. Marks b Daniel	9	– c Gould b Selvey	12
C. H. Dredge lbw b Edmonds	3	– c Daniel b Emburey	4
I. T. Botham b Edmonds	9	– c Brearley b Selvey	11
G. I. Burgess b Selvey	0	– c Smith b Emburey	35
†D. J. S. Taylor c Gould b Selvey	5	– c Radley b Edmonds	15
H. R. Moseley c Featherstone b Edmonds	30	– b Edmonds	4
D. R. Gurr c Gould b Daniel	4	– not out	3
B 1, l-b 14	15	L-b 6, n-b 2	8
1/5 2/18 3/19 4/34 5/38 6/58 7/59 8/71 9/110	118	1/56 2/163 3/170 4/184 5/193 6/206 7/251 8/255 9/262	266

Bowling: *First Innings*—Daniel 10.4–3–26–3; Selvey 17–5–33–4; Edmonds 15–3–42–3; Emburey 1–0–2–0. *Second Innings*—Selvey 20–6–59–5; Daniel 15–2–60–0; Edmonds 29–10–60–3; Emburey 33.5–7–75–2; Gatting 1–0–4–0.

Umpires: W. L. Budd and J. G. Langridge.

SOMERSET v GLOUCESTERSHIRE

Played at Taunton, May 24, 26, 27, 1980

Drawn. After a delightful innings by Gavaskar, an astonishing attacking effort by Botham dominated the game. Missed only twice when 140 and 195, he hit ten 6s and twenty-seven 4s in 48 overs, reaching 100 in 107 minutes and finally batting 184 minutes for his 228. His fourth wicket stand of 310 with Denning, who batted determinedly for 75 overs, was a record for the county. Gloucestershire never handled the seam attack well, although Zaheer and Hignell reduced the deficit to 295. After overnight rain the pitch offered sharp turn for a while on the final day, but as it eased completely Zaheer, with a superb 173 (two 6s and twenty-four 4s) in 95 overs, and Hignell, with an unbeaten hundred, saved the side comfortably, adding 254 in three and a half hours. The final irrelevant phase included all eleven Somerset players bowling, and Botham keeping wicket.

Somerset

*B. C. Rose c Sadiq b Brain	32
S. M. Gavaskar c Sadiq b Wilkins	75
P. A. Slocombe lbw b Brain	0
P. W. Denning c and b Graveney	98
I. T. Botham c Sadiq b Procter	228
V. J. Marks lbw b Procter	0
†D. J. S. Taylor not out	57
D. Breakwell not out	22
L-b 18, n-b 4	22
1/78 2/78 3/119 4/429 5/429 6/486	(6 wkts) 534

H. R. Moseley, C. H. Dredge and K. F. Jennings did not bat.

Bowling: Procter 24–5–81–2; Brain 21–0–134–2; Wilkins 18–4–112–1; Partridge 21–2–104–0; Graveney 16–4–81–1.

Gloucestershire

A. W. Stovold c Marks b Dredge	32	– c Botham b Dredge	14
Sadiq Mohammad c Dredge b Moseley	4	– b Breakwell	55
Zaheer Abbas run out	62	– c and b Jennings	173
A. J. Hignell c Taylor b Dredge	80	– not out	100
*M. J. Procter c and b Jennings	23	– (6) c Marks b Slocombe	32
M. W. Stovold c Botham b Jennings	2	– (5) lbw b Jennings	1
M. D. Partridge b Jennings	15	– not out	3
D. A. Graveney c Taylor b Jennings	1		
†A. J. Brassington c Rose b Moseley	3		
A. H. Wilkins c Taylor b Moseley	7		
B. M. Brain not out	0		
L-b 6, w 1, n-b 3	10	B 3, l-b 10, n-b 3	16
1/12 2/82 3/112 4/142 5/159 6/184 7/204 8/231 9/237	239	1/33 2/92 3/346 4/356 5/390	(5 wkts) 394

Bowling: *First Innings*—Moseley 21–3–66–3; Dredge 21–5–51–2; Jennings 25–9–87–4; Marks 14–5–25–0. *Second Innings*—Moseley 10–1–35–0; Dredge 17–4–58–1; Marks 31–13–66–0; Botham 15–4–57–0; Breakwell 16–6–39–1; Jennings 15–4–59–2; Gavaskar 7–2–29–0; Rose 5–0–25–0; Slocombe 1–0–7–1; Denning 1–0–2–0; Taylor 2–1–1–0.

Umpires: D. Shackleton and P. S. G. Stevens.

SOMERSET v GLOUCESTERSHIRE

Played at Bath, June 13, 15, 16, 1981

Drawn. A match dominated by Zaheer's remarkable 215 not out and 150 not out was eventually saved for Somerset by a memorable rearguard action from Rose and Roebuck, both of whom had sustained severe leg injuries while fielding. Zaheer, missed when 45, hit five 6s and twenty-two 4s in the first innings and one 6 and twenty-two 4s in the second. Somerset collapsed twice before Bainbridge and Wilkins, but the follow-on was averted by a brisk innings from Botham, a sturdy effort by Marks and a lively stand of 122 between Breakwell and Garner, who hit four 6s and twelve 4s in 25 overs. Although Brain was unable to bowl, Somerset's target of 349 in 200 minutes looked an unlikely one with two batsmen injured. Again Breakwell came to the rescue and, after a dedicated hour's defence from Moseley, Rose batted through the last hour and a half, hitting nineteen 4s through the attacking field. For the last threequarters of an hour he was gamely supported by the virtually immobile Roebuck, and neither batted with a runner.

Gloucestershire

B. C. Broad lbw b Botham	11	– c and b Lloyds	37
Sadiq Mohammad lbw b Botham	23	– c Denning b Marks	33
†A. W. Stovold b Moseley	40	– (5) run out	21
Zaheer Abbas not out	215	– not out	150
A. J. Hignell run out	55	– (6) not out	40
P. Bainbridge not out	3	– (3) b Moseley	12
B 1, l-b 5, w 4, n-b 4	14	B 4, l-b 2, n-b 4	10
1/30 2/36 3/224 4/346 (4 wkts dec.)	361	1/64 2/82 3/87 4/182 (4 wkts dec.)	303

S. J. Windaybank, D. A. Graveney, A. H. Wilkins, *B. M. Brain and J. H. Childs did not bat.

Bowling: *First Innings*—Garner 26–4–81–0; Botham 25–7–99–2; Richards 7–2–26–0; Moseley 15–2–56–1; Breakwell 14–4–29–0; Marks 13–2–40–0; Lloyds 3–0–16–0. *Second Innings*—Garner 10–3–20–0; Botham 9–1–45–0; Moseley 10–2–21–1; Marks 28–4–74–1; Lloyds 14–3–64–1; Richards 13–1–53–0; Denning 1–0–16–0.

Somerset

*B. C. Rose c Stovold b Wilkins	21	– (10) not out	85
J. W. Lloyds c Windaybank b Bainbridge	6	– (1) c Stovold b Bainbridge	2
I. V. A. Richards b Bainbridge	2	– c Graveney b Wilkins	37
P. W. Denning c Hignell b Wilkins	8	– (2) lbw b Wilkins	12
I. T. Botham c Stovold b Bainbridge	41	– (4) b Bainbridge	1
V. J. Marks c Sadiq b Brain	49	– (5) c Childs b Bainbridge	9
†D. J. S. Taylor c Bainbridge b Brain	18	– b Bainbridge	4
D. Breakwell c Childs b Graveney	58	– (6) lbw b Wilkins	53
J. Garner b Wilkins	90	– (8) c Sadiq b Bainbridge	16
H. R. Moseley not out	2	– (9) c Graveney b Childs	10
P. M. Roebuck absent injured		– not out	13
B 6, l-b 9, w 2, n-b 4	21	L-b 2, w 1	3
1/27 2/29 3/42 4/51 5/106 6/163 7/164 8/286 9/316	316	1/14 2/20 3/52 4/52 5/67 6/79 7/125 8/137 9/200 (9 wkts)	245

Bowling: *First Innings*—Brain 14–2–60–2; Wilkins 24–9–50–3; Childs 19–3–83–0; Bainbridge 18–3–58–3; Broad 5–1–18–0; Graveney 6–1–26–1. *Second Innings*—Wilkins 21–3–139–3; Bainbridge 20–7–68–5; Childs 11–6–15–1; Broad 3–0–15–0; Graveney 3–1–5–0.

Umpires: B. Leadbeater and P. B. Wight.

SURREY

SURREY v LEICESTERSHIRE

Played at The Oval, May 11, 13, 14, 1963

Drawn. Rain after lunch on the second and third days spoiled an interesting match which had begun in favour of Surrey. When Stewart put Leicestershire in, Loader, lively and accurate, helped to justify his captain's policy by doing the hat-trick. Off the last ball of his fifteenth over, Loader had Bird caught at slip. Then van Geloven, held at the wicket, and Pratt, clean-bowled, fell off the first two deliveries of the next over from the England bowler. Arnold, in his second county game, again made a good impression with his excellent medium-fast bowling. Leicestershire were handicapped because Boshier had to go off with leg pains, and Edrich, sound and powerful in his stroke-play, was largely instrumental in Surrey leaving off with 104 for one. Boshier did not bowl again, but Barrington failed to take full advantage of his chances when he was 94, after four hours, when rain stopped play. Stewart declared next morning, but Leicestershire, after early set-backs, saved the game, thanks to a splendid stand of 82 in an hour by Jayasinghe and Inman, and the ensuing rain.

Leicestershire

*M. R. Hallam b Arnold	16	– b Gibson	9
H. D. Bird c Barrington b Loader	32	– b Loader	2
A. Wharton c Gibson b Arnold	5	– c Long b Loader	8
S. Jayasinghe c Long b Loader	23	– c Willett b Tindall	57
C. C. Inman b Arnold	22	– not out	51
J. van Geloven c Long b Loader	0	– b Gibson	6
P. L. Pratt b Loader	0	– not out	7
†G. W. Burch c Stewart b Arnold	10		
C. T. Spencer b Gibson	35		
J. S. Savage b Gibson	6		
B. S. Boshier not out	11		
B 4, w 2	6		
1/24 2/35 3/72 4/91 5/97 6/97 7/109 8/120 9/149	166	1/3 2/19 3/19 4/101 5/126	(5 wkts) 140

Bowling: *First Innings*—Loader 20–6–36–4; Gibson 13.2–3–22–2; Lock 21–9–59–0; Arnold 14–5–22–4; Tindall 11–4–21–0. *Second Innings*—Loader 15–2–50–2; Gibson 15–2–27–2; Arnold 6–0–31–0; Lock 8–2–23–0; Tindall 3–0–9–1.

Surrey

*M. J. Stewart c Burch b Pratt	30	B. Constable not out	49
J. H. Edrich c and b Pratt	78	B 1, l-b 2	3
K. F. Barrington not out	94		
M. D. Willett lbw b Spencer	1	1/43 2/137 3/144	(3 wkts dec.) 255

R. A. E. Tindall, G. A. R. Lock, †A. Long, D. Gibson, G. G. Arnold, P. J. Loader did not bat.

Bowling: Spencer 18.5–2–62–1; Boshier 4–2–16–0; Pratt 18–3–55–2; van Geloven 25–6–49–0; Savage 20–2–70–0.

Umpires: F. Jakeman and O. W. Herman.

SURREY v LEICESTERSHIRE

Played at The Oval, May 15, 17, 18, 1965

Leicestershire won by six wickets after Stewart had set them to make 162 in two hours. Cotton shook Surrey on the first morning when he performed the hat-trick in dismissing Storey, Barrington and Tindall at 38. Then Stewart, despite a badly bruised forearm, and Gibson hit magnificently in a stand of 200, Gibson's 98 being his highest score in first-class cricket. When Leicestershire were put out by steady bowling for 215, Surrey's recovery seemed complete but rain interrupted their second innings causing them to lose valuable time. So Stewart declared hoping that Surrey would gain their first win of the season. Instead, Leicestershire hit off the runs in ninety-three minutes, thanks to three men who chiefly with hooks and pulls shared twenty-seven 4s. Jayasinghe (ten 4s) scored 64 in seventy-one minutes; Inman also knocked ten 4s and Marner six in 32. The other boundary went to Birkenshaw. Jayasinghe ran at every opportunity and really excelled himself.

Surrey

W. A. Smith b Marner	31	– c Julian b Cotton	8
J. H. Edrich c Spencer b Cotton	0	– c Birkenshaw b Savage	31
S. J. Storey lbw b Cotton	8	– c Savage b Cotton	8
K. Barrington c Greensword b Cotton	0	– lbw b Spencer	15
R. A. E. Tindall b Cotton	0	– not out	29
*M. J. Stewart c Spencer b Marner	107	– lbw b Spencer	0
D. Gibson b Marner	98	– lbw b Spencer	15
†A. Long b Marner	0		
G. G. Arnold not out	7		
D. A. D. Sydenham lbw b Savage	4		
P. I. Pocock b Cotton	4		
B 2, l-b 5, w 1, n-b 1	9	L-b 2	2
1/7 2/38 3/38 4/38 5/42 6/242 7/252 8/253 9/258	268	1/17 2/35 3/47 4/75 5/75 6/108	(6 wkts dec.) 108

Bowling: *First Innings*—Spencer 16–2–46–0; Cotton 16.1–2–38–5; Marner 25–8–66–4; Savage 22–4–58–1; Greensword 7–0–37–0; Birkenshaw 3–0–14–0. *Second Innings*—Spencer 16.2–4–41–3; Cotton 12–3–28–2; Savage 16–7–37–1.

Leicestershire

B. J. Booth b Sydenham	56	– c Barrington b Arnold	3
S. Greensword c Edrich b Arnold	6		
P. Marner c Smith b Storey	48	– b Arnold	32
S. Jayasinghe c Smith b Sydenham	6	– c Barrington b Sydenham	64
C. Inman b Gibson	17	– c Smith b Storey	49
*M. R. Hallam c Edrich b Storey	23	– not out	6
J. Birkenshaw not out	38	– not out	6
†R. Julian c Sydenham b Pocock	5		
C. T. Spencer c Storey b Pocock	0		
J. S. Savage b Arnold	1		
J. Cotton b Sydenham	0		
B 4, l-b 5, w 1, n-b 5	15	L-b 2	2
1/37 2/91 3/99 4/140 5/140 6/185 7/190 8/190 9/206	215	1/8 2/70 3/141 4/151	(4 wkts) 162

Bowling: *First Innings*—Sydenham 27.3–1–74–3; Arnold 25–8–50–2; Pocock 10–2–20–2; Gibson 15–2–47–1; Storey 13–7–9–2. *Second Innings*—Sydenham 6.3–0–39–1; Arnold 7–0–61–2; Gibson 5–0–47–0; Storey 5–1–13–1.

Umpires: John Langridge and W. J. Copson.

SURREY v NOTTINGHAMSHIRE

Played at The Oval, August 30, 31, September 1, 1967

Drawn. Rain destroyed Nottinghamshire's last chance of gaining a win in 1967 after Barrington had set them 209 in two and a half hours. Despite the County's record seventh-wicket stand of 204 by Smedley and White they also went without first-innings points. With Edwards making his only century of the season, reaching 100 in three and a half hours, Surrey scored freely on the first day. Edwards added 71 with Younis and 140 with Edrich, who hit eleven 4s in his 82. Storey occupied only eighty minutes for 60, which contained twelve 4s. Arnold took a wicket in each of his first three overs, and Nottinghamshire were 64 for six when the big stand began. Smedley batted nearly five and a half hours and White an hour less. In the second Surrey innings, when Hill offered easy runs to accelerate a declaration, Barrington passed 2,000 for the season.

Surrey

M. J. Edwards c Forbes b White	110	– c Moore b White	32
W. A. Smith b Stead	0	– c Taylor b Forbes	1
Mohammed Younis lbw b Taylor	33	– c Murray b Forbes	15
J. H. Edrich c Murray b Stead	82	– st Murray b White	22
*K. F. Barrington not out	59	– not out	48
S. J. Storey st Murray b White	60	– c Hill b Forbes	1
G. R. J. Roope not out	4	– not out	14
B 5, l-b 9, w 1, n-b 1	16	N-b 1	1
1/0 2/71 3/211 4/260 5/354	(5 wkts dec.) 364	1/8 2/36 3/60 4/65 5/90	(5 wkts dec.) 134

†A. Long, P. I. Pocock, G. G. Arnold and S. G. Russell did not bat.

Bowling: *First Innings*—Forbes 26–6–67–0; Stead 22–0–95–2; White 31–8–83–2; Taylor 25–3–61–1; Bolus 5–2–18–0; Hassan 4–0–24–0. *Second Innings*—Forbes 10–4–25–2; Stead 3–0–16–0; White 19–5–42–3; Taylor 6–3–14–0; Bolus 6–0–33–0; Hassan 1–0–3–0.

Nottinghamshire

*N. Hill b Arnold	2	– not out	0
J. B. Bolus c Long b Arnold	0	– not out	14
H. I. Moore c Barrington b Arnold	6		
M. J. Smedley c Edrich b Pocock	116		
†D. L. Murray c Younis b Russell	3		
S. B. Hassan c Long b Russell	16		
J. Parkin c Russell b Pocock	7		
R. A. White not out	116		
M. Taylor c Russell b Pocock	9		
B 2, l-b 10, n-b 3	15		
1/2 2/8 3/13 4/16 5/45 6/64 7/268 8/290	(8 wkts dec.) 290		(no wkt) 14

C. Forbes and B. Stead did not bat.

Bowling: *First Innings*—Arnold 24–6–65–3; Russell 24–4–63–2; Roope 12–3–28–0; Pocock 34.2–11–65–3; Storey 2–0–5–0; Younis 8–1–21–0; Barrington 11–4–28–0. *Second Innings*—Arnold 4–4–0–0; Russell 4–1–14–0; Pocock 0.1–0–0–0.

Umpires: W. F. Price and H. Yarnold.

SURREY v NORTHAMPTONSHIRE

Played at The Oval, May 4, 6, 7, 1968

Surrey won by eight wickets. Both sides had difficult batting conditions in the first innings. Surrey's varied attack, in which Storey, Jackman and Harman took the main honours, was the more potent. Roope and Storey pulled Surrey round after the loss of four wickets for 20 at the start of the second day. As the pitch eased they played splendidly. Although Ackerman hit hard, once slamming Harman out of the ground. Northamptonshire again failed in the second innings, and Surrey, deprived of Barrington by gastric influenza, cantered home when needing only 51 in three hours.

Northamptonshire

*R. M. Prideaux lbw b Storey	20	c Long b Storey	28
C. Milburn b Jackman	0	b Jackman	17
D. S. Steele b Pocock	13	lbw b Storey	38
H. M. Ackerman c Roope b Storey	4	c Edwards b Harman	30
Mushtaq Mohammad c Edrich b Storey	3	c Long b Jackman	0
P. Willey b Pocock	12	c Long b Harman	4
B. Crump c Edwards b Storey	14	c Long b Jackman	2
M. E. Scott c Harman b Pocock	0	c Long b Jackman	2
†L. A. Johnson b Storey	4	c Storey b Jackman	8
A. J. Durose not out	8	not out	14
H. Sully b Storey	0	st Long b Harman	1
L-b 6, n-b 3	9	B 2, l-b 6, n-b 2	10
1/0 2/34 3/34 4/42 5/43 6/55 7/56 8/60 9/87	87	1/68 2/77 3/121 4/121 5/121 6/126 7/130 8/132 9/145	154

Bowling: *First Innings*—Jackman 7–2–10–1; Roope 5–1–13–0; Pocock 21–8–27–3; Storey 19.4–12–28–6. *Second Innings*—Jackman 22–8–36–5; Roope 9–2–29–0; Pocock 18–8–37–0; Storey 11–6–21–2; Harman 14.1–9–21–3.

Surrey

J. H. Edrich c Steele b Durose	23	c Prideaux b Crump	11
M. J. Edwards lbw b Durose	19	c Johnson b Crump	18
*M. J. Stewart c Durose b Willey	12	not out	13
Younis Ahmed b Crump	1	not out	9
S. J. Storey b Scott	30		
G. R. J. Roope c Steele b Durose	60		
†A. Long c and b Crump	25		
P. I. Pocock c Prideaux b Crump	0		
R. D. Jackman not out	12		
R. Harman c Sully b Crump	1		
B 6, l-b 2	8		
1/44 2/53 3/54 4/60 5/97 6/166 7/168 8/186 9/191	191	1/20 2/29	(2 wkts) 51

K. F. Barrington absent ill.

Bowling: *First Innings*—Durose 20–2–44–3; Crump 26.3–10–42–4; Willey 7–4–20–1; Milburn 4–1–17–0; Scott 20–2–44–1; Mushtaq 5–2–16–0. *Second Innings*—Durose 7–2–15–0; Crump 10–3–22–2; Sully 4.5–0–14–0; Steele 2–2–0–0.

Umpires: J. F. Crapp and R. S. Lay.

SURREY v NOTTINGHAMSHIRE

Played at The Oval, May 20, 21, 22, 1970

Surrey won by seven wickets. The spoils belonged to Surrey, the honours to Sobers, who saved his side with dazzling centuries in both innings. Arnold and Jackman, who bowled purposefully throughout to earn six wickets, had four wickets down for 28 when Sobers began an innings of 160 which contained two straight driven 6s and twenty-eight 4s in four and three-quarter hours. In the second innings he played resolutely for two hours, being particularly tested by Pocock, but hit his final 61 in forty-seven minutes. Sobers had indifferent support both from the other batsmen and bowlers and Surrey made light of the loss of Edrich, who was struck down by influenza. They batted consistently to gain four bonus points, Edwards and Younis in the van again. Finally they were left two hours, thirty-five minutes in which to score 222, and Edwards launched them truly by hitting 79 out of an opening stand of 129. Storey and Intikhab then brought victory in dashing style by hitting the final 91 in 12 overs.

Nottinghamshire

M. J. Harris c Long b Arnold	6	– b Arnold	21
R. A. White b Jackman	5	– lbw b Jackman	11
M. J. Smedley c Storey b Jackman	2	– c Long b Jackman	0
J. B. Bolus c Long b Jackman	3	– c Arnold b Intikhab	23
*G. S. Sobers c Long b Jackman	160	– not out	103
S. B. Hassan c and b Roope	37	– c Roope b Intikhab	18
M. N. S. Taylor c Storey b Arnold	40	– c Storey b Pocock	0
C. Forbes not out	18	– c Younis b Pocock	12
D. J. Halfyard c Younis b Arnold	4	– c Roope b Intikhab	16
†D. Pullan b Jackman	0	– not out	10
B. Stead lbw b Jackman	0		
B 2, l-b 4	6	B 1, l-b 1, n-b 2	4
1/12 2/12 3/15 4/28 5/137 6/239 7/263 8/268 9/273	281	1/15 2/15 3/46 4/60 5/104 6/109 7/153 8/192	(8 wkts dec.) 218

Bowling: *First Innings*—Arnold 20–5–52–3; Jackman 20.3–7–55–6; Roope 10–1–39–1; Pocock 27–11–67–0; Intikhab 8–4–19–0; Storey 10–1–43–0. *Second Innings*—Arnold 12–3–30–1; Jackman 14–4–22–2; Roope 3–1–14–0; Pocock 23–10–48–2; Intikhab 30–8–100–3.

Surrey

*J. H. Edrich c Pullan b Halfyard	22		
M. J. Edwards c Smedley b Harris	71	– b Taylor	79
W. A. Smith c Hassan b White	22	– b Halfyard	39
Younis Ahmed c Halfyard b Stead	52	– c Pullan b Taylor	2
G. R. J. Roope not out	39		
S. J. Storey not out	56	– not out	50
Intikhab Alam (did not bat)		– not out	39
B 2, l-b 11, n-b 3	16	B 5, l-b 11	16
1/36 2/82 3/171 4/175	(4 wkts dec.) 278	1/129 2/131 3/131	(3 wkts) 225

†A. Long, G. G. Arnold, P. I. Pocock and R. D. Jackman did not bat.

Bowling: *First Innings*—Stead 15–0–50–1; Forbes 12–4–24–0; Halfyard 14–2–33–1; White 18–8–54–1; Sobers 5–1–18–0; Harris 18–3–48–1; Taylor 9–1–35–0. *Second Innings*—Stead 8–1–43–0; Halfyard 15.1–0–66–1; White 11–3–28–0; Harris 4–0–28–0; Taylor 8–2–44–2.

Umpires: J. Arnold and A. E. Fagg.

SURREY v SUSSEX

Played at Guildford, June 27, 29, 30, 1970

Drawn. Sussex without Parks, Graves and Michael Buss and further handicapped by injury to Greig in the Sunday match and subsequently to Griffith and Lenham, did well to hold Surrey. Only Stewart, who batted two hours and a half, and Roope, whose weighty driving helped them to the fourth bonus point, flourished against a persistent attack on the first day. Suttle bowled his slows economically and then with the bat retrieved a wretched start. He and Lenham added 114 in two hours and a quarter, and Griffith, who was missed before scoring, helped him to add 48 more. Griffith went on to hold the tail together and hit Intikhab for two 6s. Edwards suffered a face injury while fielding in the slips, but without him Surrey's batsmen made merry, particularly Stewart, who reached 100 in 91 balls. Though sorely handicapped by injuries, Sussex fought through to safety on the last afternoon, Griffith, who batted with a runner, playing a vital part.

Surrey

J. H. Edrich lbw b Greig	19	– c Greenidge b Bates	27
M. J. Edwards run out	37		
*M. J. Stewart c Griffith b Suttle	79	– not out	110
Younis Ahmed b Denman	22	– b Bates	27
G. R. J. Roope c Greig b Buss	66	– c sub b Denman	37
S. J. Storey c Griffith b Greig	2	– b Buss	33
Intikhab Alam c Griffith b Greig	21	– not out	5
†A. Long b Greig	0		
P. I. Pocock b Suttle	0		
R. D. Jackman b Snow	8		
R. G. D. Willis not out	6		
B 4, l-b 9, w 1, n-b 2	16	B 3, l-b 11, n-b 1	15
1/48 2/74 3/135 4/199 5/212 6/243 7/244 8/249 9/260	276	1/50 2/90 3/107 4/221	(4 wkts dec.) 254

Bowling: *First Innings*—Snow 10–0–32–1; Buss 12.2–2–35–1; Bates 13–2–63–0; Greig 17–8–28–4; Suttle 31–11–71–2; Denman 8–1–31–1. *Second Innings*—Snow 12–3–38–0; Buss 13–2–43–1; Denman 13–0–68–1; Bates 18–3–57–2; Suttle 11–3–33–0.

Sussex

G. A. Greenidge b Willis	4	– b Pocock	25
R. J. Langridge c Long b Willis	0	– c Roope b Jackman	54
J. A. Snow c Storey b Jackman	3	– c Long b Willis	0
K. G. Suttle b Willis	80	– b Willis	8
L. J. Lenham c Long b Intikhab	46		
*†M. G. Griffith b Intikhab	74	– not out	34
R. N. P. Smyth b Willis	0	– c and b Intikhab	1
A. Buss b Jackman	22	– c Edrich b Intikhab	3
J. Denman b Jackman	4	– not out	2
D. L. Bates not out	11		
A. W. Greig absent hurt	0		
B 6, l-b 11, n-b 1	18	B 6	6
1/0 2/7 3/11 4/125 5/173 6/173 7/225 8/231 9/262	262	1/58 2/70 3/97 4/109 5/113 6/121	(6 wkts.) 133

Bowling: *First Innings*—Willis 9–1–57–4; Jackman 21–2–53–3; Storey 13–2–36–0; Pocock 12–0–38–0; Intikhab 19–3–60–2. *Second Innings*—Jackman 12–2–26–1; Willis 13–4–22–2; Intikhab 19–5–63–2; Pocock 15–7–16–1.

Umpires: J. S. Buller and O. W. Herman.

SURREY v LANCASHIRE

Played at The Oval, September 12, 14, 15, 1970

Drawn. Only a remarkable win with a record number of bonus points could take Lancashire to the top of the table in the final match, and much rain made sure that could not happen. Yet five bonus points assured them of third position. They were secured despite a sterling innings by Younis. He played a lone hand, reaching 50 in 32 overs, until Pocock, driving freely and confidently, shared a ninth-wicket stand of 54 with him. In the final stages Lancashire batted weakly when Arnold made the most of some life in the dampened pitch to take five for 22.

Surrey

*J. H. Edrich c Engineer b Shuttleworth	14	†A. Long c Engineer b Shuttleworth	6
M. J. Edwards c Engineer b Sullivan	20	G. G. Arnold c Pilling b Lever	2
Younis Ahmed c Enginner b Shuttleworth	90	P. I. Pocock b Sullivan	25
G. R. J. Roope b Sullivan	2	R. D. Jackman not out	0
D. R. Owen-Thomas c Engineer b C. H. Lloyd	1	B 8, l-b 6, w 2	16
S. J. Storey c Engineer b Sullivan	8	1/33 2/56 3/62 4/63 5/82	184
Intikhab Alam b C. H. Lloyd	0	6/84 7/115 8/130 9/184	

Bowling: Lever 15–3–40–1; Shuttleworth 21–5–60–3; C. H. Lloyd 12–4–24–2; Sullivan 12.2–1–44–4.

Lancashire

D. Lloyd lbw b Jackman	11	*J. D. Bond not out	1
B. Wood c Long b Arnold	1	D. P. Hughes not out	0
H. Pilling b Arnold	0		
C. H. Lloyd lbw b Arnold	12	N-b 8	8
F. C. Hayes c Arnold b Jackman	15		
J. Sullivan c Jackman b Arnold	0	1/12 2/12 3/12 4/39 (7 wkts)	58
†F. M. Engineer b Arnold	10	5/39 6/49 7/53	

K. Shuttleworth and P. Lever did not bat.

Bowling: Arnold 11–5–22–5; Jackman 10–2–27–2; Intikhab 1–0–1–0.

Umpires: W. L. Budd and J. F. Crapp.

SURREY v ESSEX

Played at The Oval, May 1, 3, 4, 1971

Drawn. The match was evenly contested until the closing stages when Essex defended dourly to avoid defeat. At the start Surrey ran into trouble on a green pitch, but a fifth-wicket stand of 113 between Roope and Storey made the score respectable. Though Ward batted soundly for 63, Essex struggled until Hobbs transformed the innings with 71 in ninety minutes, including three 6s and nine 4s. Surrey found runs easier to get in their second innings, and Stewart set Essex to make 258 at 75 an hour, after their medium-pace bowler, Turner, had performed a late hat-trick. Essex lost seven wickets cheaply, against good spin bowling by Pocock and Waller but Francis and East resisted well.

Surrey

J. H. Edrich hit wkt b Boyce	5	– c East b Acfield	38
M. J. Edwards b Boyce	3	– run out	46
*M. J. Stewart run out	8	– c Taylor b East	38
Younis Ahmed run out	27	– not out	60
G. R. J. Roope c East b Lever	75	– c Fletcher b Turner	12
S. J. Storey run out	70	– b Turner	11
†A. Long c Taylor b East	0	– c Taylor b Turner	0
R. D. Jackman not out	14	– c Taylor b Turner	0
P. I. Pocock run out	28	– c Fletcher b Lever	28
R. G. D. Willis c East b Boyce	0		
C. E. Waller lbw b Boyce	0	– not out	16
B 1, l-b 4, n-b 7	12	L-b 5, n-b 6	11
1/11 2/13 3/29 4/80 5/193 6/193 7/199 8/240 9/240	242	1/84 2/88 3/142 4/166 5/197 6/225 7/225 8/229	(8 wkts dec.) 260

Bowling: *First Innings*—Boyce 13–1–26–4; Lever 19–1–49–1; Turner 10–2–17–0; Acfield 9–1–39–0; Hobbs 12–1–54–0; East 20–4–45–1. *Second Innings*—Boyce 8–0–41–0; Lever 16–4–53–1; Turner 18–5–54–4; Acfield 13–2–29–1; East 24–2–72–1.

Essex

B. Ward c Long b Pocock	63	– c Long b Waller	35
*†B. Taylor c and b Jackman	6	– c Willis b Pocock	33
G. J. Saville c Edrich b Willis	22	– c Edwards b Waller	18
K. W. R. Fletcher b Waller	24	– c Roope b Waller	13
B. C. Francis lbw b Pocock	7	– not out	10
K. D. Boyce c Roope b Willis	8	– c Jackman b Pocock	0
S. Turner c Roope b Waller	0	– c Long b Pocock	1
R. N. S. Hobbs c Roope b Pocock	71	– c Younis b Waller	1
R. E. East c Long b Jackman	19	– not out	43
J. K. Lever run out	6		
D. L. Acfield not out	8		
L-b 8, n-b 3	11	B 2, l-b 2	4
1/9 2/57 3/105 4/112 5/129 6/139 7/143 8/179 9/214	245	1/69 2/75 3/92 4/105 5/106 6/108 7/111	(7 wkts.) 158

Bowling: *First Innings*—Jackman 24–9–52–2; Willis 26–7–62–2; Pocock 32–12–73–3; Storey 11–3–20–0; Waller 12–7–27–2. *Second Innings*—Jackman 10–1–41–0; Willis 10–3–26–0; Pocock 26–6–59–3; Storey 3–3–0–0; Waller 21–12–28–4.

Umpires: A. E. Fagg and H. Yarnold.

SURREY v WARWICKSHIRE

Played at The Oval, May 12, 13, 14, 1971

Surrey won by six wickets. Two centuries in the match by Edrich enabled Surrey to gain an important victory in a high-scoring encounter. Apart from the early stages, when Warwickshire lost Abberley, Jameson and Kanhai for 30 runs to the fast bowler Willis, batsmen were generally on top. M. J. K. Smith hit his third century in consecutive matches in helping Warwickshire to recovery. Edrich and Edwards began Surrey's reply with a century stand; Storey and Younis also showed enterprise and Surrey took the lead and declared with only five wickets down. Jameson and Amiss scored freely before Warwickshire declared in turn, but Surrey made light of their task of scoring 257. Edrich and Edwards again began with a century stand, and the match was won in the last over.

Warwickshire

R. N. Abberley c Edwards b Willis	4	– b Jackman	4
J. A. Jameson c Long b Willis	0	– c Long b Waller	91
R. B. Kanhai c Edwards b Willis	14	– not out	32
M. J. K. Smith lbw b Storey	105	– b Jackman	17
D. L. Amiss c Waller b Pocock	42	– c Edwards b Waller	62
E. E. Hemmings c Roope b Pocock	63	– lbw b Storey	6
*†A. C. Smith b Jackman	14		
N. M. McVicker c Stewart b Storey	0		
W. Blenkiron c Edwards b Willis	44	– not out	37
L. R. Gibbs not out	6		
P. J. Lewington st Long b Storey	19		
B 1, l-b 6, n-b 1	8	L-b 6, w 1, n-b 3	10
1/2 2/5 3/30 4/113 5/234 6/235 7/235 8/290 9/295	319	1/4 2/46 3/161 4/174 5/202	(5 wkts dec.) 259

Bowling: *First Innings*—Jackman 22–5–81–1; Willis 21–5–57–4; Storey 16.3–5–34–3; Pocock 31–14–80–2; Waller 11–0–59–0. *Second Innings*—Jackman 15–4–46–2; Willis 13–3–47–0; Storey 18–8–36–1; Pocock 20–3–70–0; Waller 19–4–50–2.

Surrey

J. H. Edrich c A. C. Smith b Gibbs	111	– b Gibbs	124
M. J. Edwards b Lewington	66	– c Lewington b McVicker	68
*M. J. Stewart c M. J. K. Smith b Gibbs	8	– not out	7
Younis Ahmed not out	51	– run out	19
G. R. J. Roope c Hemmings b Lewington	21	– not out	22
S. J. Storey run out	51	– c Kanhai b Gibbs	4
†A. Long not out	7		
B 1, l-b 4, n-b 2	7	L-b 13	13
1/123 2/136 3/200 4/216 5/294	(5 wkts dec.) 322	1/140 2/181 3/222 4/225	(4 wkts) 257

R. D. Jackman, P. I. Pocock, R. G. D. Willis and C. E. Waller did not bat.

Bowling: *First Innings*—McVicker 18–5–46–0; Blenkiron 18.1–1–71–0; Gibbs 29–9–84–2; Hemmings 11–2–36–0; Lewington 12–1–43–2; Jameson 7–0–35–0. *Second Innings*—McVicker 11–1–52–1; Blenkiron 11.2–0–30–0; Gibbs 18–1–92–2; Hemmings 13–0–70–0.

Umpires: J. Arnold and O. W. Herman.

SURREY v WORCESTERSHIRE

Played at Guildford, June 19, 21, 22, 1971

Surrey won by nine wickets. Stewart put his opponents in on a rain-affected first day, and the off-spinner, Pocock, responded by performing the hat-trick on a drying pitch. Only the left-handed Headley resisted for long, batting splendidly for four hours. The pitch remained awkward when Surrey replied, and another left hander, Younis, did most to enable them to lead by 37. Back trouble prevented Turner batting in the Worcestershire second innings, and they fared poorly against the pace of Arnold and Jackman. Surrey needed only 53 to win, achieved in eighty minutes.

Worcestershire

R. G. A. Headley c Stewart b Arnold	93	– lbw b Arnold	3
*G. M. Turner retired hurt	4	– absent hurt	0
J. A. Ormrod c Edwards b Pocock	16	– c Roope b Jackman	36
E. J. O. Hemsley c Roope b Pocock	0	– lbw b Waller	14
T. J. Yardley c Storey b Pocock	0	– lbw b Arnold	11
D. E. R. Stewart c Stewart b Pocock	0	– c Stewart b Pocock	6
K. Griffith c Roope b Storey	2	– c Roope b Pocock	0
D. N. F. Slade b Waller	41	– c Long b Arnold	4
†H. G. Wilcock c Long b Arnold	0	– b Jackman	7
V. A. Holder b Jackman	1	– lbw b Jackman	0
R. G. M. Carter not out	0	– not out	1
L-b 4, n-b 2	6	B 1, l-b 4, n-b 2	7
1/71 2/71 3/71 4/73 5/82 6/136 7/136 8/139 9/163	163	1/8 2/30 3/57 4/72 5/73 6/88 7/88 8/88 9/89	89

Bowling: *First Innings*—Arnold 17–4–18–2; Jackman 8–2–16–1; Pocock 39–13–55–4; Storey 23–7–44–1; Waller 17.5–6–24–1. *Second Innings*—Arnold 10–2–25–3; Jackman 11–5–13–3; Pocock 14–3–28–2; Storey 4–4–0–0; Waller 9–4–16–1.

Surrey

M. J. Edwards c Holder b Carter	5	– lbw b Holder	15
R. M. Lewis run out	50	– not out	26
*M. J. Stewart c Hemsley b Holder	0	– not out	5
Younis Ahmed c Yardley b Hemsley	72		
G. R. J. Roope b Holder	0		
S. J. Storey c and b Carter	20		
†A. Long not out	29		
P. I. Pocock lbw b Carter	1		
G. G. Arnold b Hemsley	0		
R. D. Jackman c Hemsley b Holder	5		
C. E. Waller not out	4		
B 3, l-b 7, w 1, n-b 3	14	L-b 6, w 1	7
1/5 2/6 3/131 4/131 5/137 6/165 7/167 8/168 9/181	(9 wkts dec.) 200	1/23	(1 wkt) 53

Bowling: *First Innings*—Holder 27.1–13–36–3; Carter 20–6–36–3; Griffith 16–4–49–0; Slade 5–0–21–0; Hemsley 16–2–44–2. *Second Innings*—Holder 7–2–15–1; Carter 11–2–24–0; Hemsley 5–1–7–0.

Umpires: W. E. Alley and O. W. Herman.

SURREY v GLOUCESTERSHIRE

Played at The Oval, June 12, 14, 15, 1976

Drawn. Zaheer Abbas batted for eight hours thirty-five minutes for 216 not out and 156 not out in the cause of Gloucestershire, who for the first time could boast a batsman scoring a double century and a century in the same match. But it was not enough to produce a victory. Surrey also had a batsman of equal character in Edrich and when they were left all the last day to score 470 to win, or more to the point six hours in which to save the game, he struck the third century and his side averted defeat. Edrich battled through three hours, fifty minutes, for the most part against the spinners, and hit twenty-one 4s. Zaheer's first hundred came in three hours, and the second in just over two hours. He hit one 6 and thirty 4s and was helped by Stovold in a stand of 156 and Brown in one of 119. Surrey, already without Arnold and Pocock, lost Smith ill and Jackman toiled from lunch to the close of the innings, and then went in as nightwatchman! Zaheer hit one 6 and fourteen 4s in his second knock of 156.

Gloucestershire

Sadiq Mohammad c Roope b Baker	5	– c Aworth b Jackman	2
A. W. Stovold b Jackman	81	– c Skinner b Jackman	57
Zaheer Abbas not out	216	– not out	156
M. J. Procter b Intikhab	2	– retired hurt	23
D. R. Shepherd c Howarth b Jackman	14	– not out	19
J. C. Foat c Younis b Intikhab	0		
*A. S. Brown c Roope b Baker	39		
D. A. Graveney c Skinner b Jackman	1		
†A. J. Brassington not out	11		
B 4, l-b 13, w 1, n-b 3	21	L-b 2, w 4, n-b 1	7
1/15 2/171 3/178 4/221 5/224 6/343 7/344	(7 wkts) 390	1/2 2/153	(2 wkts dec.) 264

J. Davey and B. M. Brain did not bat.

Bowling: *First Innings*—Jackman 41–4–131–3; Baker 23–1–87–2; Roope 8–0–24–0; Butcher 3–0–19–0; Intikhab 25–5–108–2. *Second Innings*—Jackman 11–1–51–2; Baker 9–2–33–0; Roope 9–0–67–0; Butcher 3–0–15–0; Intikhab 12–1–49–0; Smith 6–0–37–0; Howarth 1–0–5–0.

Surrey

A. R. Butcher c Brown b Procter	10	– c Stovold b Graveney	23
G. P. Howarth c Procter b Graveney	49	– c Brassington b Davey	0
R. D. Jackman b Brain	15	– not out	4
G. R. J. Roope c Brassington b Brain	0	– lbw b Graveney	47
Younis Ahmed b Brain	59	– c Sadiq b Graveney	47
*J. H. Edrich c Sadiq b Brain	8	– c Zaheer b Sadiq	120
C. J. Aworth b Brain	1	– c Stovold b Graveney	33
†L. E. Skinner c Foat b Procter	6	– c Stovold b Sadiq	25
Intikhab Alam c Zaheer b Procter	15	– c Procter b Graveney	0
D. M. Smith c Brain b Procter	12	– not out	9
R. P. Baker not out	1		
L-b 1, n-b 8	9	L-b 6. w 4, n-b 7	17
1/12 2/65 3/65 4/83 5/98 6/102 7/119 8/165 9/183	185	1/2 2/89 3/204 4/204 5/281 6/286 7/290 8/321	(8 wkts) 325

Bowling: *First Innings*—Brain 22–5–74–5; Procter 18.4–6–39–4; Sadiq 2–0–14–0; Graveney 9–3–23–1; Brown 3–1–4–0; Davey 7–2–22–0. *Second Innings*—Brain 12–3–31–0; Procter 36–9–101–0; Sadiq 21–3–82–2; Graveney 46–22–77–5; Davey 9–4–17–1.

Umpires: R. Julian and P. Rochford.

SURREY IN 1977

One of the Surrey members . . . having watched the side disintegrate from 60 for one to 71 for nine against Leicestershire at The Oval, entered the office, put his pass on the counter and asked for his money back.

A humorous gesture it was thought at the time. It was only the end of May. But by the end of August others felt like joining him in his protest and it seemed that a new drive from the management reflected in a better standard in the middle would be necessary before support picked up again.

SURREY v LEICESTERSHIRE

Played at The Oval, May 28, 30, 31, 1977

Leicestershire won by eight wickets. The match was won and lost in a 37 minute period from 4.55 on the second day. In that time Surrey disintegrated from 60 for one to 71 for nine, Shuttleworth performing his first hat-trick in a career which began with Lancashire thirteen years earlier. Edrich, Intikhab and Jackman were his victims. The pitch had been a turner from the first morning and the new Kookaburra ball was in use, but these facts in no way accounted for the debacle. Each side had done reasonably well previously, ending their first innings with 33 runs separating the sides. Birkenshaw, who had taken six for 74 in winning that advantage for Leicestershire, began the slide when he had Howarth caught in the deep and after Roope had hit him for 6, he took a good return catch. Leicestershire needed only 75 runs to win when the last day started and thanks to Davison they got them easily.

Surrey

*J. H. Edrich c Dudleston b Shuttleworth	20	– b Shuttleworth	1
A. R. Butcher c Dudleston b Clift	38	– lbw b Ward	0
G. P. Howarth c and b Birkenshaw	17	– c Shuttleworth b Birkenshaw	19
Younis Ahmed c Balderstone b Birkenshaw	13	– c Higgs b Shuttleworth	0
G. R. J. Roope c Higgs b Birkenshaw	33	– c and b Birkenshaw	40
†L. F. Skinner st Dudleston b Birkenshaw	35	– c Dudleston b Shuttleworth	4
I. R. Payne b Birkenshaw	10	– c Davison b Birkenshaw	0
Intikhab Alam c Birkenshaw b Higgs	11	– lbw b Shuttleworth	0
R. D. Jackman lbw b Higgs	5	– b Shuttleworth	0
G. G. Arnold c Dudleston b Birkenshaw	17	– not out	6
P. I. Pocock not out	9	– lbw b Ward	27
B 4, l-b 3, n-b 5	12	L-b 7, n-b 3	10
1/62 2/62 3/96 4/115 5/138 6/156 7/187 8/187 9/208	220	1/0 2/60 3/60 4/66 5/70 6/71 7/71 8/71 9/71	107

Bowling: *First Innings*—Ward 9–3–23–0; Higgs 13–4–21–2; Shuttleworth 4–0–18–1; Clift 8–2–27–1; Illingworth 22–10–33–0; Birkenshaw 31–9–74–6; Balderstone 3–0–12–0. *Second Innings*—Ward 8–4–17–2; Higgs 6–1–12–0; Shuttleworth 15–5–38–5; Birkenshaw 16–7–30–3; Balderstone 1–1–0–0.

Leicestershire

D. I. Gower lbw b Jackman	24	– c Skinner b Arnold	0
J. F. Steele c Arnold b Jackman	21	– lbw b Jackman	8
J. C. Balderstone c Roope b Intikhab	67	– not out	17
B. F. Davison lbw b Butcher	21	– not out	51
K. Shuttleworth b Jackman	10		
†B. Dudleston st Skinner b Pocock	1		
J. Birkenshaw run out	17		
*R. Illingworth c Roope b Intikhab	25		
P. B. Clift not out	22		
A. Ward c and b Intikhab	19		
K. Higgs c Roope b Arnold	13		
B 3, l-b 7, n-b 3	13	L-b 2	2
1/50 2/59 3/97 4/117 5/124 6/153 7/196 8/199 9/227	253	1/0 2/10 (2 wkts)	78

Bowling: *First Innings*—Arnold 20.3–6–43–1; Jackman 19–4–46–3; Pocock 34–11–102–1; Intikhab Alam 30–18–48–3; Butcher 1–0–1–1. *Second Innings*—Arnold 8–2–18–1; Jackman 5–0–22–1; Pocock 2–0–13–0; Intikhab Alam 4.3–0–23–0.

Umpires: C. Cook and P. Rochford.

SURREY v HAMPSHIRE

Played at Guildford, June 1, 2, 3, 1977

Surrey won by eight wickets. Apart from the dismissal of Richards for nought by Jackman in his first over, there was little in this match until it had run almost half its course. The incident afterwards was perpetual during a game which finally produced 1157 runs; the first double hundred of the season; and Surrey's first Championship win. Surrey, at 139 for eight, in reply to 262 were in a poor position. Then Jackman and Pocock put on 81 and Jackman and Arnold added 68, so that Surrey led by 26. Jackman stayed two and three-quarter hours for 86 not out, hitting one 6 and thirteen 4s. Richards went cheaply a second time but Greenidge and Jesty added 147 in the last sixty-eight minutes of the second day. Greenidge scored 200 in four hours by lunch on the Friday, at which point Gilliat declared. Greenidge used the sweep and other leg-side hits for six 6s and he made room for his favourite cut for many of his twenty-six 4s in an innings of controlled aggression. Considering all this, Gilliat seemed to be generous in giving Surrey two and three-quarter hours plus a minimum of 20 overs in which to score 291 to win, an opinion which gained weight as Butcher (two 6s and eleven 4s) and Howarth (two 6s and ten 4s) gathered 168 in two hours. Only a run out parted the opening pair, after which Younis and Roope peppered the boundary on this fast scoring ground to see Surrey home with seven overs to spare.

Hampshire

B. A. Richards c Skinner b Jackman	0	– c Arnold b Butcher	7
C. G. Greenidge c Howarth b Jackman	64	– not out	200
D. R. Turner c Howarth b Butcher	28	– b Arnold	6
T. E. Jesty run out	52	– c Skinner b Arnold	60
*R. M. C. Gilliat c Roope b Pocock	45	– c Roope b Pocock	3
J. M. Rice c and b Jackman	14	– c Roope b Jackman	19
M. N. S. Taylor c Jackman b Arnold	39	– not out	10
R. B. Elms lbw b Butcher	0		
†G. R. Stephenson c Skinner b Arnold	8		
A. M. E. Roberts lbw b Arnold	2		
J. W. Southern not out	0		
B 3, l-b 4, n-b 3	10	B 5, l-b 2, w 1, n-b 3	11
1/0 2/56 3/134 4/189 5/202 6/216 7/230 8/249 9/251	262	1/9 2/25 3/183 4/186 5/275	(5 wkts dec.) 316

Bowling: *First Innings*—Arnold 13.3–3–36–3; Jackman 23–6–76–3; Butcher 12–3–43–2; Roope 2–0–16–0; Pocock 24–11–60–1; Intikhab 8–2–21–0. *Second Innings*—Arnold 20.3–4–84–2; Butcher 8–0–35–1; Pocock 19–3–65–1; Intikhab 6–2–37–0; Needham 10–1–38–0; Roope 3–0–21–0; Jackman 9–1–25–1.

Surrey

A. R. Butcher c Rice b Elms	6	– run out	93
G. P. Howarth lbw b Taylor	15	– lbw b Taylor	87
G. R. J. Roope b Elms	2	– not out	42
Younis Ahmed c Stephenson b Elms	44	– not out	61
T. M. G. Hansell c Richards b Roberts	23		
†L. E. Skinner c Richards b Taylor	29		
Intikhab Alam c Greenidge b Jesty	11		
A. Needham c Stephenson b Jesty	0		
*R. D. Jackman not out	86		
P. I. Pocock c Roberts b Rice	31		
G. G. Arnold c Elms b Rice	32		
B 2, l-b 6, n-b 1	9	B 3, n-b 5	8
1/15 2/19 3/37 4/89 5/90 6/109 7/115 8/139 9/220	288	1/168 2/210	(2 wkts) 291

Bowling: *First Innings*—Roberts 25–9–56–1; Elms 23–4–61–3; Taylor 15–5–27–2; Jesty 22–9–41–2; Southern 17–1–61–0; Richards 2–0–8–0; Rice 8.5–1–35–2. *Second Innings*—Roberts 15–2–28–0; Elms 9–1–45–0; Rice 7–1–32–0; Southern 15–1–82–0; Taylor 7–0–47–1; Jesty 5–0–27–0; Richards 3–0–18–0; Greenidge 1–0–4–0.

Umpires: J. F. Crapp and D. J. Halfyard.

SURREY v DERBYSHIRE

Played at The Oval, July 9, 11, 12, 1977

Drawn. The big event came at 5.32 on the last day but as the match was over as a contest then and Derbyshire were staying on only as a gesture, much of the occasion was lost. The occurrence was John Edrich's hundredth hundred, for which he had waited since he scored his 99th on his last outing in 1976. Of the 16 players who had got to that mark before him, three were Surrey men, Sir Jack Hobbs, Tom Hayward and Andrew Sandham. Passing the milestone much relieved Edrich, not least of all as it helped him to forget that he had given Derbyshire first innings and seen Surrey struggle from the moment that Wright and Hill began to put together an opening stand of 152. Despite a century by Roope, of which the brightest part was a straight 6-hit which brought him to three figures, Surrey were contained for five and a half hours scoring 251. Derbyshire remained on top with the help of another century, this time by Harvey-Walker in his first match of the summer for the county. Surrey, set to score 321 runs in three hours, gave up when only 80 were forthcoming from the first hour, but Edrich continued to his successful conclusion.

Derbyshire

J. G. Wright c Skinner b Jackman	86	– lbw b Baker	8
A. Hill hit wkt b Jackman	77	– b Pocock	68
*E. J. Barlow c Jackman b Baker	47	– c and b Needham	14
A. J. Borrington not out	51	– b Needham	13
H. Cartwright b Baker	46	– b Needham	0
A. J. Harvey-Walker not out	0	– not out	101
A. Morris (did not bat)		– c Younis b Pocock	0
F. W. Swarbrook (did not bat)		– not out	1
†R. W. Taylor (did not bat)		– c sub b Pocock	21
C. J. Tunnicliffe (did not bat)		– c Baker b Pocock	13
L-b 8	8	B 2, l-b 7, n-b 8	17
1/152 2/179 3/231 4/315	(4 wkts) 315	1/17 2/56 3/95 4/95 5/151 6/151 7/200 8/225	(8 wkts dec.) 256

M. Hendrick did not bat.

Bowling: *First Innings*—Jackman 20–4–46–2; Baker 19–3–75–2; Mack 5–0–29–0; Pocock 28–6–74–0; Needham 28–5–83–0. *Second Innings*—Baker 13–3–45–1; Mack 15–1–50–0; Pocock 23.5–4–65–4; Needham 34–2–65–3; Howarth 4–1–13–0; Younis 1–0–1–0.

Surrey

*J. H. Edrich c Taylor b Tunnicliffe	0	– not out	101
A. R. Butcher c Taylor b Barlow	23	– c sub b Barlow	19
G. R. J. Roope c Taylor b Tunnicliffe	104	– b Barlow	27
Younis Ahmed c and b Tunnicliffe	27	– c and b Harvey-Walker	21
G. P. Howarth st Taylor b Harvey-Walker	9	– not out	5
†L. E. Skinner c and b Barlow	0		
R. D. Jackman not out	53		
R. P. Baker not out	18		
L-b 8, w 2, n-b 7	17	L-b 6, w 1	7
1/1 2/41 3/104 4/132 5/133 6/208	(6 wkts dec.) 251	1/39 2/88 3/141	(3 wkts) 180

P. I. Pocock, A. Needham and A. J. Mack did not bat.

Bowling: *First Innings*—Hendrick 21–7–34–0; Tunnicliffe 24–9–44–3; Swarbrook 3–2–3–0; Barlow 14–2–33–2; Harvey-Walker 34–6–96–1; Morris 3–0–24–0. *Second Innings*—Tunnicliffe 8–0–34–0; Barlow 16–3–47–2; Harvey-Walker 17–1–63–1; Morris 1–0–9–0; Cartwright 5–2–10–0; Hill 2.2–0–10–0.

Umpires: D. Oslear and P. Rochford.

SURREY v KENT

Played at The Oval, July 27, 28, 29, 1977

Drawn. Kent's desire to maintain their Championship challenge was reflected in Asif's decision to give Surrey first innings. Edrich and Howarth replied with 111 for the first wicket and the batting was so consistent that Edrich was able to set a target of 244 in two and a half hours following two declarations and despite the fact that bad light and rain cut three hours from the second day. Kent's efforts to score those runs ended once Asif and Ealham were parted after putting on 71, though the slow over rate mitigated against their chances from the start. The umpires saw fit to speak to Edrich under the Law relating to Unfair Play when only eight overs had been bowled in the first forty minutes. Edrich took the honours in the earlier cricket with a century in each innings for the fourth time in his career, and in the first home match after he had completed his hundredth hundred. His first hundred contained twenty-four 4s and much good batting but the second was of less merit as Kent were throwing away runs in order to hasten the declaration. Asif himself bowled nine gentle overs for 43 runs.

Surrey

*J. H. Edrich c Johnson b Shepherd	140	– b Johnson	115
G. P. Howarth run out	56	– c Ealham Graham	4
D. M. Smith c Clinton b Hills	57		
Younis Ahmed c Clinton b Shepherd	2	– c Graham b Asif	33
Intikhab Alam lbw b Hills	0	– c Shepherd b Julien	0
R. P. Baker not out	29	– not out	0
I. R. Payne not out	4	– st Downton b Johnson	29
R. D. Jackman (did not bat)		– not out	3
B 4, l-b 8	12	B 5, l-b 2, w 1, n-b 1	9
1/111 2/252 3/262 4/263 5/266	(5 wkts dec.) 300	1/6 2/112 3/113 4/117 5/190	(5 wkts dec.) 193

†C. J. Richards, G. G. Arnold and P. I. Pocock did not bat.

Bowling: *First Innings*—Julien 9–1–28–0; Graham 16–3–35–0; Shepherd 21.1–5–54–2; Asif 3–0–20–0; Hills 15–3–49–2; Johnson 17–6–47–0; Rowe 13–2–55–0. *Second Innings*—Julien 18–3–69–1; Graham 6–3–5–1; Johnson 14–7–28–2; Shepherd 3–1–12–0; Rowe 9–1–27–0; Asif 9–0–43–1.

Kent

G. W. Johnson c Jackman b Intikhab	5	– b Jackman	13
C. S. Clinton lbw b Arnold	3	– run out	11
C. J. Tavaré lbw b Jackman	24	– not out	0
*Asif Iqbal b Arnold	47	– c Howarth b Jackman	43
A. G. E. Ealham c and b Pocock	76	– b Jackman	42
C. J. C. Rowe c Richards b Baker	41		
B. D. Julien not out	21	– not out	12
J. N. Shepherd not out	28	– c Younis b Jackman	7
B 1, l-b 3, n-b 1	5	B 5, l-b 5, n-b 1	11
1/7 2/11 3/48 4/98 5/198 6/198	(6 wkts dec.) 250	1/11 2/41 3/52 4/123 5/123	(5 wkts) 139

R. W. Hills, †P. R. Downton and J. N. Graham did not bat.

Bowling: *First Innings*—Jackman 15–1–63–1; Arnold 27–10–69–2; Intikhab 20–6–60–1; Baker 5–0–17–1; Pocock 10–1–36–1. *Second Innings*—Arnold 12–1–52–0; Jackman 11–0–49–4; Pocock 6–4–19–0; Intikhab 5–1–8–0.

Umpires: B. J. Meyer and T. W. Spencer.

SURREY v KENT

Played at The Oval, June 28, 29, 30, 1978

Kent won by an innings and 102 runs. Surrey fell foul of the best wet-wicket bowler in the world, Underwood, who returned the first nine wicket haul of the season, for 32 runs, and took thirteen for 49 in the two innings as Surrey were shot out for 95 in 50.5 overs and 75 in 39.2. Surrey lost eighteen wickets for 140 runs in four hours twenty minutes on the final day after the second had been almost washed out by rain. The conditions were "made" for Underwood, who had taken nine wickets in an innings at very low cost twice before; for 28 runs against Sussex at Hastings in 1964 and for 37 against Essex at Westcliff in 1966. Kent themselves struggled to compile a reasonable total on the first day, with Ealham playing a leading part in contributing 58 of a fourth-wicket partnership of 85 in 27 overs with Tavaré, to whom he had awarded his county cap.

Kent

R. A. Woolmer lbw b Thomas	30
C. J. C. Rowe c Baker b Thomas	14
C. J. Tavaré b Richards b Baker	64
Asif Iqbal lbw b Knight	6
*A. G. E. Ealham c Knight b Intikhab	58
C. S. Cowdrey st Richards b Baker	6
G. W. Johnson lbw b Knight	45
J. N. Shepherd c Smith b Knight	2
†P. R. Downton not out	21
D. L. Underwood not out	12
B 6, l-b 5, w 1, n-b 2	14
1/42 2/55 3/62 4/147 5/175 6/200 7/207 8/252	(8 wkts) 272

K. B. S. Jarvis did not bat.

Bowling: Jackman 25–2–70–0; Thomas 20–7–49–2; Baker 17–2–38–2; Knight 18–5–45–3; Pocock 10–2–38–0; Intikhab 10–4–18–1.

Surrey

A. R. Butcher c Ealham b Jarvis	14	– c Jarvis b Underwood	7
M. A. Lynch b Jarvis	4	– c Rowe b Underwood	11
†C. J. Richards c Shepherd b Johnson	18	– c and b Underwood	5
R. P. Baker c and b Underwood	18	– c Rowe b Underwood	0
J. H. Edrich not out	9	– c Asif b Underwood	0
*R. D. V. Knight c Rowe b Underwood	20	– c Jarvis b Underwood	2
D. M. Smith c Asif b Johnson	0	– not out	20
Intikhab Alam c Downton b Johnson	1	– c Shepherd b Johnson	4
R. D. Jackman c Woolmer b Underwood	0	– c Cowdrey b Underwood	11
P. I. Pocock c Cowdrey b Underwood	3	– c Jarvis b Underwood	2
D. J. Thomas c Downton b Johnson	3	– c and b Underwood	1
B 2, l-b 3, w 2, n-b 1	8	B 8, l-b 4	12
1/12 2/21 3/56 4/58 5/84 6/86 7/88 8/89 9/89	95	1/18 2/18 3/22 4/28 5/34 6/55 7/59 8/68 9/74	75

Bowling: *First Innings*—Jarvis 6–3–20–2; Shepherd 10–1–28–0; Underwood 19–10–17–4; Johnson 14.5–7–22–4; Rowe 1–1–0–0. *Second Innings*—Jarvis 2–2–0–0; Shepherd 1–1–0–0; Underwood 18.2–8–32–9; Johnson 18–7–31–1.

Umpires: C. G. Pepper and T. G. Wilson.

SUSSEX

SUSSEX v NORTHAMPTONSHIRE

Played at Worthing, May 8, 9, 10, 1963

Northamptonshire won by 175 runs. The match was noteworthy for the performance of Johnson, who in effecting ten catches behind the wicket equalled the record set up by A. Wilson, of Gloucestershire, in 1953. Johnson could have made eleven catches, but failed to hold a skier from Bates which swirled awkwardly in the wind. Northamptonshire gained a grip on the game when Norman (fourteen 4s) and the hard-hitting Milburn (three 6s, eleven 4s) put on 125 in ninety minutes for the second wicket and, though bowlers did better afterwards, they declared first thing on Thursday. Apart from Parks, who played attractively, the Sussex batsmen experienced difficulty against a varied attack, and Northamptonshire gained a lead of 131. Steady work by Prideaux led to Sussex being set to get 293, and this time Larter caused a breakdown, taking eight wickets for 41 which gave him a match analysis of eleven for 117.

Northamptonshire

M. Norman c Oakman b Buss	123	– c Dexter b Thomson	7
B. L. Reynolds lbw b Thomson	8	– c Parks b Buss	5
C. Milburn b Dexter	83	– c Parks b Bell	17
*R. M. Prideaux b Suttle	32	– c Oakman b Thomson	80
A. Lightfoot c Cooper b Bates	13	– b Buss	3
P. J. Watts c Parks b Bates	16	– c Bell b Suttle	9
P. D. Watts c Buss b Bates	22	– c Bell b Thomson	28
M. J. Kettle c Lenham b Dexter	19	– not out	10
M. H. J. Allen not out	0	– c Oakman b Bell	1
†L. A. Johnson c Dexter b Bates	0	– c Parks b Thomson	0
J. D. F. Larter (did not bat)		– b Bell	0
B 6, l-b 3, w 1	10	L-b 1	1
1/35 2/160 3/235 4/263 5/284 6/285 7/322 8/326 9/326	(9 wkts dec.) 326	1/12 2/12 3/39 4/52 5/58 6/127 7/150 8/151 9/161	161

Bowling: *First Innings*—Thomson 30–12–80–1; Bates 23.2–6–69–4; Buss 29–5–75–1; Bell 3–0–16–0; Dexter 21–5–60–2; Suttle 7–3–16–1. *Second Innings*—Thomson 21–9–37–4; Buss 21–6–53–2; Bates 8–1–29–0; Bell 6.2–3–18–3; Dexter 4–0–23–0; Suttle 3–3–0–1.

Sussex

A. S. M. Oakman c Johnson b Larter	17	– c Allen b Larter	2
R. J. Langridge b Kettle	0	– c Johnson b Larter	7
K. G. Suttle b P. J. Watts	27	– lbw b Larter	12
*E. R. Dexter c Allen b P. J. Watts	24	– c Johnson b Larter	18
†J. M. Parks c Prideaux b Larter	56	– c Johnson b Larter	16
L. J. Lenham c Johnson b Kettle	29	– c P. D. Watts b Larter	0
G. C. Cooper c Johnson b Kettle	6	– b Allen	41
N. I. Thomson c Lightfoot b Larter	12	– c Johnson b Larter	4
A. Buss c Johnson b P. J. Watts	3	– c Johnson b Larter	0
R. V. Bell c Johnson b P. J. Watts	6	– c and b P. J. Watts	10
D. L. Bates not out	4	– not out	1
B 2, l-b 1, n-b 8	11	W 1, n-b 5	6
1/4 2/24 3/64 4/99 5/140 6/153 7/177 8/184 9/184	195	1/0 2/4 3/14 4/41 5/60 6/98 7/106 8/112 9/116	117

Bowling: *First Innings*—Larter 19–6–76–3; Kettle 16–6–36–3; Lightfoot 8–3–22–0; P. J. Watts 8.3–1–39–4; Milburn 3–0–11–0; *Second Innings*—Larter 21.4–9–41–8; Kettle 2–0–10–0; P. J. Watts 8–3–25–1; Allen 17–7–35–1.

Umpires: W. F. Brice and D. W. Herman.

SUSSEX v LEICESTERSHIRE

Played at Hove, May 13, 14, 15, 1964

Sussex won by 174 runs a game in which they were masters throughout. On the opening day Suttle (three 6s, fourteen 4s) exceeded 20,000 runs in first-class cricket while hitting 122 out of 184. Apart from Booth, the Leicestershire batsmen failed against the bowling of Thomson and Snow. When Sussex batted again 180 in front, Dexter, in his best form, hit hard all round, paving the way to a second declaration. Leicestershire never looked like obtaining the 349 required for victory. Snow, bowling at a grand pace, dismissed three batsmen in one over.

Sussex

K. G. Suttle lbw b Savage	122	– b Savage	36
R. J. Langridge lbw b Boshier	3	– c Burch b Spencer	6
*E. R. Dexter b Savage	25	– not out	100
L. J. Lenham c Burch b Spencer	42	– not out	25
†J. M. Parks c Spencer b Boshier	42		
A. S. M. Oakman lbw b Boshier	21		
G. C. Cooper not out	1		
N. I. Thomson not out	0		
B 1, l-b 1	2	B 1	1
1/24 2/80 3/184 4/211 5/251 6/257	(6 wkts dec.) 258	1/16 2/92	(2 wkts dec.) 168

A. Buss, R. V. Bell and J. A. Snow did not bat.

Bowling: *First Innings*—Spencer 22–6–42–1; Boshier 26.4–6–81–3; van Geloven 16–4–40–0; Savage 29–6–70–2; Smith 10–3–23–0. *Second Innings*—Spencer 10–1–26–1; Boshier 11–2–28–0; van Geloven 5–0–34–0; Savage 12–1–39–1; Smith 6–0–25–0; Booth 2–0–15–0.

Leicestershire

*M. R. Hallam b Snow	2	– b Buss	5
B. J. Booth b Thomson	50	– c Bell b Snow	7
R. C. Smith c Parks b Snow	0	– c Parks b Buss	19
W. Watson c Bell b Snow	0	– b Snow	29
C. C. Inman c Oakman b Buss	2	– c Bell b Oakman	28
S. Jayasinghe hit wkt b Thomson	6	– c Lenham b Thomson	49
J. van Geloven c Suttle b Thomson	9	– c Parks b Snow	4
†G. W. Burch not out	5	– b Snow	0
C. T. Spencer b Thomson	0	– c Oakman b Buss	25
J. S. Savage b Thomson	0	– not out	4
B. S. Boshier c Parks b Thomson	1	– b Snow	1
B 3	3	N-b 3	3
1/13 2/22 3/22 4/29 5/48 6/65 7/74 8/74 9/76	78	1/12 2/14 3/58 4/107 5/112 6/112 7/135 8/164 9/173	174

Bowling: *First Innings*—Buss 12–2–34–1; Snow 14–5–25–3; Dexter 1–1–0–0; Thomson 11.2–5–14–6; Bell 10–9–2–0. *Second Innings*—Buss 15–2–37–3; Snow 20–5–69–5; Thomson 11–1–24–1; Bell 7–1–18–0; Oakman 9–1–23–1.

Umpires: L. J. Todd and P. A. Gibb.

SUSSEX v WARWICKSHIRE

Played at Worthing, June 6, 8, 9, 1964

Warwickshire won by 182 runs a match made noteworthy by the feat of Thomson, the Sussex fast-medium bowler, in taking all ten wickets in an innings. Few batsmen shone on a rain-affected pitch. Barber (eight 4s) and Smith put on 55 for the third Warwickshire wicket on an abbreviated first day, but on Monday 22 men were dismissed for an aggregate of 267 runs. Good batting by Cartwright prevented a complete Warwickshire collapse and only Suttle, Snow and Bell saved Sussex from rout against keen bowling and smart fielding. Leading by 76, Warwickshire also fared badly, Thomson bringing his match-analysis to 15 wickets for 75 runs, but Sussex needed 206 to win and, on wearing turf, offered virtually no resistance. Bannister achieved marked success and Sussex were disposed of in fifty-five minutes for 23, their lowest total for 44 years.

Warwickshire

N. F. Horner c and b Thomson	0	c Pountain b Thomson	11
R. W. Barber c Suttle b Thomson	57	c Gunn b Buss	15
K. Ibadulla c Buss b Thomson	17	lbw b Thomson	0
*M. J. K. Smith lbw b Thomson	42	c Gunn b Buss	19
J. A. Jameson b Thomson	7	c Buss b Thomson	16
T. W. Cartwright st Gunn b Thomson	54	c Cooper b Snow	24
R. E. Hitchcock lbw b Thomson	2	c Bell b Buss	0
†A. C. Smith b Thomson	2	c and b Snow	7
J. D. Bannister c Gunn b Thomson	1	b Thomson	0
R. Miller b Thomson	7	c Buss b Thomson	0
D. J. Brown not out	0	not out	25
B 2, l-b 3, n-b 2	7	B 4, l-b 4, n-b 4	12
1/10 2/48 3/107 4/122 5/133 6/151 7/155 8/163 9/181	196	1/18 2/26 3/26 4/31 5/64 6/74 7/93 8/100 9/100	129

Bowling: *First Innings*—Thomson 34.2–19–49–10; Buss 12–1–42–0; Snow 16–2–52–0; Bell 11–3–35–0; Oakman 5–2–11–0. *Second Innings*—Thomson 25.2–15–26–5; Buss 18–6–58–3; Snow 7–1–33–2.

Sussex

K. G. Suttle c M. J. K. Smith b Brown	33	c Hitchcock b Brown	8
R. J. Langridge c M. J. K. Smith b Bannister	0	c M. J. K. Smith b Bannister	1
L. J. Lenham c Ibadulla b Bannister	2	lbw b Bannister	6
*A. S. M. Oakman c Brown b Cartwright	10	c and b Bannister	0
G. C. Cooper c Hitchcock b Brown	7	c Ibadulla b Bannister	2
F. R. Pountain b Cartwright	3	b Brown	0
N. I. Thomson c M. J. K. Smith b Cartwright	8	c Brown b Bannister	4
A. Buss c and b Brown	3	b Bannister	0
J. A. Snow not out	21	c Barber b Cartwright	2
R. V. Bell run out	25	not out	0
†T. Gunn lbw b Brown	0	b Cartwright	0
B 8	8		
1/1 2/25 3/50 4/50 5/60 6/62 7/68 8/80 9/119	120	1/1 2/15 3/15 4/15 5/17 6/17 7/21 8/21 9/23	23

Bowling: *First Innings*—Brown 16.5–4–50–4; Bannister 15–7–26–2; Cartwright 26–11–36–3. *Second Innings*—Brown 6–4–7–2; Bannister 6–2–16–6; Cartwright 0.2–0–0–2.

Umpires: J. Arnold and A. E. Fagg.

SUSSEX v NOTTINGHAMSHIRE

Played at Worthing, June 10, 11, 1964

Sussex won by 114 runs. Again the pitch afforded pronounced help to bowlers and Thomson completed the week with 23 wickets for less than six runs each. Apart from Dexter, Oakman and Bell, the Sussex batsmen on the first day played apprehensively against the bowling of Cotton, from whom Corran brought off four catches at short-leg. By contrast, Bolus and Millman displayed confidence in an opening partnership of 89, but when they were parted Thomson and the left-arm bowler, Bell, finished the Nottinghamshire innings for another 44 runs. So Sussex led by a single run. A dashing not out century by Parks (twelve 4s) who, taking full advantage of an early "life", hit boldly all round, overshadowed all else in the Sussex second innings and Nottinghamshire were left to get 208 for victory. Against the pace of Thomson and Snow they found the task well beyond their powers, despite a stand of 64 by M. Hill and Gill.

Sussex

K. G. Suttle c Corran b Cotton	2	– c Millman b Davison	5
D. J. Foreman lbw b Davison	0	– c Bolus b Davison	5
*E. R. Dexter c Corran b Cotton	44	– c Corran b Davison	28
†J. M. Parks c Corran b Cotton	8	– not out	103
A. S. M. Oakman lbw b Davison	42	– b Corran	12
G. C. Cooper c Corran b Cotton	0	– c Winfield b Corran	9
F. R. Pountain c Gillhouley b Cotton	0	– c Moore b Corran	0
N. I. Thomson b Cotton	4	– lbw b Corran	0
J. A. Snow run out	0	– c Millman b Cotton	3
R. V. Bell c Davison b Wells	29	– lbw b Cotton	11
A. Buss not out	0	– c Winfield b Davison	16
B 4, n-b 1	5	B 8, l-b 6	14
1/2 2/2 3/27 4/76 5/84 6/84 7/88 8/91 9/107	134	1/5 2/27 3/58 4/103 5/125 6/131 7/135 8/140 9/172	206

Bowling: *First Innings*—Cotton 22–8–54–6; Davison 14–0–64–2; Corran 7–3–11–0; Wells 1–1–0–1. *Second Innings*—Cotton 18–6–56–2; Davison 16.2–4–60–4; Corran 14–2–42–4; Wells 2–0–14–0; Gillhouley 5–0–20–0.

Nottinghamshire

J. B. Bolus b Thomson	62	– c Dexter b Thomson	0
*†G. Millman c Oakman b Bell	37	– b Snow	8
H. M. Winfield b Thomson	11	– b Thomson	2
H. I. Moore c Suttle b Bell	4	– c Pountain b Snow	0
M. Hill c Parks b Bell	5	– c Parks b Snow	38
A. Gill c Dexter b Thomson	1	– c Parks b Snow	25
K. Gillhouley c Suttle b Bell	2	– run out	0
A. J. Corran c Suttle b Thomson	0	– c Parks b Snow	0
B. D. Wells c Thomson b Bell	6	– not out	0
I. Davison c Pountain b Thomson	0	– run out	1
J. Cotton not out	0	– c and b Thomson	4
B 1, l-b 2, n-b 2	5	B 10, l-b 3, n-b 2	15
1/89 2/106 3/115 4/120 5/125 6/125 7/127 8/127 9/127	133	1/0 2/8 3/8 4/20 5/84 6/84 7/88 8/89 9/89	93

Bowling: *First Innings*—Thomson 26–12–38–5; Snow 11–4–30–0; Oakman 8–5–13–0; Bell 16.4–5–47–5. *Second Innings*—Thomson 16.4–12–17–3; Snow 16–8–32–5; Bell 5–1–17–0; Buss 5–1–12–0.

Umpires: J. Arnold and A. E. Fagg.

SUSSEX v KENT

Played at Hastings, July 4, 6, 7, 1964

Kent won by 145 runs. They were the masters almost throughout. On the first day Denness batted attractively and Prodger scored his first century of the summer in four hours. He hit thirteen 4s and put on 121 with Dixon. Once more the Sussex batting broke down against pace, this time of Sayer. Only Langridge, who stayed three and a half hours, offered real resistance. Leading by 138, Kent readily improved their position. Richardson and Luckhurst both batting brightly, and they declared first thing on Tuesday leaving Sussex five and half hours to score 301 for victory. On a dusty pitch batsmen struggled against the varied left-arm bowling of Underwood who, taking in one spell six successive wickets for 17 runs, achieved the best analysis of his career, nine for 28. Suttle, employing aggressive methods, staved off collapse.

Kent

*P. E. Richardson b Snow	25	– c Thompson b Cooper	59
M. H. Denness lbw b Thomson	58	– lbw b Bell	13
B. W. Luckhurst c Oakman b Snow	1	– b Snow	48
R. C. Wilson c Lenham b Snow	2	– b Snow	6
S. E. Leary st Gunn b Thomson	39	– c Lenham b Snow	22
J. M. Prodger b Thomson	102	– not out	8
A. L. Dixon run out	61		
P. H. Jones not out	11		
†A. W. Catt not out	0		
B 1, l-b 4, w 1, n-b 6	12	B 2, n-b 4	6
1/54 2/56 3/78 4/93 5/165 6/286 7/311 (7 wkts dec.)	311	1/44 2/104 3/126 4/137 5/162 (5 wkts dec.)	162

D. Underwood and D. M. Sayer did not bat.

Bowling: *First Innings*—Thomson 27–6–55–3; Buss 21–3–93–0; Snow 20–3–74–3; Pountain 3–2–8–0; Bell 22–12–38–0; Oakman 12–3–26–0; Suttle 5–2–5–0. *Second Innings*—Thomson 7–0–30–0; Snow 13.2–2–38–3; Bell 11–1–47–1; Oakman 7–1–29–0; Cooper 3–0–12–1.

Sussex

K. G. Suttle c Catt b Sayer	12	– b Sayer	64
R. J. Langridge c Leary b Jones	89	– c Prodger b Underwood	6
L. J. Lenham b Sayer	0	– c Leary b Underwood	0
*A. S. M. Oakman c Prodger b Underwood	12	– c Catt b Underwood	13
G. C. Cooper c Prodger b Underwood	21	– b Underwood	25
F. R. Pountain b Sayer	2	– c Denness b Underwood	11
A. Buss b Sayer	0	– c Luckhurst b Underwood	18
J. A. Snow run out	18	– c Luckhurst b Underwood	0
N. I. Thomson b Sayer	9	– b Underwood	6
R. V. Bell not out	0	– b Underwood	0
†T. Gunn c Leary b Sayer	0	– not out	0
B 7, l-b 2, w 1	10	B 5, l-b 6, w 1	12
1/16 2/16 3/33 4/86 5/106 6/108 7/158 8/173 9/173	173	1/30 2/30 3/87 4/91 5/119 6/137 7/145 8/150 9/150	155

Bowling: *First Innings*—Dixon 14–7–27–0; Sayer 21–8–43–6; Underwood 25–13–46–2; Leary 8–2–27–0; Jones 4–2–6–1; Luckhurst 6–0–14–0. *Second Innings*—Sayer 17–4–50–1; Dixon 6–3–10–0; Underwood 14.5–6–28–9; Jones 5–2–10–0; Leary 14–3–45–0.

Umpires: L. H. Gray and R. S. Lay.

SUSSEX v SURREY

Played at Hove, July 18, 20, 21, 1964

Surrey won by ten wickets a match rendered memorable by the feat of Long, who equalled an English wicket-keeping record by holding seven catches in the first Sussex innings and set up a new one with eleven catches in the game. Sydenham, main cause of a batting breakdown stemmed only by Parks when Stewart sent Sussex in to bat on a green-looking pitch, owed much of his success to Long. Surrey began well, but lost seven wickets before taking the lead during a stand of 70 between Barrington and Harman. Barrington, whose 76 in four hours ten minutes resulted in him being frequently barracked, was unbeaten when Surrey declared 72 ahead. Again Sussex collapsed against Sydenham, who brought his match-figures to eleven wickets for 127 runs, and Surrey needed only 48 to win.

Sussex

K. G. Suttle c Long b Arnold	14	– c Long b Sydenham	23
R. J. Langridge c Sewart b Sydenham	0	– c Long b Sydenham	18
*E. R. Dexter c Barrington b Storey	14	– c Long b Harman	29
†J. M. Parks c Long b Sydenham	55	– lbw b Storey	1
G. C. Cooper c Long b Sydenham	26	– c Edwards b Sydenham	14
M. G. Griffith c Long b Arnold	0	– c Stewart b Sydenham	0
A. S. M. Oakman c Long b Sydenham	6	– c Barrington b Storey	19
F. R. Pountain lbw b Sydenham	11	– c Long b Harman	0
N. I. Thomson c Long b Storey	5	– c Barrington b Storey	4
J. A. Snow not out	26	– not out	1
R. V. Bell c Long b Sydenham	3	– c Storey b Sydenham	0
N-b 5	5	B 4, l-b 1, w 1, n-b 4	10
1/6 2/14 3/43 4/79 5/79 6/104 7/129 8/130 9/140	165	1/36 2/48 3/50 4/78 5/80 6/92 7/92 8/109 9/118	119

Bowling: *First Innings*—Sydenham 30.1–10–81–6; Arnold 19–2–62–2; Storey 11–4–17–2. *Second Innings*—Sydenham 18.3–6–46–5; Arnold 6–1–27–0; Storey 18–5–21–3; Harman 6–3–15–2.

Surrey

*M. J. Stewart lbw b Dexter	23	– not out	26
J. H. Edrich c Oakman b Snow	34	– not out	20
M. J. Edwards c Parks b Snow	14		
K. F. Barrington not out	76		
M. D. Willett c Parks b Snow	7		
R. A. E. Tindall c Parks b Thomson	9		
S. J. Storey c Oakman b Dexter	16		
†A. Long c Cooper b Pountain	17		
R. Harman c Parks b Snow	30		
G. Arnold not out	0		
B 7, n-b 4	11	L-b 2	2
1/57 2/72 3/75 4/87 5/104 6/137 7/164 8/234	(8 wkts dec.) 237		(No wkt) 48

D. A. D. Sydenham did not bat.

Bowling: *First Innings*—Snow 25–4–66–4; Thomson 30–10–50–1; Dexter 21–4–74–2; Pountain 16–5–36–1. *Second Innings*—Snow 5–0–18–0; Thomson 3–0–12–0; Oakman 2.5–0–13–0; Langridge 1–0–3–0.

Umpires: O. W. Herman and A. E. D. Smith.

SUSSEX v DERBYSHIRE

Played at Hove, August 7, 9, 10, 1965

Drawn in a highly exciting finish. The last over began with Derbyshire within five runs of the 124 needed for victory and half their wickets intact. Then Buxton was run out and with a single added A. Buss performed the hat-trick at the expense of Oates, Smith and Morgan with the remaining three balls. Few batsmen shone on a pitch which generally helped bowlers. Buxton would also have achieved a hat-trick in the first Sussex innings had not Johnson, who caught Cooper and Griffith from the two previous balls, dropped A. Buss. Derbyshire's first innings breakdown was caused by Bates, who, deputy to Snow, playing for England, took six wickets for 18 runs, the best analysis of his career.

Sussex

K. G. Suttle c Taylor b Jackson	6	– c Morgan b Jackson	39
M. Buss c Johnson b Morgan	10	– b Morgan	17
*Nawab of Pataudi c Page b Rhodes	1	– c and b Buxton	12
G. C. Cooper c Johnson b Buxton	31	– c Taylor b Jackson	27
R. J. Langridge c Morgan b Buxton	1	– c and b Jackson	2
P. J. Graves c Buxton b Jackson	1	– c Taylor b Jackson	0
M. G. Griffith c Johnson b Buxton	6	– c Morgan b Smith	18
N. I. Thomson b Buxton	17	– st Taylor b Smith	8
A. Buss c Morgan b Rhodes	20	– c Morgan b Rhodes	10
D. L. Bates not out	6	– lbw b Smith	1
†T. Gunn b Jackson	0	– not out	3
L-b 3, n-b 1	4	L-b 1, n-b 2	3
1/6 2/7 3/27 4/30 5/42 6/59 7/59 8/94 9/102	103	1/32 2/53 3/95 4/99 5/99 6/100 7/109 8/126 9/127	140

Bowling: *First Innings*—Jackson 13–1–30–3; Rhodes 15–7–13–2; Morgan 17–7–21–1; Buxton 14–5–35–4; Smith 2–2–0–0. *Second Innings*—Jackson 16–4–30–4; Rhodes 15–3–32–1; Morgan 8–2–25–1; Buxton 6–2–11–1; Smith 24.2–12–39–3.

Derbyshire

J. R. Eyre c Suttle b Thomson	23	– c Gunn b Thomson	0
I. W. Hall c Gunn b Bates	19	– b A. Buss	5
H. L. Johnson b A. Buss	20	– c Pataudi b Bates	27
†R. W. Taylor b Thomson	4	– c Suttle b Thomson	18
M. H. Page c Gunn b Thomson	1	– c Pataudi b Thomson	17
I. R. Buxton c Gunn b Bates	7	– run out	22
*D. C. Morgan c M. Buss b Bates	10	– c Griffith b A. Buss	25
W. F. Oates c M. Buss b Bates	0	– b A. Buss	0
E. Smith c M. Buss b Bates	16	– c Griffith b A. Buss	0
H. J. Rhodes c Gunn b Bates	7	– not out	0
A. B. Jackson not out	4		
B 6, l-b 3	9	B 1, l-b 5	6
1/34 2/60 3/73 4/73 5/74 6/91 7/91 8/94 9/115	120	1/0 2/20 3/25 4/71 5/72 6/119 7/120 8/120 9/120 (9 wkts)	120

Bowling: *First Innings*—A. Buss 30–8–63–1; Thomson 21–9–30–3; Bates 14.5–6–18–6. *Second Innings*—A. Buss 16–3–46–4; Thomson 16–7–30–3; Bates 13–1–38–1.

Umpires: A. E. Fagg and J. Arnold.

SUSSEX v NORTHAMPTONSHIRE

Played at Hove, May 7, 9, 10, 1966

Northampton won by ten wickets. This comfortable victory after Sussex had started with a partnership of 103 in one hour, fifty minutes between Suttle and Lenham and gone on to total over 300 was the outcome of good performances with both bat and ball. Milburn scored his second century in three Championship innings, hitting with all his known power in scoring 92 of his 137 runs in boundaries. He and Prideaux put on 141 for the first wicket, Prideaux's share being 38. Even so, Northamptonshire were 17 behind on the first innings and it took some fine off-spin bowling by Sully to put them on the path to success. He took seven wickets for 29 runs, figures which surpassed his previous best. Then Milburn and Prideaux were together in their second century stand, scoring the 127 runs needed in one hour, forty minutes.

Sussex

K. G. Suttle c Mushtaq b Larter	45	– c Mushtaq b Sully	29
L. J. Lenham c Steele b Larter	84	– c Andrew b P. J. Watts	16
R. J. Langridge c Prideaux b Sully	25	– lbw b Sully	6
†J. M. Parks b P. J. Watts	24	– c Crump b Sully	4
*Nawab of Pataudi c P. J. Watts b Scott	30	– c Larter b Sully	3
A. S. M. Oakman c P. J. Watts b Mushtaq	9	– b Scott	4
M. G. Griffith not out	38	– c Steele b Sully	3
M. A. Buss c Steele b Crump	31	– lbw b Sully	0
A. Buss b Crump	4	– c Steele b Sully	35
D. L. Bates not out	3	– not out	5
A. Jones (did not bat)		– absent ill	
B 6, n-b 6, l-b 1	13	L-b 3, n-b 1	4
1/103 2/142 3/184 4/192 5/217 6/227 7/271 8/294	(8 wkts dec.) 306	1/22 2/31 3/35 4/47 5/57 6/62 7/62 8/83 9/109	109

Bowling: *First Innings*—Larter 21.3–3–73–2; Crump 22–8–34–2; P. J. Watts 16–6–41–1; Sully 14–2–56–1; Scott 19–7–52–1; Mushtaq 18–5–37–1. *Second Innings*—Larter 4–0–19–0; Crump 5–2–10–0; P. J. Watts 3–0–6–1; Sully 23.3–9–29–7; Scott 18–7–41–1.

Northamptonshire

C. Milburn c and b A. Buss	137	– not out	68
R. M. Prideaux c Parks b Jones	38	– not out	48
B. L. Reynolds c Jones b Oakman	0		
Mushtaq Mohammad c Langridge b Oakman	38		
D. S. Steele c Pataudi b Jones	21		
P. J. Watts b Oakman	8		
B. Crump c Pataudi b Oakman	1		
H. Sully not out	20		
M. E. Scott c Parks b A. Buss	2		
*†K. V. Andrew lbw b A. Buss	7		
J. D. F. Larter b A. Buss	6		
B 3, l-b 8	11	B 10, n-b 1	11
1/141 2/146 3/194 4/230 5/251 6/252 7/253 8/265 9/275	289		(no wkt) 127

Bowling: *First Innings*—A. Buss 27.1–5–70–4; Bates 19–4–64–0; Jones 14–3–50–2; Oakman 40–13–80–4; Suttle 4–1–14–0. *Second Innings*—A. Buss 5–1–17–0; Bates 3–0–7–0; Oakman 15–5–46–0; M. A. Buss 13–3–42–0; Lenham 4–0–4–0.

Umpires: P. A. Gibb and J. Arnold.

SUSSEX v LANCASHIRE

Played at Hove, May 3, 4, 5, 1967

Drawn. Play was possible only on the first day, when Sussex established a very favourable position. This had much to do with the form of Greig, a 20-year-old South African who hit a sparkling century in his first county match. Six feet seven inches tall, and using his height to produce a lot of power in his strokes, this young man from East London completed 100 in three hours and then went on for nearly another hour, hitting twenty-two 4s in his 156. Statham and Higgs came in for their share of the punishment. Snow helped to capitalize on Greig's fine batting by taking four wickets for six runs before stumps were drawn so that Sussex were understandably annoyed at having to sit in the pavilion for the next two days watching the rain.

Sussex

A. S. M. Oakman b Higgs	6
M. A. Buss lbw b Statham	3
K. G. Suttle lbw b Lever	31
*†J. M. Parks lbw b Statham	7
A. W. Greig lbw b Savage	156
P. J. Graves lbw b Savage	32
M. G. Griffith b Statham	22
E. Lewis b Statham	21
A. Buss b Statham	17
J. A. Snow lbw b Savage	7
D. L. Bates not out	1
B 10, l-b 10, n-b 1	21
1/9 2/17 3/34 4/72 5/189 6/270 7/270 8/303 9/316	324

Bowling: Statham 27–9–70–5; Higgs 17–3–65–1; Lever 17–2–74–1; Green 7–3–13–0; Savage 23.2–5–81–3.

Lancashire

D. M. Green b Snow	8
G. Atkinson c Parks b Snow	0
H. Pilling not out	10
D. R. Worsley b Snow	0
J. S. Savage b Snow	0
L-b 3	3
1/0 2/9 3/17 4/21 (4 wkts)	21

G. Pullar, J. Sullivan, P. Lever, K. Higgs, †K. Goodwin and *J. B. Statham did not bat.

Bowling: Snow 9–6–6–4; A. Buss 8–3–12–0.

Umpires: A. E. Alderman and A. E. Rhodes.

SUSSEX v KENT

Played at Hastings, July 29, 30, 31, 1967

Kent won by an innings and 136 runs, needing only thirty-six minutes of the third day to complete their victory. This was to a large extent due to the left-arm bowling of Underwood on a ground where three years earlier he took nine for 28. This time, on a drying pitch, he captured seven wickets in each innings, finishing with fourteen for 82. During the second day he became the first bowler to take 100 wickets in the season. Sussex were 10 for six in their second innings before Griffith and Cooper stretched the game into the third day. Cowdrey, ably assisted by Denness, Shepherd and Dixon, took Kent into an impregnable position at the start. Having gone twenty-seven minutes before scoring. Cowdrey hit 118 in three and a quarter hours with the help of one 6, one 5 and eighteen 4s.

Kent

M. H. Denness c Lewis b A. Bus	65	D. L. Underwood b Greig	11
B. W. Luckhurst c Greig b Bates	6	A. Brown not out	12
J. Shepherd b Bates	58	J. N. Graham not out	0
*M. C. Cowdrey b Greig	118		
S. E. Leary c Greig b Lewis	14	B 6, n-b 3	9
R. C. Wilson c Greig b A. Buss	25		
†A. Knott b Bates	1	1/15 2/132 3/132 (9 wkts dec.)	383
A. L. Dixon b Greig	64	4/159 5/265 6/272 7/341 8/364 9/379	

Bowling: A. Buss 30–5–107–2; Bates 29–10–88–3; Greig 26–5–73–3; Lewis 19–4–77–1; Suttle 8–4–16–0; Cooper 4–1–13–0.

Sussex

L. J. Lenham c Luckhurst b Brown	8	– b Underwood	5
M. A. Buss lbw b Underwood	39	– b Underwood	2
*K. G. Suttle c Knott b Underwood	32	– c Luckhurst b Dixon	2
R. J. Langridge c Shepherd b Underwood	0	– c Cowdrey b Dixon	1
A. W. Greig b Dixon	5	– c Luckhurst b Underwood	0
G. C. Cooper c Leary b Underwood	0	– lbw b Underwood	23
†M. J. Griffith st Knott b Underwood	5	– lbw b Underwood	36
D. J. Foreman c Shepherd b Underwood	2	– c Leary b Underwood	0
E. Lewis c Denness b Underwood	15	– c Shepherd b Underwood	12
A. Buss c Luckhurst b Dixon	37	– c Shepherd b Dixon	0
D. L. Bates not out	8	– not out	0
B 2, l-b 2	4	B 11	11
1/12 2/76 3/77 4/82 5/86 6/88 7/93 8/98 9/111	155	1/2 2/9 3/9 4/9 5/10 6/10 7/76 8/76 9/85	92

Bowling: *First Innings*—Brown 5–1–20–1; Graham 12–2–28–0; Shepherd 5–2–9–0; Underwood 16–5–38–7; Dixon 12.5–3–56–2. *Second Innings*—Graham 7–5–2–0; Underwood 19.4–7–44–7; Dixon 12–4–24–3; Luckhurst 1–0–11–0.

Umpires: J. S. Buller and L. H. Gray.

SUSSEX v YORKSHIRE

Played at Eastbourne, August 23, 24, 25, 1967

Yorkshire won by 82 runs. They did not bat very well on the first day when only Padgett, who took out his bat after three and a half hours, looked sound, but a fine spell of pace bowling by Nicholson on the Thursday enabled them to establish a lead of 68. On a pitch freshened by rain and in a heavy atmosphere, Nicholson took nine wickets for the first time in his career. Seven of them came on this second day for 35 runs in 12.1 overs and the nine cost him 62. Subsequently enterprising batting enabled Yorkshire to give the bowlers five and a half hours to dismiss Sussex, who needed 350 to win. Illingworth struck the vital blows by dismissing Suttle and Parks, but even so Sussex still seemed to have a chance while Griffith and Cooper were together. They added 97 in eighty minutes. Griffith hit 6s off Cope, Wilson and Illingworth, as well as seven 4s.

Yorkshire

P. J. Sharpe c Semmence b Greig	31	– lbw b Snow	76
K. Taylor c and b M. A. Buss	7	– b A. Buss	10
D. E. V. Padgett not out	81	– lbw b M. A. Buss	17
J. H. Hampshire lbw b M. A. Buss	1	– c and b Lewis	63
R. Illingworth b M. A. Buss	0	– not out	43
R. A. Hutton st Parks b M. A. Buss	25	– c and b Lewis	4
†J. G. Binks c Greig b Lewis	7	– c Racionzer b Lewis	7
G. A. Cope lbw b M. A. Buss	1	– c Suttle b M. A. Buss	1
D. Wilson c Racionzer b Lewis	13	– c Lewis b A. Buss	51
*F. S. Trueman c Parks b Greig	24	– c Suttle b Greig	4
A. G. Nicholson c Parks b A. Buss	10		
B 5, l-b 5	10	B 3, l-b 2	5
1/18 2/56 3/61 4/61 5/99 6/116 7/119 8/142 9/199	210	1/20 2/71 3/144 4/177 5/181 6/191 7/199 8/275 9/281 (9 wkts dec.)	281

Bowling: *First Innings*—Snow 15–3–27–0; A. Buss 11.5–2–31–1; M. A. Buss 33–18–54–5; Greig 11–3–33–2; Lewis 16–1–55–2. *Second Innings*—Snow 15–2–43–1; A. Buss 16–7–32–2; M. A. Buss 31–9–81–2; Greig 12.3–2–46–1; Lewis 18–2–74–3.

Sussex

K. G. Suttle b Cope	16	– c and b Illingworth	42
A. Buss b Nicholson	17	– b Nicholson	30
A. W. Greig b Nicholson	0	– c Illingworth b Hutton	40
M. G. Griffith c Hampshire b Nicholson	36	– c Wilson b Trueman	73
*†J. M. Parks c Binks b Nicholson	38	– b Illingworth	1
G. C. Cooper st Binks b Nicholson	0	– b Trueman	36
T. B. Racionzer b Nicholson	2	– b Nicholson	3
M. A. Buss b Nicholson	11	– st Binks b Nicholson	0
D. J. Semmence c Trueman b Nicholson	1	– lbw b Trueman	0
E. Lewis not out	8	– b Hutton	17
J. A. Snow b Nicholson	2	– not out	18
B 4, l-b 3, n-b 4	11	– B 1, l-b 3, n-b 2	6
1/29 2/31 3/45 4/110 5/110 6/117 7/125 8/127 9/132	142	1/4 2/67 3/96 4/98 5/195 6/198 7/198 8/199 9/240	266

Bowling: *First Innings*—Trueman 12–3–24–0; Nicholson 23.1–5–62–9; Hutton 9–3–22–0; Cope 8–4–11–1; Wilson 5–2–12–0. *Second Innings*—Trueman 8–0–55–3; Nicholson 14.1–3–40–3; Hutton 8–0–31–2; Cope 13–3–45–0; Illingworth 19–6–67–2; Wilson 7–1–22–0.

Umpires: J. F. Crapp and F. Jakeman.

SUSSEX v GLOUCESTERSHIRE

Played at Hove, July 24, 25, 26, 1968

Gloucestershire won by four wickets. Griffith, leading Sussex for only the second time, put in Gloucestershire, who replied with the season's highest total to that point. Green led the way with his first double century, batting five hours, forty minutes and hitting two 6s and twenty-seven 4s. Milton helped in an opening partnership of 315 in four and a half hours, which beat by 64 the previous best for the county in Championship cricket by Barnett and Sinfield in 1935. Although Greig replied with a fine century (one 6, nineteen 4s) in two hours, forty minutes. Sussex followed-on 233 behind, whereupon with the help of an opening stand of 167 by Lenham and Racionzer they almost saved the game. Needing 129 runs in time enough for 24 overs, Gloucestershire got home in the last over but one. Altogether 1,227 runs were hit for the loss of 36 wickets.

Gloucestershire

D. M. Green b Griffith b A. Buss	233	– b Greig	48
*C. A. Milton lbw b A. Buss	122		
R. B. Nicholls b Jones	0	– c Suttle b Jones	15
D. Shepherd c Greig b Jones	25	– c Greig b Jones	9
M. J. Procter c Lenham b A. Buss	49	– b Greig	11
A. S. Brown lbw b Greig	3	– b Greig	8
M. Bissex not out	18	– not out	18
J. B. Mortimore not out	18	– run out	18
†B. J. Meyer (did not bat)		– not out	0
B 3, l-b 13, w 1	17	L-b 2	2
1/315 2/316 3/374 4/398 5/401 6/453	(6 wkts dec.) 485	1/34 2/55 3/74 4/89 5/98 6/126	(6 wkts) 129

D. R. Smith and J. Davey did not bat.

Bowling: *First Innings*—A. Buss 28–6–77–3; Jones 23–1–102–2; M. A. Buss 14–2–53–0; Greig 27–1–130–1; Lewis 16–1–59–0; Suttle 12–1–47–0. *Second Innings*—A. Buss 11–0–55–0; Jones 6–0–45–2; Greig 5.3–1–27–3.

Sussex

L. J. Lenham b Procter	6	– c Bissex b Mortimore	86
T. B. Racionzer c Mayer b Smith	36	– c sub b Mortimore	82
K. G. Suttle c Green b Smith	14	– b Brown	5
A. W. Greig c Meyer b Brown	117	– c Bissex b Mortimore	4
†J. M. Parks c Milton b Mortimore	17	– c Bissex b Brown	49
*M. G. Griffith c Brown b Mortimore	4	– b Brown	42
M. A. Buss b Mortimore	22	– c Bissex b Davey	13
G. C. Cooper c Meyer b Davey	2	– c and b Bissex	45
E. Lewis b Brown	5	– c Bissex b Davey	6
A. Buss not out	19	– not out	11
A. A. Jones c Meyer b Smith	4	– c Mayer b Bissex	4
L-b 5, w 1	6	L-b 13, n-b 1	14
1/10 2/55 3/64 4/107 5/119 6/175 7/190 8/212 9/235	252	1/167 2/176 3/186 4/187 5/256 6/295 7/319 8/327 9/351	361

Bowling: *First Innings*—Procter 7–0–20–1; Brown 11–3–39–2; Davey 17–1–61–1; Mortimore 21–5–63–3; Smith 15.5–4–63–3. *Second Innings*—Brown 30–6–92–3; Davey 29–2–108–2; Mortimore 35–10–81–3; Smith 16–5–45–0; Bissex 7–3–15–2; Green 2–0–6–0.

Umpires: A. Jepson and C. S. Elliott.

SUSSEX v CAMBRIDGE UNIVERSITY

Played at Horsham, July 7, 8, 9, 1971

Cambridge University won by three wickets, so gaining a useful victory on the eve of the University match, but the game will be best remembered for the efforts of Suttle. The 42-year-old left-hander in his 22nd season with the club hit a century in each innings, and it was only his second appearance of the summer. The first hundred took four and a half hours with concentration as its greatest feature, but the next day Suttle cut, drove and swept in his best style for his 48th three-figure innings. Another left-hander, Morley, helped to put on 149 for the second wicket playing in his first first-class game. Cambridge were finally asked to get 259 in just over three hours, and, without having to face Snow, who had injured his back, they succeeded in the last over. Barford, struggling to find his form, still looked unsure of himself while hitting 95 in the first innings but a second knock of 84, during a stand of 145 with the enterprising Owen-Thomas, showed him in a better light.

Sussex

G. A. Greenidge c Khan b Spencer	2	– lbw b Spencer 2
J. D. Morley lbw b Spencer	10	– lbw b Khan 50
K. G. Suttle b Khan	112	– b Khan 120
P. J. Graves c Edmonds b Spencer	76	– not out 15
R. J. Langridge c Selvey b Khan	17	– c Taylor b Selvey 1
*M. G. Griffith c Khan b Hadley	3	– lbw b Khan 25
J. A. Snow c Khan b Edmonds	17	
S. Pheasant c Khan b Edmonds	0	– not out 2
J. Denman c Steele b Spencer	42	
†A. Mansell not out	14	
M. Upton not out	2	
L-b 2, n-b 2	4	B 9, l-b 4, n-b 3 16
1/11 2/15 3/172 4/206 5/209 6/241 7/241 8/241 9/299	(9 wkts dec.) 299	1/4 2/153 3/198 4/203 5/223 (5 wkts dec.) 231

Bowling: *First Innings*—Spencer 20–6–49–4; Selvey 13–2–49–0; Hadley 15–3–52–1; Edmonds 30–5–95–2; Khan 28–9–50–2. *Second Innings*—Spencer 12–5–21–1; Selvey 15–5–28–1; Hadley 9–2–21–0; Edmonds 15–5–50–0; Khan 30–9–72–3; Steele 8–1–23–0.

Cambridge University

*Majid J. Khan c Morley b Suttle	92	– c Graves b Pheasant 5
M. T. Barford c Langridge b Upton	95	– c and b Pheasant 84
D. R. Owen-Thomas c Mansell b Denman	54	– c Morley b Pheasant 89
P. D. Johnson b Denman	0	– c Mansell b Suttle 14
C. Seager not out	16	– lbw b Suttle 17
H. K. Steele not out	10	– c and b Pheasant 8
P. H. Edmonds (did not bat)		– not out 16
M. W. W. Selvey (did not bat)		– run out 9
J. Spencer (did not bat)		– not out 8
B 3, l-b 2	5	B 4, l-b 6 10
1/140 2/225 3/231 4/247	(4 wkts dec.) 272	1/17 2/162 3/199 4/224 5/232 6/250 (7 wkts) 260

†C. R. V. Taylor and R. J. Hadley did not bat.

Bowling: *First Innings*—Snow 6–0–19–0; Denman 18–5–53–2; Pheasant 23–9–33–0; Upton 22–5–72–1; Suttle 17–5–49–1; Greenidge 5–0–31–0; Graves 2–0–10–0. *Second Innings*—Denman 17.3–2–68–0; Pheasant 27–5–88–4; Upton 8–1–48–0; Suttle 10–0–46–2.

Umpires: C. G. Pepper and G. H. Pope.

SUSSEX v HAMPSHIRE

Played at Hove, July 21, 22, 23, 1976

Sussex won by six wickets. Victory would have sent Hampshire to the top of the championship table, and when Gilliat declared, challenging Sussex to score 311 in five and a quarter hours, their prospects looked promising, especially when they took an early wicket. They had established a first innings lead of 145, the masterly Richards scoring 136 and completing his century before lunch, on his 31st birthday. His runs were made out of 213, and he hit two 6s and twenty 4s. Hampshire briskly increased their lead to 310 against a Sussex side without Greig, Snow and Knight. Miandad, however, revealed his youthful zest and class with a magnificent maiden century in England. He and the experienced Buss came together at 182 for four and paced themselves skilfully, setting a target of 88 off the final twenty overs. Miandad employed a number of audacious and unorthodox shots and hit two 6s and sixteen 4s. Buss coolly played his part in a notable Sussex victory, with 2.4 overs to spare.

Hampshire

B. A. Richards c Long b Marshall	136	– c Long b Spencer	5
P. J. Barrett lbw b Spencer	4	– c Barclay b Spencer	10
D. R. Turner c Miandad b Marshall	13	– c Barclay b Phillipson	31
T. E. Jesty c Graves b Waller	48	– run out	0
*R. M. C. Gilliat b Marshall	18	– c Long b Marshall	4
P. J. Sainsbury c Parker b Waller	6	– not out	47
N. G. Cowley c Miandad b Marshall	0	– not out	62
J. M. Rice b Spencer	71		
†G. R. Stephenson c Graves b Spencer	42		
T. M. Tremlett b Waller	4		
J. W. Southern not out	0		
B 3, l-b 5, w 1, n-b 7	16	B 4, n-b 2	6
1/10 2/43 3/194 4/213 5/228 6/228 7/234 8/242 9/351	358	1/13 2/18 3/22 4/28 5/51	(5 wkts dec.) 165

Bowling: *First Innings*—Spencer 19.3–4–68–3; Marshall 23–2–90–4; Waller 30–9–63–3; Phillipson 12–1–60–0; Barclay 6–2–18–0; Miandad 5–0–25–0; Buss 4–2–18–0. *Second Innings*—Spencer 11–4–29–2; Marshall 16–1–59–1; Waller 10–3–15–0; Phillipson 11–0–37–1; Barclay 4–0–6–0; Miandad 4–1–13–0; Buss 1–1–0–0.

Sussex

J. R. T. Barclay c Gilliat b Sainsbury	81	– b Sainsbury	63
J. D. Morley c Cowley b Jesty	8	– b Rice	9
C. P. Phillipson c Turner b Tremlett	23		
*P. J. Graves c Richards b Southern	11	– c Richards b Southern	34
Javed Miandad b Sainsbury	5	– not out	135
P. W. G. Parker c Stephenson b Southern	10	– b Sainsbury	19
†A. Long c Jesty b Cowley	22		
M. A. Buss not out	33	– not out	44
J. Spencer c Rice b Richards	2		
C. E. Waller not out	0		
B 5, l-b 7, w 1, n-b 5	18	L-b 6, n-b 1	7
1/28 2/73 3/108 4/129 5/148 6/172 7/189 8/209	(8 wkts) 213	1/17 2/88 3/123 4/182	(4 wkts) 311

R. P. T. Marshall did not bat.

Bowling: *First Innings*—Rice 17–9–24–0; Jesty 18–0–25–1; Tremlett 9–1–27–1; Sainsbury 18–10–32–2; Southern 30–7–65–2; Cowley 6–0–13–1; Richards 2–0–9–1. *Second Innings*—Rice 19.2–5–71–1; Jesty 13–2–42–0; Tremlett 1–0–6–0; Sainsbury 35–18–62–2; Southern 27–6–84–1; Cowley 15–3–39–0.

Umpires: W. L. Budd and D. L. Evans.

SUSSEX v NOTTINGHAMSHIRE

Played at Hove, August 21, 23, 24, 1976

Nottinghamshire won by 86 runs. A magnificent innings of 246 by Rice, the highest at Hove since Paynter's 322 for Lancashire in 1937, came on the opening day and proved the decisive factor throughout. The next highest score in the massive visiting total was 44 by Smedley, and despite a sound century by Graves, Nottinghamshire gained a first innings lead of 95 on a splendid batting wicket. Rice hit six beautifully struck 6s and thirty-two 4s, the ball streaking over the parched outfield to all points of the cricket compass in a stay of five hours. A swashbuckling knock of 97 by Buss saved Sussex from a heavier defeat. The left-hander batted for only eighty-eight minutes and hit 70 of his runs in boundaries. Alletson's historic innings at Hove in 1911 is still rated the greatest for entertainment, but Rice's will long be remembered.

Nottinghamshire

P. A. Todd c and b Greig	0	– c Waller b Buss	14
N. Nanan c and b Buss	31	– c Long b Spencer	15
D. W. Randall c Groome b Greig	8	– c Buss b Waller	27
C. E. B. Rice c Barclay b Waller	246	– lbw b Barclay	24
P. A. Johnson c Barclay b Buss	8	– lbw b Barclay	11
*M. J. Smedley c Phillipson b Waller	44	– c Waller b Barclay	5
†M. J. Harris c Phillipson b Waller	11	– c Groome b Waller	28
R. A. White c Long b Phillipson	14	– not out	38
P. A. Wilkinson not out	23	– c Spencer b Waller	0
K. Cooper not out	3	– c Phillipson b Waller	0
W. Taylor (did not bat)		– b Barclay	9
B 8, l-b 3, n-b 4	15	B 5, l-b 9	14
1/0 2/18 3/61 4/109 5/276 6/292 7/349 8/385	(8 wkts) 403	1/30 2/30 3/69 4/85 5/96 6/105 7/156 8/156 9/156	185

Bowling: *First Innings*—Greig 14–2–58–2; Spencer 9–1–43–0; Buss 13–3–55–2; Phillipson 13–1–55–1; Barclay 10–2–35–0; Waller 35–6–117–3; Knight 6–0–25–0. *Second Innings*—Greig 2–1–8–0; Spencer 9–1–27–1; Buss 12–5–35–1; Barclay 21.3–9–38–4; Waller 25–5–63–4.

Sussex

J. R. T. Barclay b Cooper	17	– c White b Wilkinson	0
J. J. Groome c Rice b Cooper	23	– c Todd b Rice	5
R. D. V. Knight run out	54	– b Wilkinson	10
P. J. Graves st Harris b Wilkinson	107	– st Harris b Nanan	25
J. Spencer c Johnson b Wilkinson	52	– not out	20
*A. W. Greig b Wilkinson	8	– c Rice b White	11
P. W. G. Parker not out	10	– c Johnson b White	4
M. A. Buss lbw b Wilkinson	0	– lbw b Cooper	97
†A. Long not out	9	– c Nanan b White	13
C. P. Phillipson (did not bat)		– lbw b Cooper	4
C. E. Waller (did not bat)		– c Harris b Cooper	1
B 7, l-b 16, w 3, n-b 2	28	B 1, l-b 1, n-b 2	4
1/43 2/52 3/158 4/266 5/278 6/282 7/282	(7 wkts) 308	1/0 2/12 3/16 4/41 5/49 6/101 7/168 8/170 9/178	194

Bowling: *First Innings*—Wilkinson 21–3–65–4; Rice 17–6–36–0; Cooper 20–4–71–2; White 30–6–64–0; Taylor 12–3–44–0. *Second Innings*—Wilkinson 11–2–49–2; Rice 11–4–25–1; Cooper 7.4–0–17–3; White 24–9–47–3; Taylor 1–0–10–0; Nanan 5–0–42–1.

Umpires: A. E. Fagg and D. Oslear.

SUSSEX IN 1977

Not for many a year had a season opened with such justifiably high hopes of success. Players, committee and followers of the club felt that Sussex would win one of the competitions, and the captain Tony Greig spoke confidently of the splendid spirit right throughout the camp. There was the right approach, and a very good side, he emphasized.

The way Sussex opened the campaign strengthened and confirmed these hopes and predictions. They won the first two Benson and Hedges Cup matches, the first three John Player League fixtures and the first County Championship game. Although Kent then dared to end this run of success. Sussex promptly won three matches in a row to show just how determined they were to try and make this a memorable season.

And then came the Packer affair.

The Australian TV tycoon visited the Hove County Ground and conferred with Greig in the captain's room at the top of the pavilion. Greig followed by holding the most extraordinary Press conference ever likely to be staged on the ground and the Sussex boat was then well and truly rocked.

Just what an adverse effect the whole business had on the club we do not yet know, but with Greig obviously Packer's right-hand man over here, foremost in his recruitment policy and talking with such enthusiasm of the opportunities opening out for cricket and players, plus the fact that Snow and Imran Khan had also signed up for Australian duty, Sussex were closely involved. There was uncertainty in the air, and the earlier spirit of hope and confidence disappeared. Several poor results and indifferent individual performances, including a dismal Gillette Cup display against Derbyshire, matched the wretched weather. There was previous little sunshine during the summer, and the sparkle vanished from Sussex.

Greig's spirits did not flag and although his batting and bowling figures, by his standards, were disappointing, he gave his usual tremendous effort and his magnificent fielding, in particular, set an inspiring lead. He had tried to establish a new attitude of mind in Sussex cricket – to be good winners rather than good losers. This fighting spirit enabled the side to pull round and finish a respectable eighth in the championship table and win nine John Player matches to be up among the leading clubs. This was reasonably satisfactory, but we were left to ponder what might have been without the Packer business.

SUSSEX v LANCASHIRE

Played at Hove, May 11, 12, 13, 1977

Drawn, abandoned owing to rain. The previous fixture, against the Australians, had been washed out after only a little play had been possible, and only four overs could be bowled in this match. John Langridge, one of the umpires, said that he had never seen the cricket square so saturated during his fifty years in the game, most of them as a Sussex player. The news concerning the Australian cricket "circus" broke during the match, and reporters switched from a wearying wait for play to start to attend a conference called by Greig.

Sussex

J. R. T. Barclay not out	6
K. C. Wessels not out	4
(no wkt)	10

R. D. V. Knight, Javed Miandad, *A. W. Greig, P. J. Graves, M. A. Buss, J. A. Snow, †A. Long, J. Spencer and C. E. Waller did not bat.

Bowling: Lee 2–0–6–0; Ratcliffe 2–1–4–0.

Lancashire

B. Wood, *D. Lloyd, H. Pilling, C. H. Lloyd, F. C. Hayes, J. Abrahams, J. Simmons, R. M. Ratcliffe, †J. Lyon, P. G. Lee and R. Arrowsmith.

Umpires: J. G. Langridge and B. J. Meyer.

SUSSEX v SOMERSET

Played at Hove, June 29, 30, July 1, 1977

Somerset won by an innings and 37 runs. A magnificent double century by Richards completely overshadowed all else. He drove with effortless ease and tremendous power, unleashing an exciting stream of shots to all parts of the County Ground in an innings ranking among the greatest played there. He became the first batsman to reach 1,000 runs for the season, and hit six 6s and twenty-one 4s. Somerset gained a first innings lead of 178, and the Sussex effort to stave off an innings defeat was quite undistinguished, apart from a brave seventh wicket stand of 68 in which Buss, bristling with aggression, hit 45 in company with Mendis. Two bowlers, Spencer of Sussex with five for 116, and Botham, six for 50 with match figures of ten for 161, gave a heartwarming exhibition of sheer hard work and persistency.

Sussex

J. R. T. Barclay b Botham	24	– c Richards b Botham	0
P. J. Graves c Richards b Moseley	39	– lbw b Moseley	16
R. D. V. Knight b Taylor b Botham	10	– lbw b Botham	7
Javed Miandad b Dredge	23	– b Moseley	5
*A. W. Greig c Dredge b Botham	21	– c Close b Botham	5
M. A. Buss c Kitchen b Dredge	77	– c Richards b Clapp	45
G. D. Mendis c Botham b Moseley	0	– c Moseley b Clapp	23
J. A. Snow c Kitchen b Clapp	44	– c Dredge b Botham	9
†A. Long c Rose b Botham	2	– not out	2
J. Spencer not out	7	– c Dredge b Botham	13
C. E. Waller c Close b Clapp	8	– b Botham	15
B 3, l-b 7, w 5	15	L-b 1	1
1/44 2/77 3/80 4/115 5/133 6/134 7/220 8/237 9/260	270	1/0 2/9 3/22 4/41 5/46 6/47 7/115 8/116 9/124	141

Bowling: *First Innings*—Botham 32–5–111–4; Moseley 27–6–61–2; Dredge 18–5–38–2; Clapp 15.1–6–35–2; Breakwell 5–0–10–0. *Second Innings*—Botham 23.5–10–50–6; Moseley 16–3–50–2; Dredge 13–4–38–0; Clapp 4–2–2–2.

Somerset

B. C. Rose c Greig b Snow	42
P. A. Slocombe c Waller b Spencer	14
I. V. A. Richards c Graves b Spencer	204
M. J. Kitchen c Long b Waller	51
I. T. Botham c Graves b Spencer	62
*D. B. Close c Buss b Spencer	27
†D. J. S. Taylor c and b Spencer	12
D. Breakwell c Waller b Greig	0
C. H. Dredge not out	9
H. R. Moseley not out	10
B 3, l-b 6, n-b 8	17
1/55 2/105 3/225 4/399 5/408 6/428 7/429 8/429	(8 wkts) 448

R. J. Clapp did not bat.

Bowling: Snow 24–4–68–1; Spencer 27–4–116–5; Greig 20–2–71–1; Buss 8–0–29–0; Knight 5–0–27–0; Waller 11–1–47–1; Javed 11–1–73–0.

Umpires: W. L. Budd and T. F. Brooks.

SUSSEX v KENT

Played at Hove, August 31, September 1, 2, 1977

Drawn. Underwood achieved his first hat-trick in first-class cricket during the Sussex first innings, when he took six wickets for 69. He sent back Imran and Snow with the fifth and sixth balls of one over and had Long stumped making a reckless shot off the first ball of his next. But even this exciting performance was not enough to see Kent through to a victory which would have strengthened their championship aspirations. Asif declared eight runs behind on the first innings to try to beat the weather and Kent briskly took three wickets for only 19 to live in hopes of a big haul of points, but relentless rain prevailed in the end.

Sussex

J. R. T. Barclay c Knott b Jarvis	39	– lbw b Asif	3
G. D. Mendis c Knott b Jarvis	7	– c Tavaré b Jarvis	4
R. D. V. Knight c Woolmer b Underwood	40	– c Knott b Asif	2
Javed Miandad c Knott b Shepherd	0	– not out	26
P. J. Graves c Woolmer b Underwood	10	– not out	2
*A. W. Greig c Asif b Underwood	30		
Imran Khan c Woolmer b Underwood	10		
J. A. Snow b Underwood	0		
†A. Long st Knott b Underwood	0		
J. Spencer not out	20		
R. G. L. Cheatle c Knott b Hills	34		
B 10, n-b 8	18	N-b 2	2
1/11 2/72 3/74 4/101 5/103 6/123 7/123 8/133 9/160	208	1/7 2/9 3/19 (3 wkts)	90

Bowling: *First Innings*—Jarvis 24–6–59–2; Shepherd 21–10–34–1; Hills 5.3–3–6–1; Underwood 31–9–69–6; Rowe 6–1–22–0. *Second Innings*—Jarvis 7–2–17–1; Hills 3–2–8–0; Underwood 4–3–1–0; Rowe 1–1–0–0; Asif 6–3–12–2.

Kent

G. S. Clinton lbw b Greig	19
R. A. Woolmer not out	101
C. J. Tavaré b Greig	7
*Asif Iqbal c Long b Imran	36
A. G. E. Ealham not out	24
B 5, l-b 1, n-b 7	13
1/56 2/74 3/136 (3 wkts dec.)	200

†A. P. E. Knott, J. N. Shepherd, C. J. C. Rowe, R. W. Hills, D. L. Underwood and K. B. S. Jarvis did not bat.

Bowling: Imran 13–1–52–1; Snow 11–2–22–0; Greig 13–2–44–2; Spencer 11–0–40–0; Cheatle 9.3–2–29–0.

Umpires: P. Rochford and W. L. Budd.

SUSSEX v SURREY

Played at Hove, July 26, 27, 28, 1978

A hat-trick by Pigott, the Sussex 20-year-old fast bowler, in his first season with the club, suddenly brought drama into a match which was moving peacefully towards a dull draw. He sent back Intikhab, Jackman and Pocock to make Surrey 93 for eight with only six of the final twenty overs bowled and it put Surrey's target of 250 well out of range. What made Pigott's hat-trick all the more exciting was that he had not previously taken a wicket in first-class cricket. A ninth wicket fell at 113, but in the fourteenth over that experienced campaigner Younis Ahmed was joined by Knight, batting as No. 11 as he had been ill with influenza, and the shutters were effectively put up to prevent a Sussex win. Younis's 44 not out was his side's top score. Arnold, in his best performance so far for Sussex, took five for 33, and Pigott three for 15. Runs had flowed freely for both sides in the first innings, Mendis scoring a competent 126 for Sussex and Butcher an entertaining 188 for Surrey, including seven 6s. Parker, of Sussex, played two fine innings of 67 and 99.

Sussex

K. C. Wessels b Jackman	11 – st Richards b Baker	23
G. D. Mendis c and b Intikhab	126 – b Pocock	26
P. W. G. Parker c Butcher b Jackman	67 – b Lynch	99
C. P. Phillipson not out	48 – c Baker b Intikhab	22
G. G. Arnold b Jackman	24	
Imran Khan not out	16 – run out	65
S. J. Storey (did not bat)	– not out	5
M. A. Buss (did not bat)	– not out	20
L-b 5, w 1, n-b 3	9 B 7, l-b 3, n-b 6	16
1/28 2/142 3/234 4/274	(4 wkts dec.) 301 1/54 2/58 3/125 4/251 5/251	(5 wkts dec.) 276

A. C. S. Pigott, *†A. Long and C. E. Waller did not bat.

Bowling: *First Innings*—Jackman 28–5–96–3; Thomas 11–0–48–0; Intikhab 21–8–45–1; Baker 4–0–13–0; Pocock 15.2–0–57–0; Knight 8–0–33–0. *Second Innings*—Jackman 7–3–15–0; Thomas 5–1–24–0; Intikhab 18–3–66–1; Baker 7–1–18–1; Pocock 22–4–81–1; Needham 3–1–8–0; Butcher 8–0–34–0; Lynch 4–0–14–1.

Surrey

M. A. Lynch b Imran	0 – c Buss b Arnold	7
A. R. Butcher c Imran b Buss	188 – c Buss b Arnold	29
Younis Ahmed c Wessels b Phillipson	72 – not out	44
R. P. Baker c Long b Imran	15 – c Long b Arnold	2
A. Needham c Parker b Buss	21 – b Arnold	0
†C. J. Richards c Long b Waller	6 – c Pigott b Imran	13
Intikhab Alam not out	5 – c Long b Pigott	0
R. D. Jackman b Waller	2 – c Imran b Pigott	0
P. I. Pocock (did not bat)	– lbw b Pigott	0
D. J. Thomas (did not bat)	– lbw b Arnold	12
*R. D. V. Knight (did not bat)	– not out	0
B 1, l-b 14, n-b 4	19 L-b 3, w 4, n-b 1	8
1/1 2/170 3/274 4/304 5/315 6/326	(7 wkts) 328 1/22 2/52 3/58 4/58 5/90 6/93 7/93 8/93 9/113	(9 wkts) 115

Bowling: *First Innings*—Imran 17–1–65–2; Arnold 15–3–26–0; Buss 15–6–51–2; Pigott 11–0–67–0; Storey 3–0–24–0; Phillipson 6–2–19–1; Waller 17–5–57–2. *Second Innings*—Imran 16–7–44–1; Arnold 17–6–33–5; Pigott 7–2–15–3; Waller 8–1–15–0.

Umpires: K. E. Palmer and W. L. Budd.

SUSSEX v WARWICKSHIRE

Played at Hove, July 18, 20, 21, 1981

Sussex won by five wickets. The result looked like being a dull draw when no play was possible on the last day until after lunch, but then le Roux bowled three overs at blistering pace to take four wickets for only 5 runs and the visitors added only a dozen runs to their overnight total of 114 for five. Le Roux's fine spell included a hat-trick, his third victim being Amiss, top-scorer with a polished 58, and Sussex required 168 to win in even time. Mendis and Barclay set them on the right course with a businesslike 60 off the first thirteen overs, and then Parker and Imran, pacing themselves skilfully, took their side to victory and to the top of the Championship table.

Warwickshire

*D. L. Amiss c Greig b Arnold	1	– c Gould b le Roux	58
S. H. Wootton c Gould b Imran	6	– b le Roux	0
T. A. Lloyd c and b Barclay	89	– (5) c Parker b le Roux	7
†G. W. Humpage b Imran	8	– (3) b Imran	9
Asif Din c Waller b Barclay	57	– (4) c Barclay b Greig	9
R. I. H. B. Dyer b Greig	7	– c Barclay b Imran	7
A. M. Ferreira b Arnold	36	– c Booth Jones b le Roux	21
G. C. Small b Arnold	12	– c Barclay b le Roux	0
S. P. Perryman c Phillipson b le Roux	11	– c Phillipson b le Roux	5
W. Hogg not out	1	– not out	0
D. R. Doshi run out	5	– run out	4
B 2, l-b 4, w 2, n-b 8	16	B 1, l-b 2, w 1, n-b 2	6
1/1 2/13 3/25 4/134 5/157 6/184 7/218 8/240 9/242	249	1/1 2/16 3/44 4/62 5/77 6/116 7/116 8/117 9/122	126

Bowling: *First Innings*—le Roux 22–4–71–1; Arnold 19.5–5–52–3; Imran 11–3–26–2; Greig 18–3–55–1; Barclay 16–8–15–2; Waller 11–5–14–0. *Second Innings*—le Roux 16–3–36–6; Imran 14–1–55–2; Greig 8–2–29–1.

Sussex

G. D. Mendis c Hogg b Small	12	– c Doshi b Small	32
*J. R. T. Barclay c Asif Din b Hogg	26	– c Asif Din b Small	23
T. D. Booth Jones c Small b Perryman	17	– c Dyer b Doshi	9
P. W. G. Parker c Small b Hogg	45	– lbw b Ferreira	50
I. A. Greig c Doshi b Hogg	34	– c Humpage b Hogg	7
Imran Khan c Perryman b Hogg	5	– not out	25
C. P. Phillipson c Wootton b Doshi	19	– not out	2
†I. J. Gould c Humpage b Small	18		
G. S. le Roux c Perryman b Doshi	20		
G. G. Arnold b Doshi	0		
C. E. Waller not out	0		
L-b 3, n-b 9	12	B 4, l-b 9, w 1, n-b 7	21
1/16 2/58 3/68 4/133 5/147 6/148 7/183 8/207 9/207	208	1/60 2/77 3/86 4/99 5/163	(5 wkts) 169

Bowling: *First Innings*—Small 13–0–57–2; Hogg 16–3–54–4; Perryman 12–1–35–1; Ferreira 18–4–39–0; Asif Din 1–0–4–0; Doshi 6.2–3–7–3. *Second Innings*—Hogg 15–4–49–1; Small 8–1–33–2; Ferreira 7–2–26–1; Doshi 12.5–6–40–1.

Umpires: A. Jepson and D. O. Oslear.

SUSSEX v DERBYSHIRE

Played at Eastbourne, August 12, 13, 14, 1981

Sussex won by five wickets. In a thrilling climax, Imran, who had earlier in the day taken four wickets in five balls, hit a swashbuckling unbeaten 107 to take Sussex to victory with five balls to spare. He hit three 6s and eleven 4s, reaching his 50 in only 36 minutes, and his century in 88 minutes as Sussex chased a tough target of 234 in just under two and a half hours. Earlier, Kirsten had played two fine innings for Derbyshire. This was the last day of probably the most successful ever Eastbourne Week, with crowds totalling 25,000 and enjoying fine weather, a controversial Kent victory in the John Player League, and two Sussex Championship wins producing a haul of 47 points.

Derbyshire

*B. Wood lbw b Arnold	24	– lbw b Imran	12
J. G. Wright b Greig	73	– lbw b le Roux	0
P. N. Kirsten b Greig	85	– c Waller b Wells	68
D. S. Steele b Greig	12	– lbw b Imran	59
G. Miller b Greig	0	– c Phillipson b Wells	22
A. Hill run out	5	– run out	16
K. J. Barnett c Waller b le Roux	0	– b Waller	22
†R. W. Taylor b Imran	16	– not out	11
C. J. Tunnicliffe b Arnold	12	– b Imran	0
P. G. Newman not out	0	– lbw b Imran	0
S. Oldham lbw b Arnold	7	– lbw b Imran	0
B 6, l-b 8, w 2, n-b 6	22	B 11, l-b 1, w 2, n-b 3	17
1/90 2/130 3/166 4/168 5/188 6/189 7/225 8/241 9/249	256	1/2 2/134 3/168 4/193 5/193 6/226 7/227 8/227 9/227	227

Bowling: *First Innings*—le Roux 18–3–47–1; Arnold 21.2–6–44–3; Imran 19–4–55–1; Greig 22–3–75–4; Waller 6–1–13–0. *Second Innings*—Arnold 12–4–16–0; le Roux 9–2–21–1; Imran 17.1–5–52–5; Greig 5–1–20–0; Waller 26–8–46–1; Wells 17–3–55–2.

Sussex

G. D. Mendis c Oldham b Newman	17	– lbw b Newman	1
*J. R. T. Barclay retired hurt	37		
G. S. le Roux c Wright b Newman	40		
P. W. G. Parker not out	82	– (3) c sub b Miller	41
I. A. Greig lbw b Newman	0	– c Newman b Miller	5
C. M. Wells st Taylor b Steele	11	– c Barnett b Miller	1
Imran Khan c Barnett b Steele	2	– (4) not out	107
C. P. Phillipson b Newman	0	– (7) not out	39
†I. J. Gould run out	38	– (2) c sub b Newman	29
G. G. Arnold not out	2		
L-b 2, n-b 19	21	L-b 3, w 1, n-b 8	12
1/23 2/83 3/124 4/151 5/154 6/154 7/223	(7 wkts dec.) 250	1/4 2/74 3/82 4/98 5/102	(5 wkts) 235

C. E. Waller did not bat.

Bowling: *First Innings*—Oldham 14.4–1–38–0; Newman 20–2–73–4; Steele 13–3–32–2; Miller 7–3–20–0; Tunnicliffe 21–6–47–0; Wood 7.3–2–19–0. *Second Innings*—Tunnicliffe 11–0–66–0; Newman 14.1–2–66–2; Steele 5–0–47–0; Miller 8–0–44–3.

Umpires: B. J. Meyer and R. S. Herman.

WARWICKSHIRE

WARWICKSHIRE v GLAMORGAN

Played at Birmingham, August 17, 19, 1963

Warwickshire won by an innings and 53 runs. On a drying pitch, Glamorgan collapsed against a magnificent spell of fast bowling by Webster, who took five wickets at a cost of five runs; A. Jones and Parkhouse were the only batsmen to reach double figures. Webster, a Barbados-born medical student, finished with seven for 40. M. J. K. Smith dominated the Warwickshire innings and alone faced Shepherd with any confidence. When Glamorgan batted a second time, Webster soon sent back the first three batsmen and Barber finished the match with the first hat-trick of his career. Parkhouse batted three and a quarter hours for 34 not out.

Glamorgan

A. Jones c Miller b Webster	31	– c Hitchcock b Webster	13
B. Hedges c Ibadulla b Webster	2	– b Webster	0
W. G. A. Parkhouse c Miller b Webster	20	– not out	34
A. R. Lewis c Cartwright b Edmonds	9	– b Webster	25
A. Rees b Miller	0	– lbw b Ibadulla	6
J. Pressdee c Ibadulla b Webster	1	– c Edmonds b Cartwright	1
P. M. Walker lbw b Webster	5	– c Ibadulla b Cartwright	39
†D. L. Evans c Hitchcock b Webster	1	– st A. Smith b Barber	8
D. J. Shepherd b Cartwright	4	– c Edmonds b Barber	6
*O. S. Wheatley not out	1	– b Barber	0
I. J. Jones b Webster	0	– lbw b Barber	0
L-b 4, n-b 1	5	L-b 1, n-b 1	2
1/15 2/48 3/66 4/67 5/68 6/69 7/71 8/78 9/78	79	1/1 2/14 3/43 4/51 5/54 6/114 7/124 8/134 9/134	134

Bowling: *First Innings*—Webster 17.4–4–40–7; Edmonds 10–5–17–1; Cartwright 12–8–15–1; Ibadulla 1–0–1–0; Miller 2–1–1–1. *Second Innings*—Webster 15–4–37–3; Edmonds 11–6–21–0; Cartwright 25–10–47–2; Ibadulla 12–5–13–1; Barber 5–1–14–4.

Warwickshire

N. F. Horner c Lewis b Walker	15
K. Ibadulla run out	47
W. J. Stewart c A. Jones b Pressdee	22
*M. J. K. Smith c Evans b Shepherd	112
R. W. Barber c Pressdee b Wheatley	16
T. W. Cartwright c Rees b Shepherd	13
R. E. Hitchcock lbw b Shepherd	0
†A. C. Smith c Evans b I. Jones	18
R. B. Edmonds c Pressdee b Shepherd	7
R. Miller c Evans b Shepherd	0
R. V. Webster not out	9
B 5, l-b 2	7
1/45 2/79 3/84 4/121 5/142 6/142 7/188 8/231 9/233	266

Bowling: Wheatley 14–1–55–1; I. Jones 15–3–55–1; Walker 11–2–34–1; Shepherd 38.2–3–60–5; Pressdee 14–3–55–1.

Umpires: T. W. Spencer and R. Aspinall.

WARWICKSHIRE v NOTTINGHAMSHIRE

Played at Nuneaton, June 3, 4, 5, 1964

Warwickshire won by an innings and 125 runs. Nottinghamshire were completely outclassed and their aggregate of 91 was the lowest scored against Warwickshire in any match. Bannister and Cartwright bowled splendidly in both innings and the economical Cartwright claimed nine wickets for 40 runs. A determined century by Barber, who batted for four and a quarter hours, steadied the Warwickshire innings after Cotton took three early wickets.

Nottinghamshire

J. B. Bolus c A. C. Smith b Brown	2	– c Barber b Cartwright	8
N. Hill c Cartwright b Bannister	4	– c Horner b Bannister	13
*†G. Millman b Bannister	4	– c Miller b Cartwright	8
H. I. Moore b Cartwright	5	– b Bannister	0
M. Hill c A. C. Smith b Cartwright	0	– c Barber b Bannister	2
A. Gill c Miller b Bannister	0	– c Ibadulla b Cartwright	9
K. Gillhouley c Miller b Bannister	8	– lbw b Miller	2
A. J. Corran c Ibadulla b Bannister	0	– b Cartwright	0
I. Davison b Cartwright	10	– c Jameson b Miller	6
J. Cotton c M. J. K. Smith b Cartwright	1	– not out	1
B. D. Wells not out	0	– c Jameson b Cartwright	8
1/6 2/2 3/15 4/15 5/15 6/15 7/15 8/28 9/30	34	1/18 2/24 3/24 4/26 5/39 6/40 7/42 8/42 9/49	57

Bowling: *First Innings*—Brown 5–2–7–1; Bannister 8.5–4–24–5; Cartwright 5–4–3–4. *Second Innings*—Brown 3–3–0–0; Bannister 23–12–18–3; Cartwright 23.2–12–37–5; Miller 3–1–2–2.

Warwickshire

N. F. Horner lbw b Cotton	6
R. W. Barber not out	103
K. Ibadulla c Corran b Cotton	0
*M. J. K. Smith lbw b Cotton	0
J. A. Jameson c N. Hill b Corran	41
T. W. Cartwright run out	37
R. E. Hitchcock c Millman b Wells	20
†A. C. Smith not out	7
L-b 1, n-b 1	2
1/20 2/22 3/26 4/114 5/175 6/203	(6 wkts dec.) 216

J. D. Bannister, R. Miller and D. J. Brown did not bat.

Bowling: Cotton 19–5–45–3; Davison 23–2–60–0; Corran 11–0–32–1; Wells 12–3–30–1; Gillhouley 17–4–47–0.

Umpires: J. Arnold and A. Jepson.

WARWICKSHIRE v SOMERSET

Played at Birmingham, May 12, 13, 14, 1965

Warwickshire won by three wickets. Virgin, with centuries in both innings, received valuable support from G. Atkinson and Palmer in the Somerset first innings and batted for four hours, forty minutes. Warwickshire began brightly but it was left to Amiss to pull them round against Langford. Virgin's second hundred was made at a slightly faster rate in three and three-quarter hours and allowed Somerset to ask their opponents to score 172 in under three hours. M. J. K. Smith (one 6, fourteen 4s) and Amiss (one 6, eight 4s) shared a third wicket stand of 77 in thirty-seven minutes and Stewart hit the winning four off the fourth ball of the last over.

Somerset

G. Atkinson b Miller	43	– st A. C. Smith b Edmonds	23
R. Virgin run out	124	– not out	125
P. B. Wight b Miller	7	– c Bannister b Ibadulla	65
W. E. Alley c A. C. Smith b Cartwright	11	– not out	17
R. Roe b Cartwright	3		
C. Greetham c and b Barber	14		
K. E. Palmer b Edmonds	51		
*C. R. M. Atkinson lbw b Edmonds	17		
†G. Clayton lbw b Edmonds	2		
B. Langford lbw b Edmonds	7		
F. E. Rumsey not out	2		
L-b 4	4	B 1, l-b 9	10
1/77 2/101 3/114 4/122 5/154 6/247 7/263 8/275 9/278	285	1/63 2/213 (2 wkts dec.)	240

Bowling: *First Innings*—Brown 19–4–62–0; Bannister 14–3–37–0; Cartwright 22–6–48–2; Ibadulla 7–2–13–0; Edmonds 20.4–8–54–4; Miller 16–6–41–2; Barber 9–2–26–1. *Second Innings*—Brown 10–3–18–0; Bannister 14–3–38–0; Cartwright 11–7–14–0; Edmonds 11–3–50–1; Barber 6–1–21–0; Ibadulla 13–1–60–1; Miller 6–0–29–0.

Warwickshire

R. W. Barber lbw b Alley	28	– c Clayton b Rumsey	33
K. Ibadulla c Clayton b Rumsey	42	– lbw b Palmer	1
*M. J. K. Smith c Wight b Langford	9	– b Alley	83
D. L. Amiss c Roe b Rumsey	86	– b Palmer	72
W. J. Stewart not out	5	– not out	32
T. W. Cartwright c Wight b Langford	4	– c Palmer b Langford	6
†A. C. Smith c Wight b Langford	17	– c Clayton b Rumsey	19
R. B. Edmonds c Roe b Rumsey	4	– not out	17
R. E. Miller lbw b Langford	27	– c Wight b Palmer	4
D. J. Brown c C. R. M. Atkinson b Alley	17		
J. D. Bannister b Langford	5		
B 8, l-b 3	11	B 1, l-b 5	6
1/42 2/55 3/111 4/146 5/170 6/202 7/207 8/235 9/251	255	1/2 2/72 3/149 4/176 5/208 6/216 7/224 (7 wkts)	273

Bowling: *First Innings*—Rumsey 17–2–47–3; Palmer 14–2–64–0; Alley 27.5–9–52–2; Langford 40–21–69–5; C. R. M. Atkinson 4–2–12–0. *Second Innings*—Rumsey 17.4–0–93–2; Palmer 12–0–60–3; Langford 11–1–68–1; Alley 6–0–46–1.

Umpires: W. E. Phillipson and T. Drinkwater.

WARWICKSHIRE v GLOUCESTERSHIRE

Played at Birmingham, July 7, 8, 9, 1965

Drawn. Milton and Russell gave the Gloucestershire innings a steady foundation but it was brought to a summary close by Jameson who performed the hat-trick. Warwickshire struggled against the medium pace of A. S. Brown, whose figures were partially spoiled by a ninth-wicket partnership of 48 between A. C. Smith and Webster. Gloucestershire scored freely when they batted a second time and Bissex hit thirteen 4s in his 91 made in just over two hours. Warwickshire, set to score 267 in four and a quarter hours, had made 122 for four in just over two hours when rain ended their challenge.

Gloucestershire

R. B. Nicholls b Webster	8	– c Oakes b Mence	23
C. A. Milton b Cartwright	52	– c Stewart b Mence	33
S. E. Russell c Webster b Mence	65	– c A. C. Smith b Cartwright	13
D. Brown st A. C. Smith b Mence	4	– b Webster	7
M. Bissex c Amiss b Cartwright	10	– b Webster	91
A. S. Brown b Cartwright	38	– lbw b Jameson	29
A. R. Windows not out	11	– b Webster	1
*J. B. Mortimore b Cartwright	0	– c Bannister b Cartwright	2
D. A. Allen c Stewart b Jameson	6	– c Bridge b Bannister	19
†B. J. Meyer lbw b Jameson	0	– not out	20
M. Ashenden c Cartwright b Jameson	0	– not out	2
L-b 8, w 1, n-b 2	11	B 1, l-b 4	5
1/21 2/106 3/126 4/139 5/153 6/191 7/196 8/205 9/205	205	1/41 2/69 3/69 4/90 5/170 6/192 7/203 8/203 9/232	(9 wkts dec.) 245

Bowling: *First Innings*—Webster 14–3–43–1; Bannister 17–5–26–0; Cartwright 26–8–48–4; Mence 16–2–55–2; Bridge 2–0–14–0; Jameson 4.2–2–8–3. *Second Innings*—Bannister 16–4–45–1; Webster 23–8–70–3; Mence 17–4–47–2; Cartwright 29–12–63–2; Jameson 5–3–15–1.

Warwickshire

N. F. Horner lbw b A. S. Brown	14	– b Ashenden	5
W. J. Stewart c Meyer b Ashenden	22	– c Bissex b Mortimore	28
D. L. Amiss lbw b A. S. Brown	16	– c Allen b Windows	30
J. A. Jameson c A. S. Brown b Ashenden	24	– c Nicholls b Mortimore	51
D. R. Oakes c D. Brown b A. S. Brown	13	– not out	6
T. W. Cartwright c Ashenden b Windows	17	– not out	1
*†A. C. Smith c Russell b Mortimore	33		
W. B. Bridge b A. S. Brown	3		
M. D. Mence lbw b A. S. Brown	6		
R. V. Webster c Mortimore b A. S. Brown	25		
J. D. Bannister not out	2		
B 6, l-b 3	9	L-b 1	1
1/30 2/52 3/52 4/87 5/97 6/107 7/111 8/129 9/177	184	1/21 2/41 3/100 4/119	(4 wkts) 122

Bowling: *First Innings*—A. S. Brown 34–13–50–6; Ashenden 15–2–58–2; Windows 16–3–37–1; Mortimore 5.1–4–1–1; Allen 12–3–29–0. *Second Innings*—A. S. Brown 15–4–39–0; Ashenden 5–0–18–1; Mortimore 9.1–3–23–2; Allen 6–0–15–0; Windows 7–1–26–1.

Umpires: A. E. Fagg and R. S. Lay.

WARWICKSHIRE v ESSEX

Played at Coventry, July 10, 12, 13, 1965

Drawn after rain restricted the last day to half an hour. Cartwright, who brought the ball back sharply on a helpful pitch, shot out Essex, Fletcher being the only batsman to defy him for long. Stewart, with a stubborn 39 in two hours, forty minutes, edged Warwickshire into the lead despite fine bowling by Knight. Essex seemed set for disaster against Cartwright and Bannister before rain intervened.

Essex

M. J. Bear b Brown	1	– lbw b Brown	3
G. J. Saville c Smith b Cartwright	30	– c Jameson b Bannister	3
G. J. Smith lbw b Brown	12	– c Brown b Cartwright	6
K. Fletcher lbw b Cartwright	32	– c Cartwright b Bannister	18
*T. E. Bailey c Amiss b Cartwright	2	– lbw b Cartwright	0
B. R. Knight c Oakes b Webster	5	– not out	3
†B. Taylor c Brown b Cartwright	24		
B. Edmeades c and b Cartwright	8		
R. N. S. Hobbs not out	8		
P. J. Phelan c Horner b Cartwright	3	– not out	10
G. Pritchard b Cartwright	0		
L-b 2, n-b 1	3	W 1	1
1/4 2/24 3/74 4/79 5/84 6/84 7/108 8/117 9/128	128	1/6 2/6 3/31 4/31 5/31 (5 wkts)	44

Bowling: *First Innings*—Brown 15–3–38–2; Bannister 9–4–12–0; Webster 12–3–44–1; Cartwright 19.4–12–28–7; Edmonds 5–3–3–0. *Second Innings*—Brown 8–2–15–1; Bannister 15–10–8–2; Cartwright 11–7–20–2.

Warwickshire

N. F. Horner b Knight	5
W. J. Stewart c Fletcher b Edmeades	39
D. L. Amiss c Smith b Knight	13
J. A. Jameson c Pritchard b Knight	11
D. R. Oakes c Taylor b Knight	9
*†A. C. Smith lbw b Knight	7
T. W. Cartwright c Bear b Pritchard	17
R. B. Edmonds lbw b Pritchard	23
R. V. Webster b Pritchard	5
D. J. Brown c Fletcher b Pritchard	0
J. D. Bannister not out	1
B 6, l-b 9, n-b 1	16
1/8 2/35 3/55 4/80 5/86 6/96 7/131 8/145 9/145	146

Bowling: Knight 29–8–50–5; Pritchard 11.5–3–24–4; Bailey 23–8–37–0; Edmeades 12–3–19–1.

Umpires: A. E. Rhodes and T. W. Spencer.

WARWICKSHIRE v DERBYSHIRE

Played at Coventry, August 17, 18, 19, 1966

Derbyshire won by eight wickets. Warwickshire began well and finished dismally. Not only did they allow four substantial Derbyshire partnerships to develop after getting four wickets for 24, but were then themselves bowled out for 38, their lowest score of the season. Following on 243 runs behind, they collapsed again, but A. C. Smith and Webster saved them from the second two-day defeat by the same opposition. On the last morning, however, Jackson, who had upset them in the first innings, took their last three wickets, leaving a formal task for the Derbyshire openers.

Derbyshire

L. W. Hall b Bannister	12	– not out	1
J. R. Eyre b Brown	5	– not out	5
M. H. Page c and b Brown	2		
J. F. Harvey c Bannister b Cartwright	3		
M. Hill c Bannister b Ibadulla	61		
P. E. Russell c Ibadulla b Bannister	34		
*D. C. Morgan c Ibadulla b Brown	96		
T. J. P. Eyre lbw b Ibadulla	25		
†R. W. Taylor c Jameson b Cartwright	39		
F. Smith lbw b Cartwright	0		
A. B. Jackson not out	0		
N-b 4	4	L-b 6	6
1/11 2/18 3/22 4/24 5/81 6/142 7/194 8/281 9/281	281	(no wkt)	12

Bowling: *First Innings*—Brown 24–10–47–3; Webster 13–2–39–0; Bannister 23–6–71–2; Cartwright 8.2–4–28–3; Edmonds 17–2–44–0; Ibadulla 10–0–48–2. *Second Innings*—Edmonds 1–1–0–0; A. C. Smith 1.2–0–6–0.

Warwickshire

K. Ibadulla c Taylor b Jackson	0	– b Smith	55
R. N. Abberley c Hall b Jackson	8	– c Hall b Smith	12
R. B. Edmonds c Smith b Jackson	0	– lbw b Morgan	0
A. Gordon c Russell b Jackson	4	– c Morgan b Jackson	4
*M. J. K. Smith c T. Eyre b Jackson	15	– c Taylor b T. Eyre	11
J. A. Jameson b Smith	1	– b Morgan	19
T. W. Cartwright c Hall b Jackson	3	– c Jackson b Smith	5
†A. C. Smith c Hall b Jackson	3	– c Hall b Jackson	85
R. V. Webster run out	2	– c Hall b Jackson	42
D. J. Brown c Page b Jackson	0	– c Page b Jackson	4
J. D. Bannister not out	1	– not out	2
N-b 1	1	B 8, l-b 6	14
1/0 2/0 3/13 4/18 5/19 6/28 7/32 8/34 9/37	38	1/32 2/37 3/67 4/93 5/102 6/169 7/170 8/232 9/242	253

Bowling: *First Innings*—Jackson 13.3–5–18–8; Smith 13–6–19–1. *Second Innings*—Jackson 21.2–8–31–4; Smith 53–25–65–3; T. J. P. Eyre 15–2–63–1; Morgan 29–15–66–2; Russell 2–0–14–0.

Umpires: R. S. Lay and A. E. Alderman.

WARWICKSHIRE v NORTHAMPTONSHIRE

Played at Birmingham, August 31, September 1, 1966

Warwickshire won by an innings and 89 runs. In the course of the Warwickshire innings, to which M. J. K. Smith subscribed 99, Sully, the visitors' off-spinner from Somerset, took his 100th wicket. A more remarkable achievement was reached on the second day, however, by Cartwright who needed 13 for his 100 wickets when play began and got them when he split the last Northamptonshire pair to give Warwickshire victory in two days. Andrew, the Northamptonshire captain and wicket-keeper, made his last appearance for his county.

Warwickshire

K. Ibadulla c Scott b Sully	33
R. W. Barber c Andrew b Durose	11
D. L. Amiss lbw b Scott	9
*M. J. K. Smith c Scott b Durose	99
J. A. Jameson c Reynolds b Sully	75
R. N. Abberley c Prideaux b Mushtaq	23
†A. C. Smith c Reynolds b Durose	7
T. W. Cartwright b Mushtaq	11
R. B. Edmonds b Mushtaq	19
J. M. Allen not out	0
R. V. Webster b Mushtaq	0
L-b 1, n-b 3	4
1/15 2/35 3/110 4/214 5/232 6/242 7/247 8/286 9/291	291

Bowling: Crump 12–6–25–0; Durose 26–5–59–3; Sully 50–16–106–2; Scott 20–6–49–1; Mushtaq 12.4–1–38–4; Willey 3–1–10–0.

Northamptonshire

R. M. Prideaux c Ibadulla b Edmonds	15 – c M. J. K. Smith b Cartwright	1
B. L. Reynolds c A. C. Smith b Cartwright	5 – b Cartwright	43
A. Lightfoot c Cartwright b Edmonds	31 – lbw b Cartwright	20
P. J. Watts lbw b Cartwright	5 – c Ibadulla b Edmonds	16
Mushtaq Mohammed c A. C Smith b Cartwright	0 – b Cartwright	4
P. Willey c Ibadulla b Cartwright	0 – b Edmonds	1
B. Crump b Edmonds	10 – st A. C. Smith b Cartwright	3
*†K. V. Andrew lbw b Cartwright	8 – c Abberley b Cartwright	2
M. E. Scott c Abberley b Cartwright	4 – st A. C. Smith b Edmonds	10
H. Sully lbw b Edmonds	0 – not out	4
A. J. Durose not out	0 – c A. C. Smith b Cartwright	0
B 6, l-b 4, n-b 1	11 B 2, l-b 4, w 1, n-b 2	9
1/8 2/36 3/45 4/45 5/45 6/56 7/75 8/81 9/85	89 1/8 2/64 3/73 4/82 5/82 6/85 7/102 8/107 9/113	113

Bowling: *First Innings*—Webster 8–2–17–0; Cartwright 31.5–18–40–6; Edmonds 24–16–17–4; Allan 1–0–4–0. *Second Innings*—Webster 3–0–17–0; Cartwright 20.02–4–57–7; Edmonds 9–3–12–3; Ibadulla 9–3–18–0.

Umpires: L. H. Gray and P. B. Wight.

WARWICKSHIRE v DERBYSHIRE

Played at Birmingham, June 24, 26, 27, 1967

Warwickshire won by 59 runs. Neither captain had anything good to say about the pitch after both counties had achieved their lowest scores of the season, and the matter was referred to H. C. Lock, Inspector of Pitches. Wickets fell almost exclusively to seam bowlers. Cook, an occasional Warwickshire player, batting at number ten, was top scorer for his side. Bannister and Cartwright were difficult to play, and Jackson and Rhodes were quite capable of acting for Derbyshire. The Warwickshire batting was a little more resolute at the second attempt, Ibadulla's 22 in two hours being a case in point. Seven hours were lost on the first two days.

Warwickshire

R. N. Abberley c Morgan b Jackson	4	– b Jackson	3
K. Ibadulla c Page b Rhodes	3	– b Rhodes	22
*M. J. K. Smith c Morgan b Rhodes	11	– c Page b Jackson	5
W. J. Stewart c Morgan b Rhodes	16	– c Page b Jackson	4
J. A. Jameson c Taylor b Jackson	15	– c Morgan b Jackson	0
A. Gordon c Jackson b Rhodes	9	– c Page b Rhodes	5
†A. C. Smith c Morgan b T. J. P. Eyre	0	– c Buxton b E. Smith	16
T. W. Cartwright b Jackson	10	– c Taylor b Jackson	3
J. M. Allan c Taylor b Rhodes	2	– c Taylor b Jackson	11
D. R. Cook c Taylor b Jackson	20	– not out	0
J. D. Bannister not out	4	– c Taylor b Jackson	0
B 7, n-b 5	12	B 5, l-b 2, n-b 4	11
1/9 2/11 3/22 4/45 5/65 6/66 7/70 8/74 9/89	106	1/10 2/21 3/30 4/30 5/46 6/55 7/59 8/74 9/80	80

Bowling: *First Innings*—Jackson 15.5–4–47–4; Rhodes 13–2–27–5; T. J. P. Eyre 7–2–20–1. *Second Innings*—Jackson 14.2–4–22–7; Rhodes 15–4–20–2; T. J. P. Eyre 4–1–11–0; Morgan 5–1–5–0; E. Smith 6–3–11–1.

Derbyshire

J. F. Harvey c and b Bannister	13	– c A. C. Smith b Cook	11
D. H. K. Smith c M. J. K. Smith b Bannister	7	– c A. C. Smith b Cook	4
M. H. Page lbw b Bannister	1	– c M. J. K. Smith b Cartwright	10
I. R. Buxton c A. C. Smith b Bannister	19	– c Allan b Bannister	16
*D. C. Morgan b Bannister	0	– c Abberley b Cartwright	2
J. R. Eyre lbw b Cartwright	8	– c Stewart b Cartwright	1
T. J. P. Eyre lbw b Cartwright	13	– c M. J. K. Smith b Cartwright	4
†R. W. Taylor lbw b Cartwright	1	– c A. C. Smith b Bannister	4
E. Smith b Bannister	4	– c Cartwright b Bannister	0
H. J. Rhodes b Bannister	2	– b Cartwright	2
A. B. Jackson not out	0	– not out	0
L-b 1, n-b 1	2	L-b 1, n-b 2	3
1/21 2/22 3/31 4/31 5/40 6/50 7/51 8/64 9/68	70	1/8 2/20 3/34 4/37 5/47 6/51 7/52 8/53 9/57	57

Bowling: *First Innings*—Bannister 21–5–52–7; Cook 6–2–5–0; Cartwright 14.2–10–11–3. *Second Innings*—Bannister 14.1–3–31–3; Cook 6–2–16–2; Cartwright 11–6–7–5.

Umpires: W. E. Phillipson and F. Jakeman.

WARWICKSHIRE v CAMBRIDGE UNIVERSITY

Played at Birmingham, July 5, 6, 7, 1967

Warwickshire won by 70 runs. The University were all at sea against Cartwright's medium-paced bowling and were in danger of following on until Cosh, with lusty hitting, changed the picture and inspired Cottrell, the acting captain, and Palfreman to valuable, if less spectacular emulation. Among other things, Cosh hit Gibbs, the West Indies off-spinner, for two 6s in one over. Cartwright captained a county side with only a few seniors in it. A major feature was the performance of Richardson, who scored a century in each innings. From this point onwards, he kept his place regularly in the side.

Warwickshire

R. N. Abberley c and b Acfield	97		
B. A. Richardson c Acfield b Paull	126	– b Aers	105
D. L. Amiss not out	71	– b Palfreman	2
J. A. Jameson c Palfreman b Cottrell	56	– c Aers b Palfreman	23
A. Gordon not out	6	– c Paull b Acfield	45
*T. W. Cartwright (did not bat)		– b Whitaker	31
E. E. Hemmings (did not bat)		– not out	0
L-b 3, n-b 1	4	B 4, l-b 5, n-b 1	10
1/80 2/248 3/343	(3 wkts dec.) 360	1/9 2/53 3/133 4/208 5/216	(5 wkts dec.) 216

†E. Legard, L. R. Gibbs, W. Blenkiron and R. B. Abell did not bat.

Bowling: *First Innings*—Palfreman 17–1–73–0;' Whitaker 7–3–10–0; Cottrell 23–4–79–1; Aers 29–6–100–0; Acfield 32–8–82–1; Paull 2–0–12–1. *Second Innings*—Palfreman 12–2–40–2; Whitaker 8–2–13–1; Cottrell 5–1–24–0; Aers 3.3–0–30–1; Acfield 14–3–35–1; Paull 25–8–64–0.

Cambridge University

R. D. V. Knight b Amiss b Cartwright	4	– lbw b Hemmings	26
V. P. Malalasekera lbw b Cartwright	0	– b Cartwright	4
C. P. Pyemont b Cartwright	22	– b Hemmings	18
N. J. Cosh c Amiss b Gibbs	138	– c Richardson b Gibbs	30
R. K. Paull c Abell b Hemmings	15	– b Abell	31
D. R. Aers lbw b Cartwright	1	– c Gordon b Jameson	48
*G. A. Cottrell c Richardson b Gibbs	38	– c Cartwright b Jameson	25
†D. W. W. Norris c Hemmings b Blenkiron	14	– lbw b Abell	16
A. B. Palfreman c sub b Jameson	18	– lbw b Gibbs	20
D. L. Acfield c Gordon b Abell	5	– not out	22
M. Whitaker not out	2	– b Abell	2
L-b 4	4	B 1, l-b 2	3
1/0 2/11 3/36 4/44 5/78 6/83 7/219 8/253 9/255	361	1/8 2/48 3/53 4/109 5/113 6/178 7/183 8/212 9/220	245

Bowling: *First Innings*—Blenkiron 15–5–41–1; Cartwright 19–13–17–4; Hemmings 9–2–36–1; Gibbs 24–4–88–2; Abell 16.3–3–48–1; Jameson 4–0–27–1. *Second Innings*—Blenkiron 8–1–27–0; Cartwright 18–6–35–1; Hemmings 8–2–25–2; Gibbs 25–8–71–2; Abell 24.3–7–64–3; Jameson 8–2–20–2.

Umpires: A. Jepson and R. S. Lay.

WARWICKSHIRE v HAMPSHIRE

Played at Birmingham, August 12, 14, 15, 1967

Warwickshire won by ten wickets. Since play had been reduced by more than six and a half hours owing to rain on the first two days, nothing appeared to remain for the third but the first-innings issue. This view was strengthened when Warwickshire, beginning the day 150 runs behind, could manage no better than 27 runs in the first hour. M. J. K. Smith brought about the remarkable transformation by scoring 52 in fifty-five minutes, hitting three 6s and five 4s. Hampshire retaliated by taking the next five wickets for 12 runs. Excitement mounted when they, in their turn, fell foul of Brown and Cook and were floundering at 13 for five. They were finally sunk by Cartwright and Warwickshire were left with the formality of scoring 45 in as many minutes. Prospects of rain caused them to put their best foot forward and they completed their task in twenty-five minutes.

Hampshire

*R. E. Marshall c A. C. Smith b Bannister	22	– c Richardson b Brown	0
B. L. Reed c Jameson b Brown	1	– c Amiss b Cook	3
R. M. C. Gilliat c A. C. Smith b Brown	66	– b Brown	5
D. A. Livingstone c Richardson b Bannister	0	– b Cartwright	10
P. J. Sainsbury lbw b Bannister	4	– lbw b Cook	0
R. G. Caple c A. C. Smith b Brown	14	– b Brown	0
†B. S. V. Timms b Brown	40	– c Amiss b Cartwright	4
A. T. Castell c and b Cartwright	10	– b Cartwright	3
D. Shackleton not out	14	– c sub b Cartwright	13
D. W. White b Brown	1	– c Abberley b Cartwright	4
R. M. H. Cottam b Brown	2	– not out	0
L-b 1, n-b 2	3	L-b 1, n-b 1	2
1/5 2/61 3/61 4/75 5/98 6/117 7/150 8/169 9/173	177	1/0 2/6 3/12 4/12 5/13 6/19 7/26 8/35 9/41	44

Bowling: *First Innings*—Brown 16.1–5–42–6; Bannister 20–6–57–3; Cook 16–6–29–0; Cartwright 20–6–46–1. *Second Innings*—Brown 11–2–25–3; Cook 9–3–11–2; Cartwright 9.4–7–6–5.

Warwickshire

J. M. Allan b White	11		
R. N. Abberley b Cottam	51	– not out	27
D. L. Amiss c sub b Sainsbury	29		
*M. J. K. Smith c Sainsbury b White	52		
J. A. Jameson c Timms b White	19	– not out	21
B. A. Richardson lbw b Shackleton	0		
†A. C. Smith lbw b White	4		
T. W. Cartwright run out	5		
D. R. Cook c Timms b Shackleton	0		
D. J. Brown not out	0		
J. D. Bannister b White	2		
L-b 1, n-b 3	4		
1/39 2/78 3/124 4/164 5/165 6/165 7/172 8/175 9/175	177	(no wkt)	48

Bowling: *First Innings*—Shackleton 26–12–41–2; White 19.5–4–39–5; Cottam 11–3–33–1; Castell 8–0–47–0; Sainsbury 3–0–13–1. *Second Innings*—Shackleton 3–0–23–0; White 3.2–0–18–0; Cottam 1–0–7–0.

Umpires: L. H. Gray and H. Yarnold.

WARWICKSHIRE v SCOTLAND

Played at Birmingham, August 14, 15, 16, 1968

Drawn. It was a remarkable match for two Warwickshire youngsters. First Warner, who shared a fourth-wicket partnership of 143 in ninety-five minutes with Jameson, scored a maiden century (sixteen 4s) and then Gray, a left-arm medium-fast bowler making his début, took half Scotland's first-innings wickets and finished with the astonishing analysis of 10–9–2–5. Gray's lively pace brought him four of his wickets in eleven deliveries. Blenkiron captured the other five wickets. Scotland followed on 262 behind but were saved from defeat by rain.

Warwickshire

*K. Ibadulla c Brown b Thompson	11	†C. O'Rourke not out	23
R. N. Abberley b Rhind	33		
D. P. Ratcliffe c Laing b Ellis	16	B 2, l-b 3	5
J. A. Jameson c Rhind b Barr	114		
G. S. Warner not out	118	1/18 2/48 3/79 (5 wkts dec.)	350
W. B. Bridge st Brown b Goddard	30	4/222 5/285	

R. Miller, D. R. Cook, W. Blenkiron and J. D. Gray did not bat.

Bowling: Thompson 19–3–83–1; Rhind 20–2–73–1; Barr 20–4–49–1; Ellis 9–3–36–1; Allan 21–2–76–0; Goddard 11–3–28–1.

Scotland

A. Steele c Bridge b Blenkiron	0	– c Cook b Blenkiron	6
A. M. Zuill b Gray	28	– c O'Rourke b Cook	35
L. C. Dudman c Cook b Blenkiron	27	– c Abberley b Blenkiron	4
J. G. Laing c Ratcliffe b Blenkiron	1	– c O'Rourke b Gray	2
J. M. Allan c Abberley b Gray	1	– c Jameson b Cook	0
D. Barr c and b Blenkiron	2	– not out	9
*†J. Brown not out	13	– not out	2
G. F. Goddard c O'Rourke b Gray	2		
R. Ellis c Blenkiron b Gray	0		
E. R. Thompson c Cook b Gray	0		
P. Rhind c Jameson b Blenkiron	0		
B 1, l-b 9, w 1, n-b 3	14	B 8, l-b 4, n-b 6	18
1/0 2/61 3/66 4/69 5/72	88	1/10 2/42 3/49 (5 wkts)	76
6/73 7/75 8/75 9/83		4/64 5/65	

Bowling: *First Innings*—Blenkiron 22.4–12–38–5; Cook 17–7–31–0; Miller 2–1–1–0; Ibadulla 2–1–2–0; Gray 10–9–2–5. *Second Innings*—Blenkiron 12–6–16–2; Cook 11–7–15–2; Ibadulla 2–1–1–0; Gray 13–6–25–1; Miller 2–1–1–0.

Umpires: A. Jepson and P. B. Wight.

WARWICKSHIRE v SOMERSET

Played at Birmingham, June 21, 23, 24, 1969

Drawn. Rain, which washed out most of the second day, denied Warwickshire victory after a first-innings hat-trick by Cartwright. Warwickshire found few terrors in the Somerset attack and Amiss shared valuable stands with Stewart, Kanhai and Jameson. A determined innings by Burgess held Warwickshire up after Cartwright's hat-trick and, when Somerset followed-on, Clarkson and Chappell denied Warwickshire an early breakthrough. In an exciting finish, Warwickshire needed two wickets from the last two deliveries. Brown bowled Rose but Roberts avoided an innings defeat.

Warwickshire

W. J. Stewart c Virgin b Robinson	52	T. W. Cartwright not out	18
K. Ibadulla c Chappell b R. Palmer	19	*†A. C. Smith not out	24
D. L. Amiss c Rose b Roberts	120	B 12, l-b 3, n-b 3	18
R. B. Kanhai b Chappell	47		
J. A. Jameson c Chappell b Roberts	57	1/24 2/144 3/225 (6 wkts dec.)	360
G. S. Warner c Kitchen b R. Palmer	5	4/293 5/312 6/315	

D. J. Brown, W. Blenkiron and N. M. McVicker did not bat.

Bowling: R. Palmer 25–6–91–2; Roberts 22–5–66–2; Chappell 25–6–61–1; Burgess 3–0–8–0; Robinson 14–4–49–1; Clarkson 16–2–67–0.

Somerset

*R. T. Virgin c Ibadulla b Cartwright	46	– c Amiss b Blenkiron	1
A. Clarkson c Smith b Cartwright	18	– c Warner b Cartwright	39
G. S. Chappell c Smith b Cartwright	0	– lbw b Cartwright	39
M. J. Kitchen c Brown b Cartwright	0	– c Jameson b McVicker	8
K. E. Palmer c Jameson b Blenkiron	16	– lbw b McVicker	2
P. J. Robinson c Jameson b Cartwright	1	– b Brown	3
B. C. Rose b Blenkiron	2	– b Brown	19
R. Palmer c Smith b McVicker	12	– b McVicker	0
G. Burgess b Blenkiron	62	– b McVicker	0
†C. E. P. Carter b Blenkiron	8	– not out	1
J. K. Roberts not out	1	– not out	0
L-b 2, n-b 2	4	B 4	4
1/48 2/48 3/48 4/81 5/83 6/84 7/86 8/106 9/169	170	1/1 2/70 3/87 4/89 5/89 6/89 7/89 8/111 9/116	(9 wkts) 116

Bowling: *First Innings*—Brown 19–9–36–0; Blenkiron 23–7–44–4; McVicker 13–3–56–1; Cartwright 21–10–30–5. *Second Innings*—Brown 10–3–27–2; Blenkiron 5–1–23–1; Cartwright 14–7–32–2; McVicker 10–4–30–4.

Umpires: J. S. Buller and C. S. Elliott.

WARWICKSHIRE v GLAMORGAN

Played at Birmingham, May 13, 14, 15, 1970

Warwickshire won by 75 runs. Gibbs achieved the best figures of his career in the Glamorgan second innings and brought about their first Championship defeat since September, 1968. Only M. J. K. Smith and Amiss, with a fourth-wicket partnership of 125 in just over two hours, defied Shepherd for long in Warwickshire's first innings. After a dour display by A. Jones, Glamorgan's first innings was given substance with 72 runs from the last three wickets. On a helpful pitch, Shepherd again mesmerised the Warwickshire batsmen with the exception of Kanhai, who worked for four hours, twenty minutes, for his 91. Left to score 211 in three and a half hours, Glamorgan never had a chance, as Gibbs fully exploited the conditions with his variations of pace, flight and spin. He began with five for nine in his first nine overs and ended with three wickets in eight deliveries for an analysis of eight for 37.

Warwickshire

R. N. Abberley c Walker b Cordle	13	– lbw b Shepherd	22
J. A. Jameson lbw b Nash	1	– c A. Jones b Shepherd	14
R. B. Kanhai c E. W. Jones b Williams	14	– c Williams b Walker	91
M. J. K. Smith c E. W. Jones b Shepherd	84	– c E. W. Jones b Williams	4
D. L. Amiss c R. C. Davis b Walker	67	– b Shepherd	36
K. Ibadulla c E. W. Jones b Shepherd	30	– c E. W. Jones b Walker	9
*†A. C. Smith lbw b Shepherd	6	– c R. C. Davis b Shepherd	0
W. Blenkiron lbw b Shepherd	0	– c E. W. Jones b Shepherd	0
N. M. McVicker c E. W. Jones b Cordle	2	– c E. W. Jones b Shepherd	0
L. R. Gibbs not out	3	– b Shepherd	4
W. N. Tidy b Shepherd	2	– not out	2
B 1, l-b 2, n-b 2	5	L-b 5, n-b 1	6
1/5 2/25 3/35 4/160 5/205 6/217 7/217 8/222 9/222	227	1/30 2/46 3/70 4/143 5/170 6/173 7/179 8/181 9/183	188

Bowling: *First Innings*—Nash 15–2–46–1; Williams 13–4–31–1; Shepherd 23.1–8–41–5; Cordle 20–3–53–2; Walker 10–1–41–1; R. C. Davis 2–0–10–0. *Second Innings*—Nash 9–3–21–0; Williams 26–6–53–1; Shepherd 30–12–48–7; Cordle 12–1–34–0; Walker 18–9–26–2.

Glamorgan

A. Jones lbw b Ibadulla	74	– c Kanhai b Gibbs	27
R. C. Davis c A. C. Smith b McVicker	4	– c Abberley b Blenkiron	1
K. J. Lyons b McVicker	7	– c Amiss b Blenkiron	0
D. L. Williams c Kanhai b McVicker	2	– st A. C. Smith b Gibbs	0
*A. R. Lewis c A. C. Smith b Blenkiron	35	– b Gibbs	41
B. A. Davis run out	4	– c Kanhai b Gibbs	3
P. M. Walker c Gibbs b Blenkiron	7	– lbw b Gibbs	7
†E. W. Jones not out	29	– lbw b Gibbs	0
A. E. Cordle c Blenkiron b Tidy	18	– c Ibadulla b Gibbs	18
M. A. Nash c Kanhai b McVicker	22	– c A. C. Smith b Gibbs	35
D. J. Shepherd lbw b Tidy	1	– not out	2
N-b 2	2	L-b 1	1
1/24 2/38 3/54 4/108 5/115 6/128 7/133 8/161 9/200	205	1/7 2/7 3/46 4/54 5/75 6/80 7/81 8/132 9/135	135

Bowling: *First Innings*—Blenkiron 27–10–63–2; McVicker 24–11–37–4; Ibadulla 9–1–24–1; Gibbs 20–3–54–0; Tidy 8.5–3–25–2. *Second Innings*—Blenkiron 12–3–17–2; McVicker 9–1–29–0; Ibadulla 3–0–10–0; Gibbs 16.4–5–37–8; Tidy 10–3–41–0.

Umpires: D. J. Constant and G. H. Pope.

WARWICKSHIRE v NOTTINGHAMSHIRE

Played at Birmingham, August 5, 6, 7, 1970

Warwickshire won by five wickets. The match was marred by the untimely death of the Test umpire J. S. Buller. The former Yorkshire and Worcestershire wicket-keeper collapsed in the pavilion and died during a stoppage for rain on the third day.

Bolus, who batted five and a quarter hours, and Hassan mastered the Warwickshire bowlers on a perfect pitch and shared a second-wicket partnership of 205 in just under three hours. Hassan, particularly strong on the leg side, hit one 6 and eighteen 4s. The more correct Bolus struck nineteen 4s. Rain restricted the second day to two hours and Warwickshire declared as soon as they avoided the follow-on. After a brisk opening stand of 91, Nottinghamshire asked Warwickshire to score 241 in three hours. Rain washed out five overs in the last hour but they reached their target with 14 balls to spare after Jameson (one 6 and twelve 4s) had set the pace with 74 in an hour and a half.

Nottinghamshire

M. J. Harris b Brown	16	– not out	54
J. B. Bolus not out	147	– not out	32
S. B. Hassan b Gibbs	110		
M. J. Smedley c A. C. Smith b Brown	29		
*G. S. Sobers not out	14		
B 2, l-b 4, n-b 2	8	L-b 4, n-b 1	5
1/35 2 /240 3/294 (3 wkts dec.)	324	(No wkt dec.)	91

G. Frost, R. A. White, M. N. S. Taylor, D. J. Halfyard, †D. Pullan and C. Forbes did not bat.

Bowling: *First Innings*—Brown 20–4–67–2; Blenkiron 18–8–40–0; Hemmings 9–1–42–0; Tidy 20–3–53–0; Gibbs 27–9–63–1; Jameson 8–0–28–0; Amiss 3–0–23–0. *Second Innings*—Brown 8–2–28–0; Blenkiron 7–2–20–0; Hemmings 9–3–22–0; Gibbs 10–2–16–0.

Warwickshire

R. N. Abberley c Halfyard b Taylor	45 – c Pullan b Halfyard	2
J. A. Jameson c Pullan b Halfyard	38 – c Pullan b Taylor	74
A. Gordon c Taylor b Halfyard	2 – b Taylor	17
M. J. K. Smith c Smedley b Halfyard	16 – not out	74
D. L. Amiss b Taylor	41 – b Halfyard	39
*†A. C. Smith c Pullan b Forbes	13	
E. E. Hemmings not out	8 – not out	19
D. J. Brown not out	5	
W. Blenkiron (did not bat)	– c Bolus b Halfyard	6
B 3, l-b 3, n-b 1	7 B 8, l-b 2	10
1/76 2/84 3/98 4/107 5/157 6/169	(6 wkts dec.) 175 1/3 2/90 3/109 4/195 5/213	(5 wkts) 241

L. R. Gibbs and W. N. Tidy did not bat.

Bowling: *First Innings*—Sobers 3–0–10–0; Forbes 7–2–16–1; Halfyard 28–8–62–3; Taylor 22.2–6–62–2; White 7–3–18–0. *Second Innings*—Sobers 14–1–51–0; Halfyard 21–1–94–3; Taylor 14–0–82–2; Bolus 0.4–0–4–0.

Umpires: J. S. Buller and H. Mellows.

WARWICKSHIRE v DERBYSHIRE

Played at Coventry, August 8, 10, 11, 1970

Derbyshire won by six wickets. Kanhai dominated the Warwickshire first innings with a remarkable century – the fiftieth of his career. Ward's hostile pace upset his colleagues and Kanhai scored all but six (singles by Brown and Tidy and four extras) of Warwickshire's last 126. Gibbs failed to contribute to a ninth-wicket stand of 53. Kanhai reached his hundred in two hours and batted a total of three hours, eight minutes, hitting seven 6s and twenty-six 4s. None of Derbyshire's batsmen displayed any urgency as Page anchored their first innings. Warwickshire collapsed against the left-arm spin of Swarbrook when they batted a second time and Derbyshire had ample time to score 187 for victory.

Warwickshire

J. A. Jameson c and b E. Smith	45 – c Buxton b Swarbrook	11
R. N. Abberley c Wilkins b E. Smith	21 – c and b Swarbrook	1
R. B. Kanhai not out	187 – c Wilkins b Ward	20
M. J. K. Smith c Taylor b Ward	1 – c Taylor b Ward	10
D. L. Amiss c Page b Ward	1 – b Swarbrook	58
*†A. C. Smith b Ward	0 – c Wilkins b Swarbrook	19
E. E. Hemmings c Page b Wilkins	30 – c and b Swarbrook	8
D. J. Brown c Gibbs b Ward	1 – lbw b Swarbrook	17
W. Blenkiron c Gibbs b Ward	0 – c Wilkins b E. Smith	22
L. R. Gibbs b Russell	0 – c Taylor b Ward	1
W. N. Tidy c Swarbrook b Ward	1 – not out	0
L-b 3, n-b 5	8 B 8, n-b 2	10
1/63 2/86 3/96 4/102 5/103 6/169 7/197 8/200 9/253	295 1/25 2/37 3/51 4/62 5/89 6/114 7/171 8/175 9/177	177

Bowling: *First Innings*—Ward 20.4–6–69–6; Buxton 3–1–17–0; Russell 28–8–89–1; E. Smith 11–2–55–2; Swarbrook 7–1–43–0; Wilkins 4–1–14–1. *Second Innings*—Ward 15.3–3–63–3; Buxton 7–2–17–0; Russell 13–7–19–0; Swarbrook 27–13–48–6; E. Smith 12–5–20–1.

Derbyshire

P. J. K. Gibbs c A. C. Smith b Gibbs	14	– c sub b Tidy	32
D. H. K. Smith c Abberley b Gibbs	32	– c A. C. Smith b Brown	30
M. H. Page c A. C. Smith b Blenkiron	80	– b Brown	44
C. P. Wilkins lbw b Gibbs	4	– c Gibbs b Brown	44
F. W. Swarbrook c Jameson b Brown	10		
J. F. Harvey c and b Tidy	39	– not out	16
*I. R. Buxton c Gibbs b Blenkiron	32	– not out	7
†R. W. Taylor c Kanhai b Tidy	18		
P. E. Russell not out	13		
E. Smith c M. J. K. Smith b Brown	17		
A. Ward c Hemmings b Blenkiron	10		
B 1, l-b 8, n-b 8	17	B 4, l-b 7, n-b 6	17
1/40 2/76 3/84 4/111 5/163 6/215 7/236 8/246 9/268	286	1/67 2/92 3/150 4/179	(4 wkts) 190

Bowling: *First Innings*—Brown 24–6–66–2; Blenkiron 21–4–52–3; Gibbs 32–10–75–3; Tidy 23–3–59–2; Hemmings 9–2–17–0. *Second Innings*—Brown 20–6–38–3; Blenkiron 15–5–32–0; Gibbs 27–11–49–0; Tidy 13.2–3–48–1; Jameson 2–0–6–0.

Umpires: P. B. Wight, A. S. M. Oakman (first day)
and R. K. Wilson (last two days).

WARWICKSHIRE v YORKSHIRE

Played at Birmingham, September 1, 2, 3, 1971

Warwickshire won by 22 runs. Warwickshire flayed the Yorkshire attack on a good pitch and gained eight batting points. Kanhai and Jameson (sixteen 4s) put on 140 in thirty-seven overs and then Kanhai and M. J. K. Smith added 112 in twenty-one overs for the third wicket. Kanhai batted four hours and hit twenty-one 4s. Boycott refused to let a disastrous start affect him and he went relentlessly to his twelfth century of the season. He mastered all the bowlers and carried his bat for 138 made in almost four and a half hours. Warwickshire chased runs recklessly when they batted a second time and Kanhai reached 50 in forty minutes. Left to score 284 in four and three-quarter hours, Yorkshire made a splendid start with an opening stand of 134 in two and a half hours between Boycott (one 6, one 5, seven 4s) and the more pedestrian Lumb. After Tidy claimed the first four wickets, Yorkshire failed to sustain their challenge against the spin of Gibbs and Jameson.

Warwickshire

J. Whitehouse b Old	11	– c Hampshire b Old	0
J. A. Jameson c Bairstow b Old	95	– c Bairstow b Nicholson	5
R. B. Kanhai c Hampshire b Nicholson	135	– c Johnson b Nicholson	62
M. J. K. Smith c Bairstow b Bore	45	– lbw b Nicholson	26
D. L. Amiss run out	8	– b Nicholson	23
K. Ibadulla b Nicholson	19	– lbw b Cope	1
N. M. McVicker b Old	11	– b Nicholson	37
*†A. C. Smith c Bairstow b Old	2	– c Bairstow b Hutton	0
S. J. Rouse not out	8	– c Bairstow b Hutton	0
L. R. Gibbs not out	6	– not out	3
W. N. Tidy (did not bat)		– run out	0
L-b 14	14	L-b 2, w 1, n-b 1	4
1/22 2/162 3/274 4/302 5/304 6/321 7/331 8/345	(8 wkts dec.) 354	1/0 2/26 3/89 4/94 5/96 6/149 7/156 8/156 9/160	161

Bowling: *First Innings*—Old 23–3–112–4; Nicholson 24–4–72–2; Hutton 12–1–42–0; Cope 12–3–66–0; Bore 14–2–48–1. *Second Innings*—Old 5–0–40–1; Nicholson 20–4–48–5; Hutton 18–5–38–2; Cope 8–2–14–1; Bore 5–1–17–0.

Yorkshire

*G. Boycott not out	138	– c Ibadulla b Tidy	84
R. G. Lumb c A. C. Smith b Rouse	1	– c Ibadulla b Tidy	65
P. J. Sharpe c M. J. K. Smith b McVicker	6	– c A. C. Smith b Tidy	11
J. H. Hampshire c A. C. Smith b Rouse	0	– lbw b Tidy	6
C. Johnson b McVicker	0	– lbw b Jameson	34
R. A. Hutton lbw b McVicker	4	– b Gibbs	34
†D. L. Bairstow b McVicker	9	– c Tidy b Gibbs	3
A. G. Nicholson c M. J. K. Smith b McVicker	23	– lbw b Jameson	3
C. M. Old run out	14	– b Jameson	8
G. A. Cope lbw b Gibbs	16	– not out	0
M. K. Bore lbw b Jameson	16	– c Ibadulla b Gibbs	2
L-b 1, n-b 4	5	L-b 9, w 1, n-b 1	11
1/2 2/11 3/12 4/13 5/25 6/45 7/79 8/123 9/185	232	1/134 2/159 3/167 4/170 5/223 6/230 7/249 8/255 9/255	261

Bowling: *First Innings*—McVicker 19–4–54–5; Rouse 17–4–42–2; Ibadulla 5–0–15–0; Gibbs 23–8–50–1; Tidy 15–1–65–0; Jameson 1–0–1–1. *Second Innings*—McVicker 9–1–29–0; Rouse 7–3–17–0; Gibbs 37.5–13–78–3; Ibadulla 17–5–29–0; Tidy 18–3–75–4; Jameson 12–3–22–3.

Umpires: A. Jepson and J. G. Langridge.

WARWICKSHIRE v GLOUCESTERSHIRE

Played at Birmingham, July 27, 29, 1974

Warwickshire won by an innings and 61 runs. Jameson and Kanhai, with a brutal and ruthless assault on a weakened attack, set a new world record stand for the second wicket of 465. They came together when Abberley was dismissed by the second ball of the day and created a total of five records during their five hours, twelve minutes at the crease.

The first record to go was the county's second wicket stand of 344 by J. Devey and S. P. Kinneir in 1900. At 403 they beat Warwickshire's best for any wicket made by Kanhai and K. Ibadulla in 1968. When they reached 430 they passed the English second wicket record established by J. G. Dewes and G. H. G. Doggart for Cambridge University in 1949 and the world second wicket record by B. B. Nimbalkar and K. V. Bhandarkar for Maharashtra against Kathiawar at Poona in 1948-49 went at 456. It was also the first occasion on which two Warwickshire players had completed double centuries in the same match.

The extraordinary partnership was not without blemish. Kanhai was dropped when 54 and both were dropped in the same over from the luckless Shackleton when they were just short of the world record. The cold statistics of the best innings of Jameson's career were one 6 and thirty-four 4s, while Kanhai hit one 6 and thirty 4s.

The Gloucestershire batsmen experienced an unhappy time. Hemmings caused a first innings collapse and when they batted a second time Willis and Blenkiron wreaked havoc.

Warwickshire

R. N. Abberley c Brown b Dixon	0
J. A. Jameson not out	240
R. B. Kanhai not out	213
B 7, l-b 5	12
1/0 (1 wkt)	465

*M. J. K. Smith, A. I. Kallicharran, †D. L. Murray, E. E. Hemmings, W. A. Bourne, W. Blenkiron, R. G. D. Willis and D. J. Brown did not bat.

Bowling: Dixon 17–2–91–1; Shackleton 20–2–88–0; Knight 20–2–103–0; Mortimore 31–5–87–0; Thorn 12–1–84–0.

Gloucestershire

†A. W. Stovold c Murray b Willis	49 – b Willis	9
R. D. V. Knight c Jameson b Hemmings	27 – c Hemmings b Blenkiron	5
A. J. Hignell c Willis b Hemmings	11 – c Abberley b Willis	0
M. J. Procter c Murray b Hemmings	20 – c Murray b Hemmings	46
J. C. Foat c Murray b Bourne	34 – b Blenkiron	7
M. S. T. Dunstan b Bourne	52 – c Bourne b Hemmings	32
*A. S. Brown c and b Hemmings	4 – b Blenkiron	40
P. L. Thorn not out	14 – c Murray b Willis	0
J. B. Mortimore c Kanhai b Hemmings	13 – b Willis	0
J. H. Shackleton b Blenkiron	2 – b Blenkiron	11
J. H. Dixon c Kallicharran b Hemmings	7 – not out	0
B 4, l-b 3, n-b 3	10 L-b 4, w 4, n-b 3	11
1/69 2/89 3/100 4/110 5/187 6/198 7/202 8/229 9/236	243 1/14 2/18 3/18 4/36 5/100 6/114 7/115 8/115 9/150	161

Bowling: *First Innings*—Willis 13–3–40–1; Brown 11–1–44–1; Hemmings 25.5–5–87–6; Bourne 11–2–32–2; Jameson 4–0–16–0; Blenkiron 5–1–14–1. *Second Innings*—Willis 15–6–31–4; Blenkiron 9.3–4–18–4; Brown 11–4–31–0; Hemmings 19–5–45–2; Bourne 3–0–25–0.

Umpires: A. Jepson and A. G. T. Whitehead.

WARWICKSHIRE v MIDDLESEX

Played at Birmingham, May 12, 13, 14, 1976

Warwickshire won by eight wickets. A match to be especially remembered by two players. Titmus, nearing the end of a great career, hit his first championship century for 15 years and bowled with great skill, being unfortunate to finish on the losing side. Humpage, in his first full season as Warwickshire wicket-keeper, added a second innings half-century to his 60 in the first venture. Warwickshire had just missed their fourth batting point but they gained a lead of 65 and had Middlesex on their knees at 67 for six, again in dire trouble against the pace of Brown and Willis. It was then that Titmus stood firm, reaching his century out of 133 in two hours, fifty-four minutes with one five and thirteen 4s. It was all to no avail, for although Warwickshire had only 23 overs in which to score 157, they sprinted home with 3.4 overs to spare. Jameson set a killing pace in helping to take 61 runs off the five opening overs. When he had gone, Amiss and Humpage took Warwickshire to a remarkable triumph.

Middlesex

M. J. Smith run out	36 – lbw b Willis	19
*J. M. Brearley c Humpage b Willis	6 – lbw b Brown	3
C. T. Radley b Willis	19 – lbw b Brown	16
G. D. Barlow lbw b Brown	33 – c Kanhai b Willis	1
M. W. Gatting lbw b Perryman	14 – lbw b Brown	14
P. H. Edmonds lbw b Perryman	24 – c Humpage b Willis	1
†N. P. D. Ross c Whitehouse b Willis	48 – run out	24
F. J. Titmus c Whitehouse b Brown	21 – not out	112
M. J. Vernon not out	4 – lbw b Brown	10
M. W. W. Selvey c Humpage b Willis	4 – lbw b Hemmings	9
A. A. Jones b Willis	3 – c Humpage b Brown	6
B 2, l-b 5, w 2, n-b 13	22 L-b 3, n-b 3	6
1/18 2/54 3/85 4/122 5/143 6/152 7/222 8/222 9/227	234 1/14 2/30 3/36 4/42 5/43 6/67 7/132 8/171 9/207	221

Bowling: *First Innings*—Willis 22.2–6–71–5; Brown 24–6–56–2; Perryman 20–6–41–2; Bourne 8–2–19–0; Hemmings 10–2–25–0. *Second Innings*—Willis 25–5–58–3; Brown 29.1–4–80–5; Perryman 12–6–13–0; Bourne 11–4–23–0; Hemmings 18–6–41–1.

Warwickshire

J. A. Jameson c Radley b Titmus	29	– run out	38
D. L. Amiss c Ross b Titmus	45	– not out	55
J. Whitehouse b Edmonds	24	– c Radley b Titmus	2
R. B. Kanhai c Radley b Titmus	48		
R. N. Abberley b Selvey	4		
†G. W. Humpage b Edmonds	60	– not out	54
E. E. Hemmings b Selvey	1		
W. A. Bourne lbw b Selvey	1		
R. G. D. Willis b Jones	43		
S. J. Perryman not out	3		
*D. J. Brown b Vernon	28		
B 2, l-b 7, w 1, n-b 3	13	L-b 8	8
1/74 2/89 3/129 4/155 5/159 6/167 7/169 8/246 9/295	299	1/66 2/66	(2 wkts) 157

Bowling: *First Innings*—Jones 16.4–2–41–1; Selvey 23–4–65–3; Vernon 10–0–67–1; Titmus 33–13–56–3; Edmonds 17–3–57–2. *Second Innings*—Jones 7.2–0–57–0; Selvey 5–0–41–0; Titmus 4–0–34–1; Edmonds 3–0–17–0.

Umpires: W. E. Alley and D. L. Evans.

WARWICKSHIRE v WORCESTERSHIRE

Played at Birmingham, May 29, 31, June 1, 1976

Drawn. Rain affected all three days and finally ended play half an hour early when Worcestershire, with their last man due at the wicket, were only 21 runs ahead. Warwickshire could well have won much earlier if they had held their catches. Brown's bowling dominated the Worcestershire first innings and he became the seventh bowler in his county's history to take 1,000 wickets in first-class cricket. The home opening pair, with Jameson aggressive as usual, launched a swift reply. After another hold-up for rain, Whitehouse completed his first championship century of the season in a partnership with Abberley which put on 128 and helped to take his side into a lead of 101. When Worcestershire went in again Bourne swiftly reduced them to three for 11. Thereafter the experience of Hemsley, valiantly supported by the newcomers Neale, Patel and Jones, kept the innings going until the rain closed in. Jones, a youngster from Shropshire, who had fielded brilliantly, held on for fifty minutes surrounded by fielders and actually played through 20 overs before scoring a run.

Worcestershire

G. M. Turner lbw b Brown	42	c Humpage b Bourne	4
J. A. Ormrod c Humpage b Brown	59	b Bourne	1
P. A. Neale lbw b Perryman	0	b Lewington	47
Imran Khan lbw b Perryman	2	lbw b Bourne	1
E. J. O. Hemsley c Amiss b Brown	32	lbw b Perryman	29
D. Patel b Brown	1	c Brown b Hemmings	22
B. J. R. Jones c Humpage b Perryman	11	b Perryman	2
†H. G. Wilcock lbw b Brown	21	c Bourne b Lewington	1
J. D. Inchmore lbw b Hemmings	9	c Jameson b Hemmings	6
*N. Gifford not out	17	not out	0
A. P. Pridgeon c Humpage b Brown	11		
B 4, l-b 9, n-b 2	15	B 1, l-b 6, w 1, n-b 1	9
1/70 2/71 3/73 4/137 5/141 6/147 7/166 8/179 9/194	220	1/4 2/7 3/11 4/65 5/102 6/108 7/109 8/119 9/122	(9 wkts) 122

Bowling: *First Innings*—Brown 30.4–5–81–6; Bourne 18–3–57–0; Perryman 25–9–41–3; Hemmings 21–10–26–1. *Second Innings*—Brown 12–3–32–0; Bourne 13–3–30–3; Perryman 13.1–5–16–2; Hemmings 20–12–14–2; Lewington 16–9–21–2.

Warwickshire

J. A. Jameson c Neale b Imran	32
D. L. Amiss c Turner b Inchmore	31
J. Whitehouse c Patel b Pridgeon	112
R. B. Kanhai c Gifford b Pridgeon	38
R. N. Abberley b Inchmore	46
†G. W. Humpage c Jones b Pridgeon	0
E. E. Hemmings lbw b Inchmore	23
W. A. Bourne c Ormrod b Inchmore	4
*D. J. Brown c Patel b Gifford	3
S. P. Perryman not out	0
P. J. Lewington c Turner b Gifford	0
B 9, l-b 15, n-b 8	32
1/68 2/85 3/157 4/285 5/286 6/289 7/302 8/321 9/321	321

Bowling: Inchmore 30–5–95–4; Imran 21–5–57–1; Pridgeon 23–3–79–3; Hemsley 3–0–18–0; Gifford 16.2–2–40–2.

Umpires: R. Aspinall and W. E. Phillipson.

WARWICKSHIRE v NORTHAMPTONSHIRE

Played at Birmingham, May 28, 30, 31, 1977

Warwickshire won by an innings and 21 runs. Even without Willis, a casualty with influenza, Warwickshire had the game under control by the end of the first day. Rouse in one spell claimed four wickets for 16 runs in 11 overs. Amiss hit an immaculate century which included sixteen boundaries and Kanhai, in his not out 125, had the odd experience of being credited with eight runs. Three came from a leg glance chased by the wicketkeeper and five more from a penalty imposed by the Australian umpire Brooks on Steele for using a discarded wicketkeeper's glove to field the return. Later the same umpire spoke to Sarfraz Nawaz for bowling too many short-pitched balls, one of which put Hemmings out of action. Batting again needing 197 to avoid an innings defeat, Northamptonshire capitulated to some fine bowling by Brown on a pitch which gave him little help.

Northamptonshire

R. T. Virgin c Whitehouse b Brown	9	– lbw b Brown	15
G. Cook c Whitehouse b Rouse	56	– c Kanhai b Brown	18
D. S. Steele c Humpage b Bourne	26	– b Bourne	32
*Mushtaq Mohammad c Abberley b Bourne	9	– c Humpage b Bourne	25
P. Willey c Humpage b Rouse	9	– b Rouse	22
W. Larkins lbw b Rouse	13	– c Kanhai b Rouse	19
T. J. Yardley c Humpage b Rouse	5	– c Whitehouse b Rouse	2
†G. Sharp not out	43	– c Humpage b Brown	8
Sarfraz Nawaz b Bourne	28	– c Humpage b Brown	13
A. Hodgson b Perryman	3	– not out	11
J. C. J. Dye c Hemmings b Brown	29	– c Perryman b Brown	0
B 2, l-b 10, w 4, n-b 8	24	B 1, n-b 10	11
1/16 2/62 3/84 4/98 5/142 6/145 7/150 8/185 9/192	254	1/36 2/37 3/91 4/96 5/122 6/124 7/144 8/158 9/170	176

Bowling: *First Innings*—Rouse 18–3–40–4; Brown 15.4–3–39–2; Perryman 16–4–38–1; Bourne 23–2–75–3; Hemmings 13–3–38–0. *Second Innings*—Rouse 21–5–53–3; Brown 21–1–43–5; Perryman 12–5–24–0; Bourne 12–1–45–2.

Warwickshire

D. L. Amiss c Sarfraz b Hodgson	120
K. D. Smith c Yardley b Sarfraz	20
R. N. Abberley c Cook b Dye	43
J. Whitehouse c Sharp b Dye	6
R. B. Kanhai not out	125
†G. W. Humpage c Larkins b Mushtaq	64
E. E. Hemmings retired hurt	44
W. A. Bourne c Hodgson b Dye	3
S. J. Rouse lbw b Hodgson	13
*D. J. Brown not out	1
L-b 2, n-b 10	12
1/38 2/151 3/167 4/221 5/318 6/423 7/449	(7 wkts) 451

S. J. Perryman did not bat.

Bowling: Sarfraz 30–3–124–1; Dye 27–3–110–3; Hodgson 20–6–53–2; Mushtaq 18–0–99–1; Larkins 5–0–16–0; Willey 14–1–37–0.

Umpires: D. O. Oslear and T. F. Brooks.

WARWICKSHIRE v ESSEX

Played at Birmingham, July 2, 4, 5, 1977

Essex won by eight runs. A remarkable match of 1,350 runs and five centuries, two of them by McEwan, including the fastest hundred of the season to date in ninety-five minutes, with three 6s and seventeen 4s. Warwickshire's reply was led by Whitehouse and after another feast of runs by Essex Warwickshire were left five hours in which to score 357. It proved an astutely timed declaration. Despite a brilliant century by Amiss, Warwickshire seemed out of the hunt until Hemmings hit a quick 85 in seventy-seven minutes, including two 6s and fourteen 4s. His departure was the end of Warwickshire's real hope of victory, but they fought all the way until Willis played on to Lever with seven balls left.

Essex

B. R. Hardie lbw b Brown	29	– c Humpage b Perryman	25
M. H. Denness c Humpage b Brown	95		
K. S. McEwan c Perryman b Willis	102	– b Brown	116
*K. W. R. Fletcher b Hemmings	1	– not out	40
G. A. Gooch c Humpage b Perryman	37	– not out	105
K. R. Pont c Humpage b Rouse	30		
S. Turner c Humpage b Brown	9		
R. E. East b Rouse	36		
†N. Smith c Brown b Willis	21		
J. K. Lever not out	1		
L-b 6, n-b 4	10	B 9, l-b 10, n-b 3	22
1/69 2/219 3/224 4/234 5/281 6/300 7/328 8/361 9/371	(9 wkts dec.) 371	1/96 2/207	(2 wkts dec.) 308

D. L. Acfield did not bat.

Bowling: *First Innings*—Willis 22–5–49–2; Rouse 20–4–70–2; Perryman 17–3–68–1; Brown 19–1–90–3; Hemmings 20–7–84–1. *Second Innings*—Willis 11–3–25–0; Rouse 7–0–36–0; Perryman 20–6–60–1; Brown 11–2–42–1; Hemmings 34–7–105–0; Whitehouse 5–1–18–0.

Warwickshire

D. L. Amiss c Gooch b Acfield	35	– c Hardie b Turner	100
R. N. Abberley lbw b Lever	66	– c Smith b Turner	11
J. Whitehouse not out	117	– c and b East	2
A. I. Kallicharran b East	12	– st Smith b Acfield	4
K. D. Smith lbw b Acfield	19	– c McEwan b East	34
†G. W. Humpage c Acfield b East	3	– c Lever b Turner	20
E. E. Hemmings c Smith b Acfield	47	– lbw b Turner	85
S. J. Rouse not out	14	– b Acfield	31
*D. J. Brown (did not bat)		– b Lever	24
R. G. D. Willis (did not bat)		– b Lever	6
S. P. Perryman (did not bat)		– not out	9
B 1, l-b 7, n-b 2	10	L-b 8, n-b 14	22
1/81 2/109 3/167 4/198 5/202 6/286	(6 wkts dec.) 323	1/73 2/75 3/86 4/118 5/132 6/267 7/270 8/324 9/334	348

Bowling: *First Innings*—Lever 20–4–54–1; Turner 7–1–41–0; Acfield 37–8–96–3; East 36–5–122–2. *Second Innings*—Lever 18.5–2–78–2; Turner 19–4–69–4; Acfield 34–5–84–2; East 16–5–50–2; Fletcher 5–0–45–0.

Umpires: H. D. Bird and D. J. Constant.

WARWICKSHIRE v YORKSHIRE

R. B. Kanhai's Benefit Match

Played at Birmingham, August 6, 8, 9, 1977

Drawn. This match was more noteworthy for its statistics than its outcome, too much time being lost to the weather for a genuine result. Boycott hit his 99th century; Love also confirmed his considerable promise. Whitehouse was again the mainstay of the Warwickshire reply and immediately the follow-on had been saved Kanhai declared, hoping to persuade Boycott to stage a finish. He provided the ammunition for a remarkable century in thirty-seven minutes by Old, the second fastest in the history of the game, by bowling himself. Old raced into the records with six 6s and thirteen 4s, his second 50 coming in only nine minutes, but Yorkshire declined to stage a finish. In any case the merit of a result achieved by such means would have been questionable.

Yorkshire

*G. Boycott b Perryman	104		
B. Leadbeater c Humpage b Rouse	8	– b Hemmings	21
R. G. Lumb c Humpage b Perryman	10	– c Kanhai b Hemmings	15
J. D. Love c Humpage b Savage	129	– not out	40
K. Sharp c Kanhai b Savage	48	– lbw b Whitehouse	2
†D. L. Bairstow not out	31		
G. B. Stevenson not out	0	– not out	0
C. M. Old (did not bat)		– c Kallicharran b Whitehouse	107
B 4, l-b 12, w 1, n-b 6	23	B 1, l-b 1, w 1	3
1/23 2/46 3/237 4/287 5/348	(5 wkts) 353	1/36 2/37 3/40 4/182	(4 wkts dec.) 188

G. A. Cope, S. Sylvester and M. K. Bore did not bat.

Bowling: *First Innings*—Willis 17–6–29–0; Rouse 15–2–52–1; Perryman 24–4–73–2; Savage 23–5–110–2; Hemmings 21–4–66–0. *Second Innings*—Willis 2–1–8–0; Rouse 3–1–17–0; Perryman 8–4–7–0; Hemmings 15–6–71–2; Whitehouse 12–2–55–2; Kanhai 3–0–27–0.

Warwickshire

D. L. Amiss b Bore	49		
R. N. Abberley c Old b Stevenson	20		
J. Whitehouse not out	73		
A. I. Kallicharran b Bore	23		
*R. B. Kanhai not out	31		
†G. W. Humpage (did not bat)		– not out	52
E. E. Hemmings (did not bat)		– c Bore b Old	8
S. J. Rouse (did not bat)		– not out	8
R. Le Q. Savage (did not bat)		– c Leadbeater b Boycott	1
B 3, w 1, n-b 4	8	B 1, l-b 4	5
1/29 2/94 3/139	(3 wkts dec.) 204	1/24 2/31	(2 wkts) 74

S. P. Perryman and R. G. D. Willis did not bat.

Bowling: *First Innings*—Old 13–3–34–0; Sylvester 3–0–19–0; Stevenson 17.2–2–56–1; Cope 15–4–36–0; Bore 20–8–51–2. *Second Innings*—Old 5–1–18–1; Boycott 6–2–10–1; Bairstow 6–1–20–0; Sharp 4–1–21–0.

Umpires: H. D. Bird and W. L. Budd.

WARWICKSHIRE v WORCESTERSHIRE

Played at Birmingham, August 27, 29, 30, 1977

Drawn. Delays through the weather on the third day spoiled the chance of a good finish, although both sides did their best. Amiss, scoring 251 runs in the match without being dismissed, had an outstanding game, hitting twelve boundaries in his sixth century of the season. D'Oliveira, in turn, struck vintage form to rescue his side and the eventual outcome was a challenge to Worcestershire to score 225 runs in two and three-quarter hours. They reached 138 for the loss of Turner. Jones hit his highest score of the season with aggressive support from Wilcock, who achieved success in his new role as a specialist batsman. Hemmings checked Worcestershire's bold progress with the first hat-trick of his career and both sides agreed to call it a day with three overs left.

Warwickshire

D. L. Amiss not out	160	– not out	91
R. N. Abberley c Patel b Cumbes	8	– c and b Cumbes	51
J. Whitehouse lbw b Cumbes	0	– c D'Oliveira b Holder	2
K. D. Smith c Boyns b Gifford	31	– not out	5
A. I. Kallicharran b Holder	18		
†G. W. Humpage b Boyns	34		
E. E. Hemmings lbw b Boyns	9		
S. J. Rouse b Holder	15		
*D. J. Brown b Holder	0		
S. P. Perryman not out	7		
B 8, l-b 4, n-b 8	20	B 4, l-b 5, n-b 1	10
1/17 2/18 3/86 4/125 5/205 6/250 7/284 8/289	(8 wkts) 302	1/125 2/141	(2 wkts dec.) 159

R. Le Q. Savage did not bat.

Bowling: *First Innings*—Holder 32–5–97–3; Cumbes 21–2–52–2; Boyns 23–5–70–2; Gifford 20–4–43–1; D'Oliveira 4–0–20–0. *Second Innings*—Holder 17–2–37–1; Cumbes 15–2–43–1; Boyns 11–0–36–0; Gifford 13–4–33–0.

Worcestershire

G. M. Turner b Rouse	1	– b Hemmings	17
B. J. R. Jones c Whitehouse b Rouse	8	– c Smith b Hemmings	65
D. N. Patel lbw b Rouse	0	– c Smith b Hemmings	0
S. P. Henderson c Kallicharran b Perryman	38	– not out	7
B. L. D'Oliveira c Humpage b Rouse	90	– not out	11
H. G. Wilcock b Perryman	9	– b Hemmings	48
C. N. Boyns b Perryman	0		
†D. J. Humphries c Brown b Savage	24		
V. A. Holder lbw b Rouse	15		
*N. Gifford not out	16		
J. Cumbes b Hemmings	18		
B 5, l-b 4, w 2, n-b 7	18	L-b 5, n-b 3	8
1/7 2/9 3/11 4/69 5/79 6/79 7/166 8/200 9/201	237	1/40 2/138 3/138 4/138	(4 wkts) 156

Bowling: *First Innings*—Rouse 18–11–22–5; Brown 17–4–47–0; Perryman 21–12–43–3; Savage 22–2–77–1; Hemmings 11.2–3–30–1. *Second Innings*—Rouse 11–7–17–0; Brown 3–1–7–0; Perryman 8–0–34–0; Savage 8–0–40–0; Hemmings 17–4–50–4.

Umpires D. O. Oslear and A. G. T. Whitehead.

WARWICKSHIRE v SUSSEX

Played at Birmingham, August 19, 21, 22, 1978

Drawn. Sussex were dismissed in their first innings in 67.1 overs, a surprising surrender on so placid a pitch. Willis claimed two early victims in his first eight overs and then Perryman broke through. Only Javed Miandad and Imran Khan stood between Sussex and complete rout, and the end of their stand of 84 in seventeen overs, which proved that runs could be scored, saw the return of the same uninspired pattern of batting. The last three wickets all fell with just one single needed for a second batting point. Warwickshire moved to 124 for three off 45 overs by the end of the first day, but their batting fell away on resumption. Only Smith, patient and favoured by fortune at times, held firm, and Brown gave valuable help in building a lead of 97. Sussex were heading for trouble, only 23 runs ahead with three wickets down, by the end of the second day but rain wiped out what could have been an interesting final stage.

Sussex

J. R. T. Barclay lbw b Willis	8	– b Willis	6
S. P. Hoadley b Perryman	10	– lbw b Brown	0
P. W. G. Parker lbw b Willis	12	– retired hurt	21
Javed Miandad c Brown b Willis	60	– not out	53
Imran Khan b Oliver	44	– c Amiss b Clifford	12
C. P. Phillipson b Oliver	0	– not out	8
S. J. Storey lbw b Willis	7		
*†A. Long lbw b Perryman	17		
G. G. Arnold c sub b Clifford	29		
J. Spencer c Amiss b Perryman	0		
C. E. Waller not out	0		
B 1, l-b 7, n-b 4	12	B 5, l-b 9, n-b 6	20
1/16 2/32 3/47 4/131 5/131 6/152 7/153 8/199 9/199	199	1/4 2/7 3/64	(3 wkts) 120

Bowling: *First Innings*—Willis 15–4–41–4; Brown 16–3–41–0; Perryman 16–8–31–3; Clifford 10.1–2–46–1; Oliver 10–4–28–2. *Second Innings*—Willis 10–2–42–1; Brown 9–1–25–1; Perryman 8–4–10–0; Clifford 12–7–22–1; Oliver 1–0–1–0.

Warwickshire

D. L. Amiss lbw b Arnold	27
K. D. Smith not out	132
*J. Whitehouse c Long b Barclay	9
A. I. Kallicharran c Arnold b Waller	8
T. A. Lloyd lbw b Arnold	12
†G. W. Humpage c Spencer b Waller	1
P. R. Oliver c Waller b Barclay	20
D. J. Brown b Imran	38
S. P. Perryman b Waller	1
R. G. D. Willis c Long b Arnold	14
C. Clifford b Spencer	3
B 5, l-b 12, w 2, n-b 12	31
1/38 2/79 3/96 4/129 5/132 6/168 7/240 8/241 9/285	296

Bowling: Imran 19–7–34–1; Arnold 24–9–43–3; Spencer 9.3–2–35–1; Phillipson 4–0–24–0; Waller 43–19–62–3; Barclay 20–6–43–3; Miandad 4–0–24–0.

Umpires: T. W. Spencer and P. B. Wight.

WARWICKSHIRE v WORCESTERSHIRE

Played at Birmingham, August 26, 28, 29, 1978

Drawn. After a second day on which 456 runs were scored and only one wicket fell, the outcome was inevitable on so perfect a wicket with two attacks of limited penetration. Amiss's 155, his fifth century of the season, brought a partnership of 228 – Warwickshire's highest of the summer – with the highly promising Lloyd. Worcestershire found scoring even easier. Turner hit 22 boundaries and Hemsley 15 in their third-wicket stand of 243. Amiss reached three figures again in the second innings and joined the distinguished ranks of Quaife, Wyatt, Dollery, and M. J. K. Smith by completing 20,000 runs for his county. Kallicharran also found his touch. In the end Worcestershire were left with little to do apart from play out time, being uninterested in the stiff target of 299 in two and a quarter hours.

Warwickshire

D. L. Amiss not out	155	– b Gifford	112
K. D. Smith c Turner b Watson	19	– b Pridgeon	59
T. A. Lloyd b D'Oliveira	93	– c and b Patel	38
A. I. Kallicharran not out	7	– not out	101
P. R. Oliver (did not bat)		– c Gifford b D'Oliveira	3
†G. W. Humpage (did not bat)		– not out	46
B 10, l-b 14, n-b 5	29	B 13, l-b 16, n-b 2	31
1/55 2/283	(2 wkts) 303	1/163 2/197 3/298 4/307	(4 wkts dec.) 390

*J. Whitehouse, S. J. Rouse, D. C. Hopkins, C. Clifford and S. P. Perryman did not bat.

Bowling: *First Innings*—Watson 17–3–43–1; Pridgeon 15–3–35–0; Boyns 10–0–37–0; Hemsley 13–3–41–0; Gifford 19–5–39–0; Patel 15–1–38–0; D'Oliveira 11–0–41–1. *Second Innings*—Watson 14–5–24–0; Pridgeon 19–6–43–1; Boyns 6–0–37–0; Gifford 19–2–62–1; Patel 37–6–95–1; D'Oliveira 15–4–52–1; Neale 9–0–46–0.

Worcestershire

G. M. Turner not out	202	– not out	45
J. A. Ormrod c Kallicharran b Perryman	2	– not out	35
P. A. Neale c Humpage b Perryman	70		
E. J. O. Hemsley not out	106		
B 8, l-b 5, n-b 2	15	L-b 2, w 1, n-b 1	4
1/13 2/152	(2 wkts) 395		(no wkt) 84

B. L. D'Oliveira, D. N. Patal, †D. J. Humphries, C. N. Boyns, *N. Gifford, G. G. Watson and P. A. Pridgeon did not bat.

Bowling: *First Innings*—Rouse 10–1–67–0; Perryman 36–6–98–2; Hopkins 9–1–52–0; Clifford 29–5–100–0; Oliver 16–0–63–0. *Second Innings*—Rouse 6–2–15–0; Perryman 4–1–8–0; Hopkins 5–1–9–0; Clifford 18–9–17–0; Oliver 19–5–28–0; Lloyd 2–1–3–0; Whitehouse 1–1–0–0.

Umpires: J. G. Langridge and R. Julian.

WARWICKSHIRE v WORCESTERSHIRE

Played at Birmingham, July 23, 24, 25, 1980

Worcestershire won by 96 runs. The return of fine weather inspired a high-scoring match which was given a notable send-off by Turner with a century before lunch – his eighth against Warwickshire. The spinners Doshi and Clifford shared the wickets as Worcestershire pressed on to 324 for nine before declaring. Lloyd made a century for Warwickshire, hitting fifteen 4s in his career-best 130, and former captain Whitehouse made a pleasing return with a half-century before Amiss declared 24 behind. Worcestershire created their winning position by declaring at 330 for five, after two more centuries had been reached by Ormrod and Younis. Left to score 355 in 260 minutes, Warwickshire were given a sound start by Amiss but, once he was out leg before to Alleyne for 99, their innings collapsed well short of the target.

Worcestershire

G. M. Turner st Humpage b Doshi	101	– c Amiss b Small	42
J. A. Ormrod c Oliver b Doshi	55	– b Clifford	106
P. A. Neale c Humpage b Doshi	0	– b Small	4
E. J. O. Hemsley c Humpage b Clifford	17	– lbw b Clifford	18
Younis Ahmed c Oliver b Doshi	13	– not out	121
T. S. Curtis not out	59	– lbw b Doshi	9
†D. J. Humphries c Humpage b Clifford	15	– not out	25
J. D. Inchmore c Ferreira b Clifford	13		
H. Alleyne b Clifford	1		
*N. Gifford b Doshi	27		
A. P. Pridgeon not out	8		
B 1, l-b 9, w 4, n-b 1	15	B 1, n-b 4	5
1/140 2/150 3/169 4/191 5/193 6/218 7/232 8/233 9/314	(9 wkts) 324	1/48 2/53 3/99 4/274 5/301	(5 wkts dec.) 330

Bowling: *First Innings*—Small 11–3–42–0; Hopkins 5–0–31–0; Oliver 2–0–12–0; Ferreira 10–1–38–0; Doshi 33–10–76–5; Clifford 39–12–110–4. *Second Innings*—Small 8–2–34–2; Hopkins 5–0–21–0; Ferreira 5–0–23–0; Clifford 35–5–133–2; Doshi 35–4–114–1.

Warwickshire

*D. L. Amiss b Alleyne	49	– lbw b Alleyne	99
K. D. Smith c Hemsley b Alleyne	3	– c Younis b Alleyne	10
T. A. Lloyd not out	130	– c Ormrod b Inchmore	19
†G. W. Humpage c Inchmore b Gifford	31	– b Inchmore	49
J. Whitehouse not out	50	– c Pridgeon b Gifford	16
A. M. Ferreira (did not bat)		– run out	3
P. R. Oliver (did not bat)		– b Gifford	20
D. C. Hopkins (did not bat)		– c Alleyne b Gifford	0
G. C. Small (did not bat)		– lbw b Alleyne	7
C. C. Clifford (did not bat)		– b Alleyne	6
D. R. Doshi (did not bat)		– not out	7
B 21, l-b 3, w 3, n-b 10	37	L-b 5, w 3, n-b 14	22
1/6 2/114 3/185	(3 wkts dec.) 300	1/29 2/55 3/143 4/193 5/206 6/229 7/230 8/239 9/249	258

Bowling: *First Innings*—Alleyne 22.5–6–66–2; Pridgeon 19–3–54–0; Gifford 33–4–71–1; Inchmore 12–2–46–0; Younis 5–0–26–0. *Second Innings*—Alleyne 19.2–5–63–4; Inchmore 17–2–62–2; Gifford 23–5–70–3; Pridgeon 7–1–41–0.

Umpires: W. L. Budd and D. G. L. Evans.

WARWICKSHIRE v NOTTINGHAMSHIRE

Played at Birmingham, August 22, 24, 1981

Nottinghamshire won by eight wickets. A match which began full of promise for Warwickshire when they reached a first innings total of 331 for nine, ended with a heavy defeat on the second day. Randall took charge of the Nottinghamshire innings, scoring his third century of the season and enabling Rice to declare, after 74.3 overs, at 303 for nine. Warwickshire immediately ran into trouble against Hadlee, lost half their wickets for 19 and only Oliver and Willis reached double figures as the innings folded at 49, the lowest Championship total of the season. Nottinghamshire, taking the extra half-hour, made the 78 runs needed in only 8.1 overs, Todd being undefeated with 52.

Warwickshire

D. L. Amiss c Hassen b Rice	83	– c Randall b Hadlee	1
K. D. Smith lbw b Hadlee	4	– c Hassan b Rice	3
T. A. Lloyd c French b Hadlee	32	– c Randall b Hadlee	1
†G. W. Humpage c Randall b Rice	65	– c Robinson b Cooper	6
Asif Din b Cooper	0	– c French b Hadlee	1
P. R. Oliver c French b Cooper	34	– c French b Cooper	14
A. M. Ferreira c Rice b Hadlee	40	– c Randall b Hemmings	1
G. C. Small lbw b Rice	1	– c Cooper b Hemmings	3
*R. G. D. Willis not out	33	– c Rice b Bore	11
W. Hogg b Hadlee	2	– b Bore	4
D. R. Doshi not out	12	– not out	1
B 9, l-b 12, n-b 4	25	L-b 2, w 1	3
1/23 2/130 3/134 4/141 5/235 6/236 7/242 8/283 9/297	(9 wkts dec.) 331	1/3 2/7 3/7 4/15 5/19 6/22 7/30 8/42 9/48	49

Bowling: *First Innings*—Hadlee 28–9–59–4; Rice 29–5–104–3; Cooper 20–3–70–2; Bore 8–3–20–0; Hemmings 14–2–53–0. *Second Innings*—Hadlee 9–6–8–3; Rice 6–2–8–1; Cooper 7–3–17–2; Hemmings 8–4–5–2; Bore 3.2–1–8–2.

Nottinghamshire

P. A. Todd c Smith b Hogg	13	– not out	52
R. T. Robinson run out	32	– run out	12
D. W. Randall st Humpage b Doshi	117	– (4) not out	1
B. Hassan b Ferreira	24		
*C. E. B. Rice c Small b Doshi	50		
J. D. Birch st Humpage b Doshi	20		
R. J. Hadlee b Ferreira	32	– (3) c Humpage b Small	11
†B. N. French lbw b Ferreira	1		
E. E. Hemmings c Lloyd b Doshi	2		
K. E. Cooper not out	0		
L-b 3, n-b 9	12	L-b 1, n-b 2	3
1/16 2/122 3/170 4/210 5/250 6/299 7/299 8/301 9/303	(9 wkts dec.) 303	1/62 2/75	(2 wkts) 79

M. K. Bore did not bat.

Bowling: *First Innings*—Willis 7–1–26–0; Hogg 9–1–34–1; Small 4–1–16–0; Ferreira 28–4–121–3; Doshi 26.3–6–94–4. *Second Innings*—Willis 4.1–0–32–0; Hogg 1–0–17–0; Doshi 1–0–17–0; Small 2–0–10–1.

Umpires: H. D. Bird and J. van Geloven.

WORCESTERSHIRE

TOM GRAVENEY – A CENTURY OF CENTURIES [1965]

By Neville Cardus

Thomas William Graveney who in the summer of 1964 made his hundredth hundred in first-class cricket, is one of the few batsmen today worth while our inspection if it is style and fluent strokes we are wishing to see, irrespective of the scoreboard's estimate of an innings by him. His accumulated runs, up to the moment I write this article, amount to no fewer than 38,094, averaging a little above 45. Yet he has seldom been regarded as a permanent member of the England XI; he has been for more than a decade on "trial". Nobody in his senses with half-a-notion of what constitutes a thoroughbred batsman would deny Graveney's class, his pedigree.

He came out of the Gloucestershire stable following the glamorous period of Hammond and Barnett, while the influence still pervaded the atmosphere of the County. Eleven years ago *Wisden* wrote of him in this eloquent way: "Undoubtedly no brighter star has appeared in the Gloucestershire cricket firmament since the early days of Hammond himself; some who have played with both believe that with a comparable intensity, almost ruthlessness, Graveney in time could emulate Hammond's remarkable achievements." Hammond as he matured and compiled his seven hour double-century certainly developed in mental determination. We who had seen him in his younger years realised the price we were paying for his solid durable contributions to the cause of England in Test matches – we knew that we wouldn't, except occasionally, see again the dauntless Hammond of his first raptures.

Since Hammond's glorious reign the character and economy have become tougher and tighter. Cricket everywhere, reflecting character and economy in the world at large, has tended to change from a sport and artistic spectacle to a competitive materialistic encounter, each contestant mainly setting his teeth not to lose. Batsmen not fit to tie Graveney's bootlaces, considered from the point of view of handsome stroke-embedded play, have been encouraged to oust Graveney from Test matches stern and generally unbeautiful. "Style" has become a "corny" word everywhere, so it is natural enough that we have lived to see and extol an honest artisan such as Boycott building his brick wall of an innings, what time Graveney must needs content himself scoring felicitous runs for his adopted county (incidentally going far towards winning the Championship for Worcestershire).

Were I myself Tom Graveney I shouldn't deplore my fate; I'd much rather remain a cricketer on the side of those who add to the aesthetic values and delight of those lovers of the game who find it difficult to count and work out percentages and hours of labour at the crease endured by the unblessed toilers under the sun whose presence at the wicket might not be closely observed if the scoreboard didn't dutifully and mechanically draw our attention to them.

It is true – and not to be questioned – that in Test matches against Australia Graveney has seldom done his talents justice. In some 24 innings v Australia he has failed to reach 20 twelve times and only six times gone beyond 40, with a single century put calmly together at Sydney, during the Hutton tour of 1954-55, when the rubber had already been decided in England's favour. At Lord's, in 1953, he played a royal innings with Hutton, in the face of Australia's first-innings total of 346. He was not out 78, and Hutton still in possession, when stumps were drawn on the second day with England 177 for one. Next morning in bounteous sunshine Lindwall clean bowled Graveney before another run had accrued. "Ah", said the wise heads of short memories, "he's no temperament this Graveney", forgetting at once that only a few hours since they had seen from Graveney batsmanship of the highest blood. As a fact Graveney was bowled on that morning of promise at Lord's by one of the finest balls bowled by Lindwall in his lifetime – a fast swinging yorker. "I never bowled a better," he vowed.

We should in fairness judge a man at his best. No batsman not truly accomplished is able to play a characteristic Graveney innings. Today he has no equal as a complete and stylish strokeplayer. Dexter can outshine him in rhetoric, so to say; Marshall in virtuosity of execution. But neither Dexter nor Marshall is Graveney's superior in point of effortless balance. When he is in form Graveney makes batsmanship look the easiest and most natural thing in the world. I have no rational explanation to account for his in-and-out form in Test matches – which, by the way, has not persistently been too bad. Against the West Indies in England in 1957, he scored 258 at Nottingham and 164 at Trent Bridge. No "Test match temperament"? Once on a time it was said of Hendren and W. J. Edrich that they hadn't any.

I decline to keep out of the highest class a fine batsman simply on the evidence of his half-success in Test matches. Indeed I'm not too sure nowadays that success in Test cricket most times is not an indication of dreary efficiency. It is a modern notion that anybody's talents need be measured by utility value in the "top" places of publicity. Some of the rarest artist-batsmen the game has ever nurtured have figured unobtrusively in Test matches; some of them have not appeared in Test matches at all. None the less they have adorned cricket, contributed to its memorable art, added to its summer-time appeal and delights.

Amongst these cricketers of style and pleasure can be counted L. C. H. Palairet, H. K. Foster, A. P. Day, Alan Marshal, Andy Ducat, Laurie Fishlock, George Emmett (superb stroke-playing colleague for a time of Graveney), the Hon. C. N. Bruce (as he was named), Jack Robertson – I could extend the list beginning from the days of W. G. Grace and continuing to Graveney himself and his Worcestershire captain, Donald Kenyon.

Consider cricket as a game of skill handsomely exhibited and who in the name of truth and common sense will argue that so and so's century in five hours in a Test match necessarily ranks him above, as a cricketer, Tom Graveney. Endurance and concentration, admirable factors in human nature in their proper place, don't inevitably add to the graces and allurements of any game, not even to its highly specialised technique. If some destructive processes were to eliminate all that we know about cricket, only Graveney surviving, we could reconstruct from him, from his way of batting and from the man himself, every outline of the game, every essential character and flavour which have contributed to cricket, the form of it and its soul, and its power to inspire a wide and sometimes great literature. Of how many living Test match cricketers could you say as much as this? Could you imagine Bloggs of Blankshire reminding you of the soul of cricket as he plods his computing way to a century in six hours and a half?

Graveney is one of the few batsmen today ornamenting the game, who not out at lunch, pack a ground in the afternoon. Bloggs of Blankshire sometimes empties it or keeps people away – the truth of his performances may copiously be found out from the subsequent published statistics. An innings of Graveney remains in the memory. Simply by closing our eyes we can still see, in deep winter as we browse by the fire in the twilight, a stroke by Graveney; we can see and delight in, retrospectively, the free uplift of his bat, the straight lissome poise and the rhythm of his swinging drives.

In form he hasn't need to labour; he knows the secret of artistic independence of effort. He can cut late from flexible wrists – whenever the miser of a bowler isn't pegging away on the leg stump. A fair-weather cricketer? Is it possible that any batsman not strong in mental and technical fibre could play most of his 955 innings in England, scoring more than 38,000 runs, averaging 45? No cricketer not fairly complete in character and skill could hope to score a hundred hundreds in first-class cricket.

Moreover, Graveney has often enough proved that he is capable of facing stiff problems presented by the turning ball on a nasty wicket. Not really a "Test" cricketer? – still the parrot question about him persists. Yet in Test matches Graveney has scored 3,107 runs, average 41.98. This sop I toss to the statisticians. In a world of ideal cricket, a world in which the game could freely show its class, allurement and fine subtle technique unburdened by parsimonious competitive considerations, Graveney would be a first-choice in any England XI. Really, there should for the purposes of all representative games be a certain style insisted on. Here I am an unrepentant snob; I want to see breeding in an England XI. I'd rather lose a rubber than win it by playing against the game's spirit and pride, its traditions of style and summer-time spectacle, charm and glorious change and variety.

Critics who think of Test matches as though they were of dire consequence to the nation politically, economically and what have you, have maintained that Graveney has on occasion "let England down". But nobody has claimed that Tom Graveney has ever "let cricket down". In form or out of form he has rendered tribute to the graces of cricket.

WORCESTERSHIRE v LANCASHIRE

Played at Worcester, May 26, 27, 28, 1965

Worcestershire won by 251 runs. A fighting stand of 122 by Richardson and Booth enabled Worcestershire to recover from 68 for five, after which their bowlers saw that they remained in command. Flavell, moving his fast medium deliveries either way off rain affected turf, took seven for 40 as Lancashire were shot out for 101 in 34 overs and in the second innings lasting 23 overs, Carter, stand-in for Coldwell, injured, finished things with his best figures. He took the last six wickets for seven runs in 25 balls, including a hat-trick: Howard and Greenhough caught at the wicket and Goodwin bowled.

Worcestershire

M. J. Horton c Goodwin b Statham	0	– lbw b Statham	19
C. D. Fearnley b Higgs	22	– c Statham b Greenhough	31
R. G. A. Headley c Goodwin b Statham	15	– b Howard	5
*T. W. Graveney c Howard b Greenhough	19	– c Howard b Greenhough	11
B. D'Oliveira b Greenhough	4	– c Howard b Greenhough	21
D. W. Richardson run out	82	– not out	47
†R. Booth c Sullivan b Statham	53	– b Higgs	1
N. Gifford not out	17	– lbw b Higgs	7
B. M. Brain not out	8	– b Higgs	14
B 12, l-b 10	22	L-b 9	9
1/0 2/34 3/56 4/65 5/68 6/190 7/233	(7 wkts dec.) 242	1/28 2/42 3/64 4/75 5/130 6/133 7/145 8/165	(8 wkts dec.) 165

J. A. Flavell and R. G. M. Carter did not bat.

Bowling: *First Innings*—Statham 29–9–63–3; Higgs 30–10–72–1; Greenhough 21–5–46–2; Howard 22–10–39–0. *Second Innings*—Statham 12–7–16–1; Higgs 17.3–3–58–3; Greenhough 22–6–61–3; Howard 15–8–21–1.

Lancashire

D. M. Green c Booth b Flavell	12	– c Booth b Flavell	5
G. Knox run out	1	– b Flavell	1
G. Pullar c Booth b Flavell	28	– c sub b Brain	3
J. D. Bond b Flavell	3	– b Flavell	0
J. Sullivan lbw b Flavell	13	– b Carter	15
A. M. Beddow c Graveney b Brain	15	– c D'Oliveira b Carter	13
*J. B. Statham b Flavell	1	– b Carter	11
K. Howard b Flavell	15	– c Booth b Carter	3
K. Higgs c D'Oliveira b Flavell	5	– not out	4
T. Greenhough b Brain	6	– c Booth b Carter	0
†K. Goodwin not out	0	– b Carter	0
B 1, n-b 1	2		
1/11 2/15 3/27 4/53 5/60 6/66 7/80 8/94 9/101	101	1/3 2/8 3/8 4/14 5/32 6/41 7/50 8/51 9/51	55

Bowling: *First Innings*—Flavell 17.1–2–40–7; Brain 17–1–59–2. *Second Innings*—Flavell 12–4–29–3; Brain 7–0–19–1; Carter 4.1–2–7–6.

Umpires: F. Jakeman and J. F. Crapp.

WORCESTERSHIRE v LEICESTERSHIRE

Played at Worcester, May 27, 29, 30, 1967

Drawn. In a match curtailed by rain to one day, batsmen, lacking practice, were ill at ease against both pace and slow bowling. After a blank first day, twenty-two wickets fell on the second, Lock having preferred to field. Birkenshaw, the Leicestershire off-break bowler, came out with six for 24, his best analysis and his first hat-trick. Graveney had a rare tussle with Birkenshaw and his 37 before falling to the spinner was the day's top score. Birkenshaw finished the innings by bowling Slade and Coldwell and having Flavell caught by the wicket-keeper with the last three balls. Leicestershire, troubled by the fast-medium Flavell and Coldwell, lost their last seven wickets for 57 runs, these two bowlers in the first two Championship matches on this ground having then taken 27 wickets in three innings.

Worcestershire

R. G. A. Headley b Cotton	6	– not out	17
C. D. Fearnley c Marner b Birkenshaw	15	– c Tolchard b Spencer	3
J. A. Ormrod lbw b Cotton	1	– b Cotton	3
T. W. Graveney c Lock b Birkenshaw	37		
B. L. D'Oliveira b Birkenshaw	2		
*D. Kenyon b Lock	4		
D. N. F. Slade b Birkenshaw	15	– not out	3
†R. Booth c Constant b Lock	4		
B. M. Brain not out	0		
L. J. Coldwell b Birkenshaw	0		
J. A. Flavell c Tolchard b Birkenshaw	0		
B 4, l-b 3	7		
1/6 2/10 3/38 4/54 5/63 6/67 7/80 8/91 9/91	91	1/4 2/21 (2 wkts)	26

Bowling: *First Innings*—Cotton 7–0–17–2; Spencer 8–1–13–0; Lock 19–8–30–2; Birkenshaw 17.4–5–24–6. *Second Innings*—Cotton 7–1–15–1; Spencer 4–2–10–1; Birkenshaw 2–1–1–0.

Leicestershire

M. R. Hallam b Coldwell	12
B. J. Booth c Slade b Coldwell	1
M. E. Norman b Coldwell	19
C. C. Inman c Graveney b D'Oliveira	26
P. T. Marner b Coldwell	24
D. J. Constant b Flavell	5
J. Birkenshaw b Coldwell	3
†R. W. Tolchard not out	9
*G. A. R. Lock b Coldwell	4
C. T. Spencer b Flavell	7
J. Cotton lbw b Flavell	0
N-b 1	1
1/8 2/21 3/54 4/68 5/77 6/82 7/97 8/101 9/111	111

Bowling: Flavell 15–4–38–3; Coldwell 20–3–42–6; Brain 2–0–17–0; Slade 2–2–0–0; D'Oliveira 6–2–13–1.

Umpires: W. F. Price and L. H. Gray.

WORCESTERSHIRE v SURREY

Played at Worcester, May 16, 18, 19, 1970

Drawn. A pitch of modest pace and bounce was appreciated most by Edrich, who, for the second time in his career, recorded two centuries in the same match. The first, occupying five hours ten minutes for 143 runs, was the anchor of an innings given true character only by the handsome cutting and driving of Younis in a century partnership with Edrich. In the second innings, Edrich batted more freely, taking two hours, fifty minutes over 113. Worcestershire answered Surrey's large score almost run for run, D'Oliveira taking three hours to complete his first Championship hundred since 1968. Turner and Headley, with opening stands twice topping 50, were also happy to accept the practice and indeed almost gave their side unexpected victory when scoring 84 in 15 overs towards a target of 219 in 38 overs. A vigorous innings by Cass, who hit three 6s in the match, helped Worcestershire to finish only six runs short.

Surrey

J. H. Edrich c Turner b Standen	143	– not out	113
M. J. Edwards c Gifford b Carter	1	– c Headley b Holder	25
*M. J. Stewart b Hemsley	29		
Younis Ahmed c and b Gifford	73	– c Cass b Carter	16
Intikhab Alam c Turner b Holder	12	– not out	18
G. R. J. Roope c Gifford b Slade	25	– c Hemsley b Standen	29
S. J. Storey c and b Gifford	21	– c Headley b Standen	11
†A. Long not out	35		
G. G. Arnold b Gifford	16		
P. I. Pocock c Standen b Hemsley	1		
R. D. Jackman c Cass b Gifford	0		
B 8, l-b 4, n-b 2	14	B 2, n-b 2	4
1/2 2/78 3/211 4/243 5/282 6/294 7/336 8/366 9/369	370	1/50 2/78 3/153 4/179 (4 wkts dec.)	216

Bowling: *First Innings*—Holder 23–3–61–1; Carter 23–4–66–1; D'Oliveira 10–3–23–0; Standen 15–0–58–1; Gifford 22.4–2–60–4; Hemsley 16–2–48–2; Slade 8–1–40–1. *Second Innings*—Holder 11–0–29–1; Carter 15–3–58–1; Standen 16–1–76–2; Slade 4–0–22–0; Gifford 8–0–27–0.

Worcestershire

R. G. A. Headley c and b Intikhab	30	– c Arnold b Roope	44
G. M. Turner c Younis b Pocock	66	– b Roope	52
E. J. O. Hemsley b Arnold	46	– c sub b Storey	0
B. L. D'Olive	101	– c Edwards b Storey	17
T. J. Yardley b Arnold	57	– c Edrich b Jackman	26
D. N. F. Slade not out	14	– c sub b Storey	12
†G. R. Cass not out	37	– c and b Storey	42
J. A. Standen (did not bat)		– c Roope b Jackman	0
*N. Gifford (did not bat)		– not out	5
V. A. Holder (did not bat)		– not out	5
B 1, l-b 13, w 3	17	B 9, l-b 1	10
1/56 2/138 3/167 4/297 5/317 (5 wtks dec.)	368	1/84 2/85 3/111 4/134 5/174 6/194 7/201 8/202 (8 wkts)	213

R. G. M. Carter did not bat.

Bowling: *First Innings*—Arnold 19–4–56–2; Jackman 15–1–51–0; Intikhab 17–2–71–1; Pocock 33–10–88–1; Roope 19–6–58–1; Storey 6–0–27–0. *Second Innings*—Arnold 9–0–32–0; Jackman 6–0–41–2; Roope 9–0–49–2; Pocock 2–0–17–0; Storey 11–0–47–4; Intikhab 1–0–17–0.

Umpires: A. Jepson and D. J. Constant.

WORCESTERSHIRE v NORTHAMPTONSHIRE

Played at Worcester, June 26, 28, 29, 1971

Drawn. After taking only two batting points from their previous five matches Worcestershire made adjustments to tactics and the batting order. The outcome was a remarkable success; they took seven batting points, a record for the county. Headley, surpassing his previous best score by 37 runs, was the central figure in the three century partnerships. Northamptonshire were equally at home on the perfect wicket. Steele completed his second century in successive matches and his partnership with Mushtaq yielded 184 within days of a double century stand between the same pair against Lancashire. When Worcestershire batted again Headley completed his second century of the match (the first Worcestershire player to do so since Cooper in 1946). Northamptonshire, wanting 268 in two and three-quarter hours, were saved from defeat by their captain, Watts.

Worcestershire

R. G. A. Headley b Hodgson	187	– b Steele	108
P. J. Stimpson c and b Swinburne	65	– c Watts b Breakwell	74
T. J. Yardley c Willey b Swinburne	39	– not out	36
B. L. D'Oliveira not out	56	– c Sharp b Breakwell	22
B 7, l-b 6	13	L-b 2	2
1/125 2/251 3/360	(3 wkts dec.) 360	1/147 2/205 3/242	(3 wkts dec.) 242

E. J. O. Hemsley, J. A. Ormrod, D. N. F. Slade, †H. G. Wilcock, *N. Gifford, V. A. Holder and R. G. M. Carter did not bat.

Bowling: *First Innings*—Lee 15–3–73–0; Hodgson 12.1–2–39–1; Crump 16–4–59–0; Swinburne 25–8–90–2; Mushtaq 13–3–39–0; Willey 6–0–26–0; Breakwell 8–0–21–0. *Second Innings*—Lee 14–5–37–0; Hodgson 14–4–46–0; Swinburne 10–1–35–0; Mushtaq 2–0–10–0; Breakwell 24.3–5–60–2; Steele 16–2–52–1.

Northamptonshire

P. Willey c Slade b D'Oliveira	9	– b Holder	0
H. M. Ackerman c Ormrod b Gifford	48	– c Headley b Holder	21
D. S. Steele not out	140	– c Holder b Carter	7
Mushtaq Mohammad c Wilcock b Holder	91	– c Wilcock b D'Oliveira	34
*P. J. Watts not out	39	– not out	64
B. S. Crump (did not bat)		– b Gifford	6
†G. Sharp (did not bat)		– c Yardley b Gifford	6
D. Breakwell (did not bat)		– lbw b D'Oliveira	1
A. Hodgson (did not bat)		– c Yardley b Gifford	1
J. W. Swinburne (did not bat)		– not out	0
L-b 7, n-b 1	8	B 3, n-b 2	5
1/26 2/64 3/248	(3 wkts dec.) 335	1/3 2/16 3/33 4/72 5/91 6/119 7/134 8/139	(8 wkts) 145

P. G. Lee did not bat.

Bowling: *First Innings*—Holder 20–4–69–1; Carter 14–0–71–0; D'Oliveira 11–5–23–1; Gifford 30–9–79–1; Slade 29–7–76–0; Hemsley 3–0–9–0. *Second Innings*—Holder 12–4–27–2; Carter 11–0–40–1; D'Oliveira 15–6–27–2; Gifford 18–7–33–3; Slade 4–1–13–0.

Umpires: W. L. Budd and O. W. Herman.

WORCESTERSHIRE v ESSEX

Played at Worcester, May 26, 28, 29, 1973

Drawn. Having won three of their first four Championship games, Essex tasted their first adversity of the season when Holder exploited the pace in a firm pitch and completed his best bowling figures since joining Worcestershire in 1969. His lift off a good length was disconcerting for the later Essex batsmen and the final six wickets went for 25 in forty-five minutes. Cass equalled a Worcestershire wicketkeeping record by holding six catches and so assisted the West Indian in five of his dismissals. Worcestershire also had their problems when facing the new ball, but Headley's supreme authority pulled them through the crisis and his partnership with Ormrod was worth 94 when the weather broke after the week-end and washed out the last two days.

Essex

B. E. A. Edmeades c Cass b Holder	12
B. C. Francis c Cass b Holder	4
*K. W. R. Fletcher c Cass b D'Oliveira	26
R. M. O. Cooke c Yardley b D'Oliveira	18
K. D. Boyce c Cass b Holder	17
S. Turner c Cass b Holder	3
R. E. East c Cass b Holder	4
R. N. S. Hobbs c Stewart b Brain	5
†N. Smith not out	6
J. K. Lever b Brain	0
D. L. Acfield b Holder	1
L-b 1, n-b 1	2
1/9 2/22 3/54 4/73 5/80 6/81 7/86 8/93 9/93	98

Bowling: Holder 15.3–5–20–6; Brain 14–6–29–2; D'Oliveira 13–2–35–2; Gifford 4–1–12–0.

Worcestershire

R. G. A. Headley not out	72
D. E. R. Stewart b Lever	1
R. J. Lanchbury hit wkt b Boyce	7
J. A. Ormrod not out	45
N-b 7	7
1/10 2/38	(2 wkts) 132

B. L. D'Oliveira, T. J. Yardley, I. N. Johnson, †G. R. Cass, *N. Gifford, V. A. Holder and B. M. Brain did not bat.

Bowling: Boyce 14–2–28–1; Lever 9–2–17–1; Turner 8–1–22–0; East 8–3–11–0; Hobbs 9–3–31–0; Acfield 6–3–16–0.

Umpires: R. Aspinall and H. D. Bird.

WORCESTERSHIRE v NOTTINGHAMSHIRE

Played at Worcester, September 1, 3, 4, 1973

Worcestershire won by nine wickets. Worcestershire equalled the Championship record of 25 points for a match, which Warwickshire had set at New Road earlier in the season. Turner, with his ninth first-class century of the summer, and Yardley, making a new career-highest score for the second time in the season, shared a stand of 190, Worcestershire's best of the campaign. Two wickets in successive balls by Stead were all that Nottinghamshire had to offer as Turner reached his century before lunch. Smedley and Sobers snatched a batting point for Nottinghamshire, who were later reduced to a state of despair as excellent seam bowling earned Worcestershire a lead of 250. The danger of a two-day defeat was averted by a splendid and speedy maiden century by Randall. He was supported in a partnership of 119 by Smedley, though this only gave Turner the opportunity to complete 1,000 Championship runs after joining the county on July 25 following the New Zealand tour.

Worcestershire

G. M. Turner lbw b Sobers	140	– c Sobers b Nanan	65
J. M. Parker lbw b Stead	6	– not out	37
J. A. Ormrod lbw b Stead	0	– not out	5
B. L. D'Oliveira b Sobers	8		
T. J. Yardley c Nanan b Stead	135		
Imran Khan c Todd b Edwards	23		
I. N. Johnson b Edwards	29		
†G. R. Cass not out	16		
*N. Gifford b Stead	7		
J. D. Inchmore not out	7		
B 1, l-b 7, n-b 3	11	L-b 1	1
1/27 2/27 3/217 4/227 5/288 6/338 7/360 8/369	(8 wkts dec.) 382	1/96	(1 wkt) 108

B. M. Brain did not bat.

Bowling: *First Innings*—Stead 32–6–107–4; Wilkinson 8.1–2–23–0; Birch 15–0–92–0; Sobers 15–2–57–2; White 12–1–52–0; Edwards 9.5–1–40–2. *Second Innings*—Stead 7–2–20–0; Wilkinson 4–1–12–0; Sobers 6–1–34–0; White 8–1–26–0; Edwards 2.5–0–9–0; Nanan 2–0–6–1.

Nottinghamshire

P. A. Todd b Brain	12	– c Yardley b Brain	0
R. A. White c Ormrod b Brain	0	– run out	15
D. W. Randall c Yardley b Inchmore	0	– lbw b Gifford	107
M. J. Smedley lbw b D'Oliveira	36	– lbw b Brain	84
*G. S. Sobers b Brain	25	– b Imran	24
N. Nanan c Yardley b Inchmore	1	– lbw b Gifford	5
J. D. Birch b D'Oliveira	26	– c Gifford b Inchmore	0
G. Edwards b Inchmore	10	– not out	46
B. Stead c Imran b D'Oliveira	0	– b Brain	41
P. A. Wilkinson c Yardley b Imran	14	– c Cass b Imran	19
†D. A. Pullan not out	0	– b Imran	0
L-b 4, n-b 4	8	B 2, l-b 11, n-b 3	16
1/0 2/1 3/23 4/70 5/77 6/77 7/101 8/106 9/126	132	1/1 2/40 3/159 4/206 5/231 6/233 7/248 8/331 9/355	357

Bowling: *First Innings*—Brain 11–1–33–3; Inchmore 14–2–44–3; D'Oliveira 15–5–31–3; Imran 10.5–3–16–1. *Second Innings*—Brain 21–3–44–3; Inchmore 15–4–34–1; D'Oliveira 23–7–43–0; Imran 38.3–5–123–3; Gifford 32–10–77–2; Johnson 7–0–20–0.

Umpires: A. Jepson and B. J. Meyer.

WORCESTERSHIRE v WARWICKSHIRE

Played at Worcester, April 28, 29, 30, 1976

Drawn. The marvels of an early Spring wicket playing so perfectly were appreciated by numerous batsmen in a match which produced more than 1,300 runs and five century-makers. The first hundred, complete with superb timing by D'Oliveira was perhaps the most valuable in seeing Worcestershire out of trouble after losing half their first innings wickets for 142. He struck no fewer than seventeen 4s and one 6 in two hours, thirty-five minutes and induced useful response from Wilcock, who was out only two runs short of his highest score, and Inchmore, who hit strongly for his second first-class 50. Warwickshire gained a lead of 87 following a typically whirlwind start by Jameson, who hit one 6 and fifteen 4s while reaching 97 out of 145 in two hours. The next partnership involving Amiss was worth 158, Whitehouse playing an attractive part, and the England opener went on to claim the top score of the match after batting for four hours, fifty minutes and hitting twenty boundaries. The painstaking Ormrod and the more fluent Imran then scored centuries in a third wicket partnership of 278. Imran's maiden Championship century included two 6s and fifteen 4s. Warwickshire wanted 272 in two hours fifty minutes and victory seemed almost certain when Jameson scored 101 out of 145 with Amiss in eighty seven minutes before tea. Gifford intervened powerfully as the next five wickets went for 46 runs and, although Amiss again batted well, taking his aggregate to 407 in his first four innings of the season, Warwickshire had settled for a draw before the last half hour.

Worcestershire

G. M. Turner c Humpage b Brown	11	– c Whitehouse b Willis	0
J. A. Ormrod c Abberley b Willis	9	– c Abberley b Lewington	135
P. A. Neale b Willis	16	– c Humpage b Brown	7
Imran Khan c Humpage b Rouse	12	– c Willis b Lewington	143
B. L. D'Oliveira lbw b Brown	103	– not out	31
D. Patel c Kanhai b Lewington	22	– b Hemmings	10
†H. G. Wilcock c Kanhai b Hemmings	48	– c Kanhai b Lewington	5
J. D. Inchmore c Whitehouse b Lewington	57	– c Jameson b Lewington	8
R. Senghera c Rouse b Lewington	19	– not out	0
*N. Gifford not out	11		
A. P. Pridgeon c Humpage b Brown	1		
B 1, l-b 8, n-b 4	13	B 6, l-b 3, n-b 10	19
1/26 2/26 3/47 4/73 5/142 6/217 7/241 8/290 9/314	322	1/3 2/17 3/295 4/300 5/330 6/335 7/345 (7 wkts dec.)	358

Bowling: *First Innings*—Willis 19–3–70–2; Brown 21.4–1–72–3; Rouse 15–2–58–1; Lewington 27–8–78–3; Hemmings 13–5–31–1. *Second Innings*—Willis 15–2–35–1; Brown 6–2–15–1; Rouse 17–3–58–0; Lewington 33–6–102–4; Hemmings 32–11–108–1; Jameson 10–6–21–0.

Warwickshire

J. A. Jameson c Wilcock b Imran	97	– c Imran b Gifford	101
D. L. Amiss b Imran	167	– c Pridgeon b Gifford	40
J. Whitehouse b Senghera	68	– c Senghera b Gifford	18
R. B. Kanhai not out	49	– c Gifford b Imran	9
†G. W. Humpage b Inchmore	6	– c D'Oliveira b Gifford	0
R. B. Abberley (did not bat)		– lbw b Senghera	3
E. E. Hemmings (did not bat)		– not out	37
S. J. Rouse (did not bat)		– not out	1
B 4, l-b 8, n-b 10	22	B 8, l-b 3, n-b 7	18
1/146 2/304 3/394 4/409	(4 wkts dec.) 409	1/145 2/162 3/184 4/185 5/185 6/191	(6 wkts) 227

R. G. D. Willis, *D. J. Brown and P. J. Lewington did not bat.

Bowling: *First Innings*—Inchmore 12.4–2–51–1; Pridgeon 19–4–66–0; Imran 19–1–98–2; Gifford 22–2–75–0; Senghera 30–2–97–1. *Second Innings*—Inchmore 4–0–18–0; Pridgeon 4–1–24–0; Imran 5–0–20–1; Gifford 25–5–74–4; Senghera 16–5–59–1; D'Oliveira 7–2–14–0.

Umpires: C. Cook and H. Horton.

WORCESTERSHIRE v LANCASHIRE

Played at Worcester, July 3, 5, 6, 1976

Worcestershire won by an innings and 32 runs. This victory was almost entirely due to a magnificent all-round display by Imran Khan. His first salvo was an opening spell of one hundred minutes in which he removed the leading five batsmen by extracting remarkable movement from a sunbaked pitch. Imran returned later to wind up the innings with his best figures of seven for 53. Suspicions of uneven bounce were not confirmed when Ormrod and Turner put on 97 for Worcestershire's first wicket. The stage was set for Imran's dazzling stroke play on his appearance at 181 for two. Surviving one chance at 16, he hit two 6s and fifteen 4s, while making 111 not out in three hours twenty minutes. Lancashire were ill-equipped to deal with a refreshed Imran and the probing spin of Gifford on the final morning. Lloyd, Pilling, Hughes and Simmons offered varying degrees of resistance, only for Imran to reappear with a devastating spell which cleaned up the last three wickets in 13 balls. He finished the second innings with six for 46, giving him match figures of thirteen for 99.

Lancashire

B. Wood b Imran	18	– absent hurt	0
*D. Lloyd c Wilcock b Imran	5	– b Gifford	54
H. Pilling lbw b Imran	10	– c Hemsley b Imran	34
J. Abrahams b Imran	1	– c Imran b Gifford	0
B. W. Reidy c Ormrod b Gifford	20	– c Boyns b Imran	9
F. C. Hayes b Imran	5	– b D'Oliveira	31
†F. M. Engineer b Imran	31	– b Imran	5
D. P. Hughes b Inchmore	8	– c Wilcock b Imran	35
J. Simmons c Wilcock b Inchmore	4	– not out	25
P. Lever b Imran	9	– b Imran	4
P. G. Lee not out	10	– b Imran	1
L-b 9, w 1, n-b 9	19	B 5, l-b 3, w 1, n-b 4	13
1/10 2/34 3/43 4/45 5/51 6/97 7/107 8/114 9/119	140	1/22 2/100 3/100 4/106 5/124 6/149 7/205 8/209 9/211	211

Bowling: *First Innings*—Imran 18.4–4–53–7; Inchmore 16–3–34–2; Pridgeon 10–1–24–0; Gifford 4–2–6–1; D'Oliveira 2–0–4–0. *Second Innings*—Imran 18.1–5–46–6; Inchmore 14–6–18–0; Gifford 34–18–49–2; Pridgeon 8–1–20–0; Boyns 7–1–17–0; D'Oliveira 25–9–48–1.

Worcestershire

J. A. Ormrod c and b Simmons	54
G. M. Turner c Engineer b Lever	93
P. A. Neale c Reidy b Lever	29
Imran Khan not out	111
B. L. D'Oliveira lbw b Lee	16
E. J. O. Hemsley lbw b Hughes	9
C. N. Boyns lbw b Lloyd	23
†H. G. Wilcock c Hayes b Hughes	0
J. D. Inchmore run out	13
*N. Gifford c Abrahams b Hughes	11
A. P. Pridgeon c and b Hughes	4
B 14, n-b 6	20
1/97 2/181 3/182 4/205 5/222 6/258 7/262 8/311 9/374	383

Bowling: Lever 21–1–67–2; Lee 25–5–92–1; Simmons 21–4–64–1; Hughes 41.4–13–110–4; Lloyd 9–2–30–1.

Umpires: A. E. G. Rhodes and B. J. Meyer.

WORCESTERSHIRE v GLOUCESTERSHIRE

Played at Worcester, September 8, 9, 10, 1976

Gloucestershire won by nine wickets. They clinched £1,000 for third place in the Championship. Zaheer, who struck two 6s and thirteen 4s in his eleventh Championship century of the season, completed an aggregate for the season of 2,554, the best in England since W. E. Alley scored 3,019 in 1961. Sadiq, meanwhile, reached his eighth Championship hundred of the season, including twelve 4s. This was his fourth consecutive century, the first time the feat had been achieved in England since 1949. Sadiq and Zaheer put on 191 together and, not surprisingly, Gloucestershire took a lead of 120. This would have been greater but for the unusual success of Worcestershire's last four batsmen who put on 200 runs when seven wickets had gone for 98 after they had been sent in to bat. Inchmore, with his highest innings for two years, and Wilcock amassed 122 for the eighth wicket and Pridgeon added 78 in half an hour with Gifford. Worcestershire batted badly in the second innings, losing their last four wickets in 16 balls from Brain. Gloucestershire cruised to their sixth win in the final seven Championship matches.

Worcestershire

G. M. Turner b Brain	11	– c Graveney b Procter	2
J. A. Ormrod b Brown	19	– b Davey	46
D. N. Patel b Brain	13	– c Brassington b Graveney	53
Imran Khan c Shepherd b Davey	6	– lbw b Davey	1
B. L. D'Oliveira c Stovold b Brain	23	– lbw b Brown	2
C. N. Boyns lbw b Davey	7	– b Graveney	9
R. Senghera b Graveney	7	– lbw b Brain	28
†H. G. Wilcock b Procter	43	– c Brassington b Brain	7
J. D. Inchmore c Hignell b Sadiq	75	– b Brain	6
*N. Gifford not out	48	– c Brown b Brain	0
A. P. Pridgeon not out	25	– not out	0
B 8, l-b 3, n-b 10	21	L-b 3, w 1, n-b 5	9
1/15 2/41 3/57 4/59 5/71 6/93 7/98 8/220 9/220	(9 wkts) 298	1/2 2/65 3/71 4/78 5/107 6/131 7/141 8/155 9/156	163

Bowling: *First Innings*—Procter 17–4–56–1; Brain 17–1–49–3; Davey 14–3–34–2; Brown 13–1–33–1; Graveney 19–9–37–1; Sadiq 20–4–68–1. *Second Innings*—Procter 9–1–44–1; Brain 11.2–3–20–4; Graveney 14–5–43–2; Brown 9–0–27–1; Davey 8–3–19–2; Sadiq 1–0–1–0.

Gloucestershire

Sadiq Mohammad c Wilcock b D'Oliveira	109	– b Imran	0
A. W. Stovold b Inchmore	25	– not out	4
Zaheer Abbas c Imran b Senghera	106	– not out	37
A. J. Hignell c D'Oliveira b Inchmore	56		
M. J. Procter c D'Oliveira b Inchmore	30		
D. R. Shepherd b Pridgeon	28		
D. A. Graveney c Turner b Boyns	32		
*A. S. Brown b Pridgeon	1		
†A. J. Brassington not out	4		
B 8, l-b 4, w 2, n-b 13	27	B 1, n-b 2	3
1/35 2/226 3/278 4/331 5/358 6/394 7/396 8/418 (8 wkts dec.)	418	1/1 (1 wkt)	44

B. M. Brain and J. Davey did not bat.

Bowling: *First Innings*—Imran 29–3–120–0; Inchmore 16–4–90–3; Pridgeon 10–3–27–2; Boyns 5.5–0–39–1; Gifford 18–1–62–0; Senghera 11–2–41–1; D'Oliveira 3–1–12–1. *Second Innings*—Imran 3.1–0–26–1; Inchmore 3–0–15–0.

Umpires: K. E. Palmer and P. B. Wight.

WORCESTERSHIRE v GLAMORGAN

Played at Worcester, July 6, 7, 8, 1977

Glamorgan won by eight wickets. Apart from a stand of 63 between Neale and D'Oliveira and a stinging 37 by Humphries, Worcestershire suffered yet another batting collapse in which King, who began with five maidens, and the two left-arm seamers, Nash and Wilkins met modest opposition. The Glamorgan openers, Jones and Hopkins, put on 253 in four and a half hours, Hopkins continued until he had reached 230. In all, he batted six and three-quarter hours, hitting twenty-six 4s, and was awarded his county cap to mark the highest score by a Glamorgan player since 1939. Worcestershire batted much more effectively in their second attempt. Turner hit fluently for 73, and D'Oliveira reached 156 not out, including twenty-four boundaries. Wilkins, who claimed five for 71, did much damage and Glamorgan had an hour to spare in making 69 runs.

Worcestershire

*G. M. Turner b Nash	9	– b Lloyd	73
J. A. Ormrod b King	0	– b Nash	7
P. A. Neale c King b Wilkins	41	– c King b Cordle	9
E. J. O. Hemsley b King	1	– c E. W. Jones b King	39
B. L. D'Oliveira lbw b Wilkins	34	– not out	156
D. N. Patel c Richards b King	4	– c E. W. Jones b Wilkins	21
S. P. Henderson c Richards b Wilkins	0	– b Wilkins	0
†D. J. Humphries c King b Cordle	37	– lbw b Wilkins	4
V. A. Holder c E. W. Jones b King	6	– b Wilkins	9
J. Cumbes lbw b Nash	5	– b Wilkins	0
A. P. Pridgeon not out	2	– c Hopkins b Nash	26
B 6, l-b 6, n-b 1	13	B 2, l-b 4, n-b 1	7
1/4 2/10 3/11 4/74 5/89 6/91 7/91 8/104 9/135	152	1/46 2/110 3/167 4/200 5/200 6/225 7/241 8/249 9/331	351

Bowling: *First Innings*—Nash 20–7–41–2; King 17–8–31–4; Cordle 13.4–1–40–1; Wilkins 11–4–27–3. *Second Innings*—Nash 31.1–5–86–2; King 28–6–77–1; Cordle 17–0–75–1; Wilkins 21–6–71–5; Lloyd 13–7–30–1; Richards 3–2–5–0.

Glamorgan

J. A. Hopkins lbw b Pridgeon	230	– run out	13
*A. Jones c Pridgeon b Patel	106	– not out	28
R. C. Ontong lbw b D'Oliveira	3	– lbw b Pridgeon	18
C. L. King c Hemsley b Pridgeon	44	– not out	8
M. J. Llewellyn not out	31		
B 4, l-b 7, w 1, n-b 9	21	L-b 2	2
1/253 2/282 3/368 4/435 (4 wkts dec.)	435	1/24 2/51 (2 wkts)	69

G. Richards, †E. W. Jones, M. A. Nash, A. E. Cordle, B. J. Lloyd and A. H. Wilkins did not bat.

Bowling: *First Innings*—Holder 30–6–89–0; Cumbes 21–2–101–0; Pridgeon 25.4–5–65–2; D'Oliveira 25–3–67–1; Hemsley 6–0–30–0; Patel 16–0–56–1; Henderson 1–0–6–0. *Second Innings*—Holder 5–1–9–0; Cumbes 7–2–14–0; D'Oliveira 10–2–15–0; Pridgeon 8–1–26–1; Henderson 1–0–3–0.

Umpires: H. D. Bird and C. Cook.

WORCESTERSHIRE v NORTHAMPTONSHIRE

Played at Worcester, July 9, 11, 12, 1977

Northamptonshire won by four wickets. For the third time in eight days Worcestershire lived to regret batting first after winning the toss. Griffiths, opening the Northamptonshire attack in the absence of Sarfraz, joined Hodgson in a lively start which accounted for the first four wickets. Griffiths later returned to finish the innings and achieved his best figures of five for 69. A typically patient century by Virgin kept Northamptonshire in command until Cumbes took their last three wickets to complete a hat-trick. With a lead of 76, Northamptonshire were again in a strong position when Hodgson claimed three wickets for ten runs in 19 balls. Worcestershire also lost Turner because of a badly bruised calf, but showed fighting spirit in a century partnership between D'Oliveira and the 18-year-old left hander, Henderson, who made 52. The wicket then offered increasing help to the slower bowlers and Northamptonshire struggled to victory.

Worcestershire

B. J. R. Jones lbw b Griffiths	2	– c Larkins b Hodgson	5
G. M. Turner c Cook b Hodgson	4	– retired hurt	34
P. A. Neale c Steele b Bedi	49	– c Sharp b Hodgson	5
E. J. O. Hemsley b Hodgson	19	– b Hodgson	1
B. L. D'Oliveira c Cook b Griffiths	23	– b Willey	84
S. P. Henderson c Sharp b Bedi	25	– b Mushtaq	52
†D. J. Humphries b Bedi	12	– c Mushtaq b Bedi	6
J. D. Inchmore c Sharp b Griffiths	2	– b Bedi	33
*N. Gifford b Griffiths	2	– c Cook b Willey	14
J. Cumbes b Griffiths	7	– not out	10
A. P. Pridgeon not out	3	– b Willey	0
L-b 1	1	B 3, l-b 9	12
1/5 2/9 3/58 4/91 5/109 6/134 7/137 8/137 9/144	149	1/30 2/44 3/48 4/157 5/195 6/203 7/240 8/246 9/256	256

Bowling: *First Innings*—Hodgson 12–6–26–2; Griffiths 19–6–69–5; Larkins 4–0–16–0; Mushtaq 8–2–21–0; Bedi 15–7–16–3. *Second Innings*—Hodgson 15–1–48–3; Griffiths 14–2–53–0; Bedi 24–11–39–2; Willey 35.3–11–74–3; Mushtaq 13–6–30–1.

Northamptonshire

R. T. Virgin lbw b Cumbes	107	– lbw b Gifford	27
G. Cook lbw b Inchmore	17	– b D'Oliveira	67
D. S. Steele c Henderson b Pridgeon	16	– b Gifford	1
*Mushtaq Mohammad b D'Oliveira	25	– not out	63
A. Hodgson b Pridgeon	9		
P. Willey st Humphries b Gifford	14	– b Gifford	3
W. Larkins b Gifford	12	– c and b Gifford	1
R. G. Williams not out	6	– c Humphries b Gifford	4
†G. Sharp c Hemsley b Cumbes	1	– not out	8
B. S. Bedi c Neale b Cumbes	0		
B. J. Griffiths lbw b Cumbes	0		
B 1, l-b 5, n-b 12	18	L-b 9, n-b 1	10
1/48 2/98 3/140 4/166 5/205 6/205 7/220 8/225 9/225	225	1/66 2/74 3/131 4/142 5/148 6/160	(6 wkts) 184

Bowling: *First Innings*—Inchmore 25–4–57–1; Cumbes 19.5–4–44–4; Pridgeon 20–4–49–2; D'Oliveira 9–4–18–1; Gifford 20–5–39–2. *Second Innings*—Cumbes 7–2–13–0; Inchmore 4–0–17–0; Gifford 30–7–64–5; Pridgeon 9–0–36–0; D'Oliveira 20–5–44–1.

Umpires: H. D. Bird and W. E. Phillipson.

WORCESTERSHIRE v NOTTINGHAMSHIRE

Played at Worcester, August 31, September 1, 2, 1977

Nottinghamshire won by 150 runs. At the 21st attempt, Nottinghamshire finally gained their first Championship win of the season, but largely with the co-operation of Gifford in declaring 107 behind in an effort to make up for the loss of several hours' play. Todd and Rice, who put on 111 together, and White all made fifties in the Nottinghamshire first innings, despite another strenuous performance by Holder, who took five for 62 in 35 overs. Batting again, Todd hit three 6s and nine 4s in his 66, which enabled Smedley to set a target of 240 in two and three-quarter hours. That was academic by the completion of Rice's first over, for the South African all-rounder claimed Worcestershire's first three wickets without a run on the board. At one stage, the score was 14 for five, but Turner survived the wreckage and Worcestershire were able to delay the result until well into the final hour when Holder and Gifford stayed together for 22 overs. Rice returned to take the last wicket and this gave him six for 16, his best figures for the county.

Nottinghamshire

S. B. Hassan c Gifford b Cumbes	14	– c Patel b Gifford	13
P. A. Todd c Gifford b Holder	63	– b Gifford	86
D. W. Randall c Hemsley b Boyns	6	– b Gifford	3
C. E. B. Rice c Humphries b Holder	66	– not out	22
K. Cooper c Humphries b Cumbes	0		
*M. J. Smedley c Humphries b Holder	26		
R. E. Dexter c Hemsley b Holder	0		
J. D. Birch c Turner b Holder	10	– not out	4
R. A. White not out	52		
†B. French not out	2		
L-b 11, n-b 7	18	L-b 4	4
1/20 2/45 3/156 4/163 5/163 6/165 7/181 8/244	(8 wkts dec.) 257	1/21 2/33 3/124	(3 wkts dec.) 132

D. R. Doshi did not bat.

Bowling: *First Innings*—Holder 35–11–62–5; Cumbes 36–8–80–2; Boyns 20–5–61–1; Gifford 4–0–28–0; D'Oliveira 3–0–8–0. *Second Innings*—Holder 5–2–11–0; Cumbes 4–2–4–0; Gifford 17–6–57–3; Patel 17–4–56–0.

Worcestershire

B. J. R. Jones c Rice b Doshi	38	– lbw b Rice	0
G. M. Turner c Dexter b Rice	52	– lbw b Rice	49
H. G. Wilcock c French b Doshi	0	– b Rice	0
E. J. O. Hemsley c Hassan b Doshi	23	– lbw b Rice	0
B. L. D'Oliveira not out	18	– lbw b Rice	1
†D. J. Humphries not out	15	– lbw b Doshi	6
D. N. Patel (did not bat)		– b Cooper	0
C. N. Boyns (did not bat)		– c Hassan b Doshi	10
V. A. Holder (did not bat)		– c Todd b Rice	8
*N. Gifford (did not bat)		– c Todd b White	8
J. Cumbes (did not bat)		– not out	0
L-b 3, n-b 1	4	B 3, l-b 3, n-b 1	7
1/75 2/75 3/113 4/115	(4 wkts dec.) 150	1/0 2/0 3/0 4/9 5/14 6/36 7/70 8/70 9/89	89

Bowling: *First Innings*—Rice 24–7–44–1; Cooper 15–3–46–0; Birch 9–3–23–0; Doshi 22.3–11–33–3; White 1–1–0–0. *Second Innings*—Rice 11.5–4–16–6; Cooper 8–2–24–1; Birch 2–0–4–0; Doshi 16–8–23–2; White 11–7–15–1.

Umpires: K. E. Palmer and J. van Geloven.

WORCESTERSHIRE v SURREY

Played at Worcester, July 29, 30, August 1, 1978

Drawn. Rain permitted only fifteen minutes' play on the last two days and prevented Worcestershire from gaining advantage from their sizeable total. This was based on an opening partnership of 254 in three and a quarter hours between Turner and Ormrod; both, however, were missed off the persevering Jackman before they had reached 20. Turner was the more fluent, striking one 6 and twenty-six 4s, and he was out with exactly twice as many runs as Ormrod at that stage. Ormrod then took over the leading role and finished with one 6 and twenty-two 4s in five and a half hours.

Worcestershire

G. M. Turner b Jackman	150
J. A. Ormrod c Lynch b Jackman	173
P. A. Neale lbw b Jackman	0
D. N. Patel run out	42
E. J. O. Hemsley b Wilson	25
†D. J. Humphries c Wilson b Jackman	8
G. G. Watson b Pocock	6
*N. Gifford not out	4
A. P. Pridgeon not out	1
B 13, l-b 7, n-b 9	29
1/254 2/254 3/367 4/417 5/425 6/432 7/434	(7 wkts) 438

B. J. R. Jones and J. Cumbes did not bat.

Bowling: Jackman 24–2–94–4; Wilson 13–2–76–1; Baker 6–0–42–0; Intikhab 21–4–83–0; Pocock 31–8–92–1; Younis 4–0–21–0; Lynch 1–0–1–0.

Surrey

A. R. Butcher not out	12
M. A. Lynch b Watson	4
R. P. Baker b Watson	8
Younis Ahmed not out	0
B 1, l-b 4, w 1	6
1/11 2/30 (2 wkts)	30

J. H. Edrich, A. Needham, †C. J. Richards, Intikhab Alam, *R. D. Jackman, P. I. Pocock and P. H. Wilson did not bat.

Bowling: Watson 6.2–1–12–2; Pridgeon 4–1–9–0; Gifford 1–0–3–0; Patel 1–1–0–0.

Umpires: D. L. Evans and A. G. T. Whitehead.

WORCESTERSHIRE v WARWICKSHIRE

V. A. Holder's Benefit Match

Played at Worcester, August 25, 27, 28, 1979

Warwickshire won by four wickets. Lost time was made up in a thrilling last day which produced 546 runs and finished with Warwickshire recording only their second Championship success of the season with eight balls to spare. Their orderly progress to a target of 296 in three hours forty minutes featured the foundation laying by Smith and a commendably cool partnership between Maynard and Ferreira, who were together almost throughout the last hour while putting on an unbroken 79. Worcestershire's declaration was made after some assistance from Warwickshire, who did not bowl Willis during a partnership of 147 in seventy-seven minutes between Turner, who completed his seventh century of the season, and Neale, who also reached his century before lunch, hitting three 6s and sixteen 4s in ninety three minutes. The pitch always played perfectly despite rain which washed out the first morning. Younis dominated the Worcestershire first innings with an unbeaten 152 (nineteen 4s), and Warwickshire recovered from early problems against the beneficiary, Holder. Kallicharran, with 107 not out (thirteen 4s) and Humpage, twelve 4s in his 96, put on 201 for the fifth wicket.

Worcestershire

J. A. Ormrod b Perryman	9	– c Amiss b Perryman	29
G. M. Turner c Whitehouse b Ferreira	33	– c Maynard b Clifford	108
P. A. Neale c Kallicharran b Ferreira	17	– not out	101
E. J. O. Hemsley c Smith b Ferreira	17	– not out	11
Younis Ahmed not out	152		
D. N. Patel b Clifford	19		
†D. J. Humphries b Ferreira	0		
J. D. Inchmore c Whitehouse b Clifford	24		
V. A. Holder not out	24		
L-b 5	5	B 3, l-b 5, w 2	10
1/28 2/51 3/64 4/109 5/168 6/172 7/254 (7 wkts dec.)	300	1/65 2/212 (2 wkts dec.)	259

*N. Gifford and J. Cumbes did not bat.

Bowling: *First Innings*—Willis 19–5–39–0; Perryman 31–9–115–1; Ferreira 25–6–70–4; Clifford 19.4–4–71–2. *Second Innings*—Willis 2–0–7–0; Perryman 11–1–30–1; Ferreira 7–1–29–0; Humpage 9–0–63–0; Clifford 15–0–81–1; Kallicharran 10–2–39–0.

Warwickshire

D. L. Amiss b Inchmore	21	– c Humphries b Holder	25
K. D. Smith lbw b Holder	6	– c Humphries b Patel	69
T. A. Lloyd b Holder	15	– c Gifford	21
A. I. Kallicharran not out	107	– c Hemsley b Gifford	23
*J. Whitehouse c Turner b Holder	0	– c Holder b Gifford	27
G. W. Humpage lbw b Gifford	96	– c Younis b Gifford	38
†C. W. Maynard (did not bat)		– not out	47
A. M. Ferreira (did not bat)		– not out	33
B 1, l-b 5, n-b 13	19	B 6, l-b 4, n-b 5	15
1/29 2/32 3/63 4/63 5/264	(5 wkts dec.) 264	1/55 2/119 3/149 4/150 5/198 6/219	(6 wkts) 298

R. G. D. Willis, C. C. Clifford and S. P. Perryman did not bat.

Bowling: *First Innings*—Holder 16–5–47–3; Inchmore 12–0–54–1; Cumbes 16–2–54–0; Gifford 15.5–1–64–1; Patel 9–1–26–0. *Second Innings*—Holder 9–0–33–1; Inchmore 12–0–45–0; Cumbes 3–0–13–0; Patel 18–1–101–1; Gifford 24.4–2–91–4.

Umpires: A. Jepson and J. van Geloven.

WORCESTERSHIRE v SOMERSET

Played at Worcester, June 4, 5, 6, 1980

Somerset won by eight wickets. More than 250 overs were bowled by spinners and two batsmen each scored two centuries – Ormrod for Worcestershire and Rose for Somerset – in a match which produced 1,183 runs. Ormrod faced 503 balls in nine hours to make his aggregate of 232. Rose scored at a similar pace in the first innings, but adjusted to increased demands with an unbeaten 150 (eighteen 4s) in three and a half hours when Somerset clinched victory by scoring 291 at 4.77 runs per over. Smart running for singles was the feature of his partnership of 153 with Roebuck, and then he was joined by Denning in a positive sprint, the last 119 runs coming from 18.5 overs in 59 minutes. Despite such dominance by the bat, the match also featured some sustained spin bowling, notably by Breakwell and Gifford in the first innings.

Worcestershire

G. M. Turner lbw b Gore	7	– c Roebuck b Breakwell	4
J. A. Ormrod c Denning b Breakwell	101	– not out	131
P. A. Neale b Jennings	10	– c Denning b Marks	33
E. J. O. Hemsley lbw b Moseley	19	– c and b Marks	67
Younis Ahmed c Taylor b Breakwell	74	– not out	25
D. N. Patel c Taylor b Breakwell	25		
†D. J. Humphries c Lloyds b Marks	42		
J. D. Inchmore st Taylor b Breakwell	13		
H. Alleyne not out	23		
*N. Gifford not out	0		
L-b 3, n-b 6	9	L-b 7, n-b 1	8
1/8 2/29 3/84 4/205 5/230 6/285 7/299 8/301	(8 wkts) 323	1/19 2/93 3/210	(3 wkts dec.) 268

A. P. Pridgeon did not bat.

Bowling: *First Innings*—Moseley 15–2–29–1; Gore 20–4–58–1; Jennings 10–0–38–1; Marks 30–7–109–1; Breakwell 25–5–80–4. *Second Innings*—Moseley 3–2–6–0; Gore 2–0–4–0; Marks 42–6–98–2; Breakwell 32–5–108–1; Jennings 1–0–4–0; Gavaskar 1–0–6–0; Lloyds 8–0–34–0.

Somerset

S. M. Gavaskar st Humphries b Gifford	66	– b Inchmore	11
*B. C. Rose c Pridgeon b Gifford	124	– not out	150
P. M. Roebuck c Alleyne b Gifford	30	– b Gifford	55
P. W. Denning c and b Gifford	41	– not out	60
D. Breakwell c Alleyne b Patel	13		
V. J. Marks not out	9		
B 1, l-b 12, n-b 5	18	B 4, l-b 4, n-b 7	15
1/148 2/222 3/243 4/272 5/301	(5 wkts dec.) 301	1/19 2/172	(2 wkts) 291

†D. J. S. Taylor, J. W. Lloyds, H. R. Moseley, K. F. Jennings and H. I. E. Gore did not bat.

Bowling: *First Innings*—Alleyne 5–1–22–0; Inchmore 8–0–23–0; Gifford 42.2–11–92–4; Patel 39–6–125–1; Pridgeon 5–1–21–0. *Second Innings*—Alleyne 5–0–24–0; Inchmore 13–1–58–1; Gifford 23–3–79–1; Patel 13.5–0–89–0; Pridgeon 6–0–26–0.

Umpires: R. S. Herman and K. E. Palmer.

WORCESTERSHIRE v NORTHAMPTONSHIRE

Played at Stourbridge, July 29, 30, 31, 1981

Drawn. Turner marked the return, after nineteen years, of Championship cricket to the Birmingham League club's ground by scoring a century in each innings, for the fifth time. It was here that the former New Zealand Test captain played for fifteen shillings a match and his bus fare while qualifying for Worcestershire. His first century came before lunch, made in 98 minutes out of 133, and it says much for Neale's batting that his own century in 140 minutes was almost as exhilarating. Neale's 125 contained a 6 and twenty-three 4s. Northamptonshire's response was resolute, and even Gifford's breakthrough following an opening stand of 101 failed to halt the run-chase as Allan Lamb (two 6s and eleven 4s) and Kapil Dev (six 6s and six 4s), in contrasting manner, batted superbly. Turner's second century and Patel's brisk 87 enabled Worcestershire to declare again after a morning bonanza of 186 runs. Northamptonshire, set 335 in four hours, were reduced mainly by spin to 141 for seven when the final hour was signalled, but Worcestershire's victory bid was halted by Yardley and Mallender, the former remaining unbeaten after defying his old county for more than two hours.

Worcestershire

*G. M. Turner c A. J. Lamb b T. M. Lamb	161	– c Sharp b Mallender	101
M. S. Scott c Sharp b Griffiths	43	– lbw b T. M. Lamb	10
P. A. Neale c Cook b Kapil Dev	125	– c Cook b Williams	38
D. N. Patel b Williams	21	– c and b Boyd-Moss	87
E. J. O. Hemsley c A. J. Lamb b Griffiths	2	– (6) not out	22
T. S. Curtis not out	6		
†D. J. Humphries not out	0	– c Sharp b Griffiths	20
J. D. Inchmore (did not bat)		– (5) c Yardley b Williams	14
L-b 7, w 1, n-b 10	18	B 5, l-b 7, w 4, n-b 9	25
1/198 2/242 3/323 4/342 5/374	(5 wkts dec.) 376	1/37 2/132 3/231 4/254 5/292 6/317	(6 wkts dec.) 317

J. Birkenshaw, N. Gifford and A. P. Pridgeon did not bat.

Bowling: *First Innings*—Kapil Dev 19–1–84–1; Griffiths 20–4–76–2; Mallender 14–3–48–0; T. M. Lamb 19–4–61–1; Williams 20–1–75–1; Boyd-Moss 4–0–14–0. *Second Innings*—Kapil Dev 15–1–37–0; Griffiths 11–0–55–1; Mallender 12–0–56–1; T. M. Lamb 11–0–36–1; Williams 14–1–80–2; Boyd-Moss 4–1–28–1.

Northamptonshire

*G. Cook c Pridgeon b Gifford	52	– lbw b Pridgeon	16
W. Larkins st Humphries b Gifford	43	– c Patel b Gifford	58
A. J. Lamb c Gifford b Patel	86	– (4) c Pridgeon b Patel	12
R. J. Boyd-Moss b Gifford	25	– (5) c Humphries b Gifford	10
T. J. Yardley c Turner b Patel	8	– (6) not out	65
Kapil Dev c Humphries b Birkenshaw	79	– (7) c and b Patel	4
†G. Sharp not out	44	– (8) c Birkenshaw b Patel	0
N. A. Mallender not out	10	– (9) c Birkenshaw b Curtis	7
R. G. Williams (did not bat)		– (3) b Pridgeon	4
T. M. Lamb (did not bat)		– not out	0
L-b 9, n-b 3	12	B 6, l-b 9, w 1, n-b 7	23
1/101 2/113 3/186 4/203 5/242 6/330	(6 wkts dec.) 359	1/44 2/48 3/90 4/107 5/124 6/129 7/129 8/190	(8 wkts) 199

B. J. Griffiths did not bat.

Bowling: *First Innings*—Pridgeon 16–2–55–0; Inchmore 13–0–66–0; Gifford 41–9–129–3; Patel 18–4–57–2; Birkenshaw 6–0–40–1. *Second Innings*—Inchmore 5–1–15–0; Pridgeon 9–3–26–2; Gifford 35–15–75–2; Patel 24–12–34–3; Birkenshaw 7–2–13–0; Curtis 4–2–13–1.

Umpires: W. L. Budd and K. E. Palmer.

WORCESTERSHIRE v WARWICKSHIRE

Played at Worcester, August 29, 31, September 1, 1981

Worcestershire won by six wickets. A second century of the match from Turner may have been anticipated by Warwickshire when the third declaration left Worcestershire the daunting task of scoring 347 runs at nearly 6 an over, but a century also from Patel enabled the home side to achieve their objective in a lively three and a half hours with four overs to spare. Whatever the views of those spectators who slow-handclapped Amiss's declaration as uncharitable, the Turner-Patel thrash of 200 runs in 110 minutes more than exposed the bowling inadequacies of the team firmly seated at the foot of the Championship table. Turner's fourth century in five innings in eight days made him the highest-scoring Worcestershire batsman in matches against Warwickshire, took him past 2,000 runs in the season, and it was the sixth time he made two hundreds in a match. The New Zealander hit fifteen 4s in the first innings and seventeen boundaries in the second, while Patel, who managed to outpace him during their near-faultless association, hit three 6s and nine 4s in his career-best 138. Amiss, whose sixth Championship hundred of the summer contained twenty-two 4s, was helped in a painstaking stand of 156 by Kallicharran, playing his first Championship match since June. With Lloyd and Humpage also reaching three figures, there was the rarity of six centuries in the match, in which 587 runs were scored on the third day at an average of almost 100 an hour.

Warwickshire

*D. L. Amiss b Patel	145	– run out	24
K. D. Smith c Weston b Cumbes	0	– c Humphries b Gifford	20
T. A. Lloyd c and b Pridgeon	29	– c Hemsley b Patel	120
†G. W. Humpage b Cumbes	8	– run out	111
A. I. Kallicharran not out	82	– not out	16
C. Lethbridge lbw b Cumbes	0		
P. R. Oliver b Pridgeon	11		
A. M. Ferreira not out	9		
B 9, l-b 6, w 1	16	B 4, l-b 2	6
1/2 2/61 3/84 4/240 5/245 6/271	(6 wkts dec.) 300	1/44 2/44 3/242 4/297	(4 wkts dec.) 297

G. C. Small, W. Hogg and S. P. Sutcliffe did not bat.

Bowling: *First Innings*—Pridgeon 28–6–93–2; Cumbes 34–7–96–3; Weston 6–2–21–0; Gifford 11–2–26–0; Patel 20–7–48–1. *Second Innings*—Pridgeon 7–1–13–0; Cumbes 8–1–30–0; Gifford 29.5–11–78–1; Patel 38–11–111–1; Weston 4–0–29–0; Scott 6–0–30–0.

Worcestershire

*G. M. Turner not out	147	– c Lethbridge b Hogg	139
M. S. Scott lbw b Ferreira	21	– lbw b Ferreira	12
P. A. Neale b Sutcliffe	48	– lbw b Lethbridge	0
D. N. Patel not out	24	– c Humpage b Small	138
E. J. O. Hemsley (did not bat)		– not out	38
†D. J. Humphries (did not bat)		– not out	5
B 5, l-b 3, n-b 3	11	B 3, l-b 5, w 2, n-b 5	15
1/98 2/199	(2 wkts dec.) 251	1/63 2/65 3/265 4/334	(4 wkts) 347

T. S. Curtis, M. J. Weston, N. Gifford, A. P. Pridgeon and J. Cumbes did not bat.

Bowling: *First Innings*—Hogg 10–0–58–0; Small 11–1–46–0; Ferreira 10–1–35–1; Lethbridge 7–0–34–0; Sutcliffe 22.4–1–67–1. *Second Innings*—Hogg 12–0–66–1; Small 7–0–42–1; Ferreira 14–2–86–1; Lethbridge 10–0–53–1; Sutcliffe 11–0–78–0; Kallicharran 0.5–0–7–0.

Umpires: W. E. Alley and W. L. Budd.

YORKSHIRE

YORKSHIRE v NOTTINGHAMSHIRE

Played at Bradford, August 14, 15, 16, 1963

Drawn. Rain, preventing play on the last day, robbed Yorkshire of almost certain victory. Nottinghamshire were put out for 55, on a lively pitch, Trueman ending the innings with a hat-trick, his third against Nottinghamshire and the fourth of his career. He dismissed Millman, Davison and Wells. Yorkshire went ahead with three wickets down and built a strong position when Close and Hutton added 101. Bolus, a former Yorkshire batsman, saved Nottinghamshire from a two-day defeat. He gave a fine display for three hours, forty minutes and his 114 included one 6 and thirteen 4s. He received a standing ovation from the crowd of 8,500. After his departure, Nottinghamshire lost seven wickets for 23 and Yorkshire needed 94 to win. They made 20 without loss by the close of the second day, but that was the end of the match.

Nottinghamshire

J. B. Bolus c Close b Nicholson	17	– c Boycott b Wilson	114
N. Hill c Hutton b Nicholson	0	– c Sharpe b Illingworth	46
H. M. Winfield lbw b Nicholson	15	– b Illingworth	16
H. I. Moore b Ryan	5	– c Illingworth b Wilson	19
A. Gill c Binks b Trueman	5	– c Binks b Wilson	0
*†G. Millman b Trueman	8	– c Sharpe b Wilson	6
C. Forbes b Ryan	0	– c Sharpe b Illingworth	1
A. J. Corran b Nicholson	1	– c Trueman b Nicholson	3
I. Davison c Illingworth b Trueman	3	– b Trueman	0
J. Cotton not out	0	– not out	1
B. D. Wells b Trueman	0	– c Illingworth b Trueman	4
N-b 1	1	B 1, n-b 3	4
1/4 2/20 3/35 4/42 5/42 6/45 7/47 8/52 9/55	55	1/89 2/151 3/191 4/195 5/200 6/203 7/207 8/209 9/209	214

Bowling: *First Innings*—Trueman 15.2–3–26–4; Nicholson 13–5–25–4; Ryan 7–4–3–2; Hutton 3–3–0–0. *Second Innings*—Trueman 20–3–48–2; Nicholson 10–2–19–1; Hutton 4–0–17–0; Illingworth 30–9–66–3; Wilson 23–9–39–4; Close 2–0–8–0; Ryan 2–0–13–0.

Yorkshire

J. H. Hampshire c Moore b Cotton	2	– not out	11
G. Boycott c Millman b Forbes	24	– not out	8
P. J. Sharpe c Moore b Forbes	9		
*D. B. Close c Cotton b Wells	63		
R. A. Hutton c Millman b Corran	49		
R. Illingworth b Wells	2		
F. S. Trueman b Wells	5		
†J. G. Binks b Wells	3		
D. Wilson not out	6		
M. Ryan b Wells	2		
L-b 9, n-b 2	11	N-b 1	1
1/23 2/34 3/41 4/142 5/149 6/155 7/165 8/168 9/176	(9 wkts dec.) 176		(no wkt) 20

A. G. Nicholson did not bat.

Bowling: *First Innings*—Cotton 7–1–38–1; Davison 15–3–33–0; Forbes 13–1–36–2; Corran 13–2–36–1; Wells 9.4–1–22–5. *Second Innings*—Davison 3–0–9–0; Forbes 2–0–10–0.

Umpires: C. S. Elliott and A. E. D. Smith.

YORKSHIRE v HAMPSHIRE

Played at Middlesbrough, May 19, 20, 1965

Hampshire won by 10 wickets. The game was a disaster for Yorkshire who, in their second innings, were dismissed for 23, the lowest total in their history. The pitch was lively throughout. On the first day 22 wickets fell for 253. Trueman, with a hurricane innings of 55 off 22 balls in twenty-nine minutes, saved Yorkshire from complete collapse. Shackleton, although hit by Trueman for 26 off one over, still took six for 64. Only Marshall did much for Hampshire, who led by four. Before the close, Yorkshire lost two second-innings wickets for seven runs and next morning they were demoralized by the fast bowling of White who, in one spell, took five wickets without cost and altogether claimed six for 10. Hampshire needed only 20 to inflict on Yorkshire the first defeat at Middlesbrough. Yorkshire's previous lowest total was 26 against Surrey at the Oval in 1909.

Yorkshire

G. Boycott b Shackleton	0	– lbw b White	5
J. H. Hampshire c Horton b Shackleton	10	– c Keith b Shackleton	2
D. E. V. Padgett lbw b Cottam	12	– c Keith b Shackleton	0
*D. B. Close b Shackleton	2	– c Barnard b White	1
P. J. Sharpe c Horton b Cottam	9	– c Sainsbury b White	1
R. Illingworth b Cottam	3	– b White	0
R. A. Hutton c Timms b Shackleton	22	– c Barnard b White	0
†J. G. Binks c Sainsbury b Shackleton	3	– c Keith b White	0
F. S. Trueman c Marshall b Shackleton	55	– lbw b Cottam	3
D. Wilson b Cottam	0	– not out	7
A. G. Nicholson not out	2	– c Livingstone b Cottam	0
N-b 3	3	B 4	4
1/9 2/14 3/16 4/34 5/37 6/40 7/47 8/113 9/115	121	1/7 2/7 3/7 4/7 5/8 6/8 7/12 8/13 9/23	23

Bowling: *First Innings*—Shackleton 22.5–10–64–6; White 7–4–9–0; Cottam 15–3–45–4. *Second Innings*—Shackleton 9–5–7–2; White 10–7–10–6; Cottam 1.4–0–2–2.

Hampshire

R. E. Marshall b Hutton	51	– not out	10
H. M. Barnard c and b Trueman	19	– not out	6
H. Horton c Binks b Nicholson	1		
D. A. Livingstone run out	2		
P. J. Sainsbury c Padgett b Hutton	11		
*A. C. D. Ingleby-Mackenzie c Sharpe b Hutton	6		
G. L. Keith not out	17		
†B. S. V. Timms c Hampshire b Close	3		
D. Shackleton b Close	0		
D. W. White b Nicholson	6		
R. M. Cottom b Trueman	0		
B 4, l-b 3, n-b 2	9	L-b 4	4
1/27 2/29 3/31 4/86 5/91 6/100 7/118 8/118 9/124	125	(No wkt)	20

Bowling: *First Innings*—Trueman 9.2–2–15–2; Nicholson 18–3–59–2; Hutton 16–5–33–3; Boycott 5–2–5–0; Close 1–0–4–2. *Second Innings*—Trueman 4–2–3–0; Nicholson 4–0–13–0.

Umpires: A. E. D. Smith and F. C. Gardner.

YORKSHIRE v NOTTINGHAMSHIRE

Played at Sheffield, July 16, 18, 19, 1966

65 overs. Yorkshire won by 229 runs. Yorkshire never lost the advantage created in an opening partnership of 135 by Boycott and Sharpe on the first day and they had completed victory before lunch on the third morning. Although Nottinghamshire played out their 65 overs in the first innings they could not score at a rate to bring them within reach of the Yorkshire total and Bolus alone showed confidence against the containing bowling. His dismissal early on the last day was prelude to the final surrender of batting weakened through the absence of Moore, who split his hand in a fielding accident. Boycott completed two separate centuries in a match for the first time in his career. His second innings was notably more laborious than his first and in both he was indebted to Nottinghamshire failures in catching.

Yorkshire

G. Boycott run out	103	– c Murray b Taylor	105
P. J. Sharpe c Hill b Forbes	50	– c White b Forbes	32
D. E. V. Padgett c sub b Stead	52	– run out	39
J. H. Hampshire c Smedley b Stead	13	– c Smedley b Stead	55
D. Wilson c White b Forbes	0		
*D. B. Close c Swetman b Forbes	7	– not out	8
R. Illingworth run out	2	– not out	2
J. C. Balderstone c Murray b Forbes	4		
†J. G. Binks c Murray b Forbes	0		
F. S. Trueman not out	0		
L-b 2, n-b 1	3	L-b 1, n-b 1	2
1/135 2/182 3/202 4/208 5/228 6/228 7/234 8/234 9/234	(9 wkts, 65 overs) 234	1/77 2/167 3/200 4/240	(4 wkts dec.) 243

A. G. Nicholson did not bat.

Bowling: *First Innings*—Forbes 25–2–85–5; Stead 21–2–76–2; Taylor 14–1–47–0; White 5–0–23–0. *Second Innings*—Forbes 20–3–41–1; Stead 12–1–30–1; Gillhouley 33–9–95–0; White 13–5–37–0; Taylor 13–1–38–1.

Nottinghamshire

*N. Hill c Binks b Trueman	13	– lbw b Trueman	14
M. Taylor c Illingworth b Trueman	11	– lbw b Trueman	9
J. B. Bolus run out	90	– c Close b Nicholson	10
D. L. Murray c Trueman b Close	10	– c Binks b Trueman	4
M. J. Smedley c Illingworth b Nicholson	4	– c Binks b Illingworth	12
R. A. White c Illingworth b Trueman	11	– b Wilson	10
†R. Swetman b Nicholson	11	– c Binks b Wilson	4
K. Gillhouley b Nicholson	2	– b Illingworth	4
C. Forbes not out	1	– c Balderstone b Nicholson	0
B. Stead not out	0	– not out	9
H. I. Moore (did not bat)		– absent hurt	0
L-b 2, w 1, n-b 7	10	L-b 7, w 1, n-b 1	9
1/24 2/30 3/65 4/87 5/126 6/149 7/155 8/162	(8 wkts, 65 overs) 163	1/25 2/32 3/42 4/44 5/67 6/67 7/76 8/76 9/85	85

Bowling: *First Innings*—Trueman 19–2–52–3; Nicholson 31–6–76–3; Close 15–6–25–1. *Second Innings*—Trueman 11–3–24–3; Nicholson 11.1–4–19–2; Illingworth 11–6–12–2; Wilson 11–4–21–2.

Umpires: T. W. Spencer and J. Arnold.

YORKSHIRE v KENT

Played at Harrogate, August 31, September 1, 2, 1966

Yorkshire won by 24 runs. Yorkshire entered their last Championship engagement knowing that outright victory would assure them of the title but that any other result might leave them in second place. The pitch was soft after heavy rain and first innings was a speculation but Boycott's determined batting laid the foundation for a total that proved beyond Kent's reach and left Yorkshire with an advantage of 91 when they went in again on the second day. This time they were dominated by Underwood who took seven wickets in succession on the difficult pitch, but Yorkshire's ultimate anxiety was rain that threatened abandonment of the match. Remarkable drying in a timely strong wind permitted play after lunch on the third day and though Kent had reached 143 when the fourth wicket fell the pitch gave its final favours to the spin bowlers and Yorkshire were able to complete victory in the extra half-hour.

Yorkshire

G. Boycott c Ealham b Brown	80	– c Knott b Underwood	9
P. J. Sharpe c Knott b Brown	0	– c Cowdrey b Underwood	18
D. E. V. Padgett c Knott b Underwood	31	– c and b Underwood	12
J. H. Hampshire b Underwood	29	– c Ealham b Underwood	9
*D. B. Close c Underwood b Dixon	1	– b Underwood	3
K. Taylor c Cowdrey b Brown	17	– lbw b Underwood	4
R. Illingworth c and b Brown	8	– c Knott b Brown	8
†J. G. Binks b Underwood	15	– b Underwood	3
F. S. Trueman st Knott b Underwood	4	– c Leary b Brown	18
D. Wilson c Luckhurst b Brown	14	– c Ealham b Graham	21
A. G. Nicholson not out	3	– not out	2
B 4, l-b 2, n-b 2	8	W 1, n-b 1	2
1/1 2/77 3/119 4/129 5/156 6/167 7/175 8/181 9/196	210	1/22 2/37 3/44 4/51 5/53 6/56 7/62 8/81 9/89	109

Bowling: *First Innings*—Brown 20–8–30–5; Graham 8–2–21–0; Underwood 35.5–9–105–4; Dixon 21–12–46–1. *Second Innings*—Brown 9–0–37–2; Graham 10.3–5–18–1; Underwood 20–7–30–7; Dixon 8–0–22–0.

Kent

M. H. Denness lbw b Trueman	1	– b Trueman	0
B. W. Luckhurst b Nicholson	5	– c Binks b Wilson	62
R. C. Wilson b Illingworth	22	– b Nicholson	17
*M. C. Cowdrey lbw b Trueman	1	– c Close b Illingworth	37
S. E. Leary c Hampshire b Wilson	15	– b Illingworth	39
A. Ealham lbw b Wilson	14	– c Sharpe b Wilson	1
†A. Knott c Close b Nicholson	16	– st Binks b Wilson	0
A. L. Dixon b Trueman	9	– b Illingworth	3
D. L. Underwood c Illingworth b Nicholson	0	– c Trueman b Illingworth	1
A. Brown b Trueman	19	– not out	10
J. N. Graham not out	8	– c Padgett b Illingworth	0
B 8, l-b 1	9	B 2, l-b 2, n-b 2	6
1/6 2/6 3/9 4/44 5/64 6/72 7/88 8/88 9/92	119	1/0 2/19 3/86 4/143 5/145 6/145 7/156 8/158 9/176	176

Bowling: *First Innings*—Trueman 10.5–3–25–4; Nicholson 10–3–36–3; Illingworth 7–1–26–1; Wilson 8–2–23–2. *Second Innings*—Trueman 14–4–19–1; Nicholson 19–13–31–1; Illingworth 17.5–3–55–5; Close 6–3–19–0; Wilson 17–5–46–3.

Umpires: C. G. Pepper and W. F. Simpson.

YORKSHIRE v GLOUCESTERSHIRE

Played at Harrogate, September 6, 7, 1967

Yorkshire won by an innings and 76 runs. Needing a first-innings lead to be sure of retaining the Championship, Yorkshire overwhelmed Gloucestershire to complete outright victory on the second evening. Gloucestershire won the toss and sent Yorkshire in to bat on a soft pitch, but showers delayed the anticipated drying and Boycott and Sharpe were able to score 127 for the opening partnership. Illingworth kept the innings alive until the second morning, when Wilson and Trueman put on 64 in thirty-five minutes for the last wicket. Skilful batting by Nicholls and Milton carried Gloucestershire to 66 without loss at lunch time, but the pitch afterwards became so responsive to spin that 20 wickets fell before the end of the day. Illingworth took 14 of them, his mastery so complete in the Gloucestershire second innings that he conceded only six runs from 13 overs.

Yorkshire

G. Boycott b Bissex	74
P. J. Sharpe c Russell b Bissex	75
D. E. V. Padgett c Mortimore b Allen	6
J. H. Hampshire c and b Allen	0
K. Taylor c Shepherd b Bissex	9
*D. B. Close b Bissex	0
R. Illingworth b A. S. Brown	46
R. A. Hutton c Milton b Mortimore	7
†J. G. Binks lbw b Mortimore	8
D. Wilson not out	39
F. S. Trueman c D. Brown b Mortimore	34
L-b 9, w 1, n-b 1	11
1/127 2/151 3/157 4/159 5/159 6/179 7/211 8/229 9/245	309

Bowling: Allen 24–6–62–2; Bissex 28–9–66–4; A. S. Brown 28–5–78–1; Windows 10–0–47–0; Mortimore 25.1–6–45–3.

Gloucestershire

R. B. Nicholls run out	52	c Padgett b Illingworth	16
C. A. Milton c Sharpe b Wilson	22	b Hutton	16
S. E. Russell lbw b Illingworth	0	st Binks b Illingworth	16
D. Brown lbw b Illingworth	0	c Wilson b Illingworth	1
A. S. Brown c Binks b Illingworth	0	lbw b Close	15
D. Shepherd c Trueman b Illingworth	12	c Trueman b Illingworth	0
M. Bissex lbw b Wilson	29	c Trueman b Illingworth	1
*J. B. Mortimore b Illingworth	0	c Trueman b Illingworth	0
D. A. Allen lbw b Illingworth	12	not out	5
A. R. Windows lbw b Illingworth	0	c Hampshire b Illingworth	13
†B. J. Meyer not out	4	b Close	8
L-b 2, n-b 1	3	L-b 8	8
1/66 2/67 3/67 4/71 5/81 6/96 7/96 8/118 9/118	134	1/24 2/37 3/40 4/52 5/52 6/64 7/66 8/72 9/89	99

Bowling: *First Innings*—Close 4–1–7–0; Hutton 3–0–8–0; Illingworth 23–8–58–7; Trueman 4–0–17–0; Wilson 20.4–6–41–2. *Second Innings*—Close 7.5–2–38–2; Hutton 5–2–10–1; Illingworth 13–9–6–7; Trueman 7–1–25–0; Wilson 7–3–12–0.

Umpires: A. Gaskell and R. S. Lay.

YORKSHIRE v LANCASHIRE

Played at Leeds, June 1, 3, 4, 1968

Yorkshire won by an innings and 56 runs. Lancashire were completely outplayed in a match that ended before lunch on the third day. Their batting was always subservient to bowling imaginatively handled by Trueman, who captained Yorkshire in the absence of Close through injury, whereas the one Yorkshire innings contained three substantial partnerships before Higgs hastened its end with a hat-trick that passed without immediate acclaim because it was spread over two overs. Hampshire played a vigorous innings and Padgett's century was graced by confident and polished strokes.

Lancashire

G. Atkinson c Binks b Trueman	42	– lbw b Trueman	4
G. Pullar c Binks b Trueman	2	– lbw b Trueman	35
H. Pilling c Balderstone b Wilson	8	– c Padgett b Wilson	9
†F. M. Engineer b Trueman	13	– c Hampshire b Wilson	1
D. Lloyd b Nicholson	15	– c Illingworth b Balderstone	16
*J. D. Bond c Illingworth b Trueman	12	– c Binks b Illingworth	7
D. Hughes not out	30	– c Hampshire b Illingworth	8
P. Lever c Illingworth b Nicholson	20	– b Wilson	1
K. Higgs c Hampshire b Illingworth	12	– c Binks b Wilson	19
J. B. Statham b Illingworth	10	– not out	8
J. S. Savage b Trueman	7	– b Trueman	2
L-b 1, n-b 4	5	L-b 2, n-b 4	6
1/8 2/27 3/40 4/70 5/97 6/98 7/126 8/155 9/169	176	1/3 2/11 3/29 4/31 5/38 6/48 7/69 8/76 9/103	116

Bowling: *First Innings*—Trueman 15–2–45–5; Nicholson 17–5–30–2; Wilson 24–10–47–1; Illingworth 22–11–40–2; Balderstone 2–0–9–0. *Second Innings*—Trueman 10–3–17–3; Wilson 26.2–12–32–4; Illingworth 28–13–49–2; Balderstone 3–1–12–1.

Yorkshire

G. Boycott lbw b Statham	36
P. J. Sharpe b Statham	6
D. E. V. Padgett b Lever	105
J. H. Hampshire b Lever	56
K. Taylor c Engineer b Higgs	85
D. Wilson c Higgs b Lever	2
R. Illingworth c Engineer b Higgs	49
J. C. Balderstone b Statham	0
†J. G. Binks lbw b Higgs	0
*F. S. Trueman not out	0
A. G. Nicholson absent hurt	0
L-b 7, n-b 2	9
1/17 2/84 3/179 4/245 5/251 6/341 7/348 8/348 9/348	348

Bowling: Statham 26.1–8–65–3; Higgs 24–2–82–3; Savage 11–2–47–0; Lever 24–1–84–3; Hughes 17–3–61–0.

Umpires: O. W. Herman and T. W. Spencer.

YORKSHIRE v LEICESTERSHIRE

Played at Sheffield, June 15, 17, 18, 1968

Yorkshire won by 143 runs. Yorkshire reached decisive domination on the third day when some resolute hitting by Hampshire and Illingworth permitted a declaration that left ample time for Leicestershire to be disposed of on a pitch that encouraged the faster bowlers. Trueman in particular also benefited from some spectacular catching. Boycott carried his bat through a first innings lasting nearly six hours, whereas Illingworth's century, made under different pressures, was completed in two and a half hours. He hit two 6s and eleven 4s and Hampshire hit three 6s and eight 4s. Knight's first-innings analysis of eight for 82 in a total of 297 represented an outstanding feat of bowling.

Yorkshire

G. Boycott not out	114	– c Tolchard b Knight	5
P. J. Sharpe c and b Knight	29		
D. E. V. Padgett c Norman b Spencer	42	– c Spencer b Birkenshaw	18
J. H. Hampshire c Tolchard b Knight	11	– c Birkenshaw b Matthews	96
K. Taylor b Knight	1	– b Spencer	4
R. Illingworth c Tolchard b Knight	0	– not out	100
†J. G. Binks c Spencer b Knight	9	– run out	0
R. A. Hutton lbw b Knight	1		
*F. S. Trueman c Tolchard b Knight	27		
D. Wilson c Constant b Knight	50	– not out	0
P. Stringer b Birkenshaw	2		
B 4, l-b 5, n-b 2	11	L-b 5	5
1/55 2/129 3/150 4/158 5/158 6/175 7/183 8/223 9/291	297	1/7 2/11 3/30 4/214 5/215 (5 wkts dec.)	228

Bowling: *First Innings*—Spencer 26–2–107–1; Knight 37–11–82–8; Marner 17–2–65–0; Birkenshaw 13.4–5–32–1. *Second Innings*—Spencer 19–3–74–1; Knight 21–4–63–1; Birkenshaw 12–3–49–1; Matthews 3.3–0–37–1.

Leicestershire

M. E. Norman c Padgett b Hutton	42	– c Padgett b Trueman	2
B. J. Booth c Binks b Hutton	8	– c Boycott b Trueman	26
†R. W. Tolchard c Binks b Hutton	4	– not out	17
P. T. Marner b Stringer	9	– b Trueman	0
C. C. Inman c Binks b Trueman	50	– c Sharpe b Hutton	16
*M. R. Hallam b Wilson	20	– c Binks b Trueman	0
B. R. Knight c Hampshire b Stringer	40	– lbw b Trueman	5
J. Birkenshaw not out	27	– c Stringer b Illingworth	60
D. J. Constant c Binks b Stringer	0	– c Trueman b Illingworth	0
A. Matthews b Illingworth	9	– c Sharpe b Trueman	11
C. T. Spencer b Trueman	22	– c Padgett b Illingworth	1
L-b 2, n-b 6	8	L-b 4, n-b 1	5
1/18 2/50 3/65 4/69 5/127 6/154 7/188 8/188 9/204	239	1/6 2/12 3/44 4/44 5/45 6/68 7/121 8/121 9/142	143

Bowling: *First Innings*—Trueman 15–0–62–2; Hutton 19–7–51–3; Stringer 16–6–34–3; Wilson 16–6–38–1; Illingworth 17–5–37–1; Taylor 3–1–9–0. *Second Innings*—Trueman 13–7–20–6; Hutton 10–2–62–1; Stringer 5–0–38–0; Illingworth 10.3–4–17–3; Wilson 5–4–1–0.

Umpires: T. W. Spencer and H. Mellows.

YORKSHIRE v WARWICKSHIRE

Played at Bradford, May 17, 19, 20, 1969

Warwickshire won by 5 runs. The bowling of Cartwright played the vital part in an exciting victory. He took twelve wickets for 55 runs. Few batsmen lasted long on a pitch helping all types of bowlers in each of the first innings. A notable exception was Boycott, who carried his bat for 53 in Yorkshire's innings lasting three hours. Despite this, Yorkshire lost eight wickets for 66 on the second day. Cartwright took five for 21.

Warwickshire collapsed before Nicholson and Wilson and were out for 72, leaving Yorkshire to get 121 on the last day. Although reaching 32 before a wicket fell, Yorkshire were 53 for seven, but a stand of 44 by Binks and Wilson gave them a chance. With the last two wickets falling at the same score, Warwickshire just got home. This time Cartwright claimed seven for 34.

Warwickshire

W. J. Stewart c Sharpe b Nicholson	2	– b Nicholson	34
K. Ibadulla c Binks b Nicholson	6	– lbw b Nicholson	0
D. L. Amiss b Nicholson	35	– c Binks b Nicholson	16
J. A. Jameson lbw b Hutton	22	– c Padgett b Cope	7
R. N. Abberley lbw b Close	7	– b Nicholson	0
T. W. Cartwright c Boycott b Wilson	32	– b Wilson	1
*†A. C. Smith c Sharpe b Wilson	11	– c Binks b Wilson	2
E. E. Hemmings c Binks b Old	4	– c and b Wilson	1
D. J. Brown run out	21	– lbw b Wilson	6
W. Blenkiron not out	8	– lbw b Old	0
N. M. McVicker c and b Hutton	9	– not out	0
B 1, l-b 6, n-b 3	10	B 1, l-b 2, n-b 2	5
1/6 2/17 3/71 4/71 5/88 6/109 7/117 8/150 9/150	167	1/0 2/36 3/51 4/55 5/56 6/62 7/64 8/71 9/71	72

Bowling: *First Innings*—Old 14–3–24–1; Nicholson 26–12–44–3; Hutton 17.1–8–28–2; Cope 12–4–29–0; Wilson 19–8–28–2; Close 4–3–4–1. *Second Innings*—Nicholson 21–9–22–4; Hutton 8–4–10–0; Wilson 18–12–15–4; Cope 7–2–20–1; Old 4.3–4–0–1.

Yorkshire

G. Boycott not out	53	– c Amiss b Blenkiron	5
P. J. Sharpe c Smith b Blenkiron	4	– lbw b Cartwright	29
D. E. V. Padgett c Smith b Blenkiron	7	– c Abberley b Cartwright	2
J. H. Hampshire b Brown	27	– b Cartwright	5
*D. B. Close c Abberley b Cartwright	9	– c Ibadulla b Cartwright	7
†J. G. Binks c Jameson b Blenkiron	2	– b Blenkiron	29
R. A. Hutton b McVicker	5	– c and b Cartwright	0
D. Wilson lbw b Cartwright	1	– c and b Cartwright	22
C. M. Old c McVicker b Cartwright	7	– lbw b Cartwright	2
G. A. Cope c Blenkiron b Cartwright	0	– not out	7
A. G. Nicholson c Amiss b Cartwright	0	– b Blenkiron	0
B 4	4	B 5, l-b 1, n-b 1	7
1/4 2/27 3/65 4/85 5/88 6/106 7/107 8/119 9/119	119	1/32 2/35 3/42 4/47 5/52 6/53 7/53 8/97 9/115	115

Bowling: *First Innings*—Brown 10–3–29–1; Blenkiron 16–3–36–3; Cartwright 18.4–11–21–5; McVicker 12–5–29–1. *Second Innings*—Brown 15–7–32–0; Blenkiron 9.3–2–24–3; Cartwright 21–10–34–7; McVicker 12–3–18–0.

Umpires: J. S. Buller and G. H. Pope.

YORKSHIRE v HAMPSHIRE

Played at Leeds, May 16, 17, 18, 1973

Hampshire won by seven wickets. The Headingley pitch, slightly green, helped the seam bowlers and Herman, Mottram and Taylor dismissed Yorkshire for 168, despite an innings of near perfection by Boycott. Almost out of character, forcing the ball for runs at every opportunity, Boycott scored 73 and was responsible for the collection of two bonus points. Unfortunately for Yorkshire, their fast bowler, Old, strained a muscle in his side after bowling only six overs and afterwards Hampshire dominated the game. The main mastery came from Greenidge whose driving on both sides of the wicket was powerful and a joy to watch. He hit two 6s and thirty-one 4s in his highest innings of 196 not out, and carried his bat. Yorkshire, 173 runs behind, finished the second day at 78 for four wickets. A strong rearguard action saved an innings defeat, but Hampshire, with two and a half hours to get 87 runs, were never pressed.

Yorkshire

*G. Boycott c Stephenson b Taylor	73	– b Mottram	30
R. G. Lumb c Sainsbury b Mottram	0	– c Stephenson b Mottram	0
B. Leadbeater c Stephenson b Herman	1	– b Jesty	9
J. H. Hampshire c Richards b Mottram	20	– c Turner b Jesty	84
P. J. Sharpe c Stephenson b Mottram	0	– c Gilliat b Jesty	7
C. M. Old c Greenidge b Herman	28	– not out	4
†D. L. Bairstow lbw b Taylor	0	– b Herman	21
P. Carrick c Greenidge b Herman	12	– lbw b Sainsbury	29
A. G. Nicholson not out	14	– b Taylor	15
M. K. Bore b Sainsbury	7	– c Stephenson b Sainsbury	35
A. L. Robinson b Sainsbury	2	– b Mottram	7
B 1, l-b 2, w 1, n-b 7	11	B 1, l-b 8, w 1, n-b 8	18
1/0 2/15 3/84 4/84 5/120 6/124 7/129 8/148 9/164	168	1/2 2/40 3/45 4/75 5/124 6/190 7/194 8/229 9/247	259

Bowling: *First Innings*—Herman 24–8–41–3; Mottram 11–3–45–3; Taylor 22–6–63–2; Sainsbury 5–2–8–2. *Second Innings*—Herman 24–8–37–1; Mottram 23.2–5–72–3; Jesty 26–9–41–3; Sainsbury 18–7–49–2; Taylor 14–2–42–1.

Hampshire

B. A. Richards lbw b Old	2	– lbw b Nicholson	16
C. G. Greenidge not out	196	– lbw b Robinson	1
D. R. Turner c Sharpe b Nicholson	8	– st Bairstow b Nicholson	23
*R. M. C. Gilliat lbw b Nicholson	0	– not out	33
R. V. Lewis c Robinson b Nicholson	12	– not out	11
T. E. Jesty c Sharpe b Bore	19		
P. J. Sainsbury c Bairstow b Bore	16		
M. N. S. Taylor c Bairstow b Nicholson	50		
†G. R. Stephenson b Carrick	24		
R. S. Herman c Sharpe b Bore	2		
T. J. Mottram lbw b Bore	0		
B 3, l-b 8, w 1	12	B 2, l-b 1	3
1/8 2/31 3/31 4/65 5/102 6/152 7/265 8/329 9/341	341	1/2 2/36 3/43 (3 wkts)	87

Bowling: *First Innings*—Old 6–1–17–1; Nicholson 29–5–91–4; Bore 30–11–66–4; Robinson 25–5–95–0; Carrick 23–12–60–1; Leadbeater 1–1–0–0. *Second Innings*—Nicholson 10–3–22–2; Robinson 5–1–23–1; Bore 8–1–25–0; Carrick 3–0–14–0.

Umpires: R. Julian and B. J. Meyer.

YORKSHIRE v SURREY

Played at Leeds, August 25, 27, 28, 1973

Surrey won by 42 runs. Surrey had their anxious moments, especially on the first day when their first six wickets tumbled for 69 and only a defiant display by Roope, who hit nine boundaries, enabled them to total 184. Before the close Butcher dismissed Sharpe and

Leadbeater. On Monday Jackman performed the hat trick when he removed Cooper, Bore and Cope with successive deliveries and Surrey led by 94. Possibly the pitch eased, for Surrey proceeded to master the Yorkshire attack. Edrich in steady style, made 109 (fifteen 4s) in three and three-quarter hours and Edwards with twelve 4s gave valuable help in an opening stand of 127. Edrich declared with only three wickets down leaving Yorkshire more than a day to get 342 to win. They lost Lumb overnight while getting 17, and next morning Cope and Leadbeater also went cheaply, but gradually Yorkshire recovered through some fine batting by Sharpe, Hampshire and Johnson. Even a gallant last wicket stand of 44 by Bore (two 6s) and Robinson caused Surrey trouble but in the end they claimed their second Championship win of the season over Yorkshire.

Surrey

*J. H. Edrich c Bairstow b Cooper	2	– c Bairstow b Cooper	109
M. J. Edwards c Bairstow b Robinson	5	– b Cooper	70
G. R. J. Roope c Bairstow b Hutton	81	– not out	33
Younis Ahmed c Lumb b Robinson	14	– b Bore	15
G. P. Howarth lbw b Cooper	1	– not out	1
S. J. Storey lbw b Robinson	20		
A. R. Butcher b Robinson	0		
R. D. Jackman lbw b Cooper	19		
Intikhab Alam b Cope	26		
†A. Long c Bairstow b Robinson	7		
P. I. Pocock not out	0		
B 1, l-b 3, n-b 5	9	B 4, l-b 5, n-b 10	19
1/7 2/7 3/32 4/33 5/69 6/69 7/107 8/165 9/184	184	1/127 2/171 3/233	(3 wkts dec.) 247

Bowling: *First Innings*—Cooper 21–5–49–3; Robinson 21–6–56–5; Hutton 19.3–3–56–1; Bore 3–1–9–0; Cope 3–1–5–1. *Second Innings*—Cooper 15–5–28–2; Robinson 16–1–50–0; Hutton 13–2–63–0; Bore 22–10–48–1; Cope 8–2–39–0.

Yorkshire

*P. J. Sharpe c Pocock b Butcher	12	– c Roope b Pocock	68
R. G. Lumb lbw b Jackman	20	– b Jackman	6
B. Leadbeater b Butcher	6	– b Jackman	0
J. H. Hampshire c Howarth b Butcher	9	– c Jackman b Pocock	66
C. Johnson lbw b Butcher	6	– c Edwards b Pocock	50
R. A. Hutton lbw b Storey	20	– b Intikhab	13
†D. L. Bairstow not out	7	– c Younis b Intikhab	7
H. P. Cooper c Long b Jackman	3	– lbw b Jackman	8
M. K. Bore lbw b Jackman	0	– c Butcher b Pocock	31
G. A. Cope b Jackman	0	– lbw b Butcher	3
A. L. Robinson c Long b Jackman	2	– not out	28
B 3, l-b 1, w 1	5	B 6, l-b 7, w 1, n-b 5	19
1/15 2/23 3/50 4/50 5/60 6/85 7/88 8/88 9/88	90	1/7 2/18 3/19 4/112 5/185 6/203 7/219 8/225 9/255	299

Bowling: *First Innings*—Jackman 17.5–7–47–5; Butcher 17–5–33–4; Roope 2–1–2–0; Storey 2–1–3–1. *Second Innings*—Jackman 26–6–69–3; Butcher 13–3–34–1; Storey 15–5–33–0; Intikhab 29–8–72–2; Pocock 38.5–12–71–4; Howarth 2–1–1–0.

Umpires: W. E. Alley and H. Horton.

YORKSHIRE v MIDDLESEX

Played at Middlesbrough, June 22, 24, 25, 1974

Middlesex won by eight wickets. On a slow turning pitch the limitations of the Yorkshire batsmen were exploited by Titmus, who with accurate off-spin took 14 wickets in the match and bowled Middlesex to a two-day victory. Cope, whose changed bowling action is making him a power in the Yorkshire side, also performed creditably but could not subdue the Middlesex opening batsman Featherstone. Producing a wide range of shots and hitting a century in only eighty-five minutes – equalling the time of Jameson against India at Eastbourne as the fastest of the season – he led Middlesex to a commanding first innings lead and gave Titmus scope for teasing experiment.

Yorkshire

*G. Boycott c Edmonds b Titmus	24	– lbw b Titmus	63
R. A. Hutton lbw b Marriott	0	– not out	15
P. J. Sharpe b Titmus	19	– c Radley b Titmus	37
B. Leadbeater lbw b Titmus	0	– c Featherstone b Edmonds	9
P. J. Squires c Brearley b Titmus	24	– lbw b Edmonds	3
R. G. Lumb b Titmus	7	– lbw b Titmus	4
†D. L. Bairstow c Radley b Titmus	19	– c Butcher b Titmus	0
G. A. Cope lbw b Titmus	8	– c Murray b Edmonds	0
A. G. Nicholson b Edmonds	6	– c Edmonds b Titmus	8
M. K. Bore c Murray b Edmonds	0	– b Titmus	1
A. L. Robinson not out	2	– c Edmonds b Titmus	0
B 3, l-b 3, w 1	7	L-b 2, w 1, n-b 1	4
1/4 2/43 3/43 4/54 5/74 6/87 7/101 8/108 9/109	116	1/28 2/105 3/108 4/111 5/120 6/125 7/125 8/142 9/144	144

Bowling: *First Innings*—Selvey 11–5–15–0; Marriott 8–4–18–1; Titmus 24–9–39–7; Edmonds 18.5–6–37–2. *Second Innings*—Selvey 5–2–11–0; Marriott 4–1–9–0; Titmus 40.3–13–75–7; Edmonds 34–20–38–3; Gomes 1–0–7–0.

Middlesex

N. G. Featherstone c Squires b Cope	107	– c Robinson b Cope	18
G. D. Barlow c Sharpe b Cope	27	– c Bairstow b Cope	10
*J. M. Brearley c Bairstow b Nicholson	11	– not out	26
C. T. Radley c Lumb b Cope	22	– not out	5
H. A. Gomes st Bairstow b Cope	0		
R. D. Butcher c Hutton b Cope	0		
†J. T. Murray b Nicholson	0		
P. H. Edmonds c Robinson b Cope	6		
F. J. Titmus b Cope	13		
M. W. W. Selvey not out	2		
D. A. Marriott lbw b Nicholson	7		
B 3, l-b 3, n-b 3	9	L-b 1	1
1/138 2/139 3/158 4/173 5/173 6/175 7/175 8/192 9/195	204	1/27 2/40 (2 wkts)	60

Bowling: *First Innings*—Nicholson 27.4–10–30–3; Robinson 2–0–6–0; Cope 33–9–101–7; Bore 14–5–58–0. *Second Innings*—Nicholson 5–1–22–0; Robinson 4–3–4–0; Cope 7–2–13–2; Bore 6.1–1–20–0.

Umpires: C. G. Pepper and B. J. Meyer.

YORKSHIRE v GLOUCESTERSHIRE

Played at Leeds, April 28, 29, 30, 1976

Drawn. This first Championship match on the relaid square was dominated throughout by batsmen. Hampshire, with his first century for the county on the ground, and Johnson indulged in a third-wicket partnership of 248 on the first day to set the pattern. Zaheer, missed when 67, held the Gloucestershire innings together with a classic 188 before Boycott and Lumb put together their best opening partnership – 264. Yorkshire missed several chances in Gloucestershire's second innings, during which Sadiq made a century, bringing the total of three-figure innings to six, a record for any first-class match involving Yorkshire. Only Oldham for Yorkshire and, to a lesser extent, Davey for Gloucestershire bowled with any conviction.

Yorkshire

*G. Boycott c Zaheer b Procter	30	– not out	161
R. G. Lumb c Sadiq b Brown	16	– b Childs	132
C. Johnson c Brown b Childs	102		
J. H. Hampshire not out	155		
B. Leadbeater not out	34		
†D. L. Bairstow (did not bat)		– c Shackleton b Sadiq	9
P. Carrick (did not bat)		– not out	9
L-b 4, n-b 3	7	B 4, l-b 2, n-b 4	10
1/47 2/51 3/299	(3 wkts dec.) 344	1/264 2/285	(2 wkts dec.) 321

H. P. Cooper, M. K. Bore, S. Oldham and A. L. Robinson did not bat.

Bowling: *First Innings*—Davey 16–5–49–0; Shackleton 18–2–68–0; Procter 13–2–39–1; Brown 19–1–56–1; Graveney 9–2–31–0; Sadiq Mohammad 8–1–37–0; Childs 17–1–57–1. *Second Innings*—Davey 19–5–52–0; Shackleton 18–3–56–0; Procter 10–0–37–0; Brown 12–5–19–0; Graveney 5–0–25–0; Sadiq Mohammad 6–1–34–1; Childs 10–0–57–1; Cooper 5–0–31–0.

Gloucestershire

Sadiq Mohammad c Hampshire b Cooper	13	– c and b Oldham	107
N. H. C. Cooper c Cooper b Robinson	4		
Zaheer Abbas b Cooper	188	– lbw b Oldham	4
M. J. Procter b Oldham	40	– c and b Robinson	75
†A. W. Stovold b Oldham	16	– c Johnson b Oldham	22
J. C. Foat run out	18	– not out	3
*A. S. Brown not out	28	– not out	13
D. A. Graveney not out	0		
L-b 4, n-b 10	14	B 4, l-b 4, n-b 3	11
1/13 2/20 3/139 4/210 5/290 6/319	(6 wkts) 321	1/62 2/66 3/194 4/223	(4 wkts) 235

J. H. Shackleton, J. Davey and J. H. Childs did not bat.

Bowling: *First Innings*—Robinson 23–3–74–1; Cooper 34–9–108–2; Oldham 25–7–49–2; Hampshire 1–0–7–0; Carrick 14–1–56–0; Bore 3–1–13–0. *Second Innings*—Robinson 13–3–43–1; Cooper 23–3–88–0; Oldham 17–1–50–3; Carrick 5–1–31–0; Bore 3–1–12–0.

Umpires: T. W. Spencer and H. D. Bird.

YORKSHIRE v NOTTINGHAMSHIRE

Played at Bradford, August 7, 9, 10, 1976

Yorkshire won by 95 runs. Yorkshire were given a tremendous start by their batsmen, who destroyed some indifferent Nottinghamshire bowling on the first day. Boycott made his first century since recovering from hand and back trouble, but more pleasure was gained from a maiden century by Love, who drove with particular style. Nottinghamshire in their turn, scored easily, Todd and Rice making the Yorkshire bowling look rather ordinary. The pattern continued during the Yorkshire second innings, Lumb and Squires being the main beneficiaries and a draw seemed the most likely outcome when Nottinghamshire were set 277 in three and three-quarter hours. Fine catches by Carrick and Love provided Yorkshire with the inspiration for a victory drive which gathered momentum against some wild batting. Harris hit 44 in eleven boundary strokes to illustrate Nottinghamshire's approach. A point of interest was that when Smedley and Stead were together in the second innings all fifteen men on the field were Yorkshiremen, both umpires being former Yorkshire players.

Yorkshire

*G. Boycott c Todd b Stead	141	– run out	7
R. G. Lumb c White b Wilkinson	12	– c White b Allbrook	87
J. D. Love c Harris b Wilkinson	163	– c Hassan b White	16
G. B. Stevenson c Harris b Stead	0	– c White b Allbrook	13
†D. L. Bairstow run out	22	– not out	10
C. Johnson lbw b Stead	1	– b White	2
P. J. Squires c Smedley b Wilkinson	38	– c Randall b Allbrook	70
P. Carrick not out	22	– c Harris b Wilkinson	1
G. A. Cope not out	1	– c Todd b Wilkinson	0
A. L. Robinson (did not bat)		– not out	0
B 5, l-b 6, w 2, n-b 2	15	L-b 4	4
1/44 2/287 3/287 4/350 5/351 6/351 7/409	(7 wkts) 415	1/13 2/27 3/28 4/186 5/186 6/188 7/203 8/203	(8 wkts dec.) 210

S. Oldham did not bat.

Bowling: *First Innings*—Stead 23–3–105–3; Wilkinson 23–0–98–3; Hassan 16–4–60–0; White 20–4–51–0; Allbrook 18–2–86–0. *Second Innings*—Wilkinson 17–4–48–2; White 20–5–53–2; Allbrook 30–5–99–3; Rice 3–0–6–0.

Nottinghamshire

S. B. Hassan c Cope b Carrick	12	– c Carrick b Robinson	5
P. A. Todd c Bairstow b Cope	90	– lbw b Robinson	1
D. W. Randall b Cope	40	– st Bairstow b Carrick	20
C. E. B. Rice c Bairstow b Stevenson	68	– lbw b Cope	14
N. Nanan c and b Carrick	20	– c Love b Cope	0
*M. J. Smedley not out	53	– c sub b Carrick	47
†M. J. Harris c Love b Cope	4	– b Carrick	44
R. A. White not out	25	– c Robinson b Cope	15
P. A. Wilkinson (did not bat)		– c Carrick b Cope	0
B. Stead (did not bat)		– not out	10
M. E. Allbrook (did not bat)		– c Oldham b Cope	13
B 13, l-b 20, n-b 4	37	B 4, l-b 7, n-b 1	12
1/34 2/151 3/171 4/239 5/275 6/287	(6 wkts) 349	1/8 2/9 3/40 4/40 5/46 6/105 7/139 8/143 9/154	181

Bowling: *First Innings*—Robinson 4–0–19–0; Oldham 7–1–33–0; Stevenson 8–2–15–1; Cope 42–10–104–3; Carrick 39–9–141–2. *Second Innings*—Robinson 10–4–22–2; Stevenson 4–1–12–0; Cope 18.1–7–46–5; Carrick 19–6–89–3.

Umpires: H. D. Bird and R. Aspinall.

YORKSHIRE v GLAMORGAN

Played at Middlesbrough, August 21, 23, 24, 1976

Yorkshire won by seven wickets. An innings of great professional skill by Boycott carried Yorkshire to victory in a match dominated throughout by the batsmen on a wicket of reliable bounce and gentle pace. Jones, the Glamorgan captain, became the first man since Fishlock, of Surrey, in 1937, to score a century in each innings of a Championship match against Yorkshire and in the Welsh county's second innings Richards scored an excellent, although not chanceless maiden century. Yorkshire, after some early alarms, were sustained by Bairstow who also made his first first-class century, sharing a vital partnership of 164 with Cope, promoted in the order in the face of apparent crisis. Yorkshire were set a last-day target of 318 in three and a quarter hours. It seemed an impossible task, even allowing for Glamorgan's modest attack, but Boycott, whose last 99 runs came from only 81 balls, timed his effort to perfection, the winning runs coming with ten balls to spare. In the final flurry Glamorgan paid the price for some fielding that fell well below the expected standards.

Glamorgan

*A. Jones c and b Carrick	132	– not out	156
G. P. Ellis c Stevenson b Cope	51	– lbw b Robinson	0
D. A. Francis c Bairstow b Robinson	32	– b Cope	40
J. A. Hopkins st Bairstow b Carrick	55	– st Bairstow b Cope	17
G. Richards not out	53	– not out	102
M. A. Nash st Bairstow b Carrick	0		
†E. W. Jones lbw b Carrick	2		
G. D. Armstrong lbw b Cope	0		
A. E. Cordle not out	9		
L-b 13, n-b 2	15	L-b 5	5
1/118 2/185 3/254 4/326 5/326 6/336 7/337	(7 wkts) 349	1/1 2/92 3/136	(2 wkts dec.) 320

A. H. Wilkins and A. W. Allin did not bat.

Bowling: *First Innings*—Robinson 19–7–46–1; Cooper 14–1–46–0; Stevenson 13–1–58–0; Cope 30–6–86–2; Carrick 24–5–98–4. *Second Innings*—Robinson 9–2–13–1; Cooper 8–2–26–0; Stevenson 11–2–49–0; Cope 25–5–71–2; Carrick 32–9–109–0; Squires 6.2–0–32–0; Hampshire 2–0–15–0.

Yorkshire

*G. Boycott lbw b Cordle	30	– not out	156
R. G. Lumb c E. W. Jones b Armstrong	1		
J. D. Love lbw b Nash	21	– c Francis b Wilkins	50
†D. L. Bairstow c Francis b Nash	106	– b Wilkins	10
G. A. Cope c E. W. Jones b Nash	57		
J. H. Hampshire c Cordle b Nash	6	– c E. W. Jones b Cordle	38
P. J. Squires not out	38		
P. Carrick b Wilkins	54		
G. B. Stevenson lbw b Wilkins	5	– not out	46
H. P. Cooper not out	14		
B 4, l-b 9, n-b 7	20	B 7, l-b 11	18
1/25 2/52 3/60 4/224 5/234 6/235 7/324 8/330	(8 wkts) 352	1/52 2/172 3/208	(3 wkts) 318

A. L. Robinson did not bat.

Bowling: *First Innings*—Nash 32–8–83–4; Armstrong 14–2–54–1; Cordle 22–7–77–1; Wilkins 16–0–62–2; Allin 14–1–53–0; Richards 1–0–3–0. *Second Innings*—Nash 19–0–100–0; Armstrong 9–1–52–0; Cordle 18.2–1–94–1; Wilkins 9–0–54–2.

Umpires: T. W. Spencer and R. Julian.

YORKSHIRE IN 1977

The disappointment of a sad summer for Yorkshire spilled over into an angry autumn as the selector Don Brennan waged a public campaign to replace Boycott as captain with Cope. Another member of the committee, Mel Ryan, also threatened to resign as a selector unless dramatic changes were made in the running of the team, adding to the air of crisis which hung over a sequence of unsatisfactory results.

The matter came to a head at a committee meeting at Headingley on November 9 when it was decided to reappoint Boycott as captain and engage Ray Illingworth, the Leicestershire and former England captain as team manager from April 1, 1979. After Boycott's triumphant return to Test cricket in 1977 public opinion swung solidly behind him, especially in Yorkshire.

This may have influenced the committee, who have now tried to remove some of the more onerous responsibilities from the captain. Illingworth, who left his native Yorkshire in 1968 over a contract disagreement, stated that he expects to have a happy relationship with Boycott. Following Boycott's unanimous reappointment, Brennan, who was not at the meeting, announced his resignation from the committee.

These actions focused attention on a situation which had some effect on a season during which the players lacked application in the one-day games, determination in too many Championship matches and inspiration on a general level. The most serious area of concern was the limited-overs competitions, for Yorkshire suffered some humiliating experiences. They had lost all interest in the Benson and Hedges Cup after two qualifying games, while Hampshire destroyed their challenge in the Gillette Cup with contemptuous ease. The Sunday League reflected the same unhappy picture, despite some isolated moments of success.

These served only to underline the extent to which Yorkshire contributed to their own problems, much of the bowling being conducted with bland disregard for the field placings. A number of team meetings were held without producing a satisfactory answer to an increasingly worrying situation, and the matter of making the most of obvious potential in one-day cricket should have been exercising the official mind.

YORKSHIRE v HAMPSHIRE

Played at Leeds, July 30, August 1, 2, 1977

Hampshire won by eight wickets. A weakened Yorkshire team were utterly outplayed by Hampshire's West Indian pair, Greenidge and Roberts. After Yorkshire had struggled to first innings respectability, Greenidge tore them apart hitting five 6s and twenty-seven 4s in his 208 which was made in only four and a half hours. Silvester survived this onslaught as well as anyone in his first senior game of the season. Leadbeater, who batted well throughout, and Sharp made defiant gestures, but there was no collective answer to Roberts on a pitch that was much quicker than usual, and his match haul of eight for 86 was crucial.

Yorkshire

C. W. J. Athey b Jesty	11	– c Stephenson b Rice	5
B. Leadbeater c Stephenson b Rice	63	– c Jesty b Roberts	33
J. D. Love c Rock b Roberts	18	– b Roberts	3
C. Johnson c Stephenson b Roberts	2	– c Rice b Jesty	28
K. Sharp c Taylor b Rice	16	– c Jesty b Roberts	36
†D. L. Bairstow b Taylor	0	– c Southern b Taylor	5
G. B. Stevenson c Greenidge b Rice	52	– c Stephenson b Roberts	10
*G. A. Cope not out	44	– c Cowley b Rice	0
M. K. Bore c Stephenson b Roberts	3	– c Cowley b Rice	5
A. L. Robinson b Roberts	5	– b Rice	8
S. Silvester not out	1	– not out	0
L-b 11, w 2, n-b 1	14	L-b 3, n-b 3	6
1/30 2/89 3/93 4/103 5/113 6/123 7/203 8/211 9/219	(9 wkts) 229	1/15 2/18 3/49 4/104 5/115 6/118 7/122 8/130 9/134	139

Bowling: *First Innings*—Roberts 23–9–39–4; Jesty 11–2–36–1; Rice 40–14–78–3; Taylor 22–7–57–1; Southern 4–0–5–0. *Second Innings*—Roberts 15–7–47–4; Jesty 7–1–22–1; Rice 16.4–4–48–4; Taylor 5–1–16–1.

Hampshire

C. G. Greenidge c Athey b Silvester	208	– not out	15
D. J. Rock c Love b Robinson	20	– c Bairstow b Silvester	0
D. R. Turner c Bairstow b Stevenson	13	– c Sharp b Stevenson	10
T. E. Jesty c Leadbeater b Silvester	4	– not out	7
*R. M. C. Gilliat c Robinson b Bore	6		
N. G. Cowley c Bairstow b Stevenson	0		
J. M. Rice c Bairstow b Silvester	12		
M. N. S. Taylor c Bore b Silvester	21		
†G. R. Stephenson b Stevenson	19		
A. M. E. Roberts not out	9		
J. W. Southern b Stevenson	0		
L-b 13, n-b 7	20	B 4, n-b 1	5
1/62 2/97 3/110 4/141 5/154 6/190 7/304 8/304 9/332	332	1/1 2/22	(2 wkts) 37

Bowling: *First Innings*—Stevenson 24.3–9–97–4; Robinson 25–1–75–1; Silvester 25–5–86–4; Cope 9–3–31–1; Bore 6–0–23–0. *Second Innings*—Stevenson 4–1–20–1; Silvester 4.4–0–12–1.

Umpires: W. E. Alley and A. G. T. Whitehead.

YORKSHIRE v LANCASHIRE

Played at Leeds, May 27, 28, 1978

Yorkshire, without Boycott and Old, won by an innings and 32 runs with a day to spare. On a wicket of variable bounce, which was reported as unfit for first-class cricket by the umpires, Yorkshire completely outplayed Lancashire. Although Clive Lloyd hit a brilliant half-century from 34 balls, Stevenson's best return destroyed Lancashire. He took eight for 65. Yorkshire struggled in turn, but Hampshire resisted stoutly and then Carrick scored his maiden century, Lancashire perhaps aiding him by defending too soon. A substantial Sunday crowd saw Lancashire collapse again, Cooper and Oldham gaining the rewards against opponents who appeared to lose interest in an almost impossible situation. As a result there was no cricket on the Spring Bank Holiday Monday.

Lancashire

B. Wood c Bairstow b Stevenson	18	– c Hampshire b Cooper	22
D. Lloyd c Bairstow b Stevenson	0	– c Bairstow b Oldham	6
H. Pilling lbw b Stevenson	0	– lbw b Oldham	7
C. H. Lloyd run out	58	– c Stevenson b Cooper	16
*F. C. Hayes c Bairstow b Stevenson	9	– c Bairstow b Cooper	0
D. P. Hughes c Bairstow b Stevenson	0	– c Love b Oldham	1
J. Simmons not out	24	– c Stevenson b Cooper	0
†J. Lyon c Bairstow b Cooper	5	– c Cooper b Oldham	4
R. M. Ratcliffe c Cooper b Stevenson	0	– c Bairstow b Cooper	40
C. E. H. Croft b Stevenson	4	– not out	0
W. Hogg b Stevenson	0	– b Cooper	0
L-b 3, n-b 2	5	B 4, l-b 3, w 1, n-b 1	9
1/1 2/1 3/78 4/79 5/87 6/91 7/100 8/101 9/113	123	1/12 2/55 3/59 4/60 5/60 6/60 7/60 8/99 9/105	105

Bowling: *First Innings*—Stevenson 12.1–1–65–8; Cooper 12–3–37–1; Oldham 2–0–16–0; Cope 1–1–0–0. *Second Innings*—Stevenson 15–5–42–0; Cooper 9.5–4–26–6; Oldham 14–5–28–4.

Yorkshire

R. G. Lumb c Lyon b Hogg	0
C. W. J. Athey c Hughes b Hogg	0
J. D. Love b Croft	1
*J. H. Hampshire lbw b Ratcliffe	54
K. Sharp c D. Lloyd b Hogg	3
†D. L. Bairstow c C. H. Lloyd b Croft	11
P. Carrick c Lyon b Croft	105
G. B. Stevenson c Lyon b Hogg	20
G. A. Cope c Croft b Wood	6
H. P. Cooper not out	27
S. Oldham b Croft	0
B 8, l-b 3, w 1, n-b 21	33
1/6 2/7 3/10 4/20 5/49 6/137 7/176 8/195 9/256	260

Bowling: Croft 20.5–5–58–4; Hogg 21–4–73–4; Ratcliffe 16–2–59–1; Wood 9–4–18–1; Hughes 2–0–16–0; Simmons 4–3–3–0.

Umpires: W. E. Phillipson and D. L. Evans.

YORKSHIRE v GLOUCESTERSHIRE

Played at Scarborough, September 6, 7, 8, 1978

Yorkshire won by two wickets. Yorkshire scrambled home in an exciting match reduced to one innings by rain. Gloucestershire had cause to regret electing to bat on a pitch that encouraged spin, although Stovold carried his bat throughout in a resolute if subdued innings. Procter also played well, striking the ball hard and making light of some miscalculations. Oldham was the destructive factor on the last day, profiting from poor batting as Gloucestershire collapsed. Yorkshire took a lot of time over their reply, Boycott needing two hours and four minutes and 111 deliveries to score 23. Athey was much more aggressive and Yorkshire looked to have matters comfortably in hand as they went into the 90s. Procter engineered a collapse with his off-spin, however, and it needed an innings of rare character from Carrick to give Yorkshire the points in gathering gloom and light rain.

Gloucestershire

A. V. Stovold not out	59	B. M. Brain b Oldham	2
Sadiq Mohammad c Athey b Carrick	23	J. Davey c Whiteley b Oldham	2
P. Bainbridge c Carrick b Whiteley	0	J. H. Childs b Whiteley	3
A. J. Hignell b Whiteley	0		
*M. J. Procter c Oldham b Old	50	B 7, n-b 3	10
J. C. Foat b Carrick	7		
D. A. Graveney c Bairstow b Oldham	5	1/38 2/42 3/42 4/106	161
†A. J. Brassington lbw b Oldham	0	5/123 6/144 7/146 8/148 9/154	

Bowling: Old 15–5–32–1; Stevenson 4–1–19–0; Carrick 27–11–59–2; Whiteley 20.2–7–35–3; Oldham 5–1–6–4.

Yorkshire

*G. Boycott st Brassington b Graveney	23	C. M. Old c Hignell b Brain	6
R. G. Lumb b Davey	13	G. B. Stevenson not out	7
C. W. J. Athey c sub b Procter	56	J. P. Whiteley not out	2
K. Sharp b Procter	0	L-b 9	9
J. D. Love c Procter b Graveney	9		
†D. L. Bairstow b Procter	0	1/16 2/93 3/93	(8 wkts) 162
P. Carrick b Brain	37	4/93 5/94 6/106 7/149 8/158	

S. Oldham did not bat.

Bowling: Procter 23.4–8–52–3; Brain 12–7–17–2; Davey 7–2–24–1; Childs 7–1–30–0; Graveney 12–6–30–2.

Umpires: J. van Geloven and H. D. Bird.

SPECIAL GENERAL MEETING OF YORKSHIRE MEMBERS [1979]

The controversy surrounding the deposing of Geoffrey Boycott as captain of Yorkshire and the appointment of John Hampshire as his successor continued through the autumn. Many Yorkshire members formed a Boycott Reform Group, and they forced a Special General Meeting at The Royal Hall, Harrogate, on December 9 [1978] in a battle to regain the captaincy for Boycott, who at the time was with the England team in Australia. The meeting lasted three hours, with the supporters of Boycott losing by 4,826 votes to 2,602, a majority of 2,224. The Reform Group's motion of no confidence in the Yorkshire general committee went closer. It was lost by 4,422 votes to 3,067, a majority of 1,355. The meeting produced the most serious attack on officials of the club in Yorkshire's 115 years' existence.

THE UNIVERSITIES

CAMBRIDGE UNIVERSITY

CAMBRIDGE UNIVERSITY v NORTHAMPTONSHIRE

Played at Cambridge, June 6, 8, 9, 1964

Northamptonshire won by two wickets. Brearley, who arrived after a three-hour examination, halted Northamptonshire's progress for three and a half hours after five Cambridge batsmen were dismissed for 48 runs. Northamptonshire, too, started badly, but Prideaux, P. J. Watts and Norman brought about an improvement, Watts hitting two 6s and eight 4s in a stay of under two hours. A third-wicket partnership of 101 in just over an hour between White and Brearley formed the highlight of the Cambridge second innings. Excellent leg-spin bowling by the Freshman McLachlan, who in one spell captured three wickets in three overs, made Northamptonshire fight for victory.

Cambridge University

A. R. Windows b Crump	14	– b Scott	49
D. M. Daniels b Scott	12	– b Durose	0
†M. G. Griffith c Andrew b Durose	22	– c P. J. Watts b Crump	24
R. C. White b Scott	2	– c P. J. Watts b P. D. Watts	66
I. G. Thwaites b P. J. Watts	6	– lbw b Crump	18
A. V. E. Gould b P. J. Watts	1	– b P. D. Watts	15
*J. M. Brearley c Norman b Durose	92	– c Norman b Scott	75
R. C. Kerslake lbw b Scott	7	– c Milburn b Crump	0
A. A. McLachlan c and b Crump	1	– b P. D. Watts	4
R. Roopnaraine c Prideaux b Durose	10	– c Sim b P. D. Watts	1
G. C. Pritchard not out	4	– not out	0
B 3, l-b 3	6	B 12, l-b 1, n-b 3	16
1/24 2/26 3/31 4/40 5/48 6/74 7/104 8/107 9/152	177	1/0 2/53 3/154 4/181 5/212 6/212 7/258 8/263 9/267	268

Bowling: *First Innings*—Crump 32–13–41–2; Durose 22.3–8–46–3; Scott 38–27–38–3; P. J. Watts 11–1–34–2; P. D. Watts 6–2–12–0. *Second Innings*—Crump 25–11–61–3; Durose 18–5–61–1; P. D. Watts 24.3–9–85–4; P. J. Watts 3–0–17–0; Scott 19–10–28–2.

Northamptonshire

M. Norman b Roopnaraine	30	– b Windows	21
A. M. R. Sim lbw b Windows	5	– c Brearley b McLachlan	38
C. Milburn c Griffith b Windows	0	– run out	32
R. M. Prideaux b Windows	76	– c White b Kerslake	12
A. Lightfoot b Pritchard	31	– b Kerslake	2
P. J. Watts c McLachlan b Pritchard	72	– lbw b McLachlan	24
M. E. Scott c Griffith b Pritchard	9	– c Brearley b McLachlan	3
B. Crump b Pritchard	10	– not out	39
P. D. Watts not out	3	– b McLachlan	4
*†K. V. Andrew b Windows	0	– not out	17
B 2, l-b 5, w 1, n-b 1	9	B 8, l-b 5	13
1/19 2/19 3/53 4/134 5/159 6/185 7/238 8/245 9/245	(9 wkts dec.) 245	1/39 2/77 3/89 4/113 5/113 6/128 7/140 8/151	(8 wkts) 205

A. J. Durose did not bat.

Bowling: *First Innings*—Pritchard 16–2–53–4; Windows 28.1–10–71–4; Roopnaraine 30–18–53–1; Kerslake 17–6–38–0; Thwaites 5–2–12–0; McLachlan 5–3–9–0. *Second Innings*—Pritchard 5–0–15–0; Windows 14.2–2–65–1; Roopnaraine 13–4–41–0; McLachlan 16–5–41–4; Kerslake 10–2–30–2.

Umpires: A. E. Rhodes and F. C. Gardner.

CAMBRIDGE UNIVERSITY v ESSEX

Played at Cambridge, May 5, 6, 7, 1965

Essex won by nine wickets after dismissing Cambridge for 37 which was only seven runs more than their record lowest – against Yorkshire in 1928. Essex laboured for runs on a dead pitch when play was possible after lunch on Wednesday and were only saved through a stylish display by Smith. Taking eight wickets for 88, Roopnaraine, who had a remarkable analysis, kept an immaculate length with his off-spinners. To their credit, Cambridge gave a better display with the bat at their second attempt thanks, mainly to Murray and Hughes putting on 97, but Essex needed only 14 to win.

Essex

G. Barker c Close b Hughes	50	– not out	11
M. J. Bear b Roopnaraine	21	– c and b Whitaker	0
K. Fletcher c Griffith b Roopnaraine	11	– not out	3
B. R. Knight c McAdam b Roopnaraine	8		
G. J. Smith c Hughes b Roopnaraine	68		
J. Wilcox c White b Roopnaraine	13		
*T. E. Bailey b Roopnaraine	38		
†B. Taylor b Roopnaraine	6		
B. Edmeades c White b Roopnaraine	0		
R. Hobbs c White b Hughes	0		
P. J. Phelan not out	0		
B 10, n-b 1	11		
1/45 2/83 3/83 4/91 5/115 6/205 7/223 8/223 9/226	226	1/2	(1 wkt) 14

Bowling: *First Innings*—Russell 8–4–7–0; Whitaker 11–6–22–0; White 3–0–13–0; Roopnaraine 48.2–23–88–8; Hughes 41–16–70–2; McLachlan 7–2–15–0. *Second Innings*—Russell 2–0–8–0; Whitaker 1.5–0–6–1.

Cambridge University

D. M. Daniels c Hobbs b Knight	2	– c Knight b Hobbs	17
K. McAdam c Hobbs b Bailey	22	– b Edmeades	14
*R. C. White c Taylor b Knight	7	– b Knight	4
†D. L. Murray c Fletcher b Phelan	1	– hit wkt b Edmeades	58
M. G. Griffith c Fletcher b Phelan	0	– lbw b Phelan	14
G. Hughes lbw b Bailey	0	– c Fletcher b Hobbs	48
P. A. Close c Barker b Bailey	0	– lbw b Edmeades	0
A. A. McLachlan c Taylor b Phelan	2	– lbw b Bailey	11
R. Roopnaraine b Bailey	0	– b Knight	9
S. G. Russell not out	0	– c Phelan b Knight	6
M. Whitaker b Bailey	3	– not out	4
		B 13, l-b 4	17
1/13 2/23 3/28 4/28 5/31 6/31 7/32 8/34 9/34	37	1/22 2/46 3/56 4/72 5/169 6/169 7/169 8/190 9/192	202

Bowling: *First Innings*—Knight 9–4–10–2; Edmeades 6–2–17–0; Bailey 7.2–5–3–5; Phelan 9–5–7–3. *Second Innings*—Knight 19.4–4–49–3; Edmeades 12–4–23–3; Bailey 20–7–32–1; Hobbs 20–10–25–2; Phelan 17–6–42–1; Smith 10–5–14–0.

Umpires: O. W. Herman and L. H. Gray.

CAMBRIDGE UNIVERSITY v SUSSEX

Played at Cambridge, June 9, 10, 11, 1965

Sussex won by nine wickets after rain had prevented any cricket on the first day. Apart from Daniels and Murray, Cambridge gave an inept display with the bat and A. Buss, fast-medium, finished their second innings with a hat-trick. He removed Roopnaraine with the last ball of his ninth over and Gunn, who kept wicket splendidly, caught Murray and Cutler in his tenth. With M. Buss excelling with the off drive and Suttle hitting with great power to leg, Sussex began their first innings with a stand of 82. The Nawab of Pataudi accomplished little on his first appearance of the season for the county.

Cambridge University

D. M. Daniels lbw b Cooper	40	– c M. Buss b A. Buss	31
D. Hays c Langridge b Snow	3	– b Thomson	12
M. G. Griffith c Gunn b Thomson	4	– lbw b Thomson	1
†D. L. Murray c Gunn b Snow	13	– c Gunn b A. Buss	24
*R. C. White b Snow	4	– b Thomson	5
G. Hughes b M. Buss	2	– lbw b Thomson	2
P. A. Close b Lenham b M. Buss	2	– c Pataudi b A. Buss	31
A. A. McLachlan c Suttle b M. Buss	0	– c Gunn b Snow	2
R. Roopnaraine not out	7	– b A. Buss	1
R. Cutler c Gunn b A. Buss	13	– c Gunn b A. Buss	0
S. G. Russell b M. Buss	4	– not out	0
B 2, l-b 2, n-b 1	5	L-b 3	3
1/27 2/35 3/63 4/66 5/71 6/73 7/73 8/73 9/86	97	1/39 2/43 3/44 4/58 5/64 6/107 7/109 8/110 9/110	112

Bowling: *First Innings*—Snow 13–3–22–3; A. Buss 9–1–27–1; Thomson 8–3–8–1; M. Buss 20.5–11–29–4; Cooper 5–1–6–1. *Second Innings*—Snow 8.4–1–28–1; A. Buss 10–3–27–5; Thomson 9–5–11–4; M. Buss 8–3–17–0; Cooper 4–1–21–0; Suttle 3–1–5–0.

Sussex

K. G. Suttle run out	73	– not out	4
M. A. Buss c and b Hughes	34	– c Murray b Griffith	1
L. J. Lenham c Russell b Roopnaraine	34	– not out	1
Nawab of Pataudi c Griffith b Roopnaraine	5		
R. J. Langridge b McLachlan	2		
G. C. Cooper lbw b Roopnaraine	10		
F. R. Pountain not out	40		
A. Buss b Roopnaraine	0		
†T. Gunn run out	0		
L-b 5	5	W 1	1
1/82 2/118 3/143 4/151 5/153 6/191 7/195 8/203	(8 wkts dec.) 203	1/5	(1 wkt) 7

*N. I. Thomson and J. A. Snow did not bat.

Bowling: *First Innings*—Russell 8–2–9–0; Cutler 5–0–9–0; Hughes 27–4–90–1; Roopnaraine 31.3–12–59–4; McLachlan 9–3–31–1. *Second Innings*—White 3.4–3–2–0; Griffith 3–1–4–1.

Umpires: A. E. Fagg and N. Oldfield.

CAMBRIDGE UNIVERSITY v YORKSHIRE

Played at Cambridge, May 18, 19, 20, 1966

Yorkshire won by eight wickets. The Cambridge captain took the unusual step in this match of bringing in a player who was not going to be eligible to represent the University against Oxford at Lord's. After the low scores by Cambridge in the previous matches, Brearley, who captained Cambridge in 1963 and 1964 and who was back in residence on a post-graduate course, came into the side to provide support for the less experienced batsmen. Brearley was out for 0 in the first innings, but proved his worth by scoring 101 out of the Cambridge total of 247 in the second innings. Cosh shared a stand of 114 for the fourth wicket with Brearley, but Cambridge had lost too much ground in the first innings when bowled out for 81, and Yorkshire were left with only 94 to win in two hours and ten minutes. The Yorkshire first innings had been dominated by their captain, Close, who scored 103 out of the first 147. Illingworth, whose off-breaks caused Cambridge considerable trouble, also batted well in an innings of 47.

Cambridge University

J. M. Brearley b Nicholson	0	– c Sharpe b Wilson	101
R. E. J. Chambers b Nicholson	6	– b Trueman	0
D. L. Hays b Nicholson	1	– c Binks b Nicholson	9
*†D. L. Murray c Boycott b Waring	32	– b Nicholson	34
N. J. Cosh c Close b Waring	5	– c Close b Wilson	47
V. P. Malalasekera c Wilson b Illingworth	17	– c and b Illingworth	3
G. A. Cottrell b Wilson	5	– lbw b Wilson	2
R. Roopnaraine b Wilson	0	– c Boycott b Illingworth	23
N. Sinker b Illingworth	8	– b Illingworth	1
D. L. Acfield st Binks b Illingworth	2	– not out	9
S. G. Russell not out	0	– b Trueman	3
B 3, l-b 1, n-b 1	5	L-b 12, n-b 3	15
1/5 2/6 3/27 4/43 5/53 6/66 7/70 8/70 9/80	81	1/1 2/20 3/85 4/199 5/206 6/206 7/212 8/240 9/240	247

Bowling: *First Innings*—Trueman 7–4–11–0; Nicholson 8–3–21–3; Waring 7–1–19–2; Wilson 11–6–11–2; Illingworth 12.3–8–8–3; Close 7–4–6–0. *Second Innings*—Trueman 12.4–3–29–2; Nicholson 11–6–21–2; Wilson 30–14–53–3; Illingworth 35–16–64–3; Waring 7–1–28–0; Close 10–4–19–0; Hampshire 5–0–18–0.

Yorkshire

G. Boycott c Murray b Russell	11	– b Russell	8
*D. B. Close b Roopnaraine	103		
D. E. V. Padgett run out	30		
J. H. Hampshire b Sinker	0	– c Brearley b Cosh	28
P. J. Sharpe c Cosh b Sinker	0	– not out	47
R. Illingworth c Cosh b Russell	47		
†J. G. Binks c Murray b Sinker	22		
F. S. Trueman lbw b Roopnaraine	0	– not out	12
D. Wilson lbw b Roopnaraine	6		
A. G. Nicholson not out	4		
J. Waring not out	9		
B 1, l-b 2	3	B 1	1
1/30 2/123 3/132 4/134 5/150 6/183 7/188 8/218 9/220	(9 wkts dec.) 235	1/16 2/77	(2 wkts) 96

Bowling: *First Innings*—Russell 15–3–41–2; Cottrell 8–0–35–0; Acfield 13–2–34–0; Roopnaraine 34–13–90–3; Sinker 19–5–32–3. *Second Innings*—Russell 14–4–38–1; Cottrell 12–4–33–0; Roopnaraine 3–2–5–0; Cosh 2–1–8–1; Brearley 2–1–7–0; Chambers 0.5–0–4–0.

Umpires: P. A. Gibb and J. Langridge.

CAMBRIDGE UNIVERSITY v LEICESTERSHIRE

Played at Cambridge, May 4, 6, 7, 1968

Leicestershire won by ten wickets. The Cambridge batsmen once again showed their fallibility, this time against spin. Birkenshaw took the first hat-trick of the season by dismissing Ponniah, Knight and Poulet and at one time had taken five Cambridge wickets for nine runs in eight overs. Hallam and Inman put on 169 for the third Leicestershire wicket at over a run a minute and the University were left needing 263 to avoid their second successive innings defeat. They achieved this objective through admirable batting by Knight, Palfreyman and Taylor and indeed would have escaped with a draw but for the new MCC regulation concerning 20 overs in the final hour. This allowed Leicestershire the few overs they needed to force victory. The umpires consulted MCC officials at Lord's before giving permission for the extra time.

Cambridge University

C. E. M. Ponniah c and b Birkenshaw	12	– c Marner b Cotton	3
P. G. Carling c Norman b Birkenshaw	22	– lbw b Birkenshaw	35
G. D. Raw c Dudleston b Spencer	4	– c Dudleston b Birkenshaw	10
R. D. V. Knight c Marner b Birkenshaw	0	– b Marner	83
R. Poulet b Birkenshaw	0	– b Booth	6
*G. A. Cottrell c Marner b Birkenshaw	0	– lbw b Booth	11
H. J. C. Taylor c Tolchard b Birkenshaw	1	– c Tolchard b Spencer	50
†D. W. Norris c Birkenshaw b Spencer	10	– b Cotton	5
A. B. Palfreyman c Spencer b Birkenshaw	3	– c Tolchard b Spencer	60
D. L. Acfield c Inman b Cotton	6	– not out	1
J. F. Fitzgerald not out	13	– c Hallam b Cotton	2
		B 10, l-b 5, w 1, n-b 2	18
1/31 2/38 3/38 4/38 5/38 6/38 7/40 8/50 9/52	71	1/12 2/40 3/72 4/96 5/138 6/174 7/193 8/273 9/282	284

Bowling: *First Innings*—Cotton 6.5–3–12–1; Knight 10–6–17–0; Birkenshaw 15–5–28–7; Spencer 11–5–14–2. *Second Innings*—Cotton 14.2–2–55–3; Spencer 9–2–19–2; Birkenshaw 29–9–61–2; Booth 29–7–88–2; Knight 7–2–18–0; Marner 10–1–25–1.

Leicestershire

*M. R. Hallam c Poulet b Acfield	113	– not out	11
M. E. Norman lbw b Cottrell	1		
B. J. Booth c Norris b Cottrell	17		
C. C. Inman c Acfield b Fitzgerald	92		
P. T. Marner b Fitzgerald	10		
B. Dudleston run out	7		
J. Birkenshaw c Poulet b Acfield	23		
B. R. Knight not out	49	– not out	9
†R. W. Tolchard b Acfield	1		
C. T. Spencer b Knight	16		
J. Cotton b Knight	0		
B 2, w 2, n-b 1	5	B 1, l-b 1	2
1/4 2/43 3/212 4/238 5/238 6/267 7/268 8/294 9/334	334	(no wkt)	22

Bowling: *First Innings*—Palfreyman 4–0–21–0; Cottrell 20–5–75–2; Acfield 46–17–133–3; Fitzgerald 27–6–64–2; Knight 12.1–3–36–2. *Second Innings*—Knight 2–0–12–0; Acfield 1.2–0–8–0.

Umpires: C. G. Pepper and G. H. Pope.

CAMBRIDGE UNIVERSITY v GLAMORGAN

Played at Cambridge, May 9, 11, 12, 1970

Cambridge beat the Champions by eight wickets. This was the University's first success against a county since they overcame Nottinghamshire in 1963. Set 292 to win in five and a half hours, Cambridge were indebted to Majid and Carling, who put on 225 for the second wicket, Carling hit his maiden century in four hours twenty minutes (eleven 4s) and Majid, batting against his adopted county, had sixteen 4s in his 139 not out, which took just under four hours. Eighty-five runs were needed off the last 20 overs and Cambridge achieved their objective with nine balls to spare. The University had been outplayed on the first two days. A determined innings of 94 by Jones against bowlers extracting considerable movement from the pitch enabled Glamorgan to reach 216. Then Williams exploited a damp patch and at a lively medium pace took six for 26, completely demoralising the Cambridge batsmen. A second-innings century by Lewis allowed Glamorgan to make a challenging declaration. Eifion Jones equalled an English first-class wicket-keeping record with seven victims in the Cambridge first innings.

Glamorgan

A. Jones c Knight b Owen-Thomas	94	– c Majid b Spencer	7
R. C. Davis c Knight b Jameson	1	– c Short b Spencer	3
*A. R. Lewis lbw b Spencer	6	– not out	101
G. C. Kingston c Carling b Jameson	8	– lbw b Knight	8
K. J. Lyons c Majid b Knight	17	– c Jameson b Knight	6
B. A. Davis b Wilkin	31	– b Wilkin	12
†E. W. Jones c Spencer b Johnson	28	– not out	56
A. E. Cordle c and b Owen-Thomas	12		
M. A. Nash c Jameson b Johnson	5		
D. J. Shepherd c Wilkin b Johnson	6		
D. L. Williams not out	1		
B 2, l-b 5	7	B 8, l-b 3, n-b 1	12
1/4 2/15 3/35 4/96 5/155 6/173 7/201 8/205 9/208	216	1/5 2/17 3/51 4/63 5/88	(5 wkts dec.) 205

Bowling: *First Innings*—Spencer 12–4–20–1; Jameson 20–7–56–2; Knight 14–2–35–1; Johnson 10.4–3–34–3; Wilkin 18–5–38–1; Owen-Thomas 16–4–26–2. *Second Innings*—Spencer 17–4–34–2; Jameson 14–4–32–0; Knight 11–2–39–2; Wilkin 18–6–41–1; Owen-Thomas 8–0–26–0; Johnson 3–0–21–0.

Cambridge University

*†J. I. McDowall c E. W. Jones b Williams	26	– b Williams	31
P. G. Carling c E. W. Jones b Williams	15	– c B. A. Davis b Shepherd	104
Majid Khan c Cordle b Williams	5	– not out	139
R. D. V. Knight c E. W. Jones b Cordle	0	– not out	2
D. R. Owen-Thomas st E. W. Jones b Shepherd	9		
J. R. A. Cragg c E. W. Jones b Williams	0		
R. L. Short b Williams	37		
P. D. Johnson c E. W. Jones b Nash	0		
T. E. N. Jameson c Lewis b Shepherd	22		
C. L. Wilkin not out	0		
J. Spencer c E. W. Jones b Williams	0		
B 7, l-b 9	16	B 3, l-b 12, n-b 1	16
1/36 2/48 3/49 4/51 5/51 6/75 7/82 8/130 9/130	130	1/47 2/272	(2 wkts) 292

Bowling: *First Innings*—Nash 12–4–26–1; Williams 18.5–5–26–6; Cordle 12–2–21–1; Shepherd 11–8–11–2; King 7–1–19–0; R. C. Davis 6–3–11–0. *Second Innings*—Nash 16–0–50–0; Williams 10–4–14–1; Shepherd 27.3–8–58–1; R. C. Davis 15–5–41–0; Cordle 19–4–52–0; B. A. Davis 8–2–25–0; Kingston 7–0–36–0.

Umpires: A. E. Rhodes and A. Jepson.

24-HOUR MARATHON AT CAMBRIDGE

Something unique for cricket took place on June 14/15 1973 at Parker's Piece, Cambridge. At 5 p.m. on June 14 two sides comprised of members of the Cambridge University Cricket Society took the field and at 5 p.m. the following day the same 22 players left the field having played cricket continuously except for a "lunch" break, to MCC Laws for 24 hours. As well as creating a new world record for continuous cricket the effort raised over £170 for charity.

Each side had five innings in the match and a total of 1,395 runs were scored off 367 overs. During the hours of darkness gas lights illuminated the playing area, and light coloured cricket balls, specially prepared by Alfred Reader, were used.

In the period of darkness between 1 a.m. and 4 a.m. Roger Coates scored the only century of the match. Though the light was adequate the captains, Peter Such and David Langley, agreed to suspend fast bowling during the night on the grounds of safety.

At the end of an extremely exhausting "day's" play Roger Coates, in a small ceremony, was presented with the prize for the best batting performance, by a Haig representative, and Philip Cornes received a trophy from a representative of Alfred Reader for the best bowling performance. Scores:

Langley's XI: 59, 179, 83, 200, 161. Total 682 runs.
Such's XI: 126, 254/8 dec., 121, 142/8 dec, 70/3. Total 713 runs.

Teams: Langley's XI: T. Brown, A. Ave, R. Court, J. Brett, J. Chambers, D. J. Yeandle, T. Wald, J. Preston, N. Peace, M. Coultas, D. Langley.

Such's XI: R. Coates, P. Such, P. Cornes, A. Radford, M. Williams, A. S. I. Berry, J. Burnett, P. Kinns, M. Shaw, R. Henson, M. Furneaux.

CAMBRIDGE UNIVERSITY v ESSEX

Played at Cambridge, April 28, 29, 30, 1976

Drawn. A new batting star emerged to rekindle the memory of Fenner's great past when Paul Parker, the Sussex Freshman from Collyer's School, Horsham, hit a magnificent double century – the first of the season. Batting for almost a full day Parker coped with the seven bowlers Essex used after arriving at a precarious 7 for two. He hit twenty-eight 4s and two 6s after surviving a chance early in his innings. His batting overshadowed all else although Cambridge had recovered in the first innings from 23 for five with a partnership of 108 for the sixth wicket between Jarrett and Bannister. McEwan, in tremendous early form for Essex, hit a century, and all the other senior batsmen, apart from the unfortunate Hardie, took gentle practice against an attack that threatened little on so perfect a wicket.

Cambridge University

†S. P. Coverdale c Acfield b Lever	1	– run out	2
C. N. Boyns c Smith b Lever	6	– c Smith b East	35
*T. J. Murrills c Smith b Lever	3	– c Smith b Turner	4
P. M. Roebuck lbw b Lever	4	– lbw b Turner	0
P. W. G. Parker c Pont b Gooch	2	– c Smith b Fletcher	215
D. W. Jarrett b Gooch	62	– b East	22
C. S. Bannister c Smith b Turner	50	– c Smith b Pont	48
E. J. W. Jackson c Hardie b Acfield	12	– c Gooch b Fletcher	8
P. J. Hayes c Fletcher b East	17	– c Turner b Fletcher	4
M. E. Allbrook not out	4	– not out	12
M. E. W. Brooker c McEwan b Acfield	0	– lbw b Acfield	2
L-b 8, w 1, n-b 6	15	B 8, l-b 6, w 2, n-b 2	18
1/8 2/13 3/14 4/19 5/23 6/131 7/141 8/172 9/176	176	1/7 2/7 3/81 4/91 5/152 6/247 7/330 8/337 9/357	370

Bowling: *First Innings*—Lever 14–3–33–4; Turner 14–5–19–1; Gooch 19–10–36–2; Pont 8–2–20–0; Acfield 21.3–7–31–2; East 21–11–22–1. *Second Innings*—Lever 21–6–79–0; Turner 16–6–34–2; Gooch 5–2–21–0; Acfield 29.4–7–73–1; East 27–6–81–2; Pont 12–1–35–1; Fletcher 14–4–29–3.

Essex

B. R. Hardie c Coverdale b Brooker	0
K. S. McEwan c Boyns b Brooker	131
G. A. Gooch c Murrills b Jackson	28
*K. W. R. Fletcher c Roebuck b Allbrook	58
K. R. Pont not out	64
S. Turner c sub b Hayes	54
M. K. Fosh b Brooker	23
L-b 5, n-b 5	9
1/0 2/85 3/213 4/222 5/319 6/367 (6 wkts dec.)	367

†N. Smith, R. E. East, J. K. Lever and D. L. Ackfield did not bat.

Bowling: Brooker 28.3–6–88–3; Jackson 19–3–65–1; Hayes 19–1–65–1; Allbrook 23–5–78–1; Bannister 17–5–39–0; Roebuck 1–0–18–0; Boyns 3–0–5–0.

Umpires: D. J. Constant and J. G. Langridge.

CAMBRIDGE UNIVERSITY v SURREY

Played at Cambridge, May 17, 18, 19, 1978

Drawn. Hignell, the University captain, scored a century in each innings – the first Cambridge player to achieve the feat since Prideaux. He carried the Cambridge batting on the first day as Jackman caused problems to his colleagues. Surrey replied with an unbroken partnership of 256 between Howarth and Knight, the new captain. In the second innings, Hignell received some help as he hit one 6 and twenty-three 4s. Surrey were in danger of defeat when Allbrook captured four wickets, but he then had to leave the field and the county saved the game.

Cambridge University

M. K. Fosh b Payne	26	– b Baker	9
A. M. Mubarak b Jackman	4	– b Baker	14
I. G. Peck lbw b Jackman	0	– c Knight b Baker	11
*A. J. Hignell c and b Howarth	108	– c Payne b Needham	145
N. C. Crawford c Richards b Payne	0	– b Jackman	29
A. R. Dewes c Richards b Jackman	6	– c Younis b Knight	32
N. F. M. Popplewell c Knight b Baker	12	– c Younis b Knight	1
M. G. Howat c Richards b Jackman	30	– c Roope b Knight	20
†D. J. Littlewood not out	4	– lbw b Jackman	7
M. E. Allbrook c and b Jackman	5	– c Richards b Jackman	11
M. M. Bishop b Needham	0	– not out	0
B 3, l-b 7, w 2, n-b 6	18	B 4, l-b 11, n-b 4	19
1/14 2/16 3/74 4/80 5/100 6/112 7/202 8/202 9/210	213	1/10 2/25 3/44 4/150 5/248 6/251 7/254 8/277 9/295	298

Bowling: *First Innings*—Jackman 14–5–26–5; Baker 12–3–35–1; Butcher 9–0–34–0; Payne 12–1–41–1; Needham 11.2–2–44–1; Howarth 7–3–15–1. *Second Innings*—Baker 21–4–74–3; Butcher 12–2–34–0; Payne 12–2–45–0; Needham 19–6–51–0; Roope 6–2–18–0; Jackman 12.4–3–35–3; Knight 11–2–22–3.

Surrey

G. P. Howarth not out	179	– st Littlewood b Allbrook	30
A. R. Butcher run out	31	– c and b Howat	13
*R. D. V. Knight not out	103	– not out	19
Younis Ahmed (did not bat)		– c Mubarak b Bishop	6
G. R. J. Roope (did not bat)		– b Allbrook	15
D. M. Smith (did not bat)		– c Hignell b Howat	34
R. P. Baker (did not bat)		– b Allbrook	5
I. R. Payne (did not bat)		– c Littlewood b Allbrook	1
R. D. Jackman (did not bat)		– not out	10
L-b 3, n-b 3	6	B 6, l-b 5, w 2, n-b 2	15
1/63	(1 wkt dec.) 319	1/16 2/38 3/38 4/51 5/113 6/113 7/116	(7 wkts) 148

†C. J. Richards and A. Needham did not bat.

Bowling: *First Innings*—Howat 19–0–67–0; Bishop 17–3–57–0; Popplewell 15–1–51–0; Crawford 7–0–33–0; Allbrook 21–4–56–0; Hignell 12.5–1–49–0. *Second Innings*—Howat 19–6–37–2; Bishop 8–4–13–1; Allbrook 16–5–43–4; Hignell 9–2–36–0; Popplewell 2–1–4–0; Crawford 1–1–0–0; Dewes 1–1–0–0.

Umpires: W. L. Budd and D. O. Oslear.

CAMBRIDGE UNIVERSITY v ESSEX

Played at Cambridge, April 22, 23, 24, 1981

Drawn. There could hardly have been a more eventful start to the season than this, the lone game to start on the official opening day. Mills was lbw to the first ball of the season – a gentle full toss from Lever. The University's first innings lurched from revival to collapse with regularity before all were out for 146. Essex had the better conditions in which to bat, but showed their lack of practice against an attack in which Dutton and Hodgson, both on début, captured their first wickets in first-class cricket. Pringle, of Essex and captaining Cambridge in the absence of Peck, took four wickets and then batted with some abandon in the University second innings. However, after an hour and a quarter on the third morning, the umpires called a halt, considering it unreasonable and dangerous to continue because of the extreme cold. After an early lunch they resumed in marginally warmer conditions, but there was only time for Pringle to complete his half-century and be dismissed before rain ended the match.

Cambridge University

J. P. C. Mills lbw b Lever	0	– lbw b Turner	43
A. J. Murley c Smith b Lever	14	– lbw b Acfield	15
T. D. W. Edwards c and b Turner	36	– lbw b Acfield	2
R. J. Boyd-Moss c McEwan b Turner	1	– b Acfield	0
*D. R. Pringle lbw b Turner	3	– c McEvoy b Foster	66
N. Russom c Smith b East	32	– (7) not out	47
S. J. G. Doggart c East b Turner	5	– (8) not out	1
D. C. Holliday c Smith b Pont	32		
K. I. Hodgson c McEvoy b Acfield	6		
†C. F. E. Goldie c Hardie b Acfield	3	– (6) lbw b Turner	13
R. S. Dutton not out	0		
B 1, l-b 3, w 10	14	B 2, l-b 6, w-4, n-b 5	17
1/0 2/49 3/55 4/56 5/62 6/70 7/127 8/136 9/146	146	1/53 2/59 3/59 4/72 5/101 6/201	(6 wkts) 204

Bowling: *First Innings*—Lever 9–3–20–2; Foster 13–4–53–0; Turner 11–5–20–4; Acfield 12–8–7–2; Pont 11–1–32–1; East 1.1–1–0–1. *Second Innings*—Lever 12–2–40–0; Foster 12–1–37–1; Turner 17–7–28–2; Acfield 30–12–43–3; East 26–11–39–0.

Essex

M. S. A. McEvoy c and b Dutton	53
B. R. Hardie c Edwards b Russom	13
K. S. McEwan b Pringle	16
*K. W. R. Fletcher c Pringle b Hodgson	46
K. R. Pont b Russom	37
S. Turner c Goldie b Hodgson	0
R. E. East c Russom b Hodgson	27
†N. Smith b Pringle	1
J. K. Lever b Pringle	11
D. L. Acfield lbw b Pringle	5
N. A. Foster not out	8
B 3, l-b 3, n-b 17	23
1/26 2/66 3/137 4/158 5/158 6/205 7/207 8/213 9/230	240

Bowling: Pringle 21–8–56–4; Russom 18–1–60–2; Dutton 11–0–45–1; Doggart 11–3–22–0; Hodgson 8–0–33–3; Holliday 2–1–1–0.

Umpires: D. O. Oslear and N. T. Plews.

OXFORD UNIVERSITY

OXFORD UNIVERSITY v NORTHAMPTONSHIRE

Played at Oxford, May 3, 4, 5, 1967

Drawn. A fine knock by Prideaux saved Northamptonshire after they had lost Reynolds and Milburn without a run scored. He was eventually bowled by Easter when one short of a well-deserved century. His dismissal was the beginning of a hat trick by Easter who bowled Scott and had Kettle caught. The University batting, with the exception of Toft and Barker, again failed and they were dismissed for 137 on the last day after rain had prevented any play on the second day. Confusion then arose when Oxford were asked to follow on 117 behind after the umpires had mistakingly applied the two-day ruling. The Dark Blues went for the runs in the mistaken belief that Prideaux had forfeited the second innings and were rapidly reaching the target when two telephone calls were made to Lord's to clarify the position. As a result of the information given him Ridley wisely decided to call the batsmen in twenty minutes from the end when 40 runs were needed, and the match was drawn.

Northamptonshire

*R. M. Prideaux b Easter	99
B. L. Reynolds c Goldstein b Gamble	0
C. Milburn c Toft b Gamble	0
Mushtaq Mohammad c and b Gamble	23
D. S. Steele c Walsh b Ridley	38
B. Crump b Gamble	42
M. E. Scott b Easter	0
M. J. Kettle c Barker b Easter	0
†L. A. Johnson b Easter	0
H. Sully not out	18
A. J. Durose b Easter	24
B 6, l-b 3, n-b 1	10
1/0 2/0 3/46 4/111 5/198 6/198 7/198 8/198 9/210	254

Bowling: Gamble 23–7–63–4; Easter 24–8–62–5; Heard 8–0–43–0; Ridley 28–15–40–1; Barker 13–7–36–0.

Oxford University

D. P. Toft c Durose b Sully	40	– not out	38
F. S. Goldstein c Johnson b Kettle	10	– c Reynolds b Crump	28
D. R. Walsh b Kettle	0		
A. R. Garofall c Johnson b Kettle	1		
D. A. Ashworth c Johnson b Kettle	11		
A. H. Barker run out	32	– b Kettle	12
*G. N. S. Ridley c Crump b Mushtaq	17		
N. W. Gamble c and b Sully	18		
†P. J. Burnell c Kettle b Mushtaq	1		
J. N. C. Easter b Mushtaq	2		
H. Heard not out	2		
B 1, l-b 1, n-b 1	3		
1/19 2/19 3/21 4/53 5/69 6/111 7/115 8/116 9/134	137	1/40 2/78 (2 wkts)	78

Bowling: *First Innings*—Kettle 20–8–24–4; Durose 11–4–20–0; Crump 10–5–16–0; Mushtaq 20–10–37–3; Scott 10–4–12–0; Sully 13–4–25–2. *Second Innings*—Kettle 7–2–31–1; Crump 11–6–20–1; Mushtaq 3–0–14–0; Scott 5–3–11–0; Sully 2–1–2–0.

Umpires: J. F. Crapp and J. Arnold.

OXFORD UNIVERSITY v SURREY

Played at Oxford, May 18, 20, 21, 1968

Surrey won by ten wickets. The University, still smarting from the heavy defeat in their last game, gave another dismal batting display after doing well to dismiss Surrey cheaply.

Williams bowled well, taking five for 19, and Oxford fielded superbly after rain had washed out the first day's play, but when they batted, collapsed in dramatic fashion. The first four wickets fell without a run and half the side were out for two, of which one was from a no-ball. Altogether six batsmen failed to score and the follow-on was enforced. Then Goldstein and Khan gave the Dark Blues a sound start with a stand of 50 but on Goldstein's dismissal the batting collapsed, the last five wickets adding only nine runs. Cumbes, in his cheerful way, took eight wickets for 47 in the match for Surrey.

Surrey

M. J. Edwards c Westley b Heard	25	not out	21
W. A. Smith c Westley b Niven	22	not out	17
*M. J. Stewart c Goldstein b Williams	21		
K. F. Barrington lbw b Khan	30		
Younis Ahmed c Garofall b Khan	3		
S. J. Storey b Williams	5		
†A. Long run out	7		
P. I. Pocock not out	27		
R. D. Jackman c Khan b Williams	0		
R. Harman c Goldstein b Williams	0		
J. Cumbes c Khan b Williams	2		
B 1, l-b 9, n-b 5	15		
1/44 2/60 3/96 4/113 5/120 6/122 7/145 8/155 9/157	157	(No wkt)	38

Bowling: *First Innings*—Watson 4–1–22–0; Niven 13–3–37–1; Heard 8–2–20–1; Khan 15–5–44–2; Williams 13.1–4–19–5. *Second Innings*—Watson 4–1–16–0; Niven 4–1–16–0; Goldstein 0.4–0–6–0.

Oxford University

*F. S. Goldstein c Long b Jackman	0	lbw b Storey	47
A. J. Khan c Smith b Cumbes	0	lbw b Cumbes	17
J. R. Kilbee b Jackman	0	b Cumbes	0
A. R. Garofall c Storey b Jackman	0	lbw b Pocock	12
R. L. Burchnall lbw b Harman	6	c Edwards b Pocock	9
P. R. B. Wilson c Edwards b Cumbes	0	c Edwards b Cumbes	23
A. G. M. Watson c Stewart b Harman	20	c Long b Cumbes	8
†S. A. Westley c Edwards b Pocock	0	b Pocock	2
D. Williams not out	6	b Cumbes	0
H. Heard c Jackman b Pocock	2	not out	3
R. A. Niven lbw b Harman	11	b Cumbes	0
B 1, l-b 1, n-b 3	5	B 9, l-b 4, n-b 7	20
1/0 2/0 3/0 4/0 5/2 6/30 7/31 8/31 9/33	50	1/50 2/50 3/68 4/85 5/119 6/132 7/135 8/135 9/138	141

Bowling: *First Innings*—Jackman 7–6–3–3; Cumbes 12–5–12–3; Pocock 15–11–7–2; Harman 14.1–9–23–3. *Second Innings*—Jackman 16–5–47–0; Cumbes 16.2–9–35–6; Storey 9–3–15–1; Harman 5–3–4–0; Pocock 14–5–20–3.

Umpires: L. H. Gray and H. Mellows.

OXFORD UNIVERSITY v WARWICKSHIRE

Played at Oxford, May 3, 5, 6, 1969

Drawn. Rain washed out play before the start on the last day and prevented what could have been an exciting finish in a high scoring game in which Oxford were on top. Goldstein put the county in to bat and with three wickets captured for 69 the move seemed justified, but Stewart, who scored 119 after being dropped at 1, and Cartwright with a dashing 71, helped Warwickshire to reach 310. Stuart Westley took five catches behind the wicket. Oxford's reply was remarkable. Goldstein hit a sparkling 87 in a fourth-wicket stand of 115 with Walsh and this was followed by a stand of 270 for the sixth wicket by Walsh and Stuart Westley. Walsh thrashed the bowling once he had completed a century and he raced to a double century. He was eventually caught for 207 when attempting to hit his thirty-third boundary. He also hit two 6s. Westley, 93 not out, was robbed of a possible maiden century by the weather on the last day. Their stand beat the previous best for Oxford – 236 by R. E. C. Butterworth and E. R. T. Holmes in 1927.

Warwickshire

K. Ibadulla c S. A. Westley b Heard	11
W. J. Stewart c Burchnall b Kilbee	119
D. L. Amiss b Kilbee	23
J. A. Jameson c S. A. Westley b Heard	4
R. N. Abberley c Carroll b Burton	39
G. S. Warner c Carroll b Burton	3
*†A. C. Smith c S. A. Westley b Heard	27
T. W. Cartwright c S. A. Westley b Kilbee	71
D. J. Brown c S. A. Westley b Heard	5
N. M. McVicker c Campbell b Kilbee	0
W. Blenkiron not out	3
L-b 5	5
1/24 2/60 3/69 4/142 5/158 6/193 7/285 8/285 9/294	310

Bowling: Heard 31–10–69–4; Kilbee 27.3–2–96–4; Carroll 11–3–51–0; Burton 23–7–38–2; R. B. Westley 18–4–51–0.

Oxford University

*F. S. Goldstein c sub b Jameson	87
A. Campbell c Smith b Blenkiron	4
R. L. Burchnall c Amiss b Blenkiron	0
D. R. Walsh c Cartwright b Blenkiron	207
P. R. Carroll lbw b Blenkiron	0
J. W. O. Allerton lbw b Cartwright	1
†S. A. Westley not out	93
R. B. Westley run out	0
J. R. Kilbee lbw b Blenkiron	0
M. St. J. Burton b Brown	4
H. Heard not out	3
B 3, l-b 7, n-b 4	14
1/0 2/6 3/6 4/121 5/124 6/394 7/394 8/399 9/403	(9 wkts) 413

Bowling: Brown 28–9–66–1; Blenkiron 27–6–67–5; McVicker 2–0–2–0; Ibadulla 22–7–56–0; Cartwright 28–11–76–1; Jameson 14–4–72–1; Smith 15–3–60–0.

Umpires: D. J. Constant and H. Mellows.

OXFORD UNIVERSITY v WORCESTERSHIRE

Played at Oxford, June 4, 5, 6, 1969

Worcestershire won by eight wickets. Oxford's batting frailties were again exposed when they were dismissed cheaply in their second innings after sound batting earlier had enabled Goldstein to declare. The Dark Blues produced their most consistent form of the season after Goldstein won the toss and batted, and against an ordinary attack runs came at a brisk rate. Worcestershire passed Oxford's total for the loss of only two wickets, Hemsley and Ormrod putting on 199 for the third wicket. Hemsley hit a maiden century and Ormrod also reached three figures. The Worcestershire off-spinner, Griffith, was hit for 34 off three overs in the Dark Blues first innings, but he wrecked them at the second attempt, claiming seven wickets for 41 runs.

Oxford University

*F. S. Goldstein c Yardley b Gifford	62	– c Slade b Brain	20
A. Campbell c Cass b Brain	7	– b Griffith	14
D. R. Walsh b Standen	35	– c Cass b Griffith	8
R. L. Burchnall c Headley b Slade	41	– b Standen	9
J. W. O. Allerton c Headley b Hemsley	67	– c and b Griffith	13
M. G. Heal lbw b Slade	0	– c Headley b Griffith	0
†A. H. Morgan not out	59	– c Ormrod b Standen	5
S. A. Verity c Cass b Standen	7	– c Ormrod b Griffith	15
H. Heard not out	15	– c Brain b Griffith	0
M. St J. Burton (did not bat)		– not out	10
D. J. Millener (did not bat)		– c Slade b Griffith	1
B 1, l-b 3, n-b 1	5	L-b 3, n-b 1	4
1/21 2/93 3/108 4/203 5/203 6/220 7/255	(7 wkts dec.) 298	1/25 2/48 3/57 4/74 5/75 6/79 7/83 8/88 9/98	99

Bowling: *First Innings*—Brain 25–2–98–1; Standen 29–5–92–2; Hemsley 13–3–39–1; Gifford 20–11–23–1; Slade 17–13–7–2; Griffith 3–0–34–0. *Second Innings*—Brain 11–4–8–1; Standen 23–10–46–2; Griffith 12.4–4–41–7.

Worcestershire

R. G. A. Headley c Morgan b Burton	63	– c Morgan b Millener	8
A. R. Barker c Goldstein b Heard	21	– c Burchnall b Burton	15
J. A. Ormrod c Burchnall b Burton	109	– not out	11
E. J. O. Hemsley not out	138	– not out	11
T. J. Yardley not out	8		
B 2, l-b 11	13	L-b 1	1
1/64 2/108 3/307	(3 wkts dec.) 352	1/22 2/26	(2 wkts) 46

D. N. F. Slade, †G. R. Cass, K. Griffith, J. A. Standen, *N. Gifford and B. M. Brain did not bat.

Bowling: *First Innings*—Millener 27–5–85–0; Heard 26–5–79–1; Burton 36–13–92–2; Verity 23–7–71–0; Goldstein 4–2–12–0. *Second Innings*—Millener 3–0–15–1; Burton 4–1–16–1; Heard 2.5–0–11–0; Goldstein 1–0–3–0.

Umpires: F. Jakeman and A. Jepson.

OXFORD UNIVERSITY v KENT

Played at Oxford, June 11, 12, 13, 1969

Oxford University won by one wicket. Oxford achieved their first win for two seasons in a tense and thrilling finish. Set to score 258 in three hours twenty minutes, they reached the target with the fifth ball of the last over, and with their last pair at the crease. With the scores level, Niven lifted Hooper to deep mid-off, where Leary dropped the catch and the batsmen scampered through for the winning run. Goldstein set Oxford on the way to success with a blistering 87 and Khan hit 81 not out, but Denness more than anyone kept the game alive. He kept his spinners on throughout the final 20 overs and there was time for one more over afterwards and that proved decisive. Earlier the Kent batsmen had dealt savagely with the Oxford bowling. Luckhurst (168) and Asif Iqbal (133) figured in an unbroken stand of 238 for the third wicket, and in the second innings Ealham was undefeated with 103. Oxford made a spirited reply to Kent's 401 for two declared. Goldstein and Walsh received good support from Allerton, Burchnall and Burton and the University finished only 98 behind.

Kent

*M. H. Denness lbw b Millener	37		
B. W. Luckhurst not out	168		
†D. Nicholls b Burton	59	– lbw b Niven	36
Asif Iqbal not out	133		
S. E. Leary (did not bat)		– not out	7
A. Ealham (did not bat)		– not out	103
R. A. Woolmer (did not bat)		– c Burton b Niven	8
L-b 4	4	B 2, l-b 3	5
1/65 2/163 (2 wkts dec.)	401	1/120 2/134 (2 wkts dec.)	159

A. L. Dixon, A. Brown, J. C. Dye and A. J. Hooper did not bat.

Bowling: *First Innings*—Millener 24–1–101–1; Heard 18–0–81–0; Khan 18–4–87–0; Burton 25–8–93–1; Niven 16–4–35–0. *Second Innings*—Millener 17–8–29–0; Heard 15–1–53–0; Burton 12–2–43–0; Niven 10.1–0–29–2.

Oxford University

*F. S. Goldstein c Woolmer b Hooper	76	– c Dixon b Hooper	87
A. Campbell b Dye	15	– b Hooper	22
D. R. Walsh c Ealham b Dixon	69	– st Nicholls b Hooper	9
R. L. Burchnall b Leary	37	– c Asif b Hooper	22
J. W. O'. Allerton c Dixon b Dye	45	– b Hooper	0
A. J. Khan c Luckhurst b Leary	0	– not out	81
†A. H. Morgan run out	16	– c and b Hooper	4
M. St. J. Burton c Hooper b Leary	28	– st Nicholls b Dixon	2
H. Heard c Luckhurst b Leary	5	– run out	4
D. J. Millener c Luckhurst b Dixon	3	– c Asif b Dixon	11
R. A. Niven not out	0	– not out	1
B 5, l-b 3, n-b 1	9	B 12, l-b 1, n-b 2	15
1/38 2/118 3/178 4/237 5/247 6/248 7/295 8/295 9/303	303	1/53 2/87 3/103 4/132 5/202 6/206 7/222 8/240 9/257 (9 wkts)	258

Bowling: *First Innings*—Brown 20–5–76–0; Dye 23–9–43–2; Dixon 24.4–13–39–2; Woolmer 7–2–29–0; Hooper 15–11–44–1; Leary 20–7–63–4. *Second Innings*—Dye 8–3–21–0; Brown 6–1–14–0; Dixon 24–5–80–2; Hooper 22.5–3–92–6; Leary 7–0–36–0.

Umpires: A. S. M. Oakman and C. G. Pepper.

NOTES BY THE EDITOR, 1970

MOB VIOLENCE

Now, cricket in England is threatened with mob violence. Was not a forty-five yard trench dug along the length of one side of the square in The Parks at Oxford last summer when a team of young South Africans went there to play the University? People with no interest in cricket are among those who plan to disrupt play if the South Africans carry out their tour in 1970. There is the possibility of severe damage to cricket grounds as well as bodily harm to the police on duty and to spectators.

The dispute has led to debate in the House of Lords and among those who have stated that they are against the tour taking place is Mr Dennis Howell, the Minister with special responsibility for Sport. More than one hundred Labour and Liberal MPs are apparently willing to join the anti-apartheid demonstrations. What sort of an atmosphere is this for cricket? We know that South Africa possess about the best and most attractive side in the world to-day and given normal conditions there would be splendid cricket and welcome finance to English coffers. But if money is to be poured away employing police trying to prevent ill-bred violence, how many genuine cricket lovers will want to patronise the games? Some, I feel sure, would prefer instead, a peaceful county programme with all the teams, for once, being at full strength—free from Test Match calls—in other words an authentic Championship, something we have not enjoyed for over forty years.

OXFORD UNIVERSITY v NOTTINGHAMSHIRE

Played at Oxford, May 27, 28, 29, 1970

Nottinghamshire won by eight wickets. The University's off-spinners, Burton and Johns, claimed nine Nottinghamshire first-innings wickets between them, but were let down by poor catching, which gave the county at least 60 runs. The last two wickets added 82 runs. Ridley and, to a lesser extent, Johns and Burton were the only Oxford batsmen to defy the county bowlers and the Dark Blues, all out for 142, followed on. Ridley was unbeaten with 70 and ten minutes later was back again and inspired the undergraduates to their best batting of the season. When he was finally out for 66 he had batted seven hours, forty minutes. Burchnall and Carroll showed some bold strokes in the fight back, but Nottinghamshire only wanted 105, which they easily obtained.

Nottinghamshire

M. J. Harris b Johns	31	– not out	38
G. Frost lbw b Burton	34	– c Johns b Burton	25
M. J. Smedley c Robinson b Johns	12	– lbw b Douglas-Home	28
*J. B. Bolus c Hone b Burton	30	– not out	10
S. R. Bielby c Ridley b Johns	43		
S. B. Hassan c Johns b Burton	36		
R. A. White b Johns	27		
M. N. S. Taylor c Faber b Burton	0		
D. J. Halfyard not out	47		
†D. Pullan c Burchnall b Douglas-Home	8		
B. Stead c Douglas-Home b Burton	25		
B 3, l-b 2, n-b 4	9	N-b 4	4
1/63 2/80 3/81 4/151 5/157 6/218 7/220 8/220 9/256	302	1/48 2/89 (2 wkts)	105

Bowling: *First Innings*—Hone 13–1–69–0; Douglas-Home 12–1–52–1; Johns 37–14–76–4; Burton 37–12–96–5. *Second Innings*—Hone 7.2–2–40–0; Douglas-Home 7–2–15–1; Burton 13–6–25–1; Johns 7–1–21–0; Ridley 1–1–0–0.

Oxford University

R. M. Ridley not out	70	– c Hassan b Harris	66
R. L. Burchnall c Pullan b Taylor	3	– c Harris b White	40
J. Ward c Pullan b Stead	1	– c Taylor b Stead	24
M. J. J. Faber lbw b Stead	0	– c Smedley b Taylor	14
P. R. Carroll c Bolus b Stead	1	– c Bolus b Stead	49
†G. A. Robinson lbw b Taylor	0	– b White	0
R. L. Johns b White	25	– c Harris b Halfyard	6
*M. St J. W. Burton b Halfyard	28	– c Harris b Taylor	16
D. Williams c Hassan b Taylor	1	– not out	0
A. Douglas-Home c Smedley b Taylor	1	– c Smedley b White	23
D. J. Hone run out	7	– b White	13
L-b 5	5	B 4, l-b 9	13
1/4 2/9 3/9 4/13 5/16 6/64 7/102 8/109 9/117	142	1/77 2/121 3/137 4/153 5/177 6/190 7/212 8/232 9/263	264

Bowling: *First Innings*—Stead 17–5–43–3; Taylor 19–7–24–4; Harris 12–6–15–0; White 15–4–32–1; Halfyard 14–7–23–1. *Second Innings*—Stead 23–4–58–2; Taylor 23–3–44–2; Halfyard 15–5–31–1; White 29.2–13–49–4; Harris 29–10–69–1.

Umpires: J. Arnold and C. S. Elliott.

OXFORD UNIVERSITY v WARWICKSHIRE

Played at Oxford, May 19, 20, 1971

Warwickshire won by ten wickets. Warwickshire paid their second visit to The Parks and won with a day to spare to the amazement of their captain, Alan Smith. His bowlers were hit for 309 in Oxford's first innings and then dismissed the Dark Blues for 81 at the second attempt. A seventh-wicket stand of 108 by Cushing and Peter Jones enabled the undergraduates to exceed 300 but the batting hero was undoubtedly the 22-year-old John Whitehouse, who celebrated his entry into first-class cricket with a magnificent 173. He hit thirty-five boundaries, twenty-two of them in the first 100 which came in ninety-seven minutes. Oxford collapsed in their second innings against the spin of Hemmings and Jameson who shared eight wickets and were all out in under two hours. Warwickshire needed 67 and Whitehouse and Jameson soon hit them off.

Oxford University

A. K. C. Jones lbw b Hemmings	22	– c A. C. Smith b Rouse	13
†G. A. Robinson lbw b Jameson	12	– lbw b Jameson	22
*B. May lbw b Tidy	24	– lbw b Jameson	10
D. L. Bell lbw b Blenkiron	7	– c Hemmings b Blenkiron	2
J. M. Ward lbw b Rouse	18	– c Gordon b Jameson	23
C. J. B. Ridley b Blenkiron	16	– c Jameson b Hemmings	0
V. G. B. Cushing b Rouse	74	– c Rouse b Hemmings	2
P. C. H. Jones c Rouse b Lewington	67	– c A. C. Smith b Hemmings	0
S. C. Corlett c Rouse b Tidy	24	– b Hemmings	2
A. R. Wingfield-Digby b Rouse	14	– not out	4
C. B. Hamblin not out	13	– c Gordon b Jameson	0
B 4, l-b 13, n-b 1	18	L-b 2, n-b 1	3
1/34 2/54 3/65 4/67 5/95 6/118 7/226 8/260 9/285	309	1/16 2/16 3/43 4/50 5/51 6/53 7/55 8/73 9/79	81

Bowling: *First Innings*—Blenkiron 21–4–49–2; Rouse 22–5–52–3; Hemmings 16–7–39–1; Jameson 6–1–17–1; Warner 2–1–1–0; Tidy 18.4–5–71–2; Lewington 17–5–51–1; Kallicharran 3–0–11–0. *Second Innings*—Blenkiron 7–3–6–1; Rouse 7–2–22–1; Hemmings 11–2–28–4; Jameson 10.1–2–22–4.

Warwickshire

J. A. Jameson c Robinson b Wingfield-Digby	21	– not out	30
J. Whitehouse c and b P. C. H. Jones	173	– not out	38
A. Gordon b Hamblin	16		
A. Kallicharran c Robinson b Wingfield-Digby	12		
G. S. Warner c Ridley b P. C. H. Jones	37		
E. E. Hemmings c Bell b P. C. H. Jones	1		
*†A. C. Smith not out	20		
W. Blenkiron lbw b Wingfield-Digby	4		
S. J. Rouse c Ridley b Wingfield-Digby	38		
P. J. Lewington c Ridley b Wingfield-Digby	0		
B 2	2	L-b 2	2
1/51 2/94 3/171 4/241 5/245 6/266 7/271 8/322 9/324	(9 wkts dec.) 324		(no wkt) 70

W. N. Tidy did not bat.

Bowling: *First Innings*—Wingfield-Digby 26.3–6–79–5; Hamblin 14–1–75–1; P. C. H. Jones 18–2–70–3; Corlett 10–1–45–0; Ridley 11–1–53–0. *Second Innings*—Wingfield-Digby 4–0–28–0; Hamblin 2–0–24–0; P. C. H. Jones 1.5–0–16–0.

Umpires: W. E. Alley and O. W. Herman.

OXFORD UNIVERSITY v SURREY

Played at Oxford, June 15, 16, 17, 1977

Drawn. Rain prevented any plan on the first day and the match was only kept alive by three declarations. It ended with Surrey setting Oxford to score 221 to win in two hours, twenty minutes and the University just managed to hold out with their last pair together. The match will long be remembered because Peter Wight had to operate from the bowler's end for the whole match. It was originally called off for the first two days because of the saturated state of the pitch and square and the umpires returned home. But a sudden improvement in the weather resulted in the captains deciding that play might be possible on the second day and efforts were made to summon the umpires back to Oxford. Cecil Pepper could not be contacted and a Minor Counties umpire assisted Wight on the second day and the players stood in at square leg on the third day. It was an unsatisfactory state of affairs for a first-class match.

Surrey

*J. H. Edrich c and b Wingfield-Digby	7	– c Marks b Savage	22
A. R. Butcher c Wells b Savage	25	– b Gurr	5
Younis Ahmed c Savage b Marks	54	– not out	10
D. M. Smith c Brettell b Savage	22	– b Marks	47
T. M. G. Hansell not out	8	– b Savage	8
Intikhab Alam not out	5	– st Fisher b Marks	63
I. R Payne (did not bat)		– st Fisher b Marks	4
A. Needham (did not bat)		– c Gurr b Marks	11
†C. J. Richards (did not bat)		– not out	2
R. P. Baker (did not bat)		– c and b Savage	0
L-b 5, w 1	6	B 4, l-b 1, w 1, n-b 3	9
1/3 2/40 3/104 4/118 (4 wkts dec.)	127	1/21 2/50 3/128 4/150 5/151 6/159 7/159 8/161 (8 wkts dec.)	181

A. J. Mack did not bat.

Bowling: *First Innings*—Gurr 11–3–14–0; Wingfield-Digby 16–7–16–1; Savage 18.3–2–64–2; Marks 13–4–27–1. *Second Innings*—Gurr 7–4–23–1; Wingfield-Digby 8–1–22–0; Savage 18–8–53–3; Marks 14–4–29–4; Brettell 9–1–45–0.

Oxford University

J. A. Claughton lbw b Barker	17	– c Edrich b Needham	56
R. R. C. Wells lbw b Baker	0	– b Baker	10
*V. J. Marks not out	50	– run out	44
M. L'Estrange not out	15	– c Payne b Needham	7
S. M. Clements (did not bat)		– c Baker b Needham	11
D. Kayum (did not bat)		– c Younis b Intikhab	7
†P. B. Fisher (did not bat)		– not out	0
A. R. Wingfield-Digby (did not bat)		– b Intikhab	5
D. N. Brettell (did not bat)		– b Intikhab	3
D. R. Gurr (did not bat)		– c Hansell b Intikhab	3
R. Le Q. Savage (did not bat)		– not out	0
B 5, l-b 1	6	L-b 10, w 1, n-b 7	18
1/8 2/39 (2 wkts dec.)	88	1/32 2/107 3/123 4/132 5/144 6/155 7/159 8/161 9/164 (9 wkts)	164

Bowling: *First Innings*—Mack 5–1–14–0; Baker 8.2–1–25–2; Intikhab 8–1–35–0; Needham 3–1–8–0. *Second Innings*—Mack 10–1–39–0; Baker 8–3–18–1; Intikhab 8–4–21–4; Needham 10–2–25–3; Payne 7–1–43–0.

Umpires: C. G. Pepper and P. B. Wight.

ONE-DAY CRICKET

THE GILLETTE CUP

THE KNOCK-OUT COMPETITION [1964]

The new Knock-Out competition aroused enormous interest. Very large crowds, especially in the later rounds, flocked to the matches and 25,000 spectators watched the final at Lord's where Sussex narrowly defeated Worcestershire by 14 runs in a thoroughly exciting match. It says much for this type of cricket that tremendous feeling was stirred-up among the spectators as well as the cricketers with numerous ties being decided in the closest fashion. At Lord's, supporters wore favours and banners were also in evidence, the whole scene resembling an Association Football Cup Final more than the game of cricket and many thousands invaded the pitch at the finish to cheer Dexter, the Sussex captain, as he received the Gillette Trophy from the MCC President, Lord Nugent.

Sussex emphasized their superiority in the one-day game when they beat the West Indies by four wickets in a Challenge match at Hove on September 12.

There were two points which invite criticism. Firstly, the majority of counties were loath to include even one slow bowler in their sides and relied mainly on pace and secondly the placing of the entire field around the boundary to prevent rapid scoring – Dexter used this tactic in the Final – became fairly common. The success of the spinners at Lord's may have exploded the first theory.

There is no doubt that provided the Competition is conducted wisely it will attract great support in the future and benefit the game accordingly.

THE KNOCK-OUT COMPETITION

LANCASHIRE v LEICESTERSHIRE

Played at Manchester, May 1, 2, 1963

Lancashire won by 101 runs. Rain held up the start of this opening match in the new competition, between the two bottom counties of the previous season's Championship. After a delay of three hours the Leicestershire captain, Hallam, put Lancashire in to bat, but the decision did not pay. Without undue recklessness Lancashire averaged 4.67 runs per over for the 65 overs, Grieves and Marner adding 136 for the fourth wicket. Although Hallam, like Marner, made a hard-hit century, Leicestershire found their task too heavy against the accurate pace of Statham and steady medium pace of Marner who won £50 and a gold medal as the "Man of the Match".

Lancashire

B. Booth b Pratt	50	J. B. Statham b Boshier	0
R. Entwistle hit wkt b Pratt	18	K. Higgs not out	7
J. D. Bond lbw b Pratt	7	C. Hilton not out	3
*K. Grieves c Wharton b Savage	57	L-b 4, n-b 2	6
P. Marner c Spencer b Savage	121		
G. Houlton c Spencer b Savage	1	(9 wkts) after 65 overs	304
J. Dyson b Van Geloven	6	1/42 2/62 3/82 4/218 5/225 6/264	
†G. Clayton b Savage	28	7/266 8/280 9/299	

Bowling: Spencer 15–1–48–0; Boshier 12–1–58–1; Pratt 15–2–75–3; Van Geloven 15–2–63–1; Savage 8–0–54–4.

Leicestershire

*M. R. Hallam c and b Marner	106	†R. Julian b Statham	4
H. D. Bird b Statham	7	J. S. Savage b Marner	2
A. Wharton c Clayton b Statham	0	B. S. Boshier not out	0
S. Jayasinghe c Clayton b Statham	1		
C. Inman c Entwistle b Higgs	26	L-b 5	5
J. Van Geloven b Higgs	26		
R. L. Pratt c Bond b Marner	25	1/21 2/21 3/23 4/72 5/164	203
C. T. Spencer b Statham	1	6/183 7/191 8/201 9/203	

Bowling: Statham 12–2–28–5; Higgs 15–2–48–2; Hilton 15–1–73–0; Marner 11.3–0–49–3.

Umpires: R. Aspinall and H. Yarnold.

SOMERSET v NOTTINGHAMSHIRE

Played at Taunton, May 27, 1964

Somerset won by one wicket in extraordinary fashion. They needed four to win with the last pair together when Wells began the final over; Langford took a single, Hall was nearly run out then scored a run, and Langford managed to scramble another off the last ball to equal the scores. Somerset won by the Cup rules because they had lost only nine wickets to ten. M. Hill was named man of the match for his brilliant innings of 107 in just under two hours. He hit three 6s and thirteen 4s after three Nottinghamshire wickets had fallen for 17. Sensible batting from Atkinson, Virgin and Kitchen highlighted the Somerset innings, although Davison nearly ruined their hopes of victory by taking four wickets for six runs in one spell of twelve deliveries.

Nottinghamshire

N. Hill c Virgin b Hall	9	A. J. Corran c Hall b Alley	15
J. B. Bolus b Palmer	6	I. Davison not out	14
B. Whittingham b Palmer	0	J. Cotton b Greetham	6
H. Moore c Eele b Langford	29		
M. Hill c and b Hall	107	B 5, l-b 4	9
K. Gillhouley lbw b Hall	1		
*†G. Millman c Hall b Alley	14	1/15 2/15 3/17 4/127 5/128	215
B. D. Wells b Langford	5	6/163 7/168 8/192 9/194	

Bowling: Hall 13–3–55–3; Palmer 13–3–41–2; Alley 13–5–41–2; Greetham 6.2–1–24–1; Langford 13–2–45–2.

Somerset

G. Atkinson c M. Hill b Davison	69	†P. J. Eele b Corran	4
B. Roe c M. Hill b Cotton	0	B. Langford not out	16
R. Virgin b Davison	43	G. Hall not out	1
*W. E. Alley b Davison	10	B 4, l-b 3, w 2, n-b 1	10
P. B. Wight b Davison	0		——
C. Greetham c Millman b Cotton	21	(9 wkts) after 60 overs	215
M. Kitchen c Gillhouley b Wells	41	1/3 2/109 3/120 4/120 5/127 6/161 7/167	
K. E. Palmer c Cotton	0	8/195 9/206	

Bowling: Cotton 13–2–49–3; Davison 13–2–34–4; Gillhouley 10–0–45–0; Corran 13–6–30–1; Wells 11–2–47–1.

Umpires: J. Langridge and A. E. D. Smith.

MIDDLESEX v DERBYSHIRE

Played at Lord's, May 22, 1965

Middlesex won by 10 runs after a most exciting struggle. They were put in by Derbyshire whose attack of five seamers, backed up by smart fielding, always caused trouble. Six wickets went for 70 before Titmus, the rival captain, hit seven 4s while making 40 not out. Bennett caused Derbyshire to slump after they reached 50 for one wicket. He shot out four opponents while conceding only eight runs and when they were 77 for eight the end seemed near. Then Taylor, the Derbyshire wicket-keeper, who earlier had taken three catches, hit one 6 and six 4s in his 53 not out, the top score of the match. He and Rhodes made an unbroken stand of 74, also the highest in the game, but the quota of overs ran out for this gallant pair, and Taylor had to be content with the man of the match award.

Middlesex

W. E. Russell b Jackson	2	D. Bennett c Hall b Buxton	22
J. M. Brearley lbw b Jackson	24	R. W. Hooker lbw b Morgan	9
R. A. Gale lbw b Rhodes	1	J. S. E. Price b Richardson	3
P. H. Parfitt c Taylor b Morgan	13		
E. A. Clark c Taylor b Richardson	29	B 4, l-b 7, n-b 3	14
†J. T. Murray c Morgan b Rhodes	1		——
R. A. White c Taylor b Buxton	3	1/14 2/17 3/39 4/51 5/55 6/70	161
*F. J. Titmus not out	40	7/84 8/118 9/142	

Bowling: Jackson 13–5–19–2; Rhodes 13–2–33–2; Morgan 10–0–36–2; Richardson 11.3–4–40–2; Buxton 10–5–19–2.

Derbyshire

I. W. Hall lbw b Clark	14	†R. W. Taylor not out	53
I. R. Buxton lbw b Bennett	34	G. W. Richardson c Murray b Price	2
H. L. Johnson c Russell b Bennett	1	H. J. Rhodes not out	26
M. H. Page c Titmus b Bennett	3	B 4, l-b 4, w 1	9
W. F. Oates c Murray b Bennett	9		——
*D. C. Morgan c Murray b Hooker	0	1/35 2/50 3/55 (8 wkts) after 60 overs	151
J. F. Harvey lbw b Price	0	4/64 5/65 6/66 7/66 8/77	

A. B. Jackson did not bat.

Bowling: Price 13–5–20–2; Bennett 13–7–27–4; Clark 13–4–36–1; Titmus 8–1–22–0; Hooker 13–3–37–1.

Umpires: J. Arnold and O. W. Herman.

THE 1965 FINAL

SURREY v YORKSHIRE

Played at Lord's, September 4, 1965

Yorkshire won by 175 runs. Yorkshire deservedly became the new holders of the trophy in a surprisingly one-sided match. Despite this, the 25,000 spectators, of whom over 21,000 paid, received six hours of capital entertainment. Yorkshire, spearheaded by an aggressive Boycott, broke most of the competition's records. Boycott made the highest individual score, shared in the biggest partnership with his captain and Yorkshire reached a new total. The previous highest total – 314 for seven by Sussex against Kent in 1963 – was scored off 65 overs as opposed to 60 overs. Yorkshire, sent in, began slowly but gradually Boycott, well supported by Close, completely mastered Surrey's attack. After an indifferent season and without a first-class century, he cast aside his troubles and played forcing shots all round the wicket. He struck three 6s and fifteen 4s. Close hit one 6 and seven 4s and Storey, alone of Surrey's bowlers, escaped severe punishment. Surrey's batsmen never got into their stride and the writing was on the wall when Trueman sent back Edrich, Smith and Barrington in four deliveries. Illingworth also captured three wickets in one over and Tindall played an almost lone hand. Boycott was an obvious choice as man of the match by the chairman of the England selectors, D. J. Insole.

Because of a 24-hour downpour which made part of the outfield waterlogged the previous day, the match had appeared in jeopardy. Heroic work by the ground-staff, reinforced by drying machines from The Oval, enabled the match to begin only an hour and a half late.

Yorkshire

G. Boycott c Storey b Barrington	146	D. Wilson not out	11
K. Taylor c Barrington b Sydenham	9	B 3, l-b 4, n-b 3	10
*D. B. Close c Edrich b Gibson	79		
F. S. Trueman b Arnold	24	1/22 (4 wkts) after 60 overs	317
J. H. Hampshire not out	38	2/214 3/248 4/292	

D. E. V. Padgett, P. J. Sharpe, R. Illingworth, R. A. Hutton and †J. G. Binks did not bat.

Bowling: Arnold 13–3–51–1; Sydenham 13–1–67–1; Gibson 13–1–66–1; Storey 13–2–33–0; Tindall 3–0–36–0; Barrington 5–0–54–1.

Surrey

*M. J. Stewart st Binks b Wilson	33	†A. Long b Illingworth	17
J. H. Edrich c Illingworth b Trueman	15	G. Arnold not out	3
W. A. Smith lbw b Trueman	0	D. A. D. Sydenham b Illingworth	8
K. F. Barrington c Binks b Trueman	0		
R. A. E. Tindall c Wilson b Close	57	B 4, l-b 4	8
S. J. Storey lbw b Illingworth	1		
M. J. Edwards b Illingworth	0	1/27 2/27 3/27 4/75 5/76 6/76	142
D. Gibson lbw b Illingworth	0	7/76 8/130 9/132	

Bowling: Trueman 9–0–31–3; Hutton 8–3–17–0; Wilson 9–0–45–1; Illingworth 11.4–1–29–5; Close 3–0–12–1.

Umpires: J. S. Buller and C. S. Elliott.

YORKSHIRE v CAMBRIDGESHIRE

Played at Castleford, May 25, 1967

Yorkshire won by six wickets. The match became a desperate improvisation reduced to 10 overs for each side after play had been impossible on any of the three days originally allocated. Assembling at Headingley on the new date arranged, the teams found the ground under water and when they moved to Castleford, some 12 miles away, they met further frustration through a thunderstorm. Honouring the agreement that a result would be obtained whatever the conditions, Cambridgeshire fielded in drenching rain and the cricket verged on the farcical, though some notable catches were held.

Cambridgeshire

D. H. Fairey c Close b Trueman	22	A. Ponder c Sharpe b Close	0
P. A. Shippey c Trueman b Nicholson	0	C. B. Gadsby not out	2
T. Hale c Trueman b Nicholson	1	D. Wing not out	2
*†R. A. Gautrey b Wilson	9	B 1	1
J. H. Wardle b Nicholson	0		
E. Davis c Sharpe b Wilson	6	1/8 2/15 3/24 (8 wkts, 10 overs)	43
S. W. Shippey c Taylor b Close	0	4/24 5/34 6/38 7/40	

A. R. Wilson did not bat.

Bowling: Trueman 3–1–15–1; Nicholson 3–0–11–3; Close 2–0–8–2; Wilson 2–0–8–2.

Yorkshire

J. H. Hampshire c Gadsby b Wardle	1	F. S. Trueman not out	11
K. Taylor c Hall b Wardle	20	R. Illingworth not out	1
*D. B. Close c and b Fairey	1		
D. Wilson c Gadsby b Fairey	12	1/7 2/9 3/26 4/41 (4 wkts)	46

G. Boycott, D. E. V. Padgett, P. J. Sharpe, †J. G. Binks and A. G. Nicholson did not bat.

Bowling: Fairey 3–0–8–2; Wardle 3–0–32–2; Wing 0.5–0–6–0.

Umpires: F. Jakeman and A. Jepson.

KENT v SUSSEX

Played at Canterbury, July 19, 1967

Kent won by 118 runs. A wonderful day's cricket was watched by 16,500 spectators who saw Kent emerge thoroughly deserved winners. After a bad start Luckhurst and Shepherd pulled Kent round with a second-wicket stand of 135, in which the West Indian Shepherd punished the hitherto menacing Sussex attack right from the start of his innings. When Cowdrey arrived the stage was set for a magnificent innings and he did not fail. He raced to his half-century in ten overs and after he lost Luckhurst he added 57 runs in six overs with Knott. Cowdrey hit twelve 4s in his majestic innings, which occupied only eighteen overs and except for some fine fielding by Sussex the Kent total would have been even more impressive. Sussex made a disastrous start, losing three wickets for 27 runs but Suttle and Parks took part in a fighting stand. Sayer, however, dismissed them – two vital wickets – and it was left to Greig and Griffith to provide the final resistance. Greig hooked Shepherd for 6, but at 150 became the first of three reasonably priced victims to Underwood. Sussex then faded completely and their last three wickets fell at the same total. Cowdrey was the Man of the Match.

Kent

M. H. Denness b Snow	2	A. Brown not out	3
B. W. Luckhurst b Greig	78		
J. Shepherd lbw b Bates	77	B 6, l-b 7	13
*M. C. Cowdrey b Greig	78		—
†A. Knott b A. Buss	19	1/3 2/138 3/205	(5 wkts, 60 overs) 293
A. L. Dixon not out	23	4/263 5/281	

S. E. Leary, A. Ealham, D. L. Underwood and D. M. Sayer did not bat.

Bowling: Snow 11–0–65–1; A. Buss 12–2–56–1; Greig 12–0–59–2; Bates 12–0–44–1; Suttle 12–3–47–0; Oakman 1–0–9–0.

Sussex

A. S. M. Oakman b Brown	10	A. Buss not out	6
M. A. Buss c Ealham b Dixon	11	J. A. Snow b Brown	0
K. G. Suttle b Sayer	34	D. L. Bates b Brown	0
G. C. Cooper c Luckhurst b Dixon	0		
*†J. M. Parks b Sayer	44	B 2, l-b 6	8
A. W. Greig b Underwood	33		—
M. G. Griffith c Knott b Underwood	26	1/18 2/26 3/27 4/95 5/116	175
E. Lewis c Leary b Underwood	3	6/152 7/167 8/175 9/175	

Bowling: Brown 8.3–3–17–3; Dixon 12–2–49–2; Sayer 12–0–45–2; Underwood 12–3–26–3; Shepherd 6–1–30–0.

Umpires: P. B. Wight and H. Yarnold.

MIDDLESEX v ESSEX

Played at Lord's, May 4, 6, 1968

Middlesex won by six runs. Middlesex struggled against tight bowling on a rain-interrupted first day, and only an eighth wicket stand of 46 between Hooker and Herman improved their position. Hobbs finished the innings with a hat-trick. Essex ended the first day in trouble at 31 for three, four hostile overs from Price doing the damage. In a battle of attrition on the Monday, Barker and the Essex middle several times threatened to take control, but each time a wicket fell at a vital moment. In one of the most exciting finishes in the history of the competition eight runs were needed from the last over, but Hobbs was bowled by the first ball and Turner run out off the fourth. Boyce won the match award for his medium-pace bowling and his batting.

Middlesex

W. E. Russell b Boyce	26	R. S. Herman b Hobbs	25
M. J. Harris c Fletcher b Boyce	1	J. S. E. Price c Irvine b Hobbs	0
P. H. Parfitt lbw b Boyce	10	R. W. Stewart not out	0
C. T. Radley b Edmeades	11		
*F. J. Titmus b Jorden	21	B 2, l-b 8, n-b 1	11
M. J. Smith c Turner b Edmeades	14		—
†J. T. Murray b Turner	23	1/1 2/27 3/43 4/67	(60 overs) 161
R. W. Hooker b Hobbs	19	5/87 6/103 7/115 8/161 9/161	

Bowling: Boyce 12–3–21–3; Lever 12–2–31–0; Jorden 12–2–28–1; Edmeades 12–3–20–2; Turner 11–2–39–1; Hobbs 1–0–11–3.

Essex

G. Barker c Russell b Stewart	39	R. N. S. Hobbs b Parfitt	11
M. J. Bear lbw b Price	7	J. K. Lever not out	1
†B. Taylor lbw b Price	0	S. Turner run out	1
K. W. R. Fletcher c Murray b Price	10		
B. L. Irvine c Herman b Hooker	20	L-b 2, w 1, n-b 3	6
B. E. Edmeades b Titmus	29		—
K. D. Boyce c and b Hooker	23	1/10 2/10 3/31 4/76 (59.4 overs)	155
A. M. Jorden c Price b Titmus	8	5/86 6/115 7/138 8/141 9/154	

Bowling: Price 12–5–22–3; Herman 12–5–23–0; Stewart 8–3–26–1; Titmus 12–0–35–2; Hooker 12–2–30–2; Parfitt 3.4–0–13–1.

Umpires: J. G. Langridge and A. E. Alderman.

THE 1968 FINAL

SUSSEX v WARWICKSHIRE

Played at Lord's, September 7, 1968

Warwickshire won by four wickets. This was very much the story of Cyril Washbrook's Man of the Match, A. C. Smith. At 155 for six and still 59 runs short of the Sussex total of 214, Warwickshire seemed to be fighting a losing battle. Then Smith, looking every inch the general, brought it to a successful conclusion without further loss. In forty minutes he and Amiss put on 60 runs, demonstrating in the process to the 25,000 onlookers the great charm of these matches which can change face within a very short space of time.

The seventh pair rode their luck admirably, stealing singles which produced a nervous edge in the field; two difficult chances given by Smith in an over from Bates were put down. The triumphant conclusion came with three overs to spare and was marked by Smith being carried shoulder high to receive the trophy.

Smith had also kept wicket splendidly, diving far to his left to hold a thin edge down the leg side offered by Oakman, who with M. A. Buss gave Sussex a sound start in a partnership of 54. This and a stand of 78 between Greig and Parks, made up the bulk of the Sussex innings, which was not altogether impressive considering the side's reputation in knock-out cricket.

With Cartwright and Bannister absent injured, Warwickshire used Amiss as a bowler and his medium-paced deliveries were hit for 63 runs. The Sussex attack was much stronger and when Barber and Kanhai, the real punishers of anything on the loose side, were out cheaply, it seemed to be on top. But a sound 59 in two hours, ten minutes by Stewart served Warwickshire admirably and provided the springboard from which Smith led the onslaught which ended just before seven o'clock with Warwickshire taking the Cup for the second time.

Sussex

M. A. Buss c Smith b Ibadulla	36	*M. G. Griffith not out	15
A. S. M. Oakman c Smith b Ibadulla	31	J. A. Snow not out	2
K. G. Suttle not out	3		
E. R Dexter b Ibadulla	8	L-b 11	11
A. W. Greig b Blenkiron	41		—
†J. M. Parks run out	57	1/54 2/64 3/84 4/85 (7 wkts)	214
G. C. Cooper c Barber b Blenkiron	10	5/163 6/193 7/208	

A. Buss and D. L. Bates did not bat.

Bowling: Brown 12–2–49–0; Blenkiron 12–5–40–2; Ibadulla 12–4–25–3; Amiss 12–0–63–0; Gibbs 12–3–26–0.

Warwickshire

R. W. Barber b Bates	15	R. N. Abberley b M. A. Buss	1
W. J. Stewart c Parks b Bates	59	*†A. C. Smith not out	39
J. A. Jameson c Dexter b M. A. Buss	15	B 1, l-b 10	11
R. B. Kanhai c Griffith b M. A. Buss	3		——
K. Ibadulla c Greig b M. A. Buss	28	1/34 2/64 3/73	(6 wkts, 57 overs) 215
D. L. Amiss not out	44	4/110 5/151 6/155	

W. Blenkiron, D. J. Brown and L. R. Gibbs did not bat.

Bowling: Snow 10–0–32–0; A. Buss 12–4–32–0; Bates 11–2–43–2; M. A. Buss 12–0–42–4; Greig 12–0–55–0.

Umpires: A. Jepson and A. E. Rhodes.

NOTTINGHAMSHIRE v ESSEX

Played at Nottinghamshire, July 2, 1969

Nottinghamshire won by two wickets. Amid scenes of tremendous excitement with spectators invading the pitch, an injured Nottinghamshire batsman, Frost – he damaged a hamstring while fielding – hit the fourth ball of the last over to the boundary to give his county victory. Essex, with 45 overs gone were in deep trouble at 100 for five and then Nottinghamshire lost their grip. Fletcher, missed early by the wicket-keeper, Murray, hit defiantly for 74, which included eight 4s. Stead bowled his medium-fast left-arm deliveries exceptionally well and was rewarded with two wickets in his allotted 12 overs at a cost of only 17 runs. The Essex total looked formidable and Nottinghamshire were not able to take early command in the face of some keen bowling. Indeed, with seven out for 148 the position looked ominous, but Halfyard improved matters with an adventurous knock, Forbes, and the injured Frost, who had the fleet-footed Hassan as his runner, then scampered the runs for victory.

Essex

B. Ward c Murray b Taylor	21	R. N. S. Hobbs c Forbes b White	4
*†B. Taylor c Murray b Stead	4	R. E. East not out	12
G. Barker c Murray b Forbes	5	J. K. Lever not out	1
K. W. R. Fletcher b Forbes	74		
B. L. Irvine b Stead	7	L-b 4, n-b 3	7
K. D. Boyce c Murray b Halfyard	22		——
B. E. Edmeades c Halfyard b Taylor	23	1/5 2/20 3/39 4/48 5/93	180
S. Turner run out	0	6/133 7/133 8/153 9/180	

Bowling: Stead 12–4–17–2; Forbes 12–3–47–2; Taylor 12–3–32–2; Halfyard 12–2–42–1; White 12–2–35–1.

Nottinghamshire

*J. B. Bolus run out	37	M. N. Taylor run out	8
M. J. Harris c Taylor b Lever	11	C. Forbes not out	5
R. A. White c Fletcher b Edmeades	13	D. J. Halfyard c Irvine b Turner	20
M. J. Smedley b Boyce	29	B 1, l-b 10, n-b 6	17
†D. L. Murray c Taylor b Boyce	18		——
G. Frost not out	18	1/19 2/46 3/83 4/96	(8 wkts) 182
S. B. Hassan c East b Edmeades	6	5/110 6/136 7/148 8/159	

B. Stead did not bat.

Bowling: Boyce 12–4–20–2; Lever 12–1–27–1; Edmeades 12–0–41–2; East 12–1–29–0; Turner 11.4–1–48–1.

Umpires: W. E. Alley and C. G. Pepper.

LANCASHIRE v GLOUCESTERSHIRE

Played at Manchester, July 28, 1971

Lancashire won by three wickets. This semi-final attracted a crowd officially returned at 23,520, with receipts of £9,738, and made Gillette Cup history by extending from 11 a.m. to 8.50 p.m., after an hour's delay through rain at lunch time. Winning the toss, Gloucestershire were given a solid start by Green and Nicholls who reached 57 before Green was run out. Nicholls played spendidly for 53 until he was second out at 87 when play reopened and afterwards Procter dominated a well-paced Gloucestershire innings by hitting one 6 and nine 4s in making 65 before being superbly caught behind the wicket.

Gloucestershire contained David Lloyd and Wood so well that Lancashire took 17 overs to raise the first 50 runs. Wood stayed and Pilling built well on a solid foundation, but Lancashire were in trouble when Mortimore dismissed Clive Lloyd and Engineer, and Davey accounted for Sullivan in a mid-innings slump. Play proceeded in gradually worsening light after 7.30 p.m. Bond and Simmons brought Lancashire back into the picture by adding 40 runs from seven overs for the seventh wicket after Bond had opted to play on in light that was now murky to say the least.

When Mortimore bowled Simmons at 203, with 27 needed from the last six overs, Hughes joined Bond and put the issue beyond all doubt with a magnificent onslaught against Mortimore. He hit the off-spinner for 24 runs, two 6s, two 4s and two 2s in the 56th over to make the scores level and amidst mounting tension and with lights on in the pavilion Bond got the winning run off the fifth ball of the 57th over. Hughes was given the Man of the Match award and it was well past ten o'clock before the big crowd dispersed.

Gloucestershire

R. B. Nicholls b Simmons	53	*A. S. Brown c Engineer b Sullivan	6
D. M. Green run out	21	H. Jarman not out	0
R. D. V. Knight c Simmons b Hughes	31	B 2, l-b 14, w 1, n-b 1	18
M. J. Procter c Engineer b Lever	65		——
D. R. Shepherd lbw b Simmons	6	1/57 2/87 3/113 4/150	(6 wkts) 229
M. Bissex not out	29	5 /201 6/210	

J. B. Mortimore, †B. J. Meyer and J. Davey did not bat.

Bowling: Lever 12–3–40–1; Shuttleworth 12–3–33–0; Wood 12–3–39–0; Hughes 11–0–68–1; Simmons 12–3–25–2; Sullivan 1–0–6–1.

Lancashire

D. Lloyd lbw b Brown	31	J. Simmons b Mortimore	25
B. Wood run out	50	D. P. Hughes not out	26
H. Pilling b Brown	21		
C. H. Lloyd b Mortimore	34	B 1, l-b 13, n-b 1	15
J. Sullivan b Davey	10		——
†F. M. Engineer hit wkt b Mortimore	2	1/61 2/105	(7 wkts, 56.5 overs) 230
*J. D. Bond not out	16	3/136 4/156 5/160 6/163 7/203	

P. Lever and K. Shuttleworth did not bat.

Bowling: Procter 10.5–3–38–0; Davey 11–1–22–1; Knight 12–2–42–0; Mortimore 11–0–81–3; Brown 12–0–32–2.

Umpires: H. D. Bird and A. Jepson.

THE 1971 FINAL

LANCASHIRE v KENT

Played at Lord's, September 4, 1971

Lancashire, the holders, won by 24 runs before a crowd of 25,000. This was a wonderful match played on a glorious summer's day and the result hung in the balance until almost the very end. It was possibly the best and most exciting of all the nine Gillette Cup Finals. That Lancashire triumphed for the second successive year was due to a magnificent right-handed catch at extra cover by their captain Bond; he leapt to his right and as he fell backwards he clutched a powerful drive by Asif, Kent's hero whom Ray Illingworth named the Man of the Match.

After Bond had won the toss, Lancashire lost Wood to the second ball of the match, but David Lloyd held fast while Pilling produced some splendid strokes. As Asif began with five consecutive maiden overs, Lancashire found progress difficult and though Clive Lloyd opened his score by hooking Asif for 6, the steady accurate attack of Shepherd and Underwood generally commanded respect. Engineer could muster only eight runs in fifty minutes and when he left Lancashire were 179 for seven in the 54th over. Uninhibited slogging by Simmons and Hughes brought 39 priceless runs for Lancashire from the last four overs.

The pace attack of the two England bowlers, Lever and Shuttleworth, whom Bond used discreetly, proved to be Lancashire's main weapon. Kent lost Luckhurst in the first over and with the first four batsmen going for 68 Lancashire gained control. Then came some sensible batting by Asif and Knott until the England wicket-keeper, with the ball going behind Asif who never anticipated a run, charged down the pitch only to be sent back in futile pursuit.

Following that disaster, Asif excelled with pulls, drives and cuts in a classic display, for he rarely lifted the ball until Bond brought off the catch of the day. On Asif's dismissal, the three remaining Kent wickets went down for three runs in the course of fourteen balls. Actually Asif hit his 89 out of 141 in two and a quarter hours.

Lancashire

B. Wood lbw b Dye	0
D. Lloyd b Shepherd	38
H. Pilling lbw b Dye	21
C. H. Lloyd c Ealham b Asif	66
J. Sullivan run out	8
†F. M. Engineer b Woolmer	24
*J. D. Bond b Underwood	1
J. Simmons not out	28
D. P. Hughes not out	25
L-b 8, w 1, n-b 4	13
1/0 2/45 3/104 4/122 5/145 6/150 7/179 (7 wkts, 60 overs)	224

P. Lever and K. Shuttleworth did not bat.

Bowling: Dye 12–2–51–2; Asif 12–5–36–1; Woolmer 12–1–60–1; Shepherd 12–2–38–1; Underwood 12–3–26–1.

Kent

B. W. Luckhurst c Engineer b Lever	0
D. Nicholls c D. Lloyd b Shuttleworth	4
*M. H. Denness b Wood	29
A. G. E. Ealham b Hughes	22
Asif Iqbal c Bond b Simmons	89
†A. P. E. Knott run out	15
J. N. Shepherd c Hughes b Shuttleworth	18
R. A. Woolmer b Lever	12
B. D. Julien run out	1
D. L. Underwood c Wood b Lever	0
J. C. Dye not out	0
L-b 8, w 1, n-b 1	10
1/0 2/19 3/56 4/68 5/105 6/152 7/197 8/199 9/200 (56.2 overs)	200

Bowling: Lever 11.2–4–24–3; Shuttleworth 10–2–25–2; Wood 12–1–48–1; Hughes 12–1–49–1; Simmons 11–0–44–1.

Umpires: C. S. Elliott and A. E. Fagg.

ESSEX v MIDDLESEX

Played at Westcliff, July 19, 1972

Essex won by eight wickets. On what their captain afterwards described as "an under-prepared pitch", Middlesex offered the slightest of resistance to the pace bowling of Boyce, the Man of the Match, and Lever who, sharing the wickets evenly, dismissed them inside an hour and a half for the smallest total registered in the competition by a first-class county. Only Murray reached double figures and six men were out without scoring. With Price, the Middlesex fast bowler absent with lumbago, Essex achieved the light task without much difficulty.

Middlesex

W. E. Russell c East b Boyce	0
M. J. Smith c Hobbs b Boyce	7
P. H. Parfitt c Boyce b Lever	3
C T. Radley c Saville b Boyce	0
*J. M. Brearley c Taylor b Lever	0
N. G. Featherstone lbw b Lever	8
†J. T. Murray b Boyce	12
K. V. Jones b Boyce	0
C. J. R. Black c Fletcher b Lever	0
M. W. W. Selvey c East b Lever	0
D. A. Marriott not out	0
L-b 10, n-b 1	11
1/7 2/18 3/18 4/19 5/21 6/40 7/40 8/41 9/41 (19.4 overs)	41

Bowling: Boyce 10–3–22–5; Lever 9.4–5–8–5.

Essex

B. E. A. Edmeades c Murray b Selvey	6
G. J. Saville c Murray b Selvey	8
K. W. R. Fletcher not out	15
B. Ward not out	6
B 4, l-b 2, n-b 2	8
1/10 2/24 (2 wkts, 18 overs)	43

K. D. Boyce, K. R. Pont, *†B. Taylor, S. Turner, R. N. S. Hobbs, R. E. East and J. K. Lever did not bat.

Bowling: Selvey 9–2–13–2; Jones 4–1–14–0; Marriott 3–1–3–0; Black 2–1–5–0.

Umpires: W. L. Budd and A. G. T. Whitehead.

THE 1972 FINAL

LANCASHIRE v WARWICKSHIRE

Played at Lord's, September 2, 1972

Lancashire won by four wickets, and so lifted the trophy for the third consecutive year under Jackie Bond's inspiring leadership. No one quarrelled with Basil d'Oliveira when he named Clive Lloyd the Man of the Match. Not only did the talented West Indies cricketer subdue Warwickshire when M. J. K. Smith decided to bat first – he bowled his 12 overs on the trot – but he played one of the finest innings imaginable, hitting his 126 off 42 overs in two and a half hours. Among his many wonderful strokes were three 6s and fourteen 4s.

Earlier, Whitehouse and Smith gave sound displays for Warwickshire and there was a delightful fifty by the left-handed Kallicharran, but really Warwickshire were thwarted when on Kanhai threatening trouble, Bond turned to Hughes, his left-arm slow bowler. Kanhai was tempted and fell, for he hooked a half-volley high and square and there was David Lloyd on the boundary waiting to accept it. Bond's wise use of both Hughes and Simmons proved the value of relying on a varied attack even in limited-over cricket.

Lancashire wanted 235, a target never previously accomplished by the victors batting second in a Gillette Cup match, and they succeeded with more than three overs to spare, but the excitement was maintained to the very end. Lancashire made a sedate start against some splendid bowling and fielding. They lost their openers in 10 overs for 26 and Clive Lloyd made only six runs in the next eight overs. Then he drove Brown with tremendous power and hooked the next ball for 6; these 10 runs from two strokes set him on an inspired course during which he was sustained at the other end by the fine work of Pilling and Hayes. Few of the 25,000 onlookers, plus the untold number who were glued to their TV sets, will forget Lloyd's sparkling straight drives which passed the fielders before they could move. Lancashire needed only 16 when Lloyd left and Bond was a proud man when he received the Cup in front of the pavilion.

Warwickshire

J. Whitehouse st Engineer b Hughes	68	D. J. Brown run out	5
D. L. Amiss lbw b Wood	16	S. J. Rouse run out	0
R. B. Kanhai c D. Lloyd b Hughes	14	R. G. D. Willis not out	2
*M. J. K. Smith lbw b Simmons	48	L. R. Gibbs not out	4
A. I. Kallicharran c Engineer b Sullivan	54		—
†D. L. Murray lbw b Sullivan	10	1/50 2/69 3/122 4/207	(9 wkts) 234
N. M. McVicker run out	1	5/222 6/222 7/224 8/227 9/228	

Bowling: C. H. Lloyd 12–2–31–0; Lee 10–1–48–0; Wood 12–2–27–1; Hughes 12–0–50–2; Sullivan 5–1–27–2; Simmons 9–0–39–1.

Lancashire

D. Lloyd lbw b Brown	10	†F. M. Engineer b Willis	0
B. Wood c and b McVicker	15	D. P. Hughes not out	4
H. Pilling run out	30	L-b 6	6
C. H. Lloyd lbw b Willis	126		—
F. C. Hayes c Murray b Brown	35	1/26 2/26	(6 wkts, 56.4 overs) 235
J. Sullivan not out	9	3/123 4/209 5/219 6/223	

*J. D. Bond, J. Simmons and P. Lee did not bat.

Bowling: McVicker 12–1–44–1; Willis 12–1–29–2; Brown 12–1–67–2; Rouse 10.4–0–45–0; Gibbs 10–0–44–0.

Umpires: C. S. Elliott and A. E. G. Rhodes.

YORKSHIRE v DURHAM

Played at Harrogate, June 30, 1973

Durham won by five wickets. It was the first defeat of a first-class county by a junior side since the Minor Counties joined the competition in its second year, ten years earlier. It meant that Yorkshire had not won a Gillette Cup match since they won the Cup in 1969. When Boycott won the toss and had choice of batting or bowling it seemed that everything was in their favour. Instead, the Durham opening bowlers, Wilkinson and Alan Old (Rugby international brother of the Yorkshireman) performed so steadily that only 18 runs came in the first nine overs. At this stage Wilkinson bowled Boycott and this success lifted the Durham bowlers and fieldsmen to unexpected heights. They seldom bowled a bad ball and the fielding was superb. In spite of a good innings by Johnson, Yorkshire were bowled out in 58.4 overs for only 135 runs. The Durham captain, Lander, returned the best bowling figures of his career, and was Man of the Match. Nicholson and Chris Old, with the new ball, often beat the bat in their opening spell, but they could not upset the determination and concentration of the batsmen. With plenty of time in hand, Inglis scored 47 runs in good style. Durham coasted to victory.

Yorkshire

*G. Boycott b Wilkinson	14
R. G. Lumb c Old b Lander	4
P. J. Sharpe c Cole b Inglis	12
J. H. Hampshire c Inglis b Lander	0
C. Johnson ht wkt b Greensword	44
R. A. Hutton b Lander	0
C. M. Old b March	5
†D. L. Bairstow lbw b Greensword	11
P. Carrick b Lander	18
H. P. Cooper not out	10
A. G. Nicholson b Lander	0
B 1, l-b 6	7
1/18 2/32 3/34 4/49 5/49 6/80 7/100 8/121 9/135 (58.4 overs)	135

Bowling: Wilkinson 12–3–33–1; Old 7–2–10–0; Lander 11.4–3–15–5; Inglis 8–3–23–1; March 8–3–18–1; Greensword 12–2–29–2.

Durham

R. Inglis c Cooper b Carrick	47
S. R. Atkinson c and b Carrick	14
S. Greensword not out	35
J. G. March run out	7
A. G. B. Old c Bairstow b Cooper	6
N. A. Riddell b Nicholson	15
D. W. Soakell not out	10
L-b 4	4
1/58 2/63 3/87 4/96 5/123 (5 wkts, 51.3 overs)	138

P. J. Crane, *B. R. Lander, J. S. Wilkinson and †R. Cole did not bat.

Bowling: Old 8–1–15–0; Nicholson 11.3–3–27–1; Cooper 12–3–25–1; Carrick 12–4–32–2; Hutton 8–1–35–0.

Umpires: C. S. Elliott and A. Jepson.

THE 1973 FINAL

GLOUCESTERSHIRE v SUSSEX

Played at Lord's, September 1, 1973

Gloucestershire won by 40 runs. Inspired by the captain, Tony Brown, whom Alec Bedser named the Man of the Match and the all-round brilliance of Procter, Gloucestershire deserved their first major success since 1877, when they last won the County Championship. Sussex, appearing in their fifth Gillette Cup final, a record, put up a gallant performance before a restricted crowd of 21,300 who paid £56,000. In a remarkable sequence of these finals since 1963, the side batting first has won in alternate years, and Sussex could consider themselves unfortunate in losing the toss as the light deteriorated and was quite bad in the later stages of their innings.

Moreover, Sussex were without one of their key men, Tony Buss, injured, although his deputy, Marshall, a young, quick, red-haired, left-arm bowler, performed most creditably. Gloucestershire had their anxious moments, their worst period being at the beginning when they lost their first three wickets for 27. Procter came to the rescue and he received staunch support from Shepherd and Stovold. Procter promptly struck two short balls from Michael Buss for 6 but at 106 for five Gloucestershire could not have been happy.

This was a critical stage; Brown took charge at one end while Procter, steady and sure in defence, drove and hooked at every opportunity until after batting two and a half hours, he was held at deep square leg for 94. The stand produced 74 and on Procter's departure Brown took up the assault. He hit 46 out of 68 in the last eight overs, passing his fifty when he helped himself to 14 from Spencer in the 56th over. The agile Foat, aged 20, ran like a gazelle while getting seven in a stand of 49, and finally Brown pulled Greig twice for 6, the first into the grandstand balcony.

Greenidge and Morley were not awed by Gloucestershire's formidable total of 248 and gave Sussex a sound start of 52. The side reached 155 for two in 44 overs against a varied attack in which Mortimore played an important part by bowling his 12 overs off the reel for only 32 runs. Prideaux played some grand strokes, but when Procter came back for his second spell in inferior light the issue swung clearly in Gloucestershire's favour.

The Sussex captain tried to steal a leg-bye off the last ball of the over, but the tall and agile Foat swooped in from cover and ran him out before he could get back. Graves continued to bat splendidly, but Knight and Procter were too much for the tail and Gloucestershire in the end won comfortably.

Gloucestershire

Sadiq Mohammad lbw b Buss	9	J. C. Foat b Snow	7
R. D. V. Knight b Snow	2	D. A. Graveney run out	6
Zaheer Abbas b Buss	9		
M. J. Procter c Morley b Buss	94	B 4, l-b 10, n-b 9	23
D. R. Shepherd c Griffith b Marshall	11		
†A. W. Stovold c Griffith b Snow	10	1/5 2/22 (8 wkts, 60 overs)	248
*A. S. Brown not out	77	3/27 4/74 5/106 6/180 7/229 8/248	

J. B. Mortimore and J. Davey did not bat.

Bowling: Snow 12–4–31–3; Greig 12–1–53–0; Buss 12–5–46–3; Marshall 12–3–29–1; Spencer 12–0–66–0.

Sussex

G. A. Greenidge b Knight	76	J. A. Snow b Procter	4
J. D. Morley c Zaheer Abbas b Brown	31	J. Spencer b Knight	2
R. M. Prideaux b Davey	28	R. P. T. Marshall b Procter	0
P. J. Graves not out	36		
*A. W. Greig run out	0	B 5, l-b 9	14
M. A. Buss c Graveney b Knight	5		
†M. G. Griffith b Knight	3	1/52 2/121 3/155 (56.5 overs)	208
M. J. J. Faber not out	9	4/156 5/173 6/180 7/195 8/204 9/207	

Bowling: Procter 10.5–1–27–2; Davey 10–1–37–1; Mortimore 12–3–32–0; Brown 12–1–33–1; Graveney 2–0–18–0; Knight 10–0–47–4.

Umpires: A. E. Fagg and T. W. Spencer.

HAMPSHIRE v GLAMORGAN

Played at Southampton, July 16, 1975

Hampshire won by 164 runs. Hampshire took merciless revenge for the defeat inflicted on them by Glamorgan in the County Championship the previous week. They shattered records by scoring 371 for four and left the act of winning little more than a formality. Hampshire beat the Gillette Cup best of 327 for 7 made by Gloucestershire against Berkshire at Reading in 1966 as well as setting a new figure for all limited-over cricket. That record was held by England, who scored 334 for four against India at Lord's in the World Cup. There were new records for Greenidge, who scored 177 with devastating authority for the highest individual score in one-day competitions. It beat the 173 not out which he himself made against Minor Counties (South) in the Benson & Hedges Cup at Amersham in 1973 and Boycott's Gillette Cup best of 146 for Yorkshire against Surrey in the 1965 final at Lord's. Greenidge bristled with power, but Richards (two 6s and twenty-two 4s), elegant and technically perfect, stroked his way to a hundred before lunch. The pair put on 210 and then Greenidge scored 104 runs in 20 overs. He struck seven 6s and seventeen 4s, and he was Man of the Match.

In South Africa on October 19, 1974 in the first round of the South African Gillette Cup, Eastern Province batting first against Border scored 373 for five wickets from 60 overs. R. G. Pollock going in at 48 for two, scored 222 not out and A. M. Short 115. Their partnership realised 267.

Hampshire

B. A. Richards b Ellis	129	A. M. E. Roberts not out	14
C. G. Greenidge c Hopkins b Nash	177	B 4, l-b 6, n-b 5	15
D. R. Turner lbw b Davis	19		——
T. E. Jesty b Nash	12	1/210 (4 wkts, 60 overs)	371
*R. M. C. Gilliat not out	5	2/284 3/352 4/353	

P. J. Sainsbury, A. J. Murtagh, J. M. Rice, †G. R. Stephenson and R. S. Herman did not bat.

Bowling: Nash 12–1–84–2; Cordle 12–0–81–0; Solanky 12–1–57–0; Ellis 12–1–63–1; Armstrong 6–0–38–0; Davis 6–0–33–1.

Glamorgan

A. Jones lbw b Roberts	4	M. A. Nash b Rice	0
A. L. Jones lbw b Roberts	11	A. E. Cordle c Richards b Herman	8
R. C. Davis st Stephenson b Sainsbury	25	G. D. Armstrong not out	19
*Majid J. Khan c and b Sainsbury	29		
J. A. Hopkins hit wkt b Sainsbury	12	B 2, l-b 16, w 2, n-b 3	23
G. P. Ellis c Stephenson b Jesty	25		——
J. W. Solanky c Richards b Roberts	51	1/19 2/32 3/78 (50.1 overs)	207
†E. W. Jones c Stephenson b Rice	0	4/83 5/98 6/138 7/142 8/144 9/163	

Bowling: Roberts 8.1–1–17–3; Herman 10–1–45–1; Rice 10–1–32–2; Jesty 12–2–37–1; Sainsbury 10–1–53–3.

Umpires: R. Julian and K. E. Palmer.

THE 1976 FINAL

LANCASHIRE v NORTHAMPTONSHIRE

Played at Lord's, September 4, 1976

Northamptonshire won by four wickets. Northamptonshire, for so long the Cinderella county, deserved their first honour in 98 years, winning with eleven balls to spare after as entertaining and exciting limited-over final as there has been in recent seasons.

Lancashire, badly handicapped when Wood broke a finger early in the day, fought hard to retain the Cup in a competition which they have dominated in the seventies. Hughes slogged 26 off Bedi's last over of the Lancashire innings – 4, 6, 2, 2, 6, 6 – to give them a defensible total of 195 for seven. But the absence of Wood, who retired hurt when 14, left them a bowler short and Northamptonshire took full advantage.

A splendid opening partnership of 103 between Willey and Virgin proved vital insurance against any later breakdown. Willey who hit eleven 4s, three in one over from Lever, played some fine back foot strokes through the covers. Virgin gave another solid display although he once relaxed sufficiently to hit Hughes into the pavilion.

The pitch favoured seam bowling more the longer the match continued and Lever, Lee and Ratcliffe were all testing. The Northamptonshire batsmen understandably chose Hughes as the bowler to "get after".

Hughes' tremendous display of hitting was a memorable crescendo to a good Lancashire recovery from a poor start. Dye's inswinging yorker which bowled Engineer without a run scored was a great fillip for Northamptonshire after Mushtaq had put the opposition into bat.

Early pace in the pitch aided them in the dismissal of Pilling and Hayes soon after the withdrawal of Wood when he was hit on the right hand by Dye. However, with the second line bowlers in action Lancashire fought back with a partnership of 95 between Lloyd and Abrahams.

Bedi was not introduced until the 40th over and he got rid of both the left-handers as they tried to accelerate. Simmons and Ratcliffe soon followed and it was left to Hughes to raise Lancashire hopes as Bedi was permitted to bowl the last over, even though Dye and Hodgson had overs in hand. Two of Hughes's sixes went over mid wicket and one over long on, all generously applauded by the bowler who went from three for 26 to three for 52 in a few hectic minutes.

Hughes's effort surpassed his 24 off John Mortimore in the famous twilight finish to the Old Trafford semi-final of 1971, but this time his efforts were not rewarded with a victory.

Colin Cowdrey, the adjudicator, made Willey Man of the Match.

Lancashire

B. Wood retired hurt	14	J. Simmons b Sarfraz	1
†F. M. Engineer b Dye	0	R. M. Ratcliffe c Larkins b Bedi	4
H. Pilling c Cook b Sarfraz	3	P. Lever not out	8
F. C. Hayes c and b Hodgson	19	B 1, l-b 9, w 2, n-b 1	13
*D. Lloyd b Bedi	48		——
J. Abrahams b Bedi	46	1/0 2/17 (7 wkts, 60 overs)	195
D. P. Hughes not out	39	3/45 4/140 5/143 6/148 7/157	

P. G. Lee did not bat.

Bowling: Sarfraz 12–2–39–2; Dye 7–3–9–1; Hodgson 6–3–10–1; Larkins 12–4–31–0; Willey 12–2–41–0; Bedi 11–0–52–3.

Northamptonshire

R. T. Virgin c and b Ratcliffe	53	†G. Sharp not out	10
P. Willey c Engineer b Lee	65	Sarfraz Nawaz not out	3
*Mushtaq Mohammad c Hayes b Ratcliffe	13	B 5, l-b 1, n-b 2	8
D. S. Steele c sub b Hughes	24		——
W. Larkins lbw b Lever	8	1/103 (6 wkts, 58.1 overs)	199
G. Cook c Engineer b Lee	15	2/127 3/143 4/154 5/178 6/182	

A. Hodgson, B. S. Bedi and J. C. J. Dye did not bat.

Bowling: Lever 12–3–29–1; Lee 12–4–29–2; Simmons 11.1–2–29–0; Ratcliffe 12–2–48–2; Hughes 11–0–56–1.

Umpires: A. E. Fagg and H. D. Bird.

HAMPSHIRE v NOTTINGHAMSHIRE

Played at Southampton, June 29, 1977

Hampshire won by ten wickets with 15 overs to spare. Richards and Greenidge, who before the match had been uncertain whether they would be fit to play, scored magnificent centuries as Hampshire won with complete comfort. Although both were in some discomfort, they displayed the full range of strokes and each man reached the century he deserved. Greenidge was first to the century in two hours, fifty minutes, hitting one 6 and thirteen 4s, and Richards followed a minute later, his innings containing one 6 and fifteen 4s. Whereas the batting of Richards and Greenidge was fluent and skilful, the Nottinghamshire innings was laboured, with the exception of Randall, who marked his return to cricket after an arm injury with a jaunty 41. Hassan batted with determination for three hours but there was no other major contribution. Greenidge was "Man of the Match".

Nottinghamshire

S. B. Hassan lbw b Rice	79
†M. J. Harris c Stephenson b Rice	12
D. W. Randall lbw b Elms	41
C. E. B. Rice run out	19
N. Nanan c Jesty b Rice	16
*M. J. Smedley c Cowley b Rice	11
J. D. Birch c Elms b Mottram	10
P. A. Wilkinson c Greenidge b Mottram	4
R. A. White c Elms b Mottram	8
B. Stead not out	2
W. Taylor b Roberts	0
L-b 9, w 2, n-b 2	13
1/24 2/102 3/145 4/176 5/190 6/193 7/199 8/213 9/213	(58.4 overs) 215

Bowling: Roberts 11.4–3–20–1; Mottram 12–0–54–3; Rice 10–1–37–4; Jesty 8–4–27–0; Taylor 12–2–45–0; Elms 5–0–19–1

Hampshire

B. A. Richards not out	101
C. G. Greenidge not out	106
L-b 10, n-b 3	13
(No wkt, 45.1 overs)	220

D. R. Turner, T. E. Jesty, J. M. Rice, N. G. Cowley, M. N. S. Taylor, R. B. Elms, *†G. R. Stephenson, A. M. E. Roberts and T. J. Mottram did not bat.

Bowling: Rice 8–1–19–0; Stead 6–1–27–0; Wilkinson 10.1–1–46–0; Taylor 12–0–73–0; White 7–0–27–0; Birch 2–0–15–0.

Umpires: C. G. Pepper and A. E. G. Rhodes.

KENT v MIDDLESEX

Played at Canterbury, June 29, 30, 1977

Middlesex won by two wickets in a thrilling finish. Three wickets in five balls by Jones put Kent on the rack as they slumped to 47 for five, but Asif and Shepherd staged a magnificent recovery. Jones had to leave the field with a back injury and Asif hit 52 out of 87 with seven 4s. His stand with Shepherd was worth 89 and Shepherd went on to reach a brilliant century in the final over. He hit two 6s and nine 4s in a stay of two and three-quarter hours. Gatting reached 50 in under the hour with six 4s and with Featherstone added 58. When bad light stopped play Middlesex needed 49 to win off nine overs with five wickets in hand. In the forty-five minutes play on the second morning fortunes fluctuated until Middlesex needed six runs to win off the final over with their ninth wicket pair together. In mounting excitement they scrambled home with one ball to spare. Shepherd was Man of the Match.

Kent

R. A. Woolmer c Barlow b Selvey	10
C. S. Cowdrey c Gould b Jones	9
C. J. C. Rowe c Edmonds b Selvey	1
*Asif Iqbal c Gatting b Jones	59
A. G. E. Ealham c Gatting b Jones	0
B. D. Julien c Daniel b Jones	0
J. N. Shepherd c Gould b Gatting	101
†A. P. E. Knott c sub b Jones	11
R. W. Hills c Brearley b Edmonds	7
D. L. Underwood c and b Daniel	2
K. B. S. Jarvis not out	0
B 5, l-b 18, w 2, n-b 1	26
1/18 2/20 3/47 4/47 5/47 6/136 7/166 8/185 9/210 (60 overs)	226

Bowling: Daniel 12–2–49–1; Selvey 12–2–34–2; Jones 8–2–23–5; Featherstone 12–2–31–0; Edmonds 10–1–38–1; Gatting 6–1–25–1.

Middlesex

*J. M. Brearley c Cowdrey b Julien	6
M. J. Smith c Knott b Woolmer	8
G. D. Barlow b Ealham b Asif	39
C. T. Radley lbw b Hills	33
M. W. Gatting b Julien	62
N. C. Featherstone b Julien	21
P. H. Edmonds c Asif b Jarvis	35
†I. J. Gould b Julien	1
M. W. W. Selvey not out	8
W. W. Daniel not out	1
L-b 10, w 2, n-b 1	13
1/10 2/31 3/82 4/114 5/172 6/199 7/205 8/221 (8 wkts, 59.5 overs)	227

A. A. Jones did not bat.

Bowling: Jarvis 9–1–31–1; Julien 11.5–0–45–4; Shepherd 11–1–36–0; Woolmer 12–2–36–1; Hills 10–0–33–1; Asif 6–0–33–1.

Umpires: J. F. Crapp and P. Rochford.

LANCASHIRE v GLOUCESTERSHIRE

Played at Manchester, July 19, 20, 1978

Lancashire won by seven wickets. Winning the toss, Lancashire put Gloucestershire in and saw them bat consistently to total 266 for five. Stovold gave his side a good start with a sound 45 after Sadiq had fallen to Ratcliffe at 42, but it was the stylish Zaheer who gave a crowd of 15,000 most entertainment with a delightful 73 (eight 4s) in an hour and a half. Procter was an able assistant, hitting one 6 and five 4s in his 34, and later Foat – 47 in the closing overs – and Shepherd put the finishing touches to a formidable total. Bad light held up Lancashire's reply after Kennedy had fallen to Brain without scoring, and with Abrahams also failing the home side were in trouble when play continued the following day. Hayes was bowled by Davey for 13, and at 33 for three Lancashire appeared doomed to defeat. Then the two Lloyds, David and Clive, came together to hit centuries and take their side to victory without further loss as they added a record 234 runs for the fourth wicket. David Lloyd's 121 contained one 6 and nine 4s and earned him the Man of the Match award; Clive Lloyd hit three 6s and six 4s in his share of this memorable partnership.

Gloucestershire

†A. W. Stovold b Hughes	45	D. A. Graveney not out	8
Sadiq Mohammad c Hughes b Ratcliffe	12		
Zaheer Abbas c Simmons b Hogg	73	L-b 10, n-b 6	16
*M. J. Procter c Hayes b Simmons	34		—
D. R. Shepherd not out	31	1/42 2/110	(5 wkts, 60 overs) 266
J. C. Foat c Reidy b Ratcliffe	47	3/168 4/171 5/251	

P. Bainbridge, B. M. Brain, N. H. Finan and J. Davey did not bat.

Bowling: Hogg 12–0–71–1; Ratcliffe 12–2–39–2; Reidy 12–3–39–0; Simmons 12–3–46–1; Hughes 12–2–55–1.

Lancashire

A. Kennedy c Stovold b Brain	0	C. H. Lloyd not out	119
D. Lloyd not out	121	B 4, l-b 6, n-b 2	12
J. Abrahams b Brain	2		—
*F. C. Hayes b Davey	13	1/4 2/12 3/33	(3 wkts, 57.3 overs) 267

B. W. Reidy, J. Simmons, D. P. Hughes, †J. Lyon, R. M. Ratcliffe and W. Hogg did not bat.

Bowling: Procter 11–1–33–0; Brain 12–2–42–2; Davey 10.3–1–58–1; Finan 12–2–58–0; Graveney 12–0–64–0.

Umpires: H. D. Bird and B. J. Meyer.

SOMERSET v ESSEX

Played at Taunton, August 16, 1978

Somerset won a tremendous match in which, with the scores level, they lost fewer wickets. On a fresh pitch Lever had both Richards, when 22, and Rose dropped at slip and having survived they added 84 in 23 overs. Richards, in great form which brought him the Man of the Match award, next dominated a partnership of 103 with Roebuck, who played intelligently through 30 overs, and when finally out to a superb catch he had hit one 6, one 5 and fourteen 4s in 45 overs. Marks and Breakwell helped to make the last ten overs worth a vital 79. For Essex, Gooch, missed when 15, attacked strongly through 30 overs; McEwan and then Fletcher, after a slow, fortunate start, supported him well. Hardie drove firmly and Essex needed 122 from the last eighteen overs. Slocombe ran out Hardie, but Pont, who hit two 6s, and Fletcher, who stayed 40 overs, finished with an all-out attack, the pair adding 80 in twelve overs. With 42 required off five overs, Essex looked likely winners, but then Botham ran out Pont and caught and bowled Fletcher in successive overs. After some hectic cricket, the last over arrived with 12 needed from the last two wickets. Smith hit a single and East edged a boundary before being bowled by Dredge. Dredge then produced a no-ball which, with an overthrow, brought three. Lever had to get three from the last ball, but Rose's throw just beat Smith as he tried for the third.

Somerset

*B. C. Rose c East b Pont	24	G. I. Burgess b Lever	5
P. A. Slocombe lbw b Phillip	0	D. Breakwell not out	17
I. V. A. Richards c Denness b Gooch	116	B 10, l-b 14, w 1, n-b 3	28
P. M. Roebuck c Lever b Phillip	57		—
I. T. Botham b East	7	1/2 2/86	(6 wkts, 60 overs) 287
V. J. Marks not out	33	3/189 4/208 5/247 6/255	

†D. J. S. Taylor, J. Garner and C. H. Dredge did not bat.

Bowling: Lever 12–0–61–1; Phillip 11–1–56–2; Turner 8–6–22–0; Pont 6–1–35–1; Gooch 12–0–42–1; East 11–1–43–1.

Essex

M. H. Denness c Marks b Dredge	3	R. E. East b Dredge	10
G. A. Gooch c Taylor b Garner	61	†N. Smith run out	6
K. S. McEwan b Burgess	37	J. K. Lever not out	5
*K. W. R. Fletcher c and b Botham	67		
B. R. Hardie run out	21	B 14, l-b 9, n-b 2	25
K. R. Pont run out	39		—
N. Phillip run out	1	1/9 2/70 3/127 (60 overs)	287
S. Turner b Botham	12	4/166 5/246 6/248 7/248 8/266 9/281	

Bowling: Garner 12–1–46–1; Dredge 12–0–60–2; Botham 12–1–48–2; Burgess 12–1–43–1; Breakwell 2–0–11–0; Marks 1–0–13–0; Richards 9–1–41–0.

Umpires: D. G. L. Evans and A. Jepson.

THE 1979 FINAL

SOMERSET v NORTHAMPTONSHIRE

Played at Lord's, September 8, 1979

Somerset won by 45 runs, before a capacity crowd of 25,000 who saw them gain their first victory in any competition since they were formed 104 years previously. Next day they completed a memorable double by heading the John Player League. Everything went right for Somerset, for even when Brian Rose lost the toss, Jim Watts, the Northamptonshire captain, sent them in to bat on a perfect summer's morning.

While Somerset's triumph was a team effort, two of their West Indies players achieved outstanding performances. Vivian Richards gave of his best in scoring 117 and, when Northamptonshire faced the enormous task of getting 270, Joel Garner, the 6ft 8in fast bowler, took six wickets for 29.

Richards, whom Cyril Washbrook named Man of the Match, batted superbly from the seventh to the last over; he did not offer a chance. Most of his eleven boundaries came from powerful leg hits and straight drives during an innings which lasted three hours and nine minutes. The two left-handers. Rose and Denning, gave Somerset a brisk start; both were severe on Griffiths but had to pay respect to Sarfraz. Then came a tidy spell of twelve overs off the reel by Watts, and after Tim Lamb had suffered from Richards, Willey bowled his off-spinners to good purpose, although he could not tame Richards. Botham, in his most belligerent mood, struck five hearty 4s while putting on 41 in seven overs with Richards. Just before the end of the Somerset innings, Watts broke a bone in his right hand when taking a hot return from the deep and took no further part in the match.

Immediately Northamptonshire began their task, Garner, with three slips, removed Larkins in the first over and Williams, glancing Garner to fine leg, trod on his wicket. With two men out for 13 the issue already seemed decided. Then the talented Allan Lamb joined Cook and repaired the damage to some extent as they added 113 in thirteen overs. Cook was most impressive until he tried a risky second run and failed to get home against Roebuck's swift return from long-on. Willey was another Garner victim, well caught low and wide of the off stump by Taylor. Allan Lamb maintained his pleasing aggression for nearly two and a half hours and Somerset were greatly relieved when Richards had him smartly stumped for 78 (nine 4s). Now half the wickets were down in the 48th over for 170. Next Richards held Yardley at deep extra cover and, although Sharp and Sarfraz offered token resistance, Somerset went to their inevitable victory. They took the Cup and £5,500; Northamptonshire received £2,500.

Somerset

*B. C. Rose b Watts	41
P. W. Denning c Sharp b Sarfraz	19
I. V. A. Richards b Griffiths	117
P. M. Roebuck b Willey	14
I. T. Botham b T. M. Lamb	27
V. J. Marks b Griffiths	9
G. I. Burgess c Sharp b Watts	1
D. Breakwell b T. M. Lamb	5
J. Garner not out	24
†D. J. S. Taylor not out	1
B 5, l-b 3, n-b 3	11
1–34 2–95 3–145 4/185 5/213 6/214 7/219 8/268 (8 wkts, 60 overs)	269

K. F. Jennings did not bat.

Bowling: Sarfraz 12–3–51–1; Griffiths 12–1–58–2; Watts 12–2–34–2; T. M. Lamb 12–0–70–2; Willey 12–2–45–1.

Northamptonshire

G. Cook run out	44
W. Larkins lbw b Garner	0
R. G. Williams hit wkt b Garner	8
A. J. Lamb st Taylor b Richards	78
P. Willey c Taylor b Garner	5
T. J. Yardley c Richards b Burgess	20
†G. Sharp b Garner	22
Sarfraz Nawaz not out	16
T. M. Lamb b Garner	4
B. J. Griffiths b Garner	0
*P. J. Watts absent hurt	
B 6, l-b 9, w 5, n-b 7	7
1/3 2/13 3/126 4/138 5/170 6/182 7/218 8/224 9/224 (56.3 overs)	224

Bowling: Garner 10.3–3–29–6; Botham 10–3–27–0; Jennings 12–1–29–0; Burgess 9–1–37–1; Marks 4–0–22–0; Richards 9–0–44–1; Breakwell 2–0–9–0.

Umpires: D. J. Constant and J. G. Langridge.

NOTES BY THE EDITOR, 1981

THE GILLETTE CONNECTION

A word of gratitude to Gillette, who were one of the pioneers of modern cricket sponsorship from which they have now withdrawn. So smoothly did their knockout cup overcome the objections to one-day cricket that one of their reasons for giving it up was that it had come to be associated not with anything they made but almost exclusively with cricket. Their place has been taken by the National Westminster Bank. At a dinner to mark the end of the Gillette connection, Clive Lloyd was nominated as the outstanding cricketer of their eighteen years in the game.

BENSON AND HEDGES CUP

MINOR COUNTIES (SOUTH) v HAMPSHIRE

Played at Amersham, April 28, 1973

Hampshire won by 128 runs, repeating their easy win of the previous season. Greenidge and Turner mastered the Minor Counties' bowling in a second wicket partnership of 285, the highest in one-day cricket. Greenidge, who hit two 6s and twenty-three 4s, also reached the biggest score in this class of the game. Turner hit three 6s and seventeen 4s. The loss of four wickets for 20 runs ended all the Minor Counties' hopes, though Mence and Smith batted well later. Greenidge received the Gold Award.

Hampshire

B. A. Richards c Rosier b Bond	18
C. G. Greenidge not out	173
D. R. Turner not out	123
L-b 6, w 1	7
1/36 (1 wkt, 55 overs)	321

*R. M. C. Gilliat, R. V. Lewis, T. E. Jesty, P. J. Sainsbury, M. N. S. Taylor, †G. R. Stephenson, R. S. Herman and T. J. Mottram did not bat.

Bowling: Bond 11–1–34–1; Laitt 11–1–70–0; Rosier 11–0–68–0; Mence 11–1–62–0; Smith 11–0–80–0.

Minor Counties (South)

D. S. Mackintosh c Gilliat b Herman	9
A. G. Warrington b Mottram	4
R. Pearman lbw b Mottram	0
A. R. Garofall b Taylor	17
T. K. Rosier b Herman	3
J. K. S. Edwards c Gilliat b Sainsbury	32
M. D. Mence run out	50
†F. E. Collyer c Taylor b Sainsbury	11
*J. Smith c Sainsbury b Mottram	50
D. J. Laitt c Mottram b Jesty	6
R. E. Bond not out	0
B 6, w 2, n-b 3	11
1/9 2/15 3/17 4/20 5/64 6/70 7/98 8/173 9/187 (52.1 overs)	193

Bowling: Herman 11–1–46–2; Mottram 8.1–1–28–3; Jesty 9–0–18–1; Taylor 11–3–18–1; Sainsbury 11–2–65–2; Richards 2–0–7–0.

Umpires: A. G. T. Whitehead and P. B. Wight.

LANCASHIRE v GLAMORGAN

Played at Manchester, June 13, 1975

Lancashire won by 159 runs. Winning the toss, Lancashire lost Wood with only nine runs scored from nine overs, but Pilling and David Lloyd took the total to 93 before the Lancashire captain fell to Solanky. Pilling went on to hit ten 4s and one 5 in his not out 109 and Lancashire were able to shrug off the cheap dismissal of C. H. Lloyd and Hayes when Sullivan hit 50 out of a fifth wicket partnership of 100 in 14 overs spread over forty-four minutes of attacking batsmanship. Glamorgan needed a good start, but Lever wrecked Frederick's stumps in his first over and Lee had Alan Jones caught at the wicket in his opening over. Majid then fell to a remarkable catch when he hit his rival captain full on the head at short leg in pulling Lever, only to see Pilling make the catch running in from mid-on. David Lloyd was taken to hospital with concussion, but returned and watched Glamorgan shot out for 68. Simmons picked up three victims for only five runs after Lee, Lever and Shuttleworth had prepared the way. Pilling receiving the Gold Award.

Lancashire

*D. Lloyd c A. Jones b Solanky	41	†F. M. Engineer not out	6
B. Wood b Williams	3		
H. Pilling not out	109	B 2, l-b 7, n-b 2	12
C. H. Lloyd b Davis	5		—
F. C. Hayes run out	1	1/9 2/93 (5 wkts, 55 overs)	227
J. Sullivan c Solanky b Williams	50	3/110 4/113 5/213	

J. Simmons, P. Lever, K. Shuttleworth and P. Lee did not bat.

Bowling: Cordle 11–2–36–0; Nash 11–2–27–0; Williams 11–1–63–2; Solanky 11–2–27–1; Davis 11–0–62–1.

Glamorgan

R. C. Fredericks b Lever	6	†E. W. Jones not out	0
A. Jones c Engineer b Lee	6	A. E. Cordle b Simmons	0
*Majid J. Khan c Pilling b Lever	0	D. L. Williams b Simmons	0
A. R. Lewis c Engineer b Shuttleworth	13		
M. J. Lewellyn b Lee	7	B 4, l-b 2	6
J. W. Solanky lbw b Simmons	13		—
R. C. Davis c Pilling b Wood	9	1/6 2/12 3/12 (36.5 overs)	68
M. A. Nash c Hayes b Wood	8	4/21 5/39 6/58 7/67 8/68 9/68	

Bowling: Lever 6–1–15–2; Lee 8–2–16–2; Shuttleworth 9–3–14–1; Wood 10–4–12–2; Simmons 3.5–1–5–3.

Umpires: R. Julian and C. G. Pepper.

HAMPSHIRE v GLOUCESTERSHIRE

Played at Southampton, June 22, 1977

Gloucestershire won by seven runs. There was much to excite a full house in this splendid game, yet all was overshadowed by a tremendous individual performance by Procter, the Gloucestershire captain, who ripped away the Hampshire front line batting by taking their first four wickets in five balls, including a hat-trick. At full pace Procter bowled Greenidge with the fifth ball of his third over. Then he dismissed Richards, Jesty and Rice with the first three balls of his fourth. Hampshire were 18 for four, but a match of swinging fortune saw them rally thanks to a gallant partnership of 109 between Turner and Cowley. However, Brain's return put Gloucestershire on top again and Procter, in his second spell, took two more wickets to finish with six for 13. Inevitably, he won the Gold Award, but Hampshire did well to get so close after their disastrous start. Earlier, Stovold and Sadiq particularly, had batted splendidly and their opening stand of 106 should have been the platform for a more substantial Gloucestershire score.

Gloucestershire

†A. V. Stovold c Turner b Mottram 46	J. H. Shackleton st Stephenson b Mottram 1
Sadiq Mohammad c Greenidge b Rice 76	M. J. Vernon c Jesty b Mottram 2
Zaheer Abbas c Richards b Jesty 11	B. M. Brain b Roberts 2
*M. J. Procter c Greenidge b Taylor 8	
D. R. Shepherd run out 18	B 1, l-b 8, n-b 1 10
J. C. Foat c Stephenson b Taylor 1	
M. D. Partridge b Taylor 0	1/106 2/121 3/146 4/162 (54.2 overs) 180
D. A. Graveney not out 5	5/164 6/168 7/169 8/174 9/176

Bowling: Roberts 10.2–3–20–1; Mottram 10–2–21–3; Taylor 11–1–37–3; Rice 11–0–39–1; Jesty 11–1–39–1; Murtagh 1–0–14–0.

Hampshire

B. A. Richards lbw b Procter 3	*†G. R. Stephenson b Procter 10
C. G. Greenidge b Procter 9	A. M. E. Roberts b Brain 17
D. R. Turner b Brain 49	T. J. Mottram not out 3
T. E. Jesty lbw b Procter 0	
J. M. Rice b Procter 0	L-b 9, n-b 9 18
N. G. Cowley b Shackleton 59	
M. N. S. Taylor c Stovold b Proctor 4	1/13 2/18 3/18 4/18 (54.3 overs) 173
A. J. Murtagh c Stovold b Brain 1	5/127 6/137 7/138 8/144 9/159

Bowling: Procter 11–5–13–6; Brain 10.3–4–28–3; Shackleton 11–4–33–1; Partridge 6–1–22–0; Graveney 6–0–24–0; Vernon 10–2–35–0.

Umpires: T. W. Spencer and D. J. Constant.

WORCESTERSHIRE v SOMERSET

Played at Worcester, May 23, 24, 1979

Worcestershire beat Somerset by ten wickets when the Somerset captain, Rose, sacrificed all known cricketing principles by deliberately losing the game. His declaration after one over from Holder, who bowled a no-ball to concede the only run, enabled Somerset to maintain their superior striking rate in the group.

In the end, Worcestershire and Somerset went forward when Glamorgan's final match was rained off, thus preventing the Welsh county from joining the other two teams with nine points. Rose won the battle of mathematics but lost all the goodwill which Somerset had gained by playing attractive cricket in the preceding years. Worcestershire, embarrassed if not totally angered, refunded admission money to 100 paying spectators after Turner had scored two singles to complete their victory in a match which lasted for sixteen deliveries and only twenty minutes, including the ten minutes between the innings. Worcestershire chairman, Mr Geoffrey Lampard commented: "It is a great pity when the supreme game of cricket is brought down to this level". The TCCB met at Lord's on June 1 and Somerset, for bringing the game into disrepute, were disqualified from the Benson and Hedges Cup by seventeen votes to one (Derbyshire).

Somerset

*B. C. Rose not out	0
P. W. Denning not out	0
N-b 1	1
(no wkt dec., 1 over)	1

P. M. Roebuck, I. V. A. Richards, I. T. Botham, V. J. Marks, D. Breakwell, †D. J. S. Taylor, H. R. Moseley, C. H. Dredge and K. F. Jennings did not bat.

Bowling: Holder 1–1–0–0.

Worcestershire

G. M. Turner not out	2
J. A. Ormrod not out	0
(No wkt, 1.4 overs)	2

P. A. Neale, E. J. O. Hemsley, Younis Ahmed, D. N. Patel, †D. J. Humphries, V. A. Holder, J. D. Inchmore, *N. Gifford and A. P. Pridgeon did not bat.

Bowling: Dredge 1–0–1–0; Jennings 0.4–0–1–0.

Umpires: C. T. Spencer and J. van Geloven.

NOTES BY THE EDITOR, 1980

SOMERSET'S SHAME

The old saying "It is not cricket" used to be universal when something shady was done in any walk of life, but in modern times cricket has so often blotted its copybook that one rarely hears the term these days. It certainly applied when Somerset, to ensure their passage to the Benson and Hedges Cup quarter-finals, cut short their match against Worcestershire at Worcester to exactly seventeen balls, including one no ball. It was all over in eighteen minutes, and the Somerset players left the ground fourteen minutes later.

Somerset entered the match with nine points from previous contests, and they had the faster rate of taking wickets than either of their challengers in Group A, Worcestershire and Glamorgan, both with six points. Somerset risked nothing by declaring after one over and allowing Worcestershire no chance to improve their wicket-taking rate. Somerset were within the law governing the competition – it has since been changed – but they showed no consideration to their sponsors or the spectators. Brian Rose, the Somerset captain, was condemned in the cricket world for his action, although I understand it was planned by some members of his team.

Donald Carr, secretary of the TCCB said: "Somerset's action is totally contrary to the spirit of the competition." Colin Atkinson, the Somerset president and a former captain of the county, tried unsuccessfully to have the match replayed. Within eight days, the TCCB, at an emergency meeting, banned Somerset for their "indefensible" Cup declaration, and their place was given to Glamorgan, who played and lost to Derbyshire at Cardiff.

THE 1979 FINAL

ESSEX v SURREY

Played at Lord's, July 21, 1979

Essex won by 35 runs, and carried off their first trophy since the present county club was formed 103 years earlier. They achieved it in a great match, and with the highest total ever made in a Benson and Hedges final. The main hero was Gooch, the England batsman to whom Trevor Bailey rightly gave the Gold Award. His 120 was the first century ever scored in eight Benson and Hedges finals and came in three hours and twenty-four minutes. His innings was one of high quality and memorable strokes, including three mighty 6s and eleven 4s. When he was fifth to leave, he had seen Essex amass 273 runs, following Knight's decision to take the field.

Praise must also be given to Surrey for a stout-hearted performance. Whereas Essex were at full strength, Surrey were without their key fast bowler, Sylvester Clarke, and Jackman was not really fit to play, although he made a brave and valuable contribution.

With the Lord's groundsman, Jim Fairbrother, able to provide a fast, true pitch, there were other fine batting displays besides that by Gooch. After Denness had helped Essex to take 21 from the first three overs, and partnered Gooch in an opening stand of 48 in ten overs, McEwan was at his brilliant best for ninety-eight minutes. He stroked ten boundaries while scoring 72 in a stand of 124. Then came Fletcher, the studious Essex captain, who further enriched the cricket, while Essex met some really capable bowling from Wilson, the tall young paceman, who took four for 56. Knight kept a steady length and line and eventually removed his rival captain. Intikhab delivered his mixed spin skilfully but for once Pocock had an off day and suffered accordingly.

Needing 291 to win, Surrey faced their mammoth task with admirable courage, but Essex possessed five quality bowlers and Fletcher was able to reserve some late overs for his main spearheads, Lever and Phillip. Surrey lost their opening pair, Butcher and Lynch, for 45. Knight gave the innings momentum with some splendid strokes and hit 52 in just over an hour. After a quiet beginning, Howarth hit boldly for 74 until Fletcher held a skier at mid-wicket. Surrey needed 71 from the last ten overs but, despite an unbeaten 39 from Roope, could not rise to the occasion, and their last five wickets mustered only 50 runs as the light deteriorated.

Essex

M. H. Denness c Smith b Wilson	24	N. Phillip c Howarth b Jackman	2
G. A. Gooch b Wilson	120	S. Turner not out	1
K. S. McEwan c Richards b Wilson	72	B 3, l-b 8, w 1, n-b 2	14
*K. W. R. Fletcher b Knight	34		——
B. R. Hardie c Intikhab b Wilson	4	1/48 2/172 3/239 (6 wkts, 55 overs)	290
K. R. Pont not out	19	4/261 5/273 6/276	

†N. Smith, R. E. East and J. K. Lever did not bat.

Bowling: Jackman 11–0–69–1; Wilson 11–1–56–4; Knight 11–1–40–1; Intikhab 11–0–38–0; Pocock 11–0–73–0.

Surrey

A. R. Butcher c Smith b Lever	13	†C. J. Richards b Turner	1
M. A. Lynch c McEwan b East	17	P. I. Pocock b Phillip	7
G. P. Howarth c Fletcher b Point	74	P. H. L. Wilson b Lever	0
*R. D. V. Knight c Smith b Pont	52		
D. M. Smith b Phillip	24	B 4, l-b 16, w 1, n-b 5	26
G. R. J. Roope not out	39		——
Intikhab Alam c Pont b Phillip	1	1/21 2/45 3/136 4/187 (51.4 overs)	255
R. D. Jackman b East	1	5/205 6/219 7/220 8/226 9/250	

Bowling: Lever 9.4–2–33–2; Phillip 10–2–42–3; East 11–1–40–2; Turner 11–1–47–1; Pont 10–0–67–2.

Umpires: H. D. Bird and B. J. Meyer.

TCCB DISCIPLINARY COMMITTEE

INCIDENT AT LORDS

The Disciplinary Committee took the opportunity to remind counties of their duty to ensure high standards of behaviour from their players following an incident between Imran Khan and J. M. Brearley in the Middlesex v Sussex Benson and Hedges Cup quarter-final in June [1980]. The Board asked both clubs to hold inquiries into the incident and when these were completed the Board stated:

"The Disciplinary Committee of the TCCB will not be meeting officially to discuss the incident. Both counties have taken action over the matter and fully accept the necessity to maintain the best standards of behaviour on the field of play. The incident occurred during a tense part of the game when Imran questioned the umpire on the amount of short-pitched bowling being delivered. On hearing this, Brearley made a remark to Imran which could be considered provocative and Imran reacted heatedly. Sussex have reprimanded Imran for his part and warned him as to his future conduct. It is accepted that Brearley used no bad language, but both he and Middlesex have expressed regrets that he became involved and thus contributed to an incident which otherwise would not have taken place. Both clubs have stated unequivocally that they fully support the stand taken by the Board on the question of behaviour. At all times it is the object of the Disciplinary Committee to encourage clubs to keep their own house in order in the best interests of the game. In this instance both clubs have acted responsibly and the chairman of the Disciplinary Committee is confident that the point has been made sufficiently clearly to each club."

THE 1981 FINAL

SOMERSET v SURREY

Played at Lord's, July 25, 1981

Somerset won by seven wickets to claim the Benson and Hedges Cup for the first time. On the day they were much the better side, restricting Surrey to 194 for eight, a total they passed with 10.3 overs to spare. As he makes a habit of doing, Vivian Richards, Somerset's great West Indian batsman, carried off the main honours, including the Gold Award, with a brilliant innings of 132 not out.

Having been sent in by Rose, Surrey made a hesitant start, being just 15 for one after seventeen overs, and only a good innings of 92 by their captain, Knight, gave respectability to their total. Howarth was out of form, and although Lynch and Clarke made some punishing blows they were both out too soon to stretch Somerset's target demandingly, Clarke to a superb running catch by Popplewell at mid-wicket. Garner's bowling figures were cripplingly economical.

When Somerset lost Denning and Rose in the first three overs of their innings, Richards was obliged to play himself in with some care. Having done so, he finished by treating the bowling much as he pleased. Roebuck made a useful and obdurate 22, and by the time the match ended Botham was trading strokes with Richards in a way that suggested 275 might not have been out of Somerset's reach. It was a handicap to Surrey that Clarke was not fully fit, and his appearance in the final delayed his recovery from the back injury which kept him out for most of the rest of the season.

The takings were £161,937 and the attendance 21,130.

Surrey

G. S. Clinton c Roebuck b Marks	6	G. R. J. Roope not out	14
†C. J. Richards b Garner	1	D. J. Thomas b Garner	0
*R. D. V. Knight c Taylor b Garner	92	R. D. Jackman not out	2
G. P. Howarth c Roebuck b Marks	16	B2, l-b 14, w 2, n-b 1	19
M. A. Lynch c Garner b Popplewell	22		—
D. M. Smith b Garner	7	1/4 2/16 3/63 (8 wkts, 55 overs)	194
S. T. Clarke c Popplewell b Garner	15	4/98 5/132 6/166 7/182 8/183	

P. I. Pocock did not bat.

Bowling: Garner 11–5–14–5; Botham 11–2–44–0; Dredge 11–0–48–0; Marks 11–5–24–2; Popplewell 11–0–45–1.

Somerset

*B. C. Rose b Jackman	5	I. T. Botham not out	37
P. W. Denning b Clarke	0	N-b 1	1
I. V. A. Richards not out	132		——
P. M. Roebuck c Smith b Knight	22	1/5 2/5 3/110 (3 wkts, 44.3 overs)	197

N. F. Popplewell, V. J. Marks, D. Breakwell, J. Garner, †D. J. S. Taylor and C. H. Dredge did not bat.

Bowling: Clarke 8–1–24–1; Jackman 11–1–53–1; Thomas 5.3–0–32–0; Pocock 11–1–46–0; Knight 9–0–41–1.

Umpires: H. D. Bird and B. J. Meyer.

JOHN PLAYER LEAGUE

HAMPSHIRE v MIDDLESEX

Played at Portsmouth, July 19, 1970

Middlesex won by eight wickets. Parfitt's "pocket computer" and a hard-hit 49 by Russell took Middlesex to victory in a rain-affected match. Parfitt's "computer" – a piece of paper on which he had recorded Hampshire's over-by-over score – was vital for Middlesex. He knew his side not only had to score 135 in 35 overs to win, but they also had to keep ahead of the Hampshire total for each over in case rain ended play abruptly. In fact, they always kept ahead and would have won at any stage after ten overs. Hampshire, who batted first on a damp wicket suffered two interruptions and they owed most to Livingstone and Jesty, who put on 59 in 11 overs. Middlesex found the men for the situation in Russell and Parfitt, both of whom paused to consult the "computer" every other over.

Hampshire

B. L. Reed c Featherstone b Jones	26
K. J. Wheatley c Featherstone b Connolly	0
D. R. Turner c Murray b Jones	12
*R. E. Marshall c Murray b Black	6
D. A. Livingstone not out	36
T. E. Jesty c Black b Connolly	32
A. T. Castell c Radley b Price	0
†G. R. Stephenson b Titmus	1
R. M. H. Cottam b Connolly	4
J. W. Holder not out	4
B 2, l-b 9, n-b 2	13
1/0 2/25 3/42 4/48 5/107 6/108 7/113 8/126 (8 wkts, 35 overs)	134

D. Shackleton did not bat.

Bowling: Price 8–1–22–1; Connolly 8–1–31–3; Jones 8–1–42–2; Black 8–1–20–1; Titmus 3–1–6–1.

Middlesex

W. E. Russell c Stephenson b Holder	49
M. J. Smith c Stephenson b Cottam	17
*P. H. Parfitt not out	41
C. T. Radley not out	25
L-b 6	6
1/34 2/95 (2 wkts, 31.5 overs)	138

N. G. Featherstone, †J. T. Murray, F. J. Titmus, K. V. Jones, A. N. Connolly, J. S. E. Price and C. J. R. Black did not bat.

Bowling: Shackleton 8–1–22–0; Cottam 7–0–27–1; Holder 8–0–30–1; Castell 3.5–0–27–0; Jesty 5–0–26–0.

Umpires: A. E. Fagg and C. G. Pepper.

HAMPSHIRE v KENT

Played at Bournemouth, September 6, 1970

Hampshire won by eight wickets. This was a fine last match of the season, providing the crowd of 5,000 with superb entertainment. Basking in September sunshine, they saw 441 runs scored in four hours and the full glory of Richards. When Kent batted first, Denness went cheaply, but Luckhurst and Asif attacked with power and Cowdrey felt that Kent's

220 could be a winning total. Richards was in such majestic form that Kent were powerless to stay in the game. The young South African, at the end of a three-year contract with Hampshire, rarely allowed the ball to pass the bat as he struck three 6s and fifteen 4s in his not-out 132. He used all the strokes in the book, many deployed with almost arrogant ease, others defiant, some savage and fierce. But he never slogged; this was perfect batting, aggressive but correct. Kent, although beaten, had the satisfaction of finishing runners-up to Lancashire.

Kent

M. H. Denness b Cottam	2
B. W. Luckhurst b Jesty	59
Asif Iqbal c Livingstone b Sainsbury	70
J. N. Shepherd c and b Sainsbury	19
*M. C. Cowdrey c Stephenson b Holder	24
S. E. Leary run out	1
†A. P. E. Knott not out	24
A. Brown b Cottam	3
R. A. Woolmer not out	9
L-b 8, n-b 1	9
1/10 2/135 3/141 4/162 5/171 6/188 7/193 (7 wkts, 40 overs)	220

D. L. Underwood and J. C. Dye did not bat.

Bowling: Cottam 8–0–27–2; Castell 8–1–35–0; Holder 8–0–52–1; Sainsbury 8–0–45–2; Jesty 8–0–52–1.

Hampshire

B. A. Richards not out	132
C. G. Greenidge c Brown b Dye	10
D. R. Turner b Underwood	48
*R. E. Marshall not out	23
B 4, l-b 4	8
1/20 2/156 (2 wkts, 33.5 overs)	221

D. A. Livingstone, P. J. Sainsbury, T. E. Jesty, †G. R. Stephenson, A. T. Castell, J. W. Holder and R. M. H. Cottam did not bat.

Bowling: Brown 6–1–27–0; Dye 6.5–0–56–1; Shepherd 5–0–29–0; Woolmer 8–0–57–0; Underwood 8–0–44–1.

Umpires: W. E. Alley and A. Jepson.

HAMPSHIRE v YORKSHIRE

Played at Bournemouth, September 5, 1971

Hampshire won on faster scoring rate over 34 overs. Amid scenes of confusion, Hampshire won by a margin of 0.12 runs per over. Chasing Yorkshire's 40-over score of 202 for five, to which Boycott and John Hampshire had been the principal contributors, Hampshire reached 176 for four off 34 overs – whereupon the umpires uprooted the stumps and strode towards the pavilion. The 5,000 crowd were stunned and clearly felt cheated out of a fine finish and nobody seemed to know what was happening. It was then announced that Sunday League matches must end at 6.30 if more than five overs remain unbowled. Thus if Yorkshire had squeezed in one more over the match could have continued and Boycott must be blamed for not ensuring that this happened. Yorkshire's run rate was 5.05 from 40 overs and Hampshire's 5.17 from 34. Richards had been in dazzling form, while Marshall was at the wicket when the game ended prematurely.

Yorkshire

*G. Boycott c and b Jesty 61	D. E. V. Padgett not out 0
J. H. Hampshire st Stephenson b Sainsbury . 62	
A. J. Dalton c Stephenson b Cottam 39	L-b 11, n-b 2 13
J. D. Woodford c Gilliat b Jesty 15	—
C. Johnson c Gilliat b Jesty 4	1/121 2/138 (5 wkts, 40 overs) 202
†D. L. Bairstow not out 8	3/171 4/193 5/194

R. A. Hutton, H. P. Cooper, M. K. Bore and A. G. Nicholson did not bat.

Bowling: Cottam 8–1–36–1; Castell 8–2–28–0; Sainsbury 8–0–37–1; Jesty 8–0–58–3; Holder 8–0–30–0.

Hampshire

B. A. Richards c Hampshire b Woodford... 81	T. E. Jesty not out 23
C. G. Greenidge b Nicholson 3	B 4, l-b 10, w 3, n-b 1 18
D. R. Turner run out 18	—
R. E. Marshall not out 32	1/28 2/93 (4 wkts, 34 overs) 176
*R. M. C. Gilliat run out 1	3/125 4/127

P. J. Sainsbury, A. T. Castell, †G. R. Stephenson, J. W. Holder and R. M. H. Cottam did not bat.

Bowling: Nicholson 8–1–16–1; Bore 8–1–52–0; Hutton 8–0–31–0; Cooper 5–0–16–0; Woodford 5–0–33–1.

Umpires: D. L. Evans and P. B. Wight.

KENT v LEICESTERSHIRE

Played at Folkestone, July 18, 1971

Kent won by nine wickets. Leicestershire, starting at four runs an over, ran into trouble and lost half the side for 94. Then Illingworth and Tolchard added 49 in eight overs but Underwood polished off the innings. What followed will be remembered for some fabulous Kent batting and one over, the seventh, bowled by McKenzie. He was no-balled eight times in an over, which contained 14 deliveries, under the front foot rule by Alley, the Australian-born umpire. Denness struck six 4s and a two, five of the no-balls registered, and the total had jumped dramatically by 31 runs at the end of the over. Denness, scoring powerfully all round the wicket, altogether hit one 6 and thirteen 4s in eighty-five minutes. When the hard-hitting Nicholls was dismissed Asif took up the assault. Kent won with 14 overs to spare in one of the most dramatic Sunday League matches.

Leicestershire

B. Dudleston b Woolmer 20	J. D. D. Pember c Johnson b Underwood... 2
M. E. Norman c Knott b Shepherd 31	G. D. McKenzie b Dye 2
B. F. Davison b Woolmer 12	C. T. Spencer not out 1
C. Inman b Underwood 22	
J. F. Steele c Julien b Shepherd 6	L-b 4, n-b 1 5
*R. Illingworth c Knott b Underwood 30	—
†R. W. Tolchard not out 31	1/49 2/61 3/73 (9 wkts, 40 overs) 168
P. M. Stringer c Knott b Underwood 6	4/80 5/94 6/143 7/154 8/163 9/167

Bowling: Dye 8–0–39–1; Julien 8–1–44–0; Shepherd 8–1–32–2; Woolmer 8–1–22–2; Underwood 8–2–26–4.

Kent

*M. H. Denness not out	83
D. Nicholls c Tolchard b Pember	28
Asif Iqbal not out	49
L-b 2, n-b 7	9
1/83 (1 wkt, 26 overs)	169

A. G. E. Ealham, †A. P. E. Knott, J. N. Shepherd, G. W. Johnson, R. A. Woolmer, B. D. Julien, D. L. Underwood and J. C. Dye did not bat.

Bowling: McKenzie 4–0–34–0; Spencer 4–0–28–0; Stringer 8–0–48–0; Pember 8–0–44–1; Davison 1–0–2–0; Dudleston 1–0–4–0.

Umpires: W. E. Alley and A. G. T. Whitehead.

SOMERSET v NORTHAMPTONSHIRE

Played at Taunton, June 27, 1971

Somerset won in a thrilling finish by one wicket with two balls to spare in a match reduced by rain to 36 overs each. Willey led a capable batting performance by the visitors, who had had a long trip from Worcester, and this seemed enough when Somerset slumped to 8 for three in four overs. Burgess, dropped when 31, and Clarkson restored the position with a fine stand of 70 in 17 overs. Then, as wickets fell steadily in poor light, Cartwright, in a lucky, but forthright innings, held his side together. With one over to go, Somerset were level with three wickets left. Hodgson, the most economical of the bowlers, clean bowled Moseley with his second ball and Langford was run out off the next. Cartwright, however, pushed away the fourth, just beating the throw for the deciding single.

Northamptonshire

P. Willey b Cartwright	45
H. M. Ackerman b Moseley	5
D. S. Steele b Cartwright	20
Mushtaq Mohammad c O'Keeffe b Langford	15
*P. J. Watts b Moseley	19
B. S. Crump run out	19
†G. Sharp not out	7
D. Breakwell run out	8
B 3, l-b 7, w 1	11
1/14 2/58 3/79 4/98 5/130 6/139 7/149 (7 wkts, 36 overs)	149

P. Lee, A. Hodgson and R. R. Bailey did not bat.

Bowling: Jones 8–0–26–0; Moseley 8–1–35–2; Cartwright 8–2–21–2; O'Keeffe 4–0–18–0; Burgess 7–0–36–0; Langford 1–0–2–1.

Somerset

R. T. Virgin b Bailey	6
M. J. Kitchen c Sharp b Lee	0
D. B. Close c Sharp b Lee	0
G. I. Burgess c Willey b Crump	46
A. Clarkson b Lee	41
T. W. Cartwright not out	35
†D. J. S. Taylor c Mushtaq b Hodgson	2
K. J. O'Keeffe c Watts b Willey	7
H. R. Moseley b Hodgson	1
*B. A. Langford run out	0
A. A. Jones not out	0
L-b 11, n-b 1	12
1/6 2/6 3/8 4/78 5/116 6/121 7/140 8/149 9/149 (9 wkts, 35.4 overs)	150

Bowling: Bailey 7–2–29–1; Lee 8–1–26–3; Willey 8–0–41–1; Crump 7–0–32–1; Hodgson 5.4–1–10–2.

Umpires: J. G. Langridge and A. G. T. Whitehead.

SOMERSET v SURREY

Played at Torquay, July 4, 1971

Somerset won an enthralling match, full of ups and downs, by four runs, taking three wickets for three runs in the last seven balls. Their innings was founded on a remarkable 101 not out by Virgin who was dropped four times while hitting two 6s and eleven 4s. Kitchen helped him in an opening stand that produced 90 in 22 overs. After Close had edged a ball into his face, Cartwright gave valuable help, Virgin reaching his century off the final ball. Fine batting by Edrich, Younis (70 in 24 overs), Roope and Stewart gave Surrey a good chance, but Somerset, Taylor in particular, held their catches well. Although Surrey needed only eight off seven balls with five wickets left, a good boundary catch by Virgin followed by Burgess's decisive last over swung the game finally and dramatically. The gate takings were a record £1,272, and fifteen 6s were hit.

Somerset

R. T. Virgin not out	101
M. J. Kitchen c Roope b Storey	40
D. B. Close retired hurt	12
G. I. Burgess b Hooper	0
A. Clarkson c Roope b Hooper	7
T. W. Cartwright c Hooper b Jackman	26
H. R. Moseley c Long b Jackman	6
†D. J. S. Taylor not out	9
B 7, l-b 11	18
1/90 2/116 3/132 4/177 5/186 (5 wkts, 40 overs)	219

K. J. O'Keeffe, *B. A. Langford and A. A. Jones did not bat.

Bowling: Arnold 8–0–43–0; Jackman 8–0–24–2; Pocock 8–1–28–0; Hooper 6–0–46–2; Storey 8–0–44–1; Roope 2–0–16–0.

Surrey

J. H. Edrich c Kitchen b Langford	39
M. J. Edwards c Taylor b Moseley	4
Younis Ahmed c Taylor b Burgess	70
S. J. Storey c O'Keeffe b Langford	4
G. R. J. Roope sub b Jones	35
*M. J. Stewart c Virgin b Jones	37
J. M. M. Hooper lbw b Burgess	13
P. I. Pocock not out	0
†A. Long b Burgess	1
G. G. Arnold not out	1
B 2, l-b 8, n-b 1	11
1/26 2/58 3/72 4/144 5/157 6/212 7/212 8/214 (8 wkts, 40 overs)	215

R. D. Jackman did not bat.

Bowling: Jones 8–0–39–2; Langford 8–0–47–2; Cartwright 8–2–27–0; Burgess 7–0–56–3; Moseley 8–0–35–1.

Umpires: J. F. Crapp and A. Jepson.

SOMERSET v GLOUCESTERSHIRE

Played at Taunton, August 28, 1977

Somerset won by nine wickets with 17.5 overs to spare. Gloucestershire, put in by Close, began well with an opening stand of 33 in nine overs, but a spell of three for 1 in 10 deliveries by Burgess changed the match. As he received excellent support, notably from the spinners Marks and Breakwell, only Hignell, with a fighting 50 in 29 overs extended the innings to 127. Rose and Denning, the latter ending with seven boundaries in a crisp 41 not out, put on 56 in 16 overs and then Richards played an amazing innings. Escaping a stunning chance when 7, he struck Graveney for 34 in one over, and ended with 62 in twenty-four minutes, having hit six 6s and five 4s.

Gloucestershire

Sadiq Mohammad c Richards b Burgess	16	J. H. Shackleton run out	2
†A. W. Stovold c Denning b Burgess	17	B. M. Brain b Dredge	1
Zaheer Abbas c Taylor b Jennings	12	N. H. Finan not out	1
*M. J. Procter b Burgess	0		
A. J. Hignell st Taylor b Breakwell	50	B 1, l-b 4, w 1	6
D. R. Shepherd b Jennings	9		
J. C. Foat c Kitchen b Breakwell	6	1/33 2/40 (39.4 overs)	127
D. A. Graveney c Taylor b Dredge	7	3/40 4/51 5/84 6/101 7/118 8/122 9/125	

Bowling: Burgess 8–2–20–3; Dredge 8–0–34–2; Marks 8–1–15–0; Jennings 8–0–28–2; Breakwell 7.4–0–24–2.

Somerset

B. C. Rose c Hignell b Finan	21
P. W. Denning not out	41
I. V. A. Richards not out	62
L-b 3, w 3, n-b 1	7
1/56 (1 wkt, 22.1 overs)	131

M. J. Kitchen, *D. B. Close, V. J. Marks, †D. J. S. Taylor, D. Breakwell, G. I. Burgess, C. H. Dredge, and K. F. Jennings did not bat.

Bowling: Procter 4–1–10–0; Brain 4–1–13–0; Graveney 7–0–50–0; Finan 5–0–28–1; Shackleton 2–0–17–0, Sadiq 0.1–0–6–0.

Umpires: R. Julian and W. E. Phillipson.

SOMERSET v ESSEX

Played at Taunton, September 3, 1978

Somerset, needing a tie to win the League, lost to Essex by two runs in an agonising finish, doubly poignant after their defeat in the Gillette Cup final that previous day. Essex, put in, slumped to 29 for three but recovered remarkably. Fletcher, dropped at the wicket first ball off Burgess, attacked vividly, almost with abandon in the later stages of his innings of 32 overs, and he hit seven 4s. Pont helped him to add 63 in eighteen overs; and then Hardie's assault helped produce a decisive 98 from the final eleven overs. Bold batting from Botham, in 21 overs, Richards, Roebuck, and Slocombe took Somerset to 157 for seven in 36 overs, but despite brave efforts from Dredge and Jennings, they just failed to get 11 from the last over, or five from the final two balls, to tie. Gate receipts were a record at £7,600.

Essex

A. W. Lilley c Denning b Burgess	13	B. R. Hardie b Botham	38
G. A. Gooch c Burgess b Botham	7	L-b 16, n-b 3	19
K. S. McEwan b Moseley	2		
*K. W. R. Fletcher not out	76	1/16 2/25 (5 wkts, 40 overs)	190
K. R. Pont b Dredge	35	3/29 4/92 5/190	

N. Phillip, S. Turner, R. E. East, †N. Smith and J. K. Lever did not bat.

Bowling: Botham 8–0–38–2; Moseley 8–0–20–1; Burgess 8–0–20–1; Jennings 8–0–38–0; Dredge 8–0–55–1.

Somerset

*B. C. Rose b Lever	9	C. H. Dredge b Lever	14
P. W. Denning c Smith b Phillip	8	†D. J. S. Taylor run out	4
I. V. A. Richards c Hardie b Gooch	26	H. R. Moseley run out	0
P. M. Roebuck b East	30		
I. T. Botham c McEwan b Phillip	45	B 2, l-b 12, w 1, n-b 3	18
P. A. Slocombe b Lever	20		
G. I. Burgess c and b Turner	0	1/18 2/18 3/69 4/87 (40 overs)	188
K. F. Jennings not out	14	5/139 6/140 7/157 8/177 9/185	

Bowling: Lever 8–0–38–3; Phillip 8–0–35–2; Gooch 8–0–31–1; Turner 8–0–32–1; East 8–0–34–1.

Umpires: W. E. Alley and D. J. Halfyard.

SURREY v SUSSEX

Played at The Oval, May 28, 1978

Surrey won by seven wickets. Thomas marked his entry into the 1978 John Player League competition by taking the first four wickets for one run as Sussex plumbed the depths with six wickets down and only four runs scored. After this deplorable opening they recovered a little with the help of 33 from former Surrey wicket-keeper Long, but it was not enough to make a fight of it. With just two first-class and two one-day appearances in 1977, Thomas burst back on the scene with his left-arm fast medium, dismissing Barclay and Imran Khan with the second and third balls of the match and sending back Groome with the first delivery of his second over following the run out of Mendis, Parker was his fourth victim caught at the wicket as numbers one to five in the Sussex order went back to the pavilion with "ducks". The scoreboard read nought for four after thirteen balls.

Sussex

J. R. T. Barclay c Smith b Thomas	0	G. G. Arnold c and b Payne	8
G. D. Mendis run out	0	J. Spencer not out	21
Imran Khan c Richards b Thomas	0	R. G. L. Cheatle not out	9
J. J. Groome c Howarth b Thomas	0		
P. W. G. Parker c Richards b Thomas	0	B 3, l-b 7, w 1	11
M. A. Buss b Jackman	1		
C. P. Phillipson b Pocock	16	1/0 2/0 3/0 (9 wkts, 40 overs)	99
†A. Long c Jackman b Knight	33	4/0 5/4 6/4 7/30 8/53 9/73	

Bowling: Thomas 8–4–13–4; Jackman 8–4–15–1; Knight 8–3–18–1; Payne 8–2–32–1; Pocock 8–3–10–1.

Surrey

Younis Ahmed c Cheatle b Buss	24	D. M. Smith not out	21
G. P. Howarth c Groome b Imran	10	B 1, l-b 2, w 2, n-b 3	8
*R. D. V. Knight b Arnold	2		
G. R. J. Roope not out	39	1/13 2/21 3/53 (3 wkts, 33 overs)	104

I. R. Payne, Intikhab Alam, R. D. Jackman, D. J. Thomas, †C. J. Richards and P. I. Pocock did not bat.

Bowling: Imran 8–2–21–1; Arnold 8–1–18–1; Spencer 8–2–17–0; Buss 7–1–27–1; Cheatle 1–0–5–0; Phillipson 1–0–8–0.

Umpires: H. D. Bird and D. J. Halfyard.

OTHER MATCHES

AN ENGLAND XI v SIR FRANK WORRELL'S XI

Played at Birmingham, September 8, 9, 10, 1964

Sir Frank Worrell's XI won by 193 runs. The brilliance of Kanhai overshadowed everything else in this match and helped West Indies to a fine recovery after Coldwell had taken six for 36 on a green pitch on the opening day. Kanhai hit six 6s and twenty 4s and made his 170 in two hours, fifty minutes. Moreover he did not offer a chance until he reached 135. After lunch he made 149 of 260 added in forty-two overs and his fourth-wicket stand with Butcher yielded 201 in ninety-two minutes. Dexter alone shone with the bat for the England side. His superb driving and leg strokes earned him one 6 and eleven 4s in his 84 which was largely responsible for his team gaining a first innings lead of 46. Later when they wanted 403 to win Dexter took out his bat for 110. He showed splendid judgement in chosing the ball to punish and he hit sixteen 4s.

West Indian XI

R. E. Marshall c A. C. Smith b Coldwell	7	c Dexter b Flavell	33
C. S. Smith c Brearley b Cartwright	20	c Brearley b Gifford	68
S. M. Nurse b Coldwell	29	lbw b Coldwell	69
R. B. Kanhai c Brearley b Coldwell	4	c Gifford b Coldwell	170
G. S. Sobers c Brearley b Flavell	29	not out	19
B. F. Butcher b Coldwell	0	c Gifford b Coldwell	74
*Sir Frank Worrell b Coldwell	25		
†D. L. Murray b Gifford	8	lbw b Flavell	0
L. A. King b Gifford	14		
C. C. Griffith b Coldwell	0		
L. R. Gibbs not out	0		
L-b 1	1	B 4, l-b 9, n-b 2	15
1/17 2/48 3/57 4/68 5/76 6/107 7/123 8/129 9/129	137	1/44 2/117 3/224 4/425 5/435 6/448	(6 wkts dec.) 448

Bowling: *First Innings*—Flavell 15–1–63–1; Coldwell 23–0–36–6; Cartwright 13–8–22–1; Gifford 4–1–15–2. *Second Innings*—Flavell 12.4–1–53–2; Coldwell 16–2–63–3; Cartwright 15–2–88–0; Gifford 23–2–99–1; Barber 12–2–61–0; Dexter 12–0–69–0.

An England XI

P. R. Richardson b King	31	c Sobers b King	4
J. M. Brearley b King	1	run out	3
D. Kenyon b King	1	c Murray b Worrell	12
*E. R. Dexter c Griffith b Sobers	84	not out	110
R. M. Prideaux c Smith b Sobers	12	c Murray b Marshall	21
R. W. Barber run out	18	c Kanhai b Sobers	24
T. W. Cartwright st Murray b Sobers	2	b Gibbs	2
†A. C. Smith c Griffith b Sobers	10	c Murray b Sobers	0
N. Gifford c Sobers b Gibbs	3	b Gibbs	4
L. J. Coldwell c Smith b Gibbs	0	b Gibbs	8
J. A. Flavell not out	9	st Murray b Gibbs	6
L-b 10, n-b 2	12	B 14, w 1	15
1/2 2/14 3/49 4/130 5/143 6/160 7/167 8/174 9/174	183	1/7 2/7 3/27 4/75 5/116 6/131 7/140 8/149 9/197	209

Bowling: *First Innings*—Griffith 7–1–24–0; King 10–2–32–3; Gibbs 16–2–56–2; Sobers 15–2–59–4. *Second Innings*—Griffith 2–1–3–0; King 9–1–31–1; Worrell 11–1–37–1; Marshall 7–1–16–1; Gibbs 19.5–4–60–4; Sobers 17–4–47–2.

OLD ENGLAND XI v LORD'S TAVERNERS XI

Played at Lord's, June 11, 1966

Old England XI won by three wickets. Two England stalwarts of not long ago, Compton and May, batting in their varying styles, helped to bring about the victory with thirty-seven minutes to spare. Compton, partnered at first by his former Middlesex ally, Edrich, in a stand of 33, showed many of his inimitable strokes while scoring 50 quickly and May seemed to have lost little of his lustre in contributing 43. Compton's noted "all-sorts" brought him the game's best bowling figures too, four for 62, during a Taverners' innings which would indeed have been a sorry sight but for a ninth-wicket stand of 56 between Laker and Clarke.

Lord's Taverners

J. D. Robertson c Edrich b Compton	30	E. A. Bedser c May b Ikin	20
A. H. Phebey b A. V. Bedser	5	Dr C. B. Clarke b Compton	42
B. A. Barnett b Perks	4	J. C. Laker c McIntyre b Ikin	39
L. Livingstone c McIntyre b Edrich	23	J. W. Martin not out	2
R. Benaud b Watkins	4		
J. F. Pretlove b Compton	19	1/5 2/18 3/52 4/57 5/73	190
D. Frost b Compton	2	6/81 7/92 8/118 9/174	

Bowling: A. V. Bedser 6–1–14–1; Perks 6–1–11–1; Watkins 5–0–16–1; Edrich 9–0–35–1; Wright 6–1–15–0; Compton 10.4–0–62–4; Ikin 9–1–37–2.

Old England XI

R. T. Simpson b Laker	33	A. J. McIntyre not out	3
J. G. Dewes b Laker	37	A. V. Bedser not out	4
W. J. Edrich c Pretlove b E. A. Bedser	14		
D. C. S. Compton c Pretlove b Benaud	50	L-b 3	3
P. B. H. May b Pretlove	43		
J. T. Ikin b E. A. Bedser	1	1/71 2/72 3/105 4/141	(7 wkts) 191
A. J. Watkins run out	3	5/146 6/157 7/186	

R. T. D. Perks and D. V. P. Wright did not bat.

Bowling: Martin 8–0–35–0; Livingstone 2.3–1–1–0; E. A. Bedser 18–6–43–2; Laker 10–1–28–2; Benaud 18–2–47–1; Clarke 6–1–14–0; Pretlove 5.4–0–20–1.

Umpires: T. C. Burrell and H. P. Sharp.

IRELAND v MCC

Played at Dublin, September 3, 5, 6, 1966

MCC won by 36 runs. Despite an excellent recovery in which O'Riordan, getting a fair amount of pace, took six wickets for 35 runs as MCC slumped to 67 all out in their second innings, Ireland could not avert another defeat which followed those against Middlesex and Scotland. They were "destroyed" by Bailey, the former Essex and Oxford University medium-pace bowler, who took thirteen for 57 in the match. He controlled the last day, which began with Ireland seemingly well placed, needing 90 to win with seven wickets in hand. The only score over fifty came from Pretlove, formerly of Cambridge University and Kent. He hit 81 for MCC in just over two and a half hours.

MCC

*M. H. Bushby b O'Riordan	2	hit wkt b Anderson	5
B. L. Reed c Huey b Torrens	41	c Hope b O'Riordan	11
R. A. Gale b Torrens	0	absent hurt	0
J. F. Pretlove b O'Riordan	81	c and b O'Riordan	9
M. A. Eagar c Colhoun b Lang	8	lbw b O'Riordan	0
A. R. Duff not out	30	c McCall b O'Riordan	0
†C. R. Howland run out	1	b O'Riordan	21
P. L. Bedford b Anderson	21	c Lang b Anderson	0
J. D. Piachaud c and b Anderson	7	not out	17
J. A. Bailey c Pigot b Huey	8	c Pigot b O'Riordan	0
G. H. Chesterton b Anderson	0	b Anderson	0
B 1, l-b 7, n-b 3	11	B 1, l-b 1, w 1, n-b 1	4
1/17 2/22 3/92 4/135 5/139 6/141 7/182 8/190 9/209	210	1/17 2/20 3/20 4/20 5/37 6/38 7/50 8/56 9/67	67

Bowling: *First Innings*—O'Riordan 29–7–63–2; Torrens 14–5–37–2; Lang 17–4–36–1; Huey 15–3–51–1; Anderson 4.3–1–12–3. *Second Innings*—O'Riordan 17–6–35–6; Anderson 10–2–18–3; Torrens 2–1–8–0; Huey 6–4–2–0.

Ireland

H. C. McCall c Duff b Piachaud	33	b Bailey	6
D. R. Pigot b Bailey	4	c Eager b Bailey	0
B. A. O'Brien c sub b Duff	29	c Howland b Bailey	22
I. Anderson b Bailey	44	lbw b Bailey	12
A. J. O'Riordan c Reed b Duff	8	lbw b Duff	19
D. M. Pratt b Duff	5	b Bailey	8
K. W. Hope lbw b Bailey	0	not out	0
†O. D. Colhoun st Howland b Duff	0	b Duff	0
D. Lang not out	0	b Bailey	1
R. Torrens b Bailey	4	b Bailey	0
*S. S. Huey b Bailey	0	c Eagar b Bailey	0
B 18, l-b 4	22	B 15, l-b 4, w 2, n-b 3	24
1/5 2/49 3/107 4/115 5/137 6/138 7/145 8/145 9/149	149	1/5 2/16 3/35 4/44 5/59 6/81 7/91 8/92 9/92	92

Bowling: *First Innings*—Bailey 19.2–7–33–5; Chesterton 9–7–9–0; Piachaud 22–8–46–1; Pretlove 12–7–12–0; Duff 21–9–27–4. *Second Innings*—Bailey 32.1–22–24–8; Chesterton 11–9–3–0; Piachaud 4–1–14–0; Duff 20–13–27–2.

Umpires: J. Connerton and K. Orme.

INTERNATIONAL CAVALIERS v BARBADOS

Played at Scarborough, September 3, 4, 5, 1969

International Cavaliers won by 11 runs. Pollock's fine batting in the first innings, when he reached his century in fifty-two minutes, overshadowed everything else in the match, which Cavaliers won with four minutes to spare. Pollock batted faultlessly on an easy-paced pitch. He scored his first fifty runs in twenty-six minutes, and kept up the same rate for the second fifty, employing a wide range of powerful and graceful strokes, with the cover-drive predominant. He hit 101, including nineteen 4s and a 6, off sixty-seven deliveries. His century was the fastest in England since R. M. Prideaux scored one in the same time for South v North at Blackpool in 1961 – a feat then recorded in Wisden as the quickest since 1937. In the second innings Pollock hit 61 (two 6s and six 4s) in sixty-five minutes. Barbados, who fielded seven Test players, needed 301 to win in four hours. Bynoe and Lashley shared in an opening partnership of 110 and only four wickets were down for 233, but the side failed to sustain a consistent effort.

International Cavaliers

R. C. Fredericks b Bethell	40	– c sub b Brancker	43
D. M. Green c Boxhill b Maxwell	47	– c Lashley b Maxwell	15
R. Collins c Boxhill b Edwards	58	– b Holford	28
L. Rowe b Holford	1	– run out	8
R. G. Pollock c Blades b Edwards	101	– c Lashley b Brancker	61
P. D. Swart c Boxhill b Hall	1	– c Blades b Brancker	19
J. B. Mortimore b Holford	9	– c Boxhill b Holford	20
*F. S. Trueman c Nurse b Edwards	26	– st Boxhill b Brancker	11
N. J. N. Hawke b Holford	27	– c Hall b Brancker	2
P. Trimborn c Lashley b Holford	7	– not out	18
†T. G. Evans not out	4	– not out	0
B 13, l-b 3, n-b 3	19	L-b 6	6
1/80 2/113 3/124 4/253 5/254 6/268 7/276 8/318 9/335	340	1/27 2/73 3/94 4/107 5/138 6/199 7/200 8/202 9/223 (9 wkts dec.)	231

Bowling: *First Innings*—Hall 11–0–48–1; Edwards 23–4–102–3; Bethell 6–1–19–1; Maxwell 16–4–60–1; Holford 19.2–2–92–4. *Second Innings*—Hall 3–0–11–0; Edwards 3–0–15–0; Bethell 5–1–11–0; Maxwell 8–1–26–1; Holford 21–2–78–2; Brancker 23–3–84–5.

Barbados

M. R. Bynoe c and b Swart	43	– c Rowe b Mortimore	75
P. D. Lashley c and b Trueman	46	– c and b Green	56
C. Blades c Evans b Trimborn	48	– c Fredericks b Trimborn	25
D. A. J. Holford b Mortimore	32	– c Collins b Hawke	22
*S. M. Nurse b Mortimore	5	– b Trimborn	45
A. Bethell c and b Green	6	– lbw b Trimborn	0
R. C. Brancker c Green b Swart	51	– c and b Hawke	7
†D. Boxhill c Pollock b Swart	14	– b Trimborn	2
R. Edwards c Green b Swart	16	– b Trueman	22
W. W. Hall c Fredericks b Mortimore	2	– run out	13
L. Maxwell not out	0	– not out	0
B 3, l-b 4, n-b 1	8	B 6, l-b 12, n-b 4	22
1/68 2/117 3/158 4/163 5/186 6/186 7/232 8/254 9/271	271	1/110 2/162 3/167 4/233 5/241 6/241 7/265 8/268 9/289	289

Bowling: *First Innings*—Trueman 10–1–41–1; Hawke 11–5–26–0; Trimborn 8–0–22–1; Mortimore 38–15–83–3; Swart 14.1–0–74–4; Green 8–1–17–1. *Second Innings*—Trueman 11–0–52–1; Hawke 4–0–20–2; Trimborn 19.3–3–64–4; Mortimore 23–2–89–1; Green 10–2–42–1.

Umpires: J. S. Buller and T. W. Spencer.

THE 1970 TEST MATCHES

By Norman Preston

When England were forced by the Government to cancel the tour arranged for South Africa to the United Kingdom in 1970 the authorities at Lord's through the Test and County Cricket Board devised a series of five matches against The Rest of the World. At the same time it was announced that England caps would be given to the home team and that the matches would be accorded the dignity of unofficial Test status. The counties agreed to release any of their players required for the Rest, whose sides were chosen by F. R. Brown (manager), G. S. Sobers (captain) and L. E. G. Ames (secretary-manager of Kent).

The series was sponsored by Guinness who put up a handsome silver trophy and £20,000, of which £13,000 went to the players and £7,000 to the counties. The winning team in each Test thus received £2,000 and the winners of the rubber £3,000.

The Rest won four matches and so carried off the main spoils, a curious feature being that in all five matches victory went to the side that fielded first.

Another interesting factor was the presence of five of the South African players fresh from their country's clean sweep in the four unofficial Test matches against Australia earlier in the year: E. J. Barlow, B. A. Richards, R. G. Pollock, P. M. Pollock and M. J. Procter. There were also five West Indies representatives in the successful side, G. S. Sobers, C. H. Lloyd, R. B. Kanhai, L. R. Gibbs and D. L. Murray. Pakistan supplied two, their captain Intikhab Alam, and Mushtaq Mohammad, while Australia had G. D. McKenzie and India, F. M. Engineer. Other notable overseas Test players who were available included Majid Jahangir Khan, Asif Iqbal, Younis Ahmed and Sarfraz Narwaz (Pakistan), J. N. Shepherd (West Indies) and G. M. Turner (New Zealand).

For the most part attendances at the matches were disappointing, particularly at Trent Bridge, but various circumstances militated against large crowds. First, the doubt which had always existed against the South African tour taking place, meant that advance winter bookings for the Tests were negligible. When the five hastily arranged matches were announced the country was in the midst of a General Election and in addition sporting attention and press and television publicity were switched to the World Cup Tournament in Mexico; then came the Commonwealth Games in Edinburgh, and all these things threw limelight on cricket into the background.

Nevertheless, the cricket reached a very high standard; possibly only the Australian sides of 1921 and 1948 could have risen to the heights attained by The Rest, yet England, after a frightful start on the first day of the opening match, proved worthy opponents. They won at Trent Bridge and in two other games – at Headingley and The Oval – the issue remained in the balance until the closing stages.

England had looked forward to opposing South Africa, because form showed them to be the strongest Test combination at the present time. The presence of a powerful foe was also needed in order to produce an English team to visit Australia and New Zealand the following winter. The Rest of the World certainly fulfilled those requirements. England were well aware of loopholes in their batting and this was confirmed on that first humid morning at Lord's. Sobers, with his speed and swerve, effected a collapse. England could muster only 127, Sobers taking six for 26, and he followed with a magnificent innings of 183. Barlow made 119 and the Rest totalled 546.

On the first day of the second Test at Trent Bridge, two medium paced bowlers, D'Oliveira and Greig, each took four wickets when the Rest were dismissed for 276, despite 114 not out by Clive Lloyd and 64 by Richards. But again the England batsmen struggled. Barlow distinguished himself in taking five wickets for 66 and when he followed with a brilliant innings of 142, England's final task of making 284 looked very difficult. Luckhurst rose to the occasion by staying seven hours for 113 not out and saw England home by eight wickets.

D'Oliveira, the central figure in the apartheid controversy, held the England batting together in the third Test at Edgbaston with scores of 110 and 81, but the Rest, with Lloyd getting 101, Sobers 80 and the tail hitting to good purpose, reached 563 before they closed their first innings and went on to win comfortably.

Barlow proved the man of the match in the fourth Test at Headingley with seven wickets on the first day, including four in five balls. Altogether Barlow took twelve for 142 and again Sobers shone with the bat, 114 and 59, but England fought nobly and went down by only two wickets.

So far the only disappointing performer for The Rest had been Graeme Pollock, but in the final Test at The Oval he played gloriously for 114 and thousands of white and coloured spectators cheered him and Sobers (79) while they indulged in a memorable stand of 165. This was a feast of batsmanship. Apart from Luckhurst, twice dismissed by Procter for 0, England showed up well with the bat, Boycott playing superbly for 157, and in the end only a skilful 100 by Kanhai enabled the Rest to get home with four wickets to spare.

That is a brief summary of the five Tests, but one must dwell more on the performances of the England players because these had an important bearing on the selection of sixteen men who went to Australia.

Cowdrey, after his Achilles tendon trouble of the previous summer, was still not satisfied about his fitness and form; Boycott, too, was out of form, and both asked not to be considered for the first Test. So there was no question about Illingworth continuing as captain. Once more, he proved a sound tactician and time and again he came to the rescue in the many batting crises that occurred when England faced the Rest's bowling. His scores were: 63 and 94; 97; 15 and 43; 58 and 54; 52 and 0. His Test aggregate of 476 was only surpassed in the series by Sobers, 588, though Illingworth's seven wickets cost 40 runs each. So Cowdrey, already three times vice-captain in Australia, again had to play second fiddle.

At first the batting was brittle. Alan Jones and M. H. Denness were passed over after the first match. A badly bruised finger troubled Edrich and he appeared only twice. Fortunately Boycott suddenly jumped right to the top of his form, but the only real find was Luckhurst, who made 408 runs in the first four matches. He failed in the last, but he had done enough.

As D'Oliveira showed no decline and Fletcher, a fine stylist, averaged nearly 50, they were chosen with the last batting place going to John Hampshire on the strength of his century on his Test début against West Indies the previous year at Lord's and his proven ability to get runs on Australian wickets when he was coach to Tasmania. Knott and Taylor were considered by most experts as the best pair of wicket-keepers, but a big query hung over the bowling.

The main figure was Snow; Ward had broken down after one match, but reappeared late in the season in county matches and being proclaimed fit, was selected, only to encounter more bad luck soon after getting to Australia. Lever, tried in the last Test, won his place by capturing seven wickets in the Rest's first innings, Barlow, Pollock, Sobers and Lloyd being among his victims. A place was also found for Shuttleworth – dropped after the first Test – and the remaining two places were filled by the slow left-arm bowlers, Underwood and Wilson. So two genuine spinners who might have caused a stir in Australia, P. I. Pocock (off-spin) and R. N. S. Hobbs (wrist spin) were left behind, which was sad to reflect upon, but in line with modern thinking in "the swinging seventies".

ENGLAND v REST OF THE WORLD

First Test Match

Played at Lord's, June 17, 19, 20, 22, 1970

Rest of the World won by an innings and 80 runs with a day to spare. England were so outclassed in this opening match of the series that few could have expected the four following games to be so closely contested. English hopes of victory had all but disappeared by lunch on the first day, which was a Wednesday, Thursday becoming a "rest day" because of the General Election.

The match was a personal triumph for the World XI captain, Gary Sobers, who not only wielded his collection of star players into a team straightaway, but set a remarkable personal example. He first destroyed the England batting with his best bowling in Test cricket and followed with a memorable innings of 183. This was the third occasion that the West Indies captain had made a century and taken five wickets in an innings in a Test match. No other player had done it more than once.

England's experimental batting side, with Cowdrey and Boycott requesting not to be considered because of lack of form and Edrich forced out by a hand injury, made a sorry showing on the first morning. The cloudy, humid conditions were ideal for seam and swing bowling and Sobers made the most of them after Illingworth had won the toss. With the aid of Procter and McKenzie he had England down to 44 for seven by the first interval. Jones and Luckhurst, two of three newcomers in the England side, were quickly swept aside. Jones, given an overdue chance after years of consistent scoring in county cricket, seemed overcome by the occasion. After edging the first ball of the match from McKenzie over the slips he played a rash stroke to Procter's fast delivery and lost his wicket.

This was the start of the decline not arrested until Illingworth and Underwood came together for the eight wicket. Sobers, varying pace and swing shrewdly, took wickets in his third, sixth, eight, ninth and twelfth overs. After 49 balls his figures were four for 9, his final return six for 21. Much of the England batting was spiritless. Illingworth showed that Sobers was not unplayable with the first of the rescuing innings he was to play in the series. He dealt so firmly with the bowling that there were ten 4s in his 63, which helped England to a total of 127, made in three and a half hours.

This was soon shown to be woefully inadequate. Richards, all ease and casual grace, and the more rugged Barlow put on 69 for the first wicket. Kanhai was also out before the close but by then the Rest of the World were only 13 behind.

On the Friday, Barlow and Graeme Pollock took their third-wicket stand to 131 before both were out in the space of three balls, Pollock for 55 and Barlow for 119, his seventh Test century. Barlow showed vast powers of concentration and few signs that he had come from a South African winter into a Test match with only minimal practice. He hit sixteen 4s in a stay of four hours, forty minutes.

Sobers then put the England bowling to the sword in a superb exhibition which showed him still at the peak of his powers. After Ward, England's best bowler, had removed Lloyd and Engineer with the new ball, Sobers and Intikhab made 197 together in the final two and a half hours of the day. Shuttleworth, England's new fast bowler, had Sobers dropped by Luckhurst at long leg when he was 41, otherwise Sobers gave the bowlers no encouragement. Intikhab played forcefully but was quite overshadowed.

By the close of the second day the score was 475 for six, with Sobers 147. Before a crowd of 14,500 on the Saturday he could not recapture his carefree mood of the previous evening. Yet by the time he was dismissed by Snow he had hit one 6 and thirty 4s. Snow took his 100th wicket for England when he bowled Procter but with a total of 546 the Rest of the World led by 419.

After a second failure by Jones, England made a better fight in their second innings, but were slowly spun out by Intikhab, who bowled 54 overs of leg breaks and googlies for his best Test figures of six for 113. Luckhurst used his feet well to the spinners and stayed three hours for 67, adding 101 for the third wicket with D'Oliveira, whose 78 was full of attacking strokes. Sobers accounted for Sharpe, his 200th Test victim, and by the close of the third day England were 228 for five. On Monday, Illingworth and Knott batted defiantly, taking the match into the afternoon while adding 117 in three hours. Illingworth again looked a batsman of true Test class while scoring 94 (eleven 4s). But after Sobers, in his slower style, had dismissed the England captain six short of a well deserved century, Intikhab run through the tailenders. Total attendance: 35,000.

England

B. W. Luckhurst c Richards b Sobers	1	– c Engineer b Intikhab	67
A. Jones c Engineer b Procter	5	– c Engineer b Procter	0
M. H. Denness c Barlow b McKenzie	13	– c Sobers b Intikhab	24
B. L. D'Oliveira c Engineer b Sobers	0	– c Lloyd b Intikhab	78
P. J. Sharpe c Barlow b Sobers	4	– b Sobers	2
*R. Illingworth c Engineer b Sobers	63	– c Barlow b Sobers	94
†A. P. E. Knott c Kanhai b Sobers	2	– lbw b Gibbs	39
J. A. Snow c Engineer b Sobers	2	– b Intikhab	10
D. L. Underwood c Lloyd b Barlow	19	– c Kanhai b Intikhab	7
A. Ward c Sobers b McKenzie	11	– st Engineer b Intikhab	0
K. Shuttleworth not out	1	– not out	0
L-b 5, n-b 1	6	B 4, l-b 8, n-b 6	18
1/5 2/17 3/23 4/23 5/29 6/31 7/44 8/94 9/125	127	1/0 2/39 3/140 4/148 5/196 6/313 7/323 8/334 9/338	339

Bowling: *First Innings*—McKenzie 16.1–3–43–2; Procter 13–6–20–1; Sobers 20–11–21–6; Barlow 4–0–26–1; Intikhab 2–0–11–0. *Second Innings*—McKenzie 15–8–25–0; Procter 15–4–36–1; Sobers 31–13–43–2; Barlow 7–2–10–0; Intikhab 54–24–113–6; Lloyd 1–0–3–0; Gibbs 51–17–91–1.

Rest of the World

B. A. Richards c Sharpe b Ward	35
E. J. Barlow c Underwood b Illingworth	119
R. B. Kanhai c Knott b D'Oliveira	21
R. G. Pollock b Underwood	55
C. H. Lloyd b Ward	20
*G. S. Sobers c Underwood b Snow	183
†F. M. Engineer b Ward	2
Intikhab Alam b Ward	61
M. J. Procter b Snow	26
G. D. McKenzie c Snow b Underwood	0
L. R. Gibbs not out	2
B 10, l-b 5, n-b 7	22
1/69 2/106 3/237 4/237 5/293 6/298 7/496 8/537 9/544	546

Bowling: Snow 27–7–109–2; Ward 33–4–121–4; Shuttleworth 21–2–85–0; D'Oliveira 18–5–45–1; Underwood 25.5–8–81–2; Illingworth 30–8–83–1.

Umpires: J. S. Buller and A. E. Fagg.

ENGLAND v REST OF THE WORLD

Second Test Match

Played at Nottingham, July 2, 3, 4, 6, 7, 1970

England won by eight wickets. A match of constantly changing fortunes on the first three days was finally won by England in convincing fashion to square the series against all predictions. Before the week-end the weather was damp and cool, conditions which made the game a battle between the respective sets of seam bowlers. On Monday and Tuesday the weather brightened and although England's final target was 284, batting conditions on a slow-paced pitch were the easiest of the match. Luckhurst, playing a dogged innings of 113 not out, which took him seven hours, saw England home with over four hours to spare.

Cowdrey, who made 64 in a second-wicket stand of 120 with his Kent colleague, became the highest scoring batsman in Test history; when 21 he passed Walter Hammond's aggregate of 7,249.

Lloyd and Barlow played memorable innings for the Rest of the World and Illingworth for England. The captain kept his side in the match with a knock of 97, adding 84 for the last wicket with Snow to secure a narrow lead. The two first innings followed almost identical patterns, each side recovering from 126 for six.

Despite the fine cricket played, the match failed to capture the interest of the Nottingham public, only 16,000 altogether watching the play on the five days.

Greig, the Sussex all-rounder, was the one new cap in the England side, which showed five changes. Jones, Denness, Sharpe and Shuttleworth were dropped and Ward was unfit. In came Edrich, Cowdrey, Fletcher, Brown and Greig, the last-named soon making an impression, for he took four for 59 as the World XI were bowled out for 276 on the opening day.

They were rescued from disaster by a dashing, not out 114 by Lloyd; only Richards and Procter of the other batsmen made much of a showing. D'Oliveira began a collapse when he dismissed Barlow with his second ball, Greig soon joined him in the attack and with the ball swinging freely the bowlers got on top. Richards played well for two and a half hours for 64, but when he was out only Lloyd of the specialist batsmen could handle the medium pace bowlers. He slashed, pulled and drove his way to his fourth Test century and third against England, hitting the ball with tremendous power. Three 6s and ten 4s were his chief scoring strokes in three hours and forty minutes of exhilarating strokeplay. Procter also attacked the bowling in a stand of 87, but when D'Oliveira, England's best bowler with four for 43, closed the innings at 276 five minutes before the normal time, England could be well satisfied with their day's work.

Illingworth, for England, and Barlow, for the Rest of the World, dominated the second day which began with a steadfast partnership of 78 by Edrich and Luckhurst. Barlow, the fifth bowler tried, caused a collapse when in his first seven overs he sent back Luckhurst, Cowdrey, Fletcher, Edrich and D'Oliveira for 17 runs, bemusing the batsmen with his outswing and constant changes of pace and angle. Greig hit his first three balls for 4, 3, 4 but when he went England's prospects looked bleak, for Illingworth had only Knott and the bowlers left to support him. Illingworth, handicapped by a back injury which required a manipulative operation after the match, began shakily, edging three boundaries through the slips off an anguished Barlow. Knott stayed for an hour, but the ninth wicket went at 195. Then Snow again proved himself one of Test cricket's great number eleven batsmen. He took runs calmly while Illingworth went boldly for the bowling.

The new ball, taken at 231 for nine, failed to unsettle the batsmen, who gained England an advantage of three runs before Illingworth, attempting to hit Sobers for his tenth boundary, was bowled three short of a century after a stay of three and three-quarter hours. He had given only one chance, being dropped by Sobers at short leg off Intikhab when 41.

The Rest of the World second innings revolved around Barlow, who added a score of 142 to his five England wickets. He defied the England bowlers throughout Saturday and into Monday morning while the majority of his colleagues struggled. Although Illingworth was unable to bowl he was not missed. Wickets fell steadily and a brief threat offered by Lloyd ended unluckily when he swept at Underwood and the ball rebounded high from his front pad and rolled on to the stumps.

Intikhab and Procter helped Barlow in valuable partnerships, but neither could play the major innings which the World XI needed. The last three wickets, including that of Barlow after six and a quarter hours of stern resistance, went down cheaply on Monday, leaving England plenty of time to get the runs; D'Oliveira's match figures were seven for 106 and Greig, seven for 130.

When England batted a second time, Luckhurst's unbreachable defence and Cowdrey's return to form soon removed most doubts about the eventual outcome. When Barlow finally had Cowdrey leg-before with a full toss England were 163 for two. In Monday's closing thirty minutes Luckhurst and Fletcher safely resisted the new ball and on the following morning took England smoothly to victory. Fletcher, playing his most confident Test innings in England, made 69 of a third-wicket stand of 120, batting in carefree style while the patient Luckhurst kept the other end secure.

Rest of the World

B. A. Richards c Knott b Greig	64	– b Greig	30
E. J. Barlow c Cowdrey b D'Oliveira	11	– b Greig	142
†R. B. Kanhai c Fletcher b Greig	6	– c Knott b D'Oliveira	6
R. G. Pollock b D'Oliveira	2	– lbw b D'Oliveira	0
C. H. Lloyd not out	114	– b Underwood	20
*G. S. Sobers b Greig	8	– c Knott b Greig	18
†F. M. Engineer c Knott b Greig	0	– c and b Underwood	1
Intikhab Alam c Cowdrey b D'Oliveira	12	– c and b Brown	23
M. J. Procter b Brown	43	– c Edrich b D'Oliveira	27
G. D. McKenzie c and b Brown	0	– not out	6
L. R. Gibbs b D'Oliveira	1	– b Snow	1
B 4, l-b 9, n-b 2	15	B 2, l-b 8, n-b 2	12
1/31 2/46 3/55 4/106 5/126 6/126 7/172 8/259 9/267	276	1/68 2/87 3/87 4/112 5/141 6/154 7/220 8/263 9/281	286

Bowling: *First Innings*—Snow 20–5–58–0; Brown 15–1–64–2; D'Oliveira 17.4–3–43–4; Greig 18–3–59–4; Underwood 9–4–25–0; Illingworth 4–2–12–0. *Second Innings*—Snow 19.2–2–64–1; Brown 13–0–41–1; D'Oliveira 26–9–63–3; Greig 23–7–71–3; Underwood 26–13–35–2.

England

J. H. Edrich c Engineer b Barlow	39	– c Barlow b McKenzie	17
B. W. Luckhurst b Barlow	37	– not out	113
M. C. Cowdrey c Richards b Barlow	1	– lbw b Barlow	64
K. W. R. Fletcher c Engineer b Barlow	4	– not out	69
B. L. D'Oliveira b Barlow	16		
*R. Illingworth b Sobers	97		
A. W. Greig c Gibbs b Sobers	14		
†A. P. E. Knott c Kanhai b Intikhab	21		
D. J. Brown b Procter	3		
D. L. Underwood c Sobers b Intikhab	2		
J. A. Snow not out	27		
B 1, l-b 7, n-b 10	18	L-b 14, w 3, n-b 4	21
1/78 2/82 3/86 4/106 5/109 6/126 7/179 8/191 9/195	279	1/44 2/164	(2 wkts) 284

Bowling: *First Innings*—Procter 17–6–42–1; McKenzie 21–3–60–0; Sobers 20.5–3–49–2; Gibbs 6–3–8–0; Barlow 20–5–66–5; Intikhab 19–3–36–2. *Second Innings*—Procter 20–9–23–0; Sobers 18–7–24–0; McKenzie 24–8–53–1; Intikhab 27–9–94–0; Gibbs 31–10–40–0; Barlow 14–4–20–1; Kanhai 1–0–4–0; Pollock 0.2–0–5–0.

Umpires: A. E. Fagg and C. S. Elliott.

ENGLAND v REST OF THE WORLD

Third Test Match

Played at Edgbaston, July 16, 17, 18, 20, 21, 1970

Rest of the World won by five wickets. After trailing by 269 on the first innings England did well to take the match into the final hour but could not prevent their first defeat in fourteen Test Matches at Edgbaston. The Rest of the World gained ample revenge for their Nottingham set-back, consistent batting enabling them to total 563 for nine in their first innings after dismissing England for 294.

Illingworth and Cowdrey played this match under a fierce spotlight of publicity for it was known that during its course the selectors would decide between them for the captaincy of the MCC team to Australia. The choice finally fell on Illingworth who with Cowdrey made a determined second-innings effort to deny the World XI victory. But England's batting hero was D'Oliveira who rescued the side on the first day with a superb 110 and was top scorer in the second innings with 81.

The all-round strength of the opposition proved just too much. Eight of their batsmen made 40 or more in the first innings, Lloyd and Sobers giving the Birmingham crowd a rare treat by adding 95 together in the final hour on Friday just as the England bowlers, led by Snow, had looked likely to redress the balance.

England fielded the team that won at Trent Bridge. The Rest of the World selectors made two changes, replacing McKenzie with the South African fast bowler Peter Pollock, who thus combined playing and reporting the game, and calling up the former West Indies wicket-keeper, Deryck Murray, a student at Nottingham University, to replace Engineer, whose batting had been disappointing.

Edrich and Luckhurst again gave England a steady start but Sobers, who dismissed Luckhurst, Cowdrey and Fletcher without cost to himself, then plunged the innings into crisis: but D'Oliveira was equal to it. He rescued his side from 76 for four with his fourth century for his adopted country. His second scoring stroke was a 6 and he hit so strongly that Gibbs bowled to him with a long-off and a long-on. With his short backlift D'Oliveira was particularly powerful on the leg side. Illingworth helped to add 58 for the fifth wicket and Greig contributed a watchful 55. While he and D'Oliveira were together there were hopes of a complete recovery, but Lloyd, the seventh bowler tried, caught and bowled D'Oliveira to end his stay of three and a half hours, during which he hit fifteen 4s. Procter, who then bowled Greig, soon cleared away the tail next morning to finish with five for 46, his speed and accuracy proving too much for the later batsmen.

Similarly aggressive fast bowling by Snow kept England on terms until Lloyd and Sobers came together at 175 for four. After early uncertainties against Illingworth they launched a blistering attack on the bowling. Sobers, who earlier in the day had taken his 100th Test catch, passed 7,000 runs in international cricket when he was 15 and needed only sixty-eight minutes for 50. Lloyd was not far behind as, matching each other for audacious strokes, they took complete command.

A crowd of 12,500 turned up on Saturday to see the West Indian left-handers renew their onslaught. They stayed for another half an hour, bringing their partnership to 155 in two hours, before Illingworth bowled Sobers for 80. Lloyd reached his second 100 of the series in three and a quarter hours with two 6s and ten 4s, before he, too, fell to Illingworth.

Procter then carried on the assault and hit twelve 4s in his 50 – a majestic display. When Snow bowled him for 62 much of the sparkle went from the batting. Nevertheless, Murray and Intikhab built up the second highest Test score at Edgbaston before the declaration left the England openers to play out fifty minutes in the evening.

On Monday Intikhab soon disposed of them, but England made no attempt to strive solely for a draw. Cowdrey and Fletcher played brightly from the start. It was a bad blow for England when Fletcher was needlessly run out. Cowdrey never recovered his best form after this incident but his sensible 71 gave England reason to hope. D'Oliveira punished pace and spin so freely that he made 41 in his first hour. At 271 for four, with he and Illingworth going well, England were making a great fight. Then Sobers took a hand, ending D'Oliveira's innings, which lasted for two hours, twenty minutes and included ten 4s. Illingworth and Greig soon followed so that at the start of the last day England, only 51 on with three wickets left, looked a well beaten side.

However, Knott, given an early life, prolonged the innings for a further two and a half hours, with help from Brown and Snow, the latter staying for eighty minutes while 45 runs were made for the last wicket, Knott finishing with 50 not out. The final task for the Rest of the World, 141 in three and a quarter hours, proved no mere formality. Barlow, Richards, Kanhai, Sobers and Lloyd all fell before the target was reached. At 107 for five, with Graeme Pollock injured, there were some doubts about the outcome. However, these were resolved by Procter and Intikhab, who knocked off the remaining 34 runs in quick time. Attendance: 30,000.

England

J. H. Edrich b P. M. Pollock	37	– c Sobers b Intikhab	3
B. W. Luckhurst c Murray b Sobers	28	– c Murray b Intikhab	35
M. C. Cowdrey lbw b Sobers	0	– c Murray b P. M. Pollock	71
K. W. R. Fletcher c Murray b Sobers	0	– run out	27
B. L. D'Oliveira c and b Lloyd	110	– c Barlow b Sobers	81
*R. Illingworth c Murray b Procter	15	– b Gibbs	43
A. W. Greig b Procter	55	– c and b Sobers	22
†A. P. E. Knott b Procter	21	– not out	50
D. J. Brown b Procter	13	– c Murray b Procter	32
D. L. Underwood c Sobers b Procter	1	– b Sobers	0
J. A. Snow not out	3	– b Sobers	21
L-b 7, n-b 4	11	B 14, l-b 10	24
1/56 2/56 3/66 4/76 5/134 6/244 7/258 8/282 9/290	294	1/20 2/58 3/132 4/193 5/271 6/279 7/317 8/364 9/364	409

Bowling: *First Innings*—Procter 24.1–7–46–5; P. M. Pollock 15–1–62–1; Barlow 11–2–28–0; Sobers 20–11–38–3; Intikhab 19–4–45–0; Gibbs 19–5–41–0; Lloyd 7–1–23–1. *Second Innings*—Procter 22–10–26–1; P. M. Pollock 18–5–48–1; Barlow 9–2–26–0; Sobers 51.5–20–89–4; Intikhab 63–29–116–2; Gibbs 42–16–80–1.

Rest of the World

E. J. Barlow b Snow	4	– c Knott b Snow	0
B. A. Richards c Greig b Illingworth	47	– b Underwood	32
R. B. Kanhai c Greig b Illingworth	71	– c and b Underwood	37
R. G. Pollock b Snow	40		
C. H. Lloyd b Illingworth	101	– b Illingworth	20
*G. S. Sobers b Illingworth	80	– lbw b Illingworth	7
M. J. Procter b Snow	62	– not out	25
†D. L. Murray c Fletcher b Underwood	62		
Intikhab Alam c Knott b Illingworth	45	– not out	15
P. M. Pollock not out	23		
L. R. Gibbs not out	3		
B 10, l-b 13, n-b 2	25	B 1, l-b 4	5
1/7 2/80 3/157 4/175 5/350 6/377 7/450 8/526 9/538	(9 wkts dec.) 563	1/3 2/72 3/79 4/100 5/107	(5 wkts) 141

Bowling: *First Innings*—Snow 38–6–124–4; Brown 14–2–65–0; Greig 16–0–58–0; D'Oliveira 24–8–58–0; Underwood 44–17–90–1; Illingworth 49–13–131–4; Fletcher 2–0–12–0. *Second Innings*—Snow 7–2–10–1; Brown 7–2–23–0; Underwood 15–2–52–2; Illingworth 14–4–51–2.

Umpires: J. S. Buller and A. E. Rhodes.

ENGLAND v REST OF THE WORLD

Fourth Test Match

Played at Leeds, July 30, 31, August 1, 3, 4, 1970

Rest of the World won by two wickets. There was a tremendous struggle before the Rest of the World clinched the series, their nerveless ninth-wicket pair Procter and the injured Richards steering them home after England had entered the last day slight favourites to win the match.

Needing 223 to win in the fourth innings on a pitch playing well, Sobers' side collapsed to 62 for five before recovering, thanks to a stand of 115 between the captain and Intikhab. The turning point came when Greig at second slip dropped Intikhab off Snow with the score at 82. Had that chance been accepted soon after the last day's play began the teams could well have gone to The Oval all square.

England were always striving to get on terms after a poor first-innings total of 222. Barlow was the cause with a remarkable burst of four wickets in five balls; he equalled the feat of M. J. C. Allom in the Christchurch Test in New Zealand in 1929-30. Barlow, who performed the first hat-trick in Test cricket since Gibbs achieved one for West Indies against Australia in Adelaide in 1960-61, confessed afterwards that not only was this the first of his career, but was in fact the first he had seen.

Sobers, whose team were handicapped by injuries to Richards and Kanhai on the first day, put England in on a slow-drying pitch, but this gamble was only just rewarded. England brought in three Yorkshiremen, Boycott, Wilson and Old, the last named for his first Test at the age of 21. Edrich, Brown and Underwood were omitted. The World XI showed one change, their batting being further strengthened as Peter Pollock gave way to Mushtaq Mohammad.

In the England first innings only Luckhurst, Fletcher and Illingworth scored more than 20. The position might have been worse had Sobers been properly rewarded for some magnificent bowling, but his luck was right out. Fletcher and Illingworth put on 118 for the fifth wicket to retrieve a poor start and the score reached 209 for four before a total disintegration against Barlow. Once he had broken through with the new ball he proved irresistible in a spell of five for 16. After dismissing Fletcher, whose 89 in three and a half hours included twelve 4s, Barlow sent back in successive deliveries Knott, Old and Wilson, the first two bowled and Wilson caught off bat and pad by Denness, the England twelfth man who was fielding as one of the two substitutes. Richards had damaged back muscles catching D'Oliveira and Kanhai was nursing a severely bruised hand, the result of intercepting a fierce hit from Fletcher.

The Rest of the World owed their first-innings advantage of 154 mainly to two men. Murray showed high application as a makeshift opener to score 95 and Sobers rallied his faltering side with another splendid century, his twenty-third in Tests – only Bradman has made more.

Greig produced the occasional disconcerting delivery and took three of the first four wickets. Murray batted nearly five hours and when he was fifth out only three runs were needed for the lead. Sobers ensured that a sizeable one was obtained with a knock of 114, lasting four and a half hours. When he was dismissed, swinging wildly at Snow, Sobers declared the innings to save Richards having to bat, although Kanhai had contributed 26 virtually one-handed.

As usual England came back strongly in the second innings. They were given a fine start by Boycott and Luckhurst who made 104 for the first wicket, a partnership dominated by the Yorkshireman, who timed his strokes perfectly. Cowdrey failed a second time, but Luckhurst and Fletcher then took England in front before Luckhurst's typically dogged effort was terminated by Barlow just before the close of play on Saturday. Barlow had a hand in the first five wickets to fall and he finished with twelve for 142.

On Monday, England wickets fell steadily and only a ninth-wicket stand of 60 between Illingworth and Old enabled a reasonable target to be set. The fast bowler made an extremely fortunate but highly valuable 37, seeing his captain to yet another fifty.

The evening's cricket bordered on the sensational as the England bowlers struck back with a vengeance. Snow, at a fiery pace, removed the openers and Pollock, and Illingworth accounted for Lloyd and Mushtaq who suddently abandoned a defensive role and fell to a wild sweep.

At the end of the fourth day the score was 75 for five; the Rest still needed 148 and Kanhai and Richards were injured. Batting was easier in the clearer light of the fifth morning. After Intikhab's escape at the hands of Greig he and Sobers slowly swung the game round. Illingworth switched his bowlers unavailingly and no wicket fell for two and a quarter hours. Then Snow produced a fine ball, causing Sobers to be caught at slip by Cowdrey. Intikhab, tempted by Wilson's flight, hit the last ball before lunch straight to D'Oliveira at long-off. Immediately after the interval Kanhai was out trying to cut Illingworth. At 183 for eight Richards and Procter were together with 40 needed and the new ball in the offing.

Richards, who had been off the field since the previous Thursday, survived an appeal for a close catch off bat and pad when facing Wilson. The new ball was taken at 201 but the England bowlers could do no more and with ice-cool batting the two young Springboks settled the match and the series. Attendance: 43,500.

England

G. Boycott c Murray b Barlow	15	– c Pollock b Barlow	64
B. W. Luckhurst c Intikhab b Procter	35	– c Gibbs b Barlow	92
M. C. Cowdrey c Murray b Barlow	1	– b Barlow	0
K. W. R. Fletcher c Murray b Barlow	89	– b Lloyd	63
B. L. D'Oliveira c Richards b Procter	2	– b Procter	21
*R. Illingworth c Murray b Barlow	58	– b Intikhab	54
A. W. Greig b Procter	5	– c Murray b Lloyd	0
†A. P. E. Knott b Barlow	0	– c Procter b Barlow	11
C. M. Old b Barlow	0	– c Murray b Gibbs	37
D. Wilson c sub b Barlow	0	– not out	6
J. A. Snow not out	3	– c Procter b Barlow	10
B 4, l-b 7, n-b 3	14	B 3, l-b 8, w 1, n-b 6	18
1/37 2/43 3/81 4/91 5/209 6/218 7/219 8/219 9/219	222	1/104 2/108 3/194 4/227 5/257 6/267 7/268 8/300 9/360	376

Bowling: *First Innings*—Procter 21–7–47–3; Sobers 20–11–24–0; Barlow 22.4–6–64–7; Gibbs 5–0–16–0; Intikhab 5–2–15–0; Mushtaq 12–4–27–0; Lloyd 10–2–15–0. *Second Innings*—Procter 40–14–67–1; Sobers 34–9–65–0; Barlow 32–8–78–5; Gibbs 13–2–31–1; Intikhab 18.5–6–28–1; Mushtaq 14–4–44–0; Lloyd 17–7–45–2.

Rest of the World

E. J. Barlow c Boycott b Greig	37	– c Cowdrey b Snow	6
†D. L. Murray c Snow b Wilson	95	– lbw b Snow	10
Mushtaq Mohammad lbw b Greig	4	– lbw b Illingworth	14
R. G. Pollock c Knott b Greig	3	– b Snow	8
C. H. Lloyd b Old	35	– c Luckhurst b Illingworth	20
*G. S. Sobers c Knott b Snow	114	– c Cowdrey b Snow	59
M. J. Procter c Knott b Old	27	– not out	22
Intikhab Alam c Knott b Greig	15	– c D'Oliveira b Wilson	54
R. B. Kanhai c and b D'Oliveira	26	– c Knott b Illingworth	4
L. R. Gibbs not out	0		
B. A. Richards (did not bat)		– not out	21
L-b 13, w 1, n-b 6	20	B 4, l-b 4	8
1/67 2/84 3/90 4/152 5/220 6/280 7/309 8/376	(9 wkts dec.) 376	1/6 2/25 3/49 4/58 5/62 6/177 7/182 8/183	(8 wkts) 226

Bowling: *First Innings*—Snow 28.1–7–80–1; Old 27–5–70–2; D'Oliveira 24–10–52–1; Greig 31–6–86–4; Wilson 20–5–48–1; Illingworth 8–2–20–0. *Second Innings*—Snow 27.5–5–82–4; Old 13–5–35–0; D'Oliveira 11–6–17–0; Greig 3–0–14–0; Wilson 18–9–29–1; Illingworth 21–8–41–3.

Umpires: A. E. Fagg and A. E. Rhodes.

ENGLAND v REST OF THE WORLD

Fifth Test Match

Played at The Oval, August 13, 14, 15, 17, 18, 1970

Rest of the World won by four wickets. There were four notable individual performances in a match which brought a magnificent series to a distinguished close. The quality of the cricket was such that 53,000 spectators watched play over the five days, although the series had been settled. England's defeat meant that the team batting first lost in all five games, a unique occurrence.

The Lancashire medium-fast bowler, Lever, made an impressive début for England, taking seven wickets for 83 runs in the Rest of the World first innings. In the same innings Graeme Pollock re-established his reputation as one of the world's great batsmen with a graceful century. His partnership of 165 with Sobers was a batting spectacle which will live long in the minds of those privileged to see it.

Boycott also came back into his own with a masterly innings of 157 which gave England a chance of victory. His effort meant that the World XI needed 284 to win on a wearing pitch, an uphill task even though Wilson had to bowl with two damaged fingers on his left hand strapped together. Kanhai rose to the challenge with a dedicated 100. Lloyd hit powerfully for 68 and Sobers was the master of the bowling in the closing stages, making the final stroke of a series in which he had been the dominant figure.

Lever for Greig was one of two changes made by the England selectors, who named D'Oliveira twelfth man so that Amiss of Warwickshire could be given a chance to win a place on the Australian tour. He did not quite do enough, although fighting hard in both innings. For the World team McKenzie replaced Gibbs, whose three wickets in the first four matches had cost over 100 runs apiece.

Cowdrey atoned for his double failure at Leeds by making top score of 73 in the England first innings of 294, which began badly when Luckhurst was bowled by Procter's third ball. Once he had settled in Cowdrey looked complete master of the attack. Then he went into his shell and made only 13 in his final hour. Illingworth, with his sixth half-century of the series, and Knott added 86 for the sixth wicket before McKenzie took three wickets in eight balls.

Lever soon made his mark by dismissing Barlow and Mushtaq in this first nine overs but his effort, and everything else on the second day, was overshadowed by the artistry of Pollock and Sobers, who put on 135 in the last two hours. Pollock, with only 108 runs from his previous six innings, made England pay dearly for a missed slip catch when he was 18. There were one 6 and sixteen 4s in his 114, which took just over two and a half hours.

On Saturday, the crowd rolled up to see Pollock and Sobers continue their assault; instead Lever took the limelight. Pollock who was restricted to 10 runs in forty-five minute was the first to fall to the Lancashire bowler who later also took the wickets of Sobers and Lloyd. His command of perfect length and direction made him a formidable opponent and only Procter of the later batsmen made progress against him.

England's arrears of 61 were cleared for the loss of Luckhurst, this time bowled first ball by Procter. Boycott set himself the task of seeing England to a match-winning score on a pitch beginning to take spin. He and Fletcher batted throughout the fourth morning and altogether added 154 for the third wicket in three and a quarter hours. When Boycott was fourth out at 289, caught off Lloyd, he had been in for six and a quarter hours and hit twenty-three 4s. This was Boycott at his best. Illingworth was dismissed first ball and the rest were swept aside by Sobers and McKenzie.

Nevertheless, the final task for the Rest of the World was formidable, especially when Barlow was bowled by Snow with six runs scored. On the final morning, Richards and Pollock were both bowled while yards down the pitch and Kanhai made some hair-raising strokes before deciding that it was possible to survive, although the ball was turning. His century in four hours was the foundation of the winning total.

Lloyd, more selective in his hitting than the South Africans, helped to wrest the advantage from the England bowlers by making 68 out of 123 put on in even time with Kanhai. With Wilson handicapped, the spinners were not up to the task and it was left to Snow to cause a late flutter by removing Lloyd, Kanhai and Mushtaq. Sobers proved immovable and his slash down to the third man boundary brought the winning runs and the crowd on to the field.

England

B. W. Luckhurst b Procter	0	– b Procter	0
G. Boycott c Sobers b Intikhab	24	– c Barlow b Lloyd	157
M. C. Cowdrey c Murray b Sobers	73	– b Intikhab	31
K. W. R. Fletcher c Murray b McKenzie	25	– c Barlow b Sobers	63
D. L. Amiss b Mushtaq	24	– c Murray b Lloyd	35
*R. Illingworth c Barlow b Intikhab	52	– c Mushtaq b Lloyd	0
†A. P. E. Knott not out	51	– b Sobers	15
J. A. Snow c Barlow b McKenzie	20	– c Mushtaq b Sobers	19
C. M. Old b McKenzie	0	– b McKenzie	5
D. Wilson b McKenzie	0	– b McKenzie	1
P. Lever b Barlow	13	– not out	0
B 2, l-b 7, n-b 3	12	B 5, l-b 10, n-b 3	18
1/0 2/62 3/113 4/150 5/150 6/236 7/266 8/266 9/266	294	1/0 2/71 3/225 4/289 5/289 6/319 7/323 8/343 9/343	344

Bowling: *First Innings*—Procter 20–10–22–1; McKenzie 24–7–51–4; Barlow 16.2–2–36–1; Sobers 15–5–18–1; Intikhab 44–14–92–2; Mushtaq 28–10–63–1. *Second Innings*—Procter 19–9–30–1; McKenzie 22.1–2–51–2; Barlow 16–2–42–0; Sobers 42–15–81–3; Intikhab 32–8–87–1; Mushtaq 1–0–1–0; Lloyd 18–3–34–3.

Rest of the World

E. J .Barlow c Amiss b Lever	28	– b Snow	6
B. A. Richards b Snow	14	– b Wilson	14
R. B. Kanhai c and b Wilson	13	– c Fletcher b Snow	100
R. G. Pollock b Lever	114	– b Illingworth	28
Mushtaq Mohammad b Lever	3	– c Fletcher b Snow	8
*G. S. Sobers b Lever	79	– not out	40
C. H. Lloyd c Knott b Lever	2	– c Knott b Snow	68
M. J. Procter c Boycott b Lever	51	– not out	9
†D. L. Murray b Snow	5		
Intikhab Alam c Boycott b Lever	15		
G. D. McKenzie not out	4		
L-b 14, n-b 13	27	B 2, l-b 8, w 1, n-b 3	14
1/26 2/46 3/92 4/96 5/261 6/267 7/280 8/310 9/338	355	1/7 2/41 3/92 4/215 5/241 6/265	(6 wkts) 287

Bowling: *First Innings*—Snow 32–8–73–2; Old 21–4–57–0; Wilson 18–5–58–1; Lever 32.5–9–83–7; Illingworth 15–3–57–0. *Second Innings*—Snow 23–6–81–4; Old 7–0–22–0; Wilson 24–8–70–1; Lever 10.1–2–34–0; Illingworth 23–5–66–1.

Umpires: C. S. Elliott and A. E. Fagg.

ENGLAND IN AUSTRALIA

SOUTH AUSTRALIA v MCC

Played at Adelaide, December 23, 24, 26, 27, 1962

Drawn. Cowdrey returned to form with a vengeance, scoring 307, the highest innings ever played by a touring player in Australia. In temperature of almost 100 degrees, MCC made 474 for four on the first day, Cowdrey finishing with 244. He was missed when 43 and 91, but otherwise batted faultlessly. Next day he and Graveney carried their fifth wicket stand to 344 in just under four hours, the second highest partnership for MCC in Australia. Cowdrey batted six and a half hours and hit four 6s and twenty-nine 4s, his driving being superb. Favell replied with a brisk century for South Australia, scoring 120 in two hours, fifty-four minutes and bright displays also came from Sobers, McLachlan and Dansie. The temperature dropped by over 30 degrees on the Monday. Leading by 136, MCC lost three for 23, but declared a second time and set South Australia to score 304 in four hours. After the fall of two wickets for 16, Sobers gave a great display of hitting. Rain held up play for fifty-five minutes and also ended the game an hour early. Sobers obtained twelve 4s in scoring 75 not out in sixty-three minutes and a fine finish might have occurred but for the weather.

MCC

P. H. Parfitt b Brooks	2	– c Jarman b Brooks	7
Rev. D. S. Sheppard b Sobers	81	– b Sobers	5
*E. R. Dexter c Chappell b Sobers	16	– c Chappell b Sangster	37
M. C. Cowdrey c Chappell b Dansie	307	– c McLachlan b Sobers	2
K. F. Barrington run out	52	– not out	52
T. W. Graveney not out	122	– b Sincock	35
F. J. Titmus (did not bat)		– c Lill b Dansie	4
†J. T. Murray (did not bat)		– not out	24
B 1, l-b 3, w 2	6	L-b 1	1
1/2 2/39 3/144 4/242 5/586	(5 wkts dec.) 586	1/8 2/12 3/23 4/62 5/108 6/121	(6 wkts dec.) 167

D. A. Allen, L. J. Coldwell and J. D. F. Larter did not bat.

Bowling: *First Innings*—Brooks 18–0–74–1; Sobers 25–2–124–2; Sincock 26–1–153–0; Sangster 10–0–75–0; Chappell 9–1–49–0; Dansie 10.2–1–59–1; Cunningham 2–0–28–0; McLachlan 3–0–14–0; Favell 1–0–4–0. *Second Innings*—Brooks 8–0–30–1; Sobers 9–1–44–2; Sangster 3–0–23–1; Sincock 10–0–55–1; Dansie 5–1–14–1.

South Australia

*L. Favell c Dexter b Allen	120	– c Cowdrey b Coldwell	3
K. Cunningham c Sheppard b Coldwell	15	– hit wkt b Larter	29
J. Lill c Dexter b Titmus	55	– b Coldwell	2
G. Sobers c Allen b Barrington	89	– not out	75
I. McLachlan b Allen	62	– b Larter	2
N. Dansie c and b Barrington	64	– not out	0
I. Chappell run out	2		
J. Sangster c Parfitt b Barrington	19		
†B. N. Jarman c Barrington b Titmus	11		
D. Sincock c Graveney b Titmus	0		
G. Brooks not out	2		
B 2, l-b 4, n-b 5	11	L-b 1, w 1	2
1/27 2/165 3/215 4/343 5/357 6/375 7/425 8/442 9/445	450	1/8 2/16 3/89 4/97	(4 wkts) 113

Bowling: *First Innings*—Coldwell 19–3–69–1; Larter 22–1–113–0; Dexter 15–1–60–0; Titmus 21.1–1–88–3; Allen 21–4–54–2; Barrington 18–2–55–3. *Second Innings*—Coldwell 8.7–0–65–2; Larter 5–0–23–2; Dexter 1–0–15–0; Allen 2–0–8–0.

Umpires: C. Egar and R. Joseph.

WESTERN AUSTRALIA v MCC

Played at Perth, October 29, 30, November 1, 2, 1965

MCC won by nine runs. The touring team's most consistently aggressive batsmen hit the first two centuries. Barber, driving superbly, made his 126 out of 197 in 44 overs, with twelve 4s, and Parks, who hit one 6 and twelve 4s and drove handsomely over mid-off, needed only 35 overs for his 107. Though more restrained, Russell also played fluent cricket in a second-wicket stand of 106 with Barber, and after a quiet start Smith was confidently aggressive towards the end of an unfinished stand of 175 with Parks. Kelly, formerly of New South Wales, retorted with a century in each innings and altogether held up MCC for nine and a half hours. Vernon, a left-hander with delightful attacking strokes, was another century maker in an attractive second innings of three and a quarter hours. Kelly retired hurt when 3, but he resumed at the fall of the third wicket and with Vernon put on 171. Western Australia then needed 77 in sixty-five minutes, but wickets fell as they pressed for runs and MCC rather fortunately gained a slender win on the point of time. The bowling on both sides was of moderate quality, but Jenner showed himself to be a leg-spinner of much promise.

MCC

R. W. Barber c and b Jenner	126		
J. H. Edrich c Becker b Mayne	33	– c Chadwick b Jenner	45
W. E. Russell c Becker b Mayne	81	– b Mayne	1
P. H. Parfitt b Jenner	6	– c Kelly b Jenner	48
M. C. Cowdrey c Lock b McKenzie	19	– c Vernon b Jenner	1
*M. J. K. Smith not out	67	– c Mayne b Jenner	1
†J. M. Parks not out	107	– not out	37
D. A. Allen (did not bat)		– not out	20
B 4, l-b 2, w 2	8	B 3	3
1/91 2/197 3/225 4/269 5/272	(5 wkts dec.) 447	1/2 2/77 3/81 4/87 5/103	(5 wkts dec.) 156

K. Higgs, I. J. Jones and J. D. F. Larter did not bat.

Bowling: *First Innings*—Mayne 24–1–105–2; McKenzie 21–2–88–1; Irvine 3–0–23–0; Lock 28–3–100–0; Jenner 26–4–107–2; Vernon 2–0–16–0. *Second Innings*—Mayne 7–1–33–1; McKenzie 13–1–34–0; Jenner 17–4–72–4; Lock 4–0–10–0; Kelly 1–0–4–0.

Western Australia

W. R. Playle b Allen	45	– run out	14
P. C. Kelly c Parks b Jones	119	– not out	108
M. Vernon c Parfitt b Barber	18	– b Jones	118
*B. K. Shepherd run out	15	– c and b Larter	11
G. D. McKenzie b Larter	25	– c Smith b Higgs	11
D. Chadwick not out	52	– c Parfitt b Larter	0
J. Irvine c Cowdrey b Jones	0	– run out	0
†G. C. Becker c Higgs b Jones	18	– c Higgs b Jones	6
T. Jenner c Parks b Jones	6	– b Larter	0
G. A. R. Lock c sub b Jones	0	– c Smith b Higgs	4
L. C. Mayne not out	0	– c Parks b Larter	0
B 3, l-b 1, n-b 1	5	B 7, l-b 12	19
1/91 2/124 3/153 4/200 5/243 6/243 7/275 8/288 9/288	(9 wkts dec.) 303	1/25 2/53 3/53 4/224 5/244 6/260 7/286 8/287 9/291	291

Bowling: *First Innings*—Larter 16–0–57–1; Higgs 17.2–2–61–0; Jones 19–3–59–5; Allen 37–7–80–1; Barber 12–2–32–1; Parfitt 2–0–9–0. *Second Innings*—Larter 11.3–2–49–4; Higgs 15–0–85–2; Allen 12–1–36–0; Jones 9–0–39–2; Barber 11–1–63–0.

Umpires: J. M. Meacham and N. Townsend.

AUSTRALIA v ENGLAND

Third Test Match

Played at Sydney, January 7, 8, 10, 11, 12, 1966

England won by an innings and 93 runs. Illness put Simpson out of the Australian side again, and Booth, as in Brisbane, was the captain. On a pitch which turned more and more in favour of spin bowlers the toss was the decisive event. Barber's greatest innings of the tour and his opening stand of 234 with Boycott made certain that England would not lose the advantage of batting first. Again Australia paid a heavy price for dropping Boycott early. He was missed at backward short leg off the luckless McKenzie when he was 12. In two hours before lunch he and Barber made 93 off 36 overs. In the next two hours before Boycott at last fell to Philpott's leg spin they added 141.

When Barber was second out at 303 he had batted four minutes under five hours and hit nineteen 4s in an innings of magnificent aggression, a match-winning innings. His wicket started Hawke on a splendid new ball spell which swept aside England's middle batting. In eight overs he took three for 14, and with his first ball on the second morning he also dismissed Brown. Despite his fine bowling – seven for 105 in conditions which did not materially help pace – England made an unassailable total, for Edrich scored a second successive Test century in almost four and a quarter hours. Finally Allen, who made his not out 50 in eighty-eight minutes, and Jones put on 55 for the last wicket in 12 overs.

On a wearing pitch Australia were always struggling after a second-wicket stand of 81 by Thomas and Cowper. Thomas revealed his wide range of beautiful strokes while making 51 of those runs with seven 4s in just under one and three-quarter hours. Cowper by contrast batted four hours, ten minutes for 60 and meekly played his side into the hands of the English fast bowlers, Jones and Brown. On his return to the side, after recovering from muscular trouble, Brown took three wickets in his first over with the new ball at 174 and finished with five for 63.

In the follow-on the off spin of Allen and Titmus was decisive on a broken pitch. The longest stand was 46 for the first wicket by Thomas and Lawry, but Walters was again responsible for the best batting. For two hours he played the turning ball with rare skill, and so for the third time running he came off splendidly when his side were in difficulties. Sincock, the left-arm spinner who was brought in to increase Australia's attacking spin on the Sydney pitch, had an unfortunate match as a bowler, but in both innings he batted with admirable determination.

England

G. Boycott c and b Philpott	84
R. W. Barber b Hawke	185
J. H. Edrich c and b Philpott	103
K. F. Barrington c McKenzie b Hawke	1
M. C. Cowdrey c Grout b Hawke	0
*M. J. K. Smith c Grout b Hawke	6
D. J. Brown c Grout b Hawke	1
†J. M. Parks c Grout b Hawke	13
F. J Titmus c Grout b Walters	14
D. A. Allen not out	50
I. J. Jones b Hawke	16
B 3, l-b 8, w 2, n-b 2	15
1/234 2/303 3/309 4/309 5/317 6/328 7/358 8/395 9/433	488

Bowling: McKenzie 25–2–113–0; Hawke 33.7–6–105–7; Walters 10–1–38–1; Philpott 28–3–86–2; Sincock 20–1–98–0; Cowper 6–1–33–0.

Australia

W. M. Lawry c Parks b Jones	0	– c Cowdrey b Brown	33
G. Thomas c Titmus b Brown	51	– c Cowdrey b Titmus	25
R. M. Cowper st Parks b Allen	60	– c Boycott b Titmus	0
P. J. Burge c Parks b Brown	6	– run out	1
*B. C. Booth c Cowdrey b Jones	8	– b Allen	27
D. J. Sincock c Parks b Brown	29	– c Smith b Allen	27
K. D. Walters st Parks b Allen	23	– not out	35
N. J. N. Hawke c Barber b Brown	0	– c Smith b Titmus	2
†A. T. W. Grout b Brown	0	– c Smith b Allen	3
G. D. McKenzie c Cowdrey b Barber	24	– c Barber b Titmus	12
P. L. Philpott not out	5	– lbw b Allen	5
B 7, l-b 8	15	B 3, l-b 1	4
1/0 2/81 3/91 4/105 5/155 6/174 7/174 8/174 9/203	221	1/46 2/50 3/51 4/86 5/86 6/119 7/131 8/135 9/140	174

Bowling: *First Innings*—Jones 20–6–51–2; Brown 17–1–63–5; Boycott 3–1–8–0; Titmus 23–8–40–0; Barber 2.1–1–2–1; Allen 19–5–42–2. *Second Innings*—Jones 7–0–35–0; Brown 11–2–32–1; Titmus 17.3–4–40–4; Allen 20–8–47–4; Barber 5–0–16–0.

Umpires: C. Egar and L. Rowan.

AUSTRALIA v ENGLAND

Second Test Match

Played at Perth, December 11, 12, 13, 15, 16, 1970

Drawn. Perth's first Test match was an outstandingly successful promotion. It was perfectly organised, and nearly 85,000 spectators saw it. That number was nearly twice that at Brisbane, and gate receipts in the region of £50,000 were almost three times as large. If not all the cricket was worthy of the enthusiastic people of Western Australia, the match was in the balance until the last afternoon. England again slipped from a position of strength in their first innings, and once more Australia's batting was revealed as fragile.

Boycott and Luckhurst with opening stands of 171 and 60 carried their total in ten opening partnerships to 994. Luckhurst was the leader in the first stand lasting four and a quarter hours. Boycott, so dominating in State games, had not yet got going as well in the Tests, and his stolid 70 contained only three 4s. Though the Perth boundaries are long Luckhurst managed nine in that time, and when bowled by McKenzie's break-back, after 78 overs occupying five hours, forty minutes, he had thirteen. Edrich also batted well and England were 257 for two at the close of the first day.

On the second Edrich ran himself out, and the middle batting failed. McKenzie bowled particularly well in this innings, but he was eclipsed by Snow. On a pitch which, like the one for the previous game was not nearly so fast as it can be on this ground, Snow had appreciably more life than any other quick bowler in the match. In his first 18 balls he took two for one, and early on the third day Australia were desperately placed at 107 for five. They were magnificently rescued by Redpath and G. S. Chappell, who was playing in his first Test. Redpath played thoroughly well, but by no means so surely as his less experienced partner. Redpath was disconcerted by pace; Chappell never was. Slowly but surely they pulled their side round. At tea the total was 240, and afterwards Chappell cut loose. He mauled Snow, Lever and Shuttleworth so severely that 74 were added in ten overs. When Chappell went three overs later, he had hit his last 60 in 13 overs while Redpath collected 25. In all he batted four and a quarter hours and hit ten 4s, while Redpath's innings lasted just over eight hours and included fourteen 4s.

Another indifferent batting performance, which Edrich redeemed with the aid of Illingworth and Knott, put England in peril. Though Boycott played his best Test innings to date they were 152 for five, only 109 ahead and sorely puzzled by Gleeson's varied and accurate spin, and more than five and a half hours remained. Illingworth, however, batted well while 57 were added, and finally he declared to allow Australia two hours, twenty-five minutes for their second innings. To score 245 in that time would have required exceptional batting, but Lawry could have been expected at least to make a token attempt. Only I. M. Chappell made a gesture. Lawry's batting was craven. His second run completed his 5,000 in Test cricket, his third his 2,000 against England. With that he seemed content. After sixty-eight minutes he had made only 6, and Australia spent 21 overs reaching 50. There was not a spark of enterprise about the batting of Lawry or Redpath until Fletcher and Cowdrey bowled their inaccurate leg breaks.

England

G. Boycott c McKenzie b Gleeson	70	– st Marsh b Gleeson	50
B. W. Luckhurst b McKenzie	131	– c Stackpole b Walters	19
J. H. Edrich run out	47	– not out	115
†A. P. E. Knott c Stackpole b Thomson	24	– not out	30
K. W. R. Fletcher b Walters	22	– lbw b Gleeson	0
M. C. Cowdrey c and b G. S. Chappell	40	– c Marsh b Thomson	1
B. L. D'Oliveira c Stackpole b Thomson	8	– b Gleeson	31
*R. Illingworth b McKenzie	34	– c Marsh b Stackpole	29
J. A. Snow not out	4		
K. Shuttleworth b McKenzie	2		
P. Lever b McKenzie	2		
L-b 8, w 1, n-b 4	13	B 2, l-b 3, n-b 7	12
1/171 2/243 3/281 4/291 5/310 6/327 7/389 8/389 9/392	397	1/60 2/98 3/98 4/101 5/152 6/209	(6 wkts dec.) 287

Bowling: *First Innings*—McKenzie 31.4–4–66–4; Thomson 24–4–118–2; G. S. Chappell 24–4–54–1; Gleeson 32–10–78–1; Walters 11–1–35–1; Stackpole 11–2–33–0. *Second Innings*—McKenzie 18–2–50–0; Thomson 25–3–71–1; Gleeson 32–11–68–3; Stackpole 15–3–43–1; Walters 7–1–26–1; G. S. Chappell 4–1–17–0.

Australia

K. R. Stackpole c Lever b Snow	5	– c sub b Snow	0
*W. M. Lawry c Illingworth b Snow	0	– not out	38
I. M. Chappell c Knott b Snow	50	– c sub b Snow	17
K. D. Walters c Knott b Lever	7	– b Lever	8
I. R. Redpath c and b Illingworth	171	– not out	26
A. P. Sheahan run out	2		
G. S. Chappell c Luckhurst b Shuttleworth	108		
†R. W. Marsh c D'Oliveira b Shuttleworth	44		
G. D. McKenzie c Lever b d'Oliveira	7		
J. W. Gleeson c Knott b Snow	15		
A. L .Thomson not out	12		
B 5, l-b 4, n-b 10	19	B 4, l-b 4, n-b 3	11
1/5 2/8 3/17 4/105 5/107 6/326 7/393 8/408 9/426	440	1/0 2/20 3/40	(3 wkts) 100

Bowling: *First Innings*—Snow 33.5–3–143–4; Shuttleworth 28–4–105–2; Lever 21–3–78–1; D'Oliveira 17–1–41–1; Illingworth 13–2–43–1; Boycott 1–0–7–0; Fletcher 1–0–4–0. *Second Innings*—Snow 9–4–17–2; Shuttleworth 3–1–9–0; Lever 5–2–10–1; D'Oliveira 4–2–5–0; Illingworth 4–2–12–0; Fletcher 4–0–18–0; Cowdrey 3–0–18–0.

Umpires: T. F. Brooks and L. P. Rowan.

SOUTH AUSTRALIA v MCC

Played at Adelaide, December 18, 19, 20, 21, 1970

Drawn. I. M. Chappell followed the lead of Lock in the matter of declarations, and at one time bad cricket by MCC and an apparent urge to lose rather than draw seemed likely to allow South Australia a win. Reckless batting on the last afternoon was redeemed in the final period by d'Oliveira and Underwood, who stayed with him nearly two hours. D'Oliveira began as recklessly as all others after a fine innings of four and a half hours by Boycott ended, but after tea he played excellent forceful cricket. He hit twelve 4s and batted nearly four hours. Until then it was nearly all South Australia, starting with 250 at above five an over by Richards and Woodcock. Woodcock actually outscored his brilliant partner until he was in the eighties, and his stoke play was quite as impressive until he retired hurt. Richards threw his wicket away in the day's final over after batting four hours, forty minutes on a rain interrupted day and hitting fifteen 4s.

In a depressing MCC batting performance Cowdrey struggled unhappily. Only Knott and Boycott batted with assurance though Willis hit eagerly and well. Willis also put in a splendid spell of fast bowling in the second innings, three wickets in 17 balls, after another superb century by G. S. Chappell. He reached 100 off 99 balls in under two hours and hit three 6s, all in the course of four balls from Underwood, and twelve 4s. I. M. Chappell's second declaration left MCC five hours, fifty minutes in which to make 398, and an early break-down soon put them out of the running. Hammond, a young fast bowler of much promise, and Mallett, a much more purposeful off-spinner than in the first match between these sides, bowled well for South Australia.

South Australia

B. A. Richards st Taylor b Underwood	146	– b Shuttleworth	23
A. J. Woodcock retired hurt	119	– c Taylor b Willis	52
G. S. Chappell c Taylor b Lever	20	– c Hampshire b D'Oliveira	102
J. P. Causby not out	7	– c Taylor b Willis	20
*I. M. Chappell (did not bat)		– c Undewood b D'Oliveira	17
K. G. Cunningham (did not bat)		– c Taylor b Willis	60
†R. P. Blundell (did not bat)		– c D'Oliveira b Willis	0
A. A. Mallett (did not bat)		– not out	42
T. J. Jenner (did not bat)		– not out	12
L-b 4, n-b 1	5	B 5, l-b 1, n-b 4	10
1/277 2/297 (2 wkts dec.)	297	1/38 2/44 3/93 4/187 5/278 6/279 7/287 (7 wkts dec.)	338

J. R. Hammond and K. J. McCarthy did not bat.

Bowling: *First Innings*—Lever 12–1–45–1; Willis 12–0–87–0; Shuttleworth 7–0–62–0; D'Oliveira 13–1–51–0; Underwood 14.4–2–47–1. *Second Innings*—Shuttleworth 11–0–44–1; Willis 16–2–81–4; D'Oliveira 14–1–58–2; Lever 6–0–41–0; Underwood 18–1–85–0; Hampshire 3–0–19–0.

MCC

G. Boycott not out	42	– c Cunningham b Mallett 92
*M. C. Cowdrey c Richards b Mallett	57	– c G. S. Chappell b Hammond 1
K. W. R. Fletcher c Cunningham b G. S. Chappell	14	– c Cunningham b Hammond 0
J. H. Hampshire c and b G. S. Chappell	2	– c G. S. Chappell b McCarthy 13
B. L. D'Oliveira b G. S. Chappell	20	– not out 162
A. P. E. Knott c G. S. Chappell b Mallett	42	– c Blundell b Mallett 7
†R. W. Taylor run out	16	– c Blundell b Mallett 0
P. Lever b Jenner	0	– b Hammond 7
K. Shuttleworth c Cunningham b Mallett	14	– c G. S. Chappell b Richards 24
D. L. Underwood c McCarthy b Mallett	0	– not out 13
R. G. D. Willis c G. S. Chappell b Jenner	27	
L-b 1, n-b 3	4	B 4, l-b 7, n-b 6 17
1/50 2/59 3/92 4/122 5/159 6/164 7/164 8/189 9/195	238	1/7 2/25 3/29 4/91 5/135 6/149 7/149 8/220 (8 wkts) 336

Bowling: *First Innings*—Hammond 4–0–19–0; McCarthy 10–2–31–0; G. S. Chappell 13–2–41–3; Cunningham 3–0–12–0; Jenner 21.1–3–72–2; Mallett 18–6–59–4. *Second Innings*—Hammond 14–1–61–3; McCarthy 16–1–56–1; Jenner 18–1–64–0; G. S. Chappell 10–1–42–0; Mallett 17–4–61–3; Richards 7–0–35–1.

Umpires: M. G. O'Connell and F. Godson.

AUSTRALIA v ENGLAND

Fourth Test Match

Played at Sydney, January 9, 10, 12, 13, 14, 1971

England won by 299 runs. Great batting by Boycott and superb fast bowling by Snow on a pitch taking spin, which was too slow for other pace bowlers, were too much for Australia. The latter were conclusively outplayed after the first day, on which their spin caused an English collapse helped by bad strokes. Boycott made 77 out of a first-wicket stand of 116 off 31 overs. Brilliant stroke play brought him eleven 4s. Though he fell to a catch on the boundary when hooking a long hop, England passed 200 with only two wickets down. In the next thirty-three minutes they lost four wickets while 18 were scored, and Mallett had remarkable success with his off breaks. In his first eight overs after tea he took three for 6.

England's later batsmen, however, hit back bravely, the last four wickets adding 119, and the rally was continued by the bowlers, Underwood being mainly responsible for the last six Australian wickets going on the third morning for 47. The only stand for Australia in the match was 99 by Redpath and Walters. Redpath played much more soundly than Walters, who was dropped at first slip when 3. Redpath also gave a slip catch, though a much more difficult one, when he was 6. Lever was the unfortunate bowler on both occasions.

In the second innings England lost their first three wickets for 48, during which time Boycott ran out Edrich. He made amends during stands of 133 with D'Oliveira and 95 with Illingworth. Both partners played excellently while Boycott ruthlessly broke the Australian attack. He played to a schedule which allowed Illingworth to leave over nine hours for Australia's second innings, staying six hours fifty minutes and hitting twelve 4s. The England bowlers needed less than half that time, and only Lawry, who stayed throughout an innings of four hours and a quarter of stern defence, could live against Snow. And he faced few of Snow's deliveries on the final day, when Snow took five for 20 in eight overs. His seven for 40 was his finest Test performance. The pitch was without pace, but on occasions Snow made the ball kick viciously from a worn patch and had his opponents apprehensive from first to last.

England

G. Boycott c Gleeson b Connolly	77	– not out	142
B. W. Luckhurst lbw b Gleeson	38	– c I. M. Chappell b McKenzie	5
J. H. Edrich c Gleeson b G. S. Chappell	55	– run out	12
K. W. R. Fletcher c Walters b Mallett	23	– c Stackpole b Mallett	8
B. L. D'Oliveira c Connolly b Mallett	0	– c I. M. Chappell b G. S. Chappell	56
*R. Illingworth b Gleeson	25	– st Marsh b Mallett	53
†A. P. E. Knott st Marsh b Mallett	6	– not out	21
J. A. Snow c Lawry b Gleeson	37		
P. Lever c Connolly b Mallett	36		
D. L. Underwood c G. S. Chappell b Gleeson	0		
R. G. D. Willis not out	15		
B 5, l-b 2, w 1, n-b 12	20	B 9, l-b 4, n-b 9	22
1/116 2/130 3/201 4/205 5/208 6/219 7/262 8/291 9/291	332	1/7 2/35 3/48 4/181 5/276	(5 wkts dec.) 319

Bowling: *First Innings*—McKenzie 15–3–74–0; Connolly 13–2–43–1; Gleeson 29–7–83–4; G. S. Chappell 11–4–30–1; Mallett 16.7–5–40–4; Walters 3–1–11–0; Stackpole 7–2–31–0. *Second Innings*—McKenzie 15–0–65–1; Connolly 14–1–38–0; G. S. Chappell 15–5–24–1; Gleeson 23–4–54–0; Mallett 19–1–85–2; Stackpole 6–1–17–0; Walters 2–0–14–0.

Australia

*W. M. Lawry c Edrich b Lever	9	– not out	60
I. M. Chappell c Underwood b Snow	12	– c D'Oliveira b Snow	0
I. R. Redpath c Fletcher b D'Oliveira	64	– c Edrich b Snow	6
K. D. Walters c Luckhurst b Illingworth	55	– c Knott b Lever	3
G. S. Chappell c and b Underwood	15	– b Snow	2
K. R. Stackpole c Boycott b Underwood	33	– c Lever b Snow	30
†R. W. Marsh c D'Oliveira b Underwood	8	– c Willis b Snow	0
A. A. Mallett b Underwood	4	– c Knott b Willis	6
G. D. McKenzie not out	11	– retired hurt	6
J. W. Gleeson c Fletcher b D'Oliveira	0	– b Snow	0
A. N. Connolly b Lever	14	– c Knott b Snow	0
N-b 11	11	B 2, n-b 1	3
1/14 2/38 3/137 4/160 5/189 6/199 7/208 8/208 9/219	236	1/1 2/11 3/14 4/21 5/66 6/66 7/86 8/116 9/116	116

Bowling: *First Innings*—Snow 14–6–23–1; Willis 9–2–26–0; Lever 8.6–1–31–2; Underwood 22–7–66–4; Illingworth 14–3–59–1; D'Oliveira 9–2–20–2. *Second Innings*—Snow 17.5–5–40–7; Lever 11–1–24–1; Underwood 8–2–17–0; D'Oliveira 7–3–16–0; Illingworth 9–5–9–0; Willis 3–2–1–1; Fletcher 1–0–6–0.

Umpires: L. P. Rowan and T. F. Brooks.

AUSTRALIA v ENGLAND

Fifth Test Match

Played at Melbourne, January 21, 22, 23, 25, 26, 1971

Drawn. Australia recovered some of their poise when England dropped eight catches in the first innings of a match marred by bad crowd behaviour. A stampede on the first day when I. M. Chappell reached 100, left its mark on the pitch. Fully 2,000 spectators rushed the pitch, stealing Chappell's cap, Cowdrey's white hat and a stump. Their offensive attitude towards the visitors culminated in an unsavoury demonstration in the final forty minutes, when Boycott and Edrich batted against a continuous background of booing, handclapping in unison and the banging of empty beer cans. At one time the umpires conferred but allowed play to continue.

Cowdrey returned to the side because Fletcher was injured, and disastrously, for his four missed slip catches in the first innings cost England their chance. He missed I. M. Chappell off Snow before he scored and again off D'Oliveira when he was 14. Altogether he missed five in the match.

Australia's 493 was a remarkable innings, for all the main scorers were missed at least once and some of the batting was remarkably faulty. Walters scored a high proportion of his runs off the bat's edge, as he did again in the second innings. After settling down I. M. Chappell played strongly, hitting twelve 4s in an innings of just over four hours, and Redpath again batted well in a stand of 180 after Lawry had been struck on the hand and retired. The most robust batting was by the left-handed Marsh, who thumped the ball hard for three and a quarter hours, hitting twelve 4s. He gave two chances in the sixties, but otherwise played sterling cricket for his side.

Lawry long delayed his declaration into the evening of the second day and then astonishingly deprived Marsh of the chance to become the first Australian wicket-keeper to score a Test century. Lawry's captaincy indeed gave his side little chance of squaring the series. When he had a lead of 101 his second innings was geared so low that it lasted four and a quarter hours for 169 for four. He could not have expected England to attempt the task of making 102 more runs in fifteen minutes less time on a slow pitch taking spin, particularly as Luckhurst could not bat and D'Oliveira, who had a badly bruised toe, could have done so only with a runner.

Luckhurst broke the little finger of his left hand quite early in a grand fighting innings, which pulled England round after Thomson, in helpful conditions, had them reeling at 88 for three. Despite his handicap Luckhurst stayed nearly five and a half hours to score his second century of the series, in which he hit eleven 4s. D'Oliveira, his partner while 140 were scored inside three hours, and Illingworth again played fine parts in rallying the side. D'Oliveira batted five and three-quarter hours for 117, also hitting eleven 4s, and Illingworth made 41 out of a fifth-wicket partnership of 78.

In Australia's second innings Snow was warned about his use of the bouncer by the new Test umpire, O'Connell, although he bowled considerably fewer than Thomson. In the final innings Boycott and Edrich, with only a draw to play for, scored 161 in the four hours. After 45 overs they had made 133, but when the crowd made concentration difficult they inevitably fell back on defence. In conditions helpful to spin Australia's slow bowlers failed badly.

This match attracted 184,503 people and the third day produced world record receipts of £25,070 sterling. Altogether the Test series was watched by 678,486 spectators who paid £248,354.

Australia

K. R. Stackpole c Lever b D'Oliveira	30	c Knott b Willis	18
*W. M. Lawry c Snow b Willis	56	c sub b Snow	42
I. M. Chappell c Luckhurst b Snow	111	b Underwood	30
I. R. Redpath b Snow	72	c Knott b Snow	5
K. D. Walters b Underwood	55	not out	39
G. S. Chappell c Edrich b Willis	3	not out	20
†R. W. Marsh not out	92		
K. J. O'Keeffe c Luckhurst b Illingworth	27		
J. W. Gleeson c Cowdrey b Willis	5		
J. R. F. Duncan c Edrich b Illingworth	3		
A. L. Thomson not out	0		
B 10, l-b 17, n-b 12	30	B 8, l-b 3, n-b 4	15
1/64 2/266 3/269 4/310 5/314 6/374 7/471 8/477 9/480	(9 wkts dec.) 493	1/51 2/84 3/91 4/132	(4 wkts dec.) 169

Bowling: *First Innings*—Snow 29–6–94–2; Lever 25–6–79–0; D'Oliveira 22–6–71–1; Willis 20–5–73–3; Underwood 19–4–78–1; Illingworth 13–0–59–2. *Second Innings*—Snow 12–4–21–2; Lever 12–1–53–0; Willis 10–1–42–1; Underwood 12–0–38–1.

England

G. Boycott c Redpath b Thomson	12	– not out	76
B. W. Luckhurst b Walters	109		
J. H. Edrich c Marsh b Thomson	9	– not out	74
M. C. Cowdrey c and b Gleeson	13		
B. L. D'Oliveira c Marsh b Thomson	117		
*R. Illingworth c Redpath b Gleeson	41		
†A. P. E. Knott lbw b Stackpole	19		
J. A. Snow b I. M. Chappell	1		
P. Lever run out	19		
D. L. Underwood c and b Gleeson	5		
R. G. D. Willis not out	5		
B 17, l-b 14, n-b 11	42	B 1, l-b 8, n-b 2	11
1/40 2/64 3/88 4/228 5/306 6/340 7/354 8/362 9/379	392		(No wkt) 161

Bowling: *First Innings*—Thomson 34–5–110–3; Duncan 14–4–30–0; G. S. Chappell 8–0–21–0; O'Keeffe 31–11–71–0; Gleeson 25–7–60–3; Stackpole 17.5–4–41–1; Walters 5–2–7–1; I. M. Chappell 3–0–10–1. *Second Innings*—Thomson 11–5–26–0; Walters 7–1–14–0; Gleeson 3–1–18–0; O'Keeffe 19–3–45–0; Stackpole 13–2–28–0; G. S. Chappell 5–0–19–0.

Umpires: M. G. O'Connell and L. P. Rowan.

THE GREATEST CENTENARY OF THEM ALL!

AUSTRALIA v ENGLAND

By Gordon Ross

On March 15, 1977, a few weeks before the first copies of *Wisden*, 1977, are on the bookstalls, the greatest event in cricket history will be celebrated – the one hundredth anniversary of the first Australia v England Test match, which began in Melbourne on March 15, 1877, the start of a rivalry which has become a piece of history, and has survived the ravages of one war after another, to stand the pasage of time unchallenged in national affection. The green caps of Australia (even the actual cap seems different in physical shape from any other cricketing cap!) have had a special magic about them; tradition has not tarnished a golden image; the cricket has mellowed through the years; it has lost nothing of its bouquet.

The England party touring Australia in 1877 were not the first to go there. They were, in fact, the fourth. It is generally accepted by historians that the first overseas cricket tour from England was in 1859, when a strong team under the captaincy of George Parr, sailed from Liverpool for Quebec on September 7. Financially the trip was a success, the players clearing £90 each, free of all expenses, not to mention the gifts that were bestowed upon them. News of this excursion was not long in reaching Australia. A Melbourne catering firm, Spiers and Pond, enterprisingly, sent a representative to England in the summer of 1861, and he, Mr Mallam, approached H. H. Stephenson of Surrey with a request that he would collect a team and go to Australia with an idea of pioneering cricket of international standard in that country.

STEPHENSON'S TEAM IN 1861

The terms arranged for the cricketers was £150 each and full expenses; in 1861 this represented handsome reward. A number of leading cricketers of the day lacked the adventurous spirit and declined to make the trip, but twelve did, and so shaped cricket's destiny. They were: H. H. Stephenson (captain), G. Bennett, W. Caffyn, G. Griffith, T. Hearne, R. Iddison, W. Mortlock, W. Mudie, C. Lawrence, T. Sewell, E. Stephenson and G. Wells. The tour opened in Melbourne on New Year's Day, 1862, when, it is said, twenty-five thousand people paid half-a-crown each for admission. Spiers and Pond are alleged to have made a very handsome profit from their venture; all the more surprising that it took another hundred years for sponsorship to play a major role in cricket.

Stephenson's cricketers had arduous journies to endure. They travelled to their second match in Australia, a distance of over two hundred miles, in a coach drawn by six greys – all to play a collection of gentlemen curiously titled 'The Ovens'. The Ovens were bowled out for 20 and 53, and when at the end of the scheduled contest, Griffith played a single-wicket match against eleven of them, all eleven suffered the extreme indignity of failing to score. To cap it all, when having to bowl Griffith out for nought in order to tie the match, The Ovens bowlers sent down two wides. This may have been a slightly Gilbertian cricket match, but it mattered little in the overall context of the tour. The players brought home with them such glowing reports of their treatment in Australia that no difficulty was found in raising the next side to go in the winter of 1863-64. This time George Parr was the captain and the rest of his party was G. Anderson, J. Caesar, W. Caffyn, R. Carpenter, A. Clarke, E. M. Grace, T. Hayward, J. Jackson, T. Lockyer, G. Tarrant, R. C. Tinley.

PARR'S TOUR OF 1863-64

The *Melbourne Age*, on April 25, 1864, wrote:

> "Parr's Eleven, one and all, proved themselves good men and true, and during their stay of four months in the colonies they have shown themselves worthy of their reputation. Much has been said about the comparative merits of the two Elevens which have visited Australia; but there cannot be a doubt in all unprejudiced minds, that the Eleven now leaving these shores is greatly superior to anything the colonists have before seen in point of cricketing excellence. The previous Eleven showed nothing equal to the wicket-keeping of Lockyer, the batting of Hayward and Carpenter, or the bowling of Jackson, Tarrant and Tinley, and it is more than probable that the Eleven which first visited Australia would now find their match in a Victorian Twenty-Two. The vist of this Eleven will be productive of much benefit to colonial cricketers, if for no other cause by its having led to the retention of Caffyn, the best all-round man among them; and with the aid of such a coach, Victoria will doubtless in future inter-colonial matches take her proper position."

History has not recorded why it was, in view of the fact that this tour was so obviously a success, that ten years elapsed before another English side set foot in Australia. These tours were privately arranged so that it first needed an invitation to be issued, and then it was a question of whether or not the financial arrangements were suitable to all parties. It seems that this was sometimes the stumbling block – and may have been the reason for a decade going by without a tour. It appears that an offer was made to W. G. Grace (then aged twenty-four) in the summer of 1872, but the inducement was not of a sufficiently tempting character, and the idea was abandoned, but in the spring of 1873 another offer came direct from the Melbourne Cricket Club to Mr Grace to bring out a team of his own selection, and the proposal met with considerable favour. Circumstances, we are told, tended to cripple the Captain in his task of forming a Twelve. Emmett was unable, and Alfred Shaw unwilling. Pooley was in disgrace, Pinder in domestic disarrangements, and Hill, at hand if wanted, but not required. Amateurs, as is their wont, promised, and no doubt intended, to fulfil their promise, but failed at the crisis, or Messrs Hornby and Bird might have been in the party. The final composition was nine from the South and only three from the North – W. G. Grace (captain), F. H. Boult, J. A. Bush, W. R. Gilbert, G. F. Grace, A. Greenwood, R. Humphrey, H. Jupp, James Lillywhite, M. McIntyre, W. Oscroft and James Southerton.

The team played fifteen matches; they won ten, lost three and two were drawn, which on the face of it would appear to be a reasonably successful tour, but one or two remarks made by members of the touring party gave a hint that all was not well at times. One of them wrote: "We left our country, as we fondly hoped, for our country's good. We came back to some extent wiser, if not sadder men." He went on: "Whatever shortcomings there were during the tour might have been remedied with a little conciliation on both sides, and the want of an occasional concession from one leader or the other did much to magnify a mere scratch into an open sore."

W. G. GRACE CAPTAIN IN 1873-74

The tour began on Boxing Day, 1873, twelve days after the P and O Steamship *Mirzahpore* had landed the party in Australia. Mr Grace disappointed his team sadly. He was not given to, or fond of, losing the toss, but he did on this occasion, and the Eighteen of Victoria took the bat to win by an innings and 21 runs. Australian cricket had, apparently, been under-rated. The second time the touring team met Victoria the latter had been suitably handicapped and their numbers reduced to Fifteen; this time the tourists won by seven wickets. For the third encounter Victoria were restored to their full complement of eighteen; the match was drawn. The general feeling was that cricket in Australia had improved wonderfully and was still improving; some very useful cricketers had been seen. Whatever undercurrents may have flowed beneath the surface, and although this was by no means the best side that England could have found, the trip seems to have done inestimable good for Australian cricket. The players were able to sharpen their claws ready for the next visit by a side from England, a side that was to make history.

And so to the winter of 1876-77. On Thursday, September 21, 1876, twelve English professional cricketers left Southampton for Adelaide in the P and O steamer *Poonah*. James Lillywhite of Sussex was the captain, Southerton of Surrey his first mate. Yorkshire sent five representatives – Ulyett, Hill, Emmett, Andrew Greenwood, and Armitage – Notts two – Alfred Shaw and Selby – while Surrey also furnished Jupp and Pooley – and the remaining player was Charlwood of Sussex. Even so, this was still not the absolute best that could be found. In bowling they were undeniably strong with Alfred Shaw, Hill, Emmett, Southerton, Lillywhite and Ulyett, and their fielding was rated very highly. It was considered that, in Pooley, the side had the best wicket-keeper of the day, but it was generally felt that they might have been considerably strengthened in batting, and Daft, Lockwood and Shrewsbury might conceivably have taken the places of Southerton, Armitage and Charlwood, but any chosen party by any set of selectors is always open to question when alternative suggestions are bandied about. The party arrived at King George's Sound on November 2; they played their first match on the 17th.

THE HISTORIC 1876-77 TOUR BEGINS

Alfred Shaw was one of the players whom W. G. Grace had invited on his tour, but Shaw had declined. The conditions offered for Grace's tour to the professional members were £150, and second class passage, travelling and hotel expenses, the latter item being fixed, where possible, at 7s 6d a day. Shaw declined the offer because he objected to the second class proviso. For the 1876 trip the terms were £150 and first-class passage. It was Shaw who began the tour in dramatic fashion against South Australia in Adelaide when Eleven played Twenty-Two. His analysis was 226 balls, 46 maidens, 12 runs, 14 wickets. England (as they were billed throughout the tour) scored 153, the Twenty-Two South Australians could muster only 54 and 53. The wicket was sandy and broke up early. The Australians had not yet learned the subtleties of wicket preparation; they were afraid to use the roller for fear that it would bruise and kill the grass. In later years, this Adelaide wicket became as firm as concrete and as smooth as a sheet of glass. The credit for this transformation was largely due to Jesse Hide, the old Sussex player, who obtained some clay off the mountains nearby and worked it into the soil at a remarkable expenditure of time, trouble, and elbow grease!

From the overwhelming success in Adelaide, England were brought down to earth at Sydney by Fifteen of New South Wales – England 122 and 97. New South Wales 81 and 151 for twelve, to win by two wickets. Shaw once again had impressive figures – 376 balls, 68 maidens, 53 runs, 8 wickets. England were shattered by Evans and Spofforth – they took 16 of the England wickets between them. What are usually termed Country matches followed against Twenty-Two of Newcastle and Twenty-Two of Goulburn.

The fifth match of the tour, however, was rather different; it was against Fifteen of Victoria at Melbourne. It began on Boxing Day. England were beaten, despite the continued magnificence of Shaw. This time he took 12 for 74, but Victoria's bowlers, Midwinter and Allen, were the prime architects of a victory by 31 runs. Yet this match had once been threatened with legal proceedings. Originally, two teams had been announced to make a tour that winter from England. One was projected by Mr G. F. Grace; the other was Lillywhite's. The Grace tour fell through, but the commodious Melbourne Ground had been engaged by Grace's agent. Lillywhite's agent had arranged for the East Melbourne enclosure, and the East Melbourne Club went to considerable expense in preparing for the visit. When Grace withdrew his project, Lillywhite decided to play on the Melbourne Ground. This intensely annoyed the people of East Melbourne and threats of legal proceedings, heated newspaper controversies, and general unpleasantness resulted. Finally, the dispute was settled by the East Melbourne Club accepting Lillywhite's offer of £230, with free admission to their members, numbering 500, to the tourists' matches in Melbourne.

The ecstasy at the success of the Victoria Fifteen erased all memories of rancour and bitterness. After two more country matches England faced the return match with Fifteen of New South Wales at Sydney – and total humiliation. They were bowled out for 35, of which Charlwood was run out for 20. The scores of the remaining ten were: 0, 1, 0, 0, 1, 2, 2, 7, 0, 2. The bowlers? – precisely the same two – Spofforth and Evans, and they did it again in the second innings, having ravaged the first six batsmen for a paltry 18 runs, when they were thwarted by Armitage (38) and Shaw (30), and an England total of 104 resulted. The Fifteen scored 124 and 17 for one wicket to win by 13 wickets.

THE POOLEY STORY

A return game was played immediately, starting the next day, by which time the handicapper had been at work and England met New South Wales at level weights, each side having eleven players, England this time having incomparably the better of it. Ulyett hit 94, and England scored 270. New South Wales were bowled out for 82, and were 140 for six in their second innings when the match ended, Shaw once again being head and shoulders England's most successful bowler – he took eight for 54. On this note the first part of the Australian tour ended, and the England team left for New Zealand. Not many historians could tell you off the cuff the results of any of the matches in New Zealand, but all of them will mention, as if it were a legend – the story of Pooley, and the trouble he got into. A number of versions have been given of the incident; age has a habit of over-colouring events; what is a little exaggeration here and there in the course of a hundred years! – but we must take note of what Alfred Shaw said; after all, he was there.

Here is Shaw's account of the proceedings:

> "It cannot be considered surprising that in quarters where betting was rampant, as was the case in Australia at this time, some of the members of our team, who needed very small encouragement to back their opinions and statements at any time, should be led to participate in enterprises they had better have eschewed. One of these enterprises had most unpleasant consequences to one member of the team and it led to the side being deprived of his services for the last few weeks of the tour. The victim was Ed Pooley. We were playing at Christchurch against Eighteen of Canterbury on February 26, 27, and 28, 1877. In a discussion as to the prospects of the match that occurred in an hotel bar at night, Pooley offered to take £1 to 1 shilling that he named the individual

score of every member of the local team. It is a trick familiar to cricketers, and in the old days of matches against local eighteens and twenty-twos it not infrequently worked off against the unwary. The bet being accepted Pooley named a duck as the score of each batsmen on the local side. A fair proportion of ducks was recorded, and Pooley claimed £1 each for them, while prepared to pay a shilling for the other scores. The man with whom the bet had been made said it was a catch bet on Pooley's part, and he declined to pay. The man's name was Ralph Donkin. His refusal to pay led to a scene of disorder, and brought Pooley's services with the team to an unpleasant end.

"We had to go next to Otago and at the close of the match there Pooley was arrested on a charge of 'having at Christchurch maliciously injured property above the value of £5, and also of assaulting Donkin'. For the assault he had £5 and costs to pay. In the other charge he had as partner in trouble Alf Bramall, a supernumerary attached to our team. The two were committed for trial, bail being allowed for £100, with two sureties of £50 each. We never saw Pooley again during the tour. He and his companion were tried before the Supreme Court at Christchurch on April 6th, and found not guilty. The local public thought he had been hardly used in having been taken away from the team. They subscribed £50 for division between Pooley and Bramall, and in addition they presented Pooley with a gold ring. The old Surrey wicket-keeper had to make the journey back to England alone."

Pooley's experience was only one of the trials the team faced during their stay in New Zealand, which was financially a failure; stories live of a most frightening experience in Otira Gorge, when what should have been a shallow ford was a rising torrent of water and the coach came to grief in mid-stream. The four horses were dead beat and fell down in the water and the players leapt off the coach up to their waists in rushing water to free the horses. They had to walk on, wearied and exhausted, and with saturated clothing, to find shelter for the night. The hotels were described as being of the crudest and most trying character. But from a purely cricket point of view affairs were reasonably happy. The side was in New Zealand from the first match in Auckland on January 29 until the final game at Invercargill ending on March 8. Eight matches were played against combinations of Twenty-Two and Eighteen, England winning six and drawing two. And so back to Australia for the eighteenth match of the tour – and England v Australia – Eleven each side – and the First Test Match!

THE FIRST TEST – MARCH 15, 1877

It was warm and sunny in Melbourne on March 15, 1877, when Charles Bannerman took guard and prepared to receive the first ball from Alfred Shaw in what has come to be universally regarded as the first Test Match. Bannerman did not commit his name to history purely because he scored the first run in a Test Match – he happened to make 165. Whether or not contemporary historians will fall out over the question of this being the first recognised Test match is quite immaterial; what cannot be disputed is that both sides were very much below full strength. W. G. Grace was missing to begin with. These early Australian tours were, as said earlier, organised by private individuals, and until MCC took over the management of official touring teams in 1903–04, the sides were never fully representative. But the same can be said of Australia. In spite of being the home side they had considerable difficulty in their selection. Evans, Allen and Spofforth (three bowlers who had caused the England players some problems) all declined to play, the latter stating categorically that the absence of Murdoch to keep wicket was his reason for refusing to take part.

Bannerman's was a truly remarkable performance. He scored 165 before retiring hurt after receiving a blow on the hand; the next highest score by an Australian was 18 – and this by Garrett, the number nine. Due to Bannerman's superhuman effort, Australia reached a total of 245; a collection was taken to mark Bannerman's feat and it raised one pound a run. England were 49 runs short of Australia's first innings total. Jupp, who opened, hit 63, Charlwood scored 36, and Hill, coming in at number nine, scored an unbeaten 35. England were all out for 196, but they swiftly struck back. Shaw and Ulyett, who had a comparatively quiet time in the first innings, bowled magnificently, and the Australian innings was soon in some disarray from which it was never able completely to recover. Shaw (5) and Ulyett (4) had taken the first nine wickets to fall, until James Lillywhite bowled the last man in. Australia were all out for 104; England thus needed 154 to win and were favourites to get them, but they were shattered by the bowling of Kendall, who had taken only one wicket in the first innings; this time he took seven, to finish with an aggregate of eight for 109. England's first four batsmen totalled 79 between them; the other seven contributed only 24 – there were 5 extras.

Australia had won by 45 runs. There was great jubilation but also a few uncomplimentary remarks addressed to the England cricketers. *The Australian* wrote that this was the weakest side by a long way that had ever played in the Colonies, notwithstanding the presence among them of Shaw, who was termed the premier bowler of England. It added: "If Ulyett, Emmett and Hill are fair specimens of the best fast bowling in England, all we can say is, either they have not been in the proper form in this Colony or British bowling has sadly deteriorated." *Scores and Biographies* had this to say: "The defeat of England must candidly be attributed to fatigue, owing principally to the distance they had to travel to each match, to sickness, and to high living. England were never fresh in any of their engagements, and, of course, had not near their best Eleven." But what were the facts? Well, the party had landed from its New Zealand trip only the day before the match began. The date had been fixed to allow a few days after landing, but the ship was delayed *en voyage*, and the accommodation had been so poor that some of the party had been obliged to sleep on deck. They were in no shape for a serious game of cricket, least of all Armitage, who had something of a nightmare match. In bowling to Bannerman, he tossed one ball wide over the batsman's head – a delivery which brought forth the remark that the Australians could not reach Armitage's bowling with a clothes prob! The next ball he rolled along the ground; worse still, Armitage dropped Bannerman at mid-off, off Shaw, before he had reached double figures. All in all, for the players of England, it was an unhappy match. And it was the first time that an Australian side confined to eleven players had defeated any eleven from England.

THE SECOND TEST

So nettled were the English party that they were anxious to arrange another match on level terms (eleven players each side) and this was done. On Saturday, March 31, 1877, and the Monday, Tuesday and Wednesday following, England met the Combined Australians on the Melbourne Ground. This time, Mr Spofforth sank his differences, and was in the Australian team, and with his presence in their side the local public predicted a second victory. But England won by four wickets, due principally to the splendid batting of George Ulyett, who scored 52 in the first innings and 63 in the next. This time the Australian public accused England of "kidding" in the first match in order to obtain another game and another gate. On a previous occasion when Spofforth and Evans had bowled the side out for 35, and in the next innings Armitage scored 38, a critic asked: "How can they be playing square, when they make only 35 one day between all of them, and on another day one man makes more than the whole of the team put together?"

Australia again won the toss, but their early batsmen wilted in the face of a fine piece of fast bowling by Hill, who took the first four wickets to fall, including the valuable prize of Bannerman, who had been strongly backed by the great gambling community to score a lot more runs; Hill bowled him for 19. Midwinter was top scorer for Australia with 31 and Australia were all out for 122. Spofforth, it will be remembered, had refused to play in the first match because Murdoch was not chosen to keep wicket. Spofforth, apparently, held the view that only Murdoch was able to take his bowling effectively. It seems that Blackham lost little time in proving to Spofforth how wrong he was. In Spofforth's third over, a fast delivery lifted, and Blackham, standing up, stumped Shaw brilliantly. As Kendall had previously bowled Jupp for a duck, England were 4 for two and remarks were already being made about the poor quality of the English side in derisory terms.

Throughout cricket's long and enduring history, the inherent steel-like toughness of Yorkshiremen has driven back many a foe in adversity. Yorkshire cricket is taught in a hard school, but like a golden thread it has entwined all the classical ages of cricket. Here, at Melbourne, on this March day in 1877 Yorkshire won a match for England. The scores of the five Yorkshiremen were: 49, 52, 48, 49 and 21. The scores of the other six players from Surrey, Notts and Sussex were: 0, 1, 14, 7, 2, 0. Greenwood (49), Ulyett (52), Emmett (48), Hill (49) and Armitage (21) carried England to a score of 261 and a lead of 139. The demon Spofforth had taken three for 67.

Australia batted consistently right down the card in their second innings, Gregory, the captain and number ten, scoring 43, the top score. England's attempt to score the 121 required for victory began calamitously. They were 9 for three and half the side were out for 76, but Ulyett stood in the breach once again with a magnificent 63. Hill struck the winning blow, England were home by four wickets, but even this victory did not alter the view of the Australian public that this was a weak England side, certainly the weakest of the four who had toured Australia.

They had a very high regard for the batting capabilities of Ulyett – and well they might have done – and they thought there were one or two average batsmen, but they rated Kendall ahead of any of the England fast bowlers. "We would counsel whoever may enter into future speculations for importing an England XI," advised one writer, "to bear in mind the great improvements of colonial cricket, and not to imagine that anything will do for Australia."

Only one more match of this long tour remained – against Twenty-Two of South Australia; a low scoring game was left drawn with Ulyett making another fifty. So ended a tour which had begun on November 16 in Adelaide and had continued through Sydney, Newcastle, Goulburn, Melbourne, Ballarat, Geelong, Auckland, Wellington, Taranaki, Nelson, Greymouth, Christchurch, Invercargill, Otago, Melbourne, Sandhurst, Ballarat, Ararat, and back to Adelaide, ending on April 16. In view of the conditions of travel this was an immense undertaking.

THE FUTURE

What the tour had shown was that there had been a tremendous improvement in the standards of Australian cricket. Alfred Shaw wrote at the time: "Cricket education is of a much higher type in the Colonies now; so high, in fact, that I am afraid they are the masters and we the pupils." So even a century ago we were prepared to acknowledge Australian mastery on the cricket field!

The Australians themselves had not been too sure of their own prowess until they won the match on level terms in Melbourne. Prior to this, Lillywhite and Shaw had done their best to persuade the Australians to undertake a tour of England, and had even offered to accept the financial responsibility, so sure were they that the tour would be a success; the Australians had demurred, but their victory at Melbourne brought about a change of heart, and an immediate tour was planned, as an Australian enterprise, in a financial sense.

It was only a year later that the first Australian visit was paid to England. That tour is another story. What should not be forgotten is the part played by these early heroes; their adventurous spirit in the first place, and the hazards of a tour such as was undertaken a hundred years ago. Here is a quotation from the diaries of one of them:

> "Jupp was suffering martyrdom from rheumatism, sciatica or something of the kind, and became so helpless from pains in the hips and loins that he could not walk or even get out of his berth without assistance. Selby and Shaw were as miserable from cold as two men could be. Hill appeared to be sickening for the measles or something of that kind, Ulyett said he wished himself in Sheffield, never to be tempted to go to sea again. In fact, all the party had an acute attack of the doldrums."

What they endured laid the foundation stone of one of the greatest sporting institutions the world has known. Alfred Shaw wrote at the conclusion of the tour: "Let it not be forgotten that cricket has played a most important part in this happy concord", and the two events which marked its origin were the matches that James Lillywhite and his men played in March and April A.D. 1877 at Melbourne.

It is unlikely that we *shall* ever forget – any of us.

THE FIRST TEST MATCH

LILLYWHITE'S TEAM v VICTORIA AND NSW

Played at Melbourne, March 15, 16, 17, 1877. Australia won by 45 runs.

Victoria and New South Wales

C. Bannerman (*NSW*) retired hurt	165	– b Ulyett	4
N. Thompson (*NSW*) b Hill	1	– c Emmett b Shaw	7
T. Horan (*Victoria*) c Hill b Shaw	12	– c Selby b Ulyett	20
*D. W. Gregory (*NSW*) run out	1	– b Shaw	3
B. B. Cooper (*Victoria*) b Southerton	15	– b Shaw	3
W. E. Midwinter (*Victoria*) c Ulyett b Southerton	5	– c Southerton b Ulyett	17
E. J. Gregory (*NSW*) c Greenwood b Lillywhite	0	– c Emmett b Ulyett	11
†J. M. Blackham (*Victoria*) b Southerton	17	– lbw b Shaw	6
T. W. Garrett (*NSW*) not out	18	– c Emmett b Shaw	0
T. Kendall (*Victoria*) c Southerton b Shaw	3	– not out	17
J. Hodges (*Victoria*) b Shaw	0	– b Lillywhite	8
B 4, l-b 2, w 2	8	B 5, l-b 3	8
1/2 2/40 3/41 4/118 5/142 6/143 7/197 8/242 9/245	245	1/7 2/27 3/31 4/31 5/35 6/58 7/71 8/75 9/75	104

Bowling: *First Innings*—Shaw 55.3–34–51–3; Hill 23–10–42–1; Ulyett 25–12–36–0; Southerton 37–11–61–3; Armitage 3–0–15–0; Lillywhite 14–5–19–1; Emmett 12–7–13–0. *Second Innings*—Shaw 34–16–38–5; Hill 14–6–18–0; Ulyett 19–7–39–4; Lillywhite 1–0–1–1.

James Lillywhite's Team

†H. Jupp (*Surrey*) lbw b Garrett	63	– lbw b Midwinter	4
†J. Selby (*Nottinghamshire*) c Cooper b Hodges	7	– c Horan b Hodges	38
H. Charlwood (*Sussex*) c Blackham b Midwinter	36	– b Kendall	13
G. Ulyett (*Yorkshire*) lbw b Thompson	10	– b Kendall	24
A. Greenwood (*Yorkshire*) c E. J. Gregory b Midwinter	1	– c Midwinter b Kendall	5
T. Armitage (*Yorkshire*) c Blackham b Midwinter	9	– c Blackham b Kendall	3
A. Shaw (*Nottinghamshire*) b Midwinter	10	– st Blackham b Kendall	2
T. Emmett (*Yorkshire*) b Midwinter	8	– b Kendall	9
A. Hill (*Yorkshire*) not out	35	– c Thompson b Kendall	0
*James Lillywhite (*Sussex*) c and b Kendall	10	– b Hodges	4
J. Southerton (*Surrey*) c Cooper b Garrett	6	– not out	1
L-b 1	1	B 4, l-b 1	5
1/23 2/79 3/98 4/109 5/121 6/135 7/145 8/145 9/168	196	1/0 2/7 3/20 4/22 5/62 6/68 7/92 8/93 9/100	108

Bowling: *First Innings*—Hodges 9–0–27–1; Garrett 18.1–10–22–2; Kendall 38–16–54–1; Midwinter 54–21–78–5; Thompson 17–10–14–1. *Second Innings*—Hodges 7–5–7–2; Garrett 2–0–9–0; Kendall 33.1–12–55–7; Midwinter 19–7–23–1; D. W. Gregory 5–1–9–0.

Umpires: Curtis Reid and B. Terry.

THE SECOND TEST MATCH

LILLYWHITE'S TEAM v VICTORIA AND NSW

Played at Melbourne, March 31, April 2, 3, 4, 1877. England won by four wickets.

Victoria and New South Wales

N. Thompson (*NSW*) lbw b Hill	18	– b Lillywhite	41
C. Bannerman (*NSW*) b Hill	19	– c Jupp b Ulyett	30
†J. M. Blackham (*Victoria*) c Lillywhite b Hill	5	– lbw b Southerton	26
T. W. Garrett (*NSW*) b Hill	12	– c Jupp b Lillywhite	18
T. J. D. Kelly (*Victoria*) b Ulyett	10	– b Southerton	35
W. Midwinter (*Victoria*) c Emmett b Lillywhite	31	– c Greenwood b Lillywhite	12
F. R. Spofforth (*NSW*) b Ulyett	0	– b Hill	17
W. L. Murdoch (*NSW*) run out	3	– c Shaw b Southerton	8
T. Kendall (*Victoria*) b Lillywhite	7	– b Southerton	12
*D. W. Gregory (*NSW*) not out	1	– c Ulyett b Lillywhite	43
J. Hodges (*Victoria*) run out	2	– not out	0
B 8, l-b 5, w 1	14	B 10, l-b 7	17
1/29 2/29 3/50 4/60 5/96 6/104 7/108 8/114 9/119	122	1/88 2/112 3/135 4/169 5/169 6/196 7/203 8/221 9/259	259

Bowling: *First Innings*—Shaw 42–27–30–0; Lillywhite 29–17–36–2; Hill 27–12–27–4; Ulyett 14.1–6–15–2. *Second Innings*—Shaw 32–19–27–0; Lillywhite 41–15–70–4; Hill 21–9–43–1; Ulyett 19–9–33–1; Emmett 13–6–23–0; Southerton 28.1–13–46–4.

James Lillywhite's Team

†H. Jupp (*Surrey*) b Kendall	0	– b Kendall	1
A. Shaw (*Nottinghamshire*) st Blackham b Spofforth	1	– not out	0
A. Greenwood (*Yorkshire*) b Hodges	49	– c Murdoch b Hodges	22
H. Charlwood (*Sussex*) c Kelly b Kendall	14	– b Kendall	0
J. Selby (*Nottinghamshire*) b Kendall	7	– b Spofforth	2
G. Ulyett (*Yorkshire*) b Spofforth	52	– c Spofforth b Hodges	63
T. Emmett (*Yorkshire*) c Kendall b Spofforth	48	– b Midwinter	8
A. Hill (*Yorkshire*) run out	49	– not out	17
T. Armitage (*Yorkshire*) c Thompson b Midwinter	21		
*James Lillywhite (*Sussex*) not out	2		
J. Southerton (*Surrey*) c Thompson b Kendall	0		
B 5, l-b 12, n-b 1	18	B 8, l-b 1	9
1/0 2/4 3/55 4/72 5/88 6/162 7/196 8/255 9/259	261	1/2 2/8 3/9 4/54 5/76 6/112	(6 wkts) 122

Bowling: *First Innings*—Kendall 52.2–21–82–4; Spofforth 29–6–67–3; Midwinter 21–8–30–1; Hodges 12–2–37–1; Garrett 5–2–10–0; Thompson 11–6–17–0. *Second Innings*—Kendall 17–7–24–2; Spofforth 15–3–44–1; Midwinter 13.1–6–25–1; Hodges 6–2–13–2; Garrett 1–0–7–0.

Umpires: B. Terry and S. Cosstick.

THE CENTENARY TEST MATCH

AUSTRALIA VICTORIOUS AGAIN BY 45 RUNS

By Reg Hayter

Played at Melbourne, March 12, 13, 14, 16, 17, 1977

An occasion of warmest reunion and nostalgia, the cricket continuously compelling, a result of straining credulity. Hans Ebeling, former Australian Test bowler and the inspiration of it all, should have been christened Hans Andersen Ebeling.

From Ebeling, a vice-president of the Melbourne Cricket Club, originated the suggestion to signalise 100 years of Test Cricket by a match between England and Australia on the same ground – in 1877 the Richmond Police Paddock – on which David Gregory's team beat James Lillywhite's all-round professional England side.

The Victorian Cricket Association and the Melbourne Cricket Club co-operated to bring this about and, with sponsorship from Qantas, TAA, Benson & Hedges and the Melbourne Hilton Hotel, a masterpiece of organisation resulted in an event which none fortunate enough to be present could forget. Unlucky were those who missed it.

Arrangements were made for the England team visiting India to extend their tour to play an official Test in the same month as the 1877 Test, and invitations to attend as guests were sent to the 244 living cricketers who had played for Australia or England in the series. All but 26 of these were able to accept for an event unique in history.

The oldest Australian Test player present was the 87-year-old Jack Ryder. Even though suffering from near blindness, the 84-year-old Percy Fender made the enervating air journey from Britain as the oldest English representative. He was accompanied by his grandson, Jeremy, who became his cricketing eyes. Poor health alone prevented E. J. ("Tiger") Smith and Herbert Sutcliffe to travel and, for the same reason, Frank Woolley could not leave Canada.

Of those who went to Melbourne many told unusual stories. Colin McCool was marooned in his Queensland home by floods and had to be hauled up from his front lawn by helicopter for the airport. Jack Rutherford's train broke down and he finished the journey to the airport by taxi. Denis Compton – who else? – left his passport in a Cardiff hotel and, but for the early start to the pre-flight champagne party at London Airport which enabled a good friend to test the speed limits on the M4, would have missed the plane.

Some ex-England players – Harold Larwood, Peter Loader, Tony Lock, Barry Knight, Frank Tyson – already lived in Australia and the Australian Neil Hawke flew home from England. The gradual gathering of all at the Hilton Hotel, 200 yards across the Jolimont Park from the Melbourne Oval, brought meetings and greetings of unabated happiness. Not a hitch, not one.

Fittingly, this was also Melbourne's Mardi Gras, a week called "Moomba", the aboriginal word for "let's get together and have fun". After a champagne (much was drunk between London and Melbourne and back) breakfast and an opening ceremony in which ex-Test captains accompanied the teams on to the field, the crowd were also given the opportunity of a special welcome to all the former Test players.

Greig called correctly to Greg Chappell's spin of the specially minted gold coin and chose for England to field first. Probably he felt apprehension about his batsmen facing Lillee while moisture remained in the pitch. The resolute fast-medium bowling of Willis, Old and Lever, helped by Underwood's customary left-handed accuracy and breath-takingly supported in the field, appeared to justify Greig's decision in Australia's dismissal for 138 in front of a crowd of over 61,000.

Australia, handicapped by the early departure of McCosker, who fractured his jaw when a ball from Willis flew off his hand into his face, were always on the defensive.

England's batting buckled even more swiftly against Lillee, at the zenith of his form and speed, and Walker – Australia's fielding being no whit inferior to that of England.

That was the last of the bowling mastery. On the second, third and fourth days Australia increased their first innings lead of 43 so much that their declaration left England 463 to win at 40 an hour.

Marsh, who had already beaten Grout's record of 187 Test victims, added to his triumph by his first Test century against England, and Walters joyfully rode his fortune in the manner that has charmed so many cricket admirers of the cavalier approach to batsmanship. Yet the spotlight centred on the 21-year-old David Hookes who won his place on the forthcoming tour to England with an innings straight from the fount of youth. This six feet, two inches powerful left-handed batsman, who had scored five centuries in 1976-77 Sheffield Shield cricket strode to the crease with a confidence even more apparent when he struck Greig for five 4s in an over – off, pull, cover, mid-wicket, cover.

Then it was England's turn. And, in the presence of the Queen and the Duke of Edinburgh – during an interval they drove round the ground and were hugely acclaimed – royally did they apply themselves. Well as Amiss, Greig, Knott and Brearley batted, however, the innings to remember was played by Randall, a jaunty, restless, bubbling character, whose 174 took England to the doorstep of victory. The Australian spectators enjoyed his approach as much as Indian crowds had done on the tour just finished.

Once, when Lillee tested him with a bouncer, he tennis-batted it to the mid-wicket fence with a speed and power that made many a rheumy eye turn to the master of the stroke, the watching Sir Donald Bradman. Words cannot recapture the joy of that moment.

Another time, when Lillee bowled short, Randall ducked, rose, drew himself to his full five feet eight, doffed his cap and bowed politely. Then, felled by another bouncer, he gaily performed a reverse roll. This helped to maintain a friendly atmosphere in what, at all times, was a serious and fully competitive match.

The Australians responded. When Randall was 161, umpire Brooks gave him out, caught at the wicket. Immediately Marsh intimated that he had not completed the catch before dropping the ball. After consultation, the umpire called Randall back. Would that this spirit was always so! At the end of the game Randall was awarded the first prize of 1,600 dollars as the Man of the Match. To be chosen ahead of the superb Lillee, whose colleagues chaired him from the field when he finished the match with an analysis of eleven for 165, was a feat indeed.

Some time after it was over someone discovered that the result of the 226th Test between the two countries – victory by 45 runs – was identical, to the same side and to the very run, with that of the 1877 Test on the same ground. Hans "Andersen" Ebeling had even scripted the final curtain.

Australia

I. C. Davies lbw b Lever	5	– c Knott b Greig	68
R. B. McCosker b Willis	4	– c Greig b Old	25
G. J. Cosier c Fletcher b Lever	10	– c Knott b Lever	4
*G. S. Chappell b Underwood	40	– b Old	2
D. W. Hookes c Greig b Old	17	– c Fletcher b Underwood	56
K. D. Walters c Greig b Willis	4	– c Knott b Greig	66
†R. W. Marsh c Knott b Old	28	– not out	110
G. J. Gilmour c Greig b Old	4	– b Lever	16
K. J. O'Keeffe c Brearley b Underwood	0	– c Willis b Old	14
D. K. Lillee not out	10	– c Amiss b Old	25
M. H. N. Walker b Underwood	2	– not out	8
B 4, l-b 2, n-b 8	14	L-b 10, n-b 15	25
1/11 2/13 3/23 4/45 5/51 6/102 7/114 8/117 9/136	138	1/33 2/40 3/53 4/132 5/187 6/244 7/277 8/353 9/407	(9 wkts dec.) 419

Bowling: *First Innings*—Lever 12–1–36–2; Willis 8–0–32–2; Old 12–4–39–3; Underwood 11.6–2–16–3. *Second Innings*—Lever 21–1–95–2; Willis 22–0–91–0; Old 27.6–2–104–4; Greig 14–3–66–2; Underwood 12–2–38–1.

England

R. A. Woolmer c Chappell b Lillee	9	– lbw b Walker	12
J. M. Brearley c Hookes b Lillee	12	– lbw b Lillee	43
D. L. Underwood c Chappell b Walker	7	– b Lillee	7
D. W. Randall c Marsh b Lillee	4	– c Cosier b O'Keeffe	174
D. L. Amiss c O'Keeffe b Walker	4	– b Chappell	64
K. W. R. Fletcher c Marsh b Walker	4	– c Marsh b Lillee	1
*A. W. Greig b Walker	18	– c Cosier b O'Keeffe	41
†A. P. E. Knott lbw b Lillee	15	– lbw b Lillee	42
C. M. Old c Marsh b Lillee	3	– c Chappell b Lillee	2
J. K. Lever c Marsh b Lillee	11	– lbw b O'Keeffe	4
R. G. D. Willis not out	1	– not out	5
B 2, l-b 2, w 1, n-b 2	7	B 8, l-b 4, w 3, n-b 7	22
1/19 2/30 3/34 4/40 5/40 6/61 7/65 8/78 9/86	95	1/28 2/113 3/279 4/290 5/346 6/369 7/380 8/385 9/410	417

Bowling: *First Innings*—Lillee 13.3–2–26–6; Walker 15–3–54–4; O'Keeffe 1–0–4–0; Gilmour 5–3–4–0. *Second Innings*—Lillee 34.4–7–139–5; Walker 22–4–83–1; Gilmour 4–0–29–0; Chappell 16–7–29–1; O'Keeffe 33–6–108–3; Walters 3–2–7–0.

Umpires: M. G. O'Connell and T. F. Brooks.

AUSTRALIA v ENGLAND

Second Test Match

Played at Perth, December 15, 16, 17, 19, 20, 1978

England won by 166 runs. The foundation for England's success was laid on the opening day by Boycott, in his most obdurate mood, and Gower, whose youthful genius was again revealed in his maiden century against Australia. In their contrasting but complementary styles they repaired the damage of a dismal start of 41 for three and proceeded to bat out a difficult day at 190 for three.

When Hogg dismissed Gooch and Randall for only three, it looked as if Yallop's decision to put in England in overcast conditions with a swirling wind was totally justified. Not only did Boycott and Gower end the collapse, but they survived a fierce new-ball attack forty minutes from the close. Their fourth-wicket stand of 158 in four hours eight minutes was soon broken on the second morning, but England had established a measure of control which was never seriously relaxed. Gower hit nine 4s on a slow outfield, but Boycott's only 4 – in a marathon seven and a half hours in which he faced 340 deliveries – was all run and included two overthrows. Nevertheless, it was an invaluable effort for his side.

Despite the splendid fast bowling of Hogg in both innings, which won him the Player of the Match award, England were able to extend their total to 309. Miller, who played an important all-round role, made 50. The worth of Gower and Boycott was immediately apparent when, in twenty overs, Australia slumped to 60 for four. Once again Willis, this time with Lever's support, struck early and decisive blows.

With four pace bowlers England had a formidable attack for the seaming pitch, though generally Australia batted under the sun and England under a cloud cover. Australia's plight worsened when Darling was run out by a marvellously quick pick-up and throw by Botham off the seventh ball of the last over. Only Toohey stood firm on the third day and he was unlucky to run out of partners as he approached a century. He finished 81 not out (six 4s, four and a half hours) and without his fine skill the innings would have been a disaster.

As it was, England led by 119, an advantage increased by 58 as Gooch and Boycott saw through the last 23 overs. England's policy, with a lead of 177 with two days left, was to go for the runs and leave as much time as possible for their bowlers to attack Australia who, with the pitch losing much of its pace, were becoming confident of a draw. As so often happens, however, it was easier said than done, particularly as Hogg maintained his impressive form. Used in short spells he again took five wickets, and dismissed any suggestion that Australia's bowling could be treated with contempt. Dymock, Hurst and Yardley backed him up creditably and England, sacrificing wickets in the cause of quick runs, were all out for 208. This left Australia to score 328 to win. All ten England wickets went in four hours for 150, and Hogg's haul in his first two Tests was 17 out of 33 to fall – as good a start as any new bowler could hope to make.

Australia's never-strong hopes of winning virtually disappeared with the loss of eighty-eight minutes to an unseasonable downpour. With Darling already out to a venomous kicker from Lever, they needed 317 on the final day with nine wickets in hand. The pitch was none the worse for the deluge, and England attacked with a ring of eager slips and gullies. They were rewarded in the seventh over when Gooch, at fourth slip, held a fierce cut from Hughes off Willis. Yallop and Toohey were dismissed in successive deliveries by Hendrick, and the breakthrough was achieved. Although England went through a bad patch of missed chances and half-chances – including two offered by Wood to Boycott at mid-wicket off Botham – and despite the Wood-Cosier fifth-wicket stand that yielded 83, the end was quick. Australia's last six wickets fell in 66 balls and forty-six minutes to Miller (three for 0 in 23 balls) and Lever (three for 11). The spirit of England was epitomised by Botham's last flying left-handed catch at slip – a stunning example of athleticism and reflex action.

During lunch, Brooks, Australia's senior umpire, who was severely criticised in some quarters, announced his retirement.

England

G. Boycott lbw b Hurst	77	– lbw b Hogg	23
G. A. Gooch c Maclean b Hogg	1	– lbw b Hogg	43
D. W. Randall c Wood b Hogg	0	– c Cosier b Yardley	45
*J. M. Brearley c Maclean b Dymock	17	– c Maclean b Hogg	0
D. I. Gower b Hogg	102	– c Maclean b Hogg	12
I. T. Botham lbw b Hurst	11	– c Wood b Yardley	30
G. Miller b Hogg	40	– c Toohey b Yardley	25
†R. W. Taylor c Hurst b Yardley	12	– c Maclean b Hogg	2
J. K. Lever c Cosier b Hurst	14	– c Maclean b Hurst	10
R. G. D. Willis c Yallop b Hogg	2	– not out	3
M. Hendrick not out	7	– b Dymock	1
B 6, l-b 9, w 3, n-b 8	26	L-b 6, n-b 8	14
1/3 2/3 3/41 4/199 5/219 6/224 7/253 8/295 9/300	309	1/58 2/93 3/93 4/135 5/151 6/176 7/201 8/201 9/206	208

Bowling: *First Innings*—Hogg 30.5–9–65–5; Dymock 34–4–72–1; Hurst 26–7–70–3; Yardley 23–1–62–1; Cosier 4–2–14–0. *Second Innings*—Hogg 17–2–57–5; Dymock 16.3–2–53–1; Hurst 17–5–43–1; Yardley 16–1–41–3.

Australia

G. M. Wood lbw b Lever	5	– c Taylor b Lever	64
W. M. Darling run out	25	– c Boycott b Lever	5
K. J. Hughes b Willis	16	– c Gooch b Willis	12
*G. N. Yallop b Willis	3	– c Taylor b Hendrick	3
P. M. Toohey not out	81	– c Taylor b Hendrick	0
G. J. Cosier c Gooch b Willis	4	– lbw b Miller	47
†J. A. Maclean c Gooch b Miller	0	– c Brearley b Miller	1
B. Yardley c Taylor b Hendrick	12	– c Botham b Lever	7
R. M. Hogg c Taylor b Willis	18	– b Miller	0
G. Dymock b Hendrick	11	– not out	6
A. G. Hurst c Taylor b Willis	5	– b Lever	5
L-b 7, w 1, n-b 2	10	L-b 3, w 4, n-b 4	11
1/8 2/34 3/38 4/60 5/78 6/79 7/100 8/128 9/185	190	1/8 2/36 3/58 4/58 5/141 6/143 7/143 8/147 9/151	161

Bowling: *First Innings*—Lever 7–0–20–1; Botham 11–2–46–0; Willis 18.5–5–44–5; Hendrick 14–1–39–2; Miller 16–6–31–1. *Second Innings*—Willis 12–1–36–1; Lever 8–2–28–4; Botham 11–1–54–0; Hendrick 8–3–11–2; Miller 7–4–21–3.

Umpires: T. F. Brooks and R. C. Bailhache.

AUSTRALIA v ENGLAND

Fourth Test Match

Played at Sydney, January 6, 7, 8, 10, 11, 1979

England won by 93 runs. Swiftly recovering from the shock of Melbourne, England, with a team weakened by a virus infection and heat exhaustion, retained the Ashes after staging one of Test cricket's most astonishing recoveries.

At lunch on the second day Australia seemed to have taken a giant stride towards victory and squaring the series. Hurst (five for 28), with his most effective Test bowling, had played a large part in dismissing England for a paltry 152, and Australia were 126 for one. No side could have been better placed, Hughes, however, drove the first ball of the afternoon session straight to mid-off and ended his second-wicket stand of 125 with Darling.

England's position worsened with the departure of the sick Willis after two overs – and only five in all – but Australia's control began to decline against the determination and ability of Hendrick and Botham, and Brearley's astute captaincy. Because of the heat and the absence of Willis, Brearley was obliged to manipulate his resources with a fine balance and skill. Consequently, although the much-improved Darling and Border – unbeaten in both innings – batted well, the lead was restricted to 142; large enough but manageable.

When Boycott was out leg before to Hogg off the first ball of the second innings, however, Australia's prospects again soared. It was Boycott's first "duck" for England in 67 innings since 1969 at Trent Bridge.

An enormous responsibility fell on the out-of-form Brearley and Randall, and they were not found wanting. With intense concentration they put on 111 for the second wicket in three and a half hours, and at the end of the third day England were only 9 runs in arrears with eight wickets left. Slowly but surely Randall pulled England round and the match away from Australia in the longest innings of his career. Missed at 113, 117 and 124, he batted in all for eleven minutes under ten hours with thirteen boundaries, three of which came in four deliveries when Hogg took the new ball. It was Randall's first century in Tests since his 174 in the Melbourne Centenary Test in March 1977, and it earned him his second Player of the Match award in the series.

Randall's discipline and stamina in the heat were considerable, and ultimately his innings was the match-winning effort. Gower, running a temperature, and Botham, also less than well, lent valuable support. Higgs' leg spin proved too much for the tail-end batsmen, however, and Australia were left to score 205 to win in 265 minutes, including the last arbitrary fifteen eight-ball overs.

From an early stage in the match Brearley had contended that a total of around 200–220 would be difficult to score in the last innings. It was a sound prediction. Darling and Wood started splendidly, clearly aiming to unsettle an attack deprived of Willis for all but two overs, and to deny Brearley a close-set field. Again Hendrick bowled with consummate skill, and once Darling fell to a good falling catch by Gooch at second slip, and Wood went for a single that was never safe, the trap was set. Wood drove to Botham's right hand at cover and set off. Hughes refused to accept the call and, with both batsmen at the same end, all Botham needed to do was return the ball to Taylor.

Only the left-handed Border, who batted well in both innings, escaped the spinning web of Emburey (four for 46) and Miller (three for 38). Sure in defence and quick to punish the loose ball, he was in a lonely class of his own as Brearley applied all the pressure needed with his field on top of the batsmen.

When Australia were dismissed in three and a half hours for 111, Brearley could justifiably claim he had led the greatest comeback of his career – perhaps in the long history of the Ashes. Moreover he became the first captain to retain the Ashes since Sir Len Hutton in 1954-55. For England, it was a triumph of astute captaincy, individual resolution, and highly professional teamwork. For Australia, it was a singularly disconcerting experience coming so closely after the Melbourne success. Having led on points they were knocked out in the final round.

England

G. Boycott c Border b Hurst	8	– lbw b Hogg	0
*J. M. Brearley b Hogg	17	– b Border	53
D. W. Randall c Wood b Hurst	0	– lbw b Hogg	150
G. A. Gooch c Toohey b Higgs	18	– c Wood b Higgs	22
D. I. Gower c Maclean b Hurst	7	– c Maclean b Hogg	34
I. T. Botham c Yallop b Hogg	59	– c Wood b Higgs	6
G. Miller c Maclean b Hurst	4	– lbw b Hogg	17
†R. W. Taylor c Border b Higgs	10	– not out	21
J. E. Emburey c Wood b Higgs	0	– c Darling b Higgs	14
R. G. D. Willis not out	7	– c Toohey b Higgs	0
M. Hendrick b Hurst	10	– c Toohey b Higgs	7
B 1, l-b 1, w 2, n-b 8	12	B 5, l-b 3, n-b 14	22
	——		——
1/18 2/18 3/35 4/51 5/66 6/70 7/94 8/98 9/141	152	1/0 2/111 3/169 4/237 5/267 6/292 7/307 8/334 9/346	346

Bowling: *First Innings*—Hogg 11–3–36–2; Dymock 13–1–34–0; Hurst 10.6–2–28–5; Higgs 18–4–42–3. *Second Innings*—Hogg 28–10–67–4; Dymock 17–4–35–0; Hurst 19–3–43–0; Higgs 59.6–15–148–5; Border 23–11–31–1.

Australia

G. M. Wood b Willis	0	– run out	27
W. M. Darling c Botham b Miller	91	– c Gooch b Hendrick	13
K. J. Hughes c Emburey b Willis	48	– c Emburey b Miller	15
*G. N. Yallop c Botham b Hendrick	44	– c and b Hendrick	1
P. M. Toohey c Gooch b Botham	1	– b Miller	5
A. R. Border not out	60	– not out	45
†J. A. Maclean lbw b Emburey	12	– c Botham b Miller	0
R. M. Hogg run out	6	– c Botham b Emburey	0
G. Dymock b Botham	5	– b Emburey	0
J. D. Higgs c Botham b Hendrick	11	– lbw b Emburey	3
A. G. Hurst run out	0	– b Emburey	0
B 2, l-b 3, n-b 11	16	L-b 1, n-b 1	2
1/1 2/126 3/178 4/179 5/210 6/235 7/245 8/276 9/290	294	1/38 2/44 3/45 4/59 5/74 6/76 7/85 8/85 9/105	111

Bowling: *First Innings*—Willis 9–2–33–2; Botham 28–3–87–2; Hendrick 24–4–50–2; Miller 13–2–37–1; Emburey 29–10–57–1; Gooch 5–1–14–0. *Second Innings*—Willis 2–0–8–0; Hendrick 10–3–17–2; Emburey 17.2–2–46–4; Miller 20–7–38–3.

Umpires: R. C. Bailhache and R. A. French.

AUSTRALIA v ENGLAND

Fifth Test Match

Played at Adelaide, January 27, 28, 29, 31, February 1, 1979

England won by 205 runs. Brearley added to his triumphs by taking the series, and he became the first England captain since Jardine in 1932-33 to win four Tests in a series in Australia. For Yallop it was a profoundly disappointing experience. England, put in to bat on a green and lively pitch, were twice in serious trouble, but Australia, set to make 366 in nine and a quarter hours, experienced the worst batting collapse and this cost them the match.

Yallop had called in a local football coach to motivate his side, and with England at 27 for five he had cause for great expectations. A crowd of 25,004 celebrated Hogg's record in passing Arthur Mailey's 36 wickets against England in 1920-21, and with Hurst also displaying controlled aggression, it was left to Botham to halt the slide to total disaster. He did so with a brilliant 74, including two 6s and six 4s in two hours forty minutes, and went on to demonstrate once again his considerable all-round flair with four wickets for 42. Australia, looking for a substantial lead to justify the gamble of conceding first innings, could do no better than England and finished five runs behind.

Hurst again bowled well and effectively in England's second innings, and when, despite a careful effort of over three hours by Boycott, they were down to 132 for six. Australia's revived hopes were justifiably high. Miller, who made a big advance on the tour, and Taylor represented England's last chance, and they could not have better served the needs of their side.

Batting with rare skill and application – certainly it was Taylor's innings of his life – they more than doubled the total. When Miller was out thirteen minutes from the close they had put on 135, broken an England seventh-wicket partnership record for the ground, and put England in a position of strength. Another stand of 69 with Emburey meant Taylor had stayed while 204 runs were scored, and there were many regrets when he was caught at the wicket well down the leg side off the last ball before lunch on the fourth day. With 97 he equalled his best score, and, as in the first innings with Willis, the Australians were frustrated by the resolution of batsmen in the lower half of the order. Taylor hit six boundaries and batted for six hours, but he lost the Player of the Match award to Botham on a split 3-2 vote.

With the pitch eased and well behaved, Australia, for whom Hogg bowled only nine overs on the crucial third day because of muscle soreness, were still in with a chance. However, Wood made it that much harder by running himself out again – Boycott made a direct hit at one stump from mid-on – and Darling left his leg stump exposed as he tried to whip Botham to leg.

On the final day the target was slimmed down to 284 with eight wickets left. England's hopes were largely pinned on the spin of Miller and Emburey, but Hughes and Yallop batted with such fluency that Brearley was obliged to call on Willis and Hendrick to control the scoring-rate. At once the situation changed dramatically. Hendrick dismissed Yallop with an exceptional delivery, and Gower, at square cover, made a brilliant diving catch to dismiss Hughes off the same bowler. Willis, who had not bowled with his customary fire since the second Test at Perth, suddenly regained his fire and rhythm. The rot set in with a vengeance and six wickets crashed for 15. Miller also took wickets, and in 100 astonishing minutes Australia's last eight wickets had gone.

Once again experience, strength in depth, and a sharply developed team spirit had prevailed. Nevertheless, England were honest enough to admit they had never expected such a headlong rush to victory, and Brearley was apt to describe it as freakish after paying a high compliment to his side.

England

G. Boycott c Wright b Hurst	6	– c Hughes b Hurst	49
*J. M. Brearley c Wright b Hogg	2	– lbw b Carlson	9
D. W. Randall c Carlson b Hurst	4	– c Yardley b Hurst	15
G. A. Gooch c Hughes b Hogg	1	– b Carlson	18
D. I. Gower lbw b Hurst	9	– lbw b Higgs	21
I. T. Botham c Wright b Higgs	74	– c Yardley b Hurst	7
G. Miller lbw b Hogg	31	– c Wright b Hurst	64
†R. W. Taylor run out	4	– c Wright b Hogg	97
J. E. Emburey b Higgs	4	– b Hogg	42
R. G. D. Willis c Darling b Hogg	24	– c Wright b Hogg	12
M. Hendrick not out	0	– not out	3
B 1, l-b 4, w 3, n-b 2	10	B 1, l-b 16, w 2, n-b 4	23
1/10 2/12 3/16 4/18 5/27 6/80 7/113 8/136 9/147	169	1/31 2/57 3/97 4/106 5/130 6/132 7/267 8/336 9/347	360

Bowling: *First Innings*—Hogg 10.4–1–26–4; Hurst 14–1–65–3; Carlson 9–1–34–0; Yardley 4–0–25–0; Higgs 3–1–9–2. *Second Innings*—Hogg 27.6–7–59–3; Hurst 37–9–97–4; Carlson 27–8–41–2; Yardley 20–6–60–0; Higgs 28–4–75–1; Border 3–2–5–0.

Australia

W. M. Darling c Willis b Botham	15	– b Botham	18
G. M. Wood c Randall b Emburey	35	– run out	9
K. J. Hughes c Emburey b Hendrick	4	– c Gower b Hendrick	46
*G. N. Yallop b Hendrick	0	– b Hendrick	36
A. R. Border c Taylor b Botham	11	– b Willis	1
P. H. Carlson c Taylor b Botham	0	– c Gower b Hendrick	21
B. Yardley b Botham	28	– c Brearley b Willis	0
†K. J. Wright lbw b Emburey	29	– c Emburey b Miller	0
R. M. Hogg b Willis	0	– b Miller	2
J. D. Higgs run out	16	– not out	3
A. G. Hurst not out	17	– b Willis	13
B 1, l-b 3, n-b 5	9	L-b 1, n-b 10	11
1/5 2/10 3/22 4/24 5/72 6/94 7/114 8/116 9/133	164	1/31 2/36 3/115 4/120 5/121 6/121 7/124 8/130 9/147	160

Bowling: *First Innings*—Willis 11–1–55–1; Hendrick 19–1–45–2; Botham 11.4–0–42–4; Emburey 12–7–13–2. *Second Innings*—Willis 12–3–41–3; Hendrick 14–6–19–3; Botham 14–4–37–1; Miller 18–3–36–2; Emburey 9–5–16–0.

Umpires: M. G. O'Connell and R. C. Bailhache.

AUSTRALIA v ENGLAND

First Test Match

Played at Perth, December 14, 15, 16, 18, 19, 1979

Australia won by 138 runs. It was unfortunate that Australia's victory at the end of an enthralling match was soured by Lillee's unsavoury behaviour in seeking to use an aluminium bat in the first innings despite objections from Brearley, the umpires and his own captain. He caused play to be held up for ten minutes before being persuaded by Chappell to exchange it for the traditional willow. The incident served only to blacken Lillee's reputation and damage the image of the game as well as, eventually, the reputation of the Australian authorities because of their reluctance to take effective disciplinary action.

Lillee's behaviour also partly overshadowed other individual performances more in keeping with the spirit of the game, notably the bowling of Botham and Dymock, the batting of Hughes and Border, and Boycott's gallant attempt to save England on the final day.

Although only once before had an England captain won a Test in Australia when asking the opposition to bat first – at Melbourne in 1912 – Brearley opted for that course now to support the decision to go into the match with two off-spinning all-rounders, plus Underwood who was making his first Test appearance in Perth. Brearley must have been reasonably content with his decision when Australia's first innings closed at 244. It was built in the main around Hughes, who made 99 in almost four hours and defied the remarkable bowling effort of Botham, being used as both strike and stock bowler. In 35 overs Botham took six wickets. But any feelings of satisfaction Brearley held were soon swept away as Randall and Boycott went without scoring and the first six England wickets fell for only 90 runs. Brearley rescued the situation himself, batting stubbornly for four hours ten minutes in making 64 and producing one of his best innings for his country. Dilley, on his Test début, gave him fine support, batting nearly three and a half hours for his 38 not out, and Australia's lead was limited to 16.

By the end of the third day, however, Australia appeared to be in a strong position, 174 ahead with eight second innings wickets in hand, after Wiener, with a half century in his first Test, and Laird had opened with a stand of 91. But another marathon bowling stint by Botham, refreshed after the rest day, changed the situation dramatically, and Australia owed much to Border for their eventual lead of 353 with an innings of 115 in six hours twenty four minutes. He was repeatedly in trouble against Botham early on but survived to pass 1,000 runs in Tests in eleven days short of a year. Botham, with five wickets in the innings, ended with match figures of eleven for 176 from 80 overs and five balls.

Only sixty-five minutes remained of the fourth day when England started their second innings, but it was time enough for Randall's second failure before bad light stopped play. Worse was to follow on the final day, most of the wounds self-inflicted by lack of application as England lost wickets regularly while Chappell switched his attack intelligently and Dymock responded with accurate seam bowling. Only Boycott showed the technique and determination needed to survive and he was still unbeaten, 1 short of his century, when England's last man, Willis, became Dymock's sixth victim with 14.4 of the last twenty overs left.

Australia

J. M. Wiener run out	11	– c Randall b Underwood	58
B. M. Laird lbw b Botham	0	– c Taylor b Underwood	33
A. R. Border lbw b Botham	4	– c Taylor b Willis	115
*G. S. Chappell c Boycott b Botham	19	– st Taylor b Underwood	43
K. J. Hughes c Brearley b Underwood	99	– c Miller b Botham	4
P. M. Toohey c Underwood b Dilley	19	– c Taylor b Botham	3
†R. W. Marsh c Taylor b Dilley	42	– c Gower b Botham	4
R. J. Bright c Taylor b Botham	17	– lbw b Botham	12
D. K. Lillee c Taylor b Botham	18	– c Willey b Dilley	19
G. Dymock b Botham	5	– not out	20
J. R. Thomson not out	1	– b Botham	8
B 4, l-b 3, n-b 2	9	B 4, l-b 5, w 2, n-b 7	18
1/2 2/17 3/20 4/88 5/127 6/186 7/219 8/219 9/243	244	1/91 2/100 3/168 4/183 5/191 6/204 7/225 8/303 9/323	337

Bowling: *First Innings*—Dilley 18–1–47–2; Botham 35–9–78–6; Willis 23–7–47–0; Underwood 13–4–33–1; Miller 11–2–30–0. *Second Innings*—Dilley 18–3–50–1; Botham 45.5–14–98–5; Willis 26–7–52–1; Underwood 41–14–82–3; Miller 10–0–36–0; Willey 1–0–1–0.

England

D. W. Randall c Hughes b Lillee	0	– lbw b Dymock	1
G. Boycott lbw b Lillee	0	– not out	99
P. Willey c Chappell b Dymock	9	– lbw b Dymock	12
D. I. Gower c Marsh b Lillee	17	– c Thomson b Dymock	23
G. Miller c Hughes b Thomson	25	– c Chappell b Thomson	8
*J. M. Brearley c Marsh b Lillee	64	– (7) c Marsh b Bright	11
I. T. Botham c Toohey b Thomson	15	– (6) c Marsh b Lillee	18
†R. W. Taylor b Chappell	14	– b Lillee	15
G. R. Dilley not out	38	– c Marsh b Dymock	16
D. L. Underwood lbw b Dymock	13	– c Wiener b Dymock	0
R. G. D. Willis b Dymock	11	– c Chappell b Dymock	0
L-b 7, n-b 15	22	L-b 3, w 1, n-b 8	12
1/1 2/12 3/14 4/41 5/74 6/90 7/123 8/185 9/203	228	1/8 2/26 3/64 4/75 5/115 6/141 7/182 8/211 9/211	215

Bowling: *First Innings*—Lillee 28–11–73–4; Dymock 29.1–14–52–3; Chappell 11–6–5–1; Thomson 21–3–70–2; Bright 2–0–6–0. *Second Innings*—Lillee 23–5–74–2; Dymock 17.2–4–34–6; Chappell 6–4–6–0; Thomson 11–3–30–1; Bright 23–11–30–1; Wiener 8–3–22–0; Border 2–0–7–0.

Umpires: M. G. O'Connell and D. G. Weser.

ENGLAND IN SOUTH AFRICA

SOUTH AFRICA v ENGLAND

Third Test Match

Played at Cape Town, January 1, 2, 4, 5, 6, 1965

Drawn. Long after the unenterprising cricket of this Test is forgotten, people will talk of two incidents which brought to a head the question of whether batsmen should "walk". With close-in fieldsmen convinced both times that umpire Warner was wrong to turn down appeals for catches, the first at short leg, the second by the wicket-keeper, Barlow of South Africa stood his ground and Barrington of England made his way to the pavilion. Parfitt felt he had caught Barlow when that batsman was 41 runs towards his 138 of the first day and Barrington tickled the ball to Lindsay when 49 and looking set for a big score. So both happenings could be said to have had a big bearing on the way the game went.

Certainly Barlow proved a stumbling block to England as he and Pithey progressed tediously to a stand of 172 in the afternoon and evening of the opening day after Smith lost the toss for the first time. The England players were so piqued at the Barlow incident that they did not applaud his century, an action which later produced an apology.

At 252 for one when the second day started, South Africa had laid their foundation, but they did not built on it with any urgency. After Barlow had been caught without adding to his overnight score, Pithey dawdled to his first Test century, which occupied just over six hours despite a benign pitch. Only fifty minutes of the day remained when the record crowd of 21,000 saw Goddard declare. One up in the series, England, presumably convinced that they could not win, set their minds to saving the game. This they did successfully, though the sight of stroke players like Dexter (four hours for 61) and Smith (four and a half hours over his century) chaining themselves did nothing for the image of the game.

The upshot was that South Africa had been in the field for eleven and a half hours before they batted a second time with a lead of 59 for the last half hour of the fourth day, and until half an hour from the end of the last day.

South Africa

*T. L. Goddard b Titmus	40	– c Parfitt b Price	6
E. J. Barlow c Parks b Thomson	138	– c Parks b Dexter	78
A. J. Pithey c Barber b Allen	154	– c Parks b Thomson	2
R. G. Pollock c Parks b Allen	31	– b Boycott	73
K. C. Bland run out	78	– b Boycott	64
†J. D. Lindsay lbw b Thomson	2	– b Barrington	50
D. Varnals c Smith b Titmus	19	– c Smith b Parfitt	20
S. F. Burke not out	10	– c Barber b Boycott	20
P. M. Pollock (did not bat)		– lbw b Barrington	7
H. D. Bromfield (did not bat)		– not out	12
G. Hall (did not bat)		– b Barrington	0
B 5, l-b 11, w 1, n-b 12	29	B 1, l-b 9, w 1, n-b 3	14
1/80 2/252 3/313 4/430 5/439 6/470 7/501	(7 wkts dec.) 501	1/10 2/13 3/86 4/44 5/231 6/256 7/310 8/331 9/334	346

Bowling: *First Innings*—Price 34–6–133–0; Thomson 45–19–89–2; Titmus 50.2–12–133–2; Dexter 2–0–10–0; Allen 39–13–79–2; Parfitt 8–0–28–0. *Second Innings*—Price 11–4–19–1; Thomson 14–4–31–1; Allen 17–6–27–0; Barber 1–0–2–0; Titmus 6–2–21–0; Parfitt 19–4–74–1; Dexter 17–3–64–1; Boycott 20–5–47–3; Smith 11–1–43–0; Barrington 3.1–1–4–3.

England

G. Boycott c Barlow b Bromfield	15	– not out 1
R. W. Barber lbw b Goddard	58	
E. R. Dexter c and b Bromfield	61	
K. F. Barrington b Linday b P. M. Pollock	49	– not out 14
P. H. Parfitt b Hall	44	
*M. J. K. Smith c Goddard b Bromfield	121	
†J. M. Parks c Lindsay b Barlow	59	
F. J. Titmus c Lindsay b P. M. Pollock	4	
D. A. Allen c Barlow b Bromfield	22	
N. I. Thomas c R. G. Pollock b Bromfield	0	
J. S. E. Price not out	0	
B 2, l-b 5, n-b 2	9	
1/72 2/80 3/170 4/206 5/243 6/360 7/368 8/438 9/440	442	(No wkt) 15

Bowling: *First Innings*—P. M. Pollock 39–14–89–2; Burke 29–8–61–0; Bromfield 57.2–26–88–5; Hall 31–7–94–1; Goddard 37–13–64–1; Barlow 12–3–37–1. *Second Innings*—Bland 2–0–3–0; R. G. Pollock 2–0–5–0; Pithey 2–0–5–0; Varnals 2–1–2–0.

Umpires: V. Costello and J. Warner.

SOUTH AFRICA v ENGLAND

Fourth Test Match

Played at Johannesburg, January 22, 23, 25, 26, 27, 1965

Drawn. Playing the better cricket, South Africa were denied a win by the Yorkshire grit of Boycott and perhaps by rain, which took three and a quarter hours out of the first two days. There were also costly errors by Waite, who on his return to the Test scene missed two catches and a stumping which would have cut short telling innings by Parfitt, Barber and Barrington, the latter before he had scored.

The start provided more than usual interest. After Smith, Dexter, Barrington and the manager, D. B. Carr, had looked hard and long at the pitch, Smith winning the toss decided that, for the first time since A. P. F. Chapman did 34 years earlier, South Africa on their own soil should bat first against England. Why, spectators could not fathom, and no doubt Smith & Co. had their doubts after Goddard and Barlow had scored 118 by lunch. Rain prevented the batsmen taking full toll later, so that despite a record fifth-wicket stand for South Africa of 157 in three hours, forty minutes between Pithey and Waite, the total was kept within reasonable bounds – 390 for six at the end of the second day. At this point Goddard declared.

Then, at a time when the pitch took spin, came those misses by Waite. Parfitt, dropped off Goddard when 38, went on to his seventh Test hundred. Yet South Africa, helped by a century from Goddard, his first in 62 Test innings, still had a chance of winning and except for the fortitude of Boycott after England had been set to score 314 at 78 runs an hour, they probably would have succeeded. Barber could not bat because he chipped a bone in his finger while fielding.

On the third day there was another incident involving an umpire. After a ball had rested in the hands of Waite and tossed by him to leg slip, Smith went "gardening", whereupon van der Merwe threw down the wicket. Umpire Kidson gave Smith out, but was prevailed upon by Goddard to call him back.

South Africa

*T. L. Goddard run out	60	– c Barber b Price	112
E. J. Barlow c and b Cartwright	96	– c Barber b Titmus	42
K. C. Bland c Parks b Price	55	– not out	38
A. J. Pithey c Cartwright b Titmus	95	– b Cartwright	39
R. G. Pollock c Parks b Price	4	– not out	65
†J. H. B. Waite run out	64		
P. L. van der Merwe not out	5		
P. M. Pollock not out	0		
L-b 7, n-b 4	11	L-b 7, n-b 4	11
1/134 2/189 3/222 4/226 5/383 6/389	(6 wkts dec.) 390	1/65 2/180 3/211	(3 wkts dec.) 307

H. D. Bromfield, A. H. McKinnon and J. T. Partridge did not bat.

Bowling: *First Innings*—Price 17–1–68–2; Thomson 31–3–91–0; Cartwright 55–18–97–1; Dexter 6–0–30–0; Titmus 29–2–68–1; Boycott 8–1–25–0. *Second Innings*—Price 14–1–56–1; Thomson 19–4–43–0; Cartwright 24–6–99–1; Titmus 31–4–98–1.

England

G. Boycott c Barlow b Partridge	5	– not out	76
R. W. Barber lbw b McKinnon	61		
E. R. Dexter c Waite b Goddard	38	– c R. G. Pollock b P. M. Pollock	0
K. F. Barrington c Waite b Barlow	93	– c Bromfield b McKinnon	11
P. H. Parfitt not out	122	– c Barlow b McKinnon	22
*M. J. K. Smith c R. G. Pollock b McKinnon	42	– b Bromfield	8
†J. M. Parks c Barlow b Partridge	0	– c R. G. Pollock b McKinnon	10
F. J. Titmus lbw b McKinnon	1	– c van der Merwe b P. M. Pollock	13
T. W. Cartwright b McKinnon	9	– not out	8
N. I. Thomson c Barlow b P. M. Pollock	3		
J. S. E. Price c Bromfield b P. M. Pollock	0		
B 1, l-b 5, w 1, n-b 3	10	L-b 5	5
1/7 2/78 3/144 4/244 5/333 6/333 7/338 8/350 9/374	384	1/21 2/21 3/33 4/80 5/106 6/124	(6 wkts) 153

Bowling: *First Innings*—P. M. Pollock 15–4–42–2; Partridge 30–6–92–2; Barlow 18–5–34–1; Goddard 16–4–35–1; McKinnon 51–13–128–4; R. G. Pollock 4–0–12–0; Bromfield 13–4–31–0. *Second Innings*—P. M. Pollock 12–3–27–2; Partridge 7–4–10–0; Bromfield 17–8–27–1; McKinnon 35–17–44–3; R. G. Pollock 11–2–35–0; Goddard 5–4–5–0.

Umpires: H. C. Kidson and L. M. Baxter.

ENGLAND IN WEST INDIES

WEST INDIES v ENGLAND

Second Test Match

Played at Kingston, February 8, 9, 10, 12, 13, 1968

Drawn. Until the bottle throwing riot in mid-afternoon on the third day England looked like winning comfortably. After the trouble, which necessitated seventy-five minutes' play being held over until a sixth day, they never regained their zest. In the end they struggled to avoid defeat in a final innings marked by strange umpiring. They made the mistake of agreeing to resume after the trouble had been put down. It would have been wiser and fairer to the visiting players to abandon play for the day.

Again England lost only two wickets on the first day when Edrich and Cowdrey repeated their feats of the Jamaican match. Already the pitch, criss-crossed by wide cracks, was firey and sportive. Yet in their differing ways, Edrich, boldly pugnacious, and Cowdrey, studiously watchful, they overcame it, as only two other batsmen, Nurse and Sobers, were able to do subsequently. Edrich made 96 of the first 178 in 66 overs. Cowdrey held the innings together for 96 overs and nearly six hours, a magnificent fighting innings in which he was stolidly helped by Barrington who batted for nearly four hours. The others went quickly to a combination of pace and spin.

So did the West Indies batsmen to the splendid fast bowling of Snow, who was ably supported by Brown and Jones. It was all over in 49 overs, and West Indies followed on 233 behind. Though Nurse made a fine attempt to hit them out of trouble – 73 off only 34 overs – half the side were again out for 204 when Butcher's dismissal to a diving leg-side catch by Parks sparked the riot. Sobers meanwhile had been badly missed by D'Oliveira at second slip off Brown while Graveney was having a damaged finger repaired in the pavilion. Sobers was then 7. Afterwards he played magnificently for more than six hours, and against a side upset by the rioting the later batsmen for once were able to give him the necessary support, despite the vagaries of the pitch.

Although the cracks steadily became wider there were surprisingly fewer shooters on the fifth than on the early days. The last innings was played in a feverish atmosphere, which seemed to unsettle the umpires. Cowdrey was lbw off his bat, and in forty-two minutes England were reduced to 19 for four. During the final seventy-five minutes on the extra day they barely held off the spin of Gibbs and Sobers.

England

G. Boycott b Hall	17	– b Sobers	0
J. H. Edrich c Kanhai b Sobers	96	– b Hall	6
*M. C. Cowdrey c Murray b Gibbs	101	– lbw b Sobers	0
K. F. Barrington c and b Holford	63	– lbw b Griffith	13
T. W. Graveney b Hall	30	– c Griffith b Gibbs	21
†J. M. Parks c Sobers b Holford	3	– lbw b Gibbs	3
B. L. D'Oliveira st Murray b Holford	0	– not out	13
F. J. Titmus lbw b Hall	19	– c Camacho b Gibbs	4
D. J. Brown c Murray b Hall	14	– b Sobers	0
J. A. Snow b Griffith	10		
I. J. Jones not out	0		
B 12, l-b 7, n-b 4	23	B 8	8
1/49 2/78 3/279 4/310 5/318 6/318 7/351 8/352 9/376	376	1/0 2/0 3/19 4/19 5/38 6/51 7/68 8/68 (8 wkts)	68

Bowling: *First Innings*—Hall 27–5–63–4; Griffith 31.2–7–72–1; Sobers 31–11–56–1; Gibbs 47–18–91–1; Holford 33–9–71–3. *Second Innings*—Sobers 16.5–7–33–3; Griffith 5–2–13–1; Hall 3–2–3–1; Gibbs 14–11–11–3.

West Indies

S. Camacho b Snow	5	– b d'Oliveira	25
†D. L. Murray c D'Oliveira b Brown	0	– lbw b Brown	14
R. B. Kanhai c Graveney b Snow	26	– c Edrich b Jones	36
S. M. Nurse b Jones	22	– b Snow	73
C. H. Lloyd not out	34	– b Brown	7
*G. S. Sobers lbw b Snow	0	– not out	113
B. F. Butcher c Parks b Snow	21	– c Parks b D'Oliveira	25
D. A. J. Holford c Parks b Snow	6	– lbw b Titmus	35
C. C. Griffith c D'Oliveira b Snow	8	– lbw b Jones	14
W. W. Hall b Snow	0	– c Parks b Jones	0
L. R. Gibbs c Parks b Jones	0	– not out	1
B 12, l-b 5, w 1, n-b 3	21	B 33, l-b 10, n-b 5	48
1/5 2/5 3/51 4/80 5/80 6/120 7/126 8/142 9/142	143	1/102 2/122 3/164 4/174 5/204 6/314 7/351 8/388 (9 wkts dec.)	391

Bowling: *First Innings*—Brown 13–2–34–1; Snow 21–7–49–7; Jones 14–4–39–2. *Second Innings*—Brown 33–9–65–2; Snow 27–4–91–1; Jones 30–4–90–3; D'Oliveira 32–12–51–2; Titmus 7–2–32–1; Barrington 6–1–14–0.

Umpires: D. Sang Hue and C. Jordan.

BARBADOS v MCC

Played at Bridgetown, February 22, 23, 24, 26, 1968

Drawn. MCC hit fifty boundaries on the first day and altogether eighty. Boycott had thirty-eight of them, including one 6, in an innings lasting 173 overs, during which he seldom made a false stroke. Edrich, who set the pace with twelve 4s, Milburn, who hit 13 before suffering an unlucky lbw, and D'Oliveira, eleven 4s, shared century stands with him. Despite a splendidly determined innings by Nurse, who batted 110 overs before being eighth out, Barbados followed-on 302 behind. In the second innings Bynoe batted four hours, but again Barbados were outplayed, and, if two chances offered by Sobers had not been missed, MCC might have won. Pocock's five for 84 on a perfect batting pitch was his finest performance of the tour, orthodox off-spin bowling of guile which promised him a big future in representative cricket.

MCC

G. Boycott c Sobers b Edwards	243	*T. W. Graveney not out	41
J. H. Edrich c Boxhill b Howard	73		
C. Milburn lbw b Lashley	68	L-b 1, n-b 7	8
B. L. D'Oliveira c Edwards b Howard	66		
J. M. Parks c Nurse b Howard	10	1/124 2/252 3/406 4/422 5/504 (5 wkts dec.)	578
K. F. Barrington not out	69		

†A. P. E. Knott, K. Higgs, J. A. Snow and P. I. Pocock did not bat.

Bowling: Edwards 21–8–49–1; Holder 25–6–82–0; Shepherd 27–9–87–0; Sobers 20–8–54–0; Holford 20–5–58–0; Howard 36–7–106–3; Brancker 31–9–88–0; Lashley 13–4–32–1; Bynoe 2–0–14–0.

Barbados

M. R. Bynoe lbw b Higgs	0	– not out 64
J. N. Shepherd c Knott b Snow	6	– b Higgs 4
S. M. Nurse c Knott b Pocock	144	– not out 7
P. D. Lashley lbw b Pocock	18	– b d'Oliveira 9
D. A. J. Holford c Knott b Pocock	5	– lbw b Snow 3
*G. S. Sobers c Knott b Pocock	37	– c and b d'Oliveira 56
R. C. Brancker c Milburn b Higgs	25	– run out 6
†D. Boxhill b Higgs	0	
R. Edwards not out	9	
A. Howard lbw b Pocock	17	
V. Holder lbw b Snow	0	
B 2, l-b 9, n-b 4	15	B 5, l-b 3, n-b 4 12
1/0 2/14 3/61 4/69 5/152 6/243 7/243 8/247 9/275	276	1/16 2/34 3/37 4/128 5/140 (5 wkts) 161

Bowling: *First Innings*—Higgs 28–7–77–3; Snow 22.5–6–39–2; d'Oliveira 20–5–38–0; Pocock 41–18–84–5; Barrington 6–1–23–0. *Second Innings*—Higgs 13–3–26–1; Snow 10–2–37–1; d'Oliveira 15–3–28–2; Pocock 16–4–31–0; Barrington 12–3–27–0; Milburn 2–2–0–0; Boycott 2–2–0–0.

WEST INDIES v ENGLAND

Fifth Test Match

Played at Georgetown, March 28, 29, 30, April 1, 2, 3, 1968

Drawn. Sobers, Kanhai and Gibbs took West Indies to the verge of victory in this six-day match. They were frustrated by the same three English star batsmen of the fourth Test, Cowdrey, Boycott and Knott with this time unexpected but magnificent assistance from Lock and Pocock. Snow, too, helped materially to pull England through by crowning a series of personal triumph by taking ten for 142 on a pitch too slow for his liking.

The West Indies first innings was all Kanhai and Sobers, who made all except 112 of the total and scored 250 together. Until late in the proceedings England's innings was also a two-man show. Boycott reached 100 in four hours and a half, and Cowdrey helped him to add 172. England's middle batting then broke down again, helped by some careless strokes, and at 259 for eight they were in grave danger. Lock, however, proceeded to bat with typical belligerence, and Pocock with such obstinacy that he spent nearly ninety minutes before scoring his first run. He stood firm while Lock battered all the bowlers. In the last hundred minutes of the fourth day they added 93, of which Lock drove and slammed 76.

On the next day they carried their stand to 109, England's best for the ninth wicket against West Indies. Lock, batting a few minutes longer, two and a half hours, superbly struck his highest score in first-class cricket. Sobers was again the bulwark in the West Indies second innings, in which the others failed to capitalize a dashing start by Nurse. From 86 for three Sobers steered his side to 264, batting chancelessly from around two o'clock until almost 5.30, when he ran out of partners only five short of another century. It was a great innings.

England had to bat throughout the last day. In ninety-five minutes they plunged to 41 for five, shattered by Gibbs and without any excuse to be found in the conditions, for the spinners turned the ball only slowly. All seemed lost when Knott joined Cowdrey, but he was there to stay until the end, nearly four hours later. Cowdrey and Knott scored 127 together, and, when Cowdrey's shrewd, commanding innings of 82 ended, seventy minutes remained. Somehow, Knott extracted enough help from the tail-enders to steer his side to safety. Crisis loomed when Pocock was out to a first bounce catch, but Jones managed to scramble through the final over from Gibbs. Gibbs bowled beautifully, starting with four for 12 in fourteen overs before lunch, but the honours lay largely with Knott in only his fourth Test. He had some luck at the start, missed by Murray off Gibbs, but once into his stride he was well nigh as assured as Cowdrey and no less courageous.

West Indies

S. M. Nurse c Knott b Snow	17	lbw b Snow	49
S. Camacho c and b Jones	14	c Graveney b Snow	26
R. B. Kanhai c Edrich b Pocock	150	c Edrich b Jones	22
B. F. Butcher run out	18	c Lock b Pocock	18
*G. S. Sobers c Cowdrey b Barrington	152	not out	95
C. H. Lloyd b Lock	31	c Knott b Snow	1
D. A. J. Holford lbw b Snow	1	b Lock	3
†D. L. Murray c Knott b Lock	8	c Boycott b Pocock	16
L. A. King b Snow	8	b Snow	20
W. W. Hall not out	5	b Snow	7
L. R. Gibbs b Snow	1	b Snow	0
L-b 3, w 2, n-b 4	9	B 1, l-b 2, w 1, n-b 3	7
1/22 2/35 3/72 4/322 5/383 6/387 7/399 8/400 9/412	414	1/78 2/84 3/86 4/133 5/171 6/201 7/216 8/252 9/264	264

Bowling: *First Innings*—Jones 31–5–114–1; Snow 27.4–2–82–4; D'Oliveira 8–1–27–0; Pocock 38–11–78–1; Barrington 18–4–43–1; Lock 28–7–61–2. *Second Innings*—Snow 15.2–0–60–6; Jones 17–1–81–1; D'Oliveira 8–0–28–0; Pocock 17–1–66–2; Lock 9–1–22–1.

England

G. Boycott c Murray b Hall	116	c Gibbs	30
J. H. Edrich c Murray b Sobers	0	c Gibbs b Sobers	6
*M. C. Cowdrey lbw b Sobers	59	lbw b Gibbs	82
T. W. Graveney c Murray b Hall	27	c Murray b Gibbs	0
K. F. Barrington c Kanhai b Sobers	4	c Lloyd b Gibbs	0
B. L. D'Oliveira c Nurse b Holford	27	c and b Gibbs	2
†A. P. E. Knott lbw b Holford	7	not out	73
J. A. Snow b Gibbs	0	lbw b Sobers	1
G. A. R. Lock b King	89	c King b Sobers	2
P. I. Pocock c and b King	13	c Lloyd b Gibbs	0
I. J. Jones not out	0	not out	0
B 12, l-b 14, n-b 3	29	B 9, w 1	10
1/13 2/185 3/185 4/194 5/240 6/252 7/257 8/259 9/368	371	1/33 2/37 3/37 4/39 5/41 6/168 7/198 8/200 9/206	(9 wkts) 206

Bowling: *First Innings*—Sobers 37–15–72–3; Hall 19–3–71–2; King 38.2–11–79–2; Holford 31–10–54–2; Gibbs 33–9–59–1; Butcher 5–3–7–0. *Second Innings*—Sobers 31–16–53–3; Hall 13–6–26–0; King 9–1–11–0; Gibbs 40–20–60–6; Holford 17–9–37–0; Butcher 10–7–9–0.

Umpires: C. Kippins and C. Jordan.

PRESIDENT'S XI v MCC

Played at Bridgetown, January 23, 24, 25, 26, 1974

Drawn. For the tourists the end was disappointing, for after dominating the match for three days they were held to a draw by a last-wicket partnership which occupied ninety minutes and was worth 84 runs when the last ball was bowled. Baichan, a left hander from Guyana who had made 49 in the first innings, scored 139 not out, Roberts, the number eleven, 48 not out. Until those two changed the match, Denness's team were in command despite virtually having had no match practice for four months. Their first innings total was impressive, 511 for four, with Boycott nine and a half hours, not out for 261, the highest score of his career. With Amiss, who made 109, he put on 252 for the first wicket. It was an innings of extraordinary perfection in a man coming back to batting after a break, no more than three balls beating his stroke. Yet in its perfection it was also an embarrassment for it curtailed the opportunity for practice of other players who had less than a fortnight to prepare for the first Test. To counter this, Denness shuffled his batting order when he decided to go in again despite a first innings lead of 347 runs. The President's XI had batted with so little application in the face of fast bowling by Arnold, who took five wickets, Willis and Old, that their recovery on the final day came as an even bigger surprise.

MCC

G. Boycott not out	261		
D. L. Amiss c Fredericks b Roberts	109		
J. A. Jameson lbw b Roberts	0	– c and b Barrett	87
*M. H. Denness b Padmore	41		
K. W. R. Fletcher c Fredericks b Padmore	70		
†A. P. E. Knott (did not bat)		– st Murray b Barrett	21
A. W. Greig (did not bat)		– c Murray b Barrett	0
C. M. Old (did not bat)		– c Foster b Barrett	19
P. I. Pocock (did not bat)		– c and b Padmore	0
G. G. Arnold (did not bat)		– not out	2
B 5, l-b 2, n-b 23	30	N-b 2	2
1/252 2/252 3/343 4/511	(4 wkts dec.) 511	1/109 2/109 3/110 4/121 5/131	(5 wkts dec.) 131

R. G. D. Willis did not bat.

Bowling: *First Innings*—Armstrong 26–2–106–0; Roberts 27–7–59–2; Holding 7–2–14–0; Padmore 51.3–9–149–2; Barrett 35–14–85–0; Foster 18–0–41–0; Fredericks 1–0–5–0; Greenidge 6–2–22–0. *Second Innings*—Armstrong 1–0–15–0; Roberts 7–1–32–0; Foster 7–3–15–0; Padmore 10–1–37–1; Fredericks 4–0–17–0; Barrett 6–3–13–4.

President's XI

R. C. Fredericks c Greig b Arnold	0	– c Amiss b Willis	8
C. G. Greenidge c Greig b Willis	37	– c Jameson b Willis	28
L. Baichan b Arnold	49	– not out	139
*M. L. C. Foster c Knott b Old	7	– c Willis b Pocock	7
H. S. Chang b Willis	4	– c Amiss b Pocock	64
†D. A. Murray c Jamieson b Willis	8	– b Willis	28
A. G. Barrett c Knott b Arnold	37	– c Willis b Old	0
M. A. Holding c Old b Arnold	5	– b Willis	1
A. Padmore c Amiss b Pocock	0	– b Old	7
G. D. Armstrong lbw b Arnold	0	– c Fletcher b Old	12
A. M. E. Roberts not out	0	– not out	48
B 8, l-b 1, n-b 8	17	L-b 8, n-b 18	26
1/1 2/55 3/63 4/71 5/85 6/141 7/155 8/164 9/164	164	1/10 6/60 3/171 4/248 5/250 6/251 7/252 8/265 9/284	(9 wkts) 368

Bowling: *First Innings*—Willis 15–6–35–3; Arnold 12–5–44–5; Old 15–4–47–1; Pocock 6.1–0–21–1. *Second Innings*—Willis 21–3–91–4; Arnold 18–4–73–0; Pocock 37–10–56–2; Old 23–8–56–3; Greig 15–3–53–0; Fletcher 4–1–13–0.

Umpires: S. E. Parris and C. A. Vyfhuis.

WEST INDIES v ENGLAND

Second Test Match

Played at Kingston, Jamaica, February 16, 17, 19, 20, 21, 1974

Drawn. In the end this became the great escape story – a match apparently lost by England but finally saved by Amiss who batted for the last nine and a half hours and scored 262 not out. Yet the achievement of Amiss, strongly and bravely supported by the tail, tended to hide the fact that this was another Test match in which England were put in jeopardy by the failure of the men in the first half of the batting order. When Denness won the toss on a pitch without pace or vice he must have been hoping for a score of around five hundred. Instead, before the first day was out, England had lost five wickets for 224 and were already committed to a rearguard action.

It was a day on which the bad ball became deadly. Amiss, Hayes and Greig all hit catches off long hops from slow bowlers, Jameson went a long way down the pitch to Gibbs, hit his own ankle instead of the ball and was stumped, while Boycott, hampered for much of his innings by a pulled leg muscle, was splendidly caught by Kanhai, rolling over at short mid-off, when driving at Sobers. By the end of that opening day it was almost certain that the West Indies could not lose the match. Yet in the second half of the England innings they found resistance stiffer. Admittedly Denness, who remained the last hope of a really big score went thirty-five minutes after the start next morning for 67, but Underwood, Knott and Pocock played with such determination that the last three wickets put on 67.

Even so, 353 was a moderate score which looked somewhat less than that by the time Rowe and Fredericks had scored 206 for the first West Indies wicket. Fredericks, a left-hander who played well within limitations set by himself, was the artisan of the partnership; Rowe, who at that point had scored all his ten first-class centuries before his own Jamaican crowd, was the artist. His footwork and his balance were superb. Yet from that point of depression England's bowlers, without much success to urge them on, produced a dogged defiance that actually pinned Kallicharran, Lloyd and Sobers to defence. It was a fine performance, valuable in its context, for it erased the fear of a huge West Indian score made quickly, which would in turn have lengthened the time England would have had to survive in the second innings.

By the start of the fourth day, the West Indies were pressed into making up time. The outcome was explosive. In 58 balls Julien hit 66, adding 112 with Sobers in seventy-five minutes. Sobers, who for once in his life played the role of junior partner to whoever was at the crease with him, scored 57 and at lunch West Indies, who had added 149 in two hours off only 30 overs, declared at 583 for nine. England's bowling, so efficient the evening before, had suddenly been made to look defenceless and bewildered.

By the end of that remarkable fourth day it seemd unlikely that England could survive. With ten hours left they could only retreat and the chances of their doing so successfully were reduced dramatically when Boyce had Boycott caught off a bouncer that brushed his glove in the third over.

By the time the score was 217 – West Indies had led by 230 – five wickets had gone and Amiss had only Knott and the tailenders left for company. Among those who had fallen was Hayes, thrown out by Lloyd from cover when Amiss unaccountably challenged the man who is probably the best cover point in the world. He did the same thing later with the result that Knott also was run out (each time Lloyd scored a direct hit on the stumps). Those two errors made it even more imperative that Amiss should stay and he responded magnificently. Immediately at the start of the fifth day he had a piece of luck which almost certainly cost West Indies the match. He turned the third ball of the day firmly but straight into the hands of Sobers at backward short leg. It fell out again.

Thenceforth, England played cricket of real courage as pressure built up both on the field and in the crowd. Underwood, who had been sent in as nightwatchman, did as much as anybody to inspire it, batting on another seventy-five minutes into the last day and bravely fending off bouncers, particularly from Boyce, that became too numerous to be acceptable. Again, when Knott was quickly dismissed it seemed that England, 41 ahead with three wickets left, were doomed. Then Old, not the best player of fast bowling, withstood another barrage of bouncers to use up another hundred minutes. He and Amiss put on 72 for the eighth wicket.

Yet, such was the delicate balance of time and runs that it was not until after tea that England were finally out of danger. By then Pocock had stayed with Amiss for eighty-five minutes scoring four runs. In the end England made 432 for nine, at which point, Amiss, who had never before in his first class career scored a double century, led them off the field for the last time. His was the hero's role in a classic escape.

The receipts, £36,000, were a record for Jamaica.

England

G. Boycott c Kanhai b Sobers	68	– c Murray b Boyce	5
D. L. Amiss c Kanhai b Barrett	27	– not out	262
J. A. Jameson st Murray b Gibbs	23	– c Rowe b Barrett	38
F. C. Hayes c Boyce b Sobers	10	– run out	0
*M. H. Denness c Fredericks b Boyce	67	– c Rowe b Barrett	28
A. W. Greig c Fredericks b Barrett	45	– b Gibbs	14
†A. P. E. Knott c Murray b Barrett	39	– run out	6
C. M. Old c Murray b Julien	2	– b Barrett	19
D. L. Underwood c Fredericks b Sobers	24	– c Murray b Sobers	12
P. I. Pocock c Gibbs b Julien	23	– c sub b Boyce	4
R. G. D. Willis not out	6	– not out	3
L-b 7, n-b 12	19	B 10, l-b 11, w 1, n-b 19	41
1/68 2/104 3/133 4/134 5/224 6/278 7/286 8/322 9/333	353	1/32 2/102 3/102 4/176 5/217 6/258 7/271 8/343 9/392	(9 wkts) 432

Bowling: *First Innings*—Boyce 19–2–52–1; Julien 18–3–40–2; Sobers 33–11–65–3; Barrett 39–16–86–3; Gibbs 40–16–78–1; Fredericks 21–4–70–2; Lloyd 4–2–2–0. *Second Innings*—Julien 13–2–36–0; Boyce 21–4–70–2; Gibbs 44–15–82–1; Barrett 54–24–87–3; Sobers 34–13–73–1; Fredericks 6–1–17–0; Lloyd 3–1–5–0; Kanhai 3–1–8–0; Rowe 2–1–1–0; Kallicharran 3–0–12–0.

West Indies

R. C. Fredericks b Old	94
L. G. Rowe lbw b Willis	120
A. I. Kallicharran c Denness b Old	93
C. H. Lloyd b Jameson	49
*R. B. Kanhai c Willis b Greig	39
G. S. Sobers c Willis b Greig	57
B. D. Julien c Denness b Greig	66
K. D. Boyce c Greig b Willis	8
†D. L. Murray not out	6
A. G. Barrett lbw b Willis	0
L. R. Gibbs not out	6
B 16, l-b 18, n-b 11	45
1/206 2/226 3/338 4/401 5/439 6/551 7/563 8/567 9/574	(9 wkts dec.) 583

Bowling: Willis 24–5–97–3; Old 23–6–72–2; Pocock 57–14–152–0; Underwood 36–12–98–0; Greig 49–14–102–3; Jameson 7–2–17–1.

Umpires: D. Sang Hue and C. Jordan.

WEST INDIES v ENGLAND

Third Test Match

Played at Bridgetown, March 6, 7, 9, 10, 11, 1974

Drawn. The third Test was virtually a replay of the second as England again escaped with a determined and skilful batting performance on the last day after four days of running second to West Indies. Whereas at Kingston Amiss had dominated the closing stages, in Barbados it was Fletcher whose third century in Test cricket created a draw out of a match England seemed to have lost. It was a match that started in English uncertainty, a factor which as much as the early moisture in the pitch encouraged Kanhai to put them in for the second time in three Test matches. After much debate Boycott, accepted as one of the world's best opening batsmen, emerged as the new number four – a move designed to keep him away from the new ball bouncers (although not at his request) and at the same time add muscle to the soft underbelly of the side.

The theory added up to nothing because when the team needed to be saved, as almost inevitably happened in the first innings, Greig and Knott did it, batting in their normal positions. They came together at 130 for five and added 163 runs before Knott was bowled for 87 cutting at Gibbs' off-break. After a long time of disappointing batting for England that had put his place in the side in jeopardy, he played with great assurance and certainty. Greig stayed to be ninth out after an innings of 148 that was his first major contribution to a match he was to dominate from an England point of view. He enjoyed one piece of luck when at 82 Sobers dropped him off a straightforward chance at second slip.

So England reached 395, a total not big enough but still much higher than had seemed likely. The modesty of it became apparent on a remarkable third day which produced the largest crowd ever seen in Bridgetown and far beyond the capacity of the ground to hold. Security broke down outside the ground, people swarmed over the walls, occupied the seats of ticket holders and perched on the roofs of the stands.

Yet with the exception of two invasions of the field when Rowe, the opening batsman, reached his first hundred and then his second hundred, they were splendidly behaved despite their real discomfort. Rowe, who had not previously scored a century outside Jamaica, provided the master performance of this match. He scored 302, the highest innings for West Indies against England, an honour previously held by George Headley (270 not out, Kingston 1935). It was the eleventh triple century in Test cricket. Rowe batted ten hours and ten minutes, a duration of only 140 overs, for England's over-rate was, as usual, laggardly, and hit one 6 and thirty-six 4s. If the statistics were impressive, the style was even more so. On this sort of pitch there was a languid ferocity about him that owed everything to his timing and his perfect balance. His cutting, driving and hooking were fearsome, yet there was always more poetry than brutality about his play. With Kallicharran, the left-hander who had already made a century in the first Test and who now reached 119, he put on 249 for the second wicket, another record for West Indies against England. It surpassed 228 by R. K. Nunes and George Headley at Kingston, 1929-30.

When Kanhai declared at tea-time on the fourth day at 596 for eight, he had a lead of 201. The only England player who will recall this West Indies innings with any sort of pleasure was Greig, who claimed six wickets for 164, bowling mostly off-spinners, and who thus became the first England player to take five wickets and score a century in a Test match. In addition, he had taken a catch at second slip to dismiss Sobers for nought, which in itself should have qualified for a prize. It was the first time Sobers had been dismissed for a duck in a Test Match on his home ground.

By the end of that day Greig was engaged again, for England lost their first four wickets, including that of Boycott, for 40. To negotiate the last day with the pitch apparently worn and certainly cracked, seemed a formidable task. Yet England accomplished it, largely through Fletcher's diligence and skill in playing slow bowling, through the resurgence in Knott's batting – they put on 142 together for the sixth wicket – and possibly through the inability of Gibbs to bowl properly because of a leg injury. Nobody can know what that cost the West Indies. Altogether 99 no-balls were called – 79 not being scored by the bat – a record.

England

*M. H. Denness c Murray b Sobers	24	– lbw b Holder	0
D. L. Amiss b Julien	12	– c Julien b Roberts	4
J. A. Jameson c Fredericks b Julien	3	– lbw b Roberts	9
G. Boycott c Murray b Julien	10	– c Kanhai b Sobers	13
K. W. R. Fletcher c Murray b Julien	37	– not out	129
A. W. Greig c Sobers b Julien	148	– c Roberts b Gibbs	25
†A. P. E. Knott b Gibbs	87	– lbw b Lloyd	67
C. M. Old c Murray b Roberts	1	– b Lloyd	0
G. G. Arnold b Holder	12	– not out	2
P. I. Pocock c Lloyd b Gibbs	18		
R. G. D. Willis not out	10		
L-b 5, n-b 28	33	B 7, l-b 5, n-b 16	28
1/28 2/34 3/53 4/68 5/130 6/293 7/306 8/344 9/371	395	1/4 2/8 3/29 4/40 5/106 6/248 7/248	(7 wkts) 277

Bowling: *First Innings*—Holder 27–6–68–1; Roberts 33–8–75–1; Julien 26–9–57–5; Sobers 18–4–57–1; Gibbs 33.4–10–91–2; Lloyd 4–2–9–0; Fredericks 3–0–5–0. *Second Innings*—Holder 15–6–37–1; Roberts 17–4–49–2; Gibbs 28.3–15–40–1; Julien 11–4–21–0; Lloyd 12–4–13–2; Sobers 35–21–55–1; Fredericks 6–2–24–0; Rowe 1–0–5–0; Kallicharran 1–0–5–0.

West Indies

R. C. Fredericks b Greig	32
L. G. Rowe c Arnold b Greig	302
A. I. Kallicharran b Greig	119
C. H. Lloyd c Fletcher b Greig	8
V. A. Holder c and b Greig	8
*R. B. Kanhai b Arnold	18
G. S. Sobers c Greig b Willis	0
†D. L. Murray not out	53
B. D. Julian c Willis b Greig	1
A. M. F. Roberts not out	9
B 3, l-b 8. n-b 35	46
1/126 2/375 3/390 4/429 5/465 6/466 7/551 8/556	(8 wkts dec.) 596

L. R. Gibbs did not bat.

Bowling: Arnold 26–5–91–1; Willis 26–4–100–1; Greig 46–2–164–6; Old 28–4–102–0; Pocock 28–4–93–0.

Umpires: D. Sang Hue and S. E. Parris.

GUYANA v MCC

Played at Georgetown, March 14, 15, 16, 17, 1974

Another drawn match, although Denness made enthusiastic if unrewarded efforts to get a result by declaring 67 runs behind on the first innings. It will be remembered for the batting performances of Fredericks, who scored a hundred in each innings of a match for the third time, and further centuries from Amiss and Boycott.

Less memorable was the obvious irritation and petulance that showed among MCC's players at their clear disagreement with the umpires on their interpretation of the no-ball and lbw laws. Coming after a Test match in which the bowlers of both sides had delivered ninety-nine no-balls, MCC now ran up another 31 in Guyana's first innings. All bowlers, quick or slow, were penalized, Underwood being called 13 times on the last day. Nor was there any more joy for the bowlers in the response to the numerous lbw appeals. Denness's declaration brought little reply from Lloyd, the acting captain of Guyana, who did not close his side's innings until the target had reached 270 at around a hundred an hour.

Guyana

L. Baichan c Willis b Birkenshaw	71	– c and b Willis	1
R. Etwaroo c and b Underwood	25	– c Taylor b Arnold	14
S. F. A. Bacchus b Hendrick	14	– c Hendrick b Birkenshaw	24
R. C. Fredericks c Fletcher b Birkenshaw	112	– not out	105
A. I. Kallicharran b Arnold	23	– st Taylor b Birkenshaw	0
*C. H. Lloyd c Taylor b Birkenshaw	65	– c Hayes b Underwood	24
†L. E. Skinner not out	27	– c Taylor b Underwood	8
R. C. Collymore c Fletcher b Birkenshaw	0	– run out	0
A. Persaud c Underwood b Birkenshaw	7	– run out	6
P. D. Blair b Underwood	10	– c Arnold b Fletcher	6
K. O. Cameron c Willis b Birkenshaw	6	– not out	0
L-b 6, n-b 27	33	B 6, n-b 8	14
1/81 2/126 3/127 4/171 5/341 6/347 7/347 8/360 9/382	393	1/1 2/38 3/40 4/40 5/81 6/115 7/123 8/150 9/200	(9 wkts dec.) 202

Bowling: *First Innings*—Arnold 21–3–72–1; Willis 18–1–90–0; Underwood 34–9–67–2; Hendrick 13–1–30–1; Birkenshaw 35.3–5–101–6. *Second Innings*—Arnold 5–2–11–1; Willis 3–0–26–1; Birkenshaw 33–10–84–2; Underwood 31–15–64–2; Fletcher 3–1–3–1.

MCC

G. Boycott retired ill	133		
D. L. Amiss c Skinner b Fredericks	108	– b Collymore	60
*M. H. Denness c Baichan b Persaud	7	– not out	63
F. C. Hayes lbw b Blair	30	– not out	8
K. W. R. Fletcher not out	26		
J. Birkenshaw not out	17		
B 1, l-b 1, w 1, n-b 2	5	L-b 7, n-b 1	8
1/91 2/208 3/258	(3 wkts dec.) 326	1/111	(1 wkt) 139

†R. W. Taylor, G. G. Arnold, D. L. Underwood, M. Hendrick and R. G. D. Willis did not bat.

Bowling: *First Innings*—Blair 18–2–79–1; Cameron 20–3–51–0; Collymore 36–8–89–0; Persaud 34–12–72–1; Fredericks 9–2–27–1; Lloyd 2–0–3–0. *Second Innings*—Blair 14–2–45–0; Cameron 6–0–24–0; Collymore 13–2–39–1; Persaud 6–1–23–0.

Umpires: C. Kippins and C. A. Vyfhuis.

WEST INDIES v ENGLAND

Fifth Test Match

Played at Port-of-Spain, March 30, 31, April 2, 3, 4, 5, 1974

England won by 26 runs with an hour to spare. The final Test was well and deservedly won by England on the strength of two outstanding personal performances – by Greig, who, bowling almost entirely in his new style as an off-spinner took thirteen wickets for 156, and by Boycott who in each innings played more convincingly than at any time since the first Test on the same ground. The toss at Port-of-Spain, where the pitch was more benevolent towards bowlers than anywhere else in the West Indies, was always important and it became more so this time with a sixth day added to the match. Denness won it and then saw the advantage dissipated as his side were bowled out for 267.

Of that total Boycott, his form not right but his determination as steadfast as ever, made 99 in six hours, twenty-five minutes. He should have been run out by half the length of the pitch when he had made 9, but Kanhai, who had scrambled towards fine leg from a close-in position, threw badly to the bowler's end. Everything that happened in the rest of England's innings emphasized the importance of that miss. Only Amiss of the other batsmen made a worthwhile contribution and his 44 was the effort of a man in whom tiredness was at last beginning to show. Boycott's innings was completely defensive – he once went fifty minutes without scoring – and it ended when he was caught left-handed by Murray diving far down the leg side, still one run short of his first century on the ground where he had scored 93 in the first Test. The value of this innings was emphasized by subsequent happenings as England's last six wickets fell for 63 in ninety minutes.

The uneasiness of that position increased as the West Indies moved steadily towards that total. Fredericks and Rowe put on 110 for the first wicket and at lunch time on the third day the West Indies score stood at 208 for two, Rowe 90, Lloyd 40. Oddly, it was a position from which England began to prosper. In the space of twenty balls Greig took the wickets of Lloyd, Sobers, Kanhai and Murray for six runs so that instead of being in a commanding position when they took the lead, the West Indies had only four wickets left. The chances of that being converted into a healthy credit balance disappeared when Rowe, who had withheld his strokes to bat with the same sort of caution as Boycott, was ninth out, caught off a full toss for 123. He batted over seven hours, the West Indies totalled 305 and Greig, in a spell of bowling that will rank among the best in Test history, took in the day eight for 33 in 19.1 overs.

Having been saved from annihilation, England batted doggedly, if not with much conviction, in their second innings. Again they dropped into danger as Amiss and Denness were dismissed for 44, but Fletcher stayed with Boycott in a stand of 101 for the third wicket before deterioration set in again. The next three wickets fell for seven runs, Julien claiming two for nine in nine overs. Boycott achieved his much wanted century after six and three-quarter hours and was then bowled by Gibbs in a manner that caused much controversy. He played forward to Gibbs and then stayed at the crease although the bail lay on the ground. Umpire Sang Hue from the bowler's end checked with his colleague at square-leg before giving him out. Apparently the ball had turned so much that his view of the stumps had been blocked by Boycott's front pad and he checked to make sure that it had hit the wicket.

Fortunately for England, Knott, who seemed to be less troubled than any batsman except Boycott, continued his successful run so that by the time he was lbw to Sobers for 44, the West Indies had been set a target of 226 to win. They started the last day 30 for none which meant that the chances of a West Indies win, an England win or a draw (the match had been constantly interrupted by rain) were all about even. Greig, significantly, had opened the England bowling with off-spinners.

Perhaps in the end the most decisive factor in the result was the tension that built up during the day. The England players withstood it better than those of West Indies, among whom some of the most experienced seemed to be the most vulnerable. The opening pair were the key players for they were the ones so clearly in form. Nothing much disturbed them until at 63 Rowe played back casually to Birkenshaw and was lbw. Two balls later Kallicharran was caught off bat and pad off Greig at first slip, thus finishing a series in which he had batted with extravagance, with a "pair". Immediately there followed an incident which may well have cost the West Indies the match.

Fredericks, who had been playing with great calmness and with an unerring judgement of stroke, played a ball from Birkenshaw past Boycott at square leg, ran a single and then surprisingly turned for a second run. Lloyd let him get as far as the middle of the pitch and then ran past him so that Fredericks watched himself being run out by several yards. In nine balls the West Indies had lost three wickets for two runs and the game had changed its complexion.

Greig again took charge for England, dismissing Kanhai and Lloyd, both of whom were clear victims of tension. Then the match swung again as Sobers, playing even in these circumstances with a charm that marked his pedigree, put on 50 for the sixth wicket with Murray, another player of good temperament. Sobers suddenly hit over a ball from Underwood and was bowled. Murray was caught driving at Greig and at 166 for eight West Indies seemed doomed.

Even then they came close to winning, for Inshan Ali, batting with a composure not apparent in some of his betters, was not dismissed until only 29 were needed and Denness in desperation had taken the new ball. Soon the innings ended and England had squared the series in a memorable match that never lacked interest and excitement even if it were sometimes short of quality.

Greig's eight wickets in an innings and thirteen wickets in the match were the best respective performances for England since Jim Laker's nine for 37 and nineteen in the match against Australia at Manchester in 1956. Greig also surpassed Trevor Bailey's seven for 34 at Kingston in 1954 as the best figures for England against West Indies.

England

G. Boycott c Murray b Julien	99	– b Gibbs	112
D. L. Amiss c Kanhai b Sobers	44	– b Lloyd	16
*M. H. Denness c Fredericks b Inshan	13	– run out	4
K. W. R. Fletcher c Kanhai b Gibbs	6	– b Julien	45
A. W. Greig lbw b Gibbs	19	– c Fredericks b Julien	1
F. C. Hayes c Rowe b Inshan	24	– lbw b Julien	0
†A. P. E. Knott not out	33	– lbw b Sobers	44
J. Birkenshaw c Lloyd b Julien	8	– c Gibbs b Inshan	7
G. G. Arnold run out	6	– b Sobers	13
P. I. Pocock c Lloyd b Inshan	0	– c Kallicharran b Boyce	5
D. L. Underwood b Gibbs	4	– not out	1
B 2, l-b 3, n-b 6	11	L-b 4, n-b 11	15
1/83 2/114 3/133 4/165 5/204 6/212 7/244 8/257 9/260	267	1/39 2/44 3/145 4/169 5/175 6/176 7/213 8/226 9/268	263

Bowling: *First Innings*—Boyce 10–3–14–0; Julien 21–8–35–2; Sobers 31–16–44–1; Gibbs 34.3–11–70–3; Inshan 35–12–86–3; Lloyd 4–2–7–0. *Second Innings*—Sobers 24.2–9–36–2; Julien 22–7–31–3; Lloyd 7–4–5–1; Gibbs 50–15–85–1; Inshan 34–12–51–1; Boyce 12–3–40–1.

West Indies

R. C. Fredericks c Fletcher b Pocock	67	– run out	36
L. G. Rowe c Boycott b Greig	123	– lbw b Birkenshaw	25
A. I. Kallicharran c and b Pocock	0	– c Fletcher b Greig	0
C. H. Lloyd c Knott b Greig	52	– c and b Greig	13
G. S. Sobers c Birkenshaw b Greig	0	– b Underwood	20
*R. B. Kanhai c and b Greig	2	– c Fletcher b Greig	7
†D. L. Murray c Pocock b Greig	2	– c Fletcher b Greig	33
B. D. Julien c Birkenshaw b Greig	17	– c Denness b Pocock	2
K. D. Boyce c Pocock b Greig	19	– not out	34
Inshan Ali lbw b Greig	5	– c Underwood b Greig	15
L. R. Gibbs not out	0	– b Arnold	1
B 11, l-b 4, n-b 3	18	B 9, l-b 2, n-b 2	13
1/110 2/122 3/224 4/224 5/226 6/232 7/270 8/300 9/300	305	1/63 2/64 3/65 4/84 5/85 6/135 7/138 8/166 9/197	199

Bowling: *First Innings*—Arnold 8–0–27–0; Greig 36.1–10–86–8; Pocock 31–7–86–2; Underwood 34–12–57–0; Birkenshaw 8–1–31–0. *Second Innings*—Arnold 5.3–1–13–1; Greig 33–8–70–5; Underwood 15–7–19–1; Pocock 25–7–60–1; Birkenshaw 10–1–24–1.

Umpires: D. Sang Hue and S. Ishmael.

WEST INDIES v ENGLAND

Third Test Match

Played at Bridgetown, March 13, 14, 15, 17, 18, 1981

West Indies won by 298 runs. Though put in on a pitch which was at its liveliest on the first morning, West Indies dominated a match tragically marred by the death, after play on the second evening, of Ken Barrington, assistant-manager and coach of the England team.

England made four changes from the side which lost in Trinidad, Gatting, Butcher, Bairstow and Jackman coming in for Rose, who had returned home, Miller, Downton and Old. Jackman, in his first Test, took two of the four wickets to fall in the first 21 overs. A splendid catch at second slip by Botham off Dilley removed Richards for 0, but the England bowlers were unable to take full advantage of the help given them in the first hour, and in a decreasing amount until lunch, and West Indies rebuilt through a long partnership between the left handers, Lloyd and Gomes, who added 154 in three and threequarter hours. Lloyd made scarcely a mistake in one of his best Test innings, but Gomes survived several chances and was lucky when 7 to be bowled by Dilley with one of only two no-balls called during the day.

In the last half-hour of the first day England took the wickets of Lloyd, Gomes and Murray, and in less than fifty minutes next morning finished off the innings, for 265. But in three overs their own score stood at 11 for two and, though there was temporary resistance from the middle order, the innings never recovered against the four fast bowlers, of whom Holding was at his fastest.

With a first innings lead of 143, the loss of Greenidge before the end of the second day scarcely troubled West Indies, and they batted comfortably if cautiously through the third day, which England played with heavy hearts after Ken Barrington's death in the night. The two teams, officials and a capacity crowd of 15,000 stood in silence in his memory before play began.

In the circumstances England did not do badly to limit the scoring on the third day to 245 off 79 overs. However, Richards, playing with unusual care, had reached 100 before the end, and after the rest day he and Lloyd took their sixth-wicket stand to 153, making the last 114 in 95 minutes. Lloyd declared at lunch, 522 runs ahead, and when, for the second time in the match, Holding disposed of Boycott in his first over, this time also bowling Gatting next ball, it seemed unlikely that England would take the match into the last day. Boycott was out twice in ten balls in this match, Gatting twice in three balls and Bairstow was out second ball in each innings.

However, a stand of 120 between Gooch and Gower, which featured much good batting, saved England's face. Dominated at first by Gower, the partnership was being taken over by Gooch when it ended after two and a half hours. Gooch had made 88 out of a score of 166 for five at the end of the day and next morning soon reached his second Test hundred after batting four hours twenty minutes. He survived a hard chance in the gully when 71 but otherwise made few mistakes against the fast bowlers, who worked their way through the rest of the batting. When he was eighth out to a brilliant low catch in the gully by Garner from a well-middled stroke, Emburey and Jackman effected a ninth-wicket stand which lasted nearly an hour and carried the match over until after lunch.

West Indies

C. G. Greenidge c Gooch b Jackman	14	– lbw b Dilley	0
D. L. Haynes c Bairstow b Jackman	25	– lbw b Botham	25
I. V. A. Richards c Botham b Dilley	0	– (4) not out	182
E. H. Mattis lbw b Botham	16	– (5) c Butcher b Jackman	24
*C. H. Lloyd c Gooch b Jackman	100	– (7) lbw b Botham	66
H. A. Gomes c Botham b Dilley	58	– run out	34
†D. A. Murray c Bairstow b Dilley	9	– (9) not out	5
A. M. E. Roberts c Bairstow b Botham	14	– c Bairstow b Botham	0
J. Garner c Bairstow b Botham	15		
M. A. Holding c Gatting b Botham	0		
C. E. H. Croft not out	0	– (3) c Boycott b Jackman	33
B 4, l-b 6, w 2, n-b 2	14	B 3, l-b 7	10
1/24 2/25 3/47 4/65 5/219 6/224 7/236 8/258 9/258	265	1/10 2/57 3/71 4/130 5/212 6/365 7/365 (7 wkts dec.)	379

Bowling: *First Innings*—Dilley 23–7–51–3; Botham 25.1–5–77–4; Jackman 22–4–65–3; Emburey 18–4–45–0; Gooch 2–0–13–0. *Second Innings*—Dilley 25–3–111–1; Botham 29–5–102–3; Jackman 25–5–76–2; Emburey 24–7–57–0; Willey 6–0–23–0.

England

G. A. Gooch b Garner	26	– c Garner b Croft	116
G. Boycott b Holding	0	– c Garner b Holding	1
M. W. Gatting c Greenidge b Roberts	2	– b Holding	0
D. I. Gower c Mattis b Croft	17	– b Richards	54
R. O. Butcher c Richards b Croft	17	– lbw b Richards	2
*I. T. Botham c Murray b Holding	26	– c Lloyd b Roberts	1
P. Willey not out	19	– lbw b Croft	17
†D. L. Bairstow c Mattis b Holding	0	– c Murray b Croft	2
J. E. Emburey c Lloyd b Roberts	0	– b Garner	9
R. D. Jackman c Roberts b Croft	7	– b Garner	7
G. R. Dilley c Gomes b Croft	0	– not out	7
B 1, l-b 1, n-b 6	8	B 1, l-b 3, n-b 4	8
1/6 2/11 3/40 4/55 5/72 6/94 7/94 8/97 9/122	122	1/2 2/2 3/122 4/134 5/139 6/196 7/198 8/201 9/213	224

Bowling: *First Innings*—Roberts 11–3–29–2; Holding 11–7–16–3; Croft 13.5–5–39–4; Garner 12–5–30–1. *Second Innings*—Roberts 20–6–42–1; Holding 19–6–46–2; Croft 19–1–65–3; Garner 16.2–6–39–2; Richards 17–6–24–2.

Umpires: D. M. Archer and D. Sang Hue.

ENGLAND IN WEST INDIES, 1980-81

By Michael Melford

In playing terms England's three-month tour of West Indies went no better and no worse than expected. Two-nil was not a massive defeat considering the known difference in the strength of the two sides, especially in bowling, even if England achieved the two draws only after being well behind on first innings and with the help of rain on the fourth day both in Antigua and Jamaica. Moreover, not many touring sides have been as beset by ill fortune as was this one in the first half of the tour.

When practice on good pitches was urgently required, the England party were handicapped by bad weather, turning pitches untypical of what was to come, and the withdrawal for political reasons from Guyana. In the first seven weeks after leaving home in mid-January, they played only seventeen days of cricket. When normality was about to be restored, the death of their assistant-manager, coach and friend, Ken Barrington, during the Barbados Test match came as a shattering blow. It was a shock to his countless friends throughout the world. To those who had been working away at the nets with him through the previous, mostly dispiriting, two months, it was more poignant, and they went through the next day's play almost in a daze.

The team had been in Guyana for two days when, early on February 23, they were joined by Jackman, the replacement for Willis who had returned home after breaking down in Trinidad. No attempt was made to conceal the fact that Jackman, like others in the party, had spent winters playing in South Africa. Bairstow had captained a South African province, Griqualand West, in 1977-78 after the signing of the Gleneagles Declaration which, in the next few days, was to become the subject of many interpretations, varying according to political taste.

By February 25, three days before the second Test was due to start, it was known that a radio commentator in Jamaica had suggested that the Guyana government, by admitting Jackman with his South African connections, was in contravention of the Gleneagles agreement. It was also learnt that the Guyana government was taking the matter seriously. The next day the British government stated clearly through the Minister for Sport, Hector Monro, that the Gleneagles Declaration was irrelevant in this case as it made no reference to actions by one country against the nationals of another.

However, later on February 26, the British High Commissioner in Georgetown was informed by the Guyanese Minister of Foreign Affairs that Jackman's visitor's permit had been withdrawn and that he must leave the country. A statement was issued simultaneously by the England manager, Alan Smith, in Georgetown and by the Cricket Council meeting at Lord's, saying that England would not play the second Test "as it is not longer possible for the Test team to be chosen without restrictions being imposed". In fact, it had not been envisaged that Jackman, newly arrived from an English winter, would play at all in Guyana, but injuries to Dilley and Old would probably have forced his inclusion if the match had taken place.

Alan Smith, in collaboration with the High Commissioner and with sympathy and support from other Caribbean countries, at once set in motion plans to withdraw the England party which, with press, radio and television representatives, was now over 40 strong. This was done next morning and, after a long wait at Georgetown airport, the team arrived that night in Barbados to a warm welcome.

A meeting was then convened in Bridgetown between representatives of the governments of Barbados, Montserrat, Antigua and Jamaica, the other islands where England were due to play. Five days later, at 2.00 a.m. local time on March 4, it was announced that the tour would go on.

The statement of the four governments said that the Gleneagles Declaration did not deal with sactions against nationals of another country. From Lord's, the Cricket Council reaffirmed its support for the right of cricketers to pursue their careers in South Africa, Australia or anywhere else on an individual basis. The Cricket Council also made the highly significant point that such eventualities had been thoroughly discussed with the West Indies Board during the year or more in which the tour was being planned. The team had gone only after assurances had been received that the fact that many English players earn their living in the winter by coaching and playing in South Africa would be "no stumbling block".

As the dust settled in later weeks, it became even clearer that the case of Jackman was being used by the Guyana government to make a political point. In particular, it was considered elsewhere in the Caribbean to have been largely a reprisal for Lord Avebury's adverse report on election rigging in Guyana. The main sufferers were the Guyanese cricket public, starved of cricket and, on all the evidence, bitterly disappointed to be deprived of a Test match. The previous match with Guyana had not been played owing to the waterlogged state of the Bourda Oval after days of heavy storms.

The tour had begun well enough with a victory over a Young West Indies XI at Pointe-á-Pierre in South Trinidad. Ironically the two first-class victories of the tour, here and in Montserrat, were largely won by Miller who, after Willis's early departure, became a respected vice-captain. Yet he was kept out of the last three Tests by the presence of an outstanding off-spinnger in Emburey, by Willey's success with the bat, and by his own illness in Jamaica.

Rain in St Vincent led to the cancellation of the four-day match against the Windward Islands and the less than satisfactory substitution of two one-day matches. The match against Trinidad was played on a turning pitch of negligible bounce and was also affected by rain. The innings defeat in the first Test and subsequent events in Guyana did nothing to improve England's chances, though morale stayed remarkably high considering the hopelessness of the cause.

The three weeks in the friendly atmosphere of Barbados were to be tragically marred by Ken Barrington's death. Yet after the heavy Test defeat there, the tour, in its remaining four weeks, followed a more normal pattern, not least in Jamaica, often turbulent in the past but now peaceful and orderly, despite the biggest crowds of the tour.

The last two Tests were drawn, and several batsmen ended the series with reputations enhanced. Gooch, Gower and Willey especially had met and come nearer to mastering the West Indies bowling than had seemed possible early in the tour.

This was not a great West Indies side. The batting relied too much on Clive Lloyd who, with a lowest score of 58, had his best series for a long time. Richards, successful though he was, was not quite the devastating genius of other series. Greenidge was also below par, and though Haynes often looked in the same high class, the batsmen did not destroy a modestly equipped English attack as some of their predecessors might have done.

It was in its bowling that Lloyd's side was as formidable as any in West Indies' cricket history. The four fast bowlers – Roberts, Holding, Croft and Garner – wheeled away hour after hour, intensely accurate, grudging every run and occasionally producing the extra pace and bounce that can upset the best batsmen. In the modern, unattractive fashion they did not spare the later batsmen, who received a full share of high bouncers. Yet, except in Barbados, the bowlers had little help from the pitches. Nor from the umpiring, about which there were singularly few complaints compared with that of other tours.

What the bowlers achieved, they achieved by high-class bowling supported by usually safe slip-catching. If they did not destroy the batsman immediately, they eventually forced him, by their unflagging accuracy and aggression, into some injudicious stroke. West Indies made only one change in the series, replacing the 30-year-old Roberts in the last Test by the lively and equally accurate Marshall, aged 22.

Together the fast bowlers made their side invincible, even though individually they were not all at their best. Garner was not always fully fit, Roberts lost form. But Holding frequently produced his best and fastest, and Croft, with his in-slant from very wide of the stumps and his extraordinary ability to make the ball deviate a fraction away from the batsman, took 21 wickets in the first three Tests played at 13 apiece. In the last Test he was hit for 56 in his first eight overs, mostly by Gooch in an innings of high class and high spirit.

The weight of fast bowling and the over-rate of little more than thirteen an hour was sometimes relieved by the off-spin of Richards, who bowled to some effect to the left-handed Gower and to batsmen wary of being caught off-guard by gentle spin after so much uncomfortable pace.

Against this formidable outcricket, England had, apart from the experience of Boycott, an unusually young batting side. When Rose returned home from Guyana with an eye defect and was replaced by Athey, this brought the number of players in the team aged 23 or under up to the remarkable number of five. It was in bowling that, as expected, England were outclassed. Dilley, still only 21, continued his improvement. The experienced Jackman soon settled down to bowl tidily, but in West Indian conditions, which allow little movement of the ball in the air or off the pitch, penetration was predictably lacking. The long and economical spells by Emburey, the one world-class bowler in the side, held the bowling together, but could only be a containing factor in these conditions. The fielding was usually keen and athletic; the slip catching was adequate but well below the lofty standards of 1978-79.

Botham at second slip was more fallible than in the past, and, though he took most wickets, his bowling never recovered the full rhythm of a year before. His batting, save in the one-day international in St Vincent, was found wanting in technqiue, concentration and eventually in confidence. His personal performances, in fact, could be cited as eloquent evidence of the undesirability of saddling a fast bowler and vital all-rounder with the extra burden of captaincy.

Yet it is fair to add that he did much to contribute to the harmony and good humour which existed between the two sides and between the England team and the public. Cynics would say that the first was because both sides knew each other well from playing, sometimes for the same counties, in England; and that the second owed much to the fact that England were always losing. Nevertheless, the crowds were well behaved, the team was popular, and Alan Smith, a manager in greater overall control than many of his predecessors, emerged from a difficult tour with immense credit.

By the end of it, several of the England batsmen had found a *modus vivendi* with the ever-menacing fast bowling. Boycott, though generally as consistent as ever, began to attract the "unplayable" ball, but Gooch, who had already made a splendid 116 in the Barbados Test, played an attacking innings of 153 on the first day of the Jamaica Test which few others could have played. Gower, with his advantage of seeing the ball earlier than others, played well throughout the tour and with a new maturity. If he was still out to the loose or casual stroke, he now seldom succumbed to the wildly irrational one. In his first innings of the tour, and in his last, he put his head down and batted for nearly eight hours, on the last day saving the final Test with his 154 not out. Willey, having worked out a method of holding off the fast bowlers, eventually carried the battle to them in his 102 not out in Antigua.

The weakness of the batting lay in the lack of an experienced number three. The original selection had relied too much on Rose's establishing himself in that position. Athey, the last incumbent, was doubtless a good pick for the future, but he found the opposition too much at this stage of his career.

Selection, both before and during a tour of West Indies, is all-important because so little cricket is played. Those not chosen for Tests go for weeks without playing, with a subsequent loss of all form, and it was hard to follow some of the choices. Gatting, having started the season confidently with an innings of 94, was left out of the team for the first Test and in the peculiar circumstances of this tour did not play another first-class innings for six weeks. Downton, selected to keep wicket in the first Test on an awkward low pitch in Port-of-Spain, had a successful match but did not play again for 31 days. When he recovered his Test place, he again kept very promisingly but had lost his batting. This made his innings on the last day of the series all the more admirable. Coming in at a critical moment with Holding in full cry with the new ball, he took numerous blows on the body but stuck it out and helped Gower to save the match by batting staunchly through the last three and a quarter hours. Both had celebrated their 24th birthdays only a fortnight before.

England's tour may have been ill-fated and unsuccessful in itself, but the performance at the end of these two young men seemed to symbolise a more prosperous future – given a new intake of fast or fast-medium bowlers.

ENGLAND IN NEW ZEALAND

NEW ZEALAND v ENGLAND

First Test Match

Played at Christchurch, February 25, 26, 28, March 1, 1966

Drawn. Excitement ran high in this match. Twice New Zealand, by capturing the first four England wickets cheaply, seemed to have gained the upper hand, but in the end they collapsed and were in danger of being dismissed for less than 26, the record lowest total credited to them at Auckland in 1955 in Sir Leonard Hutton's last Test.

For the first time for many years New Zealand had a new captain in Chapple, Reid having retired after setting up a world record of fifty-eight consecutive Test appearances, previously jointly held by Frank Woolley and Peter May, each with fifty-two.

Although the pitch was soft after several days of rain and lowering cloud forecast trouble for batsmen, Smith, winning the toss, decided to bat. It was the captain, with Parfitt, who extricated the side from difficulties in a stand of 113 before Puna, an Indian, appearing in his first Test, made one of several brilliant catches. As the pitch eased the tail built up the score, Allen playing well for three and threequarter hours for 88. Brown also shaped confidently for two and a quarter hours while the partnership realised 107.

Congdon kept the New Zealand innings on a firm basis and finished with the tenth Test hundred for his country against England which occupied nearly five and a half hours. Petrie signalled his return to Test cricket after five years, by playing soundly for 55 and finally Motz, two 6s and six 4s, hit magnificently so that New Zealand gained a first-innings lead of five.

Their cup of joy overflowed when by the end of the third day they had disposed of Boycott and Edrich for 32, but again they were thwarted by Smith and Parfitt and England set them to make 197 to win in two hours and twenty minutes.

Suddenly the England bowlers took charge and in nine overs Higgs claimed four wickets for five runs, but Pollard, hero of several innings in England in 1965 and Cunis, a well-built Rugby centre-threequarter, saved the day by defending successfully through the last thirty-five minutes.

Other highlights in the match were Parks' five catches behind the stumps in the first innings, equalling his own and Binks' England record and Cowdrey's easy catch at second slip from Chapple, which equalled W. R. Hammond's feat of one hundred Test catches. Moreover, Cowdrey held the ball on almost the same spot where Hammond claimed his hundredth victim.

England

G. Boycott c Petrie b Motz	4	– run out	4
W. E. Russell b Motz	30	– b Bartlett	25
J. H. Edrich c Bartlett b Motz	2	– lbw b Cunis	2
M. C. Cowdrey c Bilby b Cunis	0	– c Pollard b Motz	21
*M. J. K. Smith c Puna b Pollard	54	– c Bilby b Puna	87
P. H. Parfitt c Congdon b Bartlett	54	– not out	46
†J. M. Parks c Petrie b Chapple	30	– not out	4
D. A. Allen c Chapple b Bartlett	88		
D. J. Brown b Cunis	44		
K. Higgs not out	8		
I. J. Jones b Bartlett	0		
B 6, l-b 6, n-b 16	28	B 4, n-b 8	12
1/19 2/28 3/47 4/47 5/160 6/160 7/209 8/316 9/342	342	1/18 2/32 3/48 4/68 5/193	(5 wkts dec.) 201

Bowling: *First Innings*—Motz 31–9–83–3; Bartlett 33.2–6–63–3; Cunis 31–9–63–2; Puna 18–6–54–0; Chapple 9–3–24–1; Pollard 5–1–27–1. *Second Innings*—Motz 20–6–38–1; Bartlett 14–2–44–1; Cunis 19–3–58–1; Puna 14–6–49–1.

New Zealand

G. P. Bilby c Parks b Higgs	28	– c Parks b Brown	3
M. J. F. Shrimpton c Parks b Brown	11	– c Smith b Allen	13
B. E. Congdon c Smith b Jones	104	– c Cowdrey b Higgs	4
B. W. Sinclair c and b Higgs	23	– c Parks b Higgs	0
V. Pollard lbw b Higgs	23	– not out	6
*M. E. Chapple c Cowdrey b Jones	15	– c Parks b Higgs	0
G. A. Bartlett c Parks b Brown	0	– c Brown b Parfitt	0
†E. C. Petrie c Parks b Brown	55	– lbw b Higgs	1
R. C. Motz c Parks b Jones	58	– c Russell b Parfitt	2
R. Cunis not out	8	– not out	16
N. Puna c Smith b Jones	1		
B 7, l-b 13, n-b 1	21	B 2, l-b 1	3
1/39 2/41 3/112 4/181 5/202 6/203 7/237 8/326 9/344	347	1/5 2/19 3/21 4/21 5/22 6/22 7/22 8/32 (8 wkts)	48

Bowling: *First Innings*—Brown 30–3–80–3; Jones 28.3–9–71–4; Higgs 30–6–51–3; Allen 40–14–80–0; Boycott 12–6–30–0; Parfitt 3–0–14–0. *Second Innings*—Brown 4–2–6–1; Jones 7–3–13–0; Higgs 9–7–5–4; Allen 19–15–8–1; Parfitt 6–3–5–2; Parks 3–1–8–0.

Umpires: W. T. Martin and F. R. Goodall.

NEW ZEALAND v ENGLAND

First Test Match

Played at Christchurch, February 25, 26, 27, March 1, 1971

England won by eight wickets. The match was won and lost on the first day. On a damp, sparsely-grassed pitch the New Zealand batsmen found it most difficult to make strokes from the fast bowlers; the ball generally came through low and once Underwood had begun, the end was in sight. In conditions perfectly suited to his especial talents, he made the ball turn and sometimes lift very sharply. He captured six for 12. Dowling batted over two hours for 13; Pollard made a few assertive shots but Underwood was in supreme command and New Zealand were out for 65, their third lowest score against England.

New Zealand took three wickets for 56 by the close of play, but on the second morning Hampshire helped D'Oliveira to add 64 for the fourth wicket and Illingworth then shared a stand of 93 with D'Oliveira, who produced some magnificent strokes. He took risks on a pitch still taking turn readily but played a match-winning innings. He batted three hours and eleven minutes for his 100, which included two 6s and thirteen 4s. A strange inability to read Shrimpton's wrong-un contributed to an England collapse, the last six wickets falling while 43 were added.

New Zealand batted again after tea, and again started wretchedly, but Congdon and Turner halted the retreat and when bad light ended play thirty-seven minutes early, the score was 54 for two. Rain delayed the resumption until after lunch on the third day when Congdon and Turner showed some aggression in a stand of 77. Another collapse was halted by Pollard and Turner, who scored 52 together in conditions which still helped the bowlers. That England were left some sort of token task was mainly to the credit of Turner, who batted five hours and nine minutes before Underwood bowled him, just before close of play. Cunis helped him to add 57 for the eighth wicket; then Howarth and Cunis offered further resistance.

England, needing 89 to win, began half an hour before lunch on the final day and although Collinge, bowling with great spirit, soon took two wickets, Hampshire batted boldly and the game was won half an hour before tea. When Underwood had Shrimpton caught in New Zealand's second innings, he claimed his 1,000th wicket in first-class cricket. His match analysis of twelve for 97 pointed to his mastery of the situation.

Mr Charles Elliott (England) stood as one of the umpires at the invitation of the New Zealand Cricket Council; he was in New Zealand on a Churchill Fellowship.

New Zealand

*G. T. Dowling c Edrich b Underwood	13	– c Luckhurst b Lever	1
B. A. G. Morgan c Taylor b Shuttleworth	1	– b Shuttleworth	1
B. E. Congdon c Taylor b Shuttleworth	1	– b Underwood	55
R. W. Morgan c Luckhurst b Shuttleworth	6	– b Underwood	0
M. J. F. Shrimpton c Fletcher b Underwood	0	– c Illingworth b Underwood	8
G. M. Turner b Underwood	11	– b Underwood	76
V. Pollard b Wilson	18	– lbw b Underwood	34
†K. J. Wadsworth c Fletcher b Underwood	0	– c Fletcher b Wilson	1
R. S. Cunis b Underwood	0	– b Shuttleworth	35
H. J. Howarth st Taylor b Underwood	0	– c Illingworth b Underwood	25
R. O. Collinge not out	3	– not out	7
B 9, l-b 1, w 1, n-b 1	12	B 6, l-b 3, w 1, n-b 1	11
1/4 2/7 3/19 4/28 5/33 6/54 7/54 8/62 9/62	65	1/1 2/6 3/83 4/83 5/99 6/151 7/152 8/209 9/231	254

Bowling: *First Innings*—Lever 5–4–1–0; Shuttleworth 8–1–14–3; D'Oliveira 3–1–2–0; Underwood 11.6–7–12–6; Illingworth 6–3–12–0; Wilson 4–2–12–1. *Second Innings*—Lever 15–3–30–1; Shuttleworth 12–1–27–2; Underwood 32.3–7–85–6; Wilson 21–6–56–1; Illingworth 17–5–45–0.

England

B. W. Luckhurst c Wadsworth b Collinge	10	– not out	29
J. H. Edrich lbw b Cunis	12	– c Wadsworth b Collinge	2
K. W. R. Fletcher b Collinge	4	– c Howarth b Collinge	2
J. H. Hampshire c Turner b Howarth	40	– not out	51
B. L. D'Oliveira b Shrimpton	100		
*R. Illingworth b Shrimpton	36		
†R. W. Taylor st Wadsworth b Howarth	4		
D. Wilson c Murray b Howarth	5		
P. Lever b Howarth	4		
K. Shuttleworth b Shrimpton	5		
D. L. Underwood not out	0		
B 1, l-b 9, n-b 1	11	B 1, l-b 4	5
1/20 2/26 3/31 4/95 5/188 6/213 7/220 8/224 9/231	231	1/3 2/11 (2 wkts)	89

Bowling: *First Innings*—Collinge 12–2–39–2; Cunis 13–2–44–1; Howarth 19–7–46–4; Pollard 9–3–45–0; Shrimpton 11.5–0–35–3; Congdon 3–0–11–0. *Second Innings*—Collinge 7–2–20–2; Cunis 8–0–17–0; Howarth 4–0–17–0; Shrimpton 3–0–21–0; Pollard 3–1–9–0.

Umpires: C. S. Elliott and W. T. Martin.

NEW ZEALAND v ENGLAND

First Test Match

Played at Wellington, February 10, 11, 12, 14, 15, 1978

New Zealand won by 72 runs. After 48 years and in the 48th Test between the two countries, New Zealand beat England for the first time. Though England's form and fortune struck rock bottom in the crucial final innings, it was a great and deserved triumph for New Zealand and for Richard Hadlee, the fast bowling son of Walter Hadlee, the former Test captain and much-respected chairman of the NZ Cricket Council. Success was all the sweeter, and more exciting, because of the remarkable turn-around of the match. At tea on the fourth day the air was loaded with foreboding for New Zealand; the portents were all for the pattern of history to continue. Willis, supported by superb catching, had caused a collapse of nine for 41 in two hours and England, with time of no concern, had to score a moderate 137 to win.

Only two hours later, New Zealand gloom was transformed into joy as England, with Rose retired with a bruised right arm, tottered on the brink of defeat with eight down for 53. England, in turn, had been routed by Richard Hadlee and Collinge. The next morning, after a frustrating delay of forty minutes for rain, New Zealand took forty-nine minutes to complete a famous victory in an understandably emotional atmosphere. The crowd gathered in front of the pavilion and sang "For they are jolly good fellows", followed by three cheers.

Hadlee fittingly took the last two wickets. In the first innings he had four for 74, and in the second six for 26. Apart from one over by Dayle Hadlee, Richard Hadlee and Collinge bowled unchanged as England were dismissed for 64. England's previous lowest total against New Zealand was 181 at Christchurch in 1929-30 – the first series between the countries.

Without detracting in any way from the magnificence of Hadlee and Collinge, who took his 100th Test and 500th first-class wicket during the match – and twice dismissed the key batsman Boycott – it would be kind to draw a discreet veil over England's performance. Both Hadlee and Collinge, tore into the attack with hostility, skill and speed on a pitch of uneven bounce, and England's response once Boycott was bowled off his pads was inept in the extreme.

In some ways it was a bizarre game with a gale-force wind blowing directly down the pitch on the first day, and changing direction several times during the next four playing days. For Boycott it was a disheartening experience. On winning the toss he conceded first innings – a decision which was fully expected of either captain – and his gamble might have succeeded but for the resolve and skill of the Derbyshire left-hander, Wright, in his first Test. Surviving a strong appeal for a catch at the wicket against Willis off the first ball of the game, Wright settled into a groove of brave and skilled defiance which had an important bearing on the result. Nothing disturbed him. He waited forty-seven minutes for his first run, and ended the opening day of five hours forty minutes – there were two interruptions for rain and bad light – 55 not out. What New Zealand's fate might have been but for Wright was not difficult to imagine.

Though he was out next day without adding to his score, Wright had laid the foundation for his side's victory. Another vital contribution came from the former captain, Congdon, as he celebrated his 40th birthday. Only Wright and Congdon were able to cope with an attack in which Old excelled. All but three of Old's overs on the first day were bowled into the teeth of the gale. During the afternoon he sent down eleven overs for only 13 runs, capturing a second wicket in the bargain, and added another seven overs after tea. His considerable feat of stamina led to figures of six for 54, his best in 35 Tests.

At one nine-over stage Old had four for 11. New Zealand lost four wickets for 5 runs – thanks to some acrobatic catching by Taylor – and the total was a disappointing 228 in 502 minutes. It seemed nothing like large enough, particularly as Boycott, at his most obdurate, could not be budged. England, despite the departure of Miller – caught in two minds – in the last over, finished at 89 for two.

On the third day Boycott's hourly scoring was 10, 12, 6 (including a boundary), and 12. Congdon, used as a defensive ploy in the overs before the new ball was due in most Tests in the series, delivered seven successive maidens, and conceded only 7 runs in ten overs. When the new ball was taken after 67 overs, England were still 82 short of New Zealand's total and in the end they were led by 13 runs.

It was a trying innings for Boycott. Grit constantly got behind his contact lenses – in his own words, the wind crucified his eyes – and at 68 he was struck over his right eye attempting to hook Richard Hadlee. By then he had celebrated passing Sir Jack Hobbs's Test aggregate of 5,410 runs – when 61 – but when he was sixth out England dismally faded into nothing. Boycott batted for seven hours twenty-two minutes, faced 304 balls, and hit nine boundaries.

Wright and Anderson put on 54 for the first wicket and New Zealand were sitting comfortably until Willis found his rhythm and speed. In 31 balls he captured four for 14. With Botham in accurate support, Howarth, Congdon, Parker and Burgess were out in the course of 6 runs. New Zealand went from 82 for one to 123, but the mood of resignation to defeat was magically transformed when Boycott, going for the drive, was bowled off the twelfth ball. Bowling and catching were uplifted, and by the time the total was a paltry 18, Miller, Randall and Roope were dismissed; Rose was out of action. Despite a flurry by Botham, England at 53 for eight at the close were a beaten side and New Zealand's finest hour had arrived. They deserved the congratulations of the cricket world.

New Zealand

R. W. Anderson c Taylor b Old	28	– lbw b Old	26
J. G. Wright lbw b Botham	55	– c Roope b Willis	19
G. P. Howarth c Botham b Old	13	– c Edmonds b Willis	21
*M. G. Burgess b Willis	9	– c Boycott b Botham	6
B. E. Congdon c Taylor b Old	44	– c Roope b Willis	0
J. M. Parker c Rose b Willis	16	– c Edmonds b Willis	4
†W. K. Lees c Taylor b Old	1	– lbw b Hendrick	11
R. J. Hadlee not out	27	– c Boycott b Willis	2
D. R. Hadlee c Taylor b Old	1	– c Roope b Botham	2
R. O. Collinge b Old	1	– c Edmonds b Hendrick	6
S. L. Boock b Botham	4	– not out	0
B 12, l-b 3, w 1, n-b 13	29	B 3, l-b 8, w 2, n-b 13	26
1/42 2/96 3/114 4/152 5/191 6/193 7/194 8/196 9/208	228	1/54 2/82 3/93 4/93 5/98 6/99 7/104 8/116 9/123	123

Bowling: *First Innings*—Willis 25–7–65–2; Hendrick 17–2–46–0; Old 30–11–54–6; Edmonds 3–1–7–0; Botham 12.6–2–27–2. *Second Innings*—Willis 15–2–32–5; Hendrick 10–2–16–2; Old 9–2–32–1; Edmonds 1–0–4–0; Botham 9.3–3–13–2.

England

B. C. Rose c Lees b Collinge	21	– not out	5
*G. Boycott c Congdon b Collinge	77	– b Collinge	1
G. Miller b Boock	24	– c Anderson b Collinge	4
†R. W. Taylor c and b Collinge	8	– run out	0
D. W. Randall c Burgess b R. Hadlee	4	– lbw b Collinge	9
G. R. J. Roope c Lees b R. Hadlee	37	– c Lees b R. Hadlee	0
I. T. Botham c Burgess b R. Hadlee	7	– c Boock b R. Hadlee	19
C. M. Old b R. Hadlee	10	– lbw b R. Hadlee	9
P. H. Edmonds lbw b Congdon	4	– c Parker b R. Hadlee	11
M. Hendrick lbw b Congdon	0	– c Parker b R. Hadlee	0
R. G. D. Willis not out	6	– c Howarth b R. Hadlee	3
B 1, l-b 3, n-b 13	17	N-b 3	3
1/39 2/89 3/108 4/126 5/183 6/188 7/203 8/205 9/205	215	1/2 2/8 3/18 4/18 5/38 6/38 7/53 8/53 9/63	64

Bowling: *First Innings*—R. Hadlee 28–5–74–4; Collinge 18–5–42–3; D. Hadlee 21–5–47–0; Boock 10–5–21–1; Congdon 17.4–11–14–2. *Second Innings*—R. Hadlee 13.3–4–26–6; Collinge 13–5–35–3; D. Hadlee 1–1–0–0.

Umpires: W. R. C. Gardiner and R. L. Monteith.

NEW ZEALAND v ENGLAND

Second Test Match

Played at Christchurch, February 24, 25, 26, 28, March 1, 1978

England won by 174 runs. Despite a wretched start, England gained a swift and sweeping revenge for the Wellington defeat. Batting first on a greenish pitch England lost three men, including Boycott, in no time for 26. The recovery was started by Roope and Taylor, continued by Miller, who had to retire when struck in the face when 31, Botham, Edmonds, and finally by a recovered Miller.

It became Botham's match, and, no matter how long he plays for England, he will find it hard to equal his spectacular all-round performance. His maiden Test century, in only his fourth game for England, included one 6 and twelve 4s and was full of impressive and powerful strokes. By any standard it was a superb innings. In the second innings, when England led by 183 runs and quick runs were needed to ram home their advantage, Botham hit 30 off 36 balls. His bowling was equally convincing, with figures of five for 73 and three for 38, and he took three catches, two of which were in the sensational class.

Like Botham and Taylor, Edmonds made his highest Test score with a perfect 50 off 68 balls – probably his best innings at any level – and on the third morning Miller took four successive boundaries off Collinge before he was caught at mid-on with his score at 89. A total of 418 had been beyond England's wildest expectations after such a disastrous start and Boycott's decision to bat first, and indeed bat through to the end, was vindicated by events.

New Zealand had considerable difficulty in avoiding the follow-on – achieved only when the last pair Parker and Chatfield, were together – and they were indebted to Parker and Collinge for an eighth-wicket stand of 58. Apart from Anderson, who was severe on Old, there was little to commend in New Zealand's batting. Botham and Edmonds both bowled well, the former turning the innings by whipping out Burgess and Lees. Hadlee, the victim of a ball keeping low, went to Edmonds which meant three men out for 5 runs. Parker had an escape at 19 when Edmonds made his solitary error in a superlative display of short leg and slip catching.

England had two and a half hours batting on the fourth evening during which New Zealand bowled 22 overs and there was an unfortunate incident when Chatfield without warning, ran out Randall, the non-striker. Chatfield ran in normally, stopped, and took off the bails under-arm to the acute embarrassment of the majority of the spectators. The view in an angry English camp was that, if Chatfield had continued with his normal overarm action, Randall would still have been in his ground. In the English first innings there had been some gallery-playing action by Hadlee against two batsmen. He held the ball after completing his action, and it hardly needs adding that the game would be in a constant state of disruption if bowlers made a habit of such tactics.

New Zealand had to make 280 when Boycott declared first thing on the last morning. Within two hours England were on the point of victory, having taken five wickets for 48. Willis started the collapse by having Wright caught off the sixth ball by Roope, in the manner of a goalkeeper above his head. Wright tried to take evasive action against a short pitcher but did not have time to take his bat away.

Roope's catch set a remarkable high standard for the other slip catchers, who gave superb support to the bowling of Willis, Botham and Edmonds. However, both Willis and Botham ran foul of umpire Goodall and were officially warned for running down the pitch. Boycott protested that the marks had been made by all the right-arm bowlers throughout the previous four days.

The second caution led to Willis going round the wicket and, if anything, he became more accurate and deadly. Congdon was caught by a diving Botham – a quite superb catch – at slip, and in the next over Willis hit the off stump of Anderson and Lees with successive deliveries. To add to New Zealand's problems Burgess stood still and allowed a ball from Willis to hit his left elbow. He was forced to retire, and by the time he returned nine wickets were down and the Test was won and lost. Willis's match-winning spell was four for 9.

Botham enthusiastically came in for the kill as he succeeded Willis. He ended the seventy-seven minute resistance of Hadlee (eight 4s) by sprinting from leg slip to square leg to take a skier, and his catch at leg slip to dismiss Parker was also one to savour. In everything he did Botham was the inspired cricketer.

England

B. C. Rose c Howarth b Chatfield	11	– c Lees b Collinge	7
*G. Boycott lbw b Collinge	8	– run out	26
D. W. Randall c Burgess b Hadlee	0	– run out	13
G. R. J. Roope c Burgess b Hadlee	50	– not out	9
G. Miller c Congdon b Collinge	89		
C. T. Radley c Lees b Hadlee	15		
I. T. Botham c Lees b Boock	103	– not out	30
†R. W. Taylor run out	45		
C. M. Old b Hadlee	8	– b Collinge	1
P. H. Edmonds c Lees b Collinge	50		
R. G. D. Willis not out	6		
B 14, l-b 9, n-b 10	33	B 4, l-b 3, n-b 3	10
1/15 2/18 3/26 4/127 5/128 6/288 7/293 8/305 9/375	418	1/25 2/47 3/67 4/74 (4 wkts dec.)	96

Bowling: *First Innings*—Hadlee 43–10–147–4; Collinge 26.5–6–89–3; Chatfield 37–8–94–1; Congdon 18–11–14–0; Boock 21–11–41–1. *Second Innings*—Hadlee 6–1–17–0; Collinge 9–2–29–2; Chatfield 5–0–22–0; Congdon 2–0–18–0.

New Zealand

J. G. Wright c and b Edmonds	4	– c Roope b Willis	0
R. W. Anderson b Edmonds	62	– b Willis	15
G. P. Howarth c Edmonds b Willis	5	– c Edmonds b Old	1
*M. G. Burgess c Roope b Botham	29	– not out	6
B. E. Congdon lbw b Botham	20	– c Botham b Willis	0
J. M. Parker not out	53	– c Botham b Edmonds	16
†W. K. Lees c Miller b Botham	0	– b Willis	0
R. J. Hadlee b Edmonds	1	– c Botham b Edmonds	39
R. O. Collinge c Edmonds b Botham	32	– c Miller b Botham	0
S. L. Boock c Taylor b Edmonds	2	– c Taylor b Botham	0
E. J. Chatfield c Edmonds b Botham	3	– lbw b Botham	6
B 4, l-b 1, n-b 19	24	L-b 6, n-b 16	22
1/37 2/52 3/82 4/119 5/148 6/151 7/153 8/211 9/216	235	1/2 2/14 3/19 4/25 5/25 6/59 7/81 8/90 9/95	105

Bowling: *First Innings*—Willis 20–1–45–1; Old 14–4–55–0; Botham 24.7–6–73–5; Edmonds 34–11–38–4. *Second Innings*—Willis 7–2–14–4; Old 7–4–9–1; Botham 7–1–38–3; Edmonds 6–2–22–2.

Umpires: F. R. Goodall and R. L. Monteith.

ENGLAND IN INDIA

INDIA v ENGLAND

Second Test Match

Played at Bombay, January 21, 22, 23, 25, 26, 1964

Drawn. England were deprived of all except two of their specialist batsmen. Following Barrington's injury, an attack of stomach trouble removed Edrich, Sharpe and Mortimore before the match and Stewart at tea time on the first day. The ten-man side then consisted of two specialist batsmen, two wicket-keepers, of whom Parks reverted to his first role as specialist batsman, four quick bowlers and two spinners. Yet India played so apprehensively on the defensive that they never seriously challenged this makeshift team.

This was a spineless Indian performance, but a superb one by England, whose spirit on this testing occasion was magnificent. They put the sort of fire into their out-cricket that distinguishes the best Celtic rugger pack, and they fought splendidly with the bat. If Binks, who otherwise kept well, had stumped Borde off Titmus when he was only two, this scratch collection might even themselves have won. Borde stayed to share with Durani a fine seventh-wicket stand of 153 after the first six wickets had tumbled to Price, Titmus and Knight for 99.

England themselves were similarly in trouble when, puzzled by Chandrasekhar's googlies, they lost six for 116. Titmus, however, made his highest Test score, Price his highest in first-class cricket, and Jones stayed eighty-five minutes while the last wicket added 48. Titmus was the hub of resistance, a fighter revelling in a critical situation. He batted commandingly through 98 overs in five hours for his 84 not out. Price, his partner in a stand of 68, played only because Mortimore did not, as hoped, recover in time. From being last choice Price rose in a day to become number one choice fast bowler. He bowled throughout with such fire that he banged something out of the sluggish pitch, which no other quick bowler could do.

India still had a winning chance when leading by 67, but they remained stodgily defensive for seven hours and ten minutes; the usually aggressive Jaisimha batted almost four hours for 66. England's fragile batting side was asked to score 317 in four hours ten minutes at a rate 17 runs an hour faster than in any previous innings. They settled for a draw justifiably. Binks was another player to excel by batting three and a half hours in an opening stand of 125 with Bolus. Price, Binks and Jones, together with Chandrasekhar, had good reason to look back on their first Test with satisfaction.

India

V. Mehra lbw b Knight	9	– lbw b Titmus	35
†B. K. Kunderam c Wilson b Price	29	– c Titmus b Price	16
D. N. Sardesai b Price	12	– run out	66
V. L. Manjrekar c Binks b Titmus	0	– not out	43
*Nawab of Pataudi c Titmus b Knight	10	– b Price	0
M. L. Jaisimha c Price b Titmus	23	– c Larter b Knight	66
C. G. Borde c Binks b Wilson	84	– c Smith b Titmus	7
A. S. Durani c Binks b Price	90	– c Knight b Titmus	3
R. G. Nadkarni not out	26	– lbw b Knight	0
Rajinder Pal lbw b Larter	3	– not out	3
B. S. Chandrasekhar b Larter	0		
B 2, l-b 9, n-b 3	14	L-b 4, w 1, n-b 5	10
1/20 2/55 3/56 4/58 5/75 6/99 7/252 8/284 9/300	300	1/23 2/104 3/107 4/140 5/152 6/180 7/231 8/231	(8 wkts dec.) 249

Bowling: *First Innings*—Knight 20–3–53–2; Larter 10.3–2–35–2; Jones 13–0–48–0; Price 19–2–66–3; Titmus 36–17–56–2; Wilson 15–5–28–1. *Second Innings*—Knight 13–2–28–2; Price 17–1–47–2; Titmus 46–18–79–3; Jones 11–1–31–0; Larter 5–0–13–0; Wilson 23–10–41–0.

England

J. B. Bolus c Chandrasekhar b Durani	25	– c Pataudi b Durani	57
*M. J. K. Smith c Borde b Chandrasekhar	46	– not out	31
J. M. Parks run out	1	– not out	40
B. R. Knight b Chandrasekhar	12		
F. J. Titmus not out	84		
D. Wilson c and b Durani	1	– c Pataudi b Chandrasekhar	2
†J. G. Binks b Chandrasekhar	10	– c Borde b Jaisimha	55
J. S. E. Price b Chandrasekhar	32		
J. D. F. Larter c Borde b Durani	0		
I. J. Jones run out	5		
M. J. Stewart absent ill	0		
B 4, l-b 7, n-b 6	17	B 12, l-b 7, w 1, n-b 1	21
1/42 2/48 3/82 4/91 5/98 6/116 7/184 8/185 9/233	233	1/125 2/127 3/134	(3 wkts) 206

Bowling: *First Innings*—Rajinder Pal 11–4–19–0; Jaisimha 3–1–9–0; Durani 39–15–59–3; Borde 34–12–54–0; Chandrasekhar 40–16–67–4; Nadkarni 4–2–8–0. *Second Innings*—Rajinder Pal 2–0–3–0; Chandrasekhar 22–5–40–1; Durani 29–12–35–1; Borde 37–12–38–0; Jaisimha 22–9–36–1; Nadkarni 14–11–3–0; Sardesai 3–2–6–0; Mehra 2–1–1–0; Pataudi 3–0–23–0.

Umpires: H. E. Chowdhary and A. M. Mamsa.

INDIA v ENGLAND

Third Test Match

Played at Calcutta, January 29, 30, February 1, 2, 3, 1964

Drawn. England had 12 fit men on this occasion, Cowdrey and Parfitt having joined the team, and Jones was made twelfth man. There was more encouragement than usual for fast bowlers on the first day, and a splendid performance by Price, five wickets for 44 in 15 overs, reduced India to 169 for eight just before tea. Thanks to Nadkarni, the last two wickets added 72, and slow English batting afterwards doomed yet another match to be left drawn. Cowdrey batted six hours and twenty minutes for 107 and with two and a half hours being lost by an amazing decision of the umpires that the ground was unfit, when only one millimetre of rain fell on the third day, the English innings did not finish with a lead of 26 until the fourth day. Jaisimha then played brilliantly to reach 49 in 12 overs, but he spent another twelve overs finding his fiftieth and altogether batted five hours for 129. The final day's play was accordingly pointless, though it contained some attractive batting by Smith.

India

M. L. Jaisimha c Binks b Price	33	– c Larter b Titmus	129
†B. K. Kunderam c Binks b Price	23	– lbw b Wilson	27
D. N. Sardesai c Binks b Larter	54	– c and b Parfitt	36
V. L. Manjrekar c and b Price	25	– b Parfitt	16
R. S. Surti b Price	0		
C. G. Borde c Cowdrey b Wilson	21	– c Parks b Titmus	8
*Nawab of Pataudi c Binks b Wilson	2	– c Smith b Larter	31
A. S. Durani c Binks b Price	8	– c Cowdrey b Larter	25
R. G. Nadkarni not out	43	– not out	10
R. B. Desai lbw b Titmus	11	– not out	2
B. S. Chandrasekhar c Cowdrey b Knight	16		
L-b 1, n-b 4	5	B 7, l-b 5, n-b 4	16
1/47 2/61 3/103 4/103 5/150 6/158 7/169 8/169 9/190	241	1/80 2/161 3/217 4/218 5/237 6/272 7/289 (7 wkts dec.)	300

Bowling: *First Innings*—Knight 13.2–5–39–1; Price 23–4–73–5; Larter 18–4–61–1; Titmus 15–4–46–1; Wilson 16–10–17–2. *Second Innings*—Price 7–0–31–0; Knight 4–0–33–0; Wilson 21–7–55–1; Larter 8–0–27–2; Titmus 46–23–67–2; Parfitt 34–16–71–2.

England

J. B. Bolus c and b Durani	39	– c Jaisimha b Borde	35
†J. G. Binks c Desai b Durani	13	– b Durani	13
*M. J. K. Smith c Jaisimha b Borde	19	– not out	75
M. C. Cowdrey c Pataudi b Desai	107	– not out	13
J. M. Parks lbw b Nadkarni	30		
P. H. Parfitt c and b Desai	4		
D. Wilson st Kunderam b Chandrasekhar	1		
B. R. Knight c Manjrekar b Nadkarni	13		
F. J. Titmus b Desai	26		
J. S. E. Price not out	1		
J. D. F. Larter c Manjrekar b Desai	0		
B 5, l-b 4, n-b 5	14	B 9	9
1/40 2/74 3/77 4/158 5/175 6/193 7/214 8/258 9/267	267	1/30 2/87 (2 wkts)	145

Bowling: *First Innings*—Desai 22.5–3–62–4; Surti 6–2–8–0; Jaisimha 4–1–10–0; Durani 22–7–59–2; Borde 31–14–40–1; Chandrasekhar 21–5–36–1; Nadkarni 42–24–38–2. *Second Innings*—Desai 5–0–12–0; Pataudi 3–1–8–0; Durani 8–3–15–1; Borde 15–5–39–1; Chandrasekhar 8–2–20–0; Jaisimha 13–5–32–0; Sardesai 3–0–10–0.

Umpires: S. Roy and M. V. Nagendra.

INDIA v ENGLAND

Fourth Test Match

Played at New Delhi, February 8, 9, 11, 12, 13, 1964

Drawn. England at last were at full strength, allowing for the departure of Barrington and Stewart, and they gained a lead of 107. Up to a point they challenged hard for a win, particularly while Bolus and Edrich were sharing a brisk opening stand of 101. Titmus had given them a good opening by taking the first three wickets for 42 on the deadest and easiest batting pitch so far encountered. Mortimore also bowled artfully, and despite 105 in his first Test by Hanumant Singh off 64 overs, the finest innings of the series, India were out for a modest total.

England aimed to be 100 ahead by the end of the third day, but Cowdrey, playing his second successive Test century, batted six and a quarter hours, and India's second innings did not start until the fourth afternoon. Jaisimha then hit 32 off the first five overs and Kunderam played so surely that at the close India were 166 for two. The last day held no possible interest. It dragged wearily. Kunderam scored his second century of the series, batting 89 overs while the bowling was serious. Subsequently, in exhibition circumstances, Pataudi who was twice missed in the nineties and again soon afterwards, eclipsed Kunderam's Indian record score against England. He batted 97 overs for his first 100 and 40 against bowling far from serious for his last 103.

India

M. L. Jaisimha b Titmus	47	– st Parks b Parfitt	50
†B. K. Kunderam b Titmus	40	– lbw b Price	100
D. N. Sardesai c Parks b Mortimore	44	– b Wilson	4
*Nawab of Pataudi b Titmus	13	– not out	203
Hanumant Singh c and b Mortimore	105	– c Mortimore b Wilson	23
C. G. Borde b Price	26	– not out	67
A. S. Durani c Smith b Wilson	16		
A. G. Kripal Singh b Mortimore	0		
R. G. Nadkarni run out	34		
R. B. Desai not out	14		
B. S. Chandrasekhar run out	0		
L-b 3, n-b 2	5	B 5, l-b 9, n-b 2	16
1/81 2/90 3/116 4/201 5/267 6/283 7/283 8/307 9/344	344	1/74 2/101 3/226 4/273	(4 wkts) 463

Bowling: *First Innings*—Price 23–3–71–1; Knight 11–0–46–0; Wilson 22–9–41–1; Titmus 49–15–100–3; Mortimore 38–13–74–3; Parfitt 5–2–7–0. *Second Innings*—Price 9–1–36–1; Knight 8–1–47–0; Titmus 43–12–105–0; Mortimore 31–11–52–0; Parfitt 19–3–81–1; Wilson 41–16–74–2; Smith 13–0–52–0.

England

J. B. Bolus lbw b Kripal Singh	58
J. H. Edrich c and b Kripal Singh	41
*M. J. K. Smith c Pataudi b Kripal Singh	37
D. Wilson c Pataudi b Chandrasekhar	6
P. H. Parfitt c Kunderam b Durani	67
M. C. Cowdrey lbw b Nadkarni	151
†J. M. Parks c sub b Chandrasekhar	32
B. R. Knight c Desai b Nadkarni	21
J. B. Mortimore c Hanumant Singh b Nadkarni	21
F. J. Titmus not out	4
J. S. E. Price b Chandrasekhar	0
B 8, l-b 3, n-b 2	13
1/101 2/113 3/134 4/153 5/268 6/354 7/397 8/438 9/451	451

Bowling: Desai 9–2–23–0; Jaisimha 4–0–14–0; Kripal Singh 36–12–90–3; Chandrasekhar 34.3–11–79–3; Borde 12–2–42–0; Durani 33–4–93–1; Nadkarni 58–30–97–3.

Umpires: Satyaji Rao and Shambhu Pan.

INDIA v ENGLAND

Fifth Test Match

Played at Kanpur, February 15, 16, 18, 19, 20, 1964

Drawn. The same groundsman who had produced the drugged Delhi pitch was responsible for another defunct strip of turf, which ensured that the dull sequence of draws should be continued to the end. Pataudi won the toss for the fifth time, but gave England first innings, and they scored mightily despite much defensive bowling by Nadkarni. Smith himself set an aggressive example and on the second day Knight drove his way handsomely to a century, hitting his final 62 in one hour fifty minutes. Parfitt, his partner in a stand of 191, also played good attacking cricket after taking a long time gauging the slowness of the pitch, which accounted for much of the five hours and twenty minutes he spent reaching 121. Parks at the end was playing delightfully, and England scored their highest ever total in India.

The batting success was followed by Titmus bowling at his best and India's batsmen at their safety-first worst. On the third day they made only 136 in five and a half hours while moving to 145 for four. On the fourth they were saved from the English spinners by the resolute Nadkarni, who showed his colleagues that run-getting is more effective than obdurate defence in such circumstances. After his 52 not out he was promoted to number three and scored his first Test century. He batted for five and a half hours (107 overs) before reaching it and altogether spent eleven hours at the crease in the match. When he reached 103 out of 216, soundly supported by Sardesai, the time had come for frolic. The match was long since dead; the final proceedings allowed Sardesai and Durani cheap runs against occasional trundlers.

England

J. B. Bolus c Hanumant Singh b Nadkarni	67
J. H. Edrich c Pataudi b Borde	35
*M. J. K. Smith c Borde b Gupte	38
B. R. Knight c Manjrekar b Jaisimha	127
P. H. Parfitt lbw b Jaisimha	121
M. C. Cowdrey lbw b Pataudi	38
†J. M. Parks not out	51
J. B. Mortimore b Chandrasekhar	19
F. J. Titmus c and b Nadkarni	5
D. Wilson not out	18
B 29, l-b 9, n-b 2	40
1/63 2/134 3/174 4/365 5/458 6/474 7/520 8/531	(8 wkts dec.) 559

J. S. E. Price did not bat.

Bowling: Jaisimha 19–4–54–2; Durani 25–8–49–0; Chandrasekhar 36–7–97–1; Gupte 40–9–115–1; Borde 23–4–73–1; Nadkarni 57–22–121–2; Pataudi 3–1–10–1.

India

M. L. Jaisimha c Parks b Titmus	5	– c Cowdrey b Titmus	5
†B. K. Kunderam b Price	5	– lbw b Parfitt	55
D. N. Sardesai c Mortimore b Parfitt	79	– c Edrich b Parks	87
V. L. Manjrekar c and b Titmus	33		
Hanumant Singh c Parks b Titmus	24		
*Nawab of Pataudi b Titmus	31		
C. G. Borde b Titmus	0		
A. S. Durani b Mortimore	16	– not out	61
R. G. Nadkarni not out	52	– not out	122
B. P. Gupte c and b Titmus	8		
B. S. Chandrasekhar b Price	3		
B 5, l-b 1, n-b 4	10	B 5, l-b 11, n-b 1	17
1/9 2/17 3/96 4/135 5/182 6/182 7/188 8/229 9/245	266	1/17 2/126 3/270	(3 wkts) 347

Bowling: *First Innings*—Price 16.1–5–32–2; Knight 1–0–4–0; Titmus 60–37–73–6; Mortimore 49–31–39–1; Wilson 27–9–47–0; Parfitt 30–12–61–1. *Second Innings*—Price 10–2–27–0; Titmus 34–12–59–1; Mortimore 23–14–28–0; Parfitt 24–7–68–1; Wilson 19–10–26–0; Knight 2–0–12–0; Edrich 4–1–17–0; Bolus 3–0–16–0; Parks 6–0–43–1; Cowdrey 5–0–34–0.

Umpires: S. Bhattacharjee and S. K. Raghunatha Rao.

CRICKETERS' PEACE PLEA

The Rest of the World cricketers, among them the Nawab of Pataudi, India's captain and Hanif Mohammad, Pakistan captain, sent a telegram from Scarborough to Mr Shastri, the Indian Prime Minister and President Ayub Khan of Pakistan at the beginning of the match against an England XI. It said:

"We world cricket team wish express deep regrets at declared war between India, Pakistan. Coming from different countries, backgrounds, races, religions, we find unity on cricket field by reaching for common objective. Fervently hope both countries can meet and find amicable solution."

INDIA v ENGLAND

Second Test Match

Played at Calcutta, December 30, 31, January 1, 3, 4, 1973

India won by 28 runs. This was a memorable match in many ways. Eden Gardens, with about 70,000 spectators basking in the open stands every day, provided a spectacular setting for the match while the fascinating changes of fortune, with the outcome unpredictable till the last ball, kept the fans on their toes. The victory enabled India to draw level with England, who had won the first Test.

Eden Gardens has always been helpful to seamers and it was unfortunate that England should lose the services of Arnold, who became ill on the eve of the match. His place was taken by Old, who was so successful that he replaced Cottam in the further three tests. India made two changes, bringing in the veteran left-hander Durani in place of Sardesai, who, anyhow, had reported unfit with a pulled thigh muscle and Prasanna for Venkataraghavan.

Tight English bowling backed up by splendid fielding, in which Wood was outstanding, kept the batsmen under pressure and India could only crawl to 148 for five wickets on the first day. Between lunch and tea, they lost all the advantage of winning the toss, as four wickets fell for the addition of 47 runs to the pre-lunch score of 53 for one. The solitary wicket was that of Gavaskar, who was caught splendidly at short leg off a nasty ball from Underwood that reared from a good length spot. After lunch India slid back. Parkar offered a simple catch off Old to Knott, while Wadekar, batting fluently despite a nasty crack he had on the ribs from a ball from Old into which he ducked, lost Viswanath, caught brilliantly by Wood at gully off Cottam. Wadekar himself followed when he was unfortunately run out, almost immediately after he had taken 16 runs from an over by Underwood. Greig struck one more blow, bowling Durani with a sharp inswinger. Engineer and Solkar then halted the collapse.

The honours of the second day's play rested with India. Batting in a style true to his mood Engineer played a vital role in taking his side's score past the 200 mark. He took credit for 49 of the 62 runs added in the morning. England, starting their reply a little before lunch, lost four batsmen for 68 runs by tea, their troubles coinciding with Bedi and Chandrasekhar taking the ball. An aggressive Wood was bowled by an armer from Bedi, while Amiss, who had been let off by Durani off Chandrasekhar, was snapped up by Solkar in the leg trap. Fletcher, like Wood, tried to attack the spinners, but pulled a full toss from Prasanna into the hands of Gavaskar at short mid-on. Nine runs later Lewis went lbw to Bedi as he padded up and offered no stroke to an armer. Despite these reverses, Denness and Greig added 39 runs with apparent ease when Solkar brought off a superb catch at short leg off Chandrasekhar to send back the former. Greig and Knott then batted brightly but shortly before stumps Prasanna, straightening a delivery, forced the former to edge a high catch to extra-cover. On the next morning Old, played a significant part in England's progress from 126 for six to 174.

With his wet shirt still clinging to his back, Old gave a flying start to his side when India began their second innings, dismissing Gavaskar and Parkar. Durani, batting with Gavaskar as runner, and Viswanath retrieved the position. Despite being handicapped by a pulled thigh muscle Durani first defied the bowling and then thrust it back with aggressive strokes. His manner drew Viswanath out to play many crisp strokes. After 91 runs had been added, Fletcher took two catches to send them back. His second, off Greig, was a magnificent effort as he flung himself to his left and held the ball inches from the ground.

Greig was the cock of the walk on the next day, the fourth. He demolished the Indian innings by claiming four wickets for four runs in 33 balls. Keeping a fine length and varying his cutters with the straight ball he took five for 24, his best in Tests. Greig followed this effort by halting a batting collapse when England, mesmerised by Bedi, lost four wickets for 17 runs. He and Denness batted till the close to raise the total to 105 for four, and to raise hopes of victory.

Chandrasekhar, however, dashed these when he trapped Greig lbw with a top-spinner and then had Knott caught by Durani at mid-wicket off a pull. Picking up Denness in the next over Chandrasekhar showed figures of 4.3–2–5–3. Bedi dismissed Pocock and Underwood and it seemed all was over when Cottam put up a simple return catch, but Bedi floored this. Cottam had another escape off Chandrasekhar and profiting by these he and Old took the score to 160 by lunch. The break proved a blessing for India as in his first over after it Chandrasekhar had Cottam lbw, to bring his side an exciting victory.

India

S. M. Gavaskar c Old b Underwood	18	– lbw b Old	2
R. D. Parkar c Knott b Old	26	– c Fletcher b Old	15
*A. L. Wadekar run out	44	– lbw b Greig	0
G. R. Viswanath c Wood b Cottam	3	– c Fletcher b Old	34
A. S. Durani b Greig	4	– c Fletcher b Greig	53
E. D. Solkar b Old	19	– c Knott b Greig	6
†F. M. Engineer b Underwood	75	– c Knott b Underwood	17
S. Abid Ali b Cottam	3	– c Amiss b Old	3
E. A. S. Prasanna lbw b Cottam	6	– b Greig	0
B. S. Bedi run out	0	– not out	9
B. S. Chandrasekhar not out	1	– b Greig	1
L-b 3, n-b 8	11	B 8, l-b 2, n-b 5	15
1/29 2/68 3/78 4/99 5/100 6/163 7/176 8/192 9/192	210	1/2 2/33 3/104 4/112 5/133 6/133 7/135 8/135 9/147	155

Bowling: *First Innings*—Old 26–7–72–2; Cottam 23–6–45–3; Underwood 20.4–11–43–2; Pocock 19–10–26–0; Greig 9–1–13–1. *Second Innings*—Old 21–6–43–4; Cottam 5–0–18–0; Greig 19.5–9–24–5; Underwood 14–4–36–1; Pocock 8–1–19–0.

England

B. Wood b Bedi	11	– b Abid Ali	1
D. L. Amiss c Solkar b Chandrasekhar	11	– c Engineer b Bedi	1
K. W. R. Fletcher c Gavaskar b Prasanna	16	– lbw b Bedi	5
M. H. Denness c Solkar b Chandrasekhar	21	– lbw b Chandrasekhar	32
*A. R. Lewis lbw b Bedi	4	– c Solkar b Bedi	3
A. W. Greig c sub b Prasanna	29	– lbw b Chandrasekhar	67
†A. P. E. Knott st Engineer b Chandrasekhar	35	– c Durani b Chandrasekhar	2
C. M. Old not out	33	– not out	17
P. I. Pocock b Prasanna	3	– c and b Bedi	5
D. L. Underwood c Solkar b Chandrasekhar	0	– c Wadekar b Bedi	4
R. M. H. Cottam lbw b Chandrasekhar	3	– lbw b Chandrasekhar	13
L-b 4, n-b 4	8	B 6, l-b 5, n-b 2	13
1/18 2/37 3/47 4/56 5/84 6/117 7/144 8/153 9/154	174	1/3 2/8 3/11 4/17 5/114 6/119 7/123 8/130 9/138	163

Bowling: *First Innings*—Abid Ali 4–1–4–0; Solkar 3–1–5–0; Bedi 26–7–59–2; Chandrasekhar 26.2–5–65–5; Prasanna 16–4–33–3. *Second Innings*—Abid Ali 8–2–12–1; Solkar 1–1–0–0; Bedi 40–12–63–5; Chandrasekhar 29–14–42–4; Prasanna 9–0–19–0; Durani 4–1–14–0.

Umpires: A. M. Mamsa and J. Reuben.

INDIA v ENGLAND

Fifth Test Match

Played at Bombay (Brabourne Stadium), February 6, 7, 8, 10, 11, 1973

Drawn. India won the rubber in the series by 2-1. A good pitch, that helped the batsmen to play their strokes and then slowly turned in favour of the bowlers, found Engineer and Viswanath for India and Fletcher and Greig for England hitting centuries. Chandrasekhar set up a new record of 35 wickets for a series by an Indian bowler and Bedi and Underwood bowled extremely well to trouble the batsmen.

Durani was back in the team largely due to public opinion which reacted sharply to his being dropped for the fourth Test. Though he batted as was his wont he was unfit to run after the ball and was a burden to his side while fielding. Obviously, he could not ask for a substitute.

After Wadekar had won the toss for the fourth time in the series, India scored 250 for four wickets by stumps on the opening day. Though Old bowled Gavaskar with a fine inswinger at the start, Engineer and Wadekar added 192 runs for the second wicket. Engineer played his strokes without any inhibitions and attacked the half-volley and long hop firmly. Wadekar batted in superlative style, cutting, driving and pulling with power. The pair added 63 runs in the third hour of play, the best for India so far. In sight of his hundred, Wadekar suddenly lapsed into playing a weak drive off Birkenshaw, whom Lewis had brought on more in a moment of desperation it seemed, to give a catch to Old at mid-on. In the next over the off-spinner dismissed Engineer with a full toss which the batsman pulled into the hands of Roope at mid-on. Engineer had one escape at 70 when Roope at short leg dropped him off Underwood. One run after Engineer's exit, Underwood bowled Pataudi with an excellent delivery that whipped through straight to the stumps. The day's play ended with Durani plundering 18 runs off four balls from Underwood, with a six and three 4s.

Durani and Viswanath had lucky escapes the next morning. Durani was 21 when he snicked Old, bowling with the second new ball, to slips where Greig dropped the catch. On 39 Viswanath was beaten out of the crease by a ball from Birkenshaw, and Knott missed a catch, as the ball had gone off the inner edge of the bat, and also an easy stumping. The two batsmen then entrenched themselves to add 150 runs for the fifth wicket, which had a big say in India building up a score of 448 and making them safe from defeat. Durani scored 73 runs, playing tempestuous cover drives, square cuts and a cracking 6 over long-on off Birkenshaw. Viswanath was in a happy mood and after reaching his 50, unfolded a sequence of exciting late cuts, square and cover drives. He reached 100 comfortably and broke the hoodoo that seemed to hang over Indian batsmen who had hit a century on their Test debut but had failed to repeat the feat. The Indian innings ended forty minutes after tea, the only outstanding incident in this time being a splendid diving catch that Denness took at extra-cover off Old to send back Solkar. Denness was injured in the process and consequently batted lower in the order.

Lewis opened the England innings in his place and had the discomfiture of playing the first ball from Abid Ali on to his stumps. Roope then fell while hooking a ball from Chandrasekhar into the hands of Abid Ali at backward short leg. Underwood joined Knott as nightwatchman and halted the bowlers' successes. Underwood, however, was out early on the third day and Knott was trapped by Chandrasekhar lbw after a quick fifty, after which Greig joined Fletcher for a record stand of 254 runs for the fifth wicket against any country. After a quiet period before lunch, the two blasted the Indian bowling except that of Bedi to add 138 runs in the two hours to tea, with 71 of them in just 12 overs in the fourth hour. After getting their hundreds after tea, the pair quietened down. Fletcher played controlled strokes but Greig delighted the crowd with the grace and power of his driving and pulling. The saving grace for India was Bedi who bowled with amazing consistency, his figures at the end of the day being 40.5–15–72–2.

From 333 for five on the third day, England overhauled India's total the next day, though Chandrasekhar and Bedi prevented a big lead being taken. Chandrasekhar took three wickets, including that of Greig, to equal the Indian record of V. M. Mankad and S. P. Gupte of 34 wickets for a series. Tea was taken at the end of the innings, after which Gavaskar and Engineer put on 102 runs by stumps for the first wicket. Gavaskar excelled in straight driving. The features of the play till lunch on the last day were the fine bowling of Underwood and the batting of Viswanath and Durani. After the break the match deteriorated providing an anti-climax to the match as well as to the series. Pataudi struggled – he remained static at five for 65 minutes – for his five runs and Wadekar, deciding to play absolutely safe, declared at tea. England did not attempt to score 203 runs in ninety minutes. The only noteworthy point was Chandrasekhar setting up a new record of 35 wickets when he bowled Knott with a splendid slanted ball.

India

†F. M. Engineer c Roope b Birkenshaw	121	– b Underwood	66
S. M. Gavaskar b Old	4	– c and b Underwood	67
*A. L. Wadekar c Old b Birkenshaw	87	– not out	11
A. S. Durani c Underwood b Pocock	73	– c Knott b Pocock	37
M. A. Khan (Pataudi) b Underwood	1	– b Pocock	5
G. R. Viswanath b Arnold	113	– c Knott b Greig	48
E. D. Solkar c Denness b Old	6	– not out	6
S. Abid Ali c Roope b Arnold	15		
S. Venkataraghavan not out	11		
B. S. Bedi b Arnold	0		
B. S. Chandrasekhar c Fletcher b Old	3		
B 4, l-b 4, n-b 6	14	N-b 4	4
1/25 2/217 3/220 4/221 5/371 6/395 7/427 8/435 9/439	448	1/135 2/136 3/198 4/227 5/233	(5 wkts dec.) 244

Bowling: *First Innings*—Arnold 21–3–64–3; Old 21.2–2–78–3; Underwood 26–6–100–1; Greig 22–7–62–0; Pocock 25–7–63–1; Birkenshaw 23–2–67–2. *Second Innings*—Arnold 3–0–13–0; Old 3–1–11–0; Underwood 38–16–70–2; Greig 13–7–19–1; Pocock 27–5–75–2; Birkenshaw 12–1–52–0.

England

*A. R. Lewis b Abid Ali	0	– not out	17
G. R. J. Roope c Abid Ali b Chandrasekhar	10	– not out	26
†A. P. E. Knott lbw b Chandrasekhar	56	– b Chandrasekhar	8
D. L. Underwood c Abid Ali b Bedi	9		
K. W. R. Fletcher lbw b Bedi	113		
A. W. Greig lbw b Chandrasekhar	148		
M. H. Denness c Venkataraghavan b Bedi	29		
J. Birkenshaw b Chandrasekhar	36	– b Bedi	12
C. M. Old c and b Venkataraghavan	28		
G. G. Arnold lbw b Chandrasekhar	27		
P. I. Pocock not out	0		
B 13, l-b 5, n-b 6	24	B 3, l-b 1	4
1/0 2/38 3/67 4/79 5/333 6/381 7/397 8/442 9/479	480	1/23 2/37	(2 wkts) 67

Bowling: *First Innings*—Abid Ali 15–2–60–1; Solkar 4–0–16–0; Bedi 69–20–138–3; Chandrasekhar 46.1–8–135–5; Durani 4–0–21–0; Venkataraghavan 25–1–86–1. *Second Innings*—Solkar 2–0–4–0; Gavaskar 2–2–0–0; Chandrasekhar 9–1–26–1; Bedi 10–4–25–1; Venkataraghavan 5–1–8–0; Pataudi 1–1–0–0.

Umpires: J. Reuben and M. V. Gothoskar.

INDIA v ENGLAND

Third Test Match

Played at Madras, January 14, 15, 16, 18, 19, 1977

England won by 200 runs. The fact that England's 262 in the first innings was by far the highest total of the match and that it led to almost uninterrupted domination by them emphasized the value of the toss. The pitch, the fastest produced in many years on an Indian Test ground, was also uneven in bounce and wore rapidly. But the toss was not the only factor that gave England an easy passage. The Indian batsmen, completely lacking in confidence, submitted easily in both innings.

England, who made one change from the side that won at Calcutta – Woolmer for Barlow – themselves did not bat too expertly. They were 31 for three before a century partnership between Brearley, who batted almost throughout the day, and Greig remedied the poor start. They finished the first day at 171 for five, which was far from a satisfactory position but there was stern defiance on the next day by the tail and Tolchard, who had retired with a hand injury on the previous day.

Starting even more disastrously than England, India were 17 for three, but recovered to 58 for three by the end of the second day. The rally was inspired by Gavaskar and Patel, who both batted extremely well. The stand looked like continuing to grow on the third day but at 69, Underwood produced the classical unplayable ball to bowl Patel for 32, and Old had Gavaskar caught at slip with a deadly out-swinger.

Gavaskar's dismissal reduced India to 115 for seven, but an hour-long partnership between Kirmani and Prasanna raised the total to a more respectable level. Still, they fell 98 runs short of England.

The unfortunate "vaseline" incident took place just before the innings subsided. Lever, who took five for 59 in the innings (two of them on the previous day) was reported by umpire Reuben to be carrying on his person a strip of surgical gauze impregnated with vaseline. He considered it to be a breach of Law 46.

The MCC authorities did not deny the presence of the offending strip of gauze, but offered an explanation for its use. Their version of how it came to be discovered by the umpire did, however, conflict with that of Mr Reuben. The umpire said that it came adrift while Lever was delivering the ball. MCC, on the other hand, claimed that Lever found it a hindrance and discarded it himself.

The MCC explanation for the bowler having possession of the gauze strip was this: During the morning session, both Lever and Willis had suffered from smarting eyes because of sweat running into them from the forehead. So, on the advice of the team's physiotherapist, Mr Bernard Thomas, they went out wearing these gauze strips which were intended to divert the trickle of perspiration away from their eyes.

Ken Barrington, the MCC manager said that while there had been a technical breach of the law governing "fair and unfair play", the offence was totally unintentional. At a press conference the following day, the rest day, the captain and manager emphasized in further defence of Lever that the gauze strips were not worn until after lunch and that by then MCC had made such large inroads into the Indian innings, that such unfair methods were quite unnecessary.

Fuel had been added to the fire by Bedi, the Indian captain, stating after the incident that even at Delhi, during the first Test, he had suspicions that a polishing agent of some kind had been used.

More was to be heard of the "vaseline" incident at the end of the fourth day, on which England played themselves into a winning position. They declared their second innings at 185 for nine, to which Amiss contributed 46 and Greig a sound, determined 41. Chandrasekhar was effective for the first time since the opening day of the series and took five for 50. But in the problems that he set England's batsmen on a pitch of awkward bounce, the Indians must have seen a pointer to their own fate against Underwood in the final innings.

With a lead of 283, England gave themselves just under seven and a half hours to bowl India out again. Taking three wickets, including Gavaskar's, in his last two overs of the day, Underwood ruined a good start by India and put England well within sight of victory. India, in effect, had only six wickets left, because Vengsarkar, struck on the hand by Willis, had received an injury which would prevent him from resuming his innings.

After close of play, two statements were issued on the "vaseline" affair. The secretary of the Indian Board, Mr Ghulam Ahmed, said that the Tour Committee of the Board had considered the umpire's report and other available evidence and could not come to a definite conclusion "whether the intentions of the bowler were deliberate or not". He added that the Board had conveyed all its findings to the TCCB in London.

While this statement left the impression that the Indian Board was not satisfied one way or the other, Mr Barrington said that the Indian Board and captain Bedi "had accepted our explanation that this was not a direct infringement of the laws of the game". In a day or two, a statement came from Lord's that the TCCB was satisfied with the explanation received from Messrs Barrington and Greig.

The remnants of the Indian innings folded up on the final morning. Underwood soon added Viswanath to his bag, and Willis (three for 18) and Lever hastened the end, which came well before lunch, India were all out for 83 their lowest in a home Test.

England

D. L. Amiss lbw b Madan Lal	4	– c Amarnath b Chandrasekhar	46
R. A. Woolmer c Gavaskar b Madan Lal	22	– lbw b Prasanna	16
J. M. Brearley c and b Prasanna	59	– b Chandrasekhar	29
D. W. Randall run out	2	– c Kirmani b Chandrasekhar	0
R. W. Tolchard not out	8	– not out	10
*A. W. Greig c Viswanath b Bedi	54	– lbw b Prasanna	41
†A. P. E. Knott c Viswanath b Bedi	45	– c Patel b Prasanna	11
J. K. Lever c Kirmani b Bedi	23	– c Amarnath b Chandrasekhar	2
C. M. Old c Amarnath b Bedi	2	– c Chandrasekhar b Prasanna	4
D. L. Underwood b Prasanna	23	– st Kirmani b Chandrasekhar	8
R. G. D. Willis run out	7	– not out	4
B 5, l-b 8	13	B 14	14
1/14 2/29 3/31 4/142 5/162 6/201 7/209 8/228 9/253	262	1/39 2/54 3/83 4/83 5/124 6/135 7/141 8/169 9/180	(9 wkts dec.) 185

Bowling: *First Innings*—Madan Lal 21–5–43–2; Amarnath 14–3–26–0; Chandrasekhar 25–4–63–0; Bedi 38.5–16–72–4; Prasanna 27–11–45–2. *Second Innings*—Madan Lal 9–2–15–0; Amarnath 7–2–18–0; Bedi 13–3–33–0; Prasanna 22–5–55–4; Chandrasekhar 20.5–4–50–5.

India

S. M. Gavaskar c Brearley b Old	39	– c Woolmer b Underwood	24
M. Amarnath b Old	0	– c Woolmer b Underwood	12
G. R. Viswanath c Knott b Lever	9	– c Brearley b Underwood	6
A. V. Mankad b Lever	0	– c Old b Lever	4
B. P. Patel b Underwood	32	– c Old b Willis	4
D. B. Vengsarkar c Randall b Lever	8	– retired hurt	1
S. Madan Lal c Underwood b Willis	12	– c Knott b Willis	6
†S. M. H. Kirmani c Brearley b Lever	27	– c Brearley b Willis	1
E. A. S. Prasanna c and b Underwood	13	– c Brearley b Underwood	0
*B. S. Bedi c sub b Lever	5	– not out	11
B. S. Chandrasekhar not out	1	– b Lever	6
L-b 1, n-b 17	18	B 5, l-b 1, n-b 2	8
1/5 2/17 3/17 4/69 5/86 6/114 7/115 8/151 9/161	164	1/40 2/45 3/45 4/54 5/54 6/57 7/66 8/71 9/83	83

Bowling: *First Innings*—Willis 19–5–46–1; Old 13–4–19–2; Lever 19.5–2–59–5; Woolmer 1–0–2–0; Greig 4–1–4–0; Underwood 17–9–16–2. *Second Innings*—Willis 13–4–18–3; Old 5–1–11–0; Underwood 14–7–28–4; Lever 6.5–0–18–2.

Umpires: J. Reuben and M. S. Shivashankariah.

INDIA v ENGLAND

Fourth Test Match

Played at Bangalore, January 28, 29, 30, February 1, 2, 1977

India won by 140 runs. Tables were turned in this Test because this time India did not fritter away the advantage of batting first. The pitch, from the second day onwards, deteriorated rapidly. Other contributory factors were the return to form of Chandrasekhar and more consistent catching close to the wicket. Yajuvendra Singh, playing in his first Test, took seven catches at short leg, thus equalling the record of Victor Richardson.

The pitch, closely shaved, was even tempered on the first day and India really should have reached a larger total. The top score in their 253 was 63 by the left-handed Surinder Amarnath, playing his first Test in the series. His effort, however, would have been of little advantage had Kirmani, at number seven, not made 52. Willis, although he received no help from the pitch, took six wickets in the innings, four of them in as many overs with the second new ball.

In reply, England were all out for 195. The Indian spinners had already extracted a fair bit of spin from the pitch. Although wickets fell steadily, Amiss batted long enough to make 82, but he was lucky to survive a chance to gully, off Bedi, when only three. Further resistance came from Lever. Chandrasekhar took six for 76.

Gavaskar played an innings of great technical skill that put the India second innings on a sound footing but they slipped to 124 for five before Viswanath, who was forced to bat as low as number seven because of injury, made a masterly 79 not out. India declared at tea on the fourth day with an overall lead of 317. Underwood this time was in the forefront of the England attack taking four for 76.

At the end of the fourth day, England were 34 for four, the wickets having gone down before the total was in double figures. And it took a bit of luck for Greig and Tolchard to survive this holocaust. The collapse set in again on the last day and England declined to 61 for six before Knott played a magnificent, aggressive innings of 81 not out. Although Old and Lever each stayed with him for half an hour, the innings had been damaged too badly for England to be able to extend India. Bedi did most of the damage, taking six for 71. But for Knott's spectacular onslaught, his figures would have been even more striking.

India

S. M. Gavaskar c Underwood b Lever	4	– c Brearley b Underwood	50
A. D. Gaekwad c Tolchard b Greig	39	– b Old	9
S. Amarnath b Greig	63	– c Tolchard b Willis	14
G. R. Viswanath c Brearley b Underwood	13	– not out	79
B. P. Patel c Randall b Willis	23	– c Knott b Underwood	17
Yajuvendra Singh c Knott b Willis	8	– c Fletcher b Underwood	15
†S. M. H. Kirmani b Willis	52	– c Randall b Underwood	21
K. Ghavri c Knott b Willis	16	– c Amiss b Lever	12
E. A. S. Prasanna c Greig b Willis	6	– c Old b Willis	12
B. S. Chandrasekhar c Knott b Willis	1	– not out	0
*B. S. Bedi not out	8	– run out	15
B 8, l-b 6, n-b 6	20	B 1, l-b 6, n-b 8	15
1/9 2/102 3/124 4/134 5/153 6/170 7/236 8/240 9/249	253	1/31 2/80 3/92 4/104 5/124 6/154 7/189 8/223 9/257 (9 wkts dec.)	259

Bowling: *First Innings*—Willis 17–2–53–6; Lever 17–2–48–1; Old 12–0–43–0; Underwood 21–7–45–1; Greig 18–5–44–2. *Second Innings*—Willis 18–2–47–2; Lever 9–1–28–1; Old 10–4–19–1; Underwood 31–18–76–4; Greig 23–2–74–0.

England

D. L. Amiss c Yajuvendra b Chandrasekhar	82	– c Yajuvendra b Ghavri	0
J. M. Brearley c Viswanath b Chandrasekhar	4	– c Gaekwad b Bedi	4
K. W. R. Fletcher c Yajuvendra b Prasanna	10	– c Yajuvendra b Chandrasekhar	1
D. W. Randall c Yajuvendra b Prasanna	10	– c Gaekwad b Bedi	0
R. W. Tolchard b Chandrasekhar	0	– lbw b Chandrasekhar	14
*A. W. Greig c Yajuvendra b Chandrasekhar	2	– st Kirmani b Bedi	31
†A. P. E. Knott b Bedi	29	– not out	81
C. M. Old lbw b Prasanna	9	– lbw b Chandrasekhar	13
J. K. Lever not out	20	– c Ghavri b Bedi	11
D. L. Underwood c Yajuvendra b Chandrasekhar	12	– c Patel b Bedi	10
R. G. D. Willis lbw b Chandrasekhar	7	– st Kirmani b Bedi	0
B 3, l-b 5, n-b 2	10	B 5, l-b 6, n-b 1	12
1/13 2/34 3/64 4/65 5/67 6/137 7/146 8/154 9/175	195	1/0 2/7 3/7 4/8 5/35 6/61 7/105 8/148 9/166	177

Bowling: *First Innings*—Ghavri 13–3–31–0; Yajuvendra 1–0–2–0; Bedi 23–11–29–1; Chandrasekhar 31.2–7–76–6; Prasanna 28–10–47–3. *Second Innings*—Ghavri 4–1–4–1; Gavaskar 2–2–0–0; Bedi 21.3–4–71–6; Chandrasekhar 15–3–55–3; Prasanna 15–5–35–0.

Umpires: M. V. Nagendra and Mohamed Ghouse.

INDIA v ENGLAND

Golden Jubilee Test

Played at Bombay, February 15, 17, 18, 19, 1980

England won by ten wickets with a day to spare. With the rival sides fatigued, both mentally and physically, at the end of an arduous season, the Test match to celebrate the Golden Jubilee of the Board of Control for Cricket in India produced poor cricket. But it was redeemed by an extraordinary all-round performance by Botham, whose versatility was in full bloom. There was hardly a session on which he did not bring his influence to bear, performing the unprecedented feat of scoring a century and capturing thirteen wickets in a Test. Taylor, the England wicket-keeper, also established a new world Test record by taking ten catches in the match.

To England, after the Test series in Australia, this success, even if inspired by one man, brought welcome relief. But for India, the defeat ended an unbeaten run of fifteen Test matches, four of which they had won.

With the pitch uncharacteristically grassy, England were at no disadvantage from losing the toss; even less so as an overcast sky was a further aid to swing and cut on the opening morning. The Indians, jaded after playing sixteen tests in the past seven months, could not summon the application and discipline needed to combat these conditions and were bowled out in less than a day for 242, Botham taking six for 58 and Taylor taking seven catches. India would have fared even worse but for gallant resistance from the lower order of their batting.

Batting as indifferently as they did in Australia, England at 58 for five looked most unlikely to match India's score, let alone build on the advantage created by their bowlers. But they were only 13 runs behind when they lost their next wicket two hours twenty minutes later. Botham, batting for 206 minutes and hitting seventeen 4s, scored 114 in an innings which was responsible and yet not lacking in enterprise. His stand of 171 with Taylor was England's best-ever sixth-wicket partnership against India. Taylor remained entrenched until the third day was more than an hour old and altogether scored 43 in a stay of four and a half hours. Yet their stand could have been cut short at only 85 when umpire Hanumantha Rao upheld an appeal against Taylor for a catch behind the wicket, off Kapil Dev. Taylor hesitated and protested at the decision. Viswanath, the Indian captain, who was fielding at first slip, was as certain as the batsman that there had been no contact and persuaded the umpire to rescind his verdict.

Even on the third day there was sufficient bounce and movement off the seam to trouble the Indian batsmen. Showing little spirit, India were only 2 runs ahead with half their second-innings wickets gone, and but for an innings of 45 not out by Kapil Dev, who batted in the forthright manner of Botham, the match might not have gone into the fourth day.

The recent history of Test pitches at the Wankhede Stadium – earlier in the season both Australia and Pakistan were beaten in four days, with spinners causing the havoc – prompted England to equip themselves with two specialist spinners in Underwood and Emburey. In the event Underwood bowled only seven overs and Emburey none at all. Of the ten wickets captured by the Indians, their opening bowlers, Ghavri and Kapil Dev, took five and three wickets, respectively.

India

S. M. Gavaskar c Taylor b Botham	49	– c Taylor b Botham	24
R. M. Binny run out	15	– lbw b Botham	0
D. B. Vengsarkar c Taylor b Stevenson	34	– lbw b Lever	10
*G. R. Viswanath b Lever	11	– c Taylor b Botham	5
S. M. Patil c Taylor b Botham	30	– lbw b Botham	0
Yashpal Sharma lbw b Botham	21	– lbw b Botham	27
Kapil Dev c Taylor b Botham	0	– (8) not out	45
†S. M. H. Kirmani not out	40	– (7) c Gooch b Botham	0
K. D. Ghavri c Taylor b Stevenson	11	– c Brearley b Lever	5
S. Yadav c Taylor b Botham	8	– c Taylor b Botham	15
D. R. Doshi c Taylor b Botham	6	– c and b Lever	0
B 5, l-b 3, n-b 9	17	B 4, l-b 8, w 1, n-b 5	18
1/56 2/102 3/108 4/135 5/160 6/160 7/181 8/197 9/223	242	1/4 2/22 3/31 4/31 5/56 6/68 7/102 8/115 9/148	149

Bowling: *First Innings*—Lever 23–3–82–1; Botham 22.5–7–58–6; Stevenson 14–1–59–2; Underwood 6–1–23–0; Gooch 4–2–3–0. *Second Innings*—Lever 20.1–2–65–3; Botham 26–7–48–7; Stevenson 5–1–13–0; Underwood 1–0–5–0.

England

G. A. Gooch c Kirmani b Ghavri	8	– not out 49
G. Boycott c Kirmani b Binny	22	– not out 43
W. Larkins lbw b Ghavri	0	
D. I. Gower lbw b Kapil Dev	16	
*J. M. Brearley lbw b Kapil Dev	5	
I. T. Botham lbw b Ghavri	114	
†R. W. Taylor lbw b Kapil Dev	43	
J. E. Emburey c Binny b Ghavri	8	
J. K. Lever b Doshi	21	
G. B. Stevenson not out	27	
D. L. Underwood b Ghavri	1	
B 8, l-b 9, n-b 14	31	B 3, l-b 1, n-b 2 6
1/21 2/21 3/45 4/57 5/58 6/229 7/245 8/262 9/283	296	(no wkt) 98

Bowling: *First Innings*—Kapil Dev 29–8–64–3; Ghavri 20.1–5–52–5; Binny 19–3–70–1; Doshi 23–6–57–1; Yadav 6–2–22–0. *Second Innings*—Kapil Dev 8–2–21–0; Ghavri 5–0–12–0; Doshi 6–1–12–0; Yadav 6–0–31–0; Patil 3–0–8–0; Gavaskar 1–0–4–0; Viswanath 0.3–0–4–0.

Umpires: J. D. Ghosh and S. N. Hanumantha Rao.

ENGLAND IN PAKISTAN

NORTHERN ZONE v MCC

Played at Peshawar, February 1, 2, 3, 1967

MCC [under 25] won by an innings and 139 runs. Brearley, whose previous highest score was 169, annihilated a fair attack which had little support from the field, and achieved the rare distinction of a triple century. His 312 not out, and MCC's total, have no parallel in a day's play in any match in Pakistan. A new opening partnership of Brearley and Knott realised 208, Knott hitting his maiden first-class century. Brearley went on at ever-increasing speed, scoring three 6s and forty-one 4s. His first hundred took two hours, thirty-five minutes, the second two hours five minutes and the third only fifty minutes. The unbroken stand with Ormrod put on 234 in the final hour and three-quarters, Ormrod selflessly giving Brearley as much of the strike as he could, although he was well within range of his own best score. Hutton finished Northern Zone's first innings with his first hat-trick, and it needed good bowling by Hobbs and Fletcher to overcome some stubborn batting in the second innings.

MCC

*J. M. Brearley not out	312
†A. P. E. Knott c Intikhab Ahmad b Intikhab Alam	101
M. A. Buss c Asif Ahmad b Intikhab Alam	0
D. L. Amiss b Intikhab Alam	1
K. W. R. Fletcher c Intikhab Alam b Saifullah	18
J. A. Ormrod not out	61
B 14, l-b 4, n-b 3	21
1/208 2/213 3/242 4/280 (4 wkts dec.)	514

M. Bissex, R. A. Hutton, A. R. Windows, D. L. Underwood and R. N. S. Hobbs did not bat.

Bowling: Saifullah 12–0–70–1; Asif Ahmad 15–2–61–0; Intikhab Alam 32–4–124–3; Masood-ul-Hasan 20–2–114–0; Intikhab Ahmad 7–1–22–0; Hamid Ali 24–5–102–0.

North Zone

†Hamid Nagra c Bissex b Hobbs	21	– b Fletcher	11
Mohammad Saleem st Knott b Hobbs	7	– b Hutton	4
Kamran Rashid c Fletcher b Hutton	56	– c Buss b Hobbs	39
Masood-ul-Hasan lbw b Hobbs	16	– st Knott b Hobbs	60
Khalid Aziz (Lahore) c Brearley b Hobbs	0	– c Amiss b Fletcher	2
*Intikhab Alam c Hobbs b Bissex	1	– c Fletcher b Hobbs	32
Khalid Aziz (Peshawar) c Brearley b Hobbs	13	– lbw b Hutton	46
Intikhab Ahmad st Knott b Hobbs	0	– c Underwood b Fletcher	25
Asif Ahmad not out	4	– c Windows b Fletcher	22
Hamid Ali b Hutton	0	– not out	0
Saifullah c Brearley b Hutton	0	– b Underwood	0
B 1, l-b 5, n-b 2	8	B 1, l-b 6, n-b 1	8
1/28 2/33 3/71 4/73 5/78 6/115 7/116 8/126 9/126	126	1/7 2/49 3/71 4/94 5/107 6/183 7/213 8/244 9/249	249

Bowling: *First Innings*—Hutton 10.3–2–20–3; Windows 5–3–9–0; Hobbs 22–5–39–6; Underwood 5–1–12–0; Bissex 8–2–21–1; Buss 4–0–17–0. *Second Innings*—Hutton 8–2–33–2; Windows 4–2–6–0; Hobbs 21–5–88–3; Underwood 18.1–6–38–1; Fletcher 16–3–50–4; Bissex 4–1–6–0; Amiss 2–0–17–0; Brearley 1–0–3–0.

Umpires: Qamarudin Butt and Nazar Mohammad.

PAKISTAN v ENGLAND

Third Test Match

Played at Karachi, March 6, 7, 8, 1969

Drawn. Rioting stopped the final match of the tour early on the third day, when Knott needed only four for a first Test century. He had batted three hours, thirty-five minutes and hit one 6 and ten 4s. Milburn, who had joined the side two days before the second Test, played a storming innings to launch England on their high scoring spree. Altogether he hit one 6 and seventeen 4s and reached his 100 of 163 balls in three and a quarter hours. Graveney was more subdued during a stay of almost five hours, during which he hit nine 4s.

England

C. Milburn c Wasim b Asif Masood	139
J. H. Edrich c Saeed b Intikhab	32
T. W. Graveney c Asif Iqbal b Intikhab	105
*M. C. Cowdrey c Hanif b Intikhab	14
K. W. R. Fletcher b Mushtaq	38
B. L. D'Oliveira c Aftab b Mushtaq	16
†A. P. E. Knott not out	96
J. A. Snow b Asif Masood	9
D. J. Brown not out	25
B 5, l-b 12, n-b 11	28
1/78 2/234 3/286 4/309 5/360 6/372 7/427	(7 wkts) 502

D. L. Underwood and R. N. S. Hobbs did not bat.

Bowling: Asif Masood 28–2–94–2; Majid 20–5–51–0; Sarfraz 34–6–78–0; Intikhab 48–4–129–3; Saeed 22–5–53–0; Mushtaq 23.1–5–69–2.

Pakistan

*Saeed Ahmed, Aftab Gul, Hanif Mohammad, Mustaq Mohammad, Asif Iqbal, Majid Jahangir, Shafqat Rana, Intikhab Alam, †Wasim Bari, Asif Masood, Sarfraz Nawaz.

Umpires: Shuja-ud-Din and Daud Khan.

PAKISTAN v ENGLAND

Third Test Match

Played at Karachi, March 24, 25, 27, 28, 29, 1973

Drawn. Like the previous two Tests this one ended in a draw although it was not without its incidents, unfortunately off the field. Over one hundred minutes were lost through rioting and invasions of the field by spectators, and the match was abandoned forty-five minutes early when a dust-storm made play impossible As at Hyderabad there was a time on the last day when it seemed that there might be a victory, this time to England, but the slowness of another grassless pitch enabled Pakistan to escape. In the main it was a match of batting although none of it exciting for the bounce of the ball made stroke-play unrewarding. It was remarkable for one oddity in that Majid, Mushtaq and Amiss, who had scored a century in each of the previous Tests, were each dismissed for 99.

Majid and Sadiq laid the foundation of a big score when they put on 97 for the second wicket and when Majid eventually fell Pakistan were 297 for three. With Mushtaq, who brought his time at the crease in two innings against England to thirteen hours, he put on 121. Only a strong man could make runs quickly in these conditions and not surprisingly Intikhab with 61 provided the most enterprising batting of the innings before Pakistan declared at 445 for six.

England, who would not have wanted to face too many runs on the last day on a pitch of doubtful durability, were reassured by a second wicket stand of 130 between Amiss and Fletcher who, after a confident start, had been subdued by the accurate leg-spin of Mushtaq and Intikhab and the activities of the crowd. Strangely, Majid did not use these two together again until nearly four hours had passed on the next day, the fourth, by which time England's position had become reasonably carefree, Greig, so reliable, made 48, the captain, Lewis, 88. When the leg-spinners at last teamed up again they finished the innings in half an hour, sharing the last four wickets.

Pakistan, who theoretically should have held the initiative on the last day, lost it – and with it almost the match – in a highly effective spell by the England spinners, Gifford and Birkenshaw. Gifford bowled Talat and Sadiq and had Asif caught at extra cover, while Birkenshaw accounted for those two plunderers of England's bowling, Mushtaq and Intikhab, each for a duck. Those five wickets fell for only three runs so that Pakistan were 108 for seven with four and a half hours left.

Pakistan

Sadiq Mohammad c Denness b Gifford	89	– b Gifford	1
Talat Ali c Amiss b Gifford	33	– b Gifford	39
*Majid Khan c Amiss b Pocock	99	– b Gifford	23
Mushtaq Mohammad run out	99	– c Denness b Birkenshaw	0
Asif Iqbal c and b Pocock	6	– c Fletcher b Gifford	36
Intikhab Alam c and b Birkenshaw	61	– c Greig b Birkenshaw	0
Zaheer Abbas not out	22	– c Knott b Gifford	4
†Wasim Bari not out	17	– c Denness b Birkenshaw	41
Saleem Altaf (did not bat)		– c Knott b Birkenshaw	13
Sarfraz Nawaz (did not bat)		– not out	33
Asif Masood (did not bat)		– c Gifford b Birkenshaw	0
B 4, l-b 9, n-b 6	19	L-b 4, n-b 5	9
1/79 2/176 3/297 4/307 5/389 6/413	(6 wkts dec.) 445	1/39 2/51 3/105 4/106 5/106 6/106 7/108 8/129 9/198	199

Bowling: *First Innings*—Arnold 19–2–69–0; Greig 20–1–76–0; Pocock 38–7–93–2; Gifford 46–11–99–2; Birkenshaw 31–5–89–1. *Second Innings*—Arnold 15–2–52–0; Greig 10–2–26–0; Gifford 29–9–55–5; Birkenshaw 18.3–5–57–5.

England

B. Wood c Sarfraz b Masood	3	– c Masood b Saleem	5
D. L. Amiss c Sarfraz b Intikhab	99	– not out	21
K. W. R. Fletcher c Talat b Intikhab	54	– not out	1
M. H. Denness lbw b Masood	47		
P. I. Pocock c Sarfraz b Mushtaq	4		
*A. R. Lewis c Iqbal b Intikhab	88		
A. W. Greig b Majid	48		
†A. P. E. Knott b Majid	2		
J. Birkenshaw c Majid b Mushtaq	21		
G. G. Arnold c Mushtaq b Intikhab	2		
N. Gifford not out	4		
B 3, l-b 3, n-b 8	14	N-b 3	3
1/13 2/143 3/182 4/220 5/323 6/331 7/370 8/373 9/381	386	1/27	(1 wkt) 30

Bowling: *First Innings*—Saleem Altaf 15–3–38–0; Asif Masood 21–4–41–2; Intikhab Alam 39–8–105–4; Sarfraz Nawaz 25–3–64–0; Mushtaq Mohammad 34.3–9–73–2; Majid Khan 22–5–51–2. *Second Innings*—Saleem Altaf 5–1–16–1; Asif Masood 4–1–11–0; Sarfraz Nawaz 1–1–0–0.

Umpires: Daud Khan and Aslam Khokar.

PAKISTAN v ENGLAND

First Test Match

Played at Lahore, December 14, 15, 16, 18, 19, 1977

Drawn. A tedious five days was marred by two serious crowd disturbances and over-cautious batting on a slow pitch. Except for a brief period on the fourth afternoon when the classical slow left-arm bowling of Iqbal Qasim threatened England with the follow-on, the prospect of a result other than dreary stalemate was remote. The first innings were not completed until fifteen minutes after lunch on the last day. At that point 695 runs had been laboriously scored for nineteen wickets in twenty-two and a quarter hours play.

The first stoppage, on the second afternoon, was caused by a premature celebration of Mudassar Nazar's century, which was the longest in Test history. When he was 99 some spectators invaded the pitch. After one had been belaboured by police, running fights began. Police were chased across the ground, and four found refuge in the England dressing room. Bricks and stones were hurled in the direction of the dressing-rooms and the VIP enclosure.

Tea was taken during the trouble, and only twenty-five minutes of actual playing time were lost. Incredibly, the rioters voluntarily cleared the ground of debris.

Mudassar, the 21-year-old son of former Test opener Nazar Mohammad, now Pakistan national coach, completed his century in nine hours seventeen minutes – twelve minutes slower than the previous record by D. J. McGlew for South Africa against Australia in the 1957-58 series. In all, Mudassar batted nine minutes under ten hours for 114, with three of his twelve 4s arriving after his century. Used as the sheet anchor, Mudassar displayed remarkable concentration and unwavering resolve, and played his elected role to perfection. His record might not have lasted long if Boycott had not been beaten by a brilliant delivery which pitched middle and took the off stump when he was 63. Boycott's 50 in four hours fifty minutes was twenty minutes slower than Mudassar's 50.

The second and more serious riot, clearly with a political motivation, caused play to be abandoned fifty-five minutes before the scheduled ending on the third evening. Police fired tear gas to disperse a section of a crowd estimated at between 30,000 and 35,000. Fortunately, the next day was a rest day, but the rest of the Test suffered from a lack of atmosphere. Attendances dwindled to a few thousand and there was a considerable show of police and military strength. It was hard to concentrate in such a tense situation.

Some splendid batting, however, came from the powerfully-built Haroon Rashid, who, with Mudassar, put on 180 which passed the previous Pakistan record for the third wicket against England – established by Zaheer Abbas and Mushtaq Mohammad at The Oval in 1974. In slightly under five hours Haroon hit one 6 and seventeen 4s. Javed Miandad also livened the innings.

Cope was almost credited with a hat-trick in his maiden Test. Having dismissed Abdul Qadir and Sarfraz Nawaz with successive deliveries, he had Iqbal Qasim given out caught at slip to Brearley off the next ball. The batsman was on his way out when Brearley, uncertain of the validity of the catch, recalled him.

Pakistan batted into the third day and achieved the modest tactical position of setting England to make 208 to avoid the follow-on – the only logical way of getting a result. Yet they took England to the brink of disaster by dismissing the first six for 162, mainly by an impressive thirteen overs spell by Iqbal Qasim who removed Boycott, Roope (to an indiscreet shot), and Old at a personal cost of 23. Abdul Qadir's leg-breaks and googlies also caused trouble, but when his length began to falter the new ball was taken. It was less effective than spin.

Miller and his Derbyshire team-mate Taylor survived the crisis with 89 in three hours. Unhappily for Miller, seeking his maiden first-class century, his last partner Willis was given out, caught at backward short leg, when he was 98. Willis had stayed for ninety minutes, and Miller, though inflicted with a heavy cold and streaming eyes, had batted for six hours without serious fault, hitting ten 4s.

Pakistan

Mudassar Nazar c and b Miller	114	– c Taylor b Willis	26
Sadiq Mohammad lbw b Miller	18	– b Lever	1
Shafiq Ahmed c Rose b Old	0	– lbw b Willis	7
Haroon Rashid c and b Lever	122	– not out	45
Javed Miandad c Taylor b Lever	71	– not out	19
Wasim Raja st Taylor b Cope	24		
Abdul Qadir lbw b Cope	11		
*†Wasim Bari c Cope b Miller	17		
Sarfraz Nawaz b Cope	0		
Iqbal Qasim not out	8		
Liaqat Ali not out	0		
B 1, l-b 4, n-b 17	22	N-b 8	8
1/48 2/49 3/229 4/329 5/356 6/378 7/387 8/387 9/403	(9 wkts dec.) 407	1/15 2/40 3/45	(2 wkts) 106

Bowling: *First Innings*—Willis 17–3–67–0; Lever 16–1–47–2; Old 21–7–63–1; Miller 37–10–102–3; Cope 39–6–102–3; Boycott 3–0–4–0. *Second Innings*—Willis 7–0–34–2; Lever 3–0–13–1; Miller 10–4–24–0; Old 4–0–18–0; Cope 3–0–7–0; Randall 1–0–2–0.

England

G. Boycott b Qasim	63
*J. M. Brearley run out	23
B. C. Rose lbw b Sarfraz	1
D. W. Randall c Qasim b Liaqat	19
G. R. J. Roope b Qasim	19
G. Miller not out	98
C. M. Old c Mudassar b Qasim	2
†R. W. Taylor b Sarfraz	32
G. A. Cope lbw b Sarfraz	0
J. K. Lever c Bari b Sarfraz	0
R. G. D. Willis c Qasim b Qadir	14
B 2, l-b 8, n-b 7	17
1/53 2/55 3/96 4/127 5/148 6/162 7/251 8/251 9/253	288

Bowling: Sarfraz 34–11–68–4; Liaqat 27–11–43–1; Qadir 32.7–7–82–1; Qasim 32–12–57–3; Raja 10–2–21–0.

Umpires: Amanullah Khan and Aslam Khokhar.

CRICKET IN AUSTRALIA

SOUTH AFRICA IN AUSTRALIA AND NEW ZEALAND, 1963-64

South African cricket received a splendid boost by the achievements of the team in Australia during the three and a half months from October 1963 to February 1964. Not only did they share the series, each side winning one game with the three other Test matches drawn, but they surprised and delighted everybody by the quality of their play.

For years South African batting, with one or two exceptions, had been notable more for its dour, defensive qualities than for anything else. During this tour they showed that they possessed an array of attacking batsmen who made the team a big attraction. The selectors are to be congratulated on choosing this type of side.

When the tour began there seemed little chance that South Africa would provide much in the way of a serious challenge or attract the crowds. As the tour progressed and the players began to build their personalities the interest developed considerably. In the end the total attendances reached 500,000, the highest for a South African visit to Australia, and the profit was over £3,000.

Happy enough though they were, the South Africans were a little disappointed that they did not win the series. In the main their batting and bowling were superior to Australia's, but they were let down by poor catching. Indeed, the fielding throughout the tour was well below the high standard usually associated with South Africa.

The big successes were R. G. Pollock and Barlow, in batting, and P. Pollock and Partridge, in bowling. R. G. Pollock, a 19-year-old left-hander, established himself as a big draw. His thrilling, powerful stroke-play delighted the crowds and he hit centuries in the third and fourth Tests.

Barlow, a bespectacled, stocky player, also hit strongly, although in a less orthodox way. He scored 1,523 runs in first-class matches on the tour. Few visitors to Australia have done anything like that. He hit centuries in three of the Tests including 201 in the fourth match. The highlight of these two batsmen came during the fourth Test at Adelaide where they put on 341 for the third wicket, the highest stand ever made for South Africa. The total of 595 in the first innings was also the highest in the history of South African Test cricket. They won that match by the convincing margin of ten wickets. Australia had previously won the second test at Melbourne by eight wickets.

Generally the bowling was adequate, but it depended almost entirely on speed. P. Pollock worked up a lively pace and was considered faster than Trueman. Partridge relied more on accuracy, stamina and swing. Between them they claimed 50 Test wickets.

Two of the younger members of the party, Bland and Lindsey showed plenty of promise as batsmen. Lindsey was also a capable wicket-keeper. The side was led intelligently by Goddard, whose all-round ability did much towards the success of the tour. K. G. Viljoen proved an excellent manager.

The Australians disappointed. The absence of Davidson, who had retired, was a big handicap to the attack, but the batting was expected to be powerful. In fact, only Booth and Lawry justified themselves to the full.

Benaud gave up the captaincy after the first Test and Simpson took over. He had the satisfaction of leading his side to victory in his first game as captain, but thereafter had a difficult task in saving the series.

The South Africans went on to New Zealand where they could not maintain their top form. The three Tests were drawn, although South Africa were obviously the stronger combination. At Auckland, Sinclair scored 138, the highest Test innings by a New Zealand player in New Zealand.

AUSTRALIA v SOUTH AFRICA

First Test Match

Played at Brisbane, December 6, 7, 9, 10, 11, 1963

Drawn. There was never much hope of a definite result with one day lost through rain, but the match was made memorable by the no-balling of Meckiff for throwing and his subsequent retirement from first-class cricket. Australia made a shaky start, Simpson, Lawry and Burge being out for 88, but Booth rallied them. O'Neill, although struggling to find form, helped Booth add 120 and Benaud also shared a century stand with Booth. The bowling wilted towards the end of the day and with 153 coming in the last two hours, Australia reached 337 for five by the close. Booth went on to make 169 and the innings closed for 435.

Then came the dramatic over by Meckiff who was no-balled by Egar on his second, third, fifth and ninth deliveries. That was his only over. Egar was booed and Meckiff was carried shoulder high by a section of the crowd at the close. South Africa made a promising start, but ran into trouble against Benaud and were 157 for four at the end of the second day.

No play was possible on Monday and on the fourth day extra police were sent to the ground because of fears that the umpires, selectors and Benaud might be molested because of the Meckiff incident. There were no scenes. With little hope of victory, South Africa concentrated on saving the game. Barlow hit his first Test century, batting nearly six hours for 114. Waite also batted carefully and the Australian lead was restricted to 89. Lawry hit briskly for 87 outscoring O'Neill and Benaud declared, setting South Africa to score 234 in four hours. A little later a violent storm flooded the ground and ended the match. Afterwards Goddard entered hospital for a nasal operation. Booth suffered two chips on a knuckle while fielding.

Australia

W. M. Lawry c G. Pollock b Barlow	43	– not out	87
R. B. Simpson c Waite b P. Pollock	12	– c sub b Partridge	34
N. C. O'Neill c Barlow b P. Pollock	82	– not out	19
P. J. Burge run out	13		
B. C. Booth c Barlow b P. Pollock	169		
*R. Benaud lbw b Goddard	43		
G. D. McKenzie c P. Pollock b Goddard	39		
T. Veivers c Goddard b P. Pollock	14		
†A. T. W. Grout c Seymour b P. Pollock	6		
I. Meckiff b P. Pollock	7		
A. Connolly not out	1		
B 1, l-b 5	6	L-b 4	4
1/39 2/73 3/88 4/208 5/310 6/394 7/415 8/427 9/434	435	1/83	(1 wkt dec.) 144

Bowling: *First Innings*—P. Pollock 22.6–0–95–6; Partridge 25–3–87–0; Goddard 24–6–52–2; Barlow 9–0–71–1; Seymour 11–0–39–0; D. Pithey 23–6–85–0. *Second Innings*—P. Pollock 6–0–26–0; Partridge 17–1–50–1; Goddard 7–0–34–0; Pithey 5–0–30–0.

South Africa

*T. L. Goddard c Meckiff b Benaud	52	– not out	8
E. J. Barlow b Benaud	114	– c Simpson b McKenzie	0
P. R. Carlstein c and b Benaud	0	– not out	1
R. G. Pollock b McKenzie	25		
D. Lindsay lbw b Benaud	17		
†J. H. B. Waite lbw b Connolly	66		
P. L. Van der Merwe b O'Neill	17		
D. B. Pithey c Meckiff b Veivers	18		
P. M. Pollock lbw b Benaud	8		
M. A. Seymour b Simpson	10		
J. T. Partridge not out	3		
B 3, l-b 5, n-b 8	16	B 4	4
1/74 2/78 3/120 4/157 5/239 6/272 7/321 8/325 9/335	346	1/1 (1 wkt)	13

Bowling: *First Innings*—McKenzie 23–1–88–1; Meckiff 1–0–8–0. Connolly 19–4–46–1; Veivers 34–15–48–1; Benaud 33–10–68–5; Simpson 18.5–5–52–1; O'Neill 7–0–20–1. *Second Innings*—McKenzie 3.3–1–3–1; Connolly 1–0–2–0; Benaud 2–1–4–0.

Umpires: C. Egar and L. Rowan.

TASMANIA COMBINED XI v SOUTH AFRICANS

Played at Hobart, December 26, 27, 28, 1963

Drawn. On the first day occurred a 20-minute hold up because of a gale – a stoppage believed to be unprecedented in Australian history – and a fine century by Potter; on the second came some heavy scoring by the South Africans and the third brought a thrilling finish with the last two Combined side batsmen at the wicket. Potter alone defied the South African attack, and the gale, and his century included eleven 4s and one 6. No other batsman passed 15 in the total of 218. Centuries by Farrer and Waite ensured a good lead for the tourists, who declared 227 runs on and looked set for victory when five Combined XI wickets fell for 103. In the final over, however, Aldridge smothered the spin of the menacing Pithey and earned a draw.

Combined XI

C. Connor b Partridge	8	– c and b R. Pollock	32
B. Sheen b P. Pollock	10	– b Partridge	3
B. John c Waite b Partridge	15	– run out	5
P. J. Burge b Partridge	3	– b Partridge	10
J. Potter not out	123	– b Goddard	24
I. J. Cowley st Waite b Pithey	13	– b Pithey	41
*†L. Maddocks b Pithey	0	– b Pithey	35
B. Patterson lbw b Seymour	7	– c sub b Pithey	8
E. Richardson b P. Pollock	11	– c and b Pithey	7
G. Long run out	4	– not out	4
J. Aldridge b P. Pollock	10	– not out	0
B 2, l-b 7, n-b 5	14	B 16, l-b 2, n-b 3	21
1/21 2/26 3/37 4/50 5/97 6/99 7/122 8/150 9/168	218	1/5 2/18 3/42 4/74 5/103 6/161 7/179 8/179 9/190 (9 wkts)	190

Bowling: *First Innings*—P. Pollock 21–1–75–3; Partridge 11–2–26–3; Goddard 7–2–11–0; Seymour 14–3–42–1; Pithey 16–4–50–2. *Second Innings*—P. Pollock 5–1–10–0; Partridge 12–2–20–2; Goddard 12–4–28–1; Seymour 20–5–35–0; Pithey 14–2–39–4; R. Pollock 12–2–37–1.

South Africans

*T. L. Goddard b Patterson	95	P. L. van der Merwe c Potter b Patterson	11
E. J. Barlow c Long b Richardson	24	D. B. Pithey not out	7
W. S. Farrer b Potter	107	B 4, l-b 5, n-b 2	11
†J. H. B. Waite not out	115		
R. G. Pollock c and b Aldridge	64	1/77 2/198 3/259 (6 wkts dec.)	445
K. C. Bland c Potter b Patterson	11	4/387 5/416 6/429	

P. M. Pollock, M. Seymour, J. T. Partridge did not bat.

Bowling: Aldridge 8–0–29–1; Connor 29–2–95–0; Richardson 22–0–112–1; Long 8–0–37–0; Patterson 37–3–118–3; Potter 9–1–43–1.

WESTERN AUSTRALIA v WEST INDIES

Played at Perth, October 26, 27, 28, 29, 1968

West Indies won by six wickets. This game will be remembered by those who saw it for an incredible innings of 132 by Sobers. Coming in when the West Indies were 109 for four, he played his strokes against the Test bowlers McKenzie, Mayne and Lock with such bewildering power and certainty that he scored his runs in seven minutes under two hours, hitting twenty-five 4s. On the first day Hall and Griffith, getting some lift out of a fast pitch, broke the back of the state innings, although a solid effort by Irvine took them to 199. After Sobers and Butcher had then assured the West Indians of a big lead, Marsh, playing his first game for Western Australia, hit a robust 104 in two and three-quarter hours. The West Indies final target of 127 gave them no trouble.

Western Australia

D. Chadwick c Hendriks b Griffith	7	– c Holford b Sobers	34
R. D. Bowe c Sobers b Hall	9	– c Butcher b Hall	0
R. J. Inverarity b Griffith	0	– c Hendriks b Hall	11
C. Milburn b Hall	1	– c Hendriks b Hall	31
R. Marsh b Griffith	0	– b Sobers	104
J. T. Irvine b Carew	78	– c Fredericks b Sobers	39
†G. C. Becker c Hendriks b Griffith	10	– b Sobers	8
G. D. McKenzie c Carew b Hall	1	– not out	51
*G. A. R. Lock c Holford b King	35	– c Hendriks b Griffith	0
L. C. Mayne not out	41	– b Griffith	1
J. B. Gannon c Sobers b Holford	0	– b Griffith	0
B 4, l-b 5, n-b 8	17	L-b 5, n-b 4	9
1/22 2/23 3/24 4/25 5/27 6/37 7/39 8/87 9/198	199	1/0 2/12 3/116 4/194 5/195 6/208 7/261 8/262 9/266	288

Bowling: *First Innings*—Hall 10–3–30–3; Griffith 8–0–52–4; King 8–1–34–1; Sobers 7–0–28–0; Holford 8.5–0–37–1; Carew 3–2–1–1. *Second Innings*—Hall 10–2–44–3; Griffith 8.6–1–46–3; King 10–3–29–0; Holford 12–0–66–0; Carew 13–3–39–0; Sobers 17–3–55–4.

West Indies

R. C. Fredericks c Irvine b Gannon	49	– b Lock	40
M. C. Carew c Becker b McKenzie	19	– c sub b Lock	13
S. M. Nurse lbw b McKenzie	13		
C. H. Lloyd c Inverarity b Gannon	17	– c Irvine b Mayne	6
B. F. Butcher c Bowe b Inverarity	74	– lbw b Mayne	0
*G. S. Sobers c McKenzie b Mayne	132	– not out	16
D. A. J. Holford not out	20	– not out	47
†J. L. Hendriks c and b Lock	2		
C. C. Griffith c Marsh b Inverarity	3		
L. A. King c Lock b McKenzie	15		
W. W. Hall b McKenzie	5		
B 4, l-b 8	12	B 4, l-b 1	5
1/55 2/75 3/102 4/109 5/300 6/318 7/322 8/333 9/355	361	1/46 2/54 3/54 4/86	(4 wkts) 127

Bowling: *First Innings*—McKenzie 20.1–4–95–4; Mayne 19–1–89–1; Gannon 13–3–65–2; Lock 14–2–77–1; Inverarity 8–3–23–2. *Second Innings*—McKenzie 7–0–32–0; Mayne 11–1–35–2; Lock 8–1–41–2; Inverarity 1.3–0–4–0; Marsh 1–0–10–0.

Umpires: W. Carter and A. Foster.

COMBINED XI v WEST INDIES

Played at Perth, November 2, 3, 4, 5, 1968

Combined XI won by seven wickets. Gibbs, captaining the West Indies in place of Sobers, left the Combined XI to score 354 in four hours, ten minutes on the last day and an exciting fourth-wicket stand of 260 in two hours, thirty-six minutes between Chappell and Sheahan took them to victory with three overs left to be bowled. In a match full of exciting stroke play on a glorious wicket Butcher made a hundred in each innings and Kanhai one in the second. Milburn batted attractively for the Combined XI. On the last day Chappell made the first of his many big scores against the West Indies. At the crease just under four hours he hit twenty-three 4s; Sheahan batted two and a half hours and hit nine 4s.

West Indies

R. C. Fredericks c Milburn b Chappell	20	– c Chappell b Mayne	4
G. S. Camacho c Inverarity b Mayne	1	– c Becker b McKenzie	0
R. B. Kanhai c Inverarity b McKenzie	12	– not out	174
B. F. Butcher c Irvine b Chappell	115	– c Marsh b Mayne	172
C. H. Lloyd run out	3	– c Becker b Walters	42
D. A. J. Holford lbw b McKenzie	54	– b Mayne	4
C. A. Davis c Inverarity b Lock	15	– lbw b Mayne	17
†T. M. Findlay lbw b Lock	6	– run out	2
W. W. Hall c Milburn b Lock	15		
R. M. Edwards c Milburn b Lock	6		
*L. R. Gibbs not out	1		
L-b 4, n-b 2	6	B 3, l-b 10, n-b 4	17
1/9 2/22 3/53 4/98 5/179 6/206 7/236 8/248 9/254	254	1/0 2/12 3/128 4/165 5/382 6/406 7/432	(7 wkts dec.) 432

Bowling: *First Innings*—McKenzie 16–3–51–2; Mayne 13–1–62–1; Walters 7–0–26–0; Lock 16.5–4–54–4; Chappell 13–1–55–2. *Second Innings*—McKenzie 14–0–82–1; Mayne 17.4–0–98–4; Lock 13–0–67–0; Walters 18–0–111–1; Inverarity 2–0–2–0; Chappell 4–0–34–0; Milburn 3–0–21–0.

Combined XI

R. J. Inverarity c Findlay b Hall	11	– b Edwards	7
C. Milburn c Findlay b Davis	79	– c Findlay b Hall	18
I. M. Chappell c Findlay b Davis	23	– not out	188
R. Marsh c Findlay b Davis	0	– c Findlay b Gibbs	22
A. P. Sheahan b Davis	41	– not out	111
K. D. Walters lbw b Gibbs	43		
J. T. Irvine c Lloyd b Edwards	20		
†G. C. Becker b Hall	31		
G. D. McKenzie c Butcher b Davis	32		
*G. A. R. Lock c Camacho b Davis	32		
L. C. Mayne not out	4		
B 3, l-b 4, n-b 10	17	B 4, l-b 2, n-b 2	8
1/75 2/101 3/105 4/148 5/178 6/220 7/262 8/262 9/323	333	1/26 2/26 3/94	(3 wkts) 354

Bowling: *First Innings*—Hall 17–4–79–2; Edwards 17–1–79–1; Davis 22–1–96–6; Gibbs 20–2–62–1. *Second Innings*—Hall 6–0–51–1; Edwards 15–1–100–1; Davis 8–1–47–0; Gibbs 16–0–93–1; Holford 9–0–55–0.

Umpires: W. Carter and N. Townsend.

SOUTH AUSTRALIA v WEST INDIES

Played at Adelaide, November 8, 9, 11, 1968

South Australia won by ten wickets. The West Indies were too complacent in their approach to this game and the older players were not prepared to apply themselves to the cricket. As a result they were beaten by the young South Australian side skilfully led by Favell. In the West Indies first innings only Nurse batted with any authority, but the State were then given a fine start by Causby and I. M. Chappell who hit his second century against the touring team. The latter half of the innings was given life by a remarkable maiden century by McCarthy, a fast bowler. He and Chappell added 171 in two hours, eleven minutes for the eighth wicket – a South Australian record – and he batted only two hours, thirty-nine minutes for 127. The West Indies batsmen then got into bad trouble against some clever leg spin bowling by Jenner and again they were not prepared to fight for runs and South Australia won with a day to spare.

West Indies

R. C. Fredericks c Freeman b Jenner	46	– lbw b Freeman	12
M. C. Carew c Cunningham b Freeman	18	– c G. S. Chappell b Jenner	47
R. B. Kanhai c I. M. Chappell b Jenner	14	– c I. M. Chappell b Jenner	39
S. M. Nurse c and b Mallett	69	– lbw b McCarthy	31
C. H. Lloyd c McCarthy b Mallett	28	– c Jarman b Jenner	19
*G. S. Sobers run out	14	– b Jenner	6
C. A. Davis run out	0	– b Mallett	38
L. A. King b Freeman	2	– c Jenner b Mallett	14
†J. L. Hendriks lbw b Freeman	0	– c I. M. Chappell b Jenner	3
C. C. Griffith c Jarman b Freeman	5	– not out	10
L. R. Gibbs not out	0	– c Freeman b Mallett	3
B 2, n-b 8	10	B 6, l-b 1	7
1/45 2/80 3/95 4/166 5/186 6/187 7/189 8/190 9/202	206	1/18 2/86 3/129 4/144 5/164 6/172 7/191 8/197 9/225	229

Bowling: *First Innings*—Freeman 16.5–0–78–4; McCarthy 7–0–25–0; Cunningham 9–2–24–0; Mallett 8–2–30–2; Jenner 10–0–39–2. *Second Innings*—Freeman 13–2–39–1; McCarthy 6–0–28–1; Mallett 25.1–8–80–3; Jenner 28–2–75–5.

South Australia

P. Galloway run out	36 – not out	7
J. Causby run out	63 – not out	40
I. M. Chappell c Lloyd b Davis	123	
*L. E. Favell st Hendriks b Sobers	0	
G. S. Chappell c Griffith b Sobers	3	
K. G. Cunningham c Carew b Sobers	4	
†B. N. Jarman st Hendriks b Sobers	1	
E. W. Freeman c Lloyd b Sobers	4	
K. McCarthy c Nurse b Gibbs	127	
T. Jenner c Sobers b Davis	10	
A. A. Mallett not out	8	
B 11	11	
1/74 2/132 3/134 4/146 5/152 6/156 7/166 8/337 9/368	390	(No wkt) 47

Bowling: *First Innings*—Griffith 6–0–56–0; Sobers 26–2–107–5; King 14–2–59–0; Gibbs 27.1–4–87–1; Carew 5–1–17–0; Davis 7–0–53–2. *Second Innings*—Griffith 2–0–11–0; King 4–0–21–0; Davis 4–1–3–0; Nurse 1.4–0–12–0.

Umpires: C. J. Egar and M. G. O'Connell.

COMBINED XI v WEST INDIES

Played at Launceston, January 16, 17, 18, 1969

West Indies won by ten wickets. The Tasmanian side had been strengthened by the inclusion of Davies and Taber from New South Wales, but the match belonged to Sobers who played an unforgettable innings on the first day, hitting 121 not out in ninety-nine minutes including one six and twenty-two 4s. Butcher and Lloyd also batted well for the West Indies. The bowling of Griffith, Edwards and Sobers, who was trying out his injured right shoulder, proved too much for the Combined XI although the West Indies were held up in the second innings by another splendid innings by Hampshire, who received useful support from Davies. In four innings against the West Indians in Tasmania, Hampshire scored 268 for twice out.

West Indies

G. S. Camacho c and b Hodgetts	45 – not out	7
R. C. Fredericks c Hampshire b Hodgetts	18 – not out	14
S. M. Nurse c Taber b Hodgetts	0	
B. F. Butcher c Burrows b Davies	57	
C. H. Lloyd b Hodgetts	73	
*G. S. Sobers not out	121	
D. A. J. Holford not out	29	
L-b 3, n-b 5	8	
1/48 2/53 3/86 4/153 5/236	(5 wkts dec.) 351	(No wkt) 21

†T. M. Findlay, C. C. Griffith, R. M. Edwards and L. R. Gibbs did not bat.

Bowling: *First Innings*—Hawke 15–3–63–0; Allen 10–1–52–0; Hodgetts 19–1–92–4; Badcock 11–0–81–0; Davies 4–0–31–1; Sharman 3–0–24–0. *Second Innings*—Hampshire 3.6–0–17–0; Farrell 3–2–4–0.

Combined XI

K. Brown c Camacho b Edwards	9	– c Findlay b Griffith	12
B. Sharman c Butcher b Griffith	6	– c Sobers b Edwards	4
I. Burrows b Edwards	2	– c Nurse b Lloyd	2
†H. B. Taber c Nurse b Griffith	4	– c Sobers b Butcher	3
G. R. Davies c Camacho b Edwards	2	– c Holford b Gibbs	41
*J. H. Hampshire c Fredericks b Edwards	29	– b Butcher	92
G. Farrell b Sobers	22	– c Sobers b Gibbs	21
K. Badcock c Findlay b Sobers	17	– b Butcher	26
N. J. N. Hawke c Nurse b Holford	28	– not out	2
H. Allen b Sobers	31	– lbw b Butcher	0
B. Hodgetts not out	0	– st Findlay b Holford	0
N-b 2	2	B 9, l-b 1, n-b 3	13
1/16 2/16 3/23 4/25 5/28 6/64 7/93 8/94 9/150	152	1/14 2/20 3/20 4/98 5/132 6/204 7/213 8/215 9/215	216

Bowling: *First Innings*—Griffith 7–2–38–2; Edwards 9–4–13–4; Sobers 14–1–67–3; Holford 8–2–32–1. *Second Innings*—Griffith 5–1–22–1; Edwards 6–1–20–1; Lloyd 12–1–52–1; Gibbs 11–1–35–2; Butcher 12–1–58–4; Holford 6.4–1–16–1.

Umpires: J. Roberts and J. Guy.

AUSTRALIA v WEST INDIES

Fourth Test Match

Played at Adelaide, January 24, 25, 27, 28, 29, 1969

Drawn. For two and a half days this Test followed the identical course of the previous two before erupting to the most dramatically exciting finish. After winning the toss on a very easy paced pitch the West Indies batsmen threw their wickets away one after the other with a series of careless strokes. Even a magnificent innings by Sobers, who made 110 in two hours, twelve minutes with two 6s and fourteen 4s could not take them past 300. Sobers batted almost disdainfully and did as he wanted with the Australian attack, but this innings would have been more valuable to his side if he had come in at, say, the fall of the second wicket. For this match the West Indies had brought in Griffith and Holford for Edwards and Hall; Australia kept to their winning side.

On the second and third days Australia almost inevitably built up a huge total. Stackpole, Lawry, Chappell and Sheahan all made attractive fifties while Walters reached an efficient 110 and Australia were 257 ahead. It was now that the West Indies batsmen collectively seemed to find the determination which had been so badly lacking since Brisbane. Kanhai, Carew, who succeeded in hitting Gleeson (one for 176) out of the attack in a super innings of 90, Nurse, whose 40 was about the best innings of the match, Sobers, Lloyd and Butcher (118) all played well. But even now careless strokes cost most of them their wickets when they were well set and twenty-five minutes before tea on the fourth day the West Indies at 492 for eight were only 235 ahead with nearly a day and a half remaining.

Hendriks now joined Holford and in a ninth-wicket stand of 122 in two hours, twenty minutes they took the West Indies past 600 and almost certainly to safety. Australia's target on the last day was 360 in five and three-quarter hours. They were given such a splendid start by Lawry, Stackpole, Chappell and Walters that when the last hour began, in which 15 overs had to be bowled, Australia were 298 for three needing 62 from 120 balls. Then Chappell was lbw to Griffith and in the next fifteen minutes, Walters, Freeman and Jarman were run out by a mixture of good fielding and bad calling by Sheahan, who had a hand in all three. McKenzie then swept Gibbs to square leg and Gleeson was lbw to Griffith leaving Sheahan and Connolly, the last pair, to face 26 balls. Sobers took the new ball against Connolly, but swung it wildly down the leg side while Sheahan played two maidens from Gibbs with Australia 21 short of victory.

West Indies

R. C. Fredericks lbw b Connolly	17	– c Chappell b Connolly	23
M. C. Carew c Chappell b Gleeson	36	– c Chappell b Connolly	90
R. B. Kanhai lbw b Connolly	11	– b Connolly	80
B. F. Butcher c Chappell b Gleeson	52	– c Sheahan b McKenzie	118
S. M. Nurse c and b McKenzie	5	– lbw b Gleeson	40
*G. S. Sobers b Freeman	110	– c Walters b Connolly	52
C. H. Lloyd c Lawry b Gleeson	10	– c Redpath b Connolly	42
D. A. J. Holford c McKenzie b Freeman	6	– c Stackpole b McKenzie	80
C. C. Griffith b Freeman	7	– run out	24
†J. L. Hendriks not out	10	– not out	37
L. R. Gibbs c Connolly b Freeman	4	– b McKenzie	1
B 5, l-b 2, n-b 1	8	B 5, l-b 12, n-b 12	29
1/21 2/39 3/89 4/107 5/199 6/215 7/228 8/261 9/264	276	1/35 2/167 3/240 4/304 5/376 6/404 7/476 8/492 9/614	616

Bowling: *First Innings*—McKenzie 14–1–51–1; Connolly 13–3–61–2; Freeman 10.3–0–52–4; Gleeson 25–5–91–3; Stackpole 3–1–13–0. *Second Innings*—McKenzie 22.2–4–90–3; Connolly 34–7–122–5; Freeman 18–3–96–0; Gleeson 35–2–176–1; Stackpole 12–3–44–0; Chappell 14–0–50–0; Walters 1–0–6–0; Redpath 1–0–3–0.

Australia

*W. M. Lawry c Butcher b Sobers	62	– c sub b Sobers	89
K. R. Stackpole c Hendriks b Holford	62	– c Hendriks b Gibbs	50
I. M. Chappell c Sobers b Gibbs	76	– lbw b Griffith	96
I. R. Redpath lbw b Carew	45	– run out	9
K. D. Walters c and b Griffith	110	– run out	50
A. P. Sheahan b Gibbs	51	– not out	11
E. W. Freeman lbw b Griffith	33	– run out	1
†B. N. Jarman c Hendriks b Gibbs	3	– run out	4
G. D. McKenzie c Nurse b Holford	59	– c sub b Gibbs	4
J. W. Gleeson b Gibbs	17	– lbw b Griffith	0
A. A. Connolly not out	1	– not out	6
B 4, l-b 5, n-b 5	14	B 8, l-b 10, n-b 1	19
1/98 2/170 3/248 4/254 5/347 6/424 7/429 8/465 9/529	533	1/86 2/185 3/215 4/304 5/315 6/318 7/322 8/333 9/333	(9 wkts) 339

Bowling: *First Innings*—Sobers 28–4–106–1; Griffith 22–4–94–2; Holford 18.5–0–118–2; Gibbs 43–8–145–4; Carew 9–3–30–1; Lloyd 6–0–26–0. *Second Innings*—Griffith 19–2–73–2; Sobers 22–1–107–1; Gibbs 26–7–79–2; Holford 15–1–53–0; Carew 2–0–8–0.

Umpires: C. J. Egar and L. Rowan.

AUSTRALIA v WEST INDIES

Fifth Test Match

Played at Sydney, February 14, 15, 16, 18, 19, 20, 1969

Australia won by 382 runs. As the series had not been decided, the final Test was played over six days and it contained all the lessons of the last three matches. Australia again outclassed the West Indies, who revealed their familiar failings in all departments and particularly in the fielding. Griffith came into the West Indies side for Holford and for the last time in a Test Match partnered Hall. Sobers put Australia in and almost achieved the crucial breakthrough himself. After Stackpole had played Hall into his stumps Sobers dismissed Chappell and Redpath in the same over and Australia were 51 for three. The West Indies' chance of pressing home this advantage went when Lawry (44) drove at Sobers and was badly dropped by Nurse at second slip.

Lawry and Walters then retrieved the situation for Australia. The West Indies had one more chance of breaking the stand but Hendriks dropped a simple chance from Walters off Hall when he was 75. In all they added 336 in six and three-quarter hours, the second highest stand for Australia against the West Indies for any wicket. Lawry batted eight hours, twenty minutes hitting twelve 4s in his 151 while Walters' 242, his highest in Test cricket, took eight hours with twenty-four 4s. Freeman, Taber and Gleeson took Australia past 600.

With their chance of victory irrevocably gone the West Indies once again carelessly threw away their wickets, although they were given a fine start by Carew and Fredericks, who put on 100 in an hour and three-quarters. Then only Lloyd and Kanhai showed any fight and the West Indies finished 340 behind. But Lawry, mindful of their recovery at Adelaide, did not enforce the follow-on. Walters made another hundred, the first batsman to make a double century and a century in the same Test, and Redpath batted attractively for his first hundred in Test cricket. Eventually Lawry's declaration left the West Indies to score 735 in ten hours and although Sobers and Nurse both made defiant centuries, Australia won after only forty-three minutes play on the sixth morning.

Australia

*W. M. Lawry b Griffith	151	– c Fredericks b Griffith	17
K. R. Stackpole b Hall	20	– c Carew b Hall	6
I. M. Chappell lbw b Sobers	1	– c Hendriks b Hall	10
I. R. Redpath c Nurse b Sobers	0	– c Sobers b Gibbs	132
K. D. Walters b Gibbs	242	– c Fredericks b Gibbs	103
A. P. Sheahan c Fredericks b Griffith	27	– c Hendriks b Sobers	34
E. W. Freeman c Hendriks b Griffith	56	– c Carew b Sobers	15
G. D. McKenzie b Gibbs	19	– c Carew b Sobers	40
†H. B. Taber lbw b Hall	48	– not out	15
J. W. Gleeson c Hendriks b Hall	45	– not out	5
A. N. Connolly not out	1		
L-b 2, w 1, n-b 6	9	B 4, l-b 6, w 1, n-b 6	17
1/43 2/51 3/51 4/387 5/435 6/453 7/483 8/543 9/614	619	1/21 2/36 3/40 4/249 5/301 6/329 7/329 8/388 (8 wkts dec.)	394

Bowling: *First Innings*—Hall 35.7–3–157–3; Griffith 37–1–175–3; Sobers 28–4–94–2; Gibbs 40–8–133–2; Carew 10–2–44–0; Lloyd 2–1–7–0. *Second Innings*—Hall 12–0–47–2; Griffith 14–0–41–1; Gibbs 33–2–133–2; Sobers 26–3–117–3; Carew 5–0–26–0; Lloyd 2–0–13–0.

West Indies

R. C. Fredericks c Taber b Connolly	39	– c Taber b McKenzie	0
M. C. Carew b Taber b Freeman	64	– b Connolly	3
R. B. Kanhai c Taber b Connolly	44	– c Connolly b McKenzie	18
*G. S. Sobers c Taber b Connolly	13	– c Redpath b Gleeson	113
B. F. Butcher c Sheahan b McKenzie	10	– c Gleeson b Stackpole	31
C. H. Lloyd b McKenzie	53	– c Freeman b Stackpole	11
S. M. Nurse c Stackpole b Connolly	9	– b Gleeson	137
†J. L. Hendriks c Taber b McKenzie	1	– c Stackpole b McKenzie	16
C. C. Griffith c Freeman b Gleeson	27	– b Gleeson	15
W. W. Hall b Gleeson	1	– c Sheahan b Chappell	0
L. R. Gibbs not out	4	– not out	0
B 2, l-b 4, n-b 8	14	B 1, l-b 5, n-b 2	8
1/100 2/154 3/159 4/179 5/179 6/190 7/193 8/257 9/259	279	1/0 2/10 3/30 4/76 5/102 6/220 7/284 8/351 9/352	352

Bowling: *First Innings*—McKenzie 22.6–2–90–3; Connolly 17–2–61–4; Freeman 12–2–48–1; Gleeson 19–8–53–2; Chappell 6–1–13–0. *Second Innings*—McKenzie 16–1–93–3; Connolly 18–4–72–1; Stackpole 7–0–57–2; Gleeson 15.2–1–84–3; Freeman 2–0–16–0; Chappell 6–0–22–1.

Umpires: C. J. Egar and L. Rowan.

VICTORIA v PAKISTAN

Played at Melbourne, November 24, 25, 26, 27, 1972

Victoria won by six wickets. The Pakistanis had a further setback when Sheahan, used experimentally as an opening batsman with the Tests in mind, and Stackpole had one of the finest stands seen in Australian first class cricket for many seasons. They had a Victorian first wicket record of 270 runs against a touring team to inspire victory with three overs remaining in the match. Intikhab Alam's reasoning of setting Victoria 335 runs in 280 minutes seemed logical enough with the pitch playing low, if slowly, but Sheahan's splendid footwork, second to none among Australia's leading batsmen, and demoralising placements between the far-stretched fieldsmen earned him 143 not out in 277 minutes and the aggressive Stackpole hit a punishing 136. The tourists had some early problems against the big medium-pacer Walker, later to play a significant part in the Tests, playing to their cost at the away swinger just outside the off stump. Zaheer Abbas carried on his fine batting from Perth with 62. Asif Masood and Saleem Altaf quickly made inroads into the Victorian team to have them 3-17 before Redpath (87) and Sheahan (80) gave the innings some respectability. Majid hit his first century of the tour, sometimes brilliant, sometimes illogically dour, and the promise of things to come was evident from the left-handed opener Sadiq Mohammad in his 75.

Pakistan

Sadiq Mohammad c Walker b Duncan	11	– lbw b Walker	75
Talat Ali c Robinson b Rowan	10	– c Stackpole b Walker	17
Zaheer Abbas b Sieler	62	– b Walker	17
Majid J. Khan c Robinson b Walker	17	– not out	125
Mushtaq Mohammad c Robinson b Walker	2	– lbw b Duncan	18
Saeed Ahmed run out	5	– c Sieler b Higgs	31
Asif Iqbal c Robinson b Walker	14	– not out	25
*Intikhab Alam c Rose b Higgs	34		
Saleem Altaf not out	35		
†Masood Iqbal st Robinson b Higgs	21		
Asif Masood c Duncan b Walker	24		
B 2, l-b 3	5	L-b 1	1
1/17 2/23 3/52 4/54 5/62 6/103 7/150 8/162 9/202	240	1/38 2/69 3/152 4/205 5/254	(5 wkts dec.) 309

Bowling: *First Innings*—Rowan 13–2–51–1; Duncan 12–2–39–1; Walker 13.5–4–34–4; Higgs 14–1–76–2; Sieler 8–1–18–1; Stackpole 4–1–17–0. *Second Innings*—Rowan 10–0–52–0; Duncan 21–1–77–1; Walker 10–1–62–3; Higgs 15–1–71–1; Sieler 6–0–33–0; Stackpole 5–0–13–0.

Victoria

*K. R. Stackpole c Zaheer b Asif Masood	0	– b Intikhab	136
A. J. Sieler lbw b Saleem	0	– not out	9
A. P. Sheahan c Saeed b Asif Masood	80	– not out	143
J. W. Scholes c Masood Iqbal b Asif Masood	3	– c Majid Khan b Intikhab	3
I. R. Redpath c Mushtaq b Intikhab	87	– c and b Intikhab	15
R. Rose lbw b Intikhab	0		
†R. Robinson b Asif Masood	27	– run out	7
M. H. N. Walker lbw b Asif Masood	0		
R. Rowan c Asif Masood b Mushtaq	11		
J. R. F. Duncan not out	0		
B 2, n-b 5	7	B 5, l-b 9, n-b 8	22
1/0 2/0 3/17 4/134 5/135 6/188 7/188 8/215	(9 wkts dec.) 215	1/270 2/304 3/314 4/319	(4 wkts) 335

J. Higgs did not bat.

Bowling: *First Innings*—Asif Masood 16–4–54–5; Saleem 7–1–35–1; Asif Iqbal 5–1–10–0; Intikhab 20.1–3–72–2; Saeed 7–1–26–0; Mushtaq 6–1–11–1. *Second Innings*—Asif Masood 17–0–100–0; Saleem 13–1–54–0; Asif Iqbal 3–0–22–0; Intikhab 15–0–102–3; Saeed 2–0–15–0; Mushtaq 2–0–20–0.

Umpires: J. R. Collins and R. Figgis.

AUSTRALIA v PAKISTAN

Second Test Match

Played at Melbourne, December 29, 30, January 1, 2, 3, 1973

Australia won by 92 runs. Pakistan's lack of Test experience cost them victory after they had battled their way into a most favourable position. On a wicket heavily sedated in favour of batsmen, Pakistan needed 293 runs in five and a half hours only to collapse for 200 runs in their second innings. The run outs of Zaheer Abbas, Mushtaq Mohammad and Sarfraz Nawaz on the last day were an indication of the nervous tension the Pakistanis suffered. For a long while the game seemed destined for a draw as first Australia and then Pakistan punished the bowling.

Redpath, again opening for the injured Stackpole, made a careful 135 which assured him of his position in the team for the West Indies and G. S. Chappell a subdued 116 not out, but again Marsh struck out lustily for 74. Australia used two pace bowlers new to Test cricket, Walker, the tall Melbourne medium-paced swing bowler, and Thomson, the vigorous Sydney fast bowler, the latter appearing after only five first-class games, for Massie and Edwards.

The left-handed Sadiq Mohammad continued to grow in stature, hitting his first Test century on the ground where his brother Hanif made 104 and 93 in the drawn Test eight years previously. Zaheer Abbas made an outstanding half-century, hooking Lillee with imperiousness before being run out and the gifted Majid Khan hit the first century of his wayward Test career without Zaheer's gloss. Mushtaq Mohammad and Intikhab Alam meted out punishment until Lillee delivered bouncers at the tail-enders, compelling Intikhab to close the innings 133 runs ahead.

Centuries by Sheahan, apparently entrenched as the opener Australia had sought for several seasons, and Benaud, his first in only his second Test, carried Australia's innings past 400 again and G. S. Chappell displayed rare grace for his 62. Benaud, brother of former Test captain R. Benaud, made his 142 the day after the Australian selectors had omitted him from the third Test, and Sheahan his 127 after his announcement with Mallett he would not be available to tour the West Indies. Majid and Intikhab again batted well but the run outs and lack of application by some of the Pakistani batsmen gave Australia victory with an hour to spare.

Australia

I. R. Redpath c Saeed b Intikhab	135	– c Wasim b Saleem	6
A. P. Sheahan run out	23	– c Sarfraz b Asif Masood	127
*I. M. Chappell c Wasim b Sarfraz	66	– st Wasim b Majid	9
G. S. Chappell not out	116	– run out	62
J. Benaud c Sarfraz b Intikhab	13	– c Wasim b Saleem	142
†R. W. Marsh c Wasim b Sarfraz	74	– c Asif Iqbal b Asif Masood	3
K. J. O'Keeffe (did not bat)		– b Sarfraz	24
A. A. Mallett (did not bat)		– c Wasim b Sarfraz	8
M. H. N. Walker (did not bat)		– run out	11
J. R. Thomson (did not bat)		– not out	19
D. K. Lillee (did not bat)		– c Mushtaq b Intikhab	2
B 1, l-b 6, n-b 7	14	L-b 3, n-b 9	12
1/60 2/183 3/273 4/295 5/441	(5 wkts dec.) 441	1/18 2/251 3/288 4/298 5/305 6/375 7/391 8/392 9/418	425

Bowling: *First Innings*—Asif Masood 17–0–97–0; Saleem 9–0–49–0; Sarfraz 22.5–4–100–2; Intikhab 16–0–101–2; Majid Khan 21–2–80–0. *Second Innings*—Asif Masood 12–0–100–2; Saleem 14–0–50–2; Sarfraz 22–2–99–2; Intikhab 15.6–3–70–1; Majid Khan 17–1–61–1; Mushtaq 7–0–33–0.

Pakistan

Sadiq Mohammad lbw b Lillee	137	– c Marsh b Walker	5
Saeed Ahmed c G. S. Chappell b Walker	50	– c Mallett b Lillee	6
Zaheer Abbas run out	51	– run out	25
Majid Khan c Marsh b Walker	158	– c Marsh b Lillee	47
Mushtaq Mohammad c Marsh b O'Keeffe	60	– run out	13
Asif Iqbal c Lillee b Mallett	7	– c Redpath b Walker	37
*Intikhab Alam c Sheahan b Mallett	68	– c I. M. Chappell b Mallett	48
†Wasim Bari b Mallett	7	– b Walker	0
Saleem Altaf not out	13	– b O'Keeffe	10
Sarfraz Nawaz not out	0	– run out	8
Asif Masood (did not bat)		– not out	1
B 12, l-b 7, w 1, n-b 3	23		
1/128 2/323 3/395 4/416 5/429 6/519 7/541 8/572	(8 wkts dec.) 574	1/11 2/15 3/80 4/83 5/128 6/138 7/138 8/161 9/181	200

Bowling: *First Innings*—Lillee 16.6–1–90–1; Thomson 17–1–100–0; Walker 24–1–112–2; Mallett 38–4–124–3; O'Keeffe 23–1–94–1; I. M. Chappell 5–0–21–0; Redpath 1–0–10–0. *Second Innings*—Lillee 11–1–59–2; Thomson 2–0–10–0; Walker 14–3–39–3; Mallett 17.5–3–56–1; O'Keeffe 9–4–10–1; I. M. Chappell 3–0–16–0; G. S. Chappell 1–0–10–0.

Umpires: J. R. Collins and P. R. Enright.

AUSTRALIA v WEST INDIES

Second Test Match

Played at Perth, December 12, 13, 14, 16, 1975

West Indies won by an innings and 87 runs. This was one of the most remarkable Test matches which can ever have been played and was a complete reversal of the First in Brisbane. The West Indies batsmen and their fast bowlers found that the fastest pitch they came across in Australia exactly suited their methods and just as everything had failed in the First Test now everything came off. The two strongest memories of the match will always be Frederick's 169 and Robert's fast bowling, but Ian Chappell's 156 and Lloyd's 149 were scarcely less memorable. This match came as a sharp reminder that when everything is going right for them there is no side on earth which could stop the West Indies.

Walker came into the Australian side for Jenner, the leg spinner, and McCosker opened with Turner, Redpath dropping down to number five. The West Indies omitted Greenidge who had made a "pair" at Brisbane, and Inshan Ali and brought in their two all-rounders, Julien and Boyce, both of whom had been surprisingly short of form.

It looked a good toss for Australia to win, but Roberts soon sent back both openers, Julien and Boyce benefited from the pace and bounce, and Australia lost half their wickets for 189. Meanwhile, Ian Chappell, who had come in during the first over, was batting superbly. He had had just a little luck early on but was soon timing the ball beautifully as he hooked, pulled and drove. He was well supported by Gilmour later on and their stand of 88 came in only sixty-five minutes. Chappell's hundred took four and a half hours and it was one of the best innings that even he can have played, for he held the Australian batting together on his own. The next morning Holding finished off the innings in his second over with the second new ball when with the first, second and seventh balls of the over he bowled Chappell, Thomson and Mallett.

The West Indies had ninety minutes batting before lunch and, remarkably, Julien came out to open with Fredericks. Fredericks began by hooking Lillee's second ball for 6 off the edge although from then on he never made any sort of mistake. Runs came at a bewildering pace as he hooked and drove and cut at Thomson and Lillee. It was thrilling batting and the Australians could only stand and watch. Julien had a lot of luck as he flashed and missed, but when in the tenth over he fended Gilmour into the gully, 91 runs had already been scored. At lunch after only 14 overs the West Indies were an incredible 130 for one. Fredericks went on and on through the afternoon as one astonishing stroke was followed by the next. His hundred came in one hour, fifty-six minutes off 71 balls with one 6 and eighteen 4s and when soon after tea he drove at Lillee and was caught at slip he had made 169 out of 258.

Soon after that Kallicharran, who was batting well, hooked at Lillee and the ball flew off the edge and broke his nose. The Australian fielding had grown careless and before the end of the day Lloyd had been dropped twice and Murray once. The next day these two took their stand to 164 in two and a half hours. Murray's 50 had been exciting, and Lloyd produced his own special display of pyrotechnics which if not quite matching Fredericks' was very impressive. His 149 took three hours, thirty-eight minutes and he hit one 6 and twenty-two 4s. Later, Kallicharran, who continued his innings, and Boyce played some good strokes.

The West Indies had a lead of 256 and when in a wonderful spell of controlled fast bowling Roberts took four wickets before the close, the match was as good as over. Greg Chappell and Marsh continued their resistance for a while the next morning before Roberts dismissed them both and the last six wickets put on only another 65 runs. Roberts finished with seven for 54. It had been a match which had expressed vividly the full joy and exuberance of West Indies cricket and when compared to what went on before and afterwards its inconsistency as well.

Australia

R. B. McCosker lbw b Roberts	0 – c Rowe b Roberts	13
A. Turner c Gibbs b Roberts	23 – c Murray b Roberts	0
I. M. Chappell b Holding	156 – c sub b Roberts	20
*G. S. Chappell c Murray b Julien	13 – c Rowe b Roberts	43
I. R. Redpath c Murray b Julien	33 – lbw b Roberts	0
†R. W. Marsh c Julien b Boyce	23 – c Murray b Roberts	39
G. J. Gilmour c Julien b Gibbs	45 – c Fredericks b Roberts	3
M. H. N. Walker c Richards b Holding	1 – c sub b Julien	3
D. K. Lillee not out	12 – c Lloyd b Julien	4
J. R. Thomson b Holding	0 – b Julien	9
A. A. Mallett b Holding	0 – not out	18
B 12, l-b 5, n-b 6	23 B 13, l-b 2, n-b 2	17
1/0 2/37 3/70 4/149 5/189 6/277 7/285 8/329 9/329	329 1/0 2/25 3/45 4/45 5/124 6/128 7/132 8/142 9/146	169

Bowling: *First Innings*—Roberts 13–1–65–2; Boyce 12–2–53–1; Holding 18.7–1–88–4; Julien 12–0–51–2; Gibbs 14–4–49–1. *Second Innings*—Roberts 14–3–54–7; Holding 10.6–1–53–0; Julien 10.1–1–32–3; Boyce 2–0–8–0; Gibbs 3–1–3–0; Fredericks 1–0–2–0.

West Indies

R. C. Fredericks c G. S. Chappell b Lillee	169
B. D. Julien c Mallett b Gilmour	25
L. G. Rowe c Marsh b Thomson	19
A. I. Kallicharran c I. M. Chappell b Walker	57
I. V. A. Richards c Gilmour b Thomson	12
*C. H. Lloyd b Gilmour	149
†D. L. Murray c Marsh b Lillee	63
M. A. Holding c Marsh b Thomson	0
K. D. Boyce not out	49
A. M. E. Roberts b Walker	0
L. R. Gibbs run out	13
B 2, l-b 16, n-b 11	29
1/91 2/134 3/258 4/297 5/461 6/461 7/522 8/548 9/548	585

Bowling: Lillee 20–0–123–2; Thomson 17–0–128–3; Gilmour 14–0–103–2; Walker 17–1–99–2; Mallett 26–4–103–0; I. M. Chappell 1.4–1–0–0.

Umpires: R. R. Ledwidge and M. G. O'Connell.

TASMANIA v WEST INDIES

Played at Hobart, January 16, 17, 18, 1976

Drawn. The West Indies were still very downhearted at losing the Fourth Test and overall there was a distinct lack of effort by their players in this game. Richards was the exception and the experiment which had begun in the two-day match in Canberra of putting him in first, was continued. He batted quite magnificently, scoring a hundred in each innings. Greenidge, on one of the rare occasions he batted well in Australia, and Kallicharran also showed some beautiful strokes while Tasmania, captained by Simmons of Lancashire and with his county colleague Hughes in the side, twice batted steadily against some amiable bowling.

West Indies

L. Baichan c Doolan b Simmons	30	
I. V. A. Richards c Simmons b Leedham	160	– not out 107
R. C. Fredericks c Sellers b Simmons	17	– c Norman b Whitney 4
A. I. Kallicharran c Badcock b Simmons	0	– not out 74
C. G. Greenidge c Norman b Hughes	76	– c Leedham b Whitney 0
†D. A. Murray not out	23	
L-b 1	1	B 4, l-b 4, n-b 1 9
1/124 2/182 3/188 4/216 5/307	(5 wkts dec.) 307	1/4 2/4 (2 wkts dec.) 194

K. D. Boyce, V. A. Holder, A. M. E. Roberts, Inshan Ali and *L. R. Gibbs did not bat.

Bowling: *First Innings*—Whitney 12–2–48–0; Leedham 12–1–67–1; Badcock 10–0–55–0; Hughes 13–1–74–1; Simmons 15–3–62–3. *Second Innings*—Whitney 10–1–60–2; Leedham 7–1–47–0; Badcock 3–0–42–0; Hughes 3–1–13–0; Simmons 1.5–0–23–0.

Tasmania

†B. R. Doolan c Greenidge b Holder	5	– c Murray b Holder 82
C. F. A. Brown c Murray b Roberts	13	– c Greenidge b Boyce 7
M. J. Sellers run out	27	– c Richards b Roberts 14
S. J. Howard c Inshan b Holder	1	– c Richards b Inshan 17
M. J. Norman b Inshan	65	– st Murray b Inshan 11
R. J. Panitzki c Baichan b Gibbs	56	– not out 43
D. P. Hughes b Inshan	28	– b Inshan 7
K. B. Badcock not out	5	– not out 31
*J. Simmons b Roberts	1	
M. J. Leedham c Murray b Roberts	1	
G. R. Whitney b Roberts	0	
B 6, l-b 3, n-b 8	17	B 3, l-b 3, n-b 6 12
1/15 2/53 3/57 4/61 5/69 6/207 7/214 8/215 9/219	219	1/13 2/47 3/110 4/136 5/150 6/162 (6 wkts) 224

Bowling: *First Innings*—Roberts 8.6–3–24–4; Boyce 9–3–28–0; Holder 12–3–26–2; Inshan 20–4–81–2; Gibbs 15–3–43–1. *Second Innings*—Roberts 6–1–26–1; Boyce 7–1–28–1; Holder 9–0–44–1; Inshan 19–6–55–3; Gibbs 11–2–28–0; Kallicharran 3–0–30–0; Richards 1–0–1–0.

Umpires: K. C. Connor and L. W. Cox.

AUSTRALIA v INDIA

Second Test Match

Played at Perth, December 16, 17, 18, 20, 21, 1977

Australia won by two wickets. The pulsating finish, arrived at with 22 balls remaining, was a fitting climax to a match in which fortunes fluctuated with almost every session. Both sides approached the match with commendable enterprise and, in view of the fact that 1,468 runs were scored, the achievement of a decisive finish was remarkable.

The Australian victory was largely owed to their veteran captain, Bobby Simpson. Coming in at 65 for three in the first innings, and that only after a brief rest following a long stint in the field, Simpson rallied Australia with a dogged 176, lasting six hours forty-one minutes. Dyson, playing in his first Test, and Rixon were the only others to pass

50. Still, Australia came within near reach of India's total of 402, their highest in 27 Tests against Australia.

Considering their sound foundations, both Indian innings should have realised bigger totals. In the first, Gavaskar was again an early victim to Clark, but Chauhan and Mohinder Amarnath put on 149 for the second wicket. Another 61 were added for the third, by Amarnath and Viswanath, and at one stage India were 224 for three. India's progress was temporarily halted by a fierce spell from Thomson, during which he took three wickets in rapid succession, but they revived through a stand of 76 between Vengsarkar and Kirmani.

The second new ball again swung the balance Australia's way before India were rallied once more by the eighth-wicket pair, Madan Lal and Venkataraghavan. Trying to exploit Madan Lal's notorious weakness against the lifting ball, the Australian bowlers overworked the short ball. Madan Lal kept stepping back from his left stump and hitting them through the covers or swinging them through mid-wicket. Although crude and undignified, his method paid dividends that day.

In the second innings, India held a commanding position, with Gavaskar (127) and Mohinder Amarnath (100) staging a record second-wicket partnership of 193. After Amarnath was fourth out at 283, five more wickets went down in seventy-five minutes for only 47 runs. Although the clock was far from being on his side, Bedi declared because he did not want to risk injury to himself or Chandrasekhar.

Australia, therefore, were left six hours and forty minutes to score 339 runs for victory. The one wicket India captured before the close on the penultimate day proved a mixed blessing, for Tony Mann, who came in as night-watchman, stayed on next day to play a match-winning innings of 105 in just over three hours. The Indians suffered from their chronic weakness of being unable to bowl steadily to a left-hander. Thanks to Mann and Ogilvie, who was slow but hard to dislodge, Australia, at 195 for four, were well-placed to aim for victory. When Simpson and Toohey became so firmly entrenched, they looked to be heading for a very easy win. Only 58 runs were wanted at the start of the mandatory fifteen overs of the last hour.

However, in the second of these overs, with the margin now cut down to 44, a brilliant piece of fielding by Madan Lal, the bowler, ran out Simpson. In the same over, he produced a beautiful ball which nipped back and trapped Hughes lbw. Then, with only 9 runs wanted and almost six overs left, Toohey, who had batted with discipline and in a most accomplished manner to make 83, had a rush of blood and played a fatal, lofted drive off Bedi. There was a suggestion of panic as Rixon, in the same over, played across the line and fell lbw to Bedi, but Australia had come too near winning to be foiled.

Bedi took five wickets in each innings, and although he had previously performed the feat twelve times, this was the first instance of his capturing ten wickets in a Test match.

India

S. M. Gavaskar c Rixon b Clark	4	– b Clark	127
C. P. S. Chauhan c Gannon b Simpson	88	– c Ogilvie b Thomson	32
M. Amarnath c Gannon b Thomson	90	– c Rixon b Simpson	100
G. R. Viswanath b Thomson	38	– c Rixon b Clark	1
D. B. Vengsarkar c Rixon b Clark	49	– c Hughes b Gannon	9
B. P. Patel c Rixon b Thomson	3	– b Gannon	27
†S. M. H. Kirmani c Rixon b Thomson	38	– lbw b Gannon	2
S. Venkataraghavan c Simpson b Gannon	37	– c Hughes b Gannon	14
S. Madan Lal b Gannon	43	– b Thomson	3
*B. S. Bedi b Gannon	3	– not out	0
B. S. Chandrasekhar not out	0	– not out	0
B 1, n-b 8	9	B 1, l-b 4, n-b 10	15
1/14 2/163 3/224 4/229 5/235 6/311 7/319 8/383 9/391	402	1/47 2/240 3/244 4/283 5/287 6/289 7/327 8/328 9/330 (9 wkts dec.)	330

Bowling: *First Innings*—Thomson 24–1–101–4; Clark 17–0–95–2; Gannon 16.6–1–84–3; Mann 11–0–63–0; Simpson 11–0–50–1. *Second Innings*—Thomson 21.5–3–65–2; Gannon 18–2–77–4; Clark 18–1–83–2; Mann 8–0–49–0; Simpson 8–2–41–1.

Australia

J. Dyson c Patel b Bedi	53	– c Vengsarkar b Bedi	4
C. S. Serjeant c Kirmani b Mada Lal	13	– c Kirmani b Madan Lal	12
A. D. Ogilvie b Bedi	27	– b Bedi	47
P. M. Toohey st Kirmani b Bedi	0	– c Amarnath b Bedi	83
*R. B. Simpson c Vengsarkar b Venkat	176	– run out	39
†S. J. Rixon c Kirmani b Amarnath	50	– lbw b Bedi	23
K. J. Hughes c Patel b Bedi	28	– lbw b Madan Lal	0
A. L. Mann c Vengsarkar b Bedi	7	– c Kirmani b Bedi	105
W. M. Clark c Patel b Chandrasekhar	15	– not out	5
J. R. Thomson c Amarnath b Venkat	0	– not out	6
J. B. Gannon not out	0		
L-b 25	25	B 8, l-b 10	18
1/19 2/61 3/65 4/149 5/250 6/321 7/341 8/388 9/388	394	1/13 2/33 3/172 4/195 5/295 6/296 7/330 8/330	(8 wkts) 342

Bowling: *First Innings*—Madan Lal 15–1–54–1; Amarnath 16–2–57–1; Chandrasekhar 33.6–2–114–1; Bedi 31–6–89–5; Venkataraghavan 23–4–55–2. *Second Innings*—Madan Lal 11–0–44–2; Amarnath 3–0–22–0; Bedi 30.2–6–105–5; Chandrasekhar 15–0–67–0; Venkataraghavan 28–9–86–0.

Umpires: R. C. Bailhache and R. French.

AUSTRALIA v INDIA

Third Test Match

Played at Melbourne, December 30, 31, January 2, 3, 4, 1978

India won by 222 runs – their first win in twelve Tests on Australian soil. This achievement was due, in the main, to Chandrasekhar reaching peak form in this match. He claimed twelve wickets for 104 runs, the best match figures of his fourteen-year Test career. The capture of the first of these wickets made him only the second Indian to take 200 Test wickets. To an extent, India were lucky that a hamstring injury put Thomson out of battle for a day – the day they began their second innings with a lead of 43 runs.

True to its history, the pitch offered the bowlers lift and pace on the first morning and India lost two wickets before opening their account. A partnership of 105 between Amarnath, playing with an injured right hand, and Viswanath then stabilized the innings. Considering that this stand represented the highest point of India's prosperity during this innings, Australia caused themselves hardship by dropping Amarnath, at 43. He was missed at long-leg, hooking a bumper from Gannon. The capture of Amarnath's wicket at that stage would have reduced India to 114 for four.

Apart from a third-wicket partnership of 104 between Cosier and Serjeant, following two early blows struck by Ghavri, the Australians batted indifferently and the Indian bowling was flattered by their dismissal for only 213.

Gavaskar's third century of the series was the foundation on which India built an impressive second-innings total of 343. Viswanath made another half-century and Amarnath, whose hand injury had been aggravated and who therefore batted at number seven, again played gallantly for 41.

Australia, left to make 387 on a pitch that was yielding spin and which had become quite uneven in bounce, never looked like meeting the challenge. Chandrasekhar, whose success in the first innings was somewhat aided by the batsmen's indiscretions, this time bowled accurately and with devastating fire to hasten India towards victory.

India

S. M. Gavaskar c Rixon b Thomson	0	– c Serjeant b Gannon	118
C. P. S. Chauhan c Mann b Clark	0	– run out	20
M. Amarnath c Simpson b Clark	72	– b Cosier	41
G. R. Viswanath c Rixon b Thomson	59	– lbw b Clark	54
D. B. Vengsarkar c Simpson b Thomson	37	– c Cosier b Clark	6
A. V. Mankad c Clark b Gannon	44	– b Clark	38
†S. M. H. Kirmani lbw b Simpson	29	– c Thomson b Mann	29
K. Ghavri c Rixon b Gannon	6	– c Simpson b Clark	6
E. A. S. Prasanna b Clark	0	– c Rixon b Gannon	11
*B. S. Bedi not out	2	– not out	12
B. S. Chandrasekhar b Clark	0	– lbw b Cosier	0
L-b 3, n-b 4	7	L-b 1, n-b 7	8
1/0 2/0 3/105 4/174 5/180 6/234 7/254 8/256 9/256	256	1/40 2/89 3/187 4/198 5/265 6/286 7/294 8/315 9/343	343

Bowling: *First Innings*—Thomson 16–2–78–3; Clark 19.2–2–73–4; Gannon 14–2–47–2; Cosier 12–3–25–0; Simpson 3–1–11–1; Mann 5–1–15–0. *Second Innings*—Clark 29–3–96–4; Gannon 22–4–88–2; Cosier 12.7–2–58–2; Thomson 18–4–47–0; Mann 4–0–24–1; Simpson 3–0–22–0.

Australia

J. Dyson b Ghavri	0	– lbw b Bedi	12
G. J. Cosier c Chauhan b Chandrasekhar	67	– b Chandrasekhar	34
A. D. Ogilvie lbw b Ghavri	6	– c Chauhan b Bedi	0
C. S. Serjeant b Chandrasekhar	85	– b Chandrasekhar	17
*R. B. Simpson c Mankad b Chandrasekhar	2	– lbw b Chandrasekhar	4
P. M. Toohey c Viswanath b Bedi	14	– c Chauhan b Chandrasekhar	14
A. L. Mann c Gavaskar b Bedi	11	– c Gavaskar b Chandrasekhar	18
†S. J. Rixon lbw b Chandrasekhar	11	– c and b Chandrasekhar	12
W. M. Clark lbw b Chandrasekhar	3	– c Ghavri b Bedi	33
J. R. Thomson c Ghavri b Chandrasekhar	0	– c and b Bedi	7
J. B. Gannon not out	0	– not out	3
B 6, l-b 7, n-b 1	14	B 6, l-b 4	10
1/0 2/18 3/122 4/124 5/166 6/178 7/202 8/211 9/211	213	1/42 2/42 3/52 4/60 5/77 6/98 7/115 8/122 9/151	164

Bowling: *First Innings*—Ghavri 9–0–37–2; Gavaskar 2–0–7–0; Bedi 15–2–71–2; Chandrasekhar 14.1–2–52–6; Prasanna 10–1–32–0. *Second Innings*—Ghavri 4–0–29–0; Amarnath 3–0–10–0; Prasanna 8–4–5–0; Bedi 16.1–5–58–4; Chandrasekhar 20–3–52–6.

Umpires: M. G. O'Connell and R. French.

AUSTRALIA v INDIA

Fifth Test Match

Played at Adelaide, January 28, 29, 30, February 1, 2, 3, 1978

Australia won by 47 runs. With India putting on a record losing total in the second innings of 445, the deciding Test ended on a highly exciting note – a finale becoming an evenly fought series. The one unfortunate feature of this memorable contest was the strong feeling that crept in, albeit briefly, when, on the third day, the Indians showed displeasure over at least three umpiring decisions. The volatile Bedi expressed his criticism of the umpiring in the most strong terms.

A rare poor performance by India's spinners on the opening day gave Australia an initial advantage which they never relinquished. They would probably have won more decisively had Thomson's bowling not been lost to them after he had delivered only three and a half overs in India's first innings. He left the field at this point with a torn hamstring. Even during his brief assault, he left a deep mark on the match by taking two wickets including that of Gavaskar. India never really recovered from these setbacks.

Australia benefited from every one of the five changes made by the selectors for this Test, although four made for the inclusion of players totally new to international cricket. The presence of three left-handers also served to throw the Indian attack out of gear. Prasanna, the one Indian spinner who might have troubled the left-handers, spent most of the first innings in the pavilion with a back strain.

Australia's new opening pair of Wood and Darling, both left handers, put on 89, the home side's best start of the series. Then Yallop, another left-hander, weighed in with a century. The smartness with which he and Toohey ran between the wickets threw the Indian bowling into further disarray. With Simpson scoring a watchful century as well, Australia continued to build on the fine start and finished with a total of 505, the highest of the series by either side.

When India batted, Thomson bowled as fast and as accurately as he has ever done. Though his participation in the match was limited, it had immense bearing on the result. He removed Gavaskar and Mohinder Amarnath, the main pillars of the Indian batting, while India lost three wickets for 23 runs. There was a worthwhile partnership of 136 between Viswanath and Vengsarkar, but thereafter India never looked like matching Australia's massive total.

With six days allotted to this match, Simpson did not enforce the follow-on when India were bowled out halfway through the third day. The Indian spinners recaptured their form in the second innings, but half-centuries by Darling and Simpson saw Australia to a total of 256, which left India 493 runs to win – or more than fourteen hours to bat out for a draw. Their only comfort was that Thomson was still unfit to bowl.

India seemed doomed to a massive defeat when Gavaskar, who had already had one escape, fell at 40. Chauhan, his opening partner, was also dismissed before the end of the fourth day, at 79. The Australians could have struck one more crushing blow before stumps, but Viswanath was dropped at slip when only two.

Viswanath and Amarnath batted right through the morning of the fifth day, adding 131 before Viswanath fell to the second new ball, at 210. Amarnath carried on to make 86, and with Vengsarkar batting with composure, India continued their struggle in an encouraging manner. Both Amarnath and Vengsarkar fell in making belligerent shots, but with Gaekwad failing again, India were 348 for six at Vengsarkar's dismissal. The seventh-wicket pair, Kirmani and Ghavri, got sufficiently entrenched for the Australians to start worrying. However, the third new ball gave them the decisive breakthrough. Still India fought to the bitter end.

Australia

G. M. Wood st Kirmani b Chandrasekhar	39	– c Vensarkar b Bedi	8
W. M. Darling c Vengsarkar b Chandrasekhar	65	– b Bedi	56
G. N. Yallop c Gavaskar b Amarnath	121	– b Bedi	24
P. M. Toohey c Gavaskar b Chandrasekhar	60	– c Kirmani b Prasanna	10
*R. B. Simpson v Viswanath b Ghavri	100	– lbw b Ghavri	51
G. J. Cosier b Ghavri	1	– st Kirmani b Bedi	34
†S. J. Rixon b Bedi	32	– run out	13
B. Yardley c and b Ghavri	22	– c Vengsarkar b Ghavri	26
J. R. Thomson c Ghavri b Chandrasekhar	24	– c Amarnath b Ghavri	3
W. M. Clark b Chandrasekhar	0	– lbw b Ghavri	1
I. W. Callen not out	22	– not out	4
B 4, l-b 14, n-b 1	19	B 5, l-b 15, w 3, n-b 3	26
1/89 2/110 3/230 4/334 5/337 6/406 7/450 8/457 9/458	505	1/17 2/84 3/95 4/107 5/172 6/210 7/214 8/240 9/248	256

Bowling: *First Innings*—Ghavri 22–2–93–3; Amarnath 12–0–45–1; Bedi 34–1–127–1; Prasanna 10–1–48–0; Chandrasekhar 29.4–0–136–5; Gaekwad 5–0–37–0. *Second Innings*—Ghavri 10.5–2–45–4; Amarnath 4–0–12–0; Prasanna 34–7–68–1; Bedi 20–3–53–4; Chandrasekhar 14–0–52–0.

India

S. M. Gavaskar c Toohey b Thomson	7	– c Rixon b Callen	29
C. P. S. Chauhan c Cosier b Clark	15	– c Wood b Yardley	32
M. Amarnath c Cosier b Thomson	0	– c Callen b Yardley	86
G. R. Viswanath c Rixon b Callen	89	– c Simpson b Clark	73
D. B. Vengsarkar c Rixon b Callen	44	– c Toohey b Yardley	78
A. D. Gaekwad c Rixon b Callen	27	– c and b Yardley	12
†S. M. H. Kirmani run out	48	– b Clark	51
K. Ghavri c Simpson b Clark	3	– c sub b Callen	23
E. A. S. Prasanna not out	15	– not out	10
*B. S. Bedi c sub b Clark	6	– c Cosier b Callen	16
B. S. Chandrasekhar c and b Clark	2	– c Rixon b Simpson	2
B 4, l-b 1, n-b 8	13	B 6, l-b 11, n-b 16	33
1/23 2/23 3/23 4/159 5/166 6/216 7/226 8/249 9/263	269	1/40 2/79 3/210 4/256 5/323 6/348 7/415 8/417 9/442	445

Bowling: *First Innings*—Thomson 3.3–1–12–2; Clark 20.7–6–62–4; Callen 22–0–83–3; Cosier 4–3–4–0; Yardley 23–6–62–0; Simpson 9–0–33–0. *Second Innings*—Callen 33–5–108–3; Clark 29–6–79–2; Yardley 43–6–134–4; Simpson 23.4–6–70–1; Cosier 13–6–21–0.

Umpires: R. French and M. G. O'Connell.

AUSTRALIA v PAKISTAN

First Test Match

Played at Melbourne, March 10, 11, 12, 14, 15, 1979

Pakistan won by 71 runs. At 4.30 p.m. on the fifth and last day, Australia, with seven wickets in hand and only 77 runs needed for victory, appeared to have gained a decisive hold over an entertaining Test of changing fortunes. But then the vastly experienced Sarfraz Nawaz took charge and the match was at an end within an hour – or 65 balls and 5 runs later. Sarfraz's personal contribution of seven wickets for 1 run from 33 deliveries represented one of the greatest bowling feats in the history of Test cricket.

On the opening morning, Yallop took advantage of winning his sixth toss in the seventh Test of the summer and so gave his pace battery the opportunity to use what little early life existed in the wicket. Both openers, Majid and Mohsin, were caught as they attempted to drive – Majid by the wicket-keeper and Mohsin in the slips – and when Zaheer was bowled at 28, Hogg had completed a fiery opening spell of six overs with three wickets for a personal cost of only 9 runs. The recalled Clark then removed Asif Iqbal with a sharp, lifting delivery that carried from glove to Wright and only 40 runs were on the board. The captain, Mushtaq, slowly set about a recovery and he received solid support from Imran and Sarfraz. Although earlier erratic, Hurst later played his part with three wickets when it appeared Australia had let their advantage slip from six wickets for 99 to the eventual Pakistan total of 196.

Australia, 1 run for no wicket at the close and having included an additional batsman, appeared set for a big score. However, next morning, a between-wickets collision between openers Wood and Hilditch forced the former to retire with a sprained wrist and he did not return till the fall of the ninth wicket. Hilditch was quickly removed by Imran, and Yallop was twice dropped as he struggled to 20 in a brief partnership with Border. Both were bowled by Imran. Hughes became the eleventh Australian run out in the season's Test matches when Whatmore did not respond to a call. Nevertheless, the burly new Test batsman applied himself well for nearly three and a half hours to top score with 43 in a poor total that fell 28 runs short of Pakistan's. Hogg displayed his annoyance and livened proceedings by knocking down the stumps with his bat when he was given run out after walking from his crease before the ball was "dead". Although Hogg was recalled by the Pakistan captain, umpire Harvey refused to permit a reversal of the decision.

Pakistan used the third day to consolidate their position with aggressive batting. Mohsin cover-drove and hooked Hogg for boundaries before another fierce drive was brilliantly held by the bowler – his first catch in Test cricket. Majid and Zaheer then played glorious strokes all round the ground as they added 135 for the second wicket, taking particular toll of the new leg-spinner, Sleep. Starting the day with a delightful straight driven boundary off Hogg, Majid altogether hit sixteen 4s in his seventh Test century – 108 in three hours forty minutes. Zaheer's similarly positive approach was followed by Asif once he settled down, and Pakistan were 307 runs ahead when bad light stopped play twenty minutes early.

After rain delayed the resumption on the fourth day for an hour, Pakistan added a further 74 runs before declaring. Whatmore, substituting for Wood as opener, batted solidly for eighty minutes and shared a partnership of 49 with Hilditch who – although dropped at 26 and 59 – batted steadfastly until he became Sarfraz's second victim of the innings. At the close Australia, at 117 for two, needed 265 to win.

Within half an hour on the final morning, Yallop was foolishly run out, changing his call. This brought together Border and Hughes for a new Australia-Pakistan Tests fourth-wicket partnership which eclipsed by 2 runs the 175 of Ian Chappell and Ross Edwards in 1972-73. Combining concentration with tempered aggression, and unruffled by several dropped catches, the pair carried on steadily through the second new ball and until half an hour after tea, when Sarfraz bowled Border off a deflection with a beautiful ball that cut back sharply. Border batted six and a quarter hours and hit seven boundaries in an innings notable for his footwork.

The remainder of the innings is history. The injured Wood jabbed a catch to the wicket-keeper off the first ball. Sleep was yorked, without scoring, and Hughes – attempting to resume the run-getting – lofted a catch to mid-off. Sarfraz then removed the remaining three batsmen without scoring to complete the dismissal of all wickets except Yallop (run out) and finish with nine wickets for 86. His match figures of eleven wickets for 125 comfortably won him the Man of the Match award. The aggregate match attendance was 37, 495.

Pakistan

Majid J. Khan c Wright b Hogg	1	– b Border	108
Mohsin Kahn c Hilditch b Hogg	14	– c and b Hogg	14
Zaheer Abbas b Hogg	11	– b Hogg	59
Javed Miandad b Hogg	19	– c Wright b Border	16
Asif Iqbal c Wright b Clark	9	– lbw b Hogg	44
*Mushtaq Mohammad c Wright b Hurst	36	– c sub b Sleep	28
Wasim Raja b Hurst	13	– c Wright b Hurst	28
Imran Khan c Wright b Hurst	33	– c Clark b Hurst	28
Sarfraz Nawaz c Wright b Sleep	35	– lbw b Hurst	1
†Wasim Bari run out	0	– not out	8
Sikander Bakht not out	5		
B 2, l-b 7, w 1, n-b 10	20	B 4, l-b 6, n-b 9	19
1/2 2/22 3/28 4/40 5/83 6/99 7/122 8/173 9/177	196	1/30 2/165 3/204 4/209 5/261 6/299 7/330 8/332 9/353 (9 wkts dec.)	353

Bowling: *First Innings*—Hogg 17–4–49–4; Hurst 20–4–55–3; Clark 17–4–56–1; Sleep 7.7–2–16–1. *Second Innings*—Hogg 19–2–75–3; Hurst 19.5–1–115–3; Clark 21–6–47–0; Sleep 8–0–62–1; Border 14–5–35–2.

Australia

G. M. Wood not out	5	– c Bari b Sarfraz 0
A. M. J. Hilditch c Miandad b Imran	3	– b Sarfraz 62
A. R. Border b Imran	20	– Sarfraz 105
*G. N. Yallop b Imran	25	– run out 8
K. J. Hughes run out	19	– c Moshin b Sarfraz 84
D. F. Whatmore lbw b Sarfraz	43	– b Sarfraz 15
P. R. Sleep c Bari b Imran	10	– b Sarfraz 0
†K. J. Wright c Imran b Raja	9	– not out 1
W. M. Clark c Mushtaq b Raja	9	– b Sarfraz 0
R. M. Hogg run out	9	– lbw b Sarfraz 0
A. G. Hurst c and b Sarfraz	0	– c Bari b Sarfraz 0
B 1, l-b 5, w 2, n-b 8	16	B 13, l-b 13, n-b 9 35
1/11 2/53 3/63 4/97 5/109 6/140 7/152 8/167 9/167	168	1/49 2/109 3/128 4/305 5/305 6/306 7/308 8/309 9/310 310

Bowling: *First Innings*—Imran 18–8–26–4; Sarfraz 21.6–6–39–2; Sikander 10–1–29–0; Mushtaq 7–0–35–0; Raja 5–0–23–2. *Second Innings*—Imran 27–9–73–0; Sarfraz 35.4–7–86–9; Sikander 7–0–29–0; Mushtaq 11–0–42–0; Raja 3–0–11–0; Majid 9–1–34–0.

Umpires: R. C. Bailhache and C. E. Harvey.

AUSTRALIA v INDIA

Third Test Match

Played at Melbourne, February 7, 8, 9, 10, 11, 1981

India won by 59 runs. This was a sensational match, not only for Australia's astonishing collapse in the second innings against an Indian attack that was badly handicapped by injuries. India had come near to forfeiting the match on the previous day when their captain, Gavaskar, so sharply disagreed with an lbw decision against himself that he wanted to call off the contest. The incident took place in India's second innings, at the end of an opening partnership of 165 between Gavaskar and Chauhan. When Gavaskar was given out by umpire Whitehead, he first indicated that he had edged the ball on to his pad, and then, as he walked past Chauhan he urged him to leave the field with him. Fortunately the manager of the India team, Wing Commander S. K. Durrani, intervened, meeting the in-coming pair at the gate and ordering Chauhan to continue his innings.

With this controversial dismissal of Gavaskar, Lillee put himself level with Richie Benaud as Australia's highest wicket-taker in Test cricket, and he surpassed Benaud's record of 248 wickets a quarter of an hour later when Chauhan square-cut him to cover point.

The quality of pitches at the MCG had been a matter of criticism all season, with Greg Chappell leading the protest. On this occasion he elected to field, his decision being influenced by the extra grass the groundsman had left in the hope that it would hold the pitch togther. The move was initially rewarding, Lillee and Pascoe seizing India's first six wickets for 115 runs, but the Indians were kept in the fight by Viswanath, who, coming in at 22 for two with the innings only eleven overs old, was ninth out four and a half hours later, having made 114 in his most accomplished manner. Patil supported him in a fourth-wicket stand of 48 in as many minutes, whereafter Kirmani, 25 in 85 minutes, and

Yadav kept him company. Yadav, who resisted for 79 minutes, was struck on a toe by a yorker from Pascoe and sustained a fracture. Despite this, after taking a pain-killing injection he bowled throughout Australia's first innings. His fellow spinner, Doshi, although he did not know it at the time, toiled under a similar handicap, having been struck on the instep in the match against Victoria.

Australia also made a bad start, losing Dyson and Wood for 32 and Hughes at 81 before finding stability from a fourth-wicket partnership of 108 between Chappell and Border. Even on the second day, the pitch had lost most of what pace it had had, Chappell, who made 76, and Border, who was unbeaten that night with 95, having to graft for their runs. Batting until halfway through the third afternoon, Australia totalled 419. Border, staying just over another hour in the morning, made 124 of 265 balls, hitting twelve 4s and putting on 131 for the fifth wicket with Walters, who batted with much care for almost three and a half hours to score 78. Walters was sixth out at 356, but Australia continued to prosper through a fine innings by Marsh, who was partnered for 77 minutes by Lillee.

By the end of the third day, Gavaskar and Chauhan had reduced Australia's lead of 182 by 108, and on the fourth they added another 57 in 85 minutes before Gavaskar's contentious dismissal and dramatic walk-out. The incident disturbed the concentration of Chauhan, who, after batting in an agitated manner for another 8 runs, also succumbed to Lillee. With Vengsarkar, Man of the Match Viswanath and Patil helping towards rebuilding the innings, India at one stage were 296 for six, but the lower order surrendered quickly.

When Australia batted again, with just over an hour left to the end of the fourth day, they needed 143 to win and India were without the bowling of Kapil Dev, who had strained a thigh muscle, and Yadav, whose injury had worsened from his efforts in the first innings. Doshi, too, was in great distress, but soldiered on. Nevertheless, the weakened attack made major inroads before the day was out, with Dyson, Wood and Chappell (out first ball, bowled behind his legs) all back in the dressing-room and only 24 runs on the board.

Kapil Dev, who had batted with a runner and had not appeared on the field on the previous day, joined the fray on the final morning and bowled unchanged to take five of the seven remaining Australian wickets that fell in just over two and a quarter hours. Following Lillee's lead, Kapil Dev bowled straight and to a length and let the pitch do the rest. The ball repeatedly kept low, but the Australians, as Chappell said afterwards, were "lacking in the areas of application and determination".

India

*S. M. Gavaskar c Hughes b Pascoe	10	– lbw b Lillee	70
C. P. S. Chauhan c Yardley b Pascoe	0	– c Yardley b Lillee	85
D. B. Vengsarkar c Border b Lillee	12	– c Marsh b Pascoe	41
G. R. Viswanath c Chappell b Yardley	114	– b Lillee	30
S. M. Patil c Hughes b Lillee	23	– c Chappell b Yardley	36
Yashpal Sharma c Marsh b Lillee	4	– b Pascoe	9
Kapil Dev c Hughes b Pascoe	5	– (8) b Yardley	0
†S. M. H. Kirmani c Marsh b Lillee	25	– (7) run out	9
K. D. Ghavri run out	0	– not out	11
N. S. Yadav not out	20	– absent hurt	0
D. R. Doshi c Walters b Yardley	0	– (10) b Lillee	7
B 1, l-b 8, w 6, n-b 9	24	B 11, l-b 8, n-b 7	26
1/0 2/22 3/43 4/91 5/99 6/115 7/164 8/190 9/230	237	1/165 2/176 3/243 4/245 5/260 6/296 7/296 8/308 9/324	324

Bowling: *First Innings*—Lillee 25–6–65–4; Pascoe 22–11–29–3; Chappell 5–2–9–0; Yardley 13–3–45–2; Higgs 19–2–65–0. *Second Innings*—Lillee 32.1–5–104–4; Pascoe 29–4–80–2; Yardley 31–11–65–2; Higgs 15–3–41–0; Border 2–0–8–0.

Australia

J. Dyson c Kirmani b Kapil Dev	16	– c Kirmani b Ghavri	3
G. M. Wood c Doshi b Ghavri	10	– st Kirmani b Doshi	10
*G. S. Chappell c and b Ghavri	76	– b Ghavri	0
K. J. Hughes c Chauhan b Yadav	24	– b Doshi	16
A. R. Border b Yadav	124	– (6) c Kirmani b Kapil Dev	9
K. D. Walters st Kirmani b Doshi	78	– (7) not out	18
†R. W. Marsh c sub b Doshi	45	– (8) b Kapil Dev	3
B. Yardley lbw b Doshi	0	– (5) b Kapil Dev	7
D. K. Lillee c and b Patil	19	– b Kapil Dev	4
L. S. Pascoe lbw b Patil	3	– run out	6
J. D. Higgs not out	1	– b Kapil Dev	0
B 12, l-b 6, n-b 5	23	L-b 5, n-b 2	7
1/30 2/32 3/81 4/189 5/320 6/356 7/356 8/413 9/413	419	1/11 2/11 3/18 4/40 5/50 6/55 7/61 8/69 9/79	83

Bowling: *First Innings*—Kapil Dev 19–7–41–1; Doshi 52–14–109–3; Ghavri 39–4–110–2; Yadav 32–6–100–2; Chauhan 2–0–8–0; Patil 12.3–4–28–2. *Second Innings*—Kapil Dev 16.4–4–28–5; Doshi 22–9–33–2; Ghavri 8–4–10–2; Patil 2–0–5–0.

Umpires: M. W. Johnson and R. V. Whitehead.

SHEFFIELD SHIELD

WESTERN AUSTRALIA v NEW SOUTH WALES

Played at Perth, December 15, 17, 18, 19, 1962

New South Wales won by an innings and 45 runs. Davidson performed his first hat-trick in first-class cricket, in his third over; Misson also did well and Western Australia lost their first six wickets for 17 runs. The New South Wales innings was dominated by Simpson, who, in a display of ruthless efficiency, compiled 205 in just over six and a half hours, his first 100 having taken four and a half hours. The seventh-wicket stand with Benaud accelerated the scoring.

Western Australia

K. Gartrell c Ford b Davidson	0	– c Simpson b O'Neill	49
W. Smith c Martin b Misson	5	– c Martin b Misson	32
M. Vernon c Booth b Misson	9	– c Ford b Simpson	18
*B. Shepherd b Davidson	0	– run out	33
J. Parker b Davidson	0	– c Davidson b Benaud	13
R. Waugh c O'Neill b Davidson	0	– Harvey b Davidson	32
G. D. McKenzie c Simpson b Davidson	18	– c Martin b Davidson	25
G. A. R. Lock c Martin b Misson	24	– c Flockton b Misson	5
†B. Buggins c Booth b Benaud	49	– not out	12
D. Hoare run out	46	– lbw b O'Neill	9
H. Bevan not out	1	– b Misson	9
B 5, l-b 2	7	B 2, l-b 2	4
1/0 2/11 3/11 4/11 5/11 6/17 7/48 8/54 9/142	159	1/33 2/47 3/93 4/93 5/136 6/168 7/201 8/216 9/222	241

Bowling: *First Innings*—Davidson 17–3–40–5; Misson 11–1–54–3; Flockton 1–0–3–0; Simpson 12–3–24–0; Martin 4–0–11–0; Benaud 9.2–2–20–1. *Second Innings*—Davidson 15–3–32–2; Misson 19.5–1–54–3; Simpson 13–4–43–1; Benaud 14–3–52–1; O'Neill 13–0–56–2.

New South Wales

R. B. Simpson run out	205
G. Thomas c Shepherd b McKenzie	40
N. C. O'Neill c Buggins b Hoare	1
B. Booth c Buggins b McKenzie	4
R. N. Harvey c Shepherd b Hoare	8
A. K. Davidson c Parker b McKenzie	17
R. Flockton b Lock	44
*R. Benaud c Shepherd b Lock	64
J. Martin c Parker b Hoare	41
F. M. Misson c Buggins b Lock	0
†D. Ford not out	8
B 7, l-b 4, n-b 2	13
1/82 2/83 3/98 4/107 5/184 6/228 7/390 8/397 9/397	445

Bowling: Hoare 22.2–1–101–3; McKenzie 30–4–96–3; Bevan 21–0–117–0; Lock 27–6–103–3; Gartrell 3–0–15–0.

Umpires: A. Mackley and N. Townsend.

NEW SOUTH WALES v SOUTH AUSTRALIA

Played at Sydney, January 18, 19, 21, 1963

New South Wales won by ten wickets. Harvey's magnificent return to form and Benaud's improved bowling were outstanding features. New South Wales scored 414 runs in under five hours, before declaring. Harvey gave the Saturday crowd a treat; he pulverised the bowling, adding 120 runs in two hours between lunch and tea. His footwork was brilliant, and he played a wealth of strokes. His 231 not out, including 22 fours, came in a little under five hours. Benaud took ten wickets in the match after the left-hander Martin gained early success in South Australia's first innings. McLachlan twice fell cheaply to spin.

South Australia

*L. Favell c Martin b Davidson	0	– st Ford b Martin	55
K. Cunningham c Benaud b Martin	7	– lbw b Benaud	34
J. Lill b Benaud	73	– st Ford b Benaud	38
G. S. Sobers c Harvey b Martin	2	– b Davidson	73
I. M. McLachlan c Benaud b Simpson	8	– c Benaud b O'Neill	15
N. Dansie c Thomas b Benaud	19	– c Ford b Benaud	30
I. Chappell st Ford b Benaud	20	– c O'Neill b Martin	13
N. Hawke c Benaud b Martin	29	– c Simpson b Benaud	15
†B. N. Jarman c Ford b Benaud	6	– c Davidson b Benaud	11
D. Sincock c and b Martin	8	– not out	0
G. Brooks not out	2	– c Harvey b Benaud	0
L-b 3, w 2, n-b 1	6	B 6, l-b 2, w 2	10
1/0 2/16 3/39 4/62 5/113 6/115 7/142 8/158 9/177	180	1/81 2/105 3/143 4/170 5/255 6/255 7/283 8/287 9/294	294

Bowling: *First Innings*—Davidson 3–0–6–1; Misson 3–1–6–0; Rorke 3–0–16–0; Martin 12.2–1–43–4; Simpson 12–2–57–1; Benaud 11–1–46–4. *Second Innings*—Davidson 10–2–29–1; Misson 8–0–44–0; Rorke 4–2–8–0; Martin 16–2–61–2; Simpson 10–2–48–0; Benaud 26.3–13–52–6; O'Neill 9–0–42–1.

New South Wales

G. Thomas c Lill b Hawke	72	– not out	19
R. B. Simpson b Sobers	0	– not out	43
R. N. Harvey not out	231		
B. C. Booth st Jarman b Sobers	2		
N. C. O'Neill b Sincock	20		
A. K. Davidson c Jarman b Sobers	6		
*R. Benaud b Sincock	38		
J. Martin not out	28		
B 4, l-b 12, w 1	17	L-b 2	2
1/49 2/153 3/158 4/206 5/233 6/314 (6 wkts dec.)	414	(no wkt)	64

F. M. Misson, G. Rorke and †D. Ford did not bat.

Bowling: *First Innings*—Brooks 13–0–64–0; Sobers 21–1–120–3; Sincock 11–0–81–2; Chappell 5–1–28–0; Dansie 4–0–23–0; Hawke 14–1–73–1; McLachlan 1–0–8–0. *Second Innings*—Brooks 2–0–6–0; Sobers 4–1–14–0; Sincock 5–0–30–0; Dansie 0.2–0–4–0; Hawke 2–0–4–0; Flavell 1–0–4–0.

Umpires: E. F. Wykes and W. E. Hicks.

VICTORIA v QUEENSLAND

Played at Melbourne, February 22, 23, 25, 26, 1963

Victoria won by an innings and 28 runs. Mackay put Victoria in to bat and on a perfect pitch they hit 351 for two wickets on the opening day. They went on to their biggest Shield score since 1927-28. Lawry, who recovered from a blow on the head when he misjudged the bounce of a ball from Hall, played his most aggressive innings of the season and he and Redpath, aged 21, put on 177 in the opening stand. Redpath went on to 261 (thirty-four 4s) in eight and a quarter hours. The left-hander Cowper followed with a century. Hall, who had leg soreness, received heavy punishment. Meckiff bowled Burge first ball; but the solid Bull played another grand innings for Queensland.

Victoria

*W. M. Lawry c and b Westaway	83	I. Huntington not out	23
I. Redpath c and b Mackay	261	B 10, l-b 8, w 2, n-b 2	22
K. Stackpole c Grout b Hall	37		
J. Potter st Grout b Hill	66	1/177 2/244	(4 wkts dec.) 633
R. Cowper not out	141	3/363 4/568	

N. West, T. R. Jordon, C. Guest, I. Meckiff and A. Connolly did not bat.

Bowling: Hall 25–2–158–1; Fisher 24–1–93–0; Mackay 32–4–128–1; Hill 23–4–103–1; Westaway 19.6–0–129–1.

Queensland

S. Trimble c Lawry b Connolly	13	c Huntington b Guest	0
D. Bull b Stackpole	152	c Jordan b Meckiff	4
L. Hill b Meckiff	5	c Lawry b Connolly	41
P. J. Burge b Meckiff	0	c West b Meckiff	10
G. Bizzell c Lawry b Connolly	16	run out	16
D. Seccombe c Jordon b Stackpole	58	c Huntington b Connolly	11
*K. D. Mackay c Jordon b Connolly	78	lbw b Connolly	1
†A. T. W. Grout b Stackpole	8	b Stackpole	54
B. Fisher b Stackpole	11	c Potter b Stackpole	28
W. W. Hall c West b Stackpole	24	lbw b Meckiff	36
C. Westaway not out	11	not out	6
L-b 3, w 4, n-b 1	8	B 8, l-b 1, w 4, n-b 1	14
1/20 2/31 3/31 4/60 5/178 6/319 7/327 8/347 9/357	384	1/4 2/8 3/23 4/61 5/92 6/94 7/95 8/177 9/187	221

Bowling: *First Innings*—Meckiff 21–5–62–2; Connolly 31–5–100–3; Guest 12–1–46–0; Stackpole 29.6–8–97–5; West 2–0–7–0; Potter 3–1–21–0; Huntington 2–1–7–0; Cowper 10–4–36–0. *Second Innings*—Meckiff 14.2–7–26–3; Connolly 11–2–52–3; Guest 13–2–42–1; Stackpole 24–5–79–2; Cowper 2–0–8–0.

Umpires: W. Smyth and I. Stuart.

QUEENSLAND v NEW SOUTH WALES

Played at Brisbane, October 25, 26, 28, 29, 1963

New South Wales won on first innings. Remarkable scoring occurred on an easy pitch. Burge dominated the Queensland innings of 613 runs with a score of 283, the highest for the State in first-class cricket. He batted seven and a half hours and hit one 6 and forty-two 4s. At the end of the second day New South Wales were 42 for two. Then Simpson, maintaining extraordinary concentration and steadfast purpose, passed his first-ever century at Brisbane and went on to 359 – the second triple century in Australian post-war cricket, beating Cowdrey's 303 at Adelaide in 1962-63. Simpson batted ten and a half hours. He hit thirty-three 4s and his stand with Booth put on 241 in just over three and a half hours.

Queensland

R. Reynolds b Benaud	121		
S. Trimble c Ford b Misson	8		
D. Bull run out	28	– not out	9
P. J. Burge run out	283		
G. Bizzell b Simpson	78		
*K. D. Mackay c Booth b Lee	16		
T. R. Veivers c Martin b Benaud	17		
†A. T. W. Grout run out	22		
J. Mackay c Thomas b Lee	3		
C. Westaway not out	19	– c Ford b Booth	8
P. Allan c and b Lee	0	– not out	6
B 11, l-b 1, n-b 6	18	B 4	4
1/13 2/113 3/223 4/413 5/468 6/551 7/591 8/592 9/613	613	1/17 (1 wkt)	27

Bowling: *First Innings*—Misson 29–3–111–1; Rorke 16–1–71–0; Lee 26.2–6–107–3; Simpson 25–2–95–1; Martin 15–0–69–0; Benaud 24–5–98–2; Philpott 11–1–44–0. *Second Innings*—Lee 1–1–0–0; Martin 1–0–6–0; O'Neill 1–0–5–0; Thomas 1–0–3–0; Booth 1–0–9–1.

New South Wales

R. B. Simpson st Grout b Westaway	359
G. Thomas lbw b Allan	2
N. C. O'Neill c Westaway b J. Mackay	7
B. C. Booth c Westaway b Veivers	121
P. Philpott lbw b Veivers	40
*R. Benaud c Grout b J. Mackay	80
T. Lee c and b Westaway	15
F. M. Misson b Veivers	8
J. Martin c sub b Westaway	2
†D. Ford c Burge b Westaway	15
G. Rorke not out	4
B 1, l-b 3, n-b 4	8
1/17 2/42 3/283 4/430 5/578 6/623 7/632 8/634 9/657	661

Bowling: Allan 25–0–144–1; K. Mackay 44–5–138–0; Veivers 53.2–6–160–3; J. Mackay 29–1–112–2; Westaway 17–0–99–4.

Umpires: W. Priem and L. Rowan.

NEW SOUTH WALES v WESTERN AUSTRALIA

Played at Sydney, November 8, 9, 11, 12, 1963

New South Wales won by nine wickets. Although Western Australia lost four wickets for 69, Shepherd batted strongly for his first Sydney century. However, the total of 420 was passed by New South Wales with only one wicket down and in the second innings they lost only one for 262. Simpson, 247 not out in five and a quarter hours, and Thomas enjoyed a mammoth opening stand of 308 runs. Booth, who opened in the second innings hit a century in ninety-four minutes between lunch and tea and had reached 169 not out in two and three-quarter hours when his team won with an hour to spare.

Western Australia

A. Jones st Ford b Martin	18	– c Corling b O'Neill	34
†G. Becker b Misson	27	– lbw b Misson	1
H. Joynt c Misson b Martin	16	– c O'Neill b Benaud	11
*B. Shepherd lbw b Martin	149	– c Simpson b Martin	29
J. Inverarity b Corling	4	– run out	50
R. Waugh c and b Benaud	87	– c Corling b Misson	1
T. Jenner b Corling	2	– c Lee b Philpott	13
G. D. McKenzie c Corling b Lee	50	– b Benaud	31
K. Slater not out	49	– b Misson	58
H. Bevan b Martin	2	– b Corling	5
I. Gallash b Martin	1	– not out	4
B 3, l-b 9, w 1, n-b 2	15	B 21, l-b 8	29
1/36 2/50 3/62 4/69 5/249 6/255 7/339 8/386 9/418	420	1/13 2/15 3/57 4/122 5/131 6/182 7/184 8/230 9/254	266

Bowling: *First Innings*—Misson 13–2–48–1; Corling 23–3–46–2; Martin 24.6–3–104–5; Philpott 8–0–32–0; O'Neill 2–0–19–0; Lee 19–2–59–1; Benaud 25–5–71–1; Simpson 9–0–26–0. *Second Innings*—Misson 12.6–4–26–3; Corling 5–0–23–1; Martin 12–1–54–1; Philpott 7–0–39–1; O'Neill 12–1–52–1; Lee 12–4–25–0; Benaud 16–10–18–2.

New South Wales

G. Thomas c and b Slater	127		
R. Simpson not out	247		
P. Philpott not out	38	– not out	37
N. C. O'Neill (did not bat)		– b Gallash	43
B. C. Booth (did not bat)		– not out	169
L-b 5, n-b 8	13	B 5, l-b 5, n-b 3	13
1/308	(1 wkt dec.) 425	1/127	(1 wkt) 262

*R. Benaud, T. Lee, J. W. Martin, F. M. Misson, †D. Ford and G. E. Corling did not bat.

Bowling: *First Innings*—McKenzie 14–0–73–0; Bevan 10–0–68–0; Gallash 21–1–86–0; Slater 21–1–101–1; Jenner 9–0–76–0; Waugh 1–0–8–0. *Second Innings*—McKenzie 21–3–40–0; Bevan 4–0–29–0; Gallash 5–0–36–1; Slater 6–0–62–0; Jenner 9–0–53–0; Waugh 4–0–25–0; Shepherd 0.3–0–4–0.

Umpires: E. F. Wykes and W. E. Hicks.

VICTORIA v SOUTH AUSTRALIA

Played at Melbourne, January 1, 2, 4, 5, 1965

Victoria won by 111 runs. Lawry, 246 (run out) and 87 not out played a dominating part; he participated in another big second-wicket stand with Cowper, who contributed 87 of the 234 runs. Victoria scored 340 runs for one wicket on the opening day. Lawry and Redpath began with 142 in the second innings. A new fast left-handed bowler, Doble, sent down 35 overs for four wickets and 108 runs in South Australia's first innings.

Victoria

*W. M. Lawry run out	246	– not out	87
I. R. Redpath c and b Sellers	53	– c McAllister b Chappell	65
R. M. Cowper b Hurn	87	– run out	18
J. Potter c Jarman b Hurn	3	– not out	1
K. R. Stackpole b Sincock	0		
D. J. Anderson lbw b Sincock	0		
G. D. Watson b McCarthy	34		
†R. C. Jordon c Jarman b Hawke	31		
R. W. Rayson not out	12		
A. N. Connolly c Favell b Sincock	10		
A. Doble c Sharpe b Sellers	3		
B 4, l-b 8, n-b 1	13	L-b 1, n-b 2	3
1/157 2/391 3/394 4/395 5/395 6/395 7/460 8/466 9/483	492	1/142 2/168 (2 wkts dec.)	174

Bowling: *First Innings*—McCarthy 19–2–91–1; Hawke 33–8–99–1; Hurn 18–1–71–2; Sincock 25–1–113–3; Sellers 16.2–1–70–2; Chappell 9–1–33–0; Dansie 1–0–2–0. *Second Innings*—McCarthy 6–0–39–0; Hawke 8–0–40–0; Sellers 1–0–7–0; Hurn 9–0–45–0; Chappell 7–0–39–1; Danise 1–1–0–0; Favell 1–0–1–0.

South Australia

*L. E. Favell c Jordon b Doble	14	– b Stackpole	29
D. E. McAllister c Watson b Doble	22	– st Jordon b Cowper	43
I. M. Chappell c Jordon b Connolly	61	– b Stackpole	6
H. N. Dansie c Jordon b Doble	48	– c Cowper b Anderson	68
D. A. Sharpe c sub b Connolly	11	– c Jordon b Stackpole	0
†B. N. Jarman b Stackpole	27	– b Stackpole	0
N. J. N. Hawke c Jordon b Cowper	62	– c Jordon b Potter	5
B. M. Hurn lbw b Watson	22	– c Redpath b Potter	3
D. J. Sincock c Jordon b Doble	34	– c Lawry b Anderson	18
R. H. D. Sellers c Doble b Stackpole	16	– not out	29
K. J. McCarthy not out	13	– c Lawry b Anderson	10
B 5, l-b 2, w 4, n-b 1	12	L-b 1, w 1	2
1/26 2/57 3/134 4/153 5/180 6/197 7/245 8/309 9/317	342	1/64 2/76 3/86 4/89 5/95 6/110 7/118 8/160 9/187	213

Bowling: *First Innings*—Connolly 23–3–76–2; Doble 35–8–108–4; Watson 5–0–21–1; Cowper 22–4–62–1; Stackpole 13.1–2–42–2; Anderson 6–0–21–0. *Second Innings*—Connolly 5–0–23–0; Doble 4–1–5–0; Stackpole 18–0–79–4; Cowper 9–2–29–1; Potter 12–1–54–2; Anderson 5.3–0–21–3.

Umpires: K. Collicoat and K. Butler.

NEW SOUTH WALES v SOUTH AUSTRALIA

Played at Sydney, January 8, 9, 11, 12, 1965

New South Wales won by ten wickets. They were behind on the first innings despite a stand of 190 runs by Simpson and Thomas. In the second innings, when they needed to score 276 runs in three hours, forty minutes Simpson and O'Neill got them with fifty-two minutes to spare in a memorable opening partnership, Simpson making his second century of the match. Chappell had played an admirable rescuing century in South Australia's first innings; Shiell, a tall, young newcomer, batted stauchly for 72 and 110, though during his century innings he was missed several times.

South Australia

*L. E. Favell lbw b Corling	21	– st Taber b Martin	65
D. E. McAlister c O'Neill b Renneberg	6	– b Renneberg	0
I. M. Chappell c Simpson b Philpott	123	– c Taber b Corling	11
B. M. Hurn c Thomas b Walters	3	– lbw b Philpott	0
H. N. Dansie c Taber b Corling	31	– c Thomas b Renneberg	14
A. B. Shiell c Taber b Walters	72	– c Philpott b Simpson	110
†B. N. Jarman c Simpson b Philpott	2	– c Philpott b Corling	25
N. J. N. Hawke not out	77	– c Taber b Corling	11
D. J. Sincock st Taber b Philpott	8	– st Taber b Philpott	5
R. H. D. Sellers run out	22	– not out	14
K. J. McCarthy c and b Philpott	18	– st Taber b Philpott	5
B 3, l-b 3, w 2	8	B 4, l-b 1, w 2, n-b 1	8
1/23 2/29 3/37 4/102 5/262 6/262 7/265 8/283 9/330	391	1/6 2/25 3/46 4/134 5/155 6/156 7/228 8/248 9/250	268

Bowling: *First Innings*—Renneberg 17–1–89–1; Corling 21–2–67–2; Walters 22–3–79–2; Martin 14–2–69–0; Griffiths 10–1–29–0; Simpson 3–0–5–0; Philpott 15.3–2–45–4. *Second Innings*—Renneberg 12–0–77–2; Corling 18–3–54–3; Martin 17–0–67–1; Walters 6–0–20–0; Philpott 15.5–2–32–3; Simpson 5–0–10–1.

New South Wales

*R. B. Simpson c Sellers b Hawke	121	– not out	142
P. I. Philpott b Hawke	7		
N. C. O'Neill lbw b Hawke	0	– not out	133
G. Thomas st Jarman b Sincock	148		
B. C. Booth c Jarman b Sincock	58		
K. D. Walters c Dansie b Sincock	19		
G. E. Griffiths run out	12		
J. W. Martin not out	13		
†H. B. Taber b Chappell	2		
G. E. Corling run out	0		
D. A. Renneberg c Sellers b Sincock	1		
B 3	3	L-b 1	1
1/30 2/30 3/220 4/305 5/343 6/368 7/368 8/371 9/371	384		(no wkt) 276

Bowling: *First Innings*—McCarthy 5–0–24–0; Hawke 30–2–121–3; Hurn 9–0–50–0; Chappell 10–0–54–1; Sincock 27.7–2–98–4; Sellers 4–0–24–0; Shiell 1–0–10–0. *Second Innings*—Hawke 13–1–54–0; Hurn 9–0–72–0; Sincock 10–0–60–0; Chappell 4–0–29–0; Sellers 2–0–18–0; Dansie 3–0–20–0; Shiell 1–0–14–0; Favell 1–0–8–0.

Umpires: E. F. Wykes and P. Berridge.

SOUTH AUSTRALIA v NEW SOUTH WALES

Played at Adelaide, February, 5, 6, 8, 9, 1965

New South Wales won on the first innings. This match produced the Sheffield Shield second wicket record stand of 378 runs (five hours, seven minutes) by two young batsmen in a make-shift New South Wales eleven. L. Marks, a left-hander, hit 185 (twenty 4s) and D. Walters, a right-hander, became the youngest NSW player to reach 250 (one 6 and twenty-three 4s). Walters followed up his brilliant batting by taking seven wickets for 63 runs with well-controlled medium-paced bowling, despite a patient century by Chappell and a valuable innings by Hawke. South Australia staved off the threat of an outright defeat.

New South Wales

L. Marks c Cunningham b Hurn	185
†H. B. Taber c Sincock b Freeman	0
K. D. Walters c sub b Sincock	253
J. W. Martin lbw b Sincock	2
R. Guy c Cunningham b Sincock	8
*B. A. Rothwell st Jarman b Dansie	78
M. Hill c Shiell b Sincock	28
T. H. Lee b Hurn	2
G. E. Griffiths c Hurn b Sincock	26
D. A. Renneberg not out	0
B 3, l-b 10, n-b 6	19
1/9 2/387 3/394 4/420 5/496 6/542 7/552 8/597 9/601	(9 wkts dec.) 601

L. Ellis did not bat.

Bowling: Freeman 18–2–98–1; Hawke 27–4–101–0; Sincock 23–1–161–5; Hurn 20–0–106–2; Chappell 20–0–90–0; Dansie 3–0–13–1; Cunningham 2–0–13–0.

South Australia

*L. E. Favell c Lee b Ellis	43	– b Lee	25
J. Causby c Hill b Walters	7	– b Lee	16
I. M. Chappell c Taber b Walters	122	– lbw b Guy	15
K. G. Cunningham c Walters b Guy	0	– b Martin	58
H. N. Dansie c Griffiths b Walters	12	– b Guy	11
A. B. Shiell run out	50	– c Griffiths b Hill	29
N. J. N. Hawke not out	89	– c Martin b Walters	33
†B. N. Jarman c Griffiths b Walters	2	– lbw b Guy	60
B. M. Hurn c Martin b Walters	30	– not out	23
D. J. Sincock lbw b Walters	0	– not out	21
E. Freeman b Walters	0		
B 4, l-b 2, w 1, n-b 2	9	B 7	7
1/26 2/63 3/64 4/89 5/189 6/280 7/286 8/362 9/362	364	1/40 2/43 3/74 4/90 5/156 6/156 7/245 8/265	(8 wkts) 298

Bowling: *First Innings*—Renneberg 12–2–44–0; Ellis 16–1–64–1; Walters 22.7–3–63–7; Martin 25–7–76–0; Guy 28–7–71–1; Griffiths 14–5–28–0; Lee 6–4–9–0. *Second Innings*—Ellis 9–1–44–0; Walters 13–3–40–1; Lee 6–0–23–2; Martin 13–2–65–1; Guy 23–5–72–3; Griffiths 5–0–19–0; Hill 7–0–28–1.

Umpires: C. J. Egar and J. J. Ryan.

VICTORIA v NEW SOUTH WALES

Played at Melbourne, December 23, 24, 27 and 28, 1965

New South Wales won by nine wickets. Two double centuries were scored in this match. Thomas, whose 229 for New South Wales was an enthralling innings, took part in double-century stands with Simpson (214 in two and a half hours) and O'Neill (215 in two hours) on the same day. New South Wales gave a display of power batting. Simpson reached 113 in a three-hour effort of concentration; he was joined by Thomas after Rothwell had retired, having been struck below the right eye when he tried to hook Grant. Thomas, fighting for Test recognition, made his first double hundred in first-class cricket; tremendous power was allied to brilliant stroke play. He was dropped at 130 and 187 and was run out after periods of exhaustion in 100 degrees heat. He batted for nearly four and a half hours. In Victoria's first innings Stackpole reached 99 in an innings marked by emphatic driving and pulling; in the second innings Potter, showing his best form since his early return from the 1964 English tour, scored 221, many of the runs coming from well-placed drives.

New South Wales

*R. B. Simpson, st Jordon b Cowper	113	– not out	33
B. A. Rothwell retired hurt	3		
G. Thomas run out	229	– b Grant	8
N. C. O'Neill c Jordon b Kirby	108		
K. D. Walters b Connolly	9		
B. C. Booth c and b Kirby	26	– not out	46
J. W. Martin lbw b Connolly	8		
P. I. Philpott not out	60		
†H. B. Taber b Stackpole	20		
G. E. Corling c Redpath b Stackpole	1		
D. A. Renneberg lbw b Stackpole	1		
B 4, l-b 6, w 1, n-b 3	14	N-b 3	3
1/226 2/441 3/458 4/490 5/503 6/519 7/587 8/589 9/592	592	1/15 (1 wkt)	90

Bowling: *First Innings*—Connolly 22–2–83–2; Grant 17–0–89–0; Watson 10–0–64–0; Kirby 23–0–149–2; Stackpole 11.1–0–53–3; Cowper 26–3–117–1; Potter 3–0–23–0. *Second Innings*—Connolly 5–0–24–0; Grants 3–0–15–1; Watson 1–0–2–0; Kirby 3–0–19–0; Stackpole 3.6–0–21–0; Cowper 2–0–6–0.

Victoria

*W. M. Lawry c Taber b Walters	43	– lbw b Goring	16
L. R. Redpath b Walters	10	– lbw b Renneberg	7
R. M. Cowper c Walters b Renneberg	0	– c Philpott b Simpson	87
K. R. Stackpole b Martin	99	– c Martin b Renneberg	17
J. Potter c Philpott b Walters	34	– b Walters	221
A. P. Sheahan st Taber b Philpott	62	– c Martin b Simpson	5
G. D. Watson c and b Martin	1	– st Taber b Martin	4
†R. C. Jordon lbw b Philpott	0	– b Renneberg	20
J. W. Grant lbw b Martin	4	– c Simpson b Renneberg	15
K. Kirby not out	3	– not out	17
A. N. Connolly c Simpson b Philpott	5	– lbw b Walters	0
L-b 5	5	B 2, l-b 4	6
1/48 2/49 3/57 4/111 5/222 6/238 7/239 8/248 9/260	266	1/23 2/25 3/50 4/228 5/244 6/249 7/311 8/354 9/415	415

Bowling: *First Innings*—Renneberg 15–1–62–1; Corling 9–0–37–0; Walters 8–0–52–3; Philpott 20.3–2–72–3; Martin 12–3–38–3; Simpson 3–3–0–0. *Second Innings*—Renneberg 23–3–74–4; Corling 5–0–19–1; Walters 14.4–1–78–2; Philpott 8–1–23–0; Martin 26–2–131–1; Simpson 24–4–76–2; Booth 5–2–8–0.

Umpires: W. Smyth and J. Collins.

VICTORIA v QUEENSLAND

Played at Melbourne, January 7, 8, 10, 11, 1966

Victoria won by three wickets. Victoria ended the first innings 50 runs in arrears, after the pace bowler Allan had taken all ten wickets (15.6–3–61–10). Allan's figures were four for 32 at the end of the first day, with Victoria 76 for four. Allan next day actually took six for 14, these runs including five overthrows. The Queensland left-handed opener Bull made fine scores of 78 and 167 not out; but Queensland in the first innings lost their last nine wickets for 57. Stackpole bowled his spin mixture impressively in each innings. An opening stand of 213 runs in three and a quarter hours by Redpath, 180, and Watson, 109 had helped Victoria to recover. Redpath survived three chances during a stay of six and a quarter hours.

Queensland

D. F. Bull lbw b Stackpole	78	– not out	67
*S. C. Trimble c Sheahan b Grant	3	– c and b Stackpole	97
W. Buckle c Swanson b Stackpole	44	– c Swanson b Stackpole	0
G. M. Bizzell b Stackpole	9	– b Stackpole	2
F. Crane c Watson b Connolly	1	– b Stackpole	10
K. Ziebell c Connolly b Stackpole	9	– c and b Grant	18
J. R. Mackay b Stackpole	3	– run out	22
†L. Cooper lbw b Kirby	0	– c Sheahan b Kirby	0
P. J. Allan not out	7	– lbw b Swanson	8
J. Duncan b Kirby	4	– lbw b Kirby	0
D. Lillie c Swanson c Swanson b Kirby	13	– c and b Swanson	4
B 6, n-b 3	9	B 4, l-b 2, w 1, n-b 1	8
1/12 2/123 3/140 4/141 5/141 6/144 7/154 8/156 9/166	180	1/169 2/169 3/177 4/187 5/249 6/301 7/315 8/325 9/334	336

Bowling: *First Innings*—Connolly 13–5–36–1; Grant 13–1–49–1; Watson 4–0–9–0; Kirby 13–5–39—3; Stackpole 19–8–38–5. *Second Innings*—Connolly 19–3–56–0; Grant 12–3–34–1; Watson 7–0–33–0; Kirby 25–5–73–2; Stackpole 33–8–80–4; Swanson 10–2–31–2; Potter 2–0–19–0; Anderson 1–0–2–0.

Victoria

I. R. Redpath lbw b Allan	20	– Buckle b Mackay	180
G. D. Watson c Trimble b Allan	8	– c Mackay b Crane	109
D. Anderson c Bizzell b Allan	45	– b Ziebell	45
*J. Potter c Cooper b Allan	5	– c Cooper b Crane	24
K. R. Stackpole b Allan	1	– c Crane b Mackay	15
†R. C. Jordon b Allan	27	– c Mackay b Lillie	0
A. P. Sheahan c Cooper b Allan	0	– run out	1
J. Swanson c Crane b Allan	0	– not out	4
J. W. Grant c Crane b Allan	0	– not out	8
K. Kirby c Trimble b Allan	18		
A. N. Connolly not out	0		
L-b 4, n-b 2	6	B 1	1
1/15 2/41 3/53 4/61 5/100 6/100 7/100 7/100 9/123	130	1/213 2/247 3/345 4/371 5/375 6/375 7/376	(7 wkts) 387

Bowling: *First Innings*—Allan 15.6–3–61–10; Duncan 5–0–31–0; Mackay 1–0–12–0; Crane 9–5–20–0. *Second Innings*—Allan 11–0–63–0; Duncan 16–2–65–0; Mackay 24.6–4–78–2; Crane 10–0–47–2; Lillie 19–0–105–1; Bull 1–0–3–0; Ziebell 9–0–25–1.

Umpires: K. Butler and K. Collicoat.

SOUTH AUSTRALIA v WESTERN AUSTRALIA

Played at Adelaide, November 25, 26, 28, 29, 1966

South Australia won by five wickets. The left hander Cunningham scored a century in each innings for South Australia, giving him three Shield centuries in a row. Another feature was a furious batting display by Milburn for Western Australia, in his first century innings in Australia. Milburn hit up 129 runs in 95 minutes, having reached the century in 77 minutes. He had been missed before scoring. The consistent Lock captured four wickets in each innings with his left-arm spin.

South Australia

*L. E. Favell b Lock	41	– c and b Lock	78
G. S. Farrell c Brayshaw b Guest	6	– lbw b Lock	16
K. G. Cunningham st Edwards b Mann	107	– not out	101
H. N. Dansie b Gannon	2	– c Lock b Guest	19
G. S. Chappell c Vernon b Lock	34	– b Lock	7
A. B. Shiell c Edwards b Guest	33	– c Playle b Lock	42
†B. N. Jarman c Milburn b Brayshaw	41	– not out	4
D. Robins c Playle b Lock	9		
C. Harrison b Mann	6		
A. R. Frost c Mann b Lock	9		
J. Kowalick not out	0		
L-b 8, n-b 2	10	L-b 4, n-b 1	5
1/21 2/77 3/80 4/188 5/206 6/252 7/273 8/285 9/286	298	1/64 2/132 3/177 4/192 5/254	(5 wkts) 272

Bowling: *First Innings*—Gannon 20–3–59–1; Guest 9–0–55–2; Brayshaw 8–1–32–1; Lock 33.6–6–97–4; Mann 13–3–45–2. *Second Innings*—Gannon 8–0–32–0; Guest 5–0–26–1; Brayshaw 10–0–35–1; Lock 27–6–90–4; Mann 16.2–1–84–0.

Western Australia

W. R. Playle c and b Robins	27	– b Frost	0
P. C. Kelly b Robins	41	– c Jarman b Robins	1
*M. T. Vernon c Jarman b Harrison	6	– c Jarman b Frost	75
C. Milburn b Kowalick	129	– c Shiell b Harrison	37
D. Chadwick lbw b Dansie	13	– lbw b Frost	13
I. J. Brayshaw st Jarman b Chappell	22	– c Robins b Harrison	9
†R. Edwards b Harrison	0	– lbw b Robins	72
C. E. J. Guest c Jarman b Frost	31	– c Jarman b Chappell	31
A. Mann st Jarman b Chappell	3	– c Cunningham b Harrison	30
G. A. R. Lock not out	11	– lbw b Harrison	0
J. B. Gannon st Jarman b Chappell	2	– not out	4
B 4, l-b 2, w 1	7	L-b 3, n-b 2	5
1/67 2/78 3/82 4/171 5/231 6/232 7/275 8/279 9/280	292	1/0 2/6 3/59 4/163 5/221 6/221 7/238 8/252 9/252	277

Bowling: *First Innings*—Frost 11–0–45–1; Kowalick 11–1–58–1; Robins 12–0–68–2; Harrison 9–1–52–2; Dansie 6–0–43–1; Chappell 3.1–0–19–3. *Second Innings*—Frost 19–1–71–3; Kowalick 3–0–30–0; Robins 17–2–63–2; Harrison 19.2–2–82–4; Dansie 1–0–5–0; Chappell 6–1–21–1.

Umpires: C. J. Egar and A. T. Godson.

WESTERN AUSTRALIA v QUEENSLAND

Played at Perth, December 17, 18, 19, 20, 1966

Western Australia won by an innings and 118 runs. Lock, with splendid control, took 10 wickets in the match to equal his own record for Western Australia of 44 wickets in a first-class season; at the same time, he set his team on the way to a handsome victory. Another Englishman, Milburn, was one of three century-makers in the Western Australian innings; his 106 runs were hit in just over two hours, with fourteen 4s. Milburn scored all but 34 of the 140 runs in the opening partnership with Kelly. The Queensland opener Loxton, in his initial innings in first-class cricket, scored 100, and Burge, after retiring at 53 with a strained right shoulder, resumed to reach 101.

Western Australia

C. Milburn c and b Allan	106	C. E. J. Guest not out	13
P. C. Kelly c Crane b Paulsen	91	A. Mann not out	25
R. J. Inverarity c Cooper b Allan	114		
*M. T. Vernon c Morgan b Duncan	110	B 2, l-b 5, w 3	10
†R. Edwards c Duncan b Paulsen	73		—
I. J. Brayshaw c Crane b Allan	0	1/140 2/261 3/411 (7 wkts dec.)	554
D. McEvoy c Burge b Paulsen	12	4/417 5/471 6/515 7/519	

G. A. R. Lock and B. Yardley did not bat.

Bowling: Allan 17–1–52–3; Duncan 23–0–125–1; Morgan 21–0–103–0; Crane 25–1–115–0; Paulsen 30–2–149–3.

Queensland

S. C. Trimble c and b Lock	47	– c Edwards b Lock	20
J. Loxton c Edwards b Guest	100	– c Milburn b Yardley	4
D. J. King c Yardley b Lock	0	– not out	28
†L. Cooper c Vernon b Lock	10	– c Guest b Mann	23
*R. J. Burge not out	101	– c Milburn b Mann	35
R. Crane run out	1	– lbw b Lock	1
K. P. Ziebell c McEvoy b Lock	1	– c and b Lock	0
R. G. Paulsen st Edwards b Lock	19	– c Edwards b Mann	0
P. J. Allan c and b Mann	0	– run out	8
R. F. Duncan c Vernon b Lock	9	– c Edwards b Lock	1
O. J. Morgan c Lock b Mann	2	– c Lock b Mann	7
B 11, l-b 2, w 3	16	B 2, w 1	3
	—		—
1/85 2/85 3/120 4/216 5/219 6/220 7/266 8/271 9/286	306	1/11 2/12 3/33 4/76 5/77 6/101 7/113 8/115 9/125	130

Bowling: *First Innings*—Yardley 9–0–32–0; Brayshaw 13–2–41–0; Guest 16–3–64–1; Mann 31.5–6–68–2; Lock 43–16–85–6. *Second Innings*—Yardley 10–2–25–1; Brayshaw 4–2–5–0; Mann 16–6–39–4; Lock 21.2–5–58–4.

Umpires: N. Townsend and A. Foster.

WESTERN AUSTRALIA v SOUTH AUSTRALIA

Played at Perth, January 27, 28, 30, 31, 1967

South Australia won by 245 runs. Western Australia failed against the destructive bowling of the pace pair, Freeman and Frost. The left-handed Cunningham scored yet another century for South Australia, in the second innings. Lock's leg-spin had gained him further wickets, to make him the first bowler to complete a bag of 50 wickets in a Shield competition since the war.

South Australia

*L. E. Favell b Brayshaw	4 – c Lock b Gannon	0
J. Causby c Inverarity b Brayshaw	24 – c Inverarity b Lock	45
K. G. Cunningham c Inverarity b Gannon	3 – b Gannon	136
G. S. Chappell c Edwards b Gannon	17 – st Edwards b Mann	7
H. N. Dansie run out	44 – c Edwards b Mann	14
R. H. D. Sellers c Brayshaw b Lock	87 – lbw b Gannon	9
R. Lloyd b Mann	18 – c Edwards b Gannon	30
†B. N. Jarman not out	37 – c Mann b Gannon	25
G. Griffiths c Vernon b Lock	6 – c Edwards b Gannon	27
E. W. Freeman b Mann	1 – c Vernon b Mann	35
A. R. Frost c Kelly b Lock	5 – not out	3
L-b 1, w 1, n-b 2	4 B 2, l-b 11, w 3, n-b 2	18
1/16 2/19 3/48 4/63 5/135 6/182 7/216 8/226 9/227	250 1/0 2/72 3/91 4/143 5/165 6/244 7/268 8/293 9/308	349

Bowling: *First Innings*—Gannon 12–1–52–2; Brayshaw 12–1–50–2; Inverarity 5–0–12–0; Lock 22.7–6–67–3; Mann 15–2–55–2; Jenner 4–0–10–0. *Second Innings*—Gannon 24–4–107–6; Brayshaw 12–0–58–0; Lock 21–7–65–1; Mann 17.6–2–83–3; Jenner 7–1–18–0.

Western Australia

C. Milburn c Jarman b Frost	8 – b Cunningham	46
P. C. Kelly c Jarman b Freeman	0 – c Chappell b Frost	6
†R. Edwards b Freeman	19 – st Jarman b Griffiths	52
T. J. Jenner b Frost	31 – b Freeman	45
*M. T. Vernon lbw b Frost	8 – c Sellers b Frost	4
R. J. Inverarity b Cunningham	1 – c Jarman b Freeman	10
W. R. Playle c Favell b Cunningham	0 – c Jarman b Frost	0
I. J. Brayshaw c Dansie b Freeman	29 – c Sellers b Freeman	8
A. Mann b Griffiths	44 – not out	4
G. A. R. Lock b Dansie	25 – b Freeman	3
J. B. Gannon not out	2 – c Jarman b Freeman	0
B 2, l-b 2, n-b 1	5 B 1, n-b 3	4
1/8 2/8 3/47 4/68 5/69 6/69 7/84 8/112 9/166	172 1/7 2/17 3/47 4/50 5/77 6/183 7/175 8/177 9/182	182

Bowling: *First Innings*—Frost 12–1–41–3; Freeman 15–1–45–3; Cunningham 11–4–24–2; Sellers 1–0–6–0; Dansie 6.7–0–32–1; Griffiths 3–0–19–1. *Second Innings*—Frost 12–0–62–3; Freeman 14–1–57–5; Cunningham 2–1–3–1; Sellers 4–0–17–0; Dansie 6–0–30–0; Griffiths 4–0–9–1.

Umpires: J. M. Meachem and N. Townsend.

NEW SOUTH WALES v QUEENSLAND

Played at Sydney, November 24, 25, 27, 1967.

New South Wales won by an innings and 267 runs, thus gaining their first competition points of the season, thanks mainly to Simpson's great innings of 277; he was 243 not out at the end of the first day, and had a century opening stand with Blackman. It was the highest individual score at the Sydney Cricket Ground since Bradman's world record 452 not out in 1929-30. Renneberg smashed the Queensland batting in a devastating burst of fast bowling, taking seven for 33 in ten overs; in the second innings Gleeson bowled well and another spinner, Davies, secured six for 43.

New South Wales

O. C. Blackman b Duncan	36	†H. B. Taber not out	8
*R. B. Simpson b Morgan	277		
B. C. Booth c Crane b Paulsen	5	B 7, l-b 5, w 2, n-b 2	16
B. A. Rothwell c Paulsen b Morgan	37		
G. R. Davies c Crane b Duncan	112	1/111 2/116 (5 wkts dec.)	497
J. Benaud not out	6	3/224 4/478 5/482	

R. Collins, J. W. Gleeson, G. E. Corling and D. A. Renneberg did not bat.

Bowling: Fisher 20–0–111–0; Duncan 30–3–115–2; Morgan 21–1–107–2; Paulsen 22–2–102–1; Crane 7–0–46–0.

Queensland

S. C. Trimble b Renneberg	0	– b Gleeson	49
F. R. Crane b Renneberg	0	– b Renneberg	0
D. F. E. Bull b Corling	1	– b Gleeson	25
W. H. Buckle c Taber b Renneberg	6	– b Davies	7
*P. J. Burge b Renneberg	15	– b Davies	0
R. E. Parker b Renneberg	0	– c and b Davies	10
B. Fisher c Benaud b Corling	0	– c Renneberg b Davies	7
R. G. Paulsen c Davies b Renneberg	6	– c Simpson b Davies	7
O. J. Morgan c Taber b Renneberg	46	– c Collins b Davies	3
†L. D. Cooper not out	32	– c Davies b Gleeson	4
R. F. Duncan c and b Davies	3	– not out	0
B 2, l-b 1, n-b 2	5	B 3, l-b 1	4
1/0 2/1 3/1 4/13 5/13 6/22 7/22 8/49 9/109	114	1/0 2/75 3/82 4/82 5/84 6/96 7/103 8/106 9/116	116

Bowling: *First Innings*—Renneberg 10–1–33–7; Corling 8–0–35–2; Gleeson 9–0–17–0; Davies 5.1–1–12–1; Simpson 7–2–12–0. *Second Innings*—Renneberg 7–3–14–1; Corling 4–1–9–0; Gleeson 13.4–3–31–3; Davies 17–7–43–6; Collins 3–1–15–0.

Umpires: T. Brooks and E. F. Wykes.

QUEENSLAND v WESTERN AUSTRALIA

Played at Brisbane, February 16, 17, 18, 19, 1968

Western Australia won by 144 runs. This was a low-scoring match, but Peter Burge, playing his last game for Queensland, hit a great, fighting century in the first innings – he went lbw to Lock for four runs in the second. Inverarity played another dour innings, 64 in four hours, for Western Australia. The match provided further triumphs for the Western Australian bowlers, Lock, with his aggressive, well-controlled spin, and Mayne with his lively pace.

Western Australia

K. Slater b Allan	17	– not out	8
D. Chadwick c Duncan b Allan	24	– lbw b Duncan	18
R. J. Inverarity c Cooper b Duncan	8	– lbw b Dudgeon	64
M. T. Vernon c Burge b Morgan	2	– c Burge b Morgan	41
J. T. Irvine c Cooper b Morgan	12	– b Duncan	3
R. Edwards st Cooper b Paulsen	57	– lbw b Duncan	10
†G. C. Becker c Loxton b Morgan	0	– c and b Crane	45
I. J. Brayshaw c Cooper b Allan	43	– not out	45
G. D. McKenzie c Duncan b Paulsen	18	– c Crane b Paulsen	3
*G. A. R. Lock c Loxton b Crane	5	– c Dudgeon b Paulsen	0
L. R. Mayne not out	0	– run out	23
B 1, l-b 1, w 1, n-b 6	9	B 3, l-b 5, n-b 1	9
1/19 2/35 3/40 4/66 5/66 6/71 7/156 8/190 9/195	195	1/25 2/77 3/89 4/109 5/182 6/208 7/211 8/211 9/252	(9 wkts dec.) 269

Bowling: *First Innings*—Allan 17–1–69–3; Duncan 13–5–25–1; Morgan 16–4–40–3; Crane 12–1–42–1; Paulsen 3.4–0–10–2. *Second Innings*—Allan 2–0–8–0; Duncan 19–4–47–3; Morgan 14–1–70–1; Crane 10–2–22–1; Paulsen 22–0–85–0; Dudgeon 12–2–28–1.

Queensland

S. C. Trimble c Becker b Mayne	1	– c and b Lock	21
F. R. Crane c Inverarity b Lock	41	– b McKenzie	2
J. F. C. Loxton c Vernon b Mayne	4	– b Lock	37
*P. J. Burge b McKenzie	100	– lbw b Lock	4
R. E. Parker b Mayne	0	– b Mayne	22
K. D. Dudgeon c Becker b Lock	9	– c Edwards b Lock	15
O. J. Morgan b Lock	1	– c Edwards b Mayne	7
R. G. Paulsen lbw b Mayne	7	– st Becker b Vernon	12
P. J. Allan c Lock b Mayne	0	– lbw b Vernon	1
†L. D. Cooper not out	1	– not out	5
R. F. Duncan c Becker b Lock	0	– c Inverarity b Lock	17
B 8, l-b 2, n-b 1	11	B 1, n-b 1	2
1/13 2/22 3/36 4/88 5/162 6/163 7/174 8/174 9/174	175	1/2 2/39 3/60 4/78 5/90 6/104 7/121 8/123 9/141	145

Bowling: *First Innings*—McKenzie 14–2–54–1; Mayne 13–5–43–5; Brayshaw 8–3–14–0; Lock 21–6–33–4; Slater 3–0–20–0. *Second Innings*—McKenzie 10–1–27–1; Mayne 16–2–51–2; Brayshaw 8–3–10–0; Lock 20–7–34–5; Vernon 3.7–1–10–2.

Umpires: L. Rowan and L. Johnson.

NEW SOUTH WALES v WESTERN AUSTRALIA

Played at Sydney, November 15, 16, 17, 18, 1968

Western Australia won by an innings and 87 runs. Western Australia scored 386 runs for five wickets on the first day (five and a half hours), a hard-hit 93 by Milburn being followed by centuries from his opening partner, Chadwick (110 in three and a half hours), and Inverarity, who showed a return to form (103 in two hours, twenty minutes). The second day (Saturday) was disastrous to New South Wales. Irvine and Edwards piled on centuries, and after the closure, the home side side lost three wickets cheaply, and had their left-hander, Marks, taken to hospital after a blow on the head. Grosser was also hit, but he resumed later in the innings. In the second innings Walters and Davies made a fighting stand. For the first time in Sydney there was play on Sunday.

Western Australia

C. Milburn c Steele b Davies	93	R. Edwards not out	117
D. Chadwick c Marks b Davies	110		
R. J. Inverarity c Marks b Corling	103	L-b 5, w 1, n-b 8	14
†G. C. Becker b Renneberg	20		
J. T. Irvine c Gleeson b Renneberg	128	1/156 2/270	(6 wkts dec.) 594
R. W. Marsh c Taber b Renneberg	9	3/335 4/339 5/350 6/594	

J. D. Gannon, L. C. Mayne, *G. A. R. Lock and G. D. McKenzie did not bat.

Bowling: Renneberg 24.7–1–102–3; Corling 21–1–102–1; Walters 17–0–109–0; Gleeson 31–4–142–0; Davies 20–0–125–2.

New South Wales

L. A. Marks retired hurt	14	– absent hurt	0
A. A. Steele c Becker b McKenzie	0	– c Becker b McKenzie	8
*K. D. Walters c Inverarity b McKenzie	3	– c Milburn b McKenzie	102
B. A. Rothwell c Chadwick b Mayne	6	– c Becker b McKenzie	20
G. R. Davies b Lock	57	– not out	80
J. Rogers c Becker b McKenzie	14	– c sub b Mayne	8
T. Grosser c Irvine b Lock	48	– c Inverarity b Mayne	18
†H. B. Taber lbw b Mayne	30	– c Marsh b McKenzie	36
J. W. Gleeson b McKenzie	16	– c Marsh b Mayne	11
G. E. Corling not out	5	– c Lock b Mayne	0
D. A. Renneberg b Mayne	0	– c Marsh b Lock	12
N-b 7	7	B 2, l-b 7, n-b 3	12
1/5 2/9 3/30 4/80 5/110 6/158 7/183 8/200 9/200	200	1/13 2/61 3/74 4/200 5/256 6/258 7/275 8/275 9/307	307

Bowling: *First Innings*—McKenzie 16–4–48–4; Mayne 12.6–2–68–3; Lock 14–2–56–2; Gannon 2–0–11–0; Milburn 2–0–10–0. *Second Innings*—McKenzie 20–2–78–4; Mayne 23–5–108–4; Lock 29.4–7–59–1; Gannon 4–0–16–0; Milburn 6–0–34–0.

Umpires: E. F. Wykes and T. Brooks.

QUEENSLAND v WESTERN AUSTRALIA

Played at Brisbane, November 22, 23, 24, 25, 1968

Western Australia won by an innings and 75 runs. The dominating feature was Milburn's massive innings of 243 (four 6s and thirty-eight 4s), during which he scored 181 in two hours between lunch and tea. His opening stand with Chadwick realised 328. Inverarity and Becker scored centuries on the second day. Lock (eleven wickets in the match) drove home the advantage, despite useful batting by Surti and some delightful stroke-making by Parker in the second innings.

Western Australia

C. Milburn c and b Morgan	243	R. Edwards not out	3
D. Chadwick st Maclean b Paulsen	91		
R. J. Inverarity c Morgan b Dudgeon	108	L-b 8, w 1, n-b 4	13
†G. C. Becker c Surti b Dudgeon	112		
J. T. Irvine not out	26	1/328 2/376 3/563	(5 wkts dec.) 615
R. W. Marsh c Surti b Paulsen	19	4/580 6/612	

G. D. McKenzie, *G. A. R. Lock, L. C. Mayne and J. D. Gannon did not bat.

Bowling: Allan 21–1–86–0; Duncan 21–1–129–0; Morgan 25–3–107–1; Surti 21–4–124–0; Paulsen 15–0–114–2; Dudgeon 12–2–42–2.

Queensland

J. F. C. Loxton hit wkt b Gannon	40	– st Becker b Lock	20
G. T. Gray c Chadwick b Lock	43	– b Lock	15
M. J. Lucas c Mayne b Gannon	9	– b Mayne	1
R. F. Surti c Milburn b Mayne	77	– run out	49
K. D. Dudgeon b McKenzie	44	– c Chadwick b Lock	3
R. E. Parker c Gannon b Lock	5	– c Irvine b Lock	87
†J. A. Maclean c Inverarity b Mayne	4	– lbw b Lock	27
O. J. Morgan c Becker b Mayne	16	– c Becker b Mayne	21
R. G. Paulsen not out	18	– c McKenzie b Lock	9
*P. J. Allan c Gannon b Lock	5	– b Lock	12
J. R. F. Duncan c Milburn b Lock	0	– not out	7
B 10, l-b 7, n-b 4	21	B 3, n-b 4	7
1/50 2/64 3/184 4/190 5/199 6/215 7/241 8/265 9/281	282	1/1 2/70 3/73 4/80 5/97 6/124 7/130 8/223 9/245	258

Bowling: *First Innings*—McKenzie 18–7–41–1; Mayne 23–2–114–3; Lock 27.7–6–70–4; Gannon 8–1–25–2; Milburn 1–0–11–0. *Second Innings*—McKenzie 13–1–49–0; Mayne 11–0–66–2; Lock 21.7–6–61–7; Gannon 2–1–2–0; Milburn 7–2–33–0; Inverarity 7–0–40–0.

Umpires: L. Rowan and L. Johnson.

QUEENSLAND v NEW SOUTH WALES

Played at Brisbane, November 28, 29, 30, December 1, 1969

Queensland won by five wickets. The young left-hander, Turner, batted through the New South Wales first innings in which the pace bowler, King, took five wickets cheaply. In their second innings, the other opener, Francis, scored his maiden century in first-class cricket. Trimble was yet another opener to star; he batted splendidly for his not out century in the Queensland second innings. Their middle batting showed resistance in the first innings, despite a well-sustained effort by Renneberg.

New South Wales

B. C. Francis c Loxton b King	11	– run out	105
A. Turner not out	71	– c Paulsen b Duncan	2
R. P. Collins lbw b King	8	– c Maclean b Duncan	2
G. R. Davies lbw b King	0	– b Duncan	38
J. W. Wilson c Maclean b King	3	– run out	34
*J. Benaud b Morgan	5	– c Maclean b King	23
D. J. Colley b Maclean b Morgan	20	– c Dudgeon b Surti	15
M. D. Pawley b Paulsen	1	– c Lucas b Paulsen	5
K. J. O'Keeffe c Maclean b King	11	– not out	22
†M. J. Hendricks c King b Paulsen	8	– c Loxton b Morgan	16
D. A. Renneberg b Paulsen	0	– b Morgan	0
B 2, l-b 1, n-b 6	9	B 11, l-b 7, n-b 9	27
1/23 2/37 3/37 4/41 5/46 6/68 7/81 8/122 9/135	147	1/30 2/37 3/136 4/180 5/218 6/227 7/236 8/245 9/287	289

Bowling: *First Innings*—Duncan 8–1–18–0; King 13–1–44–5; Morgan 9–0–44–2; Paulsen 13.3–3–32–3. *Second Innings*—Duncan 20–1–58–3; King 14–1–43–1; Morgan 19.2–2–64–2; Paulsen 18–4–63–1; Surti 12–3–34–1.

Queensland

*S. C. Trimble c Benaud b Renneberg	10	– not out 114
J. F. C. Loxton b Colley	23	– c Francis b O'Keeffe 15
M. J. Lucas c Turner b Renneberg	6	– lbw b Colley 8
K. D. Dudgeon c Hendricks b Renneberg	31	– c Collins b O'Keeffe 13
R. E. Joyce c and b O'Keeffe	30	– c and b O'Keeffe 1
R. F. Surti c Collins b Colley	40	– b Colley 8
†J. A. Maclean b O'Keeffe	23	– not out 16
O. J. Morgan c Wilson b Pawley	59	
R. G. Paulsen c O'Keeffe b Collins	3	
I. H. King c Collins b Pawley	11	
J. R. F. Duncan not out	1	
B 4, l-b 2, n-b 5	11	B 5, n-b 9 14
1/14 2/20 3/68 4/74 5/131 6/154 7/171 8/174 9/230	248	1/37 2/66 3/96 4/102 5/117 (5 wkts) 189

Bowling: *First Innings*—Renneberg 28–9–54–3; Colley 22–6–48–2; O'Keeffe 17–1–65–2; Pawley 8.6–1–38–2; Davies 1–0–9–0; Collins 8–3–23–1. *Second Innings*—Renneberg 5–1–20–0; Colley 21–3–45–2; O'Keeffe 22–2–85–3; Pawley 2–0–20–0; Davies 1.5–0–5–0.

Umpires: L. Rowan and W. Priem.

VICTORIA v NEW SOUTH WALES

Played at Melbourne, December 26, 27, 28, 29, 1969

Victoria won by one wicket. This proved an attractive game in good conditions. Victoria's enthusiastic fast bowler, Thomson, took thirteen wickets in the match, his eight for 87 in the New South Wales second innings being outstanding. The captain, John Benaud, in this innings scored 134, with many powerful strokes; he was associated with Davies, 91, in a fifth-wicket stand for 204 runs. Cowper and Eastwood had given Victoria another fine start, after which the pace bowler, Colley, and the leg-spinner, O'Keeffe, were successful. The third day's play was engrossing, O'Keeffe, who bowled well but unluckily and another spinner, Davies, snaring wickets. Victoria lost eight wickets, but Watson was still there and the umpires declined to give Benaud an extra half-hour on this day. The anti-climax came next day when the Victorians fought their way out of trouble.

New South Wales

B. C. Francis c Bedford b Thomson	0	– c Bedford b Thomson 38
A. Turner c Eastwood b Rowan	5	– c Carlyon b Thomson 15
R. P. Collins c Cowper b Thomson	21	– c Eastwood b Thomson 14
G. E. Davies c Carlyon b Thomson	26	– c Carlyon b Rowan 91
J. W. Wilson b Campbell	5	– hit wkt b Thomson 0
*J. Benaud c Carlyon b Thomson	6	– c Scholes b Thomson 134
D. J. Colley run out	10	– b Thomson 0
K. J. O'Keeffe c Cowper b Campbell	2	– c Carlyon b Campbell 14
†M. Hendricks c Rowan b Thomson	32	– c Swanson b Thomson 0
J. F. Martin c Cowper b Campbell	9	– b Thomson 11
D. A. Renneberg not out	1	– not out 1
B 4, l-b 2, w 1, n-b 7	14	L-b 3, n-b 6 9
1/0 2/10 3/57 4/64 5/64 6/74 7/83 9/112	131	1/49 2/59 3/72 4/76 5/280 6/303 7/303 8/303 9/323 327

Bowling: *First Innings*—Thomson 14.3–2–54–5; Rowan 6–0–30–1; Watson 2–0–6–0; Campbell 9–3–27–3. *Second Innings*—Thomson 23.7–4–87–8; Rowan 18–2–76–1; Campbell 19–4–56–1; Bedford 9–1–37–0; Cowper 5–0–31–0; Swanson 9–1–31–0.

Victoria

K. H. Eastwood c O'Keeffe b Colley	86	c Collins b Renneberg	0
*R. M. Cowper c Hendricks b O'Keeffe	46	c Hendricks b Martin	7
P. L. A. Bedford c Hendricks b Colley	5	c Turner b Davies	30
G. D. Watson c Benaud b Collins	26	st Hendricks b Davies	68
J. W. Scholes b Martin	9	c Collins b Davies	10
J. D. Swanson hit wkt b O'Keeffe	28	b O'Keeffe	3
†N. M. Carlyon c Davies b O'Keeffe	14	c Benaud b Davies	8
L. R. Joslin c Francis b Colley	4	c Hendricks b Renneberg	12
R. K. Rowan c Hendricks b Colley	0	not out	28
B. M. Campbell not out	37	run out	1
A. L. Thomson c Benaud b O'Keeffe	18	not out	0
B 2, l-b 2, n-b 1	5	B 8, l-b 2, n-b 5	15
1/130 2/136 3/148 4/164 5/181 6/205 7/218 8/218 9/220	278	1/0 2/16 3/27 4/70 5/88 6/91 7/100 8/102 9/178	(9 wkts) 182

Bowling: *First Innings*—Renneberg 12–0–44–0; Martin 8–0–53–1; Colley 14–2–63–4; Collins 6–3–12–1; O'Keeffe 23–7–101–4. *Second Innings*—Renneberg 10–1–44–2; Martin 7–0–26–1; Colley 4–0–20–0; O'Keeffe 22.3–7–41–1; Davies 13–1–36–4.

Umpires: K. J. Butler and W. Smyth.

QUEENSLAND v SOUTH AUSTRALIA

Played at Brisbane, January 16, 17, 18, 19, 1970

Queensland won on the first innings. There was much good batting on a fast pitch. Queensland gained a lead of 14 runs after South Australia had compiled 388, with splendid batting by Chappell, Woodcock and Favell. Chappell and Woodcock took part in a third-wicket partnership of 194 in two hours, fifty minutes. In their second innings, in which Chappell gained his second century of the match, he and Favell engaged in a spectacular stand of 180 in two hours, twenty-five minutes. Queensland had recovered remarkably; after losing five wickets for 69 they profited from a stand of 137 by Maclean and Morgan. Maclean, concentrating for over six hours, scored 156.

South Australia

J. P. Causby c Maclean b Duncan	29	c Duncan b King	9
A. J. Woodcock c Maclean b Surti	96	c Graveney b Morgan	28
D. J. Sutherland c Joyce b Duncan	9	c Seib b King	10
G. S. Chappell c Buckle b Joyce	129	not out	156
*L. E. Favell c Paulsen b Morgan	76	c Seib b King	71
D. Munday b Duncan	16	b King	0
†R. P. Blundell c Maclean b King	3	c Paulsen b King	1
T. J. Jenner b Joyce	3	c Morgan b Paulsen	0
K. J. McCarthy b Morgan	6	b King	5
J. R. Hammond b Morgan	0	c Graveney b Paulsen	5
L. R. Gibbs not out	3	st Graveney b Paulsen	2
B 9, l-b 2, n-b 7	18	B 13, n-b 6	19
1/54 2/64 3/258 4/281 5/335 6/345 7/356 8/378 9/378	388	1/32 2/48 3/63 4/243 5/243 6/253 7/254 8/265 9/302	306

Bowling: *First Innings*—King 25–0–123–1; Duncan 20–4–61–3; Morgan 8.4–1–42–3; Paulsen 8–0–47–0; Joyce 17–2–60–2; Surti 5–0–37–1. *Second Innings*—King 17–1–70–6; Duncan 17–3–64–0; Morgan 8–1–27–1; Paulsen 10.3–1–56–3; Joyce 8–1–38–0; Surti 3–0–32–0.

Queensland

*S. C. Trimble c Blundell b Hammond	21	– not out	8
I. Seib b McCarthy	11	– not out	12
W. Buckle c Blundell b Mundy	6		
T. W. Graveney c Blundell b Gibbs	15		
R. F. Surti st Blundell b Gibbs	69		
R. E. Joyce c Blundell b Gibbs	8		
†J. A. Maclean c Blundell b Gibbs	156		
O. J. Morgan b Sutherland	81		
R. F. Duncan not out	16		
R. C. Paulsen not out	2		
B 6, L-b 6, n-b 5	17	W 1	1
1/27 2/39 3/45 4/61 5/69 6/206 7/375 8/396	(8 wkts dec.) 402		(No wkt) 21

I. H. King did not bat.

Bowling: *First Innings*—Hammond 14–0–71–1; McCarthy 18–3–69–1; Munday 19–4–56–1; Gibbs 31–11–84–4; Jenner 30–3–99–0; Sutherland 4–1–6–1. *Second Innings*—Hammond 2–1–5–0; McCarthy 2–0–11–0; Favell 1–0–4–0; Causby 0.3–0–0–0.

Umpires: B. Enright and L. Johnson.

RICHARDS HITS 325 IN A DAY

Barry Richards, South Australia's South African opening batsman, earned more than £150 at a sponsored dollar a run when he scored a not-out 325 for his State on the first day of their Sheffield Shield match against Western Australia in Perth on November 20, 1970.

Richards' score was only nine runs short of the day record in Australia of 334 by W. H. Ponsford at Melbourne in 1926. In 28 days Richards earned £320 for 693 runs, including 224 against MCC. He was lbw for 356, having hit one 6 and forty-eight 4s.

WESTERN AUSTRALIA v SOUTH AUSTRALIA

Played at Perth, November 20, 21, 22, 23, 1970

South Australia won by an innings and 111 runs. The match was dominated by Richards with his great innings of 356; he was with I. M. Chappell in a second-wicket partnership for 308 runs in two hours fifty minutes. Richards missed by three runs equalling the highest score in Australian first-class cricket since the war, R. B. Simpson's 359 for New South Wales against Queensland in Brisbane in 1963-4. Richards, who hit one 6 and forty-eight 4s, batted in all for six hours and twelve minutes. Against a well-balanced attack, supported by keen fielding, he scored 325 runs on the first day, in five and a half hours; 79 before lunch, 137 from lunch to tea, and 109 from tea to "stumps". His first 100 runs came in 125 minutes, and 200 in 208 minutes and 300 in 317 minutes. He was out lbw to a full toss next morning. Irvine and Inverarity showed defiance in both innings for Western Australia. Hammond bowled effectively, taking nine for 79.

South Australia

B. A. Richards lbw b Mann	356	†R. P. Blundell b Mann	0
J. J. Causby c Chadwick b Lock	38	A. A. Mallett not out	6
*I. M. Chappell st March b Lock	129	T. J. Jenner c McKenzie b Mann	5
G. S. Chappell c Marsh b McKenzie	11	N-b 4	4
K. G. Cunningham c Inverarity b Lock	13		
K. Langley run out	7	1/109 2/417 3/447 (9 wkts dec.)	575
E. W. Freeman c Irvine b Lock	6	4/551 5/553 6/563 7/563 8/564 9/575	

J. R. Hammond did not bat.

Bowling: McKenzie 19–2–101–1; Lillee 18–1–117–0; Brayshaw 12–1–69–0; Mann 20.6–1–120–3; Lock 16–1–108–4; Inverarity 8–0–56–0.

Western Australia

D. Chadwick c Blundell b Jenner	49	– c and b Hammond	2
C. Scarff c Blundell b Hammond	11	– b Cunningham	7
J. T. Irvine b Jenner	33	– c and b G. S. Chappell	57
R. J. Inverarity c G. S. Chappell b Hammond	85	– c and b G. S. Chappell	35
R. D. Meuleman retired hurt	28	– absent hurt	0
I. J. Brayshaw lbw b Freeman	22	– c Richards b Mallett	13
†R. W. Marsh c I. M. Chappell b Hammond	9	– c I. M. Chappell b Richards	19
A. L. Mann c Blundell b Hammond	2	– c I. M. Chappell b Hammond	1
D. K. Lillee c Cunningham b Hammond	12	– b Hammond	6
G. D. McKenzie b Hammond	10	– not out	18
*G. A. R. Lock not out	2	– c Hammond b Mallett	8
L-b 7, w 2, n-b 17	26	B 1, n-b 8	9
1/33 2/88 3/110 4/239 5/256 6/261 7/270 8/285 9/289	289	1/3 2/15 3/102 4/110 5/137 6/141 7/142 8/161 9/175	175

Bowling: *First Innings*—Freeman 15–1–53–1; Hammond 12.3–1–54–6; G. S. Chappell 8–1–23–0; Jenner 22–4–78–2; Mallett 18–5–37–0; Cunningham 9–2–18–0. *Second Innings*—Freeman 4–0–16–0; Hammond 9–2–25–3; G. S. Chappell 12–1–41–2; Jenner 8–0–25–0; Mallett 12.5–2–43–2; Cunningham 4–0–12–1; Richards 1–0–4–1.

Umpires: W. Carter and N. Townsend.

VICTORIA v QUEENSLAND

Played at Melbourne, December 11, 12, 13, 14, 1970

Victoria won by 138 runs. This was a grand fight back by Victoria after they had collapsed for 120 runs in their first innings, owing to the well-controlled medium-fast swing bowling of Duncan, who took eight wickets for 55 runs and thirteen wickets in the match. The left-handers, Sieler and Stephens, and also Bedford, held up the Queensland attack in the second innings. Queensland, set 204 runs in five hours to win outright, scored 31 for the first wicket, but there were two run-outs and a wretched collapse caused by the steady bowling of Connolly and Watson, the latter taking five for 23.

Victoria

K. H. Eastwood c Maclean b Dell	30 – c Maclean b Dell	0
A. J. Sieler lbw b Duncan	16 – c Dell b Duncan	97
J. W. Scholes b Duncan	1 – b Duncan	18
G. D. Watson c Maclean b Duncan	11 – c Parker b Dell	5
J. Stephens c Paulsen b Duncan	14 – c Maclean b Paulsen	48
P. L. A. Bedford c Maclean b Duncan	11 – b Paulsen	82
W. L. Stillman b Duncan	9 – c Carlson b Duncan	4
*†R. C. Jordon b Duncan	9 – run out	23
M. Walker c Parker b Duncan	6 – not out	22
A. N. Connolly c Albury b Paulsen	12 – b Duncan	5
J. Higgs not out	0 – b Duncan	0
B 1	1 B 12, l-b 2, n-b 4	18
1/20 2/22 3/57 4/63 5/77 6/87 7/101 8/106 9/120	120 1/0 2/28 3/37 4/154 5/219 6/223 7/286 8/295 9/302	322

Bowling: *First Innings*—Dell 16–4–43–1; Duncan 21–6–55–8; Albury 6–0–20–0; Surti 1–0–1–0; Paulsen 1.1–1–0–1. *Second Innings*—Dell 21–4–53–2; Duncan 28.6–7–70–5; Albury 13–0–61–0; Surti 9–1–28–0; Paulsen 28–5–86–2; Parker 1–0–6–0.

Queensland

*S. C. Trimble c Jordon b Walker	55 – b Watson	19
I. M. Seib b Walker	0 – b Watson	16
R. F. Surti c Jordon b Walker	0 – run out	10
K. E. Dudgeon c Eastwood b Connolly	16 – run out	0
P. H. Carlson c and b Connolly	61 – c Jordon b Connolly	1
R. E. Parker c Higgs b Sieler	24 – c Eastwood b Watson	3
†J. A. Maclean lbw b Walker	7 – b Watson	5
W. Albury c and b Connolly	38 – not out	3
R. G. Paulsen c Jordon b Connolly	0 – b Connolly	0
J. R. F. Duncan c Stephens b Connolly	21 – b Connolly	0
A. R. Dell not out	4 – c Jordon b Watson	0
B 1, l-b 2, n-b 10	13 B 2, l-b 3, n-b 3	8
1/8 2/8 3/75 4/81 5/123 6/148 7/191 8/191 9/224	239 1/31 2/46 3/49 4/52 5/55 6/61 7/61 8/62 9/62	65

Bowling: *First Innings*—Walker 21–6–55–4; Connolly 18.2–2–53–5; Watson 10–0–29–0; Higgs 12–3–45–0; Bedford 6–1–24–0; Sieler 6–2–20–1. *Second Innings*—Walker 4–1–11–0; Connolly 18–8–23–3; Watson 13.5–4–23–5.

Umpires: J. R. Collins and W. Smyth.

SOUTH AUSTRALIA v NEW SOUTH WALES

Played at Adelaide, February 26, 27, 28, March 1, 1971

South Australia won by 127 runs. Freeman, the former Test all-rounder, having recovered from injury, played a leading part in South Australia's conclusive victory in their last match. He took 13 wickets, including eight for 64 in the second innings. New South Wales had rallied from Freeman's early destruction in their first innings, the number eight batsman, Colley, going on to an exciting hundred. In South Australia's first innings Woodcock and I. M. Chappell each was run out for 95, after Richards had led with 55.

South Australia

B. A. Richards b Colley	55	– retired hurt	32
A. J. Woodcock run out	95	– c and b Davies	53
*I. M. Chappell run out	95	– c Crippin b O'Keeffe	38
G. S. Chappell c Taber b O'Keeffe	25	– c Benaud b Davies	52
J. P. Causby c Mackay b Renneberg	4	– c Francis b Davies	25
K. G. Cunningham c Taber b O'Keeffe	3	– c Davies b Renneberg	46
E. W. Freeman c Taber b Walters	27	– b Davies	4
A. A. Mallett c Taber b Renneberg	42	– c Taber b O'Keeffe	4
T. J. Jenner c Colley b Renneberg	26	– c Taber b Davies	0
†M. Hendricks c Mackay b Colley	7	– not out	7
J. R. Hammond not out	2	– not out	3
B 2, l-b 4, n-b 8	14	B 3, l-b 3, n-b 3	9
1/90 2/239 3/259 4/264 5/275 6/315 7/317 8/384 9/389	395	1/78 2/88 3/158 4/179 5/180 6/194 7/195 8/261 (8 wkts dec.)	273

Bowling: *First Innings*—Renneberg 14–0–97–3; Colley 21.3–2–97–2; Walters 13–2–63–1; O'Keeffe 22–5–85–2; Davies 4–0–18–0; Mackay 3–1–18–0; Crippin 2–1–3–0. *Second Innings*—Renneberg 10–0–39–1; Colley 6–2–11–0; Walters 4–0–26–0; O'Keeffe 8–0–69–2; Davies 18–0–110–5; Mackay 2–0–9–0.

New South Wales

A. Turner c Hendricks b Hammond	0	– b Freeman	6
B. C. Francis b Freeman	8	– c Hammond b Freeman	75
J. Benaud b Freeman	49	– c I. M. Chappell b Hammond	29
G. R. Davies c G. S. Chappell b Freeman	11	– c Hendricks b Freeman	32
K. D. Walters c Cunningham b Freeman	4	– c Mallett b Freeman	12
K. Mackay c G. S. Chappell b Freeman	8	– run out	5
R. Crippin c Woodcock b Mallett	44	– lbw b Freeman	1
D. J. Colley c Mallett b I. M. Chappell	101	– c Mallett b Freeman	0
K. J. O'Keeffe not out	81	– not out	12
*†H. B. Taber c Hendricks b Hammond	20	– c Cunningham b Freeman	9
D. A. Renneberg b Jenner	5	– b Freeman	0
L-b 1, w 2, n-b 14	17	B 3, l-b 1, w 3, n-b 5	12
1/0 2/39 3/63 4/68 5/82 6/85 7/179 8/276 9/332	348	1/14 2/86 3/139 4/156 5/164 6/164 7/165 8/173 9/193	193

Bowling: *First Innings*—Hammond 18–3–65–2; Freeman 7–2–41–5; Cunningham 7–1–25–0; G. S. Chappell 15–3–42–0; Jenner 18.3–1–81–1; Mallett 15–3–53–1; I. M. Chappell 8–3–24–1. *Second Innings*—Hammond 6–0–44–1; Freeman 18.5–2–64–8; Cunningham 3–0–14–0; G. S. Chappell 4–0–14–0; Jenner 10–0–36–0; Mallett 3–0–9–0.

Umpires: M. G. O'Connell and A. Godson.

WESTERN AUSTRALIA v QUEENSLAND

Played at Perth, October 30, 31, November 1, 2, 1971

Western Australia won by an innings and 93 runs. Queensland failed against well-controlled pace bowling on Perth's grassy pitch; McKenzie took seven wickets in the match. Watson, in his first innings for Western Australia, batted splendidly for just over five hours for 145 runs, having a second-wicket partnership with the new captain, Inverarity, of 184. Watson, believing that he had been caught in the gully by Allen off Neville, walked off the field. At the end of the day he was told by the umpire that it was not a catch; the umpire instructed the scorer to record Watson as "retired, out".

Western Australia

D. Chadwick c MacLean b Albury	8	A. L. Mann b Dell	9
G. D. Watson, retired, "out"	145	G. D. McKenzie c Dell b Albury	3
*R. J. Inverarity b Surti	85	D. K. Lillee not out	3
R. Edwards c MacLean b Neville	2	B 4, l-b 6, n-b 4	14
†R. W. Marsh run out	7		
L. Varis st MacLean b Dudgeon	44	1/26 2/210 3/219 (9 wkts dec.)	388
I. J. Brayshaw c MacLean b Albury	68	4/241 5/267 6/329 7/352 8/370 9/388	

R. A. L. Massie did not bat.

Bowling: Dell 19–1–70–1; Albury 23.6–1–110–3; Neville 18–2–73–1; Paulsen 12–1–46–0; Carlson 4–0–18–0; Surti 13–3–42–1; Dudgeon 4–1–15–1.

Queensland

*S. C. Trimble lbw b McKenzie	46	– c Chadwick b Lillee	4
D. Allen b Watson	20	– run out	7
B. Grace c Lillee b Watson	14	– b Lillee	12
P. H. Carlson b McKenzie	19	– b Watson	24
K. E. Dudgeon c Marsh b McKenzie	0	– c Marsh b Lillee	20
R. F. Surti lbw b Watson	6	– c Varis b McKenzie	22
†J. A. MacLean b Massie	13	– c and b McKenzie	22
W. Neville c Marsh b Massie	26	– b McKenzie	0
W. Albury c Watson b Inverarity	9	– not out	8
R. G. Paulsen c Inverarity b McKenzie	0	– c Lillee b Mann	2
A. R. Dell not out	0	– c Edwards b Inverarity	6
L-b 4, w 4, n-b 3	11	L-b 1, n-b 3	4
1/49 2/78 3/86 4/90 5/103 6/111 7/137 8/164 9/164	164	1/5 2/12 3/50 4/50 5/89 6/107 7/107 8/116 9/121	131

Bowling: *First Innings*—Lillee 10–2–33–0; Massie 14–2–47–2; McKenzie 14–4–38–4; Watson 10–3–18–3; Inverarity 4–1–17–1. *Second Innings*—Lillee 11–2–36–3; Massie 14–4–37–0; McKenzie 10–3–34–3; Watson 3–1–8–1; Inverarity 0.7–0–0–1; Mann 10–5–12–1.

Umpires: W. Carter and N. Townsend.

QUEENSLAND v VICTORIA

Played at Brisbane, October 26, 27, 28, 29, 1973

Drawn. In a match described as the most exciting on the ground since the tied Test between Australia and the West Indies, Queensland batted in dreadfully bad light and failed to gain outright victory by seven runs with three wickets standing. The game was unusual in that both Chappell and the left-handed Sieler hit centuries in each innings. Victoria began badly by losing the wickets of Stackpole and Scholes to the first two balls of the game of the former Test left arm pace bowler Dell; then Sieler and Rose set a new Victorian Shield record of 271 for the fifth wicket. It was Sieler's third first class century and Rose's first. Chappell batted with authority to enable Queensland to pass Victoria's first innings by one run and after Victoria's second poor start, Sieler and Rose made a stand of 185. Chappell and Majid Khan batted superbly for a century apiece but Victoria refused to concede defeat.

Victoria

*K. R. Stackpole b Dell	0	– c Albury b Dell	20
A. P. Sheahan c Trimble b Dell	17	– b Dell	19
J. W. Scholes c Trimble b Dell	0	– c Dudgeon b Albury	5
I. R. Redpath c Khan b Albury	19	– c Seib b Dell	1
A. J. Sieler c Chappell b Albury	157	– b Dymock	105
R. P. Rose not out	118	– c and b Dymock	88
†R. D. Robinson (did not bat)		– b Albury	21
R. J. Bright (did not bat)		– not out	20
M. H. N. Walker (did not bat)		– not out	3
L-b 1, n-b 2	3	B 3, l-b 6, n-b 2	11
1/0 2/0 3/33 4/43 5/314 (5 wkts dec.)	314	1/26 2/45 3/47 4/57 5/241 6/250 7/283 (7 wkts dec.)	293

A. G. Hurst and J. D. Higgs did not bat.

Bowling: *First Innings*—Dell 19–2–71–3; Dymock 15–4–55–0; Albury 17–0–91–2; Francke 17–1–71–0; Chappell 4–1–8–0; Carlson 3–0–15–0; Khan 1–1–0–0. *Second Innings*—Dell 23–2–106–3; Dymock 16–4–53–2; Albury 14–3–29–2; Francke 14–0–56–0; Khan 15–4–38–0.

Queensland

S. C. Trimble c Sheahan b Higgs	57	– lbw b Walker	17
I. M. Seib c Higgs b Walker	1	– c Robinson b Walker	8
Majid J. Khan c Sheahan b Hurst	4	– c Stackpole b Higgs	100
*G. S. Chappell c Bright b Hurst	180	– c Sheahan b Walker	101
P. H. Carlson b Hurst	27	– st Robinson b Higgs	5
K. E. Dudgeon c Stackpole b Higgs	7	– b Walker	17
†J. A. Maclean c Walker b Higgs	2	– c Bright b Hurst	28
F. M. Francke c Stackpole b Higgs	4	– not out	1
W. D. Albury c Robinson b Hurst	14	– not out	2
G. Dymock b Higgs	9		
A. R. Dell not out	0		
B 1, l-b 7, n-b 2	10	B 4, l-b 3	7
1/6 2/10 3/134 4/191 5/222 6/224 7/238 8/295 9/314	315	1/19 2/30 3/215 4/237 5/247 6/283 7/283 (7 wkts)	286

Bowling: *First Innings*—Hurst 27–4–89–4; Walker 26–4–91–1; Sieler 11–0–34–0; Bright 10–2–39–0; Higgs 13.1–1–52–5. *Second Innings*—Hurst 12–0–53–1; Walker 21–1–97–4; Sieler 2–0–23–0; Bright 4–0–31–0; Higgs 12–0–75–2.

Umpires: P. Enright and T. Warwick.

SOUTH AUSTRALIA v VICTORIA

Played at Adelaide, December 14, 15, 16, 17, 1973

Victoria won by 78 runs. South Australia suffered their fifth successive defeat in as many matches in the Shield competition despite magnificently aggressive centuries in both innings by their captain, I. M. Chappell. All but the first hour of the first day was lost due to rain and Chappell declared his team's innings closed soon after passing Victoria's moderate score, Chappell himself contributing 141 not out in a superb display of pulling and driving. Victoria soon lost their openers Stackpole and Rose but Sheahan and Redpath had a dazzling stand of 172 to revive their team's hopes, Sheahan finishing with 171 not out and receiving strong support from Baldry. So well did I. M. Chappell bat in the second innings that he came within two runs of gaining 100 runs in a session as he had done the previous day. Save for T. M. Chappell's sound 57, he had a poor response from his team, for no other batsman reached double figures and the last seven wickets fell while only 22 runs were scored, the pace bowlers Hurst and Walker and the spinner Bright demolishing all Chappell's earlier good work.

Victoria

*K. R. Stackpole c Curtin b Hiern	59	– lbw b Hiern	0
R. P. Rose c Woodcock b Hiern	12	– c Mallett b Barnes	7
A. P. Sheahan c Jenner b Hiern	10	– not out	171
I. R. Redpath c Hendricks b Barnes	73	– run out	88
A. J. Seiler c Curtin b Jenner	53	– c Woodcock b Barnes	0
R. J. Baldry b Jenner	5	– lbw b Hiern	51
†R. D. Robinson c Donaldson b Barnes	8		
R. J. Bright not out	6		
M. H. N. Walker c Curtin b Jenner	7		
A. G. Hurst b Jenner	18		
L-b 2, w 1, n-b 2	5	B 5, l-b 1, n-b 2	8
1/22 2/68 3/106 4/201 5/211 6/223 7/228 8/237 9/256	(9 wkts dec.) 256	1/0 2/12 3/184 4/187 5/325	(5 wkts dec.) 325

J. D. Higgs did not bat.

Bowling: *First Innings*—Hiern 14–1–64–3; Barnes 16–0–84–2; Mallett 11–2–49–0; Jenner 12.4–0–54–4. *Second Innings*—Hiern 18.1–2–87–2; Barnes 23–0–96–2; Mallett 19–2–79–0; Jenner 12–0–55–0.

South Australia

A. J. Woodcock run out	35	– c Sheahan b Walker	8
B. L. Causby st Robinson b Higgs	33	– c Redpath b Walker	6
*I. M. Chappell not out	141	– c Redpath b Hurst	130
B. G. Curtin c and b Hurst	27	– c Robinson b Walker	5
T. M. Chappell c Sieler b Walker	22	– c Bright b Hurst	57
J. S. Donaldson not out	14	– c Robinson b Hurst	3
T. J. Jenner (did not bat)		– c Sheahan b Bright	6
J. R. Barnes (did not bat)		– c Baldry b Bright	4
†M. Hendricks (did not bat)		– b Hurst	1
A. A. Mallett (did not bat)		– not out	0
B. N. Hiern (did not bat)		– b Bright	3
L-b 1, n-b 4	5	L-b 2, w 1	3
1/70 2/70 3/125 4/220	(4 wkts dec.) 277	1/8 2/43 3/49 4/204 5/210 6/212 7/218 8/222 9/222	226

Bowling: *First Innings*—Hurst 18–2–81–1; Walker 18–4–90–1; Higgs 14–1–48–1; Bright 7–0–53–0. *Second Innings*—Hurst 15–1–67–4; Walker 11–0–79–3; Higgs 4–0–26–0; Bright 3.4–1–8–3; Sieler 6–1–43–0.

Umpires: M. O'Connell and R. Bailhache.

WESTERN AUSTRALIA v NEW SOUTH WALES

Played at Perth, March 1, 2, 3, 4, 1975

Western Australia won by nine wickets. Poor batting by NSW ended their Shield aspirations. Only a stubborn half century by Turner kept Lillee and Malone at bay in the first innings, the latter appearing in his second game for the State. Marsh took six catches and completed a fine match with nine catches. He also aided his team to a first innings lead with a powerful 66 after W. J. Edwards and Laird made a good start. A brisk 77 by Rosen and McCosker gave the NSW second innings a sound start, but Malone's swinging deliveries again did their damage despite gritty efforts by Davis, O'Keeffe and Colley. Laird and Langer worked patiently against a disciplined attack to gain the desired 186 in an unfinished second wicket partnership of 151.

New South Wales

M. F. Rosen c Marsh b Malone	28	– c Marsh b Lillee	42
R. B. McCosker c Marsh b Watson	13	– c Alderman b Malone	58
A. Turner c Marsh b Watson	53	– c Alderman b Watson	11
*K. D. Walters c Marsh b Malone	6	– c Lillee b Malone	6
I. C. Davis c Marsh b Lillee	6	– c Marsh b Lillee	44
G. J. Gilmour b Malone	6	– b Malone	0
K. M. Hill b Brayshaw	20	– c sub b Malone	26
K. J. O'Keeffe b Lillee	3	– not out	32
†S. J. Rixon c Laird b Lillee	21	– c Marsh b Watson	15
D. J. Colley not out	17	– c Inverarity b Alderman	36
L. S. Pascoe c Marsh b Lillee	0	– b Alderman	0
L-b 3, n-b 2	5	L-b 3, n-b 6	9
1/31 2/51 3/61 4/82 5/99 6/129 7/137 8/151 9/178	178	1/77 2/118 3/120 4/134 5/161 6/169 7/197 8/220 9/279	279

Bowling: *First Innings*—Lillee 15-6–2–47–4; Alderman 5–0–21–0; Brayshaw 4–2–13–1; Watson 7–0–37–2; Malone 17–3–55–3. *Second Innings*—Lillee 15–1–70–2; Alderman 6.5–0–52–2; Brayshaw 2–0–5–0; Watson 12–1–48–2; Malone 26–3–87–4; Paulsen 4–0–8–0.

Western Australia

B. M. Laird c Rixon b Gilmour	24	– not out	77
W. J. Edwards c and b Gilmour	52	– c Hill b Colley	25
R. S. Langer c Rixon b Gilmour	0	– not out	72
I. J. Brayshaw c McCosker b Colley	15		
†R. W. Marsh c McCosker b O'Keeffe	66		
*R. J. Inverarity c Turner b Gilmour	2		
G. D. Watson c McCosker b Walters	24		
R. G. Paulsen c Rixon b Walters	1		
D. K. Lillee c Turner b Walters	46		
M. F. Malone c Davis b O'Keeffe	24		
T. M. Alderman not out	0		
B 1, l-b 4, w 1, n-b 12	18	L-b 1, w 1, n-b 10	12
1/69 2/84 3/85 4/113 5/159 6/169 7/227 8/257 9/272	272	1/35	(1 wkt) 186

Bowling: *First Innings*—Pascoe 14–1–79–0; Gilmour 14–2–55–4; Colley 13–1–57–1; Walters 14–6–40–3; O'Keeffe 6.3–1–23–2. *Second Innings*—Pascoe 8–0–41–0; Gilmour 10–3–35–0; Colley 11–2–46–1; Walters 2–1–3–0; O'Keeffe 12–3–25–0; Hill 4–2–24–0.

Umpires: W. Carter and D. Hawks.

WESTERN AUSTRALIA v VICTORIA

Played at Perth, November 15, 16, 17, 18, 1975

Western Australia won by four wickets. Ill-feeling ran high between the teams which have won the Sheffield Shield in the last four seasons when Walker was struck in the face by a bumper from Lillee after Hurst had delivered a series of short-pitched balls at the Western Australians. On a rain-interrupted first day Laughlin made his first century for Victoria after which Marsh declared Western Australia's innings closed 38 runs behind Victoria. Lillee was devastating, dismissing five batsmen for 58 runs, and Marsh, following his first innings' six catches, equalled A. Long's world record of 11 catches in a game in Victoria's second innings capitulation. Marsh completed a fine match with a robust 76 in ninety-nine minutes to assure his team of victory.

Victoria

*I. R. Redpath c Marsh b Alderman	11	lbw b Lillee	20
P. A. Hibbert c Marsh b Malone	12	c Alderman b Lillee	32
G. N. Yallop c Marsh b Malone	21	c Marsh b Malone	6
W. L. Stillman c Brayshaw b Alderman	48	b Malone	4
R. J. Baldry c Marsh b Lillee	60	c Marsh b Lillee	13
T. J. Laughlin c Malone b Paulsen	113	c Marsh b Lillee	29
†R. D. Robinson not out	23	c Marsh b Lillee	1
R. J. Bright c Marsh b Lillee	0	c Marsh b Paulsen	1
M. H. N. Walker c Marsh b Lillee	0	retired hurt	5
L. J. Baker not out	3	not out	4
A. G. Hurst (did not bat)		b Paulsen	6
B 4, l-b 3, w 2, n-b 2	11	W 1	1
1/19 2/29 3/69 4/106 5/247 6/292 7/292 8/292	(8 wkts dec.) 302	1/31 2/43 3/51 4/72 5/89 6/99 7/100 8/110 9/122	122

Bowling: *First Innings*—Lillee 14.3–2–85–3; Alderman 12–2–43–2; Malone 20–3–82–2; Brayshaw 6–0–23–0; Paulsen 11–1–57–1; Inverarity 1–0–1–0. *Second Innings*—Lillee 11–1–58–5; Alderman 2–1–1–0; Malone 9–2–24–2; Paulsen 11.6–3–38–2.

Western Australia

B. M. Laird lbw b Hurst	0	run out	7
W. J. Edwards b Laughlin	54	c Baker b Laughlin	26
R. S. Langer b Walker	23	b Bright	30
K. J. Hughes b Hurst	10	c Robinson b Redpath	12
*†R. W. Marsh c Robinson b Walker	36	c Laughlin b Redpath	76
R. J. Inverarity c Baldry b Walker	42	run out	0
I. J. Brayshaw c Stillman b Baker	25	not out	1
D. K. Lillee c Robinson b Baker	0		
M. F. Malone not out	19	not out	4
R. G. Paulsen not out	24		
L-b 7, n-b 24	31	L-b 4, n-b 2	6
1/2 2/38 3/56 4/120 5/145 6/205 7/209 8/224	(8 wkts dec.) 264	1/37 2/45 3/51 4/147 5/147 6/158	(6 wkts) 162

T. M. Alderman did not bat.

Bowling: *First Innings*—Walker 20–3–81–3; Hurst 21–3–80–2; Laughlin 7–0–27–1; Baker 10–1–40–2; Redpath 2–0–5–0. *Second Innings*—Hurst 13–2–46–0; Laughlin 12–3–49–1; Redpath 9–1–36–2; Bright 7.6–1–25–1.

Umpires: G. Duperouzel and D. Hawks.

SOUTH AUSTRALIA v QUEENSLAND

Played at Adelaide, February 11, 12, 13, 14, 1977

Tied. One of the most remarkable Sheffield Shield games of all time finished in a tie – 602 runs each – from the penultimate ball of the game after Queensland had seemed assured of victory with three wickets standing and requiring four runs at the start of the last over.

Carlson, Francke and Cooke were run out from the fourth, sixth and seventh balls for the tied game. The only other tied Shield game was between Victoria and New South Wales at the St Kilda Ground in Melbourne in December 1956. Hookes' innings of 185 in three hours eleven minutes and 105 in one hour forty-one minutes made him the 13th player for South Australia to make a century in each innings of a match. Maclean declared Queensland's innings closed 91 runs behind South Australia's 431 after he and Whyte had hit 161 runs in quick time for the seventh wicket. Blewett responded with a declaration soon after lunch. Queensland were three for 160 at the start of the 15 compulsory overs and then lost seven for 102 in a thrilling eighty-four minutes period; Kent made a glittering 82 and Carlson a fluent 65.

South Australia

A. J. Handrickan c Maclean b Cooke	2	– lbw b Cooke	21
*R. K. Blewett lbw b Dymock	30	– c Maclean b Cooke	10
A. M. Eaton b Cooke	0	– b Dymock	15
J. E. Nash c Maclean b Dymock	5	– c and b Francke	0
D. W. Hookes b Dymock	185	– b Carlson	105
P. Sleep c Maclean b Whyte	57	– c Maclean b Dymock	6
†R. G. Vincent b Whyte	59	– b Carlson	2
G. R. Attenborough lbw b Dymock	9		
R. M. O'Shannassy hit wkt b Dymock	48	– not out	6
D. J. Lambert not out	28		
W. Prior c Maclean b Francke	4		
L-b 1, w 1, n-b 2	4	B 1, n-b 5	6
1/2 2/2 3/14 4/75 5/234	431	1/25 2/34 3/97 (7 wkts dec.)	171
6/319 7/335 8/351 9/418		4/98 5/146 6/169 7/171	

Bowling: *First Innings*—Cooke 13–1–65–2; Dymock 25–3–109–5; Carlson 3–0–31–0; Whyte 26–2–108–2; Francke 13.3–0–73–1; Hohns 10–0–41–0. *Second Innings*—Cooke 6–0–45–2; Dymock 10–0–42–2; Francke 10–0–72–1; Whyte 2–0–2–0; Carlson 1–0–4–2.

Queensland

L. M. Richardson c Blewett b Sleep	79	– lbw b Attenborough	1
A. D. Ogilvie c Vincent b Prior	6	– c Prior b Attenborough	49
T. V. Hohns c O'Shannassy b Lambert	21	– c Vincent b Prior	25
M. F. Kent c Handrickan b Attenborough	20	– run out	82
P. H. Carlson c O'Shannassy b Attenborough	4	– run out	65
J. N. Langley lbw b Attenborough	10	– c Lambert b Attenborough	1
*†J. A. Maclean c Hookes b Sleep	82	– c Hookes b O'Shannassy	9
G. K. Whyte c Handrickan b Prior	93	– lbw b O'Shannassy	0
G. Dymock not out	10	– not out	16
F. M. Francke not out	3	– run out	0
C. J. Cooke (did not bat)		– run out	0
B 3, l-b 8, n-b 1	12	B 6, l-b 6, n-b 2	14
1/21 2/72 3/108 4/114 (8 wkts dec.)	340	1/1 2/138 3/145 4/186 5/229	262
5/130 6/157 7/318 8/333		6/237 7/237 8/261 9/262	

Bowling: *First Innings*—Prior 20–1–107–2; Attenborough 25–6–81–3; O'Shannassy 8–1–21–0; Lambert 27–7–40–1; Sleep 16–3–71–2; Hookes 2–1–1–0; Blewett 5–1–7–0. *Second Innings*—Prior 9–0–55–1; Attenborough 15.7–1–62–3; O'Shannassy 8–0–54–2; Blewett 6–1–34–0; Lambert 4–0–23–0; Sleep 2–0–20–0.

Umpires: R. C. Bailhache and M. G. O'Connell.

SOUTH AUSTRALIA v NEW SOUTH WALES

Played at Adelaide, February 18, 19, 20, 21, 1977

Drawn. All else in the game was dwarfed by the feat of Hookes in becoming the first Australian and only the second cricketer in history after T. W. Hayward of Surrey to make a century in each innings of two successive first-class matches. Following his innings of 185 and 105 against Queensland, Hookes made 135 and 156 against New South Wales. With the 18-year-old opener Handrickan, playing in only his second first-class match, Hookes added 204 in two and a quarter hours for the fourth wicket, but consistent efforts by the New South Wales batsmen enabled them to lead by 66 on the first innings; Webster, Watson, Toohey, Colley, Rixon and Hughes all passed 40. Again Hookes barred New South Wales' way for three and three-quarter hours, but Pascoe and Hourn wore down the resistance and Webster completed a grand match with 98 not out in under two hours as New South Wales sought 269 runs in 224 minutes only to lose 108 minutes through rain.

South Australia

A. J. Woodcock c Hughes b Clews	4	– c Rixon b Pascoe	16
A. J. Handrickan b Pascoe	113	– absent hurt	0
*R. K. Blewett lbw b Colley	27	– lbw b Pascoe	32
W. M. Darling c Webster b Watson	7	– not out	2
D. W. Hookes b Pascoe	135	– lbw b Watson	156
P. Sleep lbw b Pascoe	6	– lbw b Colley	0
†R. G. Vincent c and b Hourn	11	– c Hughes b Hourn	35
R. M. O'Shannassy c Border b Pascoe	0	– b Pascoe	19
G. R. Attenborough b Clews	11	– c and b Hourn	1
D. J. Lambert not out	0	– c Clews b Hourn	41
W. Prior lbw b Clews	0	– c Webster b Border	14
L-b 6, w 1, n-b 12	19	B 1, l-b 4, n-b 13	18
1/15 2/52 3/71 4/275 5/286 6/312 7/313 8/326 9/333	333	1/42 2/58 3/149 4/150 5/205 6/206 7/285 8/328 9/334	334

Bowling: *First Innings*—Pascoe 14–2–68–4; Clews 13.5–1–57–3; Watson 11–0–66–1; Colley 8–0–48–1; Hourn 10–2–44–1; Border 1–0–14–0; Webster 2–0–17–0. *Second Innings*—Pascoe 20–1–64–3; Clews 9–0–41–0; Hourn 26–1–130–3; Colley 9–1–49–1; Watson 6–1–15–1; Border 5.7–0–17–1.

New South Wales

S. E. Webster c O'Shannassy b Lambert	74	– not out	98
J. Dyson c Hookes b O'Shannassy	13	– not out	27
G. D. Watson c Attenborough b Lambert	70		
P. M. Toohey run out	54		
G. C. Hughes c sub b Lambert	48		
A. R. Border b Blewett	10		
*D. J. Colley c Hookes b Sleep	52		
†S. J. Rixon not out	50		
M. L. Clews c Vincent b Attenborough	19		
L. S. Pascoe run out	1		
D. W. Hourn b Attenborough	1		
B 2, l-b 4, n-b 1	7	L-b 1	1
1/32 2/144 3/173 4/239 5/267 6/281 7/350 8/391 9/396	399		(no wkt) 126

Bowling: *First Innings*—Prior 11–2–29–0; Attenborough 13–0–63–2; O'Shannassy 6–0–25–1; Lambert 25–1–115–3; Sleep 12–0–71–1; Hookes 8–0–41–0; Blewett 14–3–48–1. *Second Innings*—Attenborough 3–0–11–0; Prior 6–1–26–0; Lambert 2–0–11–0; O'Shannassy 9–1–37–0; Sleep 2–0–20–0; Hookes 5–0–20–0.

Umpires: A. Crafter and K. Butler.

WESTERN AUSTRALIA v TASMANIA

Played at Perth, October 29, 30, 31, November 1, 1977

Western Australia won by an innings and 14 runs. After waiting for 126 years since it conducted Australia's first Inter-Colonial match, Tasmania was accorded a most testing introduction to the Sheffield Shield competition – in the opening match of the season and against the titleholders on Western Australia's home ground. Despite the earlier loss of six players to WSC, Western Australia, under Inverarity, who resumed the captaincy after a two years' study visit to England, bristled with internationals and had great all-round strength. Tasmania were outplayed from the time they were sent in to bat on the first morning; marked inexperience contributed to an innings defeat. Apart from two fighting innings by Yorkshire professional John Hampshire, the Tasmanian batsmen were mesmerised by the leg-spin of Mann, the speed of Alderman and Gannon, and the never-ending variety of medium-pace veteran Brayshaw. In the Western Australian innings Hughes hit nine 4s during a three and a quarter hours stay for 80, and Brayshaw batted brightly for 50 after Inverarity had displayed much of his old classic style while laying the foundation of the innings.

Tasmania

†B. R. Doolan b Alderman	2	– c Wright b Alderman	17
B. W. Neill b Alderman	7	– b Mann	20
M. J. Norman b Brayshaw	8	– b Brayshaw	5
J. H. Hampshire c Inverarity b Alderman	47	– c Brayshaw b Mann	41
S. J. Howard c Wood b Mann	37	– c Brayshaw b Mann	6
T. W. Docking c Hughes b Mann	12	– c Wright b Brayshaw	1
A. J. Benneworth c Wright b Alderman	0	– b Alderman	24
*J. Simmons c and b Mann	10	– c Alderman b Mann	1
D. J. Baker c Brayshaw b Gannon	14	– c Wright b Mann	19
G. J. Cowmeadow b Gannon	0	– b Gannon	0
R. J. Sherriff not out	0	– not out	2
B 2, l-b 5, n-b 3	10	L-b 2, w 2, n-b 2	6
1/2 2/32 3/80 4/85 5/112 6/113 7/129 8/137 9/140	147	1/23 2/42 3/42 4/48 5/49 6/83 7/97 8/135 9/136	142

Bowling: *First Innings*—Alderman 15–4–32–4; Gannon 12.6–3–44–2; Brayshaw 5–3–8–1; Mann 16–4–51–3; Hagdorn 2–0–2–0. *Second Innings*—Alderman 9–4–32–2; Gannon 11–4–23–1; Brayshaw 13–6–21–2; Mann 15.5–6–43–5; Hagdorn 4–0–17–0.

Western Australia

G. M. Wood c Sherriff b Cowmeadow	55
R. I. Charlesworth c Benneworth b Baker	1
*R. J. Inverarity lbw b Baker	44
C. S. Serjeant c Baker b Cowmeadow	20
K. J. Hughes b Simmons	80
I. J. Brayshaw b Benneworth	50
A. L. Mann c Neill b Benneworth	23
†K. J. Wright not out	7
B 1, l-b 11, n-b 11	23
1/7 2/96 3/114 4/126 5/269 6/277 7/303 (7 wkts dec.)	303

K. Hagdorn, T. M. Alderman and J. B. Gannon did not bat.

Bowling: Baker 21–3–82–2; Cowmeadow 17–1–67–2; Sherriff 11–0–41–0; Benneworth 10.7–3–42–2; Simmons 14–1–48–1.

Umpires: D. Hawks and D. Weser.

QUEENSLAND v VICTORIA

Played at Brisbane, November 4, 5, 6, 7, 1977

Queensland won by five wickets. Bonus points: Queensland 15, Victoria 7. A record points total for Queensland, a fine innings by the red-bearded David Ogilvie, and a dramatic finish in which players' feelings ran high were features of Victoria's ultimate defeat. Queensland amassed 388 for six wickets on the first day, Gaskell, Cosier and Hohns vigorously assisting while Ogilvie compiled his third first-class century. Dropped at 7, he proceeded to hit twenty-nine 4s in his highest score of 194 during a stay of nearly five hours. Thomson's fine bowling – eight for 170 for the match on an unresponsive pitch – with able support from Dymock, resulted in an undistinguished Victorian first innings. Following on, Wiener hit 106 in four hours twenty minutes to become the first Victorian to score a century in his initial Shield match since Test selector Sam Loxton did so 30 years earlier, but apart from a sound supporting role by all-rounder Laughlin, five wickets fell for 31 runs after he left. Set to score 115 in one hundred minutes, Ogilvie and Gaskell scored 97 before a collapse; then captain Maclean and Carlson desperately steered Queensland to victory with two and half overs remaining – and in rapidly gathering gloom relieved only by the lightning flashes from the impending storm which hit the ground and brought total darkness within minutes of the finish. First innings time-wasting by Victoria was repeated on the final afternoon, when it attracted an umpire's warning. Queensland players and officials also severely criticised the penalizing of their side when the umpires overlooked a new ACB rule which should have allowed the Victorian innings to be continued for up to half an hour when nine wickets had fallen at the scheduled tea-break.

Queensland

A. I. Kallicharran c Maddocks b Callen	14	– b Hurst	0
M. A. Gaskell c and b Higgs	40	– c Higgs b Hurst	43
A. D. Ogilvie lbw b Laughlin	194	– c Maclean b Hurst	53
G. J. Cosier c Yallop b Wiener	41	– b Laughlin	1
T. V. Hohns c Higgs b Hibbert	44	– run out	1
P. H. Carlson c Wiener b Laughlin	33	– not out	2
*†J. A. Maclean c sub b Hurst	4	– not out	8
G. K. Whyte b Laughlin	20		
J. R. Thomson c sub b Laughlin	0		
F. M. Francke not out	4		
B 2, l-b 4, n-b 1	7	L-b 2, n-b 7	9
1/16 2/145 3/199 4/325 5/342 6/347 7/392 8/392 9/401	(9 wkts dec.) 401	1/1 2/98 3/102 4/106 5/107	(5 wkts) 117

G. Dymock did not bat.

Bowling: *First Innings*—Hurst 18–2–85–1; Callen 20–2–104–1; McArdle 3–0–10–0; Laughlin 14.2–1–71–4; Higgs 11–0–69–1; Wiener 4–0–35–1; Hibbert 3–0–20–1. *Second Innings*—Hurst 7–0–33–3; Callen 6–0–49–0; Laughlin 4–0–26–1.

Victoria

P. A. Hibbert run out	40	– c Kallicharran b Thomas	4
J. M. Wiener c Carlson b Thomson	31	– c Cosier b Dymock	106
J. K. Moss c Ogilvie b Thomson	22	– c Kallicharran b Thomson	12
D. F. Whatmore c Maclean b Dymock	8	– lbw b Thomson	4
T. J. Laughlin c Maclean b Dymock	28	– lbw b Dymock	77
*G. N. Yallop c Maclean b Francke	35	– b Carlson	14
†I. L. Maddocks lbw b Thomson	3	– c Cosier b Whyte	2
I. W. Callen c Francke b Thomson	30	– not out	13
A. G. Hurst c Francke b Dymock	19	– b Whyte	0
J. D. Higgs b Thomson	10	– b Whyte	24
B. J. McArdle not out	5	– c Francke b Dymock	10
W 1, n-b 10	11	L-b 1, w 1, n-b 5	7
1/38 2/78 3/90 4/128 5/137 6/159 7/205 8/208 9/236	242	1/9 2/34 3/50 4/67 5/218 6/229 7/242 8/249 9/249	273

Bowling: *First Innings*—Thomson 21–1–96–5; Dymock 18–5–51–3; Carlson 5–1–13–0; Francke 20–5–61–1; Whyte 8–3–10–0. *Second Innings*—Thomson 16–2–74–3; Dymock 16.5–3–53–3; Carlson 9–3–29–1; Francke 5–0–14–0; Whyte 8–2–31–3; Cosier 8–2–21–0; Hohns 12–3–44–0.

Umpires: J. M. Boyle and C. E. Harvey.

NEW SOUTH WALES v VICTORIA

Played at Sydney, November 26, 27, 28, 29, 1977

Drawn. Victorian captain Yallop played the major part in this game by hitting centuries in both innings, being ably supported by Laughlin's not out 93 in the first innings and Wiener's competent 126 in the second. However, slow batting on the third day, allied to the decision for a delayed declaration and the fact that Victoria had gone into the match with only three specialist bowlers, dissipated the advantage gained. The New South Wales batsmen, who had shown a marked lack of application in the first innings, responded to a strong call from Simpson to play out time on the final day and they finished only 67 runs behind with three wickets in hand. Toohey hit fourteen 4s in his 95 and, with the other recognised batsmen dismissed, Dyson ensured a draw by remaining undefeated with a patient 103 scored in five and a quarter hours.

Victoria

P. A. Hibbert c Border b Clews	4	– c Rixon b Watson	19
J. M. Wiener c Rixon b Watson	2	– run out	126
D. F. Whatmore c Rixon b Clews	31	– c and b Colley	0
*G. N. Yallop b Colley	105	– not out	114
P. Melville b Clews	30	– c Rixon b Hourn	9
J. K. Moss lbw b Hourn	26	– b Watson	6
T. J. Laughlin not out	93	– c Rixon b Watson	1
I. W. Callen lbw b Hourn	0	– run out	1
†I. L. Maddocks b Watson	11	– not out	26
A. G. Hurst b Colley	25		
J. D. Higgs c Rixon b Colley	1		
B 2, l-b 1, n-b 9	12	L-b 3, n-b 11	14
1/4 2/8 3/93 4/137 5/186 6/234 7/234 8/262 9/335	340	1/62 2/65 3/216 4/239 5/248 6/252 7/253	(7 wkts dec.) 316

Bowling: *First Innings*—Clews 14–1–96–3; Watson 17–2–66–2; Colley 10.7–0–84–3; Simpson 4–0–21–0; Hourn 17–4–61–2. *Second Innings*—Clews 15–3–60–0; Watson 24–3–79–3; Colley 15–0–60–1; Simpson 5–1–21–0; Hourn 18–2–82–1.

New South Wales

S. E. Webster c Maddocks b Hurst	49 – lbw b Hurst	23
A. Turner b Callen	33 – c Moss b Hurst	24
J. Dyson c Wiener b Callen	16 – not out	103
P. M. Toohey c Yallop b Hurst	39 – c Callen b Higgs	95
*R. B. Simpson b Laughlin	2 – c Wiener b Higgs	14
A. R. Border c Maddocks b Callen	56 – c Laughlin b Higgs	19
D. J. Colley c Maddocks b Hibbert	31 – c Maddocks b Callen	3
†S. J. Rixon c Hibbert b Higgs	13 – c Higgs b Laughlin	33
M. L. Clews c Maddocks b Callen	0 – not out	12
G. G. Watson not out	4	
D. W. Hourn run out	6	
B 1, l-b 1, n-b 5	7	L-b 5, n-b 2 7
1/72 2/101 3/119 4/122 5/182 6/225 7/246 8/246 9/246	256	1/41 2/52 3/189 4/239 5/264 6/269 7/321 (7 wkts) 333

Bowling: *First Innings*—Callen 18.2–4–77–4; Hurst 13–0–56–2; Laughlin 14–4–44–1; Higgs 12–1–58–1; Hibbert 5–1–14–1. *Second Innings*—Callen 20–2–85–1; Hurst 11–3–51–2; Laughlin 12–3–38–1; Higgs 21–2–107–3; Hibbert 1–0–5–0; Wiener 9–0–40–0.

Umpires: T. F. Brooks and R. A. French.

WESTERN AUSTRALIA v SOUTH AUSTRALIA

Played at Perth, November 26, 27, 28, 1977

Western Australia won by ten wickets. Against the full strength of the home side, South Australia were completely outclassed, notably in batting where only two players – Darling and the captain, Blewett – showed any of the application and resolution expected from a first-class side. In his initial appearance for the season, the twenty-year-old Darling displayed commendable control over his natural aggression to score a sound 45 in eighty-seven minutes. He followed the performance with a fine display of strokes during an unblemished second innings century in four and a quarter hours. The fast bowling of Gannon and Clark and the leg-spin of fellow-international Mann accounted for 16 wickets in the match. The best Western Australian batting again came from Serjeant – slow to begin but later aggressive with one 6 and eight 4s in his 63 – and the extremely promising Wood who followed a neat 35 by finishing the match with shots all round the wicket in the course of his undefeated 67.

South Australia

A. J. Handrickan b Clark	3 – c Serjeant b Gannon	9
W. M. Darling c Wright b Brayshaw	45 – run out	100
W. L. Stillman c Wright b Gannon	11 – c Wright b Clark	10
B. Causby c Hughes b Gannon	3 – b Mann	13
*R. K. Blewett c Wright b Gannon	62 – b Brayshaw	32
J. J. Crowe c Wright b Clark	16 – b Gannon	18
J. Benton b Clark	2 – b Gannon	0
R. Hogg b Mann	42 – c Inverarity b Mann	10
G. R. Attenborough c and b Yardley	1 – c Serjeant b Mann	0
†T. J. Robertson c Brayshaw b Gannon	1 – b Clark	0
A. T. Sincock not out	17 – not out	4
B 1, l-b 2, n-b 4	7	B 4, l-b 2, w 1, n-b 1 8
1/3 2/56 3/60 4/68 5/105 6/113 7/166 8/167 9/176	210	1/16 2/39 3/67 4/130 5/176 6/176 7/200 8/200 9/200 204

Bowling: *First Innings*—Gannon 15–2–53–4; Clark 19–2–62–3; Brayshaw 16–3–50–1; Mann 4.3–1–16–1; Yardley 7–2–22–1. *Second Innings*—Gannon 12–1–44–3; Clark 13.7–2–53–2; Brayshaw 17–6–32–1; Mann 11–3–27–3; Yardley 11–1–40–0.

Western Australia

R. I. Charlesworth lbw b Hogg	31	– not out	30
G. M. Wood c Sincock b Hogg	35	– not out	67
*R. J. Inverarity c and b Sincock	5		
C. S. Serjeant c Stillman b Attenborough	63		
K. J. Hughes c Roberston b Attenborough	19		
I. J. Brayshaw c Hendrickan b Hogg	58		
B. Yardley c Stillman b Blewett	34		
A. L. Mann c Darling b Attenborough	23		
†K. J. Wright b Attenborough	17		
W. M. Clark c Stillman b Hogg	10		
J. B. Gannon not out	1		
B 1, l-b 6, w 1, n-b 7	15	L-b 1, n-b 6	7
1/48 2/59 3/114 4/150 5/182 6/182 7/263 8/292 9/309	311		(no wkt) 104

Bowling: *First Innings*—Hogg 24–3–93–4; Attenborough 19.3–2–80–4; Sincock 15–3–63–1; Blewett 13–1–60–1. *Second Innings*—Hogg 6–0–38–0; Attenborough 7–0–26–0; Sincock 6–1–24–0; Stillman 2–0–9–0.

Umpires: B. Cook and D. Weser.

TASMANIA v QUEENSLAND

Played at Launceston, February 25, 26, 27, 28, 1978

Drawn. The first Sheffield Shield match to be conducted outside an Australian capital city attracted a good attendance, and provided entertaining cricket before last-day rain delayed play and caused a draw. Ogilvie delighted 6,000 spectators with a combination of crisp cuts and strong drives to become the first player to hit six centuries in a Shield series. His partnership with Langley produced 163 runs, and the scoring livened up further when Carlson helped add 50 in thirty-eight minutes. Undeterred, Tasmania batted with equal freedom and headed the Queensland first innings total by 10 runs; 23-year-old Hobart insurance broker Roger Woolley confirmed earlier promise by hitting a delightful 103 in two and threequarter hours. Displaying a fine array of cuts and drives and a mature choice of the right ball to hit, he became the first Tasmanian-born player to score a Shield century for his home State. Only Hohn's and Graham Whyte's seventh-wicket partnership of 100 salvaged Queensland's second innings. Tasmania – put under extreme pressure after the rain delay – did well to bat out time against fiery bowling and most aggressive fielding.

Queensland

M. Walters c Simmons b Sherriff	14	– c Doolan b Cowmeadow	10
M. A. Gaskell c Hampshire b Sherriff	9	– b Sherriff	5
A. D. Ogilvie not out	168	– c Doolan b Baker	35
J. N. Langley lbw b Simmons	65	– c Hampshire b Cowmeadow	6
P. H. Carlson b Simmons	27	– b Benneworth	24
T. V. Hohns c Doolan b Baker	23	– b Baker	53
*†J. A. Maclean not out	9	– lbw b Simmons	1
G. K. Whyte (did not bat)		– c Cowmeadow b Baker	76
D. Schuller (did not bat)		– c Sherriff b Baker	13
G. Dymock (did not bat)		– not out	1
B 1, l-b 6, n-b 7	14	L-b 2, n-b 10	12
1/21 2/34 3/197 4/256 5/315	(5 wkts dec.) 329	1/13 2/41 3/53 4/84 5/91 6/103 7/213 8/234 9/236	(9 wkts dec.) 236

J. Maguire did not bat.

Bowling: *First Innings*—Baker 19–1–76–1; Sherriff 9–0–46–2; Cowmeadow 11–0–63–0; Benneworth 13–1–47–0; Simmons 24–4–83–2. *Second Innings*—Baker 17.6–5–66–4; Sherriff 14–1–38–1; Cowmeadow 12–0–58–2; Benneworth 14–3–30–1; Simmons 17–9–32–1; Docking 2–2–0–0.

Tasmania

†B. R. Doolan c Schuller b Dymock	35	– retired hurt	1
J. H. Hampshire c Maclean b Dymock	2	– c Maclean b Maguire	22
D. Smith c and b Whyte	49	– c Ogilvie b Maguire	14
R. Woolley c Gaskell b Dymock	103	– c Maclean b Schuller	1
S. J. Howard c Maclean b Dymock	29	– c Maclean b Schuller	0
T. W. Docking c Maclean b Schuller	24	– lbw b Whyte	13
A. J. Benneworth b Whyte	7	– c Maguire b Hohns	10
D. Baker b Schuller	0	– not out	30
*J. Simmons b Maguire	46	– not out	5
G. J. Cowmeadow c Hohns b Schuller	15		
R. Sherriff not out	5		
B 7, l-b 9, n-b 8	24	L-b 3, w 1, n-b 5	9
1/8 2/61 3/179 4/230 5/238 6/253 7/260 8/291 9/331	339	1/33 2/34 3/34 4/48 5/60 6/82	(6 wkts) 105

Bowling: *First Innings*—Maguire 15.6–0–71–1; Dymock 18–2–65–4; Schuller 13–0–68–3; Whyte 10–3–66–2; Hohns 4–0–18–0; Carlson 6–2–27–0. *Second Innings*—Maguire 8–0–29–2; Dymock 4–0–9–0; Schuller 10–3–18–2; Whyte 8–1–25–1; Hohns 2–0–15–1; Carlson 1–1–0–0.

Umpires: L. Cox and A. Edsall.

NEW SOUTH WALES v VICTORIA

Played at Sydney, December 9, 10, 11, 12, 1978

Drawn. A career-best performance by left-arm spin bowler Hourn demolished a Victorian innings which stood at 262 before he took the first of nine successive wickets and ended it 35 runs later. Matthews hit a maiden Shield century and Yallop, dropped in slips at 6, produced a wide range of fine strokes, but all resistance faded as Hourn dismissed the last eight batsmen at a personal cost of 17 runs from 36 balls. Strong reservations expressed about the pitch by both captains did not materialise and New South Wales recovered from 49 for three to reach 263 on the second day, thanks to a spirited century by Border. Before becoming leg-spinner Higgs' fourth victim in the last over of the day, he hit 114, with eight 4s, in five and a half hours. For the second time in the season, Laughlin was cautioned for bowling bumpers – first unofficially and then officially by umpire Drake – and New South Wales went 18 ahead when Hourn introduced some thoroughly unorthodox strokes at number eleven. Moss replaced the injured Matthews as opener and, together with a lucky Wiener, put on 157 with a sound personal contribution of 97. However, the Victorian batting was too slow, and Yallop batted on for a further ninety minutes for 82 runs on the final morning before setting the home side 273 to win in under five hours. Hostile fast bowling by Hurst soon reduced New South Wales to 45 for three, at which stage defence became the policy of the later batting.

Victoria

J. M. Wiener c Lawson b Hourn	35	– c Hughes b Hourn	57
R. G. Matthews b Hourn	104		
D. F. Whatmore c Phillips b Lawson	30	– b Lawson	27
*G. N. Yallop c Hilditch b Hourn	100	– lbw b Border	48
J. K. Moss c Toohey b Hourn	0	– b Lawson	97
T. J. Laughlin c Dyson b Hourn	7	– c Dyson b Border	44
B. J. McArdle c Hughes b Hourn	4	– b Lawson	1
†I. L. Maddocks c Border b Hourn	3	– c Hilditch b Border	0
I. W. Callen c Toohey b Hourn	7	– c sub b Hourn	5
A. G. Hurst c Beard b Hourn	0	– not out	1
J. D. Higgs not out	1		
L-b 1 n-b 5	6	B 1, l-b 6, n-b 3	10
1/59 2/98 3/262 4/262 5/270 6/283 7/287 8/295 9/295	297	1/157 2/159 3/198 4/272 5/276 6/277 7/288 8/290	(8 wkts dec.) 290

Bowling: *First Innings*—Lawson 14–0–66–1; Watson 18–4–81–0; Beard 17–6–49–0; Hourn 16.5–0–77–9; Border 6–1–18–0. *Second Innings*—Lawson 19–1–87–3; Watson 18–3–66–0; Hourn 26.1–3–95–2; Border 9–0–32–3.

New South Wales

*A. M. J. Hilditch b Callen	8	– b Hurst	0
J. Dyson c Maddocks b Laughlin	15	– not out	26
A. R. Border c Yallop b Higgs	114	– c Wiener b Hurst	7
P. M. Toohey c Laughlin b Callen	12	– b Hurst	17
G. C. Hughes c Moss b Higgs	57	– not out	22
C. Beatty c Yallop b Higgs	15		
†R. P. Phillips b Higgs	13		
G. R. Beard c and b Wiener	30		
G. F. Lawson b Hurst	16		
G. G. Watson not out	9		
D. W. Hourn b Hurst	12		
B 6, l-b 5, n-b 3	14	N-b 1	1
1/13 2/28 3/49 4/151 5/206 6/226 7/263 8/290 9/294	315	1/0 2/17 3/45	(3 wkts) 73

Bowling: *First Innings*—Hurst 16.5–3–60–2; Callen 14–1–61–2; Laughlin 12–4–17–1; Wiener 14–4–50–1; McArdle 7–1–27–0; Higgs 25–6–86–4. *Second Innings*—Hurst 10–1–27–3; Callen 6–2–9–0; Laughlin 4–0–15–0; Wiener 3–0–16–0; Higgs 7–4–5–0.

Umpires: A. Drake and R. Harris.

TASMANIA v SOUTH AUSTRALIA

Played at Devonport, November 3, 4, 5, 6, 1979

Drawn. Tasmania lost four wickets for 60 before Boon and Smith revived the innings on the opening day, when bad light restricted play to three hours. The partnership continued to 158 – breaking an 80-year-old Tasmanian record: Smith defending as Boon forced the pace to reach 90 in three hours seven minutes with twelve 4s. When South Australia replied, Hookes was aided by dropped catches, but Rolfe, Causby and Zadow batted with ease against the limited attack. In their second innings Tasmania again collapsed, to 23 for three, but Smith and Boon once more stood firm and useful innings from Docking and Campbell ensured South Australia would bat again. Following incidents in this match, Ian Chappell was suspended by the Australian Cricket Board from playing first-class cricket for twenty-one days.

Tasmania

R. F. Jeffery c Nash b Attenborough	18 – c Nash b Prior	17
G. W. Goodman c Rolfe b Attenborough	1 – c Rolfe b Hammond	1
D. A. Smith b Mallett	85 – b Chappell	68
*B. F. Davison c Robertson b Hammond	1 – lbw b Prior	1
†R. D. Woolley b Hammond	16 – (6) c Hammond b Hookes	30
D. C. Boon lbw b Prior	90 – (4) c Rolfe b Prior	23
T. W. Docking c Rolfe b Mallett	0 – (5) b Chappell	45
R. J. Hadlee c Robertson b Prior	4 – c Causby b Mallett	17
B. M. Campbell not out	13 – not out	52
G. J. Wilson c Prior b Mallett	10 – st Robertson b Mallett	11
N. J. Majewski c Rolfe b Mallett	0 – c Rolfe b Mallett	3
L-b 10, n-b 1	11 B 8, l-b 7, n-b 2	17
1/14 2/23 3/28 4/60 5/218 6/218 7/218 8/222 9/246	249 1/18 2/18 3/23 4/66 5/131 6/182 7/211 8/213 9/261	285

Bowling: *First Innings*—Prior 26–4–76–2; Attenborough 16–10–61–2; Hammond 21–7–45–2; Hookes 4–0–16–0; Mallett 25.5–8–40–4. *Second Innings*—Prior 24–4–78–3; Attenborough 13–7–19–0; Hammond 19–7–31–1; Hookes 6–1–18–1; Mallett 35.1–14–60–3; Chappell 32–9–62–2.

South Australia

J. E. Nash c Woolley b Jeffery	18 – not out	42
D. J. Rolfe b Wilson	83	
*I. M. Chappell c Hadlee b Wilson	24 – c Hadlee b Jeffery	6
D. W. Hookes lbw b Hadlee	88 – (2) run out	9
B. L. Causby c Davison b Majewski	66	
R. J. Zadow not out	74	
J. R. Hammond c Docking b Hadlee	23 – (4) not out	1
†T. J. Robertson c Goodman b Majewski	42	
A. A. Mallett not out	8	
B 8, l-b 6, w 3, n-b 14	31 B 1, l-b 1	2
1/40 2/73 3/214 4/261 5/324 6/372 7/438	(7 wkts dec.) 457 1/44 2/51	(2 wkts) 60

W. Prior and G. R. Attenborough did not bat.

Bowling: *First Innings*—Hadlee 27–3–78–2; Wilson 23–0–98–2; Jeffery 22–2–66–1; Majewski 25–5–76–2; Goodman 7–2–35–0; Campbell 20–3–73–0. *Second Innings*—Hadlee 5–0–31–0; Jeffery 4–0–27–1.

Umpires: R. Marshall and J. Stevens.

TASMANIA v NEW SOUTH WALES

Played at Launceston, December 29, 30, 31, January 1, 1980

New South Wales won by an innings and 55 runs. Tasmania were thoroughly outclassed in a game which emphasised their bowling and fielding deficiencies as well as their inexperience of batting at first-class level. A second-wicket stand of 234 by Chappell and Dyson was notable for splendid running between the wickets and ended when Chappell's helmet fell on the stumps! McCosker and Davis both added effortless centuries, and a partnership of 190 runs in 168 mintues. Tasmania collapsed to 43 for five before a fighting stand of 114 between Boon and Woolley gave respectability to an innings wrecked by Lawson's fiery speed and ended by Holland's spin. The same two batsmen provided substance in the follow-on, as did opener Jeffery and some belated hitting from Hadlee, who earlier had produced some first-class bowling.

New South Wales

A. M. J. Hilditch c Woolley b Wilson	4	†S. J. Rixon lbw b Hadlee	1
J. Dyson c Campbell b Wilson	99	G. R. Beard not out	0
T. M. Chappell hit wkt b Majewski	144	B 14, l-b 19, n-b 4	37
I. C. Davis c Davison b Hadlee	112		
*R. B. McCosker not out	115	1/7 2/234 3/289 (6 wkts dec.)	517
K. D. Walters b Hadlee	5	4/479 5/489 5/501	

G. F. Lawson, L. S. Pascoe and R. G. Holland did not bat.

Bowling: Hadlee 33–11–58–3; Wilson 25–3–95–2; Majewski 23–3–88–1; Jeffery 16–2–81–0; Goodman 25–5–101–0; Campbell 8–1–24–0; Boon 2–0–18–0; Davison 4–0–15–0.

Tasmania

G. W. Goodman b Holland	12	lbw b Lawson	20
R. F. Jeffery lbw b Pascoe	13	c Davis b Lawson	43
R. L. Knight c McCosker b Holland	2	c McCosker b Holland	9
D. A. Smith lbw b Lawson	1	c Chappell b Holland	10
D. C. Boon lbw b Lawson	61	b Holland	32
*B. F. Davison c Rixon b Lawson	0	c Davis b Chappell	27
†R. D. Woolley c Rixon b Lawson	61	c Dyson b Pascoe	37
B. M. Campbell c McCosker b Holland	1	lbw b Pascoe	0
R. J. Hadlee not out	27	not out	33
G. J. Wilson c Rixon b Holland	0	(11) c and b Pascoe	10
N. J. Majewski c Rixon b Beard	21	(10) c Holland b Pascoe	8
B 3, l-b 2, w 1, n-b 7	13	B 2, l-b 6, w 1, n-b 12	21
1/17 2/25 3/28 4/38 5/43 6/157 7/160 8/160 9/167	212	1/57 2/80 3/80 4/122 5/134 6/196 7/196 8/197 9/207	250

Bowling: *First Innings*—Pascoe 20–3–64–1; Lawson 19–6–39–4; Beard 11–4–14–1; Holland 28–7–82–4. *Second Innings*—Pascoe 20.2–7–64–4; Lawson 14–3–43–2; Beard 16–5–23–0; Holland 26–9–84–3; Walters 2–0–15–0; Chappell 2–2–0–1.

Umpires: J. Stevens and G. Summers.

NEW SOUTH WALES v SOUTH AUSTRALIA

Played at Sydney, February 23, 24, 25, 26, 1980

New South Wales won by 98 runs. Sensational fast bowling by Pascoe brought unexpected success to the home state in a match marred by unpleasant conduct and alleged intimidation. New South Wales captain McCosker and coach Peter Philpott later submitted written complaints to the Australian Cricket Board concerning the conduct of some South Australian players. Toohey and Walters in two hours overcame a slow start and the loss of four early wickets with a brilliant unbroken stand of 166 which allowed McCosker to declare to preserve the balance of bonus points. Nash and Darling fell without addition to South Australia's overnight score of 15 but Chappell – although involved in several incidents with Pascoe and Walters – produced a delightful range of strokes in his 158. Inverarity helped him stabilise the innings with a stand of 191 in three and threequarter hours, and the visitors went 81 ahead before removing five New South Wales wickets before the close of play. South Australia needed only 167 to win with ample time available, but Pascoe, bowling with great hostility on a dead pitch, removed seven batsmen for 18 runs – a Sheffield Shield performance ranking only just behind the outstanding feats of Miller, Ironmonger and Fleetwood-Smith.

New South Wales

*R. B. McCosker c Robertson b Attenborough	82	– c Sleep b Mallett	38
J. Dyson c Nash b Mallett	30	– c Robertson b Attenborough	43
T. M. Chappell c Sleep b Attenborough	13	– c Inverarity b Mallett	3
I. C. Davis c Crowe b Mallett	1	– c Hammond b Inverarity	43
P. M. Toohey not out	100	– c and b Inverarity	34
K. D. Walters not out	72	– c Chappell b Mallett	35
G. J. Gilmour (did not bat)		– c Mallett b Hammond	24
†S. J. Rixon (did not bat)		– not out	16
L. S. Pascoe (did not bat)		– b Hammond	0
R. G. Holland (did not bat)		– c Attenborough b Hammond	6
D. W. Hourn (did not bat)		– b Mallett	0
L-b 3, n-b 1	4	L-b 6	6
1/98 2/125 3/126 4/136	(4 wkts dec.) 302	1/60 2/72 3/93 4/160 5/171 6/221 7/227 8/230 9/248	248

Bowling: *First Innings*—Prior 16–5–40–0; Attenborough 19–4–62–2; Hammond 16–2–60–0; Mallett 34–11–87–2; Sleep 13–0–49–0; Inverarity 1–1–0–0. *Second Innings*—Prior 11–1–29–0; Attenborough 25–7–62–1; Hammond 9–3–12–3; Mallett 39.2–14–73–4; Inverarity 29–8–66–2.

South Australia

J. E. Nash c Rixon b Gilmour	8	– c McCosker b Holland	11
W. M. Darling c Rixon b Pascoe	6	– lbw b Pascoe	7
*I. M. Chappell c Davis b Pascoe	158	– c Holland b Pascoe	0
R. J. Inverarity c Davis b Walters	53	– b Pascoe	7
J. J. Crowe st Rixon b Holland	20	– c Toohey b Holland	0
P. R. Sleep c McCosker b Hourn	16	– run out	24
J. R. Hammond c McCosker b Holland	19	– lbw b Pascoe	1
†T. J. Robertson not out	52	– b Pascoe	0
G. R. Attenborough c Hourn b Holland	24	– b Pascoe	16
A. A. Mallett c Toohey b Pascoe	6	– not out	0
W. Prior lbw b Holland	0	– b Pascoe	0
B 3, l-b 6, n-b 12	21	N-b 3	3
1/15 2/15 3/206 4/246 5/265 6/273 7/306 8/372 9/383	383	1/11 2/12 3/28 4/28 5/28 6/33 7/33 8/65 9/69	69

Bowling: *First Innings*—Pascoe 26–4–112–3; Gilmour 17–4–44–1; Holland 33.5–7–94–4; Walters 12–3–25–1; Hourn 22–3–87–1; Chappell 1–1–0–0. *Second Innings*—Pascoe 12.3–6–18–7; Gilmour 6–2–5–0; Holland 11–3–19–2; Hourn 4–0–24–0.

Umpires: R. G. Harris and A. S. Ward.

SOUTH AUSTRALIA v VICTORIA

Played at Adelaide, December 4, 5, 6, 7, 1980

Victoria won by nine wickets. In a low-scoring match, the turning-point occurred when, with the Victorian score at 53 for six in reply to the modest South Australian opening effort of 114, Robinson was "caught" off the bowling of Hogg. Upon umpire Wilson indicating that he considered the bowling intimidatory, a no-ball was signalled and Robinson was recalled to the crease. The innings that followed, wherein Robinson advanced his score from 2 to 120, was instrumental in carrying Victoria to an unexpectedly easy win. For Robinson, the game was a personal triumph; apart from leading his side to victory and scoring his seventh first-class century – his third against South Australia – he took eight catches and made one stumping. This performance apart, the bowlers were always on top. Callen had an impressive double. Walker and Bright bowled economically and well and, for South Australia, Hogg showed the form which restored him to the Australian Test side. Umpire Wilson was not invited to officiate in another Shield game during the season.

South Australia

J. J. Crowe c Scholes b Callen	32	– b Cosier	7
G. W. Goodman lbw b Callen	3	– c Robinson b Callen	43
D. Lovell c Robinson b Walker	7	– c Robinson b Bright	14
R. J. Zadow c Robinson b Cosier	0	– st Robinson b Bright	10
W. M. Darling c Robinson b Callen	19	– run out	15
P. R. Sleep b Callen	0	– c Robinson b Higgs	16
†K. J. Wright c Robinson b Walker	18	– lbw b Callen	3
G. R. Attenborough c Moss b Walker	14	– b Bright	10
*A. A. Mallett not out	0	– c Cosier b Callen	0
R. M. Hogg c Wiener b Walker	0	– c Robinson b Callen	14
W. Prior c Whatmore b Walker	0	– not out	14
B 1, l-b 5, n-b 15	21	B 1, l-b 4, n-b 11	16
1/13 2/38 3/39 4/72 5/72 6/88 7/107 8/114 9/114	114	1/35 2/62 3/83 4/86 5/106 6/119 7/119 8/119 9/135	162

Bowling: *First Innings*—Callen 12–5–30–4; Walker 15.5–7–29–5; Cosier 5–1–13–1; Bright 11–4–21–0; Higgs 1–1–0–0. *Second Innings*—Callen 18–4–47–4; Walker 11–2–41–0; Cosier 8–4–12–1; Bright 14.3–10–12–3; Higgs 11–1–34–1.

Victoria

J. M. Wiener c Mallett b Hogg	0	– c Goodman b Sleep	4
D. F. Whatmore b Attenborough	0	– not out	33
W. J. Scholes c Lovell b Hogg	29	– not out	16
G. N. Yallop c Zadow b Prior	13		
J. K. Moss c Wright b Hogg	5		
G. J. Cosier b Prior	1		
*†R. D. Robinson lbw b Hogg	120		
R. J. Bright lbw b Hogg	27		
M. H. N. Walker c Wright b Hogg	13		
I. W. Callen c Goodman b Mallett	3		
J. D. Higgs not out	2		
B 1, l-b 6, n-b 3	10	N-b 1	1
1/0 2/0 3/20 4/47 5/48 6/50 7/140 8/187 9/216	223	1/4	(1 wkt) 54

Bowling: *First Innings*—Hogg 25.2–4–75–6; Attenborough 16–2–44–1; Prior 17–6–56–2; Mallett 17–7–26–1; Sleep 3–1–12–0. *Second Innings*—Mallett 9–4–11–0; Sleep 8–0–33–1; Darling 1–0–2–0; Crowe 1–0–6–0; Zadow 0.2–0–1–0.

Umpires: B. E. Martin and J. F. Wilson.

WESTERN AUSTRALIA v NEW SOUTH WALES

Played at Perth, February 27, 28, March 1, 2, 1981

Western Australia won by 115 runs. The result was always likely to be crucial in determining the destiny of the Shield and Western Australia rose to the occasion. At times New South Wales were unrecognisable as the team which, earlier in the season, had outplayed the same opponents. The principal difference in the two games lay in the performance of Pascoe. Earlier, he had swept all before him; now, struggling for fitness, he went wicketless. With an even batting display, Western Australia never lost control, being particularly well served by Hughes, who was back to his best form, and the consistent Shipperd. Marsh and Yardley made vital runs when they were most needed in the second innings. A second innings collapse by New South Wales to 80 for six when chasing 386 for victory produced a valiant recovery from Dyson and Rixon, but their partnership of 159 merely delayed the inevitable Western Australian win. On an unhappy note, Dyson and Marsh, each of whom otherwise had outstanding games, became the first players to be reported and subsequently fined under the players' code of behaviour. Dyson's misdemeanour involved kicking down his stumps when given out caught in his first innings; Marsh incurred his fine for abusing umpire McConnell.

Western Australia

G. M. Wood c Walters b Lawson	38	– c Walters b Lawson	3
B. M. Laird c Dyson b Walters	21	– c Rixon b Lawson	21
G. Shipperd c McCosker b Holland	80	– run out	65
*K. J. Hughes c Rixon b Lawson	94	– lbw b Lawson	73
M. D. O'Neill run out	31	– c McCosker b Holland	6
†R. W. Marsh c Wellham b Beard	22	– not out	76
B. Yardley not out	26	– c Wellham b Beard	42
C. S. Serjeant not out	6	– st Rixon b Holland	6
D. K. Lillee (did not bat)		– not out	10
L-b 3, w 4, n-b 3	10	B 1, l-b 9, w 2, n-b 5	17
1/63 2/65 3/232 4/270 5/292 6/314	(6 wkts dec.) 328	1/13 2/61 3/165 4/180 5/182 6/220 7/298	(7 wkts dec.) 319

M. F. Malone and T. M. Alderman did not bat.

Bowling: *First Innings*—Pascoe 19.4–4–65–0; Lawson 25–5–81–2; Beard 25–7–79–1; Walters 7–2–15–1; Holland 22–4–78–1. *Second Innings*—Pascoe 13–4–33–0; Lawson 28–5–77–3; Beard 15–3–61–1; Walters 6–2–9–0; Holland 24–3–101–2; Chappell 5–0–21–0.

New South Wales

*R. B. McCosker c Alderman b Lillee	3	– b Lillee	0
J. Dyson c Wood b Yardley	25	– c Alderman b Yardley	134
T. M. Chappell lbw b Malone	71	– c Laird b Malone	1
D. M. Wellham c Marsh b Alderman	35	– c Marsh b Alderman	14
P. M. Toohey c Marsh b Malone	36	– c Marsh b Alderman	0
K. D. Walters c Hughes b Alderman	0	– c Marsh b Alderman	13
G. R. Beard run out	44	– c Laird b Yardley	4
†S. J. Rixon c Marsh b Yardley	24	– c Marsh b Malone	66
G. F. Lawson not out	4	– not out	21
R. G. Holland (did not bat)		– c Shipperd b Yardley	4
L. S. Pascoe (did not bat)		– c Marsh b Lillee	2
B 12, l-b 5, w 1, n-b 2	20	L-b 5, w 6	11
1/16 2/52 3/126 4/183 5/188 6/239 7/243 8/258	(8 wkts dec.) 262	1/6 2/19 3/53 4/53 5/71 6/80 7/239 8/243 9/258	270

Bowling: *First Innings*—Lillee 24–7–66–1; Malone 25–9–51–2; Alderman 22–4–56–2; Yardley 26.3–8–69–2. *Second Innings*—Lillee 15.2–5–41–2; Malone 11–3–35–2; Alderman 12–0–50–3; Yardley 26–5–119–3; O'Neill 2–0–14–0.

Umpires: D. G. Weser and P. McConnell.

BENSON AND HEDGES WORLD SERIES CUP

AUSTRALIA v WEST INDIES

Played at Melbourne, December 9, 1979

West Indies won by 80 runs. This match will remain in the memory of a crowd of almost 40,000 and thousands of others who watched it on television for Richards's exceptional batsmanship. Given pain-killing injections to ease a back injury, and hobbling throughout his innings, he launched a furious assault on every bowler, scoring 153 not out from 131 balls with one 6 and sixteen 4s. Haynes, who played his best innings of the season, was completely overshadowed in their partnership of 205. Australia, left with a virtually impossible task, never looked likely to get on terms.

West Indies

C. G. Greenidge c Marsh b Lillee	11
D. L. Haynes c Marsh b Thomson	80
I. V. A. Richards not out	153
A. I. Kallicharran not out	16
B 1, l-b 10	11
1/28 2/233 (2 wkts, 48 overs)	271

L. G. Rowe, C. L. King, *†D. L. Murray, A. M. E. Roberts, M. A. Holding, J. Garner and D. R. Parry did not bat.

Bowling: Lillee 10–1–48–1; Hogg 10–1–50–0; Chappell 4–0–24–0; Thomson 8–0–43–1; Bright 6–0–29–0; Hookes 1–0–10–0; Border 7–0–40–0; Wiener 2–0–16–0.

Australia

B. M. Laird b Holding	7
J. M. Wiener c and b Parry	27
A. R. Border run out	44
*G. S. Chappell c Richards b King	31
K. J. Hughes b Holding	12
D. W. Hookes c Murray b Roberts	9
†R. W. Marsh c Rowe b Roberts	13
R. J. Bright not out	19
D. K. Lillee b King	19
R. M. Hogg not out	3
B 1, l-b 6	7
1/16 2/54 3/102 4/119 5/128 6/147 7/151 8/185 (8 wkts, 48 overs)	191

J. R. Thomson did not bat.

Bowling: Roberts 8–1–33–2; Holding 10–2–29–2; Garner 10–1–26–0; King 10–0–40–2; Parry 10–0–56–1.

Umpires: K. Carmody and R. Whitehead.

AUSTRALIA v NEW ZEALAND

Third Final Match

Played at Melbourne, February 1, 1981

Australia won by 6 runs. With New Zealand needing 6 runs to tie the match off the last ball, Trevor Chappell, instructed to do so by his brother and captain, Greg, bowled McKechnie an underarm ball, which caused a furore that could haunt Australian–New Zealand cricket for a long time. Earlier in the day Greg Chappell, when 52, had refused to walk when Snedden, at deep mid-wicket, claimed what appeared to be a low but fair catch off Cairns; as neither umpire was watching the incident – they said they were looking for short runs – New Zealand's impassioned appeals for a catch were in vain. After quickly losing Border, Wood and Greg Chappell added 145 for Australia's second wicket in 34 overs, Chappell again being in his best form. When he was finally out, caught by Edgar diving forward at deep mid-wicket, it was to a similar catch to that which was earlier held by Snedden and confirmed by the television replays. This time Chappell went without hesitation. Late in the innings Kent and Marsh both made useful runs. Although Wright and Edgar gave New Zealand another excellent start, putting on 85 in 24 overs, and runs continued to come at a rate which made a New Zealand victory possible, such a result always seemed just against the odds. Edgar, with a splendid hundred to his name, was not out at the end. After some good blows by Parker, Trevor Chappell came on to bowl the last over with 15 still needed and four wickets left. Hadlee straight drove the first ball for 4 and was lbw to the second. Smith then hit two 2s before being bowled, swinging at the fifth ball, leaving New Zealand with 6 to tie off the now infamous underarm delivery.

Australia

A. R. Border c Parker b Hadlee	5
G. M. Wood b McEwan	72
*G. S. Chappell c Edgar b Snedden	90
M. F. Kent c Edgar b Snedden	33
†R. W. Marsh not out	18
K. D. Walters not out	6
B 8, l-b 3	11
1/8 2/153 3/199 4/215 (4 wkts, 50 overs)	235

K. J. Hughes, T. M. Chappell, G. R. Beard, D. K. Lillee and M. H. N. Walker did not bat.

Bowling: Hadlee 10–0–41–1; Snedden 10–0–52–2; Cairns 10–0–34–0; McKechnie 10–0–54–0; McEwan 7–1–31–1; Howarth 3–0–12–0.

New Zealand

J. G. Wright c Kent b G. S. Chappell	42
B. A. Edgar not out	102
*G. P. Howarth c Marsh b G. S. Chappell	18
B. L. Cairns b Beard	12
M. G. Burgess c T. M. Chappell b G. S. Chappell	2
P. E. McEwan c Wood b Beard	11
J. M. Parker c T. M. Chappell b Lillee	24
R. J. Hadlee lbw b T. M. Chappell	4
†I. D. S. Smith b T. M. Chappell	4
B. J. McKechnie not out	0
L-b 10	10
1/85 2/117 3/136 4/139 5/172 6/221 7/225 8/229 (8 wkts, 50 overs)	229

M. C. Snedden did not bat.

Bowling: Lillee 10–1–34–1; Walker 10–0–35–0; Beard 10–0–50–2; G. S. Chappell 10–0–43–3; T. M. Chappell 10–0–57–2.

Umpires: P. M. Cronin and D. G. Weser.

CRICKET IN SOUTH AFRICA

TRANSVAAL v AUSTRALIANS

Played at Johannesburg, November 11, 12, 14, 15, 1966

Transvaal won by 76 runs. In a spine-tingling finish the Australians tasted defeat on South African soil for the first time in 64 years. Man of the match was undoubtedly Bacher the 24-year-old Transvaal captain. Augmenting a personal match aggregate of 280 runs with five magnificent catches, he proved a real inspiration and his second innings double century eclipsed the 231 scored by Dudley Nourse against the 1935 Australians as the highest innings against an overseas touring team in South Africa. Supported by Weinstein and Lance, he set Simpson's team the stupendous task of scoring 489 runs in six hours forty minutes. The Australians fought magnificently to preserve their proud record and maintained a scoring rate in excess of a run a minute. Lawry and Veivers narrowly missed their first tour hundreds and took the score to within 110 runs of the target when the sudden loss of three wickets altered the complexion of the game and left Hawke and Hubble the responsibility of playing out time. They managed to hang on grimly until with eight minutes to go Hawke was completely beaten by Tillim's wrong 'un.

Transvaal

E. J. Barlow c Simpson b Chappell	55	– c Thomas b Hubble	3
L. J. Weinstein lbw b Hawke	14	– c Simpson b Cowper	60
*A. Bacher c Thomas b Chappell	45	– b Hawke	235
P. L. Corbett c McKenzie b Martin	69	– st Becker b Chappell	1
H. R. Lance c Simpson b Chappell	17	– b Hawke	107
R. C. White b Simpson	37	– c Thomas b McKenzie	5
D. Mackay-Coghill run out	19	– not out	0
A. F. Tillim c Becker b Hubble	38		
†S. Katz c Simpson b Hubble	13		
A. H. McKinnon c Thomas b Hawke	3		
E. Esterhuizen not out	0		
B 4, l-b 6, w 1	11	B 4, l-b 5, w 1, n-b 1	11
1/48 2/95 3/129 4/187 5/240 6/250 7/282 8/314 9/321	321	1/5 2/165 3/172 4/409 5/418 6/422 (6 wkts dec.)	422

Bowling: *First Innings*—McKenzie 20–6–52–0; Hawke 15.3–4–53–2; Hubble 10–2–35–2; Chappell 30–10–59–3; Martin 17–4–57–1; Veivers 6–1–27–0; Simpson 12–3–27–1. *Second Innings*—McKenzie 26–5–91–1; Hawke 20.4–5–85–2; Hubble 14–4–46–1; Chappell 18–8–55–1; Martin 6–1–28–0; Veivers 13–3–39–0; Simpson 6–0–33–0; Cowper 10–3–34–1.

Australians

*R. B. Simpson c Bacher b McKinnon	72	– lbw b Mackay-Coghill	38
W. M. Lawry b Lance	49	– c Barlow b Lance	93
G. Thomas b Lance	26	– c Barlow b McKinnon	6
R. M. Cowper c Bacher b McKinnon	23	– c Bacher b Mackay-Coghill	47
I. M. Chappell c Bacher b McKinnon	26	– c Weinstein b Mackay-Coghill	50
T. R. Veivers run out	28	– c Katz b Barlow	94
†G. C. Becker lbw b McKinnon	13	– lbw b Esterhuizen	3
J. W. Martin b Lance	1	– c and b Barlow	36
N. J. N. Hawke b McKinnon	0	– b Tillim	5
G. D. McKenzie not out	12	– run out	11
J. M. Hubble b Lance	0	– not out	8
B 1, l-b 2, n-b 1	4	B 10, l-b 11, w 1	22
1/111 2/137 3/171 4/176 5/228 6/236 7/242 8/242 9/242	254	1/60 2/160 3/179 4/201 5/299 6/313 7/379 8/400 9/400	413

Bowling: *First Innings*—Mackay-Coghill 15–1–63–0; Esterhuizen 5–2–15–0; Barlow 4–0–19–0; McKinnon 27–7–97–5; Tillim 3–0–12–0; Lance 18.4–6–44–4. *Second Innings*—Mackay-Coghill 26–7–65–3; Esterhuizen 19–5–49–1; Barlow 18–3–47–2; McKinnon 33–10–136–1; Tillim 14.2–2–70–1; Lance 11–1–24–1.

Umpires: L. M. Baxter and H. C. Kidson.

EASTERN PROVINCE v AUSTRALIANS

Played at Port Elizabeth, November 25, 26, 28, 29, 1966

Australians won by six wickets. In another dramatic finish Simpson square cut Pollock to the boundary to clinch a memorable victory off the fourth ball of the last over of the match. Four centuries were scored in this remarkable game. Fortunes fluctuated daily and even at the end of the third day a draw seemed a moral certainty. A fourth-wicket stand of 160 by Pollock and van der Merwe, both of whom had failed in the first innings, added zest to the game when the early Australian advantage was erased and the visitors were left with a target calling for a run a minute.

Simpson's innings was magnificent in quality and execution although Pollock's hundred (one 6 and seventeen 4s) was easily the best of the four – and the fastest by seventy-five minutes. Another valuable contribution was 102 by Fenix, who saved Eastern Province from outright disaster as his colleagues capitulated before the best bowling performance from Hubble to date. The local bowling, steady and hostile at the outset, lacked penetration and both Chappell and Watson were able to join the ranks of century makers on South African soil. The ground attendance for a Provincial match against an overseas team broke the previous record by almost 10,000.

Eastern Province

*K. Bond c Watson b Hubble	0	– c and b Simpson	0
A. Short c Martin b Hubble	11	– st Becker b Chappell	10
F. Fenix b Stackpole	102	– c Simpson b Chappell	14
R. G. Pollock run out	3	– c Chappell b Watson	120
†P. L. van der Merwe c Cowper b Hubble	7	– c Becker b Hawke	60
A. L. Wilmot st Becker b Chappell	42	– lbw b Cowper	33
D. Gradwell c Veivers b Hubble	5	– b Simpson	29
A. Hector b Hubble	8	– c Stackpole b Cowper	49
P. M. Pollock lbw b Chappell	60	– not out	28
M. Burton not out	29	– b Cowper	2
G. Den b Cowper	25	– c Simpson b Cowper	4
B 2, l-b 4	6	B 13, l-b 5, w 1	19
	298		368
1/0 2/26 3/32 4/39 5/114 6/133 7/143 8/212 9/244		1/26 2/31 3/109 4/269 5/273 6/329 7/333 8/333 9/336	

Bowling: *First Innings*—Hubble 22–2–74–5; Hawke 12–2–50–0; Watson 6–0–20–0; Martin 12–3–29–0; Chappell 23–6–61–2; Veivers 7–2–17–0; Simpson 4–0–18–0; Stackpole 4–0–14–1; Cowper 3.5–1–9–1. *Second Innings*—Hubble 5–1–10–0; Hawke 34–12–51–1; Watson 8–3–16–1; Martin 16–1–55–0; Chappell 32–8–107–2; Simpson 17–4–45–2; Stackpole 8–1–18–0; Cowper 16.3–4–47–4.

Australians

*R. B. Simpson c Fenix b Den	24	– not out	82
I. R. Redpath b P. M. Pollock	9	– c Gradwell b Den	37
R. M. Cowper b P. M. Pollock	13	– c Bond b Wilmot	5
I. M. Chappell c Den b P. M. Pollock	113	– not out	12
K. R. Stackpole run out	86	– b Hector	24
T. R. Veivers c Short b Wilmot	16		
G. Watson not out	118		
†G. C. Becker run out	16		
J. W. Martin c Wilmot b R. G. Pollock	52	– c Den b Hector	6
N. J. N. Hawke c Wilmot b Burton	9		
J. M. Hubble b R. G. Pollock	20		
B 2, l-b 14, w 2, n-b 2	20	B 4, l-b 2, n-b 2	8
1/19 2/39 3/54 4/185 5/235 6/289 7/350 8/432 9/472	496	1/88 2/93 3/143 4/153	(4 wkts) 174

Bowling: *First Innings*—P. M. Pollock 27–3–108–3; Hector 35–8–101–0; Den 17–2–71–1; Burton 52–19–89–1; Wilmot 14–2–33–1; R. G. Pollock 23–4–74–2. *Second Innings*—P. M. Pollock 17.4–2–60–0; Hector 18–2–58–2; Den 6–0–26–1; Wilmot 5–0–22–1.

Umpires: F. R. Payne and R. Stead.

SOUTH AFRICA v AUSTRALIA

First Test Match

Played at Johannesburg, December 23, 24, 26, 27, 28, 1966

South Africa won by 233 runs. The match will go down as one of the most memorable in the history of South African cricket. Australia's proud record of 64 years without defeat in Test matches in South Africa was smashed after even the most sanguine supporter had written off the Springboks' chances within an hour of play commencing.

On a ground saturated by days of rain, which only ceased 48 hours before the start, the margin and quality of victory were unbelievable. Five wickets down for 41 was the sequel to van der Merwe's decision to bat first. Lance and Lindsay stopped the rot and added 110 for the sixth wicket, but South Africa totalled only 199, of which Simpson and Lawry erased 118 before being separated. At that stage Australia were in complete command. They passed the South African total with nine wickets intact and then a dramatic collapse occurred and the lead was restricted to 126. The Springboks wiped off this deficit and taking full advantage of some amazing dropped catches – Lindsay at 10 and van der Merwe 2 being the chief beneficiaries – they soared to incredible heights while achieving the highest South African total in Test cricket.

Lindsay hit his maiden Test century and his pulsating 182 in four hours, thirty-four minutes included five 6s, one 5 and twenty-five 4s – yet the gem of the innings was Pollock's 90. On this display the young left-hander looked without peer and his timing, placing and wristwork were an object lesson for the purist. Australia now wanted a mammoth score of 495 in eight hours. The turning point came on the final morning when Simpson, set fair for a big total, ran himself out attempting a quite unnecessary run. The visitors played as a team without heart and a wonderful exhibition of controlled bowling by Goddard – his finest performance in any Test – set the seal on a South African victory. Another achievement by Lindsay was to equal the world wicket-keeping record of six wickets in an innings, set up by Grout on the same ground nine years earlier. He finished the match with eight wickets – as did Taber in an outstanding début – and also shared a seventh wicket partnership of 221 with van der Merwe.

South Africa

T. L. Goddard c Taber b Hawke	5	– c Simpson b Hawke	13
E. J. Barlow c Taber b McKenzie	13	– c Taber b Renneberg	50
A. Bacher c Cowper b McKenzie	5	– run out	63
R. G. Pollock c McKenzie b Renneberg	5	– b Cowper	90
K. C. Bland lbw b McKenzie	0	– c Simpson b Chappell	32
†J. D. Lindsay c Taber b Renneberg	69	– c Chappell b Stackpole	182
H. R. Lance b McKenzie	44	– c Simpson b McKenzie	70
*P. L. van der Merwe c Taber b Simpson	19	– c Chappell b Simpson	76
R. Dumbrill c Chappell b Simpson	19	– c Taber b Chappell	29
P. M. Pollock c Taber b McKenzie	6	– st Taber b Simpson	2
A. H. McKinnon not out	0	– not out	0
B 11, w 3	14	B 7, l-b 5, w 1	13
1/14 2/31 3/31 4/35 5/41 6/151 7/156 8/190 9/199	199	1/29 2/87 3/178 4/228 5/268 6/349 7/570 8/614 9/620	620

Bowling: *First Innings*—McKenzie 21.5–5–46–5; Hawke 8–1–25–1; Renneberg 16–3–54–2; Chappell 2–0–16–0; Veivers 9–1–13–0; Cowper 6–0–21–0; Simpson 4–1–10–2. *Second Innings*—McKenzie 39–4–118–1; Hawke 14–1–46–1; Renneberg 32–8–96–1; Chappell 21–3–91–2; Veivers 18–3–59–0; Cowper 16–2–56–1; Simpson 16.1–3–66–2; Stackpole 21–6–75–1.

Australia

*R. B. Simpson c Goddard b P. M. Pollock	65	– run out	48
W. M. Lawry c Lindsay b Goddard	98	– b McKinnon	27
I. R. Redpath c Lindsay b Barlow	41	– c van der Merwe b Barlow	21
R. M. Cowper c Lindsay b Barlow	0	– c Lindsay b Goddard	1
K. R. Stackpole c Lindsay b Barlow	0	– b Goddard	9
I. M. Chappell c Lindsay b Goddard	37	– c Lindsay b Dumbrill	34
T. R. Veivers b Lance	18	– b Goddard	55
†H. B. Taber c Lindsay b McKinnon	13	– b Goddard	7
G. D. McKenzie run out	16	– c sub b Goddard	34
N. J. N. Hawke not out	18	– c sub b Goddard	13
D. A. Renneberg c Goddard b McKinnon	9	– not out	2
L-b 5, w 2, n-b 3	10	L-b 6, w 2, n-b 2	10
1/118 2/204 3/207 4/207 5/218 6/267 7/267 8/294 9/325	325	1/62 2/97 3/98 4/110 5/112 6/183 7/210 8/212 9/248	261

Bowling: *First Innings*—P. M. Pollock 25–6–74–1; Dumbrill 18–3–55–0; Goddard 26–11–39–2; Lance 17–6–35–1; McKinnon 27.2–9–73–2; Barlow 17–3–39–3. *Second Innings*—P. M. Pollock 18–3–33–0; Dumbrill 16–6–43–1; Goddard 32.5–14–53–6; Lance 3–0–6–0; McKinnon 30–14–64–1; Barlow 15–1–47–1; R. G. Pollock 3–1–5–0.

Umpires: H. C. Kidson and L. M. Baxter.

SOUTH AFRICA v AUSTRALIA

Second Test Match

Played at Newlands, Cape Town, December 31, January 2, 3, 4, 5, 1967

Australia won by six wickets after Simpson had won the toss. Following close upon the heels of the first Test Australia enjoyed occupation of a feather-bed wicket for the first ten hours. Simpson's confident approach had its effect on his colleagues and the resultant total was more in keeping with the reputation of the side. The Australian captain's century, his first of the tour and sixth in Tests, was one of patient dedication and his half share of the 310-run foundation, in six and a half hours, placed his team in a strong position. On this occasion Simpson received good support from Redpath and Chappell and when they had been disposed of Stackpole and Watson took over, adding 128 runs in ninety-five minutes.

Shades of the first Test! Goddard, Barlow and Bacher out for 41 – and all to McKenzie. Holding the fort at the end of the second day were Pollock and Lance, the former, despite an injured leg, having six boundaries in his 28. A crowd of 19,000 saw Lance and Lindsay dismissed for the addition of only 29 runs, and the Springboks were in real trouble. The wicket-keeper's dismissal was unusual. He attempted a timid hook off Renneberg, and the ball rose sharply, struck the shoulder of the bat and rebounded fifteen yards from the batsman's forehead to Renneberg's outstretched hands as the bowler flung himself full length. Lindsay fell as if poleaxed and was carried off.

The advent of van der Merwe sent Pollock on the rampage. In the next four hours, partnered by his captain and his brother in turn, the young maestro reached his fifth Test hundred in three and a quarter hours, after facing only 139 balls. In a masterly innings he raced past his previous highest Test score (175 at Adelaide in 1963-4) to a brilliant double century after six hours at the crease (thirty 4s), during which time the score advanced from 12 for two to 343 for nine wickets. Van der Merwe contributed another sound fifty and the elder Pollock a useful 41. The remaining batsmen did little and the bid to save the follow-on failed by 39 runs.

In the second innings Australia captured the first four wickets for 64, including the gold wicket of Pollock, who was clean bowled by Simpson, who had alternated over and round the wicket. Lance and Lindsay staged their third lucrative partnership in four innings to overcome the poor start, and when the bandaged 'keeper got an edge as he attempted to drive Cowper, he gave Simpson his 90th catch in 46 Tests. Pithey and Pollock survived periodic onslaughts from McKenzie – easily the most dangerous bowler of the match. Each reached fifty and when Pollock eventually ran out of partners he had, like his brother, attained his highest Test score.

Australia lost four wickets against an attack mainly entrusted to Goddard and McKinnon, but the reliable Redpath found in Veivers a partner admirably suited to such an occasion. The winning boundary, twenty-four minutes from time, put the series on an even keel, with the intriguing prospect of a real build-up in public interest for the three remaining matches.

Australia

*R. B. Simpson c Lance b Barlow	153	– c Goddard b P. M. Pollock	18
W. M. Lawry lbw b P. M. Pollock	10	– c P. M. Pollock b Goddard	39
I. R. Redpath lbw b McKinnon	54	– not out	69
R. M. Cowper c van der Merwe b Lance	36	– c Lindsay b Goddard	4
I. M. Chappell c Lindsay b Goddard	49	– b McKinnon	7
T. R. Veivers lbw b P. M. Pollock	30	– not out	35
K. R. Stackpole c Lindsay b Barlow	134		
G. Watson c Lance b Barlow	50		
G. D. McKenzie c and b Barlow	11		
†H. B. Taber not out	2		
D. A. Renneberg b Barlow	2		
B 2, l-b 7. w 2	11	L-b 5, n-b 3	8
1/21 2/138 3/216 4/310 5/316 6/368 7/496 8/537 9/538	542	1/49 2/81 3/98 4/119	(6 wkts) 180

Bowling: *First Innings*—P. M. Pollock 22–4–84–2; Dumbrill 11–2–36–0; Goddard 42–15–79–1; Barlow 33.3–9–85–5; Pithey 22–5–59–0; McKinnon 38–16–93–1; Lance 20–1–95–1. *Second Innings*—P. M. Pollock 12–2–42–1; Goddard 29.1–10–67–2; Barlow 2–1–1–0; McKinnon 22–5–62–1.

South Africa

E. J. Barlow c Redpath b McKenzie	19	– run out	17
T. L. Goddard c Stackpole b McKenzie	7	– lbw b Simpson	37
A. Bacher b McKenzie	0	– c Simpson b McKenzie	4
R. G. Pollock c Taber b Simpson	209	– b Simpson	4
H. R. Lance c Simpson b Chappell	2	– run out	53
†J. D. Lindsay c and b Renneberg	5	– c Simpson b Cowper	81
*P. L. van der Merwe c Cowper b Simpson	50	– lbw b Chappell	18
D. B. Pithey c Taber b McKenzie	4	– c Redpath b Renneberg	55
P. M. Pollock c Stackpole b Veivers	41	– not out	75
R. Dumbrill c Chappell b McKenzie	6	– b McKenzie	1
A. H. McKinnon not out	6	– b McKenzie	8
L-b 4	4	B 5, l-b 9	14
1/12 2/12 3/41 4/66 5/85 6/197 7/242 8/258 9/343	353	1/45 2/60 3/60 4/64 5/183 6/211 7/245 8/331 9/345	367

Bowling: *First Innings*—McKenzie 33–10–65–5; Renneberg 18–6–51–1; Watson 11–2–27–0; Chappell 13–4–51–1; Simpson 24–9–59–2; Veivers 8.1–2–32–1; Stackpole 14–2–36–0; Cowper 6–0–28–0. *Second Innings*—McKenzie 39.3–11–67–3; Renneberg 24–2–63–1; Chappell 39–17–71–1; Simpson 39–12–99–2; Veivers 7–2–21–0; Stackpole 8–4–11–0; Cowper 10–2–21–1.

Umpires: H. C. Kidson and G. Goldman.

GRIQUALAND WEST v AUSTRALIANS

Played at Kimberley, February 10, 11, 13, 1967

Australians won by 376 runs. Five of the visiting batsmen made their top score of the tour in the highest total by any Australian team in South Africa. An indication of the power of the onslaught may be gleaned from the fact that 326 of the runs came in boundaries. "Lives", gratefully accepted by Simpson and Lawry, bolstered the total by 233 runs, the unfortunate bowler being the industrious Burrow who had five of six chances offered dropped off his bowling. Martin, with five 6s, spent forty-five merry minutes at the wicket, a prelude to his eleven wickets for 78 in a single day's play. The only batsman capable of reading the left-arm bowler's hand was Saggers whose valuable 57 was compiled in even time. An unusual incident was the sight of both teams taking the field at the end of the Griquas' first innings. Simpson apparently forgot to advise the home captain of his intention to enforce the follow-on and, in order to resolve the situation Watson and Taber made a token appearance at the crease.

Australians

*R. B. Simpson c Saggers b McLachlan	141		
W. M. Lawry c Schonegevel b McLachlan	107		
†G. Thomas b Hay	134		
K. R. Stackpole c McLachlan b Hay	24		
G. Watson c Burrow b Hay	8	– not out	17
T. R. Veivers b Hay	72		
H. B. Taber lbw b Hay	0	– not out	7
J. W. Martin c Burrow b McLachlan	60		
N. J. N. Hawke not out	27		
J. M. Hubble b McLachlan	5		
D. A. Renneberg c Symcox b McLachlan	22		
B 2, l-b 10, w 3, n-b 5	20	N-b 1	1
1/227 2/277 3/320 4/346 5/501 6/536 7/536 8/578 9/594	620	(No wkts dec.)	25

Bowling: *First Innings*—English 27–2–134–0; Burrow 36–4–150–0; Hay 29–2–143–5; Schonegevel 5–0–30–0; McLachlan 31–3–132–5; Draper 2–0–11–0. *Second Innings*—English 3–0–15–0; Burrows 4–1–5–0; Hay 2–1–4–0.

Griqualand West

A. McLachlan c Hawke b Hubble	20	– c Hawke b Renneberg	0
D. Dobson b Hubble	24	– b Martin	13
W. Symcox b Hubble	0	– b Renneberg	2
D. J. Schonegevel b Hubble	10	– c Simpson b Renneberg	20
*E. J. Draper b Hawke	1	– b Martin	9
B. W. Burrow c Thomas b Hawke	7	– c Hawke b Martin	21
K. Saggers st Thomas b Martin	57	– st Thomas b Martin	16
†D. Ellis c Hawke b Martin	24	– not out	4
G. Keating not out	9	– lbw b Martin	0
E. Hay b Martin	2	– lbw b Martin	0
C. English b Martin	8	– b Martin	2
B 2, l-b 7, n-b 7	16	L-b 4	4
1/28 2/29 3/51 4/52 5/63 6/81 7/1 8/157 9/166	178	1/0 2/2 3/20 4/46 5/48 6/78 7/87 8/87 9/87	91

Bowling: *First Innings*—Renneberg 3–0–24–0; Hubble 16–5–38–4; Hawke 13–3–38–2; Martin 8.4–1–48–4; Veivers 4–1–14–0. *Second Innings*—Renneberg 13–1–42–3; Martin 11.4–3–30–7; Watson 4–2–5–0; Simpson 3–1–10–0.

Umpires: T. Boggan and N. le Cordeur.

A SOUTH AFRICAN XI v AUSTRALIANS

Played at Jan Smuts Ground, Pietermaritzburg, February 17, 18, 20, 21, 1967

Drawn. In reply to an unexpectedly moderate total the Australian batting followed the pattern which had characterised the tour. The lower order men did not press home the ascendancy achieved against a five-man seam attack. In the end they led by 130. Two splendid displays by the twenty-one-year-old Richards brought his aggregate against the tourists to 385 in five completed innings. After rain had completely washed out the second day's play Richards shared with Barlow the first three-figure opening partnership against the Australians and virtually placed his team clear of defeat. Thereupon, Versfeld, Lance and Bland all failed and as McKenzie captured two more wickets the home team led by only 47 with three wickets to fall. Then Ackerman, a most promising youngster, got into his stride and with Gamsy added 139 for the eighth wicket. Ackerman dispelled any ideas his opponents may have been nursing of victory, for in two and a half hours he hit one 6 and eighteen 4s while making his second century of the season.

A South African XI

*E. J. Barlow c Cowper b McKenzie	10	– lbw b Watson	46
B. A. Richards c Redpath b Cowper	88	– b Watson	65
B. Versfeld c Thomas b McKenzie	28	– c Lawry b Martin	3
H. R. Lance c Thomas b McKenzie	5	– c Veivers b Martin	0
K. C. Bland c Veivers b Watson	29	– b Martin	7
H. M. Ackerman c Cowper b Chappell	46	– c Watson b Chappell	128
D. B. Pithey lbw b Cowper	0	– c Redpath b McKenzie	4
D. Mackay-Coghill c Watson b Martin	9	– b McKenzie	8
†D. Gamsy lbw b Martin	1	– b Martin	48
A. Hector not out	7	– not out	10
J. T. Botten not out	1		
B 13, l-b 1, n-b 1	15	B 10, l-b 4	14
1/10 2/87 3/95 4/140 5/170 6/178 7/224 8/226 9/226	(9 wkts dec.) 239	1/118 2/125 3/125 4/125 5/136 6/159 7/177 8/316 9/333	(9 wkts) 333

Bowling: *First Innings*—McKenzie 18–3–43–3; Hubble 13.5–3–37–0; Watson 14–4–29–1; Cowper 16–7–27–2; Hawke 3–0–11–0; Chappell 17–5–47–1; Martin 10–3–30–2. *Second Innings*—McKenzie 14–2–25–2; Hubble 4–1–11–0; Watson 15–3–48–2; Cowper 13–4–51–0; Hawke 5–0–26–0; Chappell 16–1–66–1; Martin 15.5–2–68–4; Veivers 9–0–24–0.

Australians

*W. M. Lawry lbw b Lance	54
I. R. Redpath b Lance	48
R. M. Cowper b Pithey	54
I. M. Chappell b Mackay-Coghill	97
T. R. Veivers c Mackay-Coghill b Barlow	30
G. Watson c Gamsy b Barlow	0
J. W. Martin c Mackay-Coghill b Hector	30
G. D. McKenzie lbw b Mackay-Coghill	11
†G. Thomas b Hector	5
N. J. N. Hawke not out	16
J. M. Hubble b Mackay-Coghill	8
L-b 7, n-b 9	16
1/97 2/114 3/205 4/249 5/251 6/298 7/326 8/337 9/345	369

Bowling: Mackay-Coghill 19–3–66–3; Botten 18–2–60–0; Hector 19–2–70–2; Barlow 9–1–27–2; Pithey 32–9–85–1; Lance 12–2–42–2; Richards 1–0–3–0.

Umpires: D. R. Fell and D. M. West.

SOUTH AFRICA v AUSTRALIA

Fifth Test Match

Played at Port Elizabeth, February 24, 25, 27, 28, March 1, 1967

South Africa won by seven wickets. Another sensation marked the start of the final match in a drama-packed series when Lawry sacrificed his wicket without having faced a ball, in attempting an impossible third run. Van der Merwe had taken the initiative by sending Australia to the wicket. The visitor's only hope of sharing the series was an outright victory and this unfortunate incident unsettled them from the start. Simpson and Chappell were also removed from the scene during the morning session and Redpath followed soon afterwards. Cowper and Stackpole added 48 fluent runs and appeared to have the position in hand until Goddard switched ends and precipitated another incredible collapse. The Springbok all-rounder dealt a death blow by dismissing three batsmen with the score at 137 in a spell reading 4–3–3–3. For good measure Trimborn ended Cowper's courageous and cultured innings and 137 for four suddenly became 137 for eight. Cowper's scalp gave

Lindsay his twenty-second wicket and the record for a series between South Africa and Australia, eclipsing the twenty-one by R. A. Saggers during the 1949-50 tour of South Africa.

After surviving an hour of McKenzie at his best, Barlow and Goddard recorded the only century opening partnership by the Springboks in the present series. They played responsible cricket but after the lunch interval, with the total at 84, Barlow survived two chances in one over. Then McKenzie made the breakthrough with three wickets for two runs in twenty-seven balls – with Lance dropped into the bargain. Goddard made his highest score in the series and also passed his 10,000 runs in first-class cricket. McKenzie was bowling excellently and gained two further successes before rain stopped play. He had an uncertain Lindsay caught and in the same over Procter was out, hit wicket when dodging a bumper. Altogether an exciting second day, before a capacity crowd enthralled by the mastery of Pollock, who scored 67 in an hour and forty-eight minutes – and was "going like a bomb!"

Pollock duly celebrated his twenty-third birthday with his sixth Test century – his fourth against Australia – in three hours (one 6, thirteen 4s) and with Cowper taking three wickets for four runs in five overs, South Africa finished 103 runs in front. Seam again proved Australia's downfall and at the close of the third day half the side had been dismissed and the visitors led by only 104 runs. At this stage it was obvious that their hopes of saving the game were hanging on the proverbial thread. When the elder Pollock captured Redpath's wicket he shared his brother's birthday celebration by taking his one hundredth Test wicket, being the third and youngest South African to attain this honour.

After batting with confidence the previous evening, Cowper (54) and Martin (20) resumed with a contrasting air of uncertainty and both lost their wickets without addition to the score. The left-arm spin bowler became Lindsay's twenty-fourth victim which took the South African 'keeper to within two wickets of Waite's world record. Watson again disappointed and it was left to McKenzie and Taber to take the lead to 175. Goddard again passed fifty and his 133 runs and six wickets for 76 were a magnificent contribution to South Africa's success. After McKenzie had again captured the wickets of the opening batsmen, giving him 24 wickets in the series, Bacher mistimed a drive, leaving Pollock and Lance to coast towards the glittering but hitherto unattainable goal. And as the ball left Lance's bat and soared high into the packed stand, the crowd of almost 12,000 acclaimed what must surely have been the greatest feat in all the years cricket has been played in South Africa. The clear-cut victory margin of three to one left no possible doubt as to the justice of the verdict.

Australia

*R. B. Simpson c Lindsay b P. M. Pollock	12	– lbw b Goddard	35
W. M. Lawry run out	0	– c Bacher b Barlow	25
I. R. Redpath c du Preez b P. M. Pollock	26	– lbw b P. M. Pollock	28
I. M. Chappell c Bacher b Procter	11	– lbw b Goddard	15
R. M. Cowper c Lindsay b Trimborn	60	– b Barlow	54
K. R. Stackpole c R. G. Pollock b Goddard	24	– c Lindsay b Trimborn	19
J. W. Martin lbw b Goddard	0	– c Lindsay b Goddard	20
G. Watson c Barlow b Goddard	0	– b P. M. Pollock	9
G. D. McKenzie c Trimborn b du Preez	14	– c R. G. Pollock b Trimborn	29
†H. B. Taber c Bacher b Procter	20	– c Goddard b Trimborn	30
D. A. Renneberg not out	0	– not out	0
W 1, n-b 5	6	L-b 2, w 1, n-b 11	14
1/4 2/17 3/27 4/89 5/137 6/137 7/137 8/137 9/173	173	1/50 2/74 3/79 4/144 5/166 6/207 7/207 8/229 9/268	278

Bowling: *First Innings*—P. M. Pollock 17–2–57–2; Procter 15.1–3–36–2; Trimborn 18–4–37–1; Goddard 10–3–13–3; Barlow 4–2–9–0; Lance 8–4–15–0; du Preez 2–2–0–1. *Second Innings*—P. M. Pollock 15–0–42–2; Procter 16–3–59–0; Trimborn 10.1–4–12–3; Goddard 36–12–63–3; Barlow 15–3–52–2; Lance 5–2–7–0; du Preez 8–4–29–0.

South Africa

T. L. Goddard c Taber b McKenzie	74	– c Taber b McKenzie	59
E. J. Barlow lbw b McKenzie	46	– c Chappell b McKenzie	15
A. Bacher c Taber b McKenzie	3	– c Martin b Chappell	40
R. G. Pollock c Cowper	105	– not out	33
H. R. Lance c Renneberg b Simpson	21	– not out	28
†J. D. Lindsay c Redpath b McKenzie	1		
M. J. Procter hit wkt b McKenzie	0		
*P. L. van der Merwe lbw b Watson	8		
J. H. du Preez lbw b Cowper	0		
P. M. Pollock c Lawry b Cowper	13		
P. H. J. Trimborn not out	0		
B 1, l-b 3, w 1	5	L-b 1, w 2, n-b 1	4
1/112 2/124 3/125 4/175 5/201 6/201 7/266 8/271 9/271	276	1/27 2/109 3/118	(3 wkts) 179

Bowling: *First Innings*—McKenzie 35–13–65–5; Renneberg 19–6–44–0; Watson 18–3–58–1; Cowper 19.3–9–27–3; Martin 17–1–64–0; Simpson 8–2–13–1. *Second Innings*—McKenzie 17–5–38–2; Renneberg 12–1–38–0; Watson 3–0–10–0; Cowper 12–4–26–0; Martin 5–0–25–0; Simpson 5–0–10–0; Chappell 7.1–2–28–1.

Umpires: H. C. Kidson and R. G. Draper.

SOUTH AFRICA v AUSTRALIA

First Test Match

Played at Newlands, Cape Town, January 22, 23, 24, 26, 27, 1970

South Africa won by 170 runs. They made an excellent start to the four-match series by inflicting the first defeat on an Australian team in sixty years of Test cricket at Newlands. Bacher, who won the toss, must have viewed his captaincy début with satisfaction. In addition to a sound fifty he handled his rampant attack with skill and matched Lawry with intelligent field placing. Four new caps were introduced by the Springboks – Richards, Irvine, Gamsy and Chevalier – and each in his own sphere justified his place. Barlow reached his fifth Test century – his fourth against Australia in eleven Tests – after five hours of industrious application. In all he batted six hours – one 6 and eleven 4s – but in common with Goddard, Richards and Pollock he had his moments of good fortune and made the most of dropped catches.

Australia began on a sensational note. With the total only five, Lawry and Chappell gave Peter Pollock his first two wickets of the series within the space of four deliveries. Then it was Procter's turn, for he combined with Barlow to dismiss Stackpole and Redpath – and the board read 39 for four, Sheahan joined the procession which gave Chevalier a wicket with his fifth Test delivery and right on time Taber was leg-before-wicket to Seymour. Australia, six down for 92, was almost unbelievable and yet the pattern persisted throughout the series when a similar collapse occurred in at least one innings of each Test.

Walters (73) played his best innings of the tour and was the only batsman to give an indication of his true ability. The second innings developed into a two-man show and in their battle to stave off defeat Lawry and Redpath received little support from their colleagues. The reason for Australia's surprisingly poor effort could only be attributed to an inane desire to play at rising deliveries outside the line, or a failure to get behind the ball. A natural sequel was for the South African bowlers to persist in this lucrative type of delivery which was supported by brilliant catching in the area behind the wicket.

Of the attack, McKenzie was unrecognizable as the man South Africa feared three years earlier, Connolly, however, was most impressive and his seven wickets were due reward for his intelligent variation of pace and swing. The spinners, Mallett and Gleeson, had a good match and no batsman at Newlands could claim to have mastered them. Luck was not on their side and it was a tribute to their skill, and to Lawry's superb field placing, that they confined the top South African batsmen to a run off every third delivery.

South Africa

B. A. Richards b Connolly	29	– c Taber b Connolly	32
T. L. Goddard c Taber b Walters	16	– c Lawry b Mallett	17
*A. Bacher lbw b Connolly	57	– lbw b Gleeson	16
R. G. Pollock c Chappell b Walters	49	– c Walters b Connolly	50
E. J. Barlow c Chappell b Gleeson	127	– c Taber b Gleeson	16
B. L. Irvine c Gleeson b Mallett	42	– c Walters b Connolly	19
M. J. Procter b Mallett	22	– c Taber b Connolly	48
†D. Gamsy not out	30	– c Taber b Gleeson	2
P. M. Pollock lbw b Mallett	1	– b Gleeson	25
M. A. Seymour c Lawry b Mallett	0	– c Lawry b Connolly	0
G. A. Chevalier c Chappell b Mallett	0	– not out	0
B 2, l-b 5, n-b 2	9	B 1, l-b 4, n-b 2	7
1/21 2/96 3/111 4/187 5/281 6/323 7/363 8/364 9/374	382	1/52 2/52 3/91 4/121 5/147 6/171 7/187 8/222 9/226	232

Bowling: *First Innings*—McKenzie 30–8–74–0; Connolly 29–12–62–2; Walters 8–1–19–2; Gleeson 45–17–92–1; Mallett 55.1–16–126–5. *Second Innings*—McKenzie 8–0–29–0; Connolly 26–10–47–5; Gleeson 30–11–70–4; Mallett 32–10–79–1.

Australia

K. R. Stackpole c Barlow b Procter	19	– c Barlow b Goddard	29
*W. M. Lawry b P. M. Pollock	2	– lbw b Procter	83
I. M. Chappell c Chevalier b P. M. Pollock	0	– b Chevalier	13
K. D. Walters c Irvine b P. M. Pollock	73	– c Irvine b Procter	4
I. R. Redpath c Barlow b Procter	0	– not out	47
A. P. Sheahan c Barlow b Chevalier	8	– b Seymour	16
†H. B. Taber lbw b Seymour	11	– lbw b Procter	15
G. D. McKenzie c R. G. Pollock b P. M. Pollock	5	– c P. M. Pollock b Chevalier	19
A. A. Mallett c Goddard b Chevalier	19	– c P. M. Pollock b Procter	5
J. W. Gleeson b Goddard	17	– b Richards	10
A. N. Connolly not out	0	– b Chevalier	25
B 5, n-b 5	10	B 7, l-b 2, n-b 5	14
1/5 2/5 3/38 4/39 5/58 6/92 7/123 8/134 9/164	164	1/75 2/130 3/131 4/136 5/161 6/188 7/198 8/228 9/239	280

Bowling: *First Innings*—Procter 12–4–30–2; P. M. Pollock 12–4–20–4; Goddard 19.4–9–29–1; Chevalier 11–2–32–2; Seymour 11–2–28–1; Barlow 1–0–15–0. *Second Innings*—Procter 17–4–47–4; P. M. Pollock 18–12–19–0; Goddard 32–12–66–1; Chevalier 31.1–9–68–3; Seymour 19–6–40–1; Barlow 6–2–14–0; Richards 6–1–12–1.

Umpires: G. Goldman and W. W. Wade.

SOUTH AFRICA v AUSTRALIA

Second Test Match

Played at Kingsmead, Durban, February 5, 6, 7, 9, 10, 1970

South Africa won by an innings and 129 runs. They made two changes in the side that gained a convincing victory at Newlands, Lance (Transvaal) and Traicos (Rhodesia) – a new Cap and a student at Natal University – replacing the spin bowlers, Seymour and Chevalier. Freeman for Mallett was the only Australian change.

The match produced a host of new records, pride of place going to Graeme Pollock for his mammoth 274 which gave him the individual record for a South African in Test matches. This was Pollock's first century on the Kingsmead ground; he reached 100 in two hours, fifty minutes and 200 in five hours, seven minutes and altogether batted three minutes under seven hours, before he played a tame return to Stackpole. He hit one 5 and forty-three 4s. His concentration never wavered and he attacked continuously and with merciless efficiency.

The total exceeded by two runs the previous highest total made by South Africa in the 170 Tests played against Australia, England and New Zealand. England's 654 for five wickets in the Timeless Test on the same ground in 1938-39 is the only score for or against these countries to surpass the latest total. Another highlight of the match was Richards' maiden Test hundred in only his second Test. In an exhibition of technical perfection the 24-year-old Natal and Hampshire batsman scored 140 of the 229 runs on the board. He reached his hundred off 116 deliveries and his only false stroke in a three-hour innings was his last one. He had Pollock as a partner for the last hour and the spectators were treated to a superb display as the pair added 103 runs for the third wicket. Between them they scored 414 runs of South Africa's gigantic total. Pollock, with Lance as his partner, also established a new South African sixth-wicket Test record of 200.

The Australians, thoroughly demoralized and with victory out of the question, failed to match the 164 they scored in the first innings at Newlands. Lawry and Stackpole put on 44 in even time and survived some hair-raising moments. The dynamic Barlow was then given the ball and in ten deliveries, with Goddard at the other end, the total slumped to 48 for four wickets. Sheahan batted beautifully, but it was a lone battle as Pollock and Procter accounted for the tail and the touring team followed-on 465 runs behind.

In the second innings Walters, Redpath and Stackpole all reached the seventies and at times the visitors' prospects seemed quite encouraging. Both Lawry and Chappell had succumbed to the fatal touch and Sheahan's batting, during a short stay, bore no resemblance to his first innings effort. In the latter stages Bacher again called on Barlow, whose figures at that point read nought for 50; the all-rounder staged a repeat performance and captured three wickets in quick succession for only four runs. This put paid to Redpath's hopes of assistance and any thoughts of an Australian recovery. Redpath was the hero of the innings but was unable to find a reliable partner and the match ended with South Africa two up and a full day to spare.

South Africa

B. A. Richards b Freeman	140
T. L. Goddard c Lawry b Gleeson	17
*A. Bacher b Connolly	9
R. G. Pollock c and b Stackpole	274
E. J. Barlow lbw b Freeman	1
B. L. Irvine b Gleeson	13
H. R. Lance st Taber b Gleeson	61
M. J. Procter c Connolly b Stackpole	32
†D. Gamsy lbw b Connolly	7
P. M. Pollock not out	36
A. J. Traicos not out	5
B 1, l-b 3, n-b 23	27
1/88 2/126 3/229 4/231 5/281 6/481 7/558 8/575 9/580	(9 wkts dec.) 622

Bowling: McKenzie 25.5–3–92–0; Connolly 33–7–104–2; Freeman 28–4–120–2; Gleeson 51–9–160–3; Walters 9–0–44–0; Stackpole 21–2–75–2.

Australia

*W. M. Lawry lbw b Barlow	15	– c Gamsy b Goddard	14
K. R. Stackpole c Gamsy b Goddard	27	– lbw b Traicos	71
I. M. Chappell c Gamsy b Barlow	0	– c Gamsy b P. M. Pollock	14
K. D. Walters c Traicos b Barlow	4	– c R. G. Pollock b Traicos	74
I. R. Redpath c Richards b Procter	4	– not out	74
A. P. Sheahan c Traicos b Goddard	62	– c Barlow b Procter	4
E. W. Freeman c Traicos b P. M. Pollock	5	– b Barlow	18
†H. B. Taber c and b P. M. Pollock	6	– c Lance b Barlow	0
G. D. McKenzie c Traicos b Procter	1	– lbw b Barlow	4
J. W. Gleeson not out	4	– c Gamsy b Procter	24
A. N. Connolly c Bacher b Traicos	14	– lbw b Procter	0
L-b 5, n-b 10	15	B 9, l-b 8, n-b 22	39
1/44 2/44 3/44 4/48 5/56 6/79 7/100 8/114 9/139	157	1/65 2/88 3/151 4/208 5/222 6/264 7/264 8/268 9/336	336

Bowling: *First Innings*—Procter 11–2–39–2; P. M. Pollock 10–3–31–2; Goddard 7–4–10–2; Barlow 10–3–24–3; Traicos 8.2–3–27–1; Lance 2–0–11–0. *Second Innings*—Procter 18.5–5–62–3; P. M. Pollock 21.3–4–45–1; Goddard 17–7–30–1; Barlow 31–10–63–3; Traicos 30–8–70–2; Lance 7–4–11–0; Richards 3–1–8–0; R. G. Pollock 3–1–8–0.

Umpires: J. G. Draper and C. M. P. Coetzee.

SOUTH AFRICA v AUSTRALIA

Fourth Test Match

Played at St George's Park, Port Elizabeth, March 5, 6, 7, 10, 1970

South Africa won by 323 runs. Bacher, in his first series as captain, was determined on a clean sweep for the first time in South Africa's history; whereas victory for the Australians could only salvage a portion of their damaged prestige. South Africa's only change was Trimborn for Trevor Goddard, who had announced his retirement from first-class cricket. McKenzie, after a three weeks' lay-off on medical advice, returned to replace Freeman.

Bacher's lucky coin worked the oracle for the fourth time in succession and Richards and Barlow gave vent to their appreciation by recording the only century opening partnership of the series. Barlow's innings was virtually without blemish, but Richards was dropped at 55 and again at 77. After toiling for three and a half hours, the great-hearted Connolly dismissed both batsmen within five minutes of each other, and Gleeson's 50th wicket of the tour was the valuable scalp of Graeme Pollock. The idol of Port Elizabeth had been dismissed for a single and three Springbok wickets had fallen for two runs in fourteen deliveries.

Gleeson suffered through at least three dropped catches, but Connolly, whose six for 47 was his best performance in 28 Tests, captured his 100th Test wicket when Traicos touched one to Taber for the wicket-keeper's fifth catch of the innings.

Procter, Pollock and Trimborn gradually made their way through the Australian batsmen but once again Redpath and Sheahan, both of whom played the short rising deliveries with confidence, put up stout resistance. Sheahan made the top score with an impressive 67 and his dismissal earned Pollock his 50th wicket in Tests against Australia, whose 212 was their highest first-innings total in the four Tests.

When South Africa batted a second time good bowling and tight field setting forced the opening batsmen to fight for every run. Richards again played the dominant part and after Barlow's dismissal ran amok and punished all the bowlers. He reached his second Test hundred out of 159 in three and a quarter hours, giving his first chance at 111, and with his score at 118 brought his total for the series to 500. A quarter of an hour later, after four hours at the crease, he played a tired stroke to Mayne and South Africa were 199 for two. Richards hit two 6s and twelve 4s. Graeme Pollock failed for the second time in front of his home crowd.

On the fourth day, with 235 for three on the board, Bacher and Irvine resumed the quest for runs. The Springbok captain had the misfortune to dislodge a bail after reaching his highest Test score, but Lindsay, celebrating a "life" at 13, found his touch and proceeded to overhaul Irvine. When Gleeson came on, the wicket-keeper took 4 off each of the last five balls of an over and reached 50 in forty-eight minutes. Two overs from Gleeson produced 35 runs and the two-hour morning session added 162 runs to the total. After lunch, by which time the wind had increased to gale force, any hope a fieldsman might have had of positioning himself under a lofted ball had disappeared. In these conditions Irvine scored his maiden Test hundred, after lives at 86, 99 and 101, in two hours, fifty-one minutes.

When Bacher declared with an unassailable lead of 569, Australia's fate was sealed. Peter Pollock pulled a hamstring in his second over but it made little or no difference for Procter and Barlow had removed the top four batsmen for 134 by the end of the fourth day. Australia's fate now rested on the shoulders of the not-out batsmen, Walters and Sheahan. Both played attractively, taking the total to 189 before Trimborn removed Sheahan. Walters had the misfortune to chop a ball from Procter on to his wicket and from that success the Springbok fast bowler, despite a severe attack of 'flu, took four wickets in a row for his best performance in seven Tests. Connolly averted the hat-trick, but Trimborn soon took his wicket and South Africa had administered the *coup de grâce*.

South Africa

B. A. Richards c Taber b Connolly	81	– c Chappell b Mayne	126
E. J. Barlow c McKenzie b Connolly	73	– c Stackpole b Walters	27
*A. Bacher run out	17	– hit wkt b McKenzie	73
R. G. Pollock c Taber b Gleeson	1	– b Mayne	4
B. L. Irvine c Redpath b Gleeson	25	– c Gleeson b Mayne	102
†J. D. Lindsay c Taber b Connolly	43	– b Connolly	60
H. R. Lance b Mayne	21	– run out	19
M. J. Procter c Taber b Connolly	26	– c Mayne b Gleeson	23
P. M. Pollock not out	4	– not out	7
P. H. J. Trimborn b Connolly	0		
A. J. Traicos c Taber b Connolly	2		
B 4, l-b 3, n-b 11	18	L-b 9, n-b 20	29
1/157 2/158 3/159 4/183 5/208 6/259 7/294 8/305 9/305	311	1/73 2/199 3/213 4/279 5/367 6/440 7/440 8/470	(8 wkts dec.) 470

Bowling: *First Innings*—McKenzie 27–7–66–0; Mayne 27–4–71–1; Connolly 28.2–9–47–6; Walters 9–1–19–0; Gleeson 32–9–90–2. *Second Innings*—McKenzie 20–3–72–1; Mayne 29–6–83–3; Connolly 36–3–130–1; Walters 5–2–14–1; Gleeson 30.2–5–142–1; Redpath 1–1–0–0.

Australia

*W. M. Lawry c Lindsay b Lance	18	– c Lindsay b Barlow	43
K. R. Stackpole c Barlow b Procter	15	– b Procter	20
I. R. Redpath c Trimborn b Procter	55	– c Barlow b Procter	37
I. M. Chappell c Procter b Trimborn	17	– c Trimborn b Barlow	14
K. D. Walters c Lindsay b Trimborn	1	– b Procter	23
A. P. Sheahan c Procter b P. M. Pollock	67	– c Lindsay b Trimborn	46
†H. B. Taber lbw b Barlow	3	– not out	30
L. C. Mayne b Procter	13	– c Lindsay b Procter	12
G. D. McKenzie c Barlow b P. M. Pollock	0	– c Lindsay b Procter	2
J. W. Gleeson c Lindsay b P. M. Pollock	8	– b Procter	0
A. N. Connolly not out	2	– c Bacher b Trimborn	3
L-b 3, w 1, n-b 9	13	L-b 2, n-b 14	16
1/27 2/46 3/80 4/82 5/152 6/177 7/191 8/195 9/208	212	1/22 2/98 3/116 4/130 5/189 6/207 7/234 8/241 9/241	246

Bowling: *First Innings*—P. M. Pollock 14–2–46–3; Procter 25.1–11–30–3; Barlow 9–1–27–1; Lance 8–1–32–1; Trimborn 17–1–47–2; Traicos 3–1–17–0. *Second Innings*—P. M. Pollock 1.1–0–2–0; Procter 24–11–73–6; Barlow 18–3–66–2; Lance 10–4–18–0; Trimborn 20.2–4–44–2; Traicos 14–5–21–0; Richards 3–1–6–0.

Umpires: C. M. P. Coetzee and A. J. Warner.

RHODESIA v INTERNATIONAL WANDERERS

Played at Salisbury, September 29, 30, October 1, 1972

Rhodesia won by 411 runs. In the return match at the Police Ground, Procter joined Carlstein with the score 57 for three and in three hours hit two 6s and thirteen 4s in his brilliant 114. Fine bowling by Procter and Clift had the Wanderers reeling. The Rhodesian captain disposed of the first three batsmen with only 13 on the board. Turner and Edrich improved the position but the 19-year-old Clift captured four good wickets whereupon Close declared, giving his side one and a half hours before close of play to attack the Rhodesians. The move paid, for McKenzie and Greig captured three good wickets for 60 before play ended. Next morning Davison and Procter restored the balance and tore the attack to shreds as they ran to their hundreds in a stand of 169 in two and a quarter hours. Procter thus became the first Rhodesian and thirteenth South African to score centuries in both innings of a first-class match. He closed his innings with an overall lead of 523 and seven and a half hours left for the visitors to bat on a wet, lively wicket after the covers had been carelessly removed. Against the pace of Procter they were not inclined to take chances. They lost six wickets for 67 and it needed only twenty-five minutes on the final morning for du Preez to take the last three wickets with his leg spin and finish a one-sided match.

Rhodesia

B. F. Barbour c Jameson b McKenzie	0	– b McKenzie	20
D. A. G. Fletcher c Parks b McKenzie	26	– c Close b McKenzie	0
S. D. Robertson c d'Oliveira b Greig	1	– lbw b Greig	5
P. R. Carlstein c and b Close	33		
*M. J. Procter c Close b d'Oliveira	114	– c McKenzie b Close	131
B. F. Davison b McKenzie	17	– c Jones b Gifford	125
J. H. du Preez c Jameson b Gifford	23	– run out	18
M. M. Benkenstein c Parks b d'Oliveira	11	– c Jameson b Gifford	35
†H. A. B. Gardiner b Gifford	4	– not out	8
P. B. Clift not out	22	– not out	14
R. H. Kaschula c Greig b d'Oliveira	7		
B 6, l-b 2, n-b 7	15	B 4, l-b 7, n-b 7	18
1/0 2/2 3/57 4/82 5/125 6/217 7/238 8/238 9/244	273	1/13 2/24 3/27 4/124 5/293 6/336 7/352	(7 wkts dec.) 374

Bowling: *First Innings*—McKenzie 17–1–79–3; Greig 21–1–60–1; d'Oliveira 20.5–3–58–3; Close 5–3–15–1; Green 4–1–5–0; Gifford 15–4–41–2. *Second Innings*—McKenzie 21–6–82–2; Greig 22–5–62–1; d'Oliveira 9–2–28–0; Close 9–1–59–1; Gifford 22–0–93–2; Jameson 8–1–32–0.

International Wanderers

G. M. Turner c Gardiner b Clift	45	– absent hurt	0
J. A. Jameson c Davison b Procter	1	– c Procter b Fletcher	15
D. M. Green c Gardiner b Procter	0	– c Robertson b Clift	22
*D. B. Close c Fletcher b Procter	10	– b du Preez	16
J. H. Edrich b Clift	32	– c Gardiner b Clift	6
B. L. d'Oliveira b Clift	7	– b Du Preez	2
†J. M. Parks c Gardiner b Clift	8	– c Robertson b du Preez	16
M. J. Kitchen c Fletcher b Procter	0	– b du Preez	0
A. W. Greig not out	9	– c Clift b du Preez	18
G. D. McKenzie not out	6	– not out	9
N. Gifford (did not bat)		– c Fletcher b du Preez	6
L-b 2, w 1, n-b 3	6	L-b 1, n-b 1	2
1/1 2/3 3/13 4/76 5/86 6/98 7/105 8/105	(8 wkts dec.) 124	1/26 2/48 3/54 4/62 5/65 6/65 7/87 8/95 9/112	112

Bowling: *First Innings*—Procter 14–9–20–4; Fletcher 5–1–18–0; Kaschula 5–3–12–0; Clift 11.3–2–53–4; Davison 5–1–15–0. *Second Innings*—Procter 3–0–13–0; Fletcher 5–0–9–1; Kaschula 3–0–8–0; Clift 10–0–41–2; du Preez 10.4–2–39–6.

Umpires: F. Kelly and K. Poole.

CRICKET IN WEST INDIES

WEST INDIES v AUSTRALIA

Third Test Match

Played at Georgetown, April 14, 15, 17, 19, 20, 1965

West Indies won by 212 runs. On the eve of the match, Kippin, one of the West Indies most experienced umpires, withdrew apparently at the insistence of the local Umpires' Association, who objected to the appointment of Jordan, of Barbados. The Association were angered because both umpires were not Guianese. The very game was threatened by this unhappy and unique situation, but it was met by appointing G. Gomez, the former Test all-rounder and now a selector, in Kippin's place. In the meantime a request was sent to Trinidad for another umpire, but although one arrived in good time, it was a tribute to Gomez's conscientious efficiency that he remained until the end. He had not previously umpired a first-class match, although he held an umpiring certificate. Gomez has been closely identified with umpiring, and an attempt to raise its standards in the West Indies.

His first duty was to order the creases to be remarked. The game started ten minutes late. The act of the local umpires caused Kippin much distress, and served only to cost West Indies cricket in general loss of prestige.

For the most part Australia waged a losing battle. In the first innings Kanhai was at his best and was not to be restrained. Hawke, however, did exceptionally well to finish with six for 72. Once again Australia were denied a solid start, and they fell 176 runs behind on the first innings. Yet the the West Indies did not make the best use of their big advantage. Their tactics were hard to understand. The first half of the second innings was conducted at a snail's pace. They then tried to finish at a gallop. Neither policy succeeded, but Australia had to get 357 to win.

By tea with only Simpson out for a total of 80, and Lawry and Cowper going well they were almost back in the game. Gibbs changed ends after the interval, and in fifteen minutes he took four wickets, putting Australia very much on the slippery slope of defeat. At the end of the day Gibbs was five for 29 in 22 overs, and Australia had only one wicket left. The next morning Gibbs needed only two more balls to complete his own and the West Indies' triumph. The pitch took some spin, but scarcely enough to account for one of Australia's most surprising and dispiriting collapses. It was the man and not the pitch which led to the final rout.

West Indies

C. C. Hunte c McKenzie b Philpott	31	– c Grout b Hawke	38
L. Davis b Hawke	28	– b McKenzie	17
R. B. Kanhai b Hawke	89	– b McKenzie	0
B. F. Butcher run out	49	– b Hawke	18
S. M. Nurse c and b Hawke	42	– st Grout b Philpott	6
G. S. Sobers c Grout b Hawke	45	– c Simpson b Philpott	42
J. S. Solomon c Grout b Hawke	0	– c Simpson b Philpott	17
J. L. Hendriks not out	31	– c Grout b Hawke	2
W. W. Hall c Mayne b Hawke	7	– not out	20
C. C. Griffith lbw b O'Neill	19	– c Thomas b Philpott	13
L. R. Gibbs b O'Neill	2	– b Hawke	1
B 7, l-b 1, w 1, n-b 3	12	L-b 3, w 1, n-b 2	6
1/56 2/68 3/203 4/210 5/290 6/290 7/297 8/309 9/353	355	1/31 2/31 3/62 4/69 5/125 6/129 7/146 8/146 9/176	180

Bowling: *First Innings*—McKenzie 23–2–92–0; Hawke 32–8–72–6; Mayne 12–1–54–0; Philpott 26–5–75–1; O'Neill 6.1–1–26–2; Simpson 7–1–23–0; Cowper 1–0–1–0. *Second Innings*—McKenzie 21–7–53–2; Hawke 20.4–7–43–4; Simpson 17–9–19–0; Mayne 2–1–6–0 Philpott 16–3–49–4; O'Neill 1–0–4–0.

Australia

R. B. Simpson b Sobers	7	– b Griffith	23
W. M. Lawry run out	20	– b Gibbs	22
R. M. Cowper c Hendriks b Gibbs	41	– st Hendriks b Gibbs	30
N. C. O'Neill b Griffith	27	– c Sobers b Gibbs	16
P. Philpott c Butcher b Sobers	5	– c Sobers b Gibbs	6
B. C. Booth c Sobers b Gibbs	37	– c Hendriks b Gibbs	0
G. Thomas b Hall	8	– st Hendriks b Solomon	5
N. J. N. Hawke c Sobers b Hall	0	– c Hendriks b Sobers	14
A. T. W. Grout run out	19	– b Sobers	8
G. D. McKenzie not out	3	– b Gibbs	6
L. Mayne b Gibbs	5	– not out	0
L-b 1, n-b 6	7	B 4, l-b 4, n-b 6	14
1/11 2/68 3/71 4/85 5/116 6/127 7/129 8/170 9/171	179	1/31 2/88 3/91 4/104 5/109 6/115 7/130 8/130 9/144	144

Bowling: *First Innings*—Hall 13–2–43–2; Sobers 12–2–38–2; Griffith 14–2–40–1; Gibbs 25.5–9–51–3. *Second Innings*—Hall 2–1–1–0; Griffith 6–1–30–1; Sobers 19–6–40–2; Gibbs 22.2–8–29–6; Solomon 9–2–30–1.

Umpires: G. Gomez and C. Jordan.

WEST INDIES v AUSTRALIA

Fourth Test Match

Played at Bridgetown, May 5, 6, 7, 8, 10, 11, 1965

Drawn. Simpson and Lawry mastered the bowling with such purpose that they batted throughout the first day for 263, and, on the next, became the first opening pair in Test history to score double centuries in the same innings. Their stand of 382, only 31 short of the world Test record, by V. Mankad (231) and P. Roy (173) for India v New Zealand, 1955-56, represented a complete transformation of all that had gone before in the series.

Griffith was cautioned for his excessive use of bumpers by Umpire Kippin, restored after the troubles at Georgetown, and the West Indies' discomfort was complete when Cowper added his century with almost disdainful ease.

Simpson declared with five wickets down at 650, and the West Indies' much shaken pride was further injured when Davis was quickly dismissed. Hunte was hit in the face attempting to hook Hawke and had to retire. The crisis brought out the vintage Kanhai. Nurse gradually won control and scored the third double century of the match. Their efforts, plus those of Hunte and Sobers, would not have been enough without a valiant half-century by Griffith.

Australia finished only 77 on, and with time running out, Simpson had no alternative but to gamble and declare early in the second innings. West Indies had to get 253 in four and a half hours. Hunte and Davis made 145 in ten minutes under three hours, a West Indies first-wicket record against Australia, but when Kanhai was out 106 were needed in ninety minutes . . . then 70 in fifty-five . . . and down to 28 in sixteen. By then Simpson had eight defending the boundary, and despite a gallant effort by Sobers the West Indies fell 11 runs short with five wickets left in as thrilling a finish as any could wish to see. The result meant the rubber for the West Indies.

Australia

W. M. Lawry c Sobers b Solomon	210	– retired hurt	58
R. B. Simpson b Hall	201	– c Nurse b Sobers	5
R. M. Cowper b Sobers	102	– c and b Hall	4
N. C. O'Neill c Kanhai b Gibbs	51	– not out	74
B. C. Booth b Gibbs	5	– c Sobers b Gibbs	17
G. Thomas not out	27	– b Gibbs	1
B. Shepherd lbw b Hall	4		
N. J. N. Hawke not out	8		
B 10, l-b 12, w 2, n-b 18	42	B 11, l-b 3, w 1, n-b 1	16
1/382 2/522 3/583 4/604 5/615 6/631	(6 wkts dec.) 650	1/7 2/13 3/160 4/175	(4 wkts dec.) 175

P. Philpott, A. T. W. Grout and G. D. McKenzie did not bat.

Bowling: *First Innings*—Hall 27–3–117–2; Griffith 35–3–131–0; Sobers 37–7–143–1; Gibbs 73–16–168–2; Solomon 14–1–42–1; Hunte 3–1–7–0. *Second Innings*—Hall 8–0–31–1; Sobers 20–11–29–1; Gibbs 18.2–4–61–2; Griffith 7–0–38–0.

West Indies

C. C. Hunte c Simpson b McKenzie	75	– c Grout b McKenzie	81
B. Davis b McKenzie	8	– c sub b Philpott	68
R. B. Kanhai c Hawke b McKenzie	129	– lbw b McKenzie	1
B. F. Butcher c Simpson b O'Neill	9	– c Booth b Philpott	27
S. M. Nurse c Simpson b Hawke	201	– lbw b Hawke	0
G. S. Sobers c Grout b McKenzie	55	– not out	34
J. S. Solomon c McKenzie b Hawke	1	– not out	6
J. L. Hendriks retired hurt	4		
W. W. Hall c Simpson b Hawke	3		
C. C. Griffith run out	54		
L. R. Gibbs not out	3		
B 13, l-b 12, w 1, n-b 5	31	B 19, l-b 3, w 2, n-b 1	25
1/13 2/99 3/299 4/445 5/448 6/453 7/474 8/539 9/573	573	1/145 2/146 3/183 4/216 5/217	(5 wkts) 242

Bowling: *First Innings*—McKenzie 47–11–114–4; Hawke 49–11–135–3; Philpott 45–17–102–0; O'Neill 26–13–60–1; Simpson 16–3–44–0; Cowper 21–6–64–0; Booth 6–2–17–0; Shepherd 3–1–6–0. *Second Innings*—McKenzie 24–6–60–2; Hawke 15–4–37–1; Philpott 24–7–74–2; Cowper 8–4–19–0; Booth 5–1–12–0; Simpson 9–4–15–0.

Umpires: C. Kippins and C. Jordan.

WEST INDIES v AUSTRALIA

Fifth Test Match

Played at Port of Spain, May 14, 15, 17, 1965

Australia won by 10 wickets with three days to spare. A pitch on which the ball often kept low produced much unexpected cricket, and Australia made by far the better use of it. Kanhai's 121 out of a total of 224 was superb, but the West Indies never really recovered from a devastating opening spell by Hawke in which he accounted for Hunte, Davis and Butcher for 11 runs.

Again Australia were indebted to Simpson and Cowper for their total of 294. The rest struggled unsuccessfully against Griffith, whose six wickets cost only 46 runs. West Indies sacrificed four wickets before they were on terms, and were finally bundled out by

McKenzie, Hawke and Sincock for a mere 131, of which Hunte, carrying his bat, made 60. McKenzie, who had given the air of a tired bowler in the early part of the series, took the last three wickets in four balls, and finished with five for 33. Simpson and Lawry hit the 63 needed for victory and the series ended as if Australia, and not West Indies, were the conquerors.

West Indies

C. C. Hunte c Grout b Hawke	1	– not out	60
B. Davis c McKenzie b Hawke	4	– lbw b Hawke	8
R. B. Kanhai c Hawke b Cowper	121	– b Hawke	9
B. F. Butcher lbw b Hawke	2	– c Cowper b Sincock	26
S. M. Nurse b McKenzie	9	– lbw b Hawke	1
G. S. Sobers b Sincock	18	– b McKenzie	8
W. V. Rodriguez c and b Sincock	9	– st Grout b Sincock	1
D. W. Allan run out	11	– c Cowper b McKenzie	7
W. W. Hall b Philpott	29	– b McKenzie	8
C. C. Griffith c Sincock b Philpott	11	– b McKenzie	0
L. R. Gibbs not out	0	– b McKenzie	0
B 4, l-b 2, w 2, n-b 1	9	B 2, w 1	3
1/2 2/18 3/26 4/64 5/100 6/114 7/162 8/202 9/217	224	1/12 2/22 3/63 4/66 5/87 6/92 7/103 8/131 9/131	131

Bowling: *First Innings*—McKenzie 14–0–43–1; Hawke 13–3–42–3; Sincock 15–1–79–2; Philpott 8.3–0–25–2; Cowper 6–0–26–1. *Second Innings*—McKenzie 17–7–33–5; Hawke 13–2–31–3; Sincock 18–0–64–2.

Australia

W. M. Lawry c Allan b Griffith	3	– not out	18
R. B. Simpson b Griffith	72	– not out	34
R. M. Cowper lbw b Sobers	69		
B. C. Booth lbw b Griffith	0		
G. Thomas c Allan b Griffith	38		
B. Shepherd c sub b Gibbs	38		
N. J. N. Hawke b Griffith	3		
P. Philpott b Gibbs	10		
A. T. W. Grout c Griffith b Gibbs	14		
D. J. Sincock not out	17		
G. D. McKenzie b Griffith	8		
B 12, l-b 3, w 1, n-b 6	22	B 4, w 1, n-b 6	11
1/5 2/143 3/143 4/167 5/222 6/230 7/248 8/261 9/270	294	(No wkt)	63

Bowling: *First Innings*—Hall 14–2–46–0; Griffith 20–6–46–6; Gibbs 44–17–71–3; Rodriguez 13–2–44–0; Sobers 37–13–65–1. *Second Innings*—Griffith 6–0–19–0; Hall 4–0–7–0; Gibbs 4–2–6–0; Sobers 2–0–8–0; Rodriguez 1–0–8–0; Kanhai 1–0–4–0.

Umpires: C. Jordan and C. Kippins.

BARBADOS v REST OF THE WORLD

Played at Kensington Oval, Bridgetown, March 8, 9, 10, 11, 1967

Rest of the World won by 262 runs with a day to spare. This match, arranged as part of the celebrations to mark Barbados attaining Independence, provided many surprises before and during play. Compared with the original choice, the Rest showed several changes owing to the withdrawal of the captain, R. B. Simpson, and K. D. Walters (Australia), the cancelling of the invitations to three South Africans, P. M. Pollock, R. G. Pollock and K. C. Bland, owing to the controversy over apartheid, and an injury to the Jamaican wicket-keeper, J. L. Hendriks. The deputies, notably Murray and Mushtaq, excelled.

Winning the toss, Sobers took the daring course of putting in the Rest to bat. The pitch was moist and considering the first five wickets fell for 122 the Rest recovered splendidly in reaching a total of 308. Mushtaq on his first appearance in the West Indies took part in a stand of 52 with Borde and with Murray unafraid of the bouncers from Hall and Griffith, the Rest reached 250 for seven wickets at the end of the first day. Mushtaq resumed confidently and Holford chipped a finger trying to take a hot return from him. A bruised finger on his left hand restricted Sobers to nine overs and threw a lot of work on Hall and Griffith.

McKenzie, who replaced Peter Pollock in the side, was responsible for The Rest's breakthrough, from which Barbados never recovered. Lawry handled his bowling skillfully and the combination of Gibbs (off-spin) and Mushtaq (leg-spin) brought about a complete rout so that The Rest led by 224.

With more than an hour left before the close and D'Oliveira unable to bowl after receiving a blow on the foot when batting to Griffith, Lawry wisely decided that The Rest should bat again and they made 47 while Hall broke Barber's leg stump and Lawry himself was taken at the wicket. Next day, Barbados fought back to such purpose that five Rest wickets were down for 89 and then came Murray who hit his third consecutive century in matches against West Indies bowling. In three hours Murray lashed the attack for 121 out of 164. As Mushtaq again shaped splendidly, Barbados finally needed 501 to win.

The pitch by this time was worn and Gibbs and Barber acquired enough lift and turn to keep the batsmen in trouble. Hunte and Bynoe fared satisfactorily against the new ball and their stand of 65 was the best of the innings. Sobers struggled forty minutes against the spin bowling for three, but Nurse played soundly and Taylor hit freely. Yet at no time did The Rest appear likely to lose the stranglehold on a most interesting game.

The three £100 prizes offered by Horlicks went to Murray (batting), Gibbs (bowling) and Mushtaq (best all-round performance).

Rest of the World

*W. M. Lawry c Taylor b Griffith	0	– c Taylor b Griffith	33
R. W. Barber c Taylor b Hall	30	– b Hall	6
R. B. Kanhai c Lashley b Hall	16	– c Taylor b Griffith	4
T. W. Graveney c Lashley b Hall	31	– b Griffith	10
C. G. Borde hit wkt b Griffith	48	– c Sobers b Brancker	15
B. L. D'Oliveira lbw b Holford	16	– lbw b Griffith	5
Mushtaq Mohammad c Bynoe b Sobers	82	– c Taylor b Sobers	57
†J. T. Murray b Hall	33	– c and b Bethell	121
G. D. McKenzie c Nurse b Holford	14	– lbw b Bethell	6
N. J. N. Hawke c Nurse b Lashley	23	– b Griffith	3
L. R. Gibbs not out	0	– not out	0
B 5, l-b 7, n-b 3	15	B 11, l-b 1, n-b 4	16
1/9 2/31 3/72 4/92 5/122 6/174 7/232 8/255 9/304	308	1/21 2/47 3/48 4/68 5/89 6/185 7/255 8/273 9/276	276

Bowling: *First Innings*—Hall 23–5–85–4; Griffith 23–3–85–2; Sobers 9–5–15–1; Holford 8–5–44–2; Brancker 19–7–33–0; Bethell 7–0–20–0; Lashley 3.4–0–11–1. *Second Innings*—Hall 12–1–52–1; Griffith 21–2–82–5; Bethell 7–0–19–2; Sobers 21–4–39–1; Brancker 24–4–65–1; Hunte 3–0–3–0.

Barbados

C. C. Hunte c Murray b Hawke	15	– c Hawke b Barber	36
M. R. Bynoe b McKenzie	8	– b Gibbs	37
P. D. Lashley c Lawry b Gibbs	10	– b Gibbs	6
S. M. Nurse lbw b McKenzie	0	– c Barber b Hawke	48
R. C. Brancker b Mushtaq	9	– c Murray b McKenzie	17
*G. S. Sobers b Gibbs	32	– c Hawke b Barber	3
A. Bethell b Mushtaq	0	– c Graveney b Hawke	6
†A. Taylor lbw b Mushtaq	3	– c Kanhai b Gibbs	46
C. C. Griffith lbw b Gibbs	0	– b Mushtaq	15
W. W. Hall run out	4	– not out	1
D. A. J. Holford not out	0	– absent hurt	0
B 1, n-b 2	3	B 17, l-b 4, n-b 2	23
1/18 2/28 3/28 4/42 5/62 6/64 7/69 8/70 9/84	84	1/65 2/81 3/82 4/99 5/146 6/160 7/171 8/228 9/238	238

Bowling: *First Innings*—McKenzie 12–3–28–2; Hawke 8–3–17–1; Gibbs 12.2–4–13–3; Mushtaq 9–2–23–3. *Second Innings*—McKenzie 23–10–49–1; Hawke 9–2–44–2; Mushtaq 12–2–27–1; Gibbs 28–10–59–3; Barber 21–9–36–2.

Umpires: J. S. Buller and C. Jordan.

WEST INDIES v INDIA

Third Test Match

Played at Georgetown, March 19, 20, 21, 23, 24, 1971

Drawn. Sobers won the toss for the third time, but West Indies progressed hesitantly against high-class spin bowling by India, who did not appear to miss the injured Prasanna. West Indies made 231 for six on the first day when only two batsmen looked capable of dominating the bowling. One was Kanhai, but he was unable to carry his assault beyond forty-five minutes, in which he made 25 runs. Lloyd's innings was developing into his best of the series when with 60 to his name, he and Sobers collided in the middle of the pitch while taking a rapid second run. The collision at high speed between two big men threw Lloyd so far off course that he could not regain his crease. Badly dazed, Lloyd had to be assisted off the field and Sobers, who sustained an injury in the neck, held on for almost half an hour but was caught at slip from the last ball of the day. Two more wickets fell cheaply on the second morning, but the Jamaican wicket-keeper, Lewis, playing in his first Test, and Gibbs staged a dour, two-hour partnership which added 84 for the ninth wicket. Gibbs' 25 was his highest Test score and Lewis was 81 not out when the West Indies innings ended at 363, about half an hour before tea.

India's innings, launched with an opening stand of 72, beat a fairly healthy pulse throughout. Lasting almost as long as West Indies', it finished 13 runs in excess of their total. Gavaskar batted with supreme ease for his 116, which took four hours, twenty-five minutes, but he had four lives, the first two in his initial 35 runs. He and Viswanath, another promising youngster who had not played in the earlier Tests because of injury, put on 112 for the third wicket. The second new ball enabled West Indies to bring about a minor collapse and India had five down for 246. Solkar was run out at 278 on the fourth morning. Again Sardesai took control and he and Abid Ali put on 61 for the seventh wicket before Sardesai was run out by a brilliant piece of fielding by Lloyd.

West Indies finished the fourth day at 63 for the loss of only one wicket, that of Fredericks, but on the last day they got into trouble as soon as they tried to force the pace. Carew holed out at long on and Bedi drifted one away to induce a fatal snick by Lloyd. Sobers groped forward to Durani within minutes of his arrival and when the appeal for a bat-and-pad catch at short-leg was turned down, Durani asked a second time. When he was rejected he threw down the ball in an unseemly gesture of anger and despair. Thereafter Sobers batted with masterly confidence and aggression to score his first century of the series. Davis, if less brilliant, collected runs fluently on a wicket which was still completely in the batsmen's favour. He, too, got into three figures and after an unbroken partnership of 170, Sobers made a courtesy declaration at tea. In the ninety minutes remaining the Indians made 123 without loss.

West Indies

R. C. Fredericks c Abid Ali b Venkataraghavan	47	– lbw b Solkar	5
M. C. Carew c Mankad b Durani	41	– c Durani b Bedi	45
R. B. Kanhai c Krishnamurthy b Bedi	25		
C. H. Lloyd run out	60	– c Krishnamurthy b Bedi	9
C. A. Davis lbw b Solkar	34	– not out	125
*G. S. Sobers c Venkataraghavan b Bedi	4	– not out	108
†D. Lewis not out	81		
K. D. Boyce c Gavaskar v Venkataraghavan	9		
G. C. Shillingford c Bedi b Venkataraghavan	5		
L. R. Gibbs run out	25		
J. Noreiga run out	9		
B 11, l-b 9, n-b 3	23	B 5, l-b 6, n-b 4	15
1/78 2/119 3/135 4/213 5/226 6/231 7/246 8/256 9/340	363	1/11 2/114 3/137 (3 wkts dec.)	307

Bowling: *First Innings*—Abid Ali 13.2–5–42–0; Solkar 17–3–34–1; Venkataraghavan 59–14–128–3; Bedi 55–18–85–2; Durani 14–3–51–1. *Second Innings*—Abid Ali 14–2–55–0; Solkar 16–4–43–1; Bedi 26–9–55–2; Venkataraghavan 20–10–47–0; Mankad 5–0–33–0; Durani 16–2–47–0; Wadekar 3–0–12–0.

India

A. V. Mankad b Noreiga	40	– not out	53
S. M. Gavaskar c Carew b Sobers	116	– not out	64
*A. L. Wadekar b Sobers	16		
G. R. Viswanath b Boyce	50		
A. S. Durani lbw b Sobers	2		
D. N. Sardesai run out	45		
E. D. Solkar run out	16		
A. Abid Ali not out	50		
S. Venkataraghavan lbw b Shillingford	12		
†P. Krishnamurthy run out	0		
B. S. Bedi lbw b Boyce	2		
B 5, l-b 6, w 1, n-b 15	27	B 4, w 1, n-b 1	6
1/72 2/116 3/228 4/244 5/246 6/278 7/339 8/370 9/374	376	(No wkt)	123

Bowling: *First Innings*—Boyce 20.4–5–48–2; Shillingford 21–2–75–1; Sobers 43–15–72–3; Gibbs 39–17–61–0; Noreiga 42–9–91–1; Carew 2–0–2–0. *Second Innings*—Boyce 2–0–12–0; Shillingford 2–0–13–0; Lloyd 3–0–20–0; Noreiga 10–0–30–0; Gibbs 1–0–4–0; Sobers 5–1–14–0; Fredericks 4–0–9–0; Davis 3–0–15–0.

Umpires: C. Kippins and R. Gosein.

WEST INDIES v INDIA

Fifth Test Match

Played at Port-of-Spain, April 13, 14, 15, 17, 18, 19, 1971

Drawn. With the series still open after the fourth Test, the final encounter was extended to six days. It was largely due to dropped catches on both sides that the final Test failed to yield a result despite the added time. The match was hard-fought, in a manner befitting the deciding Test of an interesting series. The pitch was a vast improvement on the one used for the second Test on the same ground. It yielded turn, but it turned slowly. The tendency of the ball to keep low was again apparent, although less so than in the second Test.

Winning the toss, India progressed precariously to a total of 360 which, from their point of view was not good enough for a six-day Test. Gavaskar held the innings together for almost six hours forty minutes and scored 124. There was a vital partnership of 122 runs for the fourth wicket between him and Sardesai, who seemed to have lost his touch, and batted sketchily for the first 50 of his 75 runs. He and India were lucky that a catch from a mistimed square-cut, when he was only four, was dropped at third slip. Even then, it took a brave tail-end recovery led by Venkataraghavan, who made 51, to give India a respectable total.

Though the Indian bowling maintained high levels of guile and accuracy, West Indies always looked like taking a big lead. Kanhai, foolishly run out, and Lloyd failed to make substantial contributions, but Lewis again proved hard to dislodge and, furthermore, batted with greater authority than in his previous innings. Davis made the most of an escape at 29 to score another century and Sobers scored a superb hundred, although the Indians, judging by their reactions, seemed to believe that he was caught and bowled by Bedi, when 34. Runs had, however, to be fought for and Bedi toiled gallantly on the third day, during which he sent down 42 overs. It was only towards the evening that the Indian spinners seemed to tire and Foster was able to cut loose. On the fourth day, the Jamaican all-rounder played powerfully off the back foot and West Indies gained a lead of 166. Foster was desperately unlucky to miss a well-deserved century by only one run.

India, who began their second innings with about two hours left on the fourth day, were kept in the fight by Gavaskar's vigil of eight hours and fifty minutes, in which he scored 220. The second highest score in India's innings of 427 was 54 by Wadekar. Sardesai, Viswanath and Jaisimha also made a stand, thus enabling India to bat well into the last morning. Jaisimha, however, had three escapes on the final morning and had the first of these chances been held, West Indies might have bowled out India in sufficient time to give themselves a chance. With the pitch now turning substantially, Noreiga claimed five wickets for 129 runs. Most of these runs went to Gavaskar who, even late in his innings had enough stamina left to run down the wicket and drive. What heightened the merit of his epic innings was the fact that he was suffering from severe toothache.

The clock was put further against the West Indies by a shower which extended the lunch interval by twenty minutes. Ultimately, West Indies had to make 262 in two hours, thirty-five minutes. Although Lloyd, who came in at number three, struck the ball often and with thunderous power, West Indies' hopes seemed lost when Sobers, entering at number five, with the score at 50, was bowled first ball by a rank shooter. Foster left after a partnership of 51 and Holford was sixth out at 114, in the second of the last 20 overs. West Indies put up the shutters immediately, but Wadekar did not call on his spinners and turn to attack till only 12 overs were left. Venkataraghavan bowled menacingly as soon as he was brought on and Lloyd who had made 64, and Davis were removed in successive overs. The last three batsmen, however, had only nine balls to negotiate. The ninth-wicket pair, Lewis and Dowe saw West Indies through, but one was left with the impression that India might have snatched another win had Wadekar not delayed the final offensive.

India

S. Abid Ali c Davis b Sobers	10	lbw b Sobers	3
S. M. Gavaskar c Lewis b Holford	124	b Shepherd	220
*A. L. Wadekar c Sobers b Shepherd	28	c Shepherd b Noreiga	54
D. N. Sardesai c Lewis b Holford	75	c and b Foster	21
G. R. Viswanath c Lewis b Shepherd	22	b Sobers	38
M. L. Jaisimha c Carew b Dowe	0	lbw b Shepherd	23
E. D. Solkar c sub b Dowe	3	c Sobers b Noreiga	14
S. Venkataraghavan c Carew b Shepherd	51	b Noreiga	21
†P. Krishnamurthy c Lewis b Noreiga	20	c sub b Noreiga	2
E. A. S. Prasanna c Lloyd b Holford	16	not out	10
B. S. Bedi not out	1	c Sobers b Noreiga	5
L-b 1, n-b 9	10	B 2, l-b 8, n-b 6	16
1/26 2/68 3/190 4/238 5/239 6/247 7/296 8/335 9/354	360	1/11 2/159 3/194 4/293 5/374 6/377 7/409 8/412 9/413	427

Bowling: *First Innings*—Sobers 13–3–30–1; Dowe 29–1–99–2; Shepherd 35–7–78–3; Davis 10–0–28–0; Noreiga 16–3–43–1; Holford 28.3–5–68–3; Foster 2–0–4–0. *Second Innings*—Sobers 43–15–83–2; Dowe 21–2–54–0; Shepherd 24–8–45–2; Noreiga 53.4–8–129–5; Holford 27–3–63–0; Carew 7–2–15–0; Foster 12–4–10–1; Davis 10–2–12–0.

West Indies

M. C. Carew c Wadekar b Prasanna	28	run out	4
†D. Lewis c Krishnamurthy b Bedi	72	not out	4
R. B. Kanhai run out	13	b Abid Ali	21
C. A. Davis c Solkar b Venkataraghavan	105	c Viswanath b Venkataraghavan	19
C. H. Lloyd c Venkataraghavan b Prasanna	6	c Wadekar b Venkataraghavan	64
*G. S. Sobers b Prasanna	132	b Abid Ali	0
M. L. C. Foster b Abid Ali	99	run out	18
D. A. J. Holford st Krishnamurthy b Venkataraghavan	44	c Bedi b Solkar	9
J. N. Shepherd c Abid Ali b Venkataraghavan	0	c and b Abid Ali	9
U. Dowe lbw b Venkataraghavan	3	not out	0
J. Noreiga not out	0		
B 14, l-b 8, n-b 2	24	B 9, l-b 8	17
1/52 2/94 3/142 4/153 5/330 6/424 7/517 8/522 9/523	526	1/10 2/16 3/50 4/50 5/101 6/114 7/152 8/161	(8 wkts) 165

Bowling: *First Innings*—Abid Ali 31–7–58–1; Solkar 11–1–35–0; Bedi 71–19–163–1; Prasanna 65–15–146–3; Venkataraghavan 37.3–5–100–4; Jaisimha 1–1–0–0. *Second Innings*—Abid Ali 15–1–73–3; Solkar 13–1–40–1; Venkataraghavan 5–1–11–2; Prasanna 5–0–23–0; Bedi 2–1–1–0.

Umpires: D. Sang Hue and R. Gosein.

WEST INDIES v NEW ZEALAND

First Test Match

Played at Kingston, February 16, 17, 18, 19, 21, 1972

Drawn. An astonishing innings of 223 not out by Turner saved New Zealand from an overwhelming defeat which had seemed a certainty since just before lunch on the third day when New Zealand were 108 for five in reply to West Indies 508 for four declared. Turner was then helped in a sixth-wicket stand of 220 by Wadsworth whose previous highest Test score had been 21. Statistically Turner was overshadowed by Rowe, who in his first Test made 214 and 100 not out, becoming the first batsman ever to score two separate hundreds in his first Test match. Rowe continued where he had left off for Jamaica against the New Zealanders. His was a phenomenal performance and he did not appear to have any technical weaknesses. His subsequent failures in the next three Test matches were more than anything a question of temperament. Rowe is a stockily built right hander who is a more compact batsman than most instinctive West Indian stroke players in that he seldom plays with his bat far from his pad.

In the final analysis the West Indies had only themselves to blame for not winning as Turner was badly dropped by Carew at extra cover off Gibbs when he had made 47. Sobers's captaincy also helped the New Zealanders, for when Wadsworth joined Turner, Sobers made no attempt to keep Turner away from the strike and so he was able to shield his partner with impunity. Later Sobers gave Holford, whose leg spin had caused the New Zealand batsmen a lot of trouble, surprisingly little bowling.

On another very easy paced wicket Rowe and Fredericks put the game out of New Zealand's reach on the first day after Sobers had won the toss. While Rowe batted faultlessly, Fredericks survived three difficult catches, but he hit the ball tremendously hard, particularly square on the off side, and he completed his first Test century in four and three-quarter hours. These two added 269 for the second wicket. The New Zealand selectors had left out Taylor and their attack looked sadly below standard, although Howarth was impressive.

The West Indies fast bowlers made the initial breakthrough when New Zealand went in and then Holford went through the middle order, but after surviving the catch to extra cover off Gibbs, Turner took complete charge and batted magnificently. In spite of the desperate situation he was always on the look out for runs. He took as much pressure as he could off Wadsworth and showed an impeccable technique against both pace and spin. No praise was too high either for Wadsworth who showed great guts and a beautifully straight bat. Their stand of 220 came against nine bowlers.

The West Indies lead was kept to 122 and they then tried to increase it as fast as possible to enable Sobers to declare. When the last day began Rowe was 67 not out and Sobers probably delayed his declaration to allow him to reach his second hundred. Even so New Zealand had an anxious afternoon. Holford removed Dowling and Turner immediately after lunch and only a fighting hundred by Burgess enabled them to survive an amazing game of cricket.

West Indies

R. C. Fredericks c and b Howarth	163	– b Congdon	33
M. C. Carew lbw b Congdon	43	– b Congdon	22
L. G. Rowe c Dowling b Howarth	214	– not out	100
C. A. Davis c Turner b Cunis	31	– b Howarth	41
M. L. C. Foster not out	28	– not out	13
*G. S. Sobers not out	13		
B 1, l-b 11, n-b 4	16	B 9	9
1/78 2/347 3/428 4/488 (4 wkts dec.)	508	1/44 2/57 3/155 (3 wkts dec.)	218

U. G. Dowe, †T. M. Findlay, D. A. J. Holford, L. R. Gibbs and G. C. Shillingford did not bat.

Bowling: *First Innings*—Webb 25–4–86–0; Cunis 34–3–118–1; Congdon 23–2–55–1; Alabaster 24–4–110–0; Howarth 44–6–108–2; Burgess 2–0–15–0. *Second Innings*—Webb 5–1–34–0; Cunis 20.4–2–87–0; Congdon 11–2–45–2; Howarth 17–6–43–1.

New Zealand

*G. T. Dowling lbw b Dowe	4	– b Holford	23
G. M. Turner not out	223	– b Holford	21
T. W. Jarvis b Shillingford	7	– lbw b Holford	0
M. G. Burgess b Dowe	15	– c and b Dowe	101
B. E. Congdon c and b Holford	11	– run out	16
B. F. Hastings c Sobers b Gibbs	16	– b Holford	13
†K. J. Wadsworth c Fredericks b Dowe	78	– not out	36
R. S. Cunis c Findlay b Shillingford	0	– not out	13
H. J. Howarth lbw b Holford	16		
J. C. Alabaster c Dowe b Gibbs	2		
M. G. Webb lbw b Shillingford	0		
B 10, l-b 4	14	B 5, l-b 6, n-b 2	13
1/4 2/25 3/48 4/75 5/108 6/328 7/329 8/361 9/364	386	1/50 2/51 3/96 4/131 5/135 6/214	(6 wkts) 236

Bowling: *First Innings*—Dowe 29–5–75–3; Shillingford 26.5–8–63–3; Sobers 11–3–20–0; Holford 44–18–64–2; Gibbs 45–9–94–2; Foster 14–8–20–0; Fredericks 4–1–5–0; Carew 9–0–29–0; Davis 5–3–2–0. *Second Innings*—Dowe 13–3–46–1; Shillingford 11–2–32–0; Sobers 13–5–16–0; Holford 33–12–55–4; Gibbs 21–8–42–0; Foster 9–5–12–0; Carew 4–1–6–0; Fredericks 4–0–14–0.

Umpires: D. Sang Hue (Jamaica) and J. Gayle (Jamaica).

GUYANA v NEW ZEALAND

Played at Georgetown, March 30, April 1, 2, 3, 1972

Drawn. This match will be remembered longest for two dramatic hundreds by Clive Lloyd, who showed most emphatically that he had completely recovered from the serious back injury which he had sustained playing for the Rest of the World in Australia. The lifeless Bourda wicket made a result highly unlikely and the captains did not use their imagination to try and counter this. On the first day Lloyd's driving was supreme and he reached his hundred in only two hours, eight minutes. Kallicharran also batted very fluently and then Fredericks, coming in down the order, made a typically free century. When the New Zealanders batted Turner was as immovable as ever. He batted ten hours for 259 and it was a featureless innings as this figure suggests. Congdon had been the more commanding player in a second-wicket stand of 171. Then, on the last afternoon there was time for Lloyd to make his second hundred and the sixth of the match.

Guyana

G. S. Camacho c Wadsworth b Congdon	32	– c Morgan b Webb	17
L. Baichan st Wadsworth b Alabaster	10	– c Wadsworth b Taylor	10
A. I. Kallicharran lbw b Taylor	154	– c Wadsworth b Vivian	51
C. H. Lloyd c Turner b Webb	133	– not out	104
R. C. Fredericks not out	100	– c Wadsworth b Webb	5
R. Ramnarace not out	34	– c Campbell b Vivian	11
†M. Pydanna (did not bat)		– not out	0
B 4, l-b 20, w 1, n-b 5	30	N-b 4	4
1/41 2/65 3/278 4/406	(4 wkts dec.) 493	1/22 2/32 3/161 4/191 5/202	(5 wkts) 202

S. Matthews, *L. R. Gibbs, R. C. Collymore and V. Adonis did not bat.

Bowling: *First Innings*—Webb 30–6–115–1; Taylor 24–3–66–1; Congdon 19–2–66–1; Alabaster 22–5–84–1; Morgan 8–1–39–0; Campbell 18.2–3–70–0; Vivian 3–0–23–0. *Second Innings*—Webb 9–0–32–2; Taylor 6–0–23–1; Campbell 8–1–39–0; Congdon 9–1–16–0; Morgan 11–1–53–0; Vivian 7–0–35–2.

New Zealanders

T. W. Jarvis b Adonis	0
G. M. Turner c Pydanna b Collymore	259
*B. E. Congdon c and b Collymore	103
B. F. Hastings lbw b Camacho	37
R. W. Morgan lbw b Matthews	8
G. E. Vivian c Pydanna b Collymore	1
K. O. Campbell b Collymore	18
†K. J. Wadsworth st Pydanna b Collymore	25
B. R. Taylor c Lloyd b Gibbs	15
M. G. Webb st Pydanna b Collymore	0
J. C. Alabaster not out	0
B 10, l-b 7, w 3, n-b 2	0
1/0 2/171 3/300 4/331 5/336 6/373 7/473 8/474 9/488	488

Bowling: Adonis 20–1–80–1; Matthews 29–4–77–1; Ramnarace 27–0–87–0; Gibbs 43–17–66–1; Collymore 55.2–16–115–6; Kallicharran 4–0–14–0; Fredericks 1–0–4–0; Camacho 3–0–14–1; Lloyd 11–5–12–0.

WEST INDIES v NEW ZEALAND

Fourth Test Match

Played at Georgetown, April 6, 7, 8, 9, 11, 1972

Drawn. It would be hard to imagine a duller game of cricket than this. The abiding memory was of another mammoth innings double century by Turner, the utterly lifeless pitch and the total lack of effort by either captain to open up the game. The West Indies in their team selection (they played only four specialist bowlers and included an extra batsman in Kallicharran), appeared to have settled for a draw while New Zealand, who had marginally the better of the game from a purely mathematical viewpoint, were happy to fall in with this line of thought. The West Indies played Greenidge, the Barbados opening batsman, in place of Carew, and Howard, an off-spinner also from Barbados, played in place of Inshan Ali who, it was felt, would not be suited by the pitch.

The West Indies continued their first innings until an hour into the third day, partly as a result of some rain and partly because of a bottle-throwing incident on the first day when Lloyd was run out, which also cost some time. The run out was Lloyd's own fault, but the spectators were very disappointed and angry with Davis who was Lloyd's partner at the time. A section of the crowd began to throw bottles on to the ground, but as the result of an appeal by Lloyd himself over the local radio for order and good sense to prevail, the situation did not get out of hand. The crowd were given plenty to cheer about, however, when Kallicharran made a delightful hundred in his first Test innings. It was a remarkably mature innings for he did not allow the interruptions to unsettle him and scored the last 41 on the third morning in just an hour before Sobers declared. Greenidge also made a satisfactory start in Test cricket with a good looking half century.

New Zealand's innings was a statistician's dream. Turner and Jarvis gave the bowlers nothing to hope for as they went on remorselessly and painstakingly. At the end of the third day, after 90 overs, the score stood at 163 for nought and all through the following day milestones were reached, but never was there any hint of urgency about the batting. Irritatingly both batsmen played enough shots to show what could have been done. Most of the bowling, too, was by part-time bowlers because Holder was off the field for much of the innings, while Sobers was feeling a leg injury and bowled himself hardly at all. The pair put on 387 for the first wicket, a New Zealand record, but still Turner went on and when he was out for 259 for the second time in a week he had batted for eleven hours, forty-two minutes. Even then Congdon took three and a half hours to reach 50.

This Test match was a complete negation of cricket as a game of challenge. Records were broken in the most meaningless way and for the last two days the ground was nearly empty, a bitter comment considering how little top-class cricket the Guyanese public are able to watch.

West Indies

R. C. Fredericks c Turner b Cunis	41	– not out 42
G. A. Greenidge c Wadsworth b Taylor	50	– not out 35
L. G. Rowe b Congdon	31	
C. H. Lloyd run out	43	
C. A. Davis c Wadsworth b Taylor	28	
A. I. Kallicharran not out	100	
*G. S. Sobers c Burgess b Taylor	5	
D. A. J. Holford lbw b Congdon	28	
†T. M. Findlay not out	15	
B 10, l-b 5, w 1, n-b 8	24	B 4, l-b 2, w 1 n-b 2 9
1/79 2/103 3/160 4/178 5/237 6/244 7/305	(7 wkts dec.) 365	(No wkt) 86

V. A. Holder and A. B. Howard did not bat.

Bowling: *First Innings*—Cunis 24–5–61–1; Taylor 37–7–105–3; Congdon 33–7–86–2; Howarth 38–10–79–0; Vivian 3–0–10–0. *Second Innings*—Cunis 5–0–13–0; Taylor 6–3–9–0; Morgan 9–3–10–0; Howarth 9–3–12–0; Burgess 5–3–12–0; Vivian 3–0–16–0; Turner 2–1–5–0; Jarvis 1–1–0–0.

New Zealand

G. M. Turner lbw b Howard	259
T. W. Jarvis c Greenidge b Holford	182
*B. E. Congdon not out	61
M. G. Burgess b Howard	8
B. F. Hastings not out	18
L-b 11, n-b 4	15
1/387 2/482 3/496	(3 wkts dec.) 543

R. W. Morgan, G. E. Vivian, B. R. Taylor, †K. J. Wadsworth, R. S. Cunis and H. J. Howarth did not bat.

Bowling: Holder 24–8–39–0; Sobers 42–15–76–0; Lloyd 36–11–74–0; Howard 62–16–140–2; Holford 54–24–78–1; Greenidge 14–4–34–0; Davis 25–8–42–0; Kallicharran 6–1–17–0; Rowe 5–0–28–0.

Umpires: C. Jordan (Barbados) and C. Kippins (Guyana).

BARBADOS v AUSTRALIANS

Played at Bridgetown, March 1, 2, 3, 4, 1973

Australians won by nine wickets. This match will always be remembered for an astonishing display of batting by the Chappell brothers, who put on 300 in only five minutes over three hours in the Australian first innings. It is seldom that two world class batsmen bat at their best at the same time. For those three hours there was nothing that the Barbados bowlers could do – they were without Holder who was rested for the Second Test. When Barbados batted on the first day Geoffrey Greenidge made a good hundred and held the innings together. He received some belated support from Farmer, with whom he added 126 in two hours. The two Chappells then assured the Australians of a good lead. In all Ian Chappell batted four hours, twenty-four minutes, hitting one 6, two 5s and twenty-seven 4s in his 209. Only a determined innings by Lashley in the Barbados second innings made it necessary for the Australians to bat again.

Barbados

C. G. Greenidge c O'Keeffe b Hammond	4	– b Hammond	17
G. A. Greenidge not out	148	– b Massie	21
P. D. Lashley c Marsh b G. S. Chappell	34	– c and b G. S. Chappell	76
†D. A. Murray c O'Keeffe b Jenner	33	– c Hammond b G. S. Chappell	16
N. E. Clarke b Jenner	14	– c Jenner b Massie	36
K. D. Boyce c G. S. Chappell b Jenner	44	– c Edwards b Massie	2
*D. A. J. Holford c Redpath b G. S. Chappell	0	– c Benaud b Jenner	31
S. W. Farmer c Massie b Jenner	57	– c Marsh b G. S. Chappell	0
A. B. Howard c Marsh b O'Keeffe	5	– c Hammond b Jenner	5
C. A. Selman not out	27	– c O'Keeffe b G. S. Chappell	10
A. Padmore (did not bat)		– not out	0
L-b 7, n-b 5	12	B 1, l-b 4, w 1, n-b 2	8
1/15 2/73 3/140 4/154 5/212 6/213 7/339 8/346	(8 wkts dec.) 378	1/25 2/43 3/77 4/144 5/150 6/201 7/201 8/210 9/222	222

Bowling: *First Innings*—Hammond 24–6–80–1; Massie 17–5–46–0; O'Keeffe 13–0–49–1; G. S. Chappell 27–7–60–2; Jenner 36–8–131–4; I. M. Chappell 1–1–0–0. *Second Innings*—Hammond 14–3–37–1; Massie 23–6–55–3; O'Keeffe 13–5–26–0; G. S. Chappell 16.3–3–57–4; Jenner 28–14–39–2.

Australians

I. R. Redpath c Murray b Boyce	1	– not out	39
*I. M. Chappell c G. A. Greenidge b Howard	209		
J. Benaud c Boyce b Padmore	21	– not out	22
G. S. Chappell b Selman	142		
R. Edwards lbw b Boyce	8	– b Boyce	17
K. D. Walters c Boyce b Farmer	30		
†R. W. Marsh c Murray b Howard	56		
J. R. Hammond st Murray b Holford	6		
T. J. Jenner b Padmore	0		
K. J. O'Keeffe not out	26		
R. A. L. Massie b Howard	0		
B 11, l-b 5, n-b 3	19	B 4, l-b 2	6
1/1 2/57 3/357 4/389 5/401 6/453 7/472 8/473 9/518	518	1/42	(1 wkt) 84

Bowling: *First Innings*—Selman 17–1–92–1; Boyce 25–4–97–2; Farmer 14–1–26–1; Padmore 36–2–138–2; Holford 18–0–70–1; Howard 13.3–0–76–3. *Second Innings*—Selman 7–0–26–0; Boyce 8–0–20–1; Farmer 3–0–15–0; C. G. Greenidge 1.3–0–17–0.

WEST INDIES v AUSTRALIA

Third Test Match

Played at Port of Spain, March 23, 24, 25, 27, 28, 1973

Australia won by 46 runs. In one of the most exciting of contemporary Test matches Australia won on the last afternoon just when it had looked as if Kallicharran was going to lead the West Indies to an astonishing victory after they had been left to score 334 to win on a turning wicket. West Indies suffered the big handicap of losing Rowe when he pulled the ligaments in his ankle in the field on the first day and was unable to bat in either innings.

Fredericks gave the West Indies a good start in the final innings and after a wild and irresponsible stroke by Kanhai and some predictable agonies by Lloyd against spin, Kallicharran and Foster came together. By lunch on the last day they had taken the score to 268 for four and only 66 more were needed. With Ian Chappell keeping his slips up and attacking to the last, Kallicharran played a slightly casual back shot to Walker's first ball of the afternoon and was caught behind. Soon afterwards Foster pushed O'Keeffe gently into forward short leg's hands and that was that.

For this match the West Indies left out Greenidge, moving Foster up the order to open with Fredericks and bringing in Lloyd. Lloyd had a dual purpose, for the selectors had dropped Holder, leaving Lloyd to share the new ball with Boyce who had been retained after his good bowling in the previous Test. The Queen's Park Oval wicket always favours spin and this one was no exception and so using the new ball meant doing little more than removing the shine for the spinners. Inshan Ali, whose shoulder had recovered, came back into the side in place of Holder. Australia played the same eleven as in Barbados.

The shape of the game was established on the first morning after Ian Chappell had won the toss for the third consecutive time. Within thirty-five minutes of the start Gibbs was bowling to three short legs. Australia had begun badly, losing Stackpole to the third ball of the innings, but Ian Chappell and Redpath put on 107 for the second wicket before Chappell was out in the last over before lunch. This brought in Walters, who produced the best innings of the series. Reputedly it is a difficult wicket to play strokes on and yet in the two hours between lunch and tea Walters scored exactly 100, hitting sixteen 4s. By any standards it was a magnificent innings. His driving was quite glorious and he cut and pulled with power and certainty. In all he batted for two hours, twenty-eight minutes, hitting one 6 and sixteen 4s.

West Indies made a bad start, but Kallicharran scored an attractive fifty and Kanhai produced a more careworn half century. The Australian leg-spinners, Jenner and O'Keeffe, did not bowl particularly well and the side badly missed an off spinner. There was another important innings by Murray, who took West Indies to within 52 of Australia's score.

By the time Australia went in again the ball was turning a long way, but increasingly slowly, Redpath and Walters made useful runs and there was a glorious innings of 97 by Ian Chappell, who held the innings together at a time when it seemed that the West Indies spinners would win the match. His 97 took him three hours, fifty minutes, but it was not an entirely defensive innings, for he never wasted any chance of scoring runs. He was seventh out at 231 and then some strange bowling by Gibbs allowed the last three wickets to add 50, which was slightly more than the margin between the two sides at the end.

Against the main batsmen Gibbs had been pushing the ball through with his short legs up for the catch. Now he put his fielders back on the boundary and tried to buy the remaining wickets. Walker with his huge shoulders took advantage of this and swung his bat for 23 priceless runs and he and Hammond added 33 for the last wicket. If Gibbs had gone on pushing the ball through he might have given away the odd edged single, but he would surely have restricted the batsmen to very few runs. As it was the runs he gave away made the difference between victory and defeat.

Australia

K. R. Stackpole c Foster b Boyce	0	– c Fredericks b Boyce	18
I. R. Redpath run out	66	– c Kanhai b Willett	44
G. S. Chappell c Kallicharran b Gibbs	56	– c and b Gibbs	1
K. D. Walters c Fredericks b Inshan	112	– c Gibbs b Willett	32
R. Edwards lbw b Boyce	12	– b Gibbs	14
*I. M. Chappell c and b Inshan	8	– c Fredericks b Willett	97
†R. W. Marsh b Inshan	14	– b Inshan	8
K. J. O'Keeffe run out	37	– c Kallicharran b Gibbs	7
T. J. Jenner lbw b Gibbs	2	– b Gibbs	6
M. H. N. Walker b Gibbs	0	– not out	23
J. R. Hammond not out	2	– c Kanhai b Gibbs	19
B 10, l-b 7, n-b 6	23	– B 5, l-b 7	12
1/1 2/108 3/181 4/240 5/257 6/262 7/312 8/321 9/321	332	1/31 2/96 3/99 4/156 5/185 6/208 7/231 8/231 9/248	281

Bowling: *First Innings*—Boyce 18–4–54–2; Lloyd 7–3–13–0; Gibbs 38–11–79–3; Willett 19–3–62–0; Inshan 41.1–11–89–3; Foster 6–2–12–0. *Second Innings*—Boyce 10–1–41–1; Lloyd 3–1–11–0; Gibbs 45–14–102–5; Willett 28–15–33–3; Inshan 21–2–82–1.

West Indies

R. C. Fredericks c I. M. Chappell b Jenner	16	– c Redpath b Stackpole	76
M. L. C. Foster lbw b Jenner	25	– c G. S. Chappell b O'Keeffe	34
A. I. Kallicharran c G. S. Chappell b Jenner	53	– c Marsh b Walker	91
C. H. Lloyd c and b G. S. Chappell	20	– c Stackpole b O'Keeffe	15
*R. B. Kanhai c Redpath b O'Keeffe	56	– b G. S. Chappell	14
†D. L. Murray lbw b Hammond	40	– c Redpath b Walker	7
K. D. Boyce c Marsh b O'Keeffe	12	– c I. M. Chappell b O'Keeffe	11
Inshan Ali c Marsh b Walker	15	– b Walker	2
E. T. Willett not out	4	– b O'Keeffe	0
L. R. Gibbs c O'Keeffe b Jenner	6	– not out	0
L. G. Rowe absent hurt	0	– absent hurt	0
B 17, l-b 11, w 1, n-b 4	33	B 19, l-b 13, n-b 7	39
1/33 2/44 3/100 4/149 5/206 6/230 7/265 8/267 9/280	280	1/39 2/141 3/177 4/219 5/268 6/274 7/281 8/288 9/289	289

Bowling: *First Innings*—Walker 30–8–55–1; Hammond 7–3–7–1; Jenner 38.3–7–98–4; O'Keeffe 28–10–62–2; G. S. Chappell 14–8–16–1; Stackpole 2–0–8–0; I. M. Chappell 2–1–1–0. *Second Innings*—Walker 25–6–43–3; Hammond 6–3–12–0; Jenner 15–2–46–0; O'Keeffe 24.1–5–57–4; G. S. Chappell 32–10–65–1; Stackpole 11–4–27–1.

Umpires: D. Sang Hue and R. Gosein.

GUYANA v AUSTRALIANS

Played at Georgetown, March 31, April 1, 2, 3, 1973

Australians won by 40 runs. For three days the Australians played enterprising but careless cricket and then on the last day when Guyana had a good chance of winning, having been left to score 275 in five and three-quarter hours, they fought back with all their usual determination and won a vastly entertaining cricket match. On the first day Greg Chappell played a glorious innings of 154 which took him only three and a quarter hours and contained twenty-four 4s. There were good supporting innings by Edwards and Marsh and 399 runs were scored in the day.

On the second day Guyana did even better. After an attractive opening stand of 110 between Fredericks and Camacho, Lloyd played an exhilarating innings, reaching his hundred in eighty-eight minutes with three 6s and fourteen 4s. Fredericks, too, batted magnificently, scoring 158 and adding 180 with Lloyd in one and three-quarter hours. Guyana scored 458 in the day.

On the third day the Australians again went for their strokes regardless. Edwards, Redpath, Benaud and Greg Chappell all played delightful innings, but in the end Guyana were left with a perfectly reasonable task. While Fredericks stayed they were always the likely winners. He made his second hundred of the match and this was the better innings of the two for the Australians now kept him under constant pressure. Even so he reached his hundred in only two and a quarter hours. Australia were indebted to Massie's best piece of bowling on the tour. For the first time he recovered his old control and supported by good fielding he took seven for 52, winning the match for the Australians.

Australians

I. R. Redpath c Pydanna b Blair	2	– run out	63
R. Edwards c McRae b Glasgow	74	– b Blair	56
J. Benaud c Pydanna b Glasgow	12	– lbw b Doodnauth	45
G. S. Chappell b Shivnarine	154	– b Doodnauth	77
†R. W. Marsh c McRae b Glasgow	46	– c McRae b Shivnarine	35
*I. M. Chappell run out	39	– c Doodnauth b Shivnarine	0
T. J. Jenner lbw b Shivnarine	35	– c Pydanna b Blair	23
J. R. Hammond not out	28	– lbw b Glasgow	17
D. K. Lillee c McRae b Doodnauth	1	– b Glasgow	0
J. R. Watkins not out	0	– lbw b Glasgow	6
R. A. L. Massie (did not bat)		– not out	6
B 2, l-b 6	8	L-b 2, n-b 3	5
1/2 2/23 3/187 4/277 5/317 6/344 7/375 8/384	(8 wkts dec.) 399	1/93 2/154 3/182 4/243 5/245 6/291 7/304 8/321 9/333	333

Bowling: *First Innings*—Blair 21–1–93–1; Glasgow 26–7–83–3; Lloyd 4–0–14–0; Shivnarine 18–3–77–2; Doodnauth 20–0–104–1; Fredericks 4–0–20–0. *Second Innings*—Blair 18–3–73–2; Glasgow 23–4–71–3; Shivnarine 31–5–101–2; Doodnauth 28–7–73–2; McRae 2–0–10–0.

Guyana

R. C. Fredericks c G. S. Chappell b Watkins	158	– c Marsh b Massie	118
G. S. Camacho c Massie b Jenner	55	– lbw b Massie	8
L. Baichan c Hammond b Watkins	32	– c Marsh b Hammond	3
*C. H. Lloyd c and b Watkins	124	– b Hammond	19
L. McRae c and b Watkins	5	– lbw b Massie	7
F. Bacchus not out	36	– c Benaud b Massie	31
†M. R. Pydanna st Marsh b Benaud	4	– b Massie	3
S. Shivnarine c Benaud b Hammond	14	– c G. S. Chappell b Massie	14
K. Glasgow b Hammond	6	– b G. S. Chappell	1
R. Doodnauth not out	5	– not out	8
P. D. Blair (did not bat)		– lbw b Massie	1
B 4, l-b 8, w 5, n-b 2	19	B 4, l-b 10, n-b 7	21
1/110 2/183 3/363 4/375 5/394 6/407 7/425 8/436	(8 wkts dec.) 458	1/16 2/36 3/125 4/159 5/187 6/192 7/212 8/228 9/229	234

Bowling: *First Innings*—Hammond 14–0–81–2; Massie 11–1–51–0; G. S. Chappell 11–2–21–0; Jenner 15–0–90–1; Watkins 21–1–110–4; Redpath 5–0–28–0; I. M. Chappell 4–0–28–0; Benaud 10–2–30–1. *Second Innings*—Hammond 15–1–61–2; Massie 16.4–2–52–7; G. S. Chappell 9–1–24–1; Jenner 13–0–46–0; Watkins 5–0–30–0.

WEST INDIES v INDIA

Third Test Match

Played at Port-of-Spain (Trinidad), April 7, 8, 10, 11, 12, 1976

India won by six wickets. India scored over 400 to win this Test, a feat accomplished only once before – by Australia against England, at Headingley, in 1948. Their victory was the climax of a very brave second-innings recovery.

Gavaskar and Viswanath both batted at their best to meet the big challenge in the second innings and Mohinder Amarnath was outstanding while playing the role of anchor. But India's achievement reflected poorly on the three West Indies spin bowlers who could make so little headway on a worn, turning pitch. In contrast, all three of India's spinners bowled magnificently in both innings.

West Indies built up a seemingly impregnable position over the first two days. Although Chandrasekhar had West Indies struggling at 52 for three after only seventy minutes, they recovered to score 320 for five by the end of the first day, Richards scoring 151 not out, his third century of the series. It was a masterly knock, but as in the previous Tests, he was let off by Kirmani. It was a leg-side chance from a mistimed sweep and Richards then was 72. Lloyd contributed 68 to a partnership of 124 for the fourth wicket and Julien to one of 106 for the sixth.

All five wickets that fell on the first day were claimed by Chandrasekhar and on the second day Bedi rounded up the innings in only forty-five minutes, for the addition of 39 runs, the West Indies losing wickets quickly while trying to force the pace.

Although there was no pace or bounce in the pitch, Holding bowled with great fire. He removed Gavaskar, who failed for the first time in a match in Trinidad. Viswanath made 41 in promising fashion, but was out cutting Imtiaz Ali, the leg-spinner, and at the end of the second day, India were 169 for five. Holding, armed with the second new ball, proved too much for the remaining Indian batsmen although there was a flurry of bold shots by Madan Lal and India narrowed the gap to 131.

In the remaining four hours of the day. West Indies doubled their lead at the cost of three second-innings wickets. The Indians bowled extremely well to restrict the scoring rate and while they must have hoped to make deeper inroads, they at least had the satisfaction that Richards was gone.

Runs were again hard to get on the fourth day, especially after Lloyd fell in Chandrasekhar's first over of the day, brilliantly caught at slip by Viswanath. Kallicharran, who made his only century of the series, batted very circumspectly and in about three hours that their innings was continued, West Indies could add only 139 runs.

India lost only Gaekwad (at 69) before the end of the day. The total was 134, of which 85 were made by Gavaskar, with twelve 4s. On the last day, India's target was 269 in six hours. After completing his century, Gavaskar lost his touch and eventually succumbed in trying to move back into top gear.

Mohinder Armarnath, who had helped Gavaskar to put on 108, did not have the skill to dominate and in the second hour, the scoring rate slumped to 22. Armarnath had become particularly bogged down after surviving a return chance to Imtiaz Ali, at 37. Time was still on India's side at lunch when 206 were required in four hours.

In forty-five minutes after the resumption, they added 26 and then Lloyd took the new ball, 29 overs after it was due. Julien bowled very loosely with it and with Viswanath getting after him, India now began to make rapid advance. In eight overs with the new ball, 37 runs were scored.

Viswanath was now inspired. Using his feet, he bent the spin attack to his will and his century came out of 147 runs, with thirteen 4s. The pair, who put on 159 in all, took India to within 67 of their objective and then Viswanath, backing up too far, was run out. The statutory overs began five minutes later.

India were not thrown out of their stride by Viswanath's dismissal. Patel took command of the spin attack, which collapsed under the pressure and India got home at a gallop, with seven overs to spare.

West Indies

R. C. Fredericks c Amarnath b Chandra	27	– c Solkar b Chandra	25
L. G. Rowe c Viswanath b Chandra	18	– c Kirmani b Venkat	27
I. V. A. Richards c Chandra b Bedi	177	– c Solkar b Venkat	23
A. I. Kallicharran b Chandra	0	– not out	103
*C. H. Lloyd c Gaekwad b Chandra	68	– c Viswanath b Chandra	36
†D. L. Murray b Chandra	11	– c Solkar b Bedi	25
B. D. Julien c Viswanath b Bedi	47	– c Kirmani b Venkat	6
M. A. Holding lbw b Bedi	1	– not out	17
Imtiaz Ali not out	1		
A. L. Padmore c Gavaskar b Bedi	0		
R. R. Jumadeen lbw b Chandra	0		
L-b 7, n-b 2	9	B 2, l-b 7	9
1/45 2/50 3/52 4/176 5/228 6/334 7/357 8/358 9/358	359	1/41 2/78 3/81 4/162 5/214 6/231	(6 wkts dec.) 271

Bowling: *First Innings*—Madan Lal 6–1–22–0; Amarnath 5–0–26–0; Solkar 9–2–40–0; Bedi 30–11–73–4; Chandrasekhar 32.2–8–120–6; Venkataraghavan 27–7–69–0. *Second Innings*—Madan Lal 11–2–14–0; Amarnath 11–3–19–0; Bedi 25–3–76–1; Chandrasekhar 27–5–88–2; Venkataraghavan 30.3–5–65–3.

India

S. M. Gavaskar lbw b Holding	26	– c Murray b Jumadeen	102
A. D. Gaekwad c Murray b Julien	6	– c Kallicharran b Jumadeen	28
M. Amarnath st Murray b Padmore	25	– run out	85
G. R. Viswanath b Imtiaz	41	– run out	112
E. D. Solkar b Holding	13		
B. P. Patel c Fredericks b Holding	29	– not out	49
S. Madan Lal c Richards b Holding	42	– not out	1
S. Venkataraghavan b Imtiaz	13		
†S. M. H. Kirmani lbw b Holding	12		
*B. S. Bedi b Holding	0		
B. S. Chandrasekhar not out	0		
B 11, l-b 6, w 4	21	B 10, l-b 12, w 1, n-b 6	29
1/22 2/50 3/86 4/112 5/147 6/182 7/203 8/225 9/227	228	1/69 2/177 3/336 4/392	(4 wkts) 406

Bowling: *First Innings*—Julien 13–4–35–1; Holding 26.4–3–65–6; Lloyd 1–0–1–0; Padmore 29–11–36–1; Imtiaz Ali 17–7–37–2; Jumadeen 16–7–33–0. *Second Innings*—Julien 13–2–52–0; Holding 21–1–82–0; Lloyd 6–1–22–0; Padmore 47–10–98–0; Imtiaz Ali 17–3–52–0; Jumadeen 41–10–70–2; Fredericks 2–1–1–0.

Umpires: R. Gosein and C. Vyfhuis.

WEST INDIES v PAKISTAN

First Test Match

Played at Bridgetown, February 18, 19, 20, 22, 23, 1977

Drawn. A fascinating match, in which 39 wickets fell for 1398 runs, ended with the West Indies tailenders defending stubbornly amidst high tension to avoid defeat.

Nothing in the respective first innings suggested a result other than a draw. Pakistan started confidently, reached 148 before losing their second wicket. Majid was in commanding mood before he was bowled leg stump, but Garner and Croft, the two new West Indies fast bowlers, caused a collapse which left Pakistan 269 for six at the end of the first day. Raja attacked enterprisingly in scoring his second Test century and the tailenders were responsible for a revival which gave their team an excellent total of 435. The left handed Raja's not out 117 included one 6 and twelve 4s.

The West Indies reply was faltering at 183 for five before the captain, Lloyd, and the vice-captain, Murray, came together in a vital partnership of 151. Lloyd gave a straightforward chance to second slip off Sarfraz when 42 but made no other mistake in an innings of typical power which included three 6s and twenty-one 4s. Effective hitting by Garner helped the West Indies to within 14 runs of Pakistan's total.

Fortunes swung dramatically one way and then the next over the final two days. The three West Indies fast bowlers proved so menacing in the Pakistan second innings that the ninth wicket fell at 158 in mid-afternoon on the fourth day and a victory for the home team appeared certain. At this point, their cricket fell to pieces. Their fielding and catching were shocking and Murray allowed 29 byes to pass. In the circumstances, Raja rode his luck, having been dropped four times, and with the wicket-keeper, Bari, added 133 for the last wicket, a new Pakistan Test record. The total of 291 included 68 extras, a record number for Tests, and the West Indies required a challenging 306 to win.

They suffered an early loss, but Fredericks and Richards then shifted the balance in their favour with a purposeful second wicket partnership of 130. As had happened so frequently throughout, the match took yet another, dramatic swing in the session between lunch and tea. Steady bowling by Sarfraz, Imran and Salim and a slow over-rate frustrated the impatient West Indies batsmen; both Fredericks and Richards were out trying to force the pace and a collapse set in. Pakistan captured the eighth wicket with a quarter of an hour to go before the final 20 mandatory overs began and it was left to level-headed defiance from Roberts, Holder and Croft to deny them victory.

Pakistan

Majid J. Khan b Garner	88	– c Garner b Croft	28
Sadiq Mohammad c Croft b Garner	37	– c Garner b Croft	9
Haroon Rashid c Kallicharran b Foster	33	– b Roberts	39
*Mushtaq Mohammad c Murray b Croft	0	– c Murray b Roberts	6
Asif Iqbal c Murray b Croft	36	– b Croft	0
Javed Miandad lbw b Garner	2	– c Greenidge b Croft	1
Wasim Raja not out	117	– c Garner b Foster	71
Imran Khan c Garner b Roberts	20	– c Fredericks b Garner	1
Salim Altaf lbw b Garner	19	– b Garner	2
Sarfraz Nawaz c Kallicharran b Foster	38	– c Murray b Roberts	6
†Wasim Bari lbw b Croft	8	– not out	60
B 5, l-b 6, w 1, n-b 23	35	B 29, l-b 11, n-b 28	68
1/72 2/148 3/149 4/186 5/207 6/233 7/271 8/355 9/408	435	1/29 2/68 3/102 4/103 5/108 6/113 7/126 8/146 9/158	291

Bowling: *First Innings*—Roberts 30–3–124–1; Croft 31.4–6–85–3; Holder 4–0–13–0; Garner 37–7–130–4; Foster 27–13–41–2; Richards 3–1–3–0; Fredericks 1–0–4–0. *Second Innings*—Roberts 25–5–66–3; Croft 15–3–47–4; Garner 17–4–60–2; Foster 8–2–34–1; Richards 2–0–16–0.

West Indies

R. C. Fredericks c and b Sarfraz	24	– b Sarfraz	52
C. G. Greenidge c Majid b Imran	47	– c Raja b Sarfraz	2
I. V. A. Richards c Salim b Sarfraz	32	– c Sadiq b Sarfraz	92
A. I. Kallicharran c Sarfraz b Imran	17	– c Bari b Salim	9
*C. H. Lloyd c Sadiq b Salim	157	– c Bari b Imran	11
M. L. C. Foster b Sarfraz	15	– b Sarfraz	4
†D. L. Murray c Mushtaq b Imran	52	– c Bari b Salim	20
J. Garner b Javed	43	– b Salim	0
A. M. E. Roberts c Bari b Salim	4	– not out	9
C. Croft not out	1	– not out	5
V. A. Holder absent hurt	0	– b Imran	6
B 2, l-b 6, n-b 21	29	B 2, l-b 7, w 1, n-b 31	41
1/59 2/91 3/120 4/134 5/183 6/334 7/404 8/418 9/421	421	1/12 2/142 3/166 4/179 5/185 6/206 7/210 8/217 9/217	(9 wkts) 251

Bowling: *First Innings*—Imran 28–3–147–3; Sarfraz 29–3–125–3; Salim 21–3–70–2; Javed 10.4–3–22–1; Mushtaq 5–0–27–0; Majid 1–0–1–0. *Second Innings*—Imran 32–16–58–2; Sarfraz 34–10–79–4; Salim 21–7–33–3; Javed 11–4–31–0; Majid 1–0–1–0; Asif Iqbal 1–0–8–0.

Umpires: D. Sang Hue and R. Gosein.

WEST INDIES v PAKISTAN

Second Test Match

Played at Port-of-Spain, March 4, 5, 6, 8, 9, 1977

West Indies won by six wickets. A phenomenal exhibition of fast bowling on the first day by Croft caused a Pakistan collapse and gave the West Indies an early advantage which they did not relinquish. Sarfraz (injured) and Javed were omitted from Pakistan's first Test team and replaced by two spinners, Intikhab and Qasim. The West Indies brought in Shillingford and Jumadeen for Foster and Holder.

Croft, in only his second Test, bowled with pace and accuracy throughout his two spells in the Pakistan first innings, becoming only the second West Indies fast bowler to take eight wickets in a Test innings. Ironically, the only other had been Holding whose injury created the vacancy in the team filled by Croft. Pakistan's problems began when Sadiq was forced to retire after being hit on the forearm by Croft before he had scored. Croft then dismissed Haroon, Mushtaq and Asif Iqbal cheaply before Majid and Raja came together for the best partnership of the innings – 82 for the fourth wicket. However, Majid and Imran were dismissed in quick succession in mid-afternoon and Croft's final spell proved decisive, five wickets for nine runs in 10.5 overs. Salim produced two excellent balls before the end of the day to remove Greenidge and Richards in the same over but, on the second day, Fredericks batted superbly in acting as the foundation on which the West Indies built a lead of 136. He gave one difficult chance off Intikhab when 56 but otherwise made no mistake in his eighth Test century and his first at the Queen's Park Oval. He batted six hours twenty minutes, sharing important stands with Kallicharran and Shillingford. Hard hitting by Garner and Croft late in the innings contributed more crucial runs for the West Indies at a time when Mushtaq's leg-spin threatened to limit the deficit for his team.

Pakistan hopes were lifted by a steady opening partnership of 123 in their second innings between Majid and Sadiq before the former was caught at slip off Jumadeen. The effort declined in the final series of the third day when four wickets fell for 79, including that of Sadiq whose 81 was his best innings of the tour. That the West Indies target was eventually as high as 205 was due, almost entirely, to the aggressive Raja and Imran who put on 76 for the seventh wicket. Raja's 84 in three hours represented the fourth time he had made top score in the series for his team.

Fredericks and Greenidge began so confidently for the West Indies that the first wicket put on 97 and a comfortable victory appeared certain on the final day. Instead, Imran and Salim bowled with such accuracy and determination that the struggle was intense. Imran claimed Greenidge, Richards and Shillingford in rapid succession and Kallicharran took more than half an hour to score his first run. Not until five minutes before lunch did Lloyd drive Salim to the cover boundary for only the second four of the morning. So West Indies secured victory and the lead in the series.

Pakistan

Majid J. Khan lbw b Garner	47	– c Kallicharran b Jumadeen	54
Sadiq Mohammad c and b Croft	17	– c Kallicharran b Garner	81
Haroon Rashid c Lloyd b Croft	4	– lbw b Fredericks	7
*Mushtaq Mohammad c Richards b Croft	9	– c Greenidge b Roberts	21
Asif Iqbal c Murray b Croft	0	– b Garner	12
Wasim Raja b Croft	65	– c Garner b Croft	84
Imran Khan c Fredericks b Jumadeen	1	– c Murray b Roberts	35
Intikhab Alam b Croft	0	– b Garner	12
†Wasim Bari c Murray b Croft	21	– c Fredericks b Roberts	2
Salim Altaf b Croft	1	– not out	0
Iqbal Qasim not out	0	– b Roberts	4
B 3, l-b 3, n-b 9	15	B 13, l-b 4, n-b 11	28
1/10 2/21 3/21 4/103 5/112 6/150 7/154 8/159 9/161	180	1/123 2/155 3/167 4/181 5/223 6/239 7/315 8/334 9/340	340

Bowling: *First Innings*—Roberts 17–2–34–0; Croft 18.5–7–29–8; Garner 16–1–47–1; Jumadeen 16–3–55–1. *Second Innings*—Roberts 26–4–85–4; Croft 25–3–66–1; Garner 20.1–6–48–3; Jumadeen 35–13–72–1; Fredericks 6–2–14–1; Richards 12–4–27–0.

West Indies

R. C. Fredericks c Sadiq b Mushtaq	120	– c Asif b Raja	57
C. G. Greenidge b Salim	5	– c Bari b Imran	70
I. V. A. Richards b Salim	4	– b Imran	30
A. I. Kallicharran c Bari b Intikhab	37	– not out	11
I. T. Shillingford lbw b Mushtaq	39	– c Bari b Imran	2
*C. H. Lloyd c Haroon b Intikhab	22	– not out	23
†D. L. Murray b Mushtaq	10		
J. Garner lbw b Imran	36		
A. M. E. Roberts b Mushtaq	4		
C. Croft not out	23		
R. R. Jumadeen lbw b Imran	0		
B 5, l-b 11	16	B 1, l-b 11, w 1	13
1/18 2/22 3/102 4/183 5/216 6/243 7/258 8/270 9/316	316	1/97 2/159 3/166 4/170	(4 wkts) 206

Bowling: *First Innings*—Imran 21–5–50–2; Salim 18–3–44–2; Intikhab 29–6–90–2; Majid 8–3–9–0; Qasim 10–2–26–0; Mushtaq 20–7–50–4; Raja 10–1–31–0. *Second Innings*— Imran 24–8–59–3; Salim 21–3–58–0; Intikhab 2–1–6–0; Qasim 13–6–30–0; Mushtaq 9–1–27–0; Raja 5–1–13–1.

Umpires: D. Sang Hue and R. Gosein.

WEST INDIES v AUSTRALIA

First Test Match

Played at Port-of-Spain, March 3, 4, 5, 1978

West Indies won by an innings and 106 runs. The luck ran against Australia from the start and they suffered a crushing defeat inside three days for West Indies to record their first victory over Australia at the ground. The foundations of the win were laid on the first day when West Indies' fast bowlers exploited helpful conditions to rout the opposition for 90.

Rain on the day before and on the morning of the match not only delayed the start until five minutes before lunch but also affected preparation of the pitch. Two deliveries in the only over possible before the interval, bowled by Roberts, behaved so unpredictably as to sow seeds of suspicion in the minds of the Australians, who had been sent in to bat. Croft effected the early breakthrough, dismissing Wood, Yallop, and Serjeant for nine runs in his first eight overs.

For a brief period Toohey appeared at ease, but he was struck on the face hooking at Roberts when 15 and had to be taken from the field to have stitches inserted in the wound. When he returned later, he had his thumb fractured by a ball from the same bowler, an injury which prevented his taking any further part in the match or in the following two Tests. The only resistance was provided by Cosier who attacked boldly, hitting seven boundaries through ultra-attacking fields before he was last out for 46. Australia's 90 was the lowest Test score on the ground; nine of their batsmen contributed 10 runs between them.

West Indies were left slightly more than an hour's batting before the end of the day and, in that time, their openers unleashed such a flurry of shots that they scored 79 off only fourteen overs. On his Test début, Haynes captivated a crowd of 25,000 by taking 20 off an over from Thomson, including a hook for 6, and by pulling Higgs for another 6 in the last over of the day. In that period, he also hit six 4s and Greenidge five.

On the following morning the pace was less hectic as the Australians fought to keep in the game. Haynes added only eight, and Richards and Greenidge went relatively cheaply, Thomson troubling all the batsmen with his deep breakbacks. However, the left-handers, Kallicharran and Lloyd, managed to shake free and their fourth-wicket partnership of 170 at better than a run a minute ensured West Indies a formidable lead. Kallicharran's ninth Test century was his fourth on the ground and was made without blemish. It lasted four hours twenty minutes and included seventeen 4s. Lloyd clubbed one 6 and ten 4s before playing on to Thomson, although the Australians were convinced he should have been given out, caught behind off the glove to Clark, when 26. The latter half of the West Indian innings subsided rapidly, but Australia still faced a deficit of 315 when they batted a second time.

On a pitch by now slow but true, they made a promising start. Wood and Serjeant put on 59 for the first wicket before both were lbw, and then the left-handed Yallop batted so diligently that Australia went to tea 157 for three and a reasonable total appeared likely. Afterwards Yallop opened out with a series of confident drives, especially against Croft, but attempting another had his middle stump uprooted by Roberts. That proved to be the end of the opposition. Australia's last six wickets fell for 15 runs off 26 deliveries; four to Roberts who finished with five for 56, and two to Parry, the new off-spinner. The paid attendances were 21,703 (first day), 24,211 (second), and 16,233 (third).

Australia

G. M. Wood c Haynes b Croft	2	lbw b Roberts	32
C. S. Serjeant c Murray b Croft	3	lbw b Garner	40
G. N. Yallop c Richards b Croft	2	b Roberts	81
P. M. Toohey b Garner	20	absent hurt	0
*R. B. Simpson lbw b Garner	0	b Parry	14
G. J. Cosier c Greenidge b Croft	46	lbw b Garner	19
†S. J. Rixon run out	1	c Parry b Roberts	0
B. Yardley c Murray b Roberts	2	not out	7
J. R. Thomson c Austin b Roberts	0	b Parry	4
W. M. Clark b Garner	0	b Roberts	0
J. D. Higgs not out	0	b Roberts	2
B 4, l-b 6, n-b 4	14	B 5, l-b 2, w 1, n-b 2	10
1/7 2/10 3/16 4/23 5/45 6/75 7/75 8/84 9/90	90	1/59 2/90 3/149 4/194 5/194 6/196 7/200 8/201 9/209	209

Bowling: *First Innings*—Roberts 12–4–26–2; Croft 9.1–5–15–4; Garner 14–6–35–3. *Second Innings*—Roberts 16.2–3–56–5; Croft 13–1–55–0; Garner 17–5–39–2; Parry 17–1–49–2.

West Indies

C. G. Greenidge b Yardley	43	A. M. E. Roberts st Rixon b Higgs	7
D. L. Haynes c Rixon b Higgs	61	J. Garner c Cosier b Higgs	0
I. V. A. Richards lbw b Thomson	39	C. E. H. Croft not out	4
A. I. Kallicharran b Yardley	127		
*C. H. Lloyd b Thomson	86	L-b 9, n-b 6	15
R. A. Austin c sub b Thomson	2		——
†D. L. Murray c Rixon b Higgs	21	1/87 2/143 3/143 4/313 5/324	405
D. R. Parry b Yardley	0	6/385 7/385 8/391 9/391	

Bowling: Thomson 21–6–84–3; Clark 16–3–41–0; Higgs 24.5–3–91–4; Simpson 16–2–65–0; Yardley 19–1–64–3; Cosier 13–2–45–0.

Umpires: D. Sang Hue and R. Gosein.

WEST INDIES v AUSTRALIA

Third Test Match

Played at Georgetown, March 31, April 1, 2, 3, 4, 1978

Australia won by three wickets. Events leading up to this match were so controversial and the atmosphere so emotionally charged that it was to their credit that the two teams, more particularly West Indies, managed to produce such a keen, closely-fought contest. The public, whatever their feelings on the matter that led to the resignation from the captaincy of Lloyd, a native Guyanese, responded magnificently, and fears of trouble at the ground proved ill-founded.

Lloyd's decision was triggered by the omission of Haynes, Austin, and Murray from the team that won the first and second Tests. All three were contracted to World Series Cricket. The selectors explained that they had been omitted to give new players a chance; this with the tour of India and Sri Lanka later in the year in view and as they could get no assurance from the WSC players that they would be available then. Subsequently, all WSC West Indians joined Lloyd in registering their lack of confidence in the selectors.

Such action meant that West Indies had hastily to assemble a new team. Kallicharran was named captain, and with him only Parry had played in the earlier Tests. Six of those now under him were making their Test débuts, and it was clear when West Indies were bowled out for 205 on the first day that they were psychologically unprepared for the event. Only two innings saved them from an even worse fate: one of 56 by Alvin Greenidge, who took the place of his unrelated namesake as opener, and one of 53 by the all-rounder Shivnarine, rather a surprise choice in the eleven. Everyone else faltered as Thomson and Clark shared eight wickets betwen them.

Even though they fielded an entirely new staff of fast bowlers, West Indies struck back when Australia replied. Phillip, bowling at lively pace, removed Darling and Ogilvie cheaply before the end of the first day, and Clarke and Holder followed by having Cosier, Serjeant, and Wood early on the second morning. Australia, going to lunch at 146 for six, appeared to have wasted the advantage gained for them by the bowlers on the opening day. It was at this stage that the lack of penetration in the West Indian attack was revealed and Simpson, Rixon, and Yardley put Australia ahead by 81. Simpson batted for three hours for his highest score of the series while Rixon, whose previous four innings brought him only 17, now batted enterprisingly for 54 before he fell to a brilliant catch at second slip.

The new West Indians mounted a spirited recovery in their second innings to record the highest total of the series and leave Australia with a demanding winning target. Two centuries of contrasting styles, one by Williams and one by Gomes, formed the basis of the effort but there were also important contributions from Parry, Shivnarine, and Holder. Ironically, both Williams and Gomes were in the original team, chosen to replace Haynes and Austin. Williams kept on playing his shots in spite of several narrow escapes, particularly against Thomson, and became only the tenth West Indian to score a century in his first Test. Having done that, he hooked the next ball he faced and was caught at fine leg. He hit nineteen of the 118 deliveries he faced to the boundary and batted only two and three-quarter hours. Parry, sent in as nightwatchman on the second afternoon, lent him admirable support in a stand of 77 for the third wicket.

When Williams departed, the left-handed Gomes replaced him and proceeded to build the West Indies total in a more sedate but no less assured manner. Kallicharran and Shillingford, the two most experienced batsmen, both fell cheaply, but Shivnarine joined Gomes to thwart Australia's hopes of a complete breakthrough. In fact, he outlasted Gomes who, like Williams before him, was out next ball after completing his 100 (three hours twenty-five minutes, eleven 4s). The pair added 70 for the seventh wicket, and then Shivnarine and Holder put on a further 62 for the ninth.

Australia began their second innings needing more runs than either side had ever scored against the other in the fourth innings of a Test. And when Clarke despatched Darling, Ogilvie, and Simpson inside the first forty minutes, they seemed beaten. However, Wood and Serjeant, the two Western Australians, responded to the crisis with great determination, defying everything West Indies could put against them to add 251 in four and a half hours for the fourth wicket. Both passed their first Test centuries, but they and Cosier fell in the final session of the day to leave the match evenly balanced for the final day. Serjeant, whose 124 included one 6 and eighteen 4s, top-edged a hook to be brilliantly caught at deep backward square leg; Wood, never in any bother, was finally run out for 126 (one 6 and eight 4s). Australia needed another 69 on the final day with four wickets remaining. A close fight was expected, but West Indies lacked conviction in their approach and Australia lost only one further wicket in winning.

West Indies

A. T. Greenidge lbw b Thomson	56	– b Clark	11
B. Williams lbw b Clark	10	– c Serjeant b Clark	100
H. A. Gomes b Clark	4	– c Simpson b Yardley	101
*A. I. Kallicharran b Thomson	0	– b Yardley	22
I. T. Shillingford c Clark b Laughlin	3	– c and b Thomson	16
†D. A. Murray c Ogilvie b Clark	21	– lbw b Simpson	16
S. Shivnarine c Rixon b Thomson	53	– b Cosier	63
N. Phillip c Yardley b Simpson	15	– st Rixon b Yardley	4
V. A. Holder c Laughlin b Clark	1	– lbw b Clark	31
D. R. Parry not out	21	– lbw b Clark	51
S. Clarke b Thomson	6	– not out	5
L-b 2, n-b 13	15	B 4, l-b 5, n-b 10	19
1/31 2/36 3/48 4/77 5/84 6/130 7/165 8/166 9/193	205	1/36 2/95 3/172 4/199 5/249 6/285 7/355 8/369 9/431	439

Bowling: *First Innings*—Thomson 16.2–1–57–4; Clark 24–6–64–4; Laughlin 10–4–34–1; Cosier 2–1–1–0; Simpson 3–1–34–1. *Second Innings*—Thomson 20–2–83–1; Clark 34.4–4–124–4; Yardley 30–6–96–3; Simpson 19–4–70–1; Cosier 6–1–14–1; Laughlin 7–1–33–0.

Australia

W. M. Darling c Greenidge b Phillip	15	– c Williams b Clarke	0
G. M. Wood lbw b Holder	50	– run out	126
A. D. Ogilvie c and b Phillip	4	– lbw b Clarke	0
G. J. Cosier lbw b Clarke	9	– b Phillip	0
C. S. Serjeant b Clarke	0	– c sub b Phillip	124
*R. B. Simpson run out	67	– c Murray b Clarke	4
T. J. Laughlin c Greenidge b Parry	21	– c and b Parry	24
†S. J. Rixon c Holder b Phillip	54	– not out	39
B. Yardley b Clarke	33	– not out	15
J. R. Thomson c and b Phillip	3		
W. M. Clark not out	2		
L-b 12, w 1, n-b 15	28	B 8, l-b 4, w 2, n-b 16	30
1/28 2/36 3/77 4/85 5/90 6/142 7/237 8/256 9/268	286	1/11 2/13 3/22 4/273 5/279 6/290 7/338	(7 wkts) 362

Bowling: *First Innings*—Phillip 18–0–75–4; Clarke 22–3–58–3; Holder 17–1–40–1; Gomes 3–0–8–0; Parry 15–2–39–1; Shivnarine 8–0–38–0. *Second Innings*—Clarke 27–5–83–3; Phillip 19–2–65–2; Holder 20–3–55–0; Parry 17–1–61–1; Shivnarine 18–2–68–0.

Umpires: R. Gosein and C. Vyfhuis.

WEST INDIES v AUSTRALIA

Fifth Test Match

Played at Kingston, April 28, 29, 30, May 2, 3, 1978

Abandoned as a draw after a crowd disturbance had halted play late on the scheduled final day with one West Indian wicket standing and 6.2 of the mandatory final twenty overs remaining. Even though the West Indies Board representatives, after lengthy discussions with officials of both teams, decided to extend the match into a sixth day to make up the time lost, the umpires were neither consulted nor informed about the decision. In the event, one, Gosein, who stood in all five Tests, had to be summoned from his hotel just before play was scheduled to be resumed, and he was adamant that there was no provision in the laws or the playing conditions for the match to be extended. He refused to continue, as did the stand-by umpire, John Gayle – on the same grounds – so the match was left abandoned.

The match was shrouded in controversy from the start. The Australians objected to one of the umpires originally chosen: Douglas Sang Hue, who had no-balled Yardley for throwing in the preceding match against Jamaica. The West Indies Board, while stating their faith in Sang Hue, acquiesced and Wesley Malcolm stood instead. It was ironic that it was a decision by Malcolm, who ruled Holder caught behind the wicket, that triggered the troubles. At the time, West Indies were putting up a spirited fight to save a match which they appeared to have conclusively lost earlier in the day. Holder lingered at the crease before walking towards the pavilion, apparently dissatisfied with the decision. In minutes, the crowd was hurling bottles, stones, and other debris on to the ground and the police found it impossible to quell the disturbance or clear the ground so that play could be resumed. So a series bedevilled by rancour and controversy ended unhappily.

It was a frustrating experience for Australia, who held the upper hand throughout the match. Rain delayed the start by an hour and a quarter, and a maiden Test century by Toohey allowed Australia to recover from the loss of two early wickets and end the first day 186 for three. Toohey, whose partnership of 133 with Yallop emphasized the easy-paced nature of the pitch, batted five and a quarter hours all told and hit ten 4s. He also provided Holder with his 100th Test wicket three-quarters of an hour into the second day when he snicked a catch to second slip. Holder became the seventh West Indian bowler to reach the landmark. There was no other innings to compare with Toohey's and Australia, yet again, fell away badly towards the end, Jumadeen claiming the last four wickets off 28 balls for only 8 runs.

In three-quarters of an hour before bad light halted play, West Indies were subjected to a fiery spell from Thomson and lost both openers for 28. It was the medium paced Laughlin, opening the bowling in the absence of the injured Clark and Callen, who caused the problems on the third morning, adding Murray, Kallicharran, and Foster to his bag as West Indies slumped to 63 for five. He was aided in each case by alert catching. In such a daunting position, the West Indies lower order showed resilience in helping Gomes rebuild the innings. He shared stands of 96 with Shivnarine, 46 with Phillip, and 57 with Holder, and himself ended the day 115 not out with West Indies 276 for eight, only 67 in arrears.

Gomes, whose 115 took five and a half hours and included eleven 4s, played on to Thomson's fourth ball of the fourth morning, and nor did Holder add to his overnight score. The pressure was now on Australia to score quickly enough to give their bowlers ample time to press for victory. Wood and Toohey fulfilled their purposes admirably, adding 180 in three hours for the second wicket after Wood and Ogilvie had provided a solid start of 65. Each batsmen was so dominant that each appeared certain to pass his century. Neither did, both falling in the nineties to Jumadeen. Wood was well caught at extra cover, having batted four hours twenty minutes. Toohey needed only three to become the first Australian to score centuries in each innings of a Test in the West Indies when he was beaten by the flight and stumped. In three hours he hit one six and eight 4s. Soon afterwards Simpson declared, challenging West Indies to get 369 on the final day.

Their hopes flickered only briefly while Williams and Bacchus put together 42 in three-quarters of an hour. However, they lost four wickets by lunch and a fifth soon afterwards, leaving them with an uphill fight to stave off defeat. Their captain, Kallicharran, led the way with a purposeful display, receiving crucial support from Shivnarine, who helped him add 91, and Phillip, who outlasted him after he was out with 9.5 overs remaining. Kallicharran's innings was divided into two parts. He was so intent on defence at first that he took two and a half hours to reach his first 50. His second 50 occupied only fifty-six minutes. However, when his chanceless 126 was ended and umpire Malcolm made his fateful decision against Holder, Australia were on the verge of victory. They were denied a chance of clinching it by the unfortunate crowd intervention.

Australia

G. M. Wood c Parry b Phillip	16	– c Bacchus b Jumadeen	90
A. D. Ogilvie c Shivnarine b Holder	0	– st Murray b Parry	43
P. M. Toohey c Williams b Holder	122	– st Murray b Jumadeen	97
G. N. Yallop c sub b Shivnarine	57	– not out	23
C. S. Serjeant b Holder	26	– not out	32
*R. B. Simpson c Murray b Foster	46		
T. J. Laughlin c sub b Jumadeen	35		
†S. J. Rixon not out	13		
B. Yardley b Jumadeen	7		
J. R. Thomson c Murray b Jumadeen	4		
J. D. Higgs c Foster b Jumadeen	0		
L-b 5, w 1, n-b 11	17	B 5, l-b 8, n-b 7	20
1/0 2/38 3/171 4/217 5/266 6/308 7/324 8/335 9/343	343	1/65 2/245 3/246 (3 wkts dec.)	305

Bowling: *First Innings*—Phillip 35–5–90–1; Holder 31–9–68–3; Parry 5–0–15–0; Jumadeen 38.4–6–72–4; Foster 32–11–68–1; Shivnarine 9–2–13–1. *Second Innings*—Phillip 17–1–64–0; Holder 18–2–41–0; Jumadeen 23–2–90–2; Parry 18–3–60–1; Foster 7–1–22–0; Shivnarine 3–1–8–0.

West Indies

B. Williams c Serjeant b Laughlin	17	– c Wood b Yardley	19
S. F. A. Bacchus c Yardley b Thomson	5	– c Simpson b Thomson	21
†D. A. Murray c Wood b Laughlin	12	– b Yardley	10
H. A. Gomes b Thomson	115	– c Rixon b Higgs	1
*A. I. Kallicharran c Ogilvie b Laughlin	6	– lbw b Higgs	126
M. L. C. Foster c Rixon b Laughlin	8	– run out	5
S. Shivnarine st Rixon b Higgs	53	– c Yallop c Yardley	27
D. R. Parry lbw b Higgs	4	– c Serjeant b Yardley	0
N. Phillip c Rixon b Simpson	26	– not out	26
V. A. Holder lbw b Laughlin	24	– c Rixon b Higgs	6
R. R. Jumadeen not out	4	– not out	0
L-b 1, n-b 5	6	B 14, l-b 1, n-b 2	17
1/13 2/28 3/41 4/47 5/63 6/159 7/173 8/219 9/276	280	1/42 2/43 3/43 4/59 5/88 6/179 7/181 8/242 9/258	(9 wkts) 258

Bowling: *First Innings*—Thomson 22–4–61–2; Laughlin 25.4–4–101–5; Yardley 14–4–27–0; Simpson 10–0–38–1; Higgs 19–3–47–2. *Second Innings*—Thomson 15–1–53–1; Laughlin 10–0–34–0; Higgs 38.4–10–67–3; Yardley 29–17–35–4; Simpson 11–4–44–0; Yallop 3–1–8–0.

Umpires: R. Gosein and W. Malcolm.

CRICKET IN NEW ZEALAND

NEW ZEALAND v INDIA

Second Test Match

Played at Christchurch, February 22, 23, 24, 26, 27, 1968

New Zealand won by six wickets. Deceived by the appearance of the pitch, which hinted strongly at assistance for the fast bowlers, Pataudi sent New Zealand in and at the end of the first day they were 273 for three: Murray and Dowling scored 126 for the first wicket and Congdon helped Dowling to add 82 for the second wicket. Although failing to take a wicket on a very easy pitch, Nadkarni bowled 41 overs for 54 runs. Prasanna, however, was punished severely. Dowling, 135 overnight, went on to a New Zealand Test record of 239, Burgess and Thomson – in his first Test – sharing three-figure partnerships. Dowling, dropped at 61 and 122, hit twenty-eight 4s and five 6s in an innings of just over nine hours. New Zealand reached 500 for the second time in Test matches.

Then steady bowling and India's inability to sustain concentration saw the touring team out, on the third day, for 288. There was much speculation as to whether Dowling, with a lead of 214, would enforce the follow-on, and thus risk last use of a pitch taking spin. He asked India to bat again and there was a time when New Zealand were in danger of defeat. A brilliant 63 by Engineer, and resolute batting by Surti, Pataudi and Borde took India to 230 for four, but Bartlett, in one over, bowled Pataudi and Borde, so that New Zealand, in the end, needed only 88.

By that time the Indian slow bowlers were able to turn the ball sharply, and New Zealand might have been in difficulties had Congdon not played a sensibly aggressive innings, with nine 4s in his 61.

New Zealand

B. A. G. Murray b Abid Ali	74	– b Abid Ali	0
*G. T. Dowling st Engineer b Prasanna	239	– lbw b Bedi	5
B. E. Congdon c Wadekar b Bedi	28	– not out	61
V. Pollard c Jaisimha b Bedi	1	– c Jaisimha b Prasanna	9
M. G. Burgess c Pataudi b Nadkarni	26	– lbw b Bedi	1
K. Thomson c Borde b Bedi	69	– not out	0
G. R. Bartlett c Wadekar b Bedi	22		
R. C. Motz c sub b Bedi	1		
R. O. Collinge c Pataudi b Nadkarni	11		
J. C. Alabaster c Borde b Bedi	1		
†R. I. Harford not out	0		
B 2, l-b 13, n-b 15	30	B 8, l-b 1, n-b 3	12
1/126 2/208 3/214 4/317 5/436 6/471 7/473 8/498 9/502	502	1/0 2/30 3/70 4/79 (4 wkts)	88

Bowling: *First Innings*—Kulkarni 13–3–38–0; Surti 21–4–65–0; Abid Ali 18–4–40–1; Nadkarni 66–34–114–2; Bedi 47.3–10–127–6; Prasanna 19–2–83–1; Jaisimha 2–0–5–0. *Second Innings*—Abid Ali 3–0–13–1; Jaisimha 2–0–10–0; Nadkarni 8–3–11–0; Bedi 17–9–21–2; Prasanna 8–0–18–1; Surti 2.3–1–3–0.

India

Abid Ali c and b Motz	7	– c Harford b Alabaster	16
†F. M. Engineer c Congdon b Motz	12	– c Burgess b Bartlett	63
A. L. Wadekar b Motz	15	– c Murray b Alabaster	8
R. F. Surti c Pollard b Motz	67	– lbw b Pollard	45
*Nawab of Pataudi c Murray b Pollard	52	– b Bartlett	47
M. L. Jaisimha c Murray b Collinge	1	– run out	15
C. G. Borde lbw b Motz	57	– b Bartlett	33
R. G. Nadkarni c Harford b Collinge	32	– b Bartlett	29
E. A. S. Prasanna c Dowling b Motz	7	– c Pollard b Bartlett	7
B. S. Bedi c Congdon b Collinge	3	– c Murray b Bartlett	5
U. N. Kulkarni not out	0	– not out	1
B 5, l-b 8, n-b 22	35	B 2, l-b 11, n-b 19	32
1/7 2/30 3/50 4/153 5/154 6/179 7/270 8/281 9/287	288	1/16 2/82 3/107 4/186 5/231 6/232 7/264 8/278 9/300	301

Bowling: *First Innings*—Collinge 18.2–6–43–3; Motz 21–6–63–6; Bartlett 14–1–52–0; Alabaster 15–7–36–0; Pollard 24–7–59–1. *Second Innings*—Motz 14–5–37–0; Collinge 22–4–79–0; Alabaster 31–13–63–2; Pollard 15–2–52–1; Bartlett 16.5–5–38–6.

Umpires: R. W. Shortt and D. E. A. Copps.

NEW ZEALAND v WEST INDIES

Third Test Match

Played at Christchurch, March 13, 14, 15, 17, 1969

Drawn. Only one change was made in the teams, Burgess coming back into the New Zealand eleven for Morgan. Sobers won the toss and the West Indies batted on a pitch which was slow and low of bounce on the first day. The innings was dominated to an extraordinary extent by Nurse, who made his highest Test score. In very poor light, he batted far better than at Auckland, and punished the New Zealand pace bowlers with superb drives off the back foot. In four hours, twenty-five minutes, before rain ended play, the West Indies scored 203 for one and next morning Carew went to a painstaking 91 in five hours, seven minutes before being beautifully caught by Turner at slip. The score was 326 before the third wicket fell, but in mid-afternoon Motz, in a very aggressive spell, took four for 7 in 27 balls and Nurse alone looked like staying. He spent three and a quarter hours over his first century, over six and a half hours reaching his second, and in all batted eight hours for 258, with one 6 and thirty-five 4s. It was the highest Test score made at Christchurch, and it was a magnificent display of aggressive but responsible batting.

New Zealand reached 55 before Dowling was out in the last over, but on the third day Holford and Gibbs assumed command on a pitch which took spin readily. The New Zealanders fought right down the line, but were in slow retreat all day and had to follow on 200 behind. This time Dowling and Turner shared an opening partnership of 115, an all-wicket New Zealand record against the West Indies and New Zealand knocked off their arrears with only two wickets down. There was still much turn in the pitch, but the home country, with Hastings batting particularly well, gave their most convincing display for a long time and easily saved the match. Hastings, in for four hours, forty-one minutes, deserved his first Test century. Bad light ended play forty minutes early.

West Indies

R. C. Fredericks c Turner b Motz	4	C. C. Griffith c Pollard b Taylor	8
M. C. Carew c Turner b Pollard	91	R. M. Edwards st Milburn b Yuile	0
S. M. Nurse st Milburn b Yuile	258	L. R. Gibbs not out	0
B. F. Butcher lbw b Motz	29		
C. A. Lloyd c Yuile b Motz	3	B 4, l-b 9, n-b 1	14
*G. S. Sobers b Motz	0		
D. A. J. Holford b Motz	0	1/16 2/247 3/326 4/340 5/350	417
†J. L. Hendriks c Milburn b Taylor	10	6/350 7/383 8/413 9/417	

Bowling: Motz 27–3–113–5; Cunis 22–2–93–0; Taylor 14.4–0–63–0; Pollard 18–6–64–1; Yuile 20–5–70–2.

New Zealand

*G. T. Dowling lbw b Edwards	23	– lbw b Sobers	76
G. M. Turner b Gibbs	30	– c Holford b Sobers	38
B. W. Yuile lbw b Carew	17	– b Griffith	20
B. E. Congdon b Gibbs	42	– b Sobers	43
B. F. Hastings b Holford	0	– not out	117
M. G. Burgess b Edwards	26	– c Sobers b Holford	2
V. Pollard b Holford	21	– b Carew	44
B. R. Taylor not out	43	– not out	0
R. C. Motz c Fredericks b Holford	6		
R. S. Cunis c Carew b Holford	0		
†B. D. Milburn c Holford b Gibbs	0		
B 5, l-b 3, w 1	9	B 10, l-b 14, n-b 3	27
1/55 2/63 3/95 4/117 5/119 6/160 7/182 8/200 9/216	217	1/115 2/128 3/203 4/210 5/320 6/363	(6 wkts) 367

Bowling: *First Innings*—Sobers 8–3–21–0; Griffith 5–2–15–0; Edwards 15–4–30–2; Gibbs 24.3–6–64–3; Holford 20–5–66–4; Carew 8–2–12–1. *Second Innings*—Sobers 31–8–70–3; Griffith 13.4–1–55–1; Edwards 21–6–67–0; Gibbs 19–4–42–0; Holford 25–5–82–1; Carew 9–4–24–1.

Umpires: W. T. Martin and E. A. C. MacKintosh.

CENTRAL DISTRICTS v PAKISTAN

Played at New Plymouth, January 24, 1973

(40 Overs) Central Districts won by four wickets. Central Districts took considerable satisfaction from beating Pakistan for a second time in a week. The game had a muddled start, Intikhab winning the toss and deciding to bat, but the Central captain M. J. F. Shrimpton being under the impression his side had been asked to bat first. So there were four batsmen padded by each side before the misunderstanding was cleared up and the game started. Pakistan tried to score too fast too soon and lost wickets rapidly. Central

had 15 balls left when the match was won. Pakistan 163 (Majid Khan 70; A. B. Jordan 3/20, B. Stewart 3/44, D. R. O'Sullivan 2/27); Central Districts 166/6 (D. Neal 39 not out).

NEW ZEALAND v PAKISTAN

Second Test Match

Played at Dunedin, February 7, 8, 9, 10, 1973

Pakistan won by an innings and 166 runs. Intikhab won the toss again – it was New Zealand's seventh consecutive Test lost toss – and his players made the most of this good fortune to inflict a crushing defeat on a New Zealand team which was expected to be very much in competition. New Zealand's lack of a wrist-spinner was fatal in a match dominated by the batting of Mushtaq and Asif Iqbal, the bowling of Intikhab and Mushtaq. On the first morning, Pakistan scored 107 for two, and then play ended because of rain. On the second day Mushtaq and Asif broke the Pakistan fourth-wicket record against all countries in a magnificent display which yielded 350 runs. Even while they were batting, there were hints of what was to follow; on the third day the pitch powdered rapidly, the ball being white and dusty as Intikhab spun his way brilliantly to his best Test figures, Mushtaq took up where Intikhab left off to complete a crushing defeat on New Zealand.

At 126 for three Sadiq was out after making his third consecutive big score in the Tests and New Zealand had done reasonably well, but the medium pace bowlers were put to the sword by Mushtaq and Asif after a hard-fought morning. Only 40 runs were scored in the first eighty minutes. After lunch the bowling deteriorated and only Howarth, who could turn the ball a shade, contained the batsmen. Mushtaq's century was the twenty-first in Tests by the four Mohammad brothers. He spent two and three-quarter hours over his first 50, but his subsequent half-centuries took only 100, 64 and 70 minutes. Asif made his century in three hours twenty minutes, and his third 50 came in thirty-six minutes and an indication of the dazzling display they gave once they were established, was the times for the 50s in the partnership – 67, 57, 38, 38, 17, 23, 34. In the last four hours, Pakistan scored 316 on the second day. The stand of 350 took only 274 minutes; it was the most severe thrashing New Zealand bowling had suffered for twenty years. Mushtaq hit twenty 4s, Asif one 6 and eighteen 4s.

Intikhab declared before the third day's play began and although Jarvis failed again, Turner and Congdon progressed swiftly against the medium-pace bowling. As soon as Intikhab took up the attack, the writing was on the wall. He obtained sharp turn and bounce, sometimes had the ball whipping through low and the New Zealanders, unable to go fully forward or back, resorted to the sweep shot with disastrous results. After Turner and Congdon, Wadsworth alone showed enough enterprise to challenge the bowlers. Nine of the New Zealand players had scored centuries or half-centuries in Tests, but the team was humiliated by Intikhab's skill and aggression. He was able to bring his fieldsmen in for nearly all of his long spell.

Following on, New Zealand again started briskly against medium-paced bowling which was innocuous on this pitch, but soon the spinners were at work again and the game ended after an hour on the last day. It was Intikhab's first victory in four years as a Test captain. Mushtaq became only the second Test player to make a double century and take five wickets in an innings in the same match. The first was the West Indian D. Atkinson (219 and 5/56) against Australia in 1954–55. Pollard batted vigorously for 50 in seventy-two minutes.

Pakistan

Sadiq Mohammad b Hadlee	61	*Intikhab Alam c Pollard b Howarth	3
Zaheer Abbas c Wadsworth b Hadlee	15	†Wasim Bari not out	2
Majid Khan c and b Taylor	26		
Mushtaq Mohammad c Wadsworth b Congdon	201	L-b 13, n-b 3	16
Asif Iqbal c Hastings b Taylor	175	1/23 2/81 3/126 4/476 5/500 6/504 (6 wkts dec.)	507
Wasim Raja not out	8		

Saleem Altaf, Sarfraz Nawaz and Pervez Sajjad did not bat.

Bowling: Hadlee 24–3–100–2; Taylor 22–3–91–2; Congdon 17–1–72–1; Howarth 29–6–83–1; Pollard 13–2–64–0; O'Sullivan 18–2–81–0.

New Zealand

G. M. Turner c Mushtaq b Intikhab	37	– c Mushtaq b Intikhab	24
T. W. Jarvis c Mushtaq b Sarfraz	7	– c Bari b Mushtaq	39
*B. E. Congdon c Bari b Intikhab	35	– c Khan b Mushtaq	7
B. F. Hastings c Sarfraz b Intikhab	4	– b Mushtaq	9
M. G. Burgess b Intikhab	10	– c Pervez b Intikhab	4
V. Pollard c Sarfraz b Intikhab	3	– b Intikhab	61
B. R. Taylor c Sarfraz b Intikhab	0	– run out	3
†K. J. Wadsworth b Mushtaq	45	– c Khan b Intikhab	17
D. R. Hadlee st Bari b Intikhab	1	– c Khan b Mushtaq	0
D. R. O'Sullivan c Raja b Mushtaq	4	– b Mushtaq	1
H. J. Howarth not out	4	– not out	7
B 1, l-b 2, n-b 3	6	B 5, l-b 7, n-b 1	13
1/15 2/73 3/84 4/87 5/99 6/99 7/104 8/116 9/139	156	1/48 2/57 3/78 4/88 5/92 6/127 7/150 8/159 9/169	185

Bowling: *First Innings*—Saleem 5–0–23–0; Sarfraz 5–0–20–1; Intikhab 21–3–52–7; Pervez 17–5–40–0; Mushtaq 3.5–1–15–2. *Second Innings*—Saleem 4–2–11–0; Sarfraz 4–0–16–0; Mushtaq 18–2–49–5; Intikhab 18.4–2–78–4; Raja 2–0–8–0; Pervez 3–0–10–0.

Umpires: R. W. Shortt and D. E. A. Copps.

NEW ZEALAND v PAKISTAN

Third Test Match

Played at Auckland, February 16, 17, 18, 19, 1973

Drawn. With a prudent approach to the match. Pakistan held New Zealand at arm's length and thus recorded their first Test rubber success away from home. It was a remarkable match, full of interest almost until the end. Intikhab again won the toss, but this was of little moment for the pitch played quite easily after it had given a little bounce and movement before lunch on the first day. Once more Majid Khan led the Pakistan batting, but this was a very subdued innings, compared with his earlier brilliance. He was in almost four and a half hours for 110. Taylor and Howarth commanded considerable respect as Pakistan went to 300 for seven at the close. Once more the New Zealand catching was below standard. Khan and Mushtaq scored 104 for the third wicket, then Asif Iqbal was with Khan while 86 were added. During the day Wadsworth broke the New Zealand Test wicket-keeping record of 50 (set by A. E. Dick) and in the last over he took a magnificent diving catch to give Taylor his hundredth wicket in Tests, only the second New Zealander to reach that mark. In Pakistan's second innings he took two more wickets to leave R. C. Motz's record behind.

The second day, a Saturday, was a study in contrasts. Pakistan, determined to take no chance, batted on for three hours to add 102. Saleem was undefeated for 53, made in three hours and Pervez, sharing a last-wicket stand of 48, had a personal Test best, much to his and everyone's delight. Wasim Bari stayed nearly two hours for 30 as Pakistan made the game safe. In his Test début the tall, fair-haired left-hander, Redmond, contributed a spectacular century. Diffident and unsound at first, he began to attack vigorously after the first half-hour. Strangely, the only other New Zealanders – J. E. Mills and Taylor – to make centuries on their Test débuts were also left-handers. Redmond, driving, cutting and pulling with tremendous confidence, reached his century in two hours, twelve minutes from 110 balls. He hit twenty 4s and one 5 in a scintillating display. When Khan bowled, Redmond hit all of the first five balls to the fence. At 97, he thumped a ball away to mid-wicket and it seemed a certain four. A crowd of about 300 boys and youths streamed on to the field to congratulate Redmond, but on the boundary Asif Iqbal had made a magnificent save and Redmond was only 99. This demonstration, which lasted several minutes, was without parallel in New Zealand domestic cricket. Redmond was hoisted shoulder high, a bail was souvenired, an umpire slightly injured in the jostling throng. But Redmond went to his century with another four. With Redmond was Turner, playing a flawless innings as New Zealand scored 159 for the first wicket. Once the stand was broken, Intikhab took command with another splendid display of spin bowling. On the third morning he took five for 42 as New Zealand wickets tumbled and at lunch nine were down with Hastings fighting grimly for survival and two runs still needed to avoid the follow-on.

In this crisis, Collinge batted with extraordinary solidity and aggression. Using his considerable reach, he played the spinners safely and from time to time let go with powerful attacking strokes. As soon as the batsmen had forced the removal of Sarfraz from a close leg-side catching position, their progress became easier and faster. Hastings, although not batting without blemish, won admiration for his concentration and his cutting and driving. Soon they left the New Zealand tenth-wicket record behind, and went on to beat the world record of 130 set by Rhodes and Foster almost seventy years earlier. They went past that mark when Collinge crashed Pervez through the covers, and they were not separated until they had added 151 and the totals were level. They made the runs in two hours, thirty-five minutes. Hastings batted over four and a half hours.

New Zealand made further progress by capturing three wickets for 73 before the close, but could not get wickets quickly enough on the last day to have a chance of victory. Asif was missed very early and batted another seventy minutes: New Zealand were always a little behind the striking rate needed.

It was a determined defensive action by Pakistan. The normally ebullient Mushtaq batted two hours fifty minutes for 52, Saleem an hour and three-quarters for 11 but Raja shaped well. In New Zealand's second innings Redmond was even more convincing than in the first and scored a fine 56.

Pakistan

Sadiq Mohammad c Wadsworth b Collinge	33	– Hadlee b Taylor	38
Zaheer Abbas c Turner b Taylor	10	– c Turner b Taylor	0
Majid Khan c Wadsworth b Taylor	110	– c Wadsworth b Howarth	33
Mushtaq Mohammad c Hastings b Congdon	61	– b Howarth	52
Asif Iqbal b Taylor	34	– lbw b Congdon	39
Wasim Raja c Wadsworth b Collinge	1	– b Collinge	49
*Intikhab Alam c Wadsworth b Taylor	34	– b Howarth	2
†Wasim Bari c and b Howarth	30	– lbw b Hadlee	27
Saleem Altaf not out	53	– lbw b Congdon	11
Sarfraz Nawaz c Wadsworth b Howarth	2	– c Taylor b Collinge	4
Pervez Sajjad lbw b Congdon	24	– not out	8
B 1, l-b 3, n-b 6	10	B 3, l-b 3, w 2	8
1/43 2/43 3/147 4/223 5/238 6/267 7/295 8/342 9/354	402	1/4 2/61 3/71 4/116 5/159 6/203 7/206 8/238 9/242	271

Bowling: *First Innings*—Collinge 24–2–72–2; Hadlee 17–2–100–0; Taylor 32–9–86–4; Howarth 32–5–86–2; Congdon 11.5–0–48–2. *Second Innings*—Hadlee 5.7–0–35–1; Taylor 19–5–66–2; Howarth 31–11–99–3; Collinge 7–2–19–2; Congdon 16–3–44–2.

New Zealand

R. E. Redmond c Mushtaq b Pervez	107	– c Intikhab b Raja	56
G. M. Turner c Sarfraz b Intikhab	58	– b Raja	24
*B. E. Congdon b Intikhab	24	– not out	6
B. F. Hastings b Raja	110	– not out	4
M. G. Burgess b Intikhab	2	– c Mushtaq b Raja	1
T. W. Jarvis lbw b Intikhab	0		
†K. J. Wadsworth c Sadiq b Intikhab	6		
B. R. Taylor c Khan b Pervez	2		
D. R. Hadlee b Intikhab	0		
H. J. Howarth c Khan b Mushtaq	8		
R. O. Collinge not out	68		
B 8, l-b 6, n-b 3	17	B 1	1
1/159 2/180 3/203 4/205 5/205 6/225 7/235 8/236 9/251	402	1/80 2/81 3/87 (3 wkts)	92

Bowling: *First Innings*—Saleem 20–0–58–0; Sarfraz 16–1–85–0; Intikhab 30–4–127–6; Khan 3–0–30–0; Pervez 15–3–50–2; Mushtaq 5–0–26–1; Raja 1.6–0–9–1. *Second Innings*—Saleem 4–0–17–0; Sarfraz 4–0–13–0; Raja 8–2–32–3; Khan 3–0–11–0; Sadiq 5–1–18–0.

Umpires: E. C. A. Mackintosh and W. T. Martin.

NEW ZEALAND v AUSTRALIA

Second Test Match

Played at Christchurch, March 8, 9, 10, 12, 13, 1974

New Zealand won by five wickets. Until the last hour of this fascinating match, there was no saying how it would end. No New Zealander has taken part in a more thrilling Test. Drizzle delayed the start and Congdon sent in Australia to bat. In three and a quarter hours' play Australia lost five for 128. Although Stackpole went early, the New Zealand bowlers were not sufficiently accurate at first to make the most of movement and life in the pitch. Later, they bowled with admirable control and purpose. Ian Chappell was the only batsman to discover anything false in the pitch. The ball which bowled him was short but came through strangely slowly. Howarth took a magnificent catch to dismiss Greg Chappell off another short one slashed with fearful force above Howarth's head in his gully position. Greg Chappell laboured ninety minutes for 25 and Redpath, who gave a hard chance when 3, spent three and a quarter hours over 55 runs; but it was a fascinating struggle.

On the second morning Redpath and Marsh put on 53 before Congdon deceived Marsh with a change of pace and then New Zealand pressed steadily. The attack was supported by some of the best fielding New Zealand have achieved in Test cricket.

The New Zealand batting hinged on Turner. He was certainly not at his best, for he played and missed regularly, but this was as much a tribute to the antagonistic and skilful bowling of Walker and Dymock as it was a reflection of his own frailties. Most of the others lingered long enough for the partnerships to be of some significance. Turner was 99 at the end of the second day and was on that mark for 34 balls before attaining his century in four and three-quarter hours. He was out moments later, and New Zealand had to be content with a lead of 32. Walker bowled magnificently on a pitch which allowed him to seam the ball readily and Dymock was almost his equal.

Australia began disastrously, losing Stackpole and both Chappells in half an hour with the total only 33. Ian Chappell, with his pronounced shuffle on to the line of his off stump, lost the leg one and Greg Chappell, in common with many batsmen on both sides, was out trying to cut. The lively but not excessive bounce of the ball offered fierce temptation after the Wellington match. Davis, this time with admirable restraint, and Walters, put matters right with a sound stand of 106 but before the close New Zealand were again in a strong position. Davis was caught from a fierce hook and Marsh was victim of an extraordinary caught and bowled by Dayle Hadlee – a hammer blow wide of the bowler.

After the rest day Australia resumed at 211 for six, but the innings ended at 259, mainly because of an inspired spell by D. R. Hadlee. Walters started authoritatively but Hadlee, with lively pace and sharp movement, took three for 26 in seven overs.

New Zealand needed 228 for victory and a confident-looking Parker helped Turner to score 51 for the first wicket. Then Walker had Parker and Morrison in short order and when Congdon was sadly and badly run out, New Zealand were 62 for three. Turner still batted with calm confidence and almost faultlessly. With him, in a stand of 115, was Hastings, who did not allow the situation to curb his fine attacking shots. Their vital partnership was marked by extremely good running. It was broken in the last over when Hastings thrashed at Mallett. At 177 for four, Australia needed a swift break-through on the final morning, but Coney batted ably and calmly for an hour while Turner went on to his second century in five hours thirty-eight minutes – slower but infinitely better than his first one. And he was still there to see Wadsworth hammer Greg Chappell through the covers to complete a splendid recovery.

Australia

K. R. Stackpole b Collinge	4	– c Wadsworth b Collinge	9
I. R. Redpath c and b Collinge	71	– c Howarth b R. J. Hadlee	58
*I. M. Chappell b R. J. Hadlee	20	– b Collinge	1
G. S. Chappell c Howarth b Congdon	25	– c Coney b R. J. Hadlee	6
I. C. Davis lbw b R. J. Hadlee	5	– c Congdon b R. J. Hadlee	50
K. D. Walters b R. J. Hadlee	6	– lbw b D. R. Hadlee	65
†R. W. Marsh b Congdon	38	– c and b D. R. Hadlee	4
K. J. O'Keeffe c Wadsworth b Congdon	3	– not out	23
M. H. N. Walker not out	19	– c Howarth b D. R. Hadlee	4
A. A. Mallett b Collinge	1	– c Wadsworth b R. J. Hadlee	11
G. Dymock c Congdon b D. R. Hadlee	12	– c Wadsworth b D. R. Hadlee	0
B 1, l-b 6, n-b 12	19	B 16, l-b 4, n-b 8	28
1/8 2/45 3/101 4/120 5/128 6/181 7/190 8/194 9/196	223	1/12 2/26 3/33 4/139 5/142 6/160 7/232 8/238 9/239	259

Bowling: *First Innings*—R. J. Hadlee 14–2–59–3; Collinge 21–4–70–3; Congdon 11–2–33–3; D. R. Hadlee 12.2–2–42–1. *Second Innings*—Collinge 9–0–37–2; R. J. Hadlee 20–2–75–4; D. R. Hadlee 18–5–71–4; Congdon 9–3–26–0; Howarth 11–2–22–0.

New Zealand

G. M. Turner c Stackpole b G. S. Chappell	101	– not out	110
J. M. Parker lbw b Dymock	18	– c Marsh b Walker	26
J. F. M. Morrison c Marsh b G. S. Chappell	12	– lbw b Walker	0
*B. E. Congdon c I. M. Chappell b Walker	8	– run out	2
B. F. Hastings c Marsh b Walker	19	– b Mallett	46
J. V. Coney c Marsh b Dymock	14	– c Marsh b G. S. Chappell	14
†K. J. Wadsworth c Marsh b Mallett	24	– not out	9
D. R. Hadlee c Marsh b Dymock	11		
R. J. Hadlee lbw b Walker	23		
H. J. Howarth c I. M. Chappell b Walker	0		
R. O. Collinge not out	1		
B 4, l-b 8, n-b 11	23	B 4, l-b 14, n-b 5	23
1/59 2/90 3/104 4/136 5/171 6/213 7/220 8/241 9/242	255	1/51 2/55 3/62 4/177 5/206	(5 wkts) 230

Bowling: *First Innings*—Walker 19.6–5–60–4; Dymock 24–6–59–3; G. S. Chappell 20–2–76–2; Walters 7–1–34–0; Mallett 3–1–3–1. *Second Innings*—Walker 28–10–50–2; Dymock 25–5–84–0; G. S. Chappell 15.6–5–38–1; Mallett 13–4–35–1.

Umpires: R. L. Monteith and J. B. Hastie.

NEW ZEALAND v AUSTRALIA

First Test Match

Played at Christchurch, February 18, 19, 20, 22, 23, 1977

Drawn. A splendid game held its interest until the final over. Australia were sent in on a pitch which had life before lunch, but thereafter was of easy pace, with only an occasional ball doing anything odd. New Zealand had three wickets by lunch but did not bowl nearly accurately enough to take full advantage of their opportunity. But Australia still struggled until tea – 208 for six. Then Walters, after some early mishaps, settled down to play a most assertive and attractive innings. Swift and sure in punishing the fairly frequent loose balls and sound in defence, he shared a stand of 217 with Gilmour, an Australian seventh wicket record against all countries. Gilmour gave an easy chance at 13, and had a few other narrow escapes, but drove powerfully to score his first Test century in a little over three hours. Walters, who hit two 6s and thirty 4s, batted six and a half hours for his 250, with strong, certain stroke-making. It was his best score in Tests. Altogether, Australia batted for nine hours.

New Zealand began well, Geoffrey Howarth batting fluently, but declined to 106 for three at stumps on the second day. The start of the third was delayed by rain, but an hour was added to the playing time at the end of the day. A similar arrangement held for the fourth day, after more rain.

New Zealand prospered for a while, Burgess batting most aggressively and Parker fighting hard. Although the pitch had little venom, Walker managed to get a few balls to rise. O'Keeffe bowled with admirable control, and there was a further recession which took New Zealand to 223 for seven. Edwards, playing his first Test as a replacement for Coney, who was ill, helped to begin a revival. Hedley Howarth, batting with a style and certainty far above his station, was with Dayle Hadlee at close of play when the score was 324 for eight, and 29 still needed to avoid the follow-on.

Howarth was out next day at 338. This brought in Chatfield, the player who had all but lost his life when hit by a bouncer in his only previous Test, two years earlier and he and Hadlee hit off the runs required.

Better bowling kept the Australian second innings to a fairly modest scoring rate. McCosker, after a slow start, drove freely and Chappell declared to give New Zealand a target of 350 in six and a half hours. The score was 12 without loss at close of play. The New Zealand openers went on to 70, but they were both out at the same score. Parker and Congdon added 58 in just over an hour of enterprising batting, and then Burgess joined Congdon in another pleasing and productive stand. By tea, they had taken the score to 203 for three – leaving 147 to be made from at least 27 overs, a formidable but by no means impossible task.

Some very good defensive bowling by Walker and Chappell pegged New Zealand back, and when Burgess went, trying to drive one too wide of him, New Zealand lost the initiative. The wickets fell rapidly, but Congdon, playing his one-hundredth Test innings, fought on. He gave two chances at 79 and 85, but he was still there when the eighth wicket fell, with 11 of the final 15 overs to be bowled. Congdon proceeded slowly to his seventh Test century, made in four and a half hours, and again Dayle Hadlee saw his side through a crisis. When Lillee bowled the last over, to Congdon, he had every fieldsman in a line from the wicket keeper to a point position – a ploy repeated at Auckland, so that a picture could be provided for the cover of a new book by Chappell.

Australia

A. Turner b Chatfield	3	– lbw b D. R. Hadlee 20
I. C. Davis c G. P. Howarth b R. J. Hadlee	34	– c Lees b R. J. Hadlee 22
R. B. McCosker c Parker b D. R. Hadlee	37	– not out 77
*G. S. Chappell c Turner b R. J. Hadlee	44	– c Parker b H. J. Howarth 0
G. J. Cosier b R. J. Hadlee	23	– run out 2
K. D. Walters c H. Howarth b D. Hadlee	250	– not out 20
†R. W. Marsh c Parker b H. J. Howarth	2	
G. J. Gilmour b Chatfield	101	
K. J. O'Keeffe run out	8	
D. K. Lillee c R. J. Hadlee b Chatfield	19	
M. H. N. Walker not out	10	
B 11, l-b 6, n-b 4	21	B 10, n-b 3 13
1/9 2/76 3/78 4/112 5/205 6/208 7/425 8/454 9/504	552	1/37 2/67 3/68 4/82 (4 wkts dec.) 154

Bowling: *First Innings*—R. J. Hadlee 29–1–155–3; Chatfield 31–4–125–3; D. R. Hadlee 24.5–1–130–2; H. J. Howarth 19–2–94–1; Congdon 7–0–27–0. *Second Innings*—R. J. Hadlee 13–4–41–1; Chatfield 11–1–34–0; D. R. Hadlee 3–0–28–1; H. J. Howarth 10–0–37–1; Congdon 1–0–1–0.

New Zealand

*G. M. Turner c Turner b O'Keeffe	15	– c and b O'Keeffe 36
G. P. Howarth c Marsh b O'Keeffe	42	– c Marsh b Gilmour 28
B. E. Congdon c Gilmour b Walker	23	– not out 107
J. M. Parker c Marsh b O'Keeffe	34	– c McCosker b Walker 21
M. G. Burgess c Marsh b Walker	66	– c McCosker b Walker 39
G. N. Edwards c Gilmour b O'Keeffe	34	– c Marsh b Walker 15
†W. K. Lees c Marsh b Lillee	14	– c Marsh b Lillee 3
R. J. Hadlee c Marsh b O'Keeffe	3	– c Cosier b Walker 15
H. J. Howarth b Walker	61	– b Lillee 0
D. R. Hadlee not out	37	– not out 8
E. J. Chatfield b Lillee	5	
L-b 9, w 2, n-b 12	23	L-b 12, w 1, n-b 8 21
1/60 2/65 3/91 4/189 5/193 6/220 7/223 8/265 9/338	357	1/70 2/70 3/128 4/218 5/238 6/245 7/245 8/260 (8 wkts) 293

Bowling: *First Innings*—Lillee 31.2–6–119–2; Walker 26–7–66–3; Gilmour 10–0–48–0; O'Keeffe 28–5–101–5. *Second Innings*—Lillee 18–1–70–2; Walker 25–6–65–4; Gilmour 10–0–48–1; O'Keeffe 20–4–56–1; Chappell 11–0–33–0.

Umpires: D. E. A. Copps and F. R. Goodall.

NEW ZEALAND v WEST INDIES

First Test Match

Played at Dunedin, February 8, 9, 10, 12, 13, 1980

New Zealand won by one wicket. Clear evidence of an inability to adjust to New Zealand conditions was given by West Indies' batting on the first day. Lloyd, having won the toss, made a questionable decision in batting first, for the ball often kept rather low and there was sharp movement off the pitch. Only Haynes saw the need to get on to the front foot as much as possible, and against the pace attack he batted several inches outside his crease. He was in for all the three and a half hours of an innings which yielded only 140. Four

West Indian batsmen, with their partiality for playing back, were lbw to balls cutting into them. Others lost their wickets trying to hook or cut in conditions which made such shots extremely risky. The first three wickets fell in Hadlee's first thirteen balls, for 4 runs, and after Haynes and Lloyd had fought it out for one hundred and twelve minutes there was little resistance.

The West Indian bowlers were as much at fault as their batsmen as New Zealand built up a lead of 109. They bowled much too short, unlike the New Zealanders who had made the most of the conditions by keeping the ball up. The New Zealand batsmen took a physical hammering, but they showed considerable determination in grafting for their runs. Edgar was in almost five hours for his 65, Howarth just over two hours for 33, but their stand of 67 was followed by a swift decline against fiercely hostile bowling until the late-order batsmen again came to the rescue. Cairns, a powerful hitter, took three 6s in an over from Parry which brought him 20 runs, and Hadlee had nine 4s in his 51; their eighth-wicket partnership of 54 took just 34 minutes and swung the game New Zealand's way.

There were only seventy minutes of play on the third day, which left West Indies 18 for one, and the fourth was dominated by Haynes and Hadlee. At 29 for four West Indies were in dire straits, but there were stands of 87 between Haynes and King and 64 between Haynes and Deryck Murray. The West Indian tail failed, however, and New Zealand were left needing only 104 to win. By lunch, under intense pressure, they had fought to 33 for two. About twenty minutes before lunch, Parker was given not out when Holding appealed for a catch by the wicket-keeper, which prompted Holding to demolish the stumps at the batsman's end with a full swing of the right foot. In the afternoon West Indies seemed to have the game won. Howarth was third out at 40, and fifteen minutes later New Zealand were 44 for six. Webb went at 54, but once more there was strong resistance from the tailenders. Hadlee and Cairns added 19 with Hadlee playing some fine forcing strokes; Cairns and Troup put on 27 with determination much more of a factor than finesse. At tea it was 95 for eight.

Only 1 run had been added after tea when Holding beat Cairns, but the ball touched the off stump without dislodging a bail. When Cairns was out at 100, Boock, whose best Test score was 8, saw out the last five balls of Holding's over. Garner bowled the final over. The first ball produced a bye. Boock, the non-striker, tried to make it 2 runs and turning back was almost run out. Second ball, he survived an appeal for lbw. He kept the next two out and then squeezed 2 runs backward of point to level the scores. The last ball went from his pads to backward square and the batsmen ran the leg-bye, Parry's return to the non-striker's end going wildly astray. It was the narrowest of victories, but well-earned. Hadlee, with eleven wickets for the match and a Test record of seven leg-before decisions, took his Test tally to 118, two ahead of New Zealand's previous record-holder, Richard Collinge.

West Indies

C. G. Greenidge c Cairns b Hadlee	2	– lbw b Hadlee	3
D. L. Haynes c and b Cairns	55	– c Webb b Troup	105
L. G. Rowe lbw b Hadlee	1	– lbw b Hadlee	12
A. I. Kallicharran lbw b Hadlee	0	– c Cairns b Troup	0
*C. H. Lloyd lbw b Hadlee	24	– c Lees b Hadlee	5
C. L. King c Coney b Troup	14	– c Boock b Cairns	41
†D. L. Murray c Edgar b Troup	6	– lbw b Hadlee	30
D. R. Parry b Boock	17	– c and b Hadlee	1
J. Garner c Howarth b Cairns	0	– b Hadlee	2
M. A. Holding lbw b Hadlee	4	– c Cairns b Troup	3
C. E. H. Croft not out	0	– not out	1
L-b 8, n-b 9	17	L-b 4, n-b 5	9
1/3 2/4 3/4 4/72 5/91 6/105 7/124 8/125 9/136	140	1/4 2/21 3/24 4/29 5/116 6/180 7/186 8/188 9/209	212

Bowling: *First Innings*—Hadlee 20–9–34–5; Troup 17–6–26–2; Cairns 15–5–32–2; Boock 13–4–31–1. *Second Innings*—Hadlee 36–13–68–6; Troup 36.4–13–57–3; Cairns 25–10–63–1; Boock 11–4–5–0.

New Zealand

J. G. Wright b Holding	21	– b Holding	11
B. A. Edgar lbw b Parry	65	– c Greenidge b Holding	6
*G. P. Howarth c Murray b Croft	33	– c Greenidge b Croft	11
J. M. Parker b Croft	0	– c Murray b Garner	5
P. N. Webb lbw b Parry	5	– (6) lbw b Garner	5
J. V. Coney b Holding	8	– (5) lbw b Croft	2
†W. K. Lees run out	18	– lbw b Garner	0
R. J. Hadlee c Lloyd b Garner	51	– b Garner	17
B. L. Cairns b Croft	30	– c Murray b Holding	19
G. B. Troup c Greenidge b Croft	0	– not out	7
S. L. Boock not out	0	– not out	2
B 5, l-b 2, n-b 11	18	B 7, l-b 5, n-b 7	19
1/42 2/109 3/110 4/133 5/145 6/159 7/168 8/222 9/236	249	1/15 2/28 3/40 4/44 5/44 6/44 7/54 8/73 9/100	(9 wkts) 104

Bowling: *First Innings*—Holding 22–5–50–2; Croft 25–3–64–4; Garner 25.5–8–51–1; King 1–0–3–0; Parry 22–6–63–2. *Second Innings*—Holding 16–7–24–3; Croft 11–2–25–2; Garner 23–6–36–4.

Umpires: F. R. Goodall and J. B. R. Hastie.

WELLINGTON v WEST INDIES

Played at Lower Hutt, February 16, 17, 18, 1980

West Indians lost by six wickets. This game was played on a sub-standard pitch, with sharp movement off the seam, but a side reputed to be the world's best played poorly. There were many careless strokes as the West Indians were bundled out for 102. Marshall and Garner were mainly responsible for Wellington making only 93. Haynes attacked vigorously in the tourists' second innings, and Wellington's task of making 153 seemed very difficult. However, a courageous innings by Coney took Wellington to their first win over an overseas team for 45 years. Chatfield, an occasional Test player, had the remarkable match figures of thirteen for 86.

West Indians

C. G. Greenidge c Newdick b Chatfield	4	– c Morrison b Chatfield	6
D. L. Haynes c Gray b Chatfield	3	– c Vance b Chatfield	58
L. G. Rowe b Cater	15	– b Chatfield	1
H. A. Gomes c Morrison b Cater	13	– c Gray b Cater	8
*A. I. Kallicharran c and b Chatfield	13	– b Chatfield	5
†D. A. Murray lbw b Cater	1	– c Coney b Cater	11
C. L. King b Chatfield	27	– c Reid b Cater	6
D. R. Parry not out	1	– c Vance b Chatfield	16
M. D. Marshall b Chatfield	0	– not out	13
J. Garner c Morrison b Chatfield	2	– lbw b Chatfield	3
M. A. Holding c Coney b Cater	5	– c Reid b Chatfield	0
B 6, l-b 11, n-b 1	18	B 6, l-b 9, n-b 1	16
1/7 2/12 3/35 4/41 5/49 6/88 7/93 8/93 9/97	102	1/23 2/53 3/83 4/91 5/95 6/102 7/119 8/135 9/143	143

Bowling: *First Innings*—Taylor 12–4–16–0; Chatfield 18–7–33–6; Cater 13.3–3–35–4. *Second Innings*—Taylor 8–2–20–0; Chatfield 17.4–6–53–7; Cater 12–2–54–3.

Wellington

B. A. Edgar c Garner b Marshall	14	– b Marshall	14
G. A. Newdick c Garner b Holding	2	– c and b Marshall	8
†R. H. Vance c Murray b Marshall	14	– c Murray b King	21
J. V. Coney lbw b Garner	15	– not out	69
*J. F. M. Morrison c King b Marshall	16	– hit wkt b Garner	16
R. B. Reid b Marshall	0	– not out	14
A. M. Wilson lbw b Garner	8		
E. J. Gray lbw b Marshall	0		
B. R. Taylor c Marshall b Garner	10		
S. R. Cater not out	4		
E. J. Chatfield b Garner	0		
B 4, l-b 4, n-b 2	10	B 5, l-b 7, n-b 1	13
1/19 2/19 3/49 4/65 5/65 6/78 7/78 8/86 9/93	93	1/17 2/39 3/56 4/118	(4 wkts) 155

Bowling: *First Innings*—Holding 6–2–15–1; Marshall 16–3–43–5; Garner 10–2–25–4. *Second Innings*—Holding 20–4–46–0; Marshall 17–6–40–2; Garner 15.1–5–28–1; King 6–2–19–1; Parry 1–0–9–0.

Umpires: W. R. C. Gardiner and D. A. Kinsella.

NORTHERN DISTRICTS v OTAGO

Played at Whangarei, January 12, 13, 14, 1981. Drawn.

Northern Districts

J. G. Gibson b Boock	17	– lbw b Boock	4
†M. J. E. Wright b Webb	15	– c Dawson b Boock	44
C. M. Kuggeleijn c Milburn b Boock	21	– c Milburn b Boock	6
*A. D. G. Roberts c Milburn b Webb	14	– c Walker b Boock	68
B. G. Cooper c Dawson b Boock	40	– c Milburn b Boock	22
W. P. Fowler b Webb	34	– b B. R. Blair	0
C. W. Dickeson c and b Boock	0	– lbw b Boock	35
S. R. Gillespie c B. R. Blair b Boock	26	– not out	18
P. Curtin c Rutherford b Boock	17	– c Webb b Thomson	0
S. J. Scott c B. R. Blair b Boock	1	– not out	8
K. Treiber not out	0		
B 3, l-b 7, w 2, n-b 3	15	Extras	20
1/23 2/41 3/76 4/76 5/144 6/148 7/156 8/190 9/196	200	1/13 2/27 3/80 4/109 5/110 6/164 7/213 8/217	(8 wkts dec.) 225

Bowling: *First Innings*—Webb 19–6–42–3; Thomson 15–6–33–0; B. R. Blair 11–4–18–0; Boock 37–11–84–7; Walker 8–5–8–0. *Second Innings*—Webb 20–7–49–0; Thomson 12–1–40–1; B. R. Blair 9–4–20–1; Boock 46–20–62–6; Walker 3–1–14–0; Dawson 9–4–20–0.

Otago

*I. A. Rutherford c Fowler b Gillespie	9	– st Wright b Dickeson	14
G. Blakely lbw b Dickeson	2	– c Cooper b Scott	8
†B. D. Milburn c Dickeson b Curtin	21	– c Dickeson b Gillespie	1
R. N. Hoskin c Kuggeleijn b Dickeson	57	– lbw b Scott	117
W. L. Blair b Kuggeleijn	14	– c Curtin b Kuggeleijn	5
B. R. Blair b Dickeson	2	– c sub b Dickeson	1
G. J. Dawson b Kuggeleijn	50	– not out	42
D. Walker lbw b Curtin	17	– c Gibson b Dickeson	0
G. B. Thomson b Kuggeleijn	10	– c Dickeson b Gillespie	0
S. L. Boock run out	5	– not out	0
R. J. Webb not out	0		
Extras	6	Extras	8
1/11 2/14 3/69 4/86 5/89 6/118 7/145 8/167 9/181	193	1/19 2/55 3/78 4/91 5/165 6/176 7/194 8/196	(8 wkts) 196

Bowling: *First Innings*—Treiber 6–3–10–0; Gillespie 13–4–22–1; Curtin 17–5–36–2; Dickeson 42–20–63–3; Kuggeleijn 26.3–10–46–3; Fowler 4–1–10–0. *Second Innings*—Gillespie 11–4–18–2; Curtin 8–2–29–0; Dickeson 25–9–70–3; Kuggeleijn 4–0–17–1; Fowler 6–3–8–0; Scott 15–6–46–2.

Umpires: T. A. McCall and G. I. S. Cowan.

CRICKET IN INDIA

INDIA v NEW ZEALAND

Second Test Match

Played at Calcutta, March 5, 6, 7, 8, 1965

Drawn. Everything else in this match was overshadowed by the remarkable Test début of Taylor for New Zealand. Making the most of his height, Taylor a forceful left-hander, attacked the Indian bowling freely while scoring his maiden century in first-class cricket and later he went on to take five wickets for 86 at right arm fast medium pace.

In the absence of Sardesai, injured, India called on Kunderam; they also preferred Desai and Gupte to Manjrekar and Surti and in this way strengthened their bowling, but Gupte did not come off with his wrist spin owing to erratic length and direction. New Zealand tried a leg-spinner in Vivian instead of the pacy left-handed Collinge and this move, too, did no good.

Still, New Zealand played much better cricket in this match after Reid won the toss. The captain hit four 6s and ten 4s in his spectacular 82, and Sutcliffe revealed his class by his sure defence and clean hitting while taking out his bat for 151. India faced a formidable total, but after an uncertain start (four wickets fell for 101) Borde, 62, and Pataudi began a recovery, the Nawab giving one of his best displays while making 153. New Zealand still held the upper hand and they led by 82 yet they could not leave India a reasonable task.

New Zealand

G. T. Dowling lbw b Venkataraghavan	27	c Engineer b Gupte	23
B. E. Congdon b Desai	9	c Venkataraghavan b Desai	0
R. W. Morgan c Engineer b Desai	20	b Durani	33
J. R. Reid c Borde b Venkataraghavan	82	lbw b Venkataraghavan	11
B. Sutcliffe not out	151	c Hanumant Singh b Venkataraghavan	6
B. W. Yuile b Gupte	1	lbw b Venkataraghavan	21
V. Pollard c Jaisimha b Desai	31	b Jaisimha	43
B. R. Taylor c Kunderam b Nadkarni	105	not out	0
G. E. Vivian b Desai	1	c Jaisimha b Nadkarni	43
R. C. Motz lbw b Venkataraghavan	21	c Nadkarni b Durani	0
J. T. Ward not out	1		
B 10, l-b 3	13	B 10, n-b 1	11
1/13 2/37 3/138 4/139 5/152 6/233 7/396 8/407 9/450	(9 wkts dec.) 462	1/4 2/37 3/61 4/83 5/97 6/103 7/103 8/184 9/191	(9 wkts dec.) 191

Bowling: *First Innings*—Desai 33–6–128–4; Jaisimha 20–0–73–0; Durani 10–9–49–0; Nadkarni 35–14–59–1; Gupte 16–3–54–1; Venkataraghavan 41–18–86–3. *Second Innings*—Desai 12–6–32–1; Jaisimha 15–12–21–1; Gupte 22–7–64–1; Durani 18–10–34–2; Venkataraghavan 17–11–15–3; Nadkarni 7–4–14–1.

India

M. L. Jaisimha b Motz	22	– c Morgan b Congdon	0
B. K. Kunderam b Congdon	36	– not out	12
F. M. Engineer c Pollard b Taylor	10	– c Pollard b Dowling	45
C. G. Borde c Pollard b Taylor	62		
R. G. Nadkarni b Taylor	0		
Nawab of Pataudi c Ward b Taylor	153		
Hanumant Singh c sub b Yuile	31		
S. A. Durani c sub b Yuile	20	– b Vivian	23
R. B. Desai c Ward b Yuile	0		
S. Venkataraghavan b Taylor	7	– not out	0
B. P. Gupte not out	3		
B 25, n-b 11	36	B 11, l-b 1	12
1/45 2/61 3/100 4/101 5/211 6/301 7/357 8/357 9/371	380	1/3 2/52 3/92 (3 wkts)	92

Bowling: *First Innings*—Motz 21–3–74–1; Taylor 23.5–2–86–5; Congdon 18–5–46–1; Pollard 15–1–50–0; Vivian 12–3–37–0; Reid 2–1–8–0; Yuile 14–3–43–3. *Second Innings*—Dowling 6–2–19–1; Congdon 5–0–33–1; Sutcliffe 3–2–14–0; Vivian 3–0–14–1.

Umpires: S. Ganguly and A. R. Joshi.

INDIA v NEW ZEALAND

Third Test Match

Played at Bombay, March 12, 13, 14, 15, 1965

Drawn. New Zealand missed a great opportunity of gaining the first victory in the series. Thanks mainly to a steady century by Dowling and 71 by Morgan they put together a total of 297 against some admirable fast bowling by Desai who took six of the first eight wickets.

India began their innings shortly before lunch on the second day and they were all out for 88 in under two and three-quarter hours. It was their lowest Test total in their own country and was due to the hard brick pitch allowing Taylor and Motz to bounce the ball disconcertingly. Taylor finished with five for 26 and as usual India's batting in such circumstance was irresolute.

So India followed on 209 behind, but in the terrific heat Taylor and Motz could not repeat their earlier triumphs. The turning point came when Sardesai, 20, was missed in the slips by Taylor off Congdon. That proved to be a reprieve for India as Sardesai stayed to reach 200 not out with Borde, 109, and Hanumant Singh, 75 not out, giving him splendid assistance.

The Nawab came in for severe criticism because he waited for Sardesai to complete his double century and so left New Zealand only two and a half hours at the crease when he held a lead of 254. As it was his bowlers nearly turned the tables for when the match ended New Zealand were 174 behind with only two wickets left.

New Zealand

G. T. Dowling b Desai	129	c Engineer b Jaisimha	0
B. E. Congdon c Engineer b Desai	3	c Hanumant Singh b Durani	14
B. W. Sinclair b Desai	9	c Venkataraghavan b Desai	0
R. W. Morgan b Chandrasekhar	71	b Chandrasekhar	11
B. Sutcliffe run out	4	c Durani b Chandrasekhar	1
V. Pollard c Jaisimha b Desai	26	c Borde b Durani	4
J. R. Reid lbw b Desai	22	c Borde b Chandrasekhar	10
B. R. Taylor c Hanumant Singh b Desai	8	b Venkataraghavan	21
B. W. Yuile lbw b Durani	2	not out	8
R. C. Motz not out	5		
J. T. Ward b Durani	0	not out	4
B 4, l-b 13, n-b 1	18	B 1, l-b 4, n-b 2	7
1/13 2/31 3/165 4/170 5/227 6/256 7/276 8/281 9/297	297	1/0 2/0 3/18 4/34 5/37 6/45 7/46 8/76 (8 wkts)	80

Bowling: *First Innings*—Desai 25–9–56–6; Jaisimha 17–6–53–0; Chandrasekhar 23–6–76–1; Durani 20.2–10–26–2; Venkataraghavan 32–13–46–0; Nadkarni 12–7–22–0. *Second Innings*—Desai 9–5–18–1; Jaisimha 6–5–4–1; Venkataraghavan 7–3–10–1; Chandrasekhar 14–6–25–3; Durani 7–2–16–2.

India

D. N. Sardesai c Ward b Motz	4	not out	200
M. L. Jaisimha c Ward b Taylor	4	c Ward b Pollard	47
S. A. Durani c Morgan b Taylor	4	c Ward b Taylor	6
C. G. Borde c Ward b Taylor	25	c Yuile b Taylor	109
Hanumant Singh hit wkt b Taylor	0	not out	75
Nawab of Pataudi c Ward b Congdon	9	b Motz	3
R. G. Nadkarni lbw b Congdon	7		
F. M. Engineer run out	17	c Reid b Taylor	6
R. B. Desai c Reid b Motz	0		
S. Venkataraghavan c Congdon b Taylor	7		
B. S. Chandrasekhar not out	4		
L-b 4, n-b 3	7	B 4, l-b 5, w 1, n-b 7	17
1/4 2/8 3/12 4/23 5/38 6/48 7/71 8/76 9/77	88	1/8 2/18 3/107 4/261 5/270 (5 wkts dec.)	463

Bowling: *First Innings*—Motz 15–4–30–2; Taylor 7–3–26–5; Congdon 9–5–21–2; Pollard 2–1–4–0. *Second Innings*—Motz 29.4–11–63–1; Taylor 29–5–76–3; Congdon 17–6–44–0; Yuile 28–5–76–0; Pollard 29–6–95–1; Morgan 18–3–54–0; Reid 3–1–8–0; Sutcliffe 4–0–30–0.

Umpires: M. V. Nagendra and S. Roy.

INDIA v NEW ZEALAND

Fourth Test Match

Played at New Delhi, March 19, 20, 21, 22, 1965

India won by seven wickets, thanks to the off-spin bowling of Venkataraghavan who exploited a parched pitch and took twelve wickets for 152 runs. The surface soon began to wear and New Zealand, batting first, at once realized that they had made an error in leaving out Yuile, their left-arm spinner. The conditions were not nearly so encouraging to the pace bowlers and the Indian batsmen were able to make their forcing strokes freely.

With Sardesai following up his double century of the previous match with another fine hundred, the Nawab getting a grand hundred, and Hanumant Singh and Borde also prospering India declared with a lead of 203. New Zealand battled hard to save the match, but they lost four men for 68 before Sutcliffe helped Jarvis to stem the tide. Later Collinge and Cameron played well, but India needed only 70 to win.

New Zealand

G. T. Dowling lbw b Venkataraghavan	7	– lbw b Subramanian	0
T. W. Jarvis b Venkataraghavan	34	– b Venkataraghavan	77
R. W. Morgan lbw b Venkataraghavan	82	– c Venkataraghavan b Desai	4
B. E. Congdon c Chandrasekhar b Venkataraghavan	48	– b Chandrasekhar	7
J. R. Reid b Chandrasekhar	9	– b Venkataraghavan	22
B. Sutcliffe b Venkataraghavan	2	– c Engineer b Chandrasekhar	54
B. R. Taylor c Borde b Chandrasekhar	21	– c Sardesai b Venkataraghavan	3
V. Pollard b Venkataraghavan	27	– c Engineer b Subramanian	6
J. T. Ward lbw b Venkataraghavan	11	– run out	0
R. O. Collinge not out	4	– c Engineer b Venkataraghavan	54
F. J. Cameron b Venkataraghavan	0	– not out	27
B 6, l-b 8, n-b 3	17	B 14, l-b 2, n-b 2	18
1/27 2/54 3/108 4/117 5/130 6/157 7/194 8/256 9/260	262	1/1 2/10 3/22 4/68 5/172 6/179 7/179 8/213 9/264	272

Bowling: *First Innings*—Desai 9–2–36–0; Jaisimha 5–2–12–0; Subramanian 5–2–3–0; Venkataraghavan 51.2–26–72–8; Chandrasekhar 37–14–96–2; Nadkarni 16–8–21–0; Hanumant Singh 2–0–5–0. *Second Innings*—Desai 18–3–35–1; Subramanian 16–5–32–2; Chandrasekhar 34–14–95–2; Nadkarni 19–13–10–0; Jaisimha 1–0–2–0; Venkataraghavan 61.1–31–80–4.

India

D. N. Sardesai c Jarvis b Morgan	106	– not out	27
M. L. Jaisimha c Dowling b Reid	10	– run out	1
Hanumant Singh c Congdon b Collinge	82	– not out	7
C. G. Borde c Jarvis b Cameron	87		
Nawab of Pataudi b Collinge	113	– b Reid	30
V. Subramanian b Taylor	9		
F. M. Engineer b Collinge	5	– b Taylor	2
R. G. Nadkarni not out	14		
R. B. Desai b Collinge	7		
B 23, l-b 4, w 1, n-b 4	32	L-b 4, n-b 2	6
1/56 2/179 3/240 4/378 5/414 6/421 7/457 8/465	(8 wkts dec.) 465	1/9 2/13 3/66	(3 wkts) 73

B. S. Chandrasekhar and S. Venkataraghavan did not bat.

Bowling: *First Innings*—Taylor 18–4–57–1; Collinge 20.3–4–89–4; Reid 24–4–89–1; Cameron 26–5–86–1; Morgan 15–1–68–1; Pollard 10–1–44–0. *Second Innings*—Taylor 4–0–31–1; Cameron 4–0–29–0; Reid 1–0–3–1; Sutcliffe 0.1–0–4–0.

Umpires: B. Sathyaji Rao and S. Pan.

INDIA v WEST INDIES

Second Test Match

Played at Calcutta, December 31, January 1, 3, 4, 5, 1968

West Indies won by an innings and 45 runs. This match will find a place in the history of Test cricket not because of the cricket it produced, but because of the horrible riot that broke out on the second day. The authorities had sold more tickets than there were seats and inevitably the surplus spectators tried to find accommodation on the grass round the boundaries. The constabulary mounted a baton charge, the crowd launched a counter-attack and when the outnumbered police force fled, the crowd burnt down the stands and funiture. It was indeed a frightening scene and the players, worried about their safety, were reluctant to continue the match, which came pretty close to being abandoned till assurances were received from high governmental quarters that there would be no further incidents.

The pitch was underprepared and the toss virtually decided the outcome. West Indies on the first day made 212 for four. Suspecting that batting in the second innings would be difficult, they approached their task with caution and another factor which affected the scoring rate was that the ball did not come on to the bat. Kanhai's 78 not out was a prominent feature of the day's play. He started uneasily and was twice dropped while he made 40. These errors were particularly regrettable because otherwise the Indian fielding showed a marked improvement on the Bombay performance.

The second day's play was written off because of the riot and the match was resumed after a two-day interval, the third day being the rest day. The loss of a full day's play caused West Indies to look for runs more eagerly. With Hendriks out cheaply, Sobers, who came in as late as number seven, had to play with an added sense of haste, for he had only the bowlers to support him. Hall was an able ally. Sobers attacked vigorously and scored 70 in eighty minutes.

The lack of pace in the pitch blunted the edge of the fast bowling but Sobers, in both his two spinning styles, and Gibbs, turned the ball venomously. Moreover, the ball came off at uneven heights and India did well to finish the third day at 89 for one. At this stage they needed only 102 to save the follow on and had they averted it they could have struggled to a draw. Next morning, Surti played across the line to Sobers and was lbw. Pataudi went to an imprudent hook and Borde ran himself out. Thus India collapsed and were all out just after lunch, with a deficit of 223. Dispirited and no doubt overawed by the state of the pitch, they again batted poorly and only just managed to carry the struggle into the last day. Baig's illness with a high temperature was a further handicap. The West Indies victory was a great personal triumph for Sobers and Gibbs, who each took seven wickets.

West Indies

C. C. Hunte run out	43	W. W. Hall c Subramanya b Chandrasekhar	35
M. R. Bynoe run out	19	L. R. Gibbs lbw b Chandrasekhar	1
R. B. Kanhai c Pataudi b Surti	90	C. C. Griffith not out	9
B. F. Butcher c Pataudi b Bedi	35		
C. Lloyd c Kunderan b Bedi	5	B 7, l-b 11, n-b 4	22
S. M. Nurse c Surti b Jaisimha	56		——
*G. S. Sobers c Jaisimha b Chandrasekhar	70	1/43 2/76 3/133 4/154 5/259	390
†J. L. Hendriks b Surti	5	6/272 7/290 8/362 9/371	

Bowling: Surti 30–3–106–2; Subramanya 6–1–9–0; Chandrasekhar 46–11–107–3; Bedi 36–11–92–2; Venkataraghavan 13–3–43–0; Jaisimha 6–2–11–1.

India

†B. K. Kunderan b Hall	39	– lbw b Hall	4
M. L. Jaisimha b Gibbs	37	– c and b Gibbs	31
R. F. Surti lbw b Sobers	16	– c Griffith b Sobers	31
C. G. Borde run out	11	– b Lloyd	28
*Nawab of Pataudi c Griffith b Gibbs	1	– c Griffith b Lloyd	2
Hanumant Singh c Bynoe b Gibbs	4	– b Sobers	37
V. Subramanya c Hendriks b Gibbs	12	– run out	17
S. Venkataraghavan b Sobers	18	– c Hendriks b Sobers	2
A. A. Baig b Gibbs	4	– b Gibbs	6
B. S. Bedi st Hendriks b Sobers	5	– c Bynoe b Sobers	0
B. S. Chandrasekhar not out	3	– not out	1
B 12, l-b 1, n-b 4	17	B 14, l-b 2, n-b 3	19
	——		——
1/60 2/98 3/100 4/117 5/119	167	1/4 2/23 3/89 4/105 5/108	178
6/128 7/139 8/161 9/161		6/155 7/170 8/176 9/176	

Bowling: *First Innings*—Sobers 28.5–16–42–3; Griffith 6–3–14–0; Gibbs 37–17–51–5; Hall 5–0–32–1; Lloyd 4–2–4–0; Nurse 4–1–7–0. *Second Innings*—Hall 7–0–35–1; Griffith 5–4–4–0; Sobers 20–2–56–4; Gibbs 30.4–8–36–2; Lloyd 14–5–23–2; Hunte 1–0–5–0.

Umpires: Dr I. Gopalakrishnan and S. Pan.

INDIA v NEW ZEALAND

Third Test Match

Played at Hyderabad, October 15, 16, 18, 19, 20, 1969

Drawn. This was a match of utter frustration for New Zealand, in which India were clearly outplayed, but rain, riots, and rows with the umpires lent the game drama, without pleasure. Again Dowling and Murray gave their side a great start, making 82 without loss at lunch and 106 before the first wicket fell, but Prasanna swept through the rest of the batting and New Zealand were 181 for nine at the close. The second day was washed out by rain. On the next morning, the pitch should have been cut, although it was the rest day. The umpires instructed the groundsman to cut it on the third playing morning. This was an error, and Dowling, rightly, refused to allow compensation for it by the commission of another mistake, when efforts were made to cut it on the third playing morning. India, therefore, had to bat on a pitch uncut for three days. It gave the pace bowlers more psychological than practical assistance, but on it India's reconstructed team – there were four changes in it – collapsed badly. A damp patch, well short of a length, also worried the batsmen. From 21 for one the score slumped to 50 for nine at tea, Hadlee taking four for 10 in that period; Cunis three for 9.

Venkataraghavan and Bedi, with 40 for the last wicket, batted bravely, but a youth, coming on to the field to congratulate the batsmen, was injured by a soldier and this incident provoked an ugly riot, in which gates were broken down, metal chairs flung on to the ground, fires lit in the stands, and the crowd attacked by an army unit. No play was possible in the last half-hour.

Dowling batted four hours, ten minutes for 60 but progress was slow, the Indian bowling rate dropping badly. New Zealand declared at the end of the fourth day, India thus having five and a half hours to score 268. Again the New Zealand pace bowlers were completely on top and the seventh wicket fell at 66. Over two and a quarter hours of playing time remained when the rain clouds burst, and there was a very heavy fall for half an hour, followed by hot sunshine. No real effort was made to get play started again. Instead of the covers being removed, a few workers with rags, some of them women, were given the task of removing the water from the covers and although there were official denials later, it looked very much like a deliberate go-slow policy. For perhaps the first time in cricket history a Test captain (Dowling) was on the field in bare feet, helping to remove the water. The match was abandoned twenty minutes before time, and this brought another demonstration by the crowd.

New Zealand

*G. T. Dowling run out	42	– lbw b Abid Ali	60
B. A. G. Murray c Jaisimha b Prasanna	80	– lbw b Prasanna	26
G. M. Turner c Indrajitsinh b Bedi	2	– not out	15
B. E. Congdon c Pataudi b Prasanna	3	– c Prasanna b Venkataraghavan	18
B. F. Hastings c Venkataraghavan b Prasanna	2	– c Venkataraghavan b Prasanna	21
M. G. Burgess lbw b Bedi	2	– b Abid Ali	3
B. R. Taylor c Gandotra b Prasanna	16	– b Venkataraghavan	18
D. R. Hadlee c Pataudi b Prasanna	1	– b Abid Ali	0
†K. J. Wadsworth run out	14	– lbw b Prasanna	5
R. S. Cunis c Solkar b Abid Ali	7	– not out	0
H. J. Howarth not out	5		
L-b 7	7	B 6, l-b 3	9
1/106 2/122 3/128 4/132 5/133 6/135 7/136 8/158 9/166	181	1/45 2/86 3/127 4/133 5/141 6/141 7/144 8/175 (8 wkts dec.)	175

Bowling: *First Innings*—Jaisimha 4–0–13–0; Abid Ali 12.1–5–17–1; Venkataraghavan 17–5–33–0; Bedi 34–14–52–2; Solkar 3–1–8–0; Prasanna 29–13–51–5. *Second Innings*—Jaisimha 4–2–2–0; Abid Ali 27–7–47–3; Venkataraghavan 16–3–40–2; Bedi 9–2–19–0; Prasanna 26–7–58–3.

India

S. Abid Ali b Taylor	4	– c Howarth b Taylor	5
†K. S. Indrajitsinh lbw b Cunis	7	– c Dowling b Cunis	12
A. L. Wadekar c Congdon b Hadlee	9	– c Wadsworth b Hadlee	14
M. L. Jaisimha c Hastings b Cunis	0	– c Taylor b Hadlee	0
*Nawab of Pataudi c Murray b Hadlee	0	– lbw b Cunis	9
A. Roy c Wadsworth b Hadlee	0	– c Wadsworth b Hadlee	4
A. Gandotra c Wadsworth b Howarth	18	– b Cunis	15
E. D. Solkar c Murray b Cunis	0	– not out	13
S. Venkataraghavan not out	25	– not out	2
E. A. S. Prasanna b Hadlee	2		
B. S. Bedi c Dowling b Congdon	20		
B 1, l-b 3	4	L-b 2	2
1/5 2/21 3/21 4/21 5/21 6/27 7/28 8/46 9/49	89	1/10 2/20 3/21 4/34 5/44 6/50 7/66 (7 wkts)	76

Bowling: *First Innings*—Hadlee 17–5–30–4; Taylor 10–2–20–1; Cunis 14–7–12–3; Congdon 3.2–1–7–1; Howarth 9–2–12–1; Burgess 1–0–4–0; *Second Innings*—Hadlee 10.3–2–31–3; Taylor 8–2–18–1; Cunis 12–5–12–3; Congdon 5–3–4–0; Howarth 5–2–4–0; Burgess 6–3–5–0.

Umpires: M. V. Nagendra and S. Bhattacharya.

INDIA v WEST INDIES

Third Test Match

Played at Calcutta, December 29, 30, 31, January 2, 3, 1979

Drawn. The closing stages, brought to an end by bad light, were highly exciting, West Indies saving themselves with only one wicket standing. Eleven balls remained to be bowled when the umpires decided that the light was impossible. Justice was done when the West Indians remained unbeaten, for the four overs preceding the stoppage were played in abysmal conditions. India damaged their chances of winning with a dropped slip catch and also by not hurrying through their overs in the final hour, although it was abundantly clear that the light would fail.

India won the toss for the first time in the series, but did not take advantage of the change in luck. Considering the easy pace of the pitch, their first-day score of 225 for eight represented a poor performance. Three of these wickets were claimed with the second new ball in the space of ten deliveries by Phillip. Among his victims was Gavaskar, who made a chanceless 107. A spirited 61 off 62 balls by Kapil Dev, and Venkataraghavan's stubborn resistance enabled India to scramble to 300 on the following morning.

West Indies led India by only 27 runs. They must have hoped for a much bigger advantage when they were 203 for three at the end of the second day, with Kallicharran unbeaten and in good form. The sound foundation had been laid by a century from Williams, who had two escapes before he had scored 15. Although he batted over three and a half hours, he never really looked settled. On the third day, Kallicharran was dismissed quite early by Venkataraghavan, thanks to a rousing short-leg catch by débutant Narasimha Rao. Kallicharran's dismissal threw the innings into disarray, and the collapse wrought by Venkataraghavan would have been greater but for a valuable stand of 83 between Shivnarine and Phillip.

In their second innings, India suffered an early casualty, but did not lose another wicket before Gavaskar declared, halfway between lunch and tea on the fourth day, leaving West Indies to make 335 in 365 minutes. Gavaskar remained unbeaten with 182 and became the first batsman in Test history to score two separate hundreds in a match three times. Vengsarkar's 157 not out was his first Test century and their unfinished partnership of 344, over six hours nineteen minutes, became the new record for India's second wicket against all countries. Nevertheless, a little more enterprise on their part would have enhanced India's chances of forcing home their advantage.

The inability of West Indies' bowlers to break through for over six hours was proof enough that the pitch remained in a sound state, and under the circumstances, Gavaskar's declaration was a bold one. West Indies clearly did not have the confidence to take up the challenge, and any plans they might have had for a late bid were wrecked by the dismissal of Bacchus and Gomes for only 45 runs. Furthermore, Williams had damaged a hamstring and could bat only in an emergency.

The emergency certainly did arise. At tea on the last day, West Indies seemed in a safe enough position with 143 for four. They lost one more wicket when the mandatory overs started, thirty-five minutes later. The new ball was taken in the second over of the last hour, and with it Ghavri took India to the brink of victory. He soon took three wickets and, in what transpired to be his last over, Marshall was dropped by Viswanath at first slip. That was in the twelfth over. Gavaskar was foced to take Ghavri off at this point, for the light was already dim and had the pace bowler continued, the umpires would have been forced to call off play. The dropped chance by Viswanath prolonged the ninth-wicket stand by four overs, and during the last-wicket partnership between Shivnarine – who batted most pluckily for over two hours – and Clarke, the last man faced eight deliveries. Time was lost during the closing stages by the movement of spectators behind the bowler's arm, when Shivnarine justifiably refused to take strike.

India

*S. M. Gavaskar c Bacchus b Phillip	107	– not out	182
C. P. S. Chauhan b Clarke	11		
A. D. Gaekwad c Murray b Marshall	7	– b Clarke	5
G. R. Viswanath b Phillip	32		
D. B. Vengsarkar c Williams b Parry	42	– not out	157
M. V. Narasimha Rao c Gomes b Parry	1		
K. D. Ghavri c Marshall b Phillip	5		
†S. M. H. Kirmani lbw b Phillip	0		
Kapil Dev b Parry	61		
S. Venkataraghavan lbw b Holder	7		
B. S. Bedi not out	4		
B 3, l-b 2, n-b 18	23	B 1, l-b 4, n-b 12	17
1/20 2/48 3/110 4/199 5/209 6/220 7/220 8/225 9/283	300	1/17	(1 wkt dec.) 361

Bowling: *First Innings*—Clarke 27–8–70–1; Phillip 22–6–64–4; Holder 21–5–48–1; Marshall 12–3–44–1; Parry 20.3–7–51–3; Gomes 1–1–0–0; Shivnarine 1–1–0–0. *Second Innings*—Clarke 28–4–104–1; Phillip 16–0–81–0; Marshall 13–3–45–0; Holder 20–3–59–0; Parry 13–3–50–0; Shivnarine 1–0–2–0; Gomes 1–0–3–0.

West Indies

A. B. Williams c and b Ghavri	111	– b Ghavri	11
S. F. A. Bacchus b Ghavri	26	– c and b Ghavri	20
H. A. Gomes b Venkataraghavan	8	– b Venkataraghavan	5
*A. I. Kallicharran c Narasimha Rao b Venkataraghavan.	55	– c Viswanath b Narasimha Rao	46
V. A. Holder c Narasimha Rao b Venkataraghavan	3	– b Ghavri	4
†D. A. Murray c Kapil Dev b Venkataraghavan	2	– st Kirmani b Venkataraghavan	66
S. Shivnarine c sub b Ghavri	48	– not out	36
D. R. Perry b Bedi	4	– c Gavaskar b Venkataraghavan	0
N. Phillip lbw b Kapil Dev	47	– lbw b Ghavri	0
M. D. Marshall c Kirmani b Kapil Dev	1	– lbw b Bedi	1
S. T. Clarke not out	4	– not out	0
B 5, l-b 11, n-b 2	18	B 2, l-b 2, n-b 4	8
1/58 2/95 3/197 4/210 5/213 6/218 7/230 8/313 9/318	327	1/35 2/45 3/133 4/143 5/145 6/164 7/164 8/183 9/197	(9 wkts) 197

Bowling: *First Innings*—Kapil Dev 20.4–3–88–2; Ghavri 29–5–74–3; Bedi 24–4–59–1; Venkataraghavan 33–15–55–4; Narasimha Rao 11–0–33–0. *Second Innings*—Kapil Dev 13–6–21–0; Ghavri 23–8–46–4; Venkataraghavan 30–13–47–3; Bedi 22–14–32–1; Narasimha Rao 17.1–6–43–1.

Umpires: S. N. Hanmatha Rao and P. R. Punjabi.

INDIA v WEST INDIES

Sixth Test Match

Played at Kanpur, January 2, 3, 4, 6, 7, 8, 1979

Drawn. As the series was still undecided, the duration of the final Test was extended to six days, but to no avail. With the pitch slow and with rain lopping off almost two days of play, not even the first innings were completed. India, winning the toss, batted through the first two days and well into the afternoon of the third. They declared at 644 for seven, breaking the record for their highest Test score for the second time in successive matches. However, only the size of their total was impressive. Their batting, for the most part, lacked lustre.

Viswanath batted with polish for 179, the best score of his Test career. But the centuries scored by Gaekwad and Mohinder Armarnath were featureless and too slow to be of true benefit to their side. Scoring 250, Bacchus prevented West Indies from being overwhelmed by the sheer size of their opponents' total, and his score was only 6 short of the highest by a West Indian (Rohan Kanhai) against India. Bacchus, who hit 33 4s in his innings of eight and a half hours, was playing with so much authority and brilliance when he got out in an unfortunate manner that there was every promise of his reaching a triple-century. Swivelling round to sweep, he lost his foothold on the greasy crease and broke his wicket. He gave chances at 76 and 104, but he batted with discipline and a sense of responsibility which indicated how much he had matured during the tour.

West Indies, needing 445 to avoid the follow-on, were 137 for two at the end of the third day, having lost Gomes five minutes before the close. Jumadeen came in as night-watchman and stayed till after lunch on the fourth day, having helped Bacchus add 129 runs. That Jumadeen – originally meant to bat at number eleven – was able to make 56 and resist for the best part of two and a half hours was an indictment of the play of some of the main West Indies batsmen; it was also a commentary on a pitch which was utterly lifeless. Jumadeen and Kallicharran both fell in close succession to the second new ball, leaving West Indies in a critical state. Then Murray, dogged and determined, stayed with Bacchus until bad light and drizzle brought play to a close forty-five minutes early.

The evening drizzle was prelude to a series of heavy downpours which washed out the fifth day's play and delayed the start of the sixth until after lunch. When play resumed, West Indies needed another 72 to avoid the follow-on, with six wickets in hand. The roller kept the soaked clay pitch quiet for a while; and by the time the damp came through to assist the bowlers, the gap had narrowed. Indeed it narrowed quickly, for the brilliant Bacchus lost no opportunity to exploit the openings left by aggressive field-setting.

West Indies wanted only 17 runs to make India bat again, when Bacchus became the first casualty of the short last day. Still, there was drama and excitement before West Indies were fully free of danger. Shivnarine's impetuosity made him an immediate victim, and with the ball now turning and popping, Murray – who had batted valiantly for over three and a half hours to score 44 – and Parry were caught off bat and pad. West Indies had barely avoided the follow-on when bad light rang down the curtain on this slow-moving Test match and on the series.

India

*S. M. Gavaskar c Murray b Marshall	40
C. P. S. Chauhan st Murray b Parry	79
D. B. Vengsarkar lbw b Phillip	15
G. R. Viswanath c Phillip b Parry	179
A. D. Gaekwad b Jumadeen	102
M. Amarnath not out	101
Kapil Dev c Greenidge b Jumadeen	62
†S. M. H. Kirmani c Phillip b Jumadeen	2
K. D. Ghavri not out	18
B 9, l-b 12, n-b 25	46
1/51 2/77 3/221 4/393 5/502 6/604 7/609 (7 wkts dec.)	644

S. Venkataraghavan and B. S. Chandrasekhar did not bat.

Bowling: Phillip 27–4–89–1; Marshall 34–3–123–1; Holder 43–6–118–0; Gomes 1–0–4–0; Parry 39–8–127–2; Jumadeen 45.4–4–137–3.

West Indies

A. T. Greenidge lbw b Ghavri	20
S. F. A. Bucchus hit wkt b Venkataraghavan	250
H. A. Gomes c Vengsarkar b Chandrasekhar	37
R. R. Jumadeen b Kapil Dev	56
*A. I. Kallicharran c Kirmani b Ghavri	4
†D. A. Murray c sub b Ghavri	44
S. Shivnarine c Vengsarkar b Amarnath	2
D. R. Parry c Vengsarkar b Ghavri	4
N. Phillip not out	10
M. D. Marshall not out	1
B 9, l-b 9, n-b 6	24
1/37 2/134 3/263 4/268 5/429 6/431 7/440 8/443 (8 wkts)	452

V. A. Holder did not bat.

Bowling: Kapil Dev 20–0–98–1; Ghavri 31–4–118–4; Chandrasekhar 41–10–117–1; Venkataraghavan 46.1–16–60–1; Amarnath 10–1–35–1.

Umpires: B. Satyaji Rao and P. R. Punjabi.

INDIA v PAKISTAN

Fifth Test Match

Played at Madras, January 15, 16, 17, 19, 20, 1980

India won by ten wickets. Two men shaped this decisive Indian victory – Gavaskar, with an innings of 166, the longest played in a Test match by an Indian (593 minutes), and Kapil Dev, with an outstanding all-round performance. He took eleven wickets in the match, including seven for 56 (the best figures of his Test career) in the second innings, and contributed a boisterous 84 to India's total of 430. The great-hearted bowling of Kapil Dev minimised India's self-imposed disadvantage of going into the match with only four bowlers, off-spinner Yadav having been left out.

The ball bounced more at one end than the other, but otherwise the Chepauk pitch was a better batting surface than in any recent Test on this ground. Pakistan, bowled out for 272, frittered away the advantage of winning the toss, although their batsmen did give the impression of playing with more discipline than in the previous Tests. Majid Khan ended his run of poor scores but was run out when he and Miandad looked set to enjoy a substantial partnership. Miandad batted extremely well, preventing the bowling from getting on top by running singles and 2s. Asif, too, promised much until Ghavri induced a snick with a beautiful ball, slanted across from over the wicket.

India were batting before the second morning was an hour old, and although never in deep distress, they also lost wickets regularly. At the end of the day they were 161 for four, with Gavaskar on 92. Next day, he and Sharma, the other overnight batsman, put on a century partnership which lasted until an hour after lunch, and following the dismissal in close succession of Sharma and Kirmani, he played a completely passive rôle while the flamboyant Kapil Dev hammered the tired attack.

India's innings stretched well into the morning of the fourth day, and at lunch, when Pakistan were 24 for two only thirty-eight minutes after the start of their second innings, it looked as if the match and the series would be decided before the day was out. Both Sadiq and Mudasser had fallen to loose shots, and in less than another hour, Pakistan were 58 for five. Zaheer failed yet again, out like Mudassar, glancing Kapil Dev, who took the first three wickets. Kapil Dev and Ghavri dared Majid Khan to hook, which he did profitably a couple of times before skying Ghavri to long leg. Going round the wicket, Kapil Dev had Asif caught from a square-cut, and it was only when Wasim Raja joined Miandad that resistance was at last forthcoming. Raja batted with the same abandon as the batsmen who had come to grief, but with more luck. Miandad was more discreet and built up his innings over three hours.

Pakistan still had three wickets in hand at the start of the last day and they did not concede them without a struggle. But India were left to get only 76 in the last innings, with three and threequarter hours available, and did so without loss to take a winning 2-0 lead in the series.

Pakistan

Mudassar Nazar c Kirmani b Kapil Dev	6	– c Vengsarkar b Kapil Dev	8
Sadiq Mohammad c Kirmani b Kapil Dev	46	– c Binny b Kapil Dev	0
Majid J. Khan run out	56	– c Patil b Ghavri	11
Zaheer Abbas c Kirmani b Kapil Dev	0	– c Chauhan b Kapil Dev	15
Javed Miandad c Vengsarkar b Kapil Dev	45	– c Kirmani b Doshi	52
*Asif Iqbal c Kirmani b Ghavri	34	– c Kirmani b Kapil Dev	5
Wasim Raja c Kapil Dev b Doshi	15	– c Viswanath b Doshi	57
Imran Khan run out	34	– c Doshi b Kapil Dev	29
†Wasim Bari c Binny b Ghavri	13	– lbw b Kapil Dev	15
Iqbal Qasim not out	3	– not out	19
Sikander Bakht c Vengsarkar b Ghavri	1	– b Kapil Dev	2
L-b 3, n-b 16	19	L-b 3, n-b 17	20
1/33 2/79 3/80 4/151 5/187 6/215 7/225 8/226 9/268	272	1/1 2/17 3/33 4/36 5/58 6/147 7/171 8/197 9/229	233

Bowling: *First Innings*—Kapil Dev 19–5–90–4; Ghavri 18.4–3–73–3; Binny 10–1–42–0; Doshi 26–6–48–1. *Second Innings*—Kapil Dev 23.4–7–56–7; Ghavri 14–0–82–1; Binny 13–2–33–0; Doshi 16–3–42–2.

India

*S. M. Gavaskar c Qasim b Imran	166	– not out	29
C. P. S. Chauhan c Qasim b Mudassar	5	– not out	46
D. B. Vengsarkar c Miandad b Imran	17		
G. R. Viswanath c Mudassar b Qasim	16		
S. M. Patil c Miandad b Sikander	15		
Yashpal Sharma b Qasim	46		
†S. M. H. Kirmani b Imran	2		
Kapil Dev lbw b Imran	84		
R. M. Binny not out	42		
K. D. Ghavri b Qasim	1		
D. R. Doshi c Miandad b Imran	9		
B 1, l-b 2, n-b 24	27	N-b 3	3
1/30 2/88 3/135 4/160 5/265 6/279 7/339 8/412 9/413	430		(no wkt) 78

Bowling: *First Innings*—Imran 38.2–6–114–5; Sikander 32–5–105–1; Mudassar 16–3–54–1; Qasim 37–13–81–3; Raja 2–0–19–0; Majid 9–1–30–0. *Second Innings*—Imran 5–1–20–0; Sikander 6–0–37–0; Mudassar 2–0–2–0; Qasim 4–1–12–0; Sadiq 0.5–0–4–0.

Umpires: Swaroop Kishen and M. V. Gothaskar.

CRICKET IN PAKISTAN

PAKISTAN v AUSTRALIA

Played at Karachi, October 24, 25, 27, 28, 29, 1964

Drawn. This was the last match of the Australians' long tour and in holding their own they owed everything to Simpson, who hit a century in each innings, and to fine bowling by McKenzie. Khalid Ibadulla, the Warwickshire opening batsman, distinguished himself by scoring a splendid hundred on his Test début, the first Pakistani to do so.

Pakistan introduced six new players to Test Cricket and retained only five of the team which toured UK in 1962, including Hanif Mohammad, who captained his country for the first time. Pakistan won the toss and decided to bat on a perfect pitch. Khalid Ibadulla, specially called from England, and Abdul Kadir gave the side a great start by scoring 249 in nine minutes under five hours. They beat the previous record of 162 by Hanif and Imtiaz at Madras in 1960-61. Kadir (nine 4s) missed the distinction of scoring a century in his first Test, Khalid was out off the last ball of the day, having batted five and a half hours and hit twenty 4s. Saeed in his short stay completed 2,000 runs in Test cricket. Pakistan finished the day at 284 for three.

Next morning, McKenzie, who had little luck the previous day, started a rout by taking three wickets cheaply, and when Martin dismissed Majid, Pakistan had lost four wickets in 17 balls. Undaunted by the situation, Intikhab and Asif batted beautifully; playing excellent strokes all round the wicket they put on 49 for the ninth wicket which enabled Pakistan to attain their biggest total against Australia. McKenzie with five for 22 that morning finished with six for 69.

Australia began badly when Lawry was out hooking a short ball from Majid, who took a wicket in his second over, and Redpath did not stay long. Simpson and Burge carried the score to 151 for two at the close in three hours ten minutes' play. Simpson's gallant knock which lasted six and three-quarter hours, came to an end just before tea, when Saeed had him caught. Simpson hit thirteen 4s and batted gamely with little support. His departure signalled the end, for Saeed took two more wickets and Intikhab finished the innings with Australia 62 behind. Pakistan lost Khalid before the close on the third day. Asif, going in as night watchman, played some beautiful shots and with Kadir put on 52. Instead of forcing the pace, Burki and Hanif defended and when play ended Pakistan had scored only 220 runs in five and a half hours.

After batting half an hour while 31 runs were added, Pakistan declared on the final morning, leaving Australia 342 to win in ten minutes under five hours – by no means a difficult task on a still plumb pitch. Simpson and Lawry accepted the challenge in a brisk opening stand, but Redpath had totally different ideas. He occupied thirty-seven minutes to get off the mark, and altogether batted four hours for only 40 runs. Simpson, on the other hand, hit a second hundred in three hours twenty minutes, including fifteen 4s, a great effort.

Pakistan

Khalid Ibadulla c Grout b McKenzie	166	– c Redpath b McKenzie	3
†Abdul Kadir run out	95	– hit wkt b Veivers	26
Saeed Ahmed c Redpath b Martin	7	– c sub b Martin	35
Javed Burki hit wkt b McKenzie	2	– c Grout b Cowper	62
*Hanif Mohammad c and b McKenzie	2	– c McKenzie b Booth	40
Shafqat Rana c Grout b McKenzie	0	– lbw b McKenzie	24
Nasim-ul-Ghani c Redpath b Hawke	15	– c Grout b Veivers	22
Majid Jahangir lbw b Martin	0		
Intikhab Alam c Grout b McKenzie	53	– not out	21
Asif Iqbal c Booth b McKenzie	41	– c and b Simpson	36
Pervez Sajjid not out	3		
B 9, l-b 12, n-b 3	24	B 1, l-b 6, n-b 3	10
1/249 2/266 3/284 4/296 5/296 6/301 7/302 8/334 9/383	414	1/13 2/65 3/81 4/118 5/202 6/224 7/236 8/279	(8 wkts dec.) 279

Bowling: *First Innings*—McKenzie 30–9–69–6; Hawke 20–2–84–1; Martin 36–11–106–2; Veivers 16–5–33–0; Simpson 30–8–69–0; Booth 5–2–15–0; Redpath 1–0–14–0. *Second Innings*—McKenzie 25–4–62–2; Hawke 6–2–20–0; Martin 17–4–42–1; Veivers 30–16–44–2; Simpson 20–5–47–1; Booth 13–4–18–1; Cowper 11–3–36–1.

Australia

W. M. Lawry hit wkt b Majid	7	– c Khalid b Majid	22
*R. B. Simpson c Pervez b Saeed	153	– c Khalid b Nasim	115
I. R. Redpath lbw b Intikhab	19	– not out	40
P. J. Burge c Majid b Pervez	54	– not out	28
B. C. Booth c Asif b Majid	15		
R. M. Cowper b Asif	16		
T. R. Veivers st Kadir b Saeed	25		
J. Martin b Asif	26		
†A. T. W. Grout c Asif b Saeed	0		
G. D. McKenzie lbw b Intikhab	2		
N. J. N. Hawke not out	8		
B 12, l-b 8, n-b 7	27	B 14, l-b 8	22
1/10 2/78 3/194 4/228 5/257 6/315 7/315 8/315 9/320	352	1/54 2/163	(2 wkts) 227

Bowling: *First Innings*—Majid 30–9–55–2; Asif 23.5–5–68–2; Pervez 22–5–52–1; Intikhab 28–5–83–2; Nasim 4–0–17–0; Saeed 19–5–41–3; Khalid 7–3–9–0. *Second Innings*—Majid 16–3–42–1; Asif 12–4–28–0; Pervez 8–2–17–0; Intikhab 16–3–48–0; Nasim 12–3–24–1; Saeed 13–6–28–0; Khalid 2–0–14–0; Burki 2–1–3–0; Shafqat 1–0–1–0.

Umpires: Shuja-ud-Din and Daud Khan.

PAKISTAN v COMMONWEALTH XI

Played at Karachi, March 29, 30, 31, April 1, 1968

Drawn. Perhaps stung by local criticisms of the timing of his declaration in the second "Test" at Lahore, Benaud this time surprised even his own players by asking Pakistan to make 249 in five minutes over four hours. At one point, with Hanif attacking brilliantly, Pakistan seemed to be on a good thing. He made 84 in two hours, twenty minutes, but once he left, the innings fell apart and the last hour was tensely fought with the ninth pair hanging on grimly. Intikhab, whose excellent all-round cricket became a feature of the series, played an important part in the final stages.

It was hardly surprising that Benaud left Pakistan with a reputation for infallibility. His now familiar tactics demanded a position for a declaration at the close on the first day. That he was able to do so on this occasion was due to an unbroken fourth-wicket partnership of 197 by Lewis, who has seldom shown such a rich variety of strokes, and Mushtaq. Lewis knew he had only three balls left in the last over in which to get a single and his century. It came with the last ball. Pakistan fought back with 98 by Ilyas, and when illness struck the Commonwealth on the third day they needed a long innings to get them out of a worsening position. Walker was more than equal to the occasion, and was well in command when Benaud made his closure. Benaud owed much to Allen for skilful bowling, and the end proved that a draw can still provide thrilling and absorbing cricket. The crowd were grateful for the experience.

Commonwealth XI

R. M. Prideaux c Hanif b Salim	4	– c Nasim b Intikhab	46
M. J. Edwards lbw b Intikhab	46	– c Ilyas b Intikhab	55
J. H. Hampshire c Ilyas b Salim	52	– c Asif b Intikhab	3
Mushtaq Mohammad not out	89	– c Abbas b Asif	19
A. R. Lewis not out	100	– not out	9
P. M. Walker (did not bat)		– not out	75
*R. Benaud (did not bat)		– c Nasim b Salim	11
†J. T. Murray (did not bat)		– c Wasim b Intikhab	7
K. D. Boyce (did not bat)		– b Intikhab	13
D. A. Allen (did not bat)		– b Intikhab	19
B 7, n-b 3	10	B 8, l-b 6, n-b 2	16
1/12 2/96 3/104	(3 wkts dec.) 301	1/95 2/129 3/131 4/147 5/177 6/181 7/199 8/229	(8 wkts dec.) 273

K. Shuttleworth did not bat.

Bowling: *First Innings*—Salim 19–2–65–2; Asif 19–2–72–0; Nasim 10–1–43–0; Intikhab 22–4–68–1; Saeed 14–1–43–0. *Second Innings*—Salim 21–4–52–1; Asif 16–2–45–1; Nasim 4–0–16–0; Intikhab 39–7–119–6; Saeed 12–4–25–0.

Pakistan

Mohammad Ilyas c Prideaux b Mushtaq	98	– c Edwards b Allen	12
*Hanif Mohammad c Walker b Allen	22	– b Boyce	84
Saeed Ahmed c Benaud b Allen	14	– c Benaud b Allen	14
Javed Burki b Mushtaq	47	– lbw b Walker	5
Ghulam Abbas b Boyce	15	– c and b Allen	4
Zafar Altaf run out	13	– c Boyce b Mushtaq	5
Nasim-ul-Ghani run out	15	– c Edwards b Walker	1
Intikhab Alam not out	55	– c Allen b Mushtaq	53
†Wasim Bari not out	24	– not out	6
Salim Altaf (did not bat)		– not out	11
B 1, l-b 15, n-b 7	23	B 2	2
1/54 2/74 3/176 4/194 5/209 6/229 7/258	(7 wkts dec.) 326	1/43 2/77 3/99 4/105 5/118 6/128 7/165 8/180	(8 wkts) 197

Asif Masood did not bat.

Bowling: *First Innings*—Shuttleworth 10–1–27–0; Boyce 11–0–64–1; Allen 39–9–89–2; Mushtaq 21–5–71–2; Walker 21–5–39–0; Hampshire 4–1–13–0. *Second Innings*—Shuttleworth 4–0–16–0; Boyce 7–1–21–1; Allen 22–8–60–3; Mushtaq 14–4–49–2; Walker 18–1–47–2; Hampshire 2–2–0–0; Benaud 3–2–2–0.

PAKISTAN v NEW ZEALAND

Third Test Match

Played at Karachi, October 30, 31, November 1, 3, 4, 1976

Drawn. Dropped catches, most of them by their new wicket-keeper. Shahid Israr, prevented Pakistan from translating their vast superiority into another comfortable win. All the same, a draw was a creditable result for the tourists, who had lost the first two Tests so heavily and who now found themselves playing without their captain and leading batsman, Turner, because of injury.

The enforced change in captaincy brought about no alteration in New Zealand's luck with the toss. Mushtaq won it again and Pakistan amassed a total of 565 for nine declared. The innings contained three hundreds and was notable for Majid Khan becoming the first Pakistani and the first from anywhere in 46 years to score a Test century before lunch. His innings was packed with imperious hooks and fluent, effortless cover drives. Javed scored 206 and Mushtaq registered his second century in successive Tests.

New Zealand, 67 for two at the end of the second day, recovered to score 468, more than half this total being raised by their last five wickets. Lees, the wicket-keeper, made 152, Hadlee scored a hard-hit 86 and Cairns, principally a bowler, got 52. They were helped along by Israr's errors and, possibly, by the reluctance of Pakistan's acting captain, Asif, to use Intikhab's leg-spin. Asif was in charge because Mushtaq was taken ill.

Frustrated by the resistance of the tail, Imran Khan unleashed three consecutive bumpers at Hadlee, who batted at number eight and umpire Shuja-ud-Din compelled Mushtaq to withdraw Imran from the attack.

Pakistan, 97 ahead, began their second innings midway through the morning of the fourth day and scored 290 for five before it ended. Majid again made an aggressive 50 and Javed failed by only 15 runs to perform the rare feat of scoring a double-century and a century in the same Test match. But for the risks he had to take to score quickly, he would surely have accomplished it.

Pakistan gave themselves all the last day to bowl out New Zealand and looked like doing so when four wickets were down for 93. New Zealand managed to hold out with three wickets in hand at the finish. The edge of Pakistan's attack in this innings was blunted by the absence of Sarfraz, who was also ill.

Pakistan

Sadiq Mohammad c Burgess b Hadlee	34	– c Lees b Collinge	31
Majid J. Khan c Burgess b Collinge	112	– run out	50
Zaheer Abbas b O'Sullivan	3	– c Lees b O'Sullivan	16
Javed Miandad c Hadlee b Collinge	206	– st Lees b O'Sullivan	85
*Mushtaq Mohammad c Lees b Hadlee	107	– not out	67
Asif Iqbal c Lees b Hadlee	12	– st Lees b Roberts	30
Imran Khan c O'Sullivan b Hadlee	59	– not out	4
Intikhab Alam lbw b O'Sullivan	0		
Sarfraz Nawaz lbw b Cairns	15		
†Shahid Israr not out	7		
B 3, l-b 5, n-b 2	10	L-b 4, n-b 3	7
1/147 2/151 3/161 4/413 5/427 6/524 7/525 8/548 9/565	(9 wkts dec.) 565	1/76 2/88 3/117 4/137 5/275	(5 wkts dec.) 290

Sikander Bakht did not bat.

Bowling: *First Innings*—Collinge 21–1–140–2; Hadlee 20.2–1–139–4; Cairns 28–2–142–1; O'Sullivan 35–6–131–2; Morrison 1–0–3–0. *Second Innings*—Collinge 12–0–88–1; Hadlee 12–0–75–0; O'Sullivan 17–0–96–2; Roberts 4.4–2–18–1; Morrison 2–0–6–0.

New Zealand

N. M. Parker c Shahid b Sarfraz	2	– c Imran b Intikhab	40
J. F. M. Morrison b Sarfraz	4	– c Mushtaq b Sikander	31
*J. M. Parker c Majid b Imran	24	– c Sadiq b Javed	16
A. D. G. Roberts b Imran	39	– b Sikander	45
M. G. Burgess c Javed b Sarfraz	44	– c Majid b Javed	1
R. W. Anderson lbw b Imran	8	– lbw b Imran	30
†W. K. Lees b Sikander	152	– c Asif b Imran	46
R. J. Hadlee c Shahid b Intikhab	86	– not out	30
B. L. Cairns not out	52	– not out	9
D. R. O'Sullivan c Mushtaq b Intikhab	2		
R. O. Collinge b Intikhab	3		
B 12, l-b 7, n-b 33	52	B 4, l-b 5, n-b 5	14
1/5 2/10 3/78 4/93 5/104 6/195 7/380 8/433 9/434	468	1/43 2/90 3/91 4/93 5/140 6/200 7/241	(7 wkts) 262

Bowling: *First Innings*—Sarfraz 20–1–84–3; Imran 25–4–107–3; Sikander 16–3–68–1; Intikhab 20.7–7–76–3; Mushtaq 6–2–30–0; Javed 10–3–34–0; Majid 5–2–17–0; Sadiq 1–1–0–0. *Second Innings*—Imran 21–1–104–2; Sikander 8–2–38–2; Intikhab 17–5–42–1; Javed 17–4–45–2; Majid 9–4–6–0; Mushtaq 6–3–9–0; Sadiq 1–0–4–0.

Umpires: Shuja-ud-Din and Shakoor Rana.

PAKISTAN v INDIA

First Test Match

Played at Iqbal Park, Faisalabad, October 16, 17, 18, 20, 21, 1978

Drawn. The over-prepared pitch was too slow and true to provide a finish to the first Test match ever to be played at the Iqbal Park stadium. This latest draw was the thirteenth in consecutive Tests between the two countries.

As in the three earlier series between Pakistan and India, the last of which was staged eighteen years previously, Pakistan was luckier with the toss than their rivals. The pitch was bland and easy from the very start and Pakistan, batting until tea on the second day, declared with a gigantic total of 503 for eight, their highest ever against India. It included a sparkling 176 by Zaheer Abbas and a patient, but far from staid, 154 not out by Miandad.

Parkistan had lost their first three wickets, those of Majid Khan, Sadiq Mohammad and Mushtaq Mohammad, in a short span – while they progressed from 84 to 110 – and on the second morning Asif Iqbal fell without scoring. But there was so much depth to their batting that Pakistan were never deflected from their course to a big score.

Zaheer Abbas took three hours twenty minutes to reach his century, which he did in the midst of a fiery onslaught against the second new ball, and in all he batted five and a quarter hours, hitting two 6s and twenty-four 4s. He drove with grace and exact placement on the off side and pulled violently against anything even remotely short of a length. Miandad, normally an ebullient or even impetuous batsman, played with judgement and restraint on this occasion and batted for more than seven hours. He hit three 6s and thirteen 4s. Together, Zaheer and Miandad put on 255 for the fourth wicket, the highest partnership for any wicket for either side in Test matches against each other.

Faced with an enormous score, India could do not more than play for a draw. With a sequence of big partnerships, they had made their position quite secure before lunch on the fourth day – during a stand of 166 for the fourth wicket between Viswanath and Vengsarkar. The pillars of the Indian batting were their two leading batsmen, Gavaskar and Viswanath, the former laying the foundations with a characteristic innings of 89. These two put on 101 for the third wicket, and when Gavaskar went, Viswanath took charge and scored 145 (his highest Test score). In doing so he became the first Indian to score a century against every Test-playing country.

Considering the fund of runs at their disposal, Pakistan's tactics in the field were surprisingly defensive. There was an over-abundant use of the three faster bowlers, which kept the over-rate down to about twelve an hour, and it was not unusual for Imran and Sarfraz to bowl three short-pitched balls an over. Iqbal Qasim, the left-arm spinner, was not called on until the total had passed 200, and Mushtaq directed most of his bowling, delivered from round the wicket, outside the leg stump.

With the first innings taking the best part of four days to complete and only 41 runs separating the two sides, the second innings was a mere formality. Yet Zaheer came close to achieving the rare feat of scoring two separate hundreds in a Test match, and Asif made a sparkling century.

Although the match was played for the most part in good humour, there was an unsavoury incident late on the fourth day at the start of Pakistan's second innings. During discussions that followed the warning by umpire Shakoor Rana of Mohinder Amarnath for following through into the proscribed area of the pitch, Gavaskar, the Indian vice-captain, used insulting language against the umpire concerned. Mr Rana and his colleague refused to go out the next morning until action was taken, and play was delayed by eleven minutes while a compromise was reached.

Pakistan

Majid J. Khan b Bedi	47	– c Chauhan b Prasanna	34
Sadiq Mohammad c and b Bedi	41	– c Gavaskar b Kapil Dev	16
Zaheer Abbas lbw b Prasanna	176	– c Chauhan b Gavaskar	96
*Mushtaq Mohammad c Gavaskar b Chandrasekhar	5		
Javed Miandad not out	154	– not out	6
Asif Iqbal c Chauhan b Bedi	0	– b S. Amarnath	104
Imran Khan c Vengsarkar b Chandrasekhar	32		
†Wasim Bari b Chandrasekhar	3		
Sarfraz Nawaz lbw b Chandrasekhar	18		
Sikander Bakht not out	16		
L-b 5, n-b 6	11	B 2, l-b 3, n-b 3	8
1/84 2/99 3/110 4/365 5/378 6/445 7/452 8/476	(8 wkts dec.) 503	1/54 2/60 3/226 4/264	(4 wkts dec.) 264

Iqbal Qasim did not bat.

Bowling: *First Innings*—Kapil Dev 16–2–71–0; M. Amarnath 7–0–44–0; Prasanna 42–11–123–1; Bedi 49–9–124–3; Chandrasekhar 38–6–130–4. *Second Innings*—Kapil Dev 12–3–25–1; M. Amarnath 10–1–43–0; Prasanna 14–4–34–1; Bedi 12–4–40–0; Chandrasekhar 12–1–49–0; Chauhan 5–0–26–0; Gavaskar 5–0–34–1; S. Amarnath 1.4–0–5–1.

India

S. M. Gavaskar b Qasim	89	– not out	8
C. P. S. Chauhan c Wasim b Sarfraz	46	– not out	30
S. Amarnath c Miandad b Mushtaq	35		
G. R. Viswanath b Mushtaq	145		
D. B. Vengsarkar c Wasim b Imran	83		
M. Amarnath c Wasim b Sarfraz	4		
†S. M. H. Kirmani c Qasim b Mushtaq	1		
Kapil Dev c sub b Mushtaq	8		
E. A. S. Prasanna not out	10		
*B. S. Bedi run out	1		
B 3, l-b 3, n-b 34	40	B 1, l-b 1, n-b 3	5
1/97 2/147 3/248 4/414 5/421 6/425 7/445 8/447 9/462	(9 wkts dec.) 462		(no wkt) 43

B. S. Chandrasekhar did not bat.

Bowling: *First Innings*—Imran 34.5–7–111–1; Sarfraz 37–6–105–2; Sikander 24–1–86–0; Mushtaq 27–10–55–4; Qasim 20–3–65–1. *Second Innings*—Imran 6–2–15–0; Sarfraz 2–1–3–0; Qasim 4–4–0–0; Miandad 3–1–4–0; Sadiq 4–0–16–0.

Umpires: Khalid Aziz and Shakoor Rana.

PAKISTAN v INDIA

Second Test Match

Played at Gaddafi Stadium, Lahore, October 27, 28, 29, 31, November 1, 1978

Pakistan won by eight wickets. Despite a courageous second innings recovery by India, Pakistan maintained the grip they established on the first day when they bowled out India for a meagre 199.

A grassy pitch prompted Mushtaq to put India in first. The wicket was hardly fiery, but it provided enough movement off the seam for Pakistan's pace attack to lay bare the Indian batsmen's flaws in technique. Conditions being what they were, a big innings from Gavaskar was vital to India's well-being. But in the third over, Saleem Altaf, Pakistan's veteran seam bowler, who was given the new ball in preference to Sarfraz Nawaz, produced a beautiful away-going ball to have Gavaskar caught at slip. Soon, India were reduced to 49 for four.

India were fortunate not to be overtaken by further disasters before their total reached three figures for Vengsarkar made a very shaky start and Mohinder Amarnath survived a chance at backward short leg when he was 7 and the total 88. But in the last over before lunch, at 106 for four, Amarnath turned his back on a bumper from Imran – the third of that over – and took a blow on the head. He was forced to retire. (When he resumed his innings, Amarnath trod on his wicket trying to hook yet another short-pitched delivery from Sarfraz.) Kirmani joined Vengsarkar following the injury to Amarnath and the total reached 151 before Pakistan were able to break this fifth-wicket partnership. Again, Pakistan missed an important chance by dropping Kirmani when the total was 118. Once he went, however, the innings tapered away rapidly. Vengsarkar was seventh out, having batted four hours twenty-three minutes and hit one 6 and ten 4s in his 76.

Pakistan were unperturbed by the early loss of Mudassar's wicket. A splendid 235 not out by Zaheer Abbas was the centrepiece of Pakistan's innings, but a sizeable total was guaranteed even before he came on the scene, thanks to a breezy night-watchman's innings of 85 by Wasim Bari, who completely dominated a second-wicket stand of 125 with Majid Khan.

Zaheer was in full flight again in scoring the third double-century of his Test career. The extent of his mastery can be gauged from the fact that of the 395 runs Pakistan accumulated during his six and a half hours at the wicket, his five partners mustered only 148; only Mushtaq (67) scoring more than 35. The Indians could find no way of containing Zaheer on a good wicket. The ease and fluency with which he drove, cut and pulled – he hit two 6s and 29 4s – put Pakistan well ahead of the clock and enabled Mushtaq to declare, midway through the afternoon of the third day, with an awesome lead of 340 runs.

More than half this lead was wiped out by India's opening pair, Gavaskar and Chauhan, with the highest first-wicket partnership to date in India-Pakistan Tests. Little more than eight hours remained when they were parted – and both demonstrated dissatisfaction at the decisions ruling them out, Chauhan at 93 and Gavaskar at 97. Viswanath then took charge of the situation, and though most of his partners looked vulnerable, India continued to prosper. Surinder Amarnath, who made 60, was dropped three times.

A draw looked the most likely result, even fifteen minutes before lunch on the last day when Viswanath, drawing back to cut Mudassar, was bowled for 83. India then were 406 for five and their hopes were dimmed further when Mudassar grabbed another important wicket, that of Vengsarkar, a few minutes later. It was due only to a gallant 39 not out by Kirmani that India were now able to extent Pakistan even a little. The final target was 126 runs in a shade over one hundred minutes, and with most of their batsmen well versed in the art of chasing runs after long experience in English cricket, Pakistan galloped home with 8.2 overs to spare.

India

S. M. Gavaskar c Majid b Saleem	5	– c Sarfraz b Mushtaq	97
C. P. S. Chauhan b Imran	10	– c Wasim b Javed	93
S. Amarnath c Asif b Imran	8	– c Mudassar b Mushtaq	60
G. R. Viswanath b Sarfraz	20	– b Mudassar	83
D. B. Vengsarkar c Wasim b Imran	76	– c Wasim b Mudassar	17
M. Amarnath hit wkt b Sarfraz	20	– c Qasim b Sarfraz	7
†S. M. H. Kirmani lbw b Mudassar	12	– not out	39
Kapil Dev lbw b Sarfraz	15	– c Majid b Imran	43
E. A. S. Prasanna not out	1	– c Mushtaq b Imran	4
*B. S. Bedi lbw b Sarfraz	4	– b Sarfraz	1
B. S. Chandrasekhar b Imran	0	– b Imran	4
B 17, l-b 4, n-b 7	28	B 8, l-b 4, n-b 5	17
1/15 2/19 3/48 4/49 5/151 6/186 7/192 8/194 9/198	199	1/192 2/202 3/301 4/371 5/406 6/407 7/415 8/437 9/438	465

Bowling: *First Innings*—Imran 18.5–2–54–4; Saleem 13–3–34–1; Sarfraz 16–4–46–4; Mushtaq 6–0–32–0; Mudassar 3–2–5–1. *Second Innings*—Imran 42.3–12–110–3; Saleem 16–6–36–0; Sarfraz 38–7–112–2; Mushtaq 30–6–106–2; Mudassar 4–1–4–2; Qasim 33–12–68–0; Miandad 5–1–7–1; Majid 2–0–5–0.

Pakistan

Majid J. Khan c Kirmani b Bedi	45	– c and b M. Amarnath	38
Mudassar Nazar c Gavaskar b Kapil Dev	12	– b Kapil Dev	29
†Wasim Bari c Kirmani b Bedi	85		
Zaheer Abbas not out	225	– not out	34
Asif Iqbal b Chandrasekhar	29	– not out	21
Javed Miandad b M. Amarnath	35		
*Mushtaq Mohammad run out	67		
Imran Khan not out	9		
B 12, l-b 8, w 1, n-b 1	22	L-b 6	6
1/19 2/144 3/161 4/216 5/356 6/525	(6 wkts dec.) 539	1/57 2/89	(2 wkts) 128

Sarfraz Nawaz, Iqbal Qasim and Saleem Altaf did not bat.

Bowling: *First Innings*—Kapil Dev 28–1–98–1; Gavaskar 4–1–10–0; Bedi 34–6–130–2; Chandrasekhar 21–2–109–1; M. Amarnath 21–1–76–1; Prasanna 25–2–94–0. *Second Innings*—Kapil Dev 10–1–53–1; Bedi 4–0–23–0; M. Amarnath 6–0–39–1; Viswanath 0.4–0–7–0.

Umpires: Shuja-ud-Din and Mahboob Shah.

PAKISTAN v INDIA

Third Test Match

Played at National Stadium, Karachi, November 14, 15, 17, 18, 19, 1978

Pakistan won by eight wickets. Left one hundred minutes to score 164 runs, Pakistan completed their win with seven balls to spare. The margin of victory was as much a measure of their vast batting superiority as the sharpness of their front-line pace bowlers, Imran Khan and Sarfraz Nawaz. The latter returned match figures of nine for 159, and although Imran took three fewer wickets his great pace helped to unsettle the fragile Indian batting. For the second time in his international career of eight years, Gavaskar scored two separate hundreds in a Test match. This feat and the efforts of all-rounders Kapil Dev and Ghavri prevented India from being more completely outplayed.

These performances might have been sufficient to force a draw, particularly as Pakistan's catching was erratic, but India suffered from Bedi's poor marshalling of his moderate bowling resources. For the first time in many years, India had gone into a Test match with only two spinners. The balance of their side was influenced less by the nature of the pitch than by fear of weakening the batting. As for the pitch, there was more grass on it than is normal at Karachi. Its growth was uneven, and its less pleasant features were varying pace and bounce.

India won the toss for the first time in the series, but did not fully exploit the advantage. Following partnerships of 58 and 73 for the first two wickets, they went to 179 for four. There was a further slump after Gavaskar was fifth out at 217, two more wickets going down while only 36 runs were added. India were then rallied by an eighth-wicket stand of 84 between Ghavri and Kapil Dev, in which the latter's share was a rapid 59, made off only 48 deliveries and including two 6s and eight 4s.

Pakistan, too, began soundly and then crumbled to 187 for five. For a brief period, Bedi and Chandrasekhar recaptured their old guile and devil, but the depth of Pakistan's batting enabled them to make light of this crisis. Miandad, scoring his second century of the series, put on 154 for the sixth wicket with Mushtaq Mohammad.

On the third morning, Mushtaq was removed for 78 before Pakistan drew level, and Miandad was seventh out when they were only 30 ahead. The Pakistan tail then countered so strongly that Mushtaq was able to declare with a lead of 137 runs one hour after lunch. India had lost control initially because Bedi was tardy in resting his overworked seam bowlers and trying Chandrasekhar and himself. He then went to the other extreme and bowled himself for too long – obviously in the hope of picking up the tailenders' wickets.

There was a dramatic start to India's second innings, which began with just over eight hours left in the match. Imran, bowling an opening over of lightning pace to Gavaskar, could have been most unlucky not to get the umpire's verdict when he appealed for a catch at the wicket. Then Sarfraz, in his second over, had Chauhan caught off the glove and nearly struck another blow almost immediately, getting the off-form Mohinder Amarnath to edge a simple catch before he had scored; but Zaheer dropped it.

Amarnath stayed to make 53 and helped Gavaskar to put on 117 for the second wicket. However, India collapsed hopelessly on the last morning, and with half an hour to go for lunch, they were 173 for six – only 36 ahead. Fortunately Gavaskar was still there. Two short of his hundred at lunch, he cut loose after the break against Iqbal Qasim and Sikander Bakht. He and Ghavri added 73 and India won some breathing space. Then at 246, an hour after lunch, Sarfraz went round the wicket and had Gavaskar caught behind, Bari taking a superb catch.

Imran and Sarfraz had gone flat out to break this seventh-wicket partnership and were rested once the goal was achieved. Mushtaq now turned to spin, which received rough treatment from the aggressive Kapil Dev. The new ball became due at 261, but with his main fast bowlers tired, Mushtaq delayed taking it for five overs. In doing so he nearly threw away the chance of winning, for 30 runs were added during this time. But once the new ball was taken, the innings ended abruptly.

When the mandatory overs started, Pakistan had lost one wicket, that of Majid, and needed another 137 runs to win. However, field placings designed to stop boundaries could not contain Asif – who had opened the innings – and Miandad, who was promoted up the order because Zaheer was injured. With imaginative placements and magnificent running between the wickets, the pair put on 97 from only nine overs. Although Asif was dismissed at a crucial time, Pakistan did not lose momentum through this reverse, and if their win was at all in doubt, it was settled in the sixteen over when Imran struck Bedi for two 6s and one 4.

India

S. M. Gavaskar c Sarfraz b Imran	111	– c Wasim b Sarfraz	137
C. P. S. Chauhan c Qasim b Sarfraz	33	– c Wasim b Sarfraz	0
S. Amarnath c Mushtaq b Qasim	30	– run out	14
G. R. Viswanath b Imran	0	– c Wasim b Sarfraz	1
D. B. Vengsarkar c Majid b Sikander	11	– c Wasim b Sikander	1
M. Amarnath lbw b Sarfraz	14	– b Imran	53
†S. M. H. Kirmani c Mushtaq b Sikander	14	– c Qasim b Imran	4
K. D. Ghavri c Majid b Sarfraz	42	– c Mudassar b Imran	35
Kapil Dev lbw b Sarfraz	59	– c Mushtaq b Sarfraz	34
*B. S. Bedi c Majid b Imran	4	– not out	0
B. S. Chandrasekhar not out	0	– b Sarfraz	0
B 10, l-b 6, w 1, n-b 9	26	B 9, l-b 4, w 1, n-b 7	21
1/58 2/131 3/132 4/179 5/217 6/219 7/253 8/337 9/344	344	1/5 2/122 3/143 4/147 5/170 6/173 7/246 8/297 9/299	300

Bowling: *First Innings*—Imran 32–12–75–3; Sarfraz 31.2–4–89–4; Sikander 22–6–76–2; Qasim 23–6–67–1; Mudassar 4–2–5–0; Mushtaq 3–0–6–0. *Second Innings*—Imran 28–7–76–3; Sarfraz 24–5–70–5; Sikander 10–2–42–1; Qasim 7–1–27–0; Mudassar 2–0–13–0; Mushtaq 9–0–36–0; Miandad 2–0–15–0.

Pakistan

Majid J. Khan b Kapil Dev	44	– c Chauhan b Kapil Dev	14
Mudassar Nazar c Chauhan b Chandrasekhar	57		
†Wasim Bari c Kirmani b Ghavri	3		
Zaheer Abbas c Viswanath b Bedi	42		
Asif Iqbal lbw b Chandrasekhar	1	– c Kirmani b M. Amarnath	44
Javed Miandad c Kirmani b Kapil Dev	100	– not out	62
*Mushtaq Mohammad c sub b Ghavri	78		
Imran Khan b Chandrasekhar	32	– not out	31
Sarfraz Nawaz c sub b Kapil Dev	28		
Iqbal Qasim not out	29		
Sikander Bakht not out	22		
B 5, l-b 20, w 1, n-b 19	45	B 3, l-b 9, n-b 1	13
1/84 2/104 3/153 4/155 5/187 6/341 7/374 8/408 9/447	(9 wkts dec.) 481	1/21 2/118	(2 wkts) 164

Bowling: *First Innings*—Kapil Dev 42–4–132–3; Ghavri 24–5–66–2; M. Amarnath 14–2–39–0; Chandrasekhar 25–4–97–3; Bedi 35–5–99–1; Chauhan 1–0–3–0. *Second Innings*—Kapil Dev 9–0–47–1; Ghavri 6–0–36–0; M. Amarnath 5.5–0–35–1; Bedi 4–0–33–0.

Umpires: Shuja-ud-Din and Mahboob Shah.

PAKISTAN v AUSTRALIA

First Test Match

Played at Karachi, February 27, 28, 29, March 2, 1980

Pakistan won by seven wickets in a match dominated by the spin bowlers. Off-spinner Tauseef Ahmad – on his Test début – and Iqbal Qasim made Australia struggle for their total of 225, after the visitors had elected to bat on a turning pitch. Their innings was given some respectability by Hughes, who batted three and threequarter hours for his 85, hitting one 6 and twelve 4s. Pakistan were in early trouble against Bright, but Taslim Arif and Javed Miandad initiated a recovery and, with Majid Khan hitting nine 4s in his four and a half hour stay, the home team achieved a promising total. On the third day Australia again had no answer to the spin of Qasim and Tauseef, ending the day only 23 ahead, having lost six wickets for 90. Despite a confident innings from Border, they were spun out for 140 on the fourth day, leaving Pakistan to score 73 for victory. Bright, again bowling effectively, took three wickets before the target was reached. Both Bright and Iqbal Qasim achieved career-best performances; Bright's match aggregate was ten for 111 and Iqbal Qasim returned figures of eleven for 118.

Australia

B. M. Laird lbw b Imran	6	– c Miandad by Qasim	23
G. N. Yallop c Taslim b Tauseef	12	– c Majid b Qasim	16
K. J. Hughes c Majid b Tauseef	85	– st Taslim b Tauseef	8
*G. S. Chappell st Taslim b Qasim	20	– c Taslim b Tauseef	13
D. W. Hookes c Majid b Qasim	0	– lbw b Qasim	0
A. R. Border lbw b Qasim	30	– not out	58
†R. W. Marsh c Haroon b Tauseef	13	– c Mudassar b Qasim	1
G. R. Beard b Imran	9	– b Qasim	4
R. J. Bright c Majid b Qasim	15	– c Majid b Qasim	0
D. K. Lillee not out	12	– lbw b Qasim	5
G. Dymock c Raja b Tauseef	3	– b Tauseef	0
B 8, l-b 9, n-b 3	20	B 4, l-b 5, w 1, n-b 2	12
1/8 2/39 3/93 4/93 5/161 6/177 7/181 8/199 9/216	225	1/38 2/51 3/55 4/59 5/89 6/90 7/106 8/108 9/139	140

Bowling: *First Innings*—Imran 16–4–28–2; Sarfraz 13–4–20–0; Mudassar 2–0–6–0; Qasim 30–11–69–4; Tauseef 30.2–9–64–4; Majid 2–0–13–0; Raja 2–0–5–0. *Second Innings*—Sarfraz 7–2–7–0; Mudassar 2–0–4–0; Qasim 42–22–49–7; Tauseef 34–11–62–3; Majid 1–1–0–0; Raja 4–1–6–0.

Pakistan

†Taslim Arif c Marsh b Bright	58	– b Bright	8
Haroon Rashid b Bright	6	– b Bright	10
Zaheer Abbas c Lillee b Bright	8	– not out	18
*Javed Miandad c Border b Chappell	40	– b Bright	21
Wasim Raja c sub b Chappell	0	– not out	12
Majid J. Khan c Border b Bright	89		
Mudassar Nazar c Border b Bright	29		
Imran Khan c Border b Chappell	9		
Sarfraz Nawaz c Chappell b Bright	17		
Iqbal Qasim not out	14		
Tauseef Ahmad b Bright	0		
L-b 12, n-b 10	22	L-b 3, n-b 4	7
1/34 2/44 3/120 4/121 5/134 6/210 7/238 8/266 9/292	292	1/17 2/26 3/60	(3 wkts) 76

Bowling: *First Innings*—Lillee 28–4–76–0; Dymock 5–2–5–0; Bright 46.5–17–87–7; Beard 17–8–39–0; Chappell 20–3–49–3; Yallop 2–0–14–0. *Second Innings*—Lillee 11–2–22–0; Dymock 2–0–9–0; Bright 11–5–24–3; Beard 1.1–0–14–0.

Umpires: Shakoor Rana and Mahboob Shah.

PAKISTAN v AUSTRALIA

Second Test Match

Played at Faisalabad, March 6, 7, 8, 10, 11, 1980

Drawn. Rain washed out the first day and delayed the start on the second by sixty-five minutes. The artificial methods used to restore the pitch produced a perfect batting strip on which new records were set as 999 runs were scored for the lost of just twelve wickets. For only the second time in Test history a whole side bowled; the other occasion was England v Australia at The Oval in 1884. Chappell, batting for seven hours and twenty-one minutes, scored his seventeenth Test century and shared in two record-breaking partnerships for Australia v Pakistan. With Hughes he put on 179 for the third wicket, then stayed to add 217 for the fourth with Yallop, who batted nearly eight and a half hours for his 172. Taslim Arif and Javed Miandad also set a new third-wicket record of 223 unbroken for Pakistan v Australia. Taslim, in only his third Test, batted for seven and a quarter hours, with twenty 4s, to score his unbeaten 210, remaining on the field throughout the match. Australia's 617 was their highest score against Pakistan and the first total of over 600 in a Test match in Pakistan. Yet they made an unpromising start, losing their first wicket for 1 – when Laird was out for 0 – and their second for 21; but once Hughes and Chappell came together, the runs piled up. Pakistan made a spirited reply, scoring their 382 in 435 minutes, although the game was already committed to a draw.

Australia

J. M. Wiener b Ehtesham	5
B. M. Laird c Taslim b Sarfraz	0
K. J. Hughes c Ehtesham b Tauseef	88
*G. S. Chappell lbw b Sarfraz	235
G. N. Yallop b Raja	172
A. R. Border run out	4
†R. W. Marsh lbw b Tauseef	71
G. R. Beard c Sarfraz b Tauseef	13
R. J. Bright b Raja	5
D. K. Lillee lbw b Raja	0
G. Dymock not out	0
B 11, l-b 10, n-b 3	24
1/1 2/21 3/200 4/417 5/434 6/561 7/585 8/592 9/612	617

Bowling: Sarfraz 49–13–119–2; Ehtesham 18–2–59–1; Qasim 56–11–156–0; Tauseef 34–3–77–3; Raja 30–6–100–3; Majid 22–2–66–0; Miandad 3–0–16–0.

Pakistan

†Taslim Arif not out	210
Haroon Rashid lbw b Dymock	21
Zaheer Abbas run out	19
*Javed Miandad not out	106
B 7, l-b 4, n-b 15	26
1/87 2/159	(2 wkts) 382

Mudassar Nazar, Majid J. Khan, Wasim Raja, Sarfraz Nawaz, Ehtesham-ud-Din, Tauseef Ahmad and Iqbal Qasim did not bat.

Bowling: Lillee 21–4–91–0; Dymock 20–5–49–1; Bright 33–9–71–0; Border 3–2–3–0; Beard 15–4–30–0; Hughes 8–1–19–0; Laird 2–1–3–0; Chappell 6–3–5–0; Wiener 5–1–19–0; Marsh 10–1–51–0; Yallop 3–0–15–0.

Umpires: Javed Akhtar and Khalid Aziz.

PAKISTAN v AUSTRALIA

Third Test Match

Played at Lahore, March 18, 19, 21, 22, 23, 1980

Drawn. For the third time in the series Australia won the toss, electing to bat on a perfect wicket. And once again, new records were established. Chappell scored his 5,000th Test run in this, his sixtieth Test, becoming the fifth Australian to do so. With Wiener he added 83 for the third wicket in 82 minutes. Australia were 239 for six overnight, and the next day Border achieved his fourth Test century, hitting two 6s and sixteen 4s. On the fourth day he hit yet another hundred in just under three and a half hours, with five 6s and sixteen 4s, taking his total to five centuries in twenty Tests. He was joined by Beard to put on 134 for the seventh wicket – another record for Australia v Pakistan Tests. When Chappell declared on the second afternoon, the Australians had reached a total of 407. By evening on the third day, Pakistan were still 183 behind at 224 for five, but Majid Khan's unbeaten 110 (fourteen 4s) revived the innings and, with useful contributions from Wasim Raja and Imran Khan, Javed Miandad was able to declare 13 runs ahead. Majid and Imran had added 111 for the eighth wicket, setting a new record for Pakistan v Australia. Lillee's three wickets were his first in Pakistan. When Australia replied, ten of the Pakistan team bowled, Miandad keeping wicket while Taslim Arif took his turn. Imran took two quick wickets, but the Australians batted with determination and the game ended in a draw, leaving Pakistan a 1-0 victory in the series.

Australia

J. M. Wiener lbw b Qasim	93	– c Mudassar b Imran	4
B. M. Laird b Tauseef	17	– c Taslim b Tauseef	63
K. J. Hughes b Qasim	1	– c Qasim b Imran	0
*G. S. Chappell lbw b Imran	56	– b Qasim	57
G. N. Yallop lbw b Qasim	3	– c and b Raja	34
A. R. Border not out	150	– st Mianded b Azhar	153
†R. W. Marsh b Qasim	8	– run out	13
G. R. Beard lbw b Imran	39	– c sub b Taslim	49
R. J. Bright not out	26	– not out	10
D. K. Lillee (did not bat)		– not out	1
B 4, l-b 6, n-b 4	14	L-b 4, n-b 3	7
1/50 2/53 3/136 4/153 5/204 6/218 7/298	(7 wkts dec.) 407	1/4 2/7 3/115 4/149 5/192 6/223 7/357 8/390	(8 wkts) 391

G. Dymock did not bat.

Bowling: *First Innings*—Imran 28–7–86–2; Sarfraz 28–6–67–0; Mudassar 6–1–16–0; Qasim 39–10–90–4; Tauseef 21–3–81–1; Raja 14–3–45–0; Azhar 2–1–1–0; Miandad 2–0–5–0; Majid 2–0–2–0. *Second Innings*—Imran 12–3–30–2; Sarfraz 14–5–42–0; Mudassar 2–0–20–0; Qasim 34–8–111–1; Tauseef 26–3–72–1; Raja 9–1–42–1; Azhar 1–0–1–1; Miandad 4–0–14–0; Majid 9–3–24–0; Taslim 5–0–28–1.

Pakistan

Mudassar Nazar c Yallop b Lillee	59
†Taslim Arif c Marsh b Bright	31
Iqbal Qasim c Marsh b Lillee	5
Azmat Rana c Chappell b Beard	49
*Javed Miandad c Marsh b Bright	14
Wasim Raja c Border b Lillee	55
Majid J. Khan not out	110
Azhar Khan b Bright	14
Imran Khan c Chappell b Bright	56
Sarfraz Nawaz st Marsh b Bright	5
L-b 4, w 1, n-b 17	22
1/37 2/53 3/133 4/161 5/177 6/270 7/299 8/410 9/420	(9 wkts dec.) 420

Tauseef Ahmad did not bat.

Bowling: Lillee 42–9–114–3; Dymock 24–6–66–0; Bright 56–14–172–5; Beard 10–5–26–1; Chappell 8–3–20–0.

Umpires: Amanullah Khan and Khyzar Hayat.

PAKISTAN v WEST INDIES

First Test Match

Played at Lahore, November 24, 25, 27, 28, 29, 1980

Drawn, after the loss of the third day to rain. West Indies, who were without Holding (shoulder injury) and Greenidge (stomach upset), bowled only 73 overs on the first day. Pakistan, after electing to bat on a lifeless wicket, had slipped to 95 for five by mid-afternoon, but a sixth-wicket stand of 93 between Wasim Raja and Imran Khan revived the innings. Imran became the second player (after Intikhab Alam) to achieve the double of 1,000 runs and 100 wickets in Tests for Pakistan, and on the second day he celebrated his 28th birthday by completing his maiden Test century. In 198 minutes he put on 168 for the seventh wicket with Abdul Qadir – who retired hurt at 260 for six after being hit on the shoulder by Croft – and Sarfraz Nawaz. Imran, who was named Man of the Match, then crowned his brilliant all-round performance by dismissing Bacchus in his first over.

On the fourth day Pakistan's accurate spin on a damp pitch accounted for eight of the nine wickets to fall; four to the leg-spin of Qadir and two to the off-spin of Nazir Junior. West Indies struggled once Haynes and Richards were parted, and it was thanks mainly to a sixth-wicket stand of 67 between Gomes and Murray that their first innings deficit was not greater than 72. The final day saw Pakistan going through the motions with no hope of a positive result.

Pakistan

Sadiq Mohammad c Murray b Marshall	19	– (2) lbw b Clarke	28
†Taslim Arif c Murray b Garner	32	– (1) retired hurt	8
Mansoor Akhtar c Murray b Croft	13	– b Clarke	0
*Javed Miandad c Richards b Croft	6	– run out	30
Majid J. Khan c Bacchus b Garner	4	– not out	62
Wasim Raja c Kallicharran b Richards	76	– lbw b Clarke	3
Imran Khan lbw b Marshall	123	– c Marshall b Richards	9
Abdul Qadir retired hurt	18	– c Haynes b Richards	1
Sarfraz Nawaz c Richards b Croft	55	– c Garner b Haynes	4
Iqbal Qasim b Marshall	3		
Nazir Junior not out	1		
B 1, l-b 5, w 1, n-b 12	19	B 2, l-b 3, n-b 6	11
1/31 2/65 3/67 4/71 5/95 6/188 7/356 8/368 9/369	369	1/15 2/57 3/101 4/112 5/125 6/133 7/156	(7 wkts) 156

Bowling: *First Innings*—Clarke 22–3–68–0; Croft 28–4–89–3; Marshall 22.4–4–91–3; Garner 27–6–71–2; Richards 7–0–31–1. *Second Innings*—Clarke 12–2–26–3; Croft 20–7–38–0; Marshall 15–4–30–0; Garner 9–3–17–0; Richards 11–4–19–2; Gomes 4–1–9–0; Kallicharran 1–0–4–0; Haynes 1–0–2–1.

West Indies

D. L. Haynes c Qasim b Nazir	40
S. F. A. Bacchus lbw b Imran	0
I. V. A. Richards b Nazir	75
A. I. Kallicharran c Sadiq b Qadir	11
*C. H. Lloyd c Miandad b Qasim	22
H. A. Gomes b Wasim	43
†D. A. Murray c Majid b Qadir	50
M. D. Marshall b Sarfraz	9
J. Garner c Taslim b Qadir	15
C. E. H. Croft not out	7
S. T. Clarke c Taslim b Qadir	15
B 3, l-b 6, n-b 1	10
1/1 2/118 3/119 4/143 5/158 6/225 7/255 8/275 9/276	297

Bowling: Imran 16–2–39–1; Sarfraz 13–3–40–1; Qadir 40.4–4–131–4; Qasim 12–4–18–1; Raja 10–3–21–1; Nazir 17–5–38–2.

Umpires: Khizar Hayat and Shakoor Rana.

PAKISTAN v WEST INDIES

Third Test Match

Played at Karachi, December 22, 23, 24, 26, 27, 1980

Drawn. Rain delayed the start until after lunch on the second day, when Pakistan elected to bat on the drying wicket. Their decision seemed ill advised as they lost two wickets for no score, struggled to 14 for four, and had reached only 68 for six overnight, with Zaheer Abbas also back in the pavilion after being struck on the forehead by a short ball from Croft. But recovery came through a fine captain's innings from Javed Miandad with help from Wasim Bari, who reclaimed his place in the Test side after a two-year absence. Six of Pakistan's batsmen failed to score – a new Test record. West Indies stunned by a combination of speed and spin, were reeling at 44 for five, with Richards, Kallicharran and Lloyd going in quick succession. That they achieved a first innings lead of 41 owed much to Gomes and Murray who added 99 for the sixth wicket. From 70 for one at the close on the fourth day, Pakistan slipped to 85 for five, but Man of the Match Wasim Raja batted calmly and, with stubborn tail-end resistance, Pakistan were able to bat out time, thus keeping the series alive.

Pakistan

Shafiq Ahmad lbw b Clarke	0	lbw b Garner	17
Sadiq Mohammad lbw b Croft	0	c Bacchus b Clarke	36
Zaheer Abbas not out	13	(5) lbw b Croft	1
*Javed Miandad c Lloyd b Clarke	60	c Haynes b Clarke	5
Majid J. Khan c Bacchus b Croft	0	(3) c Murray b Croft	18
Wasim Raja c Bacchus b Croft	2	not out	77
Imran Khan lbw b Garner	21	c Murray b Marshall	12
Ijaz Faqih b Marshall	0	c Murray b Marshall	8
†Wasim Bari c Murray b Clarke	23	b Garner	3
Iqbal Qasim c Richards b Clarke	0	b Croft	2
Nazir Junior b Garner	0	not out	2
L-b 1, w 1, n-b 7	9	B 4, l-b 3, n-b 16	23
1/0 2/0 3/5 4/14 5/53 6/57 7/111 8/112 9/112	128	1/30 2/76 3/78 4/82 5/85 6/122 7/146 8/150 9/178	(9 wkts) 204

Bowling: *First Innings*—Clarke 15–7–27–4; Croft 14–5–27–3; Garner 18.1–8–27–2; Marshall 14–0–38–1. *Second Innings*—Clarke 11–3–14–2; Croft 23–6–50–3; Garner 19–4–39–2; Marshall 17–1–54–2; Richards 8–2–10–0; Gomes 6–0–14–0.

West Indies

D. L. Haynes lbw b Qasim	1	S. T. Clarke b Qasim	17
S. F. A. Bacchus b Imran	16	J. Garner lbw b Imran	1
I. V. A. Richards c Zaheer b Qasim	18	C. E. H. Croft not out	3
A. I. Kallicharran b Imran	4		
*C. H. Lloyd c Miandad b Imran	1	L-b 1, w 4	5
†D. A. Murray c Miandad b Qasim	42		
H. A. Gomes c Miandad b Nazir	61	1/19 2/21 3/43 4/43 5/44	169
M. D. Marshall b Nazir	0	6/143 7/143 8/160 9/161	

Bowling: Imran 29–5–66–4; Qasim 34.1–11–48–4; Nazir 9–2–21–2; Ijaz 4–1–9–0; Raja 1–0–8–0; Majid 8–3–12–0.

Umpires: Shakoor Rana and Javed Akhtar.

PAKISTAN v WEST INDIES

Fourth Test Match

Played at Multan, December 30, 31, January 2, 3, 4, 1981

Drawn. The start of the fourth and final Test, played on a new Test ground, was delayed by the late arrival of an umpire. The match was marred on the second day by Clarke's disgraceful action in throwing a brick into the crowd. The spectators erupted and play was held up for twenty-five minutes until Kallicharran appealed to the crowd on bended knee to restore order.

The toss was won by Lloyd, who was captaining his country in Tests for the 42nd time, passing Peter May's record of 41. West Indies made an uncertain start on a worn pitch but, with useful support from Gomes and Clarke, Richards again carried the innings. Batting for six hours, he hit fifteen boundaries in his first century aginst Pakistan and the only West Indian century of the tour. From 198 for seven at the close on the first day, West Indies took their total to 249 on the second, thanks to a defiant tenth-wicket stand of 41 from Richards and Croft.

Pakistan lost both openers for 4, but Majid Khan and Javed Miandad added 100 before the close. On the third day, Wasim Raja became the tenth Pakistani player to pass 2,000 runs in Tests before Garner ended the Pakistan innings, giving his side a lead of 83 and becoming the eighth West Indian bowler to take 100 Test wickets. Richards fell, at 84, to the last ball before tea, and when play resumed ten minutes before the close – after an interruption for bad light an drizzle – Bacchus, Croft and Murray fell in quick succession, leaving West Indies vulnerable at 85 for five. Rain permitted only forty minutes of play on the fourth day and completely washed out the fifth; thus, for the first time in Pakistan, West Indies won a series – 1-0.

West Indies

D. L. Haynes b Imran	5	– st Bari b Qasim	31
S. F. A. Bacchus lbw b Imran	2	– c Zaheer b Qasim	39
I. V. A. Richards not out	120	– c Sadiq b Nazir	12
A. I. Kallicharran lbw b Imran	18	– not out	12
H. A. Gomes lbw b Qasim	32		
*C. H. Lloyd run out	9	– (7) not out	17
†D. A. Murray c Bari b Qasim	0	– (6) lbw b Nazir	0
S. T. Clarke c Miandad b Imran	28		
M. D. Marshall c Miandad b Nazir	3		
J. Garner c Nazir b Imran	2		
C. E. H. Croft lbw b Sarfraz	3	– (5) lbw b Nazir	1
B 15, l-b 6, w 3, n-b 3	27	L-b 3, w 1	4
1/9 2/22 3/58 4/134 5/146 6/153 7/198 8/201 9/208	249	1/57 2/84 3/84 4/85 5/85	(5 wkts) 116

Bowling: *First Innings*—Imran 22–6–62–5; Sarfraz 15.2–6–24–1; Qasim 28–9–61–2; Nazir 26–8–69–1; Raja 2–0–6–0. *Second Innings*—Imran 11–0–37–0; Sarfraz 5–1–15–0; Qasim 12–2–35–2; Nazir 15–3–35–3.

Pakistan

Shafiq Ahmad c Garner b Clarke	0	Sarfraz Nawaz b Garner	1
Sadiq Mohammad b Clarke	3	Iqbal Qasim c Richards b Garner	1
Majid J. Khan c Richards b Garner	41	Nazir Junior lbw b Garner	0
*Javed Miandad c Haynes b Croft	57		
†Wasim Bari run out	8	N-b 8	8
Zaheer Abbas c Murray b Marshall	8		
Wasim Raja not out	29	1/2 2/4 3/104 4/104	166
Imran Khan c Haynes b Croft	10	5/120 6/137 7/163 8/164 9/166	

Bowling: Clarke 12–1–42–2; Croft 16–3–33–2; Garner 17.2–4–38–4; Marshall 12–1–45–1.

Umpires: Khizar Hayat and Mahboob Shah.

SELECTED WISDEN ESSAYS

THE GOOGLY SUMMER [1968]

By A. A. Thomson

Sir Walter Scott, from whose part of the world my family came, began his anonymous career as a novelist with a fictional work called *Waverley* or *'Tis Sixty Years Since*. That sub-title, for no special reason, has always fascinated me. It is not so much that things which happened sixty years ago were more interesting than what happens now; indeed, I hope that as long as I retain a faculty or two, I shall be interested in most things. But, sixty years since, life was less like a ball of string the cat has done its worst with and, if you had a favourite interest, you were at liberty to pursue it without a million distractions. And if you had just passed your thirteenth birthday, and rather liked cricket, it was a wonderful world.

Not many people, especially historians, remember who was Lord Chancellor in 1908. I do. It was Lord Loreburn and I know because *John Wisden's Cricketers' Almanack* for that year tells me he was also President of the Marylebone Cricket Club, whose annual subscription, if you were allowed the privilege of paying it, appears to have been £1 10*s*. and whose refreshment department showed a profit of £463 15*s*. 9*d*. "In consequence of this satisfactory position," says the report, "it is proposed to make certain reductions in the charges." Such sublime words have never been repeated in the 1960s by anybody about the price of anything.

By 1907, about which *Wisden 1908* so richly informs us, my folk had long been settled in Yorkshire, reserving our nostalgic winter allegiance for Border rugby, but for cricket the county of our adoption was fairly satisfactory. We, in fact, felt that the only unsatisfactory item in *Wisden 1908* was that it could not record one of Yorkshire's 30 championships in 1907. The prize had gone to Nottinghamshire and, as I now look back with only mild prejudice, it had gone most deservedly. Yorkshire and a lively Worcestershire, stuffed with Fosters, tied for second place.

It was a horribly wet summer and, trust me, any man with sixty *Wisdens* on his shelves is bound to know more about the English climate than the BBC weather boys with their chatter about weak fronts and troughs of low pressure. (I have in recent seasons watched dreary pairs of opening batsmen whom the phrase "associated troughs of low pressure" would exactly fit.) So gruesome was the weather that in the Champions' two fixtures with Yorkshire only an hour and a quarter's play could be salvaged from six days. It was, as you would imagine, a bowler's, not a batsman's year. Only three made 2,000 runs and these were Hayward, Hobbs and Johnny Tyldesley, all batsmen with reasonable claims to places in an all-time world eleven. Nottinghamshire, the champions, did not boast a single batsman who made 1,000, though, to be fair, both Jack and George Gunn reached the 900s.

On the other hand 19 bowlers took 100 wickets, nine took 150, and one, George Dennett of Gloucestershire, whom I saw capture twelve in a match against my own county, took 201. The five Cricketers of the Year were all bowlers – is this a record? – though, again to be fair, one of them, Frank Tarrant, the Middlesex Australian, batted enterprisingly enough to do the double, a feat he was to repeat seven times.

The landmark in bowling, of course, was the visit of a South African team which lost the rubber in the only Test which the rain allowed to be finished, but otherwise cantered brilliantly through a long fixture list and undoubtedly earned a reputation as the most richly versatile bowling side that ever went on tour. Their four googly bowlers, R. O. Schwarz, A. E. E. Vogler, G. A. Faulkner and G. C. White, were the most formidable, the first two being chosen as *Wisden's* Cricketers of the Year, but they had four more, all exceptionally gifted, including J. H. Sinclair, medium fast, and J. J. Kotze, who bowled at terrifying speed and devoutly murmured as he galloped towards you: "O Lord, shiver his timbers". In a drier season he might have shivered more timbers than he actually did.

But it was the googly men who took the season by storm and the most intimidating thing about them was their pace off the pitch on the slow wickets of 1907. It was said that they were "like Briggs in the air and Tom Richardson off the ground". Or, in more modern terms, you must imagine, say, a West Indian bowler with an action like Lance Gibbs who could make the ball leap at your stumps like Wesley Hall. Now we know that the original inventor of the googly – why doesn't the Post Office issue a stamp? – was B. J. T. Bosanquet of Middlesex, who had exploited it with fearful success three years before in Australia, but the South African quartet were its devoted foster-parents. Bosanquet taught it to Schwarz, who also played for Middlesex, and Schwarz taught it to the others. Some of the others were cleverer still, though, so bewildering was the variety of their attack that English batsmen were never sure whether A, B, C or D gave them the most sleepless nights.

They all bowled with an action which promised a leg-break, but could make the ball whip in from the off. Schwarz was the most successful throughout the tour with 137 wickets, but Vogler, who took 119, was reckoned by the England captain, R. E. Foster, the best in the world. Schwarz on a sticky wicket was capable of breaking a yard and the batsman only had the slightest respite when the ball broke far too much. Vogler, after a short, apologetic run, would bowl with diabolically deceptive variations of flight and pace and every couple of overs would deliver a "wrong 'un" that fizzed like a Chinese cracker. He twice bowled C. B. Fry, the master of scientific batting, with a slow yorker and he did not so much swing the ball as make it quiver like a bird on the wing. Gordon White and Aubrey Faulkner were not so clever; they merely had their days of devastation, as when Faulkner took six for 17 when England were all out at Headingley for 76.

England won this match, but only after a nerve-racking struggle. The wicket was wet all through and it was a strategic error to play N. A. Knox, a bowler as timber-shivering as Kotze, but a mere passenger on so soft a pitch. Starting between showers, England scored 34 for one before lunch and then the rest of the side disintegrated before Faulkner. Breaking both ways, he completely bamboozled every batsmen except Hayward, who defended imperturbably, and Hirst, who, knowing all about wet wickets at Leeds, went out and clobbered him.

South Africa did not do much better against the superb slow left-hand bowling of Colin Blythe who, like the violinist he was, played on the batsmen's hesitations with the skill of a virtuoso. Blythe had been preferred to Rhodes, who, though he took 177 wickets that year, was rightly suspected of batting too well. Two years later he was to go in first for England. This was Blythe's finest hour, even though two months before he had taken all ten wickets in Northamptonshire's first innings, and seven in the second, making 17 for 48 in a single day. Nevertheless, the reason why I still count Rhodes the greatest of all bowlers is that he returned after the war to increase his career's bag of wickets to 4,187 and to play a vital part in England's recovery of the Ashes at the age of 48 years 10 months. Blythe, alas, alas, did not come back.

In spite of Blythe, South Africa struggled along and, with the comfort of some flabby fielding and a bit of brave banging about for the eighth wicket, they established a lead of 34. Now England were in disarray. There remained three frightful quarters of an hour before close of play and Fry had to use all his compelling charm – I can just hear him using it – to persuade his captain not to fritter away the evening with ineffective night watchmen. Fry himself and Hayward went in and survived the twilight till six-thirty. The captain almost shed tears of gratitude.

The next day the weather was worse, the wicket was vile and there were four interruptions before lunch. Fry, who made 54, was second out at 100. In his career he made 94 hundreds, six of them in succession, but none better, as he admitted to me many years later, than that 54 at Headingley. "I choose to flatter myself," he said, with a genuine modesty indistinguishable from arrogance, "that this was a good innings." The rain that ended the second day was so intense that there seemed no hope for the third day, but a windy night made play possible and the South African bowlers, especially White, made mincemeat of the rest of England's innings. They were, therefore, set only 139 to win which hardly seemed impossible, but they lost two wickets for three, survived a slip-chance and then fled from the rain.

Both sides were gluttons for punishment and, when they went out again, a pitched battle was fought for every run. Hirst and then Arnold bowled tightly at one end and Blythe, at the other, bowled even better than in the first innings. Wickets fell: three for ten, four for 16, five for 18. Faulkner and Snooke dug in, defending in a manner foreign to their lively natures, and held the broken line for an hour, but temptation became irresistible and Faulkner hit up a high catch to Foster at point. Resistance was broken, Blythe was unplayable, the end was in sight. Nineteen runs were more or less blindly hit for the ninth and tenth wickets and then Vogler sent up a towering skyer which seemed to hang aloft interminably as Johnny Tyldesley tore round the boundary. As it fell, he made a final leap, rolled over and came up, like a diver, with the ball in one hand.

With the match won, Blythe had to be helped to the pavilion. Immense concentration on every ball of 22.4 beautiful overs had drained every drop of his quivering nervous energy. Years later, Fry recalled the scene. "It wasn't so much that he took fifteen wickets in the match; it was that in 136 balls he never bowled a single one that was of less than perfect length, knowing, as we all knew, that three bad overs at any time in that innings could have lost us the match."

Of the other Cricketers of the Year two were the Nottinghamshire bowlers, Hallam and Wass, whose strongly contrasted talents formed the main reason for their county's first clear triumph in twenty-one years. Hallam was slow and Wass was fast and between them they took 319 wickets (298 in county games); twice they bowled right through a match and eight times right through an innings, and the next bowler to them in the county tables was John Gunn each of whose 37 wickets cost more than twice as much as any of Hallam's or Wass's. Nobody else in the wicket-taking line seems to have reached double figures. So much for the modern theory that you must start with three pairs of "seam" bowlers in turn, all almost exactly alike and all entitled to a stint by the clock before you put on a slow bowler to give the batsmen a chance. Imagine putting on Rhodes, Blythe or Dennett for that purpose. . . .

Hallam, a Nottinghamshire lad, had wandered a bit, first with Leicestershire and then, for six seasons, with Lancashire, but when he settled in his native shire he took on the mantle of "Dick" Attewell. He was the sort of bowler who looked easy to play from the press-box, but he made the batsman play every ball and, as P. F. Warner said, if you made a good score against Hallam, you were apt to feel a better batsman than you had ever thought you were. When chosen as a Cricketer of the Year, he was thirty-five, a pretty advanced age for the honour.

Tom Wass, also around thirty-five, was a different cup of tea, if that is the right expression. He was born at Sutton-in-Ashfield, where practically every baby born had the chance of growing up a famous cricketer. As Lascelles Hall was to Yorkshire cricketers, so Sutton-in-Ashfield was a nursery, not only for Nottinghamshire men, but for cricketers everywhere. It would have been possible to raise a formidable team of Sutton-in-Ashfield exiles scattered round the counties and, in fact, an ill-natured joke in the form of a satirical greeting card, which suggested that Sutton-in-Ashfield merely existed to be raided for players, almost caused an embittered quarrel between Nottinghamshire and Lancashire.

Tom Wass was a character. There has been in every age a fast bowler who was a rough diamond and this phenomenon is more frequently found in the north where they suspect the genuineness of their diamonds unless they are rough. His forthright comments were quoted with shocked glee round the dressing-rooms. Once when Gloucestershire scored nearly 700 against his side, he exclaimed: "If they'd only turn this flamin' wicket upside down, I'd . . . show 'em."

Tom was a grand bowler. That year he had taken six for 3 against MCC at Lord's and twice in his career he took 16 wickets in a day. On the other hand, he was neither a master-batsman nor a hawk-eyed fielder and *Wisden*, in one of its classic understatements, says that "when an easy catch goes his way the batsman has a feeling of hopefulness. . . ."

Once when playing at The Oval, he arrived at the gate, accompanied by his wife, and was told by the attendant that the lady could not be admitted free. "Right," said Tom, "if this so-and-so don't come in, then this so-and-so" – he thumped his chest – "don't play neither!" Take him for all in all, he was a cricketing character of the old school and a main reason for Nottinghamshire's well deserved victory.

Besides their two master bowlers, they had enough batting to overhaul any score the enemy might put up without being top-heavy. John Gunn, who had played for England half a dozen times and his brother, George, that wayward genius, whose playing life was to last 30 years and bring him 35,000 runs, headed the batting along with their captain, A. O. Jones, a forceful leader, an entertaining bat and one of the best three slip-fielders in the country, the other two being Braund and Tunnicliffe. The all-round fielding had no superior among the counties with the skipper at slip, John Gunn at cover, and Hardstaff (old Joe, father of the more brilliant young Joe) in the deep. Four members of this business-like eleven, George Gunn, Jack Gunn, Hardstaff and Jones, who captained MCC's 1907-08 team in Australia, were to have 38 England caps between them. One was to wait another four years for his one crowded hour of glory. His name was Edward Alletson. Their secret was teamwork, in the sense that in match after match they were able to put the same eleven into the field and their only serious setback occurred when Oates, their wicket-keeper, who had injured a hand, was replaced (for two matches only) by a capable deputy.

Remember, we were still in the Golden Age, which, when you think of Hallam and Wass and consider the figures of Haigh, whose average was only a decimal point above Hallam's, Hirst (188 wickets), Blythe (183), Tarrant (177) and Dennett (201), was, that year at any rate, a golden age of bowling. Yet there were classic batsmen in every county. Worcestershire, who shared second place with Yorkshire, had three members of the famous Foster family; H.K., G.N. and R.E., England's Test captain for the season; Surrey had Hayward, Hobbs and Hayes (who scored nearly 2,000 runs), just as Lancashire had MacLaren, Spooner and Johnnie Tyldesley. Kent, who had splendidly headed the table the year before, had a poor season, in spite of the fine bowling of Blythe and Fielder, mainly owing to an accident to K. L. Hutchings; this came from a terrific blow on the hand from J. J. Kotze, which kept him from the crease for five vital weeks.

You could go right down the county table and find players of England quality: Sussex, thirteenth, had C. B. Fry, head of the first class (and Test) averages and George Cox (senior), who took 164 wickets, while Derbyshire, the bottom county, provided in the sterling Joe Humphries, a wicket-keeper for the MCC's Australian tour. Gloucestershire, parked somewhere near the top of the table's bottom half, had the most exciting batsman in England, probably the most exciting in the game's history.

We know broadly who had impressed us with their soundness, their artistry, their elegance, or, possibly, with their combination of the excellences. But excitement? Bradman, obviously, but who to-day excites? The last England batsman to set the pulses wildly beating was E. R. Dexter. Colin Milburn excites *hopes* of excitement and I should hate to miss Roy Marshall when in town. There are others – Sobers, Kanhai, Graeme Pollock, Majid – who are exciting enough, but they are not for us every day.

In 1907 there was no argument. The most exciting batsman in the world was G. L. Jessop, captain of Gloucestershire. I had never seen him till that year, but his reputation, even among Yorkshire schoolboys, was stupendous. He had on our own ground, ten years before, hit 43 out of 54 before lunch and then, off another eight overs, taken another 58 out of 64 in a further 19 minutes. My step-Uncle Walter, who had seen every ball of this innings, recalled it as magnificent, but as also a kind of impiety, like brawling in church, because the outrage was committed against such eminent bowlers as George Hirst, Ted Wainwright, F. W. Milligan and (how dare he?) F. S. Jackson.

In the match I saw he scored at almost the same pace. From the first moment there was tension. Yorkshire began with a feeble first innings of which Rhodes, batting at No. 1, made more than half. In their reply Gloucestershire led by only three runs, in spite of masterly batting by C. L. Townsend, making his one appearance of the summer. Then Yorkshire lost six wickets quickly and were only saved by a long stand, running into the next day, between two colts, Hubert Myers and Bates, son of the more famous "Billy" Bates. Between them they also contributed more than half of the total and, with some honest thumping by Haigh, Yorkshire were able to ask Gloucestershire to make 234 to win. Three wickets fell to Hirst and then Jessop came in. He was no physical giant, but, like Bradman, short, compact and finely proportioned. What astonished us most was his stance, for he bent low to take guard; then, as the ball was delivered, he straightened . . . and struck. It is hard to describe, but it seemed like an artillery barrage. His square-cutting was as ferocious as his driving and his drives seemed propelled by a howitzer. When his successive partners had the strike, the fielders crept in; when Jessop was receiving, they retreated as from the wrath to come. Boundary followed boundary and the only time the scoring slackened was when Jessop with a hurricane sweep, sent the ball flying over the stand beyond the mid-wicket boundary and out of our ken for ever. In half an hour by my five shilling Ingersoll watch he scored 74 and when he got 15 more off four further strokes, Schofield Haigh bowled him an apocalyptic breakback. Everybody stood up on their seats and shouted, as though Mafeking had been relieved all over again. This was the beginning of the end and Rhodes easily polished off the rest.

I have two further memories of this match: one is of the heavily moustached George Dennett, who captured a dozen Yorkshire wickets with his easy rhythmic stuff. In his career he took 2,147 wickets, but never played for England, for the true but cruel reason that he was only the third best of his kind at the time. Even in this wet summer, which gave him more than 200 wickets, Blythe was preferred and, on Test performance, rightly. But I will swear that, if George was not good enough for England, the standard was incredibly high.

The other point was personal. Early the first morning I stood, gaping, with two school friends, waiting for the odd player to come out to the nets. The enemy were mostly anonymous, but . . . *him* we recognised from countless photographs and a certain impatience of step. He had a bat under his arm and, by some conjuring trick, produced three cricket balls. "Come on, boys," he said, "bowl me out."

Friend A bowled and the ball soared straight across the ground, hitting the entrance gate with a bang. Friend B, whoever he was, bowled and the ball rose, across the ground again, but higher. Then, while the batsman scanned the horizon to see where it had gone, the third bowler, unable to control a reflex action, bowled and hit G. L. Jessop's off-stump. I did not feel, as did Arthur Mailey on a similar occasion, "like a boy who had shot a dove". I was numbed. We went on bowling, if I remember rightly, till all the balls had disappeared, but the numbness, as you may perceive, has not worn off yet.

I did not need my precious 1908 *Wisden* to remind me of Jessop's vengeance. It is now regularly recorded in every *Wisden*. At Hastings Festival, playing for Gentlemen of the South against Players of the South, whose bowlers included Woolley, Fairservice, Vine, Humphreys, Albert Relf and our old friend, George Dennett, Jessop hit 191 in an hour and a half; the first 50 in 24 minutes, the second in 18 and the third in 21. And if you think his last 41 runs took a long time, you must remember that, besides his 30 fours, he hammered the ball out of the ground so often and so dangerously that the citizens must have thought it was 1066 all over again. This slowed his scoring rate and slightly spoiled his figures.

To glance through *Wisden*'s Obituary pages is not morbid; you may learn something of value, if only that man is mortal. In this year, among other good men, died H. F. Boyle, the Australian bowler who helped Spofforth to destroy England in the original Ashes match of 1882; and Harvey Fellows, who, sixty years before, bowled so fast in the Eton v Harrow match that there were 38 byes and 15 wides in the first innings and 28 byes and 4 wides in the second.

Alfred Shaw in a career of over 30 seasons took over 2,000 wickets, did the hat-trick three times, including a double one, and once captured seven for 7 against MCC in 41 overs, of which 36 were maidens. His chief assets were his steely accuracy and the benevolently bearded aspect which masked his guile. He never bowled a wide in his life.

Lastly, poor Ted Pooley, the Surrey stumper who did not keep wicket in the first of all Tests, because he happened to be languishing in gaol, through no particular fault of his own, 1,200 miles away. But that is too long a story. . . . The highest compliment ever paid him came from the tough old bruiser, Jem Mace. "Pooley," he said, "I'd rather stand up against any man in England for an hour than stand behind those stumps for five minutes. When that ball hits you, it's like hitting a brick wall."

Wisden's last words on Pooley were exquisitely compassionate: "He was in many ways his own enemy, but even to the last he had a geniality and sense of humour that to a certain extent condoned his weakness. . . ."

May heaven grant me so kindly an epitaph.

THE DREADED CYPHER [1971]

By Basil Easterbrook

A pair in a Test Match! Can anyone imagine a worse fate befalling a batsman, especially when he is fighting for a place in the MCC team to tour Australia? Such was the experience of Brian Luckhurst last August in the Final Test at The Oval where his middle stump was sent flying for 0 by Procter with the third ball of the first innings and again for 0 with the first ball of the second innings. It set me pondering on this subject of "The Dreaded Cypher".

Suppose it had happened to him on his debut for England in the first Test two months earlier at Lord's. Would the selectors have looked at him again? They cast aside Alan Jones, Sharpe and Denness for their failures in that match. Luckhurst was sensible enough to prove himself first; so he did go to Australia with my best wishes and I will tell you why.

Wisden's first edition in 1864 at one shilling for 112 pages in notebook size to slip into the slimmest pocket was the best bob's worth on the bookstalls.

On the flyleaf was a note addressed to the reader: "In offering our first edition of the Cricketer's Almanack to the patrons of the Noble Game, we have taken great pains to collect a certain amount of information, which we trust will prove interesting to all those that take pleasure in this glorious pastime. Should the present work meet with but moderate success, it is intended next year to present our readers with a variety of other matches, which the confined nature of an almanack precludes us from doing this year." A little enough acorn but what an oak grew from it!

In passing one wonders how John Wisden and Company, offering their literary sprig at their warehouse in the Haymarket, would have reacted to the 1969 edition of 1,055 pages. The original publication's collection of matches was drawn from games anywhere in the first half of the 19th century. For example, you could inspect the scorecard of a game at Lord's in July, 1806, a bare nine months after Trafalgar on page 30 and a game at The Oval in 1863, when W. G. Grace was a lad of 15, a few pages further on.

We live now in a dreary age of specialisation and the 1,000 page monsters of the 1960s deal with nothing but cricket but in 1864 you could study *Wisden* and become a mixture of Datas and Leslie Welch. On one page alone you were told the dates of the eight Crusades ranging from 1097 to 1270, the venues of the twelve battles of the Wars of the Roses, a précis of the trial of Charles the First and a final paragraph which ran "A brass bell weighing 17 cwt cast in 1699 at Woolwich Arsenal used to call and disperse the labourers, was cleft by the hammer while ringing, from the effects of the severe frost on January 4, 1861."

On another page was a potted history of English coinage going back to 1302 and all the canals in Britain above 30 miles in length. If you needed to know how to go quoiting or play Knur and Spell, or when China was first visited by Europeans, the winners of the principal horse races, the rules of the game of bowls, how to bet on cricket like a gentleman, or what time the British Museum closed, then *Wisden* 1864 was a volume you could not afford to be without.

Seen through the corrupt eyes of the second half of the 20th century, it was of course a time of innocence but the original compilers knew where their main duty and purpose lay and they also had an eye for the romance and drama of the game. Now for all cricketers like the writer who made more ducks than he has eaten baked dinners, the originators of the world's holy writ on cricket started a section called "Extraordinary Matches", which amid all the welter of feats and records has been allowed to lapse by their distinguished successors. They gave details of a match which made a man like myself feel he had his rightful place in the game without relying on the second prize of writing about it for that place. In August, 1855, the Second Royal Surrey Militia met Shillinglee in Sussex at the seat of Earl Winterton. The scorecard of the Militia's first innings was as follows:

Private Dudley b Challen junior	0
Private Plumridge b Heather	0
E. Hartnell, Esq. b Heather	0
A. Marshall, Esq. b Challen junior	0
Private Ayling b Challen junior	0
Lieut. Pontifex b Heather	0
Corporal Heyes	0
Lieut. Ball b Heather	0
Major Ridley not out	0
Sgt. Ayling run out	0
Private Newberry b Heather	0
Extras	0
Total	0

It was No. 10 who nearly ruined the whole thing. He hit one to cover point and set off like an Olympic sprinter going for the tape. Major Ridley rent the pastoral scene with a stentorial voice of command – "Go Back Sergeant." Sgt. Ayling pulled up all standing, fell base over apex and was run out by 15 yards. There were those who accused the gallant Major of moral cowardice, but I see him as a man with a sense of history. There is something aesthetically perfect about that scorecard – no catches, no stumping, no LBWs and no runs.

The Militia made 106 in their second innings, but who wants to bother with that?

From that time *Wisden* has increased tenfold in size, thirtyfold in price and a hundredfold in status, but the Pardons, Stewart Caine, S. J. Southerton and the Prestons who have built the greatest monument of print in all sporting history all stand arraigned for a serious sin of omission. They have become so intoxicated with faithfully preserving for posterity the feats of THEM, that is the handful of lucky blighters who play first-class cricket from April's end to September that they have almost completely ignored US namely, The Rest, who do not.

Individual scores of 300 or more, hundred on debut in England, most individual hundreds, they are all there in the record section extending for nearly as many pages as there were altogether in the original *Wisden*. It's sickening. Every year you are told that J. B. Hobbs hit 244 hundreds in all cricket and W. G. Grace 217 and there are columns of names running from Sir John Berry Hobbs to Brian Valentine of chaps who made 35 or more centuries in first-class cricket.

Even a young fellow like Boycott has got his name into the list obsessed with batting his life away instead of learning to pick four notes from the strings of a guitar and earning himself a £1,000 a week.

Because, let's face it, *Wisden* has made us obsessed with runs, a charge I substantiate by a reference to the simple fact that nearly 20 pages of the record section are devoted to such improbable events as C. J. Eady scoring 566 for Break-O'-Day against Wellington at Hobart in the winter of 1901-2 before a mention is made of bowling feats. And of the considerable achievement of making a duck nothing in all the 1,000 or more pages. It came to me in a blinding flash of intuition that *Wisden* is a vast conspiracy dedicated to the proposition of creating a totally false image of the game.

Any mug with enough talent and concentration can make a hundred. It requires the soul and tenacity of a martyr to score nothing and continue to score nothing. Once in 1935 at Dartmouth I made 16 out of a total of 43 against the Royal Naval College but in self defence I would point out that even Homer nodded and that if you go to the crease often enough there comes a day when you will get some runs regardless of what you do. I have remembered this innings for 35 years for I believe this is as far as I got from the circular cypher in one innings.

How much colour and interest have been withheld from lovers of cricket by *Wisden's* refusal down the years to publish a section devoted to the nought. There was Ian Peebles, for example, on an overseas MCC tour who went into the scorer's book "absent bathing 0". Hutton might easily have been one of US instead of THEM. He began with great promise – a duck in his first innings for Yorkshire seconds, a duck for the first eleven at Fenner's in 1934 and a duck in his first innings for England, against New Zealand. He deteriorated so far that he made 129 centuries and in June, 1949, by scoring 1,294 made more runs in a single month than anyone else.

Hammond made 0 in his first match against Lancashire at Cheltenham in 1920 but he slipped further than Hutton, ending his career with 167 centuries with only Hendren 170 and Hobbs 197 ahead of him in the all time list of century makers.

Philip Mead, the world's No. 4, with 153, made a duck in his first match against the Australians at Southampton in 1905. Frank Woolley, No. 6 with 145, made 0 a year later in his debut against Lancashire at Old Trafford. He soon got the taste for notoriety by making 64 in the second innings and was lost to US from then on. Old Trafford remained one of his favourite grounds and it is said that on one occasion he square cut Ted McDonald for six and the ball struck one of the pavilion towers with such force that when it rebounded back into the field of play at a tangent McDonald took it first bounce as he was walking back, said "Good shot, Frank", turned and ran in to bowl the next delivery. W. G. Grace, 126 hundreds, failed to score in his first game for the Gentlemen of the South v Players of the South at The Oval in 1865 but even at 17 he had no sense of proportion as he showed by taking thirteen wickets for 84 runs in the match.

Tom Graveney, the leading century compiler of current players, began with 0 in The Parks against Oxford in 1948 but he was another who could not keep it up.

All these with the exception of Hutton lacked the stamina to make a serious bid to be regarded as US rather than THEM, but there were players who later degenerated into household words who for a brief season did splendidly. George Dews of Worcestershire was bowled by Eric Price in both innings at Old Trafford on his debut against Lancashire and notched a notable "hat-trick" by failing to score in the first innings of his next match against Warwickshire at Dudley in 1946. Johnny Douglas, when beset by the worries of the England captaincy must more than once have pondered ruefully on how different life might have been, for, like Dews, he too started his career with a "hat-trick" of ducks. He was bowled by George Hirst in each innings in the Essex v Yorkshire match at Leyton in 1901 and failed to score in his next innings against Gloucestershire at Clifton. Morton, a Derbyshire stalwart in the early years of the century, did even better.

At Edgbaston in 1901 against Warwickshire he was clean bowled by Charlesworth twice. In his next game at Lord's he was castled a third time before he had scored and in the second innings he was run out trying to get off the mark. M. J. K. Smith got a duck for Leicestershire against Northamptonshire in his first match at Leicester in 1951 and another in his second against Derbyshire at Burton-on-Trent.

I showed this list with what I felt to be justifiable pride to a friend of mine, Michael Fordham, the well known statistician. He looked at me pityingly and said "My dear old lad, you have barely scratched the surface" and in short order came back to me with the following string of names – Ewart Astill, Sonny Avery, Wilf Barber, Gordon Barker, Les Berry, Hon. F. S. G. Calthorpe, W. A. Brown, A. W. Carr, Sam Coe, Bernard Constable, George Cox senior, A. J. Croom, Dai Davies, George Dawkes, E. W. Dawson, Ted Dexter, Desmond Eagar, George Emmett, C. B. Fry, R. A. Gale, George Geary, S. E. Gregory, J. Gunn, Arnold Hamer, Lord Hawke, A. Hearne, Clem Hill, Errol Holmes, Martin Horton, J. C. Hubble, E. Humphreys, D. R. Jardine, A. S. Kennedy, Ray Kilner, Billy Neale, Charlie Oakes, Sir T. C. O'Brien, Edgar Oldroyd, Jack Parker, Eddie Paynter, Bobby Peel, Winston Place, J. M. Read, R. R. Relf, D. W. Richardson, Jack Robertson, Water Robins, Neville Rogers, Eric Rowan, Bishop David Sheppard, A. Shipman, Reg Sinfield, Denis Smith, Ray Smith, Arthur Staples, Harold Stephenson, W. Storer, Jack Timms, Les Todd, Victor Trumper, J. Tunnicliffe, Clyde Walcott, Sir Pelham Warner, Everton Weekes, Alan Wharton, Bert Wolton, Stan Worthington and Norman Yardley. I lost a sheet or two of Michael Fordham's painstaking research so the list is not complete. It is, however, a grim enough catalogue. Of all this legion who could have swelled the ranks of US not one of THEM made less than 10,000 runs in first-class cricket. It is odd to reflect that of the 46 men who made a hundred instead of a duck on their first appearance in top-class cricket half of them made no further mark on the game and five never played at first-class level again.

We are tending perhaps to get too involved in the sheer mechanics of our theme.

There are many of cricket's best untold stories in the making of a duck. I remember one occasion when Yorkshire were playing Oxbridge. A wicket had fallen. Slowly gracefully from the pavilion emerged a slim willowly figure most beautifully attired – the next man in. His flannels could only have been cut in Savile Row; his boots were new, his pads spotless. On his head set at a carefully cultivated devil-may-care Beatty angle was a multicoloured cap. Clipped round his neck to protect his throat from the rude winds of early May which do not spare even university towns, was a silk scarf. On his way to the crease he played imaginary bowlers. With wristy cuts and flicks, perfectly timed drives, and daring late glances and hooks he despatched the imaginary ball to all parts of the ground.

The Yorkshire players watched his approach in silence. He eventually arrived at the wicket and looked all about him imperiously, like a king, come to his rightful throne. He took guard, and then spent a full minute making his block hole, shaping and patting it until it was to his satisfaction. Another look around the entire field – and he was ready to receive his first ball.

Freddie Trueman bowled it and knocked two of the three stumps clean out of the ground. As our young exquisite turned languidly and began to walk away, Freddie called to him sympathetically, "Bad luck, Sir, you were just getting settled in."

Makers of ducks have always been subject to the occupational hazard of being dropped but one of the unfairest dismissals from a team I personally encountered was down in Devon before the war. The captain of the side decided that a certain individual was failing to make runs because he was, in the skipper's choice of words, a bookworm. He wrote him a letter which began "I have decided to leave you out because it has come to my notice that midnight frequently finds you immersed in Jane Austen."

There can be mystery too in the making of a duck. One wet week-end when cricket was out of the question I played 24 frames of snooker at the Royal Hotel, Ashby-de-la-Zouch, with the late Jack Bartley, the Test Umpire.

In his playing days Jack had opened the bowling for Cheshire and in one Minor Counties fixture against Yorkshire Seconds he clean bowled the opposing captain, Col. Chichester-Constable, for a duck.

"I did it again in the second innings. The Colonel walked towards me on his way to the pavilion. As he drew level with me he grinned and looking over my shoulder addressed a greeting to a fellow called Shorthouse. The strange thing was that I do not recall a player of that name in either team. Now wasn't that odd?" said a puzzled Bartley.

The idea of writing a treatise on the making of a duck is not original. The late R. C.

Robertson-Glasgow penned one of his delightful and all too brief essays on the subject over a quarter of a century ago. In it he wrote this passage: "Even *Wisden* so rich in the scattered cypher, *Wisden* which has garnered cricket's yearly harvest, has left us to glean the 0s as best we may. They have to be picked out, like a few pearls from legions of oysters.

"True, we may read at rare intervals of whole teams shot out for 0, not even a bye flicked off the stomach past the stumper; and that is admittedly remarkable, even though, as we are apt to suspect, the outgoing side consisted of subnormal batsmen assailed by a crazy sergeant major who was bowling on a pitch of broken glass. Remarkable, yes; but not exclusive; for eleven 0s, even if one of them be perforce 0 not out, are ten too many; like eleven pies thrown by eleven comedians in one act."

Dear Crusoe, he took me under his wing when I was a fledgling cricket writer and I shall be eternally in his debt. How or when he first became Crusoe is a matter for historical research. Most of the evidence points to a day at The Parks in 1920 when Charles McGahey of Essex returning to the pavilion was asked by his skipper J. W. H. T. Douglas how he lost his wicket. McGahey replied "I was bowled out by an old —— I thought was dead, 2,000 years ago, called Robinson Crusoe."

It was in that year that Crusoe first played for Somerset under John Daniell who, at the end of the season said "Come again next summer, but don't wear that bloody straw hat."

What would Crusoe have thought about the Gillete Cup and the Player Sunday League? He would have liked them, I think. Certainly he would have entered into the spirit of the thing. But he would never have supported the throwing over of the three-day county match. "First-class cricket cannot be made just snappy. It is not a wisecrack, but an old and mellow story."

He intended to write again on the art, colour, drama, humour and heartbreak of making a duck but he never did. He gave me a few jottings on the subject once after we had dined together at a riverside hotel at Gravesend nearly 20 years ago – or perhaps it is over 20 years. "You might find them useful sometime when you have more experience and when you are less solemn about cricket," he said.

During that meal he showed me that a duck could be large and illustrious as well as an embarrassing spasm.

Miles Howell was long before my time but apparently he was playing for Surrey against Yorkshire at The Oval and Rhodes was bowling at his deadliest. Howell was just then at the top of his form, and he played the Yorkshire bowlers, mostly Rhodes, during forty-three mortal minutes, firmly and in the middle of the bat – for no runs. "Any spectator who entered the ground at any point in that innings and failed to observe the scoreboard might reasonably have thought that Howell was in the comfortable thirties or forties. But that ball would not pierce those fielders," said Crusoe. "And then he was run out, bravely answering a call from his rash partner. Run out nought; with the sweat of battle pouring from his forehead. As he remarked in the pavilion: 'Not a run; not even a little one, dammit; and I feel as if I'd sprinted to the House of Commons and back!'"

Rockley Wilson was master in charge of cricket at Winchester where he was on the staff for forty years. One day he grew mildly exasperated with a boy in the nets. This boy played across the ball and over the ball.

He played either side of it and going down on one knee to sweep played under it. Wilson who made a century in his maiden first-class match and came back out of club cricket to play for Yorkshire during school vacations in his forties said: "My dear boy, you must play one ball in the middle of your bat before you meet your Maker." This made such an impression on the boy that under Wilson's guiding hand he reached a stage when he could go to the wicket and make 15 or 20 runs every third or fourth innings.

So another promising recruit for US was lost even if he could never hope to aspire to THEM. It was a classic example of the inherent dangers of coaching. For half-way house in cricket is equivalent to the old fashioned conception of a fate worse than death. Crusoe knew that. I have before me as I write, some papers of his, yellowing a little now, and I quote again – "There are those who fancy that it is something to have scored 1 or 2 or some other disreputable and insignificant digit. They are wrong; it is nothing, or, rather, worse than 0. They have but enjoyed a span too short to show a profit, long enough to show their ineptitude.

"They have but puttered and poked and snicked in wretched incompleteness. No; give me the man who makes 0 and doesn't care. As numbers go, he has achieved nothing; but equally, because he has never started, he has left 0 unfinished."

Crusoe once whiled away a tedious train journey by compiling a list of innings of a Mr O. E. Jugg as unlikely a character as Tootling CC for whom he played. Jugg's place in the batting order at No. 10 was described as a singular promotion. Crusoe's scratch pad showed Jugg's previous six visits to the crease as:

1. v Gas, Light and Coke Company (Home) 0
   (3rd ball, snooted by a double bouncer)
2. v St Luke's Choir (Away) 0
   (without receiving a ball; fast asleep and run out by an old tenor)
3. v GPO (Home) 0
   (c and b by the head sorter)
4. v The Pirates (Home) 0
   (1st ball; shattered by a long hop)
5. v St Luke's Choir (Home) 0
   (2nd ball; LBW from behind)
6. v Gas, Light and Coke Company (Away) 0
   (1st ball; run out, after a quarrel)

Yes, Crusoe, who once said of his old friend and snicking partner Jim Bridges that they never made a century between them but they made a devil of a lot of them for other people, either bowling, or criticising from the pavilion, was *SYMPATICO* to all of US who have ever walked to the wicket with the air of men who have left lighted cigarettes in the dressing-room.

The great thing about US is that we wear our ducks like a row of medals but the other first-class lot are inclined to be terribly stuffy. Crusoe once said to one of THEM, "Ah, Prendergast, my dear fellow, how did you enjoy your duck at Lord's yesterday? I arrived just in time to see you in and out." Telling me this over coffee and cigars after that fondly remembered meal at Gravesend, Crusoe gave that great, triumphant bellow of laughter of his and said with the emphasis he did so well, "A brittle silence fell as if a bottle of the old and nutty had exploded in my pocket at a temperance rally." And off he went into another crockery shaking guffaw. What a wonderful man he was!

Gone but not forgotten. It could be said of him as of few others, "We, his fellows, loved him – and he made us laugh." What better epitaph could any man be given in this sad and sorry 20th century of ours?

Turning back to *Wisden* for a final rifling through of the batting records, I am convinced beyond a peradventure (whatever that phrase means) of the justice of my plan to be represented in this section of the Almanack. Look at the chaps who have made 35 or more centuries. There must be nearly a couple of hundred and that means there must be thousands who have made between 10 and 30 and probably millions who have made one or two. As for those who have scored their 50s and 60s it does not bear thinking about.

We would have it no other way for it gives US that warm inner glow that comes from belonging to an exclusive brotherhood. To make my point, permit me one final dip into Crusoe's cricket Thesaurus.

"The essence, the aristocracy of 0 is that it should be surrounded by large scores, that it should resemble the little silent bread-winner in a bus full of fat, noisy women. Indeed, when the years have fixed it in its place, so far from being merely the foil to jewels, it should itself grow, in the fond eye of memory, to the shape and stature of a gem."

That, as Mr Alf Garnett might say, is yer actual true philosophy of the duck.

THE MIDWINTER FILE [1971]

By Grahame Parker

A noted sportsman, Grahame Parker captained the Cambridge University XI in 1935 and appeared twice in the England [Rugby] XV, against Scotland and Ireland, in 1938. He also played county cricket for Gloucestershire before and after the last war.

W. E. Midwinter has a unique place in cricket history. He was Gloucestershire's first full-time professional, was the only cricketer to have played for Australia and England in Test Matches against each other, eight for Australia and four for England, and the first of the inter-hemisphere cricket commuters.

This is a piece of research that grew out of a reference in Haygarth's *Cricket Scores and Biographies*, Volume XIV, page 24: "He (Midwinter) was born in the Forest of Dean, near Cirencester". Throughout the last months of 1968, and during 1969, this reference grew into a file of correspondence and information an inch thick. The primary qualification in the early days of County Cricket was by birth and I felt sure the geographical inaccuracy concealed another piece of "Grace gamesmanship". I was wrong.

The cricket record books report that William Evans Midwinter was born on June 19, 1842. While England is on his death certificate, and Cirencester on his marriage certificate, there is much confusion over his place of birth. He himself told W.G. he was born in a village near Cirencester, but claims have been as diverse as Yorkshire, Gloucester, Melbourne, Bendigo, as well as Haygarth's "Cirencester in the Forest of Dean". Perhaps we should not read too much into these nineteenth century inconsistencies. The details on his birth certificate are clear enough, "born June 19, 1851, at St Briavels, Forest of Dean". His father, William John Midwinter, Farm Bailiff, of Clays Lane End, near Coleford, and his mother, Rebecca Evans, a daughter of William Evans, a farmer of the Lower Meend, St Briavels, were married at nearby St Paul's Church, Parkend by the Rev. Henry Poole on October 13, 1849. His father was born at Chedworth, near Cirencester and his mother at St Briavels.

Cirencester in the Cotswolds, 50 miles to the east of the Forest of Dean, is Midwinter country. Perhaps there was an itinerant streak in the father that was later to be strongly exhibited by the son, for there is no reference to William John Midwinter in the Forest censuses of 1841, 1851 and 1861.

We next hear of the Midwinters through a cricket reference to young William. They were in Australia at Sandhurst, present day Eaglehawk, on the Bendigo goldfields. The middle years of the last century saw much unemployment among the Forest of Dean coal miners, and many emigrated to the Colonies or tried their luck in gold rushes. Father Midwinter was first a gold miner and later a butcher.

William John Midwinter (38), gamekeeper, Rebecca Midwinter (36) and sons William (9), John (5) and daughter Jane (7), sailed from Liverpool on February 2, 1861, as unassisted passengers in the *Red Jacket* – 2,035 tons. Her Master was William Billing, she carried a crew of 65, 216 passengers and a cargo of sundries. She arrived at Melbourne on April 24.

William grew into a tall, rough, athletic boy at Sandhurst, and began a lifelong association with H. F. (Harry) Boyle, who at 15 was already showing the cricket skill and organising ability that was to make him famous as an Australian cricketer and administrator. He was playing for Sandhurst and young "Mid" for the California Gully School. Boyle formed a club of young cricketers at Sydney Flat, two miles from Sandhurst. There were only thirteen of them, but they cleared and levelled a patch of bush among the mine dumps, and it was here that Boyle, Midwinter and many other famous Victorians played their first cricket. The Midwinters lived five miles away at California

Gully in a wooden, stone slab floored shack, separated from a piece of open ground by a stone wall. The boy helped his father on his butcher's rounds but they found time to practice together here and, as with the Graces in their Downend orchard, it was the dog who did most of the fielding! In the 1890s the area became a cricket ground, appropriately named Midwinter's Oval. The shack was still standing but had been demolished progressively for firewood. Even today some rough open ground still remains, much of it occupied by two tennis courts and bungalows.

There is an unverified report that when still quite young he made 256 in an innings. The first definite reference in his cricket career is the fact that during the 1864-65 season, young Midwinter left the Sydney Flat Cricket Club for Bendigo United and although only 13, held his place in the senior club. In 1870 the Carlton Cricket Club travelled the sixty miles to Bendigo and were so impressed with Midwinter and Boyle that they invited them to play in Melbourne. During the following season they both played in a single wicket match for the Bendigo VI that surprisingly defeated Charles Bannerman's New South Wales IV. In 1873 Midwinter's name first appeared with the Melbourne CC.

W.G. took a team to Australia for the 1873-74 season. Although the party included the recently married Mrs Grace and three other Gloucestershire cricketers, G. F. Grace, J. A. Bush and W. R. Gilbert, it could not have been a happy tour. Towards the end the Englishmen were extremely unpopular with the Australians, who felt they were being fleeced, particularly in payment to W.G. It was almost twenty years before he could be enticed back. Midwinter played against them twice. Before Christmas 1873, in a game at Melbourne that drew 40,000 spectators in three days, he was caught Bush, bowled Grace, for 7. It was the second match the following March, when amid great excitement, he bowled both W.G. and G. F. Grace, that no doubt activated W.G.'s shrewd and fertile imagination.

Midwinter played his first of nine inter-state games in 1875. He was now 6 ft. $2\frac{1}{2}$ in. and 14 stone, a hard hitting batsman, a medium pace round arm spin bowler, a fine outfielder with a strong arm, one of the best quarter milers in Victoria and a fine shot and billiards player, variously nicknamed the Sandhurst Infant or the Bendigo Giant. He played in the first All Australia v All England game in Melbourne during the James Lillywhite tour of 1876-77. Spofforth, the great Australian fast bowler, refused to play in the game because his usual wicket-keeper, W. L. Murdoch had not been selected. Surprisingly England were defeated for the first time in an even-handed game against Australia. Haygarth blamed the travelling and the "high living" to which the tourists were subjected, but Charles Bannerman's first innings, 165 not out, had set up the Australian victory. Midwinter's match analysis was 6 for 101. He had now proved he was an international cricketer and decided to try his luck in England.

There is some confusion over his first journey back to England. An article written in *Cricket*, January 27, 1891, just after his death, reports his arrival at Plymouth on Tuesday, May 5, 1877. The next day the ship disembarked at London and with a rough diamond friend, Denmark Jack, he was on his way to The Oval where W.G. was playing.

In fact he sailed from Melbourne on April 21, 1877 in the S.S. *Durham*, Master F. Anderson. She was one of a line of steam and sailing ships operated by Money Wigram & Sons of Blackwell Yard, London, and on this journey she carried 246 passengers amongst whom is listed "W. Midwinter, male, 25 years, cricketer, English".

W.G. was probably expecting him, for he soon had him playing in his United South of England XI at Birmingham, Holbeck and Barrow-in-Furness. The Gloucestershire minutes of 1877 make no reference to his arrival with the County, nor do they record his departure in 1882. He played in the combined Yorkshire/Gloucestershire team which drew with a Rest of England XI at Lord's on July 17, but his first full Gloucestershire appearance was in one of the most famous games in the County's history when England were beaten at The Oval by five wickets. Midwinter's contribution was a significant 7 for 35 and 4 for 46 in the two innings. W.G. took him in hand and added a defensive dimension to his aggressive batting. This was prominently evident during the Yorkshire match later in the season, where he saved the day with a four-hour 68. A collection was taken during his innings and Mrs Grace presented him with £15. This happened to be another of those Grace testimonial games. With brotherly solicitude, E.M. raised the gate charge from 6d. to 1/- without informing his committee. Later in the season Gloucestershire beat Nottinghamshire in one of the Cheltenham Festival games early on the third day. The County then played a local XI. With broomsticks they made 299, E. M. Grace 104, Midwinter 58, to which Cheltenham, using bats, replied with 50 for 2 before time ran out. The County had been Champions in 1876 and also again – for the last time since! – in 1877.

1878 saw the first Australian tour of England. They arrived with eleven players and picked up Midwinter in this country. He had already played for the United South of England, an England XI and England v MCC before joining the Australians at Trent Bridge at May 20. They lost by an innings and 14 runs but he batted through their second innings for 16 not out in two and a half hours. The next game was the first Australian visit to Lord's. It was completed in 105 runs between 12 and 6.20 p.m. on the first day! MCC 33 and 19, Australia 41 and 12 for 1. Midwinter was top scorer with 10.

The Australian press reports of a following game against the Gentlemen at Princes, record an interesting comment that the "so-called Gentlemen Cricketers Messrs W. G. Grace and W. R. Gilbert received the sum of £60 for their services, and when Mr Conway raised an objection to it, it was asserted that W. G. Grace, G. F. Grace and W. R. Gilbert were invariably paid for playing".

And so we come to a fateful day. On Monday, June 20 the Australians were playing at Lord's. They had lost the toss and had been put in to bat. Their opening pair, Bannerman and Midwinter, were padding up, unaware that a storm was approaching them through the cloudless summer sky. On the other side of London at The Oval, W. G. Grace had found his Gloucestershire team a man short. The Champion, 6 ft. 2 in., wicketkeeper J. A. Bush, 6 ft. 2½ in. and the Coroner, E. M. Grace, 5 ft. 8 in. – to do the talking, no doubt – burst into Lord's, "persuaded" Midwinter he should be playing for Gloucestershire, bundled him into the waiting carriage and were gone. Much later Midwinter regretted what had been done, but before they had reached the Edgware Road he must have wondered how fate had dropped him into that hot, uncomfortable seat. The dust had hardly settled in the St John's Wood Road when an Australian posse set off in pursuit of the Gloucestershire hijackers. In the posse were the Australian Manager, John Conway, Midwinter's friend, Harry Boyle and David Gregory, the captain. An "unhappy altercation" took place at The Oval gates where W.G., in front of bystanders, called the Australians "a damn lot of sneaks".

The Australians were deeply hurt. Letters of increasing acidity passed between them and the County during the following weeks. The first was despatched by John Conway on June 22 from the Horse Shoe Hotel, Tottenham Court Road, and was read at the Gloucestershire Committee meeting of July 1: "Unless Mr W. G. Grace apologises for his insulting behaviour . . . we shall be compelled to erase the Gloucestershire fixture from our programme". The Committee drafted a reply regretting this fact, but added "Mr W. G. Grace did not for a moment intend his remarks to apply to Mr Conway and Mr Boyle." This brought a stinging reply from David Gregory at the Albion Hotel, Manchester. They still refused to play at Bristol. "I may state that he (W.G.) publicly insulted the whole of the Australian Eleven in most unmistakable language." He now introduced for the first time the initial cause of the storm ". . . moreover we are averse to meeting Midwinter, whose defection from us we regard as a breach of faith."

The long Gloucestershire reply tried to spread some oil on the disturbed waters, but set out their version of the Midwinter affair:

> Midwinter is a Gloucestershire man, he returned to England last year and played in all the matches which were played by Gloucestershire after his arrival in England. This year he has already played in the Colts match at Bedminster and had promised Mr Grace to play in all our County matches. This engagement of his was well known all over England, and can hardly fail to have been known to you. Mr Bush discussed this

with Mr Conway at Princes on Monday and Tuesday, the 17th and 18th of June. With the knowledge of Midwinter's engagement staring you in the face you attempted to induce him to break his promise, desert his County, and play for you by offering him a much larger sum that we could afford to pay him. Such proceedings are to say the least uncommon and go far, in our judgment, to palliate Mr Grace's stormy language at The Oval.

The Australians would not leave it there. In a letter from Leicester dated July 15, David Gregory still refused to bring his team to Bristol, but was "willing to overlook Midwinter's defection though they consider they have first claim to him, as before he came to England he asked Mr Conway to keep a place for him in the team. We started from Australia relying upon his joining us."

E. M. Grace, as Secretary, dutifully transcribed all those letters in the Minutes Book, but the page continuing W.G.'s eventual letter of apology contains only the heading "Mr W. G. Grace wrote a letter apologising to David Gregory and the Australians"! After a long search the contents of this letter came to light in an Australian report of the tour:

The Cottage,
Kingswood Hill,
Bristol.
July 21st.

Dear Sir,

I am sorry that my former expression of regret to the Australian cricketers has not been considered satisfactory. Under the circumstances, and without going further into the matter, I wish to let by-gones be by-gones. I apologise again, and express my extreme regret to Conway, Boyle and yourself, and through you to the Australian cricketers, that in the excitement of the moment I should have made use of unparliamentary language to Mr Conway. I can do no more but assure you that you will meet a hearty welcome and a good ground at Clifton.

Yours truly,
W. G. Grace.

The matter closed with W.G.'s apology. The Australians received the warmest hospitality at Bristol. Midwinter did not play against them, he had a split thumb. The Australians, with Spofforth in full blast, thrashed the County. It was Gloucestershire's first ever defeat on a home ground.

Midwinter was paid £56 for his seven games in 1878. The Gloucestershire Minutes report that he was perfectly satisfied with this arrangement. He played in all the 1879 games at the same rate of £8 a match. He had the chance of the Middlesex or Lancashire game at Clifton for his benefit and unluckily chose the latter, which was ruined by rain. It was proposed he should receive £100 as some compensation for his ruined benefit. An amendment was carried that he should receive a further £100 at the end of the 1883 season. He did not accept the bait. E.M.G. had to send this sharp reminder:

Dear Sir,

The Committee are very much surprised and annoyed that you have taken no notice of my letter to you in which I said the Committee had passed the following resolution:

"That W. Midwinter be paid the sum of £100 at the end of the season and £100 at the end of 1883 provided he plays for Gloucestershire when required to do so".

I am, yours faithfully,
Edward Mills Grace.

The reply came two days later:

Prince of Wales Hotel.
31st May 1880

To the Committee of the Gloucestershire County Cricket Club.

Gentlemen,

I beg to return you my sincere thanks for the very liberal sum of money you have kindly agreed to give me, and also to thank the Gentlemen of Gloucester CCC for the very kind treatment I have received from them since I have had the honour of playing for them.

Your obedient servant,
W. Midwinter.

In 1880 he joined the MCC staff of bowlers at Lord's. During this season he made his highest score, 103, and only century, for Gloucestershire against Surrey at Cheltenham. The Australians were again in this country and he played against them at Clifton.

He commuted between England and Australia from 1880-1882 to play six successive seasons of cricket. After completing the 1880 season for the County he returned to Australia. He sailed from London on September 29, in the *Lusitania*. The passenger list refers to him as W. Midwinter, 29 years. He travelled back to England in the same ship from Melbourne, April 26, 1881, now listed as W. Midwinter, Gent. He was in Shaw's 1881-82 England tour of Australia and played in four Tests. Back to England for 1882, he suddenly gave up his MCC bowling appointment although he had recently taken part in a quite remarkable stand for the MCC Club and Ground against Leicestershire. During his stay at the wicket the score rose from 19 for two to 472 for three in five and a half hours. He scored 187 and Barnes 266 and it is reported that he never once lost count of their joint scores. At the end of 1882 he played his last game for Gloucestershire at Clifton against – the Australians! He returned home with Murdoch's triumphant Ashes team and stood umpire for them in their games in the United States.

On his arrival home he claimed he had ceased to be a professional cricketer and "considered himself an Australian to the heart's core" and "objected to being called an Anglo Australian". These patriotic sentiments failed to impress the hard-hearted Australian critics and Censor in the Sydney Mail asked: "Are the cricketers of the Colony, and especially those of Victoria, to submit to another season of vagueness from this very slippery cricketer? One day he is an Australian and the next day an English player." All was quickly forgiven and he was soon in action for Australia against the Hon. Ivo Bligh's 1882-83 touring team. In March 1883 he was presented with a gold watch for his 92 not out for Victoria against England at Melbourne.

He returned to England with the Australians in 1884, played for them in three Tests and against Gloucestershire at Clifton and Cheltenham, on both occasions bowled out by his old friend, Woof. He was to play two more Tests for Australia against Arthur Shrewsbury's team in 1886-87. In all he played eight Tests for Australia against England and four for England against Australia.

After six years of association with the Gloucestershire amateurs it was a more refined Midwinter who finally returned to Australia than the one who had set out so hopefully in 1877.

He married Elizabeth Frances McLaughlan at St Peter's Church, Melbourne, on June 4, 1883. Her father, a carrier from Paisley, Scotland, and her mother May Downing of Kilkenny, Ireland, were married at Kyneton, Victoria, January 13, 1857.

After an unsuccessful attempt at stockbroking, he became landlord of the Clyde Hotel which still stands at the corner of Elgin and Cadogen Streets in Melbourne. Mr Christopher McCaffin, now 92, remembers as a boy being chased away from the horse drinking trough by the tall, fair-haired Billy Midwinter. He continued to take an active part in the affairs of the Carlton Club, setting a fine example to the Club's young cricketers.

His keen perception and his humorous entertaining conversation were held in high esteem. He was invited to tour England with the 1888 team, but declined on business grounds. He had moved to the Victoria, Bourke Street, but his eyesight was beginning to fail and he retired from active cricket.

The family bereavements that were to break his heart struck whilst they were living at Victoria. First his ten month old daughter, Elsie, died of pneumonia on November 22, 1888; next, August 23, 1889, his wife Elizabeth, of apoplexy and, finally, on November 2, three year old Albert Ernest.

He loved his family dearly and these sudden domestic tragedies were more than he could bear. In June 1890, whilst staying with his sister and brother-in-law, Mr and Mrs H. Hicks, at Sandhurst, he became so violent that he was removed to the Bendigo Hospital and, on August 14, to the Kew Asylum in Melbourne. He became paralysed from the waist down. Happily one of his brief periods of consciousness on November 21 coincided with a visit from his old friend Harry Boyle, on his return from the Australian 1890 tour of England. He recognised him and spoke admiringly of W.G., Arthur Shrewsbury and of Woof. He was delighted to hear that his old County had twice beaten Nottinghamshire. He died at 11 a.m. on Wednesday, December 3, 1890, aged 39. The funeral took place on Friday, December 5, attended by a great many cricketers and sportsmen among whom was a Gloucestershire representative, W. O. Tonge, who had played with Midwinter in two County matches at Clifton College during August 1880.

He was buried in the Roman Catholic compound of Melbourne General Cemetery beside his wife and children. The grave, No. L286, is difficult to find, it has no tombstone and the area surrounding it is untended.

The last word, as the first, belongs to Haygarth, in his biography of Midwinter, Vol. XIV: "May the death of no other cricketer who has taken part in great matches be like his!"

A LIFETIME WITH SURREY [1972]

STEALING SINGLES WITH JACK HOBBS

By Andrew Sandham

Sixty years, which is the total time spanned by my career with Surrey County Cricket Club as player, coach and scorer, is a very big slice out of a life-time, but I have no regrets about it. Whatever the differences in method, tactics and so on between my day and the present, I am glad that I played when I did, for I consorted with some of the "greats" and we all enjoyed the game. Cricket has been good to me in that I have met so many friends and have been enabled to visit so many countries which I would otherwise never have seen.

My keeness on cricket began at an early age. After leaving school, I turned out for my father's club, Streatham United, on Streatham Common at the age of 16. A Mr Raphael, father of J. E. Raphael, who played cricket for Oxford and Surrey, and also got a Blue for Rugby and represented England in nine Internationals between 1902 and 1906, used to watch our team occasionally and he mentioned my name to the Surrey County authorities. As a result I had annual trials at The Oval nets for three years. I remember that the first coach to see me was the famous Bobby Abel, a kindly man. Then E. H. D. Sewell became coach and later on, in 1946, when I, too, took up the position of coach, I looked up an old coaching report-book to see what he had said about me. It read: "A fair bat and a promising bowler," but I was rarely called upon to bowl in first-class cricket.

When 18 I went to Mitcham CC and a Surrey Committeeman, a Mr W. W. Thompson, spoke about me to the then County Secretary, the late W. Findlay. In December 1910, Mr Findlay strongly advised me not to become a professional cricketer; but I told him that I was sure that, if given the chance, I would make good. So I joined the County staff in 1911 at a wage of 25s a week – one golden soverign and two half-crowns.

I think my winter pay was £1 per month! But I was happy, though when I watched Tom Hayward, Jack Hobbs, Ernie Hayes and Co., I thought I would never reach their high standards. There were, if I recall, 30 players on the bowling staff, which meant that, quite apart from the first eleven, one had to be very good to get a place in the second team.

In those days when the first team were playing away, and even if a second eleven match was taking place at The Oval, members came to the nets for practice (half an hour a time). This meant that the "left overs" were continually bowling at them and at the end of the day were rather tired. We had a "kitty" and sometimes we picked up eight or ten shillings each, which at that time was a fair sum.

I was allowed to turn out for Mitcham on Saturdays and in four consecutive matches I scored a century – for Mitcham, the Young Players of Surrey, Surrey Club and Ground and Surrey second eleven against Wiltshire. As a result, I was given a game for the county eleven against Cambridge University and, in my very first first-class match, I scored 53. There was at that time a public house with a flat roof over on the gas-works side of The Oval, with six or seven tiered seats for customers who could see cricket for nothing. As the pubs were then open all day long and the beer was both cheaper and stronger, the customers by the afternoon got a bit "under the influence" and frequently gave us "the bird". I got it on my first appearance and I thought it rather hard, for I naturally wanted to do well and took only two hours for my 53. All this, too, from people who were not in the ground!

We lesser lights had to put in our own practice with the coach at 10 a.m. and then wait for any visiting players and our own first eleven players who came out for a knock and bowl to them. I remember rushing to bowl against G. L. Jessop, but after he played "forward" and the ball narrowly missed my head, I had sense enough to bowl at his legs.

Soon after my "baptism" against Cambridge, I was as usual bowling at the nets when, ten minutes before the start of a match with Lancashire, I was told that I was playing, Tom Hayward having dropped out. This was such a shock that I nearly dropped, too. In those days there was a telegraph-office on the ground and having seen the batting order, I sent my father a wire telling him the news. My father, who was a Lancashire man, had taken a few hours off from work and come to The Oval, so that he missed my telegrams. He told me that he was sitting in the crowd, but had not got a score-card. So he turned to the man next to him and asked: "Who is this lad coming in to bat?" He was shaken when he was told: "It's a second eleven lad named Sandham." I scored 60 and my father said that after I was out he left for home. I remember being nearly run out at 49 by the splendid batsman, R. H. Spooner. Come to think of it, it seems rather silly to risk a run out at 49 or 99.

In this connection, I have often been asked how Jack Hobbs and I managed to steal so many sharp runs. I guess I must have run hundreds for him, for I never called him for one! As a matter of fact, he used not to call, for I knew from his push-stroke to the off that he wanted to run. I was always a yard or so down the pitch after the ball had been delivered and as I was rather fast between wickets, he knew I would make it. I remember Herbert Sutcliffe talking to me after being in with Jack for the first time about "these short runs". I said: "Well, I know when he wants a quick run without calling, so I run." Herbie said something to the effect that he was not going to run any; they had got to stop; but I noticed that he found that he had to when coupled with Jack in Tests – and a jolly good job they made of it, too.

Incidentally I read in a newspaper article last summer the view that "Hobbs and Sutcliffe never took a chance with their running". I cannot agree with this. The fact was that, like Jack and myself this pair developed such an understanding that, though the element of risk remained, it was reduced to a minimum. I wondered at the time how the author of the article, who was born less than two years before the close of Jack's playing career, could have written with such authority. I also heard of a retired former player who said in a speech at a club dinner that "Hobbs and Sandham wouldn't have made the runs they did in these days." Well, perhaps I would not have done, who knows; but to say that Jack would not is a bit much! I looked up the person concerned in *Wisden* and I see from his birthday that he was 12 years of age when Jack retired in 1934. I fancy that, being the great batsman he was, Jack would have coped.

In 1913, I made my first first-class century, 196 against Sussex at The Oval. Curiously enough, I hit the last of my 107 centuries also against Sussex, at Hove at the age of 47 in my final game before retiring.

Many people have asked if any particular person taught me. The fact is that I must have had a natural aptitude for batting and I always watched the established players. I was always on the players balcony to see Tom Hayward and Jack Hobbs open the innings for Surrey. Tom was my idol then, though later on he frightened me, for when I was twelfth man away from home and he had made a good score, he would bark at me to get him a whisky and soda. I would say "Yes, sir," but was afraid to ask him for the money. My own fault, I suppose, but Tom had many a whisky and soda on me! He was the senior professional and "well in" with the various captains Surrey had, and what he said went.

The 1914-18 War finished Tom's career and I was destined to take his place in 1919. I wonder how many centuries Hobbs would have made during that break in first-class cricket, for I once asked him when he considered he was at his best and he said: "Before the 1914 War broke out." My association with him was broken for a time in 1921 when he was taken ill with appendicitis during a Test at Leeds against Australia. That season was a bad one for English batsmen, who had no experience against fast bowlers of the pace of Jack Gregory and Ted McDonald. What a pair for any opening batsmen to face! Incidentally, I consider that McDonald had the most graceful action I have ever seen in a fast bowler. As a result of Jack's illness, many openers were tried for England and I think about 30 men turned out for the country that year. I got my chance in the last Test at The Oval, going in at No. 5 and making 21. Being an opener, I found it rather nerve-racking to have to sit and wait until five minutes past six to take my turn at the wicket.

Odd things stick in the memory. I recall in 1921 an amateur named T. J. Moloney, who bowled under-arm, appearing in one of our trial matches. Well, he was bowling against Jack, who jokingly advanced down the pitch, only to miss and be stumped by Herbert Strudwick. A few weeks later "Struddy" said that was the worst thing he ever did, for later on Moloney played in one or two county matches and, as his mode of bowling was down the leg-side, "Struddy" experienced many narrow escapes from batsmen swinging their bats and just missing his head. "Struddy's" friend was included in the side when we went to Trent Bridge for the Whitsun Bank Holiday match, for which in those days the ground was always full before the start.

Nottinghamshire batted and after a while Moloney was put on to bowl. His was a new Surrey name to the crowd and they were curious. Well, you never heard such a howl of laughter as that which followed his first delivery. When quiet was restored and just before Moloney bowled his next ball, a man just behind me on the boundary shouted: "Keep him on, Fender. I'm going home to fetch my old woman." In actual fact, Moloney had the last laugh, for I think he took three wickets for eleven runs, all caught on the boundary.

We then went to Leicester and in due course Moloney was brought on. He bowled one ball down the leg-side wide enough for Lord, the opening batsman, to turn right round and try to hit it to the fine-leg boundary. He hit it all right, but straight to the tummy of Strudwick, who caught it as much in self-defence as anything. After that game, "Struddy" said: "If Moloney plays again, I won't", so we never saw that bowler again.

In reference to under-arm bowlers, there was one, G. H. Simpson-Hayward of Worcestershire, who was good enough to be chosen to go with the MCC to South Africa. A tall, very strong man with powerful fingers, he could spin the ball either way. The following season, when Surrey were playing Worcestershire, there was talk in our dressing-room about how to deal with him. "Struddy" said: "Well, I know which way the ball will turn, for I kept to him in South Africa." When "Struddy" went in, he was out first ball – lbw to a full-pitch!

I was a member of the 1922-23 MCC team to South Africa where at that time cricket was played on matting wickets, there being no grass pitches as now. Coming out from grass pitches, we took a long time to get used to the matting, but Jack Russell did very well and he made two separate hundreds in the last Test at Durban, a feat the more remarkable as he was far from well during that match. We were captained by one of the nicest men I played with, F. T. Mann.

In 1924-25 I was honoured again, being in the team to Australia. Though I scored a good many runs on the tour, my Test record read thus: lbw, caught on the leg-side, played on and, finally, run out. The only time I made two centuries in the same match was when I got 137 and 104 at Sydney against New South Wales during that trip. MCC were captained by A. E. R. Gilligan and he again led the side when I went to India with MCC in 1926. We played 32 matches and I missed only four of them. That was a tiring business, for there was no flying then and India was not divided, so that there were long train journeys. Nevertheless, because of this, I probably saw more of India than many people living there.

After India came a visit to the West Indies under the Hon. F. S. G. Calthorpe. I understood that the West Indies asked if MCC could send some of the older England players and Wilfred Rhodes, George Gunn and the late Joe Hardstaff (as umpire and baggage-man) were in the party. Our first Test was at Barbados on the fastest pitch I ever batted on, a view shared by the "veterans" I have mentioned. I remember the first "bouncer" I received from Learie Constantine and though I did not mind fast bowlers, I was a bit lucky to get away with this one, for I mistimed it and just cleared short-leg. Other "bouncers", which came frequently, I let go!

Meanwhile George Gunn, then 47 or 48 years old, who opened with me, put out his tongue at Learie every time he bowled him a "bouncer". George made a modest score and left me and the others to deal with an infuriated fast bowler, thoroughly roused in front of his own poeple! Over the years I have enquired of players who subsequently visited the West Indies how they found the pitch in Barbados. Their reply has been: "It may have been fast in your time. It isn't now."

Why are there no fast pitches in England today? In my early days it was agreed that the Leyton pitch and that at Taunton were the fastest in the country and allowed fast bowlers and batsmen who like fast bowling to come into their own. Nowadays fast bowlers seem to get little reward for their skills and energy. In last season's Tests with Pakistan and India, they bowled with the new ball and then gave way to the spinners, who operated from then till the end of the innings. Surely at the start of a match the batsmen and fast bowlers are entitled to expect a fast pitch to play on if there has been no rain about.

Reverting to the West Indies tour, in the last Test – also the final match of the tour – England scored 849 and 272 for nine and the West Indies 286 and 408 for five. Then it rained for, I think, two days and the game was abandoned as a draw. It was in this match that I made my highest score ever, 325; but I would not have done so but for Joe Hardstaff, who was umpiring. I started with sore toes and after reaching 100 I said to Joe: "I'm off now." But he said: "No, you stay here and talk to me. I don't know anyone out here."

Starting next day at 150 not out, I duly got to 200 and then told Joe: "I'm going now," but he always found an excuse. This time it was: "There's a new ball due. See that off." Or else there was an interval due. Anyway, by tea-time on the second day I had scored about 250 and somebody had been looking up the record by an Englishman in the West Indies. It was around 260 and Joe said "Stay here and beat that." Having managed to do so, I asked: "Are you satisfied now?" and he replied: "No, go on and make it 300" – and that's how I made my biggest score! This was all very well, but whenever a wicket fell at the other end, a sprightly newcomer came in and ran me off my feet. One of them was Les Ames, who made 149, and he was no slouch between wickets.

The following winter I went to South Africa with A. P. F. Chapman's MCC team, but unfortunately, after two matches, I was involved in a car accident – about which I knew nothing, for I was looking out of the back window at the time – and played no more on the tour. This was a considerable misfortune for the side, for it meant the loss of an opener.

I visited The Oval only occasionally in 1971, but I did go there on the last day when Glamorgan were the visitors and Surrey were trying to get another six points to win the Championship. At one time I saw a West Indian and a Pakistani batting for Glamorgan and a Pakistani bowling to them, and I thought: "Where do the young lads in the various county second elevens come in?" Mind you, I have nothing against imported cricketers, either white or black, and over the years I enjoyed playing against their countrymen. But what must county coaches think when they have a promising youngster ripe for the first eleven, an imported player is invited and the lad loses his chance? If young English cricketers are to be encouraged, surely there should be a limit to importations and I am glad this has now been done.

Another thing. Bowling tactics have changed from my early days. The advent of "in-swing" cut out off-driving and cutting, so that on-side play became the main method of scoring and drives through the covers became few and far between. This, with brave fielders standing in very close at short-leg, coupled with slower pitches, has cramped batting and no doubt bored spectators.

Fielding, I think may be better than in my time – maybe because we played till later in life and were not termed veterans at 39 or 40. It must, however, be remembered that we had to chase the ball to the far-distance boundaries, for the 75-yards boundary was not then the vogue. I remember before the 1914 War, when I was in and out of the county side, I played in a game against Oxford University at The Oval. In those days three of four of the eleven were rested for such matches and the likes of me given the chance. Tom Rushby had asked for a rest but was refused and, no doubt fed-up, did not try too hard when put on to bowl. I was at mid-on when he bowled from the Vauxhall end of a pitch well over on the gasometer side. The other boundary was a very long way away and when Tom was hit to the deep I chased the ball, thinking: "I wonder how many these lively young men have run." In fact they ran six! I had scarcely regained my position at mid-on than I was off against next ball to the same place, and again they ran six. Slightly annoyed with Tom and also out of breath, I had to pursue the next ball in the same direction though they only ran five that time! It was on my third journey that the Secretary, Mr Findlay, looked out of his office window. Next morning he sent for me and said chidingly that he was surprised to see me not running very fast – though he did apologise when I pointed out that I had chased the two previous balls while twelve runs were scored! I think this makes clear that the old-time boundaries were very long on most grounds and one had to be a tremendous thrower to get the ball back to the wicket-keeper. At present, with a fast out-field, fielders possess little chance of cutting off the four. This is a pity, because there are few things better in the game than the sight of a speedy out-fielder after the ball and picking it up near the ring. Of the many fast out-fielders of my day, I would say that Johnny Arnold, of Hampshire, was the best Englishman. He also had a fine throw.

I remember, too, those two great Australian outfieders in 1921, namely, "Nip" Pellew and J. M. Taylor. They were very fast and must have saved hundreds of runs on that tour.

Surrey in the end took the Championship last season, though I must say that I do not feel altogether happy that they got home over Warwickshire simply because they won more matches. A clear-cut points margin would have been more satisfactory all round. In the same way, I think Worcestershire's success in the Player League leaves something to be desired, for they got there by a minute fraction of a run per over averaged over the whole season. This seemed to me to be a bit rough on Essex, who scored the same number of points, even if it is in accordance with the rules of the competition. If two counties finish equal on points at the top of the table, would it not be better to have a play-off match?

COMPTON'S RECORD SEASON [1972]

IT HAPPENED 25 YEARS AGO

By Basil Easterbrook

The cricket season of 1947 came to us like a late October day of golden sunshine just before the setting in of a dark, dreary Northern winter from which at times there seemed no escape. In the quarter of a century which has followed we have seen cricket in decline.

Before the 1960s had run their course recognised England batsmen like Cowdrey and Graveney barely topped 1,000 runs for a whole season's endeavours without causing many eyebrows to be raised. On reflection, this was perhaps not to be wondered at, for those most closely connected with first-class cricket were kept occupied with rows and wrangles embracing politics, colour, the seeming impossibility of the creation of fast, true pitches, the change in public tastes; the apparent determination of first-class players to live in a cloud cuckoo land of their own devising.

The game which above all other human pastimes has inspired noble thoughts and words in profusion, has been invaded and pervaded by the general bitchiness which for all the technological advances made in a breathtakingly short space of time is, alas, the accepted pattern for living in the second half of the twentieth century. Adventure, boldness and joy had largely gone from the game. Teams are more concerned with stopping the other lot doing anything than winning themselves. There was a term for this when I was a boy. It was dog in the manger. When the spirit grows mean and over cautious inevitably performance suffers in direct ratio and this is precisely what has happened in cricket.

It helps to explain why Australian sides technically no better than England's and in some respects often not as good, have in the past twenty years survived series after series when they should have been beaten into the earth. Sunday Leagues and knock-out competitions, splendid in their way, are only palliatives not cures. If the first-class game becomes extinct the Sunday League would immediately have identical status with the long established Saturday Leagues of the North and Midlands. We shall be a nation of club cricketers as well as a nation of shopkeepers and shop stewards.

The crowd pulling power of the Sunday League, the Cavaliers, the Gillette Cup, comes from the fact that the players are first-class from a background of three-day and five-day cricket. Robertson-Glasgow put it neatly when he tried to show the impossibility of always concentrating three days cricket into one – "It is as if you approached a famous opera singer and said 'See here, madam, we are going to cut the opera from three acts to one and we want you to sing a lot faster and a lot louder to make up for the other two'."

The first-class complex concerns only 17 teams and no more than 200 players are involved at any one time. If ways and means to do this cannot be found in an island of over 50,000,000 inhabitants then it is time we stopped talking nonsense about British ingenuity and all the other qualities we pride ourselves on including a sense of history, and encouraging of all the arts and crafts known to mankind.

Of course, one likes to see cricket played against the background of a big crowd rather than a sparsely filled or virtually empty ground, but this is beside the point. First-class cricket has never been a game for a mass following and I say that in no derogatory sense. The English climate and personal economics have always made it virtually impossible that this should be so.

Nevertheless, first-class cricket is something which should always be there. The interest in a Test Match is great enough for the telephone service to provide a special number for people to ring who want to know the state of the game. That one fact alone is enough to justify the survival of the first-class game as it stands.

Cricket may have several ills but you do not cure a patient by killing him off. It is a change of heart we need rather than a change of system, for if we scrap the system which permits our best players to perform on their terms instead of being wound up like clockwork toys for over 40 overs then we sell the pass to days that are over and done. There will be no records like Compton's 3,816 runs and 18 centuries in 1947 to aim at because there will be no opportunity for any aiming to be done.

One of these years we may get another glorious summer of weather like we did in 1947 and if we do I hope our contemporary players will answer the warmth of the sun on their backs the way the boys did then. Walter Keeton, George Emmett, Jack Crapp and Denis Brookes all made six centuries, Leslie Todd, Joe Hardstaff, and Leslie Ames seven, George Cox eight, Winston Place ten. Then came Hutton and Washbrook with eleven each, Jack Robertson and Bill Edrich twelve each and far above them all on some dizzy, improbable Parnassus – Compton with eighteen.

Compton's Annus Mirabilis began with no real hint that it would be that. He made 73 and 7 for the MCC against a somewhat experimental Yorkshire side who were soundly beaten by 163 runs at Lord's on May 6. A drawn game with Surrey followed and Compton in two useful innings for MCC contributed 52 and 34. Joining Middlesex the following day, he did little with the bat in two matches, the first of which was won by Somerset by one wicket in what will always be remembered as Maurice Tremlett's game. The second against Gloucestershire was won by Middlesex in two days by an innings and 178 runs. Compton's three innings in those games were 6, 25 and 22. Compton had so far played all his cricket at Lord's and when Middlesex headed for Birmingham and their first away game Compton stayed at headquarters to help MCC beat the South Africans by 158 runs. Lindsay Tuckett got him for 18 in the first innings and caught him in the second off Ossie Dawson when Denis needed just three more runs for a hundred after a typical display of free cutting and driving.

Compton had got the taste and he took apart first the bowling of Worcestershire and then Sussex, the next two visitors to Lord's. Going in second wicket down he took out his bat for 88 in a total of 207 and in the second after a stand of 118 in eighty minutes with Bill Edrich, went on to 112 before Dick Howarth bowled him. Rain caused a long hold up on the last day but Middlesex claimed the extra half hour and Worcestershire's last two wickets to win by 234.

Whitsun brought perfect weather and 46,000 paying spectators to Lord's for the two days the game lasted. Walter Robins took the extra half hour on the Whit Monday and Middlesex scored the 21 runs they needed from their second innings without loss. Of the 380 Middlesex made in their first innings Compton scored 110 before Charlie Oakes bowled him, and his running mate all down the length of that glistening season, Bill Edrich, made 106.

When I asked Compton if he could account for his astonishing feats in 1947 he replied "Oh, don't expect me to go into a long winded technical dissertation. I was as fit as a flea, I did what came naturally and I enjoyed myself. Yes, that is what I remember best, how I loved every minute of that season."

Lovable, laughing, harum scarum Denis, it was silly of me to expect any other kind of reaction than the one I got. I will endeavour to convey what a fantastic phenomenon this man was with a bat in his hand just after World War Two before that accursed soccer injury, and the weight problems which the approach of middle age brought with them, by trying to recall just one incident in the August of 1947. Doug Wright was bowling on a Lord's pitch which had "dusted up" and was taking spin. It was the last afternoon and Middlesex were trying to chase a target not far short of 100 runs an hour. I know Middlesex did not make it but Compton scored well over 150 before he holed out to Wright on the boundary. When Wright bowled the delivery previously mentioned Compton went out of his crease like a whippet, gambling on it being a leg break and shaping to drive through the offside field. Only it wasn't a leg break. When it pitched it was as beautifully a disguised wrong 'un as the heart could wish for and I heard a voice behind me shout "Compo's gone".

It seemed a case of stating the obvious for Compo checked, reared and fell on to his chest like a demolished building – but as he did so his bat came round in a lightning sweep to send the ball, spitting in viciously from the off, to the leg side rails. That was the measure of Compton's greatness. He could do the right things superbly but when he broke all the rules the ball still ended up at the fence.

There is no better word picture of Compton than the one painted by John Arlott in his book *Vintage Summer: 1947*. "In technique, he was deficient in the straight, or near straight drive. But his control through the two wider arcs was such that he would tantalize a slow left arm bowler's cover field, or the leg side setting of an off spinner, with a degree of control few men have ever bettered. At need, he had all the strokes and, if his left foot often seemed further from the ball than the purists would approve, that gave him greater room to power his strokes, and his superb eye kept him out of such trouble as would have beset lesser cricketers who thus deviated from the text book. . . . By 1947 he had thickened physically. Before the war he had been comparatively slight: in subsequent years he developed a tendency to inconvenient weight.

"In that great summer he had come to maximum power with unimpaired mobility; powerful of shoulder and trunk, muscular in arms and legs, yet with a lazy looseness of movement and, for all his negligent air, quick and balanced on his feet. No part of his equipment was more deceptive than his speed – particularly in readjustment. He would move out to drive through the covers; the ball would, unexpectedly, move on to him and, with a mock-desperate wrench of his body and arms, he would flick it down to long leg. Or, in impish mischief, he would rock on to his back foot and, with an immensely powerful twist of the forearms – or, in even narrower space, of the wrists – drive a ball coming into his leg stump through the covers. At need he could be decorous in defence; that was never any trouble, for the germ of orthodoxy was in him, even at his most unorthodox; or, when he had abandoned the anchors, his superb natural eye and balance would retrieve the situation for him. He was an instinctively perfect timer of the ball. But the facet of his cricket which went to the heart of the average club player who watched him was his improvisation, which rectified such error as, in ordinary men, would have been fatal."

Compton ended May where he had spent it, at Lord's, playing for Middlesex against the South Africans. He had already taken 97 off them in the second innings of their game with MCC and he went out to bat on June 2 facing a total of 424 of which centuries by Bruce Mitchell and Viljoen accounted for more than half. Robertson and Brown were soon disposed of, but Compton with Edrich added 147 and then a further 103 with his brother Leslie. He was eventually stumped jumping out at Athol Rowan after four hours of sheer delight for 154 in which he hit nineteen 4s. Rowan bowled him for 34 in the second innings on a worn pitch but a not-out 133 by Edrich saw Middlesex save the match without too much difficulty.

Hampshire came next to Lord's to be beaten by an innings and 49 and Compton's contribution to a Middlesex total of 429 for six declared was a madcap 88 at two a minute. He lost his wicket to, of all people, Johnny Arnold, being stumped when running down the pitch and trying to hit the seventh bowler used by Hampshire, out of the ground.

Compton's next task was as far removed from this kind of frolicking as it could possibly be. At Trent Bridge, England in the face of South Africa's first innings 533 collapsed for 208 of which Compton made 65. Following on 325 behind on a still beautiful batting wicket England lost four wickets for 170 so that when Norman Yardley joined Compton 155 were needed to save the innings defeat and apart from Godfrey Evans there was no real batting to come. Compton and Yardley added 108 in the last hundred minutes of the day and on the final morning Yardley called for an hour's concentrated net practice from the surviving batsmen.

Yardley should have gone after adding only six to his overnight score but he was badly missed at first slip by Mitchell and he and Compton went on to a partnership of 237. When Compton gave Mitchell a slip catch off "Tufty" Mann, he had made 163 and held up South Africa for nearly five hours. It was an innings which underlined Arlott's statement that he could be decorous. Compton's critics tried to blow up to larger than life size the playboy side of his character but this was as great an innings for side as opposed to self as has yet been played in the cause of England. The tail, inspired by his example and able to take advantage of the toll in sharpness and calm that Compton's defiance had extracted, took England's score to 551. It left South Africa less than two and a half hours to get 227 to win and although Alan Melville made his second century of the match they never really attempted the task.

If they could have seen what lay ahead for them they might have been tempted to stake everything on winning this Test for they were to win none of the remaining four. Compton's next appearance for Middlesex was against Yorkshire where the potential champions had to be content with first-innings points after seven consecutive victories. Middlesex, in their only innings, declared at 350 for two when Compton was 50 not out.

Then it was Lord's Test time with the weather perfect and thousands having to be turned away on the first day after South Africa's surprising opposition at Nottingham.

This time they lost the toss and the match was decided by a mammoth third-wicket stand of 370 between Edrich and Compton. Edrich made 189 and Compton 208, his second highest score of 1947. England had a long tail and when Hutton and Washbrook went with less than a hundred on the board the responsibility for a match-winning total lay heavily upon Edrich and Compton. They faced a determined attack, splendidly supported in the field, and for a considerable time the struggle was tense. Then the Middlesex pair mastered their tormentors and *Wisden* used a phrase it has kept in cold storage these many years – "a sparkling exhibition of fluent stroke play". Compton used everything in his complete and considerable repertoire.

Still living in the memory are his brilliant sweeping of slow bowling and his powerful lofted pulled-drive. Not until twenty minutes after lunch on the second day did South Africa part the pair the popular dailies inevitably dubbed "The Terrible Twins". Edrich fell 11 short of a double century but Compton went on to 208 and was not dismissed until England's score had reached 515. He had batted ten minutes short of six hours and made his runs out of just over 400. Once again Compton had proved completely that while the stories of his forgetfulness and irresponsibility off the field grew and were not denied, when out in the middle it was very much a case of the professional soldier's belief in "on parade, on parade".

England declared at 554 for eight and although Alan Melville made 117, his fourth successive Test century against England, South Africa could do no better than reach 327. They had to follow on 227 behind and with 15 scored in their second innings play was held up for twenty minutes while the players were presented to the King and Queen and the Princesses Elizabeth and Margaret. Whether such a representative gathering of royalty intimidated the South Africans or inspired Edrich will probably always remain a matter for opinion, but on the resumption Edrich flattened Melville's middle stump with his second ball.

Two overs later he picked Viljoen's stump clean out of the ground. South Africa were clearly on the way to defeat which 80 by Mitchell and 58 by Nourse could only delay. Eventually, they made 252 which left Hutton and Washbrook the formality of going to the crease to score 26 for victory by ten wickets.

Compton rejoined Middlesex at Leeds for Bill Bowes's benefit match. The big fast bowler won the toss for Yorkshire and put Middlesex in. Compton failed twice on a pitch which retained a lot of moisture after being saturated on the Friday, the ball frequently rising alarmingly. He was caught by Hutton off Coxon for 4 and caught Coxon bowled Wardle for 15 in the second innings. Bowes's gamble backfired for although Middlesex were put out for 124 Yorkshire collapsed for 85 and Middlesex were batting again after tea on the first day. Edrich made 102 on the second day and the task of making 274 to win on a damaged surface was 88 runs out of Yorkshire's reach. It was all over in two days but it was anything but a financial failure. Over 41,000 paid around £3,000 to see two dramatic days of cricket and the popular Bowes ended the season with a benefit that topped £8,000. Compton, having failed with the bat, made a major contribution with his left arm mixture returning four for 23 and three for 28. He took the last wicket through a catch in the deep by his brother Leslie, Fred Price keeping wicket.

Denis had four days break after this match before resuming his massacre of South Africa's bowlers at Old Trafford. The Third Test was played in dull, cold thoroughly unpleasant weather. On the Saturday a bitterly cold north westerly wind blew straight down the pitch, and when I say blew, I mean strongly enough to topple one of the sight screens as well as frequently lift the bails from their grooves. South Africa had every reason to feel proud of a total of 339 in one of Manchester's most unattractive moods. They were a good side, those 1947 South Africans. Not so well equipped with all round ability as those of the sixties but very little behind. That cannot be stressed too much or too often for it puts the feats of Compton and his partner Edrich into true perspective. Nine of England's men contributed no more than 162 when their turn to bat came, but the total was 478 – 191 from Edrich and 115 from Compton, his third century in three Tests. Thus four of his first six hundreds had been taken off the Touring side and all four in succession.

Despite their lead of 139 England were a long way from victory. Nourse made a grand century when South Africa batted a second time and rain lopped three hours from the third day. In the end England had to get 129 in two and a half hours and they made them for the loss of three wickets, one of whom was Compton who, trying to keep out a nasty left arm leg break from "Tufty" Mann hit his wicket after scoring only 6.

Compton's seventh century came at Grace Road, Leicester, in a match which Middlesex won by ten wickets. An easy one-sided affair for a great team on their way to the Championship, you might assume. It was in truth a titanic achievement by Middlesex and by Compton and Edrich especially. The home side were put in to bat by Edrich, who was captaining Middlesex for the first time, and made 309, the Australian, Vic Jackson, scoring 117. Middlesex replied with 637 for four – Edrich 257, Compton 151. The two were in partnership for two hours ten minutes in which they scored 277 runs. Needing 328 to avoid an innings defeat Leicestershire refused to die gracefully. Les Berry hit 154, Maurice Tompkin 76, there was a forty here, thirties there and when the last wicket fell they were only seven short of 400.

At lunch time on the last day Leicestershire led by 17 and had six wickets standing with only eighty minutes left for play. Middlesex dropped those six wickets for 48 in thirty-five minutes and Compton did it, being easily the most successful bowler with five for 108, the last man falling to the first ball of his thirtieth over.

This left Middlesex just twenty-five minutes in which to score 66 runs. Edrich took Compton in with him and they got them in twenty-one minutes off seven overs. On the second day of the match 663 runs were scored.

Compton's next match was Gentlemen v Players, a fixture which could still draw 15,000 to Lord's in indifferent weather for a day's play. It fizzled out into a hopeless draw and in his only knock Compton was caught at the wicket by the present secretary of the MCC, Billy Griffith, off the bowling of Trevor Bailey for 11. He stayed at Lord's for the visit of Essex who gave Middlesex a good scrap for three days before losing by 102 runs. Scores: Middlesex 389 for seven declared and 356 for five declared; Essex 350 and 293. Highest individual score of a fine match was Compton's 129 in the first Middlesex innings which ended when he gave Peter Smith a return catch. He was at the crease a fraction under two hours. There was just time before the fourth Test at Leeds for Edrich and Compton to help Middlesex win at Northampton by eight wickets. Middlesex declared at 464 for five after their numbers 3 and 4 had put on 211 for the third wicket. When Compton was bowled by Partridge for 110, Edrich went on to the highest score of his career, 267 not out.

For once the Middlesex terrors played modest supporting roles to Hutton and Washbrook at Headingley. Hutton got 100 and Washbrook 75 compared with 43 by Edrich and 30 from Compton, but South Africa's batting failed twice for the first time in the series and England won by ten wickets in three days.

So Compton came to August and unknown to the world and himself nine centuries still lay ahead. He hit the first of them in Jim Langridge's benefit match at Hove which Middlesex won by nine wickets. Walter Robins declared at 401 for four as soon as Denis completed three figures for the tenth time that season. After hitting thirteen fours Denis and his "Chinamen" played the main part in putting out Sussex for 195 and making them follow on. His haul was four for 90 in 21 overs.

Lord's, Trent Bridge, Old Trafford, Hove, noble grounds all, had been fitting stages for Compton to display his genius and now he added Canterbury. Five days play at the 1947 Canterbury Festival drew 46,756 paying spectators; over 13,000 of them were there on the Thursday and they saw Compton make 106 out of a Middlesex total of 225. When Middlesex followed on Compton was caught by Leslie Ames off Harding for only 4, but Robertson and Edrich struck hundreds and the prospective champions declared. They set Kent two hours to get 232 and dropped six of their wickets to come close to winning from a near hopeless position.

Next came The Oval and the defeat of Surrey by an innings and 11 runs. The gates were closed on Saturday and 54,000 saw the three days cricket in which Compton strode the world famous enclosure like the Colossus of cricket he was. When Middlesex declared at 537 for two he was 137 not out after adding 287 in 165 minutes with Edrich without being separated. Of the four men who batted Syd Brown's 98 was the lowest score. Surrey replied with 334 and 192 and the match did nothing for the reputations of no less than thirteen bowlers. The exception was the slow-left-arm, unorthodox-over-the-wicket Compton, whose work with the ball on this occasion outstripped his batting. He took six for 94 in the first innings and six for 80 in the second, sending down nearly 53 overs. This remember was the second week in August in a season in which Compton had been the key batsman for both England and the champion county, yet neither Compton nor Robins his captain saw any reason why at such an advanced stage of the campaign he should be nursed. It is, to me, at least, a grain of comfort that in our own post-war period there were still men of giant capacity in cricket. In that match Alf Gover, Alec Bedser, Stuart Surridge, Laurie Gray and Jack Young took just three wickets between them!

Back across Westminster Bridge went Middlesex to a defeat by 75 runs by Kent that would have been much heavier had not Compton scored a glorious 168 in the fourth innings on a dusting pitch, a knock I have already touched upon. And just to make certain Compton earned his corn "Robbie" made him bowl another 55 overs in the match which brought him four more wickets!

It was now time for the fifth Test at The Oval and South Africa after three resounding defeats ended the series as they began it by coming close to victory. After four days of wonderful, fluctuating cricket the Springboks were 28 runs short with three wickets left. Bruce Mitchell on his farewell Test appearance in England made the match his by scoring 120 in the first innings and 189 not out in the second, but Compton put his stamp on the series in which great things had been done by the batsmen of both sides with innings of 53 and 113.

The series was over but a lot of cricket was left for Compton. He retraced the familiar route to Lord's for the games with Surrey and Northamptonshire which finally saw off the magnificent challenge made by Gloucestershire. Middlesex scored 462 for seven declared on the first day – thirty-five minutes were lost because of bad light. After seeing Robertson, Brown and Edrich sent back for what in 1947 Middlesex considered low scores, Compton carefully shielded F. G. Mann through a shaky start. Then the pair cut loose and in three and a quarter hours put on 304. Compton's 178 was a bewitching mixture of orthodox strokes and his own inventions. It was as if by this time he had to amuse himself with improvisations on a well worn theme to keep his interest and concentration from going altogether. Jim Laker, who was to earn his own immortality some nine years later, got him in the end, one of two wickets which cost him 105 runs. Surrey put totals of 202 and 309 in the book, but the wicket was broken when Middlesex went in to score 50; Gover got Brown for 0 and Edrich for 2, and then Compton went in to hit off the runs with Jack Robertson – after bowling 48 overs in the two Surrey innings.

Next, Northamptonshire were annihilated in two days by 355 runs, Compton playing innings of 60 and 85. This victory ensured Middlesex finishing top. The Championship secured, the season ended on a note of anti-climax for Middlesex with Lancashire coming to Lord's and winning, by 64 runs to finish third in the table for the second season running, but their win was overshadowed by Compton's feat of equalling Hobbs' 1925 record of sixteen centuries in a season. Spin and flight beat Compton early in the first innings, John Ikin bowling him for17 but in the second, with Middlesex chasing nearly 400, Compton was at his greatest. Confined to defence for long periods against bowlers who had the sweet smell of victory over the Champions, Denis fought his way grimly to three figures after spending half an hour in the nineties.

The season had brought out all the shining facets of his many sided cricket character and what could be more appropriate than that he should sign off at Lord's having made 139 and kept Lancashire from their prize for nearly three and a half hours when finally Price drew him out for Barlow to stump him. In this match watched by 60,000, he had bowled another 35 overs and added another five wickets for 95 runs to his considerable haul, but this last appearance of an unforgettable season for all connected with Lord's cast more than the first shadows of the approaching autumn.

On the first day he had to leave the field. A call to the dressing-room from the press box brought the reassuring reply "Oh, it's nothing to worry about. Denis has got a spot of knee trouble and is having some manipulative treatment." Nothing – except the first hole in the dyke.

Compton went to Hastings where on September 5 at the Central Ground the South Africans gained victory by nine wickets over the South of England, but as at Lord's a few days before the performance of a team was forgotten because of the innings of a batsman in the losing team. Compton set a new all time individual record by scoring 101 – his seventeenth century of the season. It was his twelfth hundred in 25 innings and when he reached it the game was held up for five minutes as crowd and players including his Middlesex colleagues, Edrich and Robins, went on to the field to congratulate him. It was a century to rank with the other sixteen, for the South Africans understandably were not going to give this man anything. He had already taken five centuries off them before this game and when he added another 30 in the second innings before Athol Rowan bowled him he had brought his season's aggregate against South Africa alone to 1,187 runs.

Without any comment I would like to add that over 20 years on in the enlightened era of the 1970s with its rockets orbiting to the Moon, its cannabis, its 7½ per cent bank rate, Graveney's aggregate for a whole season was 1,130 and Cowdrey's 1,093. As the man said – I suppose you cannot have everything.

The late A. A. Thomson once said to me: "Of all the seasons I wished could go on forever 1947 was the one." It is not hard to understand how "Tommy" felt. At The Oval on September 13, 15, 16 and 17, 1947, for the first time in twelve years the Champion County played The Rest of England. For only the third time the Champion county won it and for the first time a side other than Yorkshire, successful in 1905 and 1935, succeeded. Middlesex began badly, losing three wickets for 53; then Compton coming in at number five instead of his customary four, joined Edrich and they proceeded to take part an attack comprising Harold Butler, Alec Bedser, Doug Wright, Tom Goddard, and Dick Howarth. Oddly enough, both Edrich and Compton were stumped by Godfrey Evans off Goddard, Edrich for 180, Compton for a season's best 246. In their innings both batsmen beat Tom Hayward's aggregate of 3,518 runs in a season which had stood since 1906.

It was also Compton's highest innings in this country, but even in this supreme hour which lifted Compton on a pedestal in company with such as Bradman, Grace and Hobbs, the gods gave a warning that they were soon to foreclose savagely. After he had helped Edrich to add 138 on the Saturday, Compton had to retire with a recurrence of knee trouble. He resumed his innings on Monday and as the runs cascaded from his bat even those who knew just how heavily strapped his knee was found it almost impossible to accept that his freedom of movement was already restricted and would never be quite the same again although he was to thumb his nose at pain and difficulty for another seventeen years. Middlesex declared at 543 for nine; bowled out The Rest for 246 and 317 and knocked off 21 for the loss of Robertson in the first hour of the fourth day. What is remarkable is not so much the result but that Compton ignoring the knee which had driven him from the field for the second time in just over a fortnight bowled 34 overs and 4 balls and took six wickets in the match for 141 runs – the second most successful bowler in the contest.

It is among the more hackneyed phrases in sport that records are made to be broken but I wonder whether Compton's figures of 1947 will ever be surpassed. He played 50 innings, was not out in eight of them, scored 3,816 runs, made 18 centuries and had an average of 90.85. He bowled 635.4 overs and took 73 wickets. He also held 31 catches, three in one innings, for example, when Gloucestershire, the runners up, came to Lord's.

When the time came for *Wisden* to pay tribute to Compton and Edrich in their 1948 edition they turned unerringly to Robertson-Glasgow. Crusoe put them together in English cricket as Gilbert and Sullivan go together in English opera. Not was the analogy a careless one for, as he pointed out, in the art of giving pleasure to an English audience, both pairs lacked rival. Crusoe of course did not give a damn for figures. He saw the great Middlesex pair as champions in the fight against dullness and the commercial standard.

It is what they were that mattered to him far more than what they had done. In those wise and humorous eyes which I always thought to be the most striking feature in the striking whole, Compton and Edrich (and they cannot be spoken of apart in 1947) were the mirror of hope and freedom and gaiety; heroic in the manner of heroes of school stories; the inspiration, and quarry of the young, because, in a game that even then was threatening to become old in the saddest sense, they did not outgrow the habit, the ideal, the very mistakes of youth.

"Most cricketers enjoy doing well, though I could name great ones who had a queer way of showing their enjoyment," wrote Crusoe. "But Compton and Edrich are of that happy philosophy which keeps failure in its place by laughter, like boys who fall on an ice slide and rush back to try it again. . . . And they seem to be playing not only in front of us and for us, but almost literally with us. Their cricket is communicative."

That such players should break records was in Crusoe's opinion inevitable rather than relevant. It was never the slightest use trying to impress this man of many brilliant parts with statistics. I remember making the error in my salad days as a cricket writer and he made me realise the gap in our generation and our background by replying "More people have listened to Frank Sinatra than Caruso, Clark Gable received more letters of homage than Sir Henry Irving. Numbers can be such silly things." The sort of thing which delighted Crusoe was when, with easy vehemence, Compton would persuade a ball of fairish length on the leg stump to the extra cover boundary.

Robertson-Glasgow admired Edrich for his talent and his unquenchable pugnacity. He was the first to pay tribute to a cricketer who, in his words, started with a number of talents and increased them into riches. Compton was different, a cricketer apart. "Denis has genius, and, if he knows it, he doesn't care."

In his essay in *Wisden*, 1948, Crusoe wrote the following passage: "Compton cannot help it. He has the habit of batting as the sun has the habit of journeying from east to west; and the fielders are his satellites. Hardest worked of them, and most perplexed, is cover point. Other batsmen of our time have been severer on the stroke. Walter Hammond could leave the nimblest cover motionless or just flickering as by token, could use cover's toe caps as an echoing junction for the boundary; but Compton uses cover point as a game within a game, tantalises him with delayed direction and vexes him with variety. He is for ever seeking fresh by-products of the old forward stroke and has not yet, I fancy, come to the end of experiment. He finds it so amusing and so profitable. He outruns the traditional and discovers new truth. Compton is the axiom of tomorrow."

Alas, for all of us, Crusoe, you were wrong in your final sentence. Nothing in cricket that followed 1947 has remotely approached it in either stature or weather. One all time great as a writer on the game, he saw two all time great exponents of it as adornments to something that was meant not as an imitation of, but as a refreshment from, the worldly struggle.

Cricket in the two decades that followed proved unworthy of all three of them. It was to become as fearful, as joyless as so much of the world that surrounded it and its shame was greatest at the highest level of all. In the Brisbane Test of December 1958 between Australia and England a full day's play produced 106 runs and even that was not the nadir for nearly two years earlier at Karachi in a Test between Australia and Pakistan the result of a full day's labour was 95 runs. It seems that we could not possibly be talking about the same game that Percy Fender played when he scored 113 in forty-two minutes at Northampton in 1920 or when Alletson at Hove in 1911 went from 50 to 189 in half an hour.

But then, even 1947 and the Compton that enthralled me along with millions of others is already overlaid with the mists of antiquity. Compton, fielding near the wicket in a bending posture, hands palm down to his knees as if waiting for some kindred spirit to leapfrog over him – was it all a figment of my imagination?

Shortly before I wrote this article my teenage son read a piece by Cardus on Compton. He drew my attention to a sentence which ran "on the field of play, at any rate, Denis's hair was unruly beyond the pacifying power of any cream, oil or unguent whatsoever".

He looked up and shaking his head said: "I'm surprised that a writer as good as you keep telling me Sir Neville is should find it necessary to pad out an article like that." It was, I realised, another example of the generation gap. Paul had never seen Compton's portrait on hoardings up and down the land, advertising a nationally famous hair dressing, so the adroit, gentle allusion to it by Cardus was entirely without meaning for him.

When I meet Denis now, a busy, bustling character in his early fifties for ever flirting with rotundity as once he flirted with everything be it a good length, passing fair or loose as a decayed tooth, I am momentarily saddened to think that once "panting Time toiled after him in vain". Then I see him move sideways and laugh uproariously at a joke he has just told me and I know that inside he is the same person who many aver was the worst judge of when or when not to take a run the game has ever known.

I see him again with the eyes of 1947, as he was at Lord's and on the bill posters, England in a pair of pads, dark, competent, unflustered and I am glad that the most runs and centuries concentrated into one marvellous summer will remain for all time in his keeping. For once, the gods chose right.

DENIS COMPTON 1947

1.	112	v	Worcestershire	Lord's
2.	110	v	Sussex	Lord's
3.	154	v	South Africans	Lord's
4.	163	v	South Africa (1st Test)	Trent Bridge
5.	208	v	South Africa (2nd Test)	Lord's
6.	115	v	South Africa (3rd Test)	Old Trafford
7.	151	v	Leicestershire	Leicester
8.	129	v	Essex	Lord's
9.	110	v	Northamptonshire	Northampton
10.	*110	v	Sussex	Hove
11.	106	v	Kent	Canterbury
12.	*137	v	Surrey	Oval
13.	168	v	Kent	Lord's
14.	113	v	South Africans	Oval
15.	178	v	Surrey	Lord's
16.	139	v	Lancashire	Lord's
17.	101	v	South Africans	Hastings
18.	246	v	Rest of England	Oval

SHILLINGS FOR W.G. [1973]

LOOKING BACK EIGHTY YEARS

By Sir Compton Mackenzie

Wisden *is privileged to have received the last article by Sir Compton Mackenzie. It arrived a week before he died in Edinburgh on November 30, aged 89. In the last few years of his life Sir Compton was almost blind and only last summer he had a spell in hospital which left him with periodic fatigue. During his life he wrote about one hundred books. His work included novels, biographies, histories, travel books, essays, stories for children, besides numerous broadcasts and television appearances. He was born Edward Montague Compton in West Hartlepool and was educated in London at Colet Court and St Paul's School before going to Oxford University. After coming down he studied law before turning to writing and then he assumed an old family name, Mackenzie.*

Cricket is a pastime I have always enjoyed. I do not suggest that I was ever a good cricketer. I suffered, in my opinion, from the handicap of being a left-handed bowler and a right-handed batsman. I would bowl without disgracing myself, but as a batsman I was hopeless.

How well do I remember the summer of that sunblessed year, 1893. I was ten years old and eager for fun. There was the cricket match between the small boys of Broadway and the visiting team of small boys in which I took five wickets. This was a pure accident. So much embarrassed was I when put on to bowl that I concentrated on bowling straight and in order to do this I thought the surest way was to swing my arm directly over my left shoulder. The result was a series of half volleys which an experienced batsman would have hit over the boundary by stepping out and treating the delivery as a full pitch. As it was, the inexperienced batsmen I bowled against stepped back and their stumps were spreadeagled. I was entirely at a loss to understand my success as a bowler and not in the least elated by it. Only when I held a tough catch at cover point at the very end of the innings, which left the boys of Broadway victors, did I feel elated. The echo of that "well caught" from the spectators still rings in my mind's ears from eighty years ago.

I recall the Scarborough cricket week of 1893 when I was taken by Frank Goodricke, the eldest son of the manager of the Spa, to see the South of England eleven playing Yorkshire. Well do I remember the venerated figure of W. W. Read, the Surrey batsman, in his chocolate coloured cap; we were too much in awe of cricketers eighty years ago to pester them for autographs. I recall dark handsome Tom Richardson, the Surrey fast bowler, and fair handsome Lockwood; I recall the burly figure of Sir Timothy O'Brien making terrific swipes off the redoubtable Yorkshire bowler Peel; I recall F. R. Spofforth, the "demon" bowler, with his heavy drooping moustache; finally, I recall J. J. Ferris of Gloucestershire, a small left-handed bowler from Australia who only played a couple of seasons for Gloucestershire and went back to Australia in 1895. I have an impression that he took the wicket of the famous J. T. Brown; I certainly saw him take one Yorkshire wicket.

I fell into disgrace with Frank Goodricke because from where I was sitting in the pavilion I could see a football match going on. I can hear him now turning to me and saying, "This is the last time I'll bring you to Scarborough cricket week if you want to look at football." Frank Goodricke did not know that the ten-year-old boy looking at football, when the paragons of cricket were performing, was anticipating what the whole of the British public would be doing twenty years later. Two years earlier Somerset had been added to the eight first-class cricket counties. It was the bowling of S. M. J. Woods, or as we kids called him "Sammy Woods", and the perfect batting of the brothers L. C. H. and R. C. N. Palairet which kept Somerset as a new first-class county.

The summer of 1894 I spent in Britanny with several other small boys to be coached for scholarship examinations and for entrance to H.M.S. *Britannia* for the Royal Navy. What I recall from that wet summer was the destruction of my butterfly collection by the customs officials who insisted on my opening the cigar boxes, in which I was carrying them back, and scattering them all over the wet ground. So wet a summer was it that we felt we had not lost much cricket but I do recall our surprise that the top of the batting averages was Brockwell of Surrey with 39 runs an innings.

However, the year 1895 was to become a remarkable one in the history of cricket. The prodigious performance of W. G. Grace in scoring over 1,000 runs in twenty-two days in the month of May inspired the whole country with a tremendous interest in cricket and cricketers. There had been nothing like it and, moreover, more than thirty years passed before it was repeated by another Gloucestershire stalwart, W. R. Hammond, in twenty-five days.

There must have been three of four periodicals produced in 1895 devoted to cricket records and the personalities of the various cricketers. It may have been due to this interest at this time that, as I remember, five were promoted to first-class counties that year. These were Hampshire, Derbyshire, Warwickshire, Leicestershire and Essex.

It was a batsman's year. W. G. Grace was in his forty-eighth year and he had taken considerable pains to get himself into the best physical condition possible. He was by far the heaviest player taking part in the great matches and he was in his thirty-first season in first-class cricket. Moreover, he played many long innings without a mistake: 288 against Somerset at Bristol in five hours, twenty minutes; it was his hundredth century; 257 against Kent at Gravesend and The Champion was on the field during every ball of the match.

Enthusiastic crowds flocked to see him wherever he appeared and he finished that memorable summer in making 2,346 runs, the largest aggregate of the year. He was entertained at banquets in London and Bristol; a National Testimonial was organised and the *Daily Telegraph*, the paper with which I was later to have some connection, collected £5,000, by means of a shilling subscription. Schoolboys all over the country were invited to contribute. I can still recall from eighty years ago our determination not to let our pocket-money of sixpence per week be given to cigarettes until we had the necessary shilling for W.G.

One summer's evening in mid-July of this year of W.G., when I was in the Recreation ground a friend came along Gliddon Road and shouted to me to open the gate for him.

"Archie MacLaren has made 424 against Somerset," he announced as he passed through the gate.

"You liar!"

"No, really he has, and Lancashire have made 801."

I was speechless and stood gazing at the hands of the golden school clock nearing eight on that golden evening. Lancashire 801! Archie MacLaren 424! What a chap Archie MacLaren must be! It was always our custom to talk of some famous cricketers by their Christian names – Archie MacLaren, Sammy Woods, Bobby Abel, Tom Richardson and others by their initials – L.C.H. and R.C.N. (Palairet), W.W. (Read), and of course the mighty W.G. A year or two later when Worcestershire was added to the first-class counties, thanks to the redoubtable batting of old Malvernians like H. K. and R. E. Foster, it was considered a great joke to call Worcestershire, "Fostershire".

Sadly for me I did not see any of the cricket of the Scarborough Festival of 1896 because I succumbed to what was called at that time inflammation of the lungs, which meant the agony of being painted with iodine and the irritation of being told by the doctor that I was imagining the pain. My mother at this time decided to buy a bungalow called Canadian Cottage on the outskirts of Alton in Hampshire; instead of going back to school in September I went down with her to Canadian Cottage and felt myself well rewarded for the pain of that wretched iodine by the pleasure of reading at last three or four schoolboy weeklies, among them, *The Captain*, later edited by P. G. Wodehouse. A redoubtable player called Jessop was making large scores for Beccles College in East Anglia. G. L. Jessop! How lucky Gloucestershire and Cambridge University were to have him whom we used to call "The Croucher". Another of our heroes of that time was C. J. Kortright of Essex whom we believed to be the fastest bowler who ever bowled a ball.

Now with the memory of K. S. Ranjitsinhji and C. B. Fry batting at Hove and of what seemed Ranjitsinhji's ability to make it look as easy to hit the ball to the boundary as it was back to the bowler, I shall move on to 1901 when I went up to Magdalen College, Oxford. It was now being realised that golf was a menace to cricket. Instead of practice at the nets, members of the Varsity XI were going off to play golf at some place called Hinksey. At the same time junior cricketers were playing golf at Cowley long before Cowley became the heart of the Morris motor works. Then on top of the threat of golf for the future of cricket came the addition of lawn tennis, which we used to call pat-ball in those days, real tennis still being considered the only kind of tennis fit for recognition. When a half-blue was awarded for lawn tennis, professional cricket did not seem to have anything to fear from either golf or tennis.

In 1939 when war with Germany was obviously drawing nearer the second National Government invited various people to speak round the country to step up recruiting. I was invited to address the City of Bradford with Herbert Sutcliffe as my partner. I had been warned by Auckland Geddes that Bradford could be as difficult an audience as Manchester had been for him the previous week when it kept chanting "Tripe! "Tripe!" When I stepped forward on the platform of the Alhambra on that Sunday evening I said I hoped the citizens of Bradford would not suppose that I was a representative of the National Government: "What I think of the National Government could not be said on any platform or in any pulpit on a Sunday evening." When I sat down Herbert Sutcliffe turned to me and said:

"Oh my, how I wish I could speak like you."

"You don't wish nearly as much that you could speak like me as I wish I could bat like you," I replied.

As I bring to a close these reminiscences of cricket as I recall it from eighty years ago I hear on the radio that Rhodes is drawing near to a century of years and I am back hearing of the feats of Rhodes and F. S. Jackson for the White Rose of Yorkshire against the Red Rose of Lancashire.

NORFOLK AND THE EDRICH CLAN [1973]

A SPECIAL TRIBUTE TO BILL EDRICH

By Basil Easterbrook

Norfolk cricket and Bill Edrich – and surely strawberries and cream are not more synonymous – have in common an abiding endurance. There are some threads of evidence that a cricket club existed in Swaffham as far back as 1700 which means that the game has been played in this part of East Anglia for about 275 years. Nearly 100 years later Swaffham was just one of many cricket clubs in the county – Castle Acre, Downham, Norwich, Lynn, West Lexham, Brinton, Dereham, for a generous half dozen.

David J. M. Armstrong of Holt, son of the Rev. H. B. J. Armstrong, one of the most notable of Norfolk cricket enthusiasts and a legend at Lakenham for his anecdotes and humour, privately published a history of Norfolk County Cricket in 1958 in which he records a team calling itself Norfolk taking the field for the first time as far back as 1797. The match was played on Swaffham Racecourse "in the presence of an immense number of spectators from all parts of the Kingdom" between England and 33 of Norfolk. The county, despite their preponderance in numbers, were beaten by the eleven England cracks by an innings and 14 runs and in the two Norfolk innings there was but one solitary double-figure score of 14 and as many as 35 ducks!

This monumental humiliation of local talent served only to whet the appetite for cricket in Norfolk and the first quarter of the 19th century was a tale of continuing growth culminating in the formation of the County Cricket Club on January 11, 1827, at the Rampant Horse Inn, Norwich, with Lord Suffield as president. Mr Armstrong's opening chapter of early days in Norfolk cricket is studded with tales of club matches played for side stakes, some of them distinctly peculiar. One match in 1811, for example, was played for 22 bottles of cider and 22 pounds of cherries, another in 1823 between eleven married and eleven single ladies for eleven pairs of gloves. Three years before this second game Norfolk went up to Lord's to play MCC, and included in their team a man whose name had become immortal – Fuller Pilch.

At the formation of the County Club it was agreed to start with four matches the following summer, one each at Norwich, Yarmouth, Swaffham and Gunton. So great was the enthusiasm that just over five weeks later some ardent cricketers at Diss took time by the forelock and opened their season on February 20. The mere at Diss was gripped by frost of unusual severity and two teams played what was reported as a *bona fide* match on skates! The game drew a crowd of several hundred, began at 10 o'clock in the morning, and was continued until half past five.

By 1831 Norfolk were described in one periodical of the day as "Now the next club to the Marylebone". Certainly the previous summer both Norfolk and Norwich had beaten the MCC at Lord's, although MCC won the two return matches at Norwich and Dereham.

There came an historic moment in September 1833, when Yorkshire played their first-ever game and their opponents were Norfolk. The match took place at Sheffield and the Tykes immediately established the habit of winning that was to bring them 31 outright championships. The scores were Yorkshire 138 and 196; Norfolk 67 and 146. A year later Yorkshire were soundly thrashed at Norwich by 272 runs, Fuller Pilch making 87 not out and 73 in the two Norfolk innings. In 1935 the match with Yorkshire was left drawn because of rain but not before Pilch made 157 not out in Norfolk's second innings.

Now came an unexpected swing of the pendulum. The public at Yarmouth and Gunton withheld their support and in 1836 Pilch was lured away to Kent on the promise of £2 a week throughout the year. He took with him another leading Norfolk player called William Stearman. Next, Lord Suffield was thrown by his horse and killed and the drive faltered both on the field and in the committee room. The decline in the 1840s was unchecked and the County Club folded up in 1848. It was revived briefly in 1862 but by 1870 it had failed again.

It is perhaps necessary at this point to digress slightly and consider the character of the East Anglian. Local patriotism is strong in all parts of England but it is doubtful if the people of East Anglia are not the proudest of all. Progress has done less to destroy the essential character of Norfolk, Suffolk, Essex and Cambridgeshire than any other part of the United Kingdom. Their landscape, villages, churches and great country houses still retain the qualities for which they were valued in earlier centuries and even the towns are generally traditional and unspoiled.

Blickling Hall and Castle Acre Priory – where else would architectural monuments be found to surpass them? It was an early cricket match at Blickling Hall that inspired some forgotten poet to pen the lines:

Weary of play, some summer eve perchance
You will come running in from dewless lawns
The long day's sunshine on your countenance.

But there is more to Norfolk than stately piles and old monuments. The ancient wind and water mills, the harvest fields in autumn, the fishing fleet leaving or entering Yarmouth, the Broads – and driving the iron into the soul of the Norfolkman – the sea; an ambivalence brought about by a remoteness and isolation which can be both cherished and deplored. This is still splendidly evoked by Swinburne's lines:

A land that is lonelier than ruin;
A sea that is stranger than death;
Far fields that a rose never blew in,
Wan waste where the winds lack breath;
Waste endless and boundless and flowerless
But of marsh-blossoms fruitless as free,
Where earth lies exhausted, as powerless
To strive with the sea.

For me, the foregoing makes it clear why two failures were brushed aside and the dogged, uncompromising men of Norfolk started up their county cricket club once more on October 14, 1876. It certainly makes the Edrich clan entirely realistic and acceptable.

John Edrich in his book *Runs In The Family* – one of the better cricket book titles – begins his first chapter with this paragraph:

"My grandfather, Harry Edrich, of Manor Farm, Blofield, a village near Norwich, spent his days farming, cricketing and raising 13 children. One of his sons became my father, Fred, and another the father of Geoff (Lancashire), Brian (Kent and Glamorgan), Eric (Lancashire) and Bill (the famous 'W.J.' of Middlesex and England)."

What odds, one wonders would the newly arisen betting parlours on our first-class grounds offer against some future family providing players for five of England's first-class counties with two of them becoming Test stars? The greatest of them, notwithstanding John's admirable service to England, is Bill.

Lack of inches never stopped him from doing the things he set his heart on. Playing, flying, living, he extracted the last ounce from all of them, with enough success to make any two normal men envious. To see him come through the gate at Lord's and walk out to the middle was to see the personification of self-confidence and aggressiveness. There was nothing of the brute in his intelligent features, but the pugnacity was unmistakable. He walked with chest thrust out like the human fighting cock he was, but as light on his feet as a girl going to her first dancing class.

He might have been a star winger with Tottenham Hotspur but his talent at cricket was so outstanding that he wisely soon gave up his soccer. He did not play professionally for Middlesex until 1937 but in less than a season he established himself as one of the most promising players in the country in a period when there was no shortage. His fleetness of foot and his utter fearlessness made him the kind of batsman we have so often sorely needed in the years since he returned whence he came, to Norfolk, where, as late as 1970, coming up to his middle fifties, he played 18 innings and easily topped the county's batting averages.

The bowling could be nasty, fast and the ball rising but Edrich either hooked it off his eyebrows or got right behind it.

Wes Hall and Charlie Griffith would not have got under Bill's skin although I fancy he might well have got under theirs. In the war he became a pilot in Bomber Command and won the DFC, for a daylight attack – not the easiest way to earn this major decoration. Between establishing himself in first-class cricket and the outbreak of the Second World War, Bill Edrich was granted just one year – 1938, the year of Munich. Edrich seized his solitary chance characteristically to make 1,000 runs before June 1. He was the sixth man to achieve it and to date the last. Perhaps it will never be done again, although Edrich's feat was the fifth of its kind in the space of eleven years. *Fin de siècle*?

There were two other remarkable facts about it – it was done in the same season that Bradman did it for a second time, the one occasion it has been performed twice in the same May, and all Edrich's runs were made at Lord's. His innings included 104 for MCC v Yorkshire, 115 for MCC v Surrey, 182 for Middlesex v Gloucestershire and 245 for Middlesex v Nottinghamshire. When he was out against Nottinghamshire he needed just 19 more runs for his 1,000 with eight days of May still stretching ahead of him. Nottinghamshire were beaten by an innings and Middlesex did the same in the next match against Worcestershire. For Edrich it was three wasted days.

He hit a return catch to Bob Crisp the South African without scoring – his first failure in what was, for those who set store on such things, his thirteenth innings of the season. That left him two possible chances of getting the 19 runs he required, for Middlesex met the Australians on May 28, 30 and 31. All Saturday the players watched the rain falling as straight as stair rods and it did not let up on the Sunday. On the Monday play was possible all day but these were no conditions for batsmen.

The Australians, who had made six scores of over 500 in seven innings, were put out for 132 and Middlesex, battling all the way, reached 188. Edrich's share of obtaining this lead of 56 was 9. He was then bowled neck and crop by O'Reilly and when Bradman and McCabe came together in the second innings in what was the Australians' only real stand of this rain-riddled fixture Edrich seemed certain to end the month with 990 runs. Then with less than half an hour to play out the formalities of a hopelessly drawn game, Bradman declared and said to Edrich: "See if you can get those 10, Bill." There was just time for half a dozen quick overs shared by McCabe and Waite and Edrich got those 10 and helped himself to 10 more for luck. He had made 1,010 by May 31, with an average of over 84.

Edrich had his detractors, especially for the extended period he was given in the England team before he succeeded at Test level. They, the ubiquitous "they", said it was only because of his Lord's background. Well, perhaps Lord's did help him, perhaps if he had played for Somerset or Glamorgan his path to the top would have been longer and thornier, but that he would have got there in the end there can be no doubt.

The watcher from the ringside, however diligent, is always open to at least two charges, (*a*) that he has his favourites and (*b*) that he never played at top level and therefore his judgement is open to doubt.

Speaking personally, I accept those charges even if the motives behind them are often malicious so I sought a friend of both Edrich and myself who had played with him and against him. No one, I think, would question Trevor Bailey's status as a player or deny that he is a shrewd assessor now that he has become a writer on the game.

"I have always maintained that seeing this little man hook Ray Lindwall was one of the most exhilarating sights I have ever witnessed on a cricket ground" Bailey told me, adding that he rated Edrich as a great player who would have been an automatic choice for a world eleven at his peak.

"In company with most small, nimble batsmen Bill was very quick on his feet against the spinners and his cutting was of the very highest order. He also perfected a lofted stroke wide of mid-on, which was a cross between the on drive and the 'cow shot' which brought him a vast number of sixes on even the largest of grounds. As the years went by Bill lost some of his freedom and though, because of his sound technique, he was never easy to dismiss, it was possible to keep him relatively quiet by bowling a full length on and just outside his off stump – something which could never have occurred during those memorable days of 1947."

Memorable days indeed with Middlesex winning the Championship by continuous all-round cricket of brilliance and character. It was, although none knew it at the time, the last great pyrotechnic display before the game was overtaken by our egalitarian times. 1947, when Compton, Robertson and Edrich scored 32 centuries between them for Middlesex alone. 1947, when a county fixture could draw 20,000 for a day's play.

The memory of that exceptional summer of weather as well as cricket reminds me of a day when a modern player of some renown was at considerable pains to explain to Jim Sims how much more scientific the game had become since his playing days.

"Yes, mate," replied Jim Sims, "but we drew the crowds."

And why did they draw the crowds? Did they come content just to watch Compton, Edrich and the rest making their big scores? No, for while they scored heavily they still believed in the feasibility of having 400 on the board shortly after tea. Edrich was a man who knew instinctively about time and its value. Were not the last words of Elizabeth the First reported to have been: "All my possessions for a moment of time."? And there was Shakespeare lamenting "I wasted time and now doth time waste me." Whether batting all day or providing the impromptu cabaret at an all night party, Bill Edrich believed with Bacon that a man that is young in years may be old in experience if he has lost no time. Or as Quarles ended a famous passage – One to-day is worth two to-morrows.

Edrich was always for me the living symbol that a man does not have to stand six feet two in his stockinged feet to be a great cricketer. I think that it was no accident that when he finished with first-class cricket Edrich made a clean cut. Other great players like Compton, Benaud, Brown, Dexter, Yardley, Peebles, Bowes, Fingleton, Laker, Bailey and Gover – an eleven of nearly all the talents – kept in touch by writing, broadcasting or commentating on TV.

What Edrich did do, most logically and sensibly was to combine a life in commerce with playing and captaining Norfolk in the Minor Counties Competition. To give what you have to give in the right place at the right time is surely the art of living. As recently as 1970 the memories come rushing back when he made a brief reappearance at Lord's when Norfolk came to HQ on Gillette Cup business.

Cardus, of course, has not permitted such a player as Edrich to escape his matchless pen. "Edrich the born fighter, battling on with his batting, a great little driver who, on his day, could bowl fast. He would run so fast to bowl that after release of the ball his follow through propelled him somewhere near, or between, cover and gully – as though he had been sucked forward by the wind or draught of his own bowling. He was the most gallant and fearless of batsmen, whose only misgiving was that Denis Compton might any moment run him out."

Sir Neville, like myself, never had to bat against him or bowl to him and as Trevor Bailey put it as he cast his mind back more than a quarter of a century – "I did and Bill did not exactly inspire lyrical prose in my breast at the time. In those days bowling against Middlesex was more of a problem than bowling against many Test teams. Bill was a complete batsman with a magnificent defence. Few in my experience have watched the ball so closely. And, it goes without saying, he had a very wide range of attacking strokes. The harder you hit him, either with bat or ball, the greater became his determination. I never remember him flinching.

"It is hardly surprising to know he had a distinguished career in the war, not in some quiet little sinecure far removed from the main scene of the conflict but at the sharp end.

"When hostilities ended, Bill, with his DFC, a decoration never lightly awarded, returned to Middlesex and after one season decided to become an amateur. It was the early days of the social revolution when it was still considered essential to have an amateur captaining England. At that time it seemed quite probable that Bill, who was an automatic choice as player, might lead England when Wally Hammond retired. For a variety of reasons, including a disregard for the hierarchy, a certain wildness and impetuosity, and an unconventional outlook he never achieved this particular honour. However, his decision to join the amateur ranks undoubtedly cost him at least a ten thousand tax free benefit.

"Bill lived hard and played hard. He believed that life was for living and was prepared to let to-morrow take care of itself, a view which his experiences as a combat pilot had helped to develop. I always felt that he needed a 36-hour-day and inevitably there were clashes with authority from time to time, because he was a colourful, controversial and sometimes headstrong individual. I remember how he upset one rather sedate selector who simply could not understand the ethical gulf that divided the two of them, and never would. This selector was utterly and completely dedicated to cricket, to Bill it always remained a wonderful game, but he never allowed it to interfere unduly with his private life. As a result England went to Australia in 1950-51 without him, and this piece of selectorial folly could well have cost us the Ashes.

"Bill loved parties and he brought to them the same zest and enthusiasm which epitomised his cricket. He was also firmly of the opinion that a good one should never end before dawn. His party piece took the form of either a vocal, or a conjuring act.

"He had acquired his repertoire of songs during long forgotten nights in the mess and I think it is fair to say that his memory of the lyrics was considerably more impressive than his voice which was, fortunately, unique in my experience. It was an off beat, husky whisper but sufficiently penetrating to reach everyone in the room. He also had another favourite party piece involving an egg which was always far more entertaining when it failed than when successful, a view not shared by one distinguished cricket correspondent whose white tuxedo never looked quite so immaculate again."

When Trevor's fascinating reminiscences of a brother tourist came to an end I steered him carefully back to Edrich the cricketer. He saw nothing beautiful about his bowling action. A quick scurry up to the wicket followed by a slinging action (it reminded Bailey of a catapult) but he conceded Bill did propel the ball through the air at a considerable speed and with enormous zeal. Bailey, who took 2,082 wickets in something like 22 years in the first-class game, 132 of them for England, felt Edrich was essentially a shock bowler, to be used in short bursts, when he was always liable to surprise the batsman by his speed.

"His lack of height combined with his action ensured that he did not achieve much lift, in fact he tended to skid off the wicket." Bailey, a man not given to overstatement or facile praise, then added with a note of genuine admiration, the salute of one great craftsman to another – "but for a few overs he was genuinely quick".

Bailey had now dealt with his contemporary as a batsman, a bowler and an individual. To dot the i's and cross the t's did he have anything to add on Edrich as a fielder and captain?

"Originally a cover and a good mover, as one would expect from a professional soccer player, Bill gradually developed into a very effective and unspectacular first slip.

"His captaincy was in a similar mould to his slip fielding, sound rather than showy. He did not miss many tricks, but he was always willing to take a gamble if there was the slightest hope of victory."

This then was Bill Edrich who played 39 times for England and made six of his 86 centuries in Tests. In all first-class cricket he scored 36,965 runs and as in the case of his "twin" Denis Compton, Wally Hammond and Len Hutton one inevitably muses on what his figures would have been if he had been able to play at this level between 1940 and 1945. In the case of Edrich the years he lost covered the period between his 24th and 29th birthdays and he might well have retired in the company of names like Sutcliffe and Grace if not Hobbs, Woolley and Hendren. Robbed by fate as he was, he still accomplished not one but two seasons which will make his name imperishable as long as 22 men somewhere on the earth's surface can be found to play the game of cricket. Only three actual playing seasons after he achieved the now legendary feat of 1,000 in May he scored in 52 innings the remarkable aggregate of 3,539 runs which included twelve hundreds with an average of over 80. The fact that Denis Compton scored 3,816 in two innings less at an average of nearly 91 takes nothing from Edrich's marvellous follow up to 1938.

When he played his last first-class season in 1958 he was already half-way to his 43rd birthday and few could have visualised him carrying on into his middle fifties as an adornment to Minor Counties cricket. As year followed year and his name and performances continued to shine out from the middle reaches of *Wisden* those of us to whom he had given such unadulterated pleasure at Lord's were glad to know the little war horse had a whinny or two left in him.

If he has a regret it is that on his return to the county that had sired him and given him his first chance he was unable to lead Norfolk to the championship of the competition it has not won for 60 years.

The Minor Counties Championship was inaugurated in 1895 and in its first year Norfolk headed the table, sharing the title with Durham and Worcestershire. Ten years later Norfolk were outright champions after a wonderful season. Losing their first match and held to a draw in their second Norfolk, captained by the Rev. G. B. Raikes, won their remaining eight fixtures. Raikes was still captain in 1910 when Norfolk took the championship again and G. A. Stevens made 201 in the challenge match.

In 1912 Michael Falcon became captain, an office he held until the end of the 1946 season. Norfolk won seven of their eight matches but the championship was left unawarded as floods prevented the challenge match with Staffordshire being played. Ironically Norfolk with a far less impressive record won the title the following year. In a wonderful game against Staffordshire, Norfolk won by 35 runs, despite a certain Sidney Barnes taking nine for 31 in their first innings.

The outbreak of World War I caused the Minor Counties' programme to be abandoned in 1914 and it was not resumed until 1920. Between the wars Norfolk, in the opinion of its able historian Mr Armstrong, was at its strongest. Like all cricket lovers he succumbed to the temptation to pick his best eleven. In this case it is from the sides that represented Norfolk in the thirties and it comes as no surprise that three of the first six bear the name Edrich. All eleven of this team played first-class cricket at sometime or other, and here it is:

(1) D. F. Walker, (2) W. J. Edrich, (3) G. A. Edrich, (4) M. Falcon (captain), (5) M. R. Barton, (6) E. H. Edrich (wicket-keeper), (7) D. C. Rought-Rought, (8) R. C. Rought-Rought, (9) C. S. R. Boswell, (10) T. G. L. Ballance, (11) G. R. Langdale.

In this period Norfolk played 96 matches of which they won 33 outright and a further

27 on the first innings. Only 12 were lost. Yet the title at the end of the season always eluded Norfolk. Not for the first time fate took a hand against them in 1933 when, just as in 1912, the county reached the top of the Minor Counties table and in the words of the understandably disappointed Armstrong "only to be robbed, perhaps, of the title (who can tell!) by a misfortune over the challenge match, this time due to a miscalculation of points".

This is what happened: Yorkshire Second XI were credited with full points in a match with Staffordshire, when they should have had first-innings points only, the match having been reduced by rain to one day, and there having been a misunderstanding as to which of the two days had been rained off. These extra points had put Yorkshire in second place and they had then played and beaten Norfolk in what was supposed to be the Challenge Match. As a result of this victory, Yorkshire Second XI were put at the top of the table.

When the final table was being checked for insertion in *Wisden* it was found that the columns did not tally and on investigation the error was discovered. Wiltshire and not Yorkshire should have had the right to challenge Norfolk. The title was therefore left "Undecided" with Norfolk placed at the top of the table, champions in all but name.

Bill Edrich, a product of Bracondale school, made 20 out of a total of 49 against the 1932 Indian touring side and in 1935 distinguished himself against the South Africans whom he was to put to the sword in company with Compton 12 years later. At Lakenham he scored 111 for Norfolk in 165 minutes and two months later when selected for the Minor Counties he took a further 79 off the Tourists.

The degree of Edrich's virtuosity is surely plain to later generations when they learn that he continued to play for Norfolk until the end of 1936 – just two years before he scored 1,000 by the end of May. Although the title continued to elude them, sometimes by maddeningly narrow margins, Norfolk went from August 25, 1932, until July 1, 1937, without losing a single Minor Counties fixture.

When 1946 came Norfolk faced the task of building an almost new side. Walker and Ballance had been killed in action in the Second World War, Geoff Edrich and Eric Edrich had become Lancashire professionals, R. C. Rought-Rought had retired.

After one season Falcon's wonderful career came to a close. From 1906 to 1946 he took 727 wickets and scored 11,340 runs – tremendous figures for a competition so limited in fixtures as the Minor Counties.

Norfolk soldiered on into the fifties without being able to gather together a side capable of making a serious bid for honours but Eric Edrich had returned from Lancashire and in 1955 John Edrich, soon to leave for Surrey and a professional career as distinguished as Bill, topped the batting averages. As a fitting finale to the season a Norfolk XI played an All Edrich XI in which W. J. hit a century.

Before the decade was out the same W. J. Edrich was back at Lakenham. He polished off the fifties, shone steadily through the sixties and greeted the seventies by finishing top of the Norfolk batting with an average of over 35 and second in the bowling, sending down 238 overs and taking 25 wickets. He was then 54 years and seven months old. The summer of 1972 marked the 40th year since his entry into county cricket. 1972 also happened to be the centenary of the writing of the immortal song of Harrow School – "Forty Years On" by Bowen. Noble words, a haunting tune and no Harrovian of my acquaintance would object I feel sure if I quote the first verse here in tribute to one of the outstanding cricketers of my time.

Forty years on when afar and asunder
Parted are those who are singing to-day
When you look back and forgetfully wonder
What you were like in your work and your play
Then it may be there will often come o'er you
Glimpses of notes like the catch of a song
Visions of boyhood shall float them before you
Echoes of dreamland shall bear them along.

A CENTURY IN THE FIJI ISLANDS [1974]

By Philip Snow

Mr Snow captained Leicestershire 2nd XI, 1936-38. He is a former Administrator in the Colonial Service, Founder of the Fiji Cricket Association, author of Cricket in the Fiji Islands *and other works on the South Pacific, Permanent Representative of Fiji on the International Cricket Conference since 1965, and Honorary Life Member of MCC.*

Diametrically opposite England on the globe is Fiji, the farthest point to which cricket could penetrate. The Navy carried it 100 years ago. This sounds as though gunboats made Fiji British. Far from it, the chiefs asked Queen Victoria to take over Fiji. HMS *Pearl*, on February 21, 1874, played the Archipelago's then capital, Levuka, losing heavily. It was the first match – just before the independent kingdom became a Colony.

England has seldom seen Royal cricketers. A midshipman on HMS *Bacchante*'s 1881 circumnavigation, Prince George (later King George V), played against Levuka. His score significantly is not remembered. Next day he was demoted to *Bacchante*'s 2nd XI against HMS *Cleopatra*; the Press reported that "his score did not greatly affect the total". When the Prince of Wales visited Levuka in 1970 for Fiji's Independence, he was shown the ground so little productive of regal runs: the Press described him as not unamused.

Levuka had been preoccupied with commerce. With the British Administration's establishment there was incentive to contemplate British culture (not overmuch thought was given to this in a South Seas port, its public houses cluttering up the tiny beach) and recreation. Fijians saw Europeans playing: they soon wanted to participate. Hon. Jocelyn Amherst (Harrow XI) and Sir Edward Wallington (Sherborne XI and Wiltshire, an Oxford Blue, coach of an England captain in Lionel Tennyson, and latterly Queen Mary's Treasurer), both of them Aides-de-Camp to Sir William des Voeux, Governor 1878-86, encouraged them.

Quick-footed, exceptionally muscular, piercingly sharp of eye, their *forte* has been to hit everything as hard and often as possible, to catch with maximum *élan*, to bowl as swiftly as arms allow single-mindedly at the centre stump, to throw with utmost verve. Their throwing and bowling accuracy were evolutions from their spear throwing, the speed and directness of which meant the difference between life and death in their cannibal wars. Their dress – shirt and *sulu* (knee-length, side-split skirt) – contrasting with bronze, rugged, cheerful faces, their sinew, bulging calves, bootlessness, provide a spectacle unique in the cricket world, seen by only two countries, New Zealand and Australia. The larger the crowd, the greater the panache, the radiation of zest. Fijians reserve briskness of tempo for their games as a contrast to their everyday existence.

For organising Fijians, European administrators have been essential. Sir Basil Thomson (later Governor of Dartmoor and Head of Scotland Yard) and A. B. Joske (later Brewster) of Polish origin (whose widow survives at 101 in Bath), had to resist Fijian attempts to overlay the game's laws with tribal ideas for improving them, such as the crack bowler after an over resuming promptly at the other end and chiefs' inclinations to leave fielding to commoners.

J. S. Udal, Attorney-General 1890-1900, who had played for MCC (invited to go with W. G. Grace's 1873 team to Australia, he declined as he was qualifying for the Bar) and, like Wallington, for Dorset and the West of England, was influential enough to have an excellent ground made at Albert Park in the new capital, Suva. J. McC. Blackham's 1893 Australian team for England was prevented by a measles outbreak on their ship from playing Suva.

Udal, at 43 still useful, decided in 1895 to take a team the 1,000 miles to New Zealand. It consisted of six other Europeans (Sir William Allardyce, selected, could not go – he had played against Lillywhite's All England XI for the North of Scotland) and six Fijian chiefs. Ratu (Chief) Wilikonisoni Tuivanuavou bowled with distinct speed and success.

J. C. Collins carried his bat for a century – only one of 16 occasions in New Zealand's history. Playing against the leading New Zealand exponents (F. Wilding, the world's outstanding tennis player, made their only century), Fiji won 4, drew 2, lost 2.

In 1905, *en route* to England, Australia, including V. T. Trumper, R. A. Duff, C. Hill, M. A. Noble, W. W. Armstrong, F. Laver and A. Cotter, met Fiji who, batting 18 (including H. S. de Maus, New Zealand's best all-rounder a decade earlier) scored 91 to Australia's 212. Trumper, feeling unwell, hit the biggest six made on Albert Park.

Greatly daring, Mbau Island (no larger than Lord's in acreage, with a male adult population of 60) in 1908 toured Australia, 2,000 miles away. Pre-eminent as players were its two highest chiefs, both grandsons of King Ebenezer Thakombau (the only King before Cession) – Ratu Penaia Kandavulevu and his cousin, Ratu Pope E. S. Thakombau, acknowledged in Australia as of State standard. Winning 5, drawing 16, losing 5 (opponents including New South Wales, Queensland, South Australia and Victoria), Fijians' intrinsic skill needs no further underlining. It was sufficient inducement for S. E. Gregory's 1912 team from England to Australia (including C. Kellaway and E. R. Mayne) and Australia's 1913 team to Canada under A. Diamond (including C. G. Macartney, W. Bardsley, J. N. Crawford, H. L. Collins and A. A. Mailey) to play in the Islands. As the opposition was only Suva (not Fiji and including merely one Fijian), not unexpectedly they were comfortably beaten. Austin Diamond, New South Wales' leading batsman and second in Australia's 1907 averages, had worked in Fiji for the Sugar Company.

In parenthesis, just months before the First War and his own death, Rupert Brooke, a steady slow bowler in the Rugby XI, reported: "I played cricket! The Fijians play a good deal, very wildly and without great regard for the rules, but they have good eyes."

Those 1912-13 visits to Fiji have been followed by only one more match by any country's fully representative team – the West Indies in 1955. V. Y. Richardson's team to Canada (including D. G. Bradman, S. J. McCabe, Mailey, L. O'B. Fleetwood-Smith and A. F. Kippax) and D. R. Jardine's 1933 team returning from Australia were to have played in Suva had it not rained torrentially. Sitting next to Bradman in 1953 at a lunch for his birthday in a Lord's box, I was told by Sir Donald that he recalled the fastest Fijian bowler (Turanga) asking if he might feel his biceps and, on doing so, letting the interpreter know that he could not credit Bradman's reputation as the world's best batsman.

In 1924, a New Zealand team including J. S. Hiddleston, arguably then that country's best current batsman, made the first tour of Fiji, playing two matches against Fiji – not representative since the only Fijians encountered were Mbau. With such omissions Fiji, not unnaturally, lost easily. 5 wins, 3 draws, no losses (but a fright given them by Mbau) conveys a misleading result for the New Zealand side.

Another New Zealand team, the Maorilanders, captained by H. B. Massey, a Test player, made a similar tour in 1936. Two matches against Fiji were played – 1 lost, 1 won. Five Fijians were included to approach true representation: in one match the only hundred to date against a team touring Fiji was the achievement of Ratu Sir Edward Thakombau, great-grandson of King Thakombau, son of King George II of Tonga, now Fiji's Deputy Prime Minister, who had played for Auckland.

In 1938, when appointed to Fiji, I was astonished to fine Europeans and part-Europeans playing separately from Fijians and Indians. This anomaly I determined to alter as soon as I could. In 1939, when elected Secretary of the Suva Cricket Club I had this European organisation changed to the Suva Cricket Association, so constituting the first multi-racial sporting organisation of any kind in Fiji. Immediately, the most cosmopolitan side, the Central Medical School, which I was asked to coach, captained by an American Samoan and containing three Tongans, two British Samoans, one Rotuman, three Gilbertese, an Ellice Islander, two Solomon Islanders and five Fijians (the team's fastest bowler, Ratu Sir Kamisese Mara, played for Otago and became Fiji's Prime Minister on Independence 30 years later) defeated everyone.

Sir Julien Cahn only had to see the Fijians for a few minutes in 1939 before negotiating with me for an English tour. This was frustrated by the War, and then his death.

In this War, New Zealanders were in Fiji in quantity waiting to push back the Japanese and playing cricket meanwhile. P. E. Whitelaw, joint holder of the world's third wicket record, and N. Gallichan, the Test match slow left-hand bowler, achieved little; D. S. Wilson, who played in Tests on his return, and C. C. Burke, who toured Australia and England, were more successful. The New Zealand Forces, including Burke, were heavily defeated by a weakened Fiji Representative Team in 1942 (which included for the first time an Indian in top-level Fijian cricket). Amenayasi Turanga, who had politely doubted Bradman's prowess, took six for 16 in the first innings. Of Voce's build, he had his fast left-hander's bounce aimed at the batsman's shoulder. A gold-miner, he was accidentally electrocuted a fortnight later. One of the half-dozen best Fijians of all time, he was a ferocious hitter, once scoring 106 in twenty-eight minutes on a concrete pitch.

In 1946, with the backing of the leading chief, Ratu Sir Lala Sukuna, I was able to found the Fiji Cricket Association. Now fully representative Fiji teams could be established and Districts, whose Associations I had set up between 1940 and 1946, guided into regular competition.

The immediate result of the Fiji Association's foundation was organisation of a tour of New Zealand in 1948, the first truly representative Fijian one (and the second of any kind to go there in 53 years). Although there had been tests of ability against New Zealanders in Fiji conditions, Fijian prospects overseas were a risky estimate: I recall my cold feet when interviewed on deck as to our chances by the New Zealand Press arriving at dawn with Auckland's metropolitan skyline so daunting for us straight from the bush.

Starting on the right feet (mostly bare: there were 11 Fijians, with six Europeans and part-Europeans), we played all the first-class Provinces and leading Test players, W. A. Hadlee, W. M. Wallace, B. Sutcliffe, G. O. Rabone and many who were to extend England in Tests immediately afterwards. In three-day matches against the first-class Provinces Fiji won 2 and lost 3 (2 very narrowly). In the two-day matches Fiji won 4, drew 7, lost 0, and lost a one-day match. H. J. Apted, a left-hander with W. Watson's elegance, the youngest at 23, scored nearly 1,000 runs in 22 innings with an average of 46. Ilikena Lasarusa Talembulamainavaleniveivakambulaimainakulalakembalau (mercifully for New Zealand and his tremendously-in-demand autograph, known as I. L. Bula), exceeded 1,000 runs with soaring straight drives of real majesty, and M. J. Fenn, bowling slow inswingers with only one offside fielder, took 100 wickets in 700 overs – remarkable performances.

Viliame Mataika, with arm-touching-ear action, bowled Tate-like whipbacks to help us defeat Wellington early in the tour, but never played after his stretched-out bare foot had been jammed by a somnabulist traveller in a train corridor door. Ratu Sir George Thakombau, great grandson of King Thakombau, son of Ratu Pope Thakombau and now Fiji's first Governor-General since Independence, who was my Vice-captain, had a bare toe broken by a yorker half-way through the tour: it was fortunate that Ratu Sir Edward Tkakombau was able to join us then on return from Oxford. Ratu Sir Kamisese Mara was in mid-course at Oxford where injury deprived him of a Blue. His father once hit me for the highest six I have ever seen – vanishing into the sky to descend vertically into a 70-foot coconut palm's crown.

When I left Fiji in 1952, New Zealand was pressing for a repetition of the 1948 tour. Fijians, supreme guerilla fighters volunteering for the Malayan campaign, including Petero Kumbunavanua, reserve wicket-keeper in my 1948 New Zealand touring team. Selected with two other Fijians and Ratu Sir Edward Thakombau to play for Negri Sembilan State against Perak in 1952, Petero added to cricket's rare ornithological connection. Fielding at square leg and disturbed by swallows swooping on flies, he snatched one from the air and put it in his *sulu* pocket.

In 1954 P. T. Raddock (5 ft. high, he had been my 1948 wicket-keeper) with Ratu Mara, 6 ft. 5 ins. high as Vice-captain, took to New Zealand the next team – 9 Fijians, 6 Europeans and part-Europeans. They won 1, lost 3 three-day matches, won 5, lost 3 two-day matches, and won the two one-day matches. The 1948 team's performance promised first-class status for this team before the tour began. W. W. Apted, brother of

H. J. Apted (who also had a good tour), was the outstanding batsman, finishing 4th in the New Zealand averages. Bula, so evocative of Gimblett, joined the select list of those with 8 sixes in an innings when scoring 102 v Canterbury. But during this tour, unlike the 1948 tour, all the leading New Zealand players were absent (touring South Africa).

A singular accomplishment was the defeat in 1956 by Suva (not Fiji) of the West Indies captained by D. Atkinson and including J. D. Goddard, G. St A. Sobers, S. Ramadhin and A. L. Valentine. Suva's captain, Ratu Mara, opened the bowling. He told me, with the self-deprecatory touch which Fijians have in common with Europeans, that after about 30 runs had been scored quickly off him he had had a blinding flash of insight and took himself off. His replacement and the other opening bowler dismissed West Indies for 63, when to pass Suva's 91 had seemed easy.

In 1959 a modest tour was made to New South Wales Country Districts. Only one team of calibre was met: a New South Wales XI, including R. Benaud (captain), K. R. Miller, N. C. O'Neill and A. K. Davidson, was defeated in a one-day match, the Fijian fielding delighting the Sydney ground. Representing no advance on the 1908 tour by Mbau, the tour was marked by the first overseas selection of a Fiji Indian. Indians outnumber Fijians and are more prepared to take on administration than Fijians but have far to go to attain Fijians' playing standards.

Two further tours of New Zealand followed, one in 1961-62 containing 10 Fijians and 5 Europeans and part-Europeans. Astonishingly, no three-day matches were played. Nine two-day matches were lost, 8 won, 3 drawn; one one-day match lost, 1 drawn. The second, in 1967-68, managed by Josua Rambukawangga, Fiji's High Commissioner to the United Kingdom (a useful Mbauan), consisted of 11 Fijians, 3 Europeans and part-Europeans, and 2 Indians. It also played no three-day matches, won 4, lost 7 and drew 2 two-day matches, and won all 8 one-day matches.

H. J. Apted and Bula have been omnipresent in every tour since the War. Walter Hadlee considered Bula's inclusion (within the Rules as Fiji was not then playing first-class cricket and its players were therefore eligible to play for the nearest Test-playing country) for New Zealand's 1949 tour of England. After consulting me, Hadlee thought that Bula's modest knowledge of English might have led to homesickness in a long tour far away from home.

Bula holds Fiji's highest score, 246, beating the 214 not out and 196 in a fortnight of a remarkable all-rounder, Viliame Tuinaceva Longavatu who should have been seen overseas (he took 9 for 0 in 1.4 overs in 1933 in a high-grade match. I took his son, Isoa Longavatu, to New Zealand as the team's fast bowler; he had taken 10 wickets for 8 in 1941 – the best of Fiji's seven instances of 10 wickets in an innings.). The most remarkable bowling feat in Fiji's history was at Lomaloma in the Lau Archipelago (half-way between Fiji and the Kingdom of Tonga): Saiasi Vuanisokiki took 8 wickets for 0 in an 8-ball over against HMS *Leith*. A fast left-hander in Turanga's class, he would have been taken by me to New Zealand in 1948 but for an injury.

As remarkable in its way, more recently, has been 40 off 7 balls in an 8-ball over in a top-standard match scored by Nathanieli Uluiviti who had played for Auckland.

Fiji's cricket centenary, which is adding a rare connection of the game with philately by three stamps marking the event, runs parallel to a near-century of British Administration from the Island's Cession in 1874. Independence in 1970, with Fiji becoming a Dominion in the Commonwealth, was a gentle evolution from that auspicious start of the Archipelago having been given to Queen Victoria, contrasting with the usual 19th century process of colonization by conquest.

New Zealand cricket judges who have seen all Fijian sides rank the 1948 team as the best. Each team has given enjoyment to every part of New Zealand, but it has become recognised that the Fijian standard, if measured only by the lower category of opponents in subsequent tours, has not been maintained for three principal reasons. Firstly, Fijians of high standing who have been on tours, for example, Ratu Mara and the two Ratu Thakombaus, respectively Prime Minister, Deputy Prime Minister and Governor-General, have had their time heavily taken up under a preoccupation as never before, contrasted with their predecessors as high chiefs able to give time to coaching.

Secondly, Fiji's success at Rugby Football on tours beyond New Zealand and Australia to Wales, England and France have diverted attention from cricket. Thirdly, there has been insufficient progress in Fiji's improvement and, with a population doubled since 1948, increase of grounds. Beautiful and bad are not the right requisites for playing areas. Albert Park, Suva, so picturesque with its vivid colour captured in the painting in the Imperial Gallery at Lord's, is muddied-up by football and hockey, by every kind of event and festival, the huge crowds squelching the grass out by its roots in the deluges that Fiji keeps for main happenings. Like other cricket grounds in Fiji it is not, and cannot be, enclosed: income is only gained from private generosity. No sport, even football, with its undemanding outlay on equipment, can advance that way.

Other factors contribute to an uphill struggle: (1) Cricket is expensive for a country where, outside the half-dozen towns, villages are mere clusters of houses with roofs and walls of thatch shaped like haystacks: equipment is always scarce. (2) A serious obstacle lies in the distances between the 100 inhabited islands. (3) Then there is the division of island pitches between matting on either grass or concrete (4) Coaching is a quintessential requirement. So much talent waits to be steered delicately by a discerning eye – a coach without flair could extinguish the Fijian flame.

A fifth reason for Fiji's diminishing performances against New Zealand was recently explained to me by Bevan Congdon, the New Zealand captain, as being due to a sudden marked improvement in New Zealand standards.

In 1965 when the Imperial Cricket Conference became the International Cricket Conference, Fiji was the first country, with Ceylon and U.S. of America, to be admitted to the company of the Test-playing countries. England may yet see a Fiji side. One was arranged to come here in 1959 to play the Duke of Norfolk's XI, MCC at Lord's and various Counties when it became apparent that Fiji's standard had suddenly slipped and local confidence declined: postponement was considered judicious. Little but a revival of coaching is needed to restore Fiji to its first-class standard. A World Cup, particularly if on a one-day basis to which Fiji are well suited, could see them participating after not too long.

BUYING BACK ONE'S PAST [1975]

By John I. Marder
(*Past President USA Cricket Association*)

It was Oscar Wilde who once said, "No man is rich enough to buy back his past." It may have seemed that way to the inimitable Oscar, but one can always make a backward safari through time in the pages of *Wisden*. The late A. A. Thomson used to say that if he were marooned on a desert island, he would like to have the 1903 *Wisden* with him so that he could fight the battles of the 1902 Tests again. Rowland Ryder in the 1965 *Wisden* evoked the pleasure that thousands of cricket enthusiasts get out of re-living old matches and looking up the careers of bygone players. I had a friend, Karl Auty of Chicago, who kept his *Wisdens* in his bedroom. If he couldn't sleep, he would roll out the rather uniquely designed bookshelf which fitted right under his bed and pick out an interesting year to browse over. *Wisden* has mirrored the cricket world accurately since 1864 and is has unconsciously brought back another world through its advertising pages – the everyday world, where it was once possible to live very well on five pounds a week.

For the first fourteen years of its long life, the Almanack didn't accept any advertising from other firms. It was deemed sufficient in those Victorian days to list descreetly on the back pages of *Wisden*, a "List of Articles Stocked". *Wisden* in those days was one of several annuals fighting for public recognition. It was quite sufficient that if any cricketing gentleman needed any supplies, he could consult the "List" and make his wants known by a visit to the establishment.

The 1867 *Wisden* advertised a rather ingenious mechanical bowler – a Catapulta, which I believe was invented by Felix, the Kent cricketer. It was not until a few years later that a price was appended to the display. The mechanical bowler cost twelve guineas, which was rather expensive, compared with the annual fees paid to a ground bowler at the time.

Advertising in the mid Victorian era, was deemed rather vulgar and there was an upper class aversion to "persons in trade". Advertising agents were probably placed in a social niche slightly lower than a circus advance man. They were probably deemed rather a nuisance, advertising being regarded as "hawking one's wares", and not having anything like the prestige acquired in this century. The first few advertisements in the Almanack were from other cricket outfitters, which was only to be expected – and from patent medicines! These remedies were stated to be almost miraculous in their healing powers. Epilepsy, boils, sore legs, dysentery – even cancerous ulcers, were cured only by application of these magic elixirs. They were described as "pleasant tasting" too – all this for 2/6d a box! These wonder cures were of no value whatever to poor Fred Grace, who died in 1880 of congestion of the lungs, brought on, it was said, by sleeping in a damp bed. Such carelessness in regard to health and such carelessness in the attribution of magical cures to patent medicines, is typical of a credulous age. The motto of the day was "Caveat Emptor", – let the buyer beware.

In 1881 an American President was assassinated and the first Boer War began. In some ways the world news showed a curious affinity to our own day. From a sportsman's point of view, games were much less expensive than they are today. A complete cricket outfit could be bought for £2-10-0 and many famous clubs started with just such gear. Top quality bats were 21/- and balls were no problem – they were 3/- per dozen! *Wisden* seemed to be rather broad minded with their advertisers – a Mr J. D. Bartlett advertised that his premises contained "the largest stock of bats in the world", rather an ambitious claim, but no one seems to have challenged him.

Competition appears to have been fierce amongst batmakers. Cobbett's advertised that "some evilly disposed of persons are stamping our name on common and inferior goods" which seems to give the lie to the oft believed myth that the Victorians were a more sporting lot than their successors! Cobbett's warned that their bats carried a registered trademark and no Cobett bat was genuine without it. There were no fair trade laws or any consumer protection laws in those days. Cricketers couldn't be sure of the quality they were getting. Perhaps the vogue for bats with the signature of a famous cricketer dates from this period. Lawn tennis was invented in the seventies and became popular very quickly. Advertisements of the period show ladies playing in the long sweeping dresses of the period, buttoned high at the throat. One wonders how they got enough freedom of action even to play the game, no matter how innocuous it was in those early days. *Wisden* offered tennis "bats" for 25/-. Fifty-one years later a similar racquet costs 67/-. Tennis nets cost 40/- complete with poles and balls were 8/6 d a dozen.

There were many sporting newspapers during this period. After reading these advertisements one realizes the inroads that television and radio have made to our reading habits. It was a slower and pleasanter world. The *Sporting Clipper* carried the latest racing information for the venturesome punter and announced that its Saturday edition, at the unheard of price of twopence, was on the streets before the morning trains left for the neighbouring courses. One could also read *The Sportsman*, *Sporting Life*, *Bell's Life Daily* and the *Cricket and Football Times*. This was advertised at 10/- per annum and was said to have been written "by gentlemen". This brings to mind the fact that sport was dominated in those days by public schoolboys who founded the great soccer clubs of to-day, started the Rugby Union and administered the MCC.

Charles Spencer & Co. advertised a "Pangymnasticon" which was a practical home gymnasium for ten guineas. It was claimed that this outfit would greatly promote physical health. Seventy years later the successors to the firm were advertising a slip catch trainer which perhaps had more appeal for clubs suffering from a lack of good fieldsmen. Echoes of sporting days in Scotland and on the Yorkshire moors are brought to mind by the advertisement of E. M. Reilly & Co. who sold wild fowl guns for ten guineas and gamekeepers' guns for £6-10-0. First-class amateurs were always tempted after the Twelfth of August by invitations to join shooting parties and it would be a keen cricketer indeed who could resist the temptations of grouse shooting and agreeable feminine companionship.

Wisden soon carried advertising for cricket literature – the first books announced were later volumes of *Scores & Biographies* and Box's *English Game of Cricket*. There were not too many books published about the game, but Fred Gale's books were always available and there were summaries of the Oxford v Cambridge match to 1876 which were popular. Until the twenties, there was a modest annual list of cricket books which later developed into a flood. P. F. Warner turned out a book or two on his overseas tours but "tour books" did not reach real popularity until after the First World War. In 1925 *Wisden* carried announcements of M. A. Noble's book, *The Game's the Thing* and of A. C. MacLaren's study of the batting of Jack Hobbs, *The Perfect Batsman*. Both were priced at 7/6d. Tobacco advertisements came in during the eighties and it was still fashionable to advertise snuff. Virginia cigarettes were popular, one advertised brand being the "President Arthur" variety. It was doubtful if President Chester A. Arthur of the United States had authorized the use of his name.

Wisden committed one of its rare boners in 1884 when the Calendar was headed 1844. Perhaps the editor was buying back his past! The Royal Bicycle and Tricycle Agency advertised light carriages for one or two horses. This mode of transport was termed "most luxurious" and it certainly was. Motor drawn traffic was non-existent and English roads had not been improved too much since the eighteenth century. In fact they had not been improved since the stage coaches had ceased in the forties. Roads were almost chronically in disrepair. It took the twentieth century with its avalanche of motor cars to bring about an improvement in highways. Adventurous spirits could mount a "penny farthing" and attain a speed of 20 miles an hour but at the risk of their necks! By 1891 the "ordinaries" as they were termed, had disappeared from the road. Their place was taken by the "safety" models that we have known ever since. Something of a cycling craze took place in the nineties and Sugg's advertised bicycles for thirteen guineas.

E. Hawkins & Company of Brighton took many pictures of cricketers, most of them strategically posted near a potted palm or defending an obviously staged wicket. In 1886-87 Shaw and Shrewsbury took out an England team to Australia. Before 1903 these tours were arranged on a speculative basis and this team played at Bowral on January 23 and 24, 1887. Twenty-one years later, one of Australia's greatest batsmen was to be born there! Towards the end of the tour the Englishmen indulged in rather a novel match – both English and Australian players collaborating in a match between the Smokers and Non-smokers. The Non-smokers batted first and Arthur Shrewsbury and W. Bruce of Australia put on 196 for the first wicket – this against Brigge Palmer, Boyle and Lohmann. The Non-smokers showed that they did not miss a puff now and again by rolling up 803 for nine wickets. Quick to take advantage of this, the largest innings on record thus far in a first-class match, Messrs Hawkins offered pictures of the two elevens. The Smokers were proudly brandishing their cigars and pipes. The firm also advertised pictures of the Australians of 1886, taken in the field at an exposure of 1/20 sec., then deemed to be a record.

The nineties were heralded by an announcement that the International Fur Store would sell a "good fur-lined overcoat" for £10-0-0. The accompanying cut could have been used in later days to portray a capitalist – top hat, rolled fur collar and all!

Frank Bryan, who are still advertising in *Wisden*, announced that their batting gloves in future would have a protective covering for the thumb. Bryan would probably like to have buckskin leg guards for sale in the current year of grace, for 6/6d a pair. Serviceable cricket boots were 10/6d and sweaters were 4/6d. Cricket caps were 1/- each, with a few pennies extra for a monogram!

As the Victorian era drew to its close, there were slight evidences in *Wisden*. The obituaries refer to deaths in South Africa. One of the more prominent cricketers to lose his life was F. W. Milligan of Yorkshire. Some famous cricketers were at the front, but the war did not seriously interrupt the placid flow of life in England. Prices did not move upward, there was no inflation as in our more precarious days.

John Piggott could still advertise a lounge suit for 45/- and an overcoat for 12/6d. One can be sure that these coats were not fur lined! Squash was a popular game and rackets were advertised at 17/6d. Frank Sugg, the Derbyshire and Lancashire batsman, advertised extensively for some years. His trade slogan was "The Reasonable, Practical Man" and his prices sound almost incredible seventy-five years later. Running pumps were 4/6d and track suits were 1/11d. Good football boots were advertised at 9/6d a pair and batting gloves were 8/6d. Cricket entered into a Golden Age in the early part of the twentieth century. Every county had its personality and W.G., as the acknowledged "Champion" was emperor of a kingdom. This was the era of Jackson, Fry and MacLaren, Jessop, Trumper and Warner. South Africa became a cricketing power with her quartette of googly bowlers and the West Indies sent two teams to England. One could foresee their future greatness. Even Philadelphia were welcome tourists, the first and only American team to play first-class cricket. It was an exciting period for the game and the advertising in the Almanack reflected the opulence of the times.

All sorts of bats were on the market. A specially selected one would cost about 25/- and you could choose from Wisden, Gradidge, Abel, Tyldesley, Dark, Surridge and Ayres bats and many others. Wisden "Crown" cricket balls were 5/- each and leg guards, real buckskin, had advanced to 9/9d. Famous players gave their autographs to bats almost absent mindedly and in one issue of *Wisden*, C. B. Fry gave his blessing to "Imperial Drivers", "Stuart Surridge" and "J. T. Tyldesley" bats. His name on any product in the period before the First World War was eagerly sought. He was not only one of the best batsmen in England, he was also a first-class rugby player for Blackheath and played left back for Southampton when they reached the final of the FA Cup. He was the Editor of *C. B. Fry's Magazine*, which also advertised in *Wisden*. It was billed as "bringing a breezy cheerfulness to English homes". C. B. Fry gave the stamp of his own personality far beyond those times. In 1919 he was seriously proposed as King of Albania. What a monarch he would have made! There is little doubt that the Albanians would have been playing Test cricket by now instead of being part of the Chinese bloc!

The ordinary cricket ground had used horse drawn mowers for many years. There was a time indeed when the Oval turf was cropped by having sheep graze on the ground. The Staten Island CC of New York are reputed to own the grazing rights to The Oval, garnered during an exciting poker game in the 1870s, but they have not seriously requested Surrey to use their services.

It was an accepted legend in many grounds that the horses would know when the last batsman had taken his place at the crease. At Trent Bridge, when Fred Morley came in to bat for Nottinghamshire, it was said that the horse would sidle over to the mower, ready for his job! Cricketing legend died when the mowers were motorized. Ransome's had advertised horse-drawn mowers for £32-0-0. By 1909 the same firm proclaimed proudly that they had sold nearly 200 motor drawn mowers. The Automobile Age, for better or worse, was upon us. In 1903 Lord's School of Physical Culture, possibly taking advantage of a more famous "Lord's", was advertising physical culture course by mail. It was an era of biceps flexing. Whiteley's advertised "Two British Records, Foster's 287, and our Flexten home exerciser for 17/6d".

Bicycles had declined in price from ten years previously. They were advertised for eight guineas each, although motor cycles were beginning to be popular. Club secretaries may have groused when they brought grass seed at a pound a bushel, little realizing the troubles of their successors. They could console themselves by smoking "Alliance" tobacco at 5d an ounce. It was advertised as "the most exquisite blending of the finest tobaccos". Steel razors were 7/6d with ivory handles but many cricketers were beginning to use the new safety razors. Beards and moustaches were going out of style. By 1910 most cricketers looked very youthful and were cleanshaven, a style which persisted into our day. In the 1906 *Wisden*, a Mr T. N. W. took a half page advertisement to announce that he had a complete run of *Wisden* for sale. One hopes that he got a good price for his set.

During the First World War, organized cricket stopped after the season of 1914. *Wisden* shrank in size but it continued to appear, a symbol of hope for more normal times – sooner or later, the "Rolls of Honour" were fearsome but the 1916 edition carried the obituaries of A. E. Stoddard, Victor Trumper and of the "Champion" himself – W. G. Grace, dead at 67. He had seemed immortal to most cricketers. Even the enemy announced that his death was due to an air raid, which was not true.

Although first-class cricket was finished, the game was still played and other sports equipment was also advertised. Prices were little changed for the first year or two. Golf clubs were advertised at 6/6d, either woods or irons, and golf balls were 15/- a dozen. By 1918 post war inflation was beginning. Golf clubs were 8/6d and by 1919 prices really started to climb.

That year saw an experiment. County matches were restricted to two days. The trial lasted for only one year. Until one-day cricket made its debut in 1963, the first-class game was to know little change. Bats had advanced to 32/- and balls were double their pre-war price. The twenties saw matters slowly returning to normal. In fact, cricket enjoyed some of its greatest seasons with Hobbs enjoying a new career, closely followed by George Gunn, Mead, Hendren, Hearne and Frank Woolley. Wilfred Rhodes was still wheeling them over for Yorkshire and he was a playing link with the Golden Age.

Charles Pugh Ltd advertised a motor mower for thirty guineas which would cut 1,000 square yards in twenty minutes. Cricket sweaters were now 23/6d and the latest model Humber motor cycle cost £55.

The thirties were more troublesome times. An obituary in *Wisden* gave a hint of the disorders in the world, E. R. Sheepshanks of the Eton XI, who died in the Spanish Civil War. Shortage of money was chronic and *Wisden* broke new ground when a moneylender advertised his services – loans of fifty pounds and upward! With the start of the Second World War, *Wisden* again shrank in size. The wonder was that it appeared at all. The continuity of almost a hundred years was not lost. Late in 1940 the firm's factory was destroyed by enemy action but work on the Almanack went on. The article on "Public school cricket" was destroyed in the raid, the author had also suffered the loss of his notes at another place during the same raid. It was impossible to get another article ready in time for publication. Advertising came to the rescue. Four pages appeared between pp 185 and 188 of the 1941 *Wisden* instead of the article on the schools. Edward Ltd had advertised for many years but wartime restrictions made it impossible for the firm to supply their nets. They continued to advertise as usual although they had nothing to sell! Their display showed a cricket ball with the announcement, "A net regret – government regulations prevent Edwards from supplying nets for this"!

The forties were characterized by a flood of "Brylcreem" advertising featuring Denis Compton, particularly after his fine season in 1947. His face not only appeared in *Wisden*, but on Tube posters and on billboards all over the country.

Cricket schools had advertised in *Wisden* since 1928, one of the first being the Faulkner School and now Alf Gover's East Hill School became prominent. The advent of sponsored cricket inevitably lead to advertisements by Gillette, Rothman, Esso, Prudential, Haig and John Player, all of whom have done so much to popularize present day cricket.

The advertising in *Wisden* for the past hundred and eleven years is evocative of the times in which we and our fathers have lived. There is a ticket to "buy back one's past" implicit in the Almanack. A browse through the advertising pages brings memories of days far different from our own.

Wisden has seen the transition of cricket from a country pastime to a world wide sport. Amateurs have now disappeared from county cricket and one-day cricket is with us. Test cricket will inevitably widen and include some countries not yet in the charmed circle. I think particularly of Sri Lanka who will no doubt merit Test status shortly.

As we "buy back our past" we look forward to *Wisden* of 2001!

F. R. FOSTER [1976]

A PRINCE OF THE GOLDEN AGE

By Rowland Ryder

F. R. Foster was one of the most astonishing performers ever to have played the game of cricket. His career lasted from 1908 until 1914; it was all over when he was twenty-five. A dashing personality, an inspiring captain with tremendous flair, a brilliant all-rounder, his enthusiastic verve set the cricketing world ablaze. At the age of twenty-two he had accepted the captaincy of a sadly struggling Warwickshire eleven and led them to victory after victory. After that, he went to Australia, and with Sydney Barnes, shattered the Australian batting. "Before he was twenty-four" wrote P. F. Warner, "he had done enough to earn everlasting fame in the history of cricket."

Frank Rowbotham Foster was born on January 31, 1889, in Small Heath, Birmingham. He was of Lincolnshire descent, and was not related to the famous Foster family of Worcestershire. He attended what was then Solihull Grammar School, where he played his earliest cricket, and later played for Hall Green, gaining a reputation as a fastish left-arm bowler.

He got his first chance for Warwickshire in June 1908, playing against Derbyshire at Derby. He made an impressive start as a bowler, taking six wickets in the match for 52 runs. Warwickshire's next match was against Surrey, and the nineteen-year-old Frank Foster celebrated his first visit to London by capturing the wickets of Jack Hobbs and Tom Hayward. He played altogether five games in 1908, finishing with 23 wickets for seventeen runs each.

By 1909 he had become an established member of the side, under the captaincy of A. C. S. Glover; he played in seventeen matches, taking 48 wickets at 26 runs a wicket and scoring 530 runs for an average of 24: against the Australians he had the satisfaction of clean bowling Victor Trumper for 1. "F. R. Foster, one of the most promising all round cricketers in the county" ran the Warwickshire report in *Wisden*, "did admirable service with bat and ball . . . and he took more wickets than anyone except Santall." It was suggested that he might have been still more effective but for sacrificing accuracy of pitch to a higher rate of speed – a tactful way of saying that he sometimes tried to bowl too fast! Like a good many left arm bowlers, he was a right-hand batsman, and he was already showing signs that he believed in keeping the scorers occupied.

Warwickshire had a poor season in 1910. A. C. S. Glover had resigned the captaincy and his official successor, H. J. Goodwin, could play in only half the matches. That season Foster came into his own as a bowler, taking a hundred wickets for the first time. For Warwickshire he took 91 wickets at 22 runs each, and in three games for the Gentlemen against the Players he took altogether 17 wickets for 242 runs, his victims including Hobbs, Hayward, J. T. Tyldesley (twice) and Rhodes (twice). The Warwickshire report in *Wisden* described Foster as "a long way the most brillian all-round man in the county".

It seemed likely that 1911 would be even more disastrous for Warwickshire than 1910, especially as H. J. Goodwin was no longer available. Who then, should be the new captain? In desperation the committee offered the job to F. R. Foster, who, like a batsman trying to run himself out, answered "Yes", "No", and finally, "Yes" again.

Warwickshire's first match in the long dry summer of 1911 was against Surrey, and they lost by an innings early in the second day. It was this disaster which caused Foster, who had not played in the Surrey match, to change his mind and accept the captaincy.

Victories immediately followed, against Lancashire, Leicestershire and Sussex. Against Lancashire Foster showed uncanny flair by introducing the young Jack Parsons (now the Rev. Canon J. H. Parsons) – a promising batsman but hardly a first-class bowler – into the attack. The object was to capture J. T. Tyldesley's wicket. The move succeeded brilliantly. Parsons got Tyldesley caught behind and was then taken off. In Warwickshire's seventh match, against Derbyshire at Blackwell, Derbyshire needed 40 to win with five wickets to fall. At this point Foster took off Warwickshire's opening bowler Frank Field and put on A. B. Crawford – "a casual member of the side, a tall, bumpy fast bowler", as Foster described him. Crawford took two wickets and Warwickshire won by 14 runs.

By the end of June, Warwickshire had played eight matches, having won four and lost four. This was not bad going, but they were well down the Championship table and it is doubtful if, at this juncture, Foster himself had any serious hopes of winning the Championship. A new system of scoring had been introduced: there were five points for a win, three for a win on first innings and one point to the side behind, drawn matches with no decision on first innings were not counted. As the sixteen counties competing in the 1911 Championship played varying numbers of matches, positions in the table were worked out on percentages.

During the remainder of the season Warwickshire, playing like a revitalised side, and responding superbly to the leadership of their twenty-two-year-old captain, won nine of their twelve remaining matches, and they very nearly won two of the three drawn games. In doing all this they picked up fifty four points out of sixty.

July was heralded with an innings victory against Hampshire; next Warwickshire had much the better of a draw against Surrey, Foster scoring a chanceless 200 in three hours. Victories followed against Northamptonshire, Sussex and Gloucestershire. Foster scored 98 in an hour and a half against Northamptonshire, and took five for 25 in their second innings; he made 65 and took five for 52 against Sussex; in a seven wicket win against Gloucestershire he took five for 76 and three for 59; he also scored 56 and 87.

In their fourteenth Championship match Warwickshire completely outclassed Yorkshire at Harrogate. Set 257 to win Yorkshire collapsed before the bowling of Field and Foster, and were all out for 58. It is recorded that during this innings, one of the Yorkshire batsmen walked out without an appeal being made, saying that he had had enough. Foster made 60 in forty minutes and 101 in an hour and three-quarters. As a fast scorer he seems to rank second only to Jessop; his big innings were generally scored at 60 or more runs an hour.

There was a drawn game at Southampton, and then the crowds flocked to Edgbaston for the Bank Holiday match against Worcestershire. Nineteen thousand enthusiasts saw Foster score 85 in ninety minutes on the first day, and then later take four of the five wickets that fell before stumps were drawn. Worcestershire however, narrowly escaped defeat.

Next came a win against Derbyshire. Foster made 70 in as many minutes in the second innings, after which he took six for 37 in Derbyshire's total of 180. Lancashire were beaten by an innings – Foster scored 98 in a hundred minutes – and Leicestershire were defeated in two days at Hinckley.

The last match, against Northamptonshire, has passed into Warwickshire folklore. In order to win the Championship Warwickshire had to win the match. "Are you going to beat 'em, Mr Foster?" shouted a spectator, as the team left New Street station, Birmingham. "Beat 'em? We'll paralyse 'em!" he is reported to have called back.

Northamptonshire won the toss, but were all out before lunch for 73, Foster taking five for 18 in 13.2 overs. At the end of the second day, Northamptonshire with seven wickets down, needed 71 to avoid an innings defeat. Foster recounted that on that night, most of the Warwickshire team were too excited to go to bed at all. Foster himself tried to get to bed at 4 a.m., but was quickly roused to play a game of "Farmer's Glory", and he adds that the sun was shining when the team left the card table for the breakfast table. Northamptonshire lost their last three wickets in thirty-five minutes, and Warwickshire returned in triumph to New Street, where a joyous crowd awaited them. *Punch* celebrated the occasion with a full page cartoon, captioned "Two Gentlemen of Warwickshire" depicting William Shakespeare shaking hands with a beflannelled Frank Foster. "Tell Kent from me she hath lost" says Foster, and Shakespeare replies "Warwick, thou art worthy".

Warwickshire's success was indeed a splendid achievement; not since the Championship had expanded in 1895 with the introduction of new counties, had any team outside the Big Six – Kent, Lancashire, Middlesex, Nottinghamshire, Surrey and Yorkshire – won the Championship. Foster himself had played an enormous part in his county's success. Not only had his leadership revitalised the side; he was top of both batting and bowling averages, scoring 1,383 runs for an average of 44.61, and taking 116 wickets for an average of 19 runs a wicket. Foster himself, summing up Warwickshire's success in his memoirs* had this to say: "The very hot season, the dry and fast wickets, the 'keeping' of 'Tiger' Smith, the will to win, the absurd changes of bowling, the friendship between the committee and myself, the advice of R. V. Ryder, the wickets prepared by Bates our groundsman, the friendliness of all spectators, the encouragement from the crowd, the help of the new ball and the help of Frank Field at Harrogate plus the help of Fate at Northampton made Warwickshire the Champion County for the season of 1911."

Wisden chose him as one of the Five Cricketers of the Year for the 1912 issue, the others being Phil Mead, Herbert Strudwick, Jack Hearne and Warwickshire's own Septimus Kinneir. "Not since W. G. Grace in the early days of the Gloucestershire eleven" said *Wisden* in the Warwickshire report, "has so young a captain been such a match-winning force on a county side. Foster was always getting runs, always taking wickets and over and above this, he proved himself a truly inspiring leader".

Frank Foster was naturally chosen to tour Australia at the end of the season; and his bowling partnership with Sydney Barnes proved the most important factor in England winning the Ashes. The MCC team was to have been led by P. F. Warner, but, after scoring 151 in the first match, against South Australia, he became ill, and took no further part in the tour, J. W. H. T. Douglas deputising as captain. Foster opened the tour with centuries against South Australia and Victoria. He also acquired the reputation of being the best-dressed man in the team, inspiring an Australian rhymester to write:

"The flannel pants of Foster cost
A guinea clear per pair."

In the five Test matches Foster's performances as a batsman were creditable without being remarkable, his scores being 56, 21, 9, 71, 50, 15, 4 – 226 runs for an average of 32.28, his 71 being a most un-Fosterlike innings lasting nearly three hours.

It was as a bowler that he excelled himself. His greatest performance was perhaps in the third Test match. Australia in their first innings, batting on a perfect wicket, were all out for 133. "Foster was in his deadliest form" wrote *Wisden*. "He began by bowling eleven overs, six maidens for eight runs and one wicket and finished up with the remarkable average of five wickets for 36.

His final analysis read:

Overs	Maidens	Runs	Wickets
26	9	36	5

His five victims were Kelleway, Hordern, Armstrong, Clem Hill and Minnett. The left-handed Clem Hill was out first ball, stumped by "Tiger" Smith off Foster's bowling, while attempting a glide. P. F. Warner has described this planned piece of stumping as "one of the technical masterpieces of the game". "Tiger" Smith himself, who "kept" to Foster's bowling through much of the latter's career, and who recalls so vividly this Test match series, claims that Clem Hill should have been given out "stumped Smith, bowled Foster 0" in his second innings, and that he was out by about twelve inches. However, the umpire thought otherwise, and Clem Hill went on to make 98. England won this match by seven wickets and the series by four matches to one.

Foster took five for 92 in the second innings of the first Test, six for 91 in the second innings of the second Test, four for 77 and three for 38 in the fourth Test, and four for 43

* *Cricketing Memories, by Frank Foster, London Publishing Co.*

in 30.1 overs in the second innings of the fifth Test. The final figures of the Foster–Barnes combination for the five Test matches makes interesting reading:

	Overs	Maidens	Runs	Wickets	Average
Foster	275.5	58	692	32	21.62
Barnes	297	64	778	34	22.88

1912 was the year of the rain-ridden Triangular Tournament, involving England, Australia and South Africa, each country playing three Test matches against the other two, so that each country played six matches in all. Foster played in all six Tests for England. He did great things in the first Test match against South Africa, taking five for 16 in the first innings – all clean bowled, and three for 54 in the second. In general however, the pitches were too slow for him, and a third full season without a rest must have taken its toll. For Warwickshire he scored 600 runs for an average of 19.61, but considering the slow pitches, did surprisingly well with his bowling, taking 85 wickets at 16 runs a wicket.

In 1913 he was clearly not himself, and had to rest for three matches. He scored 782 runs for Warwickshire, including a century against Hampshire, but his ninety-one wickets – again on the hard fast pitches that he loved – cost over 24 runs a wicket.

In 1914, Frank Foster was back on top form. He scored 1,396 runs for an average of thirty-five, and took 117 wickets for a little over eighteen runs a wicket; his bowling figures, in fact, were slightly better than they were in 1911. Against Worcestershire, at Dudley, Foster played the innings of his life, scoring 305 not out in four hours and twenty minutes; during the course of this innings a stand of 166 with "Tiger" Smith, who made 42, lasted seventy minutes.

The last game that Foster ever played for Warwickshire was against Surrey at Edgbaston on August 27, 28 and 29. He opened the innings, both as a batsman and as a bowler, scoring 81 – "a delightful innings" says *Wisden* – and 7; taking four for 24 and five for 48 in a Warwickshire victory against a fine Surrey side. Eight of Foster's nine victims were clean bowled.

It is difficult to assess F. R. Foster in terms of cricketing greatness, owing to the comparative brevity of his career. It is chiefly as a bowler that he will be remembered; second as a dynamic captain, third, as a batsman. This at least can be said: as a bowler he went through an Australian tour with Sydney Barnes at his zenith, and wicket for wicket, proved himself his equal; as a captain, he evoked comparison with the young W. G. Grace; as an attacking batsman he was not far short of Jessop.

How did Foster bowl? This is what he wrote himself: "I took a short eight-yard run, holding the ball always in my left hand with 'seam-up' and I always delivered the ball from the very edge of the bowling crease." Foster also felt very strongly that no left-hander should ever attempt to bowl over the wicket.

This is how P. F. Warner describes Foster's action. "Bowling left-hand round the wicket with a high delivery – he was six feet tall – his action was the personification of ease. A few short steps, a graceful skip, an apparently medium-paced ball through the air, but doubling its speed as it touched the ground, he kept an exceptional length." He did in fact once bowl two consecutive maiden overs to Jessop!

And a wicket-keeper's eye view – "I remember the first time I kept to him" wrote Herbert Strudwick. "It was at Lord's in an England v The Rest match. Seymour (Kent) was batting. The first ball Mr Foster bowled appeared to be well on the leg side. Seymour shaped to play it to leg and I moved that way, but, believe me, we were both surprised when the ball flashed over the off stump, and when it went for four byes I thought I was in for a good afternoon."

Foster bowled at the leg stump, and he certainly hit the wickets pretty frequently. In 1911 74 of his 116 victims were clean bowled and 10 were lbw – a left-hander bowling at the edge of the crease could hardly expect more. Foster would seem to have developed his leg theory bowling during the Australian tour; in certain respects he did what Larwood was doing in Australia twenty-one years later; if Foster's 32 wickets, for an average of 21.62, were obtained at a slightly higher cost than Larwood's 33 wickets at 19.51, perhaps, all in all, Foster had a greater team to bowl against.

In his field placing for the Tests in Australia, Foster had a mid-off, cover and deep third man; wicket keeper, long leg, a semi-circle of four close in leg side fielders (two in front of the wicket and two behind) and a mid-on. Foster's four "death trap" fieldsmen, as he called them, were George Gunn, Frank Woolley, Bill Hitch and Wilfred Rhodes: they took nine catches off his bowling in the Tests.

As a right-handed batsman he was stylish, vigorous and attacking, though *Wisden* says that his bat was not quite straight and that he took too many risks. An unfortunate motor-cycle accident in 1915 terminated his cricket career. His book of cricketing memories was published in 1930. Frank Foster died in 1958.

He was, above all, a joyous cricketer, who played the game with splendid verve. During the wonderful summer of his achievement that lasted from May 1911 until March 1912, he was probably without equal on the cricket field. The photograph of him in the pavilion at Edgbaston, shows him at the wicket, modestly confident, cap set just so, bat upraised, left leg forward, prepared to meet all comers with a smile: F. R. Foster – Warwickshire and England.

TALES OF W. G. GRACE [1977]

JAMES GILMAN RECALLS THE PAST

By Jack Arlidge

Major James Gilman gave this interview for Wisden *a few weeks before he died in hospital on September 14, 1976, aged 97. Gilman was elected to MCC in 1900 and there are only two older surviving members, C. H. B. Fletcher and E. C. Wigan, elected in 1899.*

The legendary Dr W. G. Grace strode across the dressing room and said to a solemn faced young man: "I'm taking you in with me to open the innings", and thus began a phase in the sporting life of James Gilman which he was able to recapture in thrilling detail until his death at the age of 97 late last summer.

"It was during the reign of Queen Victoria, with the Boer War being fought, in June, 1900" he recalled. "I had been asked by Dr Grace to report to the old Crystal Palace where London County were to play the West Indians, who were making their first tour of this country.

"I was sitting in that dressing room, with famous players all round me, and the first time Grace spoke to me he asked: 'Are you nervous?', and his eyes twinkled when I replied 'I'm terrified, Sir'. He then went out to toss for innings, and it was when he came back that he told me to get padded up and open with him. It was a kind and very shrewd move, because he could see I'd have been reduced to a jelly if I'd had to wait to bat. It was typical of W.G. – his bark was worse than his bite."

Reluctant to talk about himself, still conscious of the commanding presence of Grace in those days, Major Gilman glossed over the fact that he made 63 and helped Grace to put on 136, and chuckled to remember that his famous partner was out shortly after lunch for 71.

"This wasn't at all surprising" he said. "The 'Old Man' was very keen on the catering and we had a sumptuous lunch, with hock and claret on the table. He had a real whack of the roast, followed by a big lump of cheese. He also tackled his whisky and seltzer, which was always his drink.

"A player named Constantine played for the West Indies, Sir Learie's father. They were easily beaten but Grace, in that rather squeaky voice of his, told us that he felt sure they would be very good one day. He was an astute judge of play and players."

Major Gilman, who lived at Shoreham-by-Sea in Sussex, watched the Sussex matches at the nearby County Ground in Hove right up to the time of his death, with Arthur Gilligan calling for him as he motored over from his Pulborough home. Gilman was always being asked if Grace was the autocrat of popular legend. Did he impose an iron will on players and umpires alike? Was he a cheat?

Insisting that "autocratic" was the wrong word, Major Gilman emphasised: "He would certainly stand no nonsense. He just could not abide a non-trier in the field or slackness of any sort. I remember he caught me arriving late once and said: 'You won't be coming in with me, Gilman, you'll bat number eleven.' When all was going well he called us by our Christian names, but if he was blowing hot and cold then it was by our surnames.

"Yes, he could be awkward and fiery at times, rather frightening, come to think of it, but he was basically a kind and quite considerate man. In some matches he often felt – and quite rightly too – that the crowd had come to see him play and if he suspected a decision was a bad one he would get very angry.

"He was not very happy in a match at Derby that same season of 1900 when the home side caught us on a gluepot. A slow bowler named Hulme had the 'Old Man' leg-before in the first innings – for 2 and Bestwick in the second for 0, also leg-before. I was batting at the other end so had a seat in the stalls, so to speak, to observe his reaction. The first decision did not seem a good one. Grace stalked off to the dressing room and when I went back there soon afterwards, there was a rare old rumpus. Grace had one leg out of his flannels and kept saying: 'I won't be cheated out, I've a good mind to go home.' We tried to calm him down and a whisky and seltzer came to the rescue. But the real hero was that same umpire who gave him out again!"

The awe and esteem in which Grace was held is clear, and emphasised by Major Gilman's story of the time when he was ordered to get a horse drawn cab and travel with him through London.

"Imagine my terror when the cab floor suddenly collapsed, and left us standing in the middle of Piccadilly! Grace's face was a study, but the extraordinary thing was that nobody laughed or even sniggered. There were murmurs of concern, a raising of hats by the men, sympathetic looks from the women. A dreadful moment . . ."

How did Grace compare with the great players since his day? Major Gilman, who played for Cambridge University, Middlesex and Northumberland as well as London County, and was an all-round sportsman of considerable skill and ability, felt convinced the Doctor would have been an outstanding player in any age.

"He might not have the shots of Bradman nor the flowing strokes of Hammond, but he had a shot for every ball. W.G. was an orthodox batsman whether driving, pulling or cutting. No 'shouldering arms' to a ball for him. He went out for his shots, and my old friend Herbert Strudwick, of Surrey and England, who used to live just round the corner from me at Shoreham-by-Sea, always maintained that he was a very easy batsman to keep wicket to. He rarely missed a ball! 'Struddy' rated him as one of the greatest bats he ever saw."

As a bowler, Grace did not turn the ball very much, Major Gilman remembered, but relied on length and flight. If he wasn't batting he liked to be bowling. He had amazing stamina, even in his fifties, for he was fifty-two in that match against the West Indians, and Gilman a stripling of twenty. The wickets of those days were "not too bad", but Grace might have found run-getting a little easier on modern pitches. He would certainly have become a sporting millionaire had he been playing today for, as his old opening partner recalled with a smile, "He did not do too badly as an amateur."

Major Gilman had vivid memories of other titans of cricket history. "Ranji" was a brilliant batsman, elegant and composed, skilfully caressing strokes round to leg and Gilbert Jessop, contrary to many reports of his play, was never a slogger and it was not his driving which impressed most, but his magnificent square-cutting. "I have never seen the ball cut with such power and precision."

Major Gilman followed cricket very closely and his clarity of mind and expression was remarkable. He was a kindly critic who found much to admire in present-day cricket, and his opinions were eagerly sought as he watched play from his corner seat in the committee room at the Hove County Ground, in front of which his ashes were buried, on the pitch where Grace played for Gloucestershire against Sussex in the first match ever staged there, in 1872.

His epitaph for W.G. was: "He had a great sense of mischief, but a twinkle in the eye"...

R. L. Arrowsmith writes: James Gilman, was the oldest living cricket Blue and probably the oldest first-class cricketer of any standing and the last man to open the batting in an important match with W. G. Grace. This he did for London County against the West Indians at the Crystal Palace in 1900: the match was not first-class and was the first-ever played by the West Indians in England. Gilman's share of a first-wicket stand of 136 was 63. He had been in the XI at St Paul's, but it was undoubtedly the experience of playing constantly in the next few years for London County with W.G. that made him into a good enough player to get his blue at Cambridge in 1902, his fourth year. His record for the University was not outstanding, but he fully justified his selection at Lord's. Set 272 to get in the fourth innings, Cambridge were 197 for 5 when Gilman came in to join that great batsman, S. H. Day, and they hit off the runs between them, Gilman's share being 37. He had played a few times for Middlesex in 1900 and 1901 but his first-class career ended when after 1904 London County confined themselves to club cricket. Later he played for Northumberland. He had been first-string for Cambridge in the half and had also represented them in the mile. In the last years of his life he was a constant spectator at Hove. His death leaves C. A. L. Payne, the Oxford Blue of 1906 and 1907, who has lived for many years in Vancouver, as the oldest surviving Blue.

MY LIFE REPORTING CRICKET [1980]

By Alex Bannister

(*Cricket correspondent* Daily Mail, *1947-1979*)

When I joined the *Daily Mail* from the Press Association (the news agency dubbed the "University of Fleet Street") 33 years ago, cricket had not yet been sucked into the vortex of world politics and High Court action. And if there was such a thing as player power, it was represented by the deeds of Denis Compton, Len Hutton, Alec Bedser, Bill Edrich and others on the field of play.

The one-day game was not conceived, nor was even a twinkle in the eyes of the legislators; overseas tours were long, comparatively leisurely and crammed with stuffy receptions; grounds were full in the post-war sporting boom; and there was still a division between amateur and professional. Indeed, until the abolition of the thin distinction in 1963, it was still possible to hear, as I did at Lord's, this pre-match announcement: "In the match card, for F. J. Titmus please read Titmus F. J."

At Adelaide in 1950, invitations to temporary membership of a club were extended only to the four amateurs and to those of the press who were members of MCC. It was politely declined. On board ship, the amateurs were put at a separate dining table, but the whole party travelled first-class and in style – unlike the modern trial of endurance of the jumbo jet.

Domestically the season consisted of Tests, matches with the tourists, the County Championship, prestige fixtures like Gentlemen v Players, Oxford v Cambridge, and the festivals. Pride in the swiftly disintegrating Empire remained in titles. There was the *Imperial* Cricket Conference (now the International Cricket Conference), and as late as 1953 it was the *Imperial* Cricket Memorial Gallery (The Memorial Gallery and Library). Contact between the all-powerful MCC and the working press was minimal. Selectors offered no public reasons for their decisions, and the list of secretaries read like a military gazette. The Advisory County Cricket Committee's annual meeting coincided with the University rugby match, and no-one was ever late to Twickenham for the kick-off.

Sir Don Bradman, who gave a new meaning to batting, was still leading his invincible Australians, and the West Indies were emerging as a potent force – though it was still predicted in some islands that all would collapse under a future black captain. In due course Sir Frank Worrell, a remarkable person as well as being a great cricketer, united the widely scattered and diverse cultures of the islands as no politician was able to do, before or since. His early death was a cruel blow to the entire cricket world, and I have pictured him as the perfect intermediary in the South African dispute. I remember the forthright R. W. V. Robins bluntly asking him if he ever found it a handicap to be black, especially when he was in England. Frankie's laughing response was: "Only when I'm shaving."

Twenty years passed before South Africa's racial laws blew up in cricket's face, and those attending the seemingly interminable meetings at Lord's in 1970 will never forget the ominous sight of the square behind barbed wire and under floodlights. With security guards and dogs in patrol, the ground assumed the grim appearance of a POW camp. After the 1968-69 tour of South Africa was cancelled, at the time I would have been leaving Heathrow I found myself interviewing an eleven year old at Aylesbury on why he wanted to play for Manchester United!

Pakistan, gaining full Test status in 1952, is one of the countries adamantly opposed to South Africa's re-entry. The new Muslim nation was so little known in the early years that, on an early tour there, a Commonwealth team's blazer carried the gilt-lettered world: PARKISTAN. Yet within five years Pakistan had beaten England, Australia and West Indies. The victory at The Oval was a classic case of a team, previously outplayed, being taken too lightly. A much-changed side suddenly found themselves fighting a losing battle against Fazal Mahmood, a bowler of the Bedser type on a pitch to suit him. Fazal was one of the best of his age and was a police traffic inspector. Years later, as a passenger in his jeep threading a miraculous path through a tangle of bullock carts, camel trains, cars, buses, rickshaws and wandering pedestrians. I asked him how he controlled his Karachi traffic. "You have as much chance as bowling out Hutton without stumps in the ground," he replied.

As the game might have been invented for their bubbling skills and vitalities, the rise of the West Indians was inevitable. In 1950, when they gained their first victory in England at Lord's, a very fine opening pair in Jeff Stollmeyer and Alan Rae preceded the might of the immortal Ws; Worrell, Clyde Walcott, then a wicket-keeper, and Everton Weekes. And the most experienced English batsman could not handle the novice spinners, Sonny Ramadhin and Alf Valentine.

When they arrived in England, the combined experience of "those little pals of mine, Ramadhin and Valentine", as the calypso went, was two first-class matches. It was Jack Mercer, the former Glamorgan bowler, then coaching in Jamaica, who urged the selectors to send Valentine. Mercer used to tell Valentine to spin until the blood showed from his fingers. Nobody could pick Ramadhin, and Valentine spun like a top. All John Goddard needed to do was put his slow bowlers on and they would do the rest. Valentine was charmingly vague. "When is the England captain coming in?" he asked when he was bowling out England in the Trent Bridge Test. "You dismissed him an hour ago," he was told.

Another story I associate with Jack Mercer involved Freddie Trueman on the 1953-54 tour of the West Indies. MCC were playing at Spanish Town, not far from Kingston, at a sugar plantation. Across the entrance was strung a banner exhorting the employees on the virtues of WORK, OBEDIENCE, DISCIPLINE. Trueman, who was sharing a car with Mercer and myself, looked with disgust at the banner and exploded: "I bloody well wouldn't work here!"

When West Indies won at Lord's, their supporters, singing and dancing, invaded an astonished Long Room, where I also saw an old member innocently bump into the Duke of Edinburgh, who had just opened the aforementioned Imperial Cricket Memorial Gallery. The Duke's tea spilled down the royal trousers, leaving a most unfortunate appearance. Perhaps it was just as well for his peace of mind that the member shuffled away blissfully ignorant of his gaffe.

Yet I doubt if the Duke was more taken aback than Jeff Thomson, the fire-eating Australian bowler, after his first over to Colin Cowdrey, who had just joined the England party in Australia in 1974. As England were down to twelve fit players, including two wicket keepers, Colin was pressed into premature service, although he had been in the nets for only four days. You could almost hear the dreaded Thomson's ears flap back in expectation as Colin took the pallor of an English December to the wicket. His last Test innings had been three and a half years before, but the old touch was not lost, and at the end of the over the lamb blandly approached the lion and murmured: "I don't think we have met – my name's Cowdrey."

Cowdrey in Pakistan, 1969, Hutton in the West Indies, 1954, and Peter May in Australia, 1958-59, were captains on singularly difficult tours. The unsuspecting May, comfortably England's finest post-war batsman, found himself in the centre of bitter throwing and umpiring controversies, and Hutton and Cowdrey, from the start of their misadventures, must have thought they were being committed to tip-toe barefoot through fields of broken bottles. On many occasions in the West Indies and Pakistan I had anguished doubts after filing my story. The events of the day seemed so irrational as to be the child of an overheated imagination.

Hutton found the young Trueman a frightful handful, and rumour of the most bizarre nature on a variety of themes spread through the lovely Caribbean like an unchecked forest fire. Finally there was the episode of the flamboyant Honourable Alex Bustamente, Jamaica's Chief Minister. During the final Test, with his score at 205, Hutton entered the pavilion at tea hoping to snatch a shower and a cup of tea. He was no sooner in the room than an excited official burst in and stormed: "This is the crowning insult." It transpired that Mr Bustamente's hand had been one of the several thrust out to Hutton, who had replied to the shouted congratulations with "Thank you". The interval was spent sorting the matter out, and making it clear that had he but known Mr Bustamente had been there he would have stopped. Despite a stout denial from the Chief Minister that he had been "insulted", the incident continued to be blow up out of all proportion.

More evidence that cricket was being dragged into the political maelstrom came in Pakistan. In retrospect, it is obvious that Cowdrey's tour should not have been attempted during a period of civil disorder. England arrived after a brief stay in Sri Lanka to find the itinerary changed, armed troops patrolling the streets, and a general picture of chaos and crisis. Far from bringing stability to the scene, as officialdom hoped, the Test attracted student agitators and play was constantly interrupted. Both the local Board and British diplomatists shirked the responsibility of calling a halt to the wretched and dangerous situation. Cricket was used as a political shuttlecock.

Oddly the most peaceful Test was at Dacca, which was considered to be the flash-point, because the local students took over the policing of the match. On the eve of the match their leaders conducted a serio-comical press conference at which I wondered whether I should laugh or be scared. The only casualty proved to be Cowdrey, who had £30 pinched from his pocket as he walked the width of a pavement from the bus to the ground entrance.

In the end the mob won at Karachi, with the Test abandoned on the third morning after the most serious of several riots when England were 502 for seven. Colin Milburn had scored 137 in what sadly proved to be his last Test innings and Alan Knott was within 4 runs of his maiden century for England. The team left for home that night, and I wrote my eye-witness account of the riot at home with one half of a broken stump in front of me. It was safer there.

Milburn's career effectively ended with a motor accident as his genius had started in full bloom. He had spent the winter with Western Australia and flew to what was then the east wing of Pakistan as a reinforcement when Cowdrey's fitness was in doubt. The boys prepared a welcome for him. As he came down the plane steps they sang "The green, green grass of home". They also arranged for the coach to stop at a disreputable hotel, and filed out. Colin's jaw dropped, and just as he was prepared to make a bolt for home the players returned and took him to the team's headquarters at the Inter-continental.

During a period when the side was confined to the hotel at Lahore, Roger Prideaux, then captain of Northamptonshire, slipped out to give a trial to a young student fast bowler. The nets at the Gymkhana were surrounded by barbed wire, and soldiers stood protectively by. The trialist was Sarfraz Nawaz, and it can be truthfully said that he lived up to his unconventional start.

I would not like to give the impression that all tours to Pakistan were fraught with danger. The early ones were not examples of feather-bedded luxury, but India and Pakistan can now offer comforts undreamed of at one period. At one of the less attractive centres Keith Fletcher switched on a large fan in the hope of getting rid of a colony of bats in the ceiling. Immediately a rain of mutilated bats descended on the diners below. On another occasion an England team arrived at an up-country hotel to see a corpse under a white sheet being carried away. It was the chef, knifed in a kitchen quarrel.

No cricket education can be considered half complete without a tour of India, though admittedly it can be wearing at the time. One widely held fallacy there is that anyone remotely attached to the visiting team has access to a vast pool of complimentary tickets, and is willing, nay anxious, to discuss every aspect of the game anywhere at any time. I have found strangers in my hotel room – and in the most private area – who have called in for a chat. At New Delhi, my only relief was to lock myself in the bathroom, where the light was not visible from outside, and read *Vanity Fair*, borrowed from Mike Brearley.

A Test at Calcutta is comparable to five days of the fervour of a Wembley international between England and Scotland with crowds of a comparable size. Before the 1977 match there was the astonishing sight of the grass on the pitch, such as it was, being scraped away with household scrubbing brushes.

Melbourne 1955 provided the mystery of the Damp Pitch ... except that it wasn't really a mystery. Despite official denials at the time, there could be no doubt that there was an illegal watering on the rest day. On the Saturday evening cracks had begun to appear and the pitch was worn. On Monday, after a hot Sunday, the pitch and its surrounds were damp. The Melbourne newspaper *The Age* published a story that sprinklers had been used, but among the speculation which followed was a learned explanation that the cause was a subterranean river directly under the ground. If that was right, how remarkable that the effect should be confined to a tiny area in the middle of a vast ground. There was no sinister motive, however, and the error was accepted as a groundsman's inexperience. But an England victory spared Australia no end of embarrassment.

Godfrey Evans made one of his famous catches to dismiss Neil Harvey, and in the course of 12.3 eight-ball overs Frank Tyson, who in three Tests of the series was the fastest bowler I have ever seen, and Brian Statham won the match. Tyson had seven wickets in the innings and Statham two, and I remember Sir Don Bradman, in the lounge of the Windsor Hotel, making a special effort to tell Statham that England would not have won without his brilliant support.

Inevitably in the highly competitive field of Fleet Street, a long career brings its ups and downs. Memories are the most perishable of all commodities and one's standard is measured by the last story. I have had a few successes and some failures, but I regard my part in recruiting Bradman for the two home series with Australia in 1953, the coronation year, and 1956 as my greatest coup. It happened by chance.

When teams travelled by ship I used to join the Australians at their last port of call – Malta, Naples or maybe Marseilles – and file a daily story. One morning, while waiting in a queue outside a Purser's Office, two of the Australian players told me The Don would have enjoyed making the trip. Normally I am opposed to player-writers as it can be a deception of the public and goes against my journalistic principles, but Bradman was an exception and capable of making a huge impact with his unique perception, judgement and reputation. I cabled my editor, who responded with enthusiasm and set the operation in motion.

The outcome was a dazzling success. It brought The Don, who wrote every word himself, congratulations in the fourth leader of *The Times*, and gave the newspaper a new status among the discerning public. Fully to appreciate The Don's insight and knowledge of the game it is necessary to be with him over a long period, and that was my privilege. I also understood the price he has paid for his unique fame, with incessant requests for autographs and hopeful conversations opening with, "You must remember me, we stayed at the same hotel at Leicester in 1930."

Later I had a different style of collaboration with Johnny Wardle when he was signed, in the teeth of intense competition, to reveal his troubles with Yorkshire exclusively to the *Daily Mail.* Nearing midnight I was awakened and told to go immediately to Wardle's home at Wakefield. I had two basic instructions: one, to make sure no other newspaper intervened; two, to produce three articles the next day.

After arousing the village taximan I went to King's Cross, where a rail voucher and the terms of the agreement awaited me, and then on to Wakefield station to join two others in a hired car. We parked outside Wardle's home until the family came down for breakfast, and then whisked him to the paper's offices at Sheffield. Johnny was so upset by Yorkshire's decline, and what he thought the causes to be, that the articles were simple to write. The main target of his criticism was Ron Burnet, the captain, who had been appointed to instil discipline into the side.

In the afternoon, photographs were taken at the Grand Hotel – one of Johnny at a typewriter – and as we went into the foyer, to my embarrassment, we ran into Burnet. For my part I liked both Johnny and Ron, and I felt as if I had intruded into a family quarrel. It is always to Burnet's credit that he never held a grudge and rose above the sea of disputes with dignity. In fact, I did a signed piece for him when Yorkshire won the Championship at Hove.

If Wardle was at fault, it was that his passion for Yorkshire over-boiled. When he was sent to Australia with me on Peter May's tour I found him conscientous and intelligent, as well as fearless. He was particularly useful on a tour tormented by throwing controversies, for his technical know-how was outstanding.

Of several stunts I became involved in, the most amusing was with Richie Benaud's team. Again it was aboard ship. The day before the arrival of the Australians at Tilbury I had a shore-to-ship call from J. L. Manning, a particularly demanding Sports Editor, to arrange to assemble the players at starboard stern at 1.30 p.m. precisely. A *Daily Mail* plane would then take a photograph of them, and I was to give the exact position of the ship at 1.30 p.m.; repeat, exact position.

Benaud, as always obliging, agreed, but understandably the bridge said it was not possible to give the exact position several hours in advance. Mr Manning was not to be put off within a nautical mile or two, and I lost some poundage running up the stairs to the radio room.

As the appointed time approached, the sea became choppy, there were rain squalls, and the overcoated cricketers became increasingly disenchanted with the project. "If we had weather like this we'd give Australia back to the Abbos" said one through clenched teeth. Suddenly, to my relief, a plane appeared and circled three times at a drunken angle. The picture appearing on the breakfast tables the next morning was a little out of focus, but no reader was to know that at the moment of crisis the photographer was being violently sick!

With the sixties came the time of cricket's upheavals and changed attitudes. Cricket journalism moved into sterner and more specialised dimensions. Instant judgements had to be passed on the weightiest of subjects, often after long and complicated briefings. After the International Cricket Conference had tried to thrash out the complex question of throwing I was urged by my office: "Can't you simplify it?" As generations of legislators had tried for almost a century to find the right wording I was not too ashamed to reply that it was beyond me.

I am inclined to think that if the same resolve was shown in curbing the menace of bumpers and intimidation as was applied to throwing problems, some of the recent insults to the fair name of the game would not have happened. Unfortunately an endemic weakness called self-interest and parochialism, which left the game so divided during the Packer struggle, takes over. The soft option of passing the buck to the hard-pressed umpires is seized upon avidly. There have been clearly defined regulations to stop excesses of bumpers, and I trust the experiment of the one-an-over restriction will have more success. The latest legislation represents the last chance to prevent cricket slipping into perpetual violence.

Bumpers, in fair numbers, are part of the game. Intimidation is not, and must be stamped out. One thought does occur to me: as the human frame is now infinitely bigger and stronger, is 22 yards the right length of the pitch? When 22 yards was officially drafted into the 1744 Laws, the bowling was underarm!

So swift, complete and dramatic have been the changes in the last few years, both on the field and in administration, that it almost invites ridicule to pass comparisons. Some of the old chivalry and morality, which put cricket apart from other games, has ebbed away in the tide of awards and prizes, sponsorship in its many forms, and larger appearance money. There must be some concern that the benefits of the newly developing "marketing" are not cornered by a small élite of privileged players. There is much to commend in the dedicated attitude of the players who demand more say in their affairs. Fine! As long as it is remembered that they owe a responsibility to the game at large.

Crowds are different today, and the trend is towards instant cricket and instant results. It is possible there will be little place for five-day Tests in the future, particularly in an impatient country like Australia.

On playing standards I am sure the great players of the immediate past of the class of Bradman, Hutton, May, Arthur Morris, the Ws, Compton, Martin Donnelly, Dudley Nourse, Vijay Merchant, Alec Bedser, Fred Trueman and Co. would be just as effective today. All the so-called progress of negative bowling and field placings would not have stopped Bradman. He might have been slowed down – partly because of the decline in the over-rate – but he would still have scored a staggering number of runs.

Equally Viv Richards, Sunil Gavaskar, Geoff Boycott, Barry Richards, Clive Lloyd and the other modern batting giants would have found Bedser's cut and swing and the fast bowling of Ray Lindwall and Keith Miller just as difficult. The best all-rounders I have seen are Sir Gary Sobers, Miller and Mike Procter, and Ian Botham may aspire to that class.

The Packer affair was a supreme tragedy, particularly as it had its origins in an Australian commercial TV struggle. I know all the arguments, but the over-riding disappointment to me was that negotiations were going on in secret during the nostalgic Melbourne centenary Test match. To be able to do so suggested the players involved had no affiliation whatsoever with the spirit and sentiment of their distinguished predecessors.

RADIO REFLECTIONS [1981]

By E. W. Swanton

The retirement of John Arlott, who over the course of the 35 summers since the end of the war has spread over the air more words about cricket than any other man has done, or perhaps is ever likely to do, is an appropriate time to look back to the beginnings of cricket broadcasting on Sound radio and attempt some sort of sketch of its development. The first of all cricket broadcasts concerned the first match of the first New Zealand tour to England in 1927, against Essex at the old county headquarters at Leyton. Plum Warner – and who more appropriate? – gave eye-witness accounts of each day's play, while later that summer the Rev. F. H. Gillingham, the well known cricketing parson, was in action similarly at The Oval. The very first of all sporting broadcasts had been made at Twickenham by H. B. T. Wakelam only in January, 1927. Cricket, therefore, was early in the field.

History is somewhat misty regarding the first years, for a bomb played havoc with the pre-war archives of the BBC. It it clear enough, though, that cricket was not, for a while, rated very highly as entertainment by the hierarchy. Almost up to the outbreak of war, other games, wherein the action was faster, were given wider attention. Don Bradman's first visit to England in 1930 coincided with the first coverage of Test matches, but only to the extent of periodical reports: by M. K. Foster, youngest but one of the brotherhood of seven, on the first Test, by A. C. MacLaren on the second and third, and by Aubrey Faulkner on the fourth and fifth.

An interesting sidelight on these early experiments disclosed that John Snagge, a BBC staff man from the earliest Savoy Hill days, was sent down to The Oval to help Faulkner, who was unwell. According to Snagge, and not surprisingly, he struggled a bit in an unfamiliar role. Yet on the strength of his performance he was chosen by Gerald Cock, the first head of Outside Broadcasts, to cover the boat race the following year. Thus, fortuitously, he began surely the longest of all sporting assignments, for he broadcast every race from 1931 until his retirement from the job in 1980.

Thereafter things at first moved but slowly, MCC taking much longer to appreciate the evangelistic possibilities of radio than, for instance, the equally conservative Rugby Union. Hence the story of how Howard Marshall, who was to become the first professional cricket commentator, was required in the early 1930s to hustle from Lord's round the corner to a semi-basement room in Grove End Road, where he had to compete with extraneous noises including that of a child's piano lesson in a room above. However, by 1934 Marshall was at least installed inside the ground, even though he had to tell the world about Hedley Verity's famous rout of the 1934 Australians on a turning wicket from a window in the old Tavern at square leg.

Arlott, to whose researches for the BBC publication, *Armchair Cricket*, I must make due acknowledgment, recalls his youthful memories of Marshall's rich, unmistakable voice in paying tribute to him as the innovator, "the first person to link the news-duty of the commentator with visual and human impressions". There never was a deeper, more mellifluous and attractive voice than Howard's, and when Seymour de Lotbinière became Director of Outside Broadcasts in 1935 the pair of them, along with Michael Standing, "Lobby's" deputy and himself, like Marshall, a competent club cricketer, began to explore the possibilities of the running commentary.

In the later 1930s, county cricket began to be covered in this way in addition to the Test matches, this increased activity culminating in the England-West Indies series of 1939 which was broadcast, for the first time, in its entirety ball by ball. It was then that I joined Marshall and Standing to make a commentary team of three. This comprehensive arrangement, as I recall, put something of a strain on BBC resources. It was said to have been instigated by a BBC governor who, on a winter cruise in the Caribbean, had discovered the islanders' deep fervour for the game and promised them the full treatment.

I expect I was conceited enough to think that the decision may also have owed something to my having blazed the trail the preceding winter in South Africa, where I toured with Walter Hammond's MCC side. This was the first time cricket had been broadcast in South Africa. Nor had anyone previously gone out from England to broadcast cricket home. The first reward was, in the very first Test, to fine myself with a hat-trick to describe; the second was to report the longest of all Test matches. It was Tom Goddard who woke up a few at home, dozing after their Christmas dinners, by achieving the second of only three Test hat-tricks by an Englishman in this century. As to that dreary ten-day marathon at Durban, I have a momento in the form of a letter from the BBC, saying that the great Corporation had been considering the question of some further remuneration, seeing that the match fee had been based on a duration of four days, and that they thought an extra payment of 25 guineas would be a fair arrangement. In case anyone should think this an odd computation, they pointed out that there had been no play on one of the days because of rain. Careful were the BBC in those days: my first post-war contracts offered match fees plus railway vouchers (first-class) plus expenses at the rate of one pound "for each night necessarily spent away from home".

But to less frivolous matters, and the great surge of interest in cricket after the war which broadcasting of all first-class cricket on a wide scale did so much to stimulate. Where hitherto cricket had strained to keep up in the broadcast race, now it set the pace. Rex Alston had abandoned schoolmastering at Bedford in favour of the BBC, where his first-hand sporting experience of athletics, cricket and rugby football were at once utilised. In all three activities he was a key member of the broadcast team for twenty years or more. At first Alston, Standing and I formed the Test panel, and divided between ourselves – without benefit of scorer – the lengthy coverage of many county matches as well as the Lord's classics of Univeristy Match and Gentlemen and Players.

There came, too, a fresh figure on the scene, a member of the BBC staff seconded to follow the 1946 Indian team, John Arlott. It is no stretching of the truth to compare the impact made on listeners by him with that which had been made by Neville Cardus of the *Manchester Guardian* ("Cricketer") on the cricket world a quarter of a century earlier.

With both, perhaps, the facts and the technicalities of the game sometimes ran second to the characters involved and the context of the occasion, the places and the people. John Arlott, his Hampshire tones distinctly lighter than in his later days, like Cardus, had imagination, keen powers of observation and not least the gift of words. There was an element of chance in the binding of both to cricket, Cardus being sent out for a summer's fresh air after illness, and Arlott having joined the BBC the previous year not on the sports staff but as a talks and poetry producer.

In the emergence of these two at moments when interest was booming anyway, Cardus after the first war, Arlott after the second, the game had two rare strokes of luck, for each man developed his own new following. Not least, each put across a wit and humour, which helped persuade readers and audiences that cricket was a game played by flesh-and-blood characters, to be savoured and enjoyed. For 35 years until his retirement at the end of last summer, John kept at it, for much of the period doubling broadcasting and journalism. Having worked alongside him for most of that time, it is for me a pleasure to add, in cricket's official chronicle, this appreciation to the many others he has received.

Marshall pursued other interests after the war, and though sometimes to be heard on major occasions – notably from Westminster Abbey at the Coronation – he did no more cricket broadcasting. Yet the technique which he had evolved, with the ever present advice of de Lotbinière, was aimed at by us all in our own individual ways. Howard's running commentary leading up to Len Hutton's breaking of Don Bradman's record score of 334, in The Oval Test of 1938, which is re-broadcast on nostalgic occasions, may seem a stately period-piece to some of the modern school, but most of them could profit by noting how scrupulously he observed the ground-rules.

The general picture of the occasion – the field, the weather, the crowd, the personalities and attitudes of the players, the position of the game, tactical appreciations and the options open to the captains – all these and maybe other aspects less immediate invite a wide variety of comment. By the time de Lotbinière gave his celebrated "teach-in" to the foremost outside-broadcasters in 1951, all this was called "associative material". To a large degree it makes or mars the whole performance. Yet in cricket, as in all games, the focal point is the ball, and all must be subsidiary to the bowler's approach and delivery and the batsman's reaction to it. In other words, timing is all important in commentary, and it is a cardinal sin to be late on the stroke. "The golden pause" was, I believe, first commended as one of the many attributes of the late Henry Longhurst as a television commentator on golf ("If you've nothing to say, don't say it!"); but I have always thought it also applicable to the break of a couple of seconds or more immediately before the bowler's arm comes over in the last stride and the man at the "mike", having drawn breath, reflects the speed of the ball and the nature of the stroke as he describes it all at an increased tempo to his listeners.

Nowadays, of course, the commentator of the moment has not only a statistician, perhaps Bill Frindall, on one side of him but one of the regular summarisers, Trevor Bailey, Fred Trueman or Tony Lewis maybe, on the other. If the ball bowled has had some dramatic effect, whether to the batsman's advantage or otherwise, the commentator will probably bring in one of these for his opinion, or the scorer will chip in with a relevant fact or two. Yet the man at the controls, so to speak, is still the commentator.

Marshall, as long ago as 1934, was the first man to use a scorer. At his request Lancashire lent him a young groundstaff cricketer named Arthur Wrigley for the England-Australia Test at Old Trafford – which, as England declared at 627 for nine, was a prescient move on his part. It was not, however, immediately followed up. Not until after the war (according to my memory and Michael Standing's) were scorers used, and then for a further while only for Test matches.

One important advantage the older generation of commentators had over those of today was the regular training and practice they received from broadcasting county cricket. What was then the major part of the over all coverage of cricket gave the BBC in addition the chance of trying out new material. The modern instant reports, lasting a minute or two from county grounds, demand little knowledge of the game, and one wonders how the gaps will be filled when Brian Johnston, seemingly perennial and in his particular jovial way still a highly popular element in the team, eventually follows Arlott into retirement. Though others have made acceptable contributions – and Henry Blofeld chalked up a marked success in Australia – the only other notable addition among the younger generation who comes across as combining close knowledge of the game with facility of expression is Christopher Martin-Jenkins.

Many overseas broadcasters accompanying the touring teams have added flavour to the over-all performance, notably a succession of West Indians from Learie Constantine to the present explicit, conspicuously fair-minded Tony Cozier. But for both quality and length of service, Alan McGilvray's career at the microphone stands alone. To the listeners of every Test-playing country he stands for generous-minded, unbiased, factual common sense. At any crucial moment of an England-Australia Test, the ideal recipe, for me, is to turn on the television picture, turn off the sound, and listen to Alan.

Naturally, as an old hand, one cocks a friendly yet critical ear to the Radio 3 Test programmes, and in the most important thing of all they earn surely very high marks. For they convey the feeling that they are enjoying what they are doing, and also, in so far as they conscientiously can, that this is a game played by men who, however great the financial rewards, have still for the most part some respect, diluted maybe in certain cases, for the traditional spirit of cricket. This being so, it is a valuable if tacit sanction that the cricketers know that, if they overstep the mark, commentators and critics in whom the public have confidence will not fail to say so. To this extent, apart from all else, the broadcasters fulfil an important function. It would be an evil day for cricket if its reporting over the air were to full into prejudiced, over-sensational hands.

One feels now and then that there is so much free, uninhibited talk that one cannot see the wood for the trees, and also that we are getting a slight overdose of statistical material. But, comparing the present with the past, consider how much has to be said about so little. Thirty or forty years ago one had to describe 120 balls an hour, sometimes more. There was little time for reminiscence and chit-chat when Ramadhin and Valentine were spinning England into knots at Lord's in 1950. Nowadays, fast bowlers are allowed to wander back interminable distances, and the ration can be 72 balls an hour, sometimes even less. No wonder Bill Frindall – a formidable repository of fact as were his forerunners, Arthur Wrigley and Roy Webber – is an essential member of the team. Too much dressing room jargon for the ordinary listener? On the whole, yes. And there is one perpetual irritant, the regular use of the utterly superfluous word "on" before a score. This was never, until comparatively recently, part of the language of cricket. Yet on the whole, surely, the pleasure far outweighs the pain.

SOME THOUGHTS ABOUT MODERN CAPTAINCY [1982]

By J. M. Brearley

I would not have been tempted back to cricket more than ten years ago without the allure of the captaincy of Middlesex; nor, I think, would I have continued to play without the stimulation of that job. At times, the thought of letting someone else deal with the hassles is attractive, but however good it would be for my soul to give up the reins, I doubt if I could do so willingly and still play. I think, therefore, that it is worth trying to describe the nature of captaincy, as its scope is remarkably wide.

The captain of a county cricket team is, all at once, managing director, union leader, and pit-face worker. He has almost total charge of the daily running of the concern; he is the main, if not the only, representative of the work force in the boardroom (i.e., on the committee); and he has to field, bat and maybe bowl. He conducts the orchestra and he performs: perhaps on the front deck of the violins or as second tambourine. (It varies; I've been both.) Consequently it is hard to play God, to read the Riot Act about carelessness or incompetence, when one throws one's own wicket away or plays ineptly – if not today, tomorrow or yesterday. Any conscience on this score can inhibit one's own play; the captain oscillates between pawkiness – being over-anxious about carelessness and, aware of the tendency to criticise others for slow-scoring, an inappropriate desperation for quick runs.

Social changes, together with the related changes in cricket's arrangements, have over the past fifteen or twenty years made the captain's job more, rather than less, difficult. Social hierarchies have become flatter: authority-figures are taken for granted less and criticised more. A leader has to *earn* the respect of the led. Doctors are sued more frequently for alleged incompetence: I await the day when a captain is sued for negligence by an injured close-fielder. The aristocratic tyrant has given way to the collaborative foreman, although some older players sill yearn for the old-style discipline and for the voice accustomed to command. There are, moreover, county sides in which over half the players believe that they themselves should, or could, be captain. Twenty years ago, such ambitions would have been much more circumscribed. Envy, today, is less limited, and criticism from within the team less inhibited.

Similarly, criticism from outside is more vociferous. At Old Trafford in 1981, F. S. Trueman, broadcasting on the radio, was writing Bob Willis off in extreme terms; he did not know by what right Willis was drawing his money, he had never seen such inept bowling. (I wonder even whether Trueman had the decency to be abashed when Willis took three wickets in his next over.) And because current Test players are under far more scrutiny than ever before, the captain has to bear the brunt of it on behalf of his team. D. R. Jardine was able to toss up before the start of a Test, walk back into the dressing-room – where all seventeen members of the party would be dressed in whites, opening batsmen padded up – and pin the team-sheet on the wall. He felt no need to tell the players in advance, let alone the two British pressmen, one an expert on lawn tennis, who accompanied the team on its sensational journey around Australia. Harold Larwood told me that if any journalist had dared to ask Jardine if he was considering standing down from the side, Jardine would have punched him on the jaw.

Today's press are more demanding and inquisitive. They expect answers, "quotes", and cooperation. Kim Hughes, speaking at a dinner, shortly before last summer's final Test, agreed that his team had not batted well and deserved criticism. But, he went on, some of the things said about them were such that, "if you were walking along the street and a fellow said that to you, if you had any go about you at all, you'd deck him!"

Last summer, I found an England team more embittered by the press than I'd ever known. Ian Botham refused to speak to them after his century at Leeds, and Willis was outspoken on television immediately after that match. I myself felt that rows were planted, cultivated and encouraged out of the most arid, unpromising soil by certain sections of the media. Of course there always has been some meanness in the relations between performer and critic, but the type of writing fostered by the modern craving for excitement and sensation puts today's public figures under a type of pressure unknown to their pre-war predecessors.

This same demand for excitement has, in addition, led to the revival, and proliferation, of one-day cricket, and this too has made a difference to captaincy. In all types of cricket there have to be captains, perhaps a majority, who more or less work to rule, following whatever happens to be fashionable at the time. And it is especially tempting to think of the job along these lines in limited-overs matches. One county captain used to have decided, before every Sunday League game, exactly who would bowl each over. As usual, if he has a good side, the captain who follows a rigid pattern will achieve adequate results, but this approach is a pale shadow of proper captaincy.

It is, of course, essential to have some plan or outline of policy. But situations vary enormously throughout a game, and no simple formula can fit all contingencies. The ideal captain will have a feeling for the moment when a batsman has taken the measure of one of his bowlers. He will know which bowler is least likely to be heaved to the short boundary on the leg side. He will keep some of his resources up his sleeve, but will know when to go all out for a wicket. He will gauge accurately when to stop worrying too much about saving singles and to concentrate on saving fours. In the midst of impending chaos he remains calm, juggles his bowlers sensibly, and manages to keep weak fielders out of the way. This applies in all forms of cricket: the captain remains responsible for assessing the proper balance between attack and defence. I felt Tony Greig would switch too suddenly and dramatically from one to the other.

Cricket today is less courtly than it once was. Before limited-overs cricket, slips were, in a sense, compulsory. It would have been unsporting to put all one's fielders back; just as in the air battles of the First World War it was ungentlemanly to aim at the pilot. As Bradman has admitted, it would have taken him much longer to score his runs in the modern game, and not merely because of the decline in the over-rate. We live in an era of cost-effectiveness, though occasionally a giant like Botham transcends all calculation.

Although some subtleties of the game do disappear with limited-overs cricket, there are nevertheless many occasions for the exercise of tactical judgement. However, the crucial difference is not so much tactical as psychological. There are nowadays far more close games, crucial moments, hectic situations. Many more instant and pressured decisions have to be made. County cricket used to be incredibly sedate. There was the slow rhythm of the three-day matches, with close finishes rare. Play would be held up while aeroplanes passed overhead, or until barracking died down. Bowlers rarely posed a physical threat. Aggression was low-key.

Complaints that the standard of sportsmanship have declined since those balmy days are sometimes coupled with the suggestion that the causes of the decline are financial. Players are so interested in the money available that they will stoop to get it. I would argue that the changes are mainly mis-described and certainly wrongly explained.

Off the field, too, many county captains still have much power. We have been remarkably untouched by the tide of specialisation. We have the major say in selection; and the almost total say in how much, and how, the players are to practise. The only other official closely involved with the playing staff is the coach; but his domain is mainly the Second Eleven. Moreover he is often – in our case at least – the only scout. The captain is responsible for players getting from one match to the next, and deciding who takes his car and which players. He looks after day-to-day discipline, unless a case is bad enough to go before the committee, and is involved in questions of contract and salary.

Not suprisingly, the breadth of the traditional rôle is under attack, and now the cricket manager has arrived in county cricket. He can be a help to the captain, especially in taking away many irritating little jobs, and can contribute to the whole approach of the team. But whether his contribution is worth its cost, especially when so many clubs are short of money, I rather doubt. There are, moreover, ticklish questions of priority between captain and manager. Cricket is too complex and personal to be controlled at a distance: only the captain, in the middle with his bowlers and fielders, can sensitively react to the needs of the moment. The precise rôle of the manager needs, I suspect, revaluation in some quarters.

One peculiarity of cricket amongst games and sports is that, while each individual duel is between two protagonists, bowler and batsman, these individual contests take their meaning from the overall contest between two teams. It is the captain who is primarily responsible for the fusion of the individual and the group. He is, or should be, the leader. He must try to inculcate team-spirit – the identification of the individual with the interests of the whole group – without loss of personal flair or individual opportunity.

Sometimes the need is to rediscover the expectation of winning. Last summer, England had gone twelve Tests without a win. They were dropping as many catches as they were holding; the bowlers were looking, at times, slightly half-hearted. Spirit sagged if a fielding session yielded no tangible successes. Not long after, virtually the same team was catching everything, and bowling and fielding with a new vitality. This transformation, I hasten to add, was achieved almost entirely by inspiring individual performances. The fact remains that the main shortcoming in a team may well be that it has lost the taste – even the sniff – of success.

As in other areas of mutual activity, communication is vital. Both county staff and touring party are so small that most exchanges are face to face. The problems are immediate, practical, and personal. There is no separation between management (the captain) and work-force. In industry, managers are concerned more with long-term plans and with outside organisations. They can easily be cut off from their fellow-employees, both physically and by the nature of their job. Socially and culturally, too there is often a chasm between managers and managed. On the cricket field a captain can and should be constantly in touch with the rest of the side. It was pointed out to me that I do some of this keeping in touch literally, especially with bowlers, with a hand on a player's arm or round his shoulders. I also have constant eye-contact with the fielders. This lets them know that I am aware of their efforts and feelings, that I'm satisfied or dissatisfied; and the habit of it enables me to move a fielder with a minimum of fuss.

The group is small enough to enable everyone to have a say on tactics and on the general running of the tour or of the team. A captain cannot always have six or seven players homing in on him on the field with advice at critical moments; autocracy is at times essential. But it is even more important to enable everyone to express opinions off the field, both informally and at team meetings.

At one such meeting in 1980, when Middlesex were playing below potential and there was a sense of insecurity in the side as a result of some team changes, one player said he had in the past felt a change in attitude towards him from the other players when he was dropped – as if he was no longer in quite the same sense one of them. This valid and perceptive point would have been much harder to get across had it come from an authority figure.

The spreading of the authority rôle is very important. In Australia, Bob Willis helped me, as vice-captain, by being prepared to take a tough line with players on occasion, to share the responsibility for an unpopular decision or a critical attitude. As in families, it is much better if those in charge are capable of saying both yes and no.

More broadly, the secret of motivation – easier to talk about than to achieve – is getting everyone to motivate each other and himself. In intense heat, say, and half-way through a second day in the field, bowlers need to be made to feel that the rest of the team fully value their efforts. As Rousseau said, individuals can identify not only with their personal good but with the common good.

One important asset in mutual motivation is humour, which can bring an outsider into the group, even as a butt. Through jokes, conflicts can sometimes be tactfully aired and defused. Pomposity is deflated. Humour softens the end of authority. The enemy is rendered less dangerous by nicknames – Rodney Hogg quickly became known as Quentin, Road and Hedge after other noted hogs – and team-mates are helped to feel part of the group by names that are private to it or originated within it.

The success of a team depends to some extent on compatibility and happiness, but even more on respect. Without respect, humour becomes nasty and criticism carping. On tour, one common schism is between the party-goers and the stayers-in. To the former, the latter are no fun; and what is more they don't do their share of going to the functions that are not compulsory, but at which some representatives of the team should appear. Stayers-in see the others as frivolous and excluding. One of Greig's strengths as captain was being able to stand up for either side – having been very much a party-goer himself. If players respect each other, then different social tastes do no damage.

Any group of people tends to throw up the same types. I have already mentioned fun-lover and kill-joy. In addition, there are complainers and pacifiers, the punctual and the latecomers. There are humorists and fools. The rôles that these individuals fall into may effect their performance adversely, and then the captain must try to modify the rôle if he can. For example, some people find that their only route to a sort of acceptance is to play the fool. No doubt a cricket field is not the only locus for their rôle: a poor self-image may have led them to take this way out since childhood. However, it may become prominent in their cricket, for professional cricketers are often very quick to spot a weakness and are quite ruthless at probing it. The group itself may well push such a man further into the court-jester's part.

We had such a player at Middlesex some time ago. At his previous county he had the reputation of being difficult to deal with and temperamental. His captain there was alleged to have said, when asked how overseas players fitted into the dressing-room, that he'd had no trouble with them, but that bloody "Smith"! "Smith" was a thorn in his flesh, and a figure of fun to the rest. On one occasion, "Smith" felt that he should have been bowling and not the captain, so he allowed the ball to pass by his foot and hit the boundary board before lobbing it back in. We took him on because of his undoubted talent. Besides, I rather liked him. In our pre-season practice matches, I noticed that when he bowled he tended to fall over, which provoked slightly stifled laughter, and that he presented himself as an appalling fielder, spindly and uncoordinated. This, too, provoked laughter, though I knew that we would all be irritated if it happened in competitive matches. He also made rather provocative and often odd remarks. I decided that we should not allow him to present himself as a fool, and that we should take him seriously from the start. Gradually, "Smith" spent more time on his feet than on his knees; and his fielding improved remarkably. For a while all went well, until various difficulties intervened.

There are three separate domains of captaincy; the technical (or tactical), the psychological and the administrative. These areas overlap. There is no point in having brilliant tactical ideas if your bowlers think that, coming from you, they are bound to be hogwash, or if the members of the team are pulling in different directions. Similarly, players are unlikely to remain highly motivated if they find your tactics are stupid.

How well the captain carries out his administrative rôle also affects his other rôles. He is likely to be the only representative of the players on the committee, so he has a responsibility to represent their views and, to an extent, to explain the response from the committee. A side is not likely to be well motivated if it feels that the committee has taken on or got rid of the wrong players; has grossly undervalued their services; or does not listen to their ideas. And though the captain is not the committee, he is partly responsible for good working relations between it and the playing staff.

One of the main pitfalls for a captain is an exaggeration of his own importance. He feels utterly elated when things go well, and devastated when they go badly. These swings in feeling occur along with the swings in the side's fortune, regardless of excellence or luck. Moreover, they ignore the fact that the captain's impact, though real, is limited. There are teams which would need an exceptionally bad captain to prevent them from winning, while others could be led by Napoleon and still be doomed.

The media do not encourage sanity in this area. One's own tendencies to both self-glorification and self-denigration are fanned by being hailed as a hero one day and chastised as a villain the next. This happens to any performer, but in cricket, whereas individual results are glaring, the captain's contribution is much harder to assess.

However modest the captain may appear to be, this exaggeration of one's own significance may reveal itself. He may feel more than reasonably depressed if the team has a bad day, and even if he himself has played well he may find it hard to be energetic and active. He may feel personally let down and correspondingly angry: even full of hate towards his players. Conversely, when all goes well, he loves the players and glows with pride.

OBITUARIES

ADAMS, DONALD, who died at Walton-on-Thames early in 1976, aged 95, had the distinction, curious though not unique, of obtaining his only wicket in first-class cricket by bowling W. G. Grace. This he did when, on the strength of some good bowling in the Surrey trial match in April 1902, he played a few days later for the county against London County at the Crystal Palace, opening the bowling and going in last. This was his sole appearance in first-class cricket, but he continued to play in London club cricket until well on in the 1930s.

AINSWORTH, LT-CDR MICHAEL LIONEL YEOWARD, died suddenly, while playing cricket on August 28th, 1978, aged 56. Four seasons in the Shrewsbury XI and captain in 1941, he played with considerable success for Worcestershire from 1948 to 1950. In his first innings for the county he made 71 v Kent, a month or two later 43 and 48 v Yorkshire and in the return match, which followed immediately, 85 and 32, while he finished the season with 100 exactly v Warwickshire. This brought him out top of the county averages with 34.53. The next summer, playing throughout August, he made 60 and 69 not out v Hampshire, 72 v Middlesex and 96 v Kent, an innings surprisingly ended by his being bowled by Ames, but which had much to do with his side winning by an innings. One match in 1950 concluded his county career, but he continued for many years to play for the Navy and for the Free Foresters against the University. His two highest scores in first-class cricket were 106 for Free Foresters v Cambridge in 1958 and 137 in the same match the following year. A tall man, who made full use of his height, he was a fine front-of-the-wicket batsman and a particularly good off-driver. On retiring from the Navy, he joined the staff at Ludgrove School, Wokingham, under the former Yorkshire captain, A. T. Barber.

ALEXANDER OF TUNIS, HAROLD RUPERT LEOFRIC GEORGE, FIELD-MARSHAL, EARL, who died on June 16, 1969, aged 77, was in the Harrow XI of 1910, taking part in "Fowler's Match", which Eton won at Lord's by nine runs. When Harrow were set 55 to win, R. St L. Fowler bowled his off-breaks with such telling effect that he took eight wickets for 23, the innings being all over for 45. Alexander, then the Hon. H. R. L. G. Alexander, obtained three Eton wickets for seven runs in the first innings and two for 33 in the second. In 1956, he was President of the MCC. He earned great military distinction in both World Wars, and was later Governor-General of Canada and Minister of Defence.

ALLETSON EDWARD B., who died on July 5, 1963, aged 79, was celebrated as the batsman who hit more runs in a single over than any other player in the history of the first-class game. That was for Nottinghamshire against Sussex at Hove in 1911, when he punished E. H. Killick for 34, comprising three 6s and four 4s, in an over which included two no-balls. Alletson scored 189 out of 227 in ninety minutes. Beginning quietly, he spent an hour over 50, but, by terrific driving, doubled his score in fifteen minutes and added another 89 in quarter of an hour. From seven overs he obtained 115 out of 120 and in all he hit eight 6s, twenty-three 4s, four 3s, ten 2s and seventeen singles.

While he never achieved another quite such punishing performance, he played fourteen hard-hit innings of 50 or more for his county during a professional career extending from 1906 to 1914 in which he scored 3,217 runs, average 18.47. His most successful season was that of 1913 when he made 634 runs, average 21.13, and hit Wilfred Rhodes, the Yorkshire and England left-arm slow bowler, for three 6s from following deliveries in the game at Dewsbury. He was also a useful fast bowler, as he showed when, with six wickets for 43 in the match with Kent at Trent Bridge in 1913, he helped to bring about the defeat of the eventual champions. His total of wickets was 33 at 18.90 runs each and he brought off 68 catches.

ALTHAM, HARRY SURTEES, who died from a heart attack after addressing a cricket society in Sheffield on March 11, 1965, aged 76, was among the best known personalities in the world of cricket – player, legislator, Test Selector, historian and coach. Educated at Repton, he was in the XI as opening batsman and occasional bowler for four years from 1905 to 1908, during which time *Wisden* described him as "more the made than the natural cricketer". His best season for the School, whom he captained in 1907 and 1908, was his last, when he scored 609 runs, including an innings of 150, for an average of 46.84. At Oxford, he gained a Blue in 1911 and 1912. In his first game against Cambridge he was bowled for 0 in the first innings, being the first "leg" of a hat-trick by J. F. Ireland, the Light Blue captain; but he hit 47 in the second innings, helping Oxford to victory by 74 runs. He took part in six matches for Surrey in 1912 and, when becoming a master and cricket coach at Winchester, a post he held for thirty years, threw in his lot with Hampshire. Between 1919 and 1923, he scored 710 runs, average 22.16, for Hampshire, his highest innings and only first-class century being a faultless 141 against Kent at Canterbury in 1921 after being one of five men dismissed without scoring in the first innings.

Altham collaborated with E. W. Swanton in a book, *The History of Cricket*, and he was also the author of the *MCC Cricket Coaching Book* published in 1952. Always keen on the encouragement of young players, he became chairman of the MCC Youth Cricket Association and President of the English Schools Cricket Association. When appointed chairman of the Special Committee to inquire into the future welfare of English cricket in 1949, he said: "If only we can get enough boys playing this game in England and playing it right, it is quite certain that from the mass will be thrown up in some year or another a new Compton, a new Tate, a new Jack Hobbs, and when that happens we need not worry any more about meetings with Australia."

Altham was a member of the MCC Committee from 1941 till he died, Treasurer from 1951 and President in 1959. He was chairman of the Test team Selection Committee in 1954 and, on the Committee of Hampshire for over forty years, was President of the County Club from 1946 to the date of his death.

He served in the Army during the First World War, being awarded the DSO and the MC.

AMIR ELAHI, who died on December 28, 1980, aged 72, could lay claim to two unusual distinctions: he was one of only twelve cricketers to have played for two different countries and one of the twenty oldest cricketers to have played in a Test match. He appeared once for India, against Australia at Sydney in 1947, and five times for Pakistan, all in India in 1952-53. In his last Test match, at Calcutta, he was 44. Having begun life as a medium-paced bowler, he turned to leg-breaks and googlies, and it was in this latter role that he was best known. On his first tour, to England in 1936, he met with limited success (seventeen wickets at 42.94). In Australia, too, in 1947-48, he found wickets hard to come by (eight at 65.87), as, indeed, he did when, after partition, he went with Pakistan to India (thirteen at 38.76). In the Ranji Trophy, however, he was a prolific wicket-taker (193 wickets, 24.72), mostly for Baroda, whom he helped to win the competition in 1946-47, shortly before becoming a Pakistan citizen. His finest hour with the bat (he was most at home at number eleven) was when he shared a last-wicket partnership of 104 (a Test rarity) with Zulfiqar Ahmed for Pakistan against India at Madras. Amir Elahi's share was a surprising 47. To meet him and talk about his cricketing days was always a pleasure.

ANDERSON, CECIL A. (JACK) who was shot to death by assailants at his home in Kingston, Jamaica, on April 30, 1978, was one of the most experienced and respected of cricket writers in the West Indies. His untimely death two days after his 68th birthday caused shock throughout the Caribbean. The incident occurred shortly after he had returned home after watching the third day of the Test Match between West Indies and Australia at Sabina Park. For years his cricket commentaries written with common sense and a deep devotion to the game as a whole were widely read. He became a special contributor to the *Daily Gleaner*, Jamaica in 1933, worked his way up to a sub-editor and was then transferred to the Gleaner's sister newspaper, the *Evening Star* where he was City Editor at the time of his retirement in 1976. His writing appeared in several newspapers and magazines and, for years, he was West Indian correspondent for *Wisden*. He visited England on several West Indies tours.

ASHTON, GILBERT, MC, who died at Abberley, Worcestershire, on February 6, 1981, was the eldest and also the last survivor of three brothers who played together for Cambridge and captained the University in three successive years, a record they share with the Studds. All three were soccer Blues (Gilbert captained Cambridge and the youngest, Claude, was a full international) and both Hubert and Claude were hockey Blues as well. A still older brother, Percy, was good enough to play for Essex after losing an eye in the Great War. Can any other family equal this record? Gilbert was in the Winchester XI in 1914 and 1915, when he was captain, and then went into the Royal Field Artillery, where he won the MC and was later wounded. No-one in after years watching from the boundary would have realised that he had lost his left thumb; neither in his batting nor his fielding could one detect any trace of this handicap. He got his Blue as a freshman in 1919, retained it in 1920 and was captain in 1921. This 1921 side is often spoken of as the best University side of this century, though it could be argued that the 1920 side was as strong, but in neither was Gilbert's right to a place in any doubt. He bent low over his bat in his stance, but was a fine, aggressive stroke-player and a particularly good cutter and hooker. He was also a beautiful cover-point.

Almost as soon as he went down he had, in a crisis, to take over the Headmastership of Abberley Hall, which he retained for 40 years and which was under him one of the most sought-after preparatory schools in England. For some years he used to play when possible for Worcestershire in the holidays and did enough to show what a difference he would have made could he have played regularly: his last appearance was in 1936. In 1922 he made 125 and 84 against Northamptonshire at Worcester. But probably his most notable performance was at Eastbourne in August, 1921, when A. C. MacLaren's XI (of which he was the last survivor) inflicted their first defeat on Armstrong's great Australian side. Dismissed for 43 and going in again 131 down, MacLaren's side at once began to lose wickets and it was Gilbert who, in a brilliant little innings of 36, showed for the first time in the match that the Australian bowlers were not invincible. He paved the way for the splendid partnership of 154 between his brother Hubert and that great South African cricketer, Aubrey Faulkner, which made possible a sensational victory by 28 runs.

In addition to his work as a schoolmaster, he was a magistrate and took a considerable part in public life in Worcestershire, but he never lost his interest in cricket and in particular served for years on the committee of the County Cricket Club, being its President from 1967 to 1969.

BALDWIN, HERBERT GEORGE, who died on March 7, 1969, aged 75, played as a professional batsman for Surrey from 1922 to 1930, though appearing infrequently in the Championship side. Son of H. Baldwin, the Hampshire all-rounder, "Harry" was a splendid fieldsman at cover-point. For nearly thirty years after giving up playing, he served as a first-class umpire, standing in nine Test matches between 1946 and 1953. He created a sensation in 1938 when he no-balled E. L. McCormick, the Australian fast bowler, no fewer than nineteen times in three overs in the opening match of the tour against Worcestershire at Worcester. McCormick "lost" his run-up and he apologised to Baldwin for causing him "so much trouble".

BARNES, SIDNEY GEORGE, who died suddenly at his home in Sydney on December 16, 1973, aged 57, was both a fine cricketer and a bizarre character. He played, generally as opening batsman, in 13 Test matches for Australia, hitting three centuries, and he and Sir Donald Bradman, each scoring 234, shared a world's record partnership for the fifth wicket in Test cricket when adding 405 against W. R. Hammond's team of

1946-47. Twice he toured England. In 1938 he was out of the game till towards the end of June, having fractured a wrist playing deck games on the voyage over. Even so, he scored 720 runs in 19 innings for an average of 42.35. His only Test that summer was that at The Oval when Sir Leonard Hutton hit his record-breaking 364.

His second English tour was in 1948, when he stood second in the Australian Test batting figures with an average of 82.25 and in all first-class matches put together an aggregate of 1,354, including three centuries, average 56.41. He hit 141 against England at Lord's. In that tour he came in for much criticism for his custom of fielding at point or short-leg some five yards from the bat and almost on the pitch. R. Pollard, batting for England in the Test at Old Trafford, ended the habit when he hit Barnes in the ribs with the ball from a full-blooded stroke, which resulted in him spending ten days in hospital. Following that tour Barnes dropped out of cricket for two years and began writing outspoken articles for the newspapers.

Among the peculiar occurrences in Barnes's career was the occasion in 1952 when the umpires turned down his appeal for a catch. Then captaining New South Wales against South Australia at Sydney, he began to lead his side off the field. The umpires ordered their return, whereupon Barnes, though only twenty minutes remained before the tea interval, called for drinks. In 1951-52, though chosen by the Selectors for the third Test against the West Indies, he was omitted at the insistence of the Australian Board of Control "on grounds other than cricket ability". He claimed £1,000 damages against the author of a letter to a newspaper on the subject, but the writer withdrew his criticism in court and paid the costs.

Next season, having been passed over by the Selectors for a Test against South Africa, Barnes asked to be twelfth man for New South Wales at Adelaide. There he came out with the drinks steward, attired in a grey suit with red carnation, carrying a tray with a scent spray, a portable radio and cigars which he offered to the players and umpires. He received a mixed reception from the crowd. After that season he again took to the Press Box.

In a match in England in 1948 after a strong appeal had been turned down by A. Skelding, the umpire, a dog ran on to the field. Barnes captured the animal and carried it to Skelding with the caustic comment: "Now all you want is a white stick."

He had a brief spell with Burnley, the Lancashire League club, in 1947, but the contract was ended by mutual consent before the season ended.

SYDNEY FRANCIS BARNES

Born at Smethwick, Staffordshire, April 19, 1873

Died at Chadsmoor, Staffordshire, December 26, 1967

By Sir Neville Cardus

Sydney Francis Barnes was the second son of five children of Richard Barnes who spent nearly all his life in Staffordshire and worked for a Birmingham firm for 63 years. The father played only a little cricket and Sydney Barnes averred that he never had more than three hours' coaching, but he practised assiduously to perfect the leg break after learning the off break from the Smethwick professional, Billy Ward of Warwickshire.

Most cricketers and students of the game belonging to the period in which S. F. Barnes played were agreed that he was the bowler of the century. Australians as well as English voted him unanimously the greatest. Clem Hill, the famous Australian left-handed batsman, who in successive Test innings scored 99, 98, 97 v A. C. MacLaren's England team of 1901-2, told me that on a perfect wicket Barnes could swing the new ball in and out "very late", could spin from the ground, pitch on the leg stump and miss the off. At Melbourne, in December 1911, Barnes in five overs overwhelmed Kelleway, Bardsley, Hill and Armstrong for a single. Hill was clean bowled by him. "The ball pitched outside my leg-stump, safe to the push off my pads, I thought. Before I could 'pick up' my bat, my off-stump was knocked silly."

Barnes was creative, one of the first bowlers really to use the seam of a new ball and combine "swing" so subtly with spin that few batsmen could distinguish one from the other. He made a name before a new ball was available to an attack every so many runs or overs. He entered first-class cricket at a time when one ball had to suffice for the whole duration of the batting side's innings.

He was professional in the Lancashire League when A. C. MacLaren, hearing of his skill, invited him to the nets at Old Trafford. "He thumped me on the left thigh. He hit my gloves from a length. He actually said, 'Sorry, sir!' and I said, 'Don't be sorry, Barnes. You're coming to Australia with me.'" MacLaren on the strength of a net practice with Barnes chose him for his England team in Australia of 1901-2. In the first Test of that rubber, Barnes took five for 65 in 35 overs, 1 ball, and one for 74 in sixteen overs. In the second Test he took six for 42 and seven for 121 and he bowled 80 six-ball overs in this game. He broke down, leg strain, in the third Test and could bowl no more for MacLaren, who winning the first Test, lost the next four of the rubber.

Barnes bowled regularly for Lancashire in 1902, taking more than a hundred wickets in the season, averaging around 20. *Wisden* actually found fault with his attack this year, stating that he needed to cultivate an "off break". In the late nineties he had appeared almost anonymously in the Warwickshire XI.

Throughout his career he remained mysteriously aloof, appearing in the full sky of first-class cricket like a meteor – declaring the death of the most princely of batsmen! He preferred the reward and comparative indolence of Saturday league matches to the daily toil of the county tourney. Here is one of the reasons of his absence from the England XI between 1902 and 1907. He didn't go to Australia as one of P. F. Warner's team of 1903-4 and took no part of the 1905 England v Australia rubber. The future historian of cricket may well gape and wonder why, in the crucial Test of 1902, Barnes didn't play for England at Manchester, where the rubber went to Australia by three runs only.

Barnes had bowled for England at Sheffield in the third and previous Test, taking six for 49 and one for 50. It is as likely as conjecture about cricket ever can be likely that had Barnes taken part in the famous Manchester Test of 1902 England wouldn't have lost the rubber by a hair's breadth.

He was in those days not an easy man to handle on the field of play. There was a Mephistophelian aspect about him. He didn't play cricket out of any "green field" starry-eyed idealism. He rightly considered that his talents were worth estimating in cash values. In his old age he mellowed, yet remained humorously cynical. Sir Donald Bradman argued that W. J. O'Reilly must have been a greater bowler than Barnes because he commanded every ball developed in Barnes's day – plus the "googly". I told Barnes of Bradman's remark. "It's quite true," he said, "I never bowled the 'googly'." Then with a glint in his eye, he added, "I never needed it."

Against Australia he took 106 wickets, averaged 21.58. Only Trumble and Peel have improved on these figures in Tests between England and Australia (I won't count Turner's 101 wickets at 16.53 because he bowled in conditions not known to Barnes and Trumble). Barnes had no opportunities to pick up easy victims. He played only against Australia and South Africa and, in all Test matches, his haul was 189 at 16.43 each. On matting in South Africa when South Africa's batsmanship, at its greatest, was represented by H. W. Taylor, A. D. Nourse, L. J. Tancred, J. W. Zulch, in 1913-14, he was unplayable, with 49 wickets in four Tests at 10.93 each. It was said he refused to play in the fifth match because he contended the South Africans had not carried out their promise of special reward if he took part in the tour. In the second Test at Johannesburg, Barnes took 17 wickets for 159, a record which stood until 1956 when Laker laid low Australia at Old Trafford with his unique figures of 19 for 90.

Yet against Barnes's fantastically swinging, bouncing, late-turning attack on that 1913-14 tour, "Herbie" Taylor scored 508 runs, average 50.80, perhaps the most skilful of all Test performances by a batsman. Barnes was a man of character. At Sydney on the

1911-12 tour, J. W. H. T. Douglas opened the England attack using the new ball with Frank Foster. Barnes was furious. He sulked as he sent down 35 overs for three wickets and 107 runs (in the match he took only four for 179). England lost by 146 runs.

At Melbourne, Australia batted first and Barnes this time had the new ball. We all know with what results. Australia suffered defeat – and also in the ensuing three games. The destruction wreaked by Barnes, and on his great days, was mostly done by the ball which, bowled from a splendid height, seemed to swing in to the leg stump then spin away from the pitch, threatening the off-stump. Barnes assured me that he actually turned the ball by "finger twist". The wonder of his career is that he took 77 of his 106 Australian Test wickets on the wickets of Australia when they were flawless and the scourge of all ordinarily good bowlers. He clean bowled Victor Trumper for 0 at Sydney in the 1907-8 rubber; then Fielder and J. N. Crawford in the following Test dismissed Trumper for a "pair", so Trumper was out for 0 in three successive Test innings.

Barnes remained a deadly bowler long after he went out of first-class cricket. So shrewdly did he conserve his energy that in 1928 when he was in his mid-fifties, the West Indies team of that year faced him in a club match and unanimously agreed he was the best they had encountered in the season.

For Staffordshire, in his fifty-sixth year, he took 76 wickets at 8.21 each. Round about this period, a young player, later to become famous in international company, was one of the Lancashire Second XI playing against Staffordshire. His captain won the toss and two Lancashire lads went forth to open the innings against Barnes. As this colt was number six in the batting order he put on his blazer and was about to leave the pavilion to watch Barnes "from behind". But his captain told him to go back to the dressing room and "get on his pads". "But," said the colt, "I'm not in until number six and I'd like to look at Barnes." His captain insisted. The young colt returned to the dressing room. "And there," he said "there were four of us all padded up waiting. And we were all out in the middle and back again in half an hour".

Barnes had a splendid upright action, right arm straight over. He ran on easy strides, not a penn'orth of energy wasted. He fingered a cricket ball sensitively, like a violinist his fiddle. He always attacked. "Why do these bowlers today send down so many balls the batsman needn't play?" he asked while watching a Test match many years ago. "I didn't, I never gave 'em any rest." His hatchet face and his suggestion of physical and mental leanness and keeness were part of Barnes's cricket and outlook on the game. He was relentless, a chill wind of antagonism blew from him on the sunniest day. As I say, he mellowed in full age and retirement. He came to Lord's and other grounds for Test matches, even in his ninety-fifth year, leading blind Wilfred Rhodes about. And to the end of his life he worked for his living, drawing up legal and other documents for Staffordshire County Council in the most beautiful copperplate writing he learned as a boy.

As we think of the unsmiling destroyer of all the batsmen that came his way, let us also remember Barnes immortalised in that lovely verse of Alan Ross:

"Then, elbows linked, but straight as sailors
On a tilting deck, they move. One, square-shouldered as a tailor's
Model, leans over whispering in the other's ear:
'Go easy, Steps here. This end bowling'.
Turning, I watch Barnes guide Rhodes into fresher air,
As if to continue an innings, though Rhodes may only play by ear."

Other tributes to Barnes included:

Arthur Gilligan, President of MCC: He will be mourned by cricketers the world over. He was the finest bowler there ever was and a magnificent personality after his playing days.

S. C. Griffith, Secretary of MCC: The extraordinary thing about him was that all his contemporaries considered him the greatest bowler. There was never any doubts in their minds. This must have been unique.

Wilfred Rhodes, who celebrated his 90th birthday in October, 1967, one of the greatest of cricket's all-rounders, and one of the few remaining contemporaries of Barnes in the England side: Barnes was a very fine medium-paced bowler, the best I ever played with. He had a lovely run-up to the wicket, carrying the ball in his left hand until he was only two paces from the crease and then transferring it to his right. He kept a perfect length and direction and, if you wanted to field close to the wicket say, at short leg, you could stand up to the batsman without any fear. He was quite a decent bat, far better than he was made out to be and too good for a number eleven. He was also a very good fielder.

Herbert Strudwick, the old Surrey and England wicket-keeper (now 88): He was the greatest bowler I ever kept wicket to, for he sent down something different each ball of the over. He could turn it either way in remarkable fashion and I shall never forget keeping to him for the first time in a Gentlemen v Players match at The Oval. His opening delivery pitched outside the leg stump and flew over the top of the off stump. I said to a team-mate: "What sort of bowler have we here?" I soon found out. Sydney could do almost anything with the ball. On matting wickets in South Africa where I toured with him, he was practicably unplayable.

Barnes took 14 wickets for 13 runs, less than one run apiece, playing for Staffordshire against Cheshire in 1909.

Against Northumberland he took 16 for 93 in one day. Even an All-Indian team could barely muster two runs a wicket against him in 1911 when he took 14 for 29.

Fifteen years before he was selected for England he signed for Rishton in the Lancashire League for £3 10s. a week, which included pay for his duties as groundsman. He received an extra 10s. 6d. for taking six wickets or more in a match, and 7s. 6d. for scoring 50.

Mr Leslie Duckworth, in his admirable book: *S. F. Barnes – Master Bowler*, published in July 1967, stated that Barnes in all cricket took 6,229 wickets, average 8.33 as follows:

SUMMARY OF ALL MATCHES

	Overs	*Maidens*	*Runs*	*Wickets*	*Average*
Test matches	1,313.3	358	3,106	189	16.43
County cricket	1,931.2	633	4,456	226	19.71
Other first-class matches	2,028.3	620	4,600	304	15.13
For Staffordshire	5,457.3	1,647	11,754	1,441	8.15
League and Club	12,802	3,532	27,974	4,069	6.03
	23,509.3	6,784	51,890	6,229	8.33

KEN BARRINGTON – AN APPRECIATION

By Robin Marlar

There should be no need for reticence in anyone paying tribute to Ken Barrington. He died of a heart attack in his hotel room at the Holiday Inn in Barbados on March 14, 1981, the Saturday night of the Barbados Test, while serving as assistant-manager on the England tour of the West Indies. As a player, as a friend, as a businessman and latterly as a leader of England's cricketers in the field, he was a man who always did what he could and, when the chips were on the table for all to see, one who could be relied upon to give of his best, his uttermost. The world and especially the cricketing world cannot ask for more. That is why Ken Barrington, master of the malaprop, the man who slept not like a log but "like a lark", commanded such affection all over the world. His widow, Ann, accompanied him on some of his later trips, and it is good that Ann is still involved in the game through the Lord's Taverners, to whom Ken gave so much.

Yet reticence there is, and the hesitation is on his family's account in recalling the circumstances of Ken's tragically premature death at the age of 50. However, *Wisden* is a book of record, and historians sometimes find that its early pages tell the facts but less than the whole truth.

To my mind, the story of Ken's death is as heroic as so many of his innings. It came as a great shock in the spring of 1969 to learn that the chest pains which had led him to withdraw from a double-wicket competition in Melbourne had in fact been a heart attack. After due reflection, taking into account not only his family but the fact that, at 38, batting in Test matches, always Ken's particular forte, was not going to get easier, Ken Barrington retired. Immediately the cares of carrying England's rickety batting through the uncertain and far from satisfying sixties slipped off his shoulders, like some leaden cloak. As he took to the village greens of charity cricket and to the golf courses where his game was good enough to be successfully competitive – and therefore a source of pleasure to a man who hated to be beaten – Ken Barrington's step seemed lighter and his stature in cricket enhanced. His admirers, both far and near, began to realise just how much private effort had gone into coping with "chuckers" and bouncers, as well as the vagaries of form and the whims of selectors.

None the less, a heart attack is a warning, a red light that never joins with amber and turns to green. Although he had managed tours to India, Pakistan and New Zealand, and indeed had had the well-deserved honour of leading the England party at the Melbourne Centenary Test, nothing in his managerial career had tested him quite like this final West Indian ordeal. As a player he had not only plundered bowlers on the great Indian sub-continent but, the son of a soldier who might well in other times have done tours in India of a different nature, he established such a good-humoured relationship there that win or lose, come triumph or disaster, the pressures of touring were easily absorbed. In Australia, where the results mattered more, his rôle was that of coach, so that the burdens were shared first with Doug Insole and then with Alec Bedser.

He was playing that same familiar part in the West Indies. Ironically, he had not been one of the early selections, but as an old player scarred in earlier wars against Hall and Griffith, he knew better than most the perils that a new manager, Alan Smith, and an inexperienced captain, Ian Botham, were flying into as they took on the world champions with their fast bowling quartet in the increasingly stormy Caribbean. In Guyana the heavy and persistent rain meant that the practice sessions which were his charge were suspended. They had been difficult in smaller islands like Antigua and St Vincent in the early weeks of the tour. And then he had to take the team, badly defeated in the first Test and now with their morale increasingly affected by the start of the Jackman affair, as well as their collective lack of practice and form, to the one-day beating at Berbice, while Alan Smith began to play one of his best innings with the politicians. The events of those few days deeply disturbed Barrington. He was also worried about Ann's imminent arrival if the tour was to be cancelled.

But once the party arrived safely in Barbados he seemed to relax. My own last, long and treasured conversation with him was in the happy atmosphere of a Cunarder's bridge, a party in the harbour which he himself had organised. Whatever he felt, he was full of hope for the more distant future, his absolute faith in the ability of Botham and Gatting made more significant by the summer of '81. He knew there were gaps in the England side, but he was old enough in the ways of cricket to know that they are not easily filled.

It was a little thing, at least in the context of that global conversation, that piled all the pressure back on to this caring man. At fielding practice it was Barrington who hit the ball that split Gooch's hand. Gooch was due to bat that day, and in fact played better than anyone – as he told me, without too much discomfort. However, Ken took it badly, as he was bound to do, but it was the way in which he said to Bernard Thomas, "I didn't mean to hurt him", that in retrospect gave the party's medical superintendent the first indication that events were getting out of proportion, upsetting the nervous balance. It was that night, with the Barringtons ready for bed, that the attack struck Ken down. Ann Barrington summoned Bernard Thomas, who was next door, and he knew at once that the attack had been instantaneously fatal. Next morning, when the team stood in Ken's memory, there were many tears.

My own first encounter with Ken Barrington was in 1948 when I was a boy at Harrow. Tom Barling, the new school coach, brought over from The Oval, where he had not long ceased to play for Surrey, a young leg-spinner from Reading with a West Country burr in his voice. The intention was not only to give us practice against a type of bowling that Harrow were likely to meet in the match against Eton at Lord's but also to show us what a *proper* cricketer in the making looked like. We were both seventeen. From then on his career in cricket progressed with its ration of setbacks until he became a record-breaking Test batsman, proudest of all in his unique achievement of scoring a century on every Test ground in England and in every Test-playing country.

As *Wisden* is a chronicle and as this was a man who rated only the best, it is not inappropriate that the essay on him as one of the Five Cricketers of the Year in the 1960 edition should have been written by Norman Preston and the piece on his retirement by John Woodcock, Preston's successor as Editor, in the 1970 edition. It is appropriate, too, to add to those assessments of his playing ability his ever-maturing skill as a leg-spinner. No-one ever bowled more enthusiastically in the nets on tour than Barrington, and whether they realised it or not the England players who faced him were getting practice against a player who might have done the double in the 1930s, a decade less demanding at Test level than the 1960s.

It is with his career in cricket during the last ten years of his life that this eulogy is chiefly concerned. It was at Adelaide during the difficult Australian tour of 1974-75 that Barrington first began to believe that he had a contribution to make as a coach at the highest level. He was brought up in a generation which believed as an act of faith that once a cricketer had played at Test level he knew it all. How else could he have been selected? Furthermore, and this is still a more prevalent attitude than Barrington liked, a player who makes as much of a fetish about practising as Boycott is regarded as a freak. As one who had to work out his technique, to subordinate under a layer of discipline the stroke-making ability he had acquired in his early days, Barrington by the time he retired was a batsman who, if he never knew it all, was a scholar (as well as a gentleman) compared to the players he now saw trying to cope with Lillee and Thomson at their devastating best. More than once Barrington himself had had to change his approach both in style and mind, and so he was ideally suited to the task of developing younger talent and skills.

Not every captain appreciates the need for such a rôle: or knows how to put such available experience to its best use. Ironically, it was on his last tour that Barrington really came to fulfil himself in this the last, and to my mind, most difficult of his cricketing lives. By that time he had mastered the art of subordinating self and position without losing respect or the power to contribute. "He would get me a cup of tea, suggest something which I'd reject probably because I was tired, but then I'd do it and usually it worked." This was Ian Botham during his apprentice days as captain. To the generation that is coming to full maturity Ken Barrington had become as important as the maypole; something solid. He was the "Colonel" around whom a team of cricketers could revolve while playing no part in the dance himself.

Like the maypole he was, too, a source of great happiness, with that rare gift of turning events into comic sketches as they happened. The rat hunt in the Ritz at Hyderabad is now part of cricketing legend. Some wretched rodent, unaware of the niceties of protocol, had eaten the shoulder out of the manager's England blazer in its search for nesting materials. By the time the "Colonel's" army was assembled, the entire staff of the hotel and all its brushes and brooms were ready to go into action. The villain was struck but not apprehended, and after such a warning honour was seen to have been satisfied on all sides.

Now that he is gone, it is possible that the rôle he created and played may be forgotten through want of a successor. But Ken gave so much to cricket in the 1970s that he had left a few campaigners for the cause for the remainder of the 1980s. Even now as Gooch starts or finishes a drive or Gatting hooks, a memory of Barrington the batsman is stirred. For a coach there is no finer memorial than that. It is the man, though, that his contemporaries will miss; and for this one, at least, the hole that he began to dig on the Sixth Form Ground at Harrow more than thirty years ago is never going to be filled.

BEDSER, ALEC, who died in June 1981, aged 33, in a motor accident in Johannesburg, was a right-arm medium-paced bowler who played for Border in the Currie Cup in 1971-72. Like his twin brother, Eric (they were named after the famous cricketing twins), Alec was a distinguished all-round sportsman. Another car accident, several years earlier, had curtailed his cricket career.

BENSIMON, ALFRED SAMUEL, who died in Cape Town on May 7, 1977, in his 91st year, had a short but very interesting first-class career. He played a single match for Western Province in 1931-32, making his début at the advanced age of 45, and he played three more matches for them in 1933-34 when he was over 47. He was the captain on these three occasions and bowled his leg breaks so effectively that he took 17 wickets for only 177 runs. These four matches constituted his whole first-class career. As it happened he proved a statistician's nightmare, for his younger brother, Abel, had the identical initials, A.S., and he made his first class début in 1912-13, twenty years before his elder brother; his career ended in 1923-24. Not surprisingly, it was assumed that they were one and the same person.

BLUNDEN, EDMUND, who died in January, 1974, aged 77, was a lover of cricket and author of *Cricket Country*. A celebrated poet and writer, he was professor of English literature at Tokyo University for three years from 1924, fellow and tutor of English literature at Merton College, Oxford, from 1931 to 1943, professor of English in Hong Kong in 1955 and Oxford University professor of poetry till he resigned through ill health in 1968. He kept wicket for J. C. Squire's invalids.

BOWEN, MAJOR ROWLAND, who died suddenly at his home at Buckfastleigh, Devon, on September 4th, 1978, aged 62, was one of the most learned of cricket historians. Educated at Westminster, he never claimed to have been a good player himself, but he founded in 1963 *The Cricket Quarterly* and was its Editor until he closed it down in 1971. Plenty of space in this was allotted to contemporary cricket problems, on which his views were often highly controversial, but the value of the set lies in the vast number of contributions, whether by himself or by other scholarly researchers, on abstruse points of cricket history. He himself published in 1970 *Cricket: a History*.

BRIDGES, JAMES J., who died in London on September 26, 1966, aged 79, bowled fast-medium for Somerset between 1911 and 1929. Before the 1914 war he played as a professional, but later he was one of the many popular amateurs who enjoyed cricket under the captaincy of John Daniell. He had a neat run-up and side-way action and took 685 wickets. When Jack Hobbs equalled W. G. Grace's record of 126 hundreds in 1925 at Taunton, Bridges had him caught at the wicket by M. L. Hill for 101. His bowling partner was usually R. C. Robertson-Glasgow, who tells in his *More Cricket Prints* how each considered himself the superior batsman; Daniell with rare judgement decided that they should toss for the last two places, a procedure which was regularly observed.

BROWN, GEORGE, who died in hospital at Winchester on December 3, 1964, aged 77, was a great professional all-rounder for Hampshire between 1909 and 1933 – an all-rounder in the truest sense, for he was not only a top-class left-handed batsman and medium-paced right-arm bowler, but a wicket-keeper good enough to play for England and a splendid, fearless fieldsman close to the bat. He was cremated and, at his own wish, his ashes were scattered over the County Ground at Southampton.

Born at Cowley, near Oxford, he formed, with J. Newman and A. S. Kennedy, a batting and bowling backbone for Hampshire for many years. During his career, he hit 25,649 runs, average 26.71, and took 629 wickets at 29.73 runs each. As wicket-keeper, he held 485 catches and brought off 50 stumpings for his county alone. He played behind the stumps in seven Test matches for England, first when, to strengthen the run-getting, he was called upon to replace H. Strudwick in 1921 for the last three Tests with Australia – a decision by the selectors which aroused much controversy. In five innings against Warwick Armstrong's men he did much to justify his choice by scoring 250 runs. Under the captaincy of F. T. Mann, he played four times against South Africa in South Africa in 1922-23 and was selected for the final Test with Australia in 1926, but withdrew because of a damaged thumb. He also toured the West Indies in 1909-10 and India in 1926-27 and assisted Players against Gentlemen nine times from 1919 to 1930.

Tall and of fine physique, Brown was an aggressive batsman who could when the situation demanded fill a defensive role with equal skill. He shared in a three-figure stand for every Hampshire wicket except the sixth and three of them still stand as county records: 321 for the second wicket with E. I. M. Barrett against Gloucestershire at Southampton in 1920; 344 for the third with C. P. Mead v Yorkshire at Portsmouth in 1927, and 325 for the seventh with C. H. Abercrombie v Essex at Leyton in 1913. Twice, against Middlesex at Bournemouth in 1926 and Surrey at the Oval in 1933, he carried his bat through an innings. Of his 37 centuries, the highest was 232 not out from the Yorkshire bowling in Leeds in 1920 and he exceeded 200 on two other occasions; but the display for which he will always be remembered was that at Edgbaston in 1922. Dismissed for 15, the smallest total in their first-class history, Hampshire followed-on 208 behind and seemed destined to humiliating defeat when they lost six men for 186. Then Brown played magnificently for 172 and a maiden century by W. H. Livsey helped the total to 521. Kennedy and Newman followed by dismissing Warwickshire for 158, carrying their side to a famous victory by 155 runs – a feat which brought considerable financial benefit to that intrepid Hampshire captain, the Hon. L. H. Tennyson, who, after the first-innings debacle, had accepted numerous bets at long odds!

Brown's best season was that of 1926 when, with the aid of six centuries, he reached an aggregate of 2,040 and an average of 40.00. Among his best bowling analyses were six wickets for 24 runs against Somerset at Bath and six for 48 against Yorkshire at Portsmouth, both in 1911. After his playing career ended he served for three seasons as a first-class umpire.

BROWNE, CANON FRANCIS BERNARD ROSS, who died on November 11, 1970, aged 70, enjoyed considerable success as a fast-medium right-arm bowler for Eastbourne College, Cambridge University and Sussex. For the school XI in 1916, he headed the bowling figures each season, taking 52 wickets for 8.71 runs each in 1917. He got his Blue as a Senior at Cambridge in 1922 when he finished top of the University bowling averages with 50 wickets for 12.80 runs each. In the big match at Lord's, he helped in victory for the Light Blues in an innings with 100 runs to spare by dismissing four Oxford batsmen for 53 runs, and against Warwickshire at Fenner's he took six wickets for 27 runs each in the second innings. His outstanding performance during a career with Sussex extending from 1919 to 1932 was a match analysis of 10 wickets for 79 against a powerful Yorkshire batting array at Bradford in 1925. It was a pity that he could not devote more time to county cricket. In all first-class cricket he took 252 wickets for 20.66 runs apiece and brought off 35 catches.

His action was extraordinary and was once described by *Wisden* as "a weird delivery that defies description". In the act of bowling, he appeared to cross his legs and deliver the ball off the wrong foot. This earned him the soubriquet of "Tishy" – the name of a race-horse of the time who once crossed his legs in running and was immortalised by Tom Webster, the cartoonist.

BURKE, JAMES WALLACE, the Australian opening batsman for nearly a decade during the 1950s, died by his own hand in Sydney on February 2, 1979, aged 48. In his time, this extremely likeable personality had experienced the full circle of cricket fortunes at international level; he had also excelled at competitive golf, and enjoyed good company just as much as a wide circle of friends welcomed his fellowship, keen sense of humour, and a versatile musical capacity.

By the time he was twenty, Jim Burke had achieved a highly successful schoolboy batting record with Sydney Grammar, played first-grade cricket with the Manly club at fifteen, and appeared as a New South Wales opener at 18. In his Test début against England at Adelaide two years later, he displayed ideal temperament by scoring a maiden Test century notable for neat cuts and glances. And yet, within a year, he was dropped from the Test team – the first of five such occurrences – and at 23, suffered a similar dismissal from the NSW eleven. A season in the Lancashire League with Todmorden started the fight back to international level where he became Colin McDonald's dogged but successful opening partner. In 1956, Burke was chosen with G. R. A. Langley as one of the two Australians featured among *Wisden's* five Cricketers of the Year. Although his batting was becoming increasingly dour and he had put away some of his best strokes, he scored a century before lunch at Taunton. Moving on to Bombay, he scored against India – in six hours eight minutes – the slowest Test century ever put together by an Australian. India and Pakistan were followed by a successful South African tour in 1957-58 when Burke headed the averages and was the sole Australian to reach 1,000 runs (1,041 at an average of 65.06 per innings), this including a monumental innings of nine hours thirty-eight minutes to score 189 in the Cape Town Test. Burke never fully recovered his confidence after a broken rib incurred on this tour, and his concern over the growing use of the bouncer precipitated his retirement at 28 after the England tour of P. B. H. May. His record in 24 Tests was 1,280 runs at an average of 33. In all first-class cricket, he scored 21 centuries and just over 7,600 runs at an average of 49, his record in 58 Sheffield Shield matches being 3,399 runs at 44.14 per innings. In addition, off-breaks bowled with a suggestive bent arm action gained him 101 wickets in the first-class arena.

An honorary life member of MCC, Burke became a widely known and popular radio and television commentator for the Australian Broadcasting Commission cricket service. He had been due to cover the sixth Australia v England Test which commenced a few days after his death.

BUULTJENS, EDWARD W., died in May, 1980. In 1936 he played as a bowler for Ceylon against G. O. Allen's MCC side to Australia and caught and bowled Walter Hammond, his only wicket.

CAKOBAU, RATU SIR EDWARD, who died in Suva, Fiji, on June 25, 1973, aged 64, played for Auckland and when captain of Fiji against a New Zealand touring team in 1937 he hit a century. He played for various teams when in England in 1946, turning out bare-footed in the native Fiji attire. He was President of the Fiji Cricket Association and was manager of the Fiji Rugby football touring team of 1964. Son of King George of Tonga, he became Deputy Prime Minister of Fiji when the colony was granted independence in 1970.

SIR NEVILLE CARDUS

Born April 2, 1889; Died February 27, 1975

CBE 1964; Knighted 1967

By Alan Gibson

Sir Neville Cardus died in his sleep after a very short illness. Regular readers will remember a special tribute by John Arlott to Sir Neville which appeared in the 1965 edition.

At a Memorial Service in St Paul's, Covent Garden, over 720 people joined in an occasion brimming over with joyous music and amusing talk.

The Royal Philharmonic Orchestra, conducted by James Loughran of the Hallé, offered Elgar – Serenade for Strings, and Mozart – the 2nd movements of both the Piano Concerto in A Major, and the Clarinet Concerto, Clifford Curzon played the former.

A Lancashire cricket match was recalled by Miss Wendy Hiller, who rose from a sick bed to read Francis Thompson's poem "At Lord's", and Dame Flora Robson read "Shall I Compare Thee to a Summer's Day".

The Service had great warmth and style, as had Cardus himself. Alan Gibson set the tone on the day with his tribute.

Since we are in a church, I thought it proper that we should have a text. Hear then these words from the prophet Blake (I am not sure whether Blake was one of Sir Neville's favourites, though he has recalled how enthusiastically he would join in "Jerusalem" in his days with the Ancoats Brotherhood). Blake wrote, in *Auguries of Innocence:*

"Joy and woe are woven fine,
A clothing for the soul divine;
Under every grief and pine
Runs a thread of silken twine."

On an occasion such as this, joy and woe are inseparable companions: thanksgiving for such a life, sadness that it has ended. But more than that: it was the mingling of joy and woe that made Sir Neville such a writer – the sensitivity to the human condition, not least his own; the ability to observe it, and to communicate what he saw, with detachment and yet with passion. His books are full of humour: rich comedy, sometimes almost slapstick, and yet he keeps us hovering between tears and laughter. For always he is conscious, and makes us conscious, of the fragility of happiness, of the passing of time. He loved the good moments all the more avidly because he knew they were fleeting.

There is no need to recite his achievement. His autobiographical books, the crown of his life's work, have done that already. His early cricket books gave him a reputation for "fancy" writing. The words "lyrical", "rhapsodical", were sometimes applied to him, usually by people who would not know a lyric from a rhapsody. These terms were still jostled about long after they had any possible justification, to Sir Neville's wry amusement. His mature prose was marked by clarity, balance, and indeed by restraint, though he never shrank from emotion or from beauty. Perhaps George Orwell was as good a writer of prose; or you may think of P. G. Wodehouse, or Bernard Darwin – everyone has his own favourites – but in this century it is not easy to think of many more in the same class.

I remember clearly how I was introduced to Cardus's writing. It was in August, 1935. We were on holiday in Cornwall, at St Ives, and my father was buying me a book, because of some small family service I had done. I said I would like a cricket book and the choice narrowed to two: a book of reminiscences attributed to Hendren, I think it was, and *Good Days*, by Neville Cardus. I doubt if I had heard of Cardus then, because it was difficult to get *The Manchester Guardian* in the south of England. I was inclined to Hendren, but father was inclined to Cardus. Father won. We bought *Good Days*. Father read it before I did, though I have more than made up for that since. Most of us, perhaps half a dozen times in our lives, read books – not always famous books – which change us, change our thinking, books which open doors, revelatory books. That was one of mine. It was the essay on Emmott Robinson that did it – do you remember it? – when Cardus imagined "that the Lord one day gathered together a heap of Yorkshire clay, and breathed into it, and said 'Emmott Robinson, go on and bowl at the pavilion end for Yorkshire'". And then the next bit, about how Emmott's trousers were always on the point of falling down, and he would remember to grab them just in time.

All cricket writers of the last half century have been influenced by Cardus, whether they admit it or not, whether they have wished to be or not, whether they have tried to copy him or tried to avoid copying him. He was not a model, any more than Macaulay, say, was a model for the aspiring historian. But just as Macaulay changed the course of the writing of history, Cardus changed the course of the writing of cricket. He shewed what could be done. He dignified and illuminated the craft.

It was, it has occurred to me, fortunate for cricket that Bradman and Cardus existed at the same time: fortunate for them, too, since the best of batsmen was recorded by the best of critics. Each was worthy of the other.

In the music of Sir Neville's time, at least in English music, there was never one figure quite so dominant as Bradman. Elgar, Delius and Beecham were, he wrote, "the three most original spirits known in English music since Purcell, if we leave out Sullivan". He said it with a shadow of a wink, as if to say, "and take it out of that". You remember how he described Delius, when he met him in what now seem the improbable surroundings of the Langham Hotel: "His attendant carried him into the sitting-room of his suite and flopped him down on a couch, where he fell about like a rag doll until he was arranged into a semblance of human shape. There was nothing pitiable in him, nothing inviting sympathy in this wreck of a physique. He was wrapped in a monk-like gown, and his face was strong and disdainful, every line on it grown by intrepid living." There is a picture for you; there is a piece of prose for you.

As for Sir Thomas Beecham, he is always bursting out of Cardus's pages and making his own way. It was with some difficulty that Cardus stopped his splendid Aunt Beatrice from conquering his first autobiographical book. He never quite stopped Beecham, any more than Shakespeare ever quite stopped Falstaff taking charge of Henry the Fourth.

Perhaps the most remarkable episode in the life of Cardus, going by what he said himself, and one to which we should refer here, was his conversion. I think the word is properly used: I mean his conversion to music. It was achieved by one of the minor saints; Edward German. He was watching a production of a light opera, *Tom Jones*, at the Prince's Theatre, Manchester. He had gone there because he was reading Henry Fielding, but, he says, "the music of Edward German got past my ears and entered into my mind behind my back." Only twenty months after that first experience, he was listening to the first performance of Elgar's Symphony in A Flat, and wondering, with the other musicians in the audience, how Elgar was going to cope with such a long first subject.

He used to say that he was baffled that it should have been Edward German who had first revealed the light: yet he should not have been. It was all of a piece with the man and his thought. When Beecham and MacLaren, and Bradman and Ranjitsinhji, and Elgar came within the experience of Cardus, he rose to them and did them justice – but he was capable of being moved, such was his sense of humanity, by men who were no more than good county bowlers, Emmott Robinson or Edward German.

"Joy and woe are woven fine." They are not alien, they are complementary, "A clothing for the soul divine." And in another part of that poem, Blake says

"It is right it should be so,
Man was made for joy and woe,
And when this we rightly know,
Safely through the world we go."

I am not sure whether Sir Neville Cardus would approve of that as an epitaph: but he is probably too busy to bother just now, arguing with Bernard Shaw.

CARR, ARTHUR WILLIAM, who collapsed and died after shovelling snow at his home at West Witton, Yorkshire, on February 7, 1963, aged 69, was a celebrated Nottinghamshire and England captain. Born at Mickleham, Surrey, he was educated at Sherborne were he was captain of every game except cricket. Nevertheless he earned an early reputation as a cricketer. He headed the School averages in 1910 with 638 runs at 45.47 per innings and took with fast bowling 32 wickets for 15.06 runs each; the following year, with the aid of an innings of 224, he averaged 62. While still at school he made a few appearances for Nottinghamshire and in 1913, at the age of 18, he gave a display of that strong-driving, attacking play which always characterized his cricket when he hit 169 against Leicestershire at Trent Bridge. He and G. M. Lee (200 not out) shared in a stand of 333 in just over three hours.

Not till he took over the captaincy in 1919 – a position he occupied till 1934, when he gave up, following a heart attack – did he occupy a regular place in the county eleven. Then, with improved judgement allied to his forcing methods, he became a highly valuable batsman. In each of eleven seasons he exceeded 1,000 runs, his most successful being that of 1925 when, with the help of seven centuries, including his highest – 206 against Leicestershire at Leicester – he aggregated 2,338 runs with an average of 51.95. That summer he hit no fewer than forty-eight 6s. During his first-class career, he made 21,884 runs, average 31.12, took 28 wickets at 38.17 apiece and, an exceptionally alert fieldsman anywhere near the wicket, held 361 catches.

Carr played for England on eleven occasions. He toured South Africa under F. T. Mann in 1922–23, taking part in all five Test matches: he led his country in four games against Australia in 1926 till he was superseded by A. P. F. Chapman at The Oval – a decision which aroused much controversy – and in 1929 he was recalled to the leadership for the last two matches with South Africa, replacing J. C. White, captain in the first three. In thirteen Test innings he hit 237 runs, with a top score of 63 at Johannesburg, average 19.75. He made a number of appearances for Gentlemen against Players, between 1919 and 1929.

Of somewhat stern appearance, but kind and generous at heart and a lover of cricket, Carr was a man of forthright views. He was specially outspoken in defence of H. Larwood and W. Voce, his team-mates who were principals in the "body-line" tour of Australia in 1932–33. During his long reign as captain he led Nottinghamshire to first place among the counties in 1929 – the last time they headed the Championship.

CAT, PETER, whose ninth life ended on November 5, 1964, was a well-known cricket-watcher at Lord's, where he spent 12 of his 14 years. He preferred a close-up view of the proceedings and his sleek, black form could often be seen prowling on the field of play when the crowds were biggest. He frequently appeared on the television screen. Mr S. C. Griffith, Secretary of MCC, said of him: "He was a cat of great character and loved publicity."

LORD CONSTANTINE

by John Arlott

Lord Constantine, MBE died in London on July 1, 1971. The parents of the child born in Diego Martin, Trinidad, almost seventy years before, may be in their highest ambitions have hoped that he would play cricket for the West Indies. They cannot have dreamt that he would take a major share in lifting his people to a new level of respect within the British Commonwealth; that along the way he would become the finest fieldsman and one of the most exciting all-rounders the game of cricket has known: and that he would die Baron Constantine, of Maraval in Trinidad and Tobago, and of Nelson, in the County Palatine of Lancaster, a former Cabinet Minister and High Commissioner of his native Trinidad.

Learie – or "Connie" to forty years of cricketers – came upon his historic cue as a man of his age, reflecting and helping to shape it. He made his mark in the only way a poor West Indian boy of his time could do, by playing cricket of ability and character. He went on to argue the rights of the coloured peoples with such an effect as only a man who had won public affection by games-playing could have done in the Britain of that period.

Learie Nicholas Constantine, born September 21, 1902, was the son of Lebrun Constantine, a plantation foreman who toured England as an all-rounder with the West Indian cricketers of 1900 – when he scored the first century for a West Indies team in England – and 1906. In 1923 they both played for Trinidad against British Guiana at Georgetown, one of the few instances of a father and son appearing together in a first-class match; both of them long cherished the occasion. In constant family practice the father insisted on a high standard of fielding which was to prove the foundation of his son's success.

The younger Constantine had played only three first-class matches before he was chosen for Austin's 1923 team to England when he distinguished himself largely – indeed, almost solely – by his brilliance at cover point. On that visit he learnt much that he never forgot, by no means all of it about cricket: and he recognised the game as his only possible ladder to the kind of life he wanted.

As C. L. R. James has written "he revolted against the revolting contrast between his first-class status as a cricketer and his third-class status as a man". That, almost equally with his enthusiasm for the game, prompted the five years of unremitting practice after which, in 1928, he came to England under Karl Nunes on West Indies' first Test tour as an extremely lively fast bowler, hard-hitting batsman and outstanding fieldsman in any position.

Muscular but lithe, stocky but long armed, he bowled with a bounding run, a high, smooth action and considerable pace. His batting, which depended considerably upon eye, was sometimes unorthodox to the point of spontaneous invention: but on his day it was virtually impossible to bowl at him. In the deep he picked up while going like a sprinter and threw with explosive accuracy; close to the wicket he was fearless and quick; wherever he was posted he amazed everyone by his speed and certainty in making catches which seemed far beyond reach. His movement was so joyously fluid and, at need, acrobatic that he might have been made of springs and rubber.

Although he did little in the Tests of that summer he performed the double and in public esteem was quite the most successful member of the party. He provided splendid cricketing entertainment. Everyone who ever watched him will recall with delight his particular parlour trick – when a ball from him was played into the field he would turn and walk back towards his mark: the fieldsman would throw the ball at his back, "Connie" would keep walking and, without appearing to look, turn his arm and catch the ball between his shoulder blades; no one, so far as can be ascertained, ever saw him miss.

Crowds recognised and enjoyed him as a cricketer of adventure: but the reports alone of a single match established him in the imagination of thousands who had never seen him play. At Lord's, in June, Middlesex made 352 for six and West Indies, for whom only Constantine, with 86, made more than 30, were 122 behind on the first innings. When Middlesex batted again, Constantine took seven for 57 – six for 11 in his second spell. West Indies wanting 259 to win were 121 for five when Constantine came into score 103 out of 133 – with two 6s, twelve 4s and a return drive that broke Jack Hearne's finger so badly that he did not play again that season – in an hour, to win the match by three wickets. Lord's erupted: and next day all cricketing England accepted a new major figure.

That performance confirmed the obvious, that Constantine was, as he knew he needed to be, the ideal league professional – surely the finest of all. He wanted a part-time living adequate for him to study law. England was the only place, and cricket his only means, of doing both. His batting could win a match in an hour; his bowling in a couple of overs, his catching in a few scattered moments. This was the kind of cricket nearest his heart: and he expressed himself through it. No man ever played cricket for a living – as Constantine needed to do more desperately than most professional cricketers – with greater gusto. Any club in the Lancashire leagues would have been grateful to sign him. Nelson did so with immense satisfaction on both sides. Constantine drew and delighted crowds – and won matches: Nelson won the Lancashire League eight times in his ten seasons there – an unparalleled sequence – and broke the ground attendance record at every ground in the competition. Less spectacularly, he coached and guided the younger players with true sympathy. Among the people of Nelson, many of whom had never seen a black man before, "Connie" and his wife, Norma, settled to a happy existence which they remembered with nostalgia to the end. In 1963 the Freedom of the Borough of Nelson was bestowed on the man who then was Sir Learie Constantine.

Because of his League engagements he played little more than a hundred first-class matches, in which he scored 4,451 runs at 24.32, and took 424 wickets at 20.60. In eighteen Tests between 1928 and 1939 his overall figures were poor – 641 runs at 19.42; 58 wickets at 30.10. On the other hand he virtually won two important Tests and shaped a third. At Georgetown, in 1930, when West Indies beat England for the first time, George Headley made a major batting contribution; but it was Constantine who twice broke the English batting with four for 35 and five for 87, figures not approached by any other bowler in the match. At Port of Spain in 1934-35 he levelled the series – which West Indies eventually won by one match – when, aftering scoring 90 and 31, he took two for 41 and ended his second innings three for 11 (in 14.5 overs) with the master stroke of having as great a resister as Maurice Leyland lbw with only one ball of the match remaining. In his last Test, at The Oval in 1939, when he was 37 years old, his five for 73 took West Indies to a first-innings lead.

As he grew older he grew more astute. As his pace dropped – though he was always likely to surprise with a faster ball or deal a yorker of high speed – he developed a superbly concealed slower ball; and at need he was an effective slow bowler with wrist or finger spin. He continued to play in charity matches well through his fifties when he could still make vivid strokes, bowl out good batsmen and take spectacular catches.

In his younger days some thought him bouncy or unduly colour conscious; if that were so, Nelson warmed him. It would have been strange if so dynamic and effective a cricketer had not bubbled over with confidence. Certainly, though, he gave unhestitating and helpful counsel, and generous praise to his amateur colleagues in the Nelson team. Meanwhile he fought discrimination against his people with a dignity firm but free of acrimony.

Half Learie Constantine's life was spent in England and, although his doctors had long before advised him that a lung condition endangered his life if he did not return to the warmer climate of the West Indies, he died in London. He remained in England during the Second World War as a Ministry of Labour welfare officer with West Indian workers. In 1944 he fought one of the historic cases against colour prejudice when he won damages from The Imperial Hotel in London for "failing to receive and lodge him".

He was deeply moved – and never forgot it – when the other players – all white-skinned – elected him captain of the Dominions team that beat England in the magnificent celebratory, end-of-war match at Lord's in 1946. He rose to the occasion in a fine forcing partnership with Keith Miller and his shrewd captaincy decided a narrow issue with only minutes to spare.

By then, however, his serious cricketing days were drawing to an end. He did occasional writing and broadcasting. Among his books are *Cricket in the Sun*, *Cricket and I*, *How to Play Cricket*, *Cricketers' Carnival*, *The Changing Face of Cricket* (with Denzil Batchelor), and *Colour Bar*. Years of dogged study were rewarded when he was called to the Bar by the Middle Temple in 1954. Returning to Trinidad he was elected an MP in his country's first democratic parliament; became Minister of Works in the government and subsequently High Commissioner for Trinidad and Tobago in London from 1962 until 1964. He was awarded the MBE in 1945; knighted in 1962; made an honorary Master of the Bench in 1963; and created a life peer in 1969. He served various periods as a governor of the BBC, a Rector of St Andrews, a member of the Race Relations Board and Sports Council.

A devout Roman Catholic, of easy humour and essential patience, he lived a contented domestic life with his wife and his daughter, who is now a school teacher in Trinidad. His outlook was that of a compassionate radical and he maintained his high moral standards unswervingly.

To the end of his days he recalled with joy the great moments of his cricket and the friends he had made. His wife survived him by barely two months: and Trinidad posthumously awarded him the Trinity Cross, the country's highest honour.

CRAWFORD, JOHN NEVILLE, who died on May 2, 1963, aged 76, was one of the best all-rounders of his era, although he habitually played in spectacles. Son of the Rev. J. C. Crawford and nephew of Major F. F. Crawford, both of whom played for Kent, he created such a reputation as a batsman and a bowler of varying pace at Repton that he was invited to play for Surrey in 1904 at the age of 17. He was an immediate all-round success and he and H. C. McDonell bowled unchanged through both innings of Gloucestershire at Cheltenham, Crawford taking 10 wickets for 78 and his fellow amateur 10 for 89.

Jack Crawford appeared regularly for Surrey from 1906 till 1909. Twice in succession he completed "the cricketers' double" and in 1908 failed to do so a third time by two wickets. During this period he made twelve appearances for England, going to South Africa in 1905-06 and to Australia in 1907-08, when he headed the Test bowling averages with 30 wickets for 24.79 runs each. After a mid-season dispute with Surrey in 1909 he settled in Australia, playing with distinction for South Australia and paying a visit to New Zealand with an Australian XI, in 1914. In the course of this tour he played an extraordinary innings in a two-day fixture with a South Canterbury XI at Temuka. Of a total of 922 for nine wickets, he obtained 354 – 264 of them from fourteen 6s and forty-five 4s – in five and a half hours. He and Victor Trumper put on 298 in sixty-nine minutes for the eighth wicket and he and M. A. Noble at one point added 50 in nine minutes.

Crawford returned to England following the First World War and, the disagreement having been settled, played again for Surrey from 1919 till he retired in 1921. A hard-hitting batsman, he shared a match-winning stand of 96 in thirty-two minutes with J. B. Hobbs against Kent in 1919 and the same season played what was described as the innings of his life. Going in at No. 8 against the Australian Imperial Forces side at The Oval, he hit 144 not out. When Tom Rushby, the last man, reached the wickets, Surrey needed 45 to avoid a follow-on; but Crawford attacked the bowling with such ferocity that 80 runs were added in thirty-five minutes. Rushby's share in this partnership amounted to two runs. Of Crawford, *Wisden* of the time recorded: "The way in which he drove Gregory's fast bowling was magnificent." In all first-class cricket, Crawford hit 7,005 runs average 30.19, dismissed 600 batsmen at a cost of 20.50 runs each and brought off 117 catches.

CRAWLEY, LEONARD GEORGE, a member of a notable games-playing family and himself one of the most versatile games-players of his day, died on July 9, 1981, aged 77. Though he was perhaps best known to the general public as for years golfing correspondent of *The Daily Telegraph* and one of the select body of Englishmen who have won a single in the Walker Cup, in which he appeared four times, he might well have been no less distinguished in the cricket world if he had been able to give the time to the game: in addition he had been first string for Cambridge at rackets and he was a fine shot.

Three years in the Harrow XI, he played a memorable innings of 103 at Lord's in 1921, and, getting his Blue at Cambridge as a freshman in 1923, played three years also for them. In 1925 he was 98 not out at lunch against Oxford, needing only 2 runs to equal the record of his uncle Eustace Crawley, the only man who had made a century in both the Eton and Harrow and the 'Varsity match: unfortunately he was out to the first ball after lunch. In 1922, his last year at school, and again in 1923, he had headed the Worcestershire batting averages, in 1923 actually averaging 86, but Lord Harris discovered that neither he nor the leading Worcestershire professional batsman, Fox, was properly qualified and MCC declared both ineligible for the county. This led to a famous scene in the Long Room at Lord's between Lord Deerhurst, the Worcestershire President, and Lord Harris, with J. W. H. T. Douglas, unseen it is thought by the protagonists, mimicking the actions of a boxing referee in the background.

In 1925-26 Crawley went on an MCC tour of the West Indies, then quite a minor affair, and from 1926 to 1937 played for Essex, though never for more than a few matches a season and sometimes not for that. However, in 1932 he averaged 51.87 for them and was asked whether he would be available to go to Australia that winter if wanted. Again in 1937 against Glamorgan at Pontypridd, on his first appearance of the season, he made 118, including five 6s, two of them out of the ground: no-one else made 20. But the effort left him so stiff that he was unable to take any further part in the match. A few weeks later he featured in a bizarre incident against Worcestershire at Chelmsford. The visiting captain, the Hon. C. J. Lyttelton, seeing him coming out to open and knowing that, given a chance, he would try to drive the first ball over the screen, instructed the bowler, Perks, to give him one slightly short of a length on the middle stump. Perks produced just the right ball and Crawley's bat struck it when its face was pointing straight upwards to the sky. The ball rose vertically to an astronomical height. A. P. Singleton in the gully put his hands in his pockets and said "I'm not taking that". Lyttelton looked round in desperation and finally said to Singleton, "Sandy, you've got to take it", whereupon Singleton took his hands out of his pockets and held what in the circumstances was a fine catch.

Crawley was one of the greatest drivers, straight and to the off, on his day good enough to force Maurice Tate in his prime to station a man by the screen. He was also a superb cutter, whether square or late, and if he was deficient in leg-side strokes, it did not markedly affect his ability to score fast, even against high-class bowling. In all first-class cricket he scored 5,227 runs with an average of 31.12, including eight centuries. His highest score was 222 for Essex against Glamorgan at Swansea in 1928.

CRUTCHLEY, GERALD EDWARD VICTOR, who died on August 16, 1969, aged 78, was a capital right-handed batsman. In the Harrow XI in 1908, he did much to win the fixture with Eton by ten wickets, scoring 74 runs and, with outswingers of varying pace, disposing of eight batsmen in the two innings for 46 runs. Though he achieved little as a batsman on the big occasion the next year, he took seven wickets for 33 runs and enabled Harrow to enjoy the best of a drawn game.

Going up to Oxford, he did not gain a Blue till 1912 and in that year against Cambridge he set up a curious record. Having scored 99 not out, he was found at the end of the day to be suffering from measles and had to withdraw from the match.

Business prevented Crutchley from appearing for Middlesex as often as he would have liked, but he turned out for the county whenever possible from 1910 to 1930. Among his chief feats for them was the scoring of 145 in an opening partnership of 231 with H. W. Lee (243 not out) in two and a quarter hours off the Nottinghamshire bowling at Lord's in 1921, in which season Middlesex carried off the County Championship. He held another distinction, for he was the last man to play cricket during the Canterbury Week and to act at night for the Old Stagers.

A batsman of delightfully free style, specially skilled in driving to the off, he hit 4,069 runs, including five centuries, average 22.23; took 60 wickets for 34.56 runs each and held 53 catches during his first-class career. For five years from 1957 he was President of Middlesex. As a Lieutenant in the Scots Guards during the First World War, he was wounded and held prisoner of war in Germany for almost four years.

DANIELL, JOHN, who died on January 24, 1963, aged 84, rendered splendid service to cricket and Rugby football over many years as player and administrator. He was in the Clifton XI – and the XV – in 1895, 1896 and 1897, heading the batting averages in the last year. Though he created little impression as a cricketer when he went up to Emmanuel College, Cambridge, S. M. J. Woods, the Somerset captain, included him in the county team for six games in 1898. When, the following season, Daniell hit 107 against such a powerful bowling side as Lancashire, G. L. Jessop felt compelled to award him the last place against Oxford. Daniell also played in the following two University matches and, as a lively and enthusiastic Rugby forward, he represented Cambridge from 1898 to 1900. In 1899, "The Prophet", as he was then usually known, was first chosen for England at football and he gained seven caps between then and 1904, twice being captain. A member of the Rugby Football Union Selection Committee from 1913 to 1939, he was chairman for the last eight years; he became a Vice-President of the Union in 1938, was acting-President from 1940 to 1945 and President from 1945 to 1947.

After going down from Cambridge, he was a schoolmaster for a brief spell and then took up tea-planting in India till, in 1908, he returned to England and accepted the captaincy of Somerset. A keen and highly popular leader, intolerant of "slackers", he possessed a forcefully picturesque vocabulary when things did not go as he expected; but because he was always scrupulously fair, his sometimes caustic criticism left no ill-effects. He remained Somerset captain for four seasons and then retired, but after serving in the Army in the First World War, he responded to an appeal by the county and resumed the position from 1919 to 1926.

Altogether Daniell, a hard-driving batsman at his best against off-spin bowling, scored 10,415 runs in first-class cricket, average 21.12, but it is as a fearless fieldsman at silly point, where he brought off the vast majority of his 222 catches, that he will be best remembered as a cricketer. However hard the hit, Daniell generally seemed able to hold any catch within reach. Of his nine centuries, he obtained two in one match at the age of 46 – 174 not out and 108 against Essex at Taunton in 1925.

When his playing days finally ended, Daniell served as an England cricket selector and also, to help his county in a financial crisis, acted for a time as honorary secretary to Somerset.

DENTON, WILLIAM HERBERT, the last survivor of three brothers who played together for Northamptonshire, died on April 23, 1979, aged 88. He and his identical twin J. S., who between them caused endless confusion to spectators and scorers, first appeared in 1909. By 1912, when the county, calling upon only twelve players in the Championship, came second, they had become essential members of the side. In 1913 both exceeded 1,000 runs and, from August that year until cricket was stopped by the War, they formed the regular opening pair. Both were taken prisoner in the closing months of the War and J. S. played little county cricket afterwards but W. H., after a few appearances between 1919 and 1923, resumed a regular place for the season of 1924. Unfortunately his spell as a prisoner had taken its toll of his health and, though he did much useful work, he was not the player he had been. He did not play for the county again. A small man, he had a sound defence and his footwork was neat: a large proportion of his runs were scored behind the wicket. His highest score was 230 not out, at that time a record for the county, against Essex at Leyton in 1913. Going in first he carried his bat through an innings of five hours forty minutes and was on the field throughout the match. Apart from his batting he was a fine mid-off. When Northamptonshire played Somerset in 1914, the Denton twins opened for Northamptonshire and the Rippon twins, A. D. E. and A. E. S., for Somerset – an occurrence unique in first-class cricket.

DICKENS, HENRY CHARLES, who died in November, 1966, aged 83, was the last surviving grandson of Charles Dickens. A keen cricketer, he was a member of MCC.

DONNELLY, DESMOND LOUIS, who was found dead in a London hotel bedroom on April 4, 1974, aged 53, founded in 1940 the British Empire XI which, including many famous cricketers, all unpaid, raised much money for the Red Cross. In the first season over 80,000 people watched the Empire XI's 37 matches, the Red Cross benefiting by £1,239. Donnelly afterwards joined the RAF, serving with the Desert Air Force, and following the end of the Second World War became a Member of Parliament, firstly with the Labour Party and then as an independent. A journalist, he was the author of eleven books.

DUCKWORTH, GEORGE, who died on January 5, 1966, aged 64, was an outstanding character in first-class cricket in the period between the two World Wars, a time when the game possessed far more players of popular personality than at the present time. Small of stature, but big of heart and voice, Duckworth used an "Owzat" shout of such piercing quality and volume that his appeal alone would have made him a figure to be remembered.

But Duckworth possessed many other qualities. He was one of the finest wicket-keepers the game has produced; as a batsman he could be relied upon to fight in a crisis; he possessed wit and good humour which made him an endearing companion, and he was a sound judge of a player, an ability which served his native Lancashire well as a committee man in recent years.

Duckworth, born and resident in Warrington all his life, joined Lancashire in 1922. He made his début a year later and ended his first-class career, perhaps prematurely, in 1938. He took up journalism, but hardly had time to establish himself before war broke out in 1939. Then he spent spells in hotel management and farming before his post-war career, which included journalism, broadcasting, and acting as baggage-master and scorer to MCC teams abroad, and for touring countries here. He also took Commonwealth sides to India.

Duckworth received a trial with Warwickshire before arousing the interest of his native county with whom he quickly showed his talent by the confident manner in which he kept to such varied and demanding bowlers as the Australian fast bowler, E. A. McDonald, and the spin of C. H. Parkin and R. Tyldesley. By 1924 he had gained the first of 24 Test caps for England, a total which undoubtedly would have been much higher but for the competition of L. E. G. Ames of Kent, who in the 1930s usually gained preference because of his batting prowess. In his later days with Lancashire, Duckworth also faced strong competition from Farrimond, which he resisted successfully.

In Test cricket, Duckworth claimed 59 wicket-keeping victims, and he also hit 234 runs, with 39 not out as his highest. For Lancashire his number of victims was a record 921, and his highest score 75. In all first-class matches he helped in 1,090 dismissals, 751 catches and 339 stumpings. He dismissed 107 batsmen, 77 caught and 30 stumped, in his best season, 1928.

That season completed three Championship successes for Lancashire, captained by Leonard Green, who described Duckworth as "One of the smallest, but noisiest of all cricketing artists – a man born to squat behind the wicket and provide good humour and unbounded thrills day by day in many a glorious summer".

Lancashire won the championship again in 1930, and 1934, so that Duckworth gained the honour of being a member of five championship teams. In 1949-50 Duckworth, a man of administrative ability, took his first Commonwealth team to India, Pakistan and Ceylon, and repeated the successful venture in 1950-51 and 1953-54. Then followed his duties as baggage-master and scorer, at home and abroad, where his jovial personality, wise counsel and experience were of benefit to many a team and individual cricketer. His radio and television commentaries, typically humorous and forthright, became well-known, both on cricket and on Rugby League, in which game he was a devoted follower of Warrington.

Among many tributes were:

H. Sutcliffe (Yorkshire and England): George was a delightful colleague, a great man on tours particularly. He had a vast knowledge of the game and he was always ready and willing to help any young player. As a wicket-keeper he was brilliant.

C. Washbrook (Lancashire and England): He was a magnificent wicket-keeper and a fighting little batsman. In his later years he became one of the shrewdest observers of the game and his advice was always available and eagerly sought by cricketers of every class and creed.

FAGG, ARTHUR EDWARD, died at Tunbridge Wells on September 13, 1977, aged 62. Although in a career which extended from 1932 to 1957 he scored 27,291 runs with an average of 36.05, made 58 centuries and played five times for England, it cannot be said that he ever fulfilled expectations. In the middle thirties Sutcliffe was dropping out of Test cricket and England was looking for a new opening pair. Fagg and Hutton were at once recognised as obvious candidates and Fagg, a year the senior and by some considered the better prospect, got the first chance, playing in two Tests v India in 1936 and being picked for the Australian tour that autumn. Halfway through the tour he was invalided home with rheumatic fever, a great setback to his career, and he missed the entire season of 1937. Naturally, in 1938 the selectors were cautious about playing him and, though he had a splendid season, it was not until the final Test that they picked him and then he was one of those left out.

That his health was not fully trustworthy was shown when he refused an invitation for the South African tour that winter. In 1939 he played in one Test v West Indies. Unfit for the Services during the war, he went as coach to Cheltenham and, when first-class cricket was resumed in 1946, felt so doubtful whether he could stand the strain that he decided to stay there.

In 1947 Kent persuaded him to return, but already at 32, he was moving like a veteran. Hutton and Washbrook were established as England's opening pair and his days of Test cricket were clearly over. Still, for ten years more he did splendid work for Kent and no-one watching him could fail to see that he was far more than a good county bat. Very sound, he had strokes all round the wicket and, being a fine hooker, was particularly severe on fast bowling. Against spin he was less impressive.

One record which he holds may well never be equalled. In 1938 against Essex at Colchester, he scored 244 and 202 not out, the second innings taking only 170 minutes. His fielding was never on a par with his batting and after his early years, it was difficult to place him anywhere save in the slips, where he held his share of catches without being outstanding. In the Second XI he had been trained to keep wicket and was good enough to keep on a few occasions for the county when neither Ames not Levett was available.

From 1959 to his death he was one of the First-Class umpires and from 1967 to 1976, when he retired for reasons of health, was on the panel of Test Match umpires. His long tenure of this appointment is sufficient testimony to the respect in which he was held and when at Birmingham in 1973 he threatened to withdraw after the second day because of the behaviour of some of the West Indian side who had disagreed with one of his decisions, he could be sure of public sympathy. He did not indeed appear on the field on the third morning until the second over, Alan Oakman, the Warwickshire coach, having stood during the match.

FILLISTON, JOSEPH W., who died in hospital on October 25, 1964, aged 102, five days after being knocked down by a motor-scooter, acted as umpire to the BCC Cricket Club for many years. "Old Joe" stood in the Old England v Lord's Taverners match at Lord's when over 100. In his younger days he played cricket with Dr. W. G. Grace and he helped Gentlemen of Kent defeat the Philadelphians by six wickets at Town Malling in 1889. He also played as a professional in the Staffordshire League. He liked to tell of the occasion when he gave "W.G." out leg-before in a London County game at the Crystal Palace. The Doctor, he said, refused to leave the crease and, as nobody had the courage to contradict him, he continued his innings.

FINGLETON, JOHN HENRY WEBB ("JACK"), OBE died on November 22, 1981, at the Royal North Shore Hospital in Sydney. He was 73. Born at Waverley in Sydney's Eastern Suburbs, Fingleton was educated firstly by the Christian Brothers at St Francis's School, Paddington, and then at Waverley College. Leaving school at the age of fifteen, he embarked on a career as a journalist which commenced with a cadetship at the *Sydney Daily Guardian*. Later, he was to move to the *Telegraph Pictorial* where he worked for several years prior to the Second War. At the outbreak of war, he joined the Army before being seconded to the former Prime Minister, Billy Hughes, as Press Secretary. From this time onwards, he lived and worked in Canberra. Fingleton achieved no particular distinction on the cricket field while at school, but, on joining Waverley, he quickly graduated to the first eleven of a club which included Kippax, Carter, Hendry and Mailey within its ranks. A right-hand opening batsman, Fingleton was noted more for his stubborn defence than for his aggression. The one epithet unfailingly used to describe his batting was "courageous". He was also an outstandingly gifted fieldsman, whose reputation was made in the covers but who was later to win fame with Vic Richardson, and sometimes with W. A. Brown, in South Africa in 1935-36 as part of the "O'Reilly leg-trap". Neville Cardus, for whom Jack had the greatest regard, once described the Fingleton-Brown combination as "crouching low and acquisitively, each with as many arms as an Indian God".

In 1930, when 22, Fingleton won his first cap for New South Wales and within twelve months (after only five first-class matches) he was selected for Australia. In the home series against South Africa in 1931-32, he was thrice twelfth man and he eventually won his place in the side for the final Test only because Ponsford was forced out of the selected side by illness. In a game notable for its low scoring Fingleton was second top scorer with 40. In the following summer came the "Body-line" series. Early in the season, Fingleton scored a brave century for New South Wales against the Englishmen, which was sufficient to ensure his selection for the first Test. He started the series in fine form, with scores of 26, 40 and 83, and seemed as well equipped as any to handle the novel tactics of the opposition. However, the third Test at Adelaide was a disaster for Fingleton. Australia were beaten by 338 runs, Fingleton made a "pair", and he was blamed for leaking to the newspapers details of the exchange between Woodfull and Warner which took place in the Australian dressing-room and almost led to the abandonment of the Test series. Perhaps as a repercussion, Fingleton was a surprise omission from the Australian side selected to tour England in 1934.

He was restored to the Test team for the tour of South Africa in 1935-36, a tour that was to mark the apogee of his career. Against Natal at Durban he scored 167 (the highest innings of his first-class career), during the tour he had several mammoth opening partnerships with Brown, and he concluded the series with centuries in each of the last three Test matches – 112 at Cape Town, 108 at Johannesburg and 118 in Durban. Australia won each of these games by an innings. In the following season in Australia, against an MCC side captained by G. O. Allen, he created history by scoring a fourth consecutive Test hundred at Brisbane. The achievement was later equalled by Alan Melville (whose four consecutive Test hundreds were scored between 1939 and 1947) and then surpassed by the West Indian Everton Weekes (1948-49). In the 1936-37 series, Fingleton achieved another place in the record book by sharing with Bradman, in the third Test in Melbourne, a sixth-wicket partnership of 346, a record which still stands. In 1938, Fingleton was selected in the Australian team which toured England, a Test series in which he had only moderate success. This, he was later to say, was "because I couldn't play the pull shot, I was never suited to English pitches". His Test career ended at The Oval in "Hutton's Match". For Fingleton it was a disappointing end: in the course of England's marathon innings of 903 for seven declared he sustained a leg injury which was sufficiently serious to prevent him from batting in either Australian innings.

After the Second World War Fingleton retired from first-class cricket and divided his time between Canberra, where for 34 years until his retirement in 1978 he was political correspondent for Radio Australia, and the coverage of Test matches. In Canberra he was a close friend of several Prime Ministers. Typical of these relationships was that which he enjoyed with Sir Robert Menzies, who provided him with a handsome and laudatory foreword in his book, *Masters of Cricket*. Fingleton's coverage of Tests resulted in publication of a number of books which secured for the writer a place at the forefront of Australian cricket writers. The books included *Cricket Crisis* (which involved itself principally with the Body-line series of 1932-33), *Brightly Fades the Don* (England 1948), *Brown & Company: The Tour in Australia* (Australia 1950-51), *The Ashes Crown the Year* (England 1953), *Masters of Cricket, Four Chukkas to Australia* (Australia 1958-59), *The Greatest Test of All* (Brisbane 1960), *Fingleton on Cricket* and *The Immortal Victor Trumper*. His final book – *Batting From Memory* – was to have been launched in Australia during the week of his death. In addition to his writing, Fingleton was a witty, good-humoured and perceptive commentator for the BBC and at various times a contributor to *The Times*, *The Sunday Times*, *The Observer*, and various newspapers in Australia, South Africa and elsewhere. In 1976, he was appointed OBE for services "to journalism and to cricket".

TEST RECORD

	Tests	Inns	Not Outs	Runs	Highest Inns	Avge	100s	Ct
1931-32 v South Africa	1	1	0	40	40	40.00	0	2
1932-33 v England	3	6	0	150	83	25.00	0	3
1935-36 in South Africa	5	7	1	478	118	78.33	3	4
1936-37 v England	5	9	0	389	136	44.22	2	2
1938 in England	4	6	0	123	40	20.50	0	2
Total	18	29	1	1,189	136	42.46	5	13

In his first-class career, J. H. Fingleton batted in 166 innings, was not out 13 times, and scored 6,816 runs (average 44.54), including 22 hundreds. His highest score was 167 v Natal, Durban, in 1935-36. He held 82 catches, effected 2 stumpings, and took 2 wickets (average 27.00).

Other tributes

Bill Bowes: Like all good opening batsmen, Jack Fingleton did not have much back-lift. He kept the bat close to his left foot and was rarely surprised by the quicker long half volley or yorker. He had what could be described as a "good fault" in that he tended to overdo his positioning and get too far in front of the ball instead of keeping bat and left leg side by side. This meant he had to bring the bat round the left leg to play the ball. In recent years Colin Cowdrey did the same thing, sometimes to such an extent that he occasionally had his leg stump knocked down behind his legs. It is the reason why Geoffrey Boycott takes so many knocks on the knuckles when the ball lands on the seam and lifts more than expected. When the pitch is a good one, though, this overdoing of position can bring many benefits. There are runs to be had for pushes to the on-side. And, more effectively than Boycott, Fingleton would steer the ball with accuracy through the gaps on the off-side. On true surfaces, like those found in Australia and South Africa in the 1930s, he was a dangerous opponent, full of guts; against the leg-theory bowling of Larwood during the famous "Body-line tour" of 1932-33 he never retreated. He was a reliable fieldsman in any position, especially at short leg, and possessed a strong arm. He was also a good team man. That he thought deeply about the game was envinced by his distinguished writings on cricket and cricketers.

E. W. Swanton: The number of Test cricketers whose reputations as writers on the game have come near to matching their skill on the field is very small. In this select category Jack Fingleton comes straight away to mind; but he differed from all such in that he entered first-class cricket as a well-qualified journalist rather than making his name first as a player. To a fellow cricket-writer this distinction was regularly in evidence. It was not only that his training quickened his observation and eye for detail. His judgements were always informed by careful first-hand evidence. Equally his nose unerringly sniffed a story, big or small, serious or funny. His work was lightened by various aspects of humour; it could be sly, sardonic or side-splitting. These qualities were equally appreciated by listeners on sound radio and television.

If he was not exactly an easy professional companion he was certainly a stimulating one. Some of those who, unwittingly perhaps, stepped on his corns, remained wary of him ever after. But if he was a bad enemy he was a devoted friend to a wide and diverse circle. Among his contemporaries on the field and in the press box perhaps Bill O'Reilly, Lindsay Hassett and Ian Peebles stood at the peak of his esteem. An affectionate profile of O'Reilly for *The Cricketer* was one of his last articles. He served *The Sunday Times* most ably for many years as their Australian cricket correspondent. In his own country he wrote all too little about the game, concentrating on his duties as a lobby correspondent from his base at Canberra and serving newspapers in many countries.

The first of his ten books, *Cricket Crisis*, published thirteen years afterwards in 1946, is far the best story of the Body-line tour of 1932-33, in which he was a participant and victim. There were five tour books, all lively, entertaining, wherein cricket is often merely the continuing narrative thread. It was sad that he died of a heart attack immediately upon publication of his autobiographical *Batting from Memory* – though not before he had read a highly appreciative review of it in the Melbourne *Age*, the paper whose opinion he would have valued most. In this book, as in most of his others, one had to discount an incompatibility of temperament with Sir Donald Bradman (as a man, not as a cricketer) which was damaging both to Australian cricket and even, in some degree, to their own reputations. Sir Donald, characteristically, has borne it all in silence. This qualification notwithstanding, Jack Fingleton remains surely, as cricket writer and broadcaster, the best his country has produced.

FISHER, HORACE, a left arm slow bowler, who played infrequently for Yorkshire, 1928-1936, died at his home at Overton, near Wakefield on April 16, 1974, aged 70. A contemporary of Hedley Verity, Fisher seldom played unless Verity was on Test duty. In first-class cricket he took 93 wickets, average 28.18. He was also a useful batsman at a crisis and a splendid close-to-the-wicket fieldsman. A careful man, he bowled with a low trajectory, just short of a length and he counted his overs, his maidens and the runs that were hit off him.

Fisher was the first bowler to register a hat-trick of lbw victims when he took five wickets for 12 runs against Somerset at Sheffield in 1932. The story has often been told that when umpire Alec Skelding having given out Mitchell-Innes and Andrews lbw, stared up the wicket at Luckes when the third appeal was made, uttered almost in disbelief, "As God's my judge, that's out, too", and he lifted his finger. Earlier in that same week in August, Fisher had taken six wickets for 11 runs against Leicestershire at Bradford. In 1934, Fisher toured West Indies with the Yorkshire team. A League professional for 20 years, Fisher played for various clubs in the Bradford, Huddersfield, Lancashire and Central Lancashire Leagues.

FITZROY, NEWDEGATE, COMMANDER THE HON. JOHN MAURICE, who died in hospital on May 7, 1976, aged 79, captained Northamptonshire as Commander J. M. FitzRoy from 1925 to 1927. A tall man with enormous hands, he was a fine slip and a most energetic chaser of the ball in the field; he did much to improve his side's fielding and was a splendid captain to play under. His premature retirement owing to a knee injury was greatly regretted. As a bat he was a fierce hitter who might have made more runs had he not tried to clear the boundary quite so often. As it was, he sometimes made useful scores when more esteemed batsmen had failed. In the few matches he was able to play in his last season, he made 50, the highest score of the innings and of his career, against Kent, and against Worcestershire he and T. B. G. Welch scored 86 in fifty-two minutes in an unbroken partnership to win the match with eight minutes to spare.

FOSTER, NEVILLE JOHN ACLAND, who died at Malvern on January 8, 1978, aged 87, was the youngest and the last survivor of seven brothers who did so much for Worcestershire that the side got the nickname of "Fostershire". He did not get into the eleven at Malvern and, as he spent most of his life in Malaya, his county cricket was confined to three matches in 1914 and five in 1923. In 1914 he did little, but in 1923 showed clearly in a series of useful innings, the highest of them being 40 not out against Derbyshire, that he had his share of the family eye and wrists. Unfortunately he was kept out of several matches by a strain. Later he captained the Federated Malay States. In 1908 with his brother M.K. he won the Public Schools rackets for Malvern: he was the fifth of the brothers to play in a winning pair, a record which no other family has approached.

FOWLER, REV. RICHARD HAROLD, who died on October 27, 1970, played in a few matches for Worcestershire in 1921. After taking five Gloucestershire wickets for 33 runs at Stourbridge, he was told that only his cloth had saved him from being no-balled. This doubtless accounted for the brevity of his first-class career.

FREEMAN, ALFRED PERCY, who died on January 28, 1965, aged 76, was one of the finest slow bowlers the game has known. He played as a professional for Kent from 1914 to 1936 taking 3,776 wickets at an average cost of 18.42 runs each and between 1925 and 1929 appeared in twelve Test matches for England. Only one man, W. Rhodes with 4,187 wickets, has met with greater success. Freeman's wonderfully well controlled leg-breaks, with a skilfully disguised googly or top-spinner interspersed, his well-nigh perfect length and cunning flighting frequently puzzled the most experienced opponents and on no fewer than 17 occasions he dismissed 100 or more batsmen in a season.

His most triumphant summer was that of 1928, when his victims totalled 304 for 18.15 runs each, a feat without parallel in first-class cricket, and five years later he took 298. His wickets exceeded 200 in five other seasons: 276 in 1931, 275 in 1930, 253 in 1932, 212 in 1935 and 205 in 1934. Three times – a feat unequalled by any other bowler – this short but stockily-built man, known in the cricket world as "Tich", took all 10 wickets in an innings, against Lancashire for 131 runs at Maidstone in 1929, and that despite an innings of 126 by F. Watson; against Essex for 53 runs at Southend in 1930 and against Lancashire again, this time at Old Trafford, for 79 runs in 1931. Additionally, at Hove in 1922, he disposed of nine Sussex batsmen in the first innings for 11 runs, bringing about the dismissal of the side for 47, of which E. H. Bowley obtained 24. This was one of two matches in which Freeman was responsible for 17 wickets, his second-innings analysis being eight for 56; the other was against Warwickshire at Folkestone ten years later. Three times he achieved the hat-trick, for Kent against Middlesex at Canterbury in 1920 and against Kent at Blackheath in 1934 and for MCC against South Australia at Adelaide in 1922-23.

"Tich" seldom reached in Test cricket the phenomenal success he attained in the county sphere. He toured Australia and New Zealand with A. C. MacLaren's MCC team in 1922-23 and made his first appearance for England in Australia in 1924-25. Though he did reasonably well in other matches, he took only eight wickets in two Tests and conceded 519 runs. Nor did he achieve anything of note when visiting South Africa in 1927-28, his total wickets in four Tests amounting to 14 at an average cost of 28.50. In home Tests he fared better. Against the West Indies in 1928 he headed the averages with 22 wickets at 13.72 runs apiece, including 10 for 93 at Old Trafford. For Kent against the West Indies team at Canterbury he took nine wickets in the second innings for 104 runs. He also topped the England bowling figures against South Africa the following season, dismissing 12 men for 171 runs at Old Trafford and seven for 115 in the first innings at Leeds.

When Kent, who gave him two benefits, dispensed with his services at 1936, Freeman played for a time as professional for Walsall in the Birmingham and District League. In 1949 he became one of the 26 cricket personalities to be elected to honorary life membership of the MCC.

Two celebrated leg-break bowlers paid these tributes:

D. V. P. Wright (Kent and England): I always held him to be one of the finest leg-break bowlers I ever saw. The more I bowled, the more I realised how great "Tich" was.

R. W. V. Robins (Middlesex and England): Against other than the greatest of batsmen, he was the most effective bowler I ever saw. We will never see his like again as a consistent wicket-taker. Under Percy Chapman, Freeman sometimes opened the bowling, which is astonishing in itself and almost unheard of for a leg-break bowler these days.

GEARY, GEORGE, who died at the age of 87 on March 6, 1981, after a long period of ill-health, had been in his day one of the best bowlers in the world and was also one of the last survivors of those who were playing regular county cricket before the Great War. A tall, powerful man, he bowled fast-medium well within his strength, with a short run and a beautifully easy action. His stock ball moved naturally from the off and could be deadly if the wicket helped him, as when he ruined his second benefit, against Warwickshire at Hinckley in 1936, by taking thirteen wickets for 43 (the match produced him £10). This was varied by a delivery which came straight through and, a far more dangerous ball, the leg-cutter which pitched on middle-and-leg and left the bat sharply. This was the one which the experts dreaded and which secured the all-important wicket of Bradman, caught at slip for 29, in the Nottingham Test of 1934. Apart from this he could make full use of the shine to swing the new ball. Yet with all these gifts, he will probably be remembered chiefly as a stock bowler who would peg away cheerfully all day if need be, keeping the situation under control whether or not he was getting wickets. As a batsman he never claimed to be a stylist, but he was typically effective: the more runs were needed, the more resolutely he would set himself to get them, not least by punishing ruthlessly anything which fell short of his very high standards of what first-class bowling should be. In his last season, at the age of 45, when an injury prevented him from doing his full share of bowling, he scored three centuries. He was a fine slip, but in fact his vast hands were equally tenacious anywhere: in The Oval Test of 1926, besides two blinding slip catches off Larwood, he caught a brilliant one low at mid-off off Rhodes to dismiss Arthur Richardson.

Making a few appearances for Leicestershire in 1912, he gained a regular place in 1913, and in 1914, when he took over 100 wickets, he was picked for his first representative match, the Centenary at Lord's, the Rest of England against MCC's South African team. This should have given him his one chance of seeing the great Sydney Barnes bowl, but, when he arrived in the dressing-room, he found Barnes urging the others not to play unless they received more money. *Wisden* says Barnes was prevented from playing by a strain. At this point Geary's career suffered a serious setback. Serving in the Air Force in the Great War, he was lucky not to have his leg severed by a propeller: but the damage was such that, after an unsuccessful season in 1919, he decided that he was not for the moment strong enough for county cricket and went into the Lancashire League. It was not till 1922 that he resumed a regular place in the Leicestershire side.

In 1923 he appeared in a Test trial and in 1924-25 made his first tour abroad, for Lord Tennyson's unofficial side in South Africa, where he was an outstanding success as a bowler. In 1924 he had been picked for his first Test, against South Africa, and in 1926 he played against Australia at Leeds, where Carr put his opponents in with disastrous results. According to Geary his captain's great mistake was taking his batsmen, not his bowlers, out to inspect the wicket. At any rate, when Geary came in the score, in face of a total of 494, was 182 for eight. He and Macaulay added 108, Geary making 35 not out, and, though he could not save the follow-on, he may well have rescued England from defeat. He played again in the final Test at The Oval. That winter he went with MCC to India and in 1927-28 was a member of their side in South Africa, where he took twelve for 130 in the first Test and was reckoned by the South Africans to be, on a matting wicket, the finest bowler of his type since Barnes. Unfortunately, in the second Test his right arm, which had troubled him intermittently for some years, became so bad that he could not play again until the last match, and further he missed most of the 1928 season. Indeed his career was in jeopardy. He was saved by Lord Harris, who enquired into his case and insisted upon his having the best medical treatment. An operation was performed on his elbow and was so successful that he was not only able to accept an invitation to go to Australia in 1928-29, but, with nineteen wickets at an average of 25, headed the bowling averages in the Tests. At Sydney in the second Test he followed five for 35 with an innings of 66, and in the final Test at Melbourne he had in the first innings the astonishing analysis of 81–36–105–5. In 1929 he played in the last two Tests against South Africa; in 1930 he played against Australia at Leeds, and in 1934, also against Australia, at Nottingham and Lord's. At Nottingham, coming in at 165 for six, he scored 53, including ten 4s, and helped Hendren to put on 101 in 110 minutes. In 1932 he had gone with Lord Tennyson's team to the West Indies and, as he also once took a coaching appointment in South America, he was one of the most widely travelled cricketers of his time.

His last season for Leicestershire was 1938 and then he became the professional at Charterhouse. He showed himself a great coach and in particular was one of the few who could really teach bowling. Feeling that at 65 he would be rash to undertake another three-year contract, he left Charterhouse in 1959 with great reluctance on both sides, but Rugby were desperate for help and persuaded him to come and stand behind their nets. Before the end of the first net he could bear it no longer, had his coat off and continued to bowl for another eleven years.

Few professionals have been more popular and more respected, and deservedly. No-one ever saw him out of temper: he was always cheerful and smiling and had a wonderful sense of humour which made him a splendid raconteur. E. W. Dawson said that, when he took over the Leicestershire captaincy immediately after coming down from Cambridge and utterly inexperienced, he owed everything to Geary, who, though not yet the senior professional, looked after him like a father.

In all first-class matches he made 13,500 runs (including eight centuries) with an average of 19.80 and took 2,063 wickets at 20.03.

Peter May, who was coached by Geary at Charterhouse, writes: George really fired me with the enthusiasm and ambition to play first-class cricket and to get to the top. When he told me of his great experiences in Australia and India and the wonderful friends he had made, I knew that this was something which I really wanted to follow. "You will be judged by your scores. Never give your wicket away." I shall always have the happiest memories of this great man.

GEE, HARRY, who spent a life-time in Fleet Street, was taken ill suddenly at his home at Liphook and died on January 15, 1976, aged 69. Gee joined Pardon's Cricket Reporting Agency in 1929 and for many years helped in the compilation of *Wisden.* He became a partner in the CRA in 1948 and when the Press Association, with whom Pardon's had been linked since 1880, took over the CRA in 1963, Gee was appointed PA Sports Editor. He was well known in cricket and football circles and went, on behalf of Reuter, with the MCC team to Australia and New Zealand in 1958-59.

GILBERT, EDWARD, who was the best remembered aboriginal cricketer to play first-class cricket in Australia, had been long absent from the scene of his sometimes sensational fast bowling feats of the 1930s and in ill health for many years before his death in the Wolston Park Hospital near Brisbane on January 9, 1978, aged 69. Nevertheless, this notably quiet but well spoken product of Queensland's Cherbourg Aboriginal Settlement has remained a legend down through the years. After successfully graduating through the Queensland Colts XI in 1930, Eddie Gilbert quickly reached the headlines in the 1931 Sheffield Shield match against NSW in Brisbane by his first over dismissals of Wendell Bill and Bradman without scoring. Both were caught by wicketkeeper Len Waterman within seven deliveries, but not before one ball rising from a greeen top had flicked off Sir Donald's cap and another knocked the bat from his hands! Sir Donald has since recalled that the six deliveries he faced on this occasion were the fastest experienced during his career.

Lightly built and only a little over five feet seven inches in height, Gilbert possessed exceptionally long arms and could bowl at great pace off a run sometimes no longer than four paces. It was this, allied with a somewhat whippy forearm action, which led to suggestions that his right arm bent on occasions during a pronounced arc action which finished with his hand almost touching the ground and his head at knee level. Strong advocacy for Gilbert's Test selection was nullified by the suspect action, a view several times shared and acted on by senior umpires. Nevertheless, the same officials completely accepted his delivery on most other occasions. Several films were taken without conclusive decision and controversy continued throughout Gilbert's career which was undoubtedly affected by the publicity. He faded out of the game in 1936 after showing fine form while taking six wickets in his final match – against Victoria at the Brisbane Cricket Ground in 1936. In nineteen Shield matches, he took 73 wickets at an average of 29.75, while a further fourteen wickets were gained in Queensland matches against touring MCC, West Indies and South African sides.

GILLIGAN, ALBERT HERBERT HAROLD, AFC, who died on May 5, 1978, aged 81, was the youngest and the last survivor of three distinguished cricketing brothers. Frank, the eldest, captained Oxford and played for Essex, Arthur was a notable captain of Sussex and England. Harold was in the Dulwich XI for three years and captain in the last, 1915. In 1914 he made the highest score then recorded for the school, 190 v Bedford Grammar School. Coming into the Sussex side in 1919, he played for them continuously until 1931 and, after captaining them in his brother's absence, was the official captain in 1930. In 1924-25 he was a member of S. B. Joel's unofficial side to South Africa, captained by the Hon. L. H. Tennyson, and in 1929-30, when his brother Arthur, after accepting an invitation to captain the MCC team to Australia and New Zealand, had to withdraw owing to ill-health, he was appointed to take his place.

One can pay him no higher compliment than to say that as a leader he was no less popular than his brother both with his own side and with the opposition; moreover he showed himself a shrewd captain on the field. This, though stronger than any previous English side in New Zealand, was still far short of an England side: it contained only three players who took part in the Tests in England in 1930. The captain himself had a good tour, batting particularly well in the preliminary matches in Australia. But it must be admitted that, taking his career as a whole, he was a disappointing batsman. A beautiful stylist, he would constantly through impetuosity get out to a terrible stroke just when he seemed set for a big score and, though as time went on, with much help from Albert Relf, to whose coaching he admitted a great debt, he became sounder and more consistent, he never wholly cured himself of this fault.

His figures tell their own tale. His average for his career with Sussex was only 17, he made only one century, 143 v Derbyshire at Hove in 1929, and only in three seasons, 1923, 1927 and 1929, did he score 1,000 runs. His figures for 1923 must constitute some kind of record: in 70 innings he scored 1,186 runs with an average of 17.70 and a highest score of 68. At this period he was regularly opening the batting with Bowley. Apart from his batting he was one of the great cover-points of his day and in his early years did useful work as a slow leg-spinner. After the Second War he became active behind the scenes in Surrey cricket. He served on the Committee, was for a time Honorary Treasurer and later was a Vice-President. His daughter, Virginia, married Peter May.

GIMBLETT, HAROLD, who died at his home at Verwood, Dorset, on March 30, 1978, aged 63, was the most exciting English batsman of his day. Years ago, C. B. Fry wrote of MacLaren, "Like all the great batsmen, he always attacked the bowling!" If that view was once shared by the selectors, they had abandoned it by Gimblett's time. They preferred soundness and consistency. Watching our batting in Australia in 1946-47, Macartney expressed amazement that both Gimblett and Barnett had been left at home. Gimblett played in three Tests only, two against India in 1936, the first of which at Lord's he finished with a dazzling 67 not out, culminating in five consecutive boundaries, and one against the West Indies in 1939. Those of us who saw the inexpressibly feeble English batting against Ramadhin and Valentine at Lord's in 1950 shown up for what it was by the bold tail-end hitting of Wardle, longed for an hour of Gimblett, and indeed he was picked for the next Test, but was unfortunately ill and unable to play.

The start of his career was so sensational that any novelist attributing it to his hero would have discredited the book. Given a month's trial on the Somerset staff in 1935 after a number of brilliant performaces in local matches, he was told before the period had expired that there was no future for him in county cricket and was sent home. Next day there was a last minute vacancy against Essex at Frome and he was recalled to fill it, mainly as a young man who could chase the ball in the field and perhaps bowl a few overs of mild medium pace. In fact, coming in to face Nichols, the England fast bowler, then at his best, with six wickets down for 107, he reached his 50 in twenty-eight minutes and his 100 in sixty-three, finally making 123 out of 175 in eighty minutes with three 6s and seventeen 4s. The innings won him the Lawrence Trophy for the fastest 100 of the season. In the next match, against Middlesex at Lord's, though lame and batting with a runner, he made 53 against Jim Smith, Robins, Peebles and Sims, three of them England bowlers. It was hardly to be expected that he could keep this up and his record at the end of the season was modest, but his second summer dispelled any notion that his early successes had been a fluke, as he scored 1,608 runs with an average of 32.81. People sometimes talk as if after this he was a disappointment. In fact his one set-back, apart from being overlooked by the selectors, was when in 1938, probably listening to the advice of grave critics, he attempted more cautious methods and his average dropped to 27. But can one call disappointing a man who between 1936 and his retirement in 1953 never failed to get his 1,000 runs, who in his career scored over 23,000, more than any other Somerset player, and fifty centuries, the highest 310 against Sussex at Eastbourne in 1948, and whose average for his career was over 36? Moreover after his first season he habitually went in first and yet he hit 265 sixes, surely a record.

Naturally, as time went on, his judgement improved with experience, he grew sounder and in particular became the master of the hook instead of its slave, though he never abandoned it, as did Hammond and Peter May. To the end, he might have said, as Frank Woolley used to, "When I am batting, I am the attack." Apart from his hook he was a fine cutter and driver, his off-drives often being played late and going past cover's left-hand, and like nearly all great attacking bats he freely employed the pull-drive, with which he was particularly severe on Mahomed Nissar at Lord's in 1936. Early in his career, on the fallacious grounds that a great games-player must be a great slip, he was put in the slips where he was only a qualified success. Elsewhere, a fine thrower and a good catch, he was far more successful and many will remember the catch at cover with which he dismissed K. H. Weekes in the Lord's Test in 1939.

For twenty years after his retirement he was coach at Millfield.

GRACE, DR EDGAR MERVYN, of Hilltop, Alverston, Bristol, who died on November 24, 1974, aged 88, was the son of Dr Edward Mills Grace, known in his cricketing days as "The Coroner". He was a nephew of W. G. Grace and G. F. Grace. Dr Edgar made his first appearance for the Thornbury club at the age of nine when he came in as a substitute against Cinderford and took six wickets for 24 with innocent-looking lobs. He went on to become captain of Thornbury for 37 years and altogether served the club for 79 years. In 1920, his best season, he scored well over 1,000 runs and took 146 wickets for only seven runs each. Dr Edgar's son, Gerald (G. F.) and grandson (E. M.) now carry on the family association with Thornbury.

GREEN, COLONEL LEONARD, who died on March 2, 1963, aged 73, captained Lancashire when they won the County Championship in the three years from 1926 to 1928. Though not himself a brilliant cricketer, he possessed the strength of will and good-natured tact to weld a team of individual talent into a title-winning combination. A useful batsman, besides a reliable fieldsman, he scored 3,575 runs for his county between 1922 and 1935, average 24.65. His highest innings, 110 not out against Gloucestershire at Gloucester in 1923, played a big part in a win for Lancashire by 75 runs after being 26 in arrears on first innings.

He took part in the game with Essex at Colchester in 1928 when Lancashire, needing four runs to win at the close of the second day, had to wait till the third morning to assay the task. That match led to the extra half hour being allowed on the second day if a result could thereby be achieved. It was in this fixture that the late J. W. H. T. Douglas, captaining Essex, flung up his bat, lost his grip on it and fell headlong when a short-pitched delivery from E. A. McDonald rose head-high. Anxious fieldsmen, fearing that he had been hurt, clustered around the batsman, but beat a hasty retreat as Douglas expressed his views in loud and virulent terms. When at length he arose and resumed his stance at the crease, he was informed that he was out, for the ball had struck the handle of the bat and glanced into the hands of H. Makepeace at short-leg!

After leaving Bromsgrove School, Green joined the East Lancashire Regiment, earning the Military Cross during the First World War. For many years a member of the Lancashire Committee, he became President in 1951 and 1952. He also represented the county at hockey and Rugby football.

JACK GREGORY

Born in Sydney, August 14, 1895

Died at Bega, NSW, August 7, 1973

By Sir Neville Cardus

Jack Morrison Gregory, of a famous Australian cricket family, had a comparatively brief Test Match career, for although he played in twenty-four representative games, his skill and his power were as unpredictable as a thunderstorm or a nuclear explosion. He was known mainly as a fearsome right-arm fast bowler but, also, in Test matches he scored 1,146 runs, averaging 36.96 with two centuries. He batted left-handed and gloveless.

As a fast bowler, people of today who never saw him will get a fair idea of his presence and method if they have seen Wes Hall, the West Indian. Gregory, a giant of superb physique, ran some twenty yards to release the ball with a high step at gallop, then, at the moment of delivery, a huge leap, a great wave of energy breaking at the crest, and a follow-through nearly to the batsman's door-step.

He lacked the silent rhythmic motion over the earth of E. A. (Ted) McDonald, his colleague in destruction. Gregory bowled as though against a gale of wind. It was as though he *willed* himself to bowl fast, at the risk of muscular dislocation. Alas, he did suffer physical dislocation, at Brisbane, in November 1928, putting an end to his active cricket when his age was thirty-three.

My earliest vivid impression of his fast bowling was at the beginning of the first game of the England v Australia rubber, at Trent Bridge, in 1921. The England XI had just returned from Australia after losing five Tests out of five (all played to a finish). Now, in 1921, England lost the first three encounters, taking long to recover from Gregory's onslaught at Trent Bridge.

He knocked out Ernest Tyldesley in the second innings with a bouncer which sped from cranium to stumps. Ernest's more famous brother J.T. had no sympathy; he bluntly told his brother, "Get to the off side of the ball whenever you hook, then, if you miss it, it passes harmlessly over the left shoulder." At Trent Bridge, that May morning in 1921, "Patsy" Hendren arrived with runs in plenty to his credit, largesse of runs in county matches. Gregory wrecked his wicket with an atom bomb of a breakback. Yes; it *was* a ball which came back at horrific velocity, not achieved, of course, by finger-spin, but by action.

Gregory, like Tom Richardson, perhaps the greatest of all fast bowlers ever, flung the upper part of his body over the front left leg to the offside as the arm came over, the fingers sweeping under the ball. Herbert Strudwick once told me that in the first over or two he took from Richardson he moved to the offside to "take" the ball. It broke back, shaving the leg stump, and went for four byes. Gregory, at Trent Bridge, took six wickets for 58, in England's first innings of 112; next innings McDonald took five for 52. Only once, at Lord's in 1921, did Gregory recapture the Trent Bridge explosive rapture.

In the South African summer of 1921-22 he renewed his batteries and regained combustion. Next, in Australia 1924-25, he was able to take 22 wickets in the Tests against England at 37.09 runs each. But the giant was already casting a shadow; in 1926, in England, his three Test wickets cost him 298 runs. He was not a subtle fast bowler, with the beautiful changes of pace, nuance and rhythmical deceptions of Lindwall or

McDonald (at his best). But as an announcement of young dynamic physical power and gusto for life and fast bowling, there has seldom been seen on any cricket field a cricketer as exciting as Jack Gregory.

In 1921 certain English critics made too much ungenerous palaver about Gregory's "bouncers". These "bouncers", no doubt, were awesome but not let loose with the regularity of, say, a Hall, a Griffith, not to mention other names, some playing today. In fact, no less an acute judge of the game as A. C. MacLaren declared, in 1921, that Gregory's bowling during the first deadly half hour at Trent Bridge was compact of half-volleys.

His baptism in English cricket was in 1919, with the Australian Imperial Forces team. He was already a menacing shattering fast bowler, but at Kennington Oval he was subjected to treatment such as he never afterwards had to suffer. Surrey faced a total of 436 and got into hopeless trouble. They wanted 287 to save the follow-on and five wickets went down for 26. Soon J. N. Crawford came in at number eight – a catastrophic moment – and he smote Goliath. He smote Gregory as any fast bowler has not often been smitten, except by Bradman and Dexter. Crawford actually drove a ball from Gregory, cracking and splintering his bat. When Rushby, the last man, went in Surrey still required 45 to save the follow-on. Crawford went on hitting magnificently and they added 80 in thirty-five minutes, Rushby's share being a modest two. In some two hours Crawford scored 144 not out having hit two sixes and eighteen fours. And Gregory applauded him generously.

He was a generous and likeable Australian. He gave himself to cricket with enthusiasm and relish. He enjoyed himself and was the cause of enjoyment in others. At Johannesburg in 1921 Gregory scored a century in seventy minutes v South Africa – the fastest hundred in the long history of Test cricket. He was a slip fielder of quite unfair reach and alacrity, a Wally Hammond in enlargement, so to say, though not as graceful, effortless, and terpsichorean. Gregory was young manhood in excelsis. All who ever saw him and met him will remember and cherish him.

CLARRIE GRIMMETT

Born in Dunedin, December 25, 1891,

Died in Adelaide, May 2, 1980

By W. J. O'Reilly

Born in Dunedin in the South Island of New Zealand on Christmas Day, Clarence Victor Grimmett must have been the best Christmas present Australia ever received from that country. Going to Australia in 1914, on a "short working holiday" which lasted for 66 years, he joined the Sydney club, which had its headquarters at Rushcutters Bay. Three years in Sydney District cricket were sufficient to warn him that Arthur Mailey, another great spinner, had literally been given the green light towards the New South Wales team and all fields beyond. This, and marriage to a Victorian girl, took Grimmett to Melbourne, where he played with the South Melbourne club. During his six years in Melbourne he was given only three invitations to play for Victoria, the third of which was against South Australia when, providentially, he collected eight wickets.

It was after his visit to Sydney with the Victorians, for the first Shield match after the Great War, that I managed to see him for the first time. In Sydney, in the match against New South Wales, Ted McDonald had performed outstandingly for Victoria and was consequently the cynosure of all eyes when the Victorian team, on its way home to Melbourne, played an up-country match in the mountain city of Goulburn. Not quite all eyes, however. The attention of one pair, belonging to a thirteen-year-old boy named O'Reilly, was rivetted on a wiry little leg-spinner whose name on the local score-board was "Grummett". To me, from that day onward, "Grummett" he remained, and my own endearing name for him throughout our later long association was "Grum".

We played together for the first time in an Australian team at Adelaide against Herbie Cameron's South Africans in 1931, and for the last time in the Durban Test of 1936 when Vic Richardson's Australian side became the first ever to go through a tour undefeated – a feat paralleled by Bradman's 1948 team in England. On that 1935-36 South African tour, "Grum" set an Australian record for a Test series with 44 wickets, yet he came home to be dropped forever from the Australian side. He was shoved aside like a worn-out boot for each of the five Tests against Gubby Allen's English team in Australia in 1936-37 and he failed to gain a place in the 1938 team to England, led by Bradman.

It was illogical to assume that age was the reason for his discard. He was 47, it is true, when the touring side was chosen, yet two years later, at the age of 49, he established an Australian record of 73 wickets for a domestic first-class season. Which raises, rather pointedly, the question of "why the hell was he dropped?" By now Don Bradman was Grimmett's captain for South Australia, and also Australia's captain. As such he was an Australian selector, and Bradman, it seemed, had become inordinately impressed with the spin ability of Frank Ward, a former clubmate of his in Sydney. It was Ward who was chosen for the first three Tests against Allen's side in 1936-37 and who caught the boat for England in 1938. Bradman, it seemed, had lost faith in the best spin bowler the world has seen. "Grum's" departure was a punishing blow to me and to my plans of attack. His diagnostic type of probing spin buttressed my own methods to such a degree that my reaction to his dismissal was one of infinite loss and loneliness.

Unlike Arthur Mailey, the first of the Australian spin trilogy of the inter-wars era, Grimmett never insisted on spin as his chief means of destruction. To him it was no more than an important adjunct to unerring length and tantalising direction. Grimmett seldom beat a batsman by spin alone. Mailey often did. I cannot remember Grimmett bowling a long-hop, whereas Mailey averaged one an over. So much, in fact, did inaccuracy become a feature of Mailey's success that he himself came to believe that it was an essential ingredient. Such wantonness was anathema to Grimmett, who believed that a bowler should bowl as well as he possibly could every time he turned his arm over. And Grimmett was perhaps the best and most consistently active cricket thinker I ever met.

He loved to tell his listeners that it was he who taught Stan McCabe how to use his left hand correctly on the bat handle – and I never heard Stan deny it. The "flipper" was originated by "Grum" during that Babylonian Captivity of his, and he used it to good effect in his record-breaking last season before the Second World War. He passed it on to men like Bruce Dooland and Cecil Pepper. He seldom bowled the "wrong 'un", because he preferred not to toss the ball high. On hard, true pitches he would bowl faster than his usual pace, taunting good batsmen to get to him on the half-volley. He was a genius on direction, and his talent for preying on a batsman's weakness was unequalled. He never let a batsman off the hook; once you were under his spell you were there to stay.

Grimmett joined South Australia from Victoria in 1923, just in time to bowl his way into the final Test in Sydney against Arthur Gilligan's 1924-25 England team. In his baptismal effort he took eleven wickets. In 79 Sheffield Shield games he tallied 513 wickets, an Australian record that will probably last for ever. The most successful Shield spinner in modern times, Richie Benaud, totalled 266 wickets in 73 matches, a relatively insignificant performance. Of Grimmett's 106 Test wickets against England, nearly 70 were collected on English pitches in a land where savants say leg-spinners are ineffective. One wonders what colossal figures he would have amassed had he played all his first-class cricket in England. Had he done so, you can be sure there would not be half the present insistence on pacier finger-cutting.

It was lucky for me that I preferred to bowl downwind, an unusual trait in a spinner's character. It allowed our partnership to develop and prosper. No captain ever had to worry which bowling end was whose. We competed strongly with each other and kept a critical eye on one another's performances. In Johannesburg in 1936, all-rounder "Chud" Langton hit me clean over the top of the square-leg grandstand of the old Wanderers ground. Cackling gleefully, "Grum" left no doubt in my mind that it was the biggest hit he had ever seen. Silently I was inclined to agree. In Clarrie's next over, "Chud" clouted him straight over the sightscreen and so far into the railway marshalling yards that the ball was never returned. From that delivery, until hostilities ceased for the afternoon, I never managed to get within earshot of my bowling mate.

Social life meant little to "Grum". Not until late in his career did he discover that it was not a bad idea to relax between matches. In England in 1934 I bought him a beer in the Star Hotel in Worcester to celebrate his first ten wickets of the tour. It took him so long to sink it that I decided to wait for his return gesture till some other time on the tour. Later he told me, with obvious regret, that on previous tours he had been keeping the wrong company and had never really enjoyed a touring trip. That I thought was sad, but not half as sad as I felt when, at the very zenith of his glorious career, he was tipped out of business altogether. With "Grum" at the other end, prepared to pick me up and dust me down, I feared no batsman. Our association must have been one of cricket's greatest success stories of the twentieth century.

HAIG, NIGEL ESME, who died in a Sussex hospital on October 27, 1966, aged 78, was a celebrated amateur all-rounder between the two World Wars. He did not gain a place in the XI while at Eton, but from 1912 until he retired from the game in 1934 he rendered splendid service to Middlesex, whom he captained for the last six years of his career. He was a member of the Championship-winning sides of 1920 and 1921. In addition, he played for England against Australia in the second of the disastrous Test series of 1921 and four times against the West Indies for the Hon. F. S. G. Calthorpe's MCC team of 1929-30 without achieving much success. In all first-class cricket, Haig hit 15,208 runs, average 20.83, and with swing-bowling above medium pace he obtained 1,116 wickets for 24.47 runs each.

Six times he exceeded 1,000 runs, five times he took 100 or more wickets in a season and in 1921, 1927 and 1929 he did the "cricketers' double". An agile fieldsman, he held 218 catches. His batting style was scarcely classic, but a quick eye stood him in good stead and, despite his not very powerful physique, he could hit the ball hard. The highest of his twelve centuries was 131 against Sussex at Lord's in 1920, when he, P. F. Warner, H. W. Lee and J. W. Hearne, the first four Middlesex batsmen, each reached three figures – an unprecedented occurrence in first-class cricket which was repeated for the same county by H. L. Dales, H. W. Lee, J. W. Hearne and E. Hendren against Hampshire at Southampton three years later.

Seemingly built of whipcord, Haig, a nephew of Lord Harris, bowled for long spells without apparent signs of fatigue. Among his best performances with the ball was the taking of seven wickets for 33 runs in the Kent first innings at Canterbury in 1920. This was another eventful match for Haig, for he scored 57 in the Middlesex first innings and became the "second leg" of a "hat-trick" by A. P. Freeman in the second. In 1924 Haig took six wickets for 11 runs in Gloucestershire's first innings on Packer's ground at Bristol, a game rendered specially memorable by the fact that C. W. L. Parker, the slow left-hander, twice accomplished the "hat-trick" at the expense of Middlesex. Haig was also a fine real tennis player, could hold his own with lawn tennis players of near-Wimbledon standard and was equally good at racquets, squash and golf. While serving with the Royal Field Artillery during the First World War, he won the MC.

WALTER REGINALD HAMMOND

Born at Dover, June 19, 1903

Died at his home at Durban, South Africa, July 2, 1965

By Neville Cardus

When the news came in early July of the death of W. R. Hammond, cricketers everywhere mourned a loss and adornment to the game. He had just passed his 62nd birthday and had not played in the public eye for nearly a couple of decades, yet with his end a light and a glow on cricket seemed to go out. Boys who had never seen him said, "Poor Wally"; they had heard of his prowess and personality and, for once in a while, youth of the present was not sceptical of the doings of a past master.

"Wally" indeed was cricket in excelsis. You had merely to see him walk from the pavilion on the way to the wicket to bat, a blue handkerchief peeping out of his right hip pocket. Square of shoulder, arms of obvious strength, a beautifully balanced physique, though often he looked so weighty that his sudden agility in the slips always stirred onlookers and the batsmen to surprise. At Lord's in 1938, England won the toss v Australia. In next to no time the fierce fast bowling of McCormick overwhelmed Hutton, Barnett and Edrich for 31. Then we saw the most memorable of all Wally's walks from the pavilion to the crease, a calm unhurried progress, with his jaw so firmly set that somebody in the Long Room whispered, "My God, he's going to score a century." Hammond at once took royal charge of McCormick, bouncers and all. He hammered the fast attack at will. One cover drive, off the backfoot, hit the palings under the Grandstand so powerfully that the ball rebounded half-way back. His punches, levered by the right forearm, were strong, leonine and irresistible, yet there was no palpable effort, no undignified outbursts of violence. It was a majestic innings, all the red-carpeted way to 240 in six hours, punctuated by thirty-two 4s.

I saw much of Hammond in England and in Australia, playing for Goucestershire on quiet west country afternoons at Bristol, or in front of a roaring multitude at Sydney. He was always the same; composed, self-contained, sometimes as though withdrawn to some communion within himself. He could be changeable of mood as a man; as a cricketer he was seldom disturbed from his balance of skill and poise. His cricket was, I think, his only way of self-realization. On the field of play he became a free agent, trusting fully to his rare talents.

His career as a batsman can be divided into two contrasted periods. To begin with, when he was in his twenties, he was an audacious strokeplayer, as daring and unorthodox as Trumper or Compton. Round about 1924 I recommended Hammond to an England selector as a likely investment. "Too much of a 'dasher'", was the reply. In May 1927, in his 24th year, Hammond descended with the Gloucestershire XI on Old Trafford. At close of play on the second day Lancashire were so cocksure of a victory early tomorrow (Whit Friday) that the Lancashire bowlers McDonald, Richard Tyldesley and company, arranged for taxis to be in readiness to take them to the Manchester races.

McDonald opened his attack at half-past eleven in glorious sunshine. He bowled his fastest, eager to be quick on the spot at Castle Irwell to get a good price on a "certainty". Hammond, not out overnight, actually drove the first five balls, sent at him from McDonald's superbly rhythmical arm, to the boundary. The sixth, also, would have counted – but it was stopped by a fieldsman sent out to defend the edge of the field, in front of the sight-screen – a straight deep for the greatest fast bowler of the period, bowling his first over of the day and in a desperate hurry to get to the course before the odds shortened. . . .

That day, Hammond scored 187 in three hours – four 6s twenty-four 4s. He hooked McDonald mercilessly, yes, "Wally" hooked during the first careless raptures of his youth.

As the years went by, he became the successor to Hobbs as the Monument and Foundation of an England innings. Under the leadership of D. R. Jardine he put romance behind him "for the cause", to bring into force the Jardinian theory of the Survival of the Most Durable. At Sydney, he wore down the Australians with 251 in seven and a half hours (on the 1928-29 tour); then, at Melbourne, he disciplined himself to the extent of six and three-quarter hours for 200, with only seventeen 4s; *and* then, at Adelaide, his contributions with the bat were 119 (four and a half hours) and 177 (seven hours, twenty minutes). True, the exuberant Percy Chapman was "Wally's" captain in this rubber, but Jardine was the Grey Eminence with his plotting already spinning fatefully for Australia's not distant future. In five Tests of this 1928-29 rubber, Hammond scored 905 runs, average 113.12.

Walter Reginald Hammond was born in Kent at Dover on June 19, 1903, the son of a soldier who became Major William Walter Hammond, Royal Artillery, and was killed in action in the First World War. As an infant, Walter accompanied the regiment with his parents to China and Malta. To the bad luck of Kent cricket when he was brought back to England he went to Portsmouth Grammar School in 1916 and two years later moved with his family to Cirencester Grammar School, rooting himself for such a flowering as Gloucestershire cricket had not known since the advent of W. G. Grace.

In all first-class games, Hammond scored 50,493 runs, average 56.10, with 167 centuries. Also he took 732 wickets average 30.58. In Test matches his batting produced 7,249 runs, average 58.45.

As a slip fieldsman his easy, lithe omnipresence has not often been equalled. He held 78 catches in a single season, 10 in one and the same match. He would stand at first slip erect as the bowler began to run, his legs slightly turned in at the knees. He gave the impression of relaxed carelessness. At the first sight, or hint of, a snick off the edge, his energy swiftly concentrated in him, apparently electrifying every nerve and muscle in him. He became light, boneless, airborne, He would take a catch as the ball was travelling away from him, leaping to it as gracefully as a trapeze artist to the flying trapeze.

Illness contracted in the West Indies not only kept him out of cricket in 1926; his young life was almost despaired of. His return to health a year later was a glorious renewal. He scored a thousand runs in May 1927, the season of his marvellous innings against Macdonald at Whitsuntide at Old Trafford. I am gratified that after watching this innings I wrote of him in this language: – "The possibilities of this boy Hammond are beyond the scope of estimation; I tremble to think of the grandeur he will spread over our cricket fields when he has arrived at maturity. He is, in his own way, another Trumper in the making."

Some three years before he thrilled us by this Old Trafford innings he astounded Middlesex, and everybody else on the scene, by batsmanship of genius on a terrible wicket at Bristol. Gloucestershire, in first, were bundled out for 31. Middlesex then could edge and snick only 74. In Gloucestershire's second innings Hammond drove, cut and hooked no fewer than 174 not out in four hours winning the match. By footwork he compelled the bowlers to pitch short, whereupon he massacred them. He was now hardly past his twentieth year.

Like Hobbs, he modulated, as he grew older and had to take on heavier responsibilities as a batsman, into a classic firmness and restraint. He became a classical player, in fact, expressing in a long innings the philosophy of "ripeness is all". It is often forgotten that, on a bad wicket, he was also masterful. At Melbourne, in January 1937, against Australia, on the worst wicket I have ever seen, he scored 32 without once losing his poise though the ball rose head-high, or short like a stone thrown over ice.

He could, if he had given his mind constantly to the job, have developed into a bowler as clever as Alec Bedser himself with a new ball. Here, again, he was in action the embodiment of easy flowing motion – a short run, upright and loose, a sideway action, left-shoulder pointing down the wicket, the length accurate, the ball sometimes swinging away late. I never saw him besmirching his immaculate flannels by rubbing the ball on his person, rendering it bloody and hideous to see.

He was at all times a cricketer of taste and breeding. But he wouldn't suffer boredom gladly. One day at Bristol, when Lancashire were scoring slowly, on deliberate principle, he bowled an over of ironic "grubs", all along the ground, underhand.

As a batsman, he experienced only two major frustrations. O'Reilly put him in durance by pitching the ball on his leg-stump. "Wally" didn't like it. His batting, in these circumstances, became sullen, a slow but combustible slow fire, ready to blaze and devour – as it did at Sydney, in the second Test match of the 1936-37 rubber. For a long time Hammond couldn't assert mastery over O'Reilly. For once in his lifetime he was obliged to labour enslaved. In the end he broke free from sweaty durance, amassing 231 not out, an innings majestic, even when it was stationary. We could always hear the superb engine throbbing.

The other frustration forced upon "Wally" occurred during this same 1936-37 rubber.

At Adelaide, when victory at the day's outset – and the rubber – was in England's reach at the closing day's beginning, Fleetwood-Smith clean bowled him. Another of Wally's frustrations – perhaps the bitterest to bear – befell him as England's captain. At a time of some strain in his life, he had to lead in Australia, in 1946-47, a team not at all ready for Test matches, after the long empty years of world war. Severe lumbago added to Hammond's unhappy decline.

Those cricketers and lovers of the game who saw him towards the end of his career saw only half of him. None the less they saw enough to remain and be cherished in memory. The wings might seem clipped, but they were wings royally in repose. "Wally" had a quite pretty chassé as he went forward to drive; and, at the moment his bat made impact with the ball his head was over it, the Master surveying his own work, with time to spare. First he played the game as a professional, then turned amateur. At no time did he ever suggest that he was, as Harris of Nottinghamshire called his paid colleagues, "a fellow worker".

"Wally" could have batted with any Prince of the Golden Age at the other end of the pitch – McLaren, Trumper, Hobbs, Spooner, "Ranji" – and there would have been no paling of his presence, by comparison.

Tributes to Hammond included:

A. V. Bedser (Surrey and England): I rate him the greatest all-rounder I have ever known.

C. J. Barnett (Gloucestershire and England): I played with Wally for 20 years and consider him the greatest athlete I ever knew.

W. E. Bowes (Yorkshire and England): Wally was a naturally-gifted player of most games. Tennis, golf, swimming, boxing, Soccer and billiards all came alike to him.

Sir Donald Bradman (Australia): I have never seen a batsman so strong on the off-side and as a slip fieldsman he ranked as one of the greatest. He was usually too busy scoring runs to worry about bowling, but when he did take a hand at it he caused plenty of concern. He was a much better bowler than he was given credit for.

Sir Learie Constantine (West Indies): Those of us who were fortunate enough to have watched him and played against him will always remember him.

G. Duckworth (Lancashire and England): He hardly played in a game without leaving his imprint as a batsman, fielder or bowler.

T. W. Goddard (Gloucestershire and England): He was the greatest batsman of them all, ahead of Bradman and the rest. A brilliant bowler, he was incomparable as a fielder.

H. Larwood (Nottinghamshire and England): He was a magnificent cricketer. We used to expect a "ton" from him every innings and more often than not he seemed to get it.

S. J. McCabe (Australia): Everything he did he did with the touch of a master. One could refer to him as the perfect cricketer.

A. Melville (South Africa): He was the greatest all-rounder I ever played against. He was a magnificent fielder and as a bowler I think he underestimated his capabilities.

W. A. Oldfield (Australia): Wally was majestic on the field – the perfect batting artist.

W. J. O'Reilly (Australia): He was certainly the greatest English batsman of my time, tough, hard, but always a brilliant player.

HASTINGS-BASS, CAPT. PETER ROBIN HOOD, who died on June 4, 1964, aged 43, was an outstanding cricketer, Rugby player and athlete at Stowe School, where he was wicket-keeper in 1938 and 1939, being captain the second year. He was a brilliant stand-off half in the Stowe XV who won all their school matches in 1939. His career at Oxford, for whom he ran in the quarter mile, was interrupted by the Second World War, in which he served with distinction in the Welsh Guards. He played for England in seven of the war-time Services Rugby Internationals. Widely-known as a race-horse trainer, he acted in that capacity for the Queen in 1962. In accordance with the provisions of a will, he changed his name by deed-poll from Hastings to Hastings-Bass in 1954.

HEARNE, JOHN WILLIAM, who died on September 13, 1965, aged 74, rendered admirable service as a professional for Middlesex from 1909 to 1936 and took part in 24

Test matches for England between 1912 and 1926. Joining the Lord's staff as a ground-boy in 1906, he became one of England's greatest all-rounders. In his early days he drove hard and though ill-health impaired his ability in that direction, his impeccable style and artistry in placing the ball, combined with sound defence, in which he employed a remarkably straight bat, brought him many runs. At his best on difficult pitches, he altogether scored 37,252 runs in first-class cricket, average 40.98, including 96 centuries; with skilfully-controlled leg-break and googly bowling from what surely must have been the shortest of runs-up, he took 1,839 wickets for 24.42 runs each and he held 329 catches.

"Young Jack", as he was known, was a cousin of J. T. Hearne, also of Middlesex and England fame. He received his first trial for the county in 1909, when he created a highly favourable impression with an innings of 71 against Somerset at Taunton. The following summer he hit two centuries and occasionally bowled with marked success, as against Essex at Lord's where he distinguished himself by disposing of seven men in just over five overs for two runs. Thenceforward, Hearne was an established cricketer in the world of cricket and undoubtedly one of the most immaculately attired. Five times he achieved the "cricketer's double" of 1,000 runs and 100 wickets – in 1911, 1913, 1914, 1920 and 1923 – the most successful being that of 1920 when he hit 2,148 runs and dismissed 148 batsmen: in 19 seasons his aggregate runs exceeded 1,000 and four times he passed 2,000. His highest innings was 234 not out against Somerset at Lord's and on ten other occasions he put together scores of more than 200, two of them in 1912. From the Glamorgan bowling at Lord's in 1931, he reached three figures twice in the match. Often in company with his great friend and ally on the field, "Patsy" Hendren, who in their day formed the highly valuable combination for Middlesex that D. C. S. Compton and W. J. Edrich were in later years to become, Hearne shared in many a big stand. The largest between him and Hendren was 375 for the third wicket against Hampshire at Southampton in 1923 and 325 against the same opposition at Lord's in 1919. For the second wicket, Hearne and F. A. Tarrant added 380 against Lancashire at Lord's.

Hearne began his long Test career in 1911-12, P. F. Warner successfully pressing his claims when some members of the Middlesex Committee considered him too young for so arduous a trip. In that tour he hit his only Test century, 114 at Melbourne, where he and Wilfred Rhodes joined in a second-wicket stand of 127. In the same tour Hearne and Frank Woolley put on 264 for the third MCC wicket against Tasmania at Hobart. Illness prevented him from playing in all but the opening Test in Australia in 1920-21. His full Test record was 806 runs, average 26.00, and 30 wickets for 48.73 apiece.

For all his comparatively frail physique, Hearne did not flinch from the hardest of hits in the field. At Lord's in 1928, for instance, when L. N. Constantine, with innings of 86 and 103 and a second-innings analysis of seven wickets for 57 runs, did so much towards a sensational victory by three wickets for the West Indies over Middlesex, Hearne instinctively grabbed at a return of intense ferocity from Constantine with resultant damage to his hand which put him out of the game for the remainder of the season.

Always immensely popular, with his quiet manner and subtle sense of humour, Hearne acted as coach at Lord's for many years after retiring from the field of play. In 1949 he was one of 26 former professional players honoured with life membership by the MCC.

SIR JOHN BERRY HOBBS

Born at Cambridge, December 16, 1882

Died at his home, at Hove, December 21, 1963

Knighted for his services to cricket 1953

By Neville Cardus

John Berry Hobbs, the great batsman whose first-class cricket career spanned thirty years and brought him fame everywhere as a player second to none, was born in humble surroundings at No. 4 Rivar Place, Cambridge, quite close to Fenner's, Parker's Piece and Jesus College.

Christened John Berry Hobbs because his father's name was John and his mother's maiden name Berry, John – or Jack as he was always known – was the eldest of twelve children, six boys and six girls. His father was on the staff at Fenner's and also acted as a professional umpire. When Hobbs senior became groundsman and umpire to Jesus College, young Hobbs took immense delight in watching cricket there. During the school holidays he used to field at the nets and play his own version of cricket with the College servants, using a tennis ball, a cricket stump for a bat and a tennis post for a wicket on a gravel pitch. This primitive form of practice laid the foundations of his skill. Little more than ten years old at the time, young Jack tried to produce the strokes which he had seen players employ in college matches. The narrow straight stump helped him to appreciate the importance of a straight bat, and with the natural assets of a keen eye and flexible wrists he learned to hit the ball surely and with widely varied strokes. Hobbs was self-taught and never coached, but he remembered all his life a piece of advice which his father gave him the only time the pair practised together, on Jesus College Close. Jack, facing spin bowling from his father, was inclined to stand clear of his stumps. "Don't draw away", his father told him. 'Standing up to the wicket is all important. If you draw away, you cannot play with a straight bat and the movement may cause you to be bowled off your pads."

When 12, Jack joined his first cricket team, the Church Choir Eleven at St Matthew's, Cambridge, where he was in the choir, and the first match in which he ever batted was for the choir of Jesus College who borrowed him, on their ground. He helped to form the Ivy Boys Club and they played both cricket and football on Parker's Piece.

Ranjitsinhji practised there, and Hobbs watched his beautiful wrist-play wonderingly, but the hero of Jack's boyhood was Tom Hayward, son of Dan Hayward who looked after the nets and marquees on Parker's Piece. Cricket became Jack's passion and his supreme ambition was to be good enough to play for one of the leading counties, preferably Surrey, the county of his idol, Tom Hayward. Hobbs practised morning, noon and night, and when he knew that he would be busy during the day he rose at six and practised before he went to work.

Tom Hayward first saw him bat when the noted Surrey player took a team to Parker's Piece for the last match of the summer in 1901, the season in which Jack played a few times for Cambridgeshire as an amateur.

In 1902, Hobbs obtained his first post as a professional – second coach and second umpire to Bedford Grammar School – and in the August of that year he helped Royston, receiving a fee of half a guinea for each appearance. He hit a fine century against Herts Club & Ground, so bringing immense joy to his father, but Mr Hobbs was not destined to see further progress by his son, for he died soon afterwards.

Tom Hayward was instrumental in Jack going to Surrey. A generous man, Hayward arranged a benefit for the widow Hobbs, and another friend of the family, a Mr F. C. Hutt, asked Hayward to take a good look at Jack. Hobbs was set to bat for twenty minutes on Parker's Piece against William Reeves, the Essex bowler, and Hayward was so impressed that he promised to get Jack a trial at the Oval the following spring. Mr Hutt thought that Hobbs should also try his luck with Essex, but they declined to grant him a trial, and so, in April 1903, Hobbs went to Surrey. Immediately they recognised his budding talent and engaged him. A two years' qualifying period had its ups-and-downs for Hobbs – he began with a duck when going in first for Surrey Colts at the Oval against Battersea – but soon his promise was clear for all to see. In his first Surrey Club & Ground match he made 86 against Guy's Hospital, and in his second qualifying year – 1904 – when he played several matches as a professional for Cambridgeshire, he scored 195 in brilliant style against Hertfordshire. His apprenticeship over, Hobbs commenced in 1905 the long and illustrious career with Surrey in first-class company which was to make his name known the world over and earn him a knighthood from the Queen – the first professional cricketer to receive the honour.

From the time he was awarded his county cap by Lord Dalmeny, afterwards Lord Rosebery, following a score of 155 in his first Championship match against Essex, Hobbs built up the reputation of the "Master" cricketer – a reputation perpetuated by the Hobbs Gates at The Oval and by his other permanent memorial, the Jack Hobbs Pavilion, at Parker's Piece. The tables of his achievements, given here tell eloquently how thoroughly he deserves remembrance by cricket enthusiasts, but comparisons with "W.G." will still be made.

From this point of view, Hobbs was, without argument, the most accomplished batsman known to cricket since W. G. Grace. In his career, Hobbs scored 61,237 runs with an average of 50.65 and scored 197 centuries. He played in 61 Test Matches. Other players have challenged the statistical values of Hobbs's cricket. None has, since Grace, had his creative influence.

Like "W.G.", he gave a new twist or direction to the game. Grace was the first to cope with overarm fast bowling, the first to mingle forward and back play. Hobbs was brought up on principles more or less laid down by "W.G." and his contemporaries – left leg forward to the length ball. Right foot back to the ball a shade short, but the leg hadn't to be moved over the wicket to the off. Pad-play among the Victorians was not done. It was caddish – until a low fellow, a professional from Nottingham, named Arthur Shrewsbury, began to exploit the pad as a second line of defence – sometimes, in extremity, a first.

When Hobbs played his first first-class match for Surrey on a bitterly cold Easter Monday (April 24) in 1905, the other side, captained by "W.G." was called "The Gentlemen of England". Hobbs, then 22 years and 4 months old, scored 18 and 88 – taking only two hours making the 88. Grace contemplated the unshaven youth from his position of "point". He strokes the beard and said: "He's going to be a good 'un." He could not have dreamed that 20 years later Hobbs would beat his own record of 126 centuries in a lifetime – and go on to amass 197 before retiring, and receive a knighthood for services rendered.

Hobbs learned to bat in circumstances of technique and environment much the same as those in which Grace came to his high noon. The attack of bowlers concentrated, by and large, on the off stump. Pace and length on good pitches, with varied flight. On "sticky" pitches the fast bowlers were often "rested", the damage done by slow left-hand spin or right-hand off breaks. Leg breaks were called on but rarely, then as a last resort, though already Braund, Vine and Bosanquet were developing "back-of-the-hand" trickery. Swerve was not unknown in 1905; there were Hirst, Arnold, Relf, Trott, and J. B. King "swinging" terrifically. But in those days only one and the same ball was used throughout the longest of a team's innings. And the seam was not raised as prominently as on balls made at the present time.

In 1907, two summers after Hobbs's baptism of first-class cricket, the South Africans came to this country, bringing a company of "googly" bowlers as clever as any seen since – Vogler (quick), Gordon White, Faulkner and Schwarz. Hobbs faced them only twice, scoring 18 and 41 for Surrey and 78 and 5 for C. I. Thornton's XI at Scarborough. J. T. Tyldesley, Braund, Jessop and Spooner also coped with the new witchcraft, so did George Gunn, who could cope with anything. Partly on the strength of his showing against the South Africans, Hobbs was chosen for his first overseas tour: 1907-08 in Australia.

But it was two years later, when the MCC visited South Africa, that Hobbs demonstrated quite positively that he had found the answer to the problems of the back-of-the-hand spinners. The amazing fact is that he made his demonstration on the matting wickets then used in South Africa. What is more, it was Hobbs's first taste of the mat, on which the South African spinners were at their most viciously angular. South Africa won this rubber of 1909-10 by three wins to two. In the Tests Hobbs scored 539 runs, average 67.37; double the averages of England's next best three run-makers: Thompson (33.77), Woolley (32.00), Denton (26.66) and Rhodes (25.11). It was Hobbs who first assembled into his methods all the rational counters against the ball which turned the other way. Moreover, on all kinds of pitches here and anywhere else, even on the "gluepot" of Melbourne, on the matting of South Africa, against pace, spin, swing, and every conceivable device of bowlers Hobbs reigned supreme.

His career was divided into two periods, each different from the other in style and tempo. Before the war of 1914-18 he was Trumperesque, quick to the attack on springing feet, strokes all over the field, killing but never brutal, all executed at the wrists, after the preliminary getting together of the general muscular motive power. When cricket was resumed in 1919, Hobbs, who served in the Royal Flying Corps as an Air Mechanic after a short spell in a munition factory, was heading towards his thirty-seventh birthday, and a man was regarded as a cricket veteran in 1919 if he was nearing the forties. Hobbs entering his second period, dispensed with some of the daring punitive strokes of his youthful raptures. He ripened into a classic. His style became as serenely poised as any ever witnessed on a cricket field, approached only by Hammond. He scored centuries effortlessly now; we hardly noted the making of them. They came as the hours passed on a summer day, as natural as a summer growth. An astonishing statistical fact about "The Master" is that of the 130 centuries to his name in county cricket, 85 were scored after the war of 1914-18; that is, after he had entered "middle-age". The more his years increased the riper the harvests. From 1919 to 1928 his season's yields were as follows:

1919 ..	2,594 runs	average 60.32
1920 ..	2,827 runs	average 58.89
1921 ..	312 runs	average 78.00
	(a season of illness)	
1922 ..	2,552 runs	average 62.24
1923 ..	2,087 runs	average 37.94
1924 ..	2,094 runs	average 58.16
1925 ..	3,024 runs	average 70.32
1926 ..	2,949 runs	average 77.60
1927 ..	1,641 runs	average 52.93
1928 ..	2,542 runs	average 82.00

From the time of his forty-third to his forty-sixth birthday, Hobbs scored some 11,000 runs, averaging round about the sixties. Yet he once said that he would wish to be remembered for the way he batted before 1914. "But, Jack," his friends protested, "you got bags of runs after 1919!" "Maybe," replied Hobbs, "but they were nearly all made off the back foot." Modest and true to a point. "The Master" knows how to perform within limitations. Hobbs burgeoned to an effortless control not seen on a cricket field since his departure. The old easy footwork remained to the end. At Old Trafford a Lancashire "colt" made his first appearance against Surrey. He fielded at mid-off as McDonald, with a new ball, opened the attack on Hobbs. After a few overs, the "colt" allowed a forward stroke from Hobbs to pass through his legs to the boundary. His colleagues, notably burly, redfaced Dick Tyldesley, expostulated to him – "What's matter? Wer't sleepin'?" – with stronger accessories. The "colt" explained, or excused his lapse. He had been so much "mesmerised" watching Hobbs's footwork as he played the ferocious speed of McDonald that he could not move.

It is sometimes said that Hobbs in his harvest years took advantage of the existing leg-before-wicket rule which permitted batsmen to cover their wickets with their pads against off-spin pitched outside the off-stump. True it is that Hobbs and Sutcliffe brought "the second line of defence" to a fine art. By means of it they achieved the two wonderful first-wicket stands at Kennington Oval in 1926 and at Melbourne two years later, v Australia, each time on vicious turf. But, as I have pointed out, Hobbs's technique was grounded in the classic age, when the bat was the main instrument in defence. Always was the bat of Hobbs the sceptre by which he ruled his bowlers. In his last summers his rate of scoring inevitably had to slacken – from 40 runs an hour, the tempo of his youth, to approximately 30 or 25 an hour. In 1926, at Lord's for Surrey v Middlesex, he scored 316 not out in six hours 55 minutes with 41 boundaries – a rate of more than forty an hour, not exceeded greatly these days by two batsmen together. And he was in his forty-fourth year in 1926, remember. It was in his wonderful year of 1925 that he beat "W.G.'s" record of 126 centuries, and before the summer's end gathered at his sweet will 3,024 runs, with 16 hundreds, averaging 70.32. He was now fulfilled. He often got himself out after reaching his century. He abdicated.

Those of us who saw him at the beginning and end of his career will cherish memories of the leaping young gallant, bat on high, pouncing at the sight of a ball a shade loose, driving and hooking; then, as the bowler desperately shortened his length, cutting square, the blow of the axe – a Tower Hill stroke. Then we will remember the coming of the regal control the ripeness and readiness, the twiddle of the bat before he bent slightly to face the attack, the beautifully timed push to the off to open his score – the push was not hurried, did not send the ball too quickly to the fieldsman, so that Hobbs could walk his first run. I never saw him make a bad or a hasty stroke. Sometimes, of course, he made the wrong good stroke, technically right but applied to the wrong ball. An error of judgment, not of technique. He extended the scope of batsmanship, added to the store of cricket that will be cherished, played the game with modesty, for all his mastery and produce, and so won fame and affection, here and at the other side of the world. A famous fast bowler once paid the best of all compliments to him – "It wer' 'ard work bowlin' at 'im, but it wer' something you wouldn't have missed for nothing." Let Sir Jack go at that.

The greater part of this memoir first appeared in THE GUARDIAN and is reproduced by kind permission of the Editor.

Other tributes:

Andrew Sandham: Jack was the finest batsman in my experience on all sorts of wickets, especially the bad ones, for in our day there were more bad wickets and more spin bowlers than there are to-day. He soon knocked the shine off the ball and he was so great that he really collared the bowling. He could knock up fifty in no time at all and the bowlers would often turn to me as if to say "Did you see that?" He was brilliant. Despite all the fuss and adulation made of him he was surprisingly modest and had a great sense of humour.

Herbert Strudwick: On any type of wicket, he was the best batsman in my experience, a first-class bowler if given the chance, and the finest cover point I ever saw. He never looked like getting out and he was just the same whether he made 100 or 0. I remember G. A. Faulkner after an England tour in South Africa, saying to Jack: "I only bowled you one googly." "Why," said Jack, "I did not know you bowled one." Faulkner said, "You hit the first one I bowled for 4. If you did not know it how did you know it would turn from the off?" "I didn't," answered Jack. "I watched it off the pitch."

Herbert Sutcliffe: I was his partner on many occasions on extremely bad wickets, and I can say this without any doubt whatever that he was the most brilliant exponent of all time, and quite the best batsman of my generation on all types of wickets. On good wickets I do believe that pride of place should be given to Sir Don Bradman. I had a long and happy association with Sir Jack and can testify to his fine character. A regular church-goer, he seldom missed the opportunity to attend church service on Sunday mornings both in England and abroad. He was a man of the highest integrity who believed in sportsmanship in the highest sense, teamwork, fair-play and clean-living. His life was full of everything noble and true.

Percy Fender: Jack was the greatest batsman the world has ever known, not merely in his generation but any generation and he was the most charming and modest man that anyone could meet. No-one who saw him or met him will ever forget him and his legend will last as long as the game is played – perhaps longer.

George Duckworth: My first trip to Australia in 1928 was Jack's last and I remember with gratitude how he acted as a sort of father and mother to the young players like myself. Always a boyish chap at heart, he remained a great leg-puller. When 51 he promised to come up and play in my benefit match in 1934 and despite bitterly cold weather he hit the last first-class century of his career. He told me he got it to keep warm!

Frank Woolley: Jack was one of the greatest sportsmen England ever had, a perfect gentleman and a good living fellow respected by everyone he met. I travelled abroad with him many times to Australia and South Africa, and I always looked upon him as the finest right-handed batsman I saw in the 30 years I played with and against him.

Wilfred Rhodes: He was the greatest batsmen of my time. I learned a lot from him when we went in first together for England. He had a cricket brain and the position of his feet as he met the ball was always perfect. He could have scored thousands more runs, but often he was content to throw his wicket away when he had reached his hundred and give someone else a chance. He knew The Oval inside out and I know that A. P. F. Chapman was thankful for his advice when we regained the Ashes from Australia in 1926.

HOLLIES, WILLIAM ERIC, who died suddenly on April 16, 1981, aged 68, was almost the last of the long line of leg-break and googly bowlers who played such a notable part for 50 years in English cricket. He bowled, as was then becoming fashionable, a trifle faster than many of his predecessors and turned the ball a bit less: what he lost in spin he gained in accuracy and he could well be used as a stock bowler. Like most of his type, he relied for his wickets mainly on his leg-break and top-spinner. Coached by his father, a well-known bowler in the Birmingham League, he made a modest start for Warwickshire in 1932, but in 1933 gained a regular place, which he retained until his retirement in 1957. By 1934 he had shown such promise that he was picked for the MCC side to the West Indies where, taking seven for 50 in the first innings of the third Test, he headed the Test match bowling averages. In 1935, when he took 100 wickets for the first time, a feat he accomplished on fourteen occasions, he was picked for the third Test against South Africa but was forced by injury to withdraw. After this, despite his fine record in county cricket, he was overlooked by the selectors until 1947 when he played in three Tests against South Africa. In 1948, after taking eight for 147 for Warwickshire against the Australians, he played in the final Test at The Oval and performed the feat by which he is best remembered. Bradman, coming in to prolonged applause for his last Test innings, received for his first ball a leg-break, which he played with a dead bat: the second, a perfect googly, bowled him.

But even apart from this Hollies, taking five for 131, fully justified his selection, his other victims being Barnes, Miller, Harvey and Tallon. In 1949 he played in four Tests against New Zealand and in 1950 in two against West Indies, in the first of which he took five for 63 in West Indies' first innings. That winter he was one of the MCC side to Australia and New Zealand, but the pitches did not suit him and his 21 wickets in first-class matches cost him over 40 runs each. However, in 1951 he did much to help Warwickshire win their first Championship for 40 years and he was still bowling with unabated skill in his last season, 1957, when he took 132 wickets at 18.94. Only in 1956, when he had to captain the side, did he fall below his usual standard. When he retired, he had taken far more wickets for his county than any other bowler. His most sensational performance for them was to take all ten wickets, for 49 runs, against Nottinghamshire at Edgbaston in 1946 without any assistance from the fieldsmen: seven were bowled and three lbw. In 1958 he played a few times for Staffordshire, his native county, and he continued to bowl with success in the Birmingham League until he was over sixty. No doubt his short run and easy action helped him to last, but he possessed also one of the greatest assets a bowler, and especially a bowler of his type, can have: an endlessly cheerful temperament.

In all first-class cricket this immensely popular player took 2,323 wickets at 20.94 and scored 1,673 runs with an average of 5.01, his wickets thus easily exceeding his runs. His highest score was 47 against Sussex at Edgbaston in 1954.

PERCY HOLMES

Born at Oakes, Huddersfield, November 25, 1887

Died September 3, 1971

By Sir Neville Cardus

Over decades a Yorkshire batsman has been one of the two opening an England innings in Test matches, Rhodes with Hobbs, Sutcliffe with Hobbs, Hutton with Washbrook; now

Boycott sustains the great tradition. But one of Yorkshire's most accomplished Number One (or Number Two) batsmen only once raised the curtain of an England innings v. *Australia*; his name Percy Holmes, a name as famous in Yorkshire during the 1920s and early 1930s, as Brown or Tunnicliffe, or Sutcliffe or Rhodes, or Boycott.

Holmes opened for England at Trent Bridge against Gregory and McDonald, the fearsome bowlers of Warwick Armstrong's rough-riding team, which arrived in England in 1921, having defeated J. W. H. T. Douglas's hapless England contingent five times in five Test matches, in Australia, each played to a finish. And in 1921, blessed by a glorious English summer, Armstrong's conquerors proceeded to annihilate England in the first three Test matches, three-day engagements. And the victories were settled well within the allotted time span.

Percy Holmes walked jauntily to the wicket at Trent Bridge on May 28, 1921, accompanied by D. J. Knight. England were all out for 112 and Holmes defended stoutly for ninety minutes, making top score, 30. Next innings he made no more than 8. The match was all over on the second afternoon. And this was the end of his Test match appearances until the South African season of 1927-28. He then went in first with Sutcliffe in five consecutive Test matches, at Johannesburg, Cape Town, and Durban; his scores were 0 and 15 not out; 9 and 88; 70 and 56; 1 and 63; and in the fifth game of this rubber 0 and 0.

In 1932, ten days after Holmes and Sutcliffe had made 555 together at Leyton, Holmes once again, and for the last time, received recognition from the English Selection Committee; he went in first with Sutcliffe at Lord's v India, scoring only 6 and 11. So, altogether this superb batsman played for England on seven occasions, and his modest record of 14 innings, 357 runs, average 27.46, is a complete falsification of what manner of cricketer and what manner of Yorkshire character Percy Holmes was, season after season.

His name was household in Yorkshire, as closely and proudly linked with Sutcliffe's as Tunnicliffe's with Brown's. As everybody knows – or should know – Holmes and Sutcliffe surpassed the first-wicket stand and aggregate of 554, incredibly achieved by Brown and Tunnicliffe v Derbyshire, at Chesterfield in 1898. Holmes was 44 years and troubled with lumbago in 1932, when he and Sutcliffe belaboured the Essex attack and after what the politicians call a recount, went beyond the Brown-Tunnicliffe scoreboard marathon.

Holmes, seven years to the day older than Sutcliffe, technically was perhaps Sutcliffe's better. His range of strokes was wider; he was the more versatile and impulsive batsman of the two. But Sutcliffe knew that very rare secret, which is revealed to few men, whatever their vocation. Mastery comes to him who knows his technical limitations. Again, Holmes, as a temperament, was at Sutcliffe's extreme; he was volatile, unpredictable of mood, always alive by instinct, so to say, intent on enjoyment on the cricket field, or off it. He was always first to admit that, like the rest of humans, he was fallible.

Sutcliffe seldom, if ever, admitted, as batsman, to ordinary mortal frailty. In other words, Sutcliffe found it hard to imagine that any bowler could get him out, whatever the state of the game or the wicket. One day, I saw Maurice Tate clean bowl Sutcliffe, at a game's outset – Yorkshire v Sussex. The ball was good enough to overwhelm Bradman. As Sutcliffe returned to the pavilion, I commiserated with him. "Unlucky, Herbert, to get such a ball at the beginning of the morning." But Sutcliffe reacted to my sympathy in high dudgeon. "I could have played it,' he asserted, "but a man moved in the stand, unsighting me." "I could have played it,' he repeated. I felt that I had offended Sutcliffe family pride.

Holmes, as I say, was different. At Lord's, in 1925, he actually accumulated 315 v Middlesex, in ten minutes under seven hours, with thirty-eight boundaries, as comprehensive an exhibition of stroke play as well could be imagined, all round the wicket, brilliant with late cuts and enchanting flicks to leg. Yet, when later he talked of this innings – it broke a century-old record at Lord's – and a year afterwards it was beaten by the master batsman of all (Sir Jack Hobbs) – Holmes could not account for it, at least not for the first half hour of it. He exaggerated by reckoning he was "morally out" half-a-dozen times in the first few overs. One of the Middlesex bowlers who had to cope with Holmes, in "these first few overs", confessed to me that he hadn't "so and so noticed" Holmes's insecurity. "He never missed a ball he intended to play."

Holmes was a great Yorkshire cricketer in one of the most historical periods of the county's many triumphant summers. From 1919, his real baptism to top-class cricket, till his last year of 1933, Yorkshire won the County Championship eight times. And in his prime, Yorkshire were more or less invulnerable – 1922 to 1925. These were the halcyon years, when Old Trafford, Leeds, Bradford and Sheffield would close gates at noon for a Yorkshire v Lancashire match. Nearly 80,000 people watched Lancashire v Yorkshire at Old Trafford, in 1926.

Holmes was one of the "characters", identifiable as soon as he took guard, twiddling his bat. Robertson-Glasgow, brilliant as observer as with his wit, rightly discerned in Holmes a certain aspect of "an ostler inspired to cricket". There was a curious "horsey" stable-boy air about him; he seemed to brush an innings, comb it, making the appropriate whistling sounds. He was not of the broadly soily nature of Emmott Robinson and Rhodes. I doubt if Rhodes, in his heart of hearts, really approved of Holmes's delight in a late-cut. "Cuts were never business strokes," quoth Wilfred. Roy Kilner, lovable as Maurice Leyland, would describe Percy as "a bobby-dazzler". (By nature's law of compensation, there are usually one or two rich genial spirits in the Yorkshire XI, to allow cheerfulness occasionally to creep in.)

Holmes really played cricket for fun. In a word, he was an artist, revelling in his batsmanship for its own sake. If he was furthering "The Cause" – the Yorkshire will-to-win, all very well. But he set himself to drink deeply from the sparkling wine distilled in most innings he played. In his career he scored 30,574 runs, average 42.11, including sixty-seven centuries; and I'm pretty certain that the bulk of them, the ripe bin of them, were vintage stuff.

Holmes and Sutcliffe made a most fascinating conjunction and contrast of character and technical method: Holmes was as spruce and eager to begin a Yorkshire innings as a jockey to mount his horse, using his bat as a sort of pliant persuasive whip to urge his innings along the course to the winning-post of a first-wicket century partnership.

Sutcliffe was all relaxed as he took guard. Then, very likely, he would wave, with his bat, some obtrusive member in the pavilion, even at Lord's, out of his way, wave him into crawling oblivion – and the poor exposed movable spectator could easily have been our Lord Chancellor. But, as soon as the bowler began his attacking run, Sutcliffe became almost stiff and angular with concentration. He scored with the air of a man keeping an appointment with a century, and must not be late.

Holmes often appeared to improvise; he could change stroke whenever his first glance at a ball's length had deceived him. He might move forward anticipating a half-volley; if the ball dropped shorter than its first flight advertised, he would, on swift feet, move back and cut late exquisitely. There was a certain light-footedness in his batsmanship; he could defend as obstinately as most Yorkshiremen, but even then, he gave the impression that he was defending by choice, not compulsion. He was an artist, as I say, expressing himself through cricket.

Sutcliffe, of course, was also an artist expressing himself in a different temperamental way. Never let it be thought that Sutcliffe was a tedious batsman; whether or not he was moving the score ahead, he remained an individual, lord of all that he surveyed. He was the image of supreme confidence, basking in it.

Holmes was prepared to risk the mercy and indulgence of fortune. Sutcliffe was not only surprised but scandalised, if he was bowled; Holmes accepted such a downfall as part of the common lot of cricketers and of human nature in general.

Some sixty-nine times Holmes and Sutcliffe rounded the hundred mark for Yorkshire's first wicket. Undoubtedly Holmes would, but for the omniscient presence of Hobbs, have opened for England with Sutcliffe against Australia, not once but perennially. Most of the achievements batsmen dream about came to Holmes – a century in each innings v Lancashire at Old Trafford in 1920; one thousand runs in a single month, June 1925, average 102.10; two thousand runs in a season seven times, over thirty thousand runs in his career.

But the scoreboard could not tell of his personal presence and animation. He seldom seemed static; he was always in the game. Between overs, and in the field, he was, as they say, eye-catching; but not self-consciously "producing" himself. He was as natural as could be, not aware that, as Percy Holmes, he "signed" everything he did.

His end as a cricketer arrived with an abruptness which, I am sure, tickled his mellow sense of humour. In 1932, he took part in the gigantic 555 first-wicket stand. The summer following, in 1933, he batted for Yorkshire 50 innings, scoring only 929 runs, average 19.25. This was the fall of the curtain for him. True, he was in his forty-sixth year; but somehow none of us suspected that age was on his heels and shoulders. He is a permanent chapter, not to say a whole volume, of Yorkshire's cricket history.

He had the talent – not always nurtured in the North country – to play hard for Yorkshire and, at the same time to spread over our cricket fields flashes of pleasure by his batsmanship, his nimble fielding and – best of all – by his infectious, though not demonstrative, Yorkshire nature.

HOWORTH, RICHARD, died in hospital on April 2, 1980, aged 70. A slow left-arm bowler, who kept an immaculate length and could spin and flight the ball, an attacking left-handed batsman, who usually appeared in the middle of the order but was prepared to open if wanted, and a good field close to the wicket, he did great service for Worcestershire from 1933 to 1951, scoring for them 10,538 runs at an average of 20.20, taking 1,274 wickets at 21.36 and holding 188 catches. Three times, in 1939, 1946 and 1947 he achieved the double in all matches, and he played five times for England. Born at Bacup, he appeared for Worcestershire in 1933 against the West Indians while qualifying and in the first innings was top scorer with 68. Qualified in 1934, he was disappointing, but in 1935 he jumped right to the front, heading the bowling averages with 121 wickets at 18.94, and from that time he never looked back. In 1936 he played an important part in Worcestershire's sensational victory over Yorkshire, their first since 1909; in the second innings he took five for 21. Later that summer he made the first and highest of his three centuries in county cricket – 114 in two hours and ten minutes v Kent at Dover, scored out of 180 for the first wicket – and followed it by taking, in the two innings, eight for 91. Before the War, with Verity available, there was little chance in the England side for any other slow left armer, but in 1947 Howorth was picked for the final Test v South Africa at The Oval and proved a great success. He took six wickets in the match, including one with his first ball, and was described in *Wisden* as "far the best England bowler"; he also scored 23 and 45 not out and made two fine catches in the gully. That winter he went with MCC to West Indies under G. O. Allen and played in all four Tests: so important was his steadiness to a weak attack that he was not left out of a single match. But the West Indies is not the ideal place for left-arm spin and his wickets were costly.

In his early days Howorth owed much to his captain, the Hon. C. J. Lyttelton, later Lord Cobham, who, whenever he showed signs of shortening his length and bowling too fast, insisted that he sould pitch the ball up and flight it more. When in 1951, at the age of 42, he announced his retirement after a season in which he had headed the Worcestershire bowling averages with 118 wickets at 17.97 and appeared to be bowling as well as ever, Lord Cobham, upon asking him why he was retiring, received the reply, "Because it's not as much fun as it was." Howorth played later for Stourbridge in the Birmingham League, served for many years on the Worcestershire Committee and ran a newsagent's shop across the river from the Worcester ground. He was much liked and respected, though the partial disenchantment which prompted his retirement from the first-class game was never quite thrown off.

HUBBLE, JOHN CHARLTON, who died on February 26, 1965, aged 84, was one of a trio of great wicket-keepers who, playing in succesion for Kent, spanned well over half a century. He succeeded F. H. Huish and was succeeded by L. E. G. Ames. Hubble served his county as a professional from 1904 to 1929, helping them on the last occasion they carried off the County Championship in 1913. In that time he scored over 10,000 runs and helped in the dismissal of more than 500 batsmen.

A beautiful exponent of off-side strokes, he was played until 1919 chiefly for his run-getting ability and it was not until after the First World War that he took over as regular wicket-keeper. Though a consistent batsman, he hit only five centuries in his long career, the highest being 189, put together in less than three hours, against Sussex at Tunbridge Wells in 1911. His best performance as a wicket-keeper was at Cheltenham in 1923, when he disposed of ten batsmen in the match, six in the first innings and four in the second. He held nine catches and brought off one stumping. He took part in the match with Yorkshire at Harrogate in 1904 which was declared void because the pitch had been tampered with. Holes, clearly obvious at the close of play on the first day, had been filled in before the second morning, and though play continued so that the crowd should not be disappointed, the match was not allowed to count in the Championship. Schofield Haigh, the Yorkshire and England medium-pace bowler, tried his hand at slow leg-breaks in the Kent second innings and performed the "hat-trick".

For a number of years Hubble acted as coach in South Africa.

IVERSON, JOHN BRIAN, who died in Melbourne on October 24, 1973, aged 58, was an unusual bowler who created something of a sensation during a brief career in Australian cricket. He bowled fast when at school, but took no part in cricket for twelve years afterwards. While on Army service in New Guinea, "Big Jack", as he was known, developed a peculiar method of spinning the ball, which he gripped between his thumb and middle finger. This enabled him to bowl a wide variety of deliveries, including off-breaks, leg-breaks and googlies, without any change of action. He first attracted attention in big cricket in 1949-50 when he took 46 wickets for Victoria at an average cost of 16.12. In the following autumn with W. A. Brown's team in New Zealand, he, in all matches, disposed of 75 batsmen at a cost of seven runs each and in the next Australian season, at the age of 35, he was chosen for his country against the England team captained by F. R. Brown. So perplexing did the visiting batsmen find the bowling of this tall man that in the Test series he obtained 21 wickets for 15.73 runs apiece, including six for 27 in the second innings of the third Test at Sydney. During the fourth Test at Adelaide he suffered an ankle injury when he trod on the ball. He played in only one game in each of the next two seasons and then gave up cricket altogether.

JAGGER, SAMUEL THORNTON, who died suddenly on May 30, 1964, aged 59, was a Cambridge Blue who, between 1922 and 1931, assisted Worcestershire, Sussex, Bedfordshire, Denbighshire and Wales. He headed the Malvern batting averages in both years he was in the XI, 1921 and 1922, and played as a medium-pace bowler in the University matches of 1925 and 1926. His four wickets for 34 runs in the second innings at Lord's in 1926 helped Cambridge to success by 34 runs. He also represented the University at fives. His best batting effort in first-class cricket was 41 for Worcestershire against Hampshire at Worcester in 1923, when he and the Hon. J. Coventry added 67 in three-quarters of an hour for the ninth wicket. His career with the county ended when it was found that he was not qualified to play for them. Jagger later became a house-master at Lancing.

KELLY, WILLIAM L., who died in Melbourne in December, 1968, aged 92, was manager of the Australian team in England in 1930 – Sir Donald Bradman's first tour. Kelly played for Victoria in 1908. An amusing story is told of his visit to England. During a match at The Oval, he was said to have placed a notice on the door of the Australian dressing-room which read: "Nobody admitted without manager's authority". The Oval, of course, forms part of the Duchy of Cornwall, which provided a source of revenue to the then Prince of Wales, now the Duke of Windsor. The Prince attended the match, saw the notice and told Kelly: "You can't keep me out. I'm your landlord!"

KERR, SIMON, who was found stabbed to death in a flat in Bristol on March 17, 1974, performed the extraordinary feat of scoring, when 19, five not out centuries in six innings for St. George's College, Salisbury, in 1972. (See *Wisden* 1973, page 134). The following year he paid his own fare from Rhodesia, joined the Gloucestershire ground staff and lived in the pavilion on the Bristol ground. He played for the Second XI. He was recommended to the County by M. J. Procter, the South African Test match all-rounder.

KING, JOHN BARTON, who died in a Philadelphia nursing home on October 17, 1965, aged 92, was beyond question the greatest all-round cricketer produced by America. When he toured England with The Philadelphians in 1897, 1903 and 1908, Sir Pelham Warner described him as one of the finest bowlers of all time. Very fast and powerfully built, King made the ball swerve late from leg, demonstrating that what could be done with the ball by a pitcher at baseball, at which he was expert, could also be achieved with a ball half an ounce heavier. In 1897 he took 72 wickets, average 24.20, and hit 441 runs, average 20.10. His best analysis that season was seven wickets for 13 runs at Hove where, on a good pitch, he bowled K. S. Ranjitsinhji first ball for 0 and Sussex were disposed of for 46. Six years later "Bart" King dismissed 93 batsmen for 14.91 runs each and scored 653 runs, average 28.29. At The Oval, where the Philadelphians defeated Surrey by 110 runs, he distinguished himself by scoring 98 and 113 not out and taking six wickets. Against Lancashire at Old Trafford, he followed an analysis of five wickets for 46 in the first innings by sending back nine men in the second – eight of them bowled – for 62, the remaining batsman being run out. In 1908 his record was 87 wickets in first-class games for 11.01 runs each, the best average in England that year, and he scored 290 runs, average 16.11. When Kent made a short tour of America in 1903, King played innings of 39 and 41 for Philadelphia against them and in the first county innings took seven wickets for 39 runs. He played eleven times for the USA against Canada from 1892, rarely being on the losing side, and in 1902, 1904, 1908 and 1911 held the Childs Cups for the best batting and bowling in Philadelphia cricket.

LE GROS, LT-COL PHILIP WALTER, died at the Star and Garter Home, Richmond, on February 27, 1980, aged 87. A good all-rounder, he was in the Rugby XI of 1910, being at that time a dangerous fast bowler who, in the second innings against Marlborough, took nine for 49. From 1911 to 1930 he played for Buckinghamshire and, though he bowled little after the war, was one of their leading batsmen when they won the Minor Counties Championship in 1922, 1923 and 1925. Despite a distinct stoop at the wicket, he was a stylish batsman and a strong hitter. For many years there hung in the High Wycombe pavilion a photograph of a row of cars standing by the pavilion, their windscreens smashed by Le Gros's hits. He was also a first-class squash player.

LEE, HARRY WILLIAM, for many years a reliable opening batsman for Middlesex, died in hospital on April 21, 1981, aged 90. Born in Marylebone, he had a number of trials for the county between 1911 and 1914 without any notable success, but on the outbreak of war several of the amateurs on whom the county were relying joined the forces and Lee got his chance. He took it with a faultless innings of 139 against Nottinghamshire. As soon as the season was over he joined up and in May 1915 was reported killed in action. Fortunately the report was untrue: he had in fact a badly broken thigh and was a prisoner. A few months later he was repatriated with one leg shorter than the other and was told he would never play cricket again. Happily, this too proved wrong and by the summer of 1916 he was playing for MCC against schools and making runs; when first-class cricket was resumed in 1919, no-one watching him bat, bowl or, even more, chase the ball in the field would have known he had been wounded. Meanwhile he had spent eighteen months in India, coaching and playing for the Maharajah of Cooch Behar.

He speedily made his place in the Middlesex XI secure and against Surrey at The Oval scored a hundred in each innings. In 1920, with 1,473 runs at an average of 44.63, 40 wickets at 24 runs each, and a century in the vital match against Surrey at Lord's, he played a considerable part in the county winning the Championship. Against Sussex at Lord's the first four, including himself, all made hundreds, a unique performance, and he took eleven for 68 as well. Consequently he was seriously considered for the MCC side to Australia. In 1921 he was less successful as a batsman – though he played the highest innings of his career, 243 not out against Nottinghamshire at Lord's in rather over six hours – but he had his best season as a bowler, taking 61 wickets at 21.25, including six for 53 against the Australians. Although for years he remained a valuable member of the county team, his best years were now over. Only in 1928, when he averaged 41.64, did he produce consistently his form of the first two or three seasons after the war. In 1929 for the second time he scored two hundreds in a match, on this occasion against the formidable Lancashire attack. His winters he spent usually coaching in South Africa and it was there in 1930-31, when A. P. F. Chapman's MCC side was sorely stricken with illness and injury, that he was roped in to play in the fourth Test, his sole appearance for England. In 1934 he was dropped from the Middlesex side in an endeavour to encourage younger players, but with a hundred for MCC against Oxford University and another which saved the county against Warwickshire, when he was recalled for a match or two in August, he showed that there was still a lot of cricket in him.

With an exaggerated crouch at the wicket and a tendency to score mainly on the leg side, he was not an attractive bat, but there could be no doubt of his value in a team which seldom lacked fast scorers lower in the order. He bowled slow-medium off-spinners and could also float the ball away: at one time he quite often took the new ball. He kept a good length and on a hard wicket got plenty of pace off the pitch. Against Gloucestershire at Cheltenham in 1923 he took eight for 39. From 1935 to 1946 he was a first-class umpire and from 1949 to 1953 coach at Downside. He was also author of *Forty Years of English Cricket*, an interesting book of reminiscences. Two younger brothers, Frank and Jack (who was killed in action in 1944), after starting with Middlesex did valuable work for years for Somerset. At Lord's, in 1933, the scorecard for Middlesex's first innings in their match against Somerset read "H. W. Lee c F. S. Lee b J. W. Lee 82".

LONG, HERBERT JAMES, who died on October 6, 1964, aged 85, was a London sports journalist for 50 years till retiring in 1955. Between the two world wars he reported county cricket for the *Cricket Reporting Agency* and the *Press Association* and also assisted in the preparation of *Wisden*. Through his own sports news agency, he reported football in London for many provincial newspapers. A first-rate organiser, he excelled himself at the first Wembley Cup Final in 1923 when the gates were closed on an attendance estimated at 150,000. Thousands of people remained outside the ground, but Long persuaded the police to form a path through the huge crowd so that his army of messenger boys were enabled to convey running reports of the game to the many telephones he had hired. As a fast bowler and aggressive batsman, "Bert" Long was on the Essex CCC staff in his youth and he was fond of recalling the occasion when he bowled Dr W. G. Grace in the nets at Leyton. He also played Association football for Woolwich Arsenal before they changed their name to Arsenal.

LYON, BEVERLEY HAMILTON, who died on June 22, 1970, aged 68, was one of the most astute captains of his era. Of Surrey birth, he was in the Rugby XI in 1917 and 1918, heading the batting averages in the second year, when his highest innings was 98 not out and he represented Lord's Schools against The Rest. Going up to Oxford in 1920, he gained a Blue in 1922 but failed to score in either innings in the University match, which Cambridge won by an innings and 100 runs. On the big occasion the following season, he gained some recompense, for although he scored no more than 14, an immensely powerful Oxford team this time triumphed in two days with an innings and 227 runs to spare.

In 1921, Lyon began his association with Gloucestershire. He became captain in 1929, a position which he filled for four seasons, and under his inspiring influence the county enjoyed greater success than for many years. T. W. Goddard, whose services as a fast bowler had been dispensed with by Gloucestershire, had joined the ground-staff at Lord's and become an off-break exponent. Lyon recalled him to the county and between them Goddard and the left-arm C. W. L. Parker developed into the most effective spin-bowling combination in the Championship.

Lyon also played his part as a hard-hitting batsman. He hit 1,397 runs, including three centuries, in 1929 for an average of over 33 and next season obtained 1,355 runs, average 41.00. In 1930 he hit two of his total of sixteen centuries – 115 and 101 not out – in the match with Essex at Bristol, and he enjoyed the distinction of helping his county to a tie with W. M. Woodfull's Australian team.

Lyon, known as an apostle of brighter cricket, was revolutionary in his cricket outlook. He was the originator in 1931 of the scheme by which a declaration by each side with only four byes scored in the first innings enabled maximum points to be available to the winning county after the loss of the opening two days of a Championship match through rain. This caused the Advisory County Cricket Committee to revise the regulations.

In all first-class cricket, Lyon made 10,615 runs for an average of 25.15, four times exceeding 1,000 runs in a season. He was also an excellent fieldsman, either at short-leg or in the slips.

He was the first to suggest first-class county games on Sundays, an idea which it took 36 years for the authorities to adopt. He also advanced the scheme for a knock-out competition, which came into being over 30 years afterwards.

His elder brother, M. D. Lyon, preceded him in the team at Rugby, got his Blue for two years at Cambridge and also assisted Somerset.

There was no funeral for Beverley Lyon, for he bequeathed his body to the Royal College of Surgeons.

MARRIOTT, CHARLES STOWELL, who died on October 13, 1966, aged 71, was one of the best leg-break and googly bowlers of his era. He learned his cricket in Ireland, where he was educated at St Columba's, and gained a Blue at Cambridge in 1920 and 1921, meeting with remarkable success in the University matches. In 1920, when rain prevented play on the first two days, he took seven wickets for 69 runs and in the following season he played a leading part in a triumph for the Light Blues in an innings with 24 runs to spare by dismissing seven Oxford batsmen in the match for 111 runs.

In all first-class cricket he took 724 wickets at an average cost of 24.04 runs and his bowling skill so far exceeded his ability as a batsman that his victims exceeded his aggregate of runs by 169. Cunning flighting, allied to the ability to turn the ball sharply, made him a menace to batsmen even on good pitches and when the turf gave him help, he could be well-nigh unplayable. His action was high with a free, loose arm which he swung behind his back before delivery in a manner reminiscent of Colin Blythe. From 1919 to 1921 he appeared for Lancashire and when beginning a long association with Dulwich College as master-in-charge of cricket, he threw in his lot with Kent, whom he assisted during the school holidays from 1924 to 1937.

In his first season with the Southern county he distinguished himself by taking five wickets for 31 and six for 48 in the game with Lancashire at Dover and against Hampshire at Canterbury he returned figures of five for 66 and five for 44, and he achieved many other notable performances in later years.

He met with great success on the occasion of his one appearance in a Test match for England. That was at The Oval in 1933, when he so bewildered the batsmen that he took five wickets for 37 runs in the first innings and, with second innings figures of six for 59, hurried the West Indies to defeat by an innings and 17 runs – a feat described by *Wisden* of the time as one of the best accomplished by a bowler when playing for England for the first time.

"Father" Marriott, as he was popularly known, engaged in two tours abroad. In 1924-25 he was a member of Lord – then the Hon. Lionel – Tennyson's side in South Africa and in 1933-34 he went with D. R. Jardine's MCC team to India, where, against Madras, he did the "hat-trick" for the only time in his first-class career. During the Second World War he served as an anti-aircraft gunner in the Home Guard.

MARTIN, GEOFFREY WILLIAM, who died in Launceston on March 7, 1968, aged 72, played in 22 matches for Tasmania between the 1922-23 and 1931-32 seasons. An aggressive right-hand batsman, strong in off-side strokes, he excelled in matches with MCC teams, scoring 121 at one a minute against A. E. R. Gilligan's 1924-25 side and 92 against that led by A. P. F. Chapman in 1928-29. On the latter occasion he was bowled by the Nottinghamshire fast bowler, H. Larwood, the bail travelling 67 yards 6 inches, or equal to the world record distance for a bail set up by R. D. Burrows, of Worcestershire, in 1911. Martin's career in senior grade cricket in Launceston extended over 44 years and in his last season at the age of 60 he played an innings of 63.

McCABE, STANLEY JOSEPH, who died on August 25, 1968, aged 58, following a fall from a cliff at his home in Sydney, was one of Australia's greatest and most enterprising batsmen. In 62 Test innings between 1930 and 1938 he scored 2,748 runs, including six centuries, for an average of 48.21. During a first-class career lasting from 1928 to 1942, he obtained 11,951 runs, average 49.39, reaching three figures on 29 occasions. Short and stockily-built, with strong arms, flexible wrists and excellent footwork, he was at his best when facing bowlers of pace. Though he scored most of his runs by strokes in front of the wicket, with the drive his speciality, he also hooked splendidly. In addition, he was a useful change bowler above medium pace, with the ability to send down the occasional ball which came back from the off at disconcerting speed, and an energetic and accurate fielder.

He displayed an early aptitude for cricket when, after a month in the second team at St Joseph's College, Hunter Hill, Sydney, he gained a place in the first eleven as an all-rounder at the age of 14 and held it for three years. After leaving school, he assisted Grenfell Juniors, a country district club, and in 1928 made the first of many appearances for New South Wales. His form for the State was such that he earned a place in W. M. Woodfull's team which visited England in 1930 when, having taken some time to become accustomed to unfamiliar conditions, he averaged 35 in the five Test matches and in all first-class fixtures reached 1,012 runs without hitting a century. In 1931-32 he enjoyed remarkable success in his three innings for New South Wales, scores of 229 not out against Queensland at Brisbane and 106 and 103 not out from the Victoria bowling at Sydney giving him the phenomenal Sheffield Shield average of 438. That season, too, he averaged 33.50 in five Tests with South Africa.

Against D. R. Jardine's team in 1932-33, in what is often called "the body-line tour", when England employed fast leg-theory bowling to a packed leg-side field, McCabe distinguished himself by hitting 385 runs in the five Tests, average nearly 43. His 187 not out in the first match of the series at Sydney was a remarkable exhibition of both craftmanship and courage. He made his runs out of 278 in less than four and three-quarter hours, after his earlier colleagues failed, with twenty-five 4s among his figures. His hooking of short-pitched deliveries by H. Larwood and W. Voce, the Nottinghamshire pair, was something which will for ever hold a place in Australian cricket history. In England again in 1934, he put together eight centuries – more than any of his team-mates – including 240, the highest of his career, against Surrey at The Oval and 137 in the third Test at Old Trafford. As *Wisden* of the time said of him: "He blossomed forth as an almost completely equipped batsman of the forcing type and was probably the best exponent – Bradman himself scarcely excluded – of the art of hitting the ball tremendously hard and safely".

Next season at home he became captain of New South Wales and on tour in South Africa in 1935-36 he enjoyed more success, heading the Test batting figures with 420 runs, average 84. He hit 149 in the first Test at Durban, sharing a second-wicket partnership of 161 with W. A. Brown, and 189 not out in the second meeting with South Africa at Johannesburg, where he and J. H. Fingleton put on 177 together. At Johannesburg he showed his fast-scoring ability to the full by reaching 50 in forty-two minutes.

Perhaps McCabe's most famous innings was his 232 not out in the opening Test against England at Trent Bridge in 1938 which, scored at the rate of one a minute, prompted Sir

Donald Bradman, his captain, to greet him on his return to the pavilion with the words: "If I could play an innings like that, I'd be a proud man, Stan."

S. C. Griffith, Secretary of MCC, commented upon this innings when paying a tribute to McCabe, calling it one of the best batting displays ever seen. "McCabe was a very great cricketer and a wonderful friend to all cricketers," said Mr Griffith.

Other tributes included:

Sir Robert Menzies, former Prime Minister of Australia: One of his great points was that he never bothered about averages; he enjoyed his batting. He was one of the two or three greatest batsmen I ever saw.

Sir Leonard Hutton: I knew him well. It would be hard to think of a greater Australian batsman. He had qualities that even Bradman hadn't got. I always liked to watch him bat and he was a most likeable fellow.

McGIRR, HERBERT M., who died in Nelson, New Zealand, on April 14, 1964, aged 73, was one of the most noted all-rounders to appear for Wellington. In a first-class career extending from 1914 to 1932, he scored 3,992 runs, average 28.81, and took 239 wickets with fast-medium bowling for 27.04 runs each. He toured England with T. C. Lowry's team of 1927, hitting 809 runs in all matches at 21.86 per innings and dismissing 69 batsmen for 23.98 runs apiece. McGirr played for New Zealand in two Tests against A. H. H. Gilligan's England team of 1929-30, scoring 51 in the fourth at Auckland. When he retired from first-class cricket he continued in club matches till, after making 70 at the age of 67, he slipped when taking in the milk the following morning and had to give up the game.

MONTGOMERY OF ALAMEIN, FIELD MARSHAL LORD, who died at Isington, Hampshire, on March 24, 1976, at the age of 88, was in the XI at St Paul's School in 1905 and 1906 as an opening batsman. His election to I Zingari in 1967 gave him very great pleasure. Before the battle of El Alamein he told his troops to hit Rommel's corps for six. And they did.

NEWMAN, JOHN ALFRED, who died in a Cape Town hospital on December 27, 1973, aged 89, rendered splendid all-round service to Hampshire for 25 years. He began with them in 1906 and continued till 1930. In that time he hit 15,333 runs, including nine centuries, for an average of 21.65, took 2,032 wickets at 24.20 runs apiece and held 296 catches. This lean but wiry player performed the "cricketers' double" five times between 1921 and 1928, being first to do so – on July 31 – in 1921.

For a number of years he and A. S. Kennedy virtually comprised the Hampshire bowling. Against Sussex in 1921 and in opposition to Somerset two years later, both at Portsmouth, the pair bowled unchanged through both innings. Newman, like Kennedy, of medium pace, could make the ball swing when it was new and afterwards turned to off-breaks of equally excellent length. He took 100 wickets in a season on eight occasions, his best year being 1921, when his victims numbered 177 at 21.56 runs each. He did the "hat-trick" against M. A. Noble's Australian side at Southampton in 1909: dismissed three Sussex batsmen in the course of four balls at Hove in 1923 and at Weston-super-Mare against Somerset in 1927 obtained 16 wickets for 88 runs in the match. His best all-round feat was in 1926 when he hit 66 and 42 not out and took 14 Gloucestershire wickets for 148 runs. Next summer he scored 102 and 102 not out from the Surrey bowling at The Oval when Jack Hobbs also hit two separate hundreds in the same match – a rare double performance in those days.

In 1922 Newman was the central figure in an unhappy incident at Trent Bridge, where he refused to bowl while the crowd engaged in barracking. The Hampshire captain, the Hon. L. H. (later Lord) Tennyson ordered him from the field – upon which Newman kicked down the stumps, a most unusual display of petulance from a likeable man. He continued later after an apology.

For nine seasons after retiring as a player, Newman stood as a first-class umpire and then went to live in Cape Town, where he coached for a number of years.

OAKES, ALFRED, who died at Horsham on August 16, 1965, aged 84, was an all-round sportsman in his younger days. For 60 years he lived in the cottage at the Horsham cricket ground where his sons, Charlie and Jack, who played for Sussex, were born. Pre-war county cricketers will remember the excellent pitches prepared by "Joker" Oakes for the Horsham Festival Week.

O'GORMAN, JOE G., who died at Weybridge on August 26, 1974, aged 84, was famous as the other half of a comedy act with brother Dave, but he always delighted in his cricket adventures with Surrey, which included batting with Jack Hobbs. This gave him as much pleasure as seeing his name in lights on Broadway. An all-rounder, he might well have made his mark in the game had he chosen. He played in three Championship matches for the county in 1927, sharing with Andy Sandham a partnership of 119 in sixty-five minutes, against Essex. O'Gorman hit 42 of those runs, with Sandham scoring altogether 230. A slow bowler, he took a wicket with his first ball in county cricket against Glamorgan at The Oval when he dismissed W. E. Bates, the opening batsman. For many years he and his brother played club cricket for Richmond for which club he took over 1,500 wickets.

PARSONS, THE REV. CANON JOHN HENRY, MC, who died in a Plymouth nursing home on February 2, 1981, aged 90, had a unique career. He played for Warwickshire from 1910 to 1914 as a professional: commissioned in the Great War and continuing in the Army after it, he appeared in 1919 and 1923 as Capt. J. H. Parsons: in 1924 he resumed his professional career, in 1929 he was ordained and from then to his retirement in 1934 he played again as an amateur. But for this almost complete gap of ten years, when he would normally have been in his prime, he might well have played for England. In that dismal season of 1921, when most of the batsmen who did play were cowed by the pace of Gregory and McDonald and when more slip catches were dropped than held, he would have been a strong candidate. A tall man, who made full use of his height, he was a superb driver of fast bowling, which he believed in attacking, and one of the safest slips of his day. By the time he resumed his career, English batting was fast recovering, a younger generation, Hammond, Leyland, Jardine, Chapman, was knocking at the door, and his opportunity was gone.

Born at Oxford and qualified by residence in Coventry, he had a brief trial for Warwickshire in 1910, and in 1911, with 568 runs at an average of 22.72, was a useful member of the side which so unexpectedly won the Championship. After a bad setback in the wet season of 1912, he got his thousand runs in 1913 and in 1914 was picked for the Players at The Oval, then an important match, a sign that he was regarded as potentially more than a mere county player. His few matches in 1919 and 1923 showed clearly what a loss he was and, when he returned to regular cricket in 1924, he did not disappoint expectations. In 1926-27 he was one of the leading batsmen on Arthur Gilligan's MCC side in India, not then a Test country, and in 1927 he had the splendid record for Warwickshire of 1,671 runs with an average of 50.64. This included the highest score of his career, 225 against Glamorgan at Edgbaston. Even this record he surpassed in 1931 when he averaged 63.72 in eighteen matches. In 1930 he had represented the Gentlemen at Lord's, thus joining the select band of those who played on both sides in these matches. The finale came in 1934, and perhaps no cricketer has made a more glorious exit. At Hull, under his captaincy, Warwickshire were dismissed for 45: they had to get 216 in the last innings and, thanks to Parsons who made 94 out of 121 in under two hours with three 6s and twelve 4s, they won by one wicket. It was his last match for the county.

In all first-class cricket he scored 17,983 runs with an average of 35.69, including 38 centuries. Shortly before his death a biography of him, *Cricketer Militant*, appeared written by Gerald Howat.

PEEBLES, IAN ALEXANDER ROSS, who died on February 28, 1980, aged 72, was for a short time one of the most formidable bowlers in the world and one of the few who could make Bradman look fallible. A tall man with a beautifully easy run-up and a high action, which gave him a particularly awkward flight, he bowled leg-breaks and googlies, and in an age of fine leg-spinners he was, for a while, the equal of any.

The start of his career was unusual. Coming south from Scotland in the hope of getting a chance in the cricket world, he was engaged as Secretary at the Aubrey Faulkner School of Cricket and so impressed Faulkner himself (to whose coaching he always acknowledged a great debt) and also Sir Pelham Warner that, when difficulty was found in raising a good enough Gentlemen's side against the Players at The Oval in 1927, he was given a place. On this occasion he bowled Sandham, but that was his only wicket; nor was he more successful later in the season at the Folkestone and Scarborough Festivals. However that winter he was sent with the MCC side to South Africa: ostensibly he went as secretary to the captain, but he bowled well enough to secure a place in the first four Tests and, without doing anything spectacular, made it clear that his possibilities had not been overestimated. In 1928 he played a few matches for Middlesex, but it was in 1929 that he really came to the fore, taking 120 wickets at just under 20 runs each and being one of three amateurs to take 100 wickets for the county that season – a unique performance. In 1930 he was up at Oxford, for whom he took 70 wickets, thirteen of them against Cambridge; then, after taking six wickets (including Hobbs, Sutcliffe and Leyland) for 105 for the Gentlemen v the Players, he was picked for the fourth Test at Old Trafford. Here, as soon as Peebles came on, Woodfall, who was well set, became acutely uncomfortable, on one occasion leaving a ball which just went over his middle stump; Bradman, coming in, was all but bowled first ball by Peebles, who then had him dropped in the slips and finally caught at slip for 14. The first three balls Kippax received from Peebles produced three confident but unsuccessful appeals for lbw. For such bowling three for 150 was a wholly inadequate reward. In the final Test at The Oval six for 204 may not look much, but in an Australian total of 695 it was better than anyone else. That winter Peebles went again with MCC to South Africa and both there and against New Zealand in the following summer he was one of the most effective bowlers. Already, though, the amount of bowling he had had to do in matches, followed by countless hours in the nets in winter, was affecting him: his leg-break was losing its venom, he was becoming increasingly dependent upon his googly, and his great days were passing, though he was picked for the last Test in 1934, an invitation which he had to refuse owing to injury. When, after several seasons of intermittent appearances, he returned to regular county cricket in 1939 to captain Middlesex, Peebles was really no more than a change bowler, and though he played occasionally until 1948, the loss of an eye in a war-time air-raid had, to all intents and purposes, ended his serious cricket career.

After his playing days were over he entered the wine trade and also became a notable cricket writer and journalist. When writing of players he had played with or seen, he was in the top class; to a deep knowledge of the game he added rare charm and humour. For any student of cricket history over the last 60 years, his many books are compulsory and delightful reading.

POWELL, ARCHIE, who died on December 27, 1963, aged 95, played for Gloucestershire Colts and, when catching W. G. Grace at cover point was reputed to be the only newspaper man ever to dismiss the Doctor for a "duck". Powell contributed articles on cricket and Rugby football to the *Daily Mail* for forty years. A Bristol journalist, he was a director of the *Western Daily Press*.

PRICE, WILLIAM FREDERICK FRANK, the former Middlesex and England wicket-keeper and Test match umpire, died in hospital on January 12, 1969, aged 66. A skilled performer behind the stumps, Fred Price held 648 catches and brought off 315 stumpings during a first-class career extending from 1926 to 1947. In 1937 he set up a record, since equalled but not surpassed, when he took seven catches in the Yorkshire first innings at Lord's.

After the match, a lady approached Price with congratulations upon his feat. "I was so thrilled with your performance, Mr Price", she said, "that I nearly fell over the balcony". With mock gravity, Price responded: "If you had, madam, I would have caught you as well!"

For so many years contemporary with L. E. G. Ames, 47 times capped for England, Price appeared in only one Test match, against Australia at Headingley in 1938, making two catches in the first innings. Twice he toured abroad, with the Hon. F. S. G. Calthorpe's MCC team in 1929-30, when he was sent to the West Indies as replacement for the injured Major R. T. Stanyforth, and with Sir Theodore Brinckman's side in South America in 1937-38. Price developed into a distinctly useful batsman and often opened the innings for his county. In all he scored 6,666 runs, average 17.35, three times reaching three figures. He narrowly failed to obtain two centuries in the game with Kent at Lord's in 1934, scoring 92 and 107. The previous summer, when he made his highest innings, 111 off the Worcestershire bowling at Dudley, he and E. H. Hendren (301 not out) engaged in a fifth-wicket partnership of 332.

Fearless as an umpire from 1950 to 1967, Price created a sensation when he three times no-balled G. A. R. Lock, the Surrey and England left-arm slow bowler, for throwing against V. S. Hazare's India touring team at The Oval. In the same season on the same ground when the Yorkshire batsmen, struggling to avoid defeat from Surrey, were being subjected to continuous barracking by the crowd, Price lay on the ground at square-leg till the noise subsided. "I did so," he explained afterwards, "because three times there were catcalls just as the batsman was about to play the ball. That is not my idea of British sportsmanship and under the laws of 'fair and unfair play', I will not tolerate such things on any ground, Lord's included, where I am umpiring." He officiated in eight Test matches.

F. S. Lee, the former Somerset player and Test umpire, who often "stood" with Price, paid him this tribute: "He was very conscientious, a very good umpire and a brilliant wicket-keeper, especially on the leg-side."

RATTIGAN, SIR TERENCE MERVYN, CBE, the famous play-writer, who died in Bermuda on November 30, 1977, aged 66, was, like his father and his uncle, in the Harrow XI. He won his place in 1929 as an opening bat, but next year though he played in the XI was not in the side at Lord's. He was an elegant stroke player, but unsound.

RELF, ROBERT RICHARD, who died at Reading on April 28, 1965, aged 81, played as a boy for Berkshire before qualifying for Sussex, whom he assisted as a professional all-rounder from 1905 to 1924, being one of three brothers to play for the county. He then returned to his native county, with whom he continued till the age of 63. As an all-rounder he scored 13,433 runs, including 22 centuries for Sussex, average 28.15, took 283 wickets for 38.04 runs each, and altogether held 278 catches. Capable of stern defence, he was a highly-consistent run-getter who hit well all round the wicket, with the drive probably his best stroke. His highest innings for the county was 272 not out, when he carried his bat through an innings of 433 against Worcestershire at Eastbourne in 1909, and he exceeded 200 on two other occasions. Six times he hit more than 1,000 runs in a season – from 1908 to 1913 – his best year being 1912 when in all matches he reached an aggregate of 1,804, average 32.21. He played for Players against Gentlemen at Folkestone in 1925, scoring 73.

His career with Sussex ended on an unfortunate note. Against Surrey at The Oval in 1924, he fielded while Surrey scored four runs, when rain stopped cricket. During the break, P. G. H. Fender, the Surrey captain, objected to the inclusion of Relf in the Sussex eleven on the grounds that he had played for Berkshire the previous season and thus broke his qualification. Relf was withdrawn from the side, his place being taken by J. H. Parks.

He later enjoyed great success for Berkshire, and never more so that in the 1924 Minor Counties Challenge match with Northumberland. He hit 100 in the first innings and followed by taking nine wickets for four runs apiece. From 1942 to 1960, Relf served as coach and groundsman at Leighton Park School, Reading, where his services were highly esteemed. Previously he was cricket coach to Charterhouse and Westminster.

WILFRED RHODES

By Sir Neville Cardus

Born at Kirkheaton, West Riding, October 29, 1877

Died near his home in Dorset, July 8, 1973

He had been blind since 1952

Wilfred Rhodes was Yorkshire cricket personified in the great period of the county's domination, shrewd, dour, but quick to seize opportunity. For Yorkshire he scored more than 30,000 runs, averaging 30 an innings: for Yorkshire he took 3,608 wickets at 16 runs each. When he was not playing for Yorkshire, in his spare time, so to say, he played for England and amassed 2,000 runs, average 30, and took 127 wickets, at the cost of 26.96 apiece. In his first Test match he was last in the batting order, and at Sydney in the 1903-04 rubber he took part in the most persistent and prolific Test match last-wicket partnership to this day; he helped R. E. Foster to add 130 for the tenth wicket, his share 40 not out. Eight years afterwards he went in first for England at Melbourne, and against Australia he was the partner of Hobbs in the record first-wicket stand of 323.

His career is already legendary; it does indeed read like a fairly tale. He was not 21 years old when he first bowled for Yorkshire in a match against MCC at Lord's. In the first innings he accounted for Trott and Chatteron; in the second for Trott, Chatteron, C. P. Foley, and the Hon. J. R. Tufton – six wickets for 63, a modest beginning, true. But at the season's end he had established himself as the greatest slow left-hand bowler in England with 154 wickets, average 14.60.

During the period in which Rhodes and Hobbs opened every England innings by prescriptive right, Rhodes put aside his bowling. In the Australian rubber of 1911-12 he contributed only 18 overs. But then the war came, reducing the Yorkshire attack. In 1919 Yorkshire needed again the spin and flight of Rhodes, so he picked up his bowling arts exactly where years before he had laid them down, picked them up as though he had not lost touch for a moment. He headed the bowling averages of 1919, 164 wickets, average 14.42 in 1,048 overs. He was nearly 42 by the calendar. In 1902 he had gone in last for England at Kennington Oval when 15 runs were wanted to beat Australia; George Hirst, with whom he always opened Yorkshire's attack, was holding the wicket at the other end. England won by one wicket.

Twenty-four years afterwards, Rhodes in his forty-ninth year was recalled to the England XI and was one of the main causes of Australia's defeat and England's emergence from years in the wilderness. On this, his last appearance for England, Rhodes took the wickets of Woodfull, Ponsford, Richardson (twice), Collins, and Bardsley for 79 runs. He had probably lost by then much of his old quick vitally fingered spin: but as he explained to me: "If batsmen thinks as I'm spinnin' them, then I am" – a remark metaphysical, maybe, but to the point. At Sydney, in December, 1903, on the shirt-fronted polished Bulli soil pitches of that distant halcyon day for batsmen, Australia scored 485, and the might of Australia's champions commanded the crease – Trumper, Hill, Duff, Armstrong, Gregory. Rhodes bowled 48 overs for 94 runs, five wickets. It was on this occasion that Trumper, most brilliant of all batsmen, alive or dead, made his famous remark to Rhodes – "for God's sake, Wilfred, give me a minute's rest."

Rhodes could not turn the ball on the Australian grounds of half a century ago. He prevailed by length, variations of flight, but chiefly by unceasing accuracy of pitch, always demanding close attention from the batsman, the curving arc through the air, the ball dropping on the same spot over by over, yet not on quite the same spot, each over in collusion with the rest, every ball a decoy, some balls apparently guileless, some artfully masked – and one of them, sooner or later, the master ball. He was economical in action, a few short strides, then a beautifully balanced sideways swing of the body, the arm loose and making a lovely arch. He could go on for hours; the rhythm of his action was in its easy rotation, hypnotic, lulling his victims to the tranced state in which he could work his will, make them perform strokes contrary to their reason and intention. Batsmen of Rhode's heyday frequently succumbed to his bait for a catch in the deepfield. David Denton had safe hands at long-on; and the score-sheets of the period repeated day by day the rubric – "c Denton b Rhodes". In rainy weather, "c Tunnicliffe b Rhodes" was familiar proof that Wilfred was at work on a "sticky" pitch, for Tunnicliffe was the best slip fielder of the century, a long giant with a reach into infinity.

Rhodes really was a slow bowler, not quick and low flight to the pitch, after Lock's manner. At the end of his career he proudly maintained that "Ah were never hooked and Ah were never cut," a pardonable exaggeration considering the proportion of truth in it. Rhodes seldom pitched short. "Best ball on a 'sticky' pitch is a spinnin' half-volley," such was his doctrine. And he bowled to his field with the precision of high mathematics. Ernest Tyldesley once told me that he often had no alternative but to play at least three balls an over, on a batsman's wicket, straight to mid-off, an inch off the spot where Rhodes had planted mid-off.

Rhodes made himself into a batsman by practice and hard thinking. He was one of the first batsmen to adopt the full-fronted stance, left shoulder pointing to forward leg. But it is a mistake to suppose that his batting was perpetually dour and parsimonious in strokeplay. In the Test match against the Australians at Lord's in 1912, England had first innings on a rain-damaged pitch. *Wisden* relates that Rhodes, with Hobbs as company, "so monopolised the hitting that his share of 77 runs amounted to 52". On the whole and naturally enough, Rhodes distrusted the romantic gesture. One day in conversation with him, I deplored the absence in modern cricket of the cut. "But it were never a business stroke," he maintained.

While he was actively engaged in the game he was not a man given to affability. He was known as a "natterer" on the field; and to natter in the North of England means to talk naggingly, mostly to oneself, with the intention of being overheard. At Old Trafford in the 1930s Lancashire reached a total of 500 against Yorkshire. The Lancashire captain, Leonard Green, was about to take the bowling of Rhodes when the score was 499. Green was sure in his mind that a total of 500 would never again, or not for decades, be achieved by Lancashire against Yorkshire. He therefore determined that come what may he would himself score the five hundredth run. So he blocked a ball from Rhodes, then ran like the wind. The ball was picked by by Emmott Robinson at silly-point, and hurled to the bowler's end, where it struck Rhodes on the wrist even as Green got home by the skin of his teeth. And in all the scurry and excitement Wilfred was heard to mutter, while he retrieved Robinson's violent throw. "There's somebody running up and down this wicket. Ah don't know who it is, but there's somebody runnin' up and down this wicket."

He was a great player, one of the greatest in cricket's history, not only for his all-round performances denoted by the statisticians: nearly 40,000 runs scored in 37 seasons and 4,184 wickets taken. He was great because his cricket was redolent and representative of Yorkshire county. In his old age he lost his eyesight and found his tongue. He accepted his affliction philosophically, and consoled himself by a flow of genial chatter never before heard from him. He attended cricket as long as health would permit. With an acquired sense he was able to follow the play. "He's middlin' the ball right." But it was his delight in his last years to recall the old days. I asked him what he though of Ranjitsinhji. "He were a good bat were 'Ranji'. But I always fancied myself getting him leg before doin' that leg glance of his." I tried again. "What did you think of Trumper?" "'E were a good bat were Victor." There was no advance on a "good" bat in Wilfred's vocabulary of praise. Once, though, he let himself go. I asked him his opinion of Sidney Barnes as a bowler. "The best of 'em today is half as good as Barnie." He intended this as a compliment to the champions of today.

I last saw him as his daughter, Muriel, and her husband Tom Burnley, led him out of Trent Bridge at the close of play of a Test match. More than fifty years ago he had first played for England, on the same ground, in 1899, when he was 21. Now he was going home to Canford Cliffs, Bournemouth, white stick in hand, arm in arm with his son-in-law, his face ruddy after hours sitting and listening to cricket, and whether he knew it or not, himself a permanent part of the game's history and traditions.

This memoir first appeared in THE GUARDIAN and is reproduced by kind permission of the Editor.

ROBERTSON-GLASGOW, RAYMOND CHARLES, who died suddenly on March 4, 1965, aged 63, was both a distinguished player and a celebrated cricket writer. In the Charterhouse XI in 1918 and 1919, he did specially well as opening batsman and fast-medium bowler in the second year, when he scored 537 runs, average 38.36, and took 44 wickets for 18.52 runs each, including six for 90 against Winchester. Going up to Oxford, he gained a Blue as a Freshman and played against Cambridge for four years from 1920 to 1923. He appeared for Somerset with varying frequency from 1920 till 1937 and played five times for Gentlemen v Players between 1924 and 1935.

In all first-class cricket he scored 2,083 runs, average 12.93, dismissed 464 batsmen at a cost of 25.74 runs each and held 79 catches. After his schooldays, he was better known as a tall bowler able to swing the ball appreciably, and he achieved such notable performances for Somerset as nine wickets for 38 runs in the first innings of Middlesex at Lord's in 1924; seven for 56 and seven for 50 against Sussex at Eastbourne and six for 60 and five for 87 against Gloucestershire at Bristol in 1923 and five for 47 and five for 37 against Warwickshire at Weston-super-Mare in 1930. That he did not altogether lose his batting skill he showed in 1928 when, opening the Somerset innings with A. Young, he shared in stands of 160 against Essex at Knowle and 139 against Worcestershire at Taunton in following matches. His highest innings was 80 from the Hampshire bowling at Taunton in 1920.

He was known to his host of friends as "Crusoe", a nickname which came to him as the outcome of a match between Somerset and Essex. C. P. McGahey, the Essex and England amateur, was in and out so rapidly that the next batsman, who had not been watching the play at the time, asked what had happened. "First ball," explained McGahey, "from a chap named Robinson Crusoe."

Of considerable personal charm, an infectious laugh, and possessing an infallible sense of humour which found its way into his writings when he became cricket correspondent in 1933 for *The Morning Post*", "Crusoe" was popular wherever he went. He later wrote for *The Daily Telegraph, The Observer* and *The Sunday Times*, contributed a number of articles to *Wisden* and was the author of many books, including *Cricket Prints, More Cricket Prints, 46 Not Out* – an autobiography – *Rain Stopped Play, The Brighter Side of Cricket, All In The Game* and *How To Become A Test Cricketer.*

His stories regarding the game he loved were many and various, but never ill-natured. One against him concerned the occasion when he was in the Pavilion at Lord's during the match following the University game of 1922. A friend introduced him to a certain celebrated Pressman who, as was his wont, paid little attention to his name. When the friend left them, the Pressman, endeavouring to make conversation, enquired: "Did you see Chapman's wonderful innings in the 'Varsity match?" For once "Crusoe" was speechless. A. P. F. Chapman had hit a brilliant 102 for Cambridge, a big proportion of his runs coming at the expense of Robertson-Glasgow, who sent down 43.1 overs for 97 runs and did not take a wicket!

EMMOTT ROBINSON

By Sir Neville Cardus

Born on November 16, 1883; died November 17, 1969

Emmott Robinson was as Yorkshire as Ilkley Moor or Pudsey. He was the personification of Yorkshire cricket in one of its greatest periods, the 1920s, when the county appeared to look forward towards winning the Championship by a sort of divine right. He came to first-class cricket in his late thirties – and "thrive he did though bandy".

Statistics tell us little of his essential self; in twelve seasons he scored 9,444 runs and took 892 wickets. Many cricketers have surpassed these figures; few have absorbed the game, the Yorkshire game, into their systems, their minds, nerves and bloodstreams, as Emmott did. Yorkshire cricket was, for him, a way of living, as important as stocks and shares.

With Rhodes he established the unwritten Constitution of Yorkshire cricket, the skipper content to serve in a consultative capacity. Nowadays we hear much of the supposition to the effect that first-class cricket in recent years has become "more scientific" than of yore. To speak the truth, there are few players of our latest "modern" times who would not seem to be as innocent as babes talking tactics and know-how in the company of Rhodes and Emmott.

It was these two shrewd men who evolved – with rival competition from Makepeace and Co. in Lancashire – the protective philosophy: how to close a game up, how to open it out, how to stifle the spin on a "sticky" wicket with the "dead" bat. "Loose grip on top of 'andle," said Emmott.

The shrewdness, humour, uninhibited character of North of England life was marvellously revealed and fulfilled in Yorkshire v Lancashire matches of the 1920s. Gates closed at noon; 30,000, even 40,000, partisan spectators watching. Watching for what? "Bright cricket"? Not on your life.

"We've won the toss," Harry Makepeace would announce in the Lancashire professionals' dressing-room. "Now lads, no fours before lunch." And Emmott Robinson was already polishing the new ball, holding it up to the light of day, as though investigating an egg. He bowled outswingers; for in his heyday the lbw rule rendered inswing more or less harmless. He swung the ball from middle and leg, compelling a stroke of some sort.

He was shocked if anybody "wasted new ball". After he had bowled the first over, he would personally carry the new ball, in cupped hands, to the bowler at the other end.

At Bradford in 1920, he took nine wickets in an innings against Lancashire. At a crisis for Yorkshire too! Lancashire needed only 52 to win, six wickets in hand. Then Emmott turned the game round violently. For some reason or other, I did not, in my report of the match, praise Emmott in generous enough language. I was not a convert to seam bowling in those days; and am not a bigoted convert yet. When Emmott next met me he said, "Ah suppose if Ah'd tekken all ten Lanky's wickets, tha'd have noticed me."

As a batsman he exploited pad-play to perfection. Remember that the lbw law of Emmott's halcyon years permitted a batsman to defend with his pads a ball pitching outside the off stump. If any young greenhorn, batting for Yorkshire or Lancashire, were to be bowled by an off break, he received severe verbal chastisement. "What dos't think thi pads are for?" was Emmott's outraged inquiry.

Emmott was one of the pioneer students of the "green wicket" and its habits. One day, at Headingley, rain soaked the field, then the sun shone formidably. After lunch Emmott and Rhodes walked out to inspect the pitch. Arrived there, Rhodes pressed the turf with a forefinger and said, "It'll be sticky at four o'clock, Emmott." Whereat Emmott bent down and also pressed the turf with a forefinger. "No, Wilfred," he said, "half-past."

These grand Yorkshiremen in general, and Robinson in particular, never were consciously humorous. Emmott was a terribly serious man. He could not, as Freddie Trueman did, play for a laugh. One summer at Lord's, Yorkshire got into dire trouble against Middlesex. During a tea interval I ran into Emmott. "Hey dear", he growled, "fancy, just fancy Yorkshire getting beat by Middlesex. And wheer *is* Middlesex? Is it in Lundin?" A far reaching question; because London swamps county boundaries and identities. We know what county means in Yorkshire and Lancashire.

Emmott merged his ability as cricketer into the Yorkshire XI entirely; by sheer power of will he added a technical stature which, elsewhere, might not have amounted to much. A celebrated Indian batsman, introduced to Rhodes in Rhodes's wonderfully blind old age, said he was honoured to meet so "great a cricketer". "Nay," said Wilfred, "Ah never considered myself a Star. I were just a good utility man."

Thus might Emmott have spoken; no part, no individual, was greater than the part of any Yorkshire team. "Aye," Emmott once reminded me, "and we are born and bred Yorksheer. And in thy county, tha's tekken in Ted McDonald. A TASMANIAN, mind you," as though a Tasmanian was beyond the pale.

He maintained an average of round about 24 while compiling more than 9,000 runs in his years of active service. The point about his use of the bat, aided and abetted by the broadest pads procurable, is that every stroke he ventured to make was part of a plan, designed to win the match for Yorkshire or save it.

I imagine that in all his days in the sun and rain, his keen eyes were as constantly on the clock as on the score-board. But, in the field, crouching close to the bat, he missed nothing. A lordly batsman who could hit, asked Emmott to move away a little, for the sake of self-preservation. "Thee get on with thi laikin', and Ah'll get on with mine," retorted Emmott – and for the benefit of the uninitiated I herewith translate: "laikin'" means playing; "get on with thy playing."

As I write this tribute to Emmott Robinson, with as much affection as admiration, I am bound in fairness to memory of him, to recount an incident at Old Trafford in 1927. The wicket prepared in those days, for the Lancashire and Yorkshire match, was a batsman's sleeping bed stuffed with runs. Match after match was unfinished – none the less, a grim fight for first-innings points (78,617 rabid Lancastrians and Yorkshiremen paid to watch the Lancashire v Yorkshire match at Old Trafford in 1926, fours before lunch or no fours).

Over and over did Emmott resist on this occasion in time and space, when he was, with Rhodes, salvaging his county. Suddenly, for no reason, in fact, as he later admitted, against all reason, he indulged in a most elegant late-cut towards third man. So transfixed was he by this stroke that he stood there contemplating it. And when he emerged from the realm of aesthetic contemplation to the world of unescapable reality, Wilfred Rhodes was on his doorstep and was run out. Consequently Yorkshire lost. "Fancy," he said sorrowfully to me (years after), "fancy. What could Ah'ave been thinkin' about? Me and mi cuts! But, mind you, Wilfred should never 'ave come runnin' down the pitch. Runs didn't matter with game in that sta-ate. Then counted for nowt." He was an economist. Must not waste new ball.

One Saturday Yorkshire batted all day at Lord's, scoring 350 or thereabouts. Sunday morning was drenching, a thunderstorm cleared up by noon, followed by dazzling sun. In Hyde Park near four o'clock I came upon Robinson and Rhodes. "A lovely afternoon," I said to them, in greeting. "Aye," snapped Emmott, "and a sticky wicket wa-astin at Lord's."

He was richly endowed by native qualities of character, and gave himself, heart and soul and with shrewd intelligence, to Yorkshire cricket. That's why he is remembered yet; that's why no statistics can get to the value of him. The score-board cannot reflect human nature, Yorkshire human nature, in action. He was not named Emmott Robinson for nothing.

SIMS, JAMES MORTON, who died on April 27, 1973, aged 68, was in his day a splendid leg-break and googly bowler and a more than useful batsman for Middlesex. He had been county scorer for a number of years and his death occurred while he was staying at a Canterbury hotel on the night preceding a game with Kent there. Making his début for

Middlesex in 1929, he retired from county cricket in 1952 and between those years he took 1,572 wickets at an average cost of 24.90 runs each and scored over 9,000 runs, including four centuries. He afterwards had charge of the county second eleven and served as coach till taking over the post of scorer.

Originally regarded mainly as a batsman, often opening the innings, Jim Sims developed into an all-rounder and particularly after the Second World War was relied upon chiefly for his bowling. Eight times he dismissed over 100 batsmen in a season and in 1939, with 159 victims at 20.30 runs each, he was the most prolific wicket-taker in English first-class cricket. For East against West at Kingston-upon-Thames in 1948 he enjoyed the distinction of taking all ten wickets – for 90 runs – in an innings, a feat he went close to performing 15 years earlier at Old Trafford when disposing of nine Lancashire batsmen for 92 runs. He achieved the "hat-trick" for Middlesex at the expense of A. Melville's South African team at Lord's in 1947 and in 1933 sent back three Derbyshire batsmen in the course of four balls at Chesterfield.

In his book, "Cricket Prints", the late R. C. Robertson-Glasgow wrote: "Jim Sims can unbuckle the most difficult googly in the game today." How highly this tall, lean, genial cricketer was held in the esteem of the Middlesex authorities was illustrated by their granting him two benefits in five seasons. The first in 1946 was seriously affected by rain.

He toured Australasia under E. R. T. Holmes in 1935-36 and under G. O. Allen the following winter when, though doing well in other matches, he proved costly on the hard pitches, in the two Tests for which he was called upon. He also played once each for England against South Africa, in 1935, and India, in 1936, both in England.

A humorous man, who never tired of telling stories about the game in words spoken from the side of his mouth, he was popular wherever he went. Many of them concerned his idol, "Patsy" Hendren. One regarding Sims was about the occasion when Harold Larwood, on a fiery pitch, was making the ball fly in a somewhat terrifying manner. Sims, unusually quiet, was awaiting his turn to bat when Hendren asked him: "Feeling nervous, Jim?" Said Sims: "Not exactly nervous, Patsy, just a trifle apprehensive."

On one occasion after dismissing a capable batsmen with a googly, he remarked confidentially to the nearest fieldsman: "I'd been keeping that one warm all through the winter."

Tributes to Sims included: **J. M. Brearley** (Middlesex captain): Jim helped a lot of us young players and I suppose there is no one in the side who has not benefited from his help and advice. He was a great chap to have around and everybody will miss him terribly.

L. E. G. Ames (Kent secretary-manager): I knew Jim for between 40 and 50 years and toured with him in Australia. I would say that he was one of the great characters of the game.

SMITH, CEDRIC IVAN JAMES known universally as "Big Jim" Smith, died at his home near Blackburn on February 8, 1979, aged 72. Born at Corsham, he played for Wiltshire from 1926 until 1933, but, having been on the staff of Lord's since 1926, came to the notice of the Middlesex authorities, who persuaded him to qualify for them. To the general public he was at that time unknown and his first season, 1934, was a triumph. With 172 wickets at an average of 18.88, he came sixth in the first-class bowling averages and played for the Players at Lord's. That winter he was a member of the MCC side to the West Indies, a great honour for a player with so little first-class experience. He played in all the Tests on this tour and gave some sensational displays of hitting. His only other Test match was against New Zealand at Old Trafford in 1937. He continued as a very valuable member of the Middlesex side until 1939, and in his six seasons for the county he took 676 wickets at 17.75. Standing six feet four inches and immensely strong, he had the cardinal virtue of bowling at the stumps and revelled in long spells of bowling.

Yet fine bowler and fieldsman that he was, he will surely be remembered most as a batsman whose entry always roused a hum of excitement. His principal stroke (perhaps his only one!) was to advance the left foot approximately in the direction of the ball and then swing with all his might. If the ball was well up (and the foot on the right line) it went with a low trajectory an astonishing distance. Against Gloucestershire at Bristol in 1938 he reached 50 in eleven minutes; disregarding one instance which the connivance of the bowlers rendered farcical, this is a record for first-class cricket. Against Kent at Maidstone in 1935 his 50 took fourteen minutes. In comparison to these herculean feats, his one century, 101 not out against Kent at Canterbury in 1939, was a sedate performance, taking eighty-one minutes! He added 116 for the last wicket with Ian Peebles, his own share being 98.

E. J. ("TIGER") SMITH

Born February 6, 1886; Died August 31, 1979

By Rowland Ryder

The death of Ernest James ("Tiger") Smith marks the end of an era in cricket. He had played with and against W. G. Grace; he had kept wicket for England against Australia before the First World War; and his connection with Warwickshire spanned no fewer than 75 years. He was the oldest living Test cricketer up to the time of his death.

Ernest James Smith – for over 70 years he had been known as "Tiger", although a few Warwickshire associates called him Jim – was born in Benacre Street, Birmingham; a street which has now disappeared, that area of Birmingham having been replaced by a series of ring roads, underpasses and flyovers near the centre of the city. But it used to be about a mile from the Edgbaston ground, and, four months after "Tiger" Smith was born, Warwickshire played their first match at Edgbaston.

In 1902 Edgbaston became a Test match venue, and on May 31, thanks to Wilfred Rhodes, England bowled Australia out for 36. Young Smith was working at Cadbury's then, and two years later he offered his services to Warwickshire as a wicket-keeper, although he had lost the tips of two fingers in a works accident.

He was taken on, and in 1904 played his first match for Warwickshire against the South African tourists. Right up to the end of his life he remembered the names of the South African side that came over in the googly summer of 1904, and he would rattle them off with reminiscent delight: Shalders, Tancred, Hathorn, Frank Mitchell, Sinclair, Llewellyn, Schwartz, White, S. J. Snooke, Halliwell and Kotze. *Wisden* referred to him simply as Smith, and although he played in two other games there is no reference to him in the Warwickshire report for 1904.

For a time he was seconded to the MCC. It was during this period that he met W. G. Grace, and played in several matches for and against Grace's London County Eleven. "Do you know what he'd do if he thought you weren't any good?" chuckled "Tiger". "He'd go out and buy a rabbit and put it in your cricketing bag." While he was on the ground staff, "Tiger's" duties sometimes included bowling to George Robey in the nets.

When Smith returned to Edgbaston he was apprenticed to "Dick" Lilley, who had also worked at Cadbury's before joining Warwickshire. Lilley himself, who played in 35 Test matches, 32 of them against Australia, had been for many years an opponent and close friend of J. McC. ("Old Jack") Blackham, generally considered to be the first of the great modern wicket-keepers.

"Tiger" Smith was therefore fortunate in his apprenticeship to this craft within a craft, for he was to learn from the greatest contemporary exponent in England, and indirectly from Blackham. By the year 1910 he was coming into his own, playing in nineteen of Warwickshire's twenty matches. "More than a word of praise is due to Smith," ran the Warwickshire report in *Wisden*, "who, called on to fill the vacancy created by Lilley's retirement from wicket-keeping, acquitted himself with every credit."

The next year, 1911, proved to be the most remarkable in Warwickshire's history. Under the inspiring captaincy of F. R. Foster, the side, near the bottom of the table halfway through the season, eventually won thirteen matches out of twenty and caused a cricket sensation by carrying off the Championship honours. Foster's part in this achievement was outstanding, but "Tiger" Smith himself did remarkably well, with 40 catches and five stumpings in Championship matches; eleven of his victims were off Foster's bowling. It was said that he was the only wicket-keeper who could take the left-arm bowling of Foster, whose amazing swing and speed off the pitch rendered him as much a problem to his own wicket-keepers as to the opposing batsmen. And this was during a period when there were a number of county wicket-keepers of Test match calibre playing regularly. In addition to Smith, there was Strudwick of Surrey, Huish of Kent, Dolphin of Yorkshire, Murrell of Middlesex, Humphries of Derbyshire, Buswell of Northamptonshire, Butt of Sussex, Oates of Nottinghamshire, and Brown of Hampshire – when he wasn't bowling!

Even more exciting for the young "Tiger" Smith – he was 25 in 1911 – than the winning of the Championship was the 1911-12 tour of Australia, when he was chosen as understudy to Strudwick. In the event it was Smith who kept wicket in all the Test matches, except the first; probably because he could take Foster better and read his signals to the wicket-keeper – one of which, a change in step during the run up, to indicate the slower ball, was spotted by an Australian tram conductor.

England lost the first Test. The turning point of the series was perhaps Barnes' opening spell of four wickets for 1 run in five overs in Australia's first innings of the second Test. In this innings Smith took three catches. England won the series 4-1 and Smith had eight catches and one stumping in his four Tests. Informed opinion has it that he excelled himself in the second Test. "Well, you'd got to be good at Melbourne, with forty thousand people watching you," he reminisced.

In the third Test Smith stumped the left-handed Clem Hill first ball of Foster's bowling when Hill was attempting a glide. P. F. Warner described the execution of this pre-arranged strategem as "one of the technical masterpieces of the game". Smith always contended that he did it again in the second innings, with Hill out by "about twelve inches", but the umpire thought otherwise and Hill went on to make 98.

During the ill-fated, rain-ridden Triangular Tournament of 1912, "Tiger" Smith played in all six Tests involving England, and he played in one more Test against South Africa in 1913. In the last two seasons before the first war he kept to the brilliant bowling of Percy Jeeves during the latter's brief meteoric career for Warwickshire.

When cricket was resumed after the war "Tiger" Smith was 33. He continued to play for Warwickshire until 1930. His wicket-keeping was never less than competent, and he became a sound, attacking, opening batsman. Two amazing games he played in during this period were against Hampshire in 1922 and Sussex in 1925.

In the first of these games, Hampshire were dismissed for 15 in their first innings. Following on 207 behind, they made 520 and won the match easily. Had "Tiger" stopped a ball on the leg side that went for four byes and had another fielder held a catch – the ball went through his hands and travelled to the boundary – Hampshire would have been all out for 7 in their first innings.

In the Sussex match, Warwickshire were set 391 to win in just under five hours and scored 392 for one in four hours and a quarter. All three Warwickshire batsmen made centuries: J. H. Parsons (now Canon J. H. Parsons) 124, "Tiger" Smith 139 not out and the Hon. F. S. G. Calthorpe 109 not out. Although this was not his highest score for Warwickshire – he made 177 against Derbyshire in 1927 and 173 against Kent the following year – "Tiger" always considered this innings against Sussex was the best he ever played.

In 1930 Smith retired as a player and went on the list of first-class umpires, standing in several Test matches. There was a brief period of coaching at Worcester; he was an air-raid warden during the Second World War, and in 1946 he became senior coach at Edgbaston, a position he filled with distinction until Tom Dollery succeeded him in 1955. "Tiger", now 69, continued to supervise the indoor cricket school, where he was still taking an active part up to 1970, although he had gradually handed over the reins to Derief Taylor.

By the mid-1950s he had become almost a legendary figure. "The gatemen are beginning to know me now!" was one of his favourite quips. "Is 'Tiger' watching?" members would ask one another during the course of the day's play. More often than not he *was* watching, from his seat in the corner of the players' dining-room. Often he would be joined by his team-mates of the 1920s: Norman Kilner, "Danny" Mayer, Jack Parsons, George Paine, Jack Smart; sometimes W. H. Ashdown, the great Kent cricketer of that period, would join the party from his home in Rugby.

It wasn't only with the players of the past that "Tiger" Smith discussed the game in its myriad facets. Cricketers from many counties – especially, says Leslie Deakins, since the death of C. B. Fry in 1956 – would come to "Tiger" with their batting problems. "Let's see you in the middle first," he would say, and afterwards he would diagnose the trouble. Almost invariably, because of high intelligence, experience, and a knowledge of bone and muscle structure acquired in his first war experience with the St John Ambulance Brigade, plus that indefinable intuitive flair that only the truly gifted teacher commands, he would put his finger on what was wrong and indicate the remedy. In very recent years Mike Brearley has been one of those who testified to "Tiger" Smith's remarkable powers in this direction.

He was a big, robust man, tall for a wicket-keeper, with wonderful agility in his prime. He had more than a little in common with that "kind and manly Alfred Mynn" of a former generation. Always a fighter, he had a razor-sharp sense of humour and loved "the rigour of the game". "It was 'Good morning!' before we started and 'How's that!' for the rest of the day", he said of one hard fought contest.

Once he was asked who was the best captain he had served under and he replied: "Well, any captain's a good one if you're winning." After reflection he added that F. S. G. Calthorpe was the happiest captain he had known.

He loved thinking about cricket, and in particular about the craft of wicket-keeping. In assessing Bert Oldfield and "Dick" Lilley as the greatest wicket-keepers who have ever played, he referred to "an enthusiasm greater even than dedication". He was too modest to claim that attribute for himself, but others would claim it for him.

When Field Marshal Slim spoke of the Birmingham spirit of "resilience, adaptability and a cheerful refusal to lie down under difficulties", he had summed up "Tiger" Smith in a nutshell. The seventeen-year-old boy from Benacre Street who had lost the top of two fingers in a works accident, and who asked the Edgbaston authorities for a job as wicket-keeper, possessed these qualities in good measure. Which was why he played for England at the age of 25.

SMITH, THOMAS PETER BROMLY, who died in France as a result of a brain haemorrhage following a fall while on holiday on August 4, 1967, aged 58, played with distinction as a professional all-rounder for Essex from 1929 to 1951. In that time he made 10,170 runs, average 17.98, and took 1,697 wickets – more than any other Essex bowler – for 26.63 runs each. A capital leg-break and googly exponent, he never lost his length even when at times receiving heavy punishment, as when H. T. Barlett hit him for 28 in an over in the Gentlemen v Players match at Lord's in 1938.

In 1933, Peter Smith arrived at The Oval prepared to play for England against the West Indies, only to learn that the telegram informing him of his choice had been sent by a hoaxer. Thirteen years later he did play for his country, against India on the Surrey ground, and he also took part in two Tests with Australia and one with New Zealand when a member of W. R. Hammond's MCC team in 1946-47. Though meeting with little success generally on that tour, he did achieve one notable feat, for his nine wickets for 121 against New South Wales at Sydney is still the best innings-analysis by any MCC bowler in Australia. On three other occasions he dismissed nine batsmen in an innings – for 97 runs against Middlesex at Colchester in 1947, in which game he returned match-figures of 16 for 215, for 117 v Nottinghamshire at Southend and 108 v Kent at Maidstone, both in 1948.

The summer of 1947 was a memorable one for Smith. In scoring 1,063 runs, average 23.66, and taking 182 wickets at 27.13 apiece, he completed "the double" for the only time in his career. Furthermore, he hit 163 – the best of his eight centuries – against Derbyshire at Chesterfield, the highest first-class innings in history by a batsman going in at No. 11, he and F. H. Vigar (114 not out) putting on 218 for the last wicket, which remains a record for Essex. Smith's total of wickets that year is also the largest by an Essex bowler in one season.

SMITHSON, GERALD A., who died suddenly on September 6, 1970, aged 43, played for Yorkshire in 1946 and 1947, his highest innings for the county being 169 against Leicestershire at Leicester in the second year. Conscripted as a "Bevin Boy" in the mines after the war, he received special permission, after his case had been debated in the House of Commons, to tour the West Indies with the MCC team of 1947-48, taking part in two Test matches. His picture appeared in *Wisden* 1948, page 38. In 1951 he joined Leicestershire, with whom he remained for six seasons, of which his best was that of 1952 when, by attractive left-hand batting and the aid of two centuries, he hit 1,264 runs, average 28.08. He afterwards served as coach, first at Caterham School and then at Abingdon School, and between 1957 and 1962 he also assisted Hertfordshire.

STEVENS, GREVILLE THOMAS SCOTT, who died on September 19, 1970, aged 69, was beyond question one of the outstanding amateurs of his time. A fine batsman and bowler of leg-breaks and googlies, he came to the fore when in the XI at University College School from 1917 to 1919. He attracted special attention in the last year with an innings of 466 in a house match, and that season he was accorded the signal honour for a schoolboy of inclusion in the Gentlemen's team against the Players at Lord's.

Middlesex readily appreciated his worth and they called upon his services in 1919. Upon his début in first-class cricket, he took 10 Hampshire wickets at Lord's for 136 runs, and the next summer he helped Middlesex to win the County Championship. Not surprisingly, he gained his Blue as a Freshman at Oxford in 1920 and he remained a valued member of the University side for the following three years, being captain in 1922. In 1923 he bore a major part in an overwhelming Oxford victory in an innings with 227 runs to spare over Cambridge. Caught on a pitch affected by sunshine after heavy rain, the Light Blues were dismissed in their first innings for 59, Stevens taking six wickets for 20 runs. That season, too, he shone brightly as a batsman, hitting 182 – his highest innings – for Oxford against the West Indies and 122 for the Gentlemen at Lord's.

Stevens took part in 10 Test matches for England. He helped them regain the Ashes from H. L. Collins's Australians in 1926; visited South Africa with small success in 1922 and 1927 and played twice in the West Indies in 1929, when he took 10 wickets for 195 runs in the first of the representative games.

A batsman who, considering his short back-lift, hit with surprising power, he twice exceeded 1,000 runs in a season and in all first-class cricket registered 10,361 runs, including 12 centuries, at an average of 29.69, took 676 wickets for 26.55 runs each and, as a superb fieldsman close to the wicket, held 200 catches. He would doubtless have far eclipsed this record had he been able to spare more time from business for cricket.

STRUDWICK, HERBERT, who died suddenly on February 14, 1970, a few days after his 90th birthday, held the world record for most dismissals in a career by a wicket-keeper. One of his greatest and assuredly one of the most popular players of his time, he helped to get rid of 1,493 batsmen, 71 of them in Test matches, and he established another world record which still stands by holding 1,235 catches. His stumpings numbered 258. He set up a third record in 1903 when taking 71 catches and bringing off 20 stumpings, but Fred Huish, of Kent, surpassed this eight years later.

Strudwick figured regularly behind the stumps for Surrey for 25 years and becoming scorer afterwards, served the county altogether for 60 years. He played 28 times for England between 1911 and 1926 during the period when Australia and South Africa were their only Test match opponents and would doubtless have been chosen more often had he not been contemporary with A. A. Lilley, of Warwickshire, a better batsman. Four times he toured Australia, in 1903-04, 1911-12, 1920-21 and 1924-25 and visted South Africa with MCC in 1909-10 and 1913-14. In addition, he was a frequent member of Players teams against Gentlemen. For England at Johannesburg in 1913-14, he dismissed seven South African batsmen in the match. His best performance in a single innings was six catches against Sussex at The Oval in 1904 and in a match eight victims (seven caught, one stumped) against Essex at Leyton in 1904.

No more genuine sportsman, in every sense of the word, than the teetotal, non-smoking Strudwick ever took the field for Surrey. An idol of the Surrey crowd, he was always ready to proffer helpful advice to young players. He never appealed unless sure in his own mind that a batsmen was out, and such was his keenness to save runs that he was frequently known to chase a ball to the boundary. Sir H. D. G. Leveson Gower, the former Oxford, Surrey and England captain, once wrote: "When you walk on to a certain cricket ground and you find Strudwick behind the wicket, you feel that you will not only get full value for your money, but you will participate in the cheerfulness that his presence always lends to the day."

In an article, "From Dr Grace to Peter May", in the 1959 *Wisden*, hailed by the critics as one of the best published by "The Cricketers' Bible" for many years, "Struddy", as he was affectionately known throughout the cricket world, described how hard was life as a professional cricketer in his young days. Then, one dare not stand down because of injury for fear of losing a place in the side and consequent loss of pay. Compared with that of today, the equipment of wicket-keepers was flimsy and the men behind the stumps took a lot of punishment, especially as, on the far from perfect pitches, it was difficult to gauge how the ball would come through. The article mentioned that F. Stedman, Strudwick's predecessor in the Surrey side, habitually protected his chest with a South Western Railway timetable stuffed into his shirt, and on one occasion, after receiving a more than usually heavy blow, he remarked to a nearby team-mate: "I shall have to catch a later train to-night. That one knocked off the 7.30!"

It is of interest to note that a lady set "Struddy" on the path to becoming the world's most celebrated wicket-keeper. As a choir-boy at Mitcham, his birthplace, he took part in matches under the supervision of the daughter of the vicar, a Miss Wilson. Then about 10 years old, Strudwick habitually ran in from cover to the wicket to take returns from the field. Observing how efficiency he did this, Miss Wilson once said: "You ought to be a wicket-keeper." From that point, Strudwick became one.

Not in the ordinary way regarded as much of a batsman, he hit 93 in ninety minutes, easily his largest innings, against Essex at The Oval in 1913, when he and H. S. Harrison shared an eighth-wicket partnership of 134. In the second Test match at Melbourne during the Australian tour of J. W. H. T. Douglas's 1920-21 team, he distinguished himself with innings of 21 not out and 24.

Honours bestowed upon "Struddy" included honorary membership of MCC in 1949 and life membership of Surrey, whose oil-paintings of celebrities in the Long Room at The Oval include one of him.

Tributes to Strudwick included:

A. E. R. Gilligan, under whose captaincy he played in Australia: Not only was he a magnificent wicket-keeper, but he set a fine example to the rest of the side, always being first to be ready to play. He was 100 per cent in every way.

Wilfred Rhodes, Yorkshire and England: 'Struddy was above all a wonderful man and a great player. I telephoned him just before his 90th birthday and we had a long chat over old days. I went with him on his first MCC tour to Australia in 1903-04 and then to South Africa. We were great friends.

S. C. Griffith, MCC Secretary and a former England wicket-keeper: This wonderful man and great cricketer taught me, when 14, all I ever knew about wicket-keeping at the cricket school he helped to run in South London. He was the best coach I have ever known and from that time I always numbered him among my dearest friends. Apart from his ability, he was one of the outstanding figures and personalities of the game.

Herbert Sutcliffe, Yorkshire and England: He was first of all a gentleman and a sportsman and in his capabilities as fine a player as Bertie Oldfield, the great Australian wicket-keeper. I played both with and against Strudddy and rated him absolutely first-class in every way.

HERBERT STRUDWICK

Born at Mitcham, January 28, 1880; died February 13, 1970.

By Sir Neville Cardus

Herbert Strudwick (hereinafter to be known, as he was affectionately always known, as "Struddy") served Surrey County Cricket faithfully for some sixty years; wicket-keeper for thirty years, then as a diligent scorer. He died a few days after his ninetieth birthday, and with his death a whole and lustrous chapter of cricket history at The Oval was ended.

Amongst wicket-keepers in my own experience of the game, I count Struddy with the best, in the company of "Tiger" Smith, Duckworth, Ames, "Jock" Cameron, the South African, W. A. Oldfield, Tallon, Cornford, Godfrey Evans and our present and gifted Knott. But before all else, I count Struddy as a man – in fact, to use discarded language nowadays, as a gentleman.

Few cricketers – and there have been many of rare warmth and character, off and on the field – have shared Struddy's gentle way of showing his friendliness. He was modest, often shy. With just a look in his eye he would greet you in passing; yet in a moment, he would find in you your wave-length of affection.

As wicket-keeper he was courteous as Oldfield himself. If he appealed for a catch at the wicket, it was an *appeal*, a question. An eappeal emanating from, say, the mouth of George Duckworth was a denunciation of a batsman's delinquency, as order, even a command to the umpire.

Struddy seemed to appeal almost apologetically, as though saying to the errant batsman, "So sorry. Pains me as much as yourself. But Law 42 must be observed. Better luck next time." Which reminds me that Struddy in his prime before the first world war thought nothing of standing up to the fastest of bowlers like Neville Knox and Bill Hitch. The batsman only advanced from the crease at their peril. Struddy was part and parcel, image and embodiment of Surrey cricket, in a hey-day of the county's and The Oval's renown, when Hayward, Hobbs, Hayes, Holland and Hitch strained East-Ender's powers of the accurate response to the aspirate.

I have heard it said that wicket-keeping was an easier job technically in Struddy's period than it is today – wickets were truer in texture for one thing, when the attack concentrated on the off side, giving the keeper a closer view of the ball than he can have if the ball veers to leg, the batsman's body impeding the view.

It is true that The Oval pitches were invariably firm in Struddy's high noon. Also they were very fast, enabling bounce. Struddy told me of a severe bruise he suffered from a good-length ball from J. N. Crawford, fast-medium through the air, but after pitching, it lifted explosively, and nearly cracked Struddy's breast-bone. "I once moved to the off side to take Jack Crawford, but the ball broke back inches, missed the leg stump and went for four byes."

How did Tom Richardson achieve his famous breakback, fast and acutely angular? Body action, explained Struddy. Struddy had to cope with "sticky" wickets, not generally known nowadays. The marled polished surface of lawn in dry weather became viciously collaborative with spin after rain and sun. Wickets were not covered in Struddy's years. "Razor" Smith, on a "sticky" wicket, could pitch, right fingered, on the leg stump and miss the off, Struddy taking the ball shoulder high. In 1910, "Razor" Smith took 247 wickets in the season, average 13.05. But nobody ever dreamed of asking him to play for England. The currency had not then been devalued.

Struddy played 28 times for England, between 1909 and 1926. In his career he was the cause of no fewer than 1,493 batsmen's dismissals, to use the beautiful formal phrase of the Victorians. He was one of the England team in Australia in 1911-12, 1920-21 and 1924-25. Twice he went to South Africa, with MCC teams, 1909-10, 1913-14.

It is interesting to recall the players in Struddy's first England XI v South Africa, at Johannesburg, January 1909 – Hobbs, Rhodes, Denton, F. L. Fane, Woolley, Thompson (G. J.), M. C. Bird, Buckenham, H. D. G. Leveson Gower, G. H. Simpson-Hayward, and Struddy himself. A curious fact of this England XI is that Simpson-Hayward bowled "lobs", underarm spin; and in this Johannesburg Test took six for 43 and two for 59, confounding batsmen such as Aubrey Faulkner, J. H. Sinclair, J. W. Zulch and L. A. Stricker, each as skilful as the next best of 1971. Faulkner, in fact, was a truly great batsman. Struddy always remembered Simpson-Hayward's off-spin (yes, off-spin from a right-handed lob bowler), as well as his flight and leg-break. It was later in South Africa that Struddy performed his most skilful and versatile work in Test matches. This happened in 1913-14, when in the five Tests he held fifteen catches and had eight stumpings.

The point of this achievement is that it was done coping with Sydney Barnes on a *matting* wicket. Barnes caused the ball to go through all manner of gyrations, off-spin and leg-spin, rising sharply from a good length, the pace from the mat red hot. Barnes in four Tests (he did not play in the fifth) took 49 wickets, at 10.93 each. He was quite unplayable, yet Herbert Taylor, for South Africa, scored 508 runs, average 50.80, a miracle of resourceful batsmanship against the most dangerous bowling ever.

As resourceful as Taylor in front of the wicket was Struddy behind. He was for a stumper, the right height. He was quick on his feet without demonstration and waste of physical energy. On fast grounds in England, the attack, as I have mentioned, invariably concentrated on, or outside, the off-stump, with no fieldsman behind the wicket on the leg-side. Struddy would often be seen in the swift chase (despite his flapping pads) of a hit to leg, throwing off his gloves, picking up on the run, and returning the ball rapidly and accurately. I once described him, in a report, as amongst the best outfields in the land.

On his first tour of Australia, 1903-04, he did not appear in any of the Tests and his second tour, 1911-12, engaged him in only one Test, the first of the rubber. "Tiger" Smith was then the brilliant keeper to Barnes and Frank Foster. Struddy's subsequent two visits to Australia were with unfortunate teams, captained in 1920-21 by J. W. H. T. Douglas, and by Arthur Gilligan in 1924-25. Douglas's contingent lost all five Tests, each played to a finish (as, I think, *all* Tests should be played; for, from the bowling of the first ball, we know that one team is doomed, with no chance of escape; every ball a nail in somebody's coffin!).

In the 1924-25 rubber Australia won four games, against an England XI containing Hobbs, Sutcliffe, Woolley, J. W. Hearne, Hendren, A. P. F. Chapman, Roy Kilner, J. W. H. T. Douglas, A. E. R. Gilligan, Maurice Tate and Struddy. He was in the great kill of the ancient enemy at Kennington Oval in August, 1926. England and Chapman regained the Ashes after years. On a turning pitch Hobbs and Sutcliffe amassed 172 for England's first wicket in the second innings, after Australia had led by 22. More than 100,000 watched this famous victory. Rhodes, called back to International cricket in his forty-ninth year, took six wickets in the two innings for 79. So the curtain fell on a wonderful career splendidly, even as it did on Strudwick's – as a player.

In the scorer's box, Struddy was as vigilant as ever – nobody in those days to help with the statistics. His influence on the field did not diminish in helpfulness when he was obliged to submit to increase of years. Many a young cricketer was all the better for his advice, which was never pompously or schoolmasterly given. He was a dedicated cricketer, a dedicated man, generous in praise of the Masters he had grown up with, season after season, "from W. G. Grace to Peter May".

He was always certain that Tom Richardson was the fastest and best of all fast bowlers. (In four consecutive seasons here Richardson's wickets amounted to 1,005.) Struddy would tell a rare story of a tribute to Richardson, from none other than Lockwood, regarded by Ranjitsinjhi as the "very greatest" of fast bowlers. Struddy met Lockwood, now aged and in a wheel-chair, and asked, "Bill, who was the best fast bowler of your time?" And Lockwood unhesitatingly pronounced the name of Richardson. "What about yourself?" asked Struddy, whereat Lockwood shook his head, saying, "No, I wasn't in the same parish as Tom, never mind the same street."

Naturally, Struddy regarded Jack Hobbs as the first of all batsmen of his acquaintance. He was a friend of Sir Jack, a close and abiding friend. I can say nothing better than that of Struddy of Surrey, England and Kennington Oval.

THOMSON, ARTHUR ALEXANDER, who died in hospital near Lord's on June 2, 1968, aged 74, was one of the best known and best loved writers on cricket. "A.A." or "Tommy" was born at Harrogate on April 7, 1894, and educated at Harrogate Grammar School and King's College, London. His early thoughts of entering the scholastic profession were interrupted by the First World War, when he joined the West Yorkshire Regiment and served in France and Mesopotamia. His early boyhood in Yorkshire had formed the subject of his brilliant autobiographical novel, *The Exquisite Burden* (1935), re-issued in 1963. He wrote nearly 60 books in all, including plays, novels, verse, humour and travel books, and in 1953, with *Cricket My Pleasure*, there began his long series of cricket books in which his buoyant philosophy of the game, with all its comedy and character, shone through in rich prose and mellow phrases. There then followed *Cricket My Happiness* (1954). *Pavilioned in Splendour* (1956), *The Great Cricketer* (a biography of Dr W. G. Grace) (1957 and 1968), *Odd Men In* (1958), *Hirst and Rhodes* (1959), *Cricket Bouquet* (1961), *Cricket: The Golden Ages* (1961), *Hutton and Washbrook* (1963), *Cricket: The Great Captains* (1965), *Cricket: The Wars of the Roses* (1967), and *Cricketers of My Times* (1967). He also contributed some delightful articles to *Wisden*. Probably no cricket author since Sir Neville Cardus was in his prime had a closer following. Cricket, he once declared, gave him more unalloyed pleasure over a longer period than any single thing.

He had an enormous sense of fun and a perpetual twinkle in his eye, and when, in 1958, he started writing cricket for *The Times*, and then rugger in the winter, his presence in press-boxes throughout the country could guarantee a warm fund of stories, all told with an expressive fervour, that made up for any deficiencies on the field. As an after-dinner speaker at cricket gatherings he was one of the most original and popular of the last decade, and since 1963 he had been President of the Cricket Society. During the Second World War he worked first at the Air Ministry and then as a lecturer with the Ministry of Information. In the 1966 Birthday Honours List, he was awarded the MBE for services to sports writing.

TITLEY, UEL ADDISON, who died on November 11, 1973, aged 67, appeared for the XI while at Rugby, but did not get his colours. He went up to Cambridge and for some years afterwards held an appointment in Brazil. He wrote on cricket for some years for *The Times*, but was better known as the Rugby correspondent for that newspaper. His excellent style and occasional flashes of humour earned him great respect in the football world, but his biggest achievement was the compilation of the *History of the Rugby Football Union* published in their centenary year, 1971. His unusual first name was given by his father, Samuel Titley, who said: "Everybody calls me Sam. The boy can have the other half."

WATT, ALAN EDWARD, a noted fast bowler and fearsome hitter who played for Kent between 1929 and 1939, died in Pembury hospital on February 3, 1974, aged 66. He kept the Star Inn at Matfield. Born at Limpsfield Chart, near Westerham, Watt went to Westerham School and was a bull-dog breed of cricketer. In first-class cricket he scored 4,079 runs, average 13.60 and he took 609 wickets at 28.81 runs apiece, but mere figures could not convey the delight he gave as he approached the batting crease. In those days Watt formed a trio with "Big" Jim Smith (Middlesex) and Arthur Wellard (Somerset) famed for hitting sixes.

Watt excelled with the straight drive and the pull. For his highest score, 96 against MCC at Lord's in 1932, he went in number 10, and hit one 6 and fourteen 4s, all in sixty-five minutes. Against Leicestershire at Maidstone in 1933 he struck 89 out of 124 in fifty-five minutes, including four 6s and eleven 4s. In that historic finish at Dover in 1937 when Kent set a record, which still stands, by scoring 219 in seventy-one minutes to beat Gloucestershire, Watt, 39 not out, gave such an amazing display that the last 51 runs came in ten minutes and Watt finished the contest with a straight 6 out of the ground. In 1937, also, at Folkestone, for Over Thirty against Under Thirty, he hit 77 in thirty-five minutes, striking four 6s and five 4s.

Tall and strong, Watt entered the Kent side when Tich Freeman was at his zenith and between 1928 and 1935 and for eight consecutive seasons took at least 200 wickets each year, so Watt was not required to do much more than see the shine off the ball. His best season with the ball was in 1937 when he took 108 wickets for 27.09 runs each. After Freeman retired, Watt and Leslie Todd formed a very effective opening attack during the four summers that preceded the war.

R. C. Robertson-Glasgow wrote: "Alan Watt of Kent is a cricketer for all the day. He is never known to tire, never willingly relieved of his bowling which comes very sharply from the pitch. He can swing the ball awkwardly late from leg, does not pitch just a little short for safety and fields to his own bowling with a fierce agility that is a joy to watch. He is impervious to rain. Such a man was born to be a hitter. Coming in at number 10, he hit me five or six times from the middle wicket to the square leg boundary. Suddenly, he played a relatively calm stroke, missed, and was stumped. This was difficult to understand. I asked the square leg umpire what had happened. 'Well, you see,' he answered, 'he had both feet off the ground at once'."

WAUGH, ALEC, brother of Evelyn, died in Florida on September 3, 1981, aged 83. A great lover of cricket, he was "Bobby Southcott" in A. G. Macdonnell's *England, their England*, and for 50 years seldom missed a Test match at Lord's.

WELLS, CYRIL MOWBRAY, a former Cambridge cricket and Rugby football Blue, died on August 22, 1963, aged 92. A member of the Dulwich XI from 1886 to 1890, inclusive, he was captain in the last year and when going up to Cambridge got his Blue as a Freshman. He played three times against Oxford and though achieving little in batting, he bore a big part in victory by 266 runs in 1893 when taking seven wickets for 66 runs. In that game he was concerned in a memorable incident that in all probability led to an alteration a few years later in the law governing the follow-on.

At that time the side 80 runs behind on first innings had to follow on and in this match Oxford, in reply to a total of 182, lost nine wickets for 95 when T. S. B. Wilson and W. H. Brain became associated. Three more runs were added, taking Oxford to within 84 of the Cambridge score, when a consultation between the batsmen suggested that the Dark Blues, in order that Cambridge might bat last on a pitch likely to crumble, intended to throw away their remaining wicket. Sensing the drift of the conversation, Wells decided to frustrate the plan. He immediately bowled a no-ball wide to the boundary and followed a little later with a round-arm delivery that also reached the ring, thus destroying Oxford's chance of following on. This action led to MCC increasing the deficit which meant a follow-on from 80 to 120, but when, three years later, E. B. Shine, in very similar circumstances, gave away 12 runs to prevent Oxford from following their innings, further consideration of the question became necessary. So in 1900 the Law was amended, leaving the side leading by 150 with the option of enforcing the follow-on.

Wells assisted Surrey as an amateur from 1890 to 1893 but appeared for Middlesex, the county of his birth, from 1895 to 1909. He represented Gentlemen v Players in 1892, 1893 and 1901. A free-hitting batsman, he also bowled right arm slow-medium with a deceptive delivery. He generally bowled off-breaks, but sometimes employed the leg-break and took many wickets with a ball which went straight through.

Wells played for Cambridge in the University Rugby matches of 1891 and 1892, first as full-back and then as half-back, and was half-back for England in six matches between 1893 and 1897. He also appeared for the Harlequins and Middlesex.

WHISTLER, GENERAL SIR LASHMER GORDON, who died in Cambridge Military Hospital, Aldershot, on July 4, 1963, aged 64, played for Harrow in the second of the season's "unofficial" one-day war-time matches with Eton in 1916. He scored 8 and 25 and brought off two catches. At one time it looked as though this match would not take place. Breaking bounds and other offences had resulted in half-holidays at Harrow being suspended. What was described as "a quite unpardonable comment" upon this decision was written across the School Rules in the yard and as the miscreant could not be discovered, the match was cancelled. Only at a late hour on the night before the game did the Headmaster yield to urgent representations and give permission for the team to travel to Eton. The whole-day holiday to the rest of the School was stopped.

WOOD, ARTHUR, who died on April 2, 1973, aged 74, played for Yorkshire from 1927 till 1946 and was first choice as wicket-keeper between 1927 and 1939. He helped in the dismissal of 848 batsmen – 603 caught and 245 stumped – and, a useful batsman, scored 8,579 runs for the county at an average of 21.13. His best season as a run-getter was that of 1935 when he hit 1,087, average 36.23, and put together the only century of his career, 123 not out off the Worcestershire bowling at Bramall Lane.

He gained his first Test cap a few days before his 40th birthday and I had something to do with him receiving the honour. While reporting a match at Lord's, I was sent a message in the Press Box from Sir Pelham Warner, then chairman of the England Selectors, asking me to go to the Pavilion to see him. This I did and Sir Pelham told me that he was worried because Leslie Ames was indisposed and unable to play at The Oval. He asked me if I could recommend a wicket-keeper-batsmen as replacement. At once I suggested Wood and, sure enough, he got the place. That was the match against Australia in which Len Hutton hit his record-breaking 364. Wood got 53, but the score had exceeded 500 by the time he went in. Noted for his sense of humour, he said when congratulated upon his batting success: "I was always good in a crisis."

Most celebrated of the stories about Wood concerned the game at Sheffield in 1935 when H. B. Cameron, the South African wicket-keeper, punished the Yorkshire and England slow left-arm bowler, H. Verity, for 30 runs in one over. At the end of that over, Wood told Verity: "You've got him in two minds. He doesn't know whether to hit you for six or four."

WOODFULL, WILLIAM MALDON, who collapsed and died while playing golf on a course near Brisbane on August 11, 1965, aged 67, played as opening batsman in 35 Test matches for Australia and captained them in 25. Known as "The Rock" because of his imperturbable temperament, he possessed immensely strong defence and great patience. Yet, though the back-lift of his bat was very short indeed, his weight and strength of wrist enabled him to score at a faster rate than many a more attractive player.

During a Test career extending from 1926 to 1934, he hit 2,300 runs for an average of 46.00, the highest of his seven centuries being 161 against South Africa at Melbourne in 1931–32. He shared nine three-figure stands in Test matches, three with his fellow-Victorian, W. H. Ponsford, during the tour of England in 1930 – 162 at Lord's, 159 at The Oval and 106 at Old Trafford. In all first-class cricket he hit 49 centuries, the highest of which was 284 for an Australian XI against a New Zealand XI at Auckland in 1927-28. Three times he toured England and on each occasion he well exceeded 1,000 runs. In 1926, after making 201 against Essex at Leyton in his first innings on English soil, he headed the batting figures with an aggregate of 1,809 (eight centuries), average 58.35; in 1930, as captain, he made 1,435 runs (six centuries), average 57.36 and four years later when again leading the side 1,268 runs (three centuries), average 52.83.

For Victoria, Bill Woodfull registered 16 centuries, of which the biggest was 275, not out, from the bowling of A. P. F. Chapman's MCC Team at Melbourne in 1928-29. His most prolific opening partnership for the State was 375 with Ponsford against New South Wales in 1926–27 at Melbourne.

Woodfull led Australia against D. R. Jardine's team during the notorious "body-line" tour in Australia in 1932-33. Though he achieved little against this menacing form of bowling in the first two Test matches, four innings bringing him no more than 43 runs, he displayed such grit and determination in the remaining three that he put together innings of 73, not out, 67 and 67.

He achieved distinction in another field. He was Headmaster of Melbourne High School and in the New Year's Honours list of 1963, he received the OBE for his services to education.

His quiet, unassuming demeanour won him respect and affection from team-mates and opponents alike, and tributes to him included:

R. W. V. Robins (former Middlesex and England captain): As a man he was very kindly and as a batsman he had a wonderful defence. Only once did I have the distinction of getting him out – at Lord's in the second Test in 1930. By then he had made 155 and I think he fell through sheer exhaustion!

H. Sutcliffe (former Yorkshire and England opening batsman): First-class as a man and a great fighter. As a batsman he always took such a lot of getting out and as a captain he was a fine leader.

Sir Donald Bradman (former Australian captain): He was a great gentleman, a fine citizen and an ornament to the game of cricket.

FRANK WOOLLEY

Born at Tonbridge, Kent, May 27, 1887

died in Halifax, Nova Scotia, October 18, 1978

By Norman Preston

Frank Edward Woolley, who died aged 91, was beyond doubt one of the finest and most elegant left-handed all-rounders of all time. In a first-class career extending from 1906 to 1938 he hit 58,969 runs – a total exceeded only by Sir Jack Hobbs – including 145 centuries, to average 40.75; he took 2,068 wickets for 19.85 runs each, and he held 1,015 catches, mainly at slip, a record which remains unsurpassed.

Even more impressive than the number of runs Woolley amassed was the manner in which he made them. Standing well over six feet, he was a joy to watch. He played an eminently straight bat, employed his long reach to full advantage, and used his feet in a manner nowadays rarely seen. His timing of the ball approached perfection and he generally dealt surely with all types of bowling. Master of all the strokes, he was at his best driving, cutting, and turning the ball off his legs. He was described by Sydney Pardon as the cleanest driver since F. G. J. Ford, but he often started badly and there was something wanting in his defence. As a bowler he made good use of his height and bowled with a graceful easy swing.

As a small boy he was always to be found on the Tonbridge Cricket Ground, and his natural ability as batsman and bowler attracted so much attention that, in 1903, his was engaged to take part in the morning practice and play in a match or two in the afternoon if required. In the following year he became a regular member of the Tonbridge Ground staff, which in those days was the official Kent nursery. When given his first chance in the Kent XI in 1906, he was almost unknown to the public, and his all-round form in his third match, against Surrey at The Oval, came as nothing less than a relevation. To begin with, he took three Surrey wickets, clean bowling Hayward, Hayes, and Goatly. He then made 72, and when Surrey batted again he took five wickets for 80 runs. Finally he scored 23 not out, helping to win a wonderful game for Kent by one wicket. The match established his reputation.

When Frank Woolley announced his retirement in 1938, I spent an afternoon with him at his home in Hildenborough where he talked about "My happy cricket life". In his first season with Kent they won the County Championship for the first time and altogether between 1906 and 1913 they were top four times. Now let Woolley speak for himself as he told his story to me.

"Those were the great days when plenty of amateurs could spare time for cricket. I do not believe there are so many good players in the game now as before the [First World] War. In the old days we were probably educated in cricket in a far more serious way than now. For the purpose of giving the younger people my idea of the difference, I will put up Walter Hammond, England's captain, as an example. Before 1914 there were something like 30 players up to his standard and he would have been in the England team only if at the top of his form. I make these remarks without casting the slightest reflection on Hammond. He is a grand player and one of the greatest all-round cricketers since the War – in fact, the greatest.

"I doubt whether English cricket has really recovered from the effects of the War. You see, we missed half a generation and since then young men have found many other ways of occupying their leisure hours. Still, I believe it is only a passing phase and cricket will one day produce an abundance of great players."

Unfortunately for cricket, within a year England was plunged into another war, and in my opinion the game in this country had only just shown signs of getting on its feet again with a stream of fine young players coming through, notably in the county of Kent. But to return to the Woolley interview as he saw the game 40 years ago.

"There is little wrong with the game itself. Just a question of the way it is played. It is amazing how the public steadfastly refuse to attend the third day of a match when so often the last day produces the best and most exciting cricket.

"Touching on a personal subject I have been asked if I can explain why I was dismissed so many times in the 'nineties'. The statisticians inform me that I was out 35 times between 90 and 99 and I am also told that I am credited with 89 ducks. With regard to those 'nineties', I can honestly say that with me it was never a case of the 'nervous nineties'. Lots of times I was out through forcing the game. We were never allowed to play for averages in the Kent side or take half an hour or more to get the last ten runs under normal conditions. We always had to play the game and play for the team. It is a Kent tradition.

"As a matter of fact I consider the two finest innings I ever played were in the second Test against Australia in 1921 when I was out for 95 and 93. I don't think I ever worked harder at any match during my career to get runs as I did then, nor did I ever have to face in one game such consistently fast bowlers as the Australian pair, Gregory and McDonald. Square cuts which ordinarily would have flashed to the boundary earned only two, and I believe that those two innings would have been worth 150 apiece in a county match.

I was not depressed when they got me out. I have always taken my dismissals as part of the game. In the first innings I was in the 'eighties' when I was joined by the last man, Jack Durston. It was my own fault completely that I lost my wicket. Mailey bowled me a full toss to the off; I walked down the pitch, stepping to the on to force the ball past extra cover, I missed it, and that fine wicket-keeper, H. Carter, eagerly accepted the opportunity to stump me. I was rather unlucky in the second innings when again I fell to Mailey. The ball stuck in his hand and dropped halfway on the leg side. I hit it pretty plumb between square leg and mid-on and just there was standing 'Stalky' Hendry. As I made the shot he jumped in the air and up went his right hand. The ball hit him, I think, on the wrist, and he lost his balance. The ball went up ten feet and as he was lying on the ground it fell in his lap and he caught it. He was the only man on the leg side and I think the shot would have carried for six. It was a marvellous catch.

"It is often argued that left-handed batsmen have an advantage compared with the right-handers. I do not agree. When the turf is worn the right-hand leg-break bowlers and left-arm slow bowlers are able to pitch the ball into the footholes of the bowlers who have operated at the other end. Right-handed batsmen can let these balls hit their pads, but the left-handers must use their bats. Perhaps the new [1937] lbw rule has not helped us there, but the amended law does not worry me, though in my opinion it has not improved the game. As for further extending the lbw rule I think it would make a farce of the game.

"In many quarters surprise was expressed that at the age of 51 I went in number one. Until then I had never been in first regularly, though I had always preferred that place. Beginning as a bowler made Kent place me four or five in the order, and moreover the county were always rich in opening batsmen. Consequently my wish to start the innings was denied until 1938.

"Because Kent have experienced their bad times against fast bowling [there were very few bouncers in those days] the cry has gone round that we cannot play the fast men, but I think if you search the records you will also find that Kent have hit a tremendous lot of runs off fast bowling. Again I must emphasise that Kent always endeavour to play sporting cricket, and trying to make runs off that type of bowling must sometimes have contributed to our downfall. It was never a policy of the Kent team that the pitch *must* be occupied all day after winning the toss.

"I cannot let this opportunity pass without placing on record how much I have enjoyed my cricket with Kent. If I was a youngster starting as a batsman I think I should like to play always at The Oval, but the Kent grounds, with their natural decorations of beautiful trees, members' tents flying their own colours and bedecked with flowers, lend the right tone to cricket."

After his retirement from the field, Woolley was elected a life member of MCC and Kent, and also to the county committee. He was quite active into his late 80s and in January 1971 flew to Australia to watch the last two Tests. Nine months later, in Canada, he married for a second time, his first wife having died ten years earlier. His second bride was Mrs Martha Morse, an American widow.

R. L. Arrowsmith writes:

Frank Woolley was a slow left-arm bowler with a beautiful action who took over 2,000 wickets and was at one time perhaps the best of his type in the world. He caught during his career far more catches than anyone else, except wicket-keepers, yet it is as a batsman that he is primarily remembered. Few now alive have seen a player who approached him in ease and grace, and his average rate of scoring has been exceeded only by Jessop and equalled by Trumper. His philosophy was to dominate the bowler. "When I am batting," he said, "*I* am the attack." I was lucky enough to see him innumerable times. Obviously I often saw him out for small scores, but I never saw him in difficulties. If a ball beat him, the next would probably go for four or six.

This was made possible not only by his wonderful eye and sense of timing but by his range of strokes. He had every orthodox stroke at his command and no preference for one over another. Like W.G., he simply employed the one the occasion demanded. Each of these strokes could be commended to a young player as the perfect example of how to do it. In defence, too, his back stroke, certainly in his maturer years, was a model of soundness. All types of bowler came alike to him personally, but, if he saw his partner in trouble, he would make it his business to "settle" the bowler responsible.

At Tunbridge Wells in 1924, he came in at 29 for two to join George Wood, who was in grievous difficulties with Tate, then at his best. As he passed Wood, he said: "Push a single, Mr Wood, and leave me to deal with Chubby." The single was duly obtained and Tate's next two balls were driven for four. Great trier through he was, Tate, always demonstrative, flung the ball down, exclaiming, "I can't bowl to this chap." Wood, a useful though not great bat, went on to make 49, Woolley made 87, and together they put on 103 out of a total of 190. Though Kent won by 200 runs, it is not fanciful to suggest that those two early fours had a considerable effect on the course of the match.

At Folkestone in 1928, an England XI required 286 to beat the West Indies. There was a bit of feeling in the air, and the three fast bowlers, Francis, Constantine, and Griffith, set out to intimidate the batsmen. Lee and Hammond were quickly out and Wyatt, though struggling with typical determination, was acutely uncomfortable. Woolley, as if unconscious of any trouble, set about the bowlers from the start and hit them to every corner of that large ground. Never have I seen fast bowling so massacred. He scored 151 in three hours, Wyatt compiled a gallant 75, and against all the odds the England side won by four wickets. Years later Constantine said it was the worst hammering he ever received.

The feelings of an opposing captain on such occasions were succinctly expressed by Woodfull: "He made the game look so untidy." It appeared as if the wrong bowlers were on and the fieldsmen all in the wrong places. One can see why Woolley could be a far greater menace to the opposition than players with higher averages, and why 40 years after his retirement he is mentioned in print more than any other batsman of his time except Bradman. And if some statistically minded reader says, "But wouldn't he have been a greater player had he exercised a bit more caution?" I am sure that all who saw him, and, even more, all who played with him would answer firmly, "No".

SIR FRANK WORRELL

Born in Barbados, August 1, 1924

Died in Jamaica, March 13, 1967

Knighted for his services to cricket, 1964

By Sir Learie Constantine

Sir Frank Worrell once wrote that the island of Barbados, his birthplace, lacked a hero. As usual, he was under-playing himself. Frank Maglinne Worrell was the first hero of the new nation of Barbados and anyone who doubted that had only to be in the island when his body was brought home in mid March of 1967.

Or in Westminster Abbey when West Indians of all backgrounds and shades of opinion paid their last respects to a man who had done more than any other of their countrymen to bind together the new nations of the Caribbean and establish a reputation for fair play throughout the world. Never before had a cricketer been honoured with a memorial service in Westminster Abbey.

Sir Frank was a man of strong convictions, a brave man and it goes without saying, a great cricketer. Though he made his name as a player his greatest contribution was to destroy for ever the myth that a coloured cricketer was not fit to lead a team. Once appointed, he ended the cliques and rivalries betweeen the players of various islands to weld together a team which in the space of five years became the champions of the world.

He was a man of true political sense and feeling, a federalist who surely would have made even greater contributions to the history of the West Indies had he not died so tragically in hospital of leukaemia at the early age of 42, a month after returning from India.

People in England can have little idea of the problems of West Indian cricket. It is not a question of a few countries bordering each other coming together in a joint team. Jamaica is 1,296 flying miles from Barbados and Georgetown in Guyana 462 miles from Bridgetown in Barbados.

Before that wonderful tour of Australia in 1960-61, Barbadians would tend to stick together and so would the Trinidadians, Jamaicans and Guyanans. Worrell cut across all that. Soon there were no groups, Just one team.

He told his batsmen to walk if they were given out. When Garry Sobers appeared to show his dissent with a decision, he reprimanded him. After that, everyone walked as soon as the umpire's finger went up.

So when half a million Australians lined the streets of Melbourne in their ticker tape farewell to Worrell and his men, they were not only paying a final tribute to the team's great achievements, they were recognising the capacity and potential of equals both on and off the turf.

Sir Frank started life in Barbados, worked and lived in Trinidad and died in Jamaica after doing much useful work at the University of the West Indies there. He incurred enmity by leaving his birthplace but he did not care much for insularity, cant and humbug.

He saw the many diverse elements of the West Indies as a whole, a common culture and outlook separated only by the Caribbean Sea. This is why he upset certain people in Barbados when he wrote to a newspaper there criticising the island for having the cheek to challenge the rest of the world to celebrate independence.

Worrell was strongly criticised for this action, bitterly in fact in some quarters. But being attacked did not worry him. He always had the courage to say what he felt about every issue he thought vital to the well-being of the islands.

Sadly, the news that he was dying came through as Barbados played the Rest of the World XI. But Worrell held no rancour against his homeland. He had bought a piece of land there and had intended to retire there eventually.

This willingness to speak out often got him into trouble, even at school. Cricket had come naturally to him as it does to most youngsters in the West Indies, particularly Barbados. More so with him because he was born in a house only a few yards away from the Empire cricket ground. He and his friends used to set up stumps on the outfield and play nearly all day in the holidays.

At Combermere School he fell foul of a master who accused him of hogging the crease and not letting his colleagues bat.

He was to write later: "I was unfortunate enough to have been under an endemic psychological and mental strain throughout my school days. So much so that by the time I reached the fourth form I was suffering from a persecution complex.

"These were the days when child psychology was not a subject demanded of applicants to teachers' posts. Indeed, the majority of masters did not have the experience of raising families of their own. There was no allowance for the original point of view."

Worrell was a pupil who always had an original point of view. Also, as it was becoming clear at this time, he was a cricketer with an original talent. He soon made the Barbados team and records began to flow from his bat as he moved up the order from number eleven (yes, that is where he began his career!).

He shared a partnership of 502 with John Goddard in 1943-44 and an unfinished 574 with Clyde Walcott in 1945-46. Typically he dismissed both. "The conditions were loaded in our favour," he said. "I wasn't all that delighted about it."

In 1947 he tired of living in Barbados. His mother had moved to New York and his father was away at sea most of the time so he moved to Jamaica. English people will be surprised to learn that many of Worrell's fellow Bajans have never forgiven him for this "betrayal". When will they ever learn?

He established an international reputation against the 1947-48 England touring side and at the end of that tour took the step that made him a batsman for all seasons and all wickets. He signed as professional for the Central Lancashire League side Radcliffe for a fee of £500 a year.

It was a good year to enter League cricket. The Central Lancashire League was a cricket academy and the young, talented player was bound to improve by the experience. Playing in neighbouring clubs were Bill Alley, Jock Livingston, Ray Lindwall, Cecil Pepper, Clyde Walcott, Everton Weekes, Vinoo Mankad and Dattu Phadkar.

I have always held that League cricket makes a cricketer, not only as a player but as a man. There is much to learn in the field of human relations from the kind, friendly and warm people of the North of England. Frank brought his fiancée, Velda, over and their marriage was another settling influence on him.

Worrell was not just living for the present – as I regret is the case with some of our cricketers – but he was thinking of the future. He took a course at Manchester University and qualified in economics, his chosen subject.

The flag on Radcliffe Town Hall was at half mast on the day of his death. He married his wife, Velda, at Radcliffe, and their daughter was born there. Such was the esteem in which he was held by Radcliffe that in 1964 a street near the cricket ground was named Worrell Close.

The 1950 tour of England was a triumph for him and he topped the Test batting averages with 539 runs at an average of 89.83. His best Test score of 261 was made in this season, at Trent Bridge.

Norman Yardley, the England captain of the time, told me it was impossible to set a field to him. Place the fieldsmen straight and he beat them on the wide. Place them wide and he would beat them straight.

I am not one for averages myself. I am more concerned with how a batsman made his runs and not what his average was at the end of the series. Sir Neville Cardus has written of Sir Frank that he never made a crude or an ungrammatical stroke. I agree with that. Worrell was poetry.

While Walcott bludgeoned the bowlers and Weekes dominated them, the stylist Worrell waved them away. There was none of the savage aggression of a Sobers in his batting. He was the artist. All three "Ws" were geniuses but Worrell was my favourite because he had more style and elegance. He had all the strokes and the time and capacity to use them without offence to the eye, without ever being hurried.

He was never seen playing across the line. That is why he never hooked. Players and Pressmen agreed that even when he ducked beneath a bouncer, he did so with a lack of panic and great dignity. And remember he had Lindwall and Miller to contend with!

The tour to Australia in 1951-52 was not such a success as the 1950 tour of England. Worrell himself said this was because there were too many factions in the side and John Goddard, previously showered with advice, was not helped this time by the seniors.

When Worrell took over the captaincy nine years later, he was to heed the lessons of this dismal tour. The return series in the West Indies in 1955 was again a disappointment for Worrell; he scored only 206 runs. The 1957 tour of England was a further let down. Clearly the West Indies authorities had to change their policy of always appointing a white man to captain the side.

The break was made in 1960 when Worrell, the only candidate with the outstanding qualities to do this gigantic repair job, was asked to lead the side in Australia. Everyone knows the story of that tour and how much it did to restore the good name of cricket after the "bumper" rows, "slow over rates" disputes and other ills which had been afflicting the international game.

Back in Jamaica, Worrell was acclaimed and rightly so. He was appointed Warden of the University College of the West Indies and also a Senator in Parliament.

The Indians were the next tourists to the West Indies and it was typical of the man that when their captain, Nari Contractor, was seriously injured by a blow on the head, Worrell was one of the donors of blood which saved his life.

It was not generally known that Worrell, the thirteenth West Indies captain, was a superstitous man. During the 1951 tour of Australia he was bowled first ball by Geoff Noblet. Determined to make a fresh start in the second innings, he changed every stitch of clothing, fitting himself out in a completely new gear and walked to the wicket hoping that by discarding his old clothes he would change his luck. Not a bit of it! He was out for another first baller!

As he came in, crestfallen, Clyde Walcott, the next batsman, said with a laugh: "Why do I have to face a hat trick every time I follow you?"

His finest hours in England came in 1963 when he led the West Indies to more glory. By this time he had slowed up in the field and his figure was well in excess of Miss World proportions. He was 38 (age I mean) and no longer the player he had been. He was a tired man and often told me so.

But his influence over the side as captain was such that it was unthinkable to rest him in any of the Tests. He bowled a few shrewd medium pacers with his deceptively easy delivery and when the crisis was on in the Lord's Test, the greatest Test of all time as it was called by the critics, he helped Butcher to add 110 on the Saturday afternoon. The following Monday morning the second innings collapsed.

Asked if Worrell was worried about this, another player replied: "No, he is asleep." Sir Frank had this ability to drop off at any time, particularly when there was a batting collapse. After his death, I wondered whether this had something to do with his illness which was obviously affecting him at this time, though no one knew that he was not a fit man.

As Wes Hall prepared for the final over which could have won or lost the Lord's Test, Worrell went to him with some advice. What was he saying? Bounce them? Bowl 'em straight? No, none of the obvious things. Sir Frank said calmly: "Make sure you don't give it to them by bowling no balls." Worrell was the calmest man at Lord's that day and trust him to think of a highly pertinent point which Hall, in his excitement, may have overlooked!

He announced his retirement at the end of this tour which was a triumph of leadership, technical skill and adaptability. The following year Her Majesty the Queen knighted this complete cricketer, philosopher and captain. It was a fitting end to an unforgettable career but there was one more job for him to do – manage the West Indies side against the 1965 Australian tourists.

He had groomed Sobers well for the captaincy and theirs was an unbeatable partnership. At last the West Indies were the undisputed champions in their truly national sport.

Throughout his life, Sir Frank never lost his sense of humour or his sense of dignity. Some nasty things were said and written during that 1965 tour but Sir Frank was ever the diplomat. He lost no friends, made no enemies yet won more respect. He would always come up with a smile and a loud laugh. West Indians really laugh their laughs. And Sir Frank laughed louder than most of us.

He was a happy man, a good man and a great man. The really tragic thing about his death at the age of 42 was that it cut him off from life when he still had plenty to offer the islands he loved. He was only at the beginning. Or was it that the opportunity came to him a bit too late?

OTHER TRIBUTES

S. C. Griffith (Secretary, MCC): Ever since I first saw him play during the MCC tour of the West Indies, I have thought of Frank Worrell as a great and impressive batsman and a very useful bowler. Even more than that, I have been impressed by his ever growing stature as leader of cricketers, by his tolerance and understanding and by the contribution he was making to the game. He was a great friend of mine and like countless other cricketers I shall miss him more than I can say.

P. B. H. May: The game has lost a personality we all admired. He was one of the greatest of the long line of Barbadian cricketers. One associated him with his two colleagues, Weekes and Walcott, but I regard him as the most accomplished of the trio.

Sir Donald Bradman: His name is for ever shrined on the Frank Worrell Trophy which Australia is proud to have created for permanent competition between our two countries. Players of his calibre are rare. Not only was he a truly great and stylish batsman, he was also a fine thinker with a broad outlook.

Richie Benaud: He was a great leader of men and one of the finest cricketers on and off the field in the history of the game. It is difficult to realise that the indolent drawl, the feline grace known all over the world are no more. Few men have had a better influence on cricket.

Ian Johnson: He was easily the greatest captain of modern times. He brought West Indies cricket to the top and set a wonderful example to world cricket.

Alan Barnes (Secretary, Australian Board of Control): His name is indelibly linked with the finest traditions of cricket throughout the world and particularly in the hearts of all Australian cricket lovers.

E. R. Dexter: His reputation as a cricketer is beyond dispute. I found him one of the best captains I have seen or played against.

F. S. Trueman: He was one of the nicest people I ever played against.

J. M. Kilburn: Cricket was always distinguished in the presence of Worrell – Sir Frank. His knighthood was a personal honour to a cricketer of rare quality and an acknowledgement that West Indian cricket had reached the highest level in the world. In his captaincy he won esteem and affection by the calm demeanour in which he cloaked firmness and shrewd tactics. His serenity smoothed ruffled feathers and diminished crises.

INDEX